UTAH'S CANYON COUNTRY PLACE NAMES

Stories of the cowboys, miners, pioneers,
and river runners who put names on the land.

VOLUME I
[A – L]

Steve Allen

CANYON COUNTRY PRESS

Canyon Country Press
665 Oakcrest Drive
Durango, Colorado 81301

Printed in the United States of America
First Edition
Volume I: ISBN 978-0-9884200-7-6
Volume II: ISBN 978-0-9884200-8-3

Golden Throne photograph by Harvey Halpern Wilderness Photography

Book design and production by Marin Bookworks
www.TheBookDesigner.com

For my sister Terry Allen Beck

You are always with me

Contents

Best Quotes and Stories   1

Acknowledgments   5

Introduction   7

Caveats and Disclaimers   11

How to Use This Book   13

Place name listings, A – L   15

Best Quotes and Stories

Butch Cassidy:
Beef Basin: Story by Carl Mahon.
Buckhorn Wash: Poem by Lamont Johnson: "Heavy Holstered Men."
Butch Cassidy Draw: Story by Gaylord Staveley.
Caineville: Story by Perry L. Jackson.
Freds Ridge: Story by Lula Parker Bentenson.
Horse Tanks: Story by John F. Vallentine.
Price Town: "Not Quite Dead."
Robbers Roost Flats: Story by Earnest Albert Wild.

Canyon Country Descriptions:
Aquarius Plateau: Clarence Dutton: "Described in Blank Verse."
Navajo Mountain: Clyde Kluckhohn: "This Blasted Region."
Red Rock Plateau: Clyde Kluckhohn: "A New and Strange World."
Uintah County: Unattributed: "Hold the World Together."
Vermilion Cliffs: Teddy Roosevelt: "The Lonely Wastes" and "An Incredible Wilderness."

Cowboy funnies:
Andy Mesa: Joe Taylor: "The Chipmunk Story."
Billie Flat Top: Charlie Gibbons: "I Married Your Sister."
Black Mesa: Clyde Barton: "Level This Place Out."
Burr Pass: Jack Moore: "They'd Have Caught Me."
Cathedral Valley: Charles Kelly: "A Bad Place."
Crow Seep–Robbers Roost Ranch: Pearl Baker: "Invited to Leave."
Fortknocker Canyon: Carl Mahon: "Fartknocker."
Georgie Hollow: Don Coleman. "Afore the Fog Lifted."
Neilson Wash: Joseph August Nielson: "Sore Throats."

Cowboy Stories:
Bitter Seep Wash: Wayne Gremel: "I Fell of a Ledge."
Bullock Draw: Lee Mont Swasey: "Aesop's Fable."
Cass Creek Peak: Bliss Brinkerhoff: "Frozen on their Feet."
Comb Ridge: DeReese Nielson: "Everything was Just Hamburger."
Confluence, The: Anderson Thayer: "Hiram's Eye."
Coyote Creek (Garfield Co.): Garth Noyes: "Horse Blankets."
Coyote Creek (Kane Co.): Ralph Chynoweth: "Your Mark and Brand."
Crandall Canyon: Ivan W. Young: "A Very Lucky Boy."
Desolation Canyon: George Y. Bradley: "A Terrible Wind."
Dry Valley Creek: Ralph Chynoweth: "Wooden Tongue."

Dubinky Wash: Guy Robison: "Blue Eyes."
Elsinore Town: Dona S. Hansen: "Miss Miracle."
Fish Lake: George Albert Adams: "Close Call."
Gordon Reservoir: H.L.A. Culmer: "Latigo Gordon."
Halls Crossing: Josephine Catherine Chatterly Wood: "We Did Thank Our Heavenly Father."
Harrison Spring: Erwin Oliver: "The Hand of God."
Harveys Fear Cliff: Don Coleman: "Over the Edge."
Jewkes Hollow: Joseph H. Hewkes: "Close Call."
Jacobs Chair: DeReese Nielson: "He was just stubborn."
Johnny Coldwater Spring: Erwin Oliver: "Downwind on the Mancos."
Pleasant Creek: Frederick S. Dellenbaugh. "Those Who Snore."
Pole Canyon (Piute Co.): M. Lane Warner: "The Meteor: A Supernatural Happening."
Rone Bailey Mesa: Harold Muhlestein: "Cowboy Hat Saved a Life."
Rush Beds: Ralph Chynoweth: "An Unexpected Name Derivation."
Steele Butte: Keith Durfey: "Don't Eat the Mouse."
Stove Gulch: Harvey Hardy: "Smart Dog."
Trail Cliff (San Juan Co.): Erwin Oliver: "The Last Words He Ever Spoke."
Twin Springs: Erwin Oliver: "A Cowboy at Birth."
Verdure Town: George A. Adams: "Mighty Good Horses."

Cowboy Wisdom:

Cold Springs: Vincent L. Jones: "The Government's Share."
Dark Canyon (San Juan Co.) Manti-LaSal National Forest: Erwin Oliver: "See Where I'd Been."
Smith Fork: Van Verbeck: "Keep a Man's Privacy."

Environmental:

Escalante National Monument: Wallace Stegner: "One Vast National Park."
Grand Staircase: Dr. Russell Gl Frazier: "Shouted from the Mountaintops."
Hidden Passage Canyon: Wallace Stegner: "The Loss of a Place."
Kaiparowits Plateau: Harvey Halpern: 'Cowcrapairowits Plateau—a Shame."
Lake Powell: Homer L. Dodge: "What We've Lost."
Rabbit Valley: Andrew P. Hansen. "Cattle and Sheep Destruction of the Range."
Robbers Roost Flats: Wallace Stegner: "A Lonely and Terrible Wilderness."
San Rafael Swell: H.L.A. Culmer: "Wonders of the San Rafael Swell."
Twilight Canyon: Stephen C. Jett: "The Death of Glen Canyon."
Water Canyon: (Kane Co.) Moquith Mountains: Neil M. Judd: "Bovine Progress."

Flash Floods:

North Wash: Robert Brewster Stanton. "Flash Flood."
Santa Clara Town: Mary Minerva Dart Judd: "Passed Away Like a Dream."
Warm Creek: Arthur C. Waller and Ernest Wander: "Warm Creek Flash Flood."

Inconsistent stories:

Bullion Canyon (Piute Co.): Webster Town.
Government Rapids (San Juan Co.).
Jacobs Chair (San Juan Co.).
Mollies Nipple (Kane Co.).
Montezuma Creek (San Juan Co.).
Woodenshoe Buttes (Kane Co.).

Medical:

Blue Spring Creek–Prince Shingle Mill: "An Old Indian."

Jewkes Hollow: Joseph H. Jewkes: "Mashed Flat."

Smith Fork: Charles Kelly: "Spry as a Cricket."

Straight Creek–Wolverton Mill: Barbara Ekker: "Hot Copper Wire."

Miscellaneous:

Cottonwood Gulch: Katie Lee: "Tinsel."

Crystal Geyser: Barry Goldwater: "Hard Hat!"

West Rim Trail: Robert Frothingham: "Amen."

Slot Canyons:

Bibliography Entry 1469: "First Description of a Slot Canyon, 1840."

Crystal Springs Canyon: Katie Lee: "Sequestered Gracilities."

Fiftymile Creek: "First Known Descent."

Lower Black Box: H.L.A. Culmer: "Many a Quick Pitapat."

Narrows, The (Washington Co.): Grove Karl Gilbert: "We Could Not Discover a Patch of Sky."

Parunuweap Canyon: John Wesley Powell: "We had to Swim."

Smith Fork: David D. Rust: "Broke No Bones."

Teddys Horse Pasture: Joseph L. Dudziak: "Arching."

White Canyon (San Juan Co.)–Black Hole: Kent Frost: "The Canyon has Changed!"

Willow Gulch: W. Robert Moore: "The Boulder was a Barrier No Longer."

Water:

Brushy Basin Wash: Clyde Barton: "Let Their Pants Down Quick Enough."

Buckhorn Flat (Emery Co.) Buckhorn Well: Owen McClenahan: "No Sudden Moves."

Grapevine Pass: George Peter Pectol: "Bad Water."

Mexican Seep: Owen McClenahan: "Reducing Spring."

Mussentuchit Flat: Jim Crane. "Hard Water!"

Rock Spring: (San Juan Co.): Erwin Oliver: "Pollywogs and Cow Piss."

Soda Spring (Kane Co.): D. Elden Beck: "Slick Water."

Town Descriptions:

Hanksville: Robert Coughlan: "A Speck of Stubborn Protoplasm."

Salina Town: Clarence Dutton: "Salina, a Wretched Hamlet."

Acknowledgments

This book took more than forty years of on-the-ground research and fifteen years of writing to complete. It could not have been finished without the help of and collaboration with many great people.

A special thanks to Jim Knipmeyer, my history mentor and hiking buddy, who spent many hundreds of hours helping me with this project. Jim's critical eye and depth of knowledge added immensely to the book. It could not have been done without his encouragement.

Two other historians, Brandt Hart and David Pimental, added immeasurably to the book. Brandt is the expert on San Juan River history and Dave is the authority on the Glen Canyon gold rush of the 1890s. They both provided not only historical information, but they read the manuscript several times over the years and made valuable suggestions. Jim, Brandt, Dave, and I regularly hike and run rivers together documenting history on the ground. I couldn't have better backcountry companions.

Barbara Ekker of Hanksville was there from the beginning. Her knowledge of the people and places of southern Utah is unparalleled and she graciously shared information and resources with me.

Other historians added their expertise to the book. They included Edson Alvey (deceased), JoAnne Chandler, Stefan Folias, Mike Ford, Andy Gulliford, Vaughn Hadenfeldt, Steve Jett, Tom McCourt, Will Petty, Gus Scott, Janet Burton Seegmiller, and Scott Thybony.

To the many cowboys, miners, river runners, and townspeople who took time from their busy schedules to talk with me, thanks are not enough. I hope that through your stories, the readers will glean a better understanding of what pioneer life was like in the "old" days. Each and every one of you added precious knowledge to our understanding of canyon country history.

Thank you Lisle Adams, Clyde and Karl Barton, Eric Bjørnstad, Wayne Blackburn, Bliss Brinkerhoff, Ralph Chynoweth, Emmett and Veola Clark, Don Coleman, Jim Crane, Val Dalton, Gene Dunham, Keith Durfey, Barbara Ekker, Ted Ekker, Kent Frost, Pratt Gates, Fred Goodsell, Wayne and Carrie Lou Gremel, Dee and Berneal Hatch, Lloyd Holyoak, Garn Jefferies, Cal Johnson, Sandy Johnson, Stuart Johnson, Stan Jones, Jack King, Sonny King, Katie Lee, Carl Mahon, Ione Nelson, DeReese Nielson, Newel Nielson, Garth Noyes, Erwin Oliver, Burns Ormand, Guy Pace, Roger and Debbi Reynolds, Max Robinson, Alvin and Bertha Robison, Guy and Nina Robison, John Scorup, Betty Smith, Pete Steele, Lee Mont Swasey, Dunk Taylor, Joe Taylor, Thaine Taylor, Alfonzo Turner, Ray Wareham, Kent Whittaker, Waldo Wilcox, and Dwight Williams. Brief biographies of each person I interviewed can be found in the bibliography.

Several of the people I interviewed have died. To their families, know that their stories were the ones that they told you around the campfire or in the living room. Now a larger audience has the privilege of sharing those memories that are so important to understanding the true history of southern Utah.

I was fortunate to run into many old-timers in the outback. We would talk while leaning against a pick-up truck or a corral. Unfortunately age is catching up with me and I have forgotten many names. But, I do remember Joan Anderson, Q Johnson, Mac Lafevre, Ashby Reeve, and Kevin Robison.

Jeff Grathwohl encouraged me from the start and provided needed criticism and direction in the early years of the project.

Dan and Diane Cassidy, owners of Five Quail Books in Prescott, Arizona, happily held essential books for me for indefinite periods while I was in the backcountry. Both Art Source International in Boulder, Colorado and Dumont Maps and Books of the West in Santa Fe, New Mexico let me peruse their extensive collections of maps. Pat DeCicco, owner of the Boulder Map Gallery in Boulder, Colorado, supplied many of the USGS maps. Thank you!

Mark McCarroll and Mike Pfotenhauer at Osprey Packs in Cortez, Colorado, Pete Metcalf at Black Diamond Equipment in Salt Lake City, and John Evans at Petzl Equipment in Clearfield (near Ogden) provided gear over the years. Thank you!

I spent a couple of weeks with the USGS at the Denver Federal Center. I was treated like royalty. Thank you Dale Benson, Gary Correnti, Sam Howard, and Clay Martin for all of your help.

Dozens of libraries and archives were visited all over the west. To the archivists who took an interest in the project and pointed me in the right direction, many thanks. Several libraries deserve a special and heart-felt thanks: the Daughters of Utah's Pioneers Archives in Salt Lake City; the Huntington Library in San Marino, California; the John Wesley Powell River History Museum in Green River, Utah; the Gerald R. Sherratt Library Special Collections at Southern Utah University; and the Utah State Historical Society in Salt Lake City.

Joel Friedlander of Marin Bookworks took the finished manuscript and turned it into a book. I have rarely worked with anyone as organized and professional as Joel. Many, many thanks.

For close to forty years I spent six months or more a year with a backpack on exploring Utah's magnificent canyons. I've been lucky enough to hike with hundreds of incredible people. Closest to my heart are the canyon groups California, EMDC, Kansas, and the Young Turks. From mild day hikes to month-long, hard-core expeditions; from flat-water river runs to the big water of Cataract Canyon; these groups have provided support on absolutely every level. To all of you my deepest gratitude.

California: Mike Brennan, Gail Erbe-Hamblin, Della Lewis (deceased), Tom Messenger, Lester Olin (deceased), Tony and Carol Somkin, David Saunders, Tim Tilton, Laverne Waddington, and Tina Welton.

EMDC: Tom Arnspiger, Barry and Celeste Bernards (honorary), Tom Browne, Ronni Egan, Bud Evans, Jim Finch, Harvey Halpern, Julie Marple, Don Murch, Steve Ramras (honorary), Kathie Rivers, Giles Wallace, and Ann Warner.

Ginger Harmon is the heart and soul of EMDC: our hiker "emeritus." Still going strong into her 80s, Ginger hiked literally tens of thousands of miles with me over a twenty-plus year period. Darn, we have a great time! With all my love.

Kansas: Ace Allen, Norm Beal, Greg Boyer, Fred Braun, Mary Giehl, Sharon Hunter, Bill Mahon, Amy Shima, Joro Walker, Chip Ward, and Kristy Weber.

The Young Turks—Julie Greenberg, Scott Greenberg, Eric Husby, Rob May, Tony Merten (deceased), Ann Perius-Parker (deceased), Rob Roseen, and Joe Wrona (honorary)—helped me find a new way to enjoy the canyons. Every time the going gets rough, I think of you!

Many supplied essential support on the home front. To each of you: THANKS! Ellen Meehan transcribed all of the interviews—a hard job. Byard and Nancy Peake and Kim Allen kept the home fires burning while I was gone for extended periods. Terry Anderson kept an eye on the business end of things and in an essential way made this book possible. Joe Breddan and Wendy Chase joined me in the canyons and, on the home front, provided critical support.

My parents were inveterate desert rats. My father was an expert on the deserts of Australia and the aborigines who lived there. My mother knew the people and archaeology of the northwest corner of Nevada. My desert roots run deep. Both parents died during the writing of the book. My biggest sorrow is that they didn't get to see the finished product. This book was written for and in honor of Lou and Ruth Allen.

Introduction

The realization dawned on me about twenty years ago. I'd spent years tramping all over the canyons of southern Utah and thought I knew quite a bit about them. And I did, to a point. I knew about the geology, the botany, the prehistory, and a smidgen about the history of the land I walked. In my own mind, I was an expert.

Then someone asked me about Janes Tank. I'd never heard of it. I scoured the maps. Nothing. I searched the literature. Nada. I queried my friends. Zip. Then I asked a local rancher and I got an ear full. It was an epiphany. I didn't know as much about the land as I thought I did. I'd been to Janes Tank on top of Mancos Mesa several times; I'd even camped there. But, I didn't know the name of this huge pothole that had been used by generations of cowboys as a line camp. I needed to learn more, not only about Janes Tank, but about the hundreds if not thousands of other named places in canyon country that I had been to, heard of, or read about.

I set about working on a comprehensive collection of place name derivations for the canyons, mountains, and plateaus of southern Utah. I have taken a six-prong approach.

First, I did a comprehensive literature search. I read everything I could about southern Utah, visiting libraries both local and far away, from Monticello, Utah to Washington State, and from Green River to southern California. Work took me to Colorado, Arizona, Nevada, and Idaho. I visited every major library, and many smaller ones, in those states as well. I combed the literature for every scrap of information I could find, reading books, looking through handwritten journals, perusing back issues of newspapers and magazines *ad infinitum*, shuffling through stacks of old maps, and digging through endless boxes in innumerable archives.

As research progressed, I kept finding great quotes about places. It became a game to find the earliest and best descriptions. In many cases it was heartwarming to find that the descriptions of yesteryear closely match what we see today. In others it was heart wrenching to compare today's landscapes and find the differences are so dramatic, and invariably for the worse. Those quotes became a part of the book.

Although the gathering of information for the book was started before the days of computers, the internet became an important part of the research process. An amazing variety of information is available online, from digital newspaper archives and online books and journals to extensive photo collections. And, more and more of the sources listed in the bibliography are showing up online every day.

In the old days one would have had the daunting challenge of finding historic maps scattered between many libraries and private collections. Now, there are terrific web sites with searchable map collections, making it easier to compare routes, names, and name changes over time.

The reader may wonder why one couldn't just go to the United States Geological Survey (USGS) and look at their place names records. I did, spending several weeks in their sixteen-acre map building at the Denver Federal Center. When the USGS was making topographical maps, cartographers were sent out to survey the land. They would then interview the ranchers, farmers, and townspeople about names. Unfortunately, they would only document name derivations when there was disagreement. If there was no quarrel about a name, there would be no documentation! Out of the tens of thousands of names on USGS maps, it is amazing how little controversy there was about names.

Second, I did sit-down interviews with the locals who really knew the land. Luckily I was able to talk with many of the classic old-time cowboys, those who had spent a lifetime out on the range. Other interviewees were not that old, but they grew up listening to the stories of their parents and grandparents and aunts and uncles, and they remembered them.

It was not only name derivations I was after during the interviews, it was any story about the land that could be pegged to a definite spot. At the start of interviews I would tell my subject that, as an example, we know why Cottonwood Wash received its name, but perhaps something happened there that was interesting or of historic value. Those stories, too, became a part of the book.

Third, I went out on the land. I had a *modus operandi*. In most cases, before I did an interview, I would hike the land so I would know the questions to ask. Then, after the interview, I would go back and look at the land from the perspective of the cowboy or miner or river runner whom I had interviewed. I saw so much more.

I wanted this book to be accurate. To that end, more than forty thousand miles were hiked and several vehicles were worn out over a forty-year period in order to accurately locate places. I tromped around endlessly looking for those old stock trails and inscriptions, an old line camp or line cave, a set of watering troughs I'd been told about, or an especially impressive place that had no redeeming value but for its beauty. I put them all on a map.

Fourth, I documented place name changes over time. I would often read an old diary or report about an area I knew well and would find that I didn't have a clue as to the location of certain named places. It seems that every generation needs to put a new name on the land, whether one was already in place or not. In the old days, the explorers and pioneers often did not know of previous designations. The early ranchers had the same problem. In those days, unlike today with fixed grazing allotments, cowboys and sheepherders would roam from range to range as the seasons changed in search of forage for their livestock. Each successive group would add their own name to the land.

Today, the names seem to change faster than ever. Hikers, river runners, off-road vehicle riders, artists, archaeologists, canyoneers, guides, and tour operators all have a penchant for naming and renaming. The Archway Canyon of old became today's Leprechaun Canyon. Green Canyon of old mistakenly became Donnelly Canyon, which became today's Fringe of Life Canyon. The San Rafael River of old became today's Huntington Creek while Blacks Fork or Turtle Canyon became today's San Rafael River. Even our Janes Tank is shown on the USGS maps as Jacobs Spring. The real Jacobs Spring is not labeled on the maps at all, though you can still find it a mile from Janes Tank. Its location is detailed in the book.

Fifth, the documentation of constructed stock trails became an essential part of the book. These include the major trails established or taken by the early explorers like the Don Juan María Antonia de Rivera Expedition of 1765, the Domínguez-Escalante Expedition of 1776–77, and the Parley P. Pratt Exploring Expedition to Southern Utah of 1849–50.

Trails were established slowly, each new expedition pushing farther into uncharted land or finding new or faster ways across or around convoluted terrain. Over time a dominant route would come to the forefront and a name would be put on it: the Old Spanish Trail from Santa Fe, New Mexico to southern California; the Mormon Trail from Salt Lake City to Dixie and on to California; and the Honeymoon Trail from the Arizona colonies to St. George. These, and more, have been documented.

The pioneers also left a legacy of smaller trails crisscrossing the land. Not only did these hardened settlers have to move to new locations, they had to use the land and the resources around them to support themselves and to establish their towns. They built roads and trails into the mountains or down to the valleys to gather lumber, move their livestock, fish in the creeks and lakes, mine for coal or silver or gold, or to have a way to get to their favorite hunting grounds.

The cowboys, and here we have to include the Indians who preceded them to most places, built trails almost everywhere in the canyons. Some consist of short ramps up low cliffs; others go many hundreds of feet up near-vertical walls. The height of stock trail building came in the early 1900s when the land was overgrazed and stockmen were desperate for every blade of grass they could find. That is why it is not unusual to find a stock trail that must have taken weeks to build going to a relatively small pasture. If a rancher could keep his cattle or sheep from starving for just another week or two, perhaps that would be enough to get through a season.

Sixth, inscriptions are a critical historical tool and an important part of the book. They can tell us if a person was in a particular place, on what date, and, on occasion, whom they were with. Inscriptions helped determine where the Domínguez-Escalante Expedition crossed the Colorado River in 1776, where General William Henry Ashley led his band of explorers on the Green River in 1825, the route of the fur trappers from Colorado to the Uintah Basin over the East Tavaputs Plateau in the 1830s and '40s, and the route of the Elk Mountain Mission of 1855.

An inscription helped determine if, indeed, the Old Spanish Trail—Winter Route—actually crossed the Colorado River at Spanish Bottom and exactly where the Wetherill Trail crossed the San Juan River. The derivation of the town name of Aldridge was determined by using an inscription found along the route that William Alldredge took to get there.

Locally, people take great pride in inscriptions left by their family members. In one case a series of inscriptions allowed the descendants of Llewellyn Harris to follow his travels for several days in 1894 as he made his way from the mouth of the Escalante River, along the eastern face of the Waterpocket Fold, to Muley Twist Canyon.

I have provided little information about the people who did leave their names on the rock. That is the subject of many more books. The best and most prolific writer about inscriptions is James H. Knipmeyer. His book *Butch Cassidy Was Here: Historic Inscriptions of the Colorado Plateau* (University of Utah Press, 2002) is the seminal work about inscriptions on the Colorado Plateau and provides a template for others to follow. It, though, covers only a relatively small number of inscriptions and their histories. There is much work to be done.

Famous characters put names and stories on the land, and their stories are told. Many are well known; some are legend: the Spanish friars Domínguez and Escalante; the fur trappers William Henry Ashley, Denis Julien, and Antoine Robidoux; the explorers and route-finders Kit Carson, John C. Fremont, John W. Gunnison, and Jedediah Smith; the river runners John Wesley Powell and Robert Brewster Stanton; and the early pioneers Jacob Hamblin, John D. Lee, and Nephi Johnson, Sr. come to mind. Others are infamous, and their stories, too, survive: Cap Brown, Butch Cassidy, Jack Cottrell, "Flat Nose" George Curry, Tom Dilly, Bill "Silver Tip" Wall, and Matt Warner, among many.

Best, though, the book introduces the reader to scores of less well-known people who put their stamp, and often new names, on the land: the explorers Maurico Arze and Lago Garcia, the geologists Arthur A. Baker and Charles B. Hunt; the river runners Harry Aleson, Clyde L. Eddy, Katie Lee, Otis "Dock" Marston, Norm Nevills, and Julius Stone; and the legendary cowboys Joe Biddlecome, John E. Brown, Louis M. Chaffin, Arthur Ekker, Latigo Gordon, Charlie Redd, Al and Jim Scorup, and Harve Williams.

Photographers have not only captured history on film, they too were instrumental in popularizing canyon country and, along the way, added many names to the landscape. The best include Josef and Joyce Muench, Philip Hyde, Eliot Porter, and Tad Nichols.

Let's not forget the lonely and unheralded backpacker looking for nothing but beauty in the wild mess of country called canyonlands. The first was Kent Frost. He was followed by Harry Aleson, Randall Henderson, Stan Jones, Frank E. Masland, Jr., Charlie Olajos, and Ken Sleight. More recently, rock climbers Eric Bjørnstad, Steve Bartlett, and Jeff Widen and canyoneers Bo Beck, Rick Green, David Pimental, Steve Ramras, and Dennis Turville have led the charge. And with all of them, names have proliferated.

As much as possible, I have let the people who were most intimately involved with the lands of southern Utah tell the stories in their own voice. My job was as compiler and editor; my challenge was to keep it all straight and organize it in such a way as to make sense.

Caveats and Disclaimers

One of the problems in assembling this type of material is trying to weed out fact from fiction. Napoleon perhaps said it best: "History is a set of lies agreed upon." And so it seemed when I first started working on this list. Often the stories I read or heard were quite different, even coming from people who had all been there!

What to do? Wayne County historian Barbara Ekker, who has faced this challenge many times in her writing career, told me: "Steve, it is all history. We can't check most of the stories for facts. We can just record it and leave it at that." And that is what I have done. In many cases, there are no right answers. The stories are what one person told another and another and finally someone has or is putting it down on paper. No right. No wrong. Just a story.

Although many Navajo, Paiute, and Ute names have been documented, this is primarily a book about Utah's Euroamerican pioneers and the names they put on the land. There are several good sources for Indian legends; many are noted in the bibliography. I have made every effort to attribute the correct Indian group to a certain action or story, whether it was a Navajo, Paiute, or Ute. Unfortunately, many of the early records just mention that an "Indian" was involved with the story without giving a tribal affiliation.

Many, if not most, of the pioneers, settlers, and early ranchers in southern Utah were members of The Church of Jesus Christ of Latter-day Saints, or Mormons. This book is not a Church history. It is a pioneer history.

It should be noted that quotes from those whom I interviewed are not verbatim. We talk very differently than we write, often making a verbatim story frustrating and difficult to read without editing. After the interviews, which were recorded, a word-for-word transcript was made. I would then edit the transcripts so the stories would make sense and have a flow. The interviewee would have a chance to make corrections or suggestions (or add further embellishments!).

The interviews, both original and edited versions, will make their way to local libraries and to the Utah State Historical Society and the Powell River History Museum Archives in Green River, Utah. Those interviewed also have copies.

When talking to old-timers, it was clear that "old" meant sometime pre-1900. Assume that most dates are plus or minus twenty years. For most of the facts presented, that is very much close enough. It is the story that counts.

If a place has a family name, it was sometimes hard to determine to whom the name should be credited. Was it named for granddad the pioneer, the son who built the ranch into a thriving business, or the grandson who became the mayor of the local town? There was certainly guesswork with some entries.

Discrepancies in dates are prevalent throughout the book. There is no way around it: memories fade, historians disagree, ways of determining when something happened can be different. Did a town start the day the first settler came, the day the town was surveyed and platted, the year the town got a post office, or when it was incorporated? Even in the written literature, it was common to have several dates attached to a certain incident. I was often happy to just have two sources agree on a decade.

It was often difficult to match a new or old name to a definitive place on the landscape or on the map. The early maps were notoriously inaccurate. There will invariably be mistakes of interpreting what someone else, often a century or more ago, wrote or said about a place and determining exactly where that place is today. It would often be difficult to translate verbal directions from the interviews to an exact place on the land.

For the modern-day researcher, it is often frustrating to be told about a place, but then not be provided with an accurate location. For important landmarks such as constructed stock trails, noteworthy line camps, old town and ranch sites, river camps, etc., I have added a (SAPE.)—Steve Allen Personal Experience—acronym to the appropriate entry. This tells you that I have seen that place myself. There are quite a few locations I have not visited. Though believed to be reliable, those locations are not as certain and should be recognized as such.

Often, descriptions of locations are a bit vague in this book, though in most instances, directions will get you to within a quarter of a mile or so. For those on the ground looking for constructed stock trails, you may have to do some scouting. Many stock trails are well constructed and are easy to find. Others are just shadow trails and are difficult to locate.

Many of the trails have been "cairned" (a local term used to describe a route where cairns—small stacks of rock—have been used to mark the trail). It is quite all right to knock down "cairns to nowhere." But, constructed stock trails are pieces of history we are trying to preserve. If someone has taken the time to put together the pieces and cairn in an old constructed trail, please do not knock the cairns down.

Some trails, and other features, were left out of this book at the request of local ranchers. I did not delve into reasons; I had enough respect for each and every person I talked with to understand that whatever the reason, it was important to them.

Historic inscriptions are being destroyed at an alarming rate. Perhaps the oldest inscription in southern Utah, with a date of 1776, was nearly destroyed by boaters on Lake Powell. In the Peshliki Fork of Ticaboo Creek a major inscription panel, with dates going back to the Glen Canyon gold mining boom of the 1890s, has been totally destroyed by uncaring boaters. In the 1990s historic inscriptions dating to the 1880s and '90s were destroyed in the San Rafael Swell with the blessing of state and federal authorities; they forgot to ask inscriptionologists if they were important. An inscription panel in North Wash was eradicated with power tools by someone who probably thought they were erasing modern graffiti, making it difficult for experts to determine the authenticity of one of the old inscriptions.

In this book the exact location of most of the inscriptions is not given. For the historian, it is usually enough to know that an inscription was near a certain spring or canyon or other feature; an exact location would not be helpful. For those visiting inscriptions, there are a couple of rules to keep in mind; these rules also apply to rock art. First, never touch an inscription, barehanded or otherwise; second, never chalk an inscription; and third, never make rubbings of an inscription.

Although this is not a guidebook, the information herein may lead people into the backcountry. It is the reader's responsibility to understand the risks of desert travel, be knowledgeable about desert travel, and be prepared to recognize and deal with emergency situations.

How to Use This Book

Example Entry:

Escalante River: (Garfield and Kane Counties.) GSCENM-Escalante Mountains-Glen Canyon NRA-Glen Canyon. Escalante, Calf Creek, King Bench, Red Breaks, Silver Falls Bench, Egypt, Scorpion Gulch, King Mesa, Stevens Canyon South, and Davis Gulch maps.
Also called Birch Creek and Potato Creek.
Also spelled Escalant, Escalanta, Escalente, Escalanti, Escalantis, Eskalantie, and Esklanty.

Almost all of the main entry place names are taken from USGS 7.5 Minute Series (1:24,000) topographic maps. With just a dozen or so exceptions, if it is not labeled on the map, it will not be a main entry.

The county or counties where the feature is located is shown in parentheses. Next is the federal entity that controls the land. Is it in a National Forest, a National Park, a National Monument? If it is undifferentiated Bureau of Land Management land, a designation is not used. If applicable, the physiographic area where the feature is located, such as a named plateau, mountain, or valley is given.

Then, a few helpful names are listed that will get you into the ballpark. After all, there are sixteen Water Canyons in southern Utah, with three in Kane County and four in Emery County. Which one are you looking for? In the case of a river or stream, after the federal designation and the physiographic area, the last name listed is where the waterway ends, usually at another watercourse, a lake, or in a valley.

In the example above, the Escalante River flows through Garfield and Kane counties. It starts in Grand Staircase Escalante National Monument in the Escalante Mountains and descends into Glen Canyon National Recreation Area and ends in Glen Canyon (Lake Powell).

The map list comes next. In general, the maps listed are the only ones that have that place name printed on them. In the case of watercourses, the maps are listed from the top of the drainage to the bottom. In the example above, the Escalante River starts on the Escalante map and ends on the Davis Gulch map.

The use of USGS 7.5 Minute Series maps is highly recommended. There are other excellent maps that cover the same country, but they often do not have enough detail for accuracy. USGS maps can often be purchased in local stores or online. Many of the maps can be printed directly from online sources. Do note that non-USGS maps often do not use the same elevations as the USGS maps.

The PRIVATE PROPERTY designation is important. Every effort has been made to identify private property, but land sales, exchanges, old maps, and new maps all conspire to make this an ever-changing target. Private property is just that. You are not allowed on the property without permission from the land owner. Even if the property is not noted as PRIVATE in this book, obey all posted signs. On some occasions areas of federal or state land are closed to visitors. Again, do not trespass. Example: Jasper Canyon and Virginia Park in Canyonlands National Park and Parunuweap Canyon in Zion National Park have been closed to all visitors.

Lands on all of the Indian reservations noted in this book should be considered PRIVATE PROPERTY. Some of these lands are open to visitation with the proper permits. Other areas are always closed. Web sites can be used to get information and to find out about obtaining permits.

In some areas, ranchers lock gates even though they do not own the land. Even when I know this, I do not trespass. It means that the rancher has gotten tired of uncaring visitors running stock, leaving gates open, mucking with water projects, or otherwise disrupting his livelihood. For example, both larkspur and locoweed, native plants common on western rangelands, can kill cattle when they eat it. Ranchers have found, though, that if their cattle do get into small patches of these plants, they can often tolerate them if they are not exerted. A group of hikers or a line of off-road vehicles will push the cattle and very well may kill them.

Some entries have been called by many names and without a significant source of derivation. These are listed as "Also called." The spelling of many entries has changed, or there are multiple ways of spelling a name. These are listed under "Also spelled."

Often more than one place name derivation is given, in no particular order. One name has seven different derivations! Take your pick. In some instances I do note which I believe is correct.

There are many place names that are not shown on the USGS maps. These are listed under the nearest main entry. If appropriate, they are listed in the order they are found from the top of a drainage to the bottom.

Some stories seem supernatural, silly, or impossible. During the interview process, it was common to see a twinkle in a rancher's eye as he told an unbelievable story. I leave it to the reader to determine which designation fits the story.

I frequently add the word "Town" after a place name if, in fact, it is or was a town. This is to avoid confusion. Although in real life one would not say "Escalante Town," the reader might be confused if the reference is just to Escalante. Is it the town, the river, the pasture area, or the person?

Rather than precede every distance with an "about" caveat, realize that distances are approximate. In many cases I have added the notation "as the crow flies" if a drainage is particularly sinuous. You can then measure a straight-line distance with a ruler from a given point to find the particular location.

The number immediately after a quote or a direct attribution refers to that source in the bibliography. If there are numbers after the first one, they are to references that reinforce or add to the content of the quote.

In normal writing it is appropriate to use an apostrophe in the possessive case with place names: i.e., Jane's Tank vs. Janes Tank. The USGS does not use an apostrophe and that convention has, for the most part, been used in this book. When asked why, a cartographer at the USGS told me that the apostrophe is too difficult to see on maps, so they left them out of all of their designations and in many of their publications.

I have used a method of describing springs developed for my hiking guides. I use the designations Small, Medium, or Large. This does not necessarily refer to the physical size of the springs, but to the likelihood of finding water in them. Small means the water source may dry up within days of a rain, or may be just a damp place in the sand. Medium springs run most of the time, but usually dry up in the summer months. Large springs will dry up only after prolonged drought. For backpackers trying to figure out water sources for a trip, these designations are subjective and should not be taken as gospel. The only reliable source of water is the last one you were at.

All springs are natural, but many in southern Utah have been developed by ranchers to maximize the flow of water and to pipe water away from the actual spring source to keep livestock from trampling it. Some of the water developments, such as piping, troughs, holding reservoirs, and fences are still in use. Others are no longer in use. In this book, it is possible to have a large spring that was once developed. You will most likely find water there, but not in a trough or a stock pond. As well, a spring noted as "still used" refers to the fact that it is still used by livestock.

Often the term "CCC-style troughs" is used. The Civilian Conservation Corps was responsible for developing hundreds of springs throughout southern Utah from the 1930s into the early 1940s. They had the money and man power not available to the individual rancher or to a small town. CCC-style troughs were made of tin and held off the ground using vertical posts and horizontal rails. These troughs could be made almost any length. Some are only ten feet long; others run a hundred feet or more. Many are still in use. This style trough was built into the 1950s. After World War Two most troughs were built using war surplus steel containers. Often these had protected engines or ammunition during shipping overseas and armed services numbers can still be seen.

A

Abajo Mountains: (San Juan Co.) Manti-LaSal National Forest. Abajo Mountain, Monticello Lake, Mount Linnaeus, and Shay Mountain maps.

Also called Sierra Abaja. (M.13a.)

Laurance D. Linford noted that the Navajo name is *Dzil Ditl'ooí*, or "Fuzzy Mountain." (1204~) Robert S. McPherson noted the meaning as Furry Mountain. (1338~)

Don Bernardo de Miera, the cartographer for the Domìnguez-Escalante Expedition of 1776–77, showed this as the *Sierra de Abajo*, the first time the name was used in print. (48~)

Two name derivations are given.

First, *Abajo* is Spanish for "lower" or "down," which many historians believe reflects the fact that this mountain range is below, or south of, the larger and higher La Sal Mountains. (86~)

Second, Lieutenant E.G. Beckwith of the John W. Gunnison Survey of 1853: "The [Abajo peaks are] near the junction of Grand [Colorado] and Green rivers, considerably below the fords for this [Old Spanish] trail, or, as Leroux [our guide] says, below any ford on Grand [Colorado] river known to the New Mexicans, and hence its name." (187~)

Locally these are called the Blue Mountains, named for their color when seen from a distance. John D. Lee noted them as the Blue Mountains in his diary entry for December 24, 1873, the first written record of the name. (437~)

William Henry Jackson of the Ferdinand V. Hayden Survey passed the Abajo Mountains on their eastern flank in 1875: "Our next objective was the Blue Mountains—the local name for the Abajo ... peaks in eastern Utah. It was a mysterious region reputed to be the haunt of a band of outlawed, renegade Indians.... [We] found another region of rich, abundant grass, clear mountain streams, and groves of oak and aspens.... There was luxuriant feed for our animals and plenty of clear, cool water. This was so grateful to both man and beast after the desert experiences of the past month." (952a~)

G. Nordenskiöld briefly described the Abajos in 1893: "the slopes of the Sierra Abajo (Blue Mountain), a group of lofty peaks with their luxuriant woods and rich pastures

forming as it were an oasis in the desert between Mancos [Colorado] and the Rio Colorado." (1468~)

The first Euroamerican ranchers in the Abajo Mountains area were Pat O'Donnell in 1876, then Charles "Race Horse" Johnson and Joshua B. "Spud" Hudson in 1879. (1240~) Johnson had a ranch near Durango, Colorado (1194~) and Hudson came from Texas (1741~).

—Abajo Mountain Terracing: Kent Frost noted that the man-made terraces ubiquitous throughout the Abajo Mountains were built for erosion control in the 1940s-50s: "You see, the hills have been overgrazed by the livestock so badly that nothing was left there except dirt that goes running down every time it rained. So they went in and made them there great big ditches all the way around them hillsides and divided them into little sections so the water wouldn't run off." (690~)

Abajo Peak: (San Juan Co.) Manti-LaSal National Forest-Abajo Mountains. Abajo Peak map. (11,360')

Also called Shay Mountain. (494~, 1822~)

(See Abajo Mountains for name derivation.)

Abajo Peak is the highest summit in the Abajo Mountains. Ferdinand V. Hayden of the Hayden Survey of 1876: "The view from the summit is one of more than ordinary interest, since within the circle of vision there is much that has never passed beneath the explorer's eye.... This vast area lies beneath us a silent desert, a plateau land cut by innumerable waterless cañons, and dotted with a thousand fancifully carved and brilliantly colored rocks." (849~)

—Mining Road: The road across the top of the peak was built in the 1890s to service the Gold Basin ore mill. It was improved in 1956 for the construction of a short-wave relay radio tower. (1407~, 1913~)

—East Mountain: This is one mile south of Abajo Peak (at elevation 11034). (2036~)

Abes Knoll: (Wayne Co.) Parker Mountain-Hatch Canyon. Abes Knoll map. (8,465')

Dee Hatch and Max Robinson noted that sheepman Abe Hansen camped near the knoll in the late 1800s. (844~, 1641~)

Abraham: (Washington Co.) Zion National Park-Court of the Patriarchs. Springdale East map. (6,990')

(See Court of the Patriarchs for name derivation.)

This is the tallest of the Three Patriarchs.

Acklin Peak: (Wayne Co.) Capitol Reef National Park-South Desert. Cathedral Mountain map.

Correctly spelled Akelund Peak.

Guy Pace noted that Peter Akelund (1858-1931) ran livestock in this area in the early days. (1497~)

—Constructed Stock Trail: This went up the cliffs to the east of Acklin Peak (at elevation 6526). Although signs of the trail are gone, the route can still be followed. Guy Pace quoted his father, James M. Pace, as saying: "I promised the Lord that I'd never do it again!" (1497~) Guy told of having to hack steps into the cliff to provide footing for the livestock. (1497~, 582~, SAPE.)

Acord Lakes: (Sevier Co.) Fishlake National Forest-Old Woman Plateau. Acord Lakes map.

Two name derivations are given.

First, Valentine Lewis Acord (1832-1922) settled in Castle Valley in 1875. (1641~)

Second, Barbara Ekker noted that Abraham Acord and sons Fred, Henry, and Oliver ran cattle in the area and in the San Rafael Swell starting in 1877. (606~, 1188~)

Adahchijiyanhi Canyon: (Navajo Co., Az.) Navajo Indian Reservation-Tyende Mesa-Oljeto Wash. Keet Seel Ruin and Tseyi-Hatsosi, Az. maps.

Also called Duggagei. (499~)

Laurance D. Linford noted that *Adah Ch'íjíyáhí* is Navajo for "where she fell from the cliff." (1204~) Francis Gillmor expanded on the story, telling of how Kit Carson chased the Navajo off of their tribal lands in 1863–64: "Back into the canyons they moved—the women and the children and the sheep going ahead over the rocky ridges, the men following, walking backward, and brushing out their tracks with the boughs of trees where there was sand on the trail. It was then that my mother's sister fell from the cliff.... It was night and she was running. She had seen a campfire out on the flat." (726~)

Adah Hiilini: (Coconino Co., Az. and San Juan Co., Utah.) Navajo Indian Reservation-Rainbow Plateau. Arizona map: Face Canyon. Utah map: Gregory Butte. (5,780')

Two similar name derivations are given.

First, *Adahiilíní* is Navajo for both "to flow and fall downward" and for a "waterfall" or "cascade." (2072~)

Second, Jesse C. Dyer of the USGS noted that *Adah Hiilíní* is Navajo for "waterfall ridge." (588~)

Charles L. Bernheimer named this Helen and Alice Mesa in honor of his daughters in 1921. (221~, 467~) Bernheimer, though, perhaps initially had another name in mind. From his Diary of 1921: "These series of mesas and buttes are reaching back on the south side of Sirocco

Pass [Sei Biibikoon]. The mesas lining its north rim we called [Sims—now scratched out] Helen and Alice mesas in honor of [Admiral Sims—now scratched out] our two daughters." (218~)

—Constructed Stock Trail: This goes along the east side of the buttes. (SAPE.)

Adair Hollow: (Kane Co.) Dixie National Forest-Markagunt Plateau-Pink Cliffs-Swains Creek. Strawberry Point map.

George Adair (1837-1909) had a ranch in nearby Swallow Park in the early years. Charles Kelly in 1953: "The man [Frederick S. Dellenbaugh of the Powell Survey] mentions who was a walking arsenal ... was undoubtedly George W. Adair, who had been a participant in the Mountain Meadows Massacre. He was reputed to be a tough hombre." (1061~)

Adairville: (Kane Co.) GSCENM-Paria River. West Clark Bench map. PRIVATE PROPERTY.

Also called Mace Ranch (479~), Middle Settlement (1475~), and Middletown (1599~).

Peter Shirts started a small settlement at nearby Rock House Cove in 1865. (See Rock House Cove.) Shirts and the other settlers were forced out by water problems in 1872. The town divided. One group went south with their leader, Thomas Jefferson Adair (1814-1890), and established the town of Adairville. The other group went north and established the town of Paria. By 1885 flooding forced the abandonment of Adairville. (275~, 346~, 470~, 1639~)

Stan Jones found an inscription on a gravestone near Adairville reading "Emma A., wife of J.H. Goodrich, born Jan. 11, 1845, died March 24, 1876." Jones noted that it was the only "vestige I have ever found of anything having to do with Adairville." (1022~)

Ranchers have continued to own and use the Adairville townsite. In the 1920s it was owned by Jim Tergerson. (670~) Stan Jones mentioned that Charles Hepworth owned the site in the 1970s. (1022~)

—Cottonwood Creek: Adairville is located on this small drainage. George G. Mace: "Named from the cottonwood trees found along the stream." (2053~)

—Swapp Ranch: This was two miles south of Adairville on the Paria River (at elevation 4345). (425~)

Adams Butte: (Wayne Co.) Henry Mountains-Dry Valley. Bull Mountain map. (5,080')

Guy Robison noted that the Adams family lived one-quarter mile east of the butte for many years. Several buildings still stand. (1644~, SAPE.)

Adams Canyon: (Iron Co.) Cedar Breaks National Monument-Mammoth Summit-Ashdown Creek. Brian Head map.

Hugh L. Adams (1853-1905) and family, including sons Billy R., Hugh L., and James L. were early settlers of Parowan. They had a summer ranch near Mammoth Summit. (516~)

Adams Head: (Garfield Co.) Dixie National Forest-Sevier Plateau. Adams Head map. (10,426')

Also called Adams Head Peak.

Kate B. Carter: "It was named for a Mr. Adams who used it as a lookout to watch and warn the white men of Indian attacks." (384~) The name was in place by 1879. (M.24.)

Adams Hollow: (Iron Co.) Kolob Terrace-West Fork Deep Creek. Webster Flat map.

Frank B. Adams (1868-1947), an early resident of Cedar City, had a coal mine in nearby Coal Creek. (1012~)

Adams Reservoir: (Kane Co.) Paria Canyon-Vermilion Cliffs Wilderness Area-The Cockscomb-Coyote Wash. Pine Hollow Canyon map.

This is a still-used stock reservoir. Horse and sheep corrals are nearby. (SAPE.)

Cal Johnson: "Johnny Adams had cattle all through this country years ago, in the late 1800s or early 1900s. He was there until the 1930s. He built a little pond there. He ran livestock all over the Sand Hills and down to Coyote Buttes. (See Joes Tank.) Then Trevor Leach and his dad, they had goats, got it. Then they sold it to the Northcuts." (984~)

Adams Spring: (Kane Co.) GSCENM-Park Wash. Deer Spring Point map.

This is a large, developed spring. (SAPE.)

Three name derivations are given.

First, Cal Johnson: "Old man Adams, he ran cattle up at the Swallow Park Ranch. Adams Spring is right underneath the ranch. He just lived with his cattle. That was just about in the 1870s or 1880s." (984~) This was Merle V. "Cowhide" Adams (1899-1988). He ran livestock on the Clark Benches all of his adult life. (1931~)

Second, Azra Adams (1864-1942) was one of John G. Kitchen's favorite cowboys in the 1880s-90s. Kitchen: "The best workman in the world." (1638~)

Third, George Adams (1886-1945) of Kanab bought the nearby Swallow Park Ranch in the early 1900s. (1083~, 1639~)

Adeiyi Taah Hooti: (San Juan Co., Utah and Coconino Co., Az.) Navajo Indian Reservation-Rainbow Plateau. Utah map: Gregory Butte. Arizona map: Face Canyon. (5,570')

Jesse C. Dyer of the USGS noted that *Adeiyí Taah Hóót'í* is Navajo for "ridge extending into water." (588~)

Charles L. Bernheimer called this Claras Mesa in honor of his wife. (221~, 467~) In his Diary of 1921, though, Bernheimer perhaps initially had a different name in mind: "We traveled in a southernly direction over sand flats, down washes in loose sand, knee-high along the westerly sides of the mesas which we called [Marsh—scratched out in diary] Clara's Mesas in honor of [Gen. Marsh, the chief of staff during the war—scratched out in diary] you." (218~)

Adobe Mesa: (Grand Co.) La Sal Mountains-Richardson Amphitheater. Fisher Towers and Warner Lake maps.

Also called Dobe Mesa.

Doby Brown ran livestock here for a couple of months in 1882. (1741~)

Adobe Swale: (Garfield Co.) Burr Desert-Poison Springs Canyon. Burr Point and Baking Skillet Knoll maps.

Barbara Ekker noted that a man named Doby or Dobbie ran sheep here in the early days. (606~)

—Adobe Swale Reservoir: (Burr Point map.) Alvin Robison noted that this stock pond in upper Adobe Swale was built by the CCC. (1642~)

Agate Wash: (Grand Co.) Grand Valley-Colorado River. Agate and Big Triangle maps.

Agates are found in the area. (1979~)

—Rose Ranch: (Also called Hallet Ranch.) (518~) PRIVATE PROPERTY. This was on the west side of the mouth of Agate Wash at the Colorado River (Big Triangle map). Charlie and Chloe Hallet moved to Westwater in 1892 and to the Rose Ranch in 1898. The Rose family were later owners of the ranch. (198~, 1362~, 1363~)

—Agate: (Agate map.) (Also called Agate Siding.) (347~) This was a water stop on the Denver and Rio Grande Western Railroad in the late 1800s. (1362~) (See Denver and Rio Grande Western Railroad.)

Agathla Peak: (San Juan Co.) Navajo Indian Reservation-Monument Valley. Agathla Peak map. (7,096')

Also called Agathla Needle (154~), Big Capitan (985~), The Captain (1058~, 1204~), Lava Negra (980~), and Sierra Captain (2060~).

Also spelled Agathlan Peak, Agath-sla Peak, and Algothla Peak.

Richard Van Valkenburgh, quoting Navajo Sam Jim in 1940: "We Navajos call this rock, *agalah*, much-piled-wool. It was made when the World was set on fire by

Coyote in the Holy Days. The name refers to the scraping of deer hides here by the old people." (1942~)

Robert de Roos elaborated on the story in 1965: "In the very early days, the Indians gathered at Agathlan to scrape the hides of antelope and deer. The hair, blown by the wind, adhered to the grasses and when the game animals ate the grass they died. Some wise old chief promulgated a practical blue law and dressed it up with a little romance: all the scraped hair should be placed under heavy rocks so that it would not blow away. Then, the myth promised the scraped skin would serve him well—as long as the hair remained in place under the rock." (556a~)

James H. Knipmeyer noted that an expedition led by Jose Antonio Vizcarra in 1823 traveled into Navajo country. A detachment of the expedition, led by Colonel Francisco Salazar, called it *Cerro Elevado*. (309~, 1105~)

Richard Van Valkenburg noted that Captain John Walker, while chasing a Navajo war party in 1858, named it *El Capitan*. (1942~)

It was also mentioned as *El Capitan* by Hole-in-the-Rock Expedition diarist George B. Hobbs. He saw it from the vicinity of Salvation Knoll on Cedar Mesa in 1879. (1356~)

Byron Cummings: "The Agathla Needle raises its sharp pointed crest of dark volcanic rock 1200 feet above you as you pause in its shadow and feel yourself a mere speck in this vast expanse of earth and sky." (504~)

Billie Williams Yost: "It was a place where everyone gathered. The Indians used to take their deer hides there and soak them in the bitter water, and thus they could remove the hair in a few days, making it easier to make buckskin." (2060~)

Douglas Preston: "Agathla is believed to lie at the geographical center of the [Navajo] world, and it is one of the Sun Pillars which First Woman and First Man set into place to hold up the sky." (1573~)

—First ascent: Hugh Cutler: "I climbed Agathla in 1937. Hopis climbed it to get eagle feathers—I climbed along." (512~) The first documented ascent was by Ray Garner, Jan and Herb Conn, and Lee Pedrick in 1949. (160a~, 706~)

Ahidiilini: (Coconino Co., Az.) Navajo Indian Reservation-Glen Canyon NRA-Navajo Creek. Cedar Tree Bench, Az. map.

'Ahidiilí is Navajo for a "joining of two streams," in this case, the confluence of Navajo and Kaibito creeks. (2072~)

The Domínguez-Escalante Expedition crossed Navajo Canyon at this juncture on November 11, 1776. (1944~)

The Antonio Armijo Expedition of 1829–30 camped here, "at the *Pichacho* [Peak] Springs." (69~, 805~, 855a~)

The Charles L. Bernheimer Expedition of 1921 also camped here. Bernheimer: "Because of a kingbird's nest in a niche above us I called it Kingbird Camp." (221~)

—Lower Crossing: The Navajo's Lower Crossing of Navajo Creek is at Ahidiilini. (1204~) (See Navajo Canyon—Coconino Co., Az.—Main Crossing.)

Ahlstrom Hollow: (Garfield Co.) Dixie National Forest-Paunsaugunt Plateau-East Fork Sevier River. Wilson Peak and Bryce Canyon maps.

Also spelled Alstrom. (1931~)

Maurice Newton Cope called this Ole Hollow for Ole Ahlstrom (1864-1948) in about 1900: "We arrived at Ole Hollow, made camp in an old shack and the next morning we had three feet of snow. We had 300 head of sheep die." (453~)

Airplane Spring: (Garfield Co.) Henry Mountains-The Horn. Mt. Ellen map.

A brass plaque at the spring tells the story: "So named after Col. Lorin Lavar Johnson of Payson, UT and S/Sgt Billy J. Nash of Utica, OK who died in a military air crash on Nov. 30, 1950 at a site approx. 400 yds. N.E. of this monument. Col. Johnson flew 37 combat missions over the English Channel in WWII." (1551~)

Airport Tower: (San Juan Co.) Canyonlands National Park-Island in the Sky District-White Rim. Musselman Arch map. (5,812')

Also called Square-mile Butte. (1435~)

Two name derivations are given.

First, the USGS: "So named because the rock formation gives the appearance of an airport control tower." (1931~)

Second, James H. Knipmeyer: "I can't recall all of the details on this, but on a scientific survey trip I took with the NPS [National Park Service] and GCES [Grand Canyon Environmental Services] in 1993, our guide told a story about some dare-devil pilot in the '50s or '60s (maybe Jim Hurst?) actually landing a little single-engine plane on top of the butte"! (1115~)

Aladdins Lamp Pass: (San Juan Co.) Glen Canyon NRA-Wilson Mesa. Wilson Creek map.

Also called Little Mesa (1356~) and Rabbit Ears Pass (218~).

Frank E. Masland, Jr. suggested the name in 1962: "We offer the name 'Aladdins Lamp Pass' for the pass that leads from 'Brother Lyman Canyon' on to the flat from which one drops into Wilson Creek Canyon. It is an interesting Pass, made doubly so by a solid rock that stands out clearly against the sky and that bears a striking resemblance to Aladdin's Lamp. This formation marks a pass that leads to some of the finest viewpoints between the San Juan and the Colorado." (1931~)

In early December 1879 Hole-in-the-Rock Expedition member Platte D. Lyman traversed the area from Aladdins Lamp Pass to the top of Grey Mesa while on a scouting mission: "The country here is almost entirely solid sand rock, high hills and mountains cut all to pieces by deep gulches which are in many places altogether impassable. It is certainly the worst country I ever saw." (1259~, 1356~)

Albinus Canyon: (Sevier Co.) Fishlake National Forest-Pavant Range-Sevier River. Elsinore map.

Albinus Johnson was an Elsinore pioneer. (954~)

Alcove Canyon: (San Juan Co.) Glen Canyon NRA-San Juan River. Alcove Canyon map.

Hugh D. Miser of the Kelly W. Trimble USGS Expedition of 1921 hiked up the canyon: "No trails or other signs were found to indicated that it had been previously visited by man. Its picturesqueness is most impressive and equals or surpasses the beauty of the canyon in which the famous Rainbow Natural Bridge is located. Its sandstone walls, with their buff, brown, and red colors, are as smooth as the gray granite walls of the Yosemite, and they terminate upward in gigantic rock domes which tower higher than the Washington Monument. Yet they are dented with several alcoves—some with rounded walls like the upper interior walls of a huge hollow sphere and some with straight back walls and arched roofs. To their walls there cling sparse ferns and lichens, which are fed by seeps. Rivulets leap from the rim of the canyon and join the water from springs to form a small, clear stream which runs on the rough, rocky canyon floor. The water supply maintains abundant cedars, cottonwoods, scrub oaks, grasses, and flowers. This canyon is here named Alcove Canyon." (1370~)

Randall Henderson identified this as Nevills Canyon in 1945. Before his death in 1949, guide Norman D. Nevills (1908-1949) took many tourist parties down the San Juan River. (860~)

Weldon F. Heald in 1948: "Here a miniature fall drops over a cliff into a pool banked with ferns and shaded by willow, box elder, and redbud." (1521~)

—Constructed Stock Trail: Before Lake Powell, the Navajo would cross the river with their animals and go up a constructed stock trail into the canyon. (472~) The trail does not continue up and out of the canyon. (SAPE.)

—East Alcove Canyon: This is the first canyon to the east of Alcove Canyon.

—Nevills Spring: The spring, now underwater, was on the north side of the San Juan River one-quarter mile east of the mouth of East Alcove Canyon. C. Gregory Crampton: "The spring has been named after river man Norman D. Nevills." (472~)

Alcove Spring: (San Juan Co.) Canyonlands National Park-Island in the Sky District-Trail Canyon. Upheaval Dome map.

This medium-large spring is in an alcove. (SAPE.)

—Constructed Stock Trail: This goes from the rim to the spring and then on down Trail Canyon. (SAPE.)

Aldys Hole: (Emery Co.) San Rafael Swell-The Wedge. Bob Hill Knoll map.

This is a set of medium-size potholes. (SAPE.)

Alex Spring: (Wayne Co.) Fishlake National Forest-Thousand Lake Mountain. Flat Top map.

Guy Pace noted that Alexander Smith Coleman ranched here in the early years. (1497~)

Alger Gulch: (Washington Co.) Dixie National Forest-Pine Valley Mountains-Diamond Valley. Saddle Mountain map.

John Alger (1829–1897) cut timber in the area starting in the 1860s. (803~, 887~)

Alhambra Rock: (San Juan Co.) Navajo Indian Reservation-San Juan River. The Goosenecks map. (4,849')

This dike of igneous rock was named by Herbert E. Gregory of the USGS in 1915. (101~, 1931~) Donald L. Baars noted that Alhambra was the name of a Moorish castle in Spain. (86~)

Alkali Lake: (Wayne Co.) Dixie National Forest-Boulder Mountain-Sam Legg Hollow. Government Point map.

Don Orton in 1941: "So named for the high alkaline content of the water." (2053~)

Alkali Point: (San Juan Co.) Abajo Mountains-Blanding. Bradford Canyon, Devil Mesa, Blanding South, and Blanding North maps.

Also called Alkali Mesa and Alkali Ridge. (279~)

Archaeologist John Otis Brew: "Presumably, because of the abundance of springs giving forth clear 'mountain water,' despite the name Alkali, it presents a surprisingly large number of prehistoric sites." (279~)

Alkali Ridge was heavily occupied by the Anasazi Indians. Because of this, there is one area that is designated as the Alkali Ridge National Historic Landmark. The site has been called "one of the most significant archeological sites of southwestern United States." The first archaeological survey of substance was done by Alfred V. Kidder, Neil M. Judd, Clifton Lockhart, and Byron Cummings in the summer of 1908. (505~) Cummings: "Alkali Ridge is a sandy rise of ground covered with cedar and piñon and an occasional open park of grass." (498~)

The Peabody Museum of American Archeology and Ethnology at Harvard University excavated many sites on the ridge in the early 1930s. (41~)

—Rustler Canyon: This northern tributary of Alkali Canyon is immediately west of the north end of Alkali Point (between elevations 6158T and 6167T on the Devil Mesa map). (279~)

—Blacks Ranch: (Also called Black Cabin.) This was at the north end of Alkali Point (near elevation 6321T on the Devil Mesa map). (279~)

All American Man: (San Juan Co.) Canyonlands National Park-Needles District-Salt Creek. South Six-shooter Peak map.

This well-known and absolutely amazing pictograph of a red-, white-, and blue-clad figure was named by a group of Explorer Scouts led by Canyonlands National Park Superintendent Bates Wilson in 1953. The panel dates between AD 1260 and AD 1400. (1381~, 1429~, SAPE.)

Allen Canyon: (San Juan Co.) Manti-LaSal National Forest-Ute Mountain Ute Indian Reservation-Abajo Mountains-Cottonwood Wash. Mount Linnaeus, Chippean Rocks, and Cream Pots maps. Most of this canyon is PRIVATE PROPERTY.

Correctly spelled Allan Canyon.

John and Peter Allan moved their families to the mouth of the canyon in 1887 at the behest of Bishop Francis A. Hammond to help stop the encroachment of large non-Mormon cattle herds. (1406~)

Warren K. Moorehead of the Illustrated American Exploring Expedition of 1892: "It is a wild and desolate valley, bordered by weathered cliffs, whose tops are sparsely covered with stunted piñons and cedars." (1383~)

Eugene Traughber in 1894: "Cliffs and peaks of pink, vermilion, brown, white, and yellow, rising in ledges and breaking into tier above tier, story above story, with intervening slopes covered with talus, the walls recessed with large amphitheaters, buttressed with huge spurs and decorated with towers and pinnacles, form the sides of Allen Canon and make it at once one of the grandest bits of sublime scenery of the Grand Canyon district." (1904~)

The Writers' Program of 1941: "Allen Canyon, a characteristic plateau fantasia of mesas, columns, and whorled abutments in the inevitable red sandstone, in prehistoric times sheltered a large Cliff-Dweller suburb; in historic times a band of Paiutes, who steadfastly refused to be removed to other reservations, were allotted farming lands in the canyon." (2056~)

These were the Allen Canyon Indians. Gregory C. Thompson: "The Piute village at Allen Canyon is one of the oldest settlements in Utah. Water, patches of rich soil, protection from wind, house sites in canyon walls, and adjoining hunting grounds made it [Allen Canyon Country] a desirable spot for Basket Makers and Cliff Dwellers. The Piutes and Utes found the stream flats suitable for planting corn, and early white settlers were attracted by the pasturage and the favorable conditions for small-scale irrigation. The obvious injustice of taking from the Indians land which they had used continuously for many generations led to the present arrangement; the agricultural land in Hammond, Cottonwood, and Allen Canyons and in Dry Wash is allotted to the Indians; the other lands in the Allen Canyon Country form part of the [Manti-LaSal] national forest, in which the Indians have preferential grazing rights." (774~)

Thompson again: "The Allen Canyon Indians represented all that was left of the Ute and Paiute groups that had existed in the county at an earlier time. Because it was so hard to get their children to school in Blanding and to transport supplies to their homes in Allen Canyon, people began to move closer to town. Over a period of time the community resettled on White Mesa south of Blanding." (1563~, 1526~)

Land ownership, consisting of 8,360 acres, in Allen and Cottonwood canyons wasgranted to the Paiute and Ute Indians in 1923. At present, parts of these canyons are closed to the public.

Inscriptions include Charles B. Lang, a member of the Hyde Exploring Expedition of 1893–94. (249~)

—Allen Canyon Country: This was the local name for the country defined by Allen Canyon, upper Cottonwood Wash, Dry Wash, and Hammond Canyon. Since some of this country was included in the Paiute Reservation, it was also called Paiute Basin or Paiute Park. (1931~)

—Allen Canyon Ute Cemetery: PRIVATE PROPERTY. This is the "CEM" in Cottonwood Wash one mile downcanyon from the mouth of Allen Canyon on the Cream Pots map.

—Beehives: This slickrock dome is on the east side of Allen Canyon two miles north of its mouth at Cottonwood Wash (at elevation 6386T on the Cream Pots map). (774~) It is shaped like a beehive with many small openings. The name has been in use from the late 1800s. (260~)

Allen Canyon: (San Juan Co.) Navajo Indian Reservation-Cajon Mesa-San Juan River. Navajo Canyon, Aneth, and White Mesa Village maps.

—Allans Bottom: This is at the mouth of Allen Canyon on the San Juan River (White Mesa Village map). A man named Allan settled here in 1879. Kumen Jones of the San Juan Exploring Expedition of 1879: "The company traveled 3 miles and camped on the San Juan river [at Allan Bottom]. Here they found six men who were making farms." (1356~) One of those men was John Brewer, giving the bottom another name: Brewer Bottom.

Allen Creek: (Garfield Co.) Dixie National Forest-Escalante Mountains-Upper Valley Creek. Upper Valley map.

—Allen Ranch: Pratt Gates noted that Philo Allen, Sr. (1818-1909) and family had a ranch at the mouth of Allen Creek on Upper Valley Creek. (709~) (See Allen Dump.)

—Lee Ranch: This was on the south side of Upper Valley Creek one mile downcanyon from the Allen Ranch (one-quarter mile south of elevation 6680 on the Upper Valley map). (1931~)

Allen Dump: (Garfield Co.) GSCENM-Glen Canyon NRA-Escalante Desert-Escalante River. Egypt, Red Breaks, and Sunset Flat maps.

Philo Allen, Sr. (1818–1909) is credited with bringing the first cattle into the area, in 1875. Before moving his family to Utah he was a bodyguard for the Mormon prophet Joseph Smith. (47~, 2051~)

C. Gregory Crampton: "The word 'dump' is occasionally heard in the canyon country and appears to signify a steep slope over which one must pass to reach a given destination." (471~)

Allen Well Draw: (Garfield Co.) Dixie National Forest-Awapa Plateau-Pelham Hollow. Big Lake map.

Alfonzo Turner: "That was Paul Allen. He used to work for Frank Neff. He dug that out in there for camp water. It would yield a little water in the spring with the snow melt, but it was never able to hold much water in the summer." (1914~)

Dunk Taylor: "Allen Well was a place where the sheepherders dug down and found a lot of water. And after all of the sheepherders left the country, we went in there with a Cat and right where the well was we built a big pond and it's never went dry." (1865~)

Allred Point: (Wayne Co.) Rabbit Valley-Spring Creek. Loa map. (7,247')

Also called Jack Allred Point (1188~) and Jacks Point (1734~).

Andrew Jackson "Jack" Allred (1831-1899) and family moved to the Loa area in 1876 to start a trading post at the behest of Brigham Young. After building a home near the Fremont River, the family was forced to move after the river flooded. Their new home was on Allred Point. (378~)

—Morrell Grave: This grave, marked on the map, has a plaque that reads: "Silas Warren Morrell. Died in the millrace when he was about nine months old." (1551~)

Alstrom Point: (Kane Co.) Glen Canyon NRA-Glen Canyon. Gunsight Butte and Warm Creek Bay maps. (4,580') The Alstrom (Ahlstrom?) family had a ranch at the old settlement of Paria into the early 1900s. They ran cattle on the point. (1599~)

Altar of Sacrifice: (Washington Co.) Zion National Park-Towers of the Virgin. Springdale West map. (7,505')

Also called Altar of Sacrifice Temple (1931~) and Birch Creek Peak (481~).

Eivind T. Scoyen noted that Dr. Frederick Vining Fischer named this monolith in about 1911. Scoyen: "Alter of Sacrifice, whose stains suggest barbarian atonements." (1710~)

Leo A. Borah in 1936: "I almost shuddered at sight of the Altar of Sacrifice with its realistic blood-red stains, and the superstition of the Indians, who feared to enter the canyon after nightfall, became understandable." (262~)

Alton Town: (Kane Co.) Kanab Creek-Alton Amphitheater. Alton map.

The town, an outgrowth of the small settlements of Upper Kanab, Sink Valley, and Ranch was started in 1901 by Jonathan Heaton on a piece of ground that he owned and that he called Oak Flat. Kate B. Carter noted that the town was initially called Graham for early settler Graham Duncan McDonald. (357~, 1819~) (See McDonald Canyon.)

The town was not officially named until 1908. Adonis Findlay Robinson: "Various names were suggested and discussed: Heatonville, Oaktown, Snowville, Klondyke. Charles R. Pugh … had been reading a book about the Alton Fjord in Norway, noted for its altitude. The name seemed appropriate for the new community, with its 7200-foot altitude, so he put it in the hat. A two-year old child … was allowed to draw a name from the hat, and Alton was the name drawn." (1639~, 349~, 712~, 1187~)

—Upper Kanab: PRIVATE PROPERTY. (Also called Canaan Ranch, Rounds Ranch, Roundy Ranch, Roundys Station, Upper Kanab Ranch, Vermillion Park, and Woolley Ranch.)

This small town was three miles northeast of Alton at the junction of Kanab Creek and Dry Canyon. It was initially settled by Lorenzo Wesley Roundy in 1865. Indian trouble forced abandonment a year later. The town was reestablished in 1872 when Roundy's nephew, Byron Roundy, and family moved in. In about 1873 the Mormon Church-owned Canaan Cooperative Cattle Company moved to the area after buying out most of the smaller ranches. The Roundys refused to sell, forcing the Canaan Cooperative to split their holdings. One part of the ranch was just upcanyon from the Roundy Ranch. The other part was two miles down Kanab Creek.

Others followed. In 1882 Edwin Dilworth Woolley and family moved to Upper Kanab to take charge of the Canaan Cooperative Ranch. This was called, simply, The Ranch (also called West Graham). Edwin's daughter, Mary Woolley Chamberlain: "The house was built on a side-hill commanding a wonderful view of the valley with the Pink Cliffs in the distance. The Pink Cliffs are of the same formation as Bryce's Canyon being a continuation of it, although at this time Bryce's was unknown to white man. We loved it from the beginning and that love increased as the years passed by. In the summer when it rained the water that ran down from these cliffs was as pink as they." (415~, 346~)

Woolley sold the ranch to Dan Seegmiller in 1889. By 1925 the town had been abandoned. (1716~) This is now a private ranch.

—Alton Amphitheater: This name was added to the map by USGS surveyors in the 1960s. Until that time the name was unknown to locals. (1931~)

—Smirl Mine: This coal mine is two miles south of Alton (one-half mile south-southwest of elevation 6873). For many years the mine produced most of the coal in Kane County. A fire in the mine forced closure in 1961. (743~)

—Alton Coal Field: The Alton area contains a vast amount of coal, a fact that was recognized by early settlers. Philip Klingensmith in a letter to Brigham Young in 1864: "While going down the kanyon we discovered a load of stove coal of a very excellent quality some 5 foot thick.... Brother James Williamson says it best appearance for a rich mine of any that he ever saw." (91~) From time to time—into the present—development schemes surface for mining the coal and/or building a coal powered power plant here.

Alumbed Hollow: (Sevier Co.) Fishlake National Forest-Wasatch Plateau-Salina Creek. Steves Mountain map.
Ezlan Jackman in 1942: "So named because of the small spring of alum water that springs up in the canyon and runs to the mouth of the canyon." (2053~)

Alum Cove: (Iron Co.) Dixie National Forest-Hurricane Cliffs-First Left Hand Canyon. Parowan map.
In the early days William Adams and sons gathered copper nodules and alum in the canyon. (381~)

Alunite Ridge: (Piute Co.) Fishlake National Forest-Tushar Mountains. Mount Brigham and Delano Peak maps.
In 1910 prospector Tom Gillen discovered a strange "pink spar" ore along the ridge. He sent a sample to the USGS. They determined that it was alunite, or potash, an ingredient in some fertilizers. This was the beginning of the Mineral Products Corporation, which started actively mining alunite in 1915. Tunnels were bored and a six thousand foot tramway was built that took ore eighteen hundred feet down the mountain where it was loaded on wagons and taken to the railroad at Marysvale. The mine shut down in late 1920. (332~, 333~)

Alunite Town: (Piute Co.) Sevier River-Cottonwood Creek. Marysvale map. PRIVATE PROPERTY.
This is the location of a mine that produced alunite. (323~, 1444~) (See Alunite Ridge.)

—Boltenheim Town: PRIVATE PROPERTY. (Also spelled Boltonheim.) (M.24.) This small town was two miles east-northeast of Alunite (near elevation 6186). It was started by a group of ranchers from Quebec in 1878. Curtis E. Bolton was an early resident. (1194~)

Alvey Wash: (Garfield Co.) GSCENM-Kaiparowits Plateau-Escalante Desert-Harris Wash. Death Ridge, Carcass Canyon, Dave Canyon, Canaan Creek, Escalante, and Tenmile Flat maps.
Also called Alveys Wash (1931~) and Cottonwood Wash (798~).
Alvey Wash is the upper end of Harris Wash. The dividing line is Tenmile Spring (Tenmile Flat map). (See Harris Wash.)
Escalante history teacher Edson Alvey: "Named for the Alvey brothers (Aaron, Samuel, and William) who grazed livestock there in the early days of Escalante." (55~)
Inscriptions include John Holtby, 8-21-09; P. Porter and E. Shurts, Oct. 29. 1910; Arnold Alvey, April 9, 1911; Lamon Griffin, April 2, 1924; and Layton Griffin, 5-27-44. (SAPE.)

—Kirchibal Coal Mine: This is in the western tributary of Alvey Wash that is one and one-half miles south of Coal Bed Canyon (north of elevation 6745 on the Canaan Creek map). (1931~)

—Covered Wagon Natural Bridge: This is in a western tributary of Alvey Wash that is one-quarter mile south of elevation 5675 on the Dave Canyon map. The bridge is one-quarter mile south of elevation 5765. Edson Alvey, who discovered the arch in the 1930s while herding sheep, named the bridge for the covered wagons used as shelter by sheepherders. (55~, 1956~)

—Cedar Wash Arch: This is in a western tributary of Alvey Wash that is immediately north of elevation 5491 on the Dave Canyon map. The arch is one-quarter mile southwest of elevation 5782. Robert H. Vreeland noted that it was initially named Shepherd Arch by Edson Alvey in 1932. (1956~)

Amasa Back: (Grand Co.) Colorado River-Potash. Gold Bar Canyon map.

Lloyd Holyoak noted that Amasa (also spelled Amasy) Larson ran cattle in the area starting in the 1880s. (906~)

Otho Murphy: "Amasa's Back ... was named for Amasa Larson, who aside from having run his cattle there, had a long back in proportion to the rest of his body and stood and walked in a humped position." (1420~)

Anasazi Canyon: (San Juan Co.) Navajo Indian Reservation-Glen Canyon NRA-Glen Canyon. Rainbow Bridge and Nasja Mesa maps.

Art Greene noted that Indians call this Face Canyon. (756~)

In the 1920s Norm Nevills called it Mystery Canyon. A pour-off near the mouth of the canyon contained a row of worn Moqui steps that Nevills unsuccessfully tried to climb, thus making the upper canyon a mystery. (93~, 869~)

Frank E. Masland, Jr. and Otis "Dock" Marston noted that Anasazi ruins were found in the canyon. (1931~) Marston and famed Grand Canyon explorer Harvey Butchart are credited with being the first Euroamericans into the canyon. They flew to the rim in a helicopter and used ropes to descend the canyon walls. (1917~)

Randall Henderson in 1945: "At one point a huge block of stone had fallen from above, forming a tunnel through which our boats passed. From the end of our waterway we walked 300 yards to a great domed room somewhat after the pattern of Music Temple. Here was a clear deep pool in a luxurious garden of maidenhair ferns and columbines." (860~)

Lil Diemler in 1946: "This is one of the most beautiful spots of the whole trip. We rowed thru a complete stone arch just wide enough to take the boat thru. The walls where we ate are wet from springs and covered with Maiden Hair fern and in season with columbine and pinks. There is a large pool for swimming and cold water for drinking." (557~)

Helen Kendall in 1948: "Walked back along the smooth rock canyon floor to a spot where cliff dwellers had cut steps part way up the almost perpendicular cliff. These steps, worn by time, were barely deep enough for the toe of a shoe, with nothing to hang onto along the sides, just granite-like 'slick rock' everywhere. Norman Nevills climbed up as far as he could, carrying a rope with him. Then Paul Seel climbed up to where Norman was. They then hung on like a couple of spiders." (1086~)

Inscriptions at the mouth of the canyon, before inundation, included W.H. Bush, E. Coe, E. Howard, C.W. Potter, and G.A. Sutherland, 7/14/89. All were members of the Stanton-Brown Survey of the Colorado River in 1889. (1105~)

—Constructed Stock Trail: This enters the north side of Anasazi Canyon one-quarter mile from its head (Rainbow Bridge map). (SAPE.)

—Twin Bridges: Two spectacular natural bridges were covered by the rising waters of Lake Powell. They re-emerged during the drought years of the early 2000s. Fran A. Barnes: "A pair of lovely and unique bridges cut from the monolithic sandstone of a narrow branch of Mystery Canyon now can only be viewed by the carp that proliferate in such stagnant-water side canyons of the lake." (140~)

—Rhapsody Canyon: Playing off the name of nearby Music Temple, canyoneers have used this name for the first canyon to the north of Anasazi Canyon (between elevations 3992T and 4410T on the Nasja Mesa map). (SAPE.)

Anderson Bottom: (Wayne Co.) Canyonlands National Park-Maze District-Stillwater Canyon. Cleopatras Chair map.

Also called Lower Park, Standing Rock Park, Townsite Bottom, Townsite Flat, and Town Sight Flat.

Oilman Albert Isaac Anderson (aka A.S. Anderson) entered the area in 1908 and settled on the bottom in 1910. He and his family (some say it was just Anderson and his daughter) spent a couple of years here growing crops and living in a tent. They were apparently trying to establish a town. They abandoned the bottom in 1911. One can still find the ditch Anderson built to help grow sugar cane and vegetables. In the 1950s rancher Karl Tangren built a ferry from the lower end of Queen Anne Bottom to the upper end of Anderson Bottom. (435~, 1085~, 1115~, 1734~, 1975~, SAPE.)

Charles Cutler Sharp in 1909: "a big bottom a few miles below the [Butte of the] Cross that is claimed by two Green River men who had been trying to dry farm a little during the summer. The bottom is not over ten feet above the water in the river and has as fine rich soil as there could be found anyplace.... The bottom contained several hundred acres of level land and was surrounded by the most beautiful scenery and attracted everybody that chanced to pass by." (1720~)

Inscriptions include E. Taylor, June 10, 1910, Moab Utah; Sid Wilson, 7/14/11; A.J. Tadje, Moving Pictures, Oct. 11-1914; Gib Allred and Sog Allred of Moab, 1926; and Pathe-Bray Colorado Expedition, 1927. (1761~, SAPE.)

—Tibbetts Line Camp: In the 1920s Bill Tibbetts and Tom Perkins had a line camp on the bottom. (1322~)

—Airstrip: During the 1950s an airstrip at the bottom was used by rivermen and uranium prospectors. (599~)

—The Rock: This was the John Wesley Powell name for the low butte (at elevation 4187T) in the middle of Anderson Bottom. (662~)

—Tangren Spring: This large spring is on a wall toward the north end of Anderson Bottom. Karl Tangren ranched the area and developed the spring in the 1950s. (1085~, SAPE.)

—National Park Service Cave: A cave near Tangren Spring was blasted into the cliffs in 1963. It is now used by the National Park Service for storage. (1295~)

—Anderson Bottom Trail: This constructed stock trail from the bottom to the top of the cliffs is on the northwest side of Anderson Bottom (one-half mile east-northeast of elevation 4222T). (SAPE.)

—Constructed Stock Trail: This goes from Anderson Bottom downcanyon along the river to Valentine Bottom. (SAPE.)

—The Fang: Otis "Dock" Marston in 1967: "That rock at the foot of the small cliff opposite Townsite [Anderson] Bottom is gaining the name FANG ROCK." (1286~) In 1952 William Davis noted it as the Gate of Stillwater. (528~)

Anderson Canyon: (Piute Co.) Fishlake National Forest-Sevier Plateau-Durkee Creek. Marysvale Peak and Marysvale maps.

Peter Gottfredson in 1865: "Major Andersen; this man had been a major in General Johnston's Army, which was sent to Utah in 1857." (749~)

Anderson Canyon: (Washington Co.) Dixie National Forest-Pine Valley Mountains-Dam Canyon. New Harmony map.

(See Anderson Junction for name derivation.)

Anderson Creek: (Sevier Co.) Fishlake National Forest-Fish Lake. Fish Lake map.

Max Robinson noted that the creek was most likely named for Peter Oliver Anderson (1886-1974) and family. (1641~)

Anderson Junction: (Washington Co.) Hurricane Cliffs-Interstate 15. Pintura map.

Also called Anderson, Anderson Ranch, and Anderson's Ranch.

Peter Anderson (1840-1921) and his wife, Anna, moved to Pintura in 1868. In 1884 they moved to what was then called Echo Farm, near present-day Anderson Junction. Before that the area had been called McPhersons Flat for a settler who lived here in 1858. The Anderson family had a farm and a way-station here. (14~, 273~, 338~)

Anna Anderson: "During those early pioneer years and while homesteading Anderson's Ranch, no one can picture the hardships, misery, suffering and loneliness I experienced. Always my heart yearned to run away ... to run away to the ease, comfort and luxury of my home in the old country." (41a~)

Anderson Mountain: (Iron Co.) Hurricane Cliffs-Buckskin Valley. Burnt Peak map. (8,056')

James Pace Anderson (1826–1867) arrived in Beaver in 1856. (271~)

Anderson Spring: (Iron Co.) Dixie National Forest-Markagunt Plateau. Henrie Knolls map.

This is a large, developed spring with a still-used stock reservoir.

Inscriptions on aspen trees include one that reads: "Aug. 12, 1933; Another Day Is Done." (SAPE.)

Andy Mesa: (Grand Co.) Manti-LaSal National Forest-La Sal Mountains. Warner Lake and Mount Waas maps.

Andy Swanson lived on the mesa from about 1900 to his death in 1929. Sena Taylor Flanders: "Andy was a religious fanatic. He called his home on the mesa the 'Garden of Eden' and fixed it up by building rock monuments everywhere. The circle was a religious symbol to him, evident by the vegetable and flower beds that he planted in rings and circles to protect the little gardens from animals."

Joe Taylor: "Andy Swanson was a crazy man who lived there in the early 1900s. He thought that the place was going to be the only place left when the rest of the world was destroyed. He had a boat tied to the side of his house and he had a knife in the boat so he could cut it loose in a hurry.... In the mid-1920s my mother wanted to go meet Andy Swanson. So my dad [Lester Taylor] took her and an aunt up to his house. He had a kettle on the stove with a lid on it, and the aunt says, 'Oh, what're ya cooking?' And she took the lid off the pot, and it was filled with chipmunks boiling." (1866~)

Andy Miller Flats: (Garfield Co.) Glen Canyon NRA-Narrow Canyon. Sewing Machine and Bowdie Canyon West maps.

Andy Miller ran his sheep in the area in the early years. (413~)

—Weeping Window: This formation is on Andy Miller Flats and is elevation 5216T on the Sewing Machine map. (M.44.)

—Sailor and Cobra: (Also called Cobra Rock and The Sailor.) (411~) This formation is on Andy Miller Flats and is one-half mile north of elevation 5216T on the Sewing Machine map. (M.44.)

—Window Rock Draw: This north-south drainage is immediately east of Weeping Window (Sewing Machine map). (M.44.) Inscriptions include Leland Bohleen, Jan. 30, 1931 and Elmer Jeffs, 1-4-44. (SAPE.)

—Constructed Stock Trail: This provides access into Window Rock Draw from its east side. The trail is directly west of Bohleen Butte. (SAPE.)

—Middle Finger Tower: This tower is on Andy Miller Flats and is between the Sailor and Cobra and Weeping Window. Eric Bjørnstad noted that it was named by rock climbers. (241~)

—Bohleen Butte: This is on Andy Miller Flat at elevation 5390 (Nose) on the Sewing Machine map. (M.44.) Leland Bohleen (1902-1986) ran livestock in the area in the 1930s.

—Judas Priest: This formation is one-half mile north of Bohleen Butte. (M.44.)

—Judas Priest Draw: This is immediately east of Bohleen Butte and southeast of Judas Priest. (M.44.)

—Constructed Stock Trail: This trail, used only by sheep, goes north from Andy Miller Flats to the high bench between the flats and The Block (one-quarter mile northwest of elevation 5262 on the Sewing Machine map). (SAPE.)

Aneth Town: (San Juan Co.) Navajo Indian Reservation-San Juan River. Aneth map.

Three name derivations are given.

First, Robert S. McPherson: "Aneth has had a variety of titles, including Riverview (1878–85), Holyoak (1886–around 1895), Guillette, and finally Aneth, a Hebrew word meaning 'The Answer,' given by Howard Antes, a Methodist missionary who lived there beginning in 1895." (1336~)

Second, Donald L. Baars: "It has been impossible to trace the word as either a Navajo, Spanish, or family name. The land Aneth stands on was added later to the Navajo Indian Reservation and was known as the 'Annex lands.' The Spanish word for 'annex' is *anexo* ... perhaps mispronounced in Navajo as 'aneth.' This is the only reasonable explanation for the name.... The Navajo name is *T'ááh Bíích íídii*, or 'a trader he can barely make it.'" (86~)

Third, Charles Kelly noted that to the Navajo *Aneth* means "'a good place to stay away from.' Just why it is called that is not now known but it applied to both Utes and Navajos." (1046~)

Ron McDonald noted that the town was briefly called Stulls: "This is not verified, but we believe Henry Mitchell lived in Stull County, Kansas." (1329~)

—McElmo Trading Post: PRIVATE PROPERTY. (Also called Aneth Post, Aneth Trading Post, Guillet's Store, and Riverview.) The trading post was founded in 1878 by Henry L. Mitchell on the flood plain below today's post. In 1885 high water eradicated the post, which was then rebuilt by Edgar Noland (See Cowboy Wash—Nolands Trading Post) and brothers Herman and Peter Guillette on higher ground. Francis F. Kane in 1891: "We were impressed favorably, on the whole, with Gillet." (1037~, 1596~)

Warren K. Moorehead of the Illustrated American Exploring Expedition of 1892: "We set out over the sand desert separating Gillett's trading store from Bluff City. This was the worst trip we had in the course of the expedition. We disabled two horses, came near losing our camp boy, and suffered greatly from thirst." (1383~)

The trading post has had many owners since those early days and it is now a convenience store. Some of the original walls and rock work are still visible. (SAPE.)

—Aneth Oil Field: (Also called Aneth Strip.) (1380~) This field, claimed to have been the first commercially viable oil field in southeastern Utah, was discovered by Texaco in 1957. (956~)

Angel Arch: (San Juan Co.) Canyonlands National Park-Needles District-Salt Creek. Druid Arch map.

Although cowboys from the early days certainly knew of the arch, and perhaps gave it a local name (1821~), it was not officially named until 1953. At that time Chaffee C. Young and R.E. Badger, who were the first to photograph the arch from the ground, named it. (1950~) Badger in 1965: "The Chaffee C. Youngs of Escondido, California and my wife and I were the first ones to ever photograph Angel Arch, and we were the ones who named it. Mr.

Bates Wilson, of Arches National Monument, can verify this." (92~)

Alice Higgins in 1965: "Suddenly, there against the clear blue sky, delicately soaring, was Angel Arch, a breathtaking form buttressed by a demure winged figure, together yielding a sense of peaceful grandeur." (880~)

John F. Hoffman called this Pegasus Arch, as did Kent Frost. Hoffman in 1973: "The name Angel Arch is rather well accepted. When my photo was made it seemed to suggest a horse more than an angel so this name [Pegasus Arch] was used. Angel is so damned common!!! The name I suggested has no general acceptance." (899~)

Lloyd Holyoak noted that he was probably the first to drive up to the arch, in the late 1940s. (906~)

—Cottonwood Canyon: (Also called Angel Arch Canyon.) (2019~) This is the short canyon one follows from Salt Creek to Angel Arch.

Angel Cove: (Wayne Co.) Dirty Devil River-Robbers Roost Canyon. Angel Cove map.

—Angel Trail: This is the "Pack Trail" that is immediately south of Angel Cove. Barbara Ekker: "Livestock were once herded along this trail, some of which were rushed from the area by rustlers from regions on the Henry Mountains. The livestock trail headed east down Beaver Canyon (Beaver Box), and crossed the Dirty Devil River at Angel Cove. From there the trail went up the precipitous slopes to the head of Angel Point, then east past Deadmans Hill and onto Roost Flats. It is recorded that outlaw Quimby Oliver 'Cap' Brown was one of the earliest users of the trail. Brown named the trail in the early 1870s because only an angel with wings could make it out of the Dirty Devil area and up onto the Point." (607~)

Pearl Baker: "They started up the rocky intricacies of the Angel Trail.... The loose horses were slipping on the bulging red slickrocks, losing hair and hide, the smell of burned hooves pungent on the night air. The wise old saddle horses, after the riders dismounted to lead them up the steep slopes of naked sandstone, hung back on the bridle reins, bracing and balancing themselves for the difficult climbs. Many of these steep pitches over and around which the trail snaked led down to a drop-off into a black canyon, so it behooved a man to climb fast and expertly and give a horse all the help he could." (122~)

The portion of the Angel Trail on the west side of the Dirty Devil River that is now used by hikers is not the original route to the river. Livestock was driven down Beaver Box Canyon from its head. That trail has now been made impassible by extensive erosion in the canyon. (SAPE.)

Angels Landing: (Washington Co.) Zion National Park-Zion Canyon. Temple of Sinawava map. (5,790')

Frederick S. Dellenbaugh called this the Altar of the Gods in the early 1900s. (1610~)

In 1913 the Governor of Utah, William Spring, visited Zion Canyon and for a short time locals called Angel Point "El Gobenador," a name that was later transferred to the Great White Throne. (1279~)

Claude Hirschi and Dr. Frederick Vining Fischer are credited with naming this impressive monolith in 1916. (481~, 1710~) H. Lorenzo Reid: "[Fisher] ... assigned the name, Angel's Landing, to the lesser peak that stands in front of and at the foot of, The Great White Throne. He felt that the Angels would never land on the Throne, but would reverently pause at the foot." (1610~)

R.B. Gray in 1927: "Among the boldest of the buttes is Angel's Landing, a sharp-shorn pyramidal wedge of Pompeiian red that projects far into the canyon." (754~)

—Angels Landing Trail: This was listed on the National Register of Historic Places in 1987. Several tourists have lost their lives on the trail over the years.

Angle Town: (Piute Co.) Grass Valley-Otter Creek Reservoir-Highway 62. Angle map.

Also called Grass Valley, Lower Grass Valley, North Fork, Spring Creek, and Wilmont. (289~, 1194~, 1444~, 1971~, 2063~, M.73.)

The town was started in the 1870s by early settlers of Grass Valley. (1444~) Volney King called it Clover Flat in 1883 (1096~) and it is shown as that on the 1896 USGS Fish Lake map.

Daughters of Utah Pioneer files: "The name Angle comes from the sharp right angle the road takes from the main highway into the community." (1194~)

—Old Spanish Trail: (Variation.) The Old Spanish Trail—Fish Lake Route—went along Otter Creek and by what would become Angle. (477~)

Annabella Town: (Sevier Co.) Sevier Valley-Sevier River. Annabella map.

Also spelled Anabella. (1023~)

The first settlers, Harry Dalton and Joseph Powell, arrived in 1871. (361~) In 1872 William Morrison noted this as Annabella Springs. (1391~)

Two name derivations are given.

First, M. Guy Bishop: "The settlers originally called their village Omni Point, for its proximity to Richfield (known initially as Omni).... The community's name was later changed to Annabella, probably in honor of the first two white women to live there—Anna Roberts and Isabella Dalton." (238~, 1932~, 1970~)

Second, Jean S. Greenwood: "Some claim the town was named for the heroine in a novel." (1194~)

—Annabella Canal: This was finished in 1872. (1970~)

—Annabella Reservoir: (Annabella and Water Creek Canyon maps.) (Also called Long Reservoir.)

Annies Canyon: (Kane Co.) Glen Canyon NRA-Glen Canyon. The Rincon NE, The Rincon, and Halls Crossing maps.

Also called Anns Canyon and Pool Canyon.

Two name derivations are given. It is believed that the first is correct.

First, Senator Barry Goldwater noted the naming of the canyon in his book *Delightful Journey*: "We had no sooner entered the canyon when we found a cool spring gushing from a ledge. Of course we stood under it and cooled off and drank our fill. On up the canyon we went. The passage is very narrow and crooked, with extremely high smooth walls. For a mile it twists and turns. Then three side canyons angle in and the passage widens slightly. Immediately below the junction of the three canyons, on the west wall, is the coldest spring I have ever felt. The water must be around 45 degrees. We dunked ourselves in it and after a drink of the refreshing water we took a nap. Since this canyon is unnamed, I recommend as a name Ann's Canyon. Something should be named in honor of one whose good sportsmanship is always evident, and nothing could be more like the refreshing qualities of her presence than the cool waters of our little spring tucked up there, where and if someday I have a magic lamp that could make the name permanent, I will rub the daylights out of it." (737~) The Ann was Ann Rosner. Goldwater described Rosner in his notes: "27—school teacher from Chicago—good sport—seems this is first experience with outdoors in such a big amount." (738~)

Second, Robert H. Vreeland noted that Art Greene named it for his daughter, Annie. (1946~)

Inscriptions include L. Harris, April 24, 1894. (SAPE.) In an interesting side note, Otis "Dock" Marston wrote that the inscription was "in Bates Tub Canyon near washout of Jeep road at south end of Waterpocket Fold." (29~) It is assumed that the Bates was Bates Wilson, the father of Canyonlands National Park. Perhaps he took a dip in a nearby pothole.

—Abandoned Road: A uranium-era (1950s) Jeep road went from the mouth of Halls Creek, along the face of the Waterpocket Fold, over the head of Lost Eden Canyon, and into and out of Annies Canyon before ending on the benchlands to the south at The Reef. (SAPE.) (See Iceberg Canyon–The Reef.) Arthur Chaffin noted that in the early days he used a stock trail that followed the route of the road to get supplies to the Colorado River and then across it to Gretchen Bar. (393~) The road can still be followed on foot. (SAPE.)

—Anderson Bar: (Also called Anderson Camp, Iron Rock Island, Little Anderson Bar, and Schock Bar.) This placer bar, now underwater, was on the north (or west) side of the Colorado River two miles north of the mouth of Annies Canyon (one-half mile southwest of elevation 3998T on the Halls Crossing map). William P. Anderson and Scott Lisle located the site in 1889. They called it the Ottawa Placer. Dr. William H. Schock (1846-1927) also mined here in 1898, 1908, and 1909. (466~) Inscriptions included Peter Gregersen, May 25, 1894 and C.N. Sorensen, May the 18, 1894. (466~) (See Gretchen Bar Trail below.)

—Cook Spring: This spring, now underwater, was on Anderson Bar (one-quarter mile southwest of elevation 3998T on the Halls Crossing map). It was a perennial water source. (466~)

—Gretchen Bar: Now underwater, this was on the east side of the Colorado River across from the mouth of Annies Canyon (west of elevation 4077T on the Halls Crossing map). The two-mile-long bar was first mined in 1889 and was variously named the Schock Bar or Lower Schock Bar for Dr. William H. Schock (See Iron Top Mesa), the Anderson Bar for miner William P. Anderson, and Independence Bar. Mining activity continued on the bar until at least the late 1930s. (466~)

Who was Gretchen? Harry Aleson: "No knowledge re: GRETCHEN. A simple guess would be that it originated with Dr. Schock—If he had a relative or friend by the name." (38~) Arthur Chaffin called the bar The Gressman for an early Glen Canyon miner. (399~) It is very likely that the initial name was Gressman Bar and that the name became corrupted over time to Gretchen.

—Gretchen Bar Springs: There were two good springs at Gretchen Bar. Frank Lawler: "lower end of bar is spring which would fill a 2" pipe." (1154~)

—Poor Mans Placer: Harry Aleson noted that this was the north end of Gretchen Bar and was one and one-half miles north-northwest of the mouth of Annies Canyon. (29~)

—Gretchen Bar Trail: (Also called Lake Canyon Trail.) This constructed stock trail starts on Poor Mans Placer (one-half mile south of elevation 3795T on the Halls Crossing map) and goes east up the rolling sandstone. The trail provided overland access to the extensive mining along Gretchen Bar. Built in the 1890s, the trail was upgraded with the use of a Caterpillar tractor in the 1930s. The tractor was driven from Blanding, through the Clay Hills, and joined the "Emigrant Trail" (Hole-in-the-Rock Road) near Lake Canyon. It then went overland and dropped onto Gretchen Bar. It was also used to supply the nearby Anderson or Schock Bar. Parts of it can still be followed. (466~, SAPE.)

Antelope Creek: (Coconino Co., Az.) Navajo Indian Reservation-Glen Canyon NRA-Glen Canyon. Leche-e Rock, White Dome, and Page, Az. maps.

Also called Antelope Canyon.

The Navajo name for upper Antelope Creek (above Highway 98) is *Tse Bighanilini,* or "place where water runs through rocks." It is also called The Crack.

The name for lower Antelope Canyon (below Highway 89) is *Hasdeztwazi,* or "spiral rock arches." It is also called The Corkscrew.

In 1910 A.H. Jones called this Hula Creek. (1009~)

This famous slot canyon is visited by thousands of tourists every year.

—Movies: *Broken Arrow, Planet of the Apes, Lightning Jack,* and *Beast Master Two* were filmed, in part, in Antelope Canyon.

Antelope Island: (San Juan Co., Utah and Coconino Co., Az.) Glen Canyon NRA-Lake Powell. Utah map: Warm Creek Bay. Arizona map: Page.

The Domínguez-Escalante Expedition crossed Antelope Island, or what they called San Carlos Mesa, on November 6, 1776.

Stan Jones: "Old maps all have it as San Carlos Island, and somebody in the Park Service all of a sudden changed it." (1020~)

—Wright Bar: This placer bar, now underwater, was on the north side of the Colorado River and on the southeast corner of Antelope Island (one-quarter mile south of elevation 3763 on the Page map). George M. Wright and his wife, L.C., staked a claim on the bar in 1892 and were successful in mining gold here. (467~)

—Miner's Trail: P.T. Reilly noted that a steep trail went from Wright Bar up the cliffs. Reilly also noted that Wright inscribed his name here on Nov. 15, 1892. (628~)

—Lopers Cave: This cave, now underwater, was near Wright Bar. It was named for river legend Bert Loper (1869-1949) and was often used by miners and river runners. (467~, 1612~) Inscriptions in the cave included G.M. Wright, Nov. 18, 1892; [E.R.] Monnett, Nov. 19, 1907; A.G. Turner—1876–1912; Bert Loper, 2-2-08; and J.C. Tipton, 1892–1910. (1299~)

—Galloway Cave: This cave, now underwater, was on the southwest corner of Antelope Island (three-quarters of a mile south of elevation 3922T on the Page map). Nathaniel Galloway (1853-1913) is credited with being the first to run much of the Green and Colorado rivers solo. He went from Green River, Wyoming to Needles, California in 1896–97. He inscribed his name in the cave in 1894 and 1897. (467~, 1615~) The earliest date in the cave was [G.M.] Wright, 1893.

Later, this was renamed Outlaw Cave by Norm Nevills who noted that horse thief Neal Johnson had used the cave as a hideout from the law. (869~, 1562~) P.W. Tomkins on a 1940 Norm Nevills river trip: "Pull into camp ... in cave which I have subsequently named: 'Outlaw Cave.' In this cave are the names of many early parties.... Neil Johnson, outlaw, hanged a few years ago in Nevada sojourned here." (1897~)

P.T. Reilly thought that Nevills made up the name to add color to his river trips and that Johnson was just a "shifty fellow. There is little basis for use of the term unless one considers poaching. Art Greene calls it Hislop Cave and Lou Fetzner uses Galloway Cave." (1614~) Otis "Dock" Marston: "Any Johnny-come-lately as was Nevills would not have known of any such outlaw if he did exist. The yarn appears to be pure hokum." (1300~)

Father H.B. Liebler in 1945: "well named, for there a man could hide out for an indefinite period. Invisible from land or air, with water and fish abundant. The cave is inaccessible except by way of the River and would give ample protection from the weather. There is even a natural chimney, which would draw off the smoke of one's fire." (1200a~)

Barbara Gifford in 1948: "Norm [Nevills] named it that because he thought it might have been one of [John D.] Lee's hideouts after the Mountain Meadow Massacre." (719~)

Antelope Range: (Sevier Co.) Tushar Mountains-Long Valley. Antelope Range and Marysvale Canyon maps.

—Old Spanish Trail: The trail, in order to avoid Marysvale Canyon, went across the Antelope Range. (474~) Jedediah Smith used the Antelope Range route in 1826, as did the Parley P. Pratt Exploring Expedition of 1849–50. (1762~)

—Suspect Gulch: This short drainage is part of the Marysvale Uranium District. Its top is one mile north-northeast of the Antelope Mine (one-quarter mile south of elevation 6773 on the Antelope Range map). The name was applied by miners. (1088~)

—Iron Peaks: (Also called Twin Peaks.) (332~) These hills, part of the Marysvale Uranium District, include elevation 7507 and the two summits immediately to the north on the Antelope Range map. The name was applied by miners. (1088~)

—Iron Cap Mine: This alunite mine is on the Iron Peaks. It was discovered by Billie Johnston during World War One. (332~, 1934~)

—Yellow Jacket Mine: This is a part of the Marysvale Uranium District. It is the "Quarry" north of elevation 6647 on the Antelope Range map. (1088~)

—Silica Hills: (Also called Potash Butte.) (332~) These hills, part of the Marysvale Uranium District, include elevations 7150 and 7147 on the Antelope Range map. The name was applied by miners. (1088~)

—Bullion Flat: This is a part of the Marysvale Uranium District. It is one mile south of Sage Flat (one-half mile south of elevation 6450 on the Antelope Range map). (1088~)

—Flattop: This hill, part of the Marysvale Uranium District, is at elevation 7666 (Flattop) on the Antelope Range map. The name was applied by miners. (1088~)

—Rampart Point: This is part of the Marysvale Uranium District. It is one-quarter mile north-northwest of the top of elevation 7666 (Flattop) on the Antelope Range map. The name was applied by miners. (1088~)

—Jungfrau: This hill, part of the Marysvale Uranium District, is at the "Radio Towers" immediately south of elevation 7079 on the Antelope Range map. The name was applied by miners who thought it looked like Jungfrau Mountain, one of the highest and most spectacular summits in Switzerland. (1088~)

—Prospect Ridge: This is part of the Marysvale Uranium District. It includes elevations 6678, 6910, and BM6773 on the Antelope Range map. The name was applied by miners. (1088~)

—Teacup Hill: This is part of the Marysvale Uranium District. It is elevation 7108 on the Antelope Range map. The name was applied by miners. (1088~)

—Agate Peak: This is part of the Marysvale Uranium District. It is the high point one-quarter mile northwest of elevation 6743 on the Marysvale Canyon map. The name was applied by miners. (1088~)

—The Plug: This peak, part of the Marysvale Uranium District, is one-eighth mile east of elevation 5715 on the Marysvale Canyon map. The name was applied by miners. (1088~)

Antelope Spring Draw: (Garfield Co.) Dixie National Forest-Awapa Plateau-Balsam Hollow. Big Lake, Pollywog Lake, Flossie Knoll, and Smooth Knoll maps.
Dunk Taylor: "I'll say there's antelope out there"! (1865~) Alfonzo Turner noted that when he started ranching on Parker Mountain (Awapa Plateau) there were no antelope. Then, Fish and Game reintroduced antelope to the area in the 1970s. They have proliferated and have spread over the whole area. (1914~)

—Antelope Spring: (Pollywog Lake map.) In the early 1880s the Elias H. Blackburn family had a dairy farm at the spring. (1412~) Alfonzo Turner: "It's a natural spring and about the only live water around there. The Forest Service went in and piped it out and put troughs in." (1914~) They also put a wildlife exclosure around the spring in 1974. A picturesque line shack is nearby. Inscriptions on trees date to 1922. One reads: "Let not the sun go down upon me." Another is from David Chappell, 1942. (SAPE.)

—Antelope Ditch: (Pollywog Lake map.) Sonny King noted that this ditch, still very much in evidence, was built with a team and scraper in the late 1930s and early 1940s. (1095~)

Antelope Springs: (Iron Co.) Antelope Range-Urie Hollow. Antelope Peak map.
This large spring is still used by sheepmen. Water is piped into troughs and water can no longer be found on the surface. (SAPE.)
The Indian name is *Quev-wim-pa*. (1512~)
Addison Pratt of the Jefferson Hunt Party in 1849 called this Lost Spring: "It comes out of the ground and makes quite a stream, runs a few rods and sinks again, but little grass." (1571~) William Farrer of the same expedition: "There was a spring about 14 miles from where we started [Iron Springs] in the mountains to our left a little way from the road. Capt. Hunt called it the Willow Springs." (635~)
The Howard Egan Wagon Train of 1849: "camped at [camp number] 33 a spring branch. Wood plenty feed short." (598~)

—Old Spanish Trail: The trail took a short detour to get to Antelope Spring, which was an important water source.

—Antelope Peak: (6,557') Alva Matheson: "It is the highest peak to be seen from the area of the spring which was the main watering place of a herd of antelope in the early days and from which the name was derived. It lies at the north end of what is now called the Antelope Range." (942~)

Antelope Valley: (Emery and Wayne Counties.) San Rafael Desert-Maze Road. Whitbeck Knoll, Sugarloaf Butte, and Keg Knoll maps.

Pearl Baker: "There were great herds of antelope at North Springs and in the head of Antelope Valley." (120~, 1419~) Baker described the valley: "It was just a shallow swale filled with dunes of clean-looking blow sand. Interspersed with the dunes were clusters of sand bumps along the trail, and on the higher ridges lay knolls here and there with oak brush growing around the sides and over the tops." (122~)

Muriel W. Smith: "The San Rafael had wonderful range in those days with sand grass stirrup high and other feeds as lush. Vast herds of antelope ranged the desert and hunters killed them by the wagon load to sell in Grand Junction." (1780~)

—Antelope Valley Corral: This is the "Corral" on the west side of Antelope Valley (at elevation 5653T on the Whitbeck Knoll map). Martin Robinson in 1962: "a net wire corral built by the Bureau of Land Management about 15 years ago and is used by both sheepmen and cattlemen." (1931~)

Ant Hill, The: (Wayne Co.) Fishlake National Forest-Thousand Lake Mountain. Torrey map. (9,291')

Also called The Heap.

This looks like an ant hill. At the summit is a tin plaque that reads: "Richard Chidester, Fay Deleeaw, Robert Farnsworth, Feb. 7, 1953." All were residents of Rabbit Valley. (SAPE.)

—Durfey Flats: This high, sandy meadow is one mile north of The Ant Hill (centered on elevation 8565). (1865~) (See Durfey Creek.)

Anticline Overlook: (San Juan Co.) Hatch Point-Colorado River. Shafer Basin map.

Donald L. Baars noted that from the overlook one can view the Cane Creek Anticline. An anticline is a fold in the rocks. (85~) The facilities at the overlook were built in 1963.

Antimony Creek: (Garfield Co.) Dixie National Forest-Escalante Mountains-East Fork Sevier River. Barker Reservoir, Pollywog Lake, and Antimony maps.

(See Antimony Town for name derivation.)

The Lieutenant George M. Wheeler Survey map of 1872–73 shows this as Mesa Creek. (M.76.) Clarence Dutton of the Powell Survey called it Mesa Canyon. (764~)

—Huff Mill: This sawmill, shown on the Antimony map as "Mill Ruins" in lower Antimony Canyon, was built by James Huff (1837-1903) in 1879. He is credited with discovering antimony in the canyon. (324~)

—King Ranch: Sonny King noted that the ranch, started by his grandfather in about 1910, was on Antimony Creek one mile south-southwest of Dry Lake (Pollywog Lake map). J.J. Porter in 1931: "Was prempted [?] and used as a dairy ranch by C.L. King about 1885." (1346~) A constructed stock trail leads down the hill to the ranch. (1095~, SAPE.)

—Rowan Ranch: Sonny King noted that this was on Antimony Creek one-half mile upstream from the King Ranch. It was started by Charlie Rowan in the early 1900s. (1095~, 1336~, SAPE.)

Antimony Lake: (Garfield Co.) Dixie National Forest-Awapa Plateau. Antimony map.

(See Antimony Town for name derivation.)

Sonny King noted that this natural lake is in an old volcanic crater. (1095~)

Antimony Town: (Garfield Co.) Sevier Plateau-East Fork Sevier River-Highway 62. Antimony and Deep Creek maps.

Also called North Ranch. (361~)

Albert Guiser was the first to run livestock in the area. He arrived in 1873 and left in 1876. (1969~)

Antimony was settled in May 1879 and was initially named Coyote Creek. George Washington Bean: "We dropped into a fine grassy dell, and some of our boys captured a half grown coyote, tied it up for the night and turned it over to the old Chief [*Pah-ga-ne-ap*]. Next morning, in order to 'immortalize' the spot, they cropped its ears and tail, put a paper collar on him and turned him loose to carry his marks of civilization. Thus was named Coyote Creek." (174~)

The town was renamed in 1921 for a deposit of the chemical element antimony found in nearby Coyote Creek. Sonny King told the story: "J.L. Smoot was the post master all during the depression and up until almost 1940. He didn't like the name of Coyote, so that's when they decided to rename Coyote to Antimony." (1095~)

Geologist W.M. Travers: "Antimony was discovered in Coyote Canyon in the 1880s, by the Indians, who, confusing stibnite [antimony] with lead, attempted to use it as lead.... The earliest production consisted of collecting large pieces of float [chunks of ore sitting on the surface], of which there must have been large quantities, and when this was no longer available, the high-grade pods exposed on cliff faces were mined." (1905~)

Eugene Callaghan noted that the initial discovery was in May 1879: "Mining in the early days by following the sandstone ledges and picking the 'eyes' out of the deposits was concentrated on lenses of stibnite crystal aggregates." (332~) Antimony is used mainly as an alloy to strengthen various metals.

Ant Knolls: (Garfield Co.) Henry Mountains-Shootaring Point. Lost Spring map. (4,464')
Also called Desert Ant Knolls. (663~)
The USGS: "a series of small hills which resemble ant hills." (1931~)

Antone Canyon: (Grand Co.) Roan Cliffs-Book Cliffs-Sulphur Wash. Flume Canyon and Antone Canyon maps.
John C. Cutchlow and Albert Weber: "The first name of an old time resident in the area." (1931~)

Antone Flat: (Garfield Co.) Boulder Mountain-Death Hollow. Escalante map.
Edson Alvey: "It was named for Antone Woerner, early Escalante settler." (55~) Woerner arrived in Escalante in the 1880s. (2051~)
—Boulder Mail Trail: (See Appendix Two—Boulder Mail Trail.) George C. Fraser described the section of trail that goes from Antone Flat to Pine Creek in 1922: "We descend on the summit bed with increasing steepness, toward the bottom, and there have the worst part of the Boulder Trail. A few hundred dollars in labor and dynamite would make this safe and passable, but as it is out of the National Forest, no one takes the trouble to improve it." (670~)

Antone Hollow: (Sevier Co.) Fishlake National Forest-Niotche Creek. Gooseberry Creek and Yogo Creek maps.
—Old Spanish Trail: The trail went through Salina Canyon, but if wagons were being used, or the weather was poor, a bypass to the south was taken. Going east, the bypass went up Soldier Canyon and Gooseberry Creek, over the top, down Antone Hollow to Niotche Creek, and into upper Salina Creek. (1003~)

Ant Spring: (Emery Co.) San Rafael Swell-Mussentuchit Flat. Mussentuchit Flat map.
This large, developed spring is within sight of Pissant Knoll. (SAPE.)

Anvil Rock: (San Juan Co.) Navajo Indian Reservation-Oljeto Wash. Oljeto map.
This small formation on the top of a high cliff looks like an anvil.

Apple Brush Flat: (Garfield Co.) Henry Mountains-Dugout Creek. Steele Butte map.
Horace Ekker in 1962: "Named for a small amount of apple brush found in the area." (1931~)

Aquarius Plateau: (Garfield and Wayne Counties.) Dixie National Forest. Big Lake, Jacobs Reservoir, and Pollywog Lake maps.
Also called Boulder Mountain, Boulder Range, and Wasatch Plateau. (550~, 972~)
Although the Aquarius Plateau name is only shown on three USGS 7.5 Minute Series maps, the name is locally interchangeable with Boulder Mountain. (See Boulder Mountain.)
A translated Navajo name is White Face. (1339~)
The first Euroamericans known to have explored the Aquarius Plateau were members of the Andrus Military Reconnaissance Expedition of 1866. They went up Pine Creek and ascended Boulder Mountain's west side. Captain James Andrus: "Top of the mountain comparatively flat, numerous small lakelets, groves of pine timber, growing less dense as we proceed. Surface of the country covered with black volcanic rock sometimes in huge masses or scattered in fragments over the surface." (475~, 712~)
Joseph Fish, a member of the same expedition, called it Thousand Lake Mountain, a name since transferred to a mountain to the north: "The top of the mountain was near the timber line and was covered with numerous little lakes, from which we gave it the name of Thousand Lake Mountain." (645~)
Frederick S. Dellenbaugh and Almon H. Thompson of the 1871–72 Powell Expedition traversed the Aquarius Plateau while searching for the Dirty Devil River. Dellenbaugh called it Lake Mountain Range. (547~) Thompson initially called it the Wasatch Cliffs or Wasatch Mountain. Later, impressed by the number of lakes on the plateau, he is credited with naming it for Aquarius, the waterbearer of the Zodiac. Mormon settlers, not aware of Thompson's designation, called it Boulder Mountain for its many lava boulders. (1877~)
Frederick S. Dellenbaugh: "A prettier mountain region than this could not be imagined, while the magnificent outlook to the south and east across the broken country was a bewildering sight, especially as the night enveloped it, deepening the mystery of its entangled gorges and cliffs." (541~)
Clarence Dutton of the Powell Survey: "The Aquarius should be described in blank verse and illustrated upon canvas. The explorer who sits upon the brink of its parapet looking off into the southern and eastern haze, who skirts its lava-cap or clambers up and down its vast ravines, who builds his camp-fire by the borders of its snow-fed lakes or stretches himself beneath its giant pines and

spruces, forgets that he is a geologist and feels himself a poet." (584~)

Arch Canyon: (San Juan Co.) Manti-LaSal National Forest-Dark Canyon Plateau-South Elk Ridge-Comb Wash. Kigalia Point, South Long Point, and Hotel Rock maps. Robert S. McPherson noted that the Ute name is *Tüpwi Wigagat*, or "Rock Canyon." (1335~)

Herbert E. Gregory noted that the canyon has three exceptional arches: Cathedral, Angel, and Keystone. (774~) William Henry Jackson of the Ferdinand V. Hayden Survey in 1875 passed the mouth of the canyon. (950~)

—National Monument: (Proposed.) In 1926, at the behest of the National Park Service, Frank Oastler surveyed Arch Canyon and recommended it as a national monument. (1852~)

—Perkins Ranch: PRIVATE PROPERTY. This historic ranch was immediately south of the mouth of Arch Canyon. A corral and stock pond still exist. George W. Perkins (1879-1937) and his wife, Mary Ann (1881-1947), and family ranched here in the early 1900s. (1336~, 1910~, SAPE.) Herbert E. Gregory noted that a Mr. Corswell and Joe Anderson were raising melons, corn, and alfalfa here in 1925. (761~)

—Old Highway 95: This is the obvious road cut east of the Perkins Ranch going up Comb Ridge. (See Highway 95.)

—Dreamspeaker: This spectacular 250-foot tower is a short distance below the confluence of Texas and Arch canyons (near elevation 5492T on the South Long Point map). Eric Bjørnstad noted that it was named by first ascensionist Scott Baxter in 1984. (243~)

Arches National Park: (Grand Co.) Moab-Cisco Desert. Arches National Park is reputed to contain the highest concentration of natural arches in the world. At last count the tally was over two thousand individual spans.

Juan Maria Antonio Rivera, leading an expedition in search of silver, passed by the area in 1765. Although he did not enter the area, he was able to see it from a distance.

Trapper Denis Julien entered the Devils Garden area in 1844. He left his name and a date there. (See Devils Garden.)

One of the first to mention the area was Gwinn Harris Heap of the Lieutenant Edward F. Beale Expedition of 1853. In July of that year the expedition, going west, left the Colorado River and traversed the Cisco Desert immediately north of what is now Arches National Park. Arches were visible in the distance. Heaps: "The only vegetation was a scanty growth of stunted wild sage and cacti, except at a point known as the Hole in the Rock, where

there were willows and other plants denoting the vicinity of water, but we found none on our route." (854~)

The country now included in Arches National Park was first explored and used by ranchers who started grazing their animals here in the 1870s. It can be assumed that they were the first to see many of the arches and other features.

Formal credit for the discovery of many of the arches goes to Alexander Ringhoffer who prospected in the area in 1922. He advertised the beauty of the area and was instrumental in seeing it become Arches National Monument. Official designation was by President Herbert Hoover in 1929. Neither Devils Garden nor Klondike Bluffs were within the original borders of the park.

The park was expanded in 1938, and again in 1968. In 1971 the monument was reduced in size, but it was designated a national park. In 1998 President Bill Clinton added several thousand more acres to the park. (424~)

The Arches name was first suggested by the superintendent of the Southwestern Monuments, Frank Pinkley, in July 1925: "Should a monument be made, I would suggest calling it 'the Arches National Monument.'" (869~, 424~, 644~)

Harry Goulding is credited with being the first to drive an automobile into the Windows Section of the park, in 1936. A road was graded to the area shortly thereafter. (278~)

—Old Spanish Trail: The trail passed a short distance to the west of the area. Certainly parties saw the country and some of the arches.

—Movies: The opening scenes from *Indiana Jones and the Lost Crusade* were filmed in the park. (1809~)

Argyle Canyon: (Duchesne Co.) Bad Land Cliffs-Nine Mile Creek. Jones Hollow, Lance Canyon, Minnie Maud Creek East, Wood Canyon, and Currant Canyon maps. Also called Big Canyon. (1323a~)

The original name was Bartholmeu. (1931~)

In the 1890s Benjamin Argyle (1843-1917) was one of the largest cattle raisers in the Green River area. Cattle thieves forced Argyle out of business. (1575~)

Inscriptions include HUB Warren, 1895 and EA Powel, 1899. (SAPE.)

—Harper Town: PRIVATE PROPERTY. (Also called Alger Ranch, Ellis Ranch, and Lee Ranch.) (558~, 725~) This townsite was on Nine Mile Creek one-half mile west of the mouth of Argyle Canyon (Currant Canyon map). After Preston Nutter turned the Nutter-Brock ranch (See Petes Canyon—Nutter Ranch) into a working ranch rather than a stage stop, Frank Alger took over those duties at his ranch, building a store and a post office. In 1905 the name Harper was applied to the town, which over time grew to over a hundred people. (1788~)

Inscriptions include Rob Powel, 1887; Summers, July 28, 1888; Wm. Pace, 6-6-95; and Bill Cook, July 17, 1916. (SAPE.)

—Beacon Ridge: This prominent north-south ridge is one-quarter mile west of Harper Town and is immediately south of Nine Mile Creek. (It is on the edge of the Currant Canyon map.) (725~)

—Granny Canyon: This is south of the mouth of Argyle Canyon (Currant Canyon map). (725~)

—Pig Head Rock: This is one-half mile southeast of the mouth of Argyle Canyon (Currant Canyon map). Unattributed: "The early freighters referred to the rock as 'Pig Head Rock.'" (1465~)

Armstrong Canyon: (San Juan Co.) Natural Bridges National Monument-White Canyon. Kane Gulch and Moss Back Butte maps.

Two name derivations are given.

First, John Scorup: "[Armstrong] was one of the old Texas cowboys, one of the owners of one of the Texas herds that were first down in White Canyon [in the early 1880s]." (1821~)

Second, Burl Armstrong was the photographer for an archaeological expedition into the canyon in 1907 led by Byron Cummings and Neil M. Judd. (897~)

—Zekes Trail: This is the original constructed stock trail that provided access to Owachomo Bridge. It enters Armstrong Canyon on its west side just above the mouth of Tuwa Canyon. This should not be confused with the Park Service trail shown on the Moss Back Butte map as a "Foot Trail" that is below the mouth of Tuwa Canyon. Zeke Johnson was the first ranger at Natural Bridges National Monument. His tenure lasted from 1916 to 1941.

Charles L. Bernheimer in 1919: "A party went through a few days ago and one of their horses fell down and was killed.... For man on foot there is no danger and to horse there isn't any either if he is left to himself." (218~, SAPE.)

—Original Ranger Station: The first ranger station and campground for Natural Bridges National Monument was at the top of the above-mentioned Zekes Trail (at elevation BM6022 on the Moss Back Butte map). One can still find remnants of the ranger station. (SAPE.)

Arnolds Canyon: (Duchesne Co.) Bad Land Cliffs-Argyle Creek. Wood Canyon map.

Inscriptions include Elmer Addley, March 18, 1915 and Reid Hall, 4-20-40. (SAPE.)

Arsons Garden: (Emery Co.) San Rafael Swell-Cliff Dweller Flat. Arsons Garden map.

Also called Arson Garden. (1931~)

It is believed that this was named for Joe Arson. He settled in Price in the late 1890s. (388~)

Art Canyon: (Kane Co.) Vermilion Cliffs-Cottonwood Canyon. Yellowjacket Canyon and Kanab maps.

Also called Rosencrance Canyon. (1027a~)

Arths Pasture: (Grand Co.) Tenmile Country-Bull Canyon. Gold Bar Canyon and The Knoll maps.

Also spelled Arts Pasture. (1331~)

Canyonlands National Park Superintendent Bates Wilson noted that Arth[ur] Taylor (1854-1938) was an early settler. (1931~) James H. Knipmeyer noted that Arth was one of the Taylor brothers who brought three thousand head of cattle to the La Sal Mountains in 1880. (1116~)

Asay Creek: (Garfield and Kane Counties.) Dixie National Forest-Markagunt Plateau-Sevier River. Asay Bench and George Mountain maps.

The Lieutenant George M. Wheeler Survey map of 1872–73 shows this as Asay River. (M.76.)

—Asay Town: PRIVATE PROPERTY. (Also called Asays Ranch and spelled Assies Ranch.) The townsite was one mile west of Asay Creek's junction with the Sevier River. Joseph Asay (1823-1879) and his wife, Sarah Ann (1818-1900), established a farm along the lower part of the creek in about 1872. After several years other families joined the Asay family and a small town developed. They called it Aaron after one of the Asay sons (1855-1918). In 1887, with the coming of a post office, the name was changed to Asay or Asay Town. The town was abandoned by 1900. (346~, 972~, 1445~)

Clarence Dutton's 1879 Powell Survey map shows this as Asay's. (584~) In 1884 Edwin D. Woolley called it Lower Ranch. (2047~) The 1886 USGS Kanab map shows it as Garfield.

Ash Creek: (Washington Co.) Hurricane Cliffs-Virgin River. Kolob Arch, Smith Mesa, Pintura, and Hurricane maps.

Also spelled Ashe Creek. (585~)

The Domínguez-Escalante Expedition of 1776–77 called this both the *Rio del Pilar* and *Rio de Nuestra Senora de Zaragosa*. (775~, 2043~) The expedition ascended a basalt hill opposite, or south of, the mouth of Ash Creek (at elevation 2985T on the Hurricane map). (381~)

Jedediah Smith of the South West Expedition of 1826–27 followed the creek: "I followed it a part of a day but the country becoming very Rock and hilly I was obliged to turn off ... through a rough country." (1774~, 805~)

The Parley P. Pratt Exploring Expedition to Southern Utah of 1849–50 crossed the creek, noting that it was a "large creek steep banks." (1762~)

John D. Lee named the creek in 1852: "To Ash creek 8 miles, stream 15 feet wide, 2 deep bottom narrow, yet it has abundance of excellent white ash timber on it, also large bodies of millstone grit, which upon examination proved to be of a first rate quality." (1161~) Ash, a much harder wood than the more abundant pines and firs, was in great demand. (887~)

Thomas D. Brown of the Southern Indian Mission of 1854: "Deep chasms, small ash, and cottonwood are found here on this creek." (306~) Gary Dean Young described the creek as it was seen by the first settlers: "Ash Creek was then a ditch one could jump across, but the flash-floods and erosion have caused it to become a deep canyon as it is now." (2063~)

Levi Savage told this story in 1889: "In crossing Ash Creek near town [Toquerville] the creek being high both women were tipped out of the carriage into the stream. Sister Right [Wright?] got out with out much harm but Sister Sylvester was carried down stream over the rocks. I think a full half mile, she was taken out apparently dead, but eventually revived. She was badly bruised about the face and head, by being driven over the rocks by the force of the water. One of the horses were drownded [*sic*], also." (1692~)

Inscriptions include P.R. 1777. It is unclear if this is real or fake. If real, it is unclear who was here in 1777. (1115~)

Ashdown Canyon: (Kane Co.) Kolob Terrace-North Fork Virgin River. Straight Canyon map.

(See Ashdown Creek for name derivation.)

North Fork Virgin River, near its head, runs through Ashdown Canyon.

Ashdown Creek: (Iron Co.) Cedar Breaks National Monument-Dixie National Forest-Coal Creek. Navajo Lake, Brian Head, and Flanigan Arch maps.

Also called Ashdown Gorge. (2053~)

Ann Starr: "George Ashdown, Sr. [1845-1905] owned a saw mill at head of Ashdown Gorge. Mr. Ashdown was accidently shot and killed at the mill. His sons continued operating back in the 1800s." (942~)

—Ashdown Gorge Wilderness Area: This seven thousand acre parcel was designated as a National Forest Wilderness in 1984. (1715~)

Ashton Canyon: (Iron Co.) Dixie National Forest-Upper Bear Valley. Little Creek Peak map.

Also called Ashton Draw.

The USGS noted that a man named Ashton homesteaded here in the early years. (1931~)

Aspen Lake: (Iron Co.) Kolob Terrace-Fife Creek. Webster Flat map.

This is newer name, recommended by Ira Schoppman of Cedar City. (1931~) (See Fife Creek for more on Aspen Lake.)

—Jones Hollow: This is one and one-half miles northwest of Aspen Lake. Lehi Jones (1854-1947) and his wife, Henrietta (1858-1932), and family homesteaded here. They never proved up on the land, vacating it in 1884. Lehi would later become the mayor of Cedar City. (1012~)

Aspen-Mirror Lake: (Kane Co.) Dixie National Forest-Markagunt Plateau. Henrie Knolls map.

On a calm day, aspen trees surrounding the lake are reflected in the water.

—Aspen Mirror Lake Campground: This was built by the CCC in the mid-1930s. (1715~)

Aspen Patch: (Kane Co.) GSCENM-Kaiparowits Plateau-Grove Draw. Blackburn Canyon map.

There is a large copse of aspens at the Aspen Patch. As well, there is a large, developed spring.

—Grove Draw: The Aspen Patch is at the head of an eastern tributary of Blackburn Canyon locally called Grove Draw. (SAPE.)

—Cliff: (7,641') This is the highest point on Fiftymile Mountain. It is at the head of the Aspen Patch drainage and it is shown on the map. (SAPE.)

Aspen Point: (Garfield Co.) Dixie National Forest-Boulder Mountain. Lower Bowns Reservoir map. (7,675')

—Aspen Spring: (Also called Quaking Aspen Spring.)

—Quaking Aspen Cave: In 1931 Noel Morss noted that this cave near Quaking Aspen Spring was "used as a camp ground by sheep men and called by them 'Quaking Aspen Cave.'" (1392~)

Aspen Spring: (Iron Co.) Dixie National Forest-Hurricane Cliffs-Little Creek. Cottonwood Mountain map.

This is a large, developed, and still-used spring. (SAPE.)

—Old Spanish Trail: The trail went by the spring.

—Veater Spring: This is one-quarter mile west-northwest of Aspen Spring. (1931~)

Assembly Hall Peak: (Emery Co.) San Rafael Swell-Mexican Mountain. Bottleneck Peak map. (6,395')

Old maps show this as Sawtooth Butte. (727~)

Rob Cassingham: "Assembly Hall was named for its resemblance to the original L.D.S. Assembly hall in Salt Lake City." (386~)

Atchinson Mountain: (Washington Co.) Dixie National Forest-Bull Valley Mountains-Grassy Flat. Central East map. (7,859')

This was most likely named for William Hildrith Atchison (1794-1865) and family. William and his son, John Barton Atchison (1823-1897), and family moved to St. George in 1861. They stayed for several years before moving to Panacea, Nevada. (1167~)

Atkins Well: (Mohave Co., Az.) Hurricane Cliffs-Fort Pearce Wash. Lost Spring Mountain West, Az. map. PRIVATE PROPERTY.

Ashby Reeve noted that Joe Atkin (1863-1938) was an early settler. (1608~)

Atkinville Wash: (Mohave Co., Az. and Washington Co., Utah.) Big Valley-Virgin River. Arizona map: Lizard Point. Utah maps: St. George and White Hills.

William Atkin, Sr. (1835-1900) and sons, at the behest of Brigham Young, moved to St. George in the fall of 1868. They ran sheep and cattle in the area in the 1870s-90s. (273~)

—Atkinville: (White Hills map.) (Also called Atkins Pond.) This town, consisting of just the William Atkin, Sr. family, was started in 1877. It was located at the mouth of Atkinville Wash on the Virgin River. (461~, 1141~) William Atkin, Sr.: "The place where we live is called by our name Atkinville because we were the first that took it up when it had never been used by man that anyone knows and we have made it a beautiful place and me and the boys own it all, about 160 acres." (2045~) Erosion forced the abandonment of the "town" in about 1905, though the extended Atkins family used it as a base for their livestock business until 1922.

Atomic Rock: (San Juan Co.) Grand Gulch Plateau-Red House Cliffs-Highway 95. Moss Back Butte map.

This sandstone formation looks like the mushroom cloud from an atomic explosion. At one time a sign near the highway signaled its existence. For uranium miners it was a good meeting place at the top of a long uphill grade. (SAPE.)

Auger Hole Lake: (Garfield Co.) Dixie National Forest-Aquarius Plateau. Big Lake map.

Edson Alvey: "The name was derived from the boggy nature of the meadow." (55~)

Lavern Woolsey related a story that happened near the Auger Hole: "Parley and his older brother Riley [Woolsey] had taken a number of horses to the 'Roger' [Roger Peak area] to be turned out for pasture. On the return trip the gray, one eyed horse Parley was riding bareback ran away with him and darted under a large pine tree with leg-sized limbs hanging almost to the ground. One of the limbs hooked Parley under the left ear, pulling him off the horse and the ear almost completely from his head. Riley rushed them to the ranch where their mother applied home remedy treatment, then bound the ear back in place with bandages torn from a bed sheet. The wound healed completely." (2050~)

Auger Spring: (Grand Co.) Dome Plateau-The Highlands. Cisco SW map.

The spring was heavily used by stockmen. At one time there was a line cabin (burned down), and a still extant remuda for horses. A very old fence is a short distance upcanyon from Auger Spring. (SAPE.)

Joe Taylor: "That is really called Pig's Prick Spring. The penis of a boar pig is like a corkscrew. They changed it to Auger so it wouldn't be an offensive name." (1866~)

Aurora Town: (Sevier Co.) Sevier Valley-Highway 89. Aurora map.

The first settlers, George T. Holdaway, J. Alma Holdaway, and Elliott Newell arrived in March 1875. The town was initially named Willow Bend. In 1881, when the town applied for a post office, the name was changed to Aurora at the suggestion of Numan Van Louvan. (1970~) The Willow Bend name, though, was still used for many years. It was even used on the 1896 USGS Fish Lake map.

Two name derivations are given.

First, *Aurora* means "Northern Lights." (1194~, 1970~)

Second, the town was named for the Roman Goddess of Dawn; early settlers noted that the hills around the town were particularly beautiful in the morning. (1932~)

Ila Shepherd in 1947: "Nestled in a small valley between two ranges of mountains is one of the most prosperous agricultural communities in the State of Utah. Green acres of farm land stretch from it on all sides, while through its fields to the east winds the Sevier River like a silver ribbon. Eastward are low, round-topped mountains of many shades and colors, different to anything seen elsewhere in the state. On the south and west, jagged mountains reach up, strata upon strata, showing clay and rock of the most fantastic coloring; from the highest gray to the deepest crimson, and from snow-white to the deepest blue." (1970~)

Austin Town: (Sevier Co.) Sevier Valley-Monroe-Highway 118. Annabella map.

Jimmy Hale was the first to settle in the area, arriving in 1868. A nearby sugar factory provided the impetus to establish the town. Austin was initially named Frog Town

because of the many frogs in nearby ponds. (972~, 1194~)
Mary Henderson Richen: "Supposed to have been named for Mr. Mark Austin." (2053~)

Awapa Plateau: (Garfield, Piute, and Wayne Counties.) Grass Valley-Boulder Mountain. Abes Knoll, Big Lake, Flossie Knoll, Jakes Knoll, Loa, Parker Knoll, and Polly-wog Lake maps.
Also spelled Awaga Plateau. (282~)
(See Parker Mountain.)
An 1876 map shows this as "Antelope Plateau—Fine Pine Timber." (M.61.) A map from 1879 shows it as "Wahsatch Plateau of Antelope Plateau." (M.60.)
Three similar name derivations are given.
First, John Wesley Powell noted that *Awapa* is Ute for "Many Waters." (1563~, 1566~)
Second, Luella Adams Dalton noted that it means "big or quiet waters." (516~)
Third, Rufus Wood Leigh noted that it is Paiute for "a stream or water hole among the cedars." (1174~)

Averett Canyon: (Kane Co.) GSCENM-Sheep Creek. Bryce Point, Cannonville, and Bull Valley Gorge maps.
Also called Averett Hollow. (766~)
Two similar stories are told of the death of Elijah Averett, Jr. (1845-1866).
First, Captain James Andrus of the Andrus Military Reconnaissance Expedition of 1866: "Some of our animals being unfit for service, and deeming it best to disencumber ourselves as much as possible, we sent back Elijah Averett ... [and others] having in charge 14 animals, spare equipage etc. The returning party were waylaid by Indians while crossing a deep gorge and passing up a steep ledge of rocks. The foremost man Elijah Averett being dismounted, and leading two animals, was killed at the first fire and before he could make any resistance. The party were all dismounted and leading their animals up the steep acclivity at the time the attack was made. George Isom received an arrow wound in the left shoulder." (475~)
Second, Murray A. Averett, the brother of Elijah Averett, Jr.: "Near the head of Pahreah Creek, they dismounted and walked up the hill, Averett was in the lead, and as he reached the crest of the hill he was shot by an Indian. The rest of the boys became frightened and ran. One of them stopped behind a cedar tree not far away and watched the proceedings. Elijah, Jr. was only wounded and soon sat

up. Then two Indians came up to him, and one of them took an arrow in his hand, placed the spiked end at the top of his [Elijah's] shoulder near the neck and pushed it down into his heart. Several days later the whites came back and buried him, his hat over his face." (83~)

Azansosi Mesa: (Navajo Co., Az.) Navajo Indian Reservation-Oljeto Wash. Tseyi-Hatsosi, Keet Seel Ruin, and Boot Mesa, Az. maps. (6,691')
Laurance D. Linford noted that *'Asdzáátsʹósí* is Navajo for "Slim Woman." This was the Navajo nickname for Louisa Wetherill. (1204~, 769~)

Aztec Butte: (San Juan Co.) Canyonlands National Park-Island in the Sky District-Willow Flat. Musselman Arch map. (6,312')
James H. Knipmeyer: "named for a small cliff dwelling found near its summit. In the early days all of the cliff ruins found in the Southwest were attributed to the Aztec Indians of Mexico, hence its name." (1120~)
Alfred Nestler in 1961: "Just under the east and north rim of Aztec Butte, we found a stone walled-room.... On the top of the butte itself we found a partially constructed room of stone." (1435~)
—Aztec Butte Spring: This is the "Spring" that is one-quarter mile east of Aztec Butte at the head of Trail Canyon. Alfred Nestler in 1961: "We could see a flowing spring at the base of the cliffs with a great deal of green vegetation below it. Undoubtedly this spring was the chief reason for the existence of the ancient ruins in the area [Aztec Butte]. The early cliff dwellers must have had a series of ladders or found some means of getting down to the water, for the spring canyon is a box surrounded by high sheer walls." (1435~)

Aztec Canyon: (San Juan Co.) Canyonlands National Park-Needles District-Butler Wash. Cross Canyon and Spanish Bottom maps.
This is named on early river runner Edwin T. Wolverton's map of 1929. (M.78.)

Aztec Creek: (San Juan Co.) Navajo Indian Reservation-Navajo Mountain-Forbidding Canyon. Chaiyahi Flat and Rainbow Bridge maps.
Aztec Creek runs through Forbidding Canyon.
In the 1880s Glen Canyon miners found Anasazi ruins near the mouth of the canyon. They mistakenly attributed them to the Aztec culture in Mexico. (1115~) (See Forbidding Canyon for more information.)

B

Bachelor Basin: (Grand Co.) Manti-LaSal National Forest-La Sal Mountains-Castle Creek. Warner Lake map.
This mining area was home to three hundred lonely workers, mostly bachelors. (456~)

Bacon Slide: (Wayne Co.) Henry Mountains-Birch Creek. Dry Lakes Peak map.
The William Reilly Bacon family were early settlers of Hanksville. They started logging in Sawmill Basin in the 1890s. They would push logs down the slide to a road where they could be loaded on wagons. A son, William Riley Bacon, died after drinking lye while his mother was washing clothes. (604~, 606~, 925~, 1644~)

Badger Creek: (Garfield Co.) Dixie National Forest-Paunsaugunt Plateau-East Fork Sevier River. Tropic Reservoir map.
Kate B. Carter: "Indians found numerous badgers along its course in the early days." (375~)
This may have also been called Goulding Hollow. In 1941 W.J. Shakespear noted that Goulding Hollow was at the extreme south end of Tropic Reservoir: "The water from a spring in this hollow flows in an easterly direction and was used some fifty years ago for operating a shingle mill owned by a man named Goulding." (2053~)

Badger Spring: (Coconino Co., Az.) Vermilion Cliffs National Monument-Vermilion Cliffs. Navajo Bridge, Az. map.
This developed spring, in conjunction with Twin Springs, is still used as a domestic water supply for the small settlement of Vermilion. (SAPE.)
Wayne McConkie noted that in the early days Jacob Hamblin killed a badger near the creek. He then carried the badger to the next creek and cooked it. Since the fat in the badger reacted badly with the water, it turned to soap, giving that creek its name. (461~) Hamblin was here in 1858, '59, and '60. (842~) (See Soap Creek.)
Almon Thompson of the Powell Expedition of 1871-72 called this Spring Creek: "Dry country, not very much sagebrush." (1877~)
Jesse N. Smith in 1878: "Next water [from Soap Creek] Badger Creek ... road sandy and crooked.... Very poor feed and not much fuel. The creek bed was dry but found

water for animals a little way up. It was full of mineral, apparently alkali." (1775~)
In 1882 Lorenzo Brown described the country around the creek: "The roughest and most dreary country I ever saw. No vegetation. Hills rocks and barrinness [sic] are the chief recommendations." (305~)
Lewis Barney in 1886: "Badger Creek, a little drizzling stream of water, not enough for a horse to drink without digging a hole in the sand and letting it fill up." (156~)
—Honeymoon Trail: The trail went by the spring.

Bad Land Cliffs: (Duchesne and Uintah Counties.) West Tavaputs Plateau. Maps west to east: Jones Hole, Lance Canyon, Anthro Mountain, Wood Canyon, Currant Canyon, Anthro Mountain NE, Gilsonite Draw, Cowboy Bench, Pinnacle Canyon, and Duches Hole.
The name was in place by 1878. (1567~)
Tom McCourt: "To our left was a barren, sorry excuse for a mountain, a stark, steep, blue-gray wall of shale and clay." (1324~)

Bagley Meadows: (Sevier Co.) Fishlake National Forest-Sevier Plateau-Monroe Creek. Koosharem and Monroe Peak maps.
Irvin Warnock noted that Edward Alma Bagley (1847-1929) and family moved to Greenwich in 1876. (1971~, 1444~) Sabra Jane Beckstead Hatch noted that in 1879 her husband, George A. Hatch, Sr., and Edward Bagley started a dairy here: "For eighteen years we moved up in the spring and back [to Greenwich] in the fall." (1188~)

Bagpipe Butte: (Wayne Co.) Glen Canyon NRA-Orange Cliffs. Elaterite Basin map.
This Wingate-walled monolith, with its many pinnacles, resembles a bagpipe. (607~)

Baker Bench: (Garfield Co.) Glen Canyon NRA-Escalante River. Egypt, Horse Pasture Mesa, Scorpion Gulch, and Silver Falls Bench maps.
Stockman George Baker arrived in Boulder in 1889. He ran cattle in the area starting in the late 1890s. (1168~, 1445~, 2051~)
Inscriptions include F. Baker and R. Lyman, 1912. (SAPE.)
—Ringtail Canyon: The mouth of this northern tributary of the Escalante River is one and one-half miles (as

the crow flies) downriver from the mouth of Fence Canyon (one-half mile east of elevation 4990T on the Egypt map). Steve Allen saw a ringtail cat in the canyon, a rare experience in the Escalante area.

—Constructed Stock Trail: This starts one-quarter mile south of the mouth of Ringtail Canyon on the Escalante River and goes east onto Baker Bench. Inscriptions include G.O. and G.K.O., 1932. (SAPE.)

—Main Fork Baker Canyon: (Also called West Baker Canyon.) The mouth of this northern tributary of the Escalante River is one-quarter mile upriver from the mouth of Twentyfive Mile Wash (directly north of elevation 4468T, and immediately east of elevation 5319, on the Egypt map). Dennis Turville called this Nasty Ass, a delightful acronym for "Not Another Squeeze Thank You, Another Squeeze Sucker." (653~)

—Alternate Fork of Baker Canyon: (Also called East Baker Canyon.) This eastern tributary of Main Fork Baker Canyon enters the canyon one-half mile upcanyon from the Escalante River (immediately south of elevation 5289T on the Scorpion map). Dennis Turville called this Tight Ass, "as it is a tight slot canyon through much of its extent, requiring much 'worming' (chimneying)." (653~)

—Downcanyon from Charlie Arch: This is on the east rim of Escalante Canyon immediately south of Main Fork Baker Canyon (one-eighth mile northeast of elevation 4468T on the Egypt map). Charlie Olajos, an inveterate canyon explorer, was one of the first to come to Escalante country with the express goal of backpacking. Charlie died in 1995 at the age of eighty-five. His ashes were scattered here. (SAPE.)

—Constructed Stock Trail: This sheep trail, now in poor condition, goes from the northeastern part of Baker Bench down to Moody Creek. The top of the trail is one-quarter mile south-southeast of elevation 5881T on the Horse Pasture Mesa map. (SAPE.)

Baker Dam Reservoir: (Washington Co.) Santa Clara River-Highway 18. Central West map.

Also called Baker Reservoir.

The reservoir was built in 1950–51.

Baker Pasture: (Garfield Co.) Dixie National Forest-Boulder Mountain. Deer Creek Lake map.

Also called Baker Ranch. (1931~)

(See Baker Bench for name derivation.)

The Bakers had a ranch here in the early days. (1931~)

Baker Spring: (Wayne Co.) Dixie National Forest-Boulder Mountain-Pine Creek Cove. Government Point map.

This prolific spring is the site of the Baker Cabins. Dunk Taylor noted that the Baker family homesteaded here before 1900. (1865~)

Bakeskillet Lake: (Garfield Co.) Dixie National Forest-Boulder Mountain. Jacobs Reservoir map.

This shallow lake is shaped like a baking skillet. (2053~)

Baking Skillet Knoll: (Wayne Co.) Burr Desert-Adobe Swale. Baking Skillet Knoll map. (5,480')

Two name derivations are given.

First, Barbara Ekker noted that the land is shaped like a baking skillet. Cowboys often rode to the top of the knoll to look for their livestock. (604~, 925~)

Second, Alvin Robison: "I can't remember what the whole story's about. It's about a sheepherder and something to do with the bacon." (1642~)

Balanced Rock: (Grand Co.) Arches National Park-Garden of Eden. The Windows Section map.

Also called Pinnacle Rock (898~) and Unbalanced Rock. Dick Wilson: "The balanced boulder is over 55 feet long, estimated at 3,577 tons, the weight of 1,600 automobiles." (2019~)

—Chip Off the Old Block: This was a small 'balanced' rock adjacent to Balanced Rock. It toppled in 1976.

Balanced Rock Canyon: (Kane Co.) Glen Canyon NRA-Glen Canyon. Navajo Point and Cathedral Canyon maps.

Katie Lee and friends named the canyon: "I trailed up later and when I came up on top of the rock and walked about two or three hundred feet up the slickrock and all I see is two butts straight up in the air. I think, 'What are they doing? What's the matter? Have they killed something? Is something wrong? Are they praying'? I started to laugh. And I said, 'What the hell's the matter with you guys'? And they didn't even answer me. I walked around and saw what they're trying to do. Tad [Nichols] is trying to figure out how to get his camera down under these little head-sized pieces of stone that are sitting on two and three sandstone legs or pedestals that are no thicker than my thumb. These stones have obviously rolled 'way down off of the Kaiparowits Plateau over the millennia. The sandstone, over the years, has worn out underneath the stones, leaving these little pinnacles holding these stones up off of the main slickrock, sometimes five inches, sometimes eight inches, sometimes two inches, sometimes four inches. It was the most fascinating thing I've ever seen in my life." (1163~)

Bruce Berger in 1962: "Just when we thought we had seen all the categories and the rest would be permutation, we would stumble onto something like the shelf of balanced rocks. I was familiar with that American classic. Balanced Rock, the boulder dancing on a pin ... pride of every state in the West. I was unprepared for an entire shelf of balanced rocks no more that knee-high. Wind had eroded rotten sandstone beneath an assortment of granite, gneiss, and quartzite boulders, compressing the sandstone at their weightiest points and leaving them perched on finely whittled fingers. Some rocks stood on one leg, some on two or three, and sometimes a pebble was lodged, incredibly, between the sandstone peg and the boulder. Oblong, dark, river-polished, ludicrous, these balanced rocks were more like eccentric tea tables." (216~)

Joseph L. Dudziak in 1962: "The rocks themselves are a rather minute and fragile attraction but truly amazing—small, rounded river stones balanced on tiny pedestals of sandstone. The whole place could be wrecked in a half a minute." (577~)

Bald Knoll: (Kane Co.) Sink Valley Wash-Ford Pasture. Bald Knoll map. (7,004')

J.S. Dalley: "Because of the barren condition of the knoll it is named Bald Knoll." (2053~)

Bald Knoll: (Wayne Co.) Awapa Plateau-Cedar Peak Draw. Flossie Knoll map. (9,101')

Dunk Taylor noted that little grows on the knoll. (1865~)

—Bald Knoll Reservoir: Dunk Taylor: "It was a little reservoir and they went in there and had a guy that thought he knew everything and he just made a cone in the ground, and then he put tanks out there with rocks in it and a pipe into the reservoir ... and it wouldn't let the water in quick enough and backed up and busted the dam. So it hasn't been worth much the last two or three years." (1865~)

Bald Rock Canyon: (San Juan Co.) Navajo Indian Reservation-Navajo Mountain-San Juan River. Navajo Begay and Wilson Creek maps.

Also called Bald Knob Canyon (1120~) and Bald Rock Valley (70~).

Also spelled Baldrock Canyon.

Stephen C. Jett noted that the Navajo name is *'Ata' Bikooh*, or "Canyon Between." Another name was *'Atse Bikooh,* or "First Canyon," referring to the fact that it is the first canyon reached from the end of the Navajo Mountain Road. (975~)

Many slickrock domes line the upper end of the canyon. James H. Knipmeyer noted that the canyon was "originally named Junction Canyon by surveyor William B. Douglass in 1909 because its mouth was thought to be located near the junction of the San Juan and Colorado rivers." (1116~)

Raymond Armsby in 1927: "a picturesque spot shut in by sheer walls of stone and roofed by a purple desert sky set with silver stars." (70~)

—Baldrock Crescent: The USGS noted that this is "a general name referring to the area of stripped Navajo Sandstone lying between Navajo Mountain and the San Juan River and between Forbidding and Cha canyons." (1931~) Alexander Lindsey more specifically showed this as the area of difficult slickrock that starts at Surprise Valley on the east and goes west over the heads of Lehi, Anasazi, and Moepitz canyons and ends at Oak Canyon. The Crescent includes Rainbow Point (elevation 6059) and Dougi Butte on the Rainbow Bridge map. (1202~)

Christy G. Turner in 1962: "The area between Cummings Mesa, Cha Canyon, the rivers, and north and east of the lower slopes of Navajo Mountain is here referred to as the *Baldrock Crescent*—a barren segment of the Rainbow Plateau." (1915~) Turner described the area: "[The Baldrock Crescent] is characterized as a tumbled and rugged watershed.... It is highly dissected by narrow deep canyons and tributary drainages that follow chiefly the major joints or structurally weak deposits.... The whole color scheme is dominated by the pink-orange Navajo sandstone with its degrees of brown patina. The sandstone monuments positioned above the Navajo sandstone are brilliantly white." (1918~)

The canyon group EMDC calls this UDAAR Country, an acronym for Up Down and All Around, which is certainly what one does while exploring it! (SAPE.)

—Glass Mountains: This was Zane Grey's name for the slickrock dome country between Bald Rock and Cha canyons. (1901~) Charles L. Bernheimer noted in 1920 that John Wetherill called this area Paradise Lost. (218~)

—Wetherill Trail: This is the "Pack" trail that cuts across the head of Bald Rock Canyon. It was constructed by the CCC in the 1930s. (843~) The original Wetherill Trail crossed much lower in the canyon. (See Appendix Two–Wetherill Trail.) The early explorers went down Bald Rock Canyon until near its mouth, then followed the rim back upcanyon.

—Constructed Stock Trail: This rugged trail goes from lower Bald Rock Canyon generally southwest into lower Nasja Creek. (SAPE.)

—Cha Butte: Christy G. Turner noted that this is on the upper east side of Bald Rock Canyon (at elevation 5442 [Cha] on the Navajo Begay map). (1915~)

—Redbud Canyon: (Also called Cottonwood Canyon, Dry Wash [1296~], Junction Canyon [255~], and Little Junction Canyon [1931~].) This small southern tributary of the San Juan River is one-half mile east of the mouth of Bald Rock Canyon (between elevations 4118T and 4191T on the Wilson Creek map). It was a favorite stop for river runners in the pre-Lake Powell days and is often mentioned in diaries and articles. (1162~)

Tad Nichols: "Came to Redbud Canyon.... Clear water here, filled canteens. Up at the head of Redbud, water seeps from the cliffs, which are covered with maidenhair fern, columbine, and many other plants. A botanist's paradise." (1449~)

Katie Lee: "[We] filled our canteens while standing under icewater falls in Redbud—a heavenly little grotto, verdant with that delicate tree and banks of dripping maidenhair fern, scarlet monkey flowers, and most enchanting of all, the magic flutelike song of the canyon wren." (1162~)

—Tip-top: This high point is on the lower east side of Redbud Canyon and is near elevation 4311T on the Wilson Mesa map. It was named by the canyon group EMDC. (SAPE.)

—Illusion Point: This is the long, thin point on the San Juan River (Lake Powell) squeezed between the mouths of Bald Rock and Redbud canyons. It includes elevation 3958T on the Wilson Creek map. When standing at the middle of the point, one has no sense of being surrounded by water, thus the illusion. The bend was named by the canyon group EMDC. (SAPE.)

Baldwin Hollow: (Kane Co.) GSCENM-Kaiparowits Plateau-Warm Creek. Tibbet Bench map.

George, Brent, and Angus Baldwin ran livestock south of Cannonville at the turn of the century. (186~)

Ballard Draw: (Grand Co.) Uintah and Ouray Indian Reservation-East Tavaputs Plateau-West Willow Creek. Bogart Canyon map.

(See Sego Town for name derivation.)

Balsam Hollow: (Wayne Co.) Awapa Plateau-Hare Valley. Smooth Knoll and Moroni Peak maps.

—Upper Balsam Reservoir: (Smooth Knoll map.) Dunk Taylor: "It was one of them lakes that was built in the early '30s and in a wet year it works pretty good.... We went in there and bentonited it again [made it watertight by adding a clay lining].... The water usually lasts 'til the first of July." (1865~)

—Middle Balsam Reservoir: (Smooth Knoll map.) Dunk Taylor: "Middle Balsam's not had any bentonite or any clay. It usually fills when there's run-off in the spring. And

Lower Balsam is the same way." (1865~) The reservoir was built in the 1930s and was rebuilt in 1963. (1551~)

—Lower Balsam Reservoir: (Smooth Knoll map.) This stock reservoir was built in the 1930s and was rebuilt 1961. (1551~, 1865~)

Bankhead Creek: (San Juan Co.) Manti-LaSal National Forest-Abajo Mountains-North Creek. Abajo Peak and Monticello Lake maps.

Pete Steele noted that the Bankheads were early settlers. (1821~)

—Aqueduct: In 1928 the Blue Mountain Irrigation Company piped water from the creek to the town of Monticello. (211~)

—V.C.A. Reservoir: In 1941 the Vanadium Corporation of America built a million gallon reservoir to the south of the head of Bankhead Creek (near elevation 8969T on the Abajo Peak map). (211~)

Baptist Draw: (Emery Co.) San Rafael Swell-Chute Canyon. Horse Valley map.

Lee Mont Swasey: "Joe Swasey and some other cowboys baptized their old sheep dog there by throwing him in a water hole in Baptist Draw. That was sometime between 1874 and 1930." (1853~)

Bar A Creek: (Grand Co.) La Sal Mountains-Taylor Flats-Taylor Creek. Mount Waas and Dolores Point South maps.

Joe Taylor: "There was a group called the Pittsburgh Cattle Company who ran the Bar A, and they had a cabin there in the early years. There is a spring there that's cold as ice. When the Pittsburgh Cattle Company left the Bar A area, the Taylors moved there because of the water. The Bar A is where the headquarters of the summer country has always been for the Taylor Ranch. Growing up, when school got out, we would move to the Bar A on the mountain. About once a month we'd come back, and we would buy a truck load of groceries for us and for all the sheepherders. We had a place where there were cases of canned goods and slabs of bacon, and cases of eggs and five gallon cans of honey. We milked cows and we made our own butter and our own cottage cheese. We didn't have electricity. We didn't have running water. And, we didn't even know we were deprived! It was a great world"! (1866~)

Barker Reservoir: (Garfield Co.) Dixie National Forest-Escalante Mountains-North Creek. Barker Reservoir map.

Nethella Griffin Woolsey noted that Josiah Barker, Sr. (1831-1897) moved his family to Escalante in 1884 and ran livestock in the area. (2051~)

Barney Cove: (Garfield Co.) Dixie National Forest-Sevier Plateau-Casto Canyon. Casto Canyon map.
(See Barney Lake—Garfield Co. for name derivation.)

Barney Lake: (Garfield Co.) Dixie National Forest-Aquarius Plateau. Jacobs Reservoir map.
Edson Alvey noted that Joseph S. Barney (1845-1939) moved his family to Escalante in 1878. (55~, 2051~) Scott Robinson noted that Barney ran sheep in the area. (2053~, 1346~)

Barney Lake: (Piute Co.) Fishlake National Forest-Sevier Plateau-Manning Creek. Marysvale Peak map.
This natural lake was enhanced with a dam in 1914. In 1990 the dam was rebuilt.
Lewis Barney (1808-1894) and family were pioneers of Monroe, moving there in 1864-65. They moved to Burrville in 1882. (157~)

Barney Reservoir: (Garfield Co.) GSCENM-Escalante Desert-Hole-in-the-Rock Road. Seep Flat map.
(See Barney Lake—Garfield Co. for name derivation.)
—Barney Knoll: This is one-half mile north of Barney Reservoir (at elevation 5527). (55~)

Barney Top: (Garfield Co.) Dixie National Forest-Escalante Mountains. Griffin Point and Sweetwater Creek maps. (10,574')
The Powell Expedition of 1871–72 called this Table Top Mountain. (887~)
Pratt Gates noted that Joseph S. Barney (1845-1939) and family were the first to run sheep on the top: "Two of my cousins were up there herding sheep on Barney Top. They found two Shurtz brothers dead in their tent. Apparently lightning had struck them both, right in the tent." (709~) Inscriptions on aspen trees include W. Griffin, Aug. 3rd, 1912, and Grant Twitchell, 1923. (SAPE.)
—Little Barney Top: In the old days this was the name given to the north end of Barney Top. (1346~)

Barnhurt Ridge: (Garfield Co.) Dixie National Forest-Sevier Plateau. Flake Mountain West map. (9,012')
Correctly spelled Barnhurst Ridge.
Samuel Barnhurst (1827-1890) and his wife, Anna Maria (1833-1906), and family moved to Circleville during the Black Hawk War in 1866. After being forced out, they moved to the Mammoth/Hatch area in 1889. Samuel and Anna Maria are buried in Hatch. (159~)
Jens Christian Barnhurst (1865-1947), the son of Samuel and Anna Maria, became a stalwart of the Hatch-Asay area, building homes in Hatch and Asay and running a nearby shingle mill. (158~)

Barracks, The: (Kane Co.) East Fork Virgin River-Rock Canyon. The Barracks map.
Julius S. Dalley: "named because of its resemblance to army barracks. Known as The Barracks since 1866." (2053~)
Priddy Meeks provided the first description of The Barracks after traveling down East Fork Virgin River through Long Valley in 1852: "Here the creek is closed upon by impassable high rocks, or cliffs on each side. We passed on down the bed of the creek, we supposed six miles before a chance appeared for us to leave the creek, which was gladly embraced." (1343~) (See East Fork Virgin River—Sixmile Turn.)

Barrier Creek: (Emery and Wayne Counties.) Canyonlands National Park-Horseshoe Canyon Detached Unit-Labyrinth Canyon. Head Spur, Sugarloaf Butte, Keg Knoll, and Bowknot Bend maps.
Barrier Creek goes through Horseshoe Canyon.
(See Horseshoe Canyon for name derivation.)

Bartizan, The: (Iron Co.) Cedar Breaks National Monument-Wasatch Rampart. Navajo Lake map. (9,795')
According to *Wikipedia*, a bartizan is an "overhanging, wall mounted turret projecting from the walls of medieval fortifications." This accurately describes this formation.

Bartlett Wash: (Grand Co.) Tenmile Country-Courthouse Wash. Jug Rock and Merrimac Butte maps.
Lilliston B. Bartlett moved to Moab in about 1879 and ran cattle in the area. (1116~)
—Old Spanish Trail: In 1952 Bert J. Silliman noted that the springs in upper Bartlett Wash near the abandoned Bartlett Ranch were a secondary, but nonetheless important, water source along the Old Spanish Trail. (1734~)
—Hidden Canyon: This short northern tributary of Bartlett Wash is one and three-quarters of a mile south of Brink Spring (at elevation 4898T on the Jug Rock map).

Barton Canyon: (Emery Co.) Roan Cliffs-Range Creek. Lighthouse Canyon map.
Waldo Wilcox: "That was named for Bill Barton. He worked for Preston Nutter. He built a trail down Barton Canyon. It goes from Range Creek up to Range Valley Mountain." (2011~) Jim Brown worked for Preston Nutter: "There is a cabin on the Mountains called Bill Barton Cabin." (94~)

Barton Range Canyon: (San Juan Co.) Cedar Mesa-Comb Wash. Bluff SW map.
Also called Bartons Land. (1822~)
Clyde Barton noted that his grandfather, Joseph F. Barton (1855-1926), ran livestock throughout this area from 1880 to 1905. (162~) Alice Eastwood in 1896: "When

this country is named at all it is called Barton's Range." (590~)

Barton Tebbs La Fevre Canal: (Iron Co.) Dixie National Forest-Sevier River. Panguitch NW map.

A.F. Barton, Daniel F. Tebbs, and William La Fevre were all early residents of Tebbsdale, a small and now defunct town to the north of Panguitch. (421~) (See Tebbs Hollow—Tebbsdale Town.)

Bar X Wash: (Grand Co.) Book Cliffs-Grand Valley-Bitter Creek. Jim Canyon and Bar X Wash maps.

The Bar X Cattle Company, based out of Westwater, ran livestock in the area starting before 1889. (1363~) (See Westwater–Westwater Ranch.)

Basin Canyon: (Kane Co.) GSCENM-Kaiparowits Plateau-Rogers Canyon. Basin Canyon and East of the Navajo maps.

Pratt Gates noted that this was named for a basin at the top of the canyon's east fork, which cowboys call The Basin. (709~)

In 1996 *Car and Driver Magazine* called Basin Canyon the "loneliest spot in America," noting: "Here, within a 30-mile radius, you will find no homes, few footprints, and no cable TV. What you *will* find is an astronomical number of cow-pies." (1535~)

Bastian Reservoir: (Garfield Co.) Henry Mountains-Stanton Pass. Cass Creek Peak map.

This stock reservoir was built by Antone (also spelled Anthon) Bastian and George Walgomott, owners of the nearby Trachyte Ranch, in the early years. (604~, 1644~) Bliss Brinkerhoff: "That should be Dry Lake. Old Bastion put a dam there. He was goin' to collect and store water to farm with down on Trachyte [Creek]. But the water source was never that big and the snow pack was never that big and the ground simply will not hold water. It just leaches through. So nothing more than a natural lake is there and that natural lake is Dry Lake." (291~) The reservoir has since been improved and now holds water.

Batty Pass: (Kane Co.) GSCENM-Fiftymile Bench-Escalante Desert. Big Hollow Wash map. (4,920')

Also called Battys Pass. (872~)

This is a low pass with an old uranium mining-era road and a cattle trail going through it. The remains of a rock building and a wood shed can still be seen in the pass. (SAPE.)

Three name derivations are given.

First, Pratt Gates noted that one of the earliest Escalante settlers was Philo Allen, Sr. (1818-1909). His nickname was Batty. (709~)

Second, Don Coleman noted that the cave near Batty Pass (See below) was named for a local nicknamed Batty: "This Batty would leave Escalante and he'd go down there and hide out and they even had a bush down there they called Batty Bush. I think it was a kind of tea that he drank ... Jimson weed [also known as Sacred Datura, a hallucinogen]." (441~)

Three, the Utah Geographic Place Names file noted that it was "Named for the large number of bats found in the caves." (2053~)

—Batty Pass Caves: (Also called Caveman Point.) The caves are near the end of a "Jeep Trail" on the south end of Black Ridge (one-half mile south-southwest of elevation 5339 on the Basin Canyon map). The three large caverns were excavated in the mid-1950s by brothers Bill and Cliff Lichtenhahn. They filled the caves with machinery that they used to cut and polish rock and to build lapidary machines for others. The partially completed hull of a boat they planned to use on Lake Powell sits in one cave. (47~, 55~, 2051~) John Phillips: "The Batty caves are not now notably batty but were undeniably home to batty occupants around 1964. That's when two hermits began building boats there, in preparation for the watery world of wonders that would presumably pool behind the nearby Glen Canyon Dam.... This business failed, in part because their boats were fashioned 50 percent from newspaper and in part because the liquid portion of Lake Powell never got within 18 miles of this spot." (1535~)

Bauer Canyon: (Kane Co.) Kolob Terrace-Orderville Gulch. Straight Canyon map.

This is most likely spelled Bower Gulch, named for Isaiah Bowers (1846-1926). He arrived in Orderville in the early 1880s. (1639~) Bowers ran a sawmill for the Orderville United Order and had a farm here which was called Castle Rock. (1714~)

Bauers Knoll: (Iron Co.) Cedar Valley-Eightmile Hills. Cedar City NW map.

Also spelled Bowers Knoll. (M.6)

Alowis Bauer (1831-1906) and family arrived in Cedar City in 1857. They had grazing grounds at the North Fields of Cedar City. Bauer progenitors still live in the area. (165~)

Baullies Mesa: (San Juan Co.) Cedar Mesa-Fish Creek-Picket Fork. South Long Point and Hotel Rock maps.

DeReese Nielson: "They said it was a bald-headed outlaw from Cortez, Colorado. That's what the old-timers told me.... He brought a little bunch of cattle over there to start with, and he was an old man, bald-headed, and that's how it got its name." (1451~)

Bayles Spring: (San Juan Co.) Manti-LaSal National Forest-Abajo Mountains-Allen Canyon. Mount Linnaeus map. PRIVATE PROPERTY.

This is a large spring. (SAPE.)

Grant Bayles noted that his father, Hanson Bayles (1857-1922), developed the spring in the early 1900s. (1931~)

—Allan Canyon Ranch: PRIVATE PROPERTY. This was near Bayles Spring. Cardon Jones noted that Arthur Martinez homesteaded here in the early days. (1010~) Martinez was buried in an unmarked grave on the ranch in either 1911 or 1915. (1910~) In 1916 Bishop Hanson Bayles bought the ranch. The Bayles family still has a ranch one mile northeast of the spring. (1821~, 2036~)

Bean Hill: (Iron Co.) Kanarra Mountain-Reeves Creek. Cedar Mountain map. (9,084') PRIVATE PROPERTY.

Mrs. J.A. Haslam noted that "numerous wild bean plants growing upon hill." (942~)

Bean Hill: (Piute Co.) Fishlake National Forest-Sevier Plateau. Marysvale Peak map. (10,055')

Newel Nielson: "We had what we called timber beans and bush beans and that hill was loaded with them. They're very rich feed and a herd of sheep can even bloat on them." (1458~)

Bear Canyon: (Carbon and Emery Counties.) Roan Cliffs-Range Creek. Lila Point and Lighthouse Canyon maps.

Waldo Wilcox: "They saw a bear up in there." (2011~)

Bear Canyon: (Garfield Co.) Dixie National Forest-Boulder Mountain-Oak Creek. Bear Canyon map.

Charles Kelly noted that a small bear was captured in the canyon. (1047~) Keith Durfey noted that black bears still frequent the canyon. (582~)

Bear Creek: (Garfield Co.) Dixie National Forest-Boulder Mountain-Boulder Creek. Jacobs Reservoir, Deer Creek Lake, and Boulder Town maps.

Two name derivations are given.

First, Edson Alvey: "The name was derived from black bears seen in the area." (55~)

Second, Leland Haws, the son of the original homesteader: "The homesteader, Mr. Haws, had a (bear) rough time getting into or out of his property and he called it a Bear of a creek to travel, therefore the name Bear Creek." (1931~)

—Haws Dairy: In the late 1880s Frank Haws established a dairy on Bear Creek. (381~)

Bear Creek: (Iron Co.) Dixie National Forest-Sevier River. Little Creek Peak and Panguitch NW maps.

Bear Creek runs through Upper and Lower Bear Valley.

Warren Pendleton: "It is a canyon up by Lower Bear Valley. Because of bear tracks found there in the early days it is called Bear Canyon." (1515~)

Bear Creek: (San Juan Co.) Manti-LaSal National Forest-Abajo Mountains-Indian Creek. Mount Linnaeus map.

—Forest Service Trail #018: This constructed stock trail goes from Jackson Ridge, across Bear Creek, and ends at Aspen Flat. (SAPE.)

Bear Creek: (Washington Co.) Upper Kolob Plateau-Blue Springs Reservoir. Kolob Reservoir map.

Bear Creek runs through Bear Valley.

—Kolob Mountain Ranch: PRIVATE PROPERTY. This is on Bear Creek one mile upcreek from Blue Springs Reservoir (near elevation 8297).

Bear Creek Canyon: (Emery Co.) Manti-LaSal National Forest-Gentry Mountain-Huntington Creek. Hiawatha map.

Stella McElprang noted that a bear killed a cow here in 1880. (1330~)

—Bear Creek Ranger Station: This was the first ranger station in Huntington Canyon. Built in 1909, it was at the mouth of Bear Creek. The building has since been moved to the town of Huntington. (1185~)

Bears Ears: (San Juan Co.) Manti-LaSal National Forest-Dark Canyon Plateau-South Elk Ridge. Kigalia and Woodenshoe Buttes maps. (9,058')

The Navajo, who first arrived in the Bears Ears area in about 1620 (205~), called them *Shasháá*, or the "Bears Ears" (1943~). It is unclear if the Navajo name predates that of the first Spanish explorers.

Robert S. McPherson noted that the Ute name is *Kwiyagat Nügavat*, or "Bears Ears." (1335~)

By the late 1700s Spanish explorers were using the *Las Orejas del Oso* (Ears of the Bear) name on their maps. (1336~) The Jose Antonio Vizcarra Navajo Campaign of 1823 called them *Las Orejas*. (309~)

The 1854 John C. Fremont map shows them as the *Rejas del oso*. (684~) The 1870 and 1871 Froiseth maps show these as *Ore Jas Del Oso*. (M.20., M.21.)

—First Road: The original vehicle road from Blanding to Natural Bridges went through the gap at the Bears Ears. Construction started in the mid-1920s. The first section of road went from Blanding to Cottonwood Wash and up it for several miles (some of this is now County Road 268). The second section ascended Elk Ridge just to the south of Hammond Canyon (now County Road 228). It went to the vicinity of Little Notch near Kigalia Point (now County Road 088). The road from the Bears Ears, down the cliffs, across Grand Flat, and to Natural Bridges was constructed in 1927–28. (774~)

Bear Trap Canyon: (Washington Co.) Zion National Park-La Verkin Creek. Kolob Reservoir map.

Ron Kay noted that a pioneer "cornered a wounded bear here." (1038~)

—Beartrap Canyon Wilderness: Forty acres in Bear Trap Canyon were designated as Wilderness in 2009.

Bear Trap Knoll: (Grand Co.) Uintah and Ouray Indian Reservation-East Tavaputs Plateau. Walker Point and Lion Canyon maps. (9,092')

In the old days a trap made out of poles would be set to catch bears. Nell Murbarger in 1960: "investigated several pole bear traps that hadn't been set for a quarter century." (1414~)

Bear Valley: (Sevier Co.) Sevier Plateau-The Brink. Water Creek Canyon and Koosharem maps.

Also spelled Bearvalley. (1356~)

In 1865 settlers in the new town of Panguitch found themselves on the brink of starvation. A relief party was sent to Parowan some forty miles to the west. Going up Bear Valley, their horses soon bogged down in the deep snow. In order for the expedition to continue, members laid quilts across the snow, moving them ahead one at a time as they made slow progress across the valley. The trip was successful. (1445~)

George Washington Bean: "Sunday, June 22, 1873, we struck out into the mountains on horseback. Camped that night at Brimhall Springs. Next morning we traveled up a nice narrow valley through grass which in places touched our stirrups, and at the head of the valley we found a large grizzly bear that had just been skinned; it looked as large as a cow, so they named the place 'Bear Valley,' and it still retains that name." (1971~)

—Old Spanish Trail: The trail traversed Bear Valley. The valley became the primary pioneer route from Iron County to Garfield County. (474~)

Bear Valley Junction: (Iron Co.) Sevier River-Highway 89-Highway 20. Panguitch NW map.

Also called Orton Junction for a family of that name who lived here in the early days. (854~) Another name was LeFeveres or LeFevers. (1356~)

This is the junction of Highways 89 and 20.

—Old Spanish Trail: The trail went through what is today's Bear Valley Junction, turning from south to west, up Bear Creek.

Bear Valley Guard Station: (Iron Co.) Dixie National Forest-Upper Bear Valley-Holyoak Spring. Little Creek Peak map.

This was built in the 1930s by the CCC. It is no longer used. (2021~)

Beas Lewis Flat: (Wayne Co.) Boulder Mountain-Miners Mountain. Twin Rocks map.

Also called Beason Lewis Flat. (1194~)

Beason Lewis (1836-1902) arrived in Rabbit Valley in 1873. (699~) He brought a herd of five hundred cattle to the area in 1876. (418~)

Beatty Hill: (Washington Co.) Dixie National Forest-Pine Valley Mountains. Pintura map.

(See Beatty Point for name derivation.)

Beatty Point: (Washington Co.) Zion National Park-Lee Pass. Kolob Arch map. (7,780')

Two name derivations are given.

First, Ron Kay noted that the [John T.] Beatty family were pioneers of Toquerville. At one time Beatty was the mayor of the town. (1038~, 388~)

Second, Walt and Reid Beatty were two of the first tourist guides in Zion National Park, starting in the late 19teens. Walt was the chief guide until 1927. (1279~)

—Kolob Fingers: (Also called The Finger Canyons of Kolob and The Finger Canyons of Zion.) Charles Roscoe Savage in 1875: "The road from Kanarra[ville] slopes gradually to the South.... On the left a ridge of mountains skirts the road some twenty miles. Two immense shafts of red sandstone rock point heavenward a few miles south of Kanarra. These have been called the Pillars of Hercules. The Canyons around Kanarra are full of wonderful rocky chasms and narrow passages, all composed of glaring red sand stone." (1690~)

Frank Jensen in 1964: "From [New Harmony or the Fort Harmony site], three promontories, Tucupit Point, Paria Point, and Beatty Point appear to have been thrust upward from the desert floor like the knuckles of a gigantic fist. The shadowed areas lying between the promontories are the three forks of Taylor Creek with eroded canyons 1600 feet deep." (965~)

—Icebox Canyon: This starts on the east side of Beatty Point and goes south-southeast into LaVerkin Creek, passing the east side of Nagunt Mesa and Kolob Arch on the way. Scott Patterson: "Icebox was known as Waterfalls [Canyon] and I don't know which name came first." (653~)

Beaver Bottom: (San Juan Co.) Canyonlands National Park-Stillwater Canyon. Horsethief Canyon map.

Inscriptions include Arthur Wheeler, 1893. (1115~, SAPE.)

Beaver Canyon: (Wayne Co.) Burr Desert-Dirty Devil River. Baking Skillet Knoll and Angel Cove maps.

Also called Beaver Box and Beaver Box Canyon.

Barbara Ekker noted that beavers, now gone, built dams that flooded the canyon. (607~) Darys and Horace Ekker in 1984: "The origin of this name is accounted for by the numerous beaver ponds that exist[ed] in the drainage, and by the fact that the canyon does 'box up,' a feature which provides a natural corral for the ranchers that run cattle in the area." (1931~)

The floor of the canyon has been cut by huge gullies. Alvin Robison: "In my lifetime, that's the way it's always been. But my dad, when he was a young guy and years ago, said that there was nothing but a valley in those days. It was just a big bottom all the way down to the Dirty Devil. They used to gather four, five hundred head of cows in there. That's when they had to trail everything to the railroad up in Green River. There were none of those huge gullies like they have now. The last time I was through there, I 'bout killed my horse." (1642~)

Inscriptions include A.F. Bailey, Jan. 7, 1906 and Jack Woolsey, Nov. 13, 1932. (SAPE.)

Beaver Creek: (Grand Co.) La Sal Mountains-Dolores River. Mount Waas, Dolores Point South, and Dolores Point North maps.

Bette L. Stanton: "Amasa [Larsen] settled up on Beaver Creek, on the northeast side of the La Sal Mountains. He had a cabin up there, but it is unknown if he built the structure or inherited it from some long-gone trapper." (1805~)

—Beaver Basin: (Mount Waas map.) Alden Newell told this story: "A miner named Fred McCoy had some gold claims at Beaver Basin. A company in Denver made him an offer of $75,000 for his claims. But in addition he wanted an interest in the claims and management. The Denver company wouldn't go along with his request, so he got nothing and died alone, a pauper, in his cabin in Beaver Basin." (2027~)

—Spring Canyon: This short western tributary of Beaver Creek is four miles upcanyon from the Dolores River (between elevations 5958 and 6001 on the Dolores Point North map). (1866~)

Beaver Creek: (Sevier Co.) Fishlake National Forest-Wasatch Plateau-Salina Creek. Water Hollow Ridge map. Stuart Johnson: "There is one area there that has a particular lot of beaver and beaver dams." (1003~)

Beaver Dam Mountains: (Washington Co.)

Also called Utah Hill (154~) and West Mountains (1931~). (See Beaver Dam Wash for name derivation.)

The Shivwit Indians call this *Tahokari* Mountain, or "Dry Mountain." (1931~)

—Beaver Dam Mountains Wilderness Area: This 17,600 acre Wilderness was designated in 1984. Straddling the Arizona-Utah border, there are about 15,000 acres in Arizona and about 2,600 acres in Utah.

Beaver Dam Wash: (Washington Co., Utah and Mojave Co., Az.) Acoma, Nevada-Virgin River. Utah maps: Pine Park, Docs Pass, Dodge Spring, Motoqua, West Mountain Peak, Scarecrow Peak, and Terry Benches. Arizona map: Littlefield.

The Paiute name is *Paa'uipi*, or "water wash." (82~)

Jedediah Smith of the South West Expedition of 1826–27 followed Beaver Dam Wash, which he called Pautch Creek: "The country is not so rough as on the other (E) side of the mountain but extremely barren and the [Beaver Dam] river continues wide and shoal." (1774~)

Addison Pratt was with the Jefferson Hunt Party of 1849: "We reached the Virgin River at the mouth of a dry wash where we found a grove of cottonwood and willows and some large springs. About 50 rods from the river, they formed quite a stream which ran through a mud flat near the river. Brother Hunt showed me a place where there was a beaver dam when he visited the place in 1848, but the heavy rains last winter had raised the water so high that it carried away the dam and the beavers had now left it." (1571~)

Members of the Jayhawker Party of 1849 noted this as Big Canyon. William Lewis Manly of the expedition: "Immediately in front of us was a cañon [upper Beaver Dam Wash], impassable for wagons, and down into this the trail descended." (1274~, 1211~) The Jayhawker Party turned around and found another way. But, the Henry W. Bigler party, a part of the Jayhawker Party, did descend into the canyon. Bigler: "In traveling down the canyon we passed over a place where if a horse made one false step he would have plunged hundreds of feet without any possibility of saving himself [the Jumping Off Place] ... [we] continued down the canyon ... but we soon found ourselves completely blocked up.... Some of the men descended the canyon to see if there was not a chance to make a road for our animals, in a little while they returned saying the road was extremely bad but thought by rolling a few rocks out of the way we could get along. We had two tight and steep places to ascend.... It is surprising to see where horses can go, and in ascending a very steep place, some of them fell and rolled over with their packs on." (228~)

Years later, Charles Kelly found the old trail down the Jumping Off Place: "Straight down it ran, apparently into the bowels of the earth, the longest, steepest, narrowest trail we had ever encountered in many years of desert travel. Down, down, and down we went at a snail's pace." (1071~)

John Gorham Chandler of the Lieutenant Sylvester Mowry Expedition of 1855 called this Canonwood Creek. (95~)

Amasa M. Lyman in 1857: "We were at the Cottonwood spring or the Beaver Dam so Called." (1251~)

Anson Call in 1864: "This stream is about the size of St. George North Creek. We crossed the stream and camped on the edge of Indian Thomases' farm. Here this Indian had raised good corn and we hat plenty of good Corn fodder for our animals. Bunch grass on the sand hills South of the stream. Timber is plenty here.... This Indian was desirous to have the Mormons settle in this neighborhood." (331~)

Charles Roscoe Savage in 1875: "The Beaver Dam settlement was once a small paradise, but all at once it took a notion to go down stream, and is no more." (1690~)

Don Maguire in 1878: "Beaver Dams is a mountain stream rising from some springs.... Along the stream, elder, cottonwood, and maple trees grow in considerable numbers. There were quite a number of beaver dwelling along the stream, from which it had taken its name." (1902~)

Inscriptions in upper Beaver Dam Wash include HWB. This was engraved by Henry W. Bigler, a member of the Jayhawker Party of 1849. Bigler: "Near camp are some soft rocks on which I cut the three first letters of my name and the date." (228~) Another nearby inscription is from Osborn, '49. (1071~)

Beaver Hole: (Grand Co.) Roan Cliffs-Nash Wash. Bogart Canyon map.

Longtime Cisco resident Ballard Harris noted that in the old days this country was full of beavers. (1931~)

Beaver Slide Bottom: (Grand Co.) Uintah and Ouray Indian Reservation-Gray Canyon. Three Fords Canyon map.

Waldo Wilcox: "The beavers make slides down the embankments to get to the river. Just like a kid's slide." (2011~)

Beck Hollow: (Garfield Co.) Dixie National Forest-Escalante Mountains-North Creek. Barker Reservoir map.

Pratt Gates noted that a man named Beck ran livestock in the area in the early days. (709~)

—Beck Hollow Stock Trail: This constructed stock trail is shown as a "Pack Trail." Some of it is difficult to follow. (SAPE.)

Beckwith Plateau: (Emery Co.) West Tavaputs Plateau-Book Cliffs. Blue Castle Butte, Butler Canyon, Cliff, and Jenny Canyon maps.

Also called Little Mountain.

This highland area at the southwestern corner of the West Tavaputs Plateau (the Book Cliffs) was named for Lieutenant E.G. Beckwith. He was Captain John W. Gunnison's assistant on their reconnoiter of the area in 1853. Beckwith finished Gunnison's report after Gunnison was killed during the expedition. (166~, 1419~, 1563~)

—Oil Road: This amazing road, shown as a "Pack Trail," starts near the mouth of Trail Canyon on the Price River (Jenny Canyon map) and goes generally south and east, over the top of Long Canyon (Cliff map), to the top of the Beckwith Plateau and Elliott Mesa (back to the Jenny Canyon map). It ends at a "Drill Hole" near the top of Short Canyon. (SAPE.)

Bedspring Pass: (Piute Co.) Parker Mountain-Forshea Draw. Angle map. (9,360')

Thaine Taylor: "In the summer a sheeper used to camp there.... They left an old bedspring there, hung it up in a tree, and that's how it got its name." (1868~)

Beebe Hollow: (Washington Co.) Upper Kolob Plateau-Kolob Reservoir. Kolob Reservoir map.

Also called Beebe's Canyon. (363~)

George Brimhall in about 1864: "started for Kolob, where W.A. Beebe had my cows and young stock.... We found his shantie on a very romantic spot of nearly level ground, with an excellent spring of clear water on it, wood with scattering trees of pine of about equal size." (288~) This was William Albert Beebe (1813-1884). He arrived in Washington County in 1862. He later moved to Kanab and then to Circleville. (462~)

Beebe Spring: (Garfield Co.) Dixie National Forest-Johns Valley-Rock Creek. Cow Creek map.

Gilbert R. Beebe (1863-1937) and family were residents of the nearby town of Henderson in the early 1900s. They ran a sawmill on Flake Swale. (2063~)

Beef Basin: (San Juan Co.) Dark Canyon Plateau-Gypsum Canyon. Cross Canyon, Fable Valley, House Park Butte, and Druid Arch maps.

Also called Beef Pasture. (821~)

Cattlemen started running livestock in Beef Basin in the early 1880s. Frank Silvey: "In 1883 to 1900 Jones Bros, Mel Turner, Dave Cooper, Dave Goudelock and others discovered and named ... 'Beef Basin.'" (1740~)

Fletcher B. Hammond: "It needed but one fence—from the top of the east canyon to the top of the west canyon. I helped repair that fence one time when the beef steers would jump over to get to their old feeding grounds." (821~)

Carl Mahon told this story, lightly edited, that happened in Beef Basin: "Jack Kelly took a contract to winter a bunch of steers in Beef Basin. He took them in there and they had been there for a while and here comes old Butch Cassidy and his bunch. They'd been over around Telluride or in that area and had robbed a bank and they came out there and wanted to know if they could stay a day or two. It just went to snowing like crazy and snowed and snowed.

At that time the only way out of there that they knew about was to go up Fable Valley and up by Sweet Alice Spring and then over the hill and off Trail Canyon into Dark Canyon and then back up either Peavine or Woodenshoe Canyon. Butch knew there was way too much snow to go that way and so he stayed there all winter and helped. He and his group pitched in and helped just like any other cowboys.

"Jack got sick and thought he had pneumonia. He went home in February. Butch told him, 'We probably won't be here when you get back.' Jack went to the Dugout [Ranch on Indian Creek]. They had a little store there, where the headquarters of Indian Creek Cattle Company is now. When he got there, there was Joe Bush, the old U.S. Marshall. Jack acted like he came in to spend the summer, and about the second day, why, old Bush asked him when he was going back out there. He said, 'Well, I'm not.' 'Oh yes you are,' the Marshall told him. He said, 'You get whatever groceries and things that you came after and we're going back.'

"And it liked to scare old Jack to death because he didn't want to be in the middle of it. And the cowboys had really been good to him, Butch and his bunch. So finally he decided there was a rim right up above where they were camped in Beef Basin and that he'd just ride up enough to see them and he'd take his horse and whirl and away he'd go and just let them shoot it out. He got there and Butch was gone. Whew"! (1272~, 1010~)

—Beef Basin Spring: (Fable Valley map.) This large, developed spring was often used by cowboys as a campsite. (SAPE.)

—Constructed Stock Trail: This excellent trail enters Beef Basin Wash from the east by way of a short tributary that is immediately west of elevation 7170T on the House Park Butte map. (SAPE.)

—First Road: The first road into Beef Basin started at Elephant Hill and went up Bobbys Hole. It was built for uranium exploration in the early 1950s. (1821~)

Beef Slide Canyon: (Carbon Co.) Roan Cliffs-Range Creek. Patmos Head map.

Waldo Wilcox: "Preston Nutter would bring his beef off there down into Range Creek. They could push the cows

down the slide, but they'd have to take them out another way." (2011~)

Beehive Arch: (Wayne Co.) Canyonlands National Park-Maze District-The Doll House. Spanish Bottom map.

Kent Frost guided Randall Henderson into the Maze area in 1963: "That Henderson trip was [our] first trip in there. Rosie Goldman lives in Bluff, and she is the one who got that name through the Bureau of Names and Places, in Washington, D.C. So Rosie Goldman is the one; we named it." (690~, 1429~) Frost, in suggesting the name to the USGS: "The name not only suits the shape with remarkable accuracy, but it also suits one of the two dominant cultures of the state in which it stands." (1931~)

Beehive Butte: (Grand Co.) Tenmile Country-Big Flat. The Knoll map. (5,970')

Old maps show this as Whitbeck Rock, a name that has now been applied to a larger ridge two miles to the east. (1331~) (See Whitbeck Rock.)

Inscriptions include C.W. Heler and Joe F. Sullivan, 1895. (SAPE.)

Beehive Peak: (Sevier Co.) Fishlake National Forest-Pavant Range-Red Canyon. Beehive Peak map. (9,018')

Also called Red Pyramid. (1931~)

Ernest Herbert and Blain Curtis: "Beehive Peak is a pyramid shaped peak with a striking resemblance to a red pyramid when viewed from the west, but resembling a beehive when viewed from the valley to the east." (1931~)

Irvin Warnock: "sculptured by nature to resemble the Utah State beehive symbol." (1971~)

Bee Hive Peak: (Washington Co.) Zion National Park-Towers of the Virgin. Springdale East map. (6,904')

Also called The Beehives. (1931~)

Cartographer Richard B. Roth noted that these were a "series of bumps on Terrace Top." (1931~)

Beehive Rock: (Coconino Co., Az.) Glen Canyon NRA-Glen Canyon Dam. Page, Az. map.

During construction of the Glen Canyon Dam in 1958 one face of the otherwise symmetrical Beehive Rock was removed to make room for a cableway tower. Later, the Glen Canyon Dam Visitor Center was built at the site. (2057~)

A Navajo, watching the destruction of Beehive Rock, is quoted as saying, "Something came out that looked like blood to me." The Navajo called this Round Rock and they believed that with its mutilation, an evil spirit was released that will make the dam leak and the reservoir be unsuccessful. (578~)

—Movies: *Broken Arrow*, starring John Travolta and Christian Slater, was filmed, in part, with Beehive Rock in the background. (1421~)

Begashinitani: (Navajo Co., Az.) Navajo Indian Reservation-Nokai Mesa-Nokai Canyon. Big Point and Cattle Canyon, Az. maps.

Also called Cutfinger Canyon. (1931~)

Béégashii is Navajo for "cow" or "cattle." *Béégashii Nit'ání* is "a place where cows grow up" (1931~, 2072~) or "watering place for cattle" (1204~).

Behanin Creek: (Garfield Co.) Dixie National Forest-Boulder Mountain-Pleasant Creek. Deer Creek Lake and Lower Bowns Reservoir maps.

Correctly spelled Behunin Creek.

Elijah Cutlar Behunin (1847-1933) and family moved to the Fruita area in 1886. (1419~)

—Behunin Point: This is at the head of Behunin Creek (one-quarter mile east of elevation 10802 on the Deer Creek Lake map). (337~)

—Behunin Point Trail: This is the "Pack Trail" that goes up Behunin Point (Deer Creek Lake map). (337~)

Behind the Rocks: (San Juan Co.) Spanish Valley-Highway 191. Kane Springs and Trough Springs Canyon maps. Lloyd Holyoak: "That is an old name, as far back as I can remember." (906~) Faun M. Tanner noted that the Moab Rim, to the south and west of Moab, was historically called The Rocks. Therefore, the area west of The Rocks was Behind the Rocks. (1855~)

Ward J. Roylance: "Land Behind the Rocks, a compact but exceptionally rugged region of slickrock fins and domes and labyrinthine drainage channels, a maze of strange and beautiful erosional forms." (1658~)

—Indian Fort: This is an Anasazi ruin in the eastern part of Behind the Rocks. The Indian Fort name is incised on the rock. Inscriptions include J.H. Owen, May 8/78; ME, 1884; W.H. Houck, 1892; and E.E. Shafer and C. Wilson, 2/8 96. (1115~)

—Lone Rock: (Also called Prostitute Arch.) (M.55.) This is the "Natural Arch" on a southern portion of the Behind the Rocks (near elevation 5536T on the Trough Springs Canyon map). (2019~, M.55.)

Behunin Canyon: (Washington Co.) Zion National Park-Zion Canyon. Temple of Sinawava map.

Zion National Park Superintendent P.P. Patraw in 1934 suggested the name for pioneer Isaac Behunin (1803–1881) and family. They moved to Springdale in 1863. In that year Behunin also built a small cabin in Zion Canyon. (1931~, 1891~, 2043~)

Bell Butte: (San Juan Co.) Valley of the Gods-Highway 261. The Goosenecks map. (5,351')

The butte is shaped liked a bell. The name was in use by the early 1900s. (1369~)

Bell Canyon: (Emery Co.) San Rafael Swell-Little Wild Horse Canyon. Horse Valley and Little Wild Horse Mesa maps.

Also called Cistern Canyon. (845~)

This is a newer name that is not familiar to the local ranchers.

—Ding Dang Dome: This prominent tower is halfway between Bell and Cistern canyons and is at the south end of Sinbad Country (at elevation 6107T on the Little Wild Horse Mesa map). Steve Allen named the tower while on an ascent, the name reflecting, in polite terms, the problems encountered. The canyon names below stem from Ding Dang Dome.

—Ding Canyon: This northern tributary of Little Wild Horse Canyon is immediately east of Ding Dang Dome (southwest of elevation 5468T on the Little Wild Horse Mesa map).

—Dang Canyon: This northern tributary of Little Wild Horse Canyon is immediately west of Ding Dang Dome (at elevation 5485AT on the Little Wild Horse Mesa map).

Bellevue Flats: (Emery Co.) San Rafael Swell-Red Ledges. Horn Silver Gulch map.

Lee Mont Swasey: "Bellevue Flats was named after the famous insane asylum back east.... They were going to farm this big flat and they were told that they needed to be sent to Bellevue because there was no way in —— that they were going to farm it. That was in the early 1900s." (1853~)

Bement Arch: (Kane Co.) Glen Canyon NRA-Davis Gulch. Davis Gulch map.

Bement Arch has had several names. Locally it was called Nemo Arch, Ruess Arch, or Everett Ruess Natural Window in reference to Everett Ruess, the vagabond artist who disappeared near the arch in 1934. Ruess inscribed Nemo 1934 on a wall near the arch.

Bering Monroe noted the name as Roosevelt Memorial Natural Bridge. Harry Aleson, in rejoinder, wrote: "Frankly, I never did like much connected with the Roosevelt Dynasty. After I had learned that Everett Ruess had left his 'NEMO' inscriptions both above and below the huge bridge.... I knew that he had seen it. I hoped that it might be called,—EVERETT RUESS NATURAL WINDOW." (36~, 29~)

Another name used by Monroe and Aleson was Peter Orin Barker Window. In 1945 the duo found the inscription

POB on the arch. Later they found that the arch had been visited by Barker in the early 1920s. (36~)

Members of a National Geographic Society expedition in 1955 renamed the arch for Harlon W. Bement (1916-2010), the director of the Utah State Aeronautics Commission. Bement, an avid explorer of canyon country on both foot and from the air, is credited with discovering several arches. (1382~) Jean Bennett noted that Bement himself called it Davis Arch. (208~)

Richard Negri described Bement's first view of the arch, from an airplane: "In 1954, on a return trip from Monument Valley, a storm forced Bement to swing northwest along the course of the Escalante River from where it flowed into the Colorado River. He avoided the storm and was rewarded with the view of a wonderful array of colors within the canyon. He spotted several arches that had never been recorded, including one later named Bement Arch in his honor." (1427~)

The USGS Board on Geographic Names was faced with the problem of officially naming the arch after Bement since he was still alive and land form names generally honor the dead. (47~)

Bench, The: (Piute Co.) Sevier River-Pine Creek. Marysvale map.

This is a bench above the Sevier River.

—Benchtown: This small community was at the east end of The Bench (near elevation 5938).

Bendder Pond: (Garfield Co.) Dog Valley-Granite Valley. Fremont Pass map.

This is a still-used stock pond. (SAPE.)

This was most likely named for George A. Bender. (388~)

Benson Creek: (Garfield Co.) Henry Mountains-Straight Creek. Cass Creek Peak map.

Charles B. Hunt: "[The creek was] named after Benson who was associated with [Claude] Sanford and Voight when the ranches on the north slope of Mount Hillers were started." (925~) This was in the late 1880s and early 1890s.

—Benson Spring: PRIVATE PROPERTY. This is one-quarter mile south of Benson Creek and is one and one-half miles northeast of Quaking Aspen Spring (one-quarter mile south of elevation 6484T). Garth Noyes noted that water for the nearby Cat Ranch was piped down from Benson Spring. (1473~) (See Taylor Ridges.)

—Crockett Ranch: PRIVATE PROPERTY. This was on Benson Creek one and one-half miles northeast of Benson Spring (one-quarter mile south of elevation 5670). It was started by Arthur Crockett (?-1924) in the late 1890s. Garth Noyes: "Crockett committed suicide. He hung himself. When the fellows went to cut him down, they said that he was close enough to the ground that his knees were touching. So there's always been a question on how he hung himself." (1473~) Jack King from Bicknell now owns the property. (1094~)

Benson Creek: (Iron Co.) Braffit Ridge-Parowan Canyon. Brian Head and Parowan maps.

Louella Adams Dalton: "One of the first ranches [in Iron County] was Richard Benson [1816–1896] and Phoebe Benson's [1820–1904] at the head of [Parowan] Canyon." (363~) Benson also started one of the first shingle mills in the area here. (361~)

—Sawmill: Nathan "Nattie" Benson had a sawmill in Parowan's Main Canyon just north of the Fore Bay. The Benson family has placed a plaque at the mill site. (1515~)

Berry Spring Creek: (Garfield Co.) Dixie National Forest-Paunsaugunt Plateau-Mud Spring Creek. Flake Mountain West and Bryce Canyon maps.

Two name derivations are given.

First, Gary Dean Young noted that in the mid-1870s a Mr. Berry, who was the head of the Beaver Cattle Cooperative, ran cattle in the area. (2063~)

Second, unattributed: "The creek was named by Henrie family who used to gather service berries from side hill above the creek." (2053~)

Berry Springs: (Washington Co.) Virgin River-Harrisburg Gap. Harrisburg Junction map.

Also spelled Bury's Springs. (1690~)

John W. Berry (1822–1890) was an early resident of Kanarraville. Ellen Powell Thompson noted that the spring was used for several weeks in 1872 by the Powell Expedition while they reconnoitered the surrounding country. She called it Camp Berry Spring: "The spring comes out of the rocks, warm water and impregnated with sulphur and very hard. So we shall not enjoy drinking or using it." (1763~)

Bert Avery Seep: (Wayne Co.) Henry Mountains-Blue Valley Benches. Steamboat Point map.

Charles B. Hunt: "Bert Avery was one of the earliest settlers in the region. He helped found [the now defunct town of] Clifton." (925~)

Keith Durfey told this story about Bert Avery: "He went to a dance ... one night and ended up proposing to this girl. And she said, 'No.' And he went home from the dance, got his horse, put a little pack on another horse, and left the country and never went back. He ended up over to Hanksville.... And he spent his life just around the Henry Mountains." (582~)

Inscriptions include Ivan Taft, April 27, 1912; Ernie Steele, 1931; and L. Nielson, 1939. (SAPE.)

Bertlesen Canyon: (Sevier Co.) Fishlake National Forest-Sevier Plateau-Monroe Creek. Monroe Peak map. Correctly spelled Bertelsen Canyon.

Irvin Warnock noted that Andreas Bertelsen (1829-1892) and family moved to Monroe in 1872. He built the first burr mill in the area. (1971~)

—Bertelsen Ditch: (Monroe Peak and Antelope Range maps.) Irvin Warnock noted that the ditch, surveyed by Andreas Bertelsen, was built in the 1890s. (1970~)

Bert Mesa: (Garfield Co.) Burr Desert-Dirty Devil River. Burr Point and Stair Canyon maps.

This was named for Bert Avery. (925~) (See Bert Avery Seep.)

—Oil Company Road: Alvin Robison noted that the "4WD" road from Burr Point down to Bert Mesa was built by an oil company. (1642~)

Betatakin Ruin: (Navajo Co., Az.) Navajo Indian Reservation-Navajo National Monument-Laguna Creek. Betatakin Ruin, Az. map.

Also called Kinneshon. (499~)

Part of Navajo National Monument, Betatakin, the site of a spectacular Anasazi cliff dwelling complex, was discovered by Byron Cummings, John Wetherill, and party in 1909. They named it *Betat'akin*, which is Navajo for "hillside house." Cummings is credited with being the first to excavate at Betatakin. (1654~)

Cummings on the discovery of Betatakin Ruin: "Found a large house in a big cave near the head of a side canyon.... Part of the ruin is in good condition and part has entirely fallen down. Probably there were 120 rooms or more originally.... The distinguishing feature of this house are the square kivas." (499~)

Bicknell Bottoms: (Wayne Co.) Rabbit Valley-Fremont River. Bicknell map.

Also called Thurber Bottoms.

(See Bicknell Town for name derivation.)

Romania Meeks Wise: "Bicknell Bottoms. The grass was high enough to touch the stirrups as the horsemen went riding through." (2035~)

—Red Gate: (Also called Dirty Devil Gap and The Narrows.) The Fremont River flows through the relative flats of Bicknell Bottoms and enters the Red Gate, a narrow area formed by a northern jut of Boulder Mountain and a southern jut of Thousand Lake Mountain. The Red Gate is one mile west of the junction of the Fremont River and Pine Creek (near elevation 6897). Grove Karl Gilbert of the Powell Survey named this in 1875–76. (722~, 723~)

Clarence Dutton of the Powell Survey: "The [Fremont] river leaves the [Rabbit] valley through the great gap between the [Thousand Lake] mountain and the Aquarius [Plateau], and the passage has been named the Red Gate." (584~)

—Books: Red Gate is mentioned in Hoffman Birney's fictional book *Forgotten Cañon*. (232~)

—Nielson Grist Mill: PRIVATE PROPERTY. (Also called Camp Thurber.) This was added to the Utah State Register of Historic Sites in 1971 and was listed on the National Register of Historic Places in 1975. This wood building is on the north side of Red Gap (one-eighth mile west-northwest of elevation 6884). A plaque near the mill reads, in part: "The Nielson Grist Mill on the edge of scenic country referred to by ancient Indians as 'The Land of Sleeping Rainbow.' Constructed around 1893 for Hans Peter Nielson by his son-in-law Niels Hanson [also spelled Hansen]. The mill was known as the Thurber Rolling Mill. Water for powering the mill was channeled from the Fremont River and dropped twenty-two feet through a wooden pipe to the turbine that ran the mill.

"The mill produced flour, germade [a wheat cereal], shorts, and bran, each coming from individual spouts. Farmers would receive one sack of flour for each three sacks of wheat. All forty-eight pound bags of flour were sewn by hand.... The mill made flour for the surrounding area for forty years. Improved roads, constructed in the 1930s, spelled the beginning of the end for the Thurber Rolling Mill. Since Wayne County could not grow hard wheat, which made the best bread, it became just as easy to truck in flour as hard wheat." (1551~, 1194~)

Bicknell Town: (Wayne Co.) Rabbit Valley-Fremont River-Highway 24. Bicknell map.

The town was initially named Thurber for Albert King Thurber, an Indian interpreter, Mormon Church official, and early explorer of Rabbit Valley. George Washington Bean in 1873: "[we] went to the place where Thurber is now located. A.K. Thurber liked the creek and location so well that we named the place Thurber in his honor." (749~)

Thurber started running cattle in the area in 1875 and settled here in 1879. The town was established in 1882. In 1914 easterner Thomas W. Bicknell offered a thousand volume library to any town in Utah that would change its name to Bicknell. Two towns accepted. Thurber became Bicknell. The other town, then called Grayson, became Blanding, after the maiden name of Bicknell's wife. (607~, 1047~, 1562~, 1786~, 2056~)

Betty D. Taylor grew up in Bicknell and told this story: "I was in the fourth grade when the atomic bomb was set off in Nevada, and we studied about it and we were so excited. When this was set off the whole school went out to the playground to see if we could feel the aftershocks, and which we did. It was a long ways away, but we were able to feel this when it went off. How foolish that was to go out there then, but it was an exciting time and we didn't realize that there may be some dangers from it." (1862~)

—Trenton Town: Unattributed: "Located three miles east of the present Thurber town site." (2053~) Little is known about the town.

Biddlecome Hollow: (Emery Co.) Manti-LaSal National Forest-Huntington Creek. Rilda Canyon map.

(See Biddlecome Hollow below for name derivation.)

Biddlecome Hollow: (Emery Co.) Manti-LaSal National Forest-Wasatch Plateau-Ferron Creek. The Cap and Ferron maps.

George R. Biddlecome (1844-1906) and his wife, Mary Davis (1845-1920), and family moved to Castle Dale in 1878. A couple of years later they moved to Wilsonville and, finally, in 1905, to Ferron Creek. (710~, 1195~) The Biddlecome ranch was in the first hollow east of the mouth of Biddlecome Hollow (immediately west of elevation 6575 on the Ferron map). (1967~)

In 1906 George and his daughter, Rachael, were killed while trying to cross Ferron Creek during a flash flood caused in part by a storm and by the breaching of a dam at Willow Lake. (338~, 931~) Millie Biddlecome told the story: "Ferron Creek was high. There is lots of fall in it where they crossed and no one knew just what happened but they were both drowned. They found Mr. Biddlecome that day. He still had his clothes on and his pocket knife still in his pocket. They didn't find Rachel until the next day…. They figured when they got in the water the wagon turned over." (227~)

—Behunin Coal Mine: Immediately east of the mouth of Biddlecome Hollow an old road cuts up and across the cliffs into Biddlecome Hollow. Ray Wareham noted that the road went to the Dave Behunin Coal Mine: "When you wanted coal, you made an appointment with Dave and he'd mine it out and you took your team and wagon and went up there to get loaded. When you came down, the team couldn't hold the wagon loaded with coal, so you rough-locked it. That is, you put a pole between both the front wheels and both the back wheels and then you slid down the road." (1967~)

The mine shaft—now closed with an iron gate—and other mine workings are one mile up the canyon. Inscriptions include W.J. Hansen, Aprial [*sic*] 1913 and ? Eastey, April 17, 1919. (SAPE.)

Big Bend: (Grand Co.) Arches National Park-Colorado River. Big Bend map.

This is a large bend in the Colorado River.

An inscription on the bend reads Big Bend Placer, 1894. (SAPE.)

—Big Bend Butte: Eric Bjørnstad noted that this is on the east side of the Big Bend (one-quarter mile north-north-west of elevation 5345T). On the same ridge are the Dolomite and Lighthouse towers. Podium Spire is one-half mile north-northeast of elevation 5345T. (239~)

Big Bend: (Washington Co.) Zion National Park-Zion Canyon. Temple of Sinawava map.

This bend in the North Fork Virgin River goes around The Organ and Angels Landing. In 1917 Guy Elliott Mitchell of the USGS called it Raspberry Bend. (1373~) Zion pioneer J.L. Crawford: "There's a big bend in the river, and on the shady side of the Organ between there and Angels Landing, in that cove, raspberries used to grow wild in there." (1785~)

Big Bend Draw: (Emery Co.) San Rafael Swell-Muddy Creek. Big Bend Draw map.

Big Bend Draw goes from Tea Brush Flat generally south for four miles and enters Muddy Creek at The Big Bend, which lends the draw its name.

Big Bown Bench: (Garfield Co.) GSCENM-Glen Canyon NRA-Escalante River. Silver Falls Bench, Red Breaks, and Pioneer Mesa maps.

(See Bowns Canyon for name derivation.)

—Middle Bench: This section of Big Bown Bench contains elevation 5536AT on the Silver Falls Bench map. An inscription on Middle Bench reads "Ellis Pritchett, Fairview San Pete Co. Utah., Dec. 18th, 1911." Another reads "First sheep on this Bench." This inscription was most likely from the 1880s. (441~, SAPE.)

—Trail Canyon: The head of this eastern tributary of the Escalante River is one and one-half miles northwest of Cliff Spring (east of elevation 5217T on the Silver Falls Bench map).

—Middle Bown Bench Trail: This constructed stock trail goes from the Escalante River, along the rim of the west side of Trail Canyon, to the Middle Bench section of Big Bown Bench (over elevation 5217T on the Silver Falls Bench map). (441~, SAPE.)

—Hoot Owl Canyon: This short eastern tributary of the Escalante River is between Trail Canyon and Cliff Spring (one-half mile southwest of elevation 5356T on the Silver Falls Bench map). Don Coleman: "We always called it Hoot Owl Canyon because there was always a hoot owl in there." (441~)

Big Canyon: (San Juan Co.) Abajo Mountains-Peters Canyon. Monticello Lake, Monticello North, and Church Rock maps.

The name was suggested to the USGS by Cecil Jones and Ross Musselman in 1980. (1931~)

Big Canyon: (San Juan Co.) Abajo Mountains-Westwater Creek. Mancos Jim Butte and Black Mesa Butte maps.

Karl Barton: "It's bigger than Westwater"! (162~) Herbert E. Gregory used the name in 1927. (761~)

Big Canyon: (Uintah Co.) Uintah and Ouray Indian Reservation-East Tavaputs Plateau-Desolation Canyon. Wolf Flat, Dog Knoll, and Firewater Canyon North maps.

Waldo Wilcox: "It is a big canyon"! (2011~)

Inscriptions include Will Seamount, March 21, 1911. (SAPE.)

—Cunepah Arch: This major arch is one-half mile up Big Canyon on its north wall. Ken Sleight called it Cunepah Arch, not realizing he was in Big Canyon and not in Firewater Canyon (also called Cunepah Canyon) two miles to the south. (207~)

—Skyline Sentinels: (Also called Three Sentinels.) (209~) These major pinnacles are a short distance upcanyon from Cunepah Arch and were named by Ken Sleight. (207~)

—Old Wild Horse Ben Cabin: This cabin-dugout site was used by "Wild Horse" Ben Morris in the early years. (209~) (See Duches Hole.) Waldo Wilcox noted that Ben had a still here. (2011~)

Big Dogie Canyon: (Grand and Uintah Counties.) Uintah and Ouray Indian Reservation-East Tavaputs Plateau-Hill Creek. Chicken Fork, Wolf Flat, and Flat Rock Mesa maps.

The USGS noted that this is named for a big calf, not a dog. Calves are often called "dogies" in the west. (1931~)

Big Dry Valley: (Kane Co.) Paria River-Little Creek Wood Bench. Henrieville and Slickrock Bench maps.

Ivan Willis and Sam Graff in 1963: "Big Dry Valley was named so because of its lack of water by the original homesteaders." (1931~)

—Harvey Chynoweth Ranch: PRIVATE PROPERTY. Ralph Chynoweth noted that this was in upper Big Dry Valley (one-eighth mile northwest of elevation 5980 on the Henrieville map). It was named for his father, Harvey (1893-1963). (425~)

Big Flat: (Grand Co.) Tenmile Country-Dead Horse Point State Park. The Knoll and Gold Bar Canyon maps.

Also called The Mainland. (1658~)

The Writers' Program of 1941: "A 90,000 acre livestock range developed by the U.S. Grazing Service through the drilling of two wells; powered by windmills, they provide water for 2,000 cattle and 6,000 sheep." (2056~)

Big Flat: (Piute Co.) Fishlake National Forest-Sevier Plateau. Marysvale Peak map.

—Big Flat Reservoir: Newel Nielson noted that this was built in 1934. (1458~)

Big Hill: (Emery Co.) Castle Valley-Shoemaker Wash. Cleveland map. (5,845')

This forty foot hill is notable only because it sits on an otherwise flat plain, making it a good landmark for stockmen. (SAPE.)

Big Hogan: (Navajo Co., Az.) Navajo Indian Reservation-Monument Valley. Mitten Buttes, Az. map.

This is a large natural arch. Harry Goulding: "The Big Hogan is a big cave with a hole in the top, like the smokehole in a hogan." (1380~)

Big Hole: (Emery Co.) San Rafael Swell-Pack Saddle Gulch. Chimney Rock map.

The Big Hole is a series of large potholes that almost always have water. (SAPE.) Clarence Dutton's 1879 Powell Survey map shows this as Water Pocket. (584~)

William T. Tew in 1881: "Went out in the desert. Camped by the Hole in the Rock, large tanks of water in rocks." (1871~)

—Old Spanish Trail: The Big Hole in Pack Saddle Gulch was an important stopping place along the Old Spanish Trail.

Big Hole: (Grand Co.) Colorado River-Westwater Canyon. Big Triangle map.

Big Hole was used for grazing livestock in the early 1900s. During prohibition a bootlegger resided here. (1362~)

—Constructed Stock Trail: This trail goes around the abandoned meander and exit Big Hole to the north. (SAPE.)

Big Hollow: (Wayne Co.) Awapa Plateau-Fremont River. Jakes Knoll, Moroni Peak, and Bicknell maps.

Thaine Taylor: "Big Hollow drains all of Parker Mountain clear to Antimony. So, it's a lot of drainage. Sometimes it gets pretty wild there after you get a lot of snow and it turns warm. A little water here, a little there, and you've got a lot of water flowing down there." (1868~)

—Lee Hollow: (Also called Lee Ranch.) This is the lower section of Big Hollow, from the point it opens up at its mouth to the Fremont River. Lee Brinkerhoff homesteaded here in the early years. (1931~)

Big Hollow Wash: (Kane Co.) GSCENM-Escalante Desert-Coyote Gulch. Big Hollow Wash map.

Also called Coyote Creek. (1706~)

The USGS: "The dry drain or hollow was the widest (biggest) at the point of crossing in the days of wagon travel; therefore, the name Big Hollow." (1931~)

—Big Hollow Spring: There is no spring here. There is a no-longer-functioning stock pond. (SAPE.)

Big Horn: (Garfield Co.) GSCENM-Harris Wash. Tenmile Flat map.

Edson Alvey noted that a nearby spring was used by bighorn sheep. (55~)

Bighorn Mesa: (San Juan Co.) Canyonlands National Park-Island in the Sky District. Horsethief Canyon and Upheaval Dome maps. (5,105')

—Hardscrabble Tower: (Also called Outlaw Spire.) This is on the west end of Bighorn Mesa (one-quarter mile southwest of elevation 5050T on the Horsethief Canyon map). It was named for Hardscrabble Hill, a particularly difficult section of the road that leads from Potato Bottom to Hardscrabble Bottom. (243~)

Big Horn Mountain: (Emery Co.) Book Cliffs-Price River. Jenny Canyon, Turtle Canyon, and Butler Canyon maps. Also called Buck Horn Mountain. (1931~)

Waldo Wilcox: "I'm sure it was named after bighorn sheep." (2011~)

Big Indian: (San Juan Co.) Navajo Indian Reservation-Monument Valley. Monument Pass map. (6,120')

Also called Big Chief (1931~) and Big Indian Butte (1930~).

Big Indian Valley: (San Juan Co.) Lisbon Valley-Dry Wash. Sandstone Draw and Lisbon Valley maps.

The Don Juan María Antonia de Rivera Expedition of 1765 went through Big Indian Valley. (953~)

—Big Indian Copper Mine: Don Maguire in 1892: "Big Indian creek ... carries in its float very rich copper ore, and near its head copper mines of wonderful richness have been found. I have on the table near me a sample of this ore which will run 90 percent." (1271~) The mine has been in intermittent use to the present day. (1409~)

—Big Indian Rock: (Lisbon Valley map.) A rock formation in the valley has the fanciful appearance of an Indian. In the 1920s-30s the Big Indian Copper mine was located here. (153~)

Big Lake: (Garfield Co.) Dixie National Forest-Aquarius Plateau. Big Lake map.

Also called Grass Lake. (1931~)

Alfonzo Turner noted that this natural lake was enlarged by the Forest Service. (1914~)

Julius S. Dalley: "The size of the lake, being larger than other lakes in that section of territory, gave it its name." (2053~)

This has also been called Snow Lake. The lake is fed by snow that blows off of nearby Flat Top. The deeper the snow, the deeper the lake. This name has been in use for over one hundred years. (1931~)

—Big Ditch: This was built by the CCC to bring water into Big Lake. (887~)

Big Lake: (Sevier Co.) Fishlake National Forest-Sevier Plateau. Water Creek Canyon map.

Also called Deep Lake (1931~) and Mecham Reservoir (1971~).

Irvin Warnock noted that Samuel Alvarus Mecham is credited with discovering Big Lake and, in 1885–86, constructing a ditch from the lake into Water Creek Canyon and to his farm near Annabella. (1971~)

—Mount Thurber and Mount Blue: These mountains are shown on the 1896 USGS Fish Lake map. It is most likely that Mount Thurber is one-half mile east of the south end of Big Lake (at elevation 9676). Mount Blue is most likely one-half mile south of Mount Thurber (at elevation 9694).

Bigman Spring: (Coconino Co., Az.) Navajo Indian Reservation-Cedar Tree Bench. Tse Esgizii, Az. map.

This is a large, developed spring.

The name Bigman is etched into a concrete watering trough. It is a local family name. (SAPE.)

Big Pack Mountain: (Uintah Co.) East Tavaputs Plateau-Hill Creek. Big Pack Mountain map. (6,524')

This was most likely named for brothers George W. and Ward E. Pack. They arrived in Vernal in the 1890s. (388~)

Big Plain Junction: (Washington Co.) Vermilion Cliffs-Highway 59. Smithsonian Butte map.

Big Plain is the large, relatively flat area that surrounds the junction. The junction marks the crossing of Highway 59 and the old Rockville Road which goes north to the town of Rockville.

Big Pocket: (San Juan Co.) Canyonlands National Park-Needles District-Salt Creek. South Six-shooter Peak and Cathedral Butte maps.

This large pasture area is almost completely surrounded by high cliffs. It was easy for the cowboys to keep their livestock in Big Pocket. (1821~)

Big Point: (Garfield Co.) Dixie National Forest-Awapa Plateau. Angle, Pollywog Lake, and Flossie Knoll maps. (9,428')

Also called The Point. (1096~)

The name was in place by 1892. (1096~)

—Big Point Spring: (Pollywog Lake map.) Sonny King noted that this developed spring is used to feed nearby Big Spring Pond.
(1095~)

Big Pond, The: (Emery Co.) San Rafael Swell-Crawford Draw. Twin Knolls map.

Also called Crawford Draw Reservoir.

This still-used stock reservoir was built in 1937. (1551~)

Big Ridge: (Garfield Co.) Henry Mountains-Mount Hillers. Cass Creek Peak map.

Charles B. Hunt noted that this was also called Stewart Ridge. George Stewart was in the area in the 1890s. (925~)

Big Ridge, The: (Garfield Co.) Dirty Devil Country-Orange Cliffs. Clearwater Canyon, Gordon Flats, The Pinnacle, and Fiddler Butte maps.

Many old maps show this as Land's End Plateau. (473~)

In 1928 Edwin T. Wolverton described it as "a massive island of rock." (2039~)

—Simplot Landing Strip: This is the "Landing Strip" on The Big Ridge (at elevation 6245T on the Gordon Flats map). Barbara Ekker noted that the J.R. Simplots were a wealthy Idaho family who had uranium mining interests in the area in the early 1950s. (604~)

Big Rock Candy Mountain: (Piute Co.) Tushar Mountains-Marysvale Canyon. Marysvale Canyon map. (6,979')

Also called Alum Mountain (15~), Gods Castle (384~), and Rock Candy Mountain (448~).

Harry "Haywire Mack" McClintock wrote a ballad in 1928 about the mountain while working as a brakeman for the Denver and Rio Grande Railroad:

> In the Big Rock Candy Mountain
> There's a land that's fair and bright
> Where the handouts grow on bushes
> And you sleep out every night.
> Where the box-cars all are empty
> And the sun shines every day
> On the birds and bees and cigarette trees
> And the lemonade spring. (566~)

Lemonade Spring actually exists. Fred J. Dodson: "Amber-colored water filters through the minerals and emerges as a spring—'Lemonade Springs.'" (566~) Water from Lemonade Spring was bottled and sold as a cure-all. A.M. Swanson in 1946: "The mountain has the appearance of great rolls of golden molasses candy that have been dropped on top of larger pieces of various colored candy bars and then given a liberal sprinkling of colored candy drops." (1850~)

—Candy Gulch: This is part of the Marysvale Uranium District. The head of this short western tributary of the Sevier River is on the north side of Big Rock Candy Mountain. (1088~)

—BW and H Canyon: This is part of the Marysvale Uranium District. The head of this short western tributary of the Sevier River is at the BW and H Mine. (1088~) The flat area at the mouth of the canyon on the Sevier River is called BW and H Hollow. (1934~) (See BW and H Mine.)

—Painted Gulch: This is part of the Marysvale Uranium District. The mouth of this short northern tributary of Deer Creek is one-half mile upcanyon from the Sevier River. (1088~)

Big Rocks: (Wayne Co.) Awapa Plateau-Fremont River. Moroni Peak and Bicknell maps.

The Big Rocks is a large area covered with lava rock boulders and outcrops. Informed sources say this is the local make-out spot for teens in the area. (844~)

—Jacksonville: PRIVATE PROPERTY. The first pioneers to arrive in the area stayed near the Big Rocks at a site now called Jacksonville. This was near elevation 6983 on the Bicknell map. (1865~)

—Lazenbee Bench: Dunk Taylor noted that this is the meadow area between Big Rocks and the Fremont River. Moroni Lazenbee (also spelled Lazenby and Lisenbee) was one of the first settlers here. (1865~)

Big Round Valley: (Washington Co.) Virgin River-First Narrows. White Hills map.

Anthony Atkin noted that the area above The Narrows of the Virgin River, which includes Big Round Valley, was called Lower Valley. (461~)

Big Sage: (Kane Co.) GSCENM-Kaiparowits Plateau. Carcass Canyon and Petes Cove maps.

This area is covered with Big Sagebrush (*Artemisia tridentata*). (SAPE.)

Big Spencer Flats: (Garfield Co.) GSCENM-Escalante River. Red Breaks and Tenmile Flat maps.

Edson Alvey noted that Joseph William Spencer (1859-1925), an early rancher, ran sheep in the area. (55~, 2051~)

Edson inscribed his name on a rock on the flat in 1927. (SAPE.)

Big Spring: (San Juan Co.) Manti-LaSal National Forest-Dark Canyon Plateau-North Long Point. Poison Canyon map.

The name was suggested to the USGS by John Scorup in 1979. (1931~)

Big Spring Canyon: (Wayne Co.) The Spur-Horsethief Canyon. Sugarloaf Butte and Horsethief Canyon maps.
—Big Spring: (Sugarloaf Butte map.) This large spring is in Big Spring Canyon.
—Constructed Stock Trail: Ted Ekker noted that the trail to Big Spring was constructed by the Tidwells sometime between 1926 and the mid-1940s. (623~)
—Biddlecome Corral: A log "Corral" is one mile south-southwest of Big Spring (Sugarloaf Butte map). It was built by the Biddlecomes in the early 19teens. (120~)

Big Spring Ranch: (Carbon Co.) Book Cliffs-Highway 191. Sunnyside Junction map.
Also called Sunnyside Ranch. (130~)
Lucile Richens: "So named because of the numerous large springs near the ranch buildings." (2053~)
The first settler to Big Spring was an unnamed trapper. In the early 1880s Lord Scott Elliott, an Englishman, arrived at Big Spring and started a ranch. He prospered, at one time having some thirty thousand head of stock. (1621~)
Arthur Penfold Ballard told the story of Lord Scott Elliot: "There is no 'Lord' Scott-Elliot in the English peerage. However, he came from an ancient and well-known Scotch family in Durfriesshire. In order that you may understand the situation fully I must explain that about 1880 there was a migration to Colorado Springs [Colorado] of a certain type of young Englishman, all of good physique, well educated, and with capital, who came West fired with the spirit of adventure to enter the cattle business. Scott-Elliot ... belonged to this early migration." (130~)
Harvey Hardy: "Elliott loved to drink whiskey and fight, and seemed to have the money to indulge his hobbies. I guess his Lordship did not fit in very well with his Mormon neighbors for he said to Louie [Pressit], 'Back in England they call me Lord Scott Elliott, but out here they call me a G- D- old S- of a B-.' When he left his ranch it was reported that he was going to Tasmania to raise elephants." (828~)
Drought years came and Lord Elliot's fortune dwindled and he moved back to England. The property sat idle for many years until the Denver and Rio Grande Western Railroad took it over. They piped water from Big Spring to Cedar Siding. (1621~)
—Pierson Ranch: PRIVATE PROPERTY. This was three miles east-northeast of Big Spring Ranch (one-quarter mile northeast of elevation 5874 on the Sunnyside map). (428~)

Big Sulphur Canyon: (Carbon and Duchesne Counties.) West Tavaputs Plateau-Nine Mile Canyon. Minnie Maude Creek East and Wood Canyon maps.
Also called Sulphur Canyon.
—Diversion Dam: A short distance down Nine Mile Canyon from the mouth of Big Sulphur Canyon is a diversion dam built by the Alger brothers in the 1890s. (1788~)
—Nine Mile Ranch: PRIVATE PROPERTY. This ranch and campground are in Nine Mile Canyon just below the mouth of Big Sulphur Canyon.

Big Thompson Mesa: (Garfield Co.) Henry Mountains-Grand Gulch-Long Canyon. Deer Point map. (5,402')
(See Thompson Mesa for name derivation.)

Big Triangle: (Grand Co.) Colorado River-Westwater Canyon. Big Triangle map.
The Big Triangle is formed by the junction of Coates Creek and Renegade Creek, which runs through Triangle Canyon.

Big Water Canyon: (Garfield and Wayne Counties.) Glen Canyon NRA-Horse Canyon. Elaterite Basin map.
A.C. Ekker and Pearl Baker in 1987: "Big Water Spring is just that, a great deal of water, cottonwood trees and stock drinking troughs." (1931~)

Big Wild Horse Mesa: (Emery and Wayne Counties.) San Rafael Swell-Muddy Creek. Goblin Valley, The Notch, Skyline Rim, and Little Wild Horse Mesa maps.
Also called East Wild Horse Mesa (1931~) and Wild Horse Butte.
(See Wild Horse Butte for name derivation.)

Billboard, The: (Grand Co.) Colorado River-Amasa Back. Gold Bar Canyon map.
Two name derivations are given.
First, Val Dalton: "The way I understood it, it was called that because that's as far as you can go up the river on this [east] side. They used to have something written on the rock there that the river runners used." (517~) James H. Knipmeyer: "It was so-named by river runners because of the many names, dates, and other inscriptions put there." (1116~)
Second, Lloyd Holyoak: "From the bottom of Lake Bottom down through the Billboard is a most beautiful slickrock wall. It's just gorgeous; it's covered with desert varnish. If you sit there for a couple of hours you can pick out all kinds of designs in the varnish. It's been called the Billboard as long as I can remember." (906~)

Billie Flat Top: (Kane Co.) Glen Canyon NRA-Glen Canyon. Gregory Butte map.
This is most likely named for early Glen Canyon miner William Mernard "Billy" Hay, who was quite a character.

Barbara Ekker told this story: "Billie Hay married Lennie Strauss but was later separated. He is reported to have told this story about his separation: 'she wanted me to tell her I loved her forty times a day and by—Jesus Christ a man can't do that.'" (605~)

Charlie Gibbons was asked to speak at Hays' funeral and to tell Billy's favorite joke, which he did: "It concerned a blonde woman who dressed as a ghost to scare the meanness out of her husband. Wrapped in white, the figure knocked on the door of the farm house. 'Who are you?' her husband asked. She snarled, 'I am the devil.' 'Well, come right in a make yourself at home,' her hubby replied. 'I married your sister'"! (1674~)

David D. Rust: "Billie Hay is buried in a Mormon graveyard. Always claimed the devil would never look for an Irishman there." (1674~)

—Dollar Rock Bar: This short canyon and placer bar, now mostly underwater, is on the north side of the Colorado River and is one mile east of the mouth of Rock Creek (one-half mile southeast of elevation 4206). Katie Lee: "named this for the flat little dollar sized rocks found on the bar where we had come to roll in the sun after our cold trip into Dungeon [Canyon]." (1163~)

—Nobodys Business: This short northern tributary of the Colorado River, now mostly underwater, is on the southeast end of Billie Flat Top (immediately south of elevation 4132). Katie Lee and friends named the canyon: "I had Frank [Wright] make me a grappling hook from the handles of my ski rope and I climbed up into this crazy narrow in this beautiful canyon. Mine, mine, all alone, mine … that's why it's called 'Nobodys Business.'" (1163~)

Billingsly Creek: (Kane Co.) Dixie National Forest-Markagunt Plateau-Swains Creek. Long Valley Junction map.
Correctly spelled Billingsley Creek.
Elijah R. Billingsley (1806–1888) was an Orderville pioneer. (2053~)

Billings Pass: (Wayne Co.) Fishlake National Forest-Thousand Lake Mountain. Flat Top map. (9,160')
Guy Pace noted that Lon Billings and his partners ditched water through the pass to the nearby Baker Ranch. (1497~) The highest point in Capitol Reef National Park is one-half mile east of Billings Pass.

Bill Pinney Spring: (Garfield Co.) Dixie National Forest-Sevier Plateau-Butler Wash. Casto Canyon map.
The Pinney family were early residents of Garfield County, arriving in the 1870s. (388~, 421~)

Billy Pasture: (Kane Co.) GSCENM-White Cliffs. Pine Point map.
—Constructed Stock Trail: This goes from Timber Mountain into Billy Pasture on its north side (one-half mile east of elevation 6765AT). (SAPE.)

Billy Slope Canyon: (Emery Co.) Roan Cliffs-Range Creek. Lighthouse Canyon map.
Waldo Wilcox: "It would be a bit of a guess, but I imagine that [early rancher] Bill Seamount probably slid his cattle off there. There was no trail down that canyon. I've been up in there. I'd guess that they were going to build one there." (2011~)

Billy West Canyon: (Iron Co.) Squaw Hollow-Parowan Canyon. Parowan map.
William M. West arrived in Parowan in the mid-1850s. (388~)

Binne Etteni: (Coconino Co., Az.) Navajo Indian Reservation-Navajo Creek. Inscription House Ruin, Az. map.
Also called Binne Etteni Canyon (1360~), Chilcheenta (499~), and Pinne-ettin (638a~, 769~).
William Bright noted that there are three possible meaning for *Binne Etteni*: "no face," "no waist," or "no mind." (286~)

Birch Canyon: (Garfield Co.) Dixie National Forest-Escalante Mountains-Main Canyon. Griffin Point map.
Pratt Gates noted that there are a lot of birch trees in the canyon. (709~)

Birch Canyon: (Kane Co.) Alton Amphitheater-East Fork Virgin River. Alton and Long Valley Junction maps.
—Birch Spring: (Also called Alton Spring.) (570~) Adonis Findlay Robinson noted that this spring, near a "Water Tank" on the Alton map, was used as a source of household water in Alton starting in 1914. (1639~)

Birch Creek: (Emery Co.) Manti-LaSal National Forest-Wasatch Plateau-Ferron Creek. Flagstaff Peak map.
—O'Brian Mine: This old coal mine is a short distance up Birch Creek. Ray Wareham: "The coal in it is the wrong kind of coal and it was never successful." (1967~)

Birch Creek: (Garfield Co.) Dixie National Forest-Escalante Mountains-Escalante River. Griffin Point and Wide Hollow Reservoir maps.
Birch Creek flows through Main Canyon.
Birch Creek, North Creek, and Upper Valley Creek join to form the Escalante River.
The Andrus Military Reconnaissance Expedition of 1866 called this Cottonwood Creek. (475~) Jack Hillers of the 1871–72 Powell Expedition called it Birch Creek. (884~)
Hugh Woodard in 1942: "It was so named because of the numerous Birch that are found along its coarse." (2053~)

Inscriptions include B.S. Thompson, Feb. 29, 1892. (SAPE.)

Birch Creek: (Garfield Co.) Dixie National Forest-Escalante Mountains-Johns Valley. Grass Lakes map.
—Riddle Lake: This is near the confluence of Birch and Horse creeks (one-half mile west-northwest of elevation 7817). Walter Steed: "The dam on this feature has been destroyed and the water is allowed to flow downstream in a newly built reservoir. The lake area is now grown over with brush and the name is no longer in local use." (1931~)

Birch Creek: (Kane Co.) Pink Cliffs-Oak Canyon. Skutumpah Creek map.
George G. Mace and Reed Cram in 1942: "Named for the birches found there." (2053~)

Birch Creek: (Piute Co.) Fishlake National Forest-Tushar Mountains-Sevier River. Circleville Mountain and Circleville maps.
Two name derivations are given.
First, George W. Dobson in 1941: "Named for Arthur Whittaker [correctly spelled Whitaker] a cattleman from Circleville nicknamed Bish." (2053~)
Second, birch trees line the banks of the creek. (1444~)
The Parley P. Pratt Exploring Expedition of 1849–50 went a couple of miles up the canyon, then exited to the south. They then cut along the lower slopes of Circleville Mountain and on to Fremont Pass. Robert Campbell of the expedition: "Captn [John] Brown makes report of the rout, as being impracticable but barely passible, rocky road all along for 6 miles, winding over a succession of kanyons, steep ascents and descent, cobble stones all the way, nearly perpendicular in places." (1762~)
Isaac Haight of the same expedition: "Commence to cross the Mountain ... had to let the wagons down into some deep ravines with roaps and help our cattle up out the same way had to shovel through the snow in some places." (1762~)

Birch Hollow: (Kane Co.) Clear Creek Mountain-Orderville Canyon. Clear Creek Mountain map.
Also called Birch Valley. (485~)
—Birch Valley Spring: This is the "Spring" in upper Birch Hollow. (485~)

Birch Spring: (Garfield Co.) Dixie National Forest-Sevier Plateau-Mud Spring Creek. Mount Dutton map.
Kent Whittaker noted that he developed the spring for his livestock. (2002~)

Birch Spring: (Garfield Co.) Henry Mountains-South Creek Ridge. Mount Ellen map.
This is a large, developed spring. (SAPE.)

Guy Robison believed that this should be Bert Spring, named for rancher Bert Avery. (1644~) (See Bert Avery Seep.)

Birch Spring: (Garfield Co.) Sevier Plateau-Table Mountain. Phonolite Hill map.
Also called Cannon Troughs. (1931~)

Birch Spring: (Kane Co.) Bryce Canyon National Park-Black Birch Canyon. Rainbow Point map.
Don Orton in 1941: "So named for the many birch trees on its banks." (2053~)

Birch Spring: (Sevier Co.) San Rafael Swell-Rock Springs Wash. Solomons Temple map.
This is a large, beautiful spring. (SAPE.)
Garn Jefferies noted that his grandfather, Thomas Jefferies, tried to ditch water from the spring, but there was not enough water to do anything with it. (959~)
—Cove Pasture: Jim Crane and Garn Jefferies noted that this is the pasture area below (to the east of) Birch Spring and includes the area around Solomons Temple. (478~, 959~)

Birch Spring Knoll: (Garfield Co.) Dixie National Forest-Rock Canyon. Haycock Mountain map. (8,776')
Also called Birch Mountain. (1931~)
—Birch Spring: This is a large spring with still-used troughs. The area is surrounded by aspen trees, which are often mistaken for birch trees. Inscriptions on the aspens date to 1925. (SAPE.)

Bishop Canyon: (Kane Co.) Long Canyon-East Fork Virgin River. Orderville and Glendale maps.
This was most likely named for Henry Webster Esplin (1854-1843). (485~) He was the bishop of Orderville from 1884 to 1910. (338~)

Bishopric, The: (Washington Co.) Zion National Park-Coalpits Wash. The Guardian Angels map. (7,320')
R.T. Evans of the USGS named this The Counselors in 1934: "So named for the three men, the bishop and his two counselors who, in every town or village, have charge of the local affairs of the Mormon Church." (1931~)

Bishops Tank: (Coconino Co., Az.) Glen Canyon NRA-Highway 89. Ferry Swale, Az. map.
This still-used natural stock reservoir has been enhanced with a dam. A line camp and corral used to be nearby. Inscriptions include A. Button, no date. (SAPE.)

Bitter Creek: (Garfield Co.) Henry Mountains-Tarantula Mesa-Halls Creek. Cave Flat and Bitter Creek Divide maps.
Charles B. Hunt: "The name evidently refers to the alkaline taste of the water." (925~)

Bitter Creek: (Grand Co.) Book Cliffs-Grand Valley-Ruby Canyon. San Arroyo Ridge, Bryson Canyon, Bar X Wash, Bitter Creek Well, and Westwater maps.

Also called Bitter Creek Wash (429~), Bitter Water Creek (847~), and San Arroyo Wash (1931~).

The name was used by the Ferdinand V. Hayden Survey in 1874. (M.30.)

—Sanitarium: In 1905 a sanitarium hotel was built at the mouth of Bitter Creek at the Colorado River for easterners with lung problems. The hotel burned down in 1912. (1363~)

Bitter Creek Divide: (Garfield Co.) Capitol Reef National Park-Sandy Creek. Bitter Creek Divide map.

Bitter Creek Divide marks the top of Sandy Creek, which goes north from the divide, and Halls Creek, which goes south from the divide.

—Camel's Rest: John A. Widtsoe camped in the area in 1922: "On the east ridge is the clear outline of a camel resting. The head is distinct; the neck somewhat depressed, the back with two humps very marked. This is a good land mark. Camp and place called *The Camel's Rest*." (2007~)

Bitter Seep: (Emery Co.) San Rafael Swell-Sand Bench. Short Canyon map.

This is a small seep. (SAPE.)

Ray Wareham: "Nothing will drink the water out of it. The water stinks bad." (1967~)

Bitter Seep Wash: (Emery Co.) San Rafael Swell-South Salt Wash. Emery East, Short Canyon, and Big Bend Draw maps.

Wayne Gremel: "It runs water up high [in the wash].... The water's terrible"! (780~)

Wayne told this story, edited for clarity: "I fell of a ledge last winter (2004) in Bitter Seep Wash! Old Robert Anderson had some cows out there and then he got hurt. So Joel Chance and I went out to round them up. It got dark on us. It was black and you couldn't see anything. I could see the car lights on the Interstate and I thought if I got over to where the car lights would shine I could see my way off. Well, I stepped off a ledge and fell far enough to do a flip in the air. Stupidity will beat you every time. I really smacked, boy, I thought I'd killed myself. I thought I broke my back. It was cold, the middle of the night, and I hurt so bad. I laid under a ledge for a while, until about three in the morning. I couldn't stand it any more. I thought I was gonna freeze to death. So I got up. The moon had come up by then. You could see a little bit, so I hiked up and when I got out up on top, I could see the flashlights of the search party." Carrie Lou Gremel,

Wayne's wife, finished the story: "Wayne was cold. He broke some ribs and has had a lot of eye problems since then." (780~)

Inscriptions include N.G. Jensen, Emery, no date. (SAPE.)

—Interstate 70 Construction Staging Area: Just north of Interstate 70 on Bitter Seep Wash is an area that has been furrowed. Wayne Gremel noted that this was a staging area during the construction of Interstate 70 and when they were done, they plowed the area and planted it in grass. (780~)

Bitter Spring Creek: (Garfield Co.) Capitol Reef National Park-Swap Mesa-Halls Creek. Bitter Creek Divide map.

—Bitter Spring Creek-Cave Flat Stock Trail: This constructed stock trail goes up Bitter Spring Creek, crosses Bitter Creek, and goes over the heads of Swap and Muley canyons before ending at Cave Camp, a line camp on Bullfrog Creek. (See Cave Flat.) Much of the trail is now crisscrossed by buffalo trails, making the original trail hard to follow. (925~, SAPE.)

Black Arch: (Grand Co.) Arches National Park-Devils Garden. Mollie Hogans map.

Also called Fin Canyon Arch. (898~)

Robert H. Vreeland: "It was named by Roby R. 'Slim' Mabery, a former NPS district ranger, because there always appears to be black inside the arch no matter from where it is viewed." (1949~, 869~)

Black Birch Canyon: (Kane Co.) Dixie National Forest-Willis Creek. Rainbow Point and Bryce Point maps.

The USGS noted that there are birch trees surrounding Birch Spring (Rainbow Point map). (1931~)

Blackbird Mine: (Piute Co.) Fishlake National Forest-Sevier Plateau-Manning Creek. Marysvale Peak map.

This was a manganese mine.

Black Box: (Emery Co.) San Rafael Swell-San Rafael River. Devils Hole, Drowned Hole Draw, and Mexican Mountain maps.

Also called Black Box Canyon and Upper Black Box.

Named for the high, dark walls that form the canyon, it is noteworthy that the name was in use by the 1890s.

—Upper Black Box Dam: (Proposed.) Proposals to dam the Upper Black Box at its mouth at Mexican Bend were made in 1909 and 1925. (166~, 2049~)

Black Bridge: (Uintah Co.) Uintah and Ouray Indian Reservation-Willow Creek. Big Pack Mountain NW map.

Inscriptions include H.T [Harvey Taylor], May 31, 1934. (SAPE.)

Blackburn Canyon: (Kane Co.) GSCENM-Kaiparowits Plateau-Little Valley. Blackburn Canyon map.

Also called Blackburn Draw. (664~)

Miriam B. Murphy noted that Elias Hicks Blackburn (1827-1908) moved to Loa in 1879 with his three wives and fifteen hundred head of cattle. The Blackburn family became a major force in the cattle industry and ranged their livestock from the Awapa Plateau to Bullfrog Creek, and across the San Rafael Swell to the Dirty Devil River and North Wash areas.

Inscriptions include E.T., 1919 and Harvey Eiston, Dec. 13, 1943. (SAPE.)

—First and Second Blackburn canyons: When the cowboys followed the old trail along the rim of the Straight Cliffs over the top of Blackburn Canyon, these are the first and second forks they crossed.

Blackburn Draw: (Emery and Wayne Counties.) San Rafael Desert-Dirty Devil River. Gilson Butte, Point of Rocks West, and The Notch maps.

Elias Hicks Blackburn (1827-1908) moved to Rabbit Valley in 1879. In 1882 he traversed the Blackburn Draw area while looking for a route from Loa to Glen Canyon. (338~, 1412~) Other Blackburns later settled in the Hanksville area. (1645~)

—Pioneer Road: The old Hanksville to Green River mail route went through the draw. (623~)

Blackburn Hollow: (Wayne Co.) Awapa Plateau-Fremont River. Moroni Peak and Bicknell maps.

According to Wayne Blackburn, his grandfather, Elias Hicks Blackburn (1827-1908), arrived in Rabbit Valley in 1879. (248~, 844~)

Blackburn Reservoir: (Wayne Co.) Awapa Plateau-Logging Grove. Smooth Knoll map.

Dunk Taylor noted that Wayne Blackburn ran livestock in the area. The reservoir was built in the mid-1970s. (1865~, 1914~)

—Dunky Pond: This is one mile north-northwest of Blackburn Reservoir. It was named for Dunk Taylor. (1865~)

Black Burn Trail: (Garfield Co.) Dixie National Forest-Awapa Plateau. Angle map.

Correctly spelled Blackburn Trail.

See Blackburn Draw for name derivation.

Sonny King noted that in the early days this constructed stock trail was used to get from the lowlands on the west to the Awapa Plateau on the east. (1095~)

Black Butte: (Garfield Co.) Dixie National Forest-Paunsaugunt Plateau-Blubber Creek. Tropic Reservoir map. (9,557')

Robert Ott: "It was named Black Butte because the dense growth of timber on it makes it appear black from a distance." (1931~)

Black Canyon: (Garfield Co.) Sevier Plateau-East Fork Sevier River. Antimony map.

The East Fork Sevier River flows through Black Canyon. Herbert E. Gregory noted that the canyon walls are composed of a dark-colored volcanic breccia. (764~)

—First Road: Construction on the road through the canyon was started in 1919. (1455~)

Black Cap Mountain: (Sevier Co.) Wasatch Plateau-Sevier River. Salina map. (6,597')

Clarence Dutton of the Powell Survey: "Standing prominent among these bad lands is a conical butte-like mountain of singularly perfect form ... upon it summit is a 'tip' or cap about 250 feet thick.... This mountain is called the Black Cap." (584~)

Black Creek: (Garfield Co.) Henry Mountains-Trachyte Creek. Cass Creek Peak and Black Table maps.

Emery King noted that this was also called Dark Canyon. (1931~) Garth Noyes: "There is a lot of black volcanic rock, big black rocks settin' there." (1473~)

—Trachyte Mesa: This low mesa is between the lower ends of Black and Speck creeks (Black Table map). (925~)

Black Dragon Creek: (Emery Co.) Manti-LaSal National Forest-Wasatch Plateau-Ferron Creek. Ferron Canyon map.

Ray Wareham: "The reason they call it The Dragon is that in the early days, when they were comin' over from Sanpete County, they would have to tie some logs and stuff on the back of the wagon to keep from runnin' over the horses. So that's how come it got named Dragon"! (1967~)

Black Dragon Wash: (Emery Co.) San Rafael Swell-San Rafael Reef-San Rafael River. Spotted Wolf Canyon map.

Also called Black Canyon and Black Dragon Canyon.

An article in the *Salt Lake City Daily Tribune* in 1885 noted this as Black Diamond Canyon. (1486~)

The wash was named for a Barrier Canyon Style pictograph that looks like a dragon. H.L.A. Culmer in 1909: "Black Dragon canyon is superb. It carries no stream, and for distances its gravelly bottom is as pleasant to travel upon as the shingle on the ocean beach. Its magnificent and unbroken walls, nearly 1,000 feet in height, bulge over the pathway, sometimes with an overhang of a hundred feet. Ferns and clinging vines hang from the crevices;

it is cool and shadowy in the depths; every footfall echoes with a spacious sound. For a mile or more, you wind through this cranny in the mountain and then emerge to the interior of the Swell, your course now surrounded by towers and columns of Triassic rocks. They rise in massive cliffs, in spires and minarets, in jagged sky-piercing teeth, in domes and cornices. They are of a rich orange and brown, and harmonize splendidly with the Indian red and maroon of the Permian series on which they rest. In its own unique way, Black Dragon canyon is as fine as any scenic feature in the state." (496~)

Dr. Armand J. Eardley went through the canyon in 1930: "The gorge in the Navajo [Sandstone] is spectacular. The walls are not only vertical for the full thickness of the Navajo, but for ½ mile overhanging to the extent of 75-100'." (589~)

Inscriptions include Glen Stewart, 1910; H.T. Yokey, [19]11; D.R. Seeley, 1911; Ross Petty, 1918; Archie Simonsen, 1925; and Dumas, 1940. (SAPE.)

—Old Spanish Trail: (Variation.) Black Dragon Canyon is one of the few breaks in the otherwise impregnable wall of the San Rafael Reef. A variation of the trail went through the wash.

—Black Dragon Road: Black Dragon Wash was used by travelers and ranchers from the early days to get from the San Rafael Desert to the top of the San Rafael Swell. Eric Bjørnstad noted that the road was built in 1918 to service a mining operation near its head. (240~, 641~, 1968~)

—Black Dragon Canyon Pictographs: These were listed on the National Register of Historic Places in 1980.

—Box Spring Canyon: This western tributary of the San Rafael River is one-half mile south of Black Dragon Wash (immediately south of elevation 5102T). In the early 1980s Steve Allen noted that this box canyon contains springs.

Black Dragon Reservoir: (Emery Co.) San Rafael Swell-Upper Black Box. Drowned Hole Draw map.
This stock reservoir was built in 1961. (1551~)

Black Flat: (Sevier Co.) Fishlake National Forest-UM Creek. Hilgard Mountain map.
Alfonzo Turner: "In the early days there used to be a disease in the cattle that they called Black Leg. It was mostly in calves. They used to have quite a lot of that in that area. It's quite a swampy area through there, with lots of little potholes and I figure that's what caused it. They called it Black Leg." (1914~)

Blackham Creek: (Sevier Co.) Fishlake National Forest-Yogo Creek. Hilgard Mountain and Yogo Creek maps.
Alma, John, and Sam Blackham ran sheep in the area starting in the early 1870s. (369~) Stuart Johnson noted that the Blackhams were some of the areas earliest pioneers. (1003~)

Blackhawk Mine: (Emery Co.) Wasatch Plateau-Gentry Mountain. Hiawatha map.
This coal mine was one of the first opened in the Hiawatha area. It was started in about 1908 by LeRoy Eccles and others. (1195~)

Black Hills: (Emery Co.) Little Cedar Mountain-Red Seep Wash. Buckhorn Reservoir and Hadden Holes maps.
—Old Spanish Trail: The trail went across the Black Hills. (1551~)

Black Hills: (Garfield Co.) GSCENM-Boulder Mountain-Pine Creek. Wide Hollow Reservoir and Escalante maps.
Edson Alvey noted that there was a heavy growth of scrub trees and bushes here, making the area look dark from a distance. (55~)

Black Knoll: (Kane Co.) White Cliffs-Skutumpah Terrace. Glendale map. (6,760')
Also called Corral Crater (1931~) and Corral Knoll (767~).

Black Knoll: (Sevier Co.) Sevier Valley-Sevier River. Sigurd map. PRIVATE PROPERTY.
This low knoll is covered with black lava boulders.
—Nebeker Ranch: In 1871 Henry Nebeker (1818-1891) started a ranch at Black Knoll. (1970~) Nebeker's great grandson, Roger Warren Sevy: "There was a large spring at this site which drained into the river." (1719~)
—Rocky Ford: Irvin Warnock noted that in the early days this ford near Black Knoll was one of the few good places to cross the Sevier River. (1971~)

Black Knolls: (Washington Co.) Virgin River-Middleton Wash. Washington map.
—Black Knolls Reservoir: This reservoir, used to store water coming from the Cottonwood Wash Aqueduct, was built in 1904. (1354~)

Black Lake: (Garfield Co.) Dixie National Forest-Boulder Mountain. Jacobs Reservoir map.
Lenora Hall LeFevre noted that rancher John Black (1871-1935) ran cattle in the area starting in the early 1900s. (1168~)

Black Mesa: (San Juan Co.) Comb Ridge-Cottonwood Creek. Black Mesa Butte and No-Mans Island maps.
The mesa is topped with black boulders. (162~) Although these boulders look of volcanic origin—and were for many years called "lava" by locals—they are actually

sandstone and quartzite fragments coated with desert varnish. (774~)

Clyde Barton: "One year we took sheep down onto the Black Mesa. It was getting toward evening. That sun wasn't too far from being down and we looked down there, everything was just like Eden; everything was just contented down in there. It was pretty rough country in there and dad [Karl S. Barton] says, 'Damn, you know, they said this earth was created in six days. I just wish they'd worked the other day and leveled this place out'"! (162~)

—Black Mesa Launch Complex: From 1963 to 1980 the army used Black Mesa to launch Pershing missiles to White Sands, New Mexico. They had a tent camp and a couple of prefabricated buildings on the mesa (near elevation 5618T on the Black Mesa Butte map). (162~, 1336~)

Clyde and Karl Barton ran livestock on Black Mesa for forty-three years and were there during the time they were launching missiles. Karl told this story: "One day we came down the road and found a place where there was blood in the snow and we saw where they had loaded a cow. We notified the sheriff. He sent a deputy to where their mess hall was.... We got to searching around inside the mess hall. They had big equipment for making bread and shredding cheese. The mess sergeant had taken that cow and ground it up in the cheese shredder. We found the hide and head of that cow and her unborn calf in the garbage pit. They paid us for it." (162~)

—North Road: The road up the north end of Black Mesa was built in the early 1960s. (162~)

—Black Mesa Butte: (6,016') (Black Mesa Butte map.) Karl Barton noted that this well-known landmark was called Black Hill by ranchers. (162~)

—Lonesome Mine Canyon: This is on the west edge of Black Mesa (one-quarter mile southwest of Black Mesa Butte). Karl Barton noted that Seth Shumway had a mine in the canyon. A constructed stock trail went from Black Mesa, down Lonesome Mine Canyon, to Butler Wash. (162~)

Black Mountain: (Iron Co.) Kolob Terrace-West Fork Deep Creek. Webster Flat map. (10,375')
Also called Black Hill (1012~) and Volcanic Mountain (1931~).
The USGS noted that this has also been called MacFarlane Point for an early settler who had a nearby ranch. (1931~)
Herbert E. Gregory noted that the mountain is composed of black basalt. (768~)

Stephen Vandiver Jones of the Powell Expedition of 1871-72 called this Cone Mountain: "Found a small spring at the east foot of Cone Mountain and camped. In afternoon I climbed the mountain for observations." (1023~)

—Richardson Peak: This is one mile northwest of Black Mountain (at elevation 9546). Herbert E. Gregory named the peak for geologist G.B. Richardson. He studied the area in the early 1900s. (768~)

Black Mountain: (Kane Co.) Long Valley-McDonald Canyon. Long Valley Junction and Glendale maps. (7,777')
The mountain is formed from black volcanic rock. (2053~)

Black Ridge: (Garfield Co.) Dixie National Forest-Escalante Mountains. Grass Lakes map. (8,771')
Sonny King noted that black volcanic rock is found along the ridge. (1095~)

—Burro Flat: This is on the northwest side of Black Ridge (near elevation 7317). J.J. Porter in 1931: "So named because Isaac Riddle imported a band of burros in about 1885 and they were grazed on this flat." (1346~)

Black Ridge: (Kane Co.) GSCENM-Escalante Desert-Hole-in-the-Rock Road. Basin Canyon and Big Hollow Wash maps.
Pratt Gates noted that black brush grows on the ridge. (709~)

Black Ridge: (San Juan Co.) La Sal Mountains-Kane Springs Creek. La Sal Junction and Kane Springs maps.
Lloyd Holyoak: "Black Ridge was named because of all of the Utah Juniper and pinyons that were on it. They made it look real dark, black. It was a lot darker than it is now." (906~)

Black Ridge: (Washington Co.) Hurricane Cliffs-La Verkin Creek. Smith Mesa, Kolob Arch, and Pintura maps.
Also called Big Black Ridge.
The Paiute name is *U-nav-ich,* or "Black Ridge." (1512~)
The ridge is formed from black volcanic rock. It—and the nearby Middleton Black Ridge—proved to be a major impediment to travel for the early settlers.
The Domínguez-Escalante Expedition of 1776–77 crossed the ridge. Fray Silvestre Vélez Escalante: "entered a ridge-cut entirely of black lava rock.... We continued south for a league with great hardship on account of so much rock." (261~)
John Steele named it in 1851–52: "We made our way over what we called the Black Ridge on Ash Creek." (1820~)
Mary Minerva Dart Judd in 1856: "We arrived at the foot of what is known as the Black Ridge. With quite a precipitous ascent of two miles and covered with boulders of black volcanic rock, interspersed with brush and cedar

trees, it looked impracticable for wagons. With great labor for our teams we made the summit." (367~)

Unattributed in 1861: "Down at the Black Ridge the trail ended. The wagon-boxes were let down sheer cliffs by ropes; the women and children found less precipitous places and climbed down, clinging to the rocks or to the hands of their husbands. Once down they went forward again to the rim of the basin." (1181~)

Black Ridge: (Wayne Co.) Awapa Plateau-Dog Flat Hollow. Abes Knoll and Loa maps.

Thaine Taylor noted that there is black lava rock on the ridge. (1868~)

Black Rock Canyon: (Kane Co.) Dixie National Forest-Long Valley-East Fork Virgin River. Long Valley Junction map.

Also called Lava Narrows. (1931~)

Black lava rock forms the narrows of the canyon. (1931~)

Adonis Findlay Robison noted that in 1875 Brigham Young ordered that a sawmill be moved to Black Rock Canyon. (1639~)

Black Rock Cave: (Iron Co.) Hurricane Cliffs-Parowan Valley. Paragonah map. PRIVATE PROPERTY.

In 1851 Job and Charles Hall farmed forty acres at what was then called Black Rock, which is the location of Black Rock Cave. Betsy Topham Camp: "At one time this cave was tall enough for a horse and rider to enter but has gradually settled." (336~)

Inscriptions include J.S.B., 1841; S.D., 1865; G.H. Brimhall, ? 189? GHB, 1897; Geo. H. Brimhall, 189?; Smoot Brimhall, Dec. 23, 1928; H.C. Merrill, 1935; and Rover Boys—Dave—Vic, Aug. 21, 1939. (SAPE.)

—Old Spanish Trail: The trail went just west of Black Rock Cave. With its large capacity, and an inscription from 1841, it is apparent that the cave was used as shelter by those on the trail.

Black Sage Canyon: (Coconino Co., Az.) Navajo Indian Reservation-Navajo Creek. Inscription House Ruin and Chaiyahi Rim SE, Az. maps.

Carl I. Wheat noted that the Navajo name is *Chill-izena-nashkla*. (1995~)

Blacks Canyon: (Washington Co.) Zion National Park-North Fork Virgin River. Springdale West and Springdale East maps.

Joseph S. Black was one of the areas first settlers, arriving in the early 1860s. (1931~, 2043~)

Black Steer Canyon: (San Juan Co.) Dark Canyon Plateau-Dark Canyon. Black Steer Canyon map.

Two name derivations are given.

First, Pete Steele: "Most of the steers that they had back in those days were probably brindled or pinoled or some color, and a black one was kind of unusual." (1821~)

Second, Carl Mahon: "There was a big old black steer running that area. That was his home and he was a hard son of a gun to get. I don't know if they ever got him or not. And that's where the name came from." (1272~)

Black Table: (Garfield Co.) Henry Mountains-Highway 276. Black Table map. (6,240')

Also called Black Mesa.

Charles B. Hunt noted that the name refers to the black desert varnish on the rocks of the canyon. (925~)

Black Wash: (Washington Co.) Zion National Park-North Creek. The Guardian Angels and Smith Mesa maps.

The original settler of Mountain Dell on North Creek, Joel Hills Johnson, sold his holdings to Joseph and William Black in 1865. (989~, 1141~)

Blakes Lambing Grounds: (Mohave Co., Az. and Washington Co., Utah.) Beaver Dam Mountains-Virgin River. Arizona map: Purgatory Canyon. Utah maps: White Hills and Jarvis Peak.

Benjamin Frederick Blake (1815–1884) and family arrived in St. George in 1861. They ran livestock in the Santa Clara area. (793~, 803~)

Blanding Town: (San Juan Co.) White Mesa-Highway 191. Blanding North and Blanding South maps.

Before settlers arrived, Navajos called the Blanding townsite Amidst the Sagebrush. (1337~)

Blanding, located on White Mesa and on the eastern edge of the Abajo Mountains, was first scouted as a possible townsite by Walter C. Lyman in 1880. He left the area and started a business in Salt Lake City. He returned in the late 1890s. Walter's son, Arthur R. Lyman: "In 1897, when White Mesa was a remote wilderness, Walter C. Lyman ... saw in a vision a city which was to be built at a certain part of the mesa, and he parted with his home and his business ... and moved with his family to San Juan County, Utah, to begin making the city he had seen. People who knew the country declared that no city could be made there—that it was a dry wilderness, that it had been so for centuries past, and would never be anything different." (1248~)

Walter C. Lyman's first job was to build a ditch from Johnson Creek to the Edge of the Cedars, which is at the edge of Blanding. Delays on the ditch followed and it wasn't until 1905 that the first permanent settlers arrived. They were Walter C. Lyman's son and his family, Albert R. and Mary Ellen Perkins Lyman.

The town was initially called Edge of the Cedars, or Grayson, for the Joseph A. and Nellie Grayson Lyman family. Walter C. Lyman noted that his preferred name for the new town was the biblical Sidon. In 1915 Thomas W. Bicknell offered any town in Utah a library if they would name their town after him. Two towns accepted. Thurber, west of Capitol Reef, took the name Bicknell, while Grayson changed its name to Blanding, after the maiden name of Bicknell's wife. (774~, 1238~, 1241~, 1248~, 1562~, 2056~) (See White Mesa.)

—Edge of the Cedars Museum State Park: (Also called Edge of the Cedars State Park.) The Edge of the Cedars ruin was listed on the National Register of Historic Places in 1971. This sixteen acre park in Blanding was established in 1974 and was opened to the public in 1978. (206~) The name Edge of the Cedars refers to the fact that along this geographical edge the flora changes from sagebrush to junipers (called cedars by the pioneers).

At this combination indoor/outdoor museum is an extensive Indian ruin. The first resident of Blanding, Arthur R. Lyman, initially called the ruins Soose Castle. *Soose* is Paiute for "first." Lyman's father, Walter C. Lyman, is credited with their discovery in 1897. (1248~, 1336~) The ruins were built and occupied by Anasazi Indians from AD 850 to AD 950, then abandoned. They were re-occupied from AD 1025 to AD 1125.

—Shirttail Corner: This well-known landmark is a couple of miles south of Blanding at the junction of Highways 191 and 95.

Three stories are told. The first two are similar.

First, Velda Nielson noted that in 1915 several cowboys, including Wallace "Wally" Burnham, corralled their cattle for the night at what was then called the Bend in the Road. In Blanding Ezekiel "Zeke" Johnson loaded his new car with young folks and drove south of town. Wally, hearing the car, jumped out of his bedroll in his underwear, shirttail flapping, to make sure the livestock stayed quiet. (1459~)

Second, unattributed: "One spring a large herd was being moved to the Blue Mountain [Abajo Mountains] for the summer. They camped three miles south of Blanding, holding the cattle in a lane with tarps stretched and tied across the road. Jess Thornell and Wallace [Burnham] made beds on the ground, sleeping on the side toward town. There were very few cars in San Juan County at that time and it was seldom that one was driven around at night. The cowboys with this herd were tired and went to bed early. After they were sound asleep, Zeke Johnson came down the county road joyriding. Car engines were much louder then than they are now and when the unusual noise awakened the cowboys from a sound sleep, their first thought was a fear that the cattle were stampeding. They both leaped out of bed in their shirt tails and the car headlights were right on them. Right then and there the place was named Shirt Tail Corner, and still goes by that name." (1911~)

Third, Clyde Barton: "Zeke Johnson was my wife's granddad. Shirttail Corner. He named that. He farmed down there and he got by by the shirt-tail. He was just living on his shirt-tail." (162~)

Blind Canyon: (Emery Co.) Manti-LaSal National Forest-Huntington Creek. Rilda Canyon map.

Mary Guymon noted that the canyon cannot be seen from the road. (1330~)

Blind Lake: (Wayne Co.) Dixie National Forest-Boulder Mountain. Blind Lake map.

Dwight Williams: "The reason it's called Blind Lake is you're not able to see it until you're right up on it." (2013~) Unattributed: "Snuggled in an ancient volcanic crater in the tops of the Boulder Mountain, this lake is almost hidden from view by the tall and stalwart pines." (1873~)

Blind Spring: (Piute Co.) Sevier Plateau-Steens Canyon. Phonolite Hill map.

This is a small spring. (SAPE.)

Kent Whittaker: "It is rugged country up there and I don't think there was very many people knew it was even there. There was just enough water so's I could fill a water bag." (2002~)

—Zabriskie Mine: In the early days Horace Zabriskie (1858-1943) and others had a mine near Blind Spring. (44~) There are still minor mine ruins here. (SAPE.)

Blind Spring Mountain: (Garfield Co.) Dixie National Forest-Sevier Plateau. Blind Spring Mountain map. (9,534')

Also called Blind Spring Peak. (764~)

—Blind Spring: Scott Robinson in 1942: "It is a small spring that is situated on the [north] side of Blind Spring Peak. It was so named because it is hid in a very small draw and is surrounded with brush and shrubs." (2053~)

Blind Trail Wash: (Garfield and Wayne Counties.) Henry Mountains-Wildcat Mesa-Sandy Creek. Sandy Creek Benches and Notom maps.

Charles B. Hunt: "The name was given by early settlers because of the difficulty in finding a trail onto Wildcat Mesa." (925~) Keith Durfey noted that the early route from Notom to the King Ranch on Tarantula Mesa was a long one: "Then, later on by accident, they discovered there was ... a way to go through here [Blind Trail Wash], but nobody ever knew it because it was a blind spot on the reef." (582~)

—Blind Trail Spring: This is the "Spring" in Blind Trail Wash (Sandy Creek Benches map). It is a large, developed spring. (SAPE.)

Bliss Bottom: (Grand Co.) Colorado River-Amasa Back. Gold Bar Canyon map.

James H. Knipmeyer noted that Dwight O. Bliss (1839-1930) ranched in the area in the early 1890s. (1115~)

—Middle Earth: Eric Bjørnstad noted that this climbing area is on the east side of the Colorado River immediately opposite Bliss Bottom. (242~)

Bliss Reservoir: (Garfield Co.) Henry Mountains-Thompson Creek. Clay Point map.

Also called Bliss Pond.

Bliss Brinkerhoff: "I selected this Bliss site. The Bureau of Land Management named it after me." (291~) The reservoir is no longer in use. (SAPE.)

Block Mesas: (Kane Co.) White Cliffs-Harris Mountain. Mount Carmel, Yellowjacket Canyon, and Elephant Butte maps.

Herbert E. Gregory proposed the name in 1943. (1931~)

—Esplin Point. This is on the southeast end of Block Mesas (at elevations 6824 and 6724 on the Yellowjacket Canyon map). (767~)

Block Mountain: (Emery Co.) San Rafael Swell-Home Base. Twin Knolls map. (7,425')

Lee Mont Swasey: "Block Mountain was where we knew where home was.... No matter where you're at in this area [Sinbad], Block Mountain sits there." (1853~)

Block, The: (Garfield Co.) Glen Canyon NRA-Orange Cliffs. Clearwater Canyon, Sewing Machine, and Fiddler Butte maps. (7,060')

This isolated mesa is seven miles long and up to one mile wide. It stands eighteen hundred feet above the surrounding benchlands and thirty-three hundred feet above the Colorado and Dirty Devil rivers confluence. Sheepman Leon Moynier noted that is was called The High Plateau. (1931~)

—North and South Block: The Block is divided into the North Block and South Block by a thin peninsula of land (between elevations 5567T and 6700T on the Clearwater Canyon map). The South Block was also called Horse Heaven by ranchers "as a horse can get up there and look around." (411~, SAPE.)

—Constructed Stock Trail: This interesting trail bridges the narrow ridge between the North and South blocks. (SAPE.)

—Constructed Stock Trail: This goes from The Cove to the top of the South Block. It is in a short canyon just to the south of elevation 6762T on the Fiddler Butte map. (SAPE.)

Blocks, The: (Emery Co.) San Rafael Swell-Sids Mountain. The Blocks map.

The Blocks are a series of large Navajo Sandstone buttes that stand high above the surrounding landscape. Lee Mont Swasey noted that this is an old name and that as far as he knows, no other names have been used. (1853~)

Blondie Knoll: (Kane Co.) GSCENM-Kaiparowits Plateau. Sooner Bench map. (7,546')

Two name derivations, perhaps related, are given.

First, Don Coleman: "His first name was Blondie. A horse throwed 'im and he laid there on this knoll with a broken leg for a day afore they found 'im. So that's why they named it that." (441~)

Second, James H. Knipmeyer: "It was named after LeVar 'Blondie' Chesnut, son of George Chesnut, who used to herd sheep on the plateau." (1116~)

Nearby inscriptions include Ken, 1926 and Ken Lamong, Nov. 26, 1927. (SAPE.)

Blood Mine Spring: (Piute Co.) Sevier Plateau-Steens Canyon. Phonolite Hill map.

This is a large spring. (SAPE.)

Kent Whittaker: "That was old Willis Blood (1879-1932). He had a home up the canyon. He had a mining claim there up in Steens Canyon." (2002~)

This was in the early 1900s. There are the ruins of several mine buildings near the spring. One of the buildings has an inscription from Clarence Peterson. (SAPE.)

—Mining Road: The road or trail up to the Blood Mine went from Kingston Canyon, up Steens Canyon to Blind Spring, and then around a corner and up to Blood Mine Spring. (SAPE.)

Bloody Hands Gap: (Wayne Co.) Henry Mountains-Blind Trail Wash. Notom map.

Charles B. Hunt noted that this pass was named for a "pair of hands painted with red paint on a rock wall." (925~) Keith Durfey: "There are seven hand prints there in red, upon the ledge.... [Sheepherders] corralled their sheep there and paint branded them, using linseed oil and red mineral paint. And then when you brand them, they probably got paint on their hands.... It was put on there by those sheepherders, probably eighty or ninety years ago." (582~)

Bloomington Hill: (Washington Co.) Bloomington-Virgin River. White Hills and St. George maps.

Also called Red Bluff.

Bloomington Town: (Washington Co.) Bloomington Hill-Virgin River-Interstate 15. St. George map.

The first settlers arrived in 1870. Lars James Larsen arrived in 1879 and the town was sometimes called Saint James in his honor. The town was abandoned by 1950 (371~, 487~) and was resurrected in the 1970s as a high-end housing and condominium development (14~).

—Bloomington Pictographs: These were added to the Utah State Register of Historic Sites in 1972.

Blowhard Mountain: (Iron Co.) Dixie National Forest-Pink Cliffs. Navajo Lake map. (10,657')

Wallace Adair: "Received its name from early pioneers on account of continuous and phenomenal winds in the vicinity thereof." (2053~)

Arvilla H. Day: "Named because the wind really blows hard at that place.... A crew of men were working there with livestock, possibly a fall round-up. They were talking about Blowhard Peak. Finally they peeled a tree and nailed someone's red shirt to it and dedicated it 'Blowhard Peak.'" (942~)

Blubber Creek: (Garfield Co.) Dixie National Forest-Paunsaugunt Plateau-East Fork Sevier River. Tropic Reservoir map.

Two complimentary definitions are given.

First, decaying vegetation in the water would cause it to bubble. (942~)

Second, W.J. Shakespear in 1942: "Its name is descriptive of the water blubbering or seeping up along its course." (2053~) The name was in place by 1895.

Blue Basin: (Garfield Co.) Henry Mountains-Bull Creek. Mount Ellen map.

Charles B. Hunt: "Named for blue color of Mancos Shale which forms badlands in part of Sawmill Basin." (925~)

Guy Robison: "That's on Bull Creek and there's a big spring there and the country all around it is blue clay." (1644~)

Nina Robison: "It's beautiful. And the water is wonderful, so cold that you can't hardly swallow it." (1644~)

Bluebell Creek: (Grand Co.) Uintah and Ouray Indian Reservation-East Tavaputs Plateau-Desolation Canyon. Moonwater Point and Chandler Falls maps.

Waldo Wilcox: "There were bluebells growing on the bottom." (2011~)

Bluebell Knoll: (Wayne Co.) Dixie National Forest-Boulder Mountain. Blind Lake map. (11,317')

Also called Bluebell Knob.

This is the highest summit on Boulder Mountain and in Wayne County.

Kate B. Carter noted that a species of blue larkspur grows here. (375~)

Bluebell Spring: (Iron Co.) Hurricane Cliffs-Maple Canyon. Flanigan Arch map.

Alva Matheson: "The name is given the spring because of a small swampy area containing a great concentration of wild blue bell flowers." (942~)

Blue Canyon: (San Juan Co.) Wingate Mesa-Red Canyon. Jacobs Chair, Mancos Mesa NE, and Chocolate Drop maps.

Also called Blue Canyon Wash. (1872~)

The "blue" designation is a common one for place names in southern Utah and, as in this case, refers to the blue clays of the Chinle Formation. In other instances it refers to the clays and volcanic ashes of the bentonite clays in the Mancos Shale.

—Heb Spring: This is in Blue Canyon one-quarter mile northeast of elevation 4832T on the Chocolate Drop map.

—Left Hand Fork and Right Hand Fork: Blue Canyon is split by Wingate Mesa (Chocolate Drop map): the Left Hand Fork is to the west of the mesa; the Right Hand Fork is to the south and east of the mesa.

Blue Castle: (Emery Co.) Beckwith Plateau-Blue Castle Butte. Blue Castle Butte map. (4,726')

This feature, and Blue Castle Butte (See below), are formed from a blue adobe clay. (1931~)

Blue Castle Butte: (Emery Co.) Book Cliffs-Beckwith Plateau. Blue Castle Butte map. (5,853')

(See Blue Castle for name derivation.)

—Constructed Stock Trail: This goes from Blue Castle Canyon up to the base of Blue Castle Butte. It is one mile west-northwest of the butte. (646~, SAPE.)

Blue Cove: (Kane Co.) GSCENM-Kaiparowits Plateau-Jack Riggs Bench. Lower Coyote Spring map.

Ralph Chynoweth noted that there is a lot of blue clay (Mancos Shale) in the area. (425~)

—Cove Reservoir: Ralph Chynoweth noted that this large stock reservoir is on the south end of Blue Cove (near elevation 4558). It was built by the BLM. A nearby corral and line shack were built by Ralph Chynoweth. (425~)

Blue Creek: (San Juan Co.) Manti-LaSal National Forest-Abajo Mountains-North Cottonwood Creek. Mount Linnaeus and Shay Mountain maps.

John Scorup: "The trees are a blue color from a distance." (1821~)

—Tuerto Trail: (Also called Forest Service Trail #011.) This constructed stock trail leads along this perennial stream for several miles. (See Tuerto Canyon.)

—Bayles Cabins: PRIVATE PROPERTY. The cabins, on upper Blue Creek (near elevation 9020T on the Mount Linnaeus map), were built by Boge Bayles in the 1940s. They are now owned by Val Dalton. (517~, 1821~)

Blue Flat Reservoir: (Emery Co.) San Rafael Swell-Willow Springs Wash. Mussentuchit Flat map.

Also called Lower Blue Flat Pond. (780~)

This huge stock reservoir, still used, was built in 1954. (1551~)

—Upper Blue Flat Pond: This stock reservoir is one-half mile west of Blue Flat Reservoir. (780~)

Blue Flat Reservoir: (Grand Co.) Tenmile Country-Interstate 70. Hatch Mesa map.

This still-used stock reservoir was built with pride! (SAPE.)

Blue Flats: (Emery Co.) San Rafael Swell-Mussentuchit Wash. Mussentuchit Flat and Willow Springs maps.

Jim Crane: "That's been called Blue Flats for a long time. It's for that Mancos Shale clay soil that is somewhat blue in color." (478~)

Bluefly Creek: (Garfield Co.) Dixie National Forest-Paunsaugunt Plateau-East Fork Sevier River. Wilson Peak and Bryce Canyon maps.

Kate B. Carter: "Numerous blue bottle flies noted along its course." (375~)

—Blue Fly Ranch: The Kanarra Cattle Company, a cooperative started in the early 1870s, had their headquarters near here. (186~, 363~)

Blue Gate: (Wayne Co.) Blue Valley-Fremont River. Town Point map.

Also called Caine Valley and Little Blue Valley. (164~)

Grove Karl Gilbert of the Powell Survey called the area along the Fremont River and between North and South Caineville mesas Blue Gap. (723~, 1931~)

George C. Fraser in 1915: "There is no diversification into hard and soft layers as is usual, so the erosive forces have operated equally on the entire area. The result is a maze of miniature mountain chains, peaks and valleys similar to the relief map of a very mountainous country." (668~)

Rulon Hunt, who grew up in nearby Caineville, described a boyhood sport perfected on the hills of Blue Gate: "The steep slopes of the blue clay hills offered a perfect slide for all of us who had the ambition to climb to the top with the three barrel stays we had nailed together with two boards, one on each end. This gave us a place to sit and put both feet. We had to hurry pretty fast to climb on before our contraption took off. By the time we hit the bottom we were moving fast enough and could go way out in the flat." (927~)

Blue Hills: (Grand Co.) Tenmile Country-Tenmile Wash. Dee Pass and Valley City maps.

The hills are in the blue-colored Mancos Shale clays.

Blue Jay Flat: (Sevier Co.) Fishlake National Forest-Scorups Meadows. Rex Reservoir map.

Blue Jays were common here. (2053~)

Bluejohn Canyon: (Wayne Co.) Robbers Roost Flats-Canyonlands National Park-Horseshoe Canyon Detached Unit-Horseshoe Canyon. Robbers Roost Flats, Whitbeck Knoll, and Sugarloaf Butte maps.

Joe Biddlecome named this for outlaw John "Blue John" Griffith who had one blue and one brown eye. Blue John moved to the area in 1880. (1808~) Green River pioneer LeRoy T. Harris is given credit for actually giving the nickname "Blue John" to Griffin. (1780~)

Arthur P. Ballard ran into Blue John in the town of Thompson: "Blue John was a square built, middle height, cow puncher's walk, had a shifty eye and sinister look on a weather beaten face." (130~)

Blue John built a cabin next to Bluejohn Spring in the mid-1890s. In the late 1890s he was chased out of Robbers Roost country by a Moab posse for stealing horses. Blue John headed for Dandy Crossing on the Colorado River. There he secured a boat from Cass Hite. He was last seen below California Bar and it is assumed he died on the river. (607~, 1931~)

—Movies: *127 Hours*, a movie about Aron Ralston, a young man who amputated his own arm in the canyon after a boulder rolled onto it and trapped him for 127 hours, was filmed, in part, in the canyon.

Blue Lake: (Garfield Co.) Dixie National Forest-Aquarius Plateau. Jacobs Reservoir map.

Edson Alvey: "The name was derived from the blue color of the water." (55~)

Blue Lake: (San Juan Co.) Manti-LaSal National Forest-La Sal Mountains. Mount Peale map.

Lloyd Holyoak noted that his great grandfather, Henry John Holyoak, homesteaded three sections centered on Blue Lake. The Holyoaks still own the land. Lloyd: "I think it was named Blue Lake because it was the prettiest lake on the mountain. The Blue Lake as you see it now is nothing compared to what it used to be. It used to have a lot more water than it does now. It is spring-fed and there was some of the best fishing on the La Sals there." (906~)

—Holyoak Cabins: PRIVATE PROPERTY. Lloyd Holyoak noted that cabins a short distance south of Blue Lake were part of the original Holyoak homestead: "There's a beautiful big spring there.... It's ice cold. You can't drink three swallows and that's it. Summer, winter, no matter what. Best spring on the mountain. Sweet water. My Uncle Gran built the first cabin, dad [Alvie Holyoak] built the second one, and there were two or three others built." (906~)

—Grass Lake: Lloyd Holyoak noted that this is one mile west-northwest of Blue Lake (near elevation 10502'). (906~)

Blue Notch: (Wayne Co.) Henry Mountains-Thompson Mesa-Blind Trail Wash. Notom map.

—Constructed Stock Trail: Keith Durfey noted that this goes from the Blue Notch north up the cliffs and ends on Thompson Mesa. (582~, SAPE.)

Blue Notch Canyon: (San Juan Co.) Glen Canyon NRA-Good Hope Bay. Copper Point, Mancos Mesa NE, Hite South, and Good Hope Bay maps.

Also called Blue Canyon (560a~) and Blue Pass Canyon (1931~).

The first mention of the Blue Notch name was from Bert Loper in 1909. He had a ranch in Red Canyon on the south side of Blue Notch. (1216~)

—Blue Notch: (Copper Point map.) (Also called Blue Hill.) (560a~) The Blue Notch is in the blue-tinted Chinle Formation. In the early days this was called Duckett Pass. (See Ducket Crossing.) The Duckett brothers (See Ducket Crossing) used the pass to get back and forth between White and Red canyons. (1115~)

—Blue Notch Road: The road through the notch was built in 1952–53 with help from the Atomic Energy Commission. (212~)

—The Gap: This uranium mining prospect was in lower Blue Notch Canyon (one-half mile west-northwest of elevation 4357T on the Good Hope Bay map). The name comes from a narrow area in Blue Notch Canyon known as The Gap. (1872~)

—Hite Marina: (Proposed.) The original plan was for Hite Marina to be located at Castle Butte. A branch of the highway would have gone over the Blue Notch to Castle Butte. (2018~)

Blue Peak: (Sevier Co.) Fishlake National Forest-Sevier Plateau. Koosharem map. (8,544')

Clarence Dutton's 1879 Powell Survey map shows a Blue Peak at or near this location. (584~)

Blue Pond: (Emery Co.) San Rafael Swell-Red Ledges. Buckhorn Reservoir and Cleveland maps.

This stock pond is no longer used. It is in the blue bentonite clays. (SAPE.)

Blue Spring Creek: (Garfield Co.) Dixie National Forest-Boulder Mountain-Pine Creek. Posy Lake map.

Also called Nettle Spring. (2050~)

Edson Alvey: "The name was taken from the blue spruce growing along this creek." (55~)

—CCC Forest Service Camp #18: This was on Pine Creek a short distance north of the mouth of Blue Spring Creek. It was established in 1933 and was used as a base of operations for building the Hells Backbone Road. (1551~)

—Box Ranger Station: (Also called Box Canyon Guard Station.) This was one mile southeast of the Blue Spruce Campground on the Hells Backbone Road (near elevation 8341). It was built in 1910 and was condemned in 1936. (2021~) Nothing remains. (SAPE.)

Blue Spring Creek: (Garfield Co.) Dixie National Forest-Panguitch Lake. Panguitch Lake map.

Also called Blue Creek, Blue Spring Canyon, and Blue Spring Valley.

George C. Fraser in 1915: "Its color is a deep indigo." (668~)

Mary Henderson Richens: "At the foot of the mountain and bordering the valley on the south is one of the most peculiar springs that I have ever seen. A stream which is at once large enough to operate a grist mill arises from a pond circular in form and is about 157 feet in diameter and is surrounded by bluffs. The water is bluish in color which accounts for the name of the spring." (2053~)

Linda King Newell: "The springs themselves are very deep and reach some fifty feet across and about seventy feet long. The clear water appears blue." (1445~)

—Imlay Ranch: James H. Imlay (1815-1890) homesteaded at the mouth of Blue Spring Creek in 1874. (365~, 1445~)

—Fish Hatchery: A fish hatchery was started at Blue Spring in 1908. (1444~)

—Blue Springs Ranger Station: The station, located on the south side of Panguitch Lake, was built by 1910 and closed in 1933. (2021~) It was replaced by the Panguitch Lake Ranger Station on the north shore.

—CCC Camp: A CCC camp was located here in 1933. (1715~)

—Twin Lakes: These are one-quarter mile west-northwest of Blue Spring. (365~)

—Prince Shingle Mill: In the early days William Prince (1848-1937) had a shingle mill on the creek. (1609~) This story was told: "One day at this occupation the saw fell across his [William Princes'] back almost severing the spine. An old Indian spit tobacco juice into the wound and it healed without any complications." (1581~)

Blue Spring Mountain: (Iron Co.) Dixie National Forest-Castle Valley. Panguitch Lake map. (9,890')

H. Grant Seaman: "Named with Blue Spring and Blue Spring Creek by land settlers and users. Mountain is timbered with Ponderosa Pine, Spruce, Fir and Aspen. Is a very important watershed area." (1931~)

Blue Springs: (Washington Co.) Upper Kolob Plateau-Bear Creek. Kolob Reservoir map.

This area was used for dairying in the summers by residents of St. George and surrounding towns. (273~) LeRoy Jeffers in 1922: "the welcome waters of Blue Spring. Here were great flocks of sheep which pasture on the plateau and annihilate for years the natural beauty of the forest." (960~)

Blue Spruce Campground: (Garfield Co.) Dixie National Forest-Boulder Mountain-Pine Creek. Posy Lake map.

This was built by the CCC in the mid-1930s. (1655~)

Blues, The: (Garfield Co.) GSCENM-Escalante Mountains. Upper Valley and Pine Lake maps.

Also called Blue Hills.

Ralph Chynoweth: "When you look off the top of the pass [See The Saddle below] over the Blues, that's all you can see is that blue clay, the Mancos Shale. There's not much vegetation growing in there, just blue clay." (425~)

—The Saddle: The road from Escalante to Henrieville (now Highway 12) went over The Blues. The high point was called The Saddle (elevation 7428 on the Upper Valley map). (777~) Most of the early descriptions of The Blues were from The Saddle.

Captain James Andrus of the Andrus Military Reconnaissance Expedition of 1866: "Thence up a sharp, steep, clay ridge barely wide enough at times to afford footing for our animals; one of a series of such ridges, between deep almost perpendicular gullies worn in the mountain side by storms of ages and the only one on the entire face of the mountain between Sandstone Point [Kaiparowits Plateau] and Table Mountain [Table Cliff Plateau] that is at all practicable as a trail and this is very steep difficult and dangerous. One of our animals in attempting one of the ledges was overbalanced by his pack and rolled some distance down the mountain side fortunately the side down which he fell was less steep than the opposite one or he would have been inevitably dashed to pieces. With some difficulty he was recovered, not much injured, but made more circumspect by his experience." (475~)

Jack Hillers of the 1871–72 Powell Expedition: "When I reached the top I stopped to breathe. I looked down the awful chasm—it looked wild and forbidden, the valley below being in deep shadow. Table Mountain [Table Cliff Plateau] north of it with its pink colors reflected back the golden light of the setting sun long after she had gone from my view. A wilder view I never beheld. It surpassed the Wild Scene on the Colorado at Lava Falls. What a picture for Burstadt [famed landscape artist Albert Bierstadt]." (884~)

William Derby Johnson, also of the Powell Expedition: "The divide is composed of clay shale and is 1500 feet high, very steep. The divide was cut into innumerable gulches and ridges that looked like hogs' backs, only they were more sharp. Just as we started up the divide the packs all became loose and it commenced to rain, slowly a first, then faster, until it poured down. Had a lively time coming up. The rain had made it slippery and sticky. The trail followed up a narrow ridge only two or three feet wide and outside the trail the precipice was nearly vertical for 1,000 feet, with here and there a sharp rock making its appearance in the side. But all of our trouble and vexation were repaid by the sight we saw when we reached the top of the divide. Before us lay the head of Potato Valley [Upper Valley]. It was the prettiest sight I ever saw in my life. The sun just then came out and cast a look of pleasantness upon everything." (1005~)

—Pioneer Road: Alma Barney in the early 1880s: "That same fall we made the dugway road over the Escalante Mountain and by dint of hard work got the road so we could take our wagons over the mountain." (138~) A.H. Jones in 1910: "The road from there [Henrieville] to Escalante is not good, it crosses a high divide which is made up of clay hills and gulches and it is crooked and steep." (1009~)

Blue Stem: (Carbon and Uintah Counties.) Desolation Canyon-Green River. Duches Hole map.

Also called Blue Stem Bottom.

Blue Stem is a type of bunchgrass used as forage by livestock.

Inscriptions at the north end of Blue Stem Bottom include Joseph Christianson, James Peacock, and Chris Jensen, no date. (SAPE.)

Blue Trail Creek: (Emery Co.) Manti-LaSal National Forest-Wasatch Plateau-Ferron Creek. Ferron map.

—Blue Trail: This constructed stock trail starts on Ferron Creek one-quarter mile east of the mouth of Blue Trail Creek (Ferron map). It then goes south, by elevation 6930, to the west side of Little Nelson Mountain, and on to Sage Flat (Flagstaff Peak map). (M.20.)

Blue Valley: (Wayne Co.) Caineville-Hanksville-Fremont River-Highway 24. Steamboat Point map.

Also called Dead Hills, Gaves Valley, Graves Valley, Greys Valley, The Lower Country, Painted Desert, and Valley of Graves.

Although this is shown only on one USGS 7.5 Minute Series map, locals noted that Blue Valley runs between the towns of Hanksville and Caineville. The Fremont River and Highway 24 go through the valley. Nearby and related names include Blue Mesa and Blue Flats.

Barbara Ekker: "The name came from the bluish colored mancos [shale] that is so prominent there." (607~)

John Wesley Powell called the area both Meadow Valley and Graves Valley. (1567~) In 1881 Albert King Thurber passed through the area, calling it the Dixie Hills. (1888~) Ebenezer Hanks called this Cane Valley in 1881 for all the wild cane they found in the area. (1194~) Elias Hicks Blackburn of Loa in April 1882: "We past a nice valley of 2,000 acres I named it Blue Valley from some blue banks in same." (248~)

Volney King led an exploration party through the area in 1882: "We traveled down the [Fremont] river through the blue ridge one place so steep that a horse could scarcely climb up it and so narrow that they could barely stand up it and the part we came down was very steep. We then came where the valley narrowed up to the river and we forded it and came into the blue valley. Here is 1500 acres of good land." (1096~)

Zane Grey in 1930: "It resembled a winding jewel of emerald and amethyst, set down amid barren hills of jasper and porphyry, and variegated mosaics of foothills waving away on the left, and golden racks of carved rocks, and mounds of brown clay and dunes of rusty earth. All these were stark naked, characterized by thousands of little eroded lines from top to bottom." (785~)

Hoffman Birney in 1932: "I got a big surprise from the country between the Notom Ranch [near Caineville] and Hanksville.... One drops over a divide east of Notom into a land of steel-blue shales, great flood-plain valleys where not even a clump of salt-weed grows.... The shales ... have eroded into great pyramidal dunes with surprisingly sharp ridges and hogbacks. There are rectangular buttresses and monuments, an occasional one being capped with a clastine-appearing stratum of light lemon-yellow.... The blending of colors, the pastel shades, are far superior to the Painted Desert." (231~)

Charles Kelly in 1935: "We found ourselves winding among eroded hills and mounds of decomposed shale, mostly gray or brown, streaked with every color of the rainbow. It was genuine badlands country, smeared with nature's paintbrush." (1075~)

Charles Kelly described the valley as it was when the settlers first arrived: "In those days the Dirty Devil [River] above Hanksville meandered peacefully through its long, narrow valley, its banks bordered with a thick growth of willows. Its channel was not more than a dozen steps wide and it could be waded almost anywhere.... The red alluvial soil proved rich and it was easy to plow and cultivate." (1052~)

D. Eldon Beck in 1948: "Near Caineville there is a clay formation [Mancos Shale] which is most unique in sculpturing, color and design. The nearest comparison I can give the reader of its structure is that depicted for various places on the planet Mars or the moon as visioned in the comic strip 'Buck Rogers.' It is as though a gigantic elephant had been skinned and its integument stretched over a series of ridge poles, varying in height. Not a spear of grass, not a shrub, not a tree, *nothing, nothing* alive grew or crawled over the surface. It was the land 'Lost Desolation' itself. The only change which ever comes to this land is the lights and shadows of the day and night plus the carving of a new hill by the forces of wind and water." (179~)

Jack Breed in 1952: "Beyond the cottonwoods of Caineville we crunched up the slopes of Blue Valley and prayed that the rains would leave us alone. This stretch of Mancos formation is one of the worst places in the United States for a vehicle in a storm. In pioneer days, wagons crossing it in wet weather had to stop every 100 feet to have the mud hacked from the wheels." (277~)

Ward J. Roylance in 1965: "This painted desert is a land of rare charm. Its colors are subdued pastels—yellow, grays, browns, blue-gray—with pockets here and there of multi-colored shale and clay, where the earth comes alive with a flamboyant display of Sleeping Rainbow. There is an effect of vast distance, the view being obstructed in most directions only by low, serrated ridges and plateaus, flat-topped mesas or buttes. The Henrys [Henry Mountains] alone provide impressive background relief in this wilderness of mystic beauty." (1659~)

—Ghost Towns: There were several small towns located in Blue Valley between Caineville and Hanksville. Unfortunately there is little actual information on several of the townsites, which are totally or all but gone today. As one correspondent wrote: "Blue Valley (Burgess)-Giles-Elephant and Clifton. Long gone and possibly never heard of are the names of some of these settlements. Their history is so closely interwoven that it is difficult to separate them." (1188~)

—Mesa Town: This was on the south side of the Fremont River just east of Blue Gate (at elevation 4547T on the Town Point map). The town, consisting of about ten families, was settled by the Sebron Johnson Golding family in 1894. (1419~)

—Elephant Town: This was on the north side of the Fremont River just east of Blue Gate. It was established by Orson M. Dalton and James Huntsman in 1887. Early documents called this the Neighborhood of the Elephant or The Elephant.

Two name derivations are given. First, the town was next to a hill that resembled an elephant. (925~, 1537~) Mary Henderson Richens: "Elephant. Later known as Mesa. It is about three miles east of Caineville. The place was originally named after a rocky cliff which stood out prominently in the neighborhood and which resembles an elephant." (2053~)

Andrew Jenson in 1891: "About three miles east of Cainesville, on our road to Blue Valley we come to another little cluster of houses locally called Elephant, thus named after a huge cliff somewhat resembling an elephant in shape, which stands immediately north of the village." (970a~)

Second, Bernice W. Smith: "For some reason the little hamlet was called Elephant, possibly by someone who had lived at Elephant City, an earlier settlement in Beaver County." (1194~)

Andrew Jenson: "Failure in crops caused the discontinuance of the settlement and not a vestige of it was left in 1930." (972~)

—Giles Town and Kitchentown: (See Giles Town.)

Blue Valley Benches: (Wayne Co.) Henry Mountains-Coaly Wash. Dry Lakes Peak map.
(See Blue Valley for name derivation.)

Bluff Bench: (San Juan Co.) San Juan River-Cottonwood Wash. No-Mans Island, Recapture Pocket, and Bluff maps.

In 1957 Myrtle Hunt noted that this was called Big Bench. (384~)

Robert S. McPherson noted a different name: "The League of Nations on Bluff Bench was so named because many individual ranchers ranged stock there." (1336~)

—Pioneer Road: The road from Bluff to Monticello and on north went across the bench. Albert R. Lyman: "And woe to the team which faced the shifting soil on Bluff Bench.... The road was simply a barren path through the drifting sand into which the wheels sank a disheartening

depth, coming slowly up therefrom with the miserable substance sliding from every spoke." (1240~)

Bluff Town: (San Juan Co.) San Juan River-Cottonwood Wash-Highway 191. Bluff map.
Also called Bluff City.

Laurance D. Linford noted that the Navajo name for the area where the town now sits is *tse'lagai dez'a*, or "White Rock Point." (1204~) The Ute name is *Pah saw gut*, or "Down by the River." (1335~)

Bluff was the first county seat of San Juan County. It was moved to Monticello in 1895.

In 1879 the Hole-in-the-Rock Expedition, mired at the Hole-in-the-Rock Crossing of the Colorado River, sent a scouting party of four men ahead to find a route to the San Juan River. This they did, arriving at what would become the future townsite of Bluff on December 29, 1879. They found the John Harris and Harriman families living here. The men then continued up the San Juan River to a planned townsite at the mouth of Montezuma Creek. They returned to the main expedition with the good news that they had found a route to the San Juan. Although the final destination of the Hole-in-the-Rock trekkers was to be Montezuma, they got to Bluff and simply did not have the energy to move on. (1244~) The town of Bluff, sitting between a bluff and the San Juan River, was established in April 1880.

George B. Hobbs: "Wm. Hutchings of Beaver was the man that named the place Bluff City on account of the bluffs near by." (1356~) Other settlers were laughingly told that the name was used because the site itself was one big bluff. The City was dropped from Bluff City so as not to confuse it with Council Bluffs, which was sometimes called Bluff City. (1526~)

Eliza Maria Partridge Lyman in 1881: "There are now only six men in Bluff City and plenty of Indians all around us. There is nothing but the hand of the Lord that preserves us here as well as in all places." (1253~)

Albert R. Lyman: "When the first company of settlers arrived in 1880 ... at what they called Bluff, they found themselves surrounded by a horde of inveterate thieves and murderers. The Piutes and Navajoes made life sufficiently unpleasant for the settlers, but these white desperadoes, using the country as their highway of escape from the reaching hands of the law on all sides, made it almost intolerable.... The little colony, an oasis of law in a desert of anarchy, had to meet the challenge of the menace, or give up and move away." (1237~)

The pioneers soon found that the land was not suitable for large-scale farming; the San Juan River was not usable for irrigation. When San Juan Stake President Francis Hammond moved to Bluff in 1886, he recognized that the future of the area was in the livestock industry, not in farming. The change was speedy and rewarding. (1241~, 1336~, 1356~, 1526~, 1562~, 2056~)

Frank McNitt described the town as it was in the early years: "It was an almost dry oasis, man-built, bravely planned—and in the center of nowhere. A green spot in a beautiful wide river canyon surrounded by vividly-colored sandstone." (1334~)

D.I. McLelland, in a *Rocky Mountain News* article from January 12, 1893: "It is a little Mormon settlement of twenty families. Each has a sixteen-acre tract of ground, which is in a good state of cultivation, and the inhabitants appear entirely unaffected by the [San Juan River] gold craze."

W.H. Kelly in 1895: "Nestling in a small but magnificent valley, between a high and picturesque bluff on the east and the curving sweep of the Rio San Juan on the west, across which muddy stream abruptly rises great sandstone bluffs six or seven hundred feet high, is one of the prettiest villages within our knowledge." (1082~)

Famed war correspondent Ernie Pyle in 1939: "Sand is very deep in the streets. People move slowly for there is no competition. Nobody new ever comes to Bluff." (660~)

Charles Kelly described the town in the mid-1950s: "Today Bluff is a ghost town, its remaining solidly built stone houses unoccupied." (1067~)

The town didn't start growing again until the completion of the Navajo Dam in the early 1960s brought the San Juan River under control.

As an interesting aside, in 1888 the Southern Ute Commission proposed buying all of San Juan County to be used as a Ute reservation. A government agent even amassed a list of how much each settler would get if they had to vacate the land. The attempt failed in 1894. Then, in 1906, the whole town of Bluff was offered for sale to the U.S. Government for seventy-five thousand dollars. The town was to be used as an Indian school. It is unclear as to what the few residents would have done. This idea resurfaced in the early 1930s. (1335~, 1602~)

—Gothic Mesa: The Captain John N. Macomb Expedition of 1859 was the first to apply the name Gothic Mesa to the cliffs surrounding the town of Bluff. (769~)

—Cemetery Hill: The pioneer cemetery is here. (1658~) Lucretia Lyman Ranney told this story: "Roswell Stevens, an aged man, one of the original Utah Pioneers of 1847, was the first person to die in Bluff. He was buried west of town across 'Cottonwood Wash' but the wind blew the dirt from the grave, heaping it up somewhere else. The people decided it was not a suitable place for a Cemetery so his body, in its crude wagon box-coffin was moved to a flat topped cobblestone hill north of town, where the permanent Cemetery was made. It is a dry rocky uninviting spot but the elements have no effect on the graves." (1598~)

—Old Bluff Road: This went from Bluff, along the San Juan River to Aneth. There it split; one fork went up McElmo Canyon to Cortez and Mancos; the other fork went to the Four Corners Trading Post. (See Cowboy Creek—Nolands Trading Post.) Some of this road is still in existence and can be followed, mostly on foot. (838~, SAPE.)

—Bluff Foot Bridge: (Also called Bluff Swinging Bridge and Swinging Bridge.) This is shown four miles to the east of Bluff as "Footbridge" on the Recapture Pocket map. The bridge was built in 1958 by the R.L. Manning Company to facilitate their oil drilling operations. Directly across from St. Christopher's Mission, the bridge soon became an important path for farmers and ranchers. Tourists also used the bridge to access Casa Del Eco Ruin. The bridge, deteriorating over the years, was decommissioned and torn down in 2007. There are rumors that a new bridge will be built at the old site. (838~, 839~)

Boat Bottom: (Uintah Co.) Uintah and Ouray Indian Reservation-Green River. Duches Hole map.

—Bridge: In 1898 a bridge was built across the Green River at Boat Bottom for crossing sheep. (1297~) In the early 1900s William "Billy" Miles had a ferry at the bottom. It was used mostly for sheep. The ferry was closed when the cable broke in the early 19teens (79~)

—Big Bottom: This large bottom is on the north side of the Green River and is one mile northeast of Boat Bottom. (209~)

Bobbys Hole: (San Juan Co.) Dark Canyon Plateau-Beef Basin-Cross Canyon. Cross Canyon map.

Three name derivations are given.

First, John Scorup: "The reason it is called Bobbys Hole is there's an old steer that hung out there. That was his favorite hangout, and he had a bobbed tail. Either the coyotes or the wolves had bit his tail off and that's the reason he had a bobbed tail and he was called Bobby." (1821~)

Second, Pete Steele: "I know that when cowboys from the S&S [Scorup-Somerville] Cattle Company took over that range, they had three longhorn steers that they were forever after. One was a Cedar Mesa steer and they called him 'Bobby' 'cause somebody had tipped his horns." (1821~)

Third, an unattributed source from the National Park Service noted that in the 1920s two cowboys with the name of Bobby worked for the nearby Dugout Ranch. (1116~)

—Bobbys Hole Road: The road through Bobbys Hole was built for uranium exploration in the early 1950s. (1821~) Alice Higgins in 1965: "The route was blocked by a monstrous pile called Bobby's Hell Hole Hill, where the [Jeep] trail looked like something only a suicidal mountain goat would attempt. As I resisted the impulse to faint peacefully away, we lurched forward, hood straight up, Joe [Lemon] braced and leaning out of the window like Casey Jones at the throttle, wrenching the Jeep round the turns with his tattooed arm. Somehow we reached the top, and I gave a premature sigh of relief; what goes up must come down, and that was even worse." (880~)

Bobbys Hole Canyon: (San Juan Co.) Dry Valley-Wind Whistle Ridge-Harts Draw. Hatch Rock and Harts Point North maps.

Val Dalton noted that in the old days, cowboys called this Wind Whistle Canyon and that originally Bobbys Hole was the first canyon to the west. (517~)

—Constructed Stock Trail: This goes into Bobbys Hole Canyon from the north. It starts one-half mile south of elevation 6150T on the Hatch Rock map. The trail was used by the Don Juan María de Rivera Expedition of 1765 to get into Harts Draw. (517~, 953~) Don Juan María de Rivera: "We continued to the west [on Harts Point] about three leagues through level terrain, not rocky, with some small oaks, until descending in the same direction into a very rugged canyon, very rocky and difficult with a path so very narrow that a single horse just barely fit. The path follows a terribly rigorous descent, about three escopeta [musket] shots long, which caused us great trouble, each decent loosening the cargos which shifted, not so much from the difficulty but rather from the furiousness of the North Wind which blew so hard that it stopped the horses in their tracks." (1172~, 953~)

Bob Hill Knoll: (Emery Co.) Cedar Mountain-Bull Hollow. Bob Hill Knoll map. (7,337')

Stella McElprang noted that Robert Hill moved to Huntington in 1879. He ran cattle here. (1330~)

—Bob Hill Spring: This is a large, developed spring. (SAPE.)

—Constructed Stock Trail: This goes from Wimmer Flat, past Bob Hill Spring, into the top of Bull Hollow. (SAPE.)

Bob Park Peak: (San Juan Co.) Manti-LaSal National Forest-Abajo Mountains. Mount Linnaeus map. (10,805') Robert Park was a Manti-LaSal National Forest supervisor. He died in 1951. The name was submitted to the USGS in 1952. (1931~)

Bogart Canyon: (Grand Co.) East Tavaputs Plateau-She Canyon. Bogart Canyon map.

Correctly spelled Bogert Canyon.

Harry K. Bogert used this canyon and the surrounding area for his summer range in the 1880s. (508~)

Bogus Pocket: (San Juan Co.) Abajo Mountains-Indian Creek. North Six-shooter Peak map.

Two name derivations are given.

First, Pete Steele noted that since this is not a real pocket, it is a bogus pocket. (1821~)

Second, an unattributed source from the National Park Service noted that the feed here was pretty poor, or "bogus." (1116~)

—Circus Pocket: This is next to Bogus Pocket. Pete Steele: "My dad, Percy, used to ride the rough string for the Scorup-Somerville Cattle Company 'way back when. They put him on a little horse called 'Circus' and little Circus was a real rough ridin' bronc that bucked a lot. They told dad they needed him to go up and ride that pocket. It didn't have a name at that time. He went up into there and the horse went nuts and they went 'round and 'round and 'round and the cowboys all came out laughing and saying, 'Man, you oughta seen the circus old Percy put on on old Circus.' And Circus Pocket hit and stayed forever." (1821~)

Boiling Spring: (Garfield Co.) Dixie National Forest-Escalante Mountains-Halls Creek. Griffin Point map.

Pratt Gates noted that water comes out of several springs in the immediate area. (709~)

Bolden Wash: (Emery Co.) Castle Valley-Cottonwood Creek. Castle Dale map.

Correctly spelled Boulden Wash.

Joseph Boulden (1839-1913) and his wife, Matilda (1853-1942), were Castle Dale pioneers. (970~)

Bone Flat: (Wayne Co.) Dixie National Forest-Boulder Mountain. Government Point map.

Guy Pace noted that the bones of four or so cattle were found on the flat. (1497~) The name has now been changed to Chidester Flat. Sam H. Chidester (1889–1968) was a beloved Torrey school teacher and bandmaster. He loved to camp here. (1865~)

Bone Hollow: (Iron Co.) Hurricane Cliffs-Parowan Valley. Burnt Peak and Buckhorn Flat maps.

John Pendleton: "One hard winter a herd of deer and some other animals starved to death and their bones were found there." (1515~)

Bonita Bend: (San Juan and Wayne Counties.) Canyonlands National Park-Stillwater Canyon. Cleopatras Chair map.

Also spelled Bonito Bend.

This was named by E.O. Beaman, the photographer for the Powell Expedition of 1871-72. *Bonita* is Spanish for "beautiful." (541~)

John Wesley Powell: "We pass a place where two bends of the river come together, an intervening rock having been worn away and a new channel formed across. The old channel ran in a great circle around to the right, by what was once a circular peninsula, then an island; then the water left the old channel entirely and passed through the cut, and the old bed of the river is dry. So the great circular rock stands by itself, with precipitous walls all about it, and we find but one place where it can be scaled. Looking from its summit, a long stretch of river is seen, sweeping close to the overhanging cliffs on the right, but having a little meadow between it and the wall on the left. The curve is very gentle and regular. We name this Bonita Bend." (1563~)

Boobe Hole Mountain: (Sevier Co.) Otter Creek-Plateau Valley. Mount Terrill and Boobe Hole Reservoir maps. (10,664')

Also spelled Booby Hole. (1719~)

This was most likely named for George Bube, an early resident of Circleville. (388~)

Book Cliffs: (Carbon, Duchesne, Emery, Grand, and Uintah Counties.)

Also called Book Cliff Hills (1903~), Book Mountains, Gray Mountain (419~), Brown Cliffs (1196~), Green River Mountains (1500~), and San Rafael Mountains (1195~).

The first known description of the Book Cliffs comes from Gwinn Harris Heap, a member of the Lieutenant Edward F. Beale Expedition of 1853: "The scenery was grand beyond description; the fantastic shapes of the mountains to the northward resembled in some places interminable ranges of fortifications, battlements, and towers, and in others immense Gothic cathedrals; the whole was bathed in beautiful colors thrown over the sky and mountains, and reflected in the stream by a glowing sunset." (419~)

The first time the Book Cliffs name was used to describe this long escarpment was by members of the Captain John W. Gunnison Expedition of 1853. Although the expedition diarists in general used the name Little Mountains, their topographer, Richard H. Kern, called them the Book Cliffs for their supposed resemblance to the pages of an open book. (541~, 644~)

Jacob H. Schiel of the expedition: "The Little Mountain, sometimes called Book Mountain because of its regular appearance, is several miles from the camp we erected on the right bank of the [Colorado] river. This mountain seems to be a continuation of the Roan Mountains.... The steep slopes of the mountains [Book Cliffs] are covered with a crumbling green sandstone and a red slate giving them an unusually bright coloring whose charm is nevertheless lessened by the barrenness of the entire region and the complete absence of all vegetation." (1696~)

The Powell Expedition of 1871–72 was unaware of the Book Cliffs designation. Frederick S. Dellenbaugh of the expedition: "Stretching away westward from Gunnison Butte we saw an exquisitely modeled line of cliffs, some portions being a clear azure blue. At first it was proposed to name them Henry Cliffs, but they were finally called from their colour, Azure." (1567~)

Powell noted them in his diary as the Blue Book Cliffs. (662~) Powell in 1875: "The descent [down the Book Cliffs] is not made by one bold step, for it is cut by canyons and cliffs. It is a zone several miles in width which is a vast labyrinth of canyons, cliffs, buttes, pinnacles, minarets, and detached rocks of Cyclopean magnitude, the whole destitute of soil and vegetation, colored in many brilliant tones and tints, and carved in many weird forms,—a land of desolation, dedicated forever to the geologist and the artist, where civilization can find no resting-place." (1566~)

Henry Gannett of the Ferdinand V. Hayden Survey of 1875–76 called them the Foot Hills of the Roan Cliffs: "The Grand River Valley is limited on the north by the Roan or Book Cliffs. The first name has been given them for their prevailing color, the second from the characteristic shape of the cliff, which, with its overhanging crest and slight talus, bears considerable resemblance to the edge of a bound book." (419~, M.30.)

Bootlegger Canyon: (Grand Co.) Tenmile Country-Colorado River. Gold Bar Canyon and Moab maps.

Lloyd Holyoak noted that bootleg whiskey was distilled here in the early days. (906~)

Boot Mesa: (Navajo Co., Az.) Navajo Indian Reservation-Monument Valley. Boot Mesa, Az. map. (6,650')

Also called Boot Mountain (875~, 1941~) and Rainbow Mesa (343~).

Boren Mesa: (San Juan Co.) Manti-LaSal National Forest-La Sal Mountains. Mount Tukuhnikivatz and Warner Lake maps. (9,394')
Carl J. Boren ran cattle on the mesa starting in 1878. (456~, 1856~)

Bottleneck Peak: (Emery Co.) San Rafael Swell-Sids Mountain. Bottleneck Peak map. (6,235')
Also called Sentinel Peak and The Smokestack. (1659~)
This impressive tower is incorrectly located on the map. The tower is elevation 6235. (2056~)
—Moores Canyon: This southern tributary of the San Rafael River is one mile west of Bottleneck Peak (one-quarter mile west of elevation 6245). (1318~)
—Johansen Cabin: This historic line cabin was at the mouth of Moores Canyon on the San Rafael River (near elevation 5185). The extended Johansen family were early settlers of the Castle Dale area. (1717~) The cabin has been removed.

Boulder Creek: (Garfield Co.) GSCENM-Escalante River. Deer Creek Lake, Boulder Town, Calf Creek, and King Bench maps.
Also called Boulder Valley Creek. (138~)
The creek runs from the town of Boulder to the Escalante River and was named for the lava boulders that are everywhere in the area. (607~, 2051~)
Almon H. Thompson of the 1871–72 Powell Expedition: "We are camped by a little brook that leaps from rock to rock down the mt. side, its bank grassy or lined with aspen and birch. The water is pure, clear and cold." (1877~)
—Claude V. Cutoff Road: This historic road crosses Boulder Creek one and one-half miles (as the crow flies) above its junction with Dry Hollow (one-eighth mile south of elevation 6382 on the Calf Creek map). (See Highway 12, Dry Hollow, and Haymaker Bench.)
—Constructed Stock Trail: This exits middle Boulder Creek to the south one-quarter mile northeast of elevation 5863 on the Calf Creek map. (SAPE.)
—Constructed Stock Trail: This exits lower Boulder Creek to the west one-quarter mile upcanyon from its confluence with Deer Creek (King Bench map).

Boulder Creek: (Wayne Co.) Dixie National Forest-Boulder Mountain. Blind Lake and Torrey maps.
—Riddle Sawmill: Miriam B. Murphy noted that the first sawmill in the Teasdale area was set up by Isaac Riddle (1830-1906) in this canyon in 1885. (1419~)

Boulder Mountain: (Garfield and Wayne Counties.) Blind Lake, Deer Creek Lake, Government Point, Jacobs Reservoir, and Lower Bowns Reservoir maps.
(See Aquarius Plateau for name derivation.)

Pioneers called this Forty-mile Mountain because it was forty miles across the top. (607~, 1047~, 1445~)
—Boulder Top: This is the area of Boulder Mountain that is above the 11,100' contour elevation level. (1931~)
Charles P. Berolzheimer in 1920: "The majority of the lakes are near the rim, in slightly lower ground; and there we proceeded. Every few hundred yards a new lake or pond appeared—some surrounded with tall spruce trees, others edged with rocks or long marshy grass, from its mirror-like surface. One serene body of water after another, one grove of long green grass surrounded by dark trees after another, one wide flat after another covered with grass cropped short by the sheep; black boulders of all sizes; these things did we fully appreciate and enjoy, as we rode along." (222~)

Boulder Town: (Garfield Co.) Boulder Mountain-Boulder Creek-Highway 12. Boulder Town map.
Leland Hargrave Creer: "The name Boulder was applied because of the numerous, massive, vari-colored boulders which surround the town." (489~)
William Derby Johnson of the 1871–72 Powell Expedition was one of the first to visit the area and recognize its potential: "Some six miles further lies what we afterwards called Big Boulder valley ... containing any amount of farming land, a large stream of clear water running through it to water all the land needed. This is the location for settlements." (1004~)
Nicoles Johnson and August Anderson of Richfield started using the area for cattle grazing in 1879. Anderson built a corral at what is locally called the August Corral. In 1889 Amasa Lyman, Jr. (1846-1937) and family became the first to settle permanently in Boulder. (1168~, 1445~)
Andrew Jenson: "The Boulder country may consistently be termed an oasis in the desert. The settlement covers a number of small valleys divided by mountain ridges and drained by Boulder Creek and Deer Creek, from which the settlers obtain an abundant supply of water for culinary and irrigation purposes.... Boulder would be a very desirable place to live were it not for the difficulties connected in reaching it." (489~)
Andrew Jenson again: "This valley is by no means easy of access, for in order to reach it, the traveler has to make his way over almost impassable mountain roads and dugways, almost perpendicular rocky heights and bad river crossings, but after once reaching the valley a miniature paradise opens to view." (972~)
A.M. Swanson in 1946: "This town had its place in Ripley's 'Believe it or not' as the only town in the United States that paid no taxes. The reason, the tax assessor

from Panguitch could not, would not or did not go there to make assessments." (1849~)

In 1969 the residents of Boulder temporarily changed the name of the town to Johnson's Folly in protest of President Lyndon B. Johnson's adding thousands of acres to nearby Capitol Reef National Monument.

—Anasazi Indian Village State Park. (Also called Anasazi State Park Museum, Boulder Mound, Coombs Site, and Coombs Village.) This six acre park in the town of Boulder was established in 1970. It was listed on the National Register of Historic Places in 1976.

This wonderful state park encompasses the Coombs Site, a large Indian ruin that was discovered by Ephraim Coombs in the 1920s. The Harvard Peabody Museum did the first excavation at the site in 1927, though apparently not a lot was done that year. Donald Scott in 1928: "At Boulder ... there is an extensive mound, covering in all perhaps two acres. Some excavating has been done on its south face, but so far as I could learn not very much. A number of skeletons and some pottery has been taken out, but curiously this does not seem to have incited the inhabitants to a general digging spree." (1705~) Excavation has continued intermittently to the present time. (311~, 1168~)

—Boulder Ranger Station: (Also called Baker Ranger Station.) This was built in 1911. The site of the station was acquired by the town of Boulder in 1995. (2021~)

Boundary Butte: (San Juan Co.) Manti-LaSal National Forest-Dark Canyon Plateau-North Elk Ridge. Cathedral Butte map. (7,368')

This sits on the boundary of Manti-LaSal National Forest and Canyonlands National Park.

Boundary Butte: (San Juan Co.) Navajo Indian Reservation-Glen Canyon. Gunsight Butte map. (4,497')

Also called State Line Butte. (345~)

Herbert E. Gregory in 1917: "Boundary Butte, so named from its position near the Arizona-Utah line." (769~)

—Meskin Butte: (Correctly spelled Mesken Butte.) This is one-half mile north of Boundary Butte at "Meskin 4990." (See West Canyon Creek—Mesken Bar for name derivation.)

Boundary Butte: (San Juan Co.) Navajo Indian Reservation-Nokaito Bench. Boundary Butte map. (5,438')

Laurance D. Linford noted that the Navajo name is *Gahjaa*, or "Rabbit Ears": "The 543-foot butte marked the northwestern corner of the original Navajo Reservation as defined by the Treaty of 1868." (1204~)

Bowers Knoll: (Garfield Co.) Dixie National Forest-Markagunt Plateau. Asay Bench and Henrie Knolls maps. (8,546')

Also called Black Mountain. (1931~)

Two possibly related name derivations are given.

First, Isiah Bowers bought a ranch near Castle Rock from the United Order after it disbanded in the early 1890s. (349~)

Second, J.J. Porter in 1931: "A member of Bowers family ranched near here about 1885." (1346~)

Bowery Creek: (Iron Co.) Dixie National Forest-Parowan Canyon. Brian Head, Parowan, and Red Creek Reservoir maps.

Also called The Bowery. (516~)

Bowery Creek runs through First Lefthand Canyon.

Andrew Jenson: "built by placing posts in the ground on which timbers were laid crosswise and then covered with branches of trees and other foliage, were used at an early day as places of worship by the Latter-day Saints." (972~)

Bowery Creek: (Sevier Co.) Fishlake National Forest-Fish Lake. Fish Lake map.

Rebecca M. Hales: "Fish Lake soon became a playground for the surrounding villages and ranches. A bowery was built for dancing and meetings. The Indians held their ceremonial dances there." (365~)

Joseph E. Skougaard told of the early days: "As Sevier Stake comprised not only Sevier Valley, but Grass and Rabbit valleys as well, it became customary to hold a conference each summer at the [Fish] lake, as it was a central meeting place. A large bowery was built and rude seats constructed to house the gatherings. Later a rough board floor was placed in the bowery and dances were held each evening." (357~)

In the late 1920s the Paiute and Ute Indians held their last Sun Dance near Bowery Creek. Dee Hatch, as a youngster of ten, had the privilege of seeing the Sun Dance: "They had a place out by Bowery Creek, up in the trees and the quaking aspen. They had a clearing up there, and that's the first I'd seen Indians wear braids. Some of them old-timers still had braids. We was interested and we stayed on into the night after dark. They built this fire and had a nice clearing in the trees and they started dancin' and singin' and all gathered around the campfire. Then here come the contestants out of the trees and started dancin'. They had this pole in the middle of the clearing and they'd dance up and back, up and back. They had feathers on top of the pole and they had a whistle in their mouths, and they were stripped down to the waist.... I didn't think much of it, but then I found out that was the last time they ever had a Sun Dance." (844~, 1971~)

Bowdie Canyon: (San Juan Co.) Glen Canyon NRA-Dark Canyon Plateau-Cataract Canyon. Bowdie Canyon East and Bowdie Canyon West maps.

Eugene Clyde LaRue of the William R. Chenoweth USGS Expedition of 1921 called this Cadunk Canyon. (1145~) Three name derivations are given.

First, DeReese Nielson said he remembers Franklin Jacob Adams saying that Bowdie was an outlaw. (1451~)

Second, Carl Mahon was told that Bowdie was a miner: "The story I heard was that there were some people that went in there quite a long time ago and did some panning on the river. Right there at the mouth of Gypsum Canyon, there was a great big rapid before the lake came up. They went down the Goudelock Trail [See Gypsum Canyon—Goudelock Trail] just above the mouth of Gypsum Canyon and they panned there all winter. I guess they got some pretty good gold out of there. And I think one of them was a Bowdie." (1272~)

Third, Hazel Ekker in 1966: "Lester Taylor told me that there was a Texas Cowboy came into the country and worked for the Carlisle outfit called Bowdie. He figures the [Bowdie] point was named for him." (618~)

Bowington Arch: (Garfield Co.) GSCENM-Escalante River. Calf Creek map.

(See Bowington Bench for name derivation.)

—Deer Canyon: This short northern tributary of the Escalante River is immediately east of Bowington Arch. Edson Alvey noted that the canyon is frequented by mule deer. (55~)

Bowington Bench: (Garfield Co.) GSCENM-Escalante River. Calf Creek map.

Also spelled Boynton Bench.

Edson Alvey noted that John H. Bowington was an early rancher. (56~) (See Phipps Wash for a story about Bowington.)

—Bowington Road: (See Appendix Two—Bowington Road.)

Bowknot Bend: (Emery Co.) Labyrinth Canyon-Green River. Bowknot Bend and Mineral Canyon maps.

Also called Big Bend, Double Bowknot Bend (106~), Last Bow of the Double Knot (1789~), and The Loop (1523a~).

John Wesley Powell: "We sweep around another great bend to the left, making a circuit of nine miles, and come back to a point within 600 yards of the beginning of the bend…. The men call it a 'bowknot' of river; so we name it Bowknot Bend." (1563~)

Almon H. Thompson of the 1871–72 Powell Expedition in his original diary noted it as the Bow of the Knot. (1879~) Thompson climbed out of the canyon at Bowknot Bend and described the upland area: "Weird and wild, barren and ghost-like, it seemed like an unknown world. The river is sunk. No appearance of gorge or canon a mile away. All is level to the eye, so abruptly has the river cut its channel." (1877~)

William Hiram Edwards of the Stanton-Brown Survey of 1889–90: "We soon reach 'Bow knot' or 'Fifteen mile bend,' the river going fifteen miles around and doubling back to within 300 yards." (597~)

Lute H. Johnson in 1893: "Bow Knot Loop is the name given to one of the most interesting freaks in this eccentric stream. Only 200 yards across, over a lowering sink in one of the canon walls through which the opposite wall can be seen, it is nine miles around. A great headline of the ever present red bluff is all but severed by the eccentric current. It is as though nature, wearying of the gorgeous task of walling this stream, had first resolved to shorten the route to the sea, and then, ashamed of her weakness, by extra exertion had done penance by lengthening to nine miles what might have been accomplished in a few feet. And to heighten this thought, there is the argument that the nine miles around contain more startling touches of the artistic idea followed out in the building of this canon than are to be found in any other portion of the route." (998~)

Ellsworth Kolb of the William R. Chenoweth USGS Expedition of 1921: "Reached the center of the Double Bowknot at 10:55. Time around the center loop 1 hr 20 minutes, distance 7 miles distance across neck 800 ft." (1669~)

A short distance above Bowknot Bend, on the river's left bank, is the famous inscription D. Julien, 1836 16 Mai.

—Bowknot Saddle: Powell called this saddle or neck Broken Wall. (662~) Edwin T. Wolverton called it The Narrows. (2038~) Pearl Baker noted it as The Post Office. (123~)

Colin Fletcher in 1997: "There at Bowknot Notch, looking down and along the massive trough that held the river not yet traveled, I don't think I did much thinking. It was enough to look. To absorb the colors and lineaments and conformations of rock and river. Then watch them change. For as the sun sank, rock and river underwent transformation. No sudden or drastic conversion. Just subtle shifts of emphasis. A gentle darkening. Slow seepage from day toward night." (650~)

Inscriptions include C.H. Barnes, 1903; H.T. Yokey, 1904; E. Wolverton, 9-2, 1905; E.C. LaRue, Sept. 21, 1914; and Barry Goldwater, 1940. Former Senator Goldwater ran the river in 1940 and wrote a book, *Delightful Journey,* about his experiences.

—Hiking Trail: A short trail leads up the north side of the neck of Bowknot Bend where the BLM has placed a visitor register. It is easy to hike to the saddle on the trail from the north side, but it is difficult to go down the other side as Raymond Austin Cogswell found in 1909: "Climbed down on S. side. Had a hard pull of it; had to run a long way to W. to get a chance to climb off ledge. Got a little way down; had to squeeze down a crevice and pull camera after. Risky if should lose hold." (440~)

Devergne Barber of the 1927 Pathe-Bray Expedition also had a problem going down: "Unfortunately we had brought no ropes along.... Half way down we rimmed up.... After many attempts, in which the nerve of every man was tested, by crawling on our hands and knees under an overhanging ledge, and then hanging by our hands and dropping about 12 feet, we found a place where descent to the river was possible.... Incidently, in making this drop it was necessary to fall flat on one's back for the shelf on which we fell was but a few feet wide and was followed by a sheer drop of 200 ft." (134~)

—Tower Park: This is the name the 1871–72 Powell Expedition gave to a general area immediately downriver from the south end of Bowknot Bend. John Wesley Powell: "Tower cliffs are passed; then the river widens out for several miles, and meadows are seen on either side between the river and the walls. We name this expansion of the river Tower Park." (1563~)

Julius Stone of the Stone-Galloway Expedition of 1909: "All who have visited this region speak of thousands of buttes and pinnacles, suggesting immense towers, temples, cathedrals, and almost anything the imagination pictures." (1840~)

—Jack and his Family: Pearl Baker noted that this is the tower area to the east of the Bowknot Saddle. (123~) Frank E. Masland, Jr.: "Jack and His Family is a great lonely butte and standing on its top are one large spire and one not quite so large, surrounded by a population explosion." (1310~)

—Uranium mining road: This goes partway along the bend on river right. Access to this side of the river was by way of a ferry that was a short distance downstream from the mouth of Spring Canyon. (1975~, SAPE.)

—Railroad Tunnels: (Proposed.) In 1889 Robert Brewster Stanton, while surveying for a rail line through the canyon, noted that tunnels would have to be excavated through Bow Knot Bend. (1811~)

—Dam: (Proposed.) From the *Grand Valley Times,* March 3, 1905: "It is proposed to convey water through two tunnels from the upper to the lower part of the [bowknot] bend—the capacity of such tunnels is to be 6000 cubic feet per second. By means of the said tunnels, canals, laterals, etc., it is proposed to irrigate a large acreage of land for agricultural purposes. The main object, however, is the establishment of a great electric power plant at 'The Narrows,' at Bow Knot Bend."

Bowns Canyon: (Kane Co.) Glen Canyon NRA-Glen Canyon. The Rincon NE, Stevens Canyon South, Davis Gulch, and The Rincon maps.

Also called Meadow Gulch and Navajo Creek. (466~)

William Bown, Jr. (1856-?) established the Box Bar Ranch on Sandy Creek near the town of Notom in the early 1900s. According to his grandson, Casey Bown, William used both Bown and Long canyons as winter range between 1909 and 1913. William called this once-fertile valley Meadow Canyon. (291~, 2051~)

—Bowns Trail: (See Appendix Two—Lower Desert to Halls Creek Trail.)

—Bowns Canyon to Long Canyon Trail: A constructed stock trail goes between the mouths of Bowns and Long canyons on a Kayenta Formation bench. (SAPE.)

—Bowns Cave: This huge cave is in the upper reaches of Bowns Canyon (The Rincon NE map). Ken Sleight in 1963 noted that the cave was used by outlaws to keep stolen cattle. The cave was big enough "for a thousand head." (1752~)

Box, The: (Emery Co.) Castle Valley-Molen Reef. Molen map.

Also called Ferron Box. (931~)

Mary Henderson Richens: "Ferron Creek runs through what is locally called the Box, which is perpendicular rock ledges rising to a height of about 150 feet on both sides of the creek for about two miles." (2053~)

Ray Wareham noted that the first owner of The Box he knows of was Nels Rosencrantz. Ray's grandfather, Seth Wareham, then bought the property. Ray: "We'd shear the sheep there. With the wild horses, we'd drive them and push them down a point on the north down into The Box. If you had a rider on each end, they were trapped. We had a corral there and they were trapped in that corral." (1967~)

Ray told this story: "One time, they brought a bunch of wild horses into The Box. One of them was a beautiful grey colt. Dee Nielsen wanted that colt. He didn't have any money. Ross Petty told 'im what it would take to get that colt. Nielson offered Ross some oats and some hay and a little money, but not enough. The last day the horses were gonna be there, Dee came down lookin' at that horse again. Ross said to Dee: 'We're leavin' in the morning and if you don't have that money here, that little horse is goin' over to the other side [of Ferron Mountain] and he'll be fish feed [in the fish hatchery] in a week.'

"In the morning that pretty horse was gone. He wasn't in the corral anymore, but they could see where the gate had been opened. Dee had gone down the trail on the west side of the ledge and down into the river and then they couldn't find him anymore. The water was washin' the tracks out, but they went up just a little ways and there was a whole bunch of sheep tracks, so they started followin' the sheep tracks and they found the horse just south of the Molen Cemetery tied in a bunch of whittles. Dee paid dearly for that horse! He paid about all the grain that he raised that year, and all of the wool off the sheep and everything else." (1967~)

—Paradise: PRIVATE PROPERTY. (Also called Paradise Ranch.) In 1880 Harrison Perry Fugate (1821-1902) and family homesteaded an area along the north side of Ferron Creek two miles above The Box (one-half mile south of elevation 5707), which they called Paradise. (931~) Mary Henderson Richens: "It is so named because of its pleasant surroundings. Below the settlement the bluffs close in again around the little valley in what is locally known as the Breaks." (2053~)

—Innocents Ridge: This low ridge is on the east side of Ferron Creek three-quarters of a mile north of The Box (one-half mile west of elevation 5645 on the Molen map). (1699~) Ray Wareham: "They were lookin' for dinosaurs. My dad [Ken Wareham] was foreman there, and these guys come in off of that place, and they had a dinosaur that they had dug out and they had it sealed up in plaster of Paris in a wagon, and they couldn't pull the wagon, so they got my dad to take his team and go out and pull it for 'em. They got it to Price and then it went to a museum back east…. They paid him more than he made all summer just to drag that dinosaur outta there." (1967~) Inscriptions include Hans Larsen, July 7, 1913. (SAPE.)

—Larsen Ranch: PRIVATE PROPERTY. This was directly west of The Box. (M.68.)

—Ferron Box Pictographs and Petroglyphs: These were listed on the National Register of Historic Places in 1980.

Box, The: (Garfield Co.) Dixie National Forest-Box Hollow Wilderness Area-Pine Creek. Posy Lake and Wide Hollow Reservoir maps.

In its lower reaches, Pine Creek enters a narrow defile. Edson Alvey: "So named for the steep, unscalable walls of the canyon." (56~)

The first Euroamericans known to have visited The Box were Almon H. Thompson and members of the Powell Survey. Thompson: "beautiful soft water, is 10 feet wide and runs over a rock bed…. We are camped by a little brook that leaps from rock to rock down the mountain side, its banks grassy and lined with aspen and birch. The water is pure, clear and cold." (1877~)

Thompson followed Pine Creek upcanyon until they reached a place where "the creek turns to the right and enters a close, rocky cañon." Although the Thompson party did not continue up through The Box, they did follow the general course of today's road high above its west side and over the head of The Box. (1655~)

—Constructed Stock Trail: This is the "Pack Trail" on the Posy Lake map. It is now a popular hiking trail. Pratt Gates: "They used to trail their livestock through The Box. Big herds of sheep and big herds of cattle would go through there. The sheep went pretty well, but the cattle had quite a time of it. Then, all the vegetation was gone. The water started to disappear and they finally eliminated any stock drives through there, which was the best thing that ever happened. It rejuvenated the water." (709~) Inscriptions include Peter Deuel, June 8, 1931 and Hyrum, Owen, and Vernon Porter, 9-2-33. (SAPE.)

Box, The: (Sevier Co.) Manti-LaSal National Forest-Wasatch Plateau-Muddy Creek. Flagstaff Peak map.
Also called Box Canyon.

Box Canyon: (Sevier Co.) Manti-LaSal National Forest-Wasatch Plateau. Emery West and Flagstaff Peak maps.
—Eldridges Draw: This is the top of Box Canyon (immediately east of elevation 8581 on the Emery West map). (780~)

Box Creek: (Piute and Sevier Counties.) Fishlake National Forest-Sevier Plateau-Otter Creek. Marysvale Peak and Greenwich maps.
Also called Fox Creek. (972~)
Also spelled Boxcreek. (289~)
Irvin Warnock noted that Thomas Box and family were the first settlers of the town of Box Creek (now Greenwich). (1970~) (See Greenwich Town.)

—Upper Box Creek Reservoir: Newel Nielson described how the reservoir was constructed: "The early settlers went up there and built a log crib in that channel and the story says that they put burlap sacks in the cracks and were able to store water there. And as time went on and they were able to do it, they hauled dirt and put that in front of the logs and that's how they started the reservoir." (1458~) The reservoir was rebuilt in 1953. (1971~) —Lower Box Creek Reservoir: (Greenwich map.) This was built in the 1930s. (1458~, 1971~)

Box Elder Canyon: (Kane Co.) GSCENM-Park Wash. Deer Range Point and Eightmile Pass maps.
—Stake and Rider Fence: This fence runs along the top of Box Elder Canyon. Cal Johnson: "That was a really big job. They built that clear over and down into Box Elder and all the way down clear to the Rock House [located at the south end of Kitchen Corral Point on the Eightmile Pass map]. It is astounding how they built that. You can still see the stumps they cut down to make the fence. My granddad's brother, Jed Johnson, and the Willis Littles, the Jolleys, and the Hamblins.... They were the ones who ran their cattle out there." (984~)

Box Flat: (Emery Co.) San Rafael Swell-Big Hole Wash. Devils Hole map.
Lee Mont Swasey: "There's a big cave [at the southern end of Box Flat]. And supposedly, somebody found Butch Cassidy's rifle in that cave." (1853~)
—Constructed Stock Trail: This goes from Box Flat to Jackass Flat. (1853~, SAPE.)
—Box Flat Line Camp: This was on the south side of Box Flat. (SAPE.)

Box Hollow Wilderness Area: (Garfield Co.) Dixie National Forest-Boulder Mountain.
Also called Box-Death Hollow Wilderness Area.
This 29,400 acre National Forest Wilderness was established in 1984. (887~)

Box Spring: (Garfield Co.) Henry Mountains-Pennellen Pass. Mount Ellen map.
This is a large, developed spring. (SAPE.)
Grove Karl Gilbert of the Powell Survey called this Summit Spring. (722~)

BP Spring: (Grand Co.) Uintah and Ouray Indian Reservation-East Tavaputs Plateau-Chandler Canyon. Chicken Fork map.
Two complimentary name derivations are given. In both, BP is short for Bull Prick.
First, in 1893 Red Moon (See Moon Bottom) had a run-in with rancher Preston Nutter and lashed him with a "bull-prick whip." (79~)
Second: Don Wilcox: "As the story goes, the Ute Indians used to salvage the bull penises from cattle and buffalo.... They would take the skin, clean it at the spring, and hang

it up to dry with a weight on the end. When dried, it was about four feet long, and made a very serviceable whip of tough leather. All of the Indians carried one." (935a~)

Bradford Canyon: (San Juan Co.) Alkali Point-Montezuma Creek. Bradford Canyon map.
Sylvester Bradford (1903-1982) and his wife, Thora (1904-1996), met in Blanding while teenagers, in 1919. They raised a large family in Blanding. (1911~)
—Bradford No. 5 Mine: This uranium mine in lower Bradford Canyon is one mile upcanyon from Montezuma Creek (at elevation 5358T on the Bradford Canyon map). The mine was the largest producer in Bradford Canyon. (921~)

Braffit Creek: (Iron Co.) Hurricane Cliffs-Winn Hollow. Flanigan Arch and Summit maps.
Also called Braffets Fork and Braffit Canyon.
Also spelled Braffet Creek.
Two name derivations are given.
First, George Washington Braffett (ca. 1804-1886) and his wife, Sarah, arrived in Iron County in 1850. They moved to St. George in 1879 and to Paria Town in 1880. (274~, 388~)
Second, Charles Kelly noted that Johnny Braffits was an old Indian who claimed the area. (1047~)
—Old Spanish Trail: Charles Kelly in 1943: "On a large boulder [in Braffet Canyon] was the world Gold with letters reversed, and beneath were some initials and the date 1831. On another rock nearby was cut a cross, some initials and the same date. These were probably made by early travelers over the Old Spanish Trail." (1045~)
James H. Knipmeyer noted that these inscriptions have now disappeared. (1105~)

Braffit Ridge: (Iron Co.) Benson Creek-Parowan Canyon. Parowan map. (9,100')
(See Braffit Creek for name derivation.)

Bread Knolls: (Grand Co.) Book Cliffs-Grand Valley-Death Valley. Cisco Springs map.
These brown knolls are noteworthy for their flat tops in a land of domes and triangular-shaped features. From a distance they are excellent landmarks. (SAPE.)

Breaks, The: (Emery Co.) Castle Valley-Cottonwood Creek. Hadden Holes map.
Also spelled The Brakes.
Stella McElprang noted that Fadis Hambrick had a ranch on the bottom in about 1889. (1330~)

Brian Head: (Iron Co.) Dixie National Forest-Mammoth Summit. Brian Head map. (11,307')
Also called Brians Head. (363~)
Also spelled Bryan Head. (668~)

Brian Head is the highest point in southwestern Utah and in Iron County. It was called Monument Peak or Monument Point until at least 1890.

Clarence Dutton's 1879 Powell Survey map shows this as Brin Head. (586~) His 1882 map shows it as Brian Head. (585~)

Two name derivations are given.

First, Rufus Wood Leigh noted that a member of the USGS named Brian used it as a survey point. (1174~, 942~)

Second, Lillian A. Grimshaw: "Aunt Marian Gudmusen had quite a bit to do with it. At the time we were ranching there, William Jennings Bryan was very big on the national scene. Looking from the southwest up at Monument Point, as the peak was called then, she thought the western profile resembled William Jennings Bryan's profile, or 'Bryan's Head.' She wrote to a government department; they accepted her suggestion, but misspelled the name." (942~)

—Brian Head Town: At 9,795 feet, this is the highest town in Utah. (311~)

—Brian Head Ski Area: This was started in 1964 with one chair lift and a T-bar. (887~)

Brian Spring: (Wayne Co.) Rabbit Valley-Spring Creek. Loa map.

Dee Hatch noted that Daniel Willard Brian (1880-1966) was an early settler of Rabbit Valley. (844~, 1868~)

Bridge Canyon: (Grand Co.) La Sal Mountains-Dolores River. Fisher Valley and Blue Chief Mesa maps.

Joe Taylor: "There was a sheep bridge that crossed the Dolores River at the Scarf Ranch [Utah Bottoms]." (1866~)

Bridge Canyon: (Kane Co.) Bryce Canyon National Park-Pink Cliffs-Willis Creek. Tropic Reservoir and Bryce Point maps.

Also called Bride Canyon. (1931~)

Unattributed: "So named from the Natural Bridge at it head-waters." (2053~) This is the "Natural Bridge" at the top of the canyon (Tropic Reservoir map).

—Bridge Hollow: W.J. Shakespear noted that this small canyon goes northwest into the East Fork Sevier River starting at the abovementioned "Natural Bridge." (2053~)

Bridge Canyon: (San Juan Co.) Manti-LaSal National Forest-Abajo Mountains-Peters Canyon. Monticello Lake and Monticello North maps.

Lee Bennett told this story: "As a load of whiskey was enroute to the [Blue Goose Saloon in Monticello in the 1890s] the bridge at Bridge Canyon gave way and the whiskey barrels tumbled into the arroyo. Cowboys at the scene tied their lasso ropes around the kegs and hauled them up the hillside and the load was taken to the Carlisle ranch, where a sampling party was held." (210~)

Bridge Creek: (San Juan Co.) Navajo Indian Reservation-Rainbow Bridge National Monument-Navajo Mountain-Forbidding Canyon. Rainbow Bridge map.

Also called Bridge Canyon, Bridge Chasm, and Rainbow Bridge Canyon.

Bridge Creek goes through Rainbow Bridge Canyon.

Billie Williams Yost, the daughter of early miner William F. Williams, noted that William F. called this Under the Arm Canyon: "I do not know why Bridge Canyon was known as Under the Arm Canyon, except that was the Navajo name for it." (2060~)

Zane Grey visited the canyon in 1913. In his book *The Rainbow Trail* he called the combined canyons of Bridge Creek and Forbidding Canyon by the Indian name *Nonnezoshe Boco* [also spelled Nonnezoshieboko] or "Big Arch Canyon." Grey: "It was gravel on rock bottom, tortuous, but open, with infrequent and shallow downward steps. The stream did not now rush and boil along and tumble over rock-encumbered ledges. In corners the water collected in round, green eddying pools. There were patches of grass and willow and mounds of moss.... The canyon narrowed till the walls were scarcely twenty paces apart; the color of stone grew dark red above and black down low; the light of day became shadowed, and the floor was a level, gravelly, winding lane, with the stream meandering slowly and silently." (783~)

John A. Widtsoe in 1922: "A small stream runs down the whole canyon. At first the canyon is very narrow and the cliffs high. Everything is shade. We walk in red sandstone most of the time. Beautiful pools of colored water are found all along the canyon. The sandstone is tipped up a little to form steps. In one place a parallel series of steps are formed very regularly with water running down between. Very beautiful. We name it Venus' Stairs. The canyon widens and narrows, winds and turns, is sunshiny and shady—filled with water or only a seep, with groves of willows and brush, surmounted by pinnacles and temples, or by sheer walls. It itself is a place of unusual interest." (2007~)

Lewis R. Freeman in 1922: "The entrance to Bridge Canyon proper, four miles from the mouth of Aztec Creek, proved to be almost as much of a tunnel as a gorge. Overhanging cliffs shut off completely all view of the overhead sky for a short distance, and the clear stream rippled along over sandstone that can never have known the direct light of the sun. At the end of a hundred yards the steel-trap jaws relax, and a ragged ribbon of intense cobalt blue begins broadening out until it roofs a canyon that is rather more open than that of many of the more closer-walled stretches of Aztec Creek." (682~)

Ervin S. Cobb in 1940: "Divers curious indentations worn by the weathers of a million years high upon the canyon's tan-colored mural made a fascinating sideshow here. Yonder would be a squared doorway lintel, sill and jambs all complete; and just over there a tall unfinished archway, and next along a titanic picture-frame but no picture to go in it. And then perhaps a funnel or a swirl or an arabesque or an amazing rosette, like a pastry cook's decoration for some exaggerated caramel cake." (438~)

Tad Nichols: "Bridge Canyon was narrow and shaped like a bowl at the bottom. It had been swept clean by floods, leaving nothing but a smooth rock floor with straight walls several hundred feet high.... When you walked up Bridge Creek a ways, you'd come to a string of oval tubs, scoured out and filled with beautiful spring water. The temperature of the water was just right! After that hot walk, I'd just lie down in there. Delightful." (1449~)

—Horseshoe Canyon: This northern tributary of Bridge Creek contains the Wetherill Trail (shown as a "Pack" trail immediately south of elevation 5031T). Stephen C. Jett: "Name used by the 1909 party.... Informally named for a horseshoe set into an outcrop near the canyon's head." (975~)

—Wetherill Trail: This is the "Pack" trail that goes down Bridge Creek to Rainbow Bridge. (See Appendix Two—Wetherill Trail.)

Bridge Mountain: (Washington Co.) Zion National Park-Zion Canyon. Springdale East map. (6,803')

J.L. Crawford: "Bridge Mountain gets its name from a natural arch on its face.... To residents in the late 1800s, this was Crawford Mountain, because my grandfather's [William Robinson Crawford] farm touched the lower slopes." (481~)

George C. Fraser called this Capitol Dome in 1914: "[William Robinson] Crawford showed us ... a peculiar natural bridge caused by the preservation of a bed in the cross-bedded sandstone which had resisted the weathering that removed the sandstone from underneath." (667~)

Julius V. Madsen in the late 1920s: "Bridge Mountain, on the side of which hangs a most peculiar and decidedly unique natural bridge. Unlike others of Nature's bridges, this one is tipped so that it stands on an angle of about forty degrees. It resembles the rib of a great prehistoric monster that in the remote past roamed these rugged

places. It has been called the 'Great Flying Buttress' of Zion." (1267~)

The Writers' Program of 1941: "The Bridge is named for a 'flying buttress' or natural bridge on the face of the mountain—a slender arch of stone 150 feet in length. Even through powerful glasses the bridge looks like a thread of rock that a man could put on his shoulder and carry away; its insignificant size against the wall emphasizes the colossal proportions of these monuments." (2056~)

—Saddlebagger Peak: This small peak is immediately south of Bridge Mountain. It was named by the canyon group EMDC. Since they were not able to climb Bridge Mountain, they had to settle on reaching the saddle between Saddlebagger Peak and Bridge Mountain. (SAPE.)

—G2: This peak is the second summit south of Bridge Mountain. Courtney Purcell noted this has the best views in Zion National Park. (1591~)

—CCC Camp: The Bridge Mountain CCC Camp was located under Bridge Mountain from 1934 to 1942. (486~)

Bridger Jack Mesa: (San Juan Co.) Abajo Mountains-Behind the Rocks. Kane Springs, South Six-shooter Peak, Cathedral Butte, and Harts Point South maps. (7,107')

Bridger Jack was a Ute Indian who lived in the area in the late 1800s. Frank Silvey: "Bridger Jack ... was always a friend to the white settlers around La Sal and always made his word good in any swap.... He could speak those days, considerable English, always dressed well, and was a fine looking Indian. Bridger's great weakness was gambling." (1741~)

Two stories are told of the death of Bridge Jack.

First, Cornelia Perkins: "[Bridger Jack], with his tribe, was camped at Peter's Spring [in 1897]. Wash [a Ute Indian] and his group were in close proximity. A gambling dispute between the two men became so violent that they decided to 'shoot it out.' Back to back they each stepped off twenty steps, turned and fired. Bridger Jack pointed his gun upward and fired over his assailant's head. Wash's bullet pierced Bridger Jack's heart." (1526~, 1649~)

Second, Albert R. Lyman: "Another Ute who fell at the hands of his own people, was Bridger Jack, though it must not be implied that he was other than a fine specimen of Indian, both physically and mentally. His mental genius had exalted him to the dignity of medicine man, but for some inexplicable reason, his medicine was adjudged to be bad. And for making this bad medicine, they pursued him as he ran, shooting him again and again until he fell from his horse, and then putting a sure bullet through each arm and each leg to break the evil spell of some of his bad medicine." (1240~)

—Bridger Jack Stock Trail: This rugged trail goes up the east side of the mesa towards its north end (immediately south of elevation 6747 [Cotton] on the Harts Point South map). (SAPE.) Pete Steele noted that during the Scorup-Somerville Cattle Company's reign in the late 1800s and early 1900s over Dark Canyon Plateau, they would winter horses on top of Bridger Jack Mesa. (1821~)

—Goudelock Trail: This marvelous trail starts at the Goudelock Ranch at the junction of Stevens Canyon and North Cottonwood Creek (near elevation 6091 on the Cathedral Butte map) and goes up a tributary of North Cottonwood Wash (by elevation 6036T), crosses the road, then goes up the very southeastern end of Bridger Jack Mesa. (SAPE.) (See North Cottonwood Wash—Goudelock Ranch.)

Bridger Jack Mesa: (San Juan Co.) Behind the Rocks-Highway 191-Kane Springs. Kane Springs map. (5,823')
Otho Murphy: "named after the Indian Chief [Bridger Jack] who used the flat-topped mesa with its deep water hole, for a camping place." (1420~)

Bridger Point: (Kane Co.) Paria Canyon-Vermilion Cliffs Wilderness Area-Flat Top-Paria River. Bridger Point map. (5,176')
—Constructed Stock Trail: This trail, down a sand dune, enters Bridger Canyon on its upper south side (north of elevation 5110). (SAPE.)

Briggs Hollow: (Sevier Co.) Fishlake National Forest-Mytoge Mountains-Willow Springs. Fish Lake map.
Dee Hatch, Max Robinson, and Thaine Taylor all noted that Brigham "Brigg" Reese was an early settler. (844~, 1641~, 1868~)

Brigham Plains: (Kane Co.) GSCENM-Paria River. Fivemile Valley and Lower Coyote Spring maps.
Two name derivations are given.
First, Ralph Chynoweth: "The flats are just covered with Brigham Tea [Mormon Tea] plants." (425~)
Second, Cal Johnson: "Brigham Young came down through here and off through the Nipple and down the Paria and over there to make peace with the Indians." (984~)

Brigham Tea Bench: (Garfield Co.) GSCENM-The Gulch. King Bench and Red Breaks maps.
Edson Alvey noted that this bench is covered with Brigham Tea (Mormon Tea), a favorite drink of the pioneers. (55~) Also called Mountain Rush, the plant was used as a folk remedy. (353~)
—Constructed Stock Trails: Two trails lead from the Escalante River onto Brigham Tea Bench. The first trail goes to a line shack on the north rim of the Escalante River one

mile downriver from the mouth of Boulder Creek. The line shack is shown one-half mile south-southwest of elevation 5441 on the King Bench map. (Note that the trail shown on the map going from the line shack southeast to the river is not correct. The trail actually goes down a point to the southwest of the line shack.) (SAPE.) Vaughn Short in 1964: "We climbed out of the [Escalante] canyon on a trail blasted into the rock. Not far from the top we found a little cabin. A wilder, more remote location could not be imagined. The cabin was built to shelter cowboys who ride the back country in search of cattle." (1729~, SAPE.)
The second trail starts one-half mile downriver from the line shack (one mile southwest of elevation 5264 on the King Bench map). (SAPE.)

Brimhall Double Arch: (Garfield Co.) Capitol Reef National Park-Waterpocket Fold-Halls Creek. Deer Point map.
(See Brimhall Point for name derivation.)
This was called Wingate Arch until renamed by the National Park Service in the early 1970s. Archaeologist Dr. Dean R. Brimhall (1887–1972) lived in the park until his death. (1657~, 1956~)

Brimhall Point: (Wayne Co.) Canyonlands National Park-Maze District-South Fork Horse Canyon. Spanish Bottom map.
The USGS noted that Dr. Dean R. Brimhall built a "ladder trail" into Horse Canyon from the point in order to more easily study the Harvest Scene pictograph panel. (See Horse Canyon—Wayne Co.—Harvest Scene Pictograph Panel.) The name was suggested by Canyonlands National Park Superintendent Bates Wilson in 1972. (1931~)

Brimhall Springs: (Sevier Co.) Sevier Plateau-Kings Meadow Canyon. Water Creek Canyon map.
George Washington Bean called this Cold Spring in 1873. (174~)
Irvin Warnock noted that Norman Guitteau Brimhall (1820-1907) settled in the area in 1871. The name was in place by 1873. (1971~)

Brimstone Gulch: (Kane Co.) GSCENM-Dry Fork Coyote Gulch. Egypt and Big Hollow Wash maps.
Edson Alvey noted that the names Spooky, Peek-a-boo, and Brimstone were suggested while he was exploring the area with a group of school children on Halloween day in 1935. (54~)

Brindley Flat: (Sevier Co.) Fishlake National Forest-Sevier Plateau-North Fork Box Creek. Monroe Peak map.
George Brindley (1839-1929) and family moved to Annabella in 1876 and stayed until 1879. Over the years

George and his son, Howard, and family lived variously in Koosharem and Box Creek. Howard mentioned that George and his wife moved to Box Creek in 1894. Howard had ranch land immediately north of Otter Creek Reservoir. (289~)

Brine Creek: (Sevier Co.) Sevier Plateau-Rainbow Hills-Sevier River. Sigurd map.

Lamar A. Dastrup and Tim Anderson: "Its flow [comes] from a number of very brackish salt springs.... It is unusable for stock, both because of its concentrated brackishness and because it has cut so deep into the earth that stock in many places cannot get down to the stream." (1931~)

Brink, The: (Sevier Co.) Sevier Plateau-Bear Valley. Koosharem and Water Creek Canyon maps.

(See Bear Valley for name derivation.)

Brinkerhoff Pond: (Wayne Co.) Rabbit Valley-Fremont River. Bicknell map.

(See Big Hollow—Lee Ranch for name derivation.)

Brinkerhof Spring: (Garfield Co.) GSCENM-Circle Cliffs. Bitter Creek Divide map.

Correctly spelled Brinkerhoff Spring.

This spring, hard up against the northeastern corner of the Circle Cliffs Basin, has been developed and is still used by stockmen. Willard and George Brinkerhoff brought a large herd of cattle to the area in the early 1900s. Troughs were installed in 1936. (700~, 1168~, SAPE.)

—Brinkerhoff Flats: This is the area around Brinkerhoff Spring. (1931~)

—Hutch Pasture: Charles B. Hunt noted that this pasture was two miles east-northeast of Brinkerhoff Spring (one-quarter mile northeast of elevation 5858T). (925~)

Brink Spring: (Grand Co.) Tenmile Country-Bartlett Wash. Jug Rock map.

This is a large, developed, and still-used spring. (SAPE.)

Charles T. Lupton in 1912: "Brink Spring ... has a strong flow of excellent water." (1234~)

Bert J. Silliman in 1952: "[An old Greenriver rancher] told me about Brink Springs, which now running through troughs always furnishes more water than is necessary for the cattle.... Here was a fine spring among the cedars close by to abundant pasture on the higher lands, and the halfway point between the two rivers [the Colorado and Green rivers]." (1734~) Silliman also noted that this was probably a more important spring for early travelers than the small springs at Courthouse Wash.

—Old Spanish Trail: Brink Spring was an important stopping place on the Old Spanish Trail (1538~). B. Choteau

followed the trail in the 1840s and called it Green River Spring. (805~)

Bristlecone Canyon: (Iron Co.) Dixie National Forest-Lake Creek. Flanigan Arch map.

Also called Bristlecone Ridge and Twisted Forest.

Unattributed: "Named for the trees." (942~)

Bristlecone Ridge: (Iron Co.) Cedar Breaks National Monument-Ashdown Creek. Brian Head map.

Alva Matheson: "Just under the rim of Cedar Breaks ... is a forest of bristlecone pines. These old, dry, twisted tree stumps stand on a bleak hillside with no other vegetation around them. They give proof of their struggle to grow in spite of snow and wind and especially drought, and though twisted and gnarled with as many as 120 growth rings having been counted in a quarter inch piece of wood under a magnifying glass, still have a few green branches to prove they are still alive. These bristlecone or fox tail pines, as some people call them, were standing when Christ was on the earth." (1313~)

Broadhead Lakes: (Sevier Co.) Fishlake National Forest-Boobe Hole Mountain. Mount Terrill map.

Jabez Broadhead (1841-1894) moved to the Aurora area in the early 1880s. (388~)

Brockbank Hollow: (Emery Co.) Wasatch Plateau-Huntington Creek. Hiawatha and Red Point maps.

Beulah McElprang noted that John P. Brockbank was a forest ranger based out of the Bear Creek Ranger Station in Huntington Canyon from 1909 to 1917. (1185~)

—Brockbank Ranch: PRIVATE PROPERTY. This was on the north side of Huntington Creek one-quarter mile downcanyon from the mouth of Fish Creek (Red Point map). (M.68.)

Broken Arch: (Grand Co.) Arches National Park-Fiery Furnace. Mollie Hogans map.

Unattributed: "Name comes from appearance of being cracked in the middle, but it is not broken." (2053~)

Broken Bow Arch: (Kane Co.) Glen Canyon NRA-Willow Gulch. Davis Gulch map.

Also called Gothic Arch and Honda Arch. (1672~)

In the early 1900s this was called Hondu Arch. David D. Rust: "Hondu—chaps of old Mexican Hondu—in Willow Gulch.... A Hondu is item used on end of lariat." (1673~)

The arch is in Willow Gulch. In 1923 Herbert E. Gregory, thinking he was in Fortymile Gulch, called it Fortymile Bridge. (777~)

Escalante school teacher Edson Alvey found a broken Indian bow under the arch in 1930. (1953~, 2051~) Edson in 1948: "It is a masterpiece in stone, carved by the elements from the copper, pink and white hues of Navajo sandstone. These colors change hourly and blend with the shades of green of the cottonwoods, oaks, tamaracks, and willows that grow along the crystal-clear stream of the canyon that flows at its base. One cannot help but sigh with amazement as he rounds the bend in the canyon of Willow Gulch, and comes face to face with this massive structure, which towers into the heavens and dwarfs those puny beings who look up in wonder." (53~)

Broken Pond: (Emery Co.) San Rafael Swell-Whiskey Wash. Big Bend Draw map.
Also called Broken Swale.
Wayne Gremel: "The old Broken Pond is broken. It is above what they now call the Broken Pond, which is newer." (780~)

Bromide Basin: (Garfield Co.) Henry Mountains-Crescent Creek. Mount Ellen map.
Crescent Creek starts in Bromide Basin and runs through Bromide Canyon.
Jack Sumner and Jack Butler of the 1869 Powell Expedition discovered gold in the basin in 1889. They thought that the area was also rich in bromide, giving it its name. It wasn't. The basin became the chief mining district of the Henry Mountains.
In 1892 Charles Price Edrington worked at the mine for Sumner and Butler. He called it the Cyanide Mine. (595~)

Brown Canyon: (Kane Co.) White Cliffs-John R Canyon. Cutler Point and White Tower maps.
Newman Brown (1830-1879) was an early settler of Kanab. He ran sheep in the area. He was buried at Lees Ferry. (388~)
—Brown Canyon Spring: This large spring is on the western rim of upper Brown Canyon (near elevation 6503 on the Cutler Point map). Water is piped from the spring down the cliffs into Brown Canyon. (SAPE.)

Brown Canyon: (Uintah Co.) Uintah and Ouray Indian Reservation-East Tavaputs Plateau-Hill Creek. Big Pack Mountain NW map.
(See Charlie Brown Spring for name derivation.)

Brown Creek: (Iron Co.) Dixie National Forest-Summit Creek. Flanigan Arch map.
In 1958 Calvin Connell of Parowan noted that a man named Brown had a homestead at the head of the creek. (1931~)

Browning Mine: (Emery Co.) San Rafael Swell-Quitchupah Creek. Walker Flat map.
Also called San Raphael Mine.
This was the first recorded mine in the Emery coal field.
It was discovered in 1881 by Philip Pugsley and was managed by Ira R. Browning of Castle Dale. (567~, 1233~)

Browns Canyon: (Piute Co.) Sevier Plateau-Grass Valley. Greenwich map.
One of the earliest residents of Grass Valley, George Austin Brown (1849-1920), had a farm at the mouth of Greenwich Canyon. Later, the family moved to Greenwich and had a dairy operation there. (1458~, 1971~)

Browns Canyon: (San Juan Co.) White Mesa-Recapture Creek. Blanding South map.
Also called Fast Water Canyon. (279~)
Azariah Brown (1871-1947) and family moved to the area in 1910 and homesteaded the highland area between Browns Canyon and Recapture Creek. (302~, 338~)

Browns Creek: (Garfield Co.) Henry Mountains-Straight Creek. Mount Pennell and Cass Creek Peak maps.
Two name derivations are given.
First, Charles B. Hunt noted that outlaw and rustler Quimby Oliver "Cap" Brown frequented the area in the late 1870s. (925~)
Second, Guy and Nina Robison thought that the name was misspelled and should be Bowns Creek, named for the Bowns family. (1644~) (See Bowns Canyon.)
—Browns Hole: This is the "Spring" on upper Browns Creek (at elevation 7855T on the Mount Pennell map). Inscriptions on aspen trees in the area date to July 1900. (SAPE.)

Browns Hole: (San Juan Co.) La Sal Mountains-Buck Hollow. La Sal West map. PRIVATE PROPERTY.
Doby Brown lived here for a couple of months in 1882. (1526~, 1530~)
—Tibbetts Ranch: (Also called Allred Ranch.) Amy Tibbetts and her husband, Wilford Wesley Allred, ranched here in the early 1900s. (1322~)
—Heyl Homestead: In the early 1920s George Washington Heyl (1871-1949) and family had a homestead here. (2029~)

Browns Hole: (Sevier Co.) Fishlake National Forest-Salina Creek. Gooseberry Creek and Steves Mountain maps.
—Constructed Stock Trails: Two constructed stock trails provide access from Salina Canyon, through Browns Hole, and up to the Gooseberry Creek area. The first, and no-longer-used, trail went up Dead Horse Canyon (which at one time was considered a part of Browns Hole). The second is the "Pack Trail" that starts in Salina Canyon and goes south through Browns Hole (Stevens Mountain map). It is still in use. (1874~, SAPE.)

Browns Point: (Garfield Co.) Dixie National Forest-Boulder Mountain. Lower Bowns Reservoir map. (10,937')
Correctly spelled Bowns Point.
(See Bowns Canyon for name derivation.)

The Andrus Military Reconnaissance Expedition of 1866 ascended Boulder Mountain by way of Pine Creek. They made their way across the top of the mountain and marveled at the views from Bowns Point, though they did not give it a name. (475~)

David D. Rust considered this one of the fourteen best viewpoints on the Colorado Plateau. (677~)

—Bowns Point Trail: This is the "Pack Trail" that is to the north of Bowns Point. It was in use from the early days. George C. Fraser noted going up the trail in 1915. (668~) Jack King: "There were two trails when we run sheep up there. There was one for the horses and mules and one for the sheep. Later, they improved the [Bowns Point] trail so you could take cattle up it." (1094~) (See Frisky Creek—Frisky Creek Trail.)

—Great Western Trail: The Great Western Trail goes up the Fish Creek Trail and down the Bowns Point Trail. (337~)

Brown Spring: (Kane Co.) GSCENM-Nephi Wash. Nephi Point map.

This is a large, developed spring. (SAPE.)

Two name derivations, probably related, are given.

First, Cal Johnson noted that a "Doc" Brown used the spring for his livestock. (984~)

Second, the Brown family had a ranch on Telegraph Wash five miles to the south in the early years.

—Constructed Stock Trail: This goes south from Brown Spring and upcanyon to the tablelands above. It is very old and hard to follow. (SAPE.)

Browns Rim: (San Juan Co.) Glen Canyon NRA-Glen Canyon. Copper Point and Hite South maps.

C. Gregory Crampton noted that Robert Brewster Stanton named this Mikado Flat. It was later named for John E. Brown, the first Euroamerican to run livestock in the area. He arrived in the late 1870s. (465~, 1247~) Brown would later become one of the founders of the famous Dugout Ranch in Indian Creek. (536~, 1037~) (See Dugout Ranch.)

—Jomac Hill: (Also called Jomac Mine and spelled Joe-Mack Mine.) This is on Browns Rim at elevation 5391 "Mine Adits" on the Copper Point map. The mining claim was located by J.B. Plosser and A.N. McLeon in November 1950. (1908~) Dick Sprang: "It was a producing little outfit, not great by any means, but enough to buy beans and bacon." (1797~)

Browns Wash: (Grand Co.) Book Cliffs-Tenmile Country-Gunnison Valley. Hatch Mesa, Green River NE, and Green River maps.

Also called Horse Creek. (104~, 646~)

The 1929 Edwin T. Wolverton map shows this as Soda Wash. (M.78.)

—Daly Siding: This was on Browns Wash one-half mile north-northeast of elevation 4319T on the Green River NE map. (646~) It was a siding on the Denver and Rio Grande Western Railroad in the 1880s. (See Denver and Rio Grande Western Railroad.)

—Browns Riffle: This small rapid or riffle was just below the mouth of Browns Wash on the Green River.

—Moores Bottom: (Also spelled Mohres Bottom.) This is on the east side of the Green River and one-quarter mile south of Browns Wash. In the early days the river was split into two channels by a sand island, forming Moores Riffle. (1281~) It was also called Twomile Bar or Twomile Bottom as it was two miles from Green River. (1462~)

Bruff Valley: (Emery Co.) San Rafael Swell-Chute Canyon. Horse Valley map.

Correctly spelled Brough Valley.

Guy and Nina Robison noted that the Brough family ran livestock here. (1645~)

Bruin Point: (Carbon Co.) Roan Cliffs-Range Creek. Bruin Point map. (10,184')

Also called Bruin Mountain. (1931~)

Waldo Wilcox: "Bruin Point is the highest place in Carbon County. It is at the head of Range Creek.... I always thought that there was always a storm a'brewing up there. That is just a guess. You take a wet summer and there was always a storm a'brewing up on Bruin Point." (2011~) The name was in place by 1878. (1567~)

Brumley Creek: (San Juan Co.) Manti-LaSal National Forest-La Sal Mountains-Pack Creek. Mount Tukuhnikivatz and Kane Springs maps.

Also called Brumley Hill. (1420~)

A man named Brumley operated the Gold Basin sawmill. (456~)

Lloyd Holyoak: "After you get on the top of Brumley Ridge, just before you go through the fence, there was an old adobe house. Brumley was the one that had that house. All that's left now is the rock cellar. He homesteaded up there for a long time." (906~)

—CCC Road: The road from Brumley Ridge toward Geyser Pass was built by the CCC in 1933. (1225~)

—Summerville Ranch: (Correctly spelled Somerville Ranch.) This was on the west end of Brumley Ridge (near elevation 7541T on the Mount Tukuhnikivatz map). The Somerville brothers (Andrew, James, and William S.) ran cattle in the area in the early 1900s. (73~)

Brushy Basin Wash: (San Juan Co.) Manti-LaSal National Forest-Abajo Mountains-Cottonwood Wash. Mount Linnaeus, Mancos Jim Butte, and Black Mesa Butte maps.
—Brushy Basin Wash Spring: This is the "Spring" in lower Brushy Basin Wash (Mancos Jim Butte map). Clyde Barton: "Brushy Basin. There's a spring there and there is lots of alkali water in it and there's a guy down to Blanding and he said, 'I'd just like to have bet anybody in the world that they can't come and lay down and take a drink of that water and get up and let their pants down quick enough!'" (162~) A corral is at the spring. (SAPE.)

Brushy Knoll: (San Juan Co.) Manti-LaSal National Forest-Dark Canyon Plateau-Dry Mesa. Woodenshoe Buttes and Kigalia Point maps. (8,947')
—Brushy Knoll Trail: (Also called Forest Service Trail #023.) Erwin Oliver and Pete Steele noted that this trail goes north across the top of Brushy Knoll and enters Peavine Canyon one-quarter mile below its confluence with Kigalia Canyon (at elevation 7267T on the Kigalia Point map). (1479~, 1821~, SAPE.)

Bryce Canyon: (Garfield Co.) Bryce Canyon National Park-Paunsaugunt Plateau-Pink Cliffs. Bryce Canyon map.
Paiute Indians call the area *Unka timpe-wa-wince-pock-ich*, or "red-rocks-standing-like-men-in-a-bowl-shaped-canyon." (1149~)
A Paiute legend told of the forming of Bryce Canyon: "They did something that was not good and Coyote turned them all into rocks. You can see them in that place now ... some standing in rows, some sitting down, some holding onto others. You can see their faces, with paint on them just as they were before they became rocks. The name of that place is *Angka-ku-wass-a-wits* [red painted faces]." (1445~)
The first Euroamericans known to have reached Bryce Canyon were Almon H. Thompson and Frederick S. Dellenbaugh of the 1871–72 Powell Expedition. (1711~)
Richard L. Hoxie of the Lieutenant George M. Wheeler Survey of 1872–73 saw the area from a distance: "Cliffs weathered into grotesque and strange shapes." (916~)
The Kanarra Cattle Company and several sheepmen used the Bryce Canyon area in the early 1870s, but the first permanent settler was Ebenezer Bryce (1830-1913), a rancher who moved there in 1875 from St. George with his family. They had a ranch at the mouth of the canyon. Bryce's now-classic remark about the canyon was: "Well, it's a hell of a place to lose a cow." Bryce ran cattle in the area until 1880. (384~, 1445~, 2056~)
One of the first to write about Bryce Canyon was Grove Karl Gilbert of the Powell Survey: "Up the Sevier (East Fork) a few miles and then to the left a few miles or until we came suddenly on the grandest of views. We stand on a cliff 1,000 feet high, the 'Summit of the Rim.' Just before starting down the slope, we caught a glimpse of a perfect wilderness of red pinnacles, the stunningest thing out of a picture." (763~)
T.C. Bailey in 1876: "The surface breaks off almost perpendicularly to a depth of several hundred feet—seems, indeed, as though the bottom had dropped out and left rocks standing in all shapes and forms as lone sentinels over the grotesque and picturesque scene. There are thousands of red, white, purple, and vermillion colored rocks, of all sizes resembling sentinels on the walls of castles; monks and priests with their robes, attendants, cathedrals, and congregations. There are deep caverns and rooms resembling ruins of prisons, castles, churches, with their guarded walls, battlements, spires, and steeples, niches and recesses, presenting the wildest and most wonderful scene that the eye of man ever beheld, in fact it is one of the wonders of the world." (1445~, 384~)
J. Cecil Alter in 1919: "Giant fingers of red amidst the pigmy pines suddenly become monster bananas or marshmallows in the light; and shaded groups of statuary become living models of exquisite beauty as a searching light shaft between the clouds from the sun singles out the features on this stage of pantomimics, and it commands attention like a brass band in a circus.... Here one sees a candy kitchen of creamy cones, marshmallow fingers, translucent jellies, and paste-like pinnacles; and there an art group of roughly-finished statuary—cloaked nuns stand silently in white groups amidst the bronze busts of famous men; entire families stand in reverence about the statues of departed ones; and even the dissolving talus creeps downward from such as these in respectful silence—no loose and bounding rocks to break in upon the vespers." (49~)
Wesley E. King in 1920: "I'll say that it has been a rendezvous—a Latin-Quarter—of Nature's sculptors. Want to see a front, side or rear view of the Little Corporal, or of Shakespeare or T.R. or of the Pope? Want to see a regiment or a division of soldiers, or marines on parade? Want to see some fine old castles with ramparts, turrets, moats adorning statuary and winding wooded approaches? Want to see some sphinxes, obelisks and monuments, some Italian gardens with deep recesses, dark chambers, sleeping lions or charging elephants? And then do you want to see from the heights above some nine square miles of the finest lace made from sandstone by the winds and rains of the ages? Well, if you do, and will follow me,

I'll show you all this and more, in and around Bryce canyon." (1097~)

Famed war correspondent and self-proclaimed desert rat Ernie Pyle in 1939: "Bryce Canyon had better get busy and sue Walt Disney for plagiarism, or vice versa. Either Walt is copying Nature, or Nature is copying Walt. Bryce Canyon is a Silly Symphony standing still.... Fantastic is the word for Bryce Canyon. It just doesn't seem real. It's as tho Nature decided to stop being so serious, and took half a day off and made crazy stuff and daubed it up with pretty colors and had a wonderful time." (1593~)

Buck Lee in 1940: "Probably the world's finest array of color is found here, where the elements, wind, water, heat and frost have done their best to give this glorious array of formation and color. It is said that every year new formations can be seen showing the elements still at work. Among the hundreds of gorgeously colored imaginary cities and castles in Bryce Canyon, the Victorian Arch stands out as one of the most celebrated designs, carved by the storms of ages. In this mass of grotesque figures representing all the figures of fairyland, the Queen stands above them all, presiding in dignity over her realm. Holy temples, castles, Pink Cliffs, faults, arches, peepholes, graceful figures, all are found in the natural sculpturing in Bryce Canyon. Some have referred to it as a 'Canyon of Fire' for its flaming brilliance. Under the light-giving sun it has a brilliance rarely seen. Again a little 'Bit of Heaven' for it is a glorious inspiration to stand on its rim and look down into its mysterious depths." (354~)

Maurice Howe in 1941: "Bryce, where Mother Nature's subtle fingers wrought flames in stone and topped them with angels, snowy white; then sensing incompleteness, made all the beast and birds in wondrous art and spilled the paint pots of the gods upon her handiwork, scattered seeds of pine and cedar, and left the scene for man to contemplate." (2056~)

Jonreed Lauritzen in 1947: "For the symphonist it is an abstraction of light and color spreading into wide areas of repetitive tone, rising in crescendoes of torrential brilliance. For the artist it is a study in prismatic harmonies, its shades running from dark umbres [umber] through purples, reds, yellows, creams, orange, white-lemon; the interplay of color, the reverberation of light from surface to surface making the whole seem living, translucent, as though suffused with inner fires. For the poet it is literature in stone. Characters of Shakespeare and Homer and Danté and Milton and Dickens tower on the stage, frozen in grimaces and smiles, and frowns, and in grace and droll and tortured attitudes." (1149~)

—Bryce Canyon Lodge: This was built by the Union Pacific Railroad and was finished in 1925. (1711~)

—Serviceberry Trail: In the old days Indians had a trail going from the Paria River area up the cliffs to the present location of Bryce Canyon Lodge. It was called *Te-ar-ump-Paw,* or "Service Berry Trail" for the plethora of those plants found in the canyon. (1512~)

—Rim Road: This road follows along the rim of Bryce Canyon and goes from viewpoint to viewpoint. It was finished in 1934.

—Bryce Canyon Spring: (Also called Bryce Spring.) This is on Bryce Creek to the south of Bristlecone Point (near elevation 6882 on the Bryce Point map). The town of Tropic pipes water out of the spring. (1278~)

Bryce Canyon National Park: (Garfield Co.) Paunsaugunt Plateau-Pink Cliffs.

In 1919 the Utah legislature suggested that Congress protect what is now Bryce Canyon as Temple of the Gods National Monument. In 1923 President Warren G. Harding proclaimed it as Bryce Canyon National Monument. The monument designation was changed to Bryce Canyon National Park in 1928.

Bryce Point: (Garfield Co.) Bryce Canyon National Park-Paunsaugunt Plateau-Pink Cliffs. Bryce Point map. (8,296')

Bryce Canyon National Park Superintendent P.P. Paltrow in 1934: "It commands the best view of the Ebenezer Bryce homestead (where the man for whom the canyon was named settled in 1875)." (1931~)

Weldon F. Heald in 1948: "From a narrow, jutting peninsula of rock you look down over a semicircular, bowl-shaped basin three miles across. From the rim to the floor a thousand feet below, the steep sides bristle with myriads of standing rock figures clustered together in mass formations. There are fluted columns, pilasters, heroic statues, monuments, hoodoos, and skyscrapers by the thousand etched in a complicated pattern of sunshine and shadow. And the whole basin is suffused and flowing with brilliant color. Bright salmon-pink shades imperceptibly into orange; yellow to ivory and pure white. Blues and violets blend into browns and reds. All the colors run, diffuse, and mingle with each other as if stirred in a giant mixing bowl." (1521~)

Bryson Wash: (Grand Co.) Book Cliffs-Grand Valley-Interstate 70-Bitter Creek. Bryson Canyon, Harley Dome, and Bitter Creek Well maps.

The Lee and M.A. Bryson family lived near Westwater from the 1880s into the early 1900s. (388~, 1363~)

—False Canyon: The mouth of this western tributary of Bryson Canyon is right where Bryson Canyon exits the Book Cliffs (immediately east of elevation 5820 on the Bryson Canyon map). (1634~)

—Oblong Point: This is on the southwest side of the mouth of False Canyon (at elevation 5836 on the Bryson Canyon map). (1634~)

Bubbling Spring Canyon: (Navajo Co., Az.) Navajo Indian Reservation-Shonto Plateau-Long Canyon. Betatakin Ruin map.

Stephen C. Jett noted that the Navajo name is *Ha'nilhoshi,* or "Water Gushes Up." (975~) Arroyo cutting has eliminated the spring.

Teddy Roosevelt in 1913: "We camped in Bubbling Spring Valley. It would be hard to imagine a wilder or more beautiful spot: if in the Old World, the valley would surely be celebrated in song and story; here it is one among many others, all equally unknown. We camped by the bubbling spring of pure cold water from which it derives its name.... The valley was walled in by towering cliffs, a few of them sloping, most of them sheer-sided or with the tops overhanging; and there were isolated rock domes and pinnacles. As everywhere round about, the rocks were of many colors, and the colors varied from hour to hour, so that the hues of sunrise differed from those of noonday, and yet again from the long lights of sunset. The cliffs seemed orange and purple; and again they seemed vermilion and umber; or in the white glare they were white and yellow and light red." (1648~)

Buckacre Point: (Garfield Co.) Dirty Devil Country-The Big Ridge. Fiddler Butte and Stair Canyon maps. (5,697')

—Old Spanish Trail: (Variation.) Edwin T. Wolverton in 1928 believed that a variation of the Old Spanish Trail—Winter Route—went over Buckacre Point: "The trail must go over a high ridge and around the face of a high point called Buckacre." (2039~)

—Two Step Canyon: This short eastern tributary of the Dirty Devil River is a couple of miles north-northwest of Buckacre Point (immediately south of elevation 4643T on the Stair Canyon map). Bob Bordasch noted that one must surmount two difficult steps to ascend the canyon. (SAPE.)

Buckaroo Flat: (Garfield Co.) GSCENM-Escalante Desert-Hole-in-the-Rock Road. Sunset Flat map.

The term Buckaroo not only means "cowboy," it implies a cowboy who is better than most other cowboys in both deed and dress.

Buckboard Flat: (San Juan Co.) Manti-LaSal National Forest-Abajo Mountains-Horsehead Peak. Abajo Peak map.

In 1942 Buck Lee noted that pioneers left a broken-down buckboard on the flat. (2053~)

—Buckboard Camp: (Also called Buckboard Forest Camp.) (211~) This campsite on Buckboard Flat was closed in 1954. Reasons cited were that the land was slanted, making it difficult to camp (2069~) and that pollution from the camp was able to enter Monticello's domestic water supply. The campground was moved to its present location a short distance to the north of Buckboard Flat and immediately east of Taylor Spring (Monticello Lake map). (211~)

Buck Canyon: (San Juan Co.) Canyonlands National Park-Island in the Sky District-Colorado River. Musselman Arch and Monument Basin maps.

Howard Lathrop wintered his buck sheep in the canyon in the 1940s. (1147~) (See Lathrop Canyon.)

—Constructed Stock Trail: This goes from the White Rim, down the North Fork of Buck Canyon, to the Colorado River. (SAPE.)

—Big Bottom: This is on the south side of the Colorado River between Buck and Lathrop canyons (Monument Basin map). A constructed stock trail exits the bottom on its south end. (SAPE.)

Buck Canyon: (Uintah Co.) East Tavaputs Plateau-Seep Ridge-Willow Creek. Agency Draw NE map.

Inscriptions include Leon Simmons, 1926; C.C., 1929; Lee Potts, 1931; and A. Curry, Mar. 5, 1932. (SAPE.)

Buck Canyon: (Wayne Co.) Dirty Devil Country-Dirty Devil River. Point of Rocks East, Point of Rocks West, and Angel Cove maps.

Barbara Ekker noted that the canyon had "fantastic deer hunting." (604~)

—Stock Trail: Ranchers accessed the canyon by way of the Lower Sand Slide. (See Lower Sand Slide.)

Buck Creek: (San Juan Co.) Tank Mesa-San Juan River. Bluff map.

Also called Buck Canyon Wash. (444~)

—Sand Island: (Also called Sand Island Flats.) This island is immediately south of the mouth of Buck Creek on the San Juan River. It is the site of a BLM ranger station and a popular river launch area.

—Sand Island Petroglyph Panel: This was listed on the National Register of Historic Places in 1981.

—Joseph F. Barton Store: Located at Sand Island, this was started in 1884. (1240~)

—Sand Island Crossing: This was an often-used ford of the San Juan River by Indians, settlers, and cattlemen. (1241~)

Buckeye Reef: (Washington Co.) Tucumseh Hill-Interstate 15. Hurricane map.

The Silver Reef mining area consisted of two distinct ridges, or reefs: White Reef and Buckeye Reef. (See Silver Reef Town for information on White Reef.) John Barbee is credited with discovering Buckeye Reef after spiritualist Tom McNally told him where to look. (625~)

Buckeye Reservoir: (Montrose Co., Colo.) Manti-LaSal National Forest-La Sal Mountains-Carpenter Ridge. Buckeye Reservoir, Colo. map.

The reservoir was constructed from 1908 to 1913. (926~)

—Buckeye Flat: (Also called Buckeye Park.) This pasture area is to the northwest of the reservoir. Buckeye Creek runs through the flat. Leigh Ann Hunt: "Buckeye was named for the shape of the Buckeye Park area which is shaped like Ohio." (926~)

—Deep Creek Ditch: This started at Deep Creek and went generally south over Geyser Creek, across Pine Flat, and into Buckeye Creek. The water then went over the state line and down the creek to the town of Paradox, Colorado. The ditch was built in the late 1890s. (926~)

Buck Hollow: (Garfield Co.) Dixie National Forest-Boulder Mountain-Lost Creek. Posy Lake and Wide Hollow Reservoir maps.

Pratt Gates: "A lot of deer used to be in there. It was a good place to go get a deer." (709~)

Buckhorn Basin: (Grand Co.) La Sal Mountains-Waring Canyon. Fisher Towers map.

Two stories are told.

First, Joe Taylor: "That's Lockhart Basin, not Buckhorn Basin. Lockhart was an outlaw and he had a hideout up there in the early 1900s. My dad [Lester Taylor] called Lockhart an old tough. My dad rarely, rarely said anything negative about another human being. He was very non-judgmental about others, but he called Lockhart an old tough, and that was pretty strong language for dad." (1866~)

Second, Jean Akens noted that Louis B. Lockhart moved to the area to mine in 1894. In 1901 Lockhart was shot to death. Lockhart was not well thought of, but it is unknown if he was a cattle rustler or not. (13~, 456~)

Buckhorn Flat: (Emery Co.) San Rafael Swell-Cedar Mountain-The Wedge. Buckhorn Reservoir and Bob Hill Knoll maps.

Two name derivations are given.

First, Joe Curtis in 1941: "It was named because of the brush that grows there called buckhorn brush." (2053~)

Second, Thomas E. Bryson in 1941: "Name originated from numerous deer antlers in vicinity." (2053~)

Orville C. Pratt in 1848: "The country continues as almost all the way heretofore, sandy, hilly and utterly barren. Water is also scarce.... I can hardly conceive of what earthly use a large proportion of this country was designed for"! (1572~)

The William Lewis Manly Expedition of 1849 crossed Buckhorn Flat. Manly: "plain itself was black and barren ... [and] it seemed to have no end." (1274~)

Joseph Benjamin Jewkes in 1894: "As we continued our journey across Buckhorn Flat we drove through the worst windstorm I ever experienced. The sand blew so heavily that we could not see a hundred yards and finally the horses rebelled. They could no longer face that sand barrage, but would turn completely around. Seeking the only possible shelter for our teams, we drove them down into a wash while we remained all day and the next night in our wagons wrapped in quilts.... We could scarcely stand to open our eyes." (981~)

The Writers' Program of 1941: "Buckhorn Flat, a 50,000 acre plain as level as a dance floor." (2056~)

—Old Spanish Trail: The trail went across Buckhorn Flat.

—Rail route: In 1881 the Denver and Rio Grande Western Railroad built a narrow gauge railbed across Buckhorn Flat. Sections of the railbed can still be seen. (See Denver and Rio Grande Western Railroad.)

—Buckhorn Well: (Buckhorn Reservoir map.) (Also called Buckhorn Flat Well.) The well was drilled by the BLM in 1945 as a water source for the MK Tunnels. (See below.) The water is now used for livestock. (624~) Owen McClenahan: "This water lies in the Gypsum Formation and is so hard that if soap flakes were mixed with it, it would curdle. A man can drink it for about two days only; after that time, he has to avoid any sudden moves." (1318~)

—Buckhorn Corral: (Bob Hill Knoll map.) This huge corral is still used during round-ups.

—MK Tunnels: These are on the west side of Buckhorn Wash and are one mile southeast of Buckhorn Corral. From 1948 to 1952 the Department of Defense, in a top secret project, blasted and bored holes deep into the sandstone cliffs. They then set off huge dynamite blasts above the tunnels, apparently trying to determine how strong the sandstone was for possible future military use. The contractor was Morrison Knudson, giving the name MK Tunnels.

Morrison Knudson would let the locals know when the blasts were going to happen and many would take in the sight. During construction a small town, called Shanty Town, sprung up near Buckhorn Well.

Bert J. Silliman: "The canyon of Buckhorn Wash on account of its isolated situation miles away from the nearest habitation has been selected by the Government for experiments with heavy charges of high explosives with especial reference to the behavior and resistance of sandstones to the impact and shock in tunnels and other structures designed to be bomb proof." (1734~)

Buckhorn Flat: (Iron Co.) Parowan Valley-Fremont Wash. Buckhorn Flat map.

John D. Lee in 1851: "The valley on entering it seemed rather forbidding to a farmer especially. Scarce any thing to be seen but sage and greasewood.... This name originated from the fact that a Buck Horn was found in the bottom of the spring about 4 feet deep—water brackish." (1159~)

—Buckhorn Spring: (Also called Buckhorse Spring.) (305~) The Paiute name is *Chee-ava-pa,* referring to a type of edible plant of unknown type. (1512~)

Addison Pratt of the Jefferson Hunt Party of 1849 called this First Creek as it was the first one they came to while traveling south down Parowan Valley. (1571~) The Howard Egan Wagon Train of 1849 called it Spring No. 26. (598~) Joseph Cain's "Mormon Way-bill" of 1851 called it North Kanyon Creek, noting that it had "good feed, no wood, the road rough and steep." (330~)

—Buckhorn Springs Town: In 1870 John Eyre and family moved to the area and started the small community of Buckhorn Springs. It was abandoned in the late 1920s because of water problems. (942~, 972~) Betsy Topham Camp: "The town derived its name from the fact that the first settlers coming to the spring saw a large set of deer antlers or horns left by a deer hunter who had dressed his buck at this convenient place.... The horns were secured to a large pole and for many years stood as a symbol to the townspeople and passerby that this was an oasis in the desert for tired and weary travelers." (336~)

—First television: Philo Farnsworth, who was raised in the town of Buckhorn Springs, is considered the Father of Television, which he invented in the late 1920s. (336~)

Buckhorn Reservoir: (Emery Co.) Cedar Mountain-Buckhorn Flat. Buckhorn Reservoir map.

(See Buckhorn Flat—Emery Co. for name derivation.)

The first reservoir was constructed by Joseph W. Powell in 1901. One scheme, never fulfilled, was to use water from the reservoir to farm Buckhorn Flat. (2049~)

Buckhorn Wash: (Emery Co.) San Rafael Swell-San Rafael River. Buckhorn Reservoir, Bob Hill Knoll, and Bottleneck Peak maps.

Also called Buckhorn Draw.

Two name derivations are given.

First, see Buckhorn Flat—Emery Co.

Second, Thomas E. Bryson in 1941: "Named from general shape of main draw and branching draws." (2053~)

James H. Knipmeyer noted that members of the 1854 John C. Fremont Expedition may have explored Buckhorn Wash. They may have left an inscription, J.H., 1854, B.L., in the canyon. (1105~)

The earliest description comes from Oliver B. Huntington of the Elk Mountain Mission of 1855 in a brief reference: "We came to a large gulch in rocks with nearly perpendicular banks a hundred feet high. We camped at the head of this gulch, where we found a little water standing in the rocks." (930~, 641~)

In the 1880s to early 1900s the canyon was used by horse thieves and outlaws and was part of an "Outlaw" Trail. (641~)

Lamont Johnson noted Buckhorn Wash in his epic poem "Heavy Holstered Men" about Butch Cassidy and his outlaw bunch:

> One posse left from Huntington and one from Castle Dale.
> To seek among the craggy cliffs a vanished outlaw trail;
> and deep in Buckhorn Draw that night a gun fight rattled out, each posse thought they'd found their game and put the thieves to rout....
> But, what they didn't know was this, they never had a chance.
> The outlaw band had taken care of every circumstance;
> For Butch and Lay had stationed men on three well scattered trails,
> with relay horses just in case their first way out should fail. (994~)

Inscriptions include John Justensen, 1886; John T. Reid, Nephi, Sept. 11th 1887; W.J. Powell, Jr., 1894; Ben Justensen and Warren Allred, 1894; C. Reynolds, Feb. 3, 1896; William J. Seeley, Feb. 3, 1896; and Matt Warner, 1920. Warner in his younger years was an outlaw and cattle thief who rode the hard trail with the likes of Butch Cassidy. After a stint in jail, he became a respected lawman in Price. (1968~, SAPE.)

—Buckhorn Wash Rock Art Site: This was listed on the National Register of Historic Places in 1980. It is one of the most famous Barrier Canyon Style rock art panels in southern Utah. It was noted by diarists as early as 1877. (1015~) The Writers' Program of 1941: "Buckhorn Wash, a narrow defile with low rock walls. During the rainy season, the wash is a trough from raging torrents, but in summer it is a dry stream bed. A frieze of petroglyphs, two feet high and a thousand feet long, has eluded erosion on the canyon walls." (2056~)

The panel was restored in 1996. Inscriptionologist James H. Knipmeyer: "Many old, historic inscriptions were removed when the restoration work was done. It was determined by state and federal sources that the names were of recent origin, and some were, but many names with dates in the 1880s and 1890s had been documented by archaeologists as early as 1934. These should not have been removed." (1115~)

—Marsing Pond: This no-longer-functioning stock pond was at the top of a northeastern tributary of Buckhorn Wash. The tributary is immediately west of elevation 5889 and the pond was one-quarter mile west-southwest of elevation BM5906 on the Bob Hill Knoll map. (1931~) The Marsings are a ranching family from Green River.

—San Rafael River Bridge: (Bottleneck Peak map.) (Also called San Rafael Bridge and Swinging Bridge.)

In 1921 an oil company built a road from Buckhorn Flat, through Buckhorn Wash, to the San Rafael River. A bridge—no longer standing—was constructed. The road continued south to Sinbad Country. A geology report from 1928 noted that the road was rarely used and was the best route to Sinbad Country.

In 1935 the CCC improved the road and in 1937 built the still-standing, but no-longer-used, suspension bridge. This bridge was listed on the National Register of Historic Places in 1996. (641~, 710~, 727~) A new bridge was built in the late 1990s.

—Sinbad Cowboy Stock Corral: (Also called Judd Corral.) This is one mile east of the Swinging Bridge (one-quarter mile west of elevation 5250 on the Bottleneck Peak map). The corral was built by Paul Judd in the early 1900s. (1717~)

—Old Spanish Trail: (Variation.) A variation of the trail went up Black Dragon Canyon and then through Buckhorn Wash to join the trail at Buckhorn Flat.

Buck Knoll: (Kane Co.) White Cliffs-Skutumpah Terrace. Glendale map. (6,738')
Also called Buck Crater. (767~)

Buckmaster Draw: (Emery Co.) San Rafael Swell-San Rafael River. Jessies Twist and Spotted Wolf Canyon maps.
Two name derivations are given.

First, a man named Buckmaster mined here during the uranium years of the 1950s-60s.

Second, Unattributed: "John W. Buckmaster (1847–1917) was a Civil War veteran, serving with the Cavalry. Apparently Buckmaster Draw north of Elgin [Green River] was named after him." (1780~)

—Snow Mine: This is at the north end of Buckmaster Draw at the "Air Shaft," "Mine Shaft," and "Mine Dump" (Jessies Twist map). The original uranium mining claims were located by J.W. Warf of Price. His prospects were on the lower end of Buckmaster Draw and consisted of shallow pits. Snow Mine was developed in the 1950s and became a major producer of uranium and vanadium. The mine stayed in production into the 1970s. (1906~)

Buck Mesa: (San Juan Co.) Canyonlands National Park-Island in the Sky District. Upheaval Dome map. (5,625')
Also called Deer Mesa. (1931~)

The names of Steer and Buck mesas have been swapped on the Upheaval Dome map. Del Taylor: "My father [A.T. 'Del' Taylor] led a few year-old steers off the mesa on the map marked Buck Mesa into Upheaval Canyon down one of the slides below the trail from on top to Grays pasture." (1864~)

Buck Pasture Mountain: (Washington Co.) Zion National Park-La Verkin Creek. Kolob Arch map. (8,030')
Allen Taylor pastured his male, or buck, sheep here. (1038~, 2053~) (See Taylor Creek.)

—Smith Cabin: This was one-half mile east of Buck Pasture Mountain (one-quarter mile west of elevation 7922).

Buck Ridge: (Kane Co.) GSCENM-Kaiparowits Plateau-Llewellyn Canyon. Blackburn Canyon map.
Don Coleman: "Best deer huntin' of years ago, so the old-timers said that ever was. Big bucks. Big, big, bucks." (441~)

Buckskin Gulch: (Kane Co.) Paria Canyon-Vermilion Cliffs Wilderness Area-Paria River. Eightmile Pass, Pine Hollow Canyon, West Clark Bench, and Bridger Point maps.
Also called Buckskin Creek and Kaibab Gulch. (1931~)

The name comes from Buckskin Mountain, which is now called the Kaibab Plateau. (324~) Jacob Hamblin called it Deer Mountain while leading a mission to the Hopi Indians in 1858. (454~) The Buckskin Mountain name was used by Andrew Smith Gibbons of the same expedition. (714~)

Anthony W. Ivins in 1929: "[In October 1875] I first came into the Kaibab Forest. At that time it was commonly known as the Buckskin Mountain because of the fact that the Indians brought many deer skins into the settlements for trade which were taken from deer killed upon this mountain." (944~)

Will C. Barnes in 1934: "Here the settlers and Indians all came to secure buckskins from the many deer always found in this region." (155~)

Neil M. Judd in about 1920: "The south margin of the Paria is bordered by cedars and piñons, and from this green fringe the sandy surface slopes away gently to the north and there ends abruptly at Buckskin Gulch, thirty feet wide and three hundred feet deep. Aboriginal steps lead down into the gorge." (1030~)

Inscriptions include Sam Pollock, Dec. 12, 1924 and Dell Judd, Fall '59. (SAPE.)

Buckskin Spring: (Emery Co.) San Rafael Reef-Wild Horse Creek. Goblin Valley map.

Alvin Robison: "Alton Morrell and I went in there and fenced that, dug it out, put a pipeline in to some troughs so the cattle could water from them. The uranium miners got onto that water and they'd go there and they started takin' the water for their drill rigs and drinkin' it, too. That spring didn't make enough water for miners and cattle. Alton Morrell didn't like that. He said, 'I'll fix 'em.' He went and dumped some Epsom Salts in the water, and it wasn't long 'til they couldn't drink that water any more." (1642~)

Buckskin Valley: (Iron Co.) Hurricane Cliffs–Showalter Mountain-Fremont Canyon. Burnt Peak map.

John C. Fremont traversed Buckskin Valley in 1853–54. (1445~)

Buck Spring: (Garfield Co.) Henry Mountains-Butt Canyon. Ant Knoll map.

(See Butt Canyon for name derivation.)

This is a large spring.

Nearby inscriptions date to 1930. (SAPE.)

Buck Spring: (Grand Co.) Dome Plateau-Colorado River. Dewey map.

This is a medium-size spring. (SAPE.)

—Constructed Stock Trail: This vague trail, most likely used just for sheep, is on the west side of Buck Spring Canyon. (SAPE.)

Buffalo Pond: (Wayne Co.) Antelope Valley-Maze Road. Whitbeck Knoll map.

Buffalo were released in the Jeffery Well area in 1941. The buffalo soon scattered, with several heading to Buffalo Pond country. They were seen there grazing with a herd of a hundred antelope. (864~) (See Jeffery Well.)

Bug Canyon: (San Juan Co.) Great Sage Plain-Montezuma Creek. Bug Canyon map.

A name derivation can be guessed at. Cattleman Billy Graham named the canyon. (1526~)

—Bug Lake: In 1900 T. Mitchell Prudden used this name for the stock pond at the mouth of Bug Canyon . (1588~)

Bullard Spring: (Wayne Co.) Rabbit Valley-Pine Creek. Bicknell map.

Guy Pace noted that Ezra Nelson Bullard, Sr. (1865-1946) was an early rancher. (1497~)

Bullberry Creek: (Piute Co.) Fishlake National Forest-Tushar Mountains-West Canal. Circleville map.

Thomas Thomas: "It derived its name from the bullberry brush that surrounds the spring." (2053~) Muriel W. Smith: "Bullberries were a small, red, delicious berry about the size of a currant." (1780~)

Bullberry Hollow: (Garfield Co.) Dixie National Forest-Box Hollow Wilderness Area-Lost Spring Creek. Posy Lake and Wide Hollow Reservoir maps.

Also called Blueberry Hollow. (1931~)

Pratt Gates: "There used to be a lot of bullberries up in there." (709~)

Bullberry Spring: (Emery Co.) San Rafael Swell-Sinbad Country. Hunt Draw map.

This is a small spring. (SAPE.)

Bull Bottom: (Emery Co.) Labyrinth Canyon-Green River. Tenmile Point map.

This was initially called Willys Bottom, Nigger Bill Bottom, or Nigger Bottom. (121~) Ned Chaffin: "He wasn't the Nigger Bill that they named the canyon after around Moab. I think this Nigger Bill worked for old Bishop Meeks over out of Wayne County area." (411~)

—Constructed Stock Trail: This spectacular trail leads down to Bull Bottom. It was constructed by rancher Andy Moore. Wiladeane Chaffin Wubben Hills: "The trail to the bottom [Bull Bottom] was very bad, and I always got off of my horse and walked because it was a straight drop-off.... Later Chad Moore put some bulls down in that bottom and it became known as Bull Bottom." (1430~, 580~, 1084~, SAPE.)

—Placer Bottom: This is on the east side of the Green River and is one mile downriver from Bull Bottom (one-half mile west of elevation 4264T). There was a placer mining operation on the bottom in the 1950s. Gene Dunham: "Placer Bottom was one of the real good bootlegging canyons. There is a little spring coming off that side canyon to the east. I tried to ride a horse through it once and turned the horse upside down." (580~)

Bull Canyon: (Emery Co.) West Tavaputs Plateau-Desolation Canyon. Chandler Falls map.

Waldo Wilcox: "That is where they put their bulls." (2011~)

—Lee Ranch: Ed Lee had a ranch at the mouth of Bull Canyon in the early days. (1837~)

Bull Canyon: (Grand Co.) Dome Plateau-Colorado River. Dewey map.

Also called Bull Draw. (1866~)

—Constructed Stock Trail: This comes into the canyon from the southeast. Construction is most noticeable near the mouth of the canyon. (SAPE.)

Bull Canyon: (Grand Co.) Manti-LaSal National Forest-La Sal Mountains-Fisher Creek. Mount Waas and Fisher Valley maps.

—Fisher Point: This is at the head of Bull Canyon (at elevation 8971 [Cairn] on the Mount Waas map). (924~)

—Fisher Ridge: This is one mile south of the head of Bull Canyon (at elevation 9139T on the Mount Waas map). (See Fisher Towers for name derivation.)

Bull Canyon: (Uintah Co.) East Tavaputs Plateau-Willow Creek. Wolf Point map.

Inscriptions include Herbert McElroy, Sept. 22, 1902 and David + Morse Lee, Vernal Utah, Sept. 22, 1938. (SAPE.)

Bull Creek: (Garfield and Wayne Counties.) Henry Mountains-Fremont River. Mount Ellen, Dry Lakes Peak, Bull Mountain, Steamboat Point, Hanksville, and The Notch maps.

(See Bull Mountain for name derivation.)

In the early days this was called Hanks Creek. (366~, 2053~) (See Hanksville.)

—Ninas Hill: This is on the west side of Bull Creek one mile east-southeast of Sidehill Springs (one-half mile east-northeast of elevation 5429T on the Dry Lakes Peak map). It was named by archaeologists in 1977 for Nina Robison, the owner of nearby Fairview Ranch. (961~)

Bull Dog Canyon: (San Juan Co.) Manti-LaSal National Forest-Abajo Mountains-Recapture Creek. Abajo Peak and Blanding North maps.

The first sawmill in the Abajos was set up in Bull Dog Canyon in 1887 (or 1889) by Willard Butt and C.R. Christensen. (1549~) Cornelia Perkins: "Lumber for the first sluice gates in Bluff came from the Blue Mountains. It had been cut with a rip saw by Parley R. Butt ... between Bulldog and Devil Canyon." (1526~)

Albert R. Lyman told this story: "At the mouth of Bulldog a man who married his sister, took refuge from the law forbidding such marriage. The two were protected by John Scott, who, first with a revolver and then with a shotgun, tried to bluff Sheriff Willard Butt out of marching the wrongly married man away to court, but in each case with the Sheriff's threat to 'cut you right square in two with this gun,' John dropped his weapons as if they were hot, and [the Sheriff] departed with his man." (1240~)

Bulldog Creek: (Garfield Co.) Henry Mountains-Straight Creek. Cass Creek Peak map.

The creek was named after Bulldog Peak. Bliss Brinkerhoff: "You get to one place and it kinda looks like an old bulldog settin' out there, lookin' at you." (291~) Garth Noyes: "It's at the end of Middle Mountain [Mount Pennell]. It just sticks out like a bulldog." (1473~)

Bulldog Knolls: (Washington Co.) Beaver Dam Mountains-Bulldog Canyon. Jarvis Peak map.

—Tabeau Peak: This is the southernmost summit of the Bulldog Knolls (at elevation 4482T). Frenchman Jean Baptiste Tabeau was on the John C. Fremont Expedition of 1843–44. (260~) He was killed while the expedition rested at Mountain Meadows. (1828~)

Kit Carson was with the expedition: "We moved our camp a mile. In looking among the mules, a Canadian [Tabeau] of the party missed one of his mules.... In a few hours he was missed.... I was sent with three men to seek him.... [We] saw where he fell from his horse [and a] great deal of blood was seen. [We] knew that he was killed.... I was grieved on account of the death of the Canadian. He was a brave, noble-souled fellow. I had been in many an Indian fight with him and I am confident, if he was not taken unawares, that he surely killed one or two before he fell." (351a~)

Bullet Canyon: (San Juan Co.) Cedar Mesa-Grand Gulch. Cedar Mesa North and Pollys Pasture maps.

This was initially called Graham Canyon after Charles Cary Graham. He helped Charles McLoyd on his relic hunting expeditions into the region from 1890 to 1893. Charles Graham used the name in his diary of 1891. (519~, 1389a~)

James H. Knipmeyer was told by Pete Steele that "in the lower part of Bullet, the canyon is pretty much of a straight shot to its junction with Grand Gulch. For a half-mile or more you can see a small natural arch high on the west wall of Grand Gulch, as if 'someone had shot a huge rifle, making a bullet hole in the distant wall.'" (1115~)

Inscriptions include Harry French of the Hyde Exploring Expedition. He left his name in 1894. (249~)

—Bullet Canyon Spring: (Also called Bullet Junction Spring.) This is at the mouth of Bullet Canyon (Pollys Pasture map). (249~)

—Jail House Spring: This is in Bullet Canyon two miles upcanyon from its mouth (Pollys Pasture map). It was named for a nearby ruin of that name. (249~)

—Bullet Canyon Trail: Graham and McLoyd are credited with building the first stock trail into Bullet Canyon, in 1890. It enters the canyon a short distance from Jail House Spring. (249~)

—South Fork Bullet Canyon: This is the major southern tributary of Bullet Canyon; its southern rim backs into Polly Mesa. Its head is at elevation 6439T on the Cedar Mesa North map. Two constructed stock trails enter the canyon, on the north and south sides a short distance downcanyon from the "Spring." They lead to a spring that was once developed with CCC-style watering troughs. (SAPE.)

Bull Flat: (Garfield Co.) GSCENM-The Cockscomb. Canaan Peak map.

Ralph Chynoweth: "Sam Graff, in the summertime, would take his sheep and go down into the Bull Flats area because it was flat and open. Somebody, maybe the Soil Conservation Service, put some reservoirs in there years ago." (425~)

Bullfrog: (Garfield Co.) Glen Canyon NRA-Lake Powell-Highway 276. Bullfrog map.

Also called Bullfrog Marina.

(See Bullfrog Creek for name derivation.)

This is the second largest marina on Lake Powell; Wahweap is the biggest.

Bullfrog Creek: (Garfield Co.) Henry Mountains-Glen Canyon NRA-Glen Canyon. Mount Pennell, Cave Flat, Ant Knoll, Clay Point, and Hall Mesa maps.

Also called Hanson Creek. (777~)

This was called Pine Alcove Creek by Richard L. Hoxie of the Lieutenant George M. Wheeler Survey of 1872–73. That name was still in use as late as 1924. The name Alcove Creek was used by the Powell expeditions. (466~, 1028~, 1567~, 1901~)

Two name derivations are given.

Charles Russell in 1908: "At Bullfrog creek we encountered the most formidable rapids we had yet seen in Glen canyon. On the bank beside the rapids is a huge bullfrog, some thirty feet high, eroded from the sandstone. This gives the name to the creek and rapid." (1670~)

Second, Charles B. Hunt: "There are a few hardy frogs at some of the seeps between the dry stretches of this 45-mile long valley." (925~) Bliss Brinkerhoff: "If you ever slept along Bullfrog, you've got it. There's only one name that you could give it." (291~)

The Elias H. Blackburn family of Loa was using the Bullfrog Creek area for winter range by the early 1880s. (1412~)

Charles Kelly told an interesting story that happened at the mouth of Bullfrog Creek: "Man from Salt Lake built a steamer about mouth of Bull Frog. Went to Salt Lake to get bolt for 15 cents. Drove [the steamer] up a mile and tied to bank. The steamer sank." (1067~)

George C. Fraser gave a brief description of upper Bullfrog Creek in 1915: "From the [Pennellen] Saddle we descended into a sandstone gorge draining westerly but dry. There was no water in it until the sandstone was cut through." (668~)

—George Keller Trail: This constructed stock trail goes from Bullfrog Creek, up a side canyon, to Tarantula Mesa. The bottom of the trail starts one mile northwest of Cave Flat Reservoir (one-half mile north of elevation 6784T on the Cave Flat map) and goes north onto the mesa. It is difficult to find. (582~, SAPE.) George Keller was the foreman of a local ranch. (See Keller Knoll.)

—Big Bar: (Also called High Bar.) This placer bar, now underwater, was on the south (or east) side of the Colorado River at the mouth of Bullfrog Creek (Halls Crossing map). (466~)

—Bullfrog Rapid: This rapid on the Colorado River was just below the mouth of Bullfrog Creek. David Jordan Rust in 1923: "Our first thrill came when we saw the Bull Frog Rapids. As we approached the dashing waves, shivers ran circles around my spine. When it was past there came a calm like that after a great storm." (1683~)

Harry McDonald: "That is a bad place. There is rocks in that [river] as large as a quarter of the room here, almost, and lots of them." (1327~)

Bullhead Bench: (Wayne Co.) Rabbit Valley-Spring Creek. Moroni Peak and Loa maps.

Thaine Taylor: "The way I heard it, the guys that used to be there were pretty bullheaded." (1868~)

Bull Hollow: (Emery Co.) Labyrinth Canyon-Green River. Tenmile Point map.

Ted Ekker noted that ranchers kept their bulls here. (623~)

—Constructed Stock Trail: This enters the canyon from the north one-quarter mile up from the river (one-quarter mile east-southeast of elevation 4602T). (SAPE.)

—Constructed Stock Trail: This goes from the Green River south to the flats above. It is one mile to the southeast of the mouth of Bull Hollow (to the north and west of elevation 4305T). (SAPE.)

Bull Hollow Wash: (Emery Co.) Cedar Mountain-Buckhorn Reservoir. Bob Hill Knoll, Cow Flats, and Cleveland maps.

—Bull Hollow Spring: (Cleveland map.) This large spring was once developed. (SAPE.)

Bullion Canyon: (Piute Co.) Fishlake National Forest-Tushar Mountains-Pine Creek. Mount Belknap and Mount Brigham maps.

Also called Bullion City Canyon.

Pine Creek flows through Bullion Canyon.

The first gold strike in Utah was in Bullion Canyon in 1854 by a miner named Hewitt. The area was very remote and although news of the find quickly spread, prospectors were slow to come. It wasn't until 1870 that mining started in earnest. (378~)

Clarence Dutton of the Powell Survey: "Immense ravines, rivaling those of the Wasatch in depth, but narrower and with steeper sides, have deeply cleft the great tabular mass, and subdivided it into huge pediments, which from below appear like individual mountains. The finest gorge is named Bullion Cañon [Pine Creek], in the jaws of which the little village of Marysvale is situated." (584~)

—Bully Boy Mine: PRIVATE PROPERTY. (Also called Bully Boy and Webster Mine.) This gold mine is on the south side of Bullion Canyon and is one mile east of Bullion Falls at the "Mine" (one-half mile west-northwest of elevation 9067 on the Mount Brigham map). In 1865 Jacob Hess found gold in Bullion Canyon. Tracing it to its source, he found what would become the Bully Boy Mine in 1868. (332~, 1194~)

—Bullion City: (Also called Miner's Park.) This town in Bullion Canyon was a short distance to the east of the mouth of Warnick Gulch. It was established in 1869 in response to the gold boom. At its height, it had over sixteen hundred residents. For a short time it was the county seat of Piute County. By the early 1880s the mines had played out and the town was essentially abandoned. (1194~)

—Webster Town: This mining town was on Webster Flat in Bullion Canyon two miles west of Bullion City. Local lore noted that it was started during the mining boom of the 1890s to service the Homestead, Miner's Relief, Great Western, and Niagra mines. (346~) It should be noted, though, that it is shown on a map of 1879. (M.24.) The town never did well and was slowly abandoned.

—Bullion Falls: (Mount Brigham map.) In 1873 William Derby Johnson in noted the "several magnificent falls, nearly two hundred feet high." (1005~) In 1873 artist Thomas Moran visited the falls, later doing a painting of them entitled "Mary's Veil." (1203~)

Bull Mountain: (Garfield Co.) Henry Mountains-Mount Ellen. Bull Mountain map. (9,187')

Grove Karl Gilbert of the Powell Survey called this Jukes Butte for Professor J. Beete Jukes, a member of his party. He also called it Northeast Butte. (723~, 923~, 1824~) The Jukes Butte name was in use until at least the mid-1920s. (1683~)

Charles B. Hunt noted that Bull Mountain was a corruption of the original name, which was Bowl Mountain. (925~) The Bowl Mountain name was used by Powell in 1878 (1567~) and stayed in use until at least 1918 (371~, 723~).

Two name derivations are given.

First, Kate B. Carter: "It is said that early pioneers made bowls from the surrounding trees." (375~)

Second, Nina Robison: "The mappers called it Bowl Mountain because it was settin' like a bowl. And the natives thought it looked like a buffalo bull and so they are the ones that named it Bull Mountain." (1644~)

—Reservoir Basin: This is on the northeast flank of Bull Mountain (southwest of elevation 5411T). Charles B. Hunt noted that at one time it contained a reservoir used by the Granite Ranch. (925~)

—Cottrell Bench: Guy Robison noted that this is on the northern slopes of Bull Mountain (the area to the northeast of elevation 5955T). John "Jack" Cottrell owned the Fairview·Ranch. (1644~) (See Collie Wash—Fairview Ranch.)

Bulloch Canyon: (Kane Co.) Kolob Terrace-North Fork Virgin River. Straight Canyon map.

David D. Bulloch (1844-1928) noted that in 1871 he and his brother were the first to bring range cattle onto nearby Cedar Mountain. His wife, Alice Bladin Bulloch, noted a "mountain ranch" dairy. It may have been at this location. (376~) (See North Fork Virgin River—Bulloch Cabin.)

Bullock Draw: (Emery Co.) San Rafael Swell-South Fork Coal Wash. The Blocks map.

Dee Anne Finken noted that the draw was used to hold bulls. (641~) Lee Mont Swasey: "It is fenced off, so they'd take the bulls into Bullock and lock them in until it was time to breed the cows so the calves would come at a certain time. So it's really 'lock the bulls.'" (1853~)

Lee told this story: "There is one big pothole, 10 to 12 feet in diameter in the canyon. I was bringin' cows up in the rain, and the trail takes the slickrock around the pothole. One old cow slipped on the wet sandstone and fell into the pothole. 'What am I going to do'? I got out my rope and roped 'er, and the horse couldn't pull 'er out. The hole was deep enough that with the cow in the bottom, she could look out, but the walls were undercut. I couldn't pull her out, and you don't leave a cow in a pothole. So, I spent the next three hours throwing rocks into the pothole until she could get her footing and then get out." (1853~)

Bulloch Gulch: (Washington Co.) Zion National Park-Orderville Canyon. Temple of Sinawava map.

Thomas Bullock (1816-1885) was an early settler. The name was applied in 1934. (1931~) C. Esplin noted that the original name was Lower Herd Canyon: "The original Bullock family used and owned the most of the canyon exclusively and so was soon to be known as 'Bullock Canyon' by everyone in the area." (1931~)

Bull Pasture: (Wayne Co.) Dirty Devil Country-Larry Canyon. Angel Point and Burr Point maps.

Ted Ekker: "There is a little seep there.... A beautiful place to put a bunch of horses; they couldn't get out of there. All [one] had to do was put up just one little old Cedar tree and he had 'em." (623~)

—Bull Pasture Trail: This is the "Pack Trail" that goes into Bull Pasture from the east (Angel Point map). (See Larry Canyon.)

Bullpen Mountain: (Washington Co.) Zion National Park-La Verkin Creek. Kolob Reservoir map. (7,091')

In the early days, this was used as a bull pasture. (1038~)

Bullpen Swale: (San Juan Co.) Alkali Point-Alkali Canyon. Bradford Canyon and McCracken Spring maps.

The name was recommended to the USGS by ranchers Max Dalton, Ashton Harris, and Jesse Grover in 1980. (1931~)

Bull Ridge: (Kane Co.) Glen Canyon NRA-Kaiparowits Plateau. Navajo Point map. (7,447')

—Panorama Point: This viewpoint is on the very northeast end of Bull Ridge (at elevation 7561). The name was given by Clyde Kluckhohn in 1928. (1100~)

Bull Roost: (Wayne Co.) Awapa Plateau-Cedar Peak Draw. Flossie Knoll, Jakes Knoll, and Smooth Knoll maps.

Thaine Taylor: "In the fall when they was gatherin' cattle, those bulls would have usually drifted down in there." (1868~)

Dunk Taylor: "Them old bulls, they kinda cut themselves out of the herd and don't follow the cows like they should, and they'd drift down there, and that's the reason it's got its name: Bull Roost." (1868~)

Bull Run Canyon: (Garfield Co.) GSCENM-Kaiparowits Plateau-Alvey Wash. Carcass Canyon and Dave Canyon maps.

Don Coleman: "Bull Run Canyon was where the wild cattle used to run. There was a wild bull out there that could just flat outrun a horse. So they named him Bull Run. They'd run 'im down and they could never catch 'im. He'd get down in the rough and he'd hide on 'em and they didn't get 'im out for years and years." (441~)

Bull Rush Peak: (Garfield Co.) Dixie National Forest-Sevier Plateau. Bull Rush Peak map. (9,377')

Kent Whittaker noted that there were lots of bull rushes at the head of Bull Rush Creek. (2002~)

—Bull Rush Spring: E.C. Bird in 1942: "Bullrush Spring is a small spring surrounded with bullrush and bullberry brush from which it derived its name." (2053~)

—Trachyte Upheaval: Stephen Vandiver Jones of the Powell Expedition of 1871-72 gave this name to the cliffs at the mouth of Bull Rush Creek. (1023~)

Bull Spring: (Sevier Co.) Fishlake National Forest-Dipping Vat Draw. Boobe Hole Reservoir map.

This is a large, developed, and still-used spring. (SAPE.)

Bull Valley: (San Juan Co.) Glen Canyon NRA-Dark Canyon Plateau-Beef Basin. Teapot Rock and Cross Canyon maps.

Robert S. McPherson: "[This] is where Al and Jim Scorup temporarily separated male from female cattle; newborn animals went to Calf Canyon, not far from Beef Basin." (1336~)

Bull Valley Gorge: (Kane Co.) GSCENM-Sheep Creek. Rainbow Point and Bull Valley Gorge maps.

Also called Bull Valley, Bull Valley Canyon, Bull Valley Creek (324~, 766~), and Squaw Creek (1931~).

In 1871 Jacob Hamblin called this "a deep rock gorge." (816~)

—Bull Valley Gorge Pick-up Truck: This vehicle, now famous because of its proximity to the road, was wrecked by Hart Johnson, Max Henderson, and Clarkie Smith. All were killed. (984~)

—Bull Valley: This is the local name for the upper part of the canyon, above the gorge. (1931~)

Bunchground Canyon: (Grand Co.) Manti-LaSal National Forest-La Sal Mountains-Professor Creek. Fisher Valley and Fisher Towers maps.

Joe Taylor: "A bunch ground is where you gather the cattle; you bunch them up together. When you're a cowboy, you say, 'Where are we going to bunch today? What bunch ground are we going to use'? It's very important in cowboy lingo." (1866~)

Bunker Creek: (Iron Co.) Dixie National Forest-Blue Spring Creek. Brian Head and Panguitch Lake maps.
Two possibly related name derivations are given.
First, H. Grant Seaman: "Named for an early day user. John Bunker grazed livestock, primarily sheep." (942~)
Second, Don Orton in 1941: "So named for a man by the name of Bunker who operated a sawmill near the stream." (2053~)

Bunting Canyon: (Kane Co.) Vermilion Cliffs-Kanab Creek. Kanab map.
Elsie Chamberlain Carroll noted that James Lovett Bunting (1832–1923) arrived in Kanab in 1870 and had a farm at the mouth of the canyon. (349~, 2053~)
—Lamb Point: This is at the head of Bunting Canyon (at elevations 6385 and 6377). (767~)

Burkholder Draw: (Grand Co.) La Sal Mountains-Rill Creek. Warner Lake and Rill Creek maps.
Joseph Burkholder (1844-1938), a rancher and prospector from the Telluride area, moved to Moab in 1879. (338~, 1420~, 1546~, 1855~)

Burned Ridge: (Garfield Co.) Henry Mountains-Bull Creek Pass. Mount Ellen map.
Charles B. Hunt: "an old name for a ridge on the west side of Mount Ellen, evidently referring to a forest fire." (925~)

Burning Hills: (Kane Co.) GSCENM-Kaiparowits Plateau. East of the Navajo, Smoky Hollow, Needle Eye Point, and Sit Down Bench maps.
After driving through the Burning Hills one becomes certain of the name derivation: colors and textures run rampant here. The drive through the Burning Hills is one of the most spectacular in Grand Staircase-Escalante National Monument. (SAPE.)
Dr. Russell G. Frazier in the early 1940s: "My describing this geological phenomena would be like a geologist describing a rare medical case and from a geologist's point of view, about as comprehensive.... For eight hundred feet up the mountain, the sandstone had been melted and burned. Some of the rock had the appearance of a cinder cone. In other places it had melted and dripped like wax from a burning candle, while an adjacent section of rock would only be colored from the surrounding heat. The whole mass having a highly multi colored, glazed surface. It looked for the world like some one had held a giant blow torch against the face of the mountain. Red was the predominating color with all of the hues of the rainbow scrambled up together. The cowboys who have seen this phenomena call it 'The Rock Candy Mountain.'" (674~)

Burnt Cabin Spring: (Carbon Co.) West Tavaputs Plateau-Dry Creek. Bruin Point map.
This is a large spring.
The cabin is no longer here. (SAPE.)

Burnt Cabin Spring: (Dolores Co., Colo.) Cedar Point-Monument Canyon. Burnt Cabin Spring, Colo. map.
In 1881 Indians burned a line shack and killed a couple of cowboys here. (536~)

Burnt Flat: (Piute Co.) Fishlake National Forest-Sevier Plateau. Marysvale Peak map.
—Burnt Flat Reservoir: Newel Nielson noted that the reservoir was built in 1934. (1458~)

Burnt Flat Gulch: (Kane Co.) Pink Cliffs-Highway 9-Miners Gulch. Orderville, Clear Creek Mountain, and Mount Carmel maps.
Also spelled Bernt Flat.
William B. Fawcett noted that a sawmill was near the junction of Burnt Flat Gulch and Miners Gulch from 1930 to 1935. (636~)

Burnt Hollow: (Garfield Co.) Dixie National Forest-Sevier Plateau-Circle Valley. Mount Dutton and Junction maps.
Also called Burnt Spring Canyon. (2053~)
George W. Dobson in 1941: "It derived its name because someone started a fire there at one time, which destroyed a large amount of timber." (2053~)
—Burnt Hollow Trail: (Mount Dutton map.) Kent Whittaker noted that this was built by the Forest Service and is also called the Government Trail. (2002~, SAPE.)

Burnt Knoll: (Garfield Co.) Awapa Plateau-Cedar Peak Draw. Flossie Knoll map. (9,232')
Don Orton in 1941: "So named by Ernest Brinkerhoff because while herding sheep one summer lightning struck the knoll three times in as many minutes, searing the knoll of all vegetation." (2053~)

Burnt Ridge: (Kane Co.) GSCENM-Kaiparowits Plateau-Lake Canyon. Sooner Bench map.
Don Coleman: "Burnt Ridge was named right after a fire." (441~)

Burnt Spring: (San Juan Co.) Mancos Mesa-Moqui Canyon. Burnt Spring map.
Val Dalton noted that this is incorrectly labeled on the map. The real Burnt Spring is two miles northeast of the Burnt Spring shown on the map (one-half mile west-northwest of elevation 5329T). Val: "The cowboys had to burn it every year to clear the vegetation off or there wouldn't be any water there." (517~, SAPE.)
The Burnt Spring labeled on the map was called Red Cone Spring or Red Tank by cowboys. It is shown as Red Cone

Spring on the 1938 map by Herbert E. Gregory. (774~) In 1955 Jim Scorup called it Red Rock Spring. (1931~)

—Soup Hole: This pothole, used to water livestock, is one-eighth mile north-northeast of elevation 5376T. Val Dalton: "The water in it looks like soup all of the time. It's not very good looking water." (517~, SAPE.)

Burr Canyon: (Garfield Co.) Capitol Reef National Park-Circle Cliffs-Halls Creek. Wagon Box Mesa map.

—Burr Trail: This sixty-seven-mile-long road starts in Boulder, cuts through the heart of the Circle Cliffs Basin, goes down Burr Canyon, and ends at Bullfrog Basin. The road started as a sheep trail that was used by stockman John Atlantic Burr (1846-1914) in the late 1880s. Back then, the only part of the trail that received his name was the section that went down Burr Canyon.

John Atlantic Burr's unusual middle name was in honor of his birth while his parents were crossing the Atlantic Ocean. His father was Charles Clark Burr for whom Burrville was named.

Legend has it that John Atlantic Burr died alone on the desert while trying to remedy a urinary tract blockage with a piece of wire. But, another source noted that he died at home in Monticello. It is known that he died of uremia, often caused by a urinary tract blockage. (388~)

Emmett Clark told a story he heard about using the trail: "Pack mules, goin' up that trail, and they had 'em tied to one another and one of 'em slipped and fell and pulled the whole herd of 'em down." (426~)

Burns Ormand: "There was a trail you could get down, but God Almighty, sometimes they even killed their mules agoin' down over it. They'd roll with the pack on down in the rocks and get killed." (1487~)

Bliss Brinkerhoff: "No, they didn't have a constructed trail. They just sent the animals up the face of that. It'd take 'em all day or maybe two days to get a herd of sheep up over that. They'd start just a workin' them up and then they left the sheep to work themselves up. You couldn't get cattle up the Burr Trail, so they'd go to Muley Twist and come back up through Wagon Box [Mesa]." (291~) (See Muley Twist Canyon—Halls Road.)

The switchbacks we now drive through Burr Canyon were graded in during the uranium boom in 1953 (another source says 1948). That project, financed by the Atomic Energy Commission, cost fifty thousand dollars.

Inscriptions include D.J. Teeples, Jan. 4, 1914. (1115~)

—Burr Trail Corral: This is at the top of the Burr Trail switchbacks (one-half mile north of elevation 5736AT). It was built about 1900. (521~, 604~, 699~, 1476~)

Burr Creek: (Sevier Co.) Sevier Plateau-Otter Creek. Koosharem and Burrville maps.

Also called Battle Creek. (962~, 1931~)

(See Burrville for name derivation.)

Burr Desert: (Wayne Co.) Dirty Devil River-Highway 95. Angel Cove, Bull Mountain, and Baking Skillet Knoll maps.

There is some confusion as to whether this huge grazing area was named for J.B. Buhr, the owner of the nearby Granite Ranch, or for John Atlantic Burr, a rancher from the Escalante area. The first name derivation is most likely correct.

First, Barbara Ekker: "J.B. Buhr came from New York for health reasons. He was a German and a tailor and he made beautiful 'riding habits' for his wife. Grandma Edna Ekker said she'd ride into town from their Granite Ranch and she was the envy of everyone in town." (606~)

Pearl Baker: "J.B. Buhr, a tailor from Denver, brought a herd of cattle and a band of good mares with a fine stallion named Major into the Roost in the early 1890s. He had suffered for years from asthma, and he and his two brothers had invested in the livestock, hoping a life in the open air would improve his health." (122~) Buhr started the Granite Ranch south of Hanksville. It became a haven for outlaws and rustlers. (See Granite Creek—Granite Ranch.)

Second, John Atlantic Burr ran livestock from Escalante to Glen Canyon and in the Henry Mountains. It is unclear if he also ran stock in the Burr Desert area. (1750~, 1938~) (See Burr Canyon—Burr Trail.)

Ben Wetherill described the Burr Desert area in 1897: "Desolation begins with the crossing of the [Colorado] River everything has been over run with sheep till nothing but bare rocks and sand beds remain." (1988~)

Zane Grey described the area in 1930 as viewed from the Henry Mountains: "Here was a dropping away of the green-covered mountain foothills and slopes to the ragged, wild rock and clay world, beginning with scarfs of gray wash and rims of gorge and gateways of blue canyons, and augmenting to a region that showed Nature at her most awful, grim and ghastly, tortuous in line, rending in curve, twisting in upheaval, a naked spider-web of the earth, cut and washed into innumerable ridges of monotonous colors, gray, drab, brown, mauve, and intricate passageways of darker colors, mostly purple, mysterious and repelling. Down in there dwelt death for plant, animal, and man. For miles not one green speck! And then far across that havoc of the elements which led on to a boundless region of color—white jagged rents through miles of hummocky ground, and streaked by washes of gray and red and yellow, on to vast green levels, meadow-like at such a distance, which stretched away to the obstructing zigzag wall of stone, the meandering White Bluffs [San Rafael Reef]." (785~)

Burro Canyon: (Garfield Co.) Dixie National Forest-Escalante Mountains-Henderson Canyon. Pine Lake map. Also called Pasture Canyon. (1931~)

Burro Pass: (Grand Co.) Manti-LaSal National Forest-La Sal Mountains-Wet Fork Mill Creek. Mount Waas map. (11,200')

The Don Juan María Antonio de Rivera Expedition of 1765 is believed to have come through a pass between Mount Waas and Mount Peale. It very well may have been Burro Pass. (1172~)

Burro Seep: (Wayne Co.) Hans Flats-Spur Fork. Head Spur map.

This is a large spring. (SAPE.)

When Joe Biddlecome visited this spring in about 1910 he found a burro pawing for water. (120~)

—Constructed Stock Trail: This is on the east side of the canyon one-quarter mile below its head and leads down the cliffs to the spring. It was built by Joe Biddlecome in the early 1900s. (120~, SAPE.)

Burrows Flat: (Garfield Co.) Dixie National Forest-Markagunt Plateau. Asay Bench map.

James Bascom Burrows (1861-1956), a Texas cowboy, moved to the area in 1890. He operated a sawmill on Burrows Flat from 1910 to 1913. (832~)

—Burrow Flat Spring: PRIVATE PROPERTY. This is the large, developed spring on the flat. A Mormon fence corral is nearby. (SAPE.)

Burr Pass: (Wayne Co.) San Rafael Desert-Robbers Roost Flats. Robbers Roost Flats map. (5,850')

(See Burr Desert for name derivation.)

Burr Pass was first used by cowboys working for J.B. Buhr of the Granite Ranch. They had a line shack in the pass where they would leave supplies.

Pearl Baker noted that Jack Moore built a dugout home at the pass in the 1890s. It was then called The Dugout. (122~) Moore, a cattle rustler, was later killed in Wyoming. (186~) Pearl Baker, quoting Jack Moore: "They sure liked me in Texas. In fact a bunch of them followed me clear across the state to get me to go back and if Minnie hadn't been faster than any horse they had, they'd have caught me, too." (107~)

Burr Point: (Wayne Co.) Burr Desert-Dirty Devil River. Burr Point map. (5,578')

Also called Dirty Devil Overlook. (1658~)

(See Burr Desert for name derivation.)

—Dead Man Knoll: Barbara Ekker: "Near Burr Point is a place called Dead Man Knoll. Clive Meacham [a longtime resident of Hanksville] writes that the Lowery brothers owned a herd of sheep that they wintered at Burr Point. There was a small pox epidemic and one of the Lowery boys died in his sheep camp. The law wouldn't let the family take him home for burial so he was interned where he died and his camp burnt." (606~)

Burr Top: (Garfield Co.) Dixie National Forest-Aquarius Plateau. Jacobs Reservoir map. (10,440')

(See Burr Canyon for name derivation.)

Burrville: (Sevier Co.) Grass Valley-Otter Creek-Highways 24 and 62. Burrville map.

Also called Cedar Grove.

George Washington Bean ran livestock in the area in the early 1870s. In 1874 Charles Clark Burr (1817-1903) of Payson moved to the area. The town was named for his family. (962~, 1047~)

Charles Kelly noted that the first permanent Euroamerican settlers of the area included the outlaw brothers Bill and Tom McCarty, and Porter Rockwell, famous as the leader of Brigham Young's Avenging Angels. They settled in what is now Burrville in 1874. (1047~)

George Teancum Bean told the story of the first year in Burrville when he was seventeen years old: "The winter came on early and was the most severe one I think Burrville has ever had.... We had an awful blizzard for two weeks, and the snow blowed and drifted so we could not move around but little ... to add to our grief, poor little Willie took sick and died. We could not get out to get him out nor get a coffin.... My Bro Will and I would each morning ride the mules trying to tramp a road so we could get our team and wagon out, but it would drift so we could hardly tell where our tracks were. So, for 8 days we would carry little Willie out of the house on a board, (end-gate) and put him in our granery for the day, and evening we would let our fire go down and we would then carry him into the house for the night." (173~)

—Cedar Grove: (Also called Red Cedar Grove.) (2070~) A Daughters of Utah Pioneers Monument erected near Cedar Grove in 1959 reads: "June 15, 1875 Brigham Young called Albert K. Thurber and George W. Bean, Indian interpreters, Wm. B. Page, William Nex and others to explore Grass Valley for settlement and make peace with the Indians. Chief *Tabioonah* accompanied the party and acted as guide and peacemaker. They camped near Fish Lake June 22nd where they explained their mission to a group of Indian braves led by Chief *Pah-Ga-Ne-Ap*.

The Indians from the surrounding territory met at Cedar Grove July 1, 1875 where the chiefs pledged Peace with a handshake. This Pledge was never broken." (1551~) Cedar Grove is a couple of miles north of Burrville. (2053~) It was added to the Utah State Register of Historic Sites in 1976.

Burts Spring: (Garfield Co.) Henry Mountains-Big Thompson Mesa-Long Canyon. Deer Point map.

Guy and Nina Robison thought that this was most likely named for rancher Bert Avery. (1645~) (See Bert Avery Seep.)

Bush Head: (Coconino Co., Az.) Vermilion Cliffs National Monument-Paria Plateau-Paria River. Water Pockets, Az. map. (6,104')

—Bush Head Canyon: This starts at Bush Head and goes north into the Paria River. Bob Whitaker: "Bush Head [Canyon] features lush green vegetation and several deep pools at the upper end which are reachable on an undeveloped trail." (2001~)

Butch Cassidy Draw: (Garfield Co.) Dixie National Forest-Sevier Plateau-Red Canyon. Casto Canyon and Wilson Peak maps.

Gaylord Staveley: "It is said that Cassidy's Hole-in-the-Wall Gang was once boxed in here by a posse from nearby Panguitch, but that their ringleader bluffed out the lawmen with a rather eloquent speech about the sadness of posse horses having to plod home with empty saddles to wives and children who needed their menfolk alive, not dead. The pitch succeeded." (1817~)

Butler Canyon: (Garfield Co.) Cedar Point-North Wash. Stair Canyon, Turkey Knob, Black Table, and Hite North maps.

Alvin Robison noted that this is locally called Buzzard Canyon. (1642~) Pearl Baker noted that Monte Butler lived in the area in the 1890s. (122~)

—West Fork Butler Canyon: This canyon complex is west of the main fork of Butler Canyon.

—Andrew Ekker Canyon: (Also called Middle Fork West Butler Canyon, Never Again Canyon, and Shenanigans Canyon.) This is the middle fork of upper West Fork Butler Canyon (immediately west of elevation 5143T on the Stair Canyon map). It was named for stockman Andrew Ekker (1881-1965) of Hanksville.

The Shenanigans name came from canyoneer Tom Jones. Stefan Folias: "IRISH/BUTLER THEME: **shenanigans**—tricky or questionable practices or conducts." (653~) The name accurately describes the shenanigans and body contortions needed to get through this slot canyon.

Butler Canyon: (Grand Co.) Roan Cliffs-Book Cliffs-Suluar Mesa-Gray Canyon. Butler Canyon map.

—Farrer Bottom: This is on the east side of the Green River one mile north of Butler Canyon (one-half mile north of elevation 4948). Waldo Wilcox noted that Green River pioneer John Thomas Farrer, Sr. (1831-1917) ran livestock here starting in 1879. (2011~)

—Farrer Trail: This constructed stock trail goes generally southeast up the initial cliff band from Farrer Bottom. An easy route, not a trail, goes to the top of Suluar Mesa (by elevation 5272). The trail was built by John Thomas Farrer, Sr. (2011~, SAPE.)

—Coal Canyon: This eastern tributary of the Green River is immediately south of Butler Canyon (between elevations 5324 and 5459). (859~)

—Constructed Stock Trail: This starts one-half mile downriver from the mouth of Coal Canyon and goes east up the initial cliff band. From there a route, not a trail, goes to the top of Suluar Mesa. (SAPE.)

Butler Creek: (Garfield Co.) Dixie National Forest-Panguitch Creek. Red Creek Reservoir and Fivemile Ridge maps.

Butler Creek runs through Myers Valley.

—Butlerville: (Also called Butlersville.) (M.24., M.29.) Brothers James, John L., and Thomas Butler, and their families, arrived in Panguitch in 1864. They left during Indian hostilities, but returned in 1871 and, in partnership, started a ranch in what they called Butler Valley. The ranch became a well-known stopping place for travelers and was often called Butlerville. (515~, 516~) The Lieutenant George M. Wheeler Survey map of 1872–73 shows the ranch as Bullersville. (M.76.)

Butler Valley: (Kane Co.) GSCENM-The Cockscomb-Cottonwood Creek. Butler Valley map.

Wallace Ott: "It was named after a fellow named 'Butler' who lived in this country." (1493~) The name was in place by 1881. (665~)

—CCC Corral: This "Corral" and "Well" are at the south end of Butler Valley. Ralph Chynoweth: "The CCs built that corral back in the '30s.... They also built that well there at the CCs Corral. They had a windmill and everything." (425~)

Butler Wash: (Garfield Co.) Dixie National Forest-Sevier Plateau-Sevier River. Casto Canyon and Panguitch maps.

Unattributed: "This wash derived its name from a member of the Butler family at the time of the first settlement of Panguitch in 1866 who claimed the lands on the Sevier River where this wash enters the river." (2053~) (See Butler Creek—Butlerville.)

Butler Wash: (Garfield Co.) Henry Mountains-Poison Spring Canyon. Mount Ellen, Raggy Canyon, Turkey Knob, and Baking Skillet Knoll maps.

Charles B. Hunt noted that Jack Butler, along with Jack Sumner, discovered the Bromide Basin Gold Mine. (925~)

—Airport Bench: Kevin Robison noted that an old airstrip, now used by LifeFlight, is to the south of Butler Wash near elevation 6312T on the Raggy Canyon map. Airport Bench is the area to the north of the airstrip and to the south of Butler Wash (at elevations 6181T and 6405T on the Raggy Canyon map). (1646~)

Butler Wash: (San Juan Co.) Canyonlands National Park-Needles District-The Grabens-Red Lake Canyon. House Park Butte, Druid Arch, Cross Canyon, and Spanish Bottom maps.

Fran Barnes noted that this was named for Monte Butler, a member of the Wild Bunch. He roamed the area in the late 1890s. (143~)

—Constructed Stock Trail: This enters the upper end of Butler Wash (near elevation 6718T on the House Park Butte map). It does not continue through the canyon. (SAPE.)

—Starvation Pocket: This pasture is on a small tributary of Butler Wash that is one-quarter mile southeast of elevation 6127T on the Druid Arch map.

Butler Wash: (San Juan Co.) Comb Ridge-San Juan River. Hotel Rock, Bluff SW, and San Juan Hill maps.

Also called The Butler (1240~), Butler Canyon, Butler Creek, Butler's Gulch, Butler Creek Wash (73~, 490~, 1250~), and Valley of the Butler (1241~).

Members of the San Juan Exploring Expedition of 1879 named the wash for expedition member John Butler. He was one of the first to explore the area. (774~, 1239~, 1241~) The name was in use by the time the Hole-in-the-Rock Expedition crossed Butler Wash in early 1880. Expedition member Platte D. Lyman: "Today went 4 miles to the Butler Gulch most of thet way on the rock." (1259~) Warren K. Moorehouse of the Illustrated American Exploring Expedition in 1892: "As we entered the valley ... we were struck with its weird and desolate appearance, stretching, as it does, as far as the eye can see, naked of all vegetation except stunted sagebrush and grease wood, hemmed in on the east by high precipitous cliffs of red sandstone, with curious knobs and needles jutting upwards and weathered into fantastic shapes and designs." (1383~)

T. Mitchell Prudden in 1903: "Butler Wash is a narrow, dry, shallow valley, having on its western side the sloping uplift of a great fault [Comb Ridge]." (1589~)

Inscriptions include J.L. Butler, Aug. 2, 1879; Chas. McAlister, Nov. 21, 1887; J.G. Hutchison, Nov. 2, 1887; and M. Basham, 1890. (838~) James H. Knipmeyer noted that famed cowboy "Latigo" Gordon left his name and the date 1896 on a wall in Butler Wash. (1105~, 1112~)

—Rope Spring: Karl and Clyde Barton noted that this spring is in a short eastern tributary of upper Butler Wash (at elevation 5361T on the Hotel Rock map). Karl Barton: "They used to have a sheep camp there. That's where they brought sheep off to water from up in the Cheese and Raisins." (162~) Karl noted that until Wilbur Loss blasted a good trail up the cliffs, stock could only go down the trail.

—Hobbs Wash: This short western tributary of lower Butler Wash is crossed by Highway 163. It starts at elevation 4572 on the Bluff SW map. (956~) San Juan Exploring Expedition member George B. Hobbs (1856-1921) camped in the wash: "Night overtaking us, we camped in this small canyon, this being the third night without food. I cut my name in the rock with the date I was there [Jan. 1, 1880], not knowing that I would survive the journey." (1356~) The inscription site was destroyed when the highway was realigned in the early 1960s. (1115~) The Hobbs family has erected a monument to Hobbs near the wash.

—Lower Butler Wash Road: (Also called Butler Wash Dugway, River Road, and San Juan Hill Alternative.) This old road starts on the top of the cliffs on the east side of the canyon one mile up Butler Wash from the San Juan River. At one time this spectacular road went down the canyon and around the corner just above the San Juan River to The Rincon. (See San Juan Hill.)

The road, perhaps first built as a stock trail, was in use shortly after the Hole-in-the-Rock Expedition made its way over San Juan Hill in early 1880. The road was improved during the gold mining boom of the 1890s when it became a often-used thoroughfare to the river and to The Rincon.

There is no consensus as to when the road section along the river washed out. Some think it disappeared during the big flood of 1911. But, Brandt Hart noted that several inscriptions with dates after that can still be seen on the cliff above where the road used to go. These include Ana Jones, April 5, 1931; Perry Holt 1947; and the date 1951. These are now only visible by boat, giving credence to the idea that the road was at least somewhat usable until that date. (838~, 1335~) Other inscriptions along this stretch of road include F.B. Obannon, Albuquerque, N.M., April 20 18??; C. Saunders, Feb. 15, 1887; C.E. Allen, H.M. Mann, Feb. 16, 03; and W.B. Allred, no date. (838~) Brandt Hart noted that early pioneers found Paiute Jim Joe and family living on the San Juan River near the mouth of the canyon. As well, a lime kiln was located at the mouth of the canyon in the early days. (838~, 1237~) Sydney Goddard, a member of the Hole-in-the-Rock Expedition, left his name, but no date, in the canyon near the Lower Butler Wash Road. Certainly he was there in 1880. It is unclear how he got into the canyon. Was it by way of the Lower Butler Wash Road? Another possibility is that he used an old constructed stock trail that comes into the canyon on its west side a short distance up from the river. (838~, SAPE.) This trail was used by San Juan County sheriff Dick Butt in the early days to capture some outlaws camped at the bottom of the canyon. (1237~)

Butt Canyon: (Garfield Co.) Henry Mountains-Thompson Mesa-Bullfrog Creek. The Post and Ant Knoll maps. Bliss Brinkerhoff and Dwight Williams noted that the canyon is misnamed. It should be Buck Canyon. Bliss Brinkerhoff: "That's Buck Canyon. Them old-timers fenced off the canyon and they would just throw their bucks [sheep] in there until they got ready to take 'em out to the herd." (291~, 2013~)

—The Crotch: This is the local name for the road junction at the head of Butt Canyon (at elevation 5041T on The Post map). (2007~)

Butterfly Flat: (Garfield Co.) Dixie National Forest-Awapa Plateau. Big Lake and Pollywog Lake maps.
Dunk Taylor: "There wasn't any water in there, then, but since then we went in there with a Cat and developed this stock pond. It's never been out of water since we did that. It's kind of a neat country.... There was a lot of butterflies out there." (1865~) Alfonzo Turner: "There used to be a lot of butterflies around that lake looking for water." (1914~)

—Bear Pond: This is on the east side of Butterfly Flat. Dunk Taylor: "Me and Elwood [Morrell] went by there one day in the summertime and just as we rode up over the bank, we saw a set of wet bear tracks going out the other side, so we called it the Bear Pond." (1865~)

Buttes of the Cross: (Wayne Co.) Glen Canyon NRA-Millard Canyon Benches. Cleopatras Chair map. (5,642')
Also called Cross Butte (111~) and Mount of the Cross (1768~).
Almon H. Thompson of the 1871–72 Powell Expedition called it Stonehead Cross. (1877~)

John Wesley Powell, in his original diary entry for 1871, called it The Cross. (662~) In his later writings, Powell changed the name slightly: "Off to the south we see a butte in the form of a fallen cross. It is several miles away, but it presents no inconspicuous figure on the landscape and must be many hundreds of feet high, probably more than 2,000. We ... name it 'The Butte of the Cross'.... And just here we climb out once more, to take another bearing on the Butte of the Cross. Reaching an eminence, from which we can overlook the landscape, we are surprised to find that our butte, with its wonderful form, is indeed two buttes, one so standing in front of the other that, from our last point of view, it gave the appearance of a cross." (1563~)

Franklin A. Nims of the Stanton-Brown Survey of 1889: "We paused in wonderment to gaze upon a gigantic mass of gray and red sandstone, 'The Mountain of the Cross.' On passing it, however, we discovered it to be two distinct buttes one thousand feet apart." (1464~) Nims also called this Cruz. (1463~)

James A. McCormick of the James S. Best Expedition of 1891 called it Crescent Castle: "We came in sight of Crescent Castle, so named because of the great crescent of the body of the cliff." (1320~)

Button Canyon: (Kane Co.) GSCENM-Kaiparowits Plateau-Reese Canyon. Collet Top map.
Also called Button Creek.
The Charles N. Button family were Kanab pioneers. (388~)

Butts Canyon: (San Juan Co.) Manti-LaSal National Forest-Dark Canyon Plateau-South Elk Ridge-Arch Canyon. Kigalia Point and South Long Point maps.
The Butt family has had a long history in San Juan County. Parley R. Butt (1862-1940) was on the San Juan Exploring Expedition of 1879. Famed war correspondent Ernie Pyle described meeting Parley Butt in 1939: "He's a character if I've ever seen one. He was in the Mormon scouting party that first penetrated southeastern Utah. He was a member of the fated group that made Mormon history by their experiences at the 'Hole in the Rock'.... Parley Butt was in Bluff in '78. He must be close to 80 now ... a lovable rascal. Ugly as a mud fence (aw, don't get nervous; he won't mind), with huge queer gold teeth in his lower jaw. He doodles around with a fly swatter.... When I said good-by to him he said, 'Well, give my regards to all the good looking people in the world.' I kinda doubt if a guy like that will ever die." (1592~)

Willard (Dick) Butt (1858-1919), Parley's brother, was also a member of the Hole-in-the-Rock Expedition and was responsible for minding the eighteen hundred head of livestock on the trip. The brothers ran dairy cows in the Bluff area in the 1890s. (1526~, 1860~)

A resident of Bluff, Willard Butt was elected sheriff in the 1890s during a period when the area was overrun by al l manner of criminals. He is credited with cleaning up the area. (1407~) Albert R. Lyman: "He left a mighty good taste in the mouths of the people of San Juan." (1241~)

BW and H Mine: (Piute Co.) Big Rock Candy Mountain-Sevier River. Marysvale Canyon map.

Merrill G. 'Doc' Utley: "The name of the group, B.W. & H., was derived from the surname initials of the three individuals from Joseph, Ut., who made the original locations [in 1900–01]. James Billingsly, James Wells and Brognard Hopkins." (1934~)

C

Cabbage Valley: (Iron Co.) Hurricane Cliffs-Shurtz Canyon. Cedar Mountain map.

Mrs. J.A. Haslam: "The wild cabbage plant has a little yellow flower in early summer. It is good feed for animals." (942~)

—Thompson Mine: This coal mine is in upper Cabbage Valley one and one-half miles north of Pine Spring Knoll (three-quarters of a mile northwest of elevation 10135). It started production in 1906. (570~)

Cabin Spring: (San Juan Co.) Canyonlands National Park-Island in the Sky District-Grays Pasture. Musselman Arch map.

This medium-size and once developed spring was used by ranchers starting in the late 1800s. (SAPE.)

Cable Mountain: (Washington Co.) Zion National Park-Zion Canyon. Temple of Sinawava map. (6,940')

William and David Flanigan built a cable trolley for bringing lumber from Cable Mountain down to the Zion Canyon floor in 1901. The original cable was fashioned from telegraph wires. Frank Jensen: "The old terminal was built of hand-hewn logs which later burned and were replaced with sawed logs. The telegraph wires eventually gave way to a steel cable, and steel pulleys were substituted for the wooden ones." (968~)

A sawmill atop Cable Mountain provided logs, and a shingle mill at the bottom of the cable was established in 1907. The last load of wood was sent down the cable in 1929 and the cable was removed in 1930. (1982~)

—Zion Ledges: This is the area around the sawmill at the top of Cable Mountain. (1191~)

Cache Valley Wash: (Grand Co.) Arches National Park-Dome Plateau-Salt Wash. Big Bend and The Windows Section maps.

Also spelled Cash Valley. (278~)

James H. Knipmeyer was told by George White in about 1965 that "the valley and wash received their names from the fact early settlers came down Salt Valley from Thompson and then up Cache Wash by wagon on their way to the Castle valley area. However, when they came to the rough divide separating Cache Valley Wash from the Colorado River, they had to 'cache' their wagons and large equipment back in the valley and pack on down to the river." (1116~)

—Constructed Stock Trail: Two constructed stock trails exit Cache Valley. The first goes out the head of the canyon (one-half mile southeast of elevation 4950T on the Big Bend map), goes over a divide, and descends Dry Wash to the Colorado River. (1866~, SAPE.) (See Dry Wash and Stearns Creek.)

The second trail starts in Cache Valley one mile southeast of Delicate Arch (one-eighth mile east of elevation 4535T on the Big Bend map) and goes generally north and east onto Dome Plateau. This very old trail is difficult to locate and follow. (SAPE.)

Cad Bench: (Kane Co.) GSCENM-Paria River. Bull Valley Gorge and Deer Range Point maps.

Ralph Chynoweth: "The bench was named for Cad Smith. He ran cattle out there in the early days." (425~)

Caddy Creek: (Iron Co.) Dixie National Forest-Butler Creek. Red Creek Reservoir and Fivemile Ridge maps.

A pioneer named Williamson had a nearby ranch. His son's name was Caddy. (2053~)

Cads Crotch: (Kane Co.) GSCENM-The Cockscomb. Butler Valley, Horse Flat, and Deer Range Point maps.

(See Cad Bench for name derivation.)

Caine Springs: (Wayne Co.) San Rafael Swell-Salt Wash. Caine Springs map.

This is a large spring area. (SAPE.)

Caineville: (Wayne Co.) Fremont River-Highway 24. Caineville map.

Also spelled Cainesville (1657~) and Kanesville (1196~).

Elijah Cutlar Behunin (1847-1933) and family were the first settlers of Caineville, arriving in 1882. Elijah is credited with naming the new town. (1891~)

Two name derivations are given. It is believed that the second is correct.

First, Andrew Jenson: "Thus named in honor of John T. Caine, Utah's representative to Congress." (972~)

Second, Don Orton in 1942: "So named by [Behunin's] wife for the wild canes growing there." (2053~)

Ethel Jensen: "So it was the [George B.] Rust family settled down at the world's end [Caineville in 1884] in obscure isolation where the way of life was substitution, or due without. Their neighbor settlers were friendly, equally poor, and also did without. The first winter the problem of eating would have been much more acute but for the wild unbranded cattle that roamed the Henries. To any one with a good rifle, a steady nerve, and a quick eye, the strays were fair game.... These wild cattle may have stemmed from the Johnson Army strays or from the outlaw herds." (962~)

The town did not last long in its first incarnation. C. Gregory Crampton noted the demise of many of the small towns in Blue Valley, including Aldridge, Caineville, Elephant, Giles, Kitchentown, and Mesa: "Depletion of the range up-country and the ploughing of banks practically to the water's edge increased the volume of floods and the result was a severe lowering of the streambed. By the turn of the century, Mormons along the Fremont below the [Capitol] reef found that much of their farm land had caved away to be washed downstream and that the river itself was dropping below the level of the headgates. The result was a contraction of the original frontier of the settlement as people began to move away." (699~)

Charles Kelly, quoting an unnamed old-timer in 1935: "When I first came out here the bottoms all along the Dirty Devil [Fremont River] used to be good land. The stream was as crooked as a yellow dog's hind leg, lined with brush and willows. There never were any floods in those days and the river ran quiet and easy like. The farmers began cutting down willows and straightening the channel to make it easier to irrigate. That gave the stream more fall and it wasn't long until it began to cut down through the silt. Then the sheep came in, ate off all the grass and pulled up the roots. We began to have floods." (1075~)

Ethel Jensen: "Floods, that so relentlessly plagued the lower Wayne settlements, were not without a cause. The surrounding area was sparsely vegetated and the un unabsorbent clay and rock formations was no deterrent to the summer downpours that in minutes filled the idle gullies and washes that led to the Dirty Devil [Fremont]. A contributing factor was the continuous overgrazing of the lands adjacent to the Boulder mountain. Cattlemen, with large herds, had depleted other grazing areas of the state, and now invaded the lush Boulder range. Cattle, by the thousands, roamed this rich pastureland. This added to the years of drought during the late '80s and early '90s, thus creating a situation that made flooding inevitable.... When the settlers first came to Caineville, the river banks were low and the water clear and sparkling. But with each passing summer, an increase in the volume of flood water

was noted. The 'Big Flood' was in September 1896. For the people of Caineville, everything from that date was either before the 'Big Flood' or after the 'Big Flood.'" (962~) Another cataclysmic flood that spelled the doom of the Blue Valley towns was on September 9, 1909. Ethel Jensen: "Calamities are not wholly without an antidote, and the settlers found a combative one in the flood itself. The advertised 'losts' of the settlement were by the jokesters found in ridiculous posture riding the crest of the recent flood. Even the hives of bees belonging to George B. [Rust] that had been swept away came back to him in risible jest. A man from down river, catching George B. in a crowd reported in mock solemnity, 'saw your bees go by my place, the other day. The hives were all upright, sailing merrily along, the bees going in and out, making honey, and humming like crazy. We hainta goin' ta sting no more.' But beneath all this horseplay, and bombastic dialogue, settlers knew they were through—finished. They had neither the will nor the money to carry on their battle with the river." (962~)

In recent years the area has seen a mild resurgence as farming techniques have improved. (607~, 925~)

Perry L. Jackson told this story about his father, Jeremiah, who lived in Caineville for a short time near the turn of the century: "While Jerry and [his wife] Chloe lived in Caineville, he occasionally shawed [*sic*] horses for the infamous Butch Cassidy Gang. Jerry would come out to the blacksmith shop and see two or three horses tied up to the fence. He would shoe them and tie them back up again. The next morning he would go back to the shop, and the horses would be gone, and a twenty-dollar gold piece would by lying on the anvil." (948a~)

—Caineville Wash: The Andrus Military Reconnaissance Expedition of 1866 called this Castle Creek. Early settlers spelled it Caneville Wash, but somewhere along the line others started calling it American Wash. Old-timers don't know where that name came from, though a likely source is the various shades of red-, white-, and blue-banded shales in the area. (SAPE.) Another name was South Wash, since it drained the southern part of the San Rafael Swell. (962~, 1641~)

—Saw Blade: This was the name for a distinctive escarpment five miles south-southwest of Caineville on the south side of Highway 24 (just north of elevation 5165T). (2053~)

Cain Hollow: (Grand Co.) La Sal Mountains-Castle Valley-Placer Creek. Warner Lake and Rill Creek maps. Also called Spring Creek. (1931~) Correctly spelled Cane Hollow.

Joe Taylor noted that cane grows in the hollow. (1866~)

Calf Canyon: (Carbon Co.) West Tavaputs Plateau-Desolation Canyon. Steer Ridge Canyon map.

Waldo Wilcox: "The ranchers would put their yearlings in there. That goes back to when the Seamounts were there." (2011~) (See Rock Creek—Carbon Co.)

Calf Canyon: (Emery Co.) Roan Cliffs-Range Creek. Lighthouse Canyon map.

Waldo Wilcox: "It was named Calf Canyon because they put their calves in there." (2011~)

Calf Canyon: (Emery Co.) San Rafael Swell-Buckhorn Wash. Bob Hill Knoll and Bottleneck Peak maps. Also called Calf Wash.

Owen McClenahan: "In this canyon the cowmen put their calves when they wanted to wean them." (1318~)

An old inscription near the mouth of the canyon states: "Hotel 50 cents. Beer." (SAPE.)

Calf Canyon: (Garfield Co.) Glen Canyon NRA-Waterhole Flat-Cataract Canyon. Teapot Rock map. Also called Calf Pasture Canyon. (615~)

Richard F. Negri noted that the Chaffin family ran cattle in the area from the early 1920s to the mid-1940s. (1430~) Ned Chaffin: "We used to put our calves in this canyon when we weaned them." (606~) Arthur Ekker: "There are a few good meadows at top where calves were put to feed. It is a short canyon." (602~)

—Constructed Stock Trail: This provides access from the upper pasture area of Calf Canyon to the lower pasture area. It is one-quarter mile northwest of elevation 5208. (SAPE.)

—Calf Canyon Line Camp: This is near the junction of the main and north forks of Calf Canyon (one-eighth mile southwest of elevation 5442T). (SAPE.)

—Calf Canyon Tank: This pothole is in lower Calf Canyon (one-quarter mile southwest of elevation 5527T). The tank, at the very edge of a huge cliff, is accessed by a constructed stock trail. Only a couple of animals could get to the tank at a time. (SAPE.)

Calf Canyon: (Garfield Co.) GSCENM-Kaiparowits Plateau-Alvey Wash. Dave Canyon map.

Don Coleman: "They used to wean their calves and put 'em up in Calf Canyon. They had a fence near the mouth and they couldn't get out." (441~) The fence has been removed. (SAPE.)

Calf Canyon: (San Juan Co.) Bluff Bench-San Juan River. Bluff map.

Myrtle Hunt noted that calves were herded into the canyon during the day while the cows were taken elsewhere to graze. (384~)

Inscriptions include Wm. Nix, 1893; Anna M. Bayles, June 18, 1893; John N. Brice, Feb. 4, 18??; C.H. Sitzer, June 4, 1893; G.N. Smith, Oct. 16-10; and Ellis R. Voorhies, Mar. 29, 191?. (838~, 1115~, SAPE.)

Calf Canyon: (San Juan Co.) Dark Canyon Plateau-Beef Basin-Beef Basin Wash. House Park Butte and Fable Valley maps.

Robert S. McPherson: "[Bull Valley] is where Al and Jim Scorup temporarily separated male from female cattle; newborn animals went to Calf Canyon." (1336~)

—Iron Spring: This is the "Spring" in lower Calf Canyon (at elevation 6259T on the Fable Valley map). (1664~)

Calf Canyon: (Wayne Co.) Poverty Flat-Sulphur Creek. Torrey and Twin Rocks maps.

Max Robinson noted that Ephraim P. Pectol found his famous buffalo hide Indian shield in the early 1930s here. (1641~) The shield was given to the Navajo Tribe in 2005.

Calf Creek: (Garfield Co.) GSCENM-Escalante River. Calf Creek map. Also called Sand Creek. (26~)

Edson Alvey noted that the canyon was used for weaning calves by early ranchers. (55~)

—Calf Creek Falls: These two extraordinary water falls, usually labeled Upper and Lower, are in the middle part of Calf Creek. They are both popular hiking destinations. Claire Noall in 1957: "Calf Creek ... falls over the rim of the plateau to present itself in winsome grace, a scene which must be courted if its delicate beauty is to be shared. We willingly walked up the creek bed to stand beside the pool into which the exquisite fall cascades from a rare height." (384~)

—Calf Creek Recreation Area: This BLM campground was built in 1963. It provides access to Lower Calf Creek Falls. (2051~)

—Cottonwood Canyon: The mouth of this northern tributary of the Escalante River is one-half mile upriver from Calf Creek (immediately west of elevation 5672). (1931~, 2051~)

Calf Mesa: (Emery Co.) San Rafael Swell-Cottonwood Wash. Mexican Mountain map. (4,890')

Betty Smith noted that they used to graze calves here. (1764~) Owen McClenahan: "In the early days, cowmen weaned their calves there. There was no way for them to get off the mesa when they fenced the trail with a pile of pinion logs." (1318~)

—Dexter Mine: This is on the south side of Calf Mesa. Len Wilson and Hap and Nolan Olsen patented the mine, which was a large producer of uranium ore from 1950 to 1957. Owen McClenahan: "While they were mining for uranium, they found clusters of red crystals, each of which was about a half inch in diameter. They were soft and would fall apart if left in the sun for a long period of time. After a year or so, mineralogists found they had discovered a new mineral which was named Dexterite after the name of their claim. There is no known value to the mineral." (1318~, 641~)

Calf Pasture Point: (Kane Co.) GSCENM-White Cliffs. Deer Spring Point map. (6,911')
Cartographer Bennett A. Rush noted that this was also called Adams Pasture Point. A Mr. Adams used to pasture his calves here in the summer. (1931~)
Cal Johnson: "Jim Ott used that for weanin' their calves and put 'em out there. There's pretty good feed and it's an area that they can fence off by itself." (984~)

Calico Peak: (Kane Co.) GSCENM-Paria River. Calico Peak map. (5,882')
Jack Breed in 1949: "Since no name for the towering butte was known, members of the [National Geographic Society] Expedition gave it one suggested by the brightly colored dresses Navajo matrons wear." (275~)

Callings Hollow: (Garfield Co.) Dixie National Forest-Sevier Plateau-Circle Valley. Mount Dutton map.
Kent Whittaker noted that the Callings family lived here in the early years. (2002~)

Cameron Reservoir: (Wayne Co.) Awapa Plateau-Sage Flat Draw. Moroni Peak map.
Dee Hatch noted that Lee Cameron Brinkerhoff (1879-1930) was an early sheepman. (844~) Thaine Taylor: "He was raised in Bicknell and had a few sheep and they dug that pond to take care of his sheep down in there." (1868~)

Cameron Troughs: (Garfield Co.) Dixie National Forest-Black Rock Valley. Panguitch Lake map.
This is a large spring with troughs. (SAPE.)
John Cameron (1847–1926) hauled water from this spring for use at his sawmill in the mid-1890s. (1346~, 2053~)

Cameron Wash: (Garfield Co.) Dixie National Forest-Escalante Mountains-Johns Valley. Pine Lake, Tropic Canyon, and Flake Mountain East maps.
Scott Robinson noted that John Cameron (1847-1926) and family lived here and had a sawmill nearby. (2053~)
—Zabriskie Sawmill: Orrel and George Zabriskie had a sawmill here from 1923 to 1932. (1455~)

Campbell Canyon: (Garfield Co.) Bryce Canyon National Park-Pink Cliffs-Paria River. Bryce Canyon, Tropic Canyon, and Cannonville maps.
Also called Campbell Creek.

Bryce Canyon National Park Superintendent P.P. Paltrow in 1934: "Ralph Allen Campbell [1833-1916] moved to Tropic in 1897. He located at Campbell Spring in 1898. There he had a house, corrals, and a stock reservoir." (1931~, 1346~)
—Oastler Castle: This natural arch in Campbell Canyon was named for Dr. Frank Oastler. He was on an advisory board to the National Park Service in the 1930s. (202~)

Camp Creek: (Iron Co.) Zion National Park-Hurricane Cliffs. Kolob Arch and Kanarraville maps.
Mrs. J.A. Haslam: "attractive place for camping in the early days." (942~)
—Stock Trail: A stock trail goes through the canyon. (778~)

Campers Spring: (Wayne Co.) San Rafael Swell-Middle Desert Wash. Fruita NW map.
This is a large, streambed spring. A sign at the spring notes that the water is for livestock only. (1551~)

Camp Flat: (Garfield Co.) GSCENM-Kaiparowits Plateau. Carcass Canyon map.
The camp itself is in a nice grove of pinyon and juniper trees on the north side of the flat adjacent to the Smoky Mountain Road. Nearby is a developed spring and stock tank. (SAPE.)
Don Coleman: "The ranchers would take their pack horses and they'd bring grain for their sheep herders out to Camp Flat and then they would camp out there the first night from Escalante.... They'd have maybe fifteen head of mules carrying grain for the horses they herded sheep with, and also food for the old sheepherders." (441~)

Camp Jackson Reservoir: (San Juan Co.) Manti-LaSal National Forest-Abajo Mountains-Johnson Creek. Abajo Peak map.
In 1896 Captain George A. Jackson established Camp Jackson, a small mining town, near the Dream Mine at the head of Johnson Creek. Robert S. McPherson: "Within a few months [of establishing Camp Jackson], Jackson lay dead in the snow halfway between Piute Springs and Cross Canyon. An accident occurred when he reached into his sled to get his shotgun. The trigger caught on a blanket, sending a load of buckshot into his face." (1336~)
By the early 1900s the mines had closed and Camp Jackson was essentially abandoned. (1882~)
Marvin Lyman told this story about the last Camp Jackson resident: "Louie Saylor ... came in with the mining boom probably about 1893.... It was reported that he was a bank teller in Telluride, Colorado, and he embezzled some money and went to the Blue Mountains in San Juan County to get away from the law. He stayed there

the rest of his life and after everybody was gone, he still lived there. The cowboys took care of him and saw that he had food.... He became old and finally they had to come and get him and take him to Monticello where he died [in 1945]." (1258~)

In about 1925 Monticello rancher Will Young bought Camp Jackson. His son, Lloyd: "Camp Jackson is a delightful spot in the National Forest. It provided a good horse pasture and nice potatoes grow there. Its cool springs and reservoirs (beaver dams), its location on the sunny side of the Blue, its quivering aspen groves, and a host of other qualities make it a pleasant place to be." (2068~)

Camp Spring: (Garfield Co.) GSCENM-Kaiparowits Plateau-Right Hand Collet Canyon. Death Ridge map.

This is a medium-size, wash-bottom spring.

The camp itself is just off the road near two large juniper trees. A spring is nearby. The camp was often used by stockmen. (55~, SAPE.)

Camp Spring: (Washington Co.) Shivwits Band Paiute Reservation-Beaver Dam Mountains-Santa Clara River. Shivwits map.

This is a large spring with troughs. (SAPE.)

—Old Spanish Trail: This was an often-used camping spot on the Old Spanish Trail. Anthony W. Ivins noted that it was the only water between Santa Clara and the Beaver Dams. (1447~) Ivins told this story: "At Camp Spring ... Magets, a noted Indian of the pioneer days, said that while concealed in the rocks [around the spring], he saw two miners, who were returning from the gold fields of California, kill and bury a third member of their party, after taking from his person a quantity of gold which he carried. It was later discovered that this same Indian had killed a lone prospector at Camp Spring, from whom he took ten twenty dollar gold pieces." (946~)

Orville C. Pratt in 1848: "Camped today ... at a little spring on the hill.... Grass fair but scarcity of water for animals." (1572~) Addison Pratt of the Jefferson Hunt Party in 1849 noted it as Sulphur Springs. (1571~)

Joseph Cain's "Mormon Way-bill" of 1851 called it Camp Springs, with the note "feed good." (330~) Amasa M. Lyman stopped here in 1857: "Travelled [*sic*] on to the Camp Springs." (1251~) Captain Randolph B. Marcy in 1859: "Two miles before reaching the springs the road leaves the Santa Clara. Good Grass." (1276~)

In 1864 Captain George F. Price led a military expedition from Salt Lake City to find the head of navigable waters of the Colorado River. His troop stopped at Camp Spring

and left behind several inscriptions which joined inscriptions from earlier pioneers. (805~)

Canaan Gap: (Washington Co.) Little Creek Mountain-Highway 59. Smithsonian Butte and Little Creek Mountain maps.

(See Canaan Mountain for name derivation.)

Canaan Mountain: (Washington Co.) Vermilion Cliffs-Lower Mountain. Smithsonian Butte and Hildale maps.

Kate B. Carter noted that this was named for the biblical Canaan "because it seemed to be so fruitful and desirable." (375~)

—Canaan Mountain Summit: This is on the southwest edge of Canaan Mountain (at elevation 7363 on the Smithsonian Butte map). Herbert E. Gregory called it Overlook Point. (767~)

—Zion Butte: This is one mile west-southwest of Canaan Mountain Summit (at elevation 7259 on the Smithsonian Butte map). It was named by Courtney Purcell. (1591~)

—Canaan Ranch: PRIVATE PROPERTY. (Smithsonian Butte map.) The Lieutenant George M. Wheeler Survey map of 1872–73 shows this as Maxwell's Water. (M.76.) William Bailey Maxwell pioneered ranches near Hildale and Moccasin.

The Mormon Church started this ranch as a cooperative effort in 1870. (375~) Also called the Canaan Cooperative Stock Company, it became the largest of the Mormon ranching cooperatives. Major outposts included Alton, Moccasin, Parashont, and Pipe Spring. The Canaan Cooperative Stock Company sold out to B.F. Saunders in 1895. (469~)

—Sawmill Cable: (Also called The Windlass.) (1591~) This braided steel cable drops from Canaan Mountain, down the Vermilion Cliffs, to the Canaan Springs area. It is one-half mile northwest of Canaan Spring (one-eighth mile west of elevation 7168 on the Smithsonian Butte map). Logs cut at nearby Sawmill Spring were lowered down the cliffs.

—The Box: This is the flat area one-eighth mile west-northwest of the Sawmill Cable. (1591~)

Canaan Peak: (Garfield Co.) Dixie National Forest-Kaiparowits Plateau. Canaan Peak map. (9,293')

Also called Kaiparowits Peak. (324~, 584~)

The Paiute name is *Kaiva'aipetsi*, or "mountain boy." Diane Austin: "Mountain Boy is said to be son of Table Cliff Plateau." (82~)

The Andrus Military Reconnaissance Expedition of 1866 called this Sandstone Point. (475~)

Three name derivations are given.

First, and most popular: The Canaan Cooperative Stock Company, based out of St. George, ran cattle in the area in the early years. They arrived in the Alton area in the mid-1870s. (56~, 1639~)

Second, it was originally named Cannon Peak and the name has become corrupted over time. George Q. Cannon was a Mormon apostle. The nearby town of Cannonville was named for him. (441~)

Third, Nethella Griffin Woolsey claimed that Almon H. Thompson of the 1871–72 Powell Expedition named it *Canaan*, which is Hebrew for "low mountain." (2051~) James H. Knipmeyer: "Nothing in Thompson's diaries substantiates this assertion." (1116~)

Inscriptions on aspen trees on the mountain include Reed Wooley, July 11, 1938. (SAPE.)

—Winter Spring: This large spring and stock pond are on the north side of Canaan Creek and the northeast side of Canaan Peak (three-quarters of a mile northwest of elevation 8530). (1551~, SAPE.)

Candland Mountain: (Emery Co.) Manti-LaSal National Forest-Huntington Creek. Candland Mountain map. (10,270')

David Candland (1819-1902), a Mt. Pleasant pioneer, arrived in the early 1860s. (1213~) His son, William D. Candland (1858-1940), established the Candland Sheep Company in 1889. He became well-known for his Rambouillet sheep. The company folded in 1938. (66~)

Cane Spring Desert: (Garfield Co.) Little Rockies-Hoskinnini Mesa. Hall Mesa, Lost Spring, and Bullfrog maps.

Inscriptions include Early Behunin, May 1911. (SAPE.)

—Cane Spring: (Bullfrog map.) This spring no longer exists. It was often used by early travelers. (925~) Nora Cundel in 1940: "a group of twisted willows, having a small creek close by, and a spring right among the trees." (507~) Inscriptions include J.H. Moosman, Escalante, Utah 1903; D.J. Allen, March 10, 1909; Marion Cook, Nov. the 11, 1909; Daniel Cook, March 17, 1910; Parley Coleman, March 1913; and Clinton Torgensen, Dec. 6, 1926. (SAPE.)

—Cane Spring Well: (Lost Spring map.) This is a large, developed spring. (SAPE.)

Cannonville: (Garfield Co.) Paria River-Highway 12. Cannonville map.

The town was established in 1877 by residents of Clifton, a town that was abandoned because of water problems. George Q. Cannon (1827-1901) was a Mormon apostle. Andrew J. Hansen: "Locally the name of the place was

'Shot Gun,' it being explained that it was not near large enough for a 'Cannon.'" (1186~)

—Clifton Town: This town was one mile south of Cannonville near the mouth of Henrieville Creek on the Paria River. The first settlers were David O. Littlefield, Orley D. Bliss, and William Jasper Henderson, Sr. They arrived in the fall of 1876. The town's proximity to the Pink Cliffs gave the town its name, though locally it was called Woodenshoe. (876~, 2053~)

John H. Davies: "There was insufficient water there to make a permanent town feasible. Because of this some of the people moved up the creek from the east and founded Henrieville, and the remainder of them moved up the Pahreah Creek and settled Cannonville." (523~)

—Promise Rock: William Jasper Henderson: "There is a large red sandstone rock about one fourth of a mile below the town site of Clifton. It is about one thousand feet long, five hundred feet wide and three hundred feet high.... It was on top of this rock, Aunt Vilda said, that uncle John asked her to marry him. They were married on top of this rock in the spring of 1877, and since that time it has been called the Promise Rock." (876~)

—New Clifton Town: Some families quickly became disenchanted with the town of Clifton and moved north to Henderson Creek where they started the town of New Clifton. (1445~, 1639~, 1711~, 2043~)

Canyon Country:

This is not labeled on the maps.

The Rufus B. Sage 1846 map of Utah shows the area in the vicinity of The Confluence of the Grand (Colorado) and Green Rivers both as Cañon Country and Stupendous Cañons. (1685~, M.63.) This may have been the first time the term Canyon Country was used in print.

J.A. McCormick used the Canyon Country name during the James S. Best Expedition of 1891.

T. Mitchell Prudden in 1896: "It is a region for the most part bare, brown, and desolate, thrown here and there into wild relief by barren ridges, mountain peaks, and short jumbled ranges. Over the more level parts of it, in some earlier time, great streams or sudden floods have scored and ploughed the surfaces, leaving gigantic cañons and gorges and broad lake basins, now wholly dry, among which rise abruptly the picturesque and imposing remnants of the elder surfaces as plateaus, table-lands, and mesas. The tops of the mesas and table-lands are frequently clad with dense growths of piñon, juniper, and cedar, while on the lower levels scattered tufts of grass, the hardy sagebrush, and the greasewood make shift to gather what little moisture they may need from the deep recesses of the soil. But wherever a spring pours out upon the barren surfaces, all plant life is welcome which does not too much fear the sun, and for a little space the desert plays the garden, for what uses man or nature may decree." (1590~)

Canyonlands National Park: (San Juan and Wayne Counties.)

Canyonlands National Park was the brainchild of Bates Wilson, who would eventually become its first superintendent. Initially the area now encompassing Canyonlands National Park was studied with the idea of breaking each area—Needles, Island in the Sky, and Land of Standing Rocks—into its own separate park. Leo Diederich suggested combining all three areas into the "Canyonlands," a term he is credited with coining.

Secretary of the Interior Stewart Udall, in promoting the park, wrote: "As far as the eye can see, the canyonlands country of southeastern Utah presents an array of visual wonders. Over millions of years, the mighty lashes of wind and water gouged canyons, striped rock layers until they bled in a fury of color, eroded the land into startling pinnacles and arches, and sliced away at the plateaued surface." (1316~)

The National Park, encompassing 257,640 acres, was established in September 1964 by President Lyndon Johnson. It was enlarged with the addition of the detached Horseshoe Canyon section in 1971. (1316~, 1855~, 2049~)

Canyonlands Overlook: (San Juan Co.) Hatch Point-Colorado River. Shafer Basin map.

This provides a stupendous view of the Colorado River and Canyonlands National Park.

Canyon Pond: (Emery Co.) San Rafael Swell-Sand Bench. Short Canyon map.

This is a very large and still-used stock reservoir in a very pretty setting. (SAPE.)

Wayne Gremel: "We call that the Bass Pond.... They stocked bass in it." (780~)

Inscriptions at the pond date to 1920.

—Constructed Stock Trail: This goes west from Canyon Pond up to Sand Bench. (SAPE.)

Cap, The: (Emery Co.) Manti-LaSal National Forest-Wasatch Plateau. The Cap map. (9,665')

This small mesa lies on top of, or "caps," North Horn Mountain.

Capitol Reef: (Wayne Co.) Capitol Reef National Park-Waterpocket Fold. Twin Rocks, Fruita, and Golden Throne maps.

White Navajo Sandstone above the reds and browns of the Kayenta Formation andthe Wingate Sandstone made the numerous huge slickrock domes look like the National Capitol in Washington D.C., giving the area the first part of its name. Miners coming back from the Australian gold rush noted that the area looked like the gold-bearing ridges near Bendigo, Australia, which to them resembled coral reefs, giving the area the second part of its name. (607~, 1562~, 1769~, 2056~)

The first Euroamericans to see the Capitol Reef area were members of the John C. Fremont Expedition of 1853-54. The expedition traversed Cathedral Valley and went over Thousand Lake Mountain. The Andrus Military Reconnaissance Expedition of 1866 followed the Fremont River, but did not recognize its importance. Miners left their inscriptions on a wall in Capitol Gorge in 1871. (See Capitol Wash.)

Grove Karl Gilbert of the Powell Survey, on a geological reconnaissance, passed through Capitol Reef and the areas that would become Torrey, Fruita, and Pleasant Creek. (1047~) Gilbert called it the Howell Fold. (723~)

Clarence Dutton of the Powell Survey described the area while looking down on it from the crest of Boulder Mountain: "It is a sublime panorama. The heart of the inner Plateau Country is spread out before us in a bird's-eye view. It is a maze of cliffs and terraces lined off with stratification, of crumbling buttes, red and white domes, rock platforms gashed with profound cañons, burning plains barren even of sage—all glowing with bright colors and flooded with blazing sunlight. Everything visible told of ruin and decay. It is the extreme of desolation, the blankest solitude, a superlative desert." (584~)

Don Maguire in 1892: "Red sandstone constitutes the country rock and has been worn away by the winds, the rains and the storms until the rocky cliffs have taken the most fantastic shapes and the erosions have formed narrow cañons with walls that run up perpendicularly to thousands of feet in height.... Never have I seen such awful walls of rock, such narrow passes or such majestic beauty as fill this part of Utah." (1271~)

A.M. Swanson in 1946: "All forces of nature have joined in from the great powers of glacial epochs to the might of the molten magma rivers, together with the wind and the rain and the sun and the upheavals of the earth's crust, to create Wayne Wonderland to the satisfaction of the sovereigns of all forces, until they were pleased and said it was good." (1850~)

A couple of features on the top of the reef are worth noting.

—The Crown: This three-pronged tower, on the very top of the Capitol Reef and visible from Highway 24, is elevation 7238 on the Twin Rocks map. (745~)

—The Horns: These are on the very top of Capitol Reef and are one-quarter mile northwest of The Crown. (745~)

—Abbey Window: This arch is on the very top of Capitol Reef and is three-quarters of a mile northwest of The Crown (one-eighth mile southeast of elevation 7011). It was named by former Capitol Reef National Park Ranger Fred Goodsell for his friend, writer Edward Abbey (1927-1989). (745~)

Capitol Reef National Park: (Garfield and Wayne Counties.)

In the 1920s and '30s locals started promoting the Capitol Reef area as a tourist destination, labeling it Wayne's Wonderland in reference to its location in Wayne County. Ephraim Portman Pectol, a resident of Caineville, often traveled to Torrey through Capitol Wash and grew to love the area. He, along with his brother-in-law, Joseph Hickman, became advocates for a Wayne Wonderland State Park. (1419~, 1657~) A small area around the site of Fruita was set aside as a state park in 1926.

In 1937 President Franklin Roosevelt designated the area as the 37,060 acre Capitol Reef National Monument. Dwight Eisenhower added 3,040 acres in 1958. Lyndon Johnson, in the last ninety minutes of his term in office in 1969, added another 215,056 acres by proclamation. His additions included the southern portion of the Waterpocket Fold and the Cathedral Valley area to the north. On December 18, 1971 Richard Nixon signed a bill that changed the monument into Capitol Reef National Park with a total of 241,904 acres. (699~, 1419~)

Capitol Wash: (Wayne Co.) Miners Mountain-Capitol Reef National Park-Capitol Reef-Pleasant Creek. Grover and Golden Throne maps.

Also called Capital Wash, Capitol Gorge, and Temple Creek. (584~, 974a~, 992~, 2007~)

Although the first wagon road through the Waterpocket Fold followed the course of the Fremont River, the route was not popular. One source noted that wagons had to cross the Fremont over fifty times.

In 1882 Volney King and others did a reconnaissance of Capitol Wash to see if the route was worth improving and found that "there could be a road through that way with a great expense.... We made our way ... down it which is 6

miles in length with walls of rock on either side hundreds of feet high and some places only room for a wagon to pass. It bore the mark of great floods." (1096~)

In 1884 Elijah Cutlar Behunin and crew built a road through the wash. It took them eight days to traverse the three and one-half mile long gorge. The route immediately became popular. Albert R. Lyman noted that Josephine Catherine Chatterly Wood took a wagon through the gorge in 1884, calling it the Gates of Hell. (1242~)

Several descriptions of the route through the gorge in the early days exist. Ethel Jensen described a trip taken by a relative in 1886: "The winter sun had yet to climb the canyon walls when Eliza [Rust] drove into the gargantuan gorge filled with its wild and startling spectacles of erosion, domes of pale gold, pinnacles delicately carved, giant arches splashed with cappaghbrown towering walls, copper sheeted, and more. That decades hence, this geological marvel would exhaust mans empurpled superlatives in his attempt to describe its mystical wonderment. Eliza did not know or care. On this fearful raw morning she was not inclined to be aesthetical. The man aped [sic] alcoves, so boldly striped red and gold were passed unnoticed.... To her, this was a dreadful ole hole. And no place to get hung up with a crippled horse or a broken wheel. For more than six bone wrenching jolting miles Eliza guided the team through the garbled and all but inextricable defile. Not until the wheels of the wagon dug into the deep half frozen sand, near Pleasant Creek, did she give a sigh of relief." (962~)

Ephraim Pectol and family traversed the canyon in 1888: "a very narrow gorge with ledges on either side several hundred feet high at the entrance, but lowering as one passes on down. Those tall ledges were frightening. All we could see was the sky above us for miles through it. Our little caravan would have been doomed had a bad storm been encountered while traveling this route.... One cannot comprehend the beauty of the trees and wild flowers we found along the way." (318a~)

Unattributed in 1893: "a most beautiful and wonderful cañon six or eight miles long, and so crooked as to make it a great surprise to us, both for its beauty and extent. Its walls towered hundreds of feet above us, while the cañon at places narrowed down to only a little more than the trackage for a wagon. In some respects it rivals the noted canyons on railway lines so well advertised in the West." (1688~)

Emmett Clark described going through the gorge: "It was the only way you'd get to the other side of the reef. And boy, it was difficult going. If it ever rained or snowed, it was real difficult to get down through there. And those floods'd come. At times you wasn't even sure there was a flood around, but all at once a wall of water'd hit you and you had to pull out of the wash. It was very difficult going down through there." (426~)

In 1913 a telephone line was run through the wash. Washed out by a flash flood in 1926, it was not rebuilt. While the line is no longer here, many of the old pipe standards are still in place. (581~, SAPE.)

Capitol Gorge remained the main vehicle route through Capitol Reef until 1963 when Highway 24 along the Fremont River was constructed. The Capitol Gorge road was closed and has now become a popular hike. (745~, 1047~, 1476~, 1884~)

Along the course of the gorge are many historic inscriptions. The oldest are from J.A. Call and Wal. Bateman, Sept. 20, 1871. The men, residents of Cedar City, were on their way to the Colorado River to locate placer claims. (1115~) One of the most interesting inscriptions is "Cass Hite is A —-" Following those words are a pecked image of a horse and a man facing away. Or as James H. Knipmeyer interprets the inscription: "Cass Hite is a Horses Ass!" (1105~)

—Calf Canyon: The mouth of this western tributary of Capitol Wash is one-half mile south of its junction with Pleasant Creek (one-eighth mile north of elevation 5831AT on the Golden Throne map). Keith Durfey noted that his father, Golden, used to put his calves here. (582~)

Cappies Rock Spring: (Washington Co.) Vermilion Cliffs-South Mountain-Broad Hollow. Hildale map.

This medium-size spring was once developed. (SAPE.)

Carbon County:

The county seat is Price.

Carbon County was established by dividing Emery County in 1894. Unattributed in 1948: "The name of no county in Utah is more peculiarly descriptive of its region than that of Carbon County. The underlying coal deposits are not only the primary source of County wealth but throughout the history of the county have been a major influence in its development." (1621~, 1330~, 1932~)

Carcass Canyon: (Garfield Co.) GSCENM-Kaiparowits Plateau-Right Hand Collet Canyon. Carcass Canyon map. Don Coleman: "They had a bunch of sheep out there and when they went back to find 'em, they had been snowed in and all they found was a lot of their carcasses." (441~)

Carcass Creek: (Wayne Co.) Dixie National Forest-Boulder Mountain-Fremont River. Blind Lake, Grover, and Twin Rocks maps.

Also spelled Carcas Creek. (2069~)

Two similar name derivations are given.

First, Don Orton in 1941: "So named because a severe epidemic of typhoid was caused by the many carcasses of dead sheep that found their way into the creek bed." (2053~)

Second, Barbara Ekker: "Livestock are frequently lost along this creek because its bed is rocky and steep. Animals that go down to drink sometimes slip and fall and are unable to get out and eventually die. Their carcasses are found and therefore the name." (607~)

—Perkins Ranch: In the mid- to late 1880s Benjamin Perkins (1844-1926) had a ranch on Carcass Creek. He moved to this remote area to avoid prosecution for polygamy. (1235~)

Carcass Wash: (Kane Co.) GSCENM-Fiftymile Bench-Fortymile Gulch. Sooner Bench map.

Edson Alvey noted that animals crossing the wash would fall to their deaths. (55~)

—Boy Scout Tragedy: In June 1963 a group of Explorer Scouts from Salt Lake City were being shuttled to the Hole-in-the-Rock where they were to take a river trip through Glen Canyon. The driver lost control of the truck they were in and rolled down the hill. Thirteen young men lost their lives and twenty-six were injured in the accident. (1551~)

Carlyle Wash: (Emery Co.) San Rafael Swell-Moroni Slopes-Last Chance Wash. The Frying Pan and Salvation Creek maps.

Garn Jefferies noted that this was named for Carlyle Baker (1909-1976): "Carlyle drilled a well and hit water and they had a big storage tank out there for the cows." (959~)

Wayne Gremel: "I guess we named that. The BLM had a well out on the Moroni Slopes [Last Chance Well on The Frying Pan map]. Carlyle Baker had the Baker Ranch [See Rock Springs Wash–Baker Ranch] up on the Mussentuchits.... We would travel up and down that wash and we just got to calling it Carlyle Wash." (780~)

Carpenter Basin: (San Juan Co.) Manti-LaSal National Forest-La Sal Mountains-Cottonwood Canyon. Mount Tukuhnikivatz map.

Thomas Carpenter was the manager of the Pittsburgh Land and Cattle Company starting in 1887. In 1895 it was reorganized as the La Sal Cattle Company and in 1898 as the Cunningham and Carpenter Livestock Company. Carpenter sold out in 1915 to a consortium of Bluff cattlemen who resurrected the La Sal Cattle Company name. (73~, 186~, 456~)

Carrol Canyon: (San Juan Co.) Abajo Mountains-Bulldog Canyon. Blanding North map.

Correctly spelled Carroll Canyon.

James Franklin Carroll (1870-1959) and family had a farm in Recapture Canyon below the mouth of Carroll Canyon starting in the 19teens. (1911~)

Carrot Top Arch: (San Juan Co.) Navajo Indian Reservation-Cummings Mesa-Mountain Sheep Canyon. Cathedral Canyon map.

Also spelled Carrottop Arch.

Stan Jones' nickname for his red-headed wife, Alice, was Carrottop. (1020~)

Carter Canyon: (Washington Co.) Dixie National Forest-Pine Valley Mountains-Wide Canyon. Saddle Mountain map.

Hazel B. Bradshaw: "William Carter [1821-1896], pioneer of 1847, had built a summer home for his family on the southern slopes of Pine Valley Mountain." (367~)

Carter Peak: (Sevier Co.) Sage Flat-Lost Creek. Aurora map. (6,718')

Also called Carter Mountain.

Edmund Durfee Carter (1854–1915) was an early settler of Salina. (388~)

Carter Spring: (Sevier Co.) Sevier Plateau-Cedar Mountain-Kings Meadow. Sigurd map. PRIVATE PROPERTY. (See Carter Peak for name derivation.)

Casa Colorado Rock: (San Juan Co.) Dry Valley-Hatch Wash. Sandstone Draw map. (6,414')

Also called Red House and Red Rock.

The Don Juan María de Rivera Expedition passed by Casa Colorado Rock in October 1765. (953~)

The name was applied by members of the Captain John N. Macomb Expedition of 1859. (477~) John Strong Newberry of the expedition: "Everywhere over the second plateau are scattered buttes and pinnacles, wrought ... by the erosion which has swept from this surface all traces but these of the immense mass of sedimentary rocks which once covered it. Of these one of the most striking seen from our route is the Casa Colorado [House of Red Color].... It is a detached butte, some 300 feet in height, composed of red sandstone." (1266~)

Charles H. Dimmock was with the Macomb Expedition. He called it *El Tenejal*, or "Place of the Tanks." (559~, 1269~)

William Henry Jackson of the Ferdinand V. Hayden Survey in 1875: "The only object that warranted setting up the photographic outfit was a group of red sandstone bluffs with great dome-shaped caves." (952a~)

C. Gregory Crampton: "This prominent landmark, a striking red sandstone rock rising two hundred feet above an elevated base, was so-named because its several sculptured caves and alcoves resembled the windows of a giant house." (477~)

—La Tinaja: (Also called El Tinejal and The Tank.) This large pothole on the south side of Casa Colorado Rock was an essential stopping place along the Old Spanish Trail. John Strong Newberry in 1859: "La Tenejal, a deep excavation in the red sandstone, which retains so large a quantity of surface-water, and for so long a time, as to become an important watering-place on the Spanish trail." (1266~)

Casa Del Eco Mesa: (San Juan Co.) Navajo Indian Reservation-San Juan River. White Rock Point, Hogan Mesa, Bluff, and Recapture Pocket maps.

Also spelled Casa Del Echo Mesa (1383~) and Caso del Elico (1596~).

—Casa Del Eco Ruin: (Also called Bluff Ruin, Fifteen Room Ruin, Sixteen Room Ruin, Seventeen Room Ruin, and Seventeen Window Ruin.) This famous Anasazi cliff dwelling is in the cliffs that form the eastern edge of Casa Del Eco Mesa. William Henry Jackson of the Ferdinand V. Hayden Survey in 1875 is credited with naming the ruin, and the mesa: "We discovered on the other side of the [San Juan] river ... a great circular cave.... After many attempts to find a practicable ford, we crossed the river and found the cave to be about two hundred feet in height.... The great dome over all echoed and reëchoed with marvelous distinctness every word we said. Below the Casa del Eco, as we named this ruin." (952a~) *Casa del Echo* is Spanish for "House of the Echo."

John Frank Sleeper in 1890: "Now imagine a cave 300 feet long, 150 feet deep and 250 feet from the sandstone arch to the earth below.... In the back of the cave is a bench in the rock 5 or 6 feet above the base of the sand stone. This bench is 12 feet wide in the widest part, running out at both ends upon this bench are the old ruins. Fourteen rooms in all. The front wall and partitions were above a foot thick, laid up of flat rock and chinked with mud. In this were the imprints of their hands showing all the wrinkles as plain as the day they were put there." (509~, 1117~)

Inscriptions include E. [Edwin] A. Barber [a member of the Ferdinand V. Hayden Survey in 1875]; H.M. Thornton, July 1879 [a member of the San Juan Exploring Expedition of 1879]; J.L. Butler, July 29, 1879; J. Plat, Apr. 2nd, 1883; Hyrum Ivins, 1886; W.C. McBride, Feby. 24, 91; WWR, 1892; L.W. Gunckel, I.A. Survey 5/92 [Illustrated

American Exploring Expedition]; M. Brown and M.C. Wood, 1892; A.G. Curtis, Durango, 1-13-93; JER [Rogers], 1894; and F. Eringard, 1894. As well, brothers G., N., and S.W. Honaker signed their names with no date, but assumed to be in the 1890s during the San Juan gold rush. (1115~, 838~, SAPE.)

Cascade Canyon: (Kane Co.) Glen Canyon NRA-Glen Canyon. Navajo Point, Nasja Mesa, and Rainbow Bridge maps.

Also called Kluckhohn Canyon. (1163~)

Katie Lee: "It used to be called 68 mile. Tad [Nichols] named it Cascade because it had so many little shelves and cascades all of the way down.... One cascade after another." (1163~)

Cascade Creek: (Piute Co.) Fishlake National Forest-Tushar Mountains-Bullion Canyon. Mount Brigham map.

Gold was discovered in the area in the late 1860s or early 1870s. Several mines, including the Cascade, Glen Erie, Gold Strike, and Shamrock were located here. (332~)

Cascade Falls: (Kane Co.) Dixie National Forest-Pink Cliffs. Navajo Lake map.

Also called Cascade Springs. (2020~)

(See Navajo Lake.)

Cass Creek Peak: (Garfield Co.) Henry Mountains-Mount Hillers. Cass Creek Peak map. (9,428')

Grove Karl Gilbert of the Powell Survey called this Bulldog Peak, a name that would later be applied to a nearby summit. (722~, 925~) It was named for miner Cass Hite (1845-1914). (607~) (See Hite Town.)

Bliss Brinkerhoff: "My dad [Willard A.] said that one cold winter they got caught up at the foot of Cass Creek Peak with a herd of sheep. There was about two feet of snow and they were snowed in and couldn't move their sheep. For three weeks they'd drag old dead trees and some brush to the sheep to keep them eatin'. He said that it was so cold that winter that when it began to break and they got down a little lower into the desert, they found cattle that had froze standin' there, and they hadn't thawed out yet. Those cattle were standing on their feet, frozen. I don't think he was exaggerating because I've rode down there when it's been eleven below zero in the middle of the day and that's the warmest part of the day." (291~)

—Cass Creek: (Also called Mine Canyon.) This runs west from the south side of Cass Creek Peak. (925~, 1537~)

—Cass Creek Reservoir: Garth Noyes: "The BLM built a reservoir and then ran a pipeline down into the winter range on Cow Flat and that area ... in the '30s or '40s." (1473~)

Castle, The: (Wayne Co.) Capitol Reef National Park-Highway 24. Twin Rocks map. (6,387')

Also called Split Rock (776~) and The Temple (1931~). This butte of Wingate Sandstone is often pictured in publications. It was named by the National Park Service for its "distinctive turreted appearance." (1116~)

—Navajo Knobs: This is a recent name for a couple of Navajo Sandstone outcrops that are one-half mile northwest of The Castle (at elevation 6979).

—Ford Hill: This hill on Highway 24 is immediately west of the Capitol Reef National Park Visitor Center. Charles Kelly noted that a part of the old road went up the hill. It received its name because a Ford Model T could not pull the grade. (1047~)

Castle Arch: (San Juan Co.) Canyonlands National Park-Needles District-Horse Canyon. South Six-shooter Peak map.

Robert H. Vreeland: "It was discovered in 1949 by photographers Ray and Virginia Garner.... They named it for its likeness, from one angle, to a castle, with the arch forming a flying buttress." (1950~) Virginia Garner: "A great castle of pink and white sandstone rose high above the wall of the canyon. A long buttress ran out from it and here in the rimrock the wind had carved Castle Arch, as we promptly named it. Far below, the deep greens of the serpentine canyon floor added complementary color to the scene; a scene so spectacular that it will undoubtedly someday become one of the outstanding scenic attractions of the Southwest." (705~)

Castle Butte: (San Juan Co.) Glen Canyon NRA-Glen Canyon. Good Hope Bay map. (4,527')

William Derby Johnson of the Powell Expedition of 1871–72 called this Shinumo Butte. (1004~) Robert Brewster Stanton called it Castle Dome in 1897. (1812~) Local cowboys called it Canyon Butte in 1937. (560a~)

Charles Eggert in 1957: "A great butte rises from the river's edge like a great sentinel marking the entrance to Glen Canyon. Here, atop this massive rock pedestal the mighty Indian god, Ta-vwoats must have stood, arms outstretched, pointing the way to Paradise, for if anywhere, that place was below—through the 147 miles of Glen Canyon." (599~)

Inscriptions include JWR, 1893. (SAPE.)

—Castle Butte Bar: (Also called Adams Bar and Red Canyon Bar.) This placer bar, now underwater, was on the east side of the Colorado River and one mile southwest of Castle Butte. Henry Reems located the bar. It was later worked by Frank Adams and Bert Loper. In the 1890s there was extensive gold mining on the bar. (465~)

—Staveley River Guides: In 1964 Gaylord and Joan Staveley ran one of the first marinas and guide services on the still-filling Lake Powell at Castle Butte. (1525~) The original plan was for the Hite Marina to be placed at Castle Butte. A branch of the highway would have gone over Blue Notch to the butte. (2018~)

Castle Butte: (San Juan Co.) Valley of the Gods-Lime Creek. Cigarette Spring Cave map.

Buck Lee in 1942: "It resembles a large castle hence the name." (2053~)

Castle Cliff: (Washington Co.) Beaver Dam Mountains-Castle Cliff Wash. Castle Cliff map.

Addison Pratt of the Jefferson Hunt Party in 1849: "Began to descend [from Utah Hill] a verry rough canion [Castle Cliff Wash], the rocks are flinty and sharp.... There is a solitary looking vegitable of the prickley pear order called prickley pine [Joshua tree].... They often grow in one columnar shape, and these we would often mistake for Indians." (1571~)

Anson Call noted this as Joshuay Canyon in 1864: "The road traveled down Joshuay Kanyon, and to the Beaver Dams is hard and good." (331~)

The cliff itself is interesting. A way station was built here in the early days. Water was caught in cisterns at the bottom of the cliff.

—Old Spanish Trail: The trail went by Castle Cliff.

Castle Creek: (Garfield and Kane Counties.) Dixie National Forest-Sevier River. Asay Bench and George Mountain maps.

In 1893 Thomas Chamberlain called this simply Castle. He ran sheep in the area. (416~)

—Castle Rock: (Asay Bench map.) In the 1880s Clarissa Terry ran a dairy farm for the United Order at the base of Castle Rock. (349~)

Castle Creek: (Iron Co.) Dixie National Forest-Mammoth Creek. Brian Head and Panguitch Lake maps. PRIVATE PROPERTY.

Also called Sidney Creek.

Upper Castle Creek runs through Sidney Valley (Brian Head map).

Lower Castle Creek runs through Castle Valley (Panguitch Lake map).

H. Grant Seaman: "Castle-like mountain formations named by early users." (942~) Unattributed: "At the valley's eastern edge is a definite stretch of rim-rocks and forms a base of Blue Spring Mountain. The rim-rock in places forms miniature castles. Hence the name Castle Valley.... The late Ira W. Hatch operated a sheep and dairy ranch here for a long time." (2053~)

Castle Creek: (San Juan Co.) Clay Hills-Highway 276-San Juan River. Clay Hills, Burnt Spring, Mikes Mesa, Nokai Dome, and No Mans Mesa North maps.

Also called Castle Canyon (761~), Castle Rock Canyon (1626~), Castle Wash (1105~), and Spring Gulch (1796~). Dan Lehi noted that the Navajo call this Mikes Canyon for Paiute Jim Mike who ran his horses here. (1170~) The name has now been attached to nearby Mikes Canyon and Mikes Mesa.

Two similar name derivations are given. Both refer to the San Juan Exploring Expedition of 1879 led by George B. Hobbs.

First, Albert R. Lyman: "Castle Wash got its name from the first Mormon scouts in 1879. [An Anasazi cliff dwelling] wall used to cover the mouth of the cave, and the dwellers there could challenge anyone passing up or down the wash. [The cave] has been used for years by cowmen to store salt and other things, and is but a vestige of what it was in 1879." (1248~)

Hobbs described the cave in 1879: "The next morning we ... came upon a Cliff Dwellers' dwelling, in which there were 7 rooms, the bake oven being in such a perfect state of preservation that by cleaning out the dust it would be ready to bake bread in at this late day." (1356~) The cave is near Green Water Spring (one-eighth mile south of elevation 5591AT on the Clay Hills map).

Second, Hoffman Birney in 1931: "[the Mormon scouts followed an ancient trail] to a seven-room dwelling in a cavern in the cañon wall. They camped there that night, sheltered by walls that had been reared half a dozen centuries before.... The ruin stood near the junction of three great cañons and the men recorded the spot as Castle Fork, the name suggested by the shape of a high butte of eroded sandstone." (235~)

Albert R. Lyman in 1936: "Castle Gulch was bare as a man's hand, not a snoot-full of feed in its whole length." (1249~)

Inscriptions include Hole-in-the-Rock Expedition members J. Smith, 1880; and E.L. Lyman and Joseph Libbywhite, March 5, 1880. (1105~, SAPE.) Other inscriptions include F.H. Miner, Ouray Colo., Feb. 24/87 and I.W. Shupe, Moab, Utah May 29, 1888. (1112~, 1118~, SAPE.)

—Bedrock Spring: Erwin Oliver noted that this prolific spring on Castle Creek is one mile west of Green Water Spring (just south of elevation 5405T on the Burnt Spring map). (1479~) Charles L. Bernheimer called it Bed Rock Spring in 1929 and noted that it had excellent water. (218~)

—Muleshoe Rim: Val Dalton and Erwin Oliver noted that this rim is to the north of Castle Creek and Highway 276 and is two and one-half miles west of Green Water Spring (at elevations BM5240 and 5549AT on the Burnt Spring map). The rim is shaped like a mule shoe. (517~, 1479~)

—Muleshoe Canyon: This northern tributary of Castle Creek is immediately east of the Muleshoe Rim (between elevations 5549AT and 5705T on the Burnt Spring map). (168~)

—North Fork: This northern tributary of Castle Creek is two miles west of Muleshoe Canyon (between elevations 5411T and 5563T on the Burnt Spring map). (1356~)

—Constructed Stock Trail: This used to go down Castle Wash (from the present-day Highway 276) to Zahns Camp on the San Juan River. In the 1950s uranium miners Ed Smart and Fred Baker built a road down Castle Wash to their claims near the San Juan River. Evidence of this road is apparent here and there in the canyon, especially below Johnnies Hole. (11~, SAPE.)

—Spring Gulch: The lower part of the canyon, near the San Juan River, was called Spring Gulch or Spring Creek by ranchers and geologists and is labeled that on old maps. (774~, 1370~)

—Castle Creek Crossing: This historic crossing of the San Juan River started one-quarter mile north of the mouth of Castle Creek and exited just north of the mouth of Copper Canyon (No Mans Mesa map). (472~)

Castle Dale Town: (Emery Co.) Castle Valley-Cottonwood Creek-Highway 10. Castle Dale map.

Also called Cottonwood Creek and Reid Townsite. (1553~)

This is the county seat of Emery County.

There are many castle-like sandstone formations in the vicinity. Although stockmen arrived in the early 1870s, the town was not established until Mormon missionaries arrived in 1877. Their initial intention was to call the town Castle Vale, but somehow in the process of getting a post office, the name was inadvertently changed to Castle Dale. It was called Lower Castle Dale until 1882; Orangeville was Upper Castle Dale. (710~, 970~, 1196~, 1330~, 1531~, 1561~)

Castle Dome: (Washington Co.) Zion National Park-Zion Canyon. Temple of Sinawava map. (7,060')

Ron Kay: "Named by Stephen S. Johnson, a lecturer and real estate salesman from New Jersey in 1922 because it resembles the dome of a castle." (1038~)

Castle Rock: (Grand Co.) La Sal Mountains-Richardson Amphitheater. Fisher Towers map. (6,656')

Eric Bjørnstad noted that this 400-foot tower, which gives Castle Valley its name, is a popular rock climbers' destination. First ascensionist Layton Kor, who climbed the monolith in 1961, is credited with giving the tower its more popular name, Castleton Tower, the name coming from the nearby town of Castleton. (243~) (See Castle Valley—Castleton Town.)

—Chevrolet Ad: In 1964 Chevrolet filmed an ad with one of their vehicles precariously perched on top of Castleton Tower. (239~, 1806~) Guide Lin Ottinger wrote to James H. Knipmeyer in 1965: "The car and accompanying model were lifted to the top of the tower by helicopter. However, by the conclusion of the shoot the winds had gusted up to the point where it was deemed too dangerous to get the female model back down. SUPPOSEDLY, the director had somehow foreseen just this possibility and warm clothing, a sleeping bag and blankets, and food and water had been placed in the car's trunk. After an undoubtedly scary, but relatively comfortable night atop the tall rock spire, the young lady was helicoptered safely down the next morning." (1115~)

—Movies: *Slaughter of the Innocents* was filmed, in part, with Castle Rock in the background. (1809~)

Castle Rock: (Kane Co.) Glen Canyon NRA-Lake Powell. Warm Creek Bay map. (4,321')

Also called Lone Rock. (1931~)

Father Escalante of the Domìnguez-Escalante Expedition of 1776–77 described the rock, though he did not name it: "Today we stopped ... close to a multitude of earthen embankments, small mesas, and peaks of red earth which look like ruins of a fortress at first sight." (1944~)

Edwin G. Woolley, diarist for the Utah Territorial Militia of 1869: "There are several large castellated rocks, which we call Castle Group." (2048~) Howard B. Carpenter used the Castle Rock name in 1901. (345~)

—Castle Spring: This spring, now underwater, was three-quarters of a mile northwest of Castle Rock. C. Gregory Crampton in 1960: "This spring has been developed as a watering place for winter range cattle. A pipe feeds a steady, if small, flow of water into two adjoining tanks." (465~)

Castle Rock: (San Juan Co.) Navajo Indian Reservation-Monument Valley. Monument Pass map. (6,000')

Also called The Castle and Cathedral Rock. (956~)

Famed war correspondent Ernie Pyle in 1939: "The Castle stands 1400 feet high above the surrounding flats, and that on its level top you could build a whole city." (1593~)

Castle Rock Campground: (Sevier Co.) Fishlake National Forest-Tushar Mountains-Joe Lott Creek. Marysvale Canyon map.

A castle-like rock formation stands above the campground.

—Belknap Ranger Station: This was at what is now Castle Rock Campground. (M.68.)

Castle Valley: (Grand Co.) La Sal Mountains-Colorado River-Highway 128. Warner Lake, Rill Creek, Fisher Towers, and Big Bend maps.

Also called Castle Land (1566~), Little Castle Valley (509~, 1695~), and Rock Creek (1838a~).

The town and valley were named for Castle Rock (Fisher Towers map), which towers fifteen hundred feet above the valley floor.

The Don Juan María Antonia de Rivera Expedition of 1765 traversed the valley after dropping off of the Porcupine Rim. Rivera: "[we went through] big valleys [Castle Valley] of very sandy terrain although some with pear cactus. It looks like winding-layered mineral because it has no growth nor fuelwood." (953~)

Frank C. Kendrick of the Stanton-Brown Survey in 1889: "There is the finest scenery here that we have yet seen. Castles & towers of every imaginable kind." (1838a~)

—Castleton Town: This ghost town in Castle Valley is near the "Cemetery" two miles east of Round Mountain (Warner Lake map). It was initially established as a ranch community. The first known settler was Doby Brown. He arrived in the early 1880s. A post office was established in 1882. The town grew in the late 1880s after gold was discovered in nearby Miners Basin. By 1910 the mines had played out and the cattle boom had subsided. The town was abandoned, though it wasn't officially closed until 1967. (346~, 644~, 1530~, 2056~)

—Pace Hill: This is one mile from the mouth of Castle Valley along the main access road (at elevation 4305T on the Big Bend map). The nearby Pace Brothers Ranch was started by John E. Pace in 1888 (99~, 456~, 1627~) or in 1891 (509~).

—The Red Hills: These are at the mouth of Castle Valley (at elevations 4550T and 5163T on the Big Bend map). The name seems to be of recent vintage.

Castle Valley: (Carbon and Emery Counties.)

By the mid-1700s Spanish explorers had traversed Castle Valley, calling it San Rafael Country. (1195~)

Jedediah Smith of the South West Expedition visited the valley in 1826: "I then moved on South having a high range of Mountains on the West [Wasatch Plateau] and crossing a good many small streams running East into a large valley [Castle Valley].... But having learned that the valley was very barren and Rock I did not venture into it. The country is here extremely rough." (1774~) Smith made it south of present-day Castle Dale, then turned west, following the present course of Interstate 70 up Ivie Creek.

The William Wolfskill Expedition of 1830–31 found that the valley had already been named St. Joseph's Valley. (368~, 600~)

The first Mormon settlers of the area, borrowing a name from the Indians, called it Blow Valley for its ceaseless winds. (1195~, 1330~)

Settlement started in the early 1870s with the arrival of cattle ranchers and sheepmen from Mt. Pleasant. In 1875 Orange Seely and his brothers built a road from Mt. Pleasant to Castle Dale and are credited with building the first houses here. (970~)

Almon H. Thompson of the Powell Survey: "Castle Valley [is] a long, narrow depression lying between the eastern escarpment of the Wasatch Plateau and the San Rafael Swell. It is nearly 60 miles in length from north to south, and has an average elevation of 6,000 feet above the sea." (1567~)

Edward A. Geary: "The erosional formations of the San Rafael Swell are the main source of the name Castle Valley. The 'castles' form a dramatic southeastern skyline extending from Window Blind Butte (7,030') to the San Rafael Knob (7,921'), especially striking at sunrise and sunset." (710~)

Casto Canyon: (Garfield Co.) Dixie National Forest-Sevier Plateau-Sevier River. Flake Mountain West, Casto Canyon, and Panguitch maps.

Also called Casto Wash.

Two name derivations are given.

First, Mrs. Irvin Warnock noted that George E. Casto (1849-1929), a Sevier Stake official, settled at the mouth of the canyon in the 1880s. (1972~, 1931~)

Second, Herbert E. Gregory: "Casto Bluff and Casto Canyon were named for a pioneer settler, Abel N. Casto. On some maps this word is misspelled 'Castro.'" (585~, 764~) Clarence Dutton of the Powell Survey called it Castro Wash. (585~)

George C. Fraser followed the stock trail through the canyon in 1915: "The combination of color and sculpture in this canyon surpasses in beauty and interest any other we have seen." (668~)

—Casto Canyon Spring: This large spring in Casto Canyon is one-eighth mile east of the mouth of Hancock Canyon (Casto Canyon map). (SAPE.)

—Casto Bluff: Scott Robinson noted that this "rough, ledgy, abrupt" bluff is at the head of Casto Canyon. (2053~)

—John L. Sevy Swale: Mathew Evans in 1941: "It is a small grassy swale running from the mouth of Castro Canyon east for about 3 miles opening up on East Fork Bench. This swale is used for grazing sheep and cattle during the summer.... It derived its name from John L. Sevy who ranged sheep and homesteaded in this vicinity." (2053~)

Catamount Canyon: (Sevier Co.) Fishlake National Forest-Browns Hole. Yogo Creek and Gooseberry Creek maps.

There are wild cats in the area. (1931~)

Cataract Canyon: (Garfield, San Juan, and Wayne Counties.) Canyonlands National Park and Glen Canyon NRA-Colorado River. Maps start at the head of Cataract Canyon and go downriver to its end at Mille Crag Bend: Spanish Bottom, Cross Canyon, Teapot Rock, Bowdie Canyon East, Clearwater Canyon, Bowdie Canyon West, and Sewing Machine.

Also called Cascade Cañon. (630~)

The Cataract Canyon section of the Colorado River begins at The Confluence of the Colorado and Green rivers and ends about forty miles later at Mille Crag Bend. It is the deepest gorge in Utah, measuring 2,100-feet at the mouth of Clearwater Canyon.

The first John Wesley Powell Expedition named the canyon on July 23, 1869. John Wesley Powell: "We come at once to difficult rapids and falls, that, in many places are more abrupt than in any of the canyons through which we have passed, and we decide to name this Cataract Canyon." (1566~)

John F. Steward of the 1871–72 Powell Expedition described his first view of Cataract Canyon from the cliffs above The Confluence: "Turning our eyes to the south our line of vision falls in the Canyon of Cataracts, which we are soon to enter. The acute salient angles of the sloping walls beset the river upon either side, turning its course at each place and forcing it toward the opposite wall, where it struggles through a narrow rocky channel. The roar of its mad waters seems to warn of its dangers." (1830~)

Francis M. Bishop of the 1871–72 Powell Expedition provided a succinct description: "The rocks are huge masses of ragged angular limestone that lash the immense volume of water, rushing over and around them, into a perfect fury, making the very walls tremble in their rage." (236~)

Franklin A. Nims of the Stanton-Brown Survey of 1889 described not the rapids, but the beauty of the canyon itself, after first noting that they had taken two weeks to get through the cataracts: "We were always mindful of the various changes of the fantastic and some times weird scenes that met our view. Some of the large perpendicular cliffs appeared to have been cleft by an immense circular saw, leaving marks identical to those on a piece of green timber; again others bore traces of delicate and finely drawn designs likened to ancient tapestry; these were harmonious and rich in coloring. Then came a succession of castellated turrets, battlements, spires, pinnacles, etc., which greet us high above in the air." (1464~)

Robert Brewster Stanton gave a dry, yet foreboding, description in 1890: "Cataract Cañon, in its 41 miles, has 75 rapids and cataracts, and 57 of these are crowded into 19 miles, with falls in places of 16 to 20 feet. Being thrown into the water bodily almost every day, and working in water almost up to one's armpits for weeks at a time, guiding the boats through whirlpools and eddies, and when not thus engaged, carrying sacks of flour and greasy bacon on one's back over bowlders half as high as a house, is not the most pleasant class of engineering work to contemplate." (1813~)

A *Salt Lake Herald* article from November 22, 1891, author unknown, about the Stanton-Brown Survey of 1889, described the rapids: "The rapids in this magnificent canyon, with their unceasing roar and tumult, their great churns incessantly going, their atomizing processes throwing into the air thin filmy mists, form indeed a cataract.... Tumbling amidst the boulders on either side, the middle of the stream may show for a distance a sheet of water smooth as ice, and of silver sheen—in another place rifts, as though a shelving ledge were just beneath the surface—and yonder a whirling eddy, exhibiting, as it were, the waters in a waltz. Little imitations of Scylla and Charybdis—the rock and the maelstrom—appear in not infrequent stretches; and it requires a sharp eye and a steady nerve to pilot any craft through so turbulent and wild a course."

Phil Foote (See Tidwell Bottom) claimed to have run Cataract Canyon in 1893: "I went to Green River, staid there two days and went down to Wheeler's ranch and from there by way of Cataract canyon to Cass Hite's place and remained their four months prospecting. Our outfit was the third to go through that canyon and our trip was indeed a rough one. There are seventy-five rapids in twenty-one miles and the way we plunged over them was a caution. When we got about half way through the canyon our boat got beyond our control and we lost all. With nothing to eat we set to work and constructed a raft and finished our journey taking two days. At one time we plunged under water fully twenty-five feet." (418a~)

Lute Johnson, date unknown but most likely in the late 1890s: "Break Niagara into a series of a score of falls extending from its present brink to the head of the whirlpool rapids; convert the buildings of the cities on its banks into granite boulders and pile them into the river, and drop all between canyon walls three thousand feet high, and you would form some conception of Cataract Canyon." (997~)

Brothers Ellsworth and Emery Kolb, who ran the river in 1911–12, called Cataract Canyon "The Graveyard of the Colorado" for the several lives and many injuries and adventures that had happened along this stretch of the Colorado River. (1113~)

Clyde L. Eddy expanded on this in 1929: "Nine expeditions were destroyed during the twenty years between 1889 and 1909 while attempting to pass through Cataract Canyon.... On two occasions sole survivors of shipwrecked parties escaped the river and found their way to the Hite Ranch at the foot of Cataract, arriving there half dead from hunger." (593~)

E.L. Holt in 1927: "We were now in the very heart of the Cataract Canyon.... The walls rose to a height of at least 2000 feet. It was the narrowest deepest chasm we had yet seen and beneath those towering cliffs we felt as pygmies, creeping about with our feeble strength at the bottom of the canyon. It was truly a gloomy place, with the fierce river, the giant walls, and the separation from any known path to the outside world which lay above us." (904~)

Senator Barry Goldwater in 1940: "This canyon is a gorgeous sight—Its depth at places is appalling and at every bend new vistas of beautiful red sandstone cliffs present themselves." (738~)

Arthur A. Baker in 1946: "Much of the southern part of the Green River Desert-Cataract Canyon region has strikingly beautiful scenic effects resulting from the erosion of rocks of various colors and differing degrees of resistance to erosion. Deep narrow canyons, broad grassy flats bounded by nearly vertical walls, small alcoved canyons, wide platforms surmounted by buttes, mesas, and high spires, and high unscalable cliffs horizontally banded with different colors are features of this landscape. The vast panoramas observed through the clear air of this semiarid region from vantage points on the rim of the upland surface and the more restricted views from points on the rims of lower cliffs or from the summits of canyon walls are equaled at few places in the country. The view of Cataract Canyon from many places on the canyon rim is especially impressive, as numerous rapids can be seen at the bottom of the deep narrow gorge, and the roar from the rapids is clearly audible." (100~)

River guide Kenneth I. Ross in 1956: "It has none of the serene elegance of Glen Canyon and few of the architectural glories of Grand Canyon, but it enchants with an eerie magnificence of its own which is compounded of physical splendor, titanic energies and especially, the mood it imposes upon its beholders. Close-pressing walls of Permian rock, carved by the elements into shapes beyond fantasy, tower a vertical half mile overhead and outline jagged rims against a winding ribbon of sky.... Vastness, color, light and shadow, living sound and elemental turmoil all blend to create a mood—to give Cataract Canyon an awesome personality which attracts with an hypnotic compulsion." (1652~)

—Brown Betty Rapid: (Also called Rapid 1.) This is the first of the rapids encountered in Cataract Canyon. It is one mile below Spanish Bottom (east of elevation 4643T on the Spanish Bottom map). George W. Gibson, the cook for the Stanton-Brown Survey of 1889, named one of their boats the Brown Betty for a popular dessert at that time. The expedition flipped the boat at the rapid. Although the boat survived the accident, it was destroyed on a rock further downriver. (201~, 1767~, 1975~) Expedition organizer Frank M. Brown called this the Black Betty in his diary. (299~) Otis "Dock" Marston is credited with naming the rapid in 1962.

E.L. Holt ran Brown Betty Rapid in 1927: "Downstream we shot like a ship in a tornado, then came a sensation of a loss of all support, then up and up shot the boat, the water tumbling over the gunwales." (904~)

Devergne Barber in 1927: "No one slept much last night as we are yet unused to the crashing of the water over the great boulders. It is a noise hard to describe. In the distance it resembles thunder, but on getting closer it changes its tone to a menacing roar. Great waves pile up and fall over each other in their apparent hurry to reach the Gulf." (134~)

—Mile-Long Rapids: (Also called Rapids 13, 14, 15, 16, 17, and 18; Capsize Rapid; Hell to Pay Rapid; One Mile Rapid; and Three-quarter-mile Rapid.) This series of famous Colorado River rapids start one-eighth mile downriver from the mouth of Range Canyon. Rapid 15 is also called Best Rapid. The James S. Best Expedition of 1891 was exploring the mining possibilities in the canyon. They flipped a boat here. Spending a week at the site, they had plenty of time to leave inscriptions. One states: "Camp #7, Hell to Pay, No. 1 Sunk and Down." Another inscription from the same expedition reads: "Col. Grand Canyon Mg Imp. Co. July 6 22, 1891 No. 1 Wrecked." The Grand Canyon Mining and Improvement Company was the official name of the James S. Best Expedition. Individual members of the expedition also left their names or initials, including Js. Best, H. McD (Harry McDonald), Jacobs (John H. Jacobs), and W.H.E. (William Hiram Edwards). (465~, 1105~, 1975~, SAPE.) Other inscriptions include F.G. Faatz, Aug. 27, 1892 and G.M. Wright, Sep. 16, 1892. (1105~, SAPE.)

—Big Drop Rapid: (Also called The Big Drops, Kolb Rapids, and Rapids 21, 22, and 23) (1631~) This is probably the most famous and most deadly sequence of rapids on the Colorado River and certainly in Cataract Canyon. Rapid 21, the first of the series, is also called Big Drop 1. Rapid 22, the second of the series, is also called Big Drop 2, Little Niagra, and The Maelstrom.

Rapid 23 is the most famous of the three and is also called Big Drop 3, Devils Gut, and Satans Gut. (564~, 1113~) River guide Kenneth I. Ross is often credited with naming the rapid. Ross in 1956: "Most notable of these is Satan's Gut which drops 20 feet in no more than 30 yards—a churning fabric of interwoven currents draped over a nightmare slope of boulders." (1652~)

Robert O. Collins: "After successfully shooting the slot between the rocks and the explosion wave in the middle of the third part of the Big Drop, a passenger [who was with Kenneth I. Ross on a trip in August 1952] exclaimed it was like passing through 'Satan's Gut.'" (442~)

Otis "Dock" Marston in 1973: "In recent years the unfortunate name SATANS GUT has been applied to the lower of the three rapids." (1292~)

Many luminaries have described The Big Drops.

Stephen Vandiver Jones of the Powell Expedition of 1871–72: "The water falls almost straight down 4 or 5 feet and the descent is 20 or more feet within 3/8 of a mile. Named these 'Ross Falls.'" (1023~)

Bert Loper called this, in passing, the Big Drop in 1907, becoming the first to use that name: "I found out that we had 85 thousand feet [cfs] of water and in the big drop the river was a fury." (1223~)

Doris Nevills in 1940: "This rapid is the most terrifying thing I've seen yet. It has the most terrific roar imaginable. You can't hear a person shouting at the top of his voice even though he is only 20 feet away. The water dashes over these huge rocks with an inhuman violence." (1436~)

Robert O. Collins: "Men have marveled at the Grand Canyon but have feared Cataract.... Cataract Canyon is unique, the biggest drop along any comparable stretch of the Colorado River, embracing some of the wildest, most challenging, and violent white water on Western rivers." (442~)

Robert H. Webb: "Of the fourteen deaths recorded in the river history of Canyonlands National Park, eleven occurred in the Big Drops.... Unless one is a highly experienced guide who has recently seen the river, or is a river runner with suicidal tendencies, scouting is mandatory." (1975~)

Inscriptions include "Cat. Camp 2 E.C. & E.L. Kolb, 10-28-1911." (See Appendix One—Ellsworth and Emery Kolb Expedition of 1911.) Another reads "Capsized No. 3, 7.15. [19]40, Nevills." (1115~, SAPE.)

—Hells Half Mile: (Also called Rapid 27.) This once formidable rapid was just below the mouth of Imperial Canyon. It was named by Robert Brewster Stanton in 1889. Nathaniel Galloway of the Stone-Galloway Expedition of 1909: "We passed that part of the river to-day which Stanton named 'Hells Half Mile.' But he was off in the distance. There is more than half a mile of it, possibly that's the hell of it." (701~)

—Dark Canyon Rapid: This is now underwater. Before inundation, it was considered the most difficult rapid in Cataract Canyon. Ellsworth Kolb of the William R. Chenoweth USGS Expedition of 1921: "The rapid has not improved with age, in fact it's much worse; has about 50 rocks badly placed on the south side and has a dangerous turn, filled with great rocks." (1669~)

Cat Canyon: (Emery Co.) Castle Valley-San Rafael River. Hadden Holes map.

—Sitterud Bundle: Lee Mont Swasey: "The famous Sitterud Bundle was found there." (1853~) LaVar Sitterud found this archaeological artifact in 1968. It is an elk hide bundle of artifacts used by Fremont Indians in about AD 1350. The bundle contained stone tools, including knives, scrapers and drills as well as cordage, a snare, and food items. The bundle is now in the Museum of the San Rafael in Castle Dale. (214~)

Cat Canyon: (Emery Co.) San Rafael Swell-Muddy Creek. Copper Globe, Big Bend Draw, and Ireland Mesa maps. Dee Anne Finken noted that the canyon was used by ranchers to herd their cattle from the Copper Globe area to Muddy Creek. (641~)

This is not quite correct. Two short falls in the lower canyon prevented cattle from following Cat Canyon from top to bottom. Sheep were able to do this, though.

Cattle were brought into Cat Canyon from Muddy Creek via the Dizzy Trail. (See Dizzy Trail Canyon for details.) That avoided the short drops in lower Cat Canyon. Once in Cat Canyon the cattle were herded upcanyon for about three miles. They exited onto The Dikes by way of a constructed stock trail (one-quarter mile to the southwest of elevation 6123 on the Big Bend Draw map). Various trails then led to the upland areas. Livestock would also be taken up Kimball Draw and into upper Cat Canyon, following the general route of the present-day dirt road. (SAPE.)

—Mystery Metal: This is in a small northern tributary of Cat Canyon that is one-quarter mile east of elevation 6740 on the Copper Globe map. When asked for an explanation, Ray Wareham told the story: "The Johnson brothers were in there for quite a while and they took a lot of sheet metal and a welder and they were goin' to make a huge reservoir. They got it about all welded together. They stretched an inch-thick cable across the canyon and they were going to lean this metal up and catch the water. There was ten acres of slickrock right there. The water just pours off them. They got just about done and the welder kicked out on 'em, so they come back to Salina to get another welder, and when they went back out, there'd been a flood come down through there and it'd wrecked everything they'd made and so they lost it." (1967~, SAPE.)

—Blackum Trail: This constructed stock trail, no longer used, starts one-quarter mile down Muddy Creek from the mouth of Cat Canyon and goes east up to the highland areas. The trail also crosses Muddy Creek and goes west up to Lone Tree Wedge. (See Lone Tree Wedge.) Wayne Gremel: "People by the name of Blackum ran sheep in this country years ago and they built it." (780~, SAPE.) This was "Red" Blackum for whom Red Canyon was named. (641~)

—New Trail: Wayne Gremel noted that this replaced the section of the Blackum Trail that went east up the cliffs. The New Trail starts one-eighth mile downcanyon from Poncho Wash (one-quarter mile east-southeast of elevation 5677 on the Ireland Mesa map) and goes east up the initial cliff band and then to The Dike. Wayne noted that Dewey Jensen and Elmer Adley built the trail. (780~) Inscriptions include Dewey Jensen, 1972. (SAPE.)

—The Mail Box: The Mail Box was on Muddy Creek one mile downstream from the mouth of Cat Canyon. Wayne and Carrie Lou Gremel noted that Dermus Jensen (born 1912) and his brother, Dewey Jensen (born 1918) used to run livestock on Muddy Creek. Carrie Lou Gremel:

"As the story goes ... along about February or March 1958 someone told Dermus Jensen that one of Dewey's Hereford cows was crawling with lice and was along the Muddy Creek on the desert. Dewey and Fay were living at Dragerton at the time. Dermus loaded up Topsey, a white mare owned by Jens Jensen. He took along a five gallon can and a fruit jar of de-lousing powder. Unloading at The Wedge he rode down the Blackum Trail where sure enough he found the lousy cow with TI on her right hip. Dermus roped the cow and tied her to a tree. He then mixed up the powder with water from the Muddy in the 5 gal. can, and with a rag on a long stick he gave her a good dousing. It was getting late by the time he turned the cow loose so he put the 5 gal. can in the tree with the jar inside. He left a note in the jar.... During the following years, all kinds of paper from toilet paper to notes written on brown paper bags were left in the jar. At one time there were two jars in the bucket. This five gallon can became known as the 'Mail Box.' In 1972 a book was left in the Mail Box for notes and it was brought into Emery about 1982." (780~)

Thanks to Carrie Lou, several of the entries were recorded. They include: "Dewey and Dermus/Two Black Dogs/ Feed Fair/Weather Fair/Going Down the Creek; Here again/Birds are singing/Nice Day/Is going to be Warm/ Horses Floride and Blue Father/No dogs today/Going down to turn cow loose that I tied up yesterday." (780~)

Cathedral Butte: (San Juan Co.) Manti-LaSal National Forest-Dark Canyon Plateau-North Elk Ridge. Cathedral Butte map. (7,940')

Also called Birthday Cake and Salt Creek Mesa Butte. (1800~)

Cathedral Canyon: (San Juan Co.) Navajo Indian Reservation-Cummings Mesa-Glen Canyon. Cathedral Canyon map.

Katie Lee: "Very soon we're confronted with long, dark, cold pools, god knows how deep, and walls so tight against us we can't swing our arms for a stroke. Then the gravel, then bigger and sharper rocks.... On to more stringy pools, up over boulders slick with algae into an immense cathedral.... I wanted to call it Cathedral Canyon, but was sure someone else had already named it. Apparently not. Cathedral it is to this day." (1162~)

Again, Katie Lee: "In one [amphitheater] there was this great big rock pile that stood up at half the height of this room, with the flaking off where the river had come down around and washed everything away except that. And the overhang was almost closing off the light. In the center was this great big podium and its top looked like a book, a bible, had fallen open. The pages were leaves of sandstone. I said, 'My God, this place is Mother Nature's little cathedral. This is where she does all her secret things.'" (1163~)

Joseph L. Dudziak in 1962: "Entered a canyon of truly magnificent proportions—truly cathedral-like; in sheer size, this must be the greatest! There were great undercut alcoves on the sweeping curves of the stream. Sometimes very little sky was visible." (577~)

Eliot Porter in 1963: "In Cathedral Canyon ... the floor disappears into a water-filled trough.... Swimming through it is a dreamlike adventure. Shivering, we glide along like seals ... through still depths into an inscrutable solitude ... in a journey reminiscent of Xanadu, 'through caverns measureless to man'.... At the end a wisp of a waterfall drops from unseen heights overhead, slipping over a smooth and algaed chute into a slatey pool." (1556~)

Cathedral in the Desert: (Kane Co.) Glen Canyon NRA-Clear Creek. Davis Gulch map.

An early visitor, Mrs. Howd Veater from Escalante, thought the canyon looked like a cathedral with pennons hanging along the walls and suggested the name. (1382~)

J. Allan Crocket in 1956: "It is actually a tremendous cavern, the most impressive single natural feature I have ever seen." (491~)

Stephen C. Jett in 1963: "Some of us hiked up it, and although it was a pretty canyon, we began to wonder why all the praise. But then we found the reason. Around a bend, the canyon suddenly narrowed and headed in a tremendous alcove similar to but much larger and more symmetrical than Music Temple in Glen Canyon. Overhanging walls encircled us, and to enter this huge sanctuary was a moving experience.... A beautiful pool adorned the alcove, a small waterfall cascading into it adding a soft musical sound to the otherwise complete silence." (976~)

Jean Bennett in 1964: "We passed one spectacular amphitheater after another, but finally around a particularly sharp bend we saw one of Nature's most perfect masterpieces.... On one wall water fell from a sharp cleft in the rock into a clear pool below. Moss and ferns covered the lower walls and the cool, clean smell of damp earth was everywhere.... As we were watching, a bright shaft of light appeared sending its magic finger into the grotto and contrasting with the shadowy walls draped with streaks of stain." (208~)

Fred Griffin, Jr. in 1966: "As we faced the waterfall, it seemed indeed, Nature's altar, lighted by a window to Heaven. In this place I thought no attitude of mind or heart would be possible, except one of worship.... There

is nothing left to say except that I felt like falling on my knees in thankfulness for having been permitted this experience, and in contrition for the blindness of men who permit the destruction of such handiworks of God." (790~)

David Brower in 1964: "Everywhere you looked you knew what a setting meant to a place. And in the Cathedral, whether you looked up at evening or in the morning at this miracle of color and design, or whether you looked at the gardens by the altar or the stream that flowed from the nave, you knew what this place meant to its setting. There would never be anything like it again." (1199~)

Harry Aleson in 1964: "This must be the most beautiful spot in any of the side canyons of the Escalante River. Music Temple would be dwarfed by The Cathedral in the Desert. There is a very large, water-smooth and level floor with green moss patches on the golden sands in subdued light." (22~)

Steve Allen in 1997, after having seen the Cathedral before inundation in the 1960s: "And what a wonderful place it was! The tan Navajo walls, streaked with a thick patina of brown-and-black desert varnish, curved skyward in Gothic arcs that nearly met at the top, leaving just a thin slit of sunlight to illuminate the small stream that ran down from the chancel, through the nave, and disappeared under a wall beyond the narthex. With the filling of Lake Powell, the cathedral was inundated and we lost a very special place." (47~)

Tad Nichols in 1999: "The first time I saw Cathedral in the Desert [in the 1950s], I couldn't believe it.... After following the stream bottom, you saw a rock wall ahead of you that you thought you were going to walk into. You went into sort of an entrance there, and you turned a corner, and the place hit you like that. It had a lovely waterfall at the end of it with a great big pool. In front of the pool was a sandbar covered with a light green moss, which was beautiful. It complemented the rest of the color of the canyon.... You can't do justice to that place by talking, even by pictures. You had to stand there and see it and feel it. I'm sorry most people couldn't do that." (1449~)

Cathedral Mountain: (Washington Co.) Zion National Park-Zion Canyon. Temple of Sinawava map. (6,930')

Ron Kay noted that this was named by Stephen S. Johnson in 1922 for its cathedral-like shape. (1038~)

Cathedral Mountain: (Wayne Co.) Capitol Reef National Park-Cathedral Valley. Cathedral Mountain map. (6,924')

Also called Walters Castle. (1873~)

This is the most famous cluster of "cathedrals" in Cathedral Valley. Charles Kelly called these the Pillars of Hercules in 1945. (1077~)

In 1960 Harry Aleson called a tower in Cathedral Valley "Waters' Tower." It is assumed that since Cathedral Mountain is the largest tower of the group, this was his "Waters' Tower." Aleson: "We made a side trip to photo Waters' Tower, named by the Jackson Brothers in honor of Herman Waters, formerly President of Telluride Power Co. of SLC." (26~)

Cathedral Valley: (Wayne Co.) Capitol Reef National Park-Middle Desert. Cathedral Mountain map.

Also called Little Egypt, Middle Desert (1657~), The Sinbad, Upper Valley (1873~), and West Cathedral Valley (1077~).

The John C. Fremont Expedition of 1853–54 traversed the Cathedral Valley area. (1105~) Expedition diarist Solomon Nunes Carvalho produced a stylized steel engraving of the valley entitled "Natural Obelisks." (1559~)

The valley was named by Capitol Reef National Monument's first caretaker, Charles Kelly: "To stockmen it was just a bad place to hunt for cows." (1077~)

C. Gregory Crampton: "The eroded formations ... with their fluted and domed shapes resemble the cathedrals of the old world. Hence the name." (473~)

Joyce Muench: "Fluted and domed in green, like tarnished copper, they were ages in the building. Ornate weathering has shaped statues set in niches. Filigree decorations adorn every exposed cornice. Robed saints, hooded monks, angels and cherubims are not hard to find in the confusion of forms.... True, the elongated 'doors,' carved in vertical embroidery from roof to basin floor, will never open to admit a congregation, but there are alcoves, roomy chapels without roofs, through which desert incense drifts." (1397~)

Ward J. Roylance: "Here the Gothic arch and vertical lines combine in an endless flow of elegant, upward-sweeping, three-dimensional forms. These arched and fluted forms are graceful and noble in the ultimate sense, with symmetry and harmony that approach the divine ideal. Emotion and a touch of mysticism are indispensable in fully appreciating the art of Cathedral Valley." (1657~)

—Valley of the Moon: Unattributed: "The upper valley, because of its shape, is known as The Valley of the Moon." (1873~)

—Cathedral Valley Corral: This corral in Cathedral Valley was listed on the National Register of Historic Places in 1999. It is one-half mile southeast of Needle Mountain (one-quarter mile east of elevation 6436). The corral was built in about 1900. (1419~)

—Cathedral Valley Line Shack: (Also called Morrell Cabin and Morrell Line Cabin.) This cabin in Cathedral Valley was listed on the National Register of Historic Places in 1999. It is three-quarters of a mile southwest of Needle Mountain (one-quarter mile west of elevation 6436). The cabin was built in the 1920s on Thousand Lake Mountain. Lesley Morrell moved the cabin to its present location in about 1935. (1419~)

Cathedral Wash: (Coconino Co., Az.) Glen Canyon NRA-Vermilion Cliffs-Colorado River. Navajo Bridge and Lees Ferry, Az. maps.

This was also called Twomile Wash because it is two miles from Lees Ferry. (1612~)

—Cathedral Rock: (Navajo Bridge map.) (Also called Church Rock and Sunset Rock.) (1357~)

Cat Pasture: (Kane Co.) GSCENM-Escalante Desert-Hole-in-the-Rock Road. Big Hollow Wash, Basin Canyon, and Egypt maps.

Also called The Cat (1931~) and Wildcat Pasture (55~).

Pratt Gates noted that there used to be many bobcats in the area. (709~)

Catstair Canyon: (Kane Co.) GSCENM-Sand Gulch. West Clark Bench and Fivemile Valley maps.

Also called Catstairs Gorge and Sand Gulch. (765~)

James H. Knipmeyer: "It received it name because only a cat could wind its way through the tight curves." (1115~)

Herbert E. Gregory in 1948 noted that Catstairs Gorge was "a narrow, remarkably rough defile." (765~) C. Gregory Crampton noted that an Indian route went over The Cockscomb in the vicinity of Catstair Canyon. (476~)

Cat Well: (Kane Co.) GSCENM-Hole-in-the-Rock Road. Basin Canyon map.

Also called Wildcat Well. (55~)

Pratt Gates: "There were some sheep troughs there when I was a kid. This was the division between the sheep and the cattle. The well was put in in the 1950s." (709~)

Causeway, The: (San Juan Co.) Manti-LaSal National Forest-Abajo Mountains-Elk Ridge. Mount Linnaeus and Chippean Rocks maps.

Also called The Saddle.

The Causeway is the high ridge that joins the Abajo Mountains and Elk Ridge. It was a popular route used by early cattlemen. County Road 225 now crosses the ridge. The name was proposed by Herbert E. Gregory in 1936. (1931~)

—Skyline Trail: (Also called West Mountain Trail.) This is the "Pack Trail" on the Mount Linnaeus map that starts at The Causeway (at elevation 8214T), goes east between Bob Park Peak and Mount Linnaeus, and ends on Jackson Ridge. Kent Frost noted that this was a major cattle trail across the Abajo Mountains. (690~) Inscriptions carved into aspen trees along the trail date to 1921. Many are Spanish names, reflecting the years when sheep were the primary stock run on the mountain. (SAPE.)

Cave Arch: (Wayne Co.) Canyonlands National Park-Maze District-Ernies Country. Elaterite Basin map.
Robert H. Vreeland: "It was named Cave Arch [by local cowboys] because it is located on the lip of an enormous cave." (1951~)

Cave Canyon: (Coconino Co., Az.) Navajo Indian Reservation-Colorado River. Lees Ferry, Az. map.
The canyon was named for Hislop Cave. (See Threemile Bar—Hislop Cave.)

Cave Canyon: (San Juan Co.) Alkali Point-Montezuma Creek. Bradford Canyon, McCracken Spring, Bug Canyon, and Hatch Trading Post maps.
Also called Cave Gulch.
Cleal Zemira Bradford: "Originally, seven separate towers had stood as sentry at the head of Cave Canyon. Their guard duty, or spiritual assignment, had seemingly ended when the Anasazi Indians left for canyons and mesas to the south.... Eventually, time wind and storm took its toll. Five of the rock structures had eroded to weather and little remained other than rubble." 1911~) The name was in place by 1907. (1031~)

Cave Flat: (Garfield Co.) Henry Mountains-Bullfrog Creek. Mount Pennell and Cave Flat maps.
This large flat area is a favorite roaming ground for the Henry Mountain buffalo herd. Charles B. Hunt noted that one particular area was known as Cave Camp and was often used by range riders. (925~)
Bliss Brinkerhoff: "Bullfrog had good water and there's a ledge that comes and kinda curves and there's just a little shelter or part of a cave. Just across the creek they had a place where they could fence and put their horses overnight. It's not actually a cave, but yet, it'll surprise you when it's rainin' and stormin'. The way it lays, during storms, there is about six or eight feet of dryness under that ledge. Back in the old days Clip Farnsworth was abreakin' a horse. He got on it one morning right above what we call The Cave. The horse lit in to buckin' and headed for that ledge and Clip was just barely able to get out of the saddle when the horse went over the ledge. It landed in the bottom and killed himself." (291~)

Cave House: (Uintah Co.) Uintah and Ouray Indian Reservation-East Tavaputs Plateau-Willow Creek. Wolf Point map.
This is not a house in a cave; rather, it is a ranch, built in stages from the 1920s to the 1950s, that is tucked neatly into a dense copse of trees. (SAPE.)
Inscriptions include Morse Lee, Vernal Utah, March 23, 1939.

Cave Lakes Canyon: (Kane Co.) Vermilion Cliffs-Three Lakes Canyon. Kanab and White Tower maps. PRIVATE PROPERTY.
Jesse L. Nusbaum in 1922: "Cave Lakes Cañon derives its name from two grottoes in its walls, both of which contain springs copious enough to spread out and form considerable pools under their overhanging roofs. The larger cave is 100 feet wide at the mouth and extends back about 300 feet into the red sandstone cliff; the 'lake' is not more than 7 or 8 feet deep, but it furnishes a never-failing water supply for the fields below." (1474~) The name was in place by 1872. (546~, 1877~)
The town of Kanab obtained their fresh water from the canyon in the old days. (770~) Cal Johnson noted that his wife's father, Q. Robinson, homesteaded at Cave Lakes: "In fact Q. Robinson gave Kanab its first culinary water. They piped it from [Cave Lakes Canyon] in the old wooden, eight inch pipe with wire wrapped around the wood." (984~)
Inscriptions include F.S. Dellenbaugh C.R. Ex Buffalo. N.Y. Jan. 25 and H [enry] Kiesel, 1873. Dellenbaugh and Kiesel were members of the Powell Survey; Dellenbaugh was the chronicler and Kiesel was a draftsman. (1105~, 1115~, 1877~)
—DuPont Cave: The canyon is most famous for DuPont Cave. General T. Coleman Du Pont financed a Museum of the American Indian Expedition, led by Jesse L. Nusbaum, to the cave in the fall of 1920. (1474~) Frederick S. Dellenbaugh: "General du Pont, for recognition of his interest—the cave was named after him and is known locally as Cave du Pont." (546~)
—The Meadows: This pasture area is one mile up Cave Lakes Canyon from its junction with Three Lakes Canyon (immediately south of elevation 5691 on the White Tower map). Jesse L. Nusbaum: "Up Three Lakes Canyon to its junction with Cave Lake Cañon. Another mile up the barren reaches of the latter brings one to the 'Meadows,' a fertile widening of the valley in which Mormon pioneers, attracted by abundant water and fine natural pasturage, settled more than forty years ago." (1474~) The name was in place by 1874. (687~)

Cave Point: (Kane Co.) GSCENM-Fiftymile Bench-Hole-in-the-Rock Road. Sooner Bench map. (5,412')
Also called Cave Ridge.
Edson Alvey: "The name was taken from numerous caves west of the ridge." (55~)
—Cave Spring: Edson Alvey noted that this was called Joe Predence Spring: "The name was derived from a Basque by the name of Prudencio Zaballa who operated a whiskey still in former days. He was called Joe Predence, locally." (55~)

Cave Spring: (Kane Co.) Glen Canyon NRA-Grand Bench. Mazuki Point map.
This large spring, once developed, is under a large overhang. At last count, the water there was not potable. (SAPE.)
—Constructed Stock Trail: This leads down the cliffs to the spring. (SAPE.)

Cave Spring: (San Juan Co.) Canyonlands National Park-Needles District-Salt Creek. The Loop map.
Also called Cowboy Cave.
This was listed on the National Register of Historic Places in 1988.
First used by the Anasazi, the cave later became an important line camp for cowboys on the range. When the area was designated a national park, the first rangers lived in the cave. The national park now uses the cave as an outdoor museum. (866~, 1429~, 1821~)
W. Robert Moore in 1962: "Cave Spring is no imposing landmark. It isn't even much of a spring. The cave is an eroded undercut in the base of a sandstone cliff, the spring only a tiny puddle of water in a stone depression. It accumulates from an almost imperceptible drip that comes from a crack in the rocks." (1381~)
Inscriptions include ones from Al and Jim Scorup. They ran livestock in the area starting in the 1890s. (1105~)

Caves Spring: (Grand Co.) Dome Plateau-Squaw Park-Yellow Jacket Canyon. Cisco SW map.
(See Squaw Park.)
There are several very large caves on the south face of a long escarpment. Joe Taylor noted that one of them contains a fine spring that was developed by CCC. The caves were favored by stockmen starting in the early days. (1866~)
An important inscription is from J.D. Smith, 1844, R.M.F.T. Co. This is from Jedediah Smith of the Rocky Mountain Fur Trading Company. (1110~) Other inscriptions near the spring include G.H. Ross, 1891; R.A. Dunn, 1898; W. Holeman, Dec. 6, 1899; and M.R. Walker, Jan. 14, 1900. One unattributed inscription states: "To Hell with Sheep Hearders [*sic*]." Another states "God Dam Cowboys." (1866~, SAPE.)

CCC Pond: (Emery Co.) Castle Valley-Desert Lake. Cleveland map.
This still-used stock pond was built by the CCC. (SAPE.)

Cedar: (Emery Co.) Cedar Mountain-Denver and Rio Grande Western Railroad. Cedar map.
This was a water and switching station for the Denver and Rio Grande Western Railroad. For several years in the 1940s and '50s a group of railroad section employees had homes here. (1931~) Unattributed: "The next stop is a little higher and the soil is adapted to desert trees, and the name of CEDAR is fitting." (606~) (See Denver and Rio Grande Western Railroad.)

Cedar Breaks National Monument: (Iron Co.) Markagunt Plateau. Brian Head and Navajo Lake maps.
Also called The Breaks. (376~)
Herbert E. Gregory: "To the Piutes the giant alcove [that forms Cedar Breaks] was *Uncapicunump*—the circle of painted cliffs." (768~, 1512~)
Cedar Breaks National Monument was established by President Franklin D. Roosevelt on August 22, 1933. It encompasses 5,836 acres. (384~)
Two related name derivations are given.
First, unattributed: "The name comes from 'Cedar,' a misnomer for the Juniper trees common in the area, and 'Breaks' was an early term meaning badlands." (942~)
Second, Timothy W. Canaday: "The term 'breaks' refers to the abrupt edge of the Markagunt Plateau in this region and was used by pioneers and settlers to describe high-elevation areas that quickly descend, or 'break' to lower elevations." (338~) The name was in place by 1869. (376~)
In the early 1900s Charles Adams, an Irishman, ran livestock in the Cedar Breaks Visitor Center area, giving the area the name Little Ireland or New Ireland. (338~, 363~)
J. Cecil Alter in 1927: "Had there been a sputtering of nature's original excavating machines still digging away in the depths, augmented by a busy swarm of masons, sculptors and painters fixing up the place, the group of rollicking flower pickers in our party could not have turned from the sparkling meadows and lined up more interestedly on the brink of the bowl, there to ejaculate their unfeigned surprise and admiration." (50~)
Jonreed Lauritzen in 1947: "Here a vast mountainside has been shorn of its mantle of green by centuries of swift erosion, leaving a wide arena striped and splotched and radiant with color. Artists have tried to count its earth

colors—a seemingly futile conceit, for its tonal nuances are as indistinguishable as the qualities of a great spirit. This is no happy-hunting ground for the collector of statistics. It is purely visual impression of symphonic beauty." (1149~)

Herbert E. Gregory in 1950: "In general appearance Cedar Breaks is a broad, high walled semi-circular alcove—a great amphitheater that incloses many smaller recesses similar in form. Its steeply sloping sides are furrowed and seemingly supported by buttress-like ridges that rise from the floor to the rim. The alcove is drained by innumerable steep, sharply incised stream channels—the runways of ephemeral streams.... Along the stream courses, on the interstream ridges, and on the bounding walls, the bare rocks have been carved into picturesque architectural forms, made more attractive by vivid coloring." (768~)

Luella Adams Dalton in 1962: "Cedar Breaks is one of nature's masterpieces. Its wonderful cliffs of varied colors; rose, coral, lavender, white ambers and gold are blended in such perfect harmony. It is a veritable symphony in color, bordered by stately Engelmann spruce, and grassy nooks and valleys full of large white and blue columbine, larkspur and gentians; wild flower gardens by the acres. It's some of the most picturesque, beautiful country in all the world." (516~)

—Cedar Breaks Lodge: This is at the south end of Cedar Breaks (Navajo Lake map) on what was called Buckskin Knob. It was built in the early 1920s by the Union Pacific Railroad Company. (887~)

—CCC Camp: This was one-half mile northeast of Cedar Breaks Lodge and was in use from 1933 to 1935. (339~)

—Cabin Flat: This is on Mammoth Creek one mile east of Cedar Breaks Lodge. William Lowder: "There used to be a nice cabin in the flat and that is why it got its name." (1515~)

Cedar Camp Canyon: (Grand Co.) East Tavaputs Plateau-Meadow Canyon. Cedar Camp Canyon map.
The Cedar Camp, located at the head of the canyon at Cedar Camp Spring, was built by the BLM. After the land was given to the State of Utah, the camp was removed. (1931~) The spring itself is large and is developed with still-used troughs. (SAPE.)

Cedar Canyon: (Iron Co.) Kolob Terrace-Cedar Valley. Webster Flat, Flanigan Arch, and Cedar City maps.
(See Coal Creek—Iron Co. for name derivation.)
Crow Creek goes through upper Cedar Canyon and Coal Creek goes through lower Cedar Canyon.

Cedar Canyon: (San Juan Co.) Glen Canyon NRA-Mancos Mesa-Glen Canyon. Chocolate Drop, Mancos Mesa, and Knowles Canyon maps.
Charles L. Bernheimer in 1929: "It has no cedar." (218~)
—Mancos Canyon: Sandy Johnson noted that this is the long unnamed tributary to the north of Cedar Canyon. It is immediately north of Jacobs Spring and Johnny Coldwater Spring (Mancos Mesa map). (1002~)
—Cedar Tank: Val Dalton noted that this large pothole, used to water livestock, is two and one-quarter miles up Cedar Canyon from Jacobs Spring (one-quarter mile south of elevation 4914T on the Mancos Mesa map). A stock trail exits the canyon to the south of the tank. (517~, SAPE.) Herbert E. Gregory in 1927: "Tony my horse jumped into rock pool [Cedar Tank] and soaked the camera." (761~)
—The Squeeze: Val Dalton noted that this is a very narrow place between the rim of Red Canyon and the head of Cedar Canyon (one-half mile northwest of elevation 5975T on the Chocolate Drop map). The Exxon Road traverses The Squeeze. (517~) (See Mancos Mesa—Exxon Road.)

Cedar City: (Iron Co.) Hurricane Cliffs-Cedar Valley-Interstate 15 and Highways 14 and 56. Cedar City map.
Also called Little Muddy. (2053~)
Also spelled Ceedar City. (58~)
Paiute Indians call this *we-see-ap-to*, or "grove of scrub cedars." (311~)
John Urie: "The name was given because of the abundance of Cedar Trees [juniper trees] that abounded all over the country." (1013~) Kate B. Carter: "This town was known at once by its name because of the beautiful cedar trees on the chosen spot." (354~) George A. Smith is credited with naming the community. (1715~)
The Domínguez-Escalante Expedition of 1776–77 passed a few miles west of what would become Cedar City. (1944~)
The Parley P. Pratt Exploring Expedition to Southern Utah of 1849–50 explored the area. Pratt noted that it was a "firstrate good place we were sent to find as a location for our next Southern Colony." (1762~)
Brigham Young decided that the area should be used as a base for iron smelting. To that end, in November 1851 he sent a contingent of thirty settlers, under the direction of Henry Lunt, to what would become Cedar City. The first camp was one mile north of the present townsite. Since the pioneers lived in their wagons, it was called Wagon Box Camp.
In 1852 a *Deseret News* article called this Brother Dame's Settlement, named for Dixie pioneer William Horne

Dame. (1776~) By mid-1852 a small town had arisen and was initially called Coal City or Coal Creek Settlement for the creek the town was built on.

The settlers soon built Cedar Fort and the name was changed. The fort enclosed a half acre of land and was made of rock and logs fourteen inches thick. By 1857 there were more than seven hundred people in the new town. (306~, 357~, 1013~, 1192~, 1628~)

Louisa Barnes Pratt in 1857: "The people in Cedar had built a new town, close to the brow of the mountains. Having been troubled with floods, they thought best to build on higher land. Their buildings were adobies, some very high and nicely finished.... Great was the poverty of Cedar City." (360~)

—Frontier Homestead State Park Museum: (Also called Iron Mission State Park.) This eleven acre park in Cedar City, established in 1973, has exhibits covering the pioneer history of the area from the early 1850s to the 19teens with an emphasis on the Iron Mission.

—Walker Fort: (Also called Shirts Settlement.) A *Deseret News* article on December 11, 1852 noted this settlement. Lucile Richens: "Seems to have been named for the Indian Chief, Walker. Was located 6 miles south of Cedar Fort." (2053~)

Cedar Creek: (Emery Co.) Castle Valley-Huntington Creek. Poison Spring Bench and Huntington maps.

J. Albert Jones: "In the mouth of the canyon there was many large cedar [juniper] trees growing very thrifty along its banks so they called the stream 'Cedar Creek,' and the canyon 'Cedar Creek Canyon.'" (1015~)

Grove Karl Gilbert of the Powell Survey called this Bessie Creek for his one-year-old daughter. (722~)

—Cordingly Hollow: These are the first small drainages immediately east of the mouth of Cedar Creek. William Cordingly and family moved to Huntington in 1880. (1015~)

Cedar Creek: (Garfield and Wayne Counties.) Henry Mountains-Sweetwater Creek. Mount Ellen, Dry Lakes Peak, Stevens Mesa, and Town Point maps.

—Constructed Stock Trail: In 1921 David D. Rust told of a stock trail "down steep rough trail via cedar creek to cottonwoods on Dry Wash." (1672~)

Cedar Mesa: (San Juan Co.) Grand Gulch Plateau-Glen Canyon NRA. Cedar Mesa North, Cedar Mesa South, Kane Gulch, Pollys Pasture, Slickhorn Canyon East, and Snow Flat Spring Cave maps.

Also called Cedar Base (1356~), Cedar Range (490~), and Grand Gulch Plateau (774~).

Although Cedar Mesa is labeled on only six maps, by common usage it is a much larger area that goes from the Red House Cliffs to the west, Highway 95 to the north, Comb Wash to the east, and the San Juan River to the south. Locally, the Grand Gulch Plateau and Cedar Mesa names are interchangeable.

Robert S. McPherson noted that the Navajo name is '*Atsi' Dahididlo'ii*, or "Hanging Meat Mesa": "This landmark obtained its name from a hunter who tied his deer meat in a tree to cool and dry before cutting into smaller pieces." (1335~)

The Cedar Mesa name came from what pioneers called cedar trees. They were actually juniper trees. The name was first used by the Hole-in-the-Rock Expedition. George B. Hobbs in February 1880: "Five days I spent in these cedars and gulches with the snow up to my chin." (257~) Platte D. Lyman crossed the mesa in March 1880: "What we call the Cedar Ridge extending 30 miles each way and nearly everywhere covered with a dense growth of cedar and pinion pine." (1259~)

B.D. Critchlow of the Denver and Rio Grande Survey of 1880–81: "The country was terribly rough and the trail led along the crests of ridges up the face of almost perpendicular slopes and around and across the heads of canyons, while at different points a view of the country could be obtained. As far as the eyes could reach nothing but a bed of sandstone was to be seen while in every direction the walls of cañons could be traced." (490~)

—Books: Buck Lee noted that this was also called the Enchanted Mesa, a name used by Zane Grey in his book *Riders of the Purple Sage*. (784~, 2053~)

Cedar Mountain: (Emery Co.) Castle Valley-Price River-Book Cliffs. Flattop Mountain, Chimney Rock, Bob Hill Knoll, and Cow Flats maps. (7,665')

Also called Cedar Ridge (M.41.), Red Plateau (M.76a.), and Reds Plateau (M.74.).

The mountain is covered with juniper trees, which are locally called cedars. Early explorers called this the Red Plateau for the color of its south-facing cliffs. An 1876 map shows it as the Low Rocky Cedar Ridge. (M.61.)

Virl Winder: "I homesteaded Cedar Mountain. It was a nice, quiet place to be. Although in stormy weather or when everything was wet, the mosquitoes were bad. In the evenings you could hear the coyotes howling. There are lots of lizards, snakes, and sometimes you might find scorpions on the rocks." (1155~)

—Cedar Mountain Recreation Area: (Bob Hill Knoll map.) This consists of a Viewpoint and Picnic Area. The facilities were built by the Castle Valley Job Corps in 1966. (1551~)

Cedar Mountain: (Emery Co.) San Rafael Swell-Moroni Slopes. The Frying Pan, Salvation Creek, Ireland Mesa, and Mussentuchit Flat maps. (7,075')

—Harlequin Pinnacle: This is on the east side of Cedar Mountain (at elevation 6620 on The Frying Pan map). It was named for the distinct color difference between its sides.

Cedar Mountain: (Iron Co.) Cedar Canyon-Ellies Canyon. Cedar City, Cedar Mountain, Kolob Reservoir, and Webster Flat maps. Most of Cedar Mountain is PRIVATE PROPERTY.

Also called Lone Tree Mountain. (1931~)

In 1871 David Bulloch was the first to run livestock on Cedar Mountain: "I was the first man to go over Cedar Mountains on snow shoes, and lay out in the snow two nights in that high altitude, without bed or blanket." (376~)

Cedar Park: (San Juan Co.) Montezuma Canyon-Tank Canyon. Bug Canyon map.

The name was recommended to the USGS by ranchers Max Dalton and Jim Scorup in 1980. (1931~)

Cedar Peak: (Wayne Co.) Awapa Plateau-Cedar Peak Draw. Flossie Knoll map. (8,873')

Dunk Taylor noted that the peak has cedar [juniper] trees on it. (1865~)

—Cedar Peak Lake: Don Orton in 1941: "So named because of a sparse growth of cedar at one end of the lake." (2053~)

Cedar Point: (Garfield Co.) Poison Spring Canyon-North Wash. Stair Canyon and Turkey Knob maps. (6,016')

—Alvin Seeps: Kevin Robison noted that this large, developed spring is on the southwest edge of Cedar Point (one-quarter mile north-northeast of elevation 5018T on the Turkey Knob map). Kevin's father, Alvin Robison, developed the spring. (1646~, SAPE.)

—Robison Reservoir: Kevin Robison noted that this stock reservoir is on the south edge of Cedar Point (one-half mile south of elevation 5503 on the Stair Canyon map). It was built by Kevin and his father, Alvin Robison, in the early 1960s. (1646~)

—Andrew Seeps: Kevin Robison noted that this developed spring is on the south edge of Cedar Point one-half mile east of Robison Reservoir (three-quarters of a mile east-southeast of elevation 5503 on the Stair Canyon map). It is at the head of Andrew Ekker Canyon. It was named for Andrew Ekker of Hanksville. (1646~)

Cedar Point: (San Juan Co.) Glen Canyon NRA-Cedar Mesa. The Goosenecks map. (6,220')

Cowboy Billy Graham is credited with naming this. (1526~)

Cedar Ridge Canyon: (Carbon Co.) West Tavaputs Plateau-Desolation Canyon. Cedar Ridge Canyon and Firewater Canyon North maps.

Ed F. Harmston told this story in 1913: "just below [Cedar Ridge Canyon] Black Tiger [a horse] again falls off the trail [See Firewater Canyon for the beginning of the story], rolling about 200 ft. down a precipitous slope and stopping just at the brink of a precipice 100 ft. sheer drop into the river the boys get him back on the trail without any further mishap." (833~)

—Constructed Stock Trail: This goes from the river and out the top of the canyon. The lower section of trail is mostly washed out. (SAPE.)

Cedar Spring: (San Juan Co.) Navajo Indian Reservation-Monument Valley. Goulding map.

Paiutes used to camp in a cedar [juniper] grove near the spring. Harry Goulding noted that he put in the original water troughs. (1380~)

Cedar Valley: (Iron Co.)

Also called Rush Lake Valley. (M.34.)

Arvilla H. Day: "Named for Cedar (Juniper) trees growing on nearby hills." (942~)

This valley, about thirty miles long and eight miles wide, was first written about by the Dominguez-Escalante Expedition of 1776–77. They called it *Rio del Señor San José*. Father Escalante: "We descended to a beautiful valley and we stopped at nightfall near a small river in one of its valleys which have extensive pasture lands.... It is very rich in pasturage; it has large valleys and medium sized marshes and enough very good soil for a town for seasonal planting.... Very near ... is a great deal of lumber, pine nut wood and royal pine and several good sites for cattle and sheep ranches." (81~)

The Parley P. Pratt Exploring Expedition to Southern Utah of 1849–50 crossed the valley. Robert Campbell of the expedition: "pass through extensive beautiful bottom, rich in feed, hundreds of acres on the bottom, sandy knolls dug up by Gophers, wire grass dense & thick, excellent bottom." (1762~)

Captain James H. Simpson in 1859: "These valleys [Cedar and Rush valleys] are very sparsely watered, and though the soil in itself has all the elements of fertility, yet for want of the necessary moisture, for agricultural purposes, except in a small number of areas containing but a few acres which can be irrigated, it is utterly worthless." (1749~)

Kate Denniston Kane, the wife of Thomas L. Kane, in 1874: "Our morning drive to Cedar City [from Parowan] was uninteresting; volcanic rocks, sage brush, rabbit brush and greasewood; on the plain the hills dotted with unpicturesque stunted colors." (375~)

Cedar Wash: (Kane Co.) GSCENM-Rock Springs Creek. Slickrock Bench map.

Ivan Willis and Sam Graff in 1963: "So named because of the abundance of scrub cedars [junipers] growing along the wash." (1931~)

Cement Crossing: (Emery Co.) San Rafael Swell-Big Hole Wash. Dry Mesa map.

Betty Smith: "We called that Cement Crossing 'cause someone had been there and poured some cement across a spring that was at Cement Crossing. We named it Cement Crossing 'cause there was some concrete there." (1764~)

—Old Spanish Trail: The trail traversed this area. (1270~)

Center Creek: (Garfield Co.) Dixie National Forest-Escalante Mountains-East Fork Sevier River. Grass Lakes and Antimony maps.

Two name derivations are given. Both are accurate.

First, Sonny King: "There are three creeks that start near each other. This is the center one. They are North Creek, Center Creek, and a creek that starts at Pacer Lake." (1095~)

Second, Scott Robinson in 1942: "It was so named because of being the center or between the East Fork of the Sevier River and Poison Creek." (2053~)

Center Creek: (Iron Co.) Dixie National Forest-Sidney Peaks-Parowan Canyon. Brian Head and Parowan maps. Also called Parowan Creek.

Also spelled Centre Creek. (750~)

Center Creek runs through Second Left Hand Canyon.

Addison Pratt of the Jefferson Hunt Party in 1849 called this Third Creek because it was the third creek his party crossed after entering Parowan Valley. (1571~) It was called 3rd Stream in Joseph Cain's "Mormon Way-bill" of 1851, with the notation that it had "good feed and wood." (330~)

Members of the Parley P. Pratt Exploring Expedition to Southern Utah of 1849–50 explored the canyon. Isaac Haight of the expedition: "Br. [Samuel] Gould and [Edward] Everett went up it and report large quantity of the best pine timber fit for hewing, Sawing House logs and fence polls.... The creek bottoms are wide and practible

for a good road it ascends gradually to the hed of the canion." (1762~)

Central Town: (Sevier Co.) Sevier River-Interstate 70. Annabella map.

Jean S. Greenwood: "Situated near the center of Sevier County on Highway 89 is the little community of Central." (1194~)

The first settlers of Central, William A. Stewart and Joseph Evans, arrived in the winter of 1873. Vilate Hawley Anderson: "William Morrison of Richfield, who was probate judge of Sevier County, was called to lay out the town site about 1875, and it was his privilege of giving the town its name. He gave it the name of Inverury [also spelled Inveraray], which was an old Scotch name and the name of the city in Scotland from which he came. [*Inverury* is Scottish for "between two waters."] At the time of dedication of our new Chapel, which was completed in 1940, the name was changed from Inverury to Central, by which it is now known." (1970~)

—Little Denmark and Stringtown: Leland Gray noted that the southwest part of town was called Little Denmark for its many Danish residents and the north part of town was called Stringtown. Leland Gray: "I guess it got that name because it took up the north half mile of the settlement." (2063~)

Central Town: (Washington Co.) Pine Valley Mountains-Santa Clara River-Highway 18. Central East and Central West maps.

Also called Eight Mile Flat because the location was eight miles from Pine Valley. (273~, 1803~)

Arthur F. Bruhn: "[It was] given the name Central because of the village's location approximately midway between Veyo and Pine Valley." (311~) Kate B. Carter: "Centrally located between Enterprise, Gunlock, Veyo and Pine Valley." (375~)

The town was started by Peter E. Beckstrom, Henry L. Holt, James Chadburn, and M.E. Bracken in 1909. (273~)

—Old Spanish Trail: The trail went by what would become Central.

Cha Canyon: (San Juan Co.) Navajo Indian Reservation-Navajo Mountain-San Juan River. Navajo Begay and Wilson Creek maps.

Also called Beaver Creek, Beaver Creek Canyon, Cha Brook, Cha Creek, and Cha Wash.

Jim Mike noted that the Paiute name for Beaver Creek is *Kapurats*, or "lots of water running." (1353~) In 1909 archaeologist Byron Cummings called it *Natan* or "Corn" Canyon. (499~) Christy G. Turner called it *Chawboko* in 1961. (1916~)

Donald Baars noted that *Cha* is Navajo for "beaver." (86~) The name was in place by 1916.

Hugh D. Miser in 1921: "This fork [Cha Canyon's main fork] which heads in the north base of Navajo Mountain, presents some of the wildest scenery found on the tributaries of the San Juan. The canyon, like most others in the vicinity, is narrow; its walls are vertical, inaccessible cliffs and boulder-strewn slopes; the canyon floor is dotted here and there by dense thickets of shrubbery and trees; and the creek draining it has two low falls from which it plunges into large, deep pools." (1370~)

Zane Grey in 1923: "Beaver Cañon ... was a cañon the like of which I had never seen. It was almost a bright red. The walls were half a mile high and so cracked, rent and ruined that it seemed the checkered cliffs and splintered shafts would come toppling down on us. The slopes below the wall were a chaos of blocks of rocks, reaching almost to the stream bed that wound through the middle of the cañon.... It was an abyss of decay, death and desolation." (782~)

—Grey Buttes: These are on the west side of upper Cha Canyon (between elevations 4884T and 5571T on the Nasja Begay map). Christy G. Turner: "We rode the Rainbow Trail until reaching Cha Canyon at noon. Here, turning north and proceeding along a well-worn stock trail, we pass by what is locally termed, the Grey Buttes." (1918~)

—Wetherill Trail: This is the "Pack" trail that crosses middle Cha Canyon (Navajo Begay map). (See Appendix Two—Wetherill Trail.)

—Constructed Stock Trail: This led from the Colorado River up the west fork of Cha Canyon to the Wetherill Trail. (1021~, 1369~)

—Cha Bay: This is the area at the mouth of Cha Canyon. The name was proposed by Alan Silverstein in 2004 and accepted by the USGS Board on Geographic Names in 2005. (1138~)

—Thirteen-foot Rapid: (Also called Thirteen-and-One-Half-Foot Rapids.) This was on the San Juan River at the mouth of Cha Canyon. In 1924 Hugh D. Miser named the rapid, noting that it was the largest rapid on the San Juan River, measuring thirteen feet in height. (1370~) C. Gregory Crampton: "Thirteen-foot Rapids ... is a sharp drop over a boulder–strewn bed." (472~)

Norman D. Nevills took credit for being the first to run Thirteen-foot Rapid, in the mid-1930s: "The descent of the [San Juan] canyon with no trouble whatsoever, and the boater was shot through every rapid encountered, including the 'Thirteen Foot,' declared by previous boatmen to be impassable at any stage of the water." (1437~)

Chaffin Spring: (Wayne Co.) Fishlake National Forest-Thousand Lake Mountain. Flat Top map.

Guy Pace and Max Robinson noted that George Chaffin (1845-1899) had a sawmill here in the 1890s. (1497~, 1641~)

Chaistla Butte: (Navajo Co., Az.) Navajo Indian Reservation-Capitan Valley. Agathla Peak, Az. map. (6,098')

The 1892 USGS Marsh Pass map shows this as Cha e_ Kla Rock.

In 1901 Howard B. Carpenter called it Turret Butte. (345~)

Herbert E. Gregory noted it in 1908 as *Chaezkla*, or "Little Captain," referring to Agathla Peak (El Capitan) three miles to the north. (759~) Gregory noted that *Cha-ez-kla* is Navajo for "beaver rincon." (769~)

Douglas Preston: "a magic witch's finger pointing skyward.... [In Navajo myth it] is the world's doomsday clock: it will fall when the end of the world arrives." (1573~)

Chaiyahi Creek: (Coconino Co., Az.) Navajo Indian Reservation-Navajo Mountain-Navajo Creek. Chaiyahi Rim NE, Chaiyahi Rim SE, and Chaiyahi Rim SW, Az. maps. Three name derivations are given.

First, *Ch'áyahi* is Navajo for "armpit" or "underarm." This refers to the upper crossing of Navajo Creek. (2016~, 2072~)

Second, Navajo Ernest Nelson: "At the place called *Ch'ááyáhii* the Navajos shot one of the Paiutes that was a second lieutenant in his underarm with an arrow. That is how the place got its name *Báyóòdzin Bi' Chááyá Biish*." (1231~)

Third, Stephen C. Jett noted that Navajo Floyd Laughter told him that *Ch'ayahi Bikooh*, or "Underarm Canyon" refers to a man who used a crutch. The man was Ch'ayahi, and he lived in the canyon at the turn of the century and did use a crutch. (975~)

Carl I. Wheat called what is today's Trampled Water Canyon "Sand Trampled Over Water Canyon" and noted that it went all the way to Navajo Creek. He called upper Chaiyahi Creek, from the mouth of Trampled Water Canyon east, Little Finger Canyon. (1996~)

Inscriptions include R.E. Alrod [Allred?], Oct. 1883. (1115~)

Chandler Canyon: (Grand and Uintah Counties.) Uintah and Ouray Indian Reservation-East Tavaputs Plateau-Desolation Canyon. Chicken Fork, Moonwater Point, and Chandler Falls maps.

John F. Steward of the 1871–72 Powell Expedition: "We have called it 'Chandler's Falls' and the little Creek upon the opposite side 'Chandler Creek' (following my wife's maiden name), and so they are placed upon the map." (1830~)

Jack Hillers of the same expedition: "A brook comes in on the left. Clear, sparkling water comes down over the rocks, boiling. It is started by some springs. Called it Chandler Fall and Chandler Creek." (884~)

Waldo Wilcox: "A big old crick runs in Chandler. All the water comes up within three or four miles of the mouth. One of the springs looks like a big old pipe shooting water out of the ledge. Everybody wanted to farm that. But it wasn't good soil." (2011~)

—Old Cabin: Two stories are told about the old cabin at the mouth of Chandler Canyon. First, Waldo Wilcox: "Dick Tomlinson built that old cabin. There were two Dick Tomlinsons. He was on this [south] side of the mountain [Tavaputs Plateau], the other was on the other [north] side of the mountain. This was the Uintah Basin Tomlinson. After he left, Dell Barney lived in it. Then the house burned down. Then during World War Two there was a deserter living there. He built another cabin." (2011~)

Second, George E. Stewart: "In the days of prohibition, Ben Morris, the husband of Josie Morris, the sister of Queen Ann of Brown's Park, run a 'still' at the mouth of Chandler; manufactured a fairly good grade of bootleg whiskey." (1832~) Stewart also mentioned that in the 1890s outlaw Joe Walker had a ranch here: "He stole horses and drove them there [to Chandler Creek] where they were cared for by an old man and his boy. When he had gathered a big enough herd, Walker drove them away to sell on distant markets." (1837~)

Inscriptions at the mouth of the canyon include the initials of Denis Julien. He most likely carved the inscription in about 1839. (See Appendix One—Denis Julien.)

—Get Away Ferry: This ferry across the Green River was at the mouth of Chandler Creek and operated from 1896 to 1900. C. Gregory Crampton: "It was just large enough to carry two horses and outlaws used it to make their getaway. Anyone in pursuit would have to swim across and recover the boat." (468~)

—Teapot Arch: Jean Bennett in 1965: "A striking rock formation on the right [Chandler] canyon wall has been named Teapot Arch." (207~)

—McCook Spring: Jean Bennett: "a delightful, clear spring flowing out of the stream bank into Chandler Creek near its mouth or a mile or so up." (468~)

—Chandler Creek-Desolation Canyon Trail: (Chandler Falls map.) This "Foot Trail" starts at Chandler Canyon and goes along the east side of the river. George E. Stewart: "In places where the river cuts into the ledges, this

trail has been hued out of the rock. There are gaps in the trail along the ledge and these have been timbered in such a way that if a posse were on the trail of a person who knew about this passage out, one blow of an ax, or anything knocking timber out from under the bridge, would leave a gap in the trail which would take hours to fix." (1832~)

Chaol Canyon: (Coconino Co., Az.) Navajo Indian Reservation-Navajo Creek. Horsethief Mesa and Cedar Tree Bench, Az. maps.

Kaibito Creek runs through Chaol Canyon.

Leon Wall noted that *Chá'o_* is Navajo for a "pinyon pine." (1962~, 769~)

Charley Flat: (Emery Co.) San Rafael Swell-Crawford Draw. Twin Knolls and Arsons Garden maps.

Charley Swasey (1851-1923) ran cattle throughout the San Rafael Swell in the early years. (511~, 641~, 1853~)

—Charley Holes: (Twin Knolls map.) These natural sandstone tanks are easily accessed by livestock. (SAPE.)

Charlie Brown Spring: (Uintah Co.) Uintah and Ouray Indian Reservation-East Tavaputs Plateau-Horsecorn Canyon. Wolf Flat map.

This is a large, natural spring. A stock trail leads down the cliffs to it. (SAPE.)

Charles Brown arrived in Hill Creek in the 1890s. (520~)

Checkerboard Mesa: (Kane Co.) Zion National Park-White Cliffs-Clear Creek. Springdale East map. (6,640')

Also called Quilted Mountain.

Unattributed: "So named because of the multitudinous check lines in cross-bedded white stone." (2053~) J.L. Crawford: "The checkerboarding phenomenon results from vertical weather cracks and horizontal bedding planes, and generally occurs on north facing slopes." (481~)

Cheese and Raisins: (San Juan Co.) Comb Ridge-Cottonwood Wash. Hotel Rock and Black Mesa Butte maps.

John Scorup: "That's old Albert R. Lyman. He was one of the old settlers in Blanding ... he was out gatherin' cattle and that's what they had for lunch." (1821~) Karl Barton: "That's all they had to eat, was cheese and raisins." (162~) Albert R. Lyman told the story: "Lem Redd coming into camp in the afternoon found two of the cowboys munching on the top of the fare. One of them rather sheepishly said, 'Brother Redd, won't you have some cheese and raisins with us?' Lem snorted 'Cheese'n raisins, cheese'n raisins, all you boys do is sit in camp and eat cheese'n raisins.'" (1602~)

Cheesebox Canyon: (San Juan Co.) Dark Canyon Plateau-White Canyon. Woodenshoe Buttes and The Cheesebox maps.

—The Cheesebox: (The Cheesebox map.) (Also called Bell Butte [878~] and Wedding Cake [888~].) This small tower is shaped like an old fashion cheese box.

—Outlaw Crossing: (Also called Hideout Trail and Outlaw Trail.) This constructed stock trail is one of the four named crossings of White Canyon. (The others are Soldier Crossing, Duckett Crossing, and Gravel Crossing.) It crosses White Canyon to the west of The Cheesebox. On the west side of White Canyon it starts near milepost 75 (elevation BM5653 on The Cheesebox map) and drops down a precipitous cliff. It then goes up White Canyon for one mile and exits to the north. This was an often-used trail for those taking livestock from The Hideout to Fry Canyon and the Moss Back Butte area. (1002~) The trail is difficult to find and follow. (SAPE.)

Cheney Spring Canyon: (Iron Co.) Hurricane Cliffs-Spirit Peak. Summit map.

A Mr. Cheney was an early rancher in the Parowan area. (363~) This was most likely Elam Cheney (1854-1926). (388~)

Cherry Canyon: (San Juan Co.) Manti-LaSal National Forest-Dark Canyon Wilderness-Woodenshoe Canyon. Woodenshoe Buttes map.

Erwin Oliver noted that there are lots of chokecherries growing in the head of the canyon. (1479~)

—Cherry Canyon Trail: John Scorup noted that this constructed stock trail goes down Cherry Canyon. (1821~) I was unable to locate the trail. (SAPE.)

—West Flat: Erwin Oliver noted that this flat area is between the upper forks of Cherry Canyon (at elevations 8156 and 8221T). (1479~)

Cherry Creek: (Garfield Co.) Dixie National Forest-Escalante Mountains-Main Canyon. Griffin Point map.

Pratt Gates noted that there is an abundance of chokecherries in the canyon. (709~)

—Cherry Creek Mine: Pratt Gates noted that G.H. Frandsen of Panguitch opened the mine and, because ore was so hard to get out, only mined for a couple of years, from 1962 to 1964. (709~, 570~)

Two mines are named Cherry Creek, one on the south side of Cherry Creek and one on the north. The mine on the north (Old Cherry Creek Mine) has a caved portal.

Cherry Creek: (Garfield Co.) Dixie National Forest-Sevier Plateau-Cottonwood Creek. Cow Creek map.

Scott Robinson in 1942: "It derived its name from the wild [choke] cherry brush that grow at the head of this creek." (2053~)

Cherry Flat: (Garfield Co.) GSCENM-Kaiparowits Plateau-Little Valley Wash. Canaan Creek map.

Don Coleman: "Cherry Flat has some wild chokecherries on it." (441~)

Cherry Hollow: (Garfield Co.) Dixie National Forest-Escalante Mountains-Water Canyon. Griffin Point map.

Two name derivations are given.

First, Pratt Gates: "Cherry Hollow is a steep, rough canyon and the reason they named it that is because there's a lot of chokecherries in it. And lots of bears." (709~)

Second, Scott Robinson: "George Woodard, nicknamed 'Cherry' was herding sheep in this hollow and lost a few which were later found and returned back to George 'Cherry' Woodard by a nearby herder who gave it the name of Cherry Hollow." (2053~)

—Cherry Creek Mine: Edson Alvey noted that this coal mine in Cherry Hollow was at one time owned by a man named Case. (55~)

Cherry Meadow Canyon: Roan Cliffs-Range Creek. Lighthouse Canyon map.

Waldo Wilcox: "There was a bunch of chokecherry trees there. They cut them down before my time and built a fence there. That fence is still there. There was a Cherry Meadow Ranch there and old Preston Nutter had that. There were cabins and corrals. Pretty much nothing is left. The only thing there is an old stake and rider fence. There up against the ledge were some good springs, so they built the fence to hold the horses in near the springs and the slough grass there." (2011~)

Chesler Park: (San Juan Co.) Canyonlands National Park-Needles District-Chesler Canyon. Druid Arch map.

Two probably related name derivations are given. It is believed that the second is correct.

First, Ray Garner in 1950: "Chesler Park, a place of hidden beauty surpassing anything we had yet seen. It was named for an old cowman. To us it was a garden spot lost among the standing rocks.... In every direction there were vistas of breath-taking beauty. A carpet of lush green grass accentuated the tones of the red, pink, and white formations, and the sweeping blue dome of the sky was hung with great white clouds." (705~)

Jack Breed in 1952: "Chesler, named for a rancher who drove cattle into it in 1885, is little more than three miles square but as lovely a spot as the West affords. Its warmly colored walls rise 600 feet, shutting it off from everything but the clear, blue sky. On its floor lies a blanket of thick grass, patched with acres of yellow wild mustard." (277~) Second, Clyde L. Denis noted that there is "neither mention of an individual named Chesler in local histories nor is there any record of a Chesler in the area in or around the time that the name was probably attached to this section of the Needles." Denis noted, though, that a nearby inscription from H. Shisler, Feb. 6, [18]92 (See Lower Red Lake Canyon) led him to believe that "The existence of references to Shisler and none to Chesler, suggests 'Chesler' might have come into being as the garbled version of another man's name and that H. Shisler was the original eponymous cowman." (555~)

W.G. Carroll in 1956: "This is one of the most beautiful spots I have encountered ... and one of the most inaccessible." (350~)

Inscriptions include Bill Frawley, February 1887 and Rufus Allen, Mar. 2, 1924. (1112~)

—Gilbeys Tower: This is in the middle of Chesler Park (on the ridge of elevation 5998T). Eric Bjørnstad: "Gilbey's Tower was named as a memorial to Scott Gilbert, who was killed at the age of 21 while attempting a winter ascent of the Grand Central Couloir of Mt. Kitchner, in the Canadian Rockies." (239~)

—Joint Trail: This is the "Pack" trail that is one mile southwest of Gilbeys Tower (one-eighth mile west-north-west of elevation 5984T). The trail goes through a tight crack, or joint, in a large sandstone cliff.

—Anthill Mesa: This is at the top of Chesler Canyon (at elevation 6417T). The highest point on the mesa top is shaped like an anthill. A very old constructed stock trail descends the south side of Anthill Mesa and goes to Starvation Pocket. It passes one-eighth mile east of elevation 6127T. (SAPE.)

Chessmen Canyon: (Iron Co.) Cedar Breaks National Monument-Ashdown Creek. Brian Head map.

There is a fanciful similarity of the rock formations to chess men. (942~)

Chicken Creek: (San Juan Co.) Manti-LaSal National Forest-La Sal Mountains-La Sal Creek. Mount Peale and La Sal East maps.

In the old days sharp-tailed grouse, or prairie chickens, were found in profusion here. (2053~)

Chicken Spring: (Piute Co.) Awapa Plateau-Okerlund Draw. Jakes Knoll map.

Alfonzo Turner: "I was there before they developed the spring. In the '30s the CCC or the WPA [Works Progress Administration] went in there and dug out the spring

and rocked it up and piped it out to watering troughs." (1914~)

Thaine Taylor: "There's only a very few places where there's live water on Parker Mountain [Awapa Plateau] and Chicken Spring is one of them. There was always chickens up in there, sage grouse. You could depend on goin' and gettin' a chicken fry there. I've done that myself." (1868~)

Chimney Canyon: (Emery Co.) San Rafael Swell-Muddy Creek. The Frying Pan and Hunt Draw maps.

Also called The Chimney. (1931~)

Steve Allen: "The name Chimney Canyon has been attributed to both the brick-colored walls of the Moenkopi Formation in the canyon's lower reaches and to a prominent, chimney-like tower near its head." (46~, 845~)

Wayne Gremel: "People from Wayne County called that Calf Canyon. They used to put cattle off there and wean the cattle and push 'em off a little ledge and they couldn't get back, so it was called Calf Canyon. And the Emery [Town] people called it Chimney Canyon. Here about thirty years ago a cartographer [from the USGS] came and visited. They changed the name officially to Chimney Canyon because it's got a rock chimney in it." (780~)

Chimney Meadow: (Iron Co.) Parowan Valley-Interstate 15. Paragonah map.

Luella Adams Dalton: "Someone built an old house with a big fireplace and long after the house was gone the old chimney still stood guard. So the meadow got the name of Chimney Meadow." (516~)

Chimney Park: (San Juan Co.) Manti-LaSal National Forest-Dark Canyon Plateau-North Elk Ridge-Notch Canyon. Poison Canyon and Chippean Rocks maps.

Pete Steele noted that the canyon has several towers that look like chimneys. (1821~) This is especially evident when looking down into the head of the canyon.

Chimney Rock: (Emery Co.) Cedar Mountain-Summerville Wash. Chimney Rock map. (6,661')

Thomas E. Bryson in 1941: "Named from general shape of rock formation. This rock is one of the famous land marks of Emery Co. It looms up above the surroundings and can be seen for miles in any direction." (2053~) The name was in place by 1918. (324~)

—Chinese Work Camp: A railroad grade, never used, was built through this portion of the San Rafael Swell in 1881. Chinese laborers were used during construction. One of their camps was along the old railroad grade below Chimney Rock (one-eighth mile southwest of elevation 5688). (45~, 1764~) (See Denver and Rio Grande Western Railroad.)

—Mining Road: A steep and no-longer-passable uranium mining road goes up the cliffs from the west side of Chimney Rock to the top of Cedar Mountain. The road, and a mining camp near the top of the cliffs, were built in the 1950s. (SAPE.)

Chimney Rock: (Emery Co.) San Rafael Swell-Sids Mountain. The Blocks map. (7,406')
Lee Mont Swasey: "I always knew it as Sinbad Rock." (1853~)

Chimney Rock: (Kane Co.) Big Dry Valley-Little Creek Wood Bench. Henrieville map.
Ralph Chynoweth: "That rock must be fifty or sixty feet high and it stands right out in the middle of Big Flat. Cowboys would meet over at Chimney Rock." (425~)
Inscriptions include Sears Willis, 1918; and Harold and Reno Ahlstrom and Sam Pollock, no date. (SAPE.)
—Harvey Chynoweth Ranch: PRIVATE PROPERTY. Ralph Chynoweth noted that in the early years George and Charlie Baldwin homesteaded one mile east of Chimney Rock (near elevation 5980). In the late 1940s, Ralph's father, Harvey, bought the ranch. (425~)

Chimney Rock: (Kane Co.) GSCENM-Escalante Desert-Coyote Gulch. King Mesa map.
This one hundred-foot-tall pinnacle stands tall above the surrounding desert and was a magnet and meeting place for ranchers. Inscriptions include P. Osborn, 1895; John Duel, Aug. 1897; Hy Porter, March 8, 1903; I.A. Porter, Feb. 1904; E. Wooley, March 7th, 1908; and Horace Hall, Xmas 1912. (1112~, SAPE.)
—Arch Rock: This small dome a short distance to the southwest of Chimney Rock is covered with inscriptions including MKS, 1900; Roley Shirts, Feb. 3, 1906; Riley Woolsey, 1906; W.E. Wooley, Nov. 24, 1912; Wm. Mitchell, Jan. 17, 1919; Joe Hunt, Feb. 7, 1919; and Lester Heaps, Jan. 29, 1927. (SAPE.)

Chimney Rock: (Kane Co.) GSCENM-Kaiparowits Plateau-White Rocks. Lower Coyote Spring map. (4,642')
Julius S. Dalley: "The name was given because of a resemblance to a chimney." (2053~) Ralph Chynoweth noted that this has also been called Message Rock because it was used as a message board by Indians. (425~)
Inscriptions include Mike Little, Jan. 16, 1898; Blain Cox and Roy Veater, 1915; Art Chynoweth, 1917; Sam Belock, 1919; and Ken Goulding, 1933. (SAPE.)

Chimney Rock: (Wayne Co.) Canyonlands National Park-Maze District-Land of Standing Rocks. Spanish Bottom map.
Also called Candle Stick Rock (696~) and Candlestick Spire (100~).

Chimney Rock Canyon: (Wayne Co.) Capitol Reef National Park-Meeks Mesa-Spring Canyon. Flat Top, Torrey, and Twin Rocks maps.
Locally called Chimney Canyon.
—Chimney Rock: (Twin Rocks map.) Ephraim Pectol and family moved to Caineville in 1888: "Down over Sand Creek, Sulphur Creek, past the twin rocks, on down to Chimney Rock, the majestic red sandstone Rock which stands out away from the main ledge alone very much resembling a chimney hill." (318a~)
—CCC Camp: The present-day Chimney Rock parking lot was the location of a CCC camp from 1938 to 1947. (1476~)
—Chimney Rock Stock Trail. Now a hiking trail, this was constructed by early Fruita settlers to get their livestock into Spring and Chimney Rock canyons. (See Meeks Mesa.)
—The Fluted Wall: This is the historic name for the Moenkopi Formation wall that runs along the north side of Highway 24 for several miles on both sides of Chimney Rock. Charles Kelly noted that it was named by Clarence Dutton of the Powell Survey in 1880. (1047~)
—Pandoras Box: (Also called Wiggum.) (1548~) This mouth of this southern tributary of Chimney Rock Canyon is two and one-quarter miles north-northwest of Twin Rocks (immediately east of elevation 7509 on the Twin Rocks map). Steve Brezovec and Ryan Cornia named the canyon. (653~)

Chimney Spring: (Piute Co.) Fishlake National Forest-Sevier Plateau. Marysvale map.
This large spring was once developed with watering troughs. (SAPE.)

China Neck: (Garfield Co.) Glen Canyon NRA-Orange Cliffs-The Golden Stairs. Elaterite Basin map.
Two complimentary name derivations are given.
First, A.C. Ekker and Pearl Baker noted that this is a thin neck of bare, light-colored sandstone, making it a graceful neck of land. (1931~) Wiladeane Chaffin Wubben Hills: "We used to take cattle up the Golden Stairs Trail and over the ridge from Ernie Country to Big Water which was hard to do because of the narrow Chinle stratum neck." (1430~)
Second, David Day: "The most striking thing about the narrow neck of land is that it is composed of a monolithic block of pure white sandstone while the rest of the mesa is mostly made of crumbly reddish-brown shale. The contrast is such that the bridge looks almost as if it were made of white porcelain; hence the name China Neck." (534~)

Chinatown Wash: (Washington Co.) Hurricane Cliffs-Virgin River. Hurricane map.

Chinatown was in the lower end of the wash near the Virgin River.

Two similar name derivations are given.

First, Andrew Karl Larson noted that while building the Hurricane Canal in the early 1890s, workmen lived in the wash. When someone noted that the encampment looked like Chinatown, the name stuck. (1141~)

Second, Ashby Reeve noted that many Chinese worked at the mines at Silver Reef. When work stopped there, the Chinese were hired to work on the Hurricane Canal. There was an encampment of Chinese along the creek. (1608~)

—Robbers Roost: Ashby Reeve noted that this is an area to the east of Chinatown Wash along the Virgin River. In the early years workers on the Hurricane Canal found an area of rocks and camped there. The area was apparently not the home of robbers, but looked like it should have been. (1608~) Alice Stratton: "Robber's Roost is a timeless camp. Only a violent earthquake could dislodge the giant boulder that leans, forming a natural cavern to protect men from the elements." (1843~)

Chinle Creek: (Apache Co., Az. and San Juan Co., Utah.) Navajo Indian Reservation-Canyon De Chelly National Monument-San Juan River. Arizona maps: Chinle, Many Farms, Many Farms NE, Little Round Rock, Dancing Rocks, Rock Point, Mexican Water SW, and Mexican Water. Utah maps: Moses Rock and San Juan Hill.

Also called and spelled The Chelle, Chinalee Creek, Chinlee Wash, Chin-li Wash, Keenly Wash, and Shinlee Wash. Donald L. Baars noted that *Chinle* is Navajo for "at the mouth of the canyon" or a "place where the water flows out of the mountain." (86~)

Don Bernardo de Miera, the cartographer of the Domínguez-Escalante Expedition of 1776–77, showed the headwaters of Chinle Creek as *Chegui*. The expedition did not visit Chinle Creek. The information came from other sources. (310~)

The Antonio Armijo Expedition of 1829–30 called this Chelli Creek. (69~, 805~) A U.S. War Department map from 1850 shows it as the *Rio de Chelly*. (M.71.)

In 1853 Major Henry L. Kendrick called it *Rio de Cheillez*: "Here the river enters a deep and very remarkable cañon, rent in the rocks of an ancient date. This cañon, some of the Indians told us, extends to the Colorado [San Juan]." (1087~)

Indian agent Henry L. Dodge in 1853 is credited with being the first Euroamerican to go all the way through the canyon: "I ... passed through the cañon of Chella following that stream to its confluence with the San Juan.... We returned to the valley of the Chella, which we found to be a wide rich valley, extensively cultivated in corn and some wheat.... [We were] doubtless the first Americans that ever passed entirely through the cañon." (562~, 310~)

The 1857 Rogers and Johnson map shows this as *Rio de Chelly*. (M.36.) In 1873 John D. Lee's diary noted it as the *De Chille*. (437~)

William Henry Jackson of the Ferdinand V. Hayden Survey in 1875 called this DeChelly Creek and Chin-li Wash. He described the mouth of the canyon: "Our camp was not a pleasant one—nothing but sand and sagebrush, with a landscape of bare red rocks. It was all right, however, for photography." (952a~) From his diary: "Just before sunset rode up a couple of miles into the canon of the DeChelly. Bold & rocky. Great caves in which there were walls & ruins & opposite a row of 6 or 8 little cliff houses. The canon is well nigh enpassable, tho' not so very narrow.... In very dry seasons when the bed of the stream is perfectly dry, one might travel entirely in the wash." (950~)

Inscriptions include A. [Albert] M. Rogers. Although there is no date, it is known that he was a prospector who traveled this country in the early 1890s. (838~, 1115~, SAPE.)

—Pioneer Route: Those going from the San Juan area to the Monument Valley-Navajo Mountain areas traversed Chinle Canyon. (1115~)

—River Ford: (Also called Chinle Crossing, Moki Crossing, Mule Ear Crossing [See Mule Ear], and Rincon Crossing.) Hugh D. Miser of the Kelly W. Trimble USGS Expedition of 1921: "A ledge of rock reaches across the bed of the [San Juan] river just above the mouth of Chinle Creek. It was formerly used by pack trains in fording the river at this place." (1370~)

James H. Knipmeyer: "The river ford was diagonal between Comb and Chinle [washes], and then they just followed up the wash to where it broke through the Comb [Ridge] and allowed access to Monument Valley." (1115~)

The use of the crossing subsided after the building of the first Mexican Hat (Goodridge) bridge in 1909. (975~)

—Constructed Stock Trail: This trail, and a newer uranium-era road, go up the cliffs to the northeast from the mouth of the canyon. (SAPE.)

—Diamond Mine: In 1872 con-men advanced the story that diamonds could be found near the mouth of Chinle Creek. It was later found that they had salted the area with diamonds to attract investors. (952a~, 1935~)

Evidence of this mining activity, including the remnants of several structures, can still be found near the mouth of the creek. (SAPE.)

—Constructed Stock Trails: At least eight constructed stock trails, built by Navajo, are located on both sides of Chinle Creek in its lower three miles. (838~, SAPE.)

—Bluff Dam Site: (Proposed.) (Also called Bluff Reservoir.) (1146~) Hugh D. Miser: "A notable narrows occurs in San Juan Canyon just inside its entrance, about 1 1/2 miles below the mouth of Chinle Creek.... A dam site at this locality, known as the Bluff dam site, has been mapped by the United States Bureau of Reclamation [in 1914]." (1370~) The dam, if it had been built, would have inundated the town of Bluff. (78~)

—Books: In his novel *Thief of Time* Tony Hillerman's Many Ruins Canyon is Chinle Wash. (838~)

Chipman Peak: (Iron Co.) Parowan Valley-Black Mountains. Jack Henry Knoll map. (7,966')

William Lowder: "The Chipman brothers ran their cattle there." (1515~) This was Washburn Chipman (1829-1926), William Chipman (1833-1891), and James Chipman (1839-1922).

Chippean Rocks: (San Juan Co.) Manti-LaSal National Forest-Abajo Mountains. Chippean Rocks and Cream Pots maps.

Also spelled Chipene Ridge. (1911~)

Two name derivations are given.

First, this is a Ute name. Translation unknown.

Second, local ranch owner Will Petty heard a story about the name coming from the Chaffin family of ranchers from Wayne County. (1533~)

—Chippean Trail: This is the "Pack Trail" that starts on the north end of Chippean Ridge, crosses Chippean Canyon, and exits a short distance up Deep Canyon (Chippean Rocks map). The trail ends at Bayles Spring (Mount Linnaeus map). The trail, unused for many years, is nearly impossible to follow. (1821~, SAPE.)

—Chippean Ridge Road: The road that goes down Chippean Ridge, which is on the west side of Chippean Canyon, was built in 1946. (1860~)

Chocolate Drop: (San Juan Co.) Wingate Mesa-Red Canyon. Chocolate Drop map. (5,163')

Erwin Oliver: "It looks just like one of them old-fashioned chocolates." (1479~)

Chocolate Drops: (Wayne Co.) Canyonlands National Park-Maze District-South Fork Horse Canyon. Spanish Bottom map.

Pearl Baker noted that this was named by Arthur Ekker and his son, A.C. (1931~)

In 1965 Kent Frost suggested the name Handcarts and Wagons: "So named for the resemblance to the handcarts and wagons used by many of the first settlers in Utah." (1931~)

Chokecherry Creek: (Garfield Co.) Fishlake National Forest-Tushar Mountains-Sevier River. Circleville Mountain and Circleville maps.

The Parley P. Pratt Exploring Expedition of 1849–50 crossed the creek near its head, calling it 3rd Kanyon as it was the third they'd had to cross after ascending Birch Creek to the north. Robert Campbell of the expedition: "Descend into 3rd Kanyon, where the wagons camped. Plenty timber ... make a temporary bridge over the creek.... Snow very deep, being drifted all along where we pass thro' men a head breaking road, shoveling the snow." (1762~)

Solomon Nunes Carvalho of the John C. Fremont Expedition of 1853–54 described going up the canyon: "We were surrounded by very deep snows; but as it was necessary to proceed, the whole party started to penetrate through what appeared to be a pass, on the Warsatch [Tushar] Mountains. The opening to this depression [Chokecherry Creek] was favorable, and we continued our journey until the mountains seemed to close around us, the snow in the canon got deeper, and further progress on our present course was impossible.... We commenced the ascent of this tremendous mountain, covered as it were, with any icy pall of death, Col. Fremont leading and breaking a path; the ascent was so steep and difficult, that it was impossible to keep on our animals; consequently, we had to lead them, and travel on foot.... In this manner, alternately toiling and resting, we reached the summit.... When I surveyed the distance, I saw nothing but continued ranges of mountains of everlasting snow, and for the first time, my heart failed me." (385~, 1762~)

Chokecherry Creek: (Iron Co.) Dixie National Forest-Sandy Creek. Little Creek Peak and Panguitch NW maps.

Also called Wide Hollow. (1931~)

—Chokecherry Spring: (Little Creek Peak map.) Don McIntosh in 1941: "Name descriptive because of the chokecherry brush which surround the spring." (2053~).

Chokecherry Hollow: (Sevier Co.) Fishlake National Forest-Wasatch Plateau-Salina Creek. Water Hollow Ridge map.

Stuart Johnson: "People used to go and pick chokecherries there." (1003~)

Chokecherry Point: (Garfield Co.) Dixie National Forest-Boulder Mountain. Grover map. (10,770')

Also called Tantalus Point. (668~)

Almon H. Thompson of the 1871–72 Powell Expedition climbed to the top of the point and left his name in a can on the summit. (668~) Photographer Joseph Muench helped turn this point into a favorite locale for photographers. (1395~)

—Chokecherry Trail: This is the "Pack Trail" that is immediately south of Chokecherry Point. George C. Fraser in 1915: "The trail was faint, but easy, because [Walter E.] Hanks had worked over the roughest places.... Climbing was pretty steep and we had to walk some." (668~)

John Campbell: "This old road was one of the original crossing points on to the [Boulder] Top used by loggers to access the spruce trees killed by insects. One marvels that logging trucks ever traveled this steep rocky stretch." (337~)

Choprock Bench: (Garfield Co.) Glen Canyon NRA-Escalante River. Horse Pasture Mesa, Egypt, and Silver Falls Bench maps.

Also spelled Chop-Rock Bench.

—Choprock Canyon: (Also called Wide Canyon.) (19~) The mouth of this eastern tributary of the Escalante River is three miles (as the crow flies) downriver from the mouth of Harris Wash (one-half mile east of elevation 5293T on the Silver Falls Bench map).

Burns Ormand noted that ranchers still call this Wide Mouth Canyon "'Cause it was real narrow and then it widened out where it went on to the [Escalante] creek." (1487~)

Burns affixed his inscription on a nearby wall in 1927. Other inscriptions include S. Clark, 1881; Charles Hall, 1881 Ma21; William Osborn, 1894; F. Baker, 1912; Evadean Crosby, Jan. 10, 1918; M.D. Liston, April 8, 1919; and Zenis McNelly, Nov. 20, 1919. (1115~, SAPE.)

—South Fork Choprock Canyon: (Also called Chopslot, East Fork Choprock Canyon, and Moe Slot.) The mouth of the canyon is three-quarters of a mile up from the Escalante River (immediately south of elevation 5264T on the Silver Falls Bench map). Dennis Turville: "Jenny Hall and Mike Bogart named it Kaleidoscope [Canyon], since the canyon seemed different at every turn." (653~)

—Poison Ivy Fork of Choprock Canyon: This is the north fork of Choprock Canyon (one-half mile east of elevation 6015T on the Silver Falls Bench map). The canyon, narrow and poison ivy-choked throughout, is topped by three small natural bridges. It was named by Jim Finch and Ginger Harmon. (SAPE.)

—Wide Mouth Line Camp: This large overhang is one-half mile up the canyon from the Escalante River. It was used by cowboys. (SAPE.)

—Choprock Trail: This constructed stock trail exits Choprock Canyon on its east side one-quarter mile upcanyon from the Escalante River. The trail, still easy to find, goes south to Neon Canyon. (SAPE.) Cowboys had to "chop the rock" while building the stock trail out of the canyon. Burns Ormand: "The trail went up out of the canyon and it was just chopped around this ledge, kinda cut in there with a pick and an ax. They drilled some holes in the rock, put oak pegs in, and then laid logs along there and made the trail around." (1487~) (This section of the trail has now collapsed.) Burns Ormand: "The first time I ever went down there, one of our cows had walked off of that trail. It went to eat some limbs out in this big cottonwood tree and slipped and fell clear down into where that tree forks, and she was just hangin' up there. She was dead when we come along there." (1487~)

—Neon Canyon: The mouth of this northern tributary of the Escalante River is three-quarters of a mile downriver (as the crow flies) from the mouth of Fence Canyon (one-quarter mile west of elevation 5270T on the Egypt map). Its most singular feature, the Golden Cathedral, is a large triple natural bridge a short distance up the canyon. The canyon was named for the show that occurs when light streams through the bridges and hits the large pool below. (874~) Jack Dykinga noted that he thought photographer John Telford named the canyon.

Dennis Turville called this Edge of the Earth Canyon: "When we were on an early reconnaissance of the canyon, I looked back at my friends walking along the rim and thought they looked like they were walking on the edge of the earth." (653~)

Scott Patterson noted that this was called Caverns Hollow: "I've seen an old photograph labeled Caverns Hollow in one of the museums in Southern Utah.... Also, Caverns Hollow is mentioned in some of the trip reports from the earlier runs of the Escalante River when Lake Powell began to fill." (1518~)

—Constructed Stock Trail: This exits Neon Canyon to the north one-eighth mile up from its mouth and goes to Choprock Canyon. Don Coleman noted that he did some blasting on this trail many years ago. (441~, SAPE.)

—Constructed Stock Trail: This starts on the Escalante River just south of the mouth of Neon Canyon and goes northeast onto Baker Bench. (SAPE.)

Chris Otteson Hollow: (Emery Co.) Wasatch Plateau-Huntington Creek. Hiawatha and Red Point maps.

Christian Otteson (1861-1936) moved to Huntington in 1879. An apiarist, he became locally famous for winning an award at the 1903 St. Louis World Fair for his honey. (1195~)

Chris Pond: (Emery Co.) San Rafael Swell-Mulligan Wash. Big Bend Draw map.

Carrie Lou Gremel: "That was Chris Christiansen." (780~)

—Lame Duck Pond: Wayne Gremel: "And just a little south and west [of Chris Pond] is Lame Duck Pond. We were riding along there one day and some ducks flew up and one of them hit a tree. A day or two later I came by and he was swimming around, but he was crippled, so we called it Lame Duck Pond." (780~)

Chriss Lake: (Garfield Co.) Dixie National Forest-Boulder Mountain. Deer Creek Lake map.

Also called Chriss Reservoir.

Correctly spelled Chris Lake.

Chris Moosman (1866-1958) moved his family to Boulder in 1896. (1168~, 1487~) The dam has been breached and has not been repaired. (SAPE.)

Chris Spring: (Kane Co.) Moquith Mountains-Sand Canyon Wash. Yellowjacket Canyon map.

This large spring was once developed.

William L. Crawford, while herding sheep in 1900, noted that a sheepherder named Chriss was using the same area. (483~) Herbert E. Gregory noted that this was Christian Heaton. Gregory also mentioned the "feeding" corrals at Chris Spring. These are the "Corrals" one mile southwest of Chris Spring. A pipe went from the spring, down the cliffs, to the corrals. (758~, SAPE.)

Christensen Spring: (Sevier Co.) Fishlake National Forest-Sevier Plateau-Big Lake. Water Creek Canyon map.

This large spring was once developed. Water from the spring was piped to Big Lake.

Irvin Warnock noted that the Christensen family had a cabin near the spring and ran dairy cows here in the summer. (1971~) This was most likely Albert Christian Christiansen (1841–1897). (388~)

Christiansen Wash: (Emery and Sevier Counties.) Old Woman Plateau-Castle Valley. Emery West, Emery East, Mesa Butte, and Walker Flat maps.

Also called Dripping Vat Creek. (1233~)

Casper Christiansen (1837-1924) and family had a ranch in the area in the late 1870s. (186~) They helped settle the nearby town of Emery. (2056~)

—Lewis Ranch: This historic ranch was on lower Christiansen Creek three miles south of Emery (one-quarter mile south of elevation 6161 on the Emery West map). (567~)

Christiersen Spring: (Sevier Co.) Fishlake National Forest-Sevier Plateau. Koosharem map.

This is a large, developed, and still-used spring. (SAPE.) It was most likely named for the extended Christensen family, early settlers of Sevier County. (388~)

Christmas Ridge: (Grand Co.) Book Cliffs-Crescent Flat. Hatch Mesa and Crescent Junction maps. (5,855')

—Constructed Stock Trail: This goes from Thompson Pass south onto Christmas Ridge (Crescent Junction map). Construction is most obvious near the top. (SAPE.)

—Constructed Stock Trail: This goes up Christmas Ridge on its north side (one-quarter mile southwest of elevation 5855 on the Crescent Junction map). Construction is visible only at the top. (SAPE.)

Chucker Spring: (Garfield Co.) Henry Mountains-Shitamaring Creek. Copper Creek Benches map.

Correctly spelled Chukar Spring.

This is a large spring. (SAPE.)

Chukars are a type of partridge that are common in the Henry Mountains.

Chuck Lake: (Garfield Co.) Dixie National Forest-Boulder Mountain. Government Point map.

Dunk Taylor thought, but was not positive, that a sheepherder named it after seeing a woodchuck there. (1865~)

Church Mesa: (Washington Co.) Zion National Park-Heaps Canyon. Temple of Sinawava map. (7,395')

Haden Wells Church (1817–1875) arrived in St. George in 1861. He was the first school teacher there. (382~, 1141~)

Church Rock: (Navajo Co., Az.) Navajo Indian Reservation-Comb Ridge. Church Rock, Az. map. (5,692')

Also called Church Rock Pillar.

The Antonio Armijo Expedition of 1829–30 noted this as "the rock *artenesales*." (69~, 805~, 855a~)

Charles H. Dimmock of the Captain John N. Macomb Expedition of 1859 sketched Church Rock, with the notation "Red & White Sandstone Butte." (1269~)

Herbert E. Gregory in 1917: "A volcanic neck that rises abruptly from the floor of Tyende Valley to a height of about 300 feet has a rectangular ground plan and a pointed tower that have suggested the name Church Rock." (769~)

Church Rock: (San Juan Co.) Dry Valley-Highway 191. Church Rock map. (6,254')

Also called The Church.

Ethan Pettit of the Elk Mountain Mission of 1855 passed near Church Rock: "There is a big rock on the west side of Pusley vally [Dry Valley] that looks like a large building with a Cupelo and belfry on the top." (1532~)

William Henry Jackson of the Ferdinand V. Hayden Survey in 1875 did not name the rock, but did make a sketch of it in his diary. (950~)

In 1915 a Forest Service manuscript noted that it was "Named for resemblance to church." (2053~) Enid C. Howard in 1972: "Old timers in the area, called it 'The Whiskey Jug.'" (911~)

James H. Knipmeyer noted an inscription from R. Fey, June 11, 1877. (1115~) Other inscriptions include G.N. Harmon, 1916; Norris Shumway, Nov. 28, 1928; and the missive: "Good Bye Little Darling, Good Bye" and the initials W.H., 1917. (SAPE.)

—Old Spanish Trail: The trail went to the west of Church Rock, which was an excellent landmark.

Chute, The: (Emery Co.) San Rafael Swell-Muddy Creek. Hunt Draw map.

This is a narrow and deep section of Muddy Creek that is about eight miles long. It is a favorite destination for hikers, and for boaters during the rare years when the water is high enough.

—Music Canyon: This eastern tributary of Muddy Creek is directly across The Chute of Muddy Creek from The Pasture (between elevations 5508T and 5612T on the Tomsich Butte map). It is in the middle of The Chute. Lloyd Bush: "At one point, there is a dark cavern with remarkable acoustics, and Laurie [Ness], who has a beautiful voice, began to sing. This led to a discussion as to what to name the canyon. We narrowed it down to 'Music' or 'Melody,' and Music finally won out." (318~)

Chute Canyon: (Emery Co.) San Rafael Swell-Little Wild Horse Creek. Horse Valley and Little Wild Horse Mesa maps.

For many years this was the route of an often-used road through the southern San Rafael Reef. Cars could just fit through the tightest spots.

Inscriptions include Diamond Ruff, 1888; Thomas, 1888; S. Robinson, March 8, 1898; and Warren Allred, '99. (1112~, SAPE.)

—Morgan Cabin: A small tin shack near the top of the canyon was a landmark for several decades. It has now been removed. It was built by Bud and Millie Hanni. (166~, 606~) An inscription at the cabin site reads "Morgan's Cabin 1952." (SAPE.)

—Chute Buttress: This is on the west side of Chute Canyon where it enters the San Rafael Reef from the north (at elevation 6508 [Chute] on the Horse Valley map). It was named by Steve Allen.

Chynoweth Canyon: (Kane Co.) GSCENM-Kaiparowits Plateau-Wahweap Creek. Horse Flat and Lower Coyote Spring maps.

Ralph Chynoweth: "There is a hollow coming out of Wahweap Creek and up in the head of the hollow there are some troughs. That is called Chynoweth Canyon. That was my granddad, Sampson 'Sam' Chynoweth [1878-1947]. He went in there and developed that spring and hooked them troughs up and its still called Chynoweth Canyon." (425~)

There are two springs in Chynoweth Canyon, both in the Left Fork. The first is immediately south of elevation 5203 on the Lower Coyote Spring map. A constructed stock trail goes to the spring, and down the canyon to Wahweap Creek.

The second, large and developed, is high in the Left Fork (one-eighth mile north-northeast of elevation 5168 on the Lower Coyote Spring map). A constructed stock trail, coming in from the north, goes to the spring, but does not continue down the canyon. (SAPE.)

—Line Camp: This is on Wahweap Creek a short distance north of the mouth of Chynoweth Canyon. An old school bus and a corral are at the site. (SAPE.)

Cigarette Spring Cave: (San Juan Co.) Cedar Mesa-Cigarette Spring. Cigarette Spring Cave map.

Also called Cave Spring and Cigareet Cave.

This huge cave was a favorite for cowboys and travelers for getting out of the weather, either hot or cold. A medium-size spring is in the cave.

In 1905 H.L.A. Culmer, while on an expedition to visit the natural bridges in White Canyon, called it St. George's Cave, named for guide George Perkins. (494~)

John F. Cargill in 1909: "Our first night's camp ... was made in one of these caves, large enough to shelter ourselves and horses and many others besides.... A sufficient reason for camping within this shelter, rather than in the open, is because of a spring containing the only drinkable water for many miles." (341~)

Initially visitors to the new Natural Bridges National Monument followed the old Hole-in-the-Rock (Emigrant) Trail from Bluff. The trip took several days and Cigarette Spring was a convenient camp spot along the way. The spring was made a part of Natural Bridges National Monument in 1908, but was returned to the BLM when the monument changed its boundary in the early 1960s. The troughs were installed by the Works Progress Administration (WPA). (See Snow Flat Spring Cave.)

DeReese Nielson: "When we camped there, we used to put our horses in there and put bars across that old trail so they couldn't get out, because they'd run away from us." (1451~)

—Cigareet: Cowboys called the highland area between Road and Lime canyons Cigareet or Cigarette Mesa. (1529~) The name was in place by 1909. (1921~)

—Cigareet Ponds: These stock ponds are two and one-quarter miles northwest of Cigarette Spring (one-half mile northwest of elevation 5769). DeReese Nielson helped dig the ponds, noting that they used a Fresno scrapper and a couple of mules. (1451~)

—Dead Bull Flat: (Correctly called Dead Ball Flat.) In 1905 H.L.A. Culmer used the Dead Bull Flat name for the area below Cigarette Spring Cave. (494~) Winston Hurst provided the derivation: "where Bill Ball was killed in 1886 in an ambush by the two horse thieves he was chasing." (935~)

Cinderella Reservoir: (Emery Co.) San Rafael Swell-Horn Silver Gulch. Horn Silver Gulch map.

Also called Cinderella Pond. (1330~)

Ray Wareham noted that the CCC built the pond: "It was a natural pond and they just increased it." (1967~) Lee Mont Swasey: "The old road used to go around and down this hill to where the pond is now. There was a Scotsman who said that there was a mighty hill in Scotland called Cinderella, and it didn't hold a candle to this one! I guess that the hill is in the bentonite clays. I can imagine trying to pull a team and wagon up outta there. They changed the road and came up at Jack's Twist, and then later on built the road where it is now. But that's how Cinderella got its name; because of its proximity to Cinderella Hill." (1853~)

Circle, The: (Sevier Co.) Fishlake National Forest-Sevier Plateau-Cove Mountain. Water Creek Canyon map.

Olive N. Gleave noted that The Circle was a well-known landmark. (1971~)

—The Slide: This is the "Pack Trail" immediately west of Water Creek going up Chicken Gulch to The Circle. (1971~)

Circle Cliffs: (Garfield Co.) Capitol Reef National Park-GSCENM. Maps starting on the west and going clockwise: Lamp Stand, Bear Canyon, Bitter Creek Divide, Wagon Box Mesa, The Post, Deer Point, Horse Pasture Mesa, Silver Falls Bench, Pioneer Mesa, King Bench, and Steep Creek Bench.

The Circle Cliffs Basin is part of the Circle Cliffs Upwarp. This asymmetric anticline is about fifty miles in length and parallels the Waterpocket Fold on its west side. The basin itself is the eroded remains of the upwarp and is most noted for being surrounded by the high Wingate Sandstone walls of the Circle Cliffs.

The Lieutenant George M. Wheeler Survey of 1872–73 called the country between the Waterpocket Fold and the Escalante River, which includes the Circle Cliffs, the Impracticable Ridges. (M.76.) The Circle Cliffs were named by Grove Karl Gilbert of the Powell Survey. (925~, 1893~)

Ward J. Roylance: "Here is a glorious displace of the fabled Sleeping Rainbow, where nature stores a permanent supply of colors that sometimes appear in the sky for precious, fleeting moments. Here, too, is an ancient graveyard of petrified forest giants, long buried but now exposed for all to see." (1661~)

—Tit Mesa: This is on the northeast side of the Circle Cliffs at elevation 7640 (Bitter) on the Bear Canyon map. It was named by Grove Karl Gilbert. (722~)

—Oil: The first oil exploration in the Circle Cliffs Basin was by the Ohio Oil Company in 1921. (888~)

—Uranium: The uranium mining boom in the basin started in the early 1950s with the construction of the switchbacks up Burr Canyon, which allowed easy access from the east. At its height, there were over three thousand mining claims in the area. (699~)

Circle Spring: (Kane Co.) GSCENM-Kaiparowits Plateau. Collett Top map.

Also called Circle Seep.

This medium-size spring was once developed. (SAPE.) Edson Alvey noted that the spring flows from a circular alcove. (55~)

Circle Valley: (Garfield Co.) Sevier Plateau-Sevier River. Mount Dutton, Junction, Circleville, Piute Reservoir, and Bull Rush Peak maps.

Also called Circleville Valley. (188~)

The Parley P. Pratt Exploring Expedition to Southern Utah traversed the area in 1849–1850. (188~) Oluf Christian Larsen in 1865: "We finally reached a large valley in a circular shape surrounded by high mountains, with the river flowing through its center. This valley we called Circle Valley." (1136~)

—Old Spanish Trail: The trail went through Circle Valley. (474~)

Circleville: (Piute Co.) Sevier River-Circle Valley-Highway 89. Circleville map.

Also called Circle Valley.

Kent Whittaker noted that the town is entirely circled by mountains. (2002~)

The Parley P. Pratt Exploring Expedition to Southern Utah of 1849–50 came through Circle Valley. Robert Campbell of the expedition provided the first description:

"We took up the s west branch of the Sevier [River], where there is a few hundred acres in places with rich feed. Land black and loamy, but considerable saleratus [salt]." (1762~)

Lewis Barney was one of the explorers who found the site of Circleville and was one of the first settlers: "This place we called Circleville, this happened before 1865." (156~)

William Morley "Red Bill" Black described the earliest Mormon history of Circleville: "At the Spring Stake conference in 1865 some families were called from Ephraim to go to Circle Valley and make a settlement. My name headed the list.... Circle Valley was looked upon as a favored spot, and a rapid influx of settlers followed the call. A county was organized and a central city laid out.... Then suddenly came the Black Hawk war, with its suffering and sorrow ... the settlers of Circle Valley for months were in a state of siege." (67~)

Oluf Christian Larsen continued the description in 1865: "No matter where we go in the world all is not smiles and sunshine, and so it was in Circleville for we found it to be a very windy place and the open prairie proved to be a very uncomfortable place, especially at night sitting around the campfire baking our bread, frying our meat and cooking our coffee or tea, dust and sand covering everything." (1136~)

Although the settlers built forty-five log houses by 1865, the Indian threat grew too great and the town was abandoned in 1866. Walter Clement Powell of the Powell Expedition of 1871-72: "[passed] through the deserted town of Circleville, a settlement broken up by the Indians a few years ago. The place seemed haunted with its vacant adobes, with staring doors and windows." (1570~) The settlers started to return to the area in 1873. (368~, 1628~)

—Old Spanish Trail: The trail went through what would become Circleville.

Circleville Canyon: (Garfield Co.) Sevier Plateau-Sevier River-Highway 89. Bull Rush Peak and Circleville maps.

The Parley P. Pratt Exploring Expedition to Southern Utah of 1849–50 noted this as "an impassable Kanyon ... the river rushing like a torrent between Perpendicular rocks." (1762~)

In 1872 B. Franklin called it Vulcan's Canyon. (666~) Edwin D. Woolley noted it as Circle Valley Cañon in 1884. (2047~) Kerry Boren noted that it was also called the Sevier River Canyon. (264~)

—Pioneer Road: The first road through the canyon was built in 1865. Edward Tolton in 1865: "At present the road is barely passable, and will require considerable more labor to make it easy for teams, but we are sanguine of seeing these obstacles removed, and the great thoroughfare of the south traveling along this route into 'Dixie,' at no distant day." (1896~)

—Butch Cassidy Boyhood Home: PRIVATE PROPERTY. Kerry Boren: "About three miles south of the little town of Circleville, Utah, in the south end of Circle Valley, near the mouth of Circleville Canyon ... was the childhood home of Robert Leroy Parker. The cabin was built in 1865 by Charles Van Vleet, John James, and Gardner Potter. The Parker family moved into it in 1879. Though the family stayed, Robert Leroy Parker moved out at the age of 18 in 1884." (264~)

Circleville Mountain: (Beaver and Piute Counties.) Fishlake National Forest-Tushar Mountains. Circleville Mountain map. (11,331')

The 1885 USGS Beaver map shows this as Midge Crest.

Cisco Desert: (Grand Co.) Colorado River-Book Cliffs. Also called Grand Valley Desert.

The Cisco Desert name is not used on the USGS topographic maps, but it is a name in common and local use. It refers, in general, to the area between the Colorado River and the Book Cliffs and runs from the Colorado border west to Gunnison Valley (Green River). On the south side this bumps into Tenmile Country; there is no absolute boundary between the areas. The Cisco Desert is the seemingly endless flats on either side of Interstate 70.

The Captain John W. Gunnison Expedition crossed the Cisco Desert in 1853. Jacob H. Schiel was with the expedition: "Before reaching the Green River we traveled for days over a black, clayey and absolutely sterile ground.... We found layers which form isolated standing hills of strange forms and sometimes remarkable heights. Some of them almost assume the form of high domes or houses with colossal chimneys standing beside them. And where the dirty, black formations stand close together, one believes they can see the ruins of a town whose residents lie buried under their crumbling houses of adobe or have left that desolate, barren part of the country." (1696~)

Solomon Nunes Carvalho traversed the area with the John C. Fremont Expedition of 1853–54: "The divide between Grand and the Green River, (the eastern and western forks of the Colorado) is barren and sterile to a degree. At the season that we crossed, there was no water between the two rivers, a distance of about forty miles.... The descent into the valley of the Green River was over most dangerous projections of different strata of rock, thrown into its present state by some convulsion of nature." (385~)

Cisco Springs: (Grand Co.) Book Cliffs-Danish Flat. Cisco Springs map.

(See Cisco Town for name derivation.)

This is a large area of wash-bottom springs in Dry Canyon Wash. Nearby are a couple of sheep corrals and a 1950s or later mining camp. (SAPE.)

Cisco Town: (Grand Co.) Interstate 70-Highway 128-Colorado River. Cisco map.

Also spelled Sisco. (1838a~)

Two name derivations are given.

First, Rufus Wood Leigh noted that *Cisco* is a Spanish word that refers to the coal seams in the area. (1174~)

Second, Mary A. Johnson: "*Cisco* is an Indian name for a kind of fish." (1193~)

This small town was established by the Denver and Rio Grande Western Railroad in 1883 as a place where ranchers could bring their sheep and cattle for transport. At that time the townsite was next to the narrow-gauge line, about two miles north of the present townsite of Cisco. The town moved after the introduction of the standard-gauge railroad in 1890 and the attendant moving of the tracks. (456~, 2056~) (See Denver and Rio Grande Western Railroad.)

Ballard Harris, an early resident of Cisco: "Did you know Cisco used to be called 'Little Chicago,' back in the ol' bootleg days when whiskey was runnin'?... There was dances and everybody sold whiskey there." (1805~)

—Movies: *Thelma and Louise* and *Vanishing Point* were filmed, in part, in Cisco. (1421~)

—Pioneer Road: In 1898 a wagon road was built from Cisco to Moab along the Colorado River. A ferry was installed at Dewey for crossing the river. (257~)

—Helium Mine: In the 19teens Cisco became an important locale for the war effort; it had the only helium mine in the United States. (11~)

—Cisco Landing: (Also called Cisco Pumphouse.) (1838a~) This is a popular takeout for those running Westwater Canyon. Lloyd M. Pierson noted that the Colonel William Wing Loring Expedition of 1857-58 camped here. (1545~)

—Morris Ranch: PRIVATE PROPERTY. This was on the west side of the Colorado River one and one-half miles south-southeast of Cisco Landing (one-quarter mile northwest of elevation 4150T on the Big Triangle map). (518~)

—Sieber Ranch: PRIVATE PROPERTY. (Also called Revoir Ranch and Sieber Bottom.) This was on the west side of the Colorado River one-half mile southeast of the Morris Ranch (one-eighth mile southeast of elevation 4150T on the Big Triangle map). (518~)

—Fish Ford: (Also called Fish Ford Landing.) This boat ramp and camping area is on the west bank of the Colorado River three miles south of Cisco Landing (one-eighth mile south of elevation 4245T on the Big Triangle map). It is mostly used by fishermen.

Cistern Canyon: (Emery Co.) San Rafael Swell-Sinbad Country-Hunt Draw. Horse Valley, Tomsich Butte, Little Wild Horse Mesa, and Hunt Draw maps.

Old maps show this as Boulder Canyon because of a huge chockstone near the head of the canyon. Horses could not go under the boulder. (166~, 925~)

—Ramp Canyon: The mouth of the canyon is one and three-quarters of a mile southwest of Bullberry Spring (southeast of elevation 5450T on the Hunt Draw map). It was named by Steve Allen for the technical crux of the canyon, a steep, thin ramp.

—Quandary Canyon: The mouth of the canyon is one and one-half miles west-southwest of the mouth of Ramp Canyon (at elevation 4802T on the Hunt Draw map). It was named by Steve Allen after a problematic descent. A uranium mining road leads to the top of the canyon and then goes a short distance down it and eventually into upper Knotted Rope Canyon.

—Dripping Spring: (Also called Stinking Spring.) (845~) This is the spring area at the mouth of Quandary Canyon. An Atomic Energy Commission map from the early 1950s named the spring and shows Quandary Canyon as Dripping Spring Canyon. (M.65.)

—Knotted Rope Canyon: The mouth of this northern tributary of Muddy Creek is one mile north-northwest of its junction with Salt Wash. Its head is one-half mile east of elevation 4888T on the Hunt Draw map. A knotted rope used to hang through Wayne's Wriggle, a hole at the top of the cliff. BLM wildlife biologist Wayne Luddington of Price followed several bighorn sheep through the hole, giving the feature its name. This route was used by uranium miners. Much evidence of their tenure abounds. (SAPE.)

—Mining activity: There is evidence of exploratory holes being drilled in both upper Quandary and upper Knotted Rope canyons. Horace Ekker told of drilling the holes while looking for uranium near the Pick [Hidden Splendor] Mine in the early 1950s: "The company was Interstate Mining and Exploration out of New York.... They acquired a group of claims up here on the Muddy right next to this Pick Mine.... Well, we went in there by helicopter and flew those rigs ... on top of that mesa and drilled down. We drilled seven holes back behind that Pick formation to ease up the ore. We never got one earthly thing. We spent $350,000 there and never got a smell." (620~)

City Creek: (Piute Co.) Fishlake National Forest-Tushar Mountains-Piute Reservoir. Delano Peak and Piute Reservoir maps.

This was named for the town of City Creek (now Junction). (1444~)

E.C. Bird: "derived its name from being the main source of the city water supply." (2053~) The name was in place before 1865. (156~)

—Thompson Reservoir: This is near the Junction Airport (Piute Reservoir map). Thomas Thomas in 1941: "was so named because Ambrose Thompson built the ditch that runs from City Creek and empties into this reservoir." (2053~)

Clarence Creek: (Garfield Co.) Dixie National Forest-Sevier Plateau-West Fork Hunt Creek. Flake Mountain West map.

Unattributed: "So named because Clarence Showalter [ca. 1876-1941] ranged sheep in this canyon about 1890 to 1900." (2053~, 1346~)

Clark Lake: (San Juan Co.) Manti-LaSal National Forest-La Sal Mountains-Boren Mesa. Mount Tukuhnikivatz map.

Lloyd Holyoak: "The Clarks had a ranch over in Castle Valley." (906~)

Clark Lake: (Wayne Co.) Dixie National Forest-Boulder Mountain. Blind Lake map.

Also called Alex Clark Lake.

Emmett Clark noted that this natural lake was named for Alexander Clarke (1872-1963) of Grover. He is credited with building many trails throughout Dixie National Forest. (426~, 2051~)

Clarks Canyon: (Iron Co.) Hurricane Cliffs-Parowan Valley-Cedar Valley. Enoch map.

Estella J. Grimsaw: "The canyon is named for the three Clark brothers, Porter, Collins, and Edgar, who owned the meadowland west of the canyon." (942~)

—Clarks Spring: This is in Clarks Canyon. Ivar D. Jones: "Myron Jones and son Ivar, piped the water from the spring through a wooden pipe to water a garden in the summer of 1920." (942~)

Clark Valley: (Carbon Co.) Book Cliffs-Highway 123. Pine Canyon, Sunnyside, and Sunnyside Junction maps.

Jean S. Greenwood: "One of the first to settle there [before 1898] was a man named Clark who owned a well-stocked cattle ranch. There were houses, stables, granaries, and a blacksmith's shop on the place." (1195~)

A prolonged drought forced abandonment of the ranch for several years. In 1906 Orson Dimick and John Higginson settled on the ranch. (1621~)

—Kiz Town: This town was on the west side of Clarks Valley near the "Cemetery" on the Sunnyside Junction map. The Clark Ranch became the future site of Kiz Town. By 1926 the town was large enough for its own post office. Jean S. Greenwood: "In selecting a suitable name, [George] Mead proposed the name of Kiz in honor of [Lydia] Kiziah Dimick [1861-1935], the pioneer woman of Clarks Valley who was known as Aunt Kiz." (1195~) Because of a lack of water for agriculture, the town slowly disbanded and by 1940 was abandoned.

Clause Pond: (Piute Co.) Parker Mountain-Nicks Point. Angle map.

Correctly spelled Claus Pond.

Thaine Taylor and Alfonzo Turner noted that Claus William Deleeuw (1904-1994) ran stock in the area in the 1960s. (1868~, 1914~, 338~)

Clawson Town: (Emery Co.) Castle Valley-Highway 10. Castle Dale map.

Edward Johannes Jorgensen noted that he was the first person to move to what became Clawson, in 1894. (377~) The town of Clawson was founded on what was then called North Flat in 1897 after the Ferron North Ditch was completed. It brought water from Ferron Creek to the area. Early names for the town included Silver Dell, Poverty Flat, North Flat, and Kingville or Kingsville (for settler Guy King). (972~) By 1902, irrigation-induced alkali problems forced the residents to move the town, which was two miles east of the present site of Clawson. (2053~) Naomi Jensen told the story of how the new site was chosen: "Bishop Nelson, his counselors, and some others got into his buggy to look the situation over. He had a new buggy and new harness and a lively team of horses, and when he came to the hill ... he stopped the team to look around, but when he went to start again, the clip on the singletree broke. Bishop Nelson got out of the buggy, wired it together and started out again, but had only gone a few feet when the other clip on the singletree broke off in the same manner. So he got out of the buggy and said, 'this is proof enough for me. This is the place.'" (1330~) Apostle Rudger Clawson (1857-1943) helped organize a Mormon Church Ward in the town in 1904. (710~, 1330~)

Clay Canyon: (Garfield Co.) Henry Mountains-Big Thompson Mesa-Bullfrog Creek. Deer Point and Clay Point maps.

Charles B. Hunt: "[The] name refers to the badland, clay hills along this tributary to Bullfrog Creek." (925~)

Clay Creek: (Garfield Co.) Dixie National Forest-Escalante Mountains-East Fork Sevier River. Pine Lake, Sweetwater Creek, and Flake Mountain East maps.

Also called Lower Pine Creek. (1455~)

Clay Creek runs through Pine Canyon.

William Gladstone Steel in 1926: "Flows through a sticky clay." (1819~) The name was in place by 1915. (668~)

Clay Creek: (Kane Co.) Dixie National Forest-Paunsaugunt Plateau-East Fork Sevier River. Podunk Creek and Tropic Reservoir maps.

Hyrum Barton in 1941: "It is so named because of the clay soil." (2053~) George G. Mace in 1942: "The name is indicated by the clay formation there." (2053~)

Clay Draw: (San Juan Co.) Manti-LaSal National Forest-Abajo Mountains-Spring Creek. Monticello Lake map.

Irving J. Witkind noted this as Vega Creek in 1954. (2036~)

Clay Dugway Spring: (Wayne Co.) Fishlake National Forest-Thousand Lake Mountain. Flat Top map.

This large spring is along a steep part of an old road—the Clay Dugway—that goes to the top of Flat Top. (SAPE.)

Clay Flat: (Kane Co.) Block Mesas-Yellowjacket Canyon. Mount Carmel map.

The name was in place by 1895. (416~)

—Shearing Corral: From the late 1890s into the early 1900s there was a sheep shearing corral on Clay Flat. (483~)

Clay Flats: (Sevier Co.) San Rafael Swell-Limestone Cliffs. Johns Peak and Willow Springs maps.

Jim Crane: "That name is wrong! I want to set it straight! It has always been called The Frying Pan." (478~) Garn Jefferies: "A road goes across Clay Flats, comin' from the [Jefferies] ranch. Boy, it's bad when it gets wet"! (959~)

Clay Hills Crossing: (San Juan Co.) Glen Canyon NRA-San Juan River. Mikes Mesa map.

Also called Navajo Ford. (472~)

This historic crossing of the San Juan River was part of an old Indian trail that went from the area near Goulding's Trading Post, by Train and Organ rocks, under Monitor Butte, and down Piute Wash. From there it crossed the river at Clay Hills Crossing and went along the base of the Red Cliffs.

The Captain John N. Macomb Expedition of 1859 called this Navajo Crossing. (1943~)

In the 1860s the chief of the Navajo, Hoskinnini, used the crossing while being pursued by Kit Carson, giving it another name: Hoskinnini Crossing. (501~) The route was also used by gold miners in the 1890s.

In 1954–55 uranium miners built the present-day road that goes from Highway 276 to the crossing. Today, Clay Hills Crossing is the standard exit for boaters going down the San Juan River. (1021~, 1370~, 1407~)

—Recompense: This San Juan River placer bar was on the left bank of the river between Clay Hills Crossing and Piute Farms. It was also called The Cottonwoods and Hoskinnini Camp. (472~)

Clay Hills Divide: (San Juan Co.) Red House Cliffs-Highway 276. Clay Hills map. (5,220')

Also called Clay Hills Pass. (774~)

The Clay Hills are an area of rolling hills in the vicinity of Clay Hills divide. The first Euroamericans known to have crossed the Clay Hills and discover Clay Hills Divide were members of the Hole-in-the-Rock Expedition in 1880. Cornelius Isaac Decker of the expedition: "We called it Clay Hill it had so much hard blue clay on it." (1356~) The expedition was following what they described as an "Indian Trail" over the pass. To get wagons over the pass took them eight days of difficult road construction.

David E. Miller: "Here was another drop of approximately a thousand feet, and a road had to be built all the way. However, this was a different kind of road work. Sticky blue clay was not pleasant to work with, but it was easier than the solid rock that had confronted the expedition during most of its journey." (1356~)

Expedition member Samuel Rowley: "Here we made another halt, to build the road down Clay Hill.... When the road was finished, we started down. A snow storm made our progress very miserable.... We'd come to the top of a hill, then detach the lead horses and the wives would drive them down the hill, while the men brought the wagons down with one pair of horses.... When we arrived at the bottom again, our oxen were gone and darkness was upon us and we had to camp for the night. We were at the bottom of the hill without wood and very little water. It was dark and still snowing." (1014~)

Josephine Catherine Chatterly Wood in 1882: "This country is beautiful but such a terrible road through a steep winding canyon. The mountains are all colors and very beautiful." (2041~)

Neil M. Judd in 1924: "The Clay Hills rise as an unscalable barrier of blue and gray shales and sheer sandstone cliffs. A single narrow gateway leads through and beyond this barrier." (1028~)

Charles L. Bernheimer in 1929: "As we approached the Clay Hills, if romantically inclined, we could have gone into ecstasy. The 'painted desert' in all its glory grew more brilliant as we advanced. Dark chocolate layers of rock 600 feet deep formed buttresses rippled and banded. Above these were the Chinle formation Badlands, and I have never seen them more pronounced in color and structure. The higher portions were landed in green, sea-green, turquoise blue, orange, lemon, purple, indigo blue and dark brown.... The rocks were vicious looking. Nature had done its most cruel work. It had mashed things up, baked the masses into new forms, and had torn them asunder mercilessly.... Color photography would have been welcome. We were helpless and descriptive words are futile.... It was like dwelling in a rainbow. All its colors and hundreds of demi-tone shadings gamboled around us. I shall never forget Clay Hills Pass." (218~)

An inscription, often credited to the Hole-in-the-Rock pioneers, reads "Make Peace With God." (1115~, SAPE.)

—Clay Hills Spring: The Hole-in-the-Rock Expedition discovered a spring near Clay Hills Pass, which they called Oak Spring. Later, after the oaks died, it was renamed Clay Hills Spring. It is a short distance to the northeast of the pass. (1356~)

—Uranium Miner's Cave. This cave, and the incredible rock trail leading to it, are one-half mile west of Clay Hills Divide (one-quarter mile northwest of elevation 6547T). (818~) Inscriptions include Hole-in-the-Rock Expedition member S.S. Smith, March? 1880. (1115~, SAPE.)

—The present road (Highway 276) across Clay Hills Divide parallels some sections of the Hole-in-the-Rock Road. It was initially graded by the Skelly Oil Company in 1952 while building a road to the top of Nokai Dome. It wasn't paved until the 1970s. (466~, 1407~, 1562~)

Clay Hole Wash: (Kane Co.) GSCENM-Kitchen Corral Wash. Nephi Point and Eightmile Pass maps.

Also called Jennies Clay Hole (1831~) and Jenny Clay Hole (369~).

Julius S. Dalley: "Named for the fact that burros watered there; the female being a Jenny." (2053~)

—Jennys Clay Hole: This spring is in the upper part of the canyon (Nephi Point map). Cal Johnson: "There's quite a lot of water there in Jenny Clayhole. It isn't good drinking water; it is good cow water. It's pretty slick if you drink it." (984~)

—Honeymoon Trail: This went through Clay Hole Wash. (984~, 1831~)

Clayhole Wash: (Mohave Co., Az.) Hurricane Cliffs-Fort Pearce Wash. Lost Spring Mountain West and Rock Canyon, Az. maps.

Ashby Reeve noted that there was a lot of clay in the water here. Ashby told of the early days when they would watch as wild horses would come to the wash and fill up.

Once belly full, and unable to run fast, the cowboys would jump out and catch them. (1608~)

Clay Point: (Garfield Co.) Henry Mountains-Bullfrog Creek. Clay Point map. (5,032')

Bliss Brinkerhoff noted that the point is composed of the clay-like Mancos Shale. (291~)

—Clay Point Reservoir: An abandoned mining road leads to this collapsed stock pond. Ranchers call it Link Lyman Pond for a local rancher. It was built in the late 1950s. (291~, SAPE.)

—Pot Pond: This stock reservoir is one mile south of Clay Point Reservoir (near elevation 4926AT). Bliss Brinkerhoff: "I was with three Bureau of Land Management fellers and three or four of us cowboys and we were picking out the sites for Bliss Pond and the Brown Pond. We were walkin' along and we went over the ledge and down to the site where we wanted to build this Pot Pond. I was the last one, bein' short-legged, goin' down this canyon and just afore we got there I looked on the ledge right above our heads and there set this Indian pot. I though, 'Well, there's no way in the world that I'm goin' to get that bowl. I'm the last one of seven guys here and somebody's going to see that thing.' All six of 'em walked past. When I got even with it I reached up and took the bowl and I had it in my hand and I said, 'Hey, you guys, how come you didn't want this Indian bowl? It's almost perfect.' They all stopped in their tracks and looked around and old Nick Gonatakes said, 'Hey, you ain't supposed to be takin' up that kind of stuff.' I says, 'I know it, but if I put it back down I know some Bureau of Land Management fellers'll be here before morning.' So that's why the pond is named Pot Pond." (291~)

—Blue Point: Charles B. Hunt noted that the southeast end of Clay Point is called Blue Point (at elevation 5153T on the Lost Spring map). (925~)

Clay Seep: (Emery Co.) Cedar Mountain-Cottonwood Wash. Cow Flats map.

This is a medium-size, wash-bottom seep. (SAPE.)

Clayton Spring: (Garfield Co.) Dixie National Forest-Escalante Mountains-Antimony Creek. Barker Reservoir map.

Nethella Griffin Woolsey noted that this was named for rancher Albert Clayton. (2051~)

Pratt Gates: "You can't believe the taste of it. It's so good. It's just as cold as cold as could be." (709~)

—Clayton Ranger Station: (Also called Clayton Station.) Sonny King: "Right at Clayton Springs was an old guard station. Years and years ago they had an old log cabin there and they called it the Clayton Ranger Station. They would use it in the summertime. It was really beautiful." (1095~) The station was built in 1909 at a cost of four hundred dollars. (887~)

Clear Creek: (Garfield and Iron Counties.) Dixie National Forest-Panguitch Lake. Red Creek Reservoir and Panguitch Lake maps.

Wallace Adair noted that the water in the creek is exceptionally clear. (2053~)

Clear Creek: (Kane Co.) Glen Canyon NRA-Escalante River-Lake Powell. Davis Gulch map.

Stockmen and early explorers to the lower Escalante Canyon, tired of drinking the often dirty river water, relished the "champagne-clear" water flowing from springs in Clear Creek Canyon. (47~, 1382~) (See Cathedral in the Desert.)

—Clear Creek Trail: (See Appendix Two—Lower Desert to Halls Creek Trail.)

Clear Creek: (Kane and Washington Counties.) Clear Creek Mountain-Zion National Park-Pine Creek. Clear Creek Mountain, The Barracks, and Springdale East maps.

William Adair and John H. Watson in 1942: "This creek was so named because of its clear water." (2053~)

—Keyhole Canyon: (Also called The Jughandle.) The mouth of this northern tributary of Clear Creek is one and one-quarter miles (as the crow flies) west of the north end of Checkerboard Mesa (immediately west of elevation 6848 on the Springdale East map). Dennis Turville noted that another name was Starfish Canyon: "Named by locals who thought it looked like a starfish on the Zion map." (653~) Jonathan Zambella: "The Jughandle ... was renamed the Keyhole, by Rick Praetzel in 1996 due to its entry wall formation at the first rappel which looks like a skeleton key hole." (653~)

—Aires Butte: (Also called Mount Aires.) This is immediately west of Keyhole Canyon (at elevation 6492 on the Springdale East map). (1591~)

—South Aires Butte: This is one-quarter mile south of Aires Butte. (1591~)

—Ant Hill: This is one-half mile north of Clear Creek and one and one-half miles west-northwest of the north end of Checkerboard Mesa (at elevation 6641 on the Springdale East map). (1591~)

—Scarlet Begonias: This summit is one-half mile north of the Ant Hill (at elevation 6995 on the Springdale East map). (1570a~)

—Clear Creek Ranch: PRIVATE PROPERTY. This was started in the late 1870s. Several ranches are now located along the creek. (2053~, SAPE.)

Clear Creek: (Sevier Co.) Fishlake National Forest-Ivie Creek. Hilgard Mountain, Johns Peak, and Old Woman Plateau maps.

Also called Clear Creek Canyon.

Inscriptions include M.W. Molen, May 1, 1876. (SAPE.)

—Clear Creek Guard Station: Jim Crane: "Six or seven years ago the Forest Service decided they didn't want to maintain the guard station any more. So they let us use it. We thought that was the easiest thing they ever did for us. We used it for a base camp and put our salt and stuff in there ... but then it burned down." (478~)

Clear Creek Canyon: (Sevier Co.) Fishlake National Forest-Tushar Mountains-Interstate 70-Sevier River. Trail Mountain and Marysvale Canyon maps.

Jedediah Smith of the South West Expedition of 1826–27 went through Clear Creek Canyon: "I ascended a small creek." (1774~)

Gwinn Harris Heap of the Lieutenant Edward F. Beale Expedition of 1853 called it Beaver Creek. (854~) George Washington Bean, Silas S. Smith, and party explored the canyon in 1863. (176~)

J.N. in 1874: "The scenery in the canyon, for wild sublimity, beauty and grandeur, is probably scarcely surpassed.... Soon after passing the head of the canyon the eye of the traveler is struck with admiration at the wonderful and ponderous character of his surroundings.... The masonry of nature assumes the most fantastic forms; now towering skyward to giddy heights, and again forming into natural battlements, reminding one of the historic feudal strongholds of the 'old World,' while other strange formations would bring forcibly to mind the remains of ancient monasterial architecture, which attract the curiosity seeking of the present generation." (1466~)

An inscription in the canyon from 1826 is thought to have been left by a member of Jedediah Smith's South West Expedition. The inscription has apparently disappeared. Other inscriptions include Andell?, Jun 26, 1877; Geo. Chesley, April ?, 187?; and JWEPO, Ap 21, 1887. (SAPE.)

—Pioneer Road: A road through the canyon was built in 1874 at a cost of eight thousand dollars. (1466~)

—Railroad Grade: In 1880 the Denver and Rio Grande Western Railroad started construction of a railroad through Clear Creek Canyon. Many miles of narrow gauge railbed were built. Before rails were laid, though, the route was abandoned for one that went farther north, through Price. (712~, 1659~) (See Denver and Rio Grande Western Railroad.)

—Lott Ranch: This was on the north side of Clear Creek one-quarter mile west of the mouth of Skinner Canyon.

Joe Lott and family homesteaded here from the early 1880s into the early 1900s. (1551~)

—Centennial Cabin: This cabin, now on the site of the old Lott Ranch, was moved to the area from Junction in 1995. The cabin, built in the mid-1880s, is similar to the cabin (now gone) that Lott built. (1551~)

Clearwater Canyon: (Garfield Co.) Glen Canyon NRA-Orange Cliffs-Cataract Canyon. Clearwater Canyon map. Stephen Vandiver Jones of the 1871–72 Powell Expedition described the lower canyon: "At first the cañon seemed to be the rocky bed of a torrent, not unlike others we had seen, but after climbing 2 or 3 steep walls a scene of beauty presented itself more wonderful than anything I ever saw. The walls rose on either side for 3000 feet. The narrow rocky valley was full of small trees and flowers. A tiny rivulet trickled down, sometimes lost, sometimes pent by the boulders into deep clear pools.... It seemed a paradise in the midst of a wilderness, and we called it 'Eden Cañon.'" (1023~)

Almon H. Thompson, also of the Powell Expedition: "We have had grand scenes and beautiful scenes, but none where beauty, grandeur and sublimity were so combined in one glance.... It would be a wondrous beautiful glen anywhere, but it is doubly so in this almost barren region." (1877~)

Ellsworth Kolb of the William R. Chenoweth USGS Expedition of 1921: "camped at a beautiful side canyon with clear pools, coming in from the north. I suggest calling it Chenoweth Canyon, but he [Chenoweth] overrules it and calls it Clearwater." (1669~)

Buzz Holmstrom in 1937: "at the mouth of Clearwater Creek.... This creek has the first water I have seen since the San Rafael River, and is clear and good to drink." (903~)

—Willow Tank: This natural pond at the base of a pour-off is in a small western tributary of upper Clearwater Canyon that is one mile southeast of Gunsight Butte (one-eighth mile north of elevation 5655T). The spring was developed by the Chaffin family. (615~) A constructed stock trail leads to the pond. Inscriptions include A. [Andy] H. Miller, 1895; Ford Weber, 1922; and Leland Bohleen, Ma 3, 1930. (SAPE.)

—Cottonwood Spring: This natural pond at the base of a small pour-off is in Clearwater Canyon three-quarters of a mile (as the crow flies) south of the road (one-half mile west-northwest of elevation 5441T). A stock trail, now collapsed, went around the pond and down the cliff. It was built by Faun Chaffin and Joe Biddlecome in the 1920s. (100~, 411~) Inscriptions include Ned Chaffin, Aug. 17, 1930. (SAPE.)

—Crowbar Tank: This pothole is in a northern tributary of Clearwater Canyon whose mouth is one and one-half miles upcanyon from the Colorado River (at the top of the cliff one-quarter mile southeast of elevation 5441T). Ned Chaffin: "Faun and Clell [Chaffin] and I shot a trail into this large natural tank. While Clell was moving a large rock, the rock rolled over and tore the crowbar from his hands. Both the rock and the crowbar went over the rim into the unaccessible canyon below so the tank where we lost the crowbar became Crowbar Tank." (606~)

—Eyes of Clearwater: This double natural arch in Clearwater Canyon was named by Joe Wrona in 1999. (SAPE.)

—Sidewalk Spring: (Also called Sidewalk Seep.) (1672~) This small spring is in a short western tributary of Clearwater Canyon that is two miles north-northeast of Red Point (one-quarter mile west-northwest of elevation 5470T). (615~) Ned Chaffin: "This is more of a seep than a spring. To get to this water it is necessary to cross the solid sandstone for some distance. The rock here is exceptionally smooth, like a sidewalk (almost)." (606~) A nearby, and very old, corral identifies the spring area. (SAPE.)

—1908 Emergency Exit: In October 1908 Karl Keller and William J. Law wrecked their boat in Cataract Canyon just below the mouth of Clearwater Canyon. Keller drowned. Law, unable to continue downriver by boat, found a way out of the canyon to the west a short distance below Clearwater Canyon. After eleven days he finally made it to civilization. (896~) It is most likely that the Law emergency exit was by way of a steep gully located one mile below Clearwater Canyon (immediately south of elevation 5404T on the Bowdie Canyon West map). At the top of the gully, and unrelated to Law's adventure, is an old inscription reading "God Bless Our Home" and the name Geo. Larsen, no date. (SAPE.)

Cleft Arch: (San Juan Co.) Canyonlands National Park-Needles District-Lavender Canyon. Cathedral Butte map. Also called Triangle Arch. (1403~, 1931~) This was named by members of a National Geographic Society expedition in 1961. (1381~) Fran Barnes: "The arch is named after the vertical lengthwise crack or 'cleft' in the span that can be seen only while standing in its opening." (147~)

Cleopatras Chair: (Wayne Co.) Glen Canyon NRA-Orange Cliffs. Cleopatras Chair map. (6,520') Also called Cleopatras Needle. (560~) Edwin T. Wolverton called this the Star and Crescent. (1736~)

Hazel Ekker in 1965: "As to the chair, Mr. Wolverton was one of the first ones to call it Cleopatra's Chair as I recall." (617~)

Frank E. Masland, Jr. in 1966: "From all angles, Cleopatra's Chair sits atop the world—as did the lady." (1310~)

Cleveland Canal: (Emery Co.) Castle Valley-Huntington. Huntington, Cleveland, and Poison Spring Bench maps. (See Cleveland Town for name derivation.)

This was built under the direction of Cleveland Town founder Samuel N. Alger between 1885 and 1889. It diverted water from Huntington Creek to Cleveland over a distance of twenty-five miles. (373~, 710~)

Cleveland-Lloyd Dinosaur Quarry: (Emery Co.) Cedar Mountain-Cottonwood Wash. Cow Flats map.

This is a BLM-managed quarry on the north side of Cedar Mountain. Dinosaur bones were found by cowboys on what was then called Cow Flat in the early 1920s. In 1939 Lee Stokes, a Princeton student originally from Cleveland, Utah led a University of Utah group to the location and serious and scientific recovery work started. The area was designated a National Natural Landmark in 1966. The Visitor Center was constructed in 1968. (386~, 710~, 1330~, 2056~)

Cleveland Reservoir: (Emery Co.) Manti-LaSal National Forest-Huntington Creek. Candland Mountain map. Also called Cleveland Lake.

(See Cleveland Town for name derivation.)

N.C. Oveson in 1941: "Named because it holds water used by Cleveland residents." (2053~) The dam for the reservoir was built in 1909 and rebuilt in 1985.

Cleveland Town: (Emery Co.) Castle Valley-Sand Wash. Cleveland map.

The town was established in 1884 by the Sam N. Alger and Henry W. Oviatt families. It was named in honor of President Grover Cleveland. (710~, 1330~)

Cliff: (Emery Co.) San Rafael Swell-Denver and Rio Grande Western Railroad. Cliff map. Also called Cliff Siding. (21.B.)

This was a stopping place on the Denver and Rio Grande Western Railroad. Unattributed: "The railway is opposite and rather close to the highest headlands of the Beckwith Plateau, and what could be a more appropriate name than CLIFF." (606~) (See Denver and Rio Grande Western Railroad.)

Cliff: (Garfield Co.) Glen Canyon NRA-Waterpocket Fold. Stevens Canyon North map.

This high point on the Waterpocket Fold is shown as "Cliff" at elevation 6745.

—Cliff Spring: (Also called Diz Spring.) This medium-large pothole is on the edge of Stevens Canyon one-eighth mile south-southwest of Cliff. It has a short constructed stock trail leading to it. David D. Rust in 1941: "To Monument Point (maybe high point of Water Pocket). Tanks of water and good pasture for animals near high bald-head." (1672~, SAPE.)

—Lower Cliff Spring: (Also called Lower Diz Spring.) This large, reed-filled pothole is one-quarter mile southeast of Cliff Spring. A constructed stock trail leads to it. (SAPE.)

Cliff Arch: (Kane Co.) Glen Canyon NRA-Coyote Gulch. King Mesa map.

Robert H. Vreeland: "As one of the largest jughandles in the United States, this arch deserves special mention.... Local people call this Jug Handle Arch because of its likeness to a handle of a jug or pitcher." (1953~)

D. Eldon Beck in 1943: "We named this arch the 'Dellenbaugh Arch.' Dellenbaugh was also associated with Major Powell." (178~) It was renamed by a National Geographic Society expedition in 1955. W. Robert Moore of the expedition: "We named it Cliff Arch because of the unusual manner in which the bandlike buttress clings against the canyon wall." (1382~)

Cliff Canyon: (San Juan Co.) Navajo Indian Reservation-Navajo Mountain-Aztec Creek. Rainbow Bridge map. Also called Cliff Canyon Brook. (221~)

Indian trader William F. Williams visited the canyon in the 1880s. His daughter, Billie Williams Yost, quoted William F.: "It was named [Broken Leg Canyon] because a party of white prospectors were jumped there by Paiute Indians early in 1884. They were all killed except one fellow. He escaped and got as far as that canyon, then slipped and broke his leg. Next morning a couple of prospectors ... found him and brought him out." (2059~)

John Wetherill and Charles L. Bernheimer named it Cliff Canyon during the Charles L. Bernheimer Expedition of 1922. Bernheimer: "Cliff Canyon, so named by us because of the continuous twelve hundred foot high almost exclusively smooth surface." (221~)

Inscriptions include Buck Moore, 1929 and Bob Wilson, 5-22-30. (SAPE.)

—Sunset Pass: (Also called The Saddle and Yabut Pass.) This is at the head of Cliff Canyon (one-quarter mile northwest of elevation 7330T). The pass was discovered by the Charles L. Bernheimer Expedition of 1922. They are credited with making a rough trail from the pass into Cliff Canyon. (843~) Bernheimer described their descent into the canyon: "We all walked, the most awful sliding and slipping and mussing in sand gravel and broken slate like clinkers. The animals did the same." (218~)

The Samuel I. Richardson family, who built the original Rainbow Lodge, were responsible for dramatically improving the trail in the mid-1920s into one that they could comfortably use to take tourists from the lodge to Rainbow Bridge. (1625~)

Bill Williams ran the Rainbow Lodge in 1931: "They say this is the worst trail in America, and I ain't saying it ain't." (627~)

Wilmot R. Evans in 1931: "And then we stood on the rim of Cliff Canyon and looked down two thousand feet at as wild a scene as ever greeted human eyes. In some places the walls dropped sheer almost half a mile. And away beyond the mouth of the canyon there stretched as far as the eye could see into the distant purple haze, interminable masses of tangled rock thrown together in the wildest confusion. And down into these awful depths and through those seemingly impassable cliffs led our way." (627~)

J.B. Priestly in 1937: "The scenery of this trail cannot be adequately photographed, drawn, painted or described. It is as if the Grand Canyon had been cut up and then thrown about the landscape. If that conveys nothing, you must imagine yourself traveling, at all angles, between colossal sandstone cliffs, golden, orange, rust-brown, vermilion, magenta, sometimes smoothly sliced off for 500 feet or so, sometimes like 1000-foot bastions of burnished copper, sometimes tortured into weird pinnacles. And you travel nearly all day, and every few minutes the whole thing looks different, with the sunlight working miracles at every turn. It is the landscape of some mad Arabian Nights story.... It is not merely the stupendous size of everything, making you feel like a fly that has wandered into a normal-sized gorge or glen. It is not even the fantastic towering shapes of rock, though they are impressive enough, that do the trick. You have to add to these the color, or, rather, the wild riot of colors, making every other kind of mountain scenery you have known seem by comparison to be a dingy affair of grays and blacks." (90~)

Randall Henderson and a group of seventy-two Sierra Club hikers went through the pass in 1940. Henderson: "From this point what a panorama! If you can imagine the coloring of Bryce Canyon combined with the rugged majesty of Grand Canyon you have a picture that approaches the view from Rainbow trail [at Sunset Pass]. It is a landscape of cliffs and turrets and canyons and domes as far as the eye can see—all daubed and streaked and splashed with the pastels of the painted desert." (867~)

Winona J. Holloway, who ran the Rainbow Lodge in the early 1950s, described going through Sunset Pass, or what she called The Window: "At the top of a very sharp ridge an opening has been blasted and widened enough for a horse and rider to get through. After the gap, the trail turns sharply to the right and goes up a little rise. As you turn the last point you look out on nothing but blue. Everyone who rode the trail remembers that spot. Who can forget coming out on top and looking out through 'The Window' to what appears to be nothing beyond"? (900~) (See Dome Canyon—Half Dome Trail.)

—First Water: This is the first reliable water for those hiking from Rainbow Lodge down Cliff Canyon. It is one-half mile up Cliff Canyon from where the trail turns northeast over Redbud Pass (one-quarter mile north of elevation 5191AT). (843~) Charles L. Bernheimer described Cliff Canyon and First Water in 1922: "We got down [into Cliff Canyon from The Saddle] only to find that Cliff Canyon was bone dry, vegetation withered, an awful and inspiring sickroom of Dam Nature.... But what can one expect of the 'corner of the earth which God forgot'? A dread gradually came upon us that we may not find any water at all in Cliff Canyon.... Two hours travel in Cliff Canyon brought us to a little pin hole in the cliff out of which a bit of moisture oozed. The men were safe, but how about the animals? This pinhole spring changed all this and when one or two miles further we saw the reflection of a water pool, our rejoicing was a treat to behold. It was a little stream that showed on the surface and then disappeared in the sand, coming out later on. We pitched camp among cedar and cottonwood and called it Cliff Camp. The water was delicious." (218~)

In 1940 Randall Henderson may have been the first to suggest, inadvertently, the name: "We found water seeping from the sands in the bottom of the gorge, the first opportunity we had had since leaving the [Rainbow] lodge to replenish our canteens." (867~)

Winona Johnson Holloway noted that they called this Hummingbird Spring "because these little creatures hovered there to drink." (900~) In 1978 Rob Schultheis noted that it was also called Eightmile Camp because it is eight miles from the Rainbow Lodge site. (1700~)

—Painted Rock Camp: This is at the junction of Cliff and Red Bud Pass canyons. The name was given by Charles L. Bernheimer in 1922: "We named it Painted Rock Camp because of drawings [pictographs] in three colours, red, yellow, and black, on the rock face near by." (221~)

Wilmot R. Evans in 1931: "There was a big cliff that had a niche with lunetted [shaped like the moon] top like an alcove in a church wall. Pictographs of familiar and strange animals appeared. [Guide] Bill [Wilson] called one a five-legged pig, and it looked like that. But pigs were unknown in this country and the pictograph pig was probably meant for a bear." (627~)

—Constructed Stock Trail. This exits lower Cliff Canyon one-half mile east of its junction with Aztec Creek and goes north to the top of the cliffs (near elevation 4388T). Only one short section of construction is left. (SAPE.)

Cliff Dweller Flat: (Emery Co.) San Rafael Swell-Sagebrush Bench. Arsons Garden and Drowned Hole Draw maps.

Also called Cliff Dweller Peak. (195~)

Two name derivations are given.

First, Lee Mont Swasey: "I have not found the Cliff Dweller ... in this area it usually would mean an Indian granary." (1853~)

Second, this was most likely named for the nearby Swasey Cabin. In the early days, before the cabin was built, the Swasey family lived in a nearby cave, which they called the Cliff Dweller. (510~) (See Eagle Canyon—Swasey Cabin.)

Cliff Dwellers Lodge: (Coconino Co., Az.) Vermilion Cliffs-Alt. Highway 89. Emmett Wash, Az. map. PRIVATE PROPERTY.

In 1927 Blanche Russell was driving through the area and her car broke down. While waiting for repairs she explored the area and fell in love with it. Buying land here, she and her husband, Bill, built several stone houses in the early 1930s.

After Bill died, Jack Church bought the property. In 1949 Art Greene, a well-known Glen Canyon river runner and guide, bought the property and built the present-day Cliff Dwellers Lodge. (1394~, 1551~)

—Honeymoon Trail: This went right by what is now Cliff Dwellers Lodge. Inscriptions include Alma N. Iversen, from Pleasant Grove to Arizona, A.D. Mar 23rd, 1876; and L. Jensen, March 23, 1876. (SAPE.)

Cliff Spring: (Garfield Co.) Glen Canyon NRA-Silver Falls Creek. Silver Falls Bench map.

This large spring was once developed.

This is also called Ormond Spring for rancher Burns Ormond. He developed the spring. (441~) Burns called it Bowns Bench Seep. (1487~) The original troughs built by Burns are still there, as is a more recent cattle tank.

Inscriptions near the spring date to 1930. (SAPE.)

Clints Canyon: (Kane Co.) GSCENM-Kaiparowits Plateau-John Henry Canyon. Nipple Butte and Tibbet Bench maps.

—Clints Spring: (Tibbet Bench map.) This is a large, wash-bottom spring. (SAPE.)

Clipper Western Canal: (Emery Co.) Castle Valley-Orangeville. Red Point and Castle Dale maps.

Edward A. Geary noted that this was built in 1878 to bring water to Orangeville. (712~)

Clover Flat: (Sevier Co.) Fishlake National Forest-Sevier Plateau. Koosharem map.

Also called Doe Flat. (1930~)

Cloyds Pond: (Emery Co.) San Rafael Swell-The Wedge. Buckhorn Reservoir map.

Also called Wedge Pond #1.

Lee Mont Swasey: "That's probably Cloyd Fillmore [1914-1994]. He ran sheep and lived in Lawrence." (1853~) The pond was built in 1954. (1551~)

Cly Butte: (Navajo Co., Az.) Navajo Indian Reservation-Monument Valley. Mitten Buttes, Az. map.

Laurance D. Linford noted that the Navajo name is *Tl'aaʼí*, or "Left Handed." (1204~)

Jack Breed in 1945: "Cly Butte was named for an old Indian saddle maker who lived near by and was buried at its base." (276~) Cly died in 1934 and was buried at the North Window. (1931~) (See North Window.)

Harry Goulding: "Hosteen Cly was a saddle maker. He made squaw and buck saddles, made them out of ... cedar.... He was a very good saddle maker." (1380~)

Clyde and Neils Pond: (Emery Co.) San Rafael Swell-South Salt Wash. Big Bend Draw map.

This is a still-used stock pond. (SAPE.)

Wayne Gremel noted that Clyde and Neils Morrison ran livestock in the area: "Their dad was the biggest stock person in Emery at one time." (780~)

Clydes Spring Canyon: (Wayne Co.) Glen Canyon NRA-Horsethief Canyon. Horsethief Canyon map.

This is a large spring. (SAPE.)

Barbara Ekker: "The spring was named for Clyde Tidwell, who ran cattle with his father, Tom Tidwell, and brothers Frank, Keep, and Rowland Tidwell from the mid-20s to the mid-40s." (604~)

Clyde had a still here. Evidence of the still abounds. (604~, 607~, 1644~, SAPE.) (See Tidwell Bottoms.)

Frank E. Masland, Jr.: "Clydes isn't much of a canyon." (1310~)

—Dangerous Dan Camp: This is an old name for a high area above Clydes Spring and Millard canyons (at elevation 6190 [Clyde] on the Horsethief Canyon map). (615~)

—Horsethief Trail: The trail, after going up Horsethief Canyon, went up Clydes Spring Canyon. (1890~)

Coal Bed Canyon: (Garfield Co.) GSCENM-Kaiparowits Plateau-Alvey Wash. Canaan Creek map.

Also called Canaan Creek, Coal Canyon, Heaps Wash, and Willow Creek.

Edson Alvey in 1965: "This canyon has abundant coal deposits and was the site of a commercial coal mine." (1931~)

There are four historic coal mines in Coal Bed Canyon. All were started by local residents. They are shown on the map as mine shafts. From east to west:

—Schow Mine: This is on the south side of the canyon. It was started by Andrew P. Schow (1839-1913) and was active from 1893 to 1930. (570~, 1792~) Near the mouth of the canyon is an inscription from Andrew Schow, no date. (SAPE.)

—Shurtz Mine: (Also spelled Shirts Mine.) Nethella Griffin Woolsey noted that the first coal mine in the canyon was established in 1901 by Don Shultz (1859-1931). The mine is on the south side of the canyon and was in operation from 1913 to 1928. (2051~, 570~) E. (Edwin) Shurtz left his name on a wall near the mouth of the canyon with a date of Oct. 29, 1910. (SAPE.)

—Richards Mine: This is on the south side of the canyon. It was in operation from 1913 to 1928. (570~) Morgan Richards left his name on a wall near the mouth of the canyon as well as the inscription: "Get Good Coal at Richard's Mine only for $." (SAPE.)

—Christiansen Mine: This is on the north side of the canyon. It was active from 1893 to 1930. (570~)

Herbert E. Gregory: "The sites have been selected with reference to the thickness of beds, stability of roof, and access to feasible wagon routes. Pick, shovel, and hand drill are the tools used by the miners, who work when coal is needed." (777~)

Coal Bed Canyon: (San Juan Co.) Great Sage Plain-Cedar Park-Montezuma Creek. Horsehead Point and Bug Canyon maps.

The name was in use by 1900. (1588~)

—West Cliff House No. 8 Mine: This uranium mine is in Coal Bed Canyon two miles above its confluence with Bigwater Canyon (at elevation 6005T on the Horsehead Point map). Owned by the United States Vanadium Corporation, the mine was located in 1940 and produced ore until the late 1950s. (921~)

—The Island: This is the cowboy name for the short butte in the abandoned meander at the mouth of Coal Bed Canyon (at elevation 5336T on the Bug Canyon map). The name dates from before 1900. (1588~)

Coal Bed Mesa: (Garfield Co.) Henry Mountains-Saleratus Wash. Ant Knoll map.

Charles B. Hunt: "Named for the Stanton mine coal bed at the head of Hansen Creek." (925~)

—Stanton Coal Mine: Bliss Brinkerhoff noted that the mine is at the "Prospect" on the north end of Coal Bed Mesa. (291~) Robert Brewster Stanton used coal from the mesa to fire the boilers of a dredge he built in Glen Canyon. (925~, 1795~) (See Stanton Canyon.)

Coal Bench: (Garfield Co.) GSCENM-Paria River-East Valley. Cannonville and Henrieville maps.

The Andrus Military Reconnaissance Expedition of 1866 noted this as Coal Point. (475~) Ralph Chynoweth: "There's coal up there. The older people out here call it the Wood Bench, but the new name they got up there is Coal Bench. The old-timers would go up there and cut wood." (425~)

Coal Canyon: (Grand Co.) Book Cliffs-Cottonwood Wash. Calf Canyon, Cisco Springs, and Flume Canyon maps.

At a sheep camp a short distance up the canyon are inscriptions from Ben Garcia and Victor Salazar, no dates. (SAPE.)

Coal Canyon: (Grand Co.) Book Cliffs-Green River. Bobby Canyon South and Tusher Canyon maps.

—Black Diamond Coal Mine: (Also called Farrer Mine.) (646~) John Thomas Farrer, Sr., one of the founders of Green River Town, started the Black Diamond Coal Mine in the upper canyon (at the "Prospects" on the Bobby Canyon South map) in the late 1890s. Farrer: "I hired expert miners to timber it and run a 350-foot tunnel, and another tunnel for air. The coal vein was six feet thick. I had a road built, steel laid and cabins built, all nicely fixed." (1779~)

Inscriptions include Ierneya? 1/29/03. (SAPE.)

Coal Canyon: (Iron Co.) Parowan Valley-Little Salt Lake. Parowan Gap map.

A coal mine a short distance up the canyon on its west side dates to the early 1900s. (SAPE.)

Coal Canyon: (Kane Co.) Pink Cliffs-Slide Canyon. Skutumpah Creek map.

Ralph Chynoweth: "In the wintertime the old-timers would go out there and mine the coal to keep warm. There is a coal vein there." (425~)

Coal Cliffs: (Emery Co.) San Rafael Swell-Molen Reef. Emery East, Emery NE, Emery SE, Mesa Butte, and Short Canyon maps.
Coal was first discovered in Castle Valley by the Captain John W. Gunnison Expedition of 1853. The earliest settlers discovered the Wasatch Plateau Coal Field, which encompasses the southern end of the Coal Cliffs, in 1874. Mining started in 1875. (570~) The name was in place by 1878. (1567~)

Coal Creek: (Carbon Co.) Book Cliffs-Price River. Deadman Canyon and Wellington maps.
Sam Gilson mined coal in the canyon in the late 1800s.

Coal Creek: (Grand Co.) Uintah and Ouray Indian Reservation-Roan Cliffs-Gray Canyon. Walker Point, Lion Canyon, Three Fords Canyon, and Butler Canyon maps.
Coal Creek marks the boundary between the Uintah and Ouray Indian Reservation on the north and BLM lands to the south. Waldo Wilcox: "There was a little vein of coal up in there." (2011~)
—Hy Johnson Lower Camp: This line camp on the Uintah and Ouray Indian Reservation is several miles upcanyon from the Green River. Still in use, it was developed by Hy Johnson in the early 1900s. Nearby inscriptions include E.D., 1906 and F.D., 1917. (SAPE.)
—Coal Creek Dam: (Proposed.) (Also called Buell Dam.) In 1911 O.S. Buell proposed building a dam just below Coal Creek. Ed F. Harmston in 1913: "This dam is to be 200 ft. high, the high water contour to be 180 ft.... It is planned to use it for both irrigation and power purposes, the land to be irrigated amounting to 165,000 acres." (833~)
Waldo Wilcox: "It was a fellow from back east. My granddad, Jim McPherson, said that it was just a promotion deal. They bought up a bunch of land on Elgin Flat [near Green River Town] and they were going to build a dam and then take water clear to the Colorado state line. They dug clear to bedrock. They did their assessment work. It is worth stopping and looking at it." (2011~)
Damsite workers built several stone-walled buildings near the mouth of Coal Creek. These buildings and a corral are still extant. (200~, SAPE.) Ed F. Harmston in 1913: "The power company has done considerable trenching, built two rock houses, and considerable trail and road, but no permanent work upon the dam." (833~)
Inscriptions near the buildings include Zelph, Jim, Tora, Wilber, and W.J. McPherson, Oct. 11, 1915. (SAPE.) The McPhersons had a ranch upriver at the mouth of Florence Creek. (See Florence Creek—McPherson Ranch.)

—Coal Creek Rapids: These are just below the mouth of Coal Creek. Elwyn Blake in 1926: "Our worst rapid for the day, and possibly the worst in Desolation Canyon, was Coal Creek rapid, which we ran successfully." (253~)

Coal Creek: (Iron Co.) Hurricane Cliffs-Cedar Canyon. Flanigan Arch and Cedar City maps.
Coal Creek goes through lower Cedar Canyon.
The Indian name is *Wap-pa-no-quint*. William R. Palmer: "*Wap* or *O-wap* means cedars, *pa* is water, and *no-qint* running. The translation ... is, therefore, a stream of water running through cedars." (1512~)
Orville C. Pratt in 1848: "Camped on the Maretains Cr. [Coal Creek]. Good water and fair grass. But had to make wood of sage.... And from what I have seen it seems the most desirable part of Mexico or California for agricultural purposes." (1572~)
Addison Pratt of the Jefferson Hunt Party of 1849 called this the Little Muddy: "This runs into the desert and sinks. There is cottonwood timber on this creek." (1571~)
John Urie of the Parley P. Pratt Exploring Expedition to Southern Utah of 1849–50: "The Creek was named 'Little Muddy' from its muddy appearance." (1013~) The expedition also called it Muddy Creek. (1762~)
The Howard Egan Wagon Train of 1849 noted it as "the muddy creek [Camp] No. 31. a bad creek to cross. Wood plenty, feed short." (598~)
James G. Bleak in 1851: "about this time coal was discovered near what was known as the 'Little Muddy', from its turbid waters and afterwards named Coal Creek." (258~)
Some of the first residents of Cedar City initially called it Cottonwood Creek for the cottonwood trees found along its banks. (1159~)
George Brimhall described the canyon as it was in 1852: "We started up Cove canyon [Coal Creek], where we found some specimens of stone coal. Sometimes the route was very steep and dangerous. This gulch is situated on the east side of the valley, and is almost destitute of wood of any kind. We climbed up to about the cloud line, finding various stratas of earth and rocks, blue clay and talc. All at once we found ourselves standing on a vast cone.... Here was a sublime sight, indeed." (288~)
Later, residents noted coal in the canyon and changed the name to Coal Creek. Construction of a road up the canyon started in 1852, as did coal mining. Mining continued on and off until 1969. (367~, 800~, 1727~)
—Old Spanish Trail: The trail crossed the creek near the mouth of the canyon.
—Jensen and Adams Mine: (Also called Jones and Bullock Mine and Macfarlane Mine.) This prolific coal mine

is on the south side of Coal Canyon and is one-eighth mile west of the mouth of Crow Creek (Flanigan Arch map). It was started by Heber Jensen and Frank B. Adams in 1890. (570~, 768~, SAPE.)

—Milt's Stage Stop: This well-known restaurant is in the cluster of buildings on the north side of Coal Creek opposite the mouth of Right Hand Creek (Flanigan Arch map). (1727~)

—Lawrence Canyon: The mouth of this southern tributary of Coal Creek is south of The Red Hill (immediately east of elevation 5883 on the Cedar City map). (1931~)

Coal Hollow: (Sevier Co.) Fishlake National Forest-Wasatch Plateau-Salina Creek. Water Hollow Ridge and Steves Mountain maps.

A. Milton Musser in 1874: "A short distance as of this latter place is Salina Canyon, where some very important coal discoveries have been made. These carboniferous ledges are said to be of anthracite formation, and to be almost inexhaustible, the seams varying from twenty-five to six feet in thickness." (974~)

—Coal Hollow Mine: This is the "Mine" in Coal Hollow (Steves Mountain map). The original name was the Kearn and Duggins Mine. It was intermittently active from 1910 to 1923. (567~, 1794~)

Coal Mine Wash: (Wayne Co.) North Caineville Reef-Muddy Creek. Factory Butte and Skyline Rim maps.

—Factory Butte Coal Mine: This is one mile north of Coal Mine Wash (between elevations 4709AT and 4811T on the Factory Butte map). The mine opened in 1908 and was in intermittent use until at least 1945. The coal was used for local needs. (569~, 923~, 925~) Rulon Hunt: "To get the winter's supply of coal, Caineville and surrounding towns would mine what they needed out of a coal mine located three miles north of Factory Butte. They would haul it with team and wagon." (927~) In 1977 the mine was reopened and enlarged and the coal was shipped to the Nevada Power Company at Moapa, Nevada. The mine closed in 1984.

Coalpits Wash: (Washington Co.) Zion National Park-Virgin River. The Guardian Angels and Springdale West maps.

Also called Coal Pits Cañon (1373~) and Coalpits Creek (163~).

This was not named for coal in the canyon; rather, the black lava rock looks like coal. (1038~) The name was in place by 1917.

Coal Pit Wash: (Garfield Co.) Haycock Mountain-Rock Canyon. Haycock Mountain and Hatch maps.

Also called Jump-up Wash and Little Coal Pit Wash. (1931~)

J.J. Porter in 1931: "W. Panguitch settlers burnt charcoal for blacksmith purposes in early days." (1346~)

Coal Wash: (Emery Co.) San Rafael Swell-Ivie Creek. Walker Flat map.

—Hidden Valley Coal Mine: This now-defunct coal mine is in this short canyon. (1551~)

Coal Wash: (Emery Co.) San Rafael Swell-North Salt Wash. Sid and Charley and Horn Silver Gulch maps.

Also spelled Cole Wash. (1734~)

Three name derivations are given.

Dee Anne Finken noted two name derivations.

First, a seam of tar sands may have been mistaken for coal.

Second, it is misnamed; it should have been named Cold Wash for its wintertime temperatures. (641~)

Third, Warren Allred: "It was named because there was signs of coal there." (2053~)

—Pioneer Road: (See Appendix Two—San Rafael Swell Pioneer Road.)

—Old Spanish Trail: (Variation.) The Old Spanish Trail—Winter Route—went through Coal Wash. Early ranchers reported finding an inscription from 1777 and markings on the wall showing two crosses and a cross in a circle. (1737~)

Coaly Wash: (Wayne Co.) Henry Mountains-Town Wash. Dry Lakes Peak and Steamboat Point maps.

Thin layers of coal are found along the wash and in its upper reaches in Jet Basin. (800~, 925~, 1055~, 1644~)

Coates Creek: (Grand Co.) Big Triangle-Colorado River. Marble Canyon and Big Triangle maps.

Also spelled Coach Creek (518~, 2053~) and Coats Creek (1931~).

The Ferdinand V. Hayden Survey in 1874 called this Granite Creek. (M.30.) Lucile H. Mahannah noted that it was named for the Coates family. (1931~) This was most likely the W.H. Coates family. (388~)

Coates Hollow: (Garfield and Piute Counties.) Sevier Plateau-Kingston Hollow. Phonolite Hill and Junction maps.

Kent Whittaker noted that the Cyrus Milford Coates family homesteaded here in the early days. (2002~)

Cobra Arch: (Kane Co.) Paria Canyon-Vermilion Cliffs Wilderness Area-Buckskin Gulch. West Clark Bench map. Robert H. Vreeland noted that Brent Owens named the arch for its shape and that cowboys called it Under the Dive Arch, because it is located under The Dive. (1955~)

Cocks Comb: (Garfield Co.) Henry Mountains-Highway 276. Cass Creek Peak and Black Table maps. (7,708') Grove Karl Gilbert of the Powell Survey called this Jerry Butte; Jerry Sorenson was one of his horse packers. It was later called Sawtooth Ridge for its rugged crest. (722~, 723~, 925~, 1537~)

Garth Noyes noted that they called it the Hogs Back: "Before they put the road up through there, the old trail went up on top of the ridge and then you had just a narrow hogback for half a mile there." (1473~)

Cockscomb, The: (Kane Co.) GSCENM-Cottonwood Creek. Canaan Peak, Butler Valley, Horse Flat, Calico Peak, Fivemile Valley, West Clark Bench, and Pine Hollow Canyon maps.

Also called Grey Bluffs.

Also spelled Coxcomb. (1728~)

Julius S. Dalley in 1941: "So named because subterranean upheaval has toppled the earth on end leaving the ragged rock formation resembling a great cock's comb." (2053~)

Ronald Shofner in 1970: "Coxcomb is an apt description of the upturned, exposed strata piercing the sky for the length of the [Cottonwood] canyon. The west wall is massive; white Navajo sandstone sliced here and there by knife-like canyons incised by small tributaries of Cottonwood Creek. In places the Navajo sandstone has a frosting of brilliant maroon Carmel [Formation] sandstone which is saturated with iron oxide ... causing the walls to be streaked blood-red." (1728~) The name was in place by the early 1880s. (1188~)

Cocks Comb: (Wayne Co.) Dixie National Forest-Boulder Mountain. Blind Lake map.

Also called The Comb (1931~) and Fish Creek Peak (970a~).

Grove Karl Gilbert of the Powell Survey called this White Crag in 1875. Gilbert later renamed it Wheeler's Crag for Powell Survey topographer O.D. Wheeler. Gilbert also called it Ragged Edge. (722~)

Coffee Pot Rock: (Grand Co.) La Sal Mountains-Porcupine Rim. Rill Creek map. (6,370')

Joe Taylor: "Its an old, old name.... It's like an old coffee pot, not a new coffee pot. Sheepherders would meet there." (1866~)

Cohab Canyon: (Wayne Co.) Capitol Reef National Park-Capitol Reef-Fremont River. Fruita map.

Also called Easter Canyon. (699~)

The name is short for Cohabitation Canyon. Myth has it that the canyon was used as a hideout by polygamists and their wives after Congress passed the anti-polygamy Edmunds Act in 1882. (1047~) According to Bradford J. Frye, though: "Cohab Canyon, however, was an unlikely hideout for a number of reasons. The western entrance, closest to Fruita, is approached by an exposed, switchback trail, which would force polygamists to 'flee' up a very steep slope in obvious view of approaching lawmen. The eastern entrance to the canyon, south of the Hickman Natural Bridge trailhead, would have been a more likely route. But even if this entrance was used, there really isn't a good, sheltered location anywhere in the canyon to remain hidden for any length of time." (699~)

Horatio Morrill, though probably never in Cohab Canyon, did write a poignant poem in 1887 about the trials of the families broken up by the Edmunds Bill:

> I think old Edmunds naughty
> to Make that dreadful bill
> To break up Mormon families
> As he is doing still
> I'd like to know if he has got
> A little child like mine
> that He would turn out in the cold
> No more their pa to be.
> If that is so I'd like to say
> My papa's not the man
> To disown his little children
> Though Old Edmunds thinks he can.
> I think He would much rather
> Go to the dismal Pen
> And that would be more noble
> Than the cruel Edmunds bill. (1388~)

—Pectols Pyramid: This monolith is one-quarter mile southeast of the mouth of Cohab Canyon (at elevation 6207T). Charles Kelly noted that Ephraim Portman Pectol (1875–1947) was instrumental in getting Capitol Reef designated as a national monument. He is often called the father of Capitol Reef National Park. (1047~)

Cold Spring: (Piute Co.) Fishlake National Forest-Sevier Plateau-Vale Creek. Marysvale Peak map.

Newel Nielson: "Very cold water. Someone died there. They were working in the timber and he went and took a big drink of that water and it was cold enough to kill him." (1458~)

Cold Spring: (Sevier Co.) Fishlake National Forest-Lost Creek. Mount Terrill map.

This large spring has terrific views all around. (SAPE.)

Cold Spring: (Wayne Co.) Henry Mountains-Birch Creek. Dry Lakes Peak map.

Guy Robison: "It's exceptionally cold. It's so cold. It's colder than ice. A horse can get down in there. It's rough, but they drink in sips it's so cold, and so do you. I don't know how come it's that cold. But in summertime it is just as cold as ice." (1644~)

Cold Springs: (San Juan Co.) Manti-LaSal National Forest-Abajo Mountains-South Peak. Abajo Peak map.

Gayle Turley: "The area's early cowboys had often taken their cattle there to graze. They would milk the cows and store it in the cold spring water." (1913~)

Clyde Barton: "Dad [Karl Steven Barton] had some pure bred sheep and he got a permit at Cold Springs. Once there was an old hobo going through this country and he asked dad if he could herd sheep for him for a while. So dad let him herd sheep up there at Cold Springs. One lamb was born with his hind leg just up to its hock and that old hobo made a wooden leg for that lamb and that lamb, of course, limped, but when he came off the mountain, he was just as big and fat as any of them." (162~)

Vincent L. Jones ran sheep in the area after World War Two: "I ran three thousand [sheep there]. The coyotes were getting their share and the government was getting its share, and the coyotes were getting my share, so I decided it was time to quit." (1025~)

Coldwater Spring: (San Juan Co.) Wingate Mesa-Wilson Canyon. Mancos Mesa NE map.

Carl Mahon, who named the spring while working for the BLM, noted that it was developed for use by bighorn sheep. (1272~)

Coleman Hollow Wash: (Garfield Co.) Henry Mountains-Tarantula Mesa-Sweetwater Creek. Steele Butte map.

A man named Coleman ran horses on Tarantula Mesa in the early years. (582~, 925~) (See South Creek—Garfield Co.—King Ranch.)

Coleman Reservoir: (Duchesne Co.) Myton-Eightmile Flat. Crow Knoll map.

This is a still-used stock reservoir. (SAPE.)

Coleman Reservoir: (Wayne Co.) Dixie National Forest-Boulder Mountain. Torrey map.

Sam Coleman and family moved to Teasdale in 1882. To water his ranch, Sam built the reservoir. He also operated a shingle mill on nearby Bullberry Creek. (1419~, 2013~)

Coleman Wash: (Emery Co.) Cedar Mountain-Price River. Cedar and Grassy maps.

The Coleman family were some of the earliest residents of the town of Woodside. (1188~)

Collet Top: (Kane Co.) GSCENM-Kaiparowits Plateau. Collet Top map. (6,458')

Reuben Collett (1839-1920) moved to the Escalante area in 1877. (55~, 441~, 2051~)

Clarence Dutton and Almon H. Thompson of the Powell Survey called this Last Chance Creek, a name that was used until at least 1938. (467~, 585~, 1901~) Locally it was called Twentyfive Mile Wash. (1931~)

—Big Sage: Edson Alvey noted that this pasture is between the right and left forks of Collet Canyon (near elevation 5606 on the Seep Flat map). (55~)

Collier Hollow: (Sevier Co.) Fishlake National Forest-Old Woman Plateau-Convulsion Canyon. Acord Lakes map.

The Collier family were early residents of the town of Emery. (388~)

Collie Wash: (Wayne Co.) Henry Mountains-Dry Valley. Bull Mountain and Hanksville maps.

Nina Robison noted that this is misnamed. It should be Coaly Wash. Guy Robison: "There's a little shownin' of coal up at the head of the wash ... and it's been mined a little bit." (1644~)

In 1964 Darys Ekker noted that this should be spelled Colley Wash. (1931~)

—Fairview Ranch: PRIVATE PROPERTY. This historic ranch is one-quarter mile west of upper Collie Wash (near elevation 5215T on the Sawmill Basin Road on the Bull Mountain map). Barbara Ekker: "This ranch was once one of the largest ranches located on the eastern slopes of the Henrys and was named for its attractive views." (607~) It was established by Albert Frazer "Dade" Tomlinson in about 1888 on what is now called Cottrell Bench, which is two miles north of the present site of the Fairview Ranch. (1780~)

Bette L. Stanton: "They named their new spread Fairview. From the ranch location they had a 'fair view' across the Burr Desert to the [Robbers] Roost, and north to the colorful San Rafael Desert and beautiful Book Cliff Mountains. West from the ranch stretched the awesome red canyons of Capitol Reef, backed by the hazy Thousand Lake Mountains." (1805~)

The demise of "Dade" Tomlinson is still a mystery. He and one of his cowboys, John "Jack" Cottrell, were taking a herd of horses to Telluride in 1890. Nina Robison: "Jack Cottrell came back riding one of Tomlinson's horses. And he must've had a good explanation." (1644~)

Cottrell's story was that he and Tomlinson had been attacked by thieves and Tomlinson was killed. After returning to the Fairview Ranch, Cottrell stayed on and eventually married the widow Tomlinson. Charles Kelly noted that on his death bed Cottrell admitted killing Tomlinson for his ranch, money, and wife. (1072~) This has not been verified.

George D. Beebe: "Jack Cottrell, a deputy US Marshall was at the [Tomlinson] Ranch often but he was as bad as the other rustlers. [After Tomlinson's death or murder] Jack Cottrell became a steady visitor at the ranch and Lida [Tomlinson] married him. He abused the boys till they left home. He drank up everything she had. They had seven children.... She left him in 1902." (196~)

Bette L. Stanton: "[In 1902] Jack Cottrell appeared to have left the country. One day in October he rode out and never returned. Lida thought he had deserted the family, but years later Mirt [Tomlinson] confessed ... that he had run him off, as Jack had been abusing one of the girls.... Mirt said he followed Cottrell with intentions of killing him, but by the time he caught up with him some one else had already put a bullet through him." (1805~)

Pearl Baker told the story of why Lida Tomlinson abandoned the Fairview Ranch: "One morning Mirt, her oldest boy, started down to the corral under the hill to milk the cow. He was followed a little later by Bill, his three-year-old brother. Running back to see what Bill was settling up such a howl about, Mirt found a big bobcat holding him by the seat of the pants. Mrs. Tomlinson heard the commotion, ran out with a gun and killed the cat. But that settled it—she moved her family into Hanksville." (122~) The next owner, Charlie Gibbons, moved the ranch to its present location in 1908. He is credited with naming the ranch. Vern Pace was the next owner, proving up on the land in 1918. (122~, 925~)

Guy Robison, when asked to relate a funny story about the ranch: "There was a bunch of college kids [in 1976–77]. They were making all kinds of tests. They painted rocks up on the mountain and then they'd go check 'em to see how much they slid in a year. Once, they were over here where there's just a little wash in the ground. They wanted to find out how long it took to make a wash like that. While they was standin' there figurin' it out, we had a little cloudburst on the flat. And it filled in their wash and made another wash there that was twice as big! So they stopped tryin' to figure out how long it took to make a wash. That was, to me, kinda funny." (1644~, 961~)

Collins Canyon: (San Juan Co.) Grand Gulch Plateau-Grand Gulch. Red House Spring map.
Also called Collins Spring Canyon.
James H. Knipmeyer noted that Collins was an early-day cowboy from the Bluff area. (1116~) H.L.A. Culmer in 1905: "This canyon is sometimes called Trail Canyon, as it is one of the few ways of getting down into Grand Gulch." (494~) In 1920 Nels C. Nelson called it Cartier Canyon. L.P. Cartier helped finance an expedition, led by Nelson, which became known as the Cartier Archaeological Expedition. (1433~)
—Collins Trail: This constructed stock trail goes from the top of the canyon into Grand Gulch. It is now a popular hiking trail. (1457~) The trail was built in the early 1900s. H.L.A. Culmer: "It is in vain to look down into the great gulch upon the tantalizing stream that appears and disappears from time to time in its depths for there is no scaling its dizzying walls. A year or two ago, however, some cattlemen ventured to make a trail down one of the ravines that come in from the west midway along its course [Collins Canyon], and at last succeeded in entering the solitudes of this stupendous chasm. It was along this dangerous trail we groped our way one early morning in April, 1905." (493a~)
—Collins Cave: This huge cave is on the east side of Collins Canyon one-quarter mile down from the present-day trailhead. It was often used by cattlemen to cache feed and food and as a place to bed down. After Franklin Jacob Adams purchased the Grand Gulch range in 1918, the cave was called Adam's Cache for several years. (1033~, 1901~)
Sandy Johnson: "My Granddad Fuller and Harrison Oliver used to pack grain in there for the cowboys in the wintertime. They'd go in the cave and dig the sand down about two feet and then lay a tarp down. Then they'd put down the bags of grain and throw a tarp over them and put that sand back over 'em so the mice couldn't dig it up. That was in the 1930s." (1002~)
—False Trail Canyon: The mouth of this short western tributary of Grand Gulch is one-eighth mile upcanyon from the mouth of Collins Canyon (one-quarter mile west of elevation 5253T). There is no trail out of the canyon.

Collins Creek: (Piute Co.) Fishlake National Forest-Sevier Plateau-Manning Creek. Marysvale Peak map.
Charles M. Collins, a miner, lived at Alunite Town in the 19teens. (388~)

Colorado River: (Utah counties north to south: Grand, San Juan, Wayne, Garfield, and Kane.)

The Colorado River starts on the western slopes of Longs Peak in Colorado's Rocky Mountain National Park. After going through or touching four states (Colorado, Utah, California, and Arizona), and Northern Mexico, this two thousand-mile-long river ends in the Gulf of Mexico.

Richard Firmage: "Colorado ('Red') was among the river's early names—so called for its color, laden with silt from the plateau country—and this name became common on Spanish documents by the 1770s." (644~, 1386~)

Many names have been applied to the river.

In 1540 Francisco Vasquez de Coronado led an expedition to find Cibola, a rumored city made of gold. The expedition came in two parts. Hernando de Alarcón, carrying supplies for Coronado, took two ships up the Colorado River for two hundred and twelve miles from the Gulf of Mexico. Alarcón called the river the *Buenaguia*, or "Good Guide" or "Leader."

Coronado himself took a contingent of 335 Spanish and 1300 local Indians and headed inland. The large group then split into smaller groups. Coronado sent Pedro de Tovar to the north and west. Tovar learned from the local Indians that there was a big river to the west. On Tovar's return, Coronado then sent Garcia Lopez de Cardenas and party to look for the river. They are credited with being the first to see the Grand Canyon.

A second group, led by Melchior Diaz, went overland in search of Alarcón on the Colorado River. Diaz did get to the Colorado River in the vicinity of the Gila River, but did not find Alarcón. Unaware of Alarcón's designation, Diaz named it the *Rio del Tizon* or "River of the Firebrand" in reference to the firebrands the Mohave Indians carried. (81~, 154~, 629~)

In 1604 Don Juan de Oñate called it the *Rio Grande de la Bueña Esperanza*, or the "River of Good Hope." (154~) A member of the Oñate expedition, Fray Francisco de Escobar: "We named it *Buena Esperanza*, because of reaching it on the day of the Expectation or Hope of the most blessed delivery of the Virgin Mary, our Lady." (823~) Father Escobar talked to local Indians. They told him: "From its source to where the river ends in the sea or port ... they said it was thirty days' travel." (823~)

Spanish explorer Alonso de Posada noted it in his report of 1686 as both *Colorado* and the *El Grande*. (1558~)

The Don Juan María de Rivera Expedition of 1765, as one of its goals, was looking for Melchior Diaz's *Rio de el Tison*. With the help of a Paiute guide, they intersected the river near present-day Moab. (1172~)

A Spanish map from 1767, while not specifically naming the river, noted the *Rio colorado del Norte cuio origen se ignora*, which loosely translated means a "river of the color red with unknown origins." (81~)

Padre Francisco Garcés visited the lower Colorado River in 1776, calling it the *Rio de los Martyrs*, or the "River of Martyrs." (154~)

The Domìnguez-Escalante Expedition of 1776–77 called it both the *El Río Grande de los Cosninas* or simply the *El Río Grande*. (81~, 1944~) Don Bernardo de Miera, the cartographer for expedition, showed it variously as the *Rio Colorado*, the *Rio de Zaguagana*, and the *Rio de S. Rafael*. (81~, 48~, 1172~)

The Jonathan Carver map of 1778 shows it as the *Coloredo River*. (M.10a.)

The John Melish map of 1816 shows it as the Colorado River of the West (M.45.), as does the Irvins map of 1836 (M.35.).

The Jedediah S. Smith Expedition of 1826 called it the *Seeds Keeden*, or "Prairie Hen," a name others had applied to the Green River. Smith called it both the Seedskeeder and Green River in 1827.

Trapper Daniel T. Potts called it the *Leichadu* in 1827. (2044~)

The A. Delavault map of 1827 shows it as the *Rio Zayuananas*. (M.15.)

The Antonio Armijo Expedition of 1829–30 noted: "the *Rio Grande*, known in the Californias as the *Colorado*." (69~, 805~)

Thomas J. Farnham noted it as the Sheetskadee in 1841. (633~)

John C. Fremont called it the Rio Colorado of the Gulf of California in 1845. (M.18.)

In 1851 Lorenzo D. Aldrich crossed the lower river, calling it the Colorado River. (16~)

The Mitchell map of 1851 shows it as the Rio Colorado of California. (M.47.)

The Joseph Meyer map of 1852 shows it as Red River. (M.46.)

Gwinn Harris Heap of the Lieutenant Edward F. Beale Expedition of 1853 called it both the Grand River and the *Avonkarea* or "Blue River, Utah Tongue." (854~)

The Captain John W. Gunnison Expedition of 1853–54 called it the *Nah-un-kah-rea*, or "Blue River." (854~, 1696~)

In 1858 Joseph Christmas Ives called it both the Colorado River and Big Cañon. (1637~) Lovell White in 1870: "No better name has yet been found than Big Cañon." (2004~)

Later explorers called it the Grand River and it is commonly recorded that way in diaries and books from the nineteenth and early twentieth centuries.

Senator Barry Goldwater: "It has also gone under the names of Rio Colorado del Norte, Rio Colorado del Occidente, Red River of the West, Red River of California, and the Indian name of Hackatai." (736~)

John Wesley Powell noted in his book about the Powell Surveys that the Colorado River started at the confluence of the Green and Grand. It wasn't until an act of Congress in 1921 that the name of the whole river, from its start in Colorado to its end at the Gulf of Mexico, was changed to Colorado. (805~, 1563~, 1840~, 1855~)

Colt Mesa: (Garfield Co.) GSCENM-Circle Cliffs. Horse Pasture Mesa map. (6,170')

Don Coleman: "A colt got ledged up there and somebody happened to see it. They went up there and caught it and led it back off. It was about dead. After that they always called it Colt Mesa. Then the old-timers would wean their colts and put 'em up on the mesa in the wintertime." (441~)

—Constructed Stock Trail: A trail, now improved into a mining road, went to the top of the mesa on its northwest side. (SAPE.)

Columbia Town: (Carbon Co.) Book Cliffs-East Carbon City-Highway 124. Sunnyside map.

This coal mining town was founded in 1922 by the Columbia Steel Company, a subsidiary of the United States Steel Corporation. (1621~) In 1973 it combined with another coal mining town, Dragerton, to become East Carbon City. (1282~) (See East Carbon City.)

Columbine Ridge: (Iron Co.) Cedar Breaks National Monument-Lavender Canyon. Brian Head map.

Columbine flowers grow in profusion here. (942~)

Comb Ridge: (San Juan Co.) Cedar Mesa-Comb Wash. Maps north to south. Utah: Hotel Rock, Bluff NW, Bluff SW, San Juan Hill, Moses Rock, and Mexican Hat SE. Arizona: Garnet Ridge, Rooster Rock, Red Point, Baby Rocks, and Agathla Peak.

Also called The Comb (1198~, M.32.), Comb Reef (556a~, 1238~), Coombs Reef (818a~), Great Comb Reef (935~), McComb Ridge (490~), and Rip Rap Cliff (6~).

Also spelled Combe Ridge.

Robert S. McPherson noted that the Navajo name is *Tse'k'aan*, or "Rocks Standing Up." The points on the ridge represent the four arrowheads that protect the Navajo. (1338~)

William Henry Jackson of the Ferdinand V. Hayden Survey in 1875: "Its eastern side a remarkable wall, some 400 feet in height, inaccessible throughout its whole length with the exception of one place where the Indians have made a way for themselves [See "the fifth route" below]." (951~)

George B. Hobbs of the Hole-in-the-Rock Expedition in 1880: "This wash derives its name from a perpendicular cliff about thirty miles long on its east side which is scalloped out resembling a comb to some extent." (1356~)

John F. Cargill in 1909: "The dry creek bed [Comb Wash] is walled in on the easterly side by a range of precipitous, dark, and savage cliffs rising hundreds of feet, and composed of a long succession of pinnacles of remarkable uniformity of outline. They look not unlike the teeth of an enormous comb, which suggests their title, Comb Range." (341~)

Francis F. Kane in 1891: "It presents an extraordinary appearance, the bluffs that enclose the wash on the east being caused apparently by a continuous faulting of the red sandstone." (1037~)

T. Mitchell Prudden in 1903: "The valley, from one to five or six miles wide, is shallow and dry and is bordered on the east by the serrated summit of the great fault [Comb Ridge] which, running from the divide between Abajo Mountain and Elk Ridge, turns southwesterly, crossing the San Juan and runs in the direction of Marsh Pass. On the west the country rises from the valley of Comb Wash in lofty brown and barren swells up to the high mesa at the foot of Elk Ridge." (1589~)

Enid C. Howard in 1971: "This weathered and polished natural wonder looks like a dinosaurian lizard, with naked backbone exposed. Its topmost edge has the jaunty ripple of a cockscomb, and the brilliant red of the Wingate walls adds to the illusion.... The west side of the Ridge is an awesome thing, a formidable wall that plunges straight down 800 feet to the [Comb] wash. It is as though a giant had wielded a knife to cut the west face of the Ridge, then, as if to appease the traveler for this impassable barrier, soothed the surface of the wash with a meandering stream, coloring it with the soft green of cottonwood trees and grassy slopes that nestle against the ruffled talus at the foot of the burnished red walls." (910~)

The history of the roads and trails built by the pioneers over Comb Ridge is interesting. All noted here are north of the San Juan River and are listed north to south.

—The first route went across the north end of Comb Ridge. (Hotel Rock map.) (See Trail Canyon.)

—The second route is now sometimes called the Old Highway. This was an Indian trail. It went through what is called The Notch. (Hotel Rock map.) (See County Road 240.)

Clyde Barton described building the Old Highway down the cliffs: "When they first started that, we went up there and watched. They just chiseled back enough of the cliff to make a place to stand on. Then they'd lower the workers off of the top in half-barrels. They'd drill holes and load them with powder and they'd pull them up out of there and blast it. Whiting and Hayman was the name of the construction company that did that." (162~)

—The third route is called the Posey Trail or Old Posey's Get Away. It is also called the Cowboy Trail. Robert S. McPherson noted that the Ute name is *Gava Pöö*, or "Horse Trail." (1335~)

This spectacular constructed stock trail was built by cowboys in the 1880s. It is immediately north of the present Highway 95 road cut through Comb Ridge (at elevation 5611T on the Hotel Rock map). It was named for Paiute Chief Posey. Dan Thrapp in 1942: "More than once Posey had been chased up the [Comb] wash and, for all the pursuers knew, vanished in thin air by using this hidden trail." (1885~)

Charles L. Bernheimer in 1929: "It was very steep in places very rough; but we pronounced it a very good trail." (218~)

Clyde Barton: "The upper part is the scariest, where you first break over Comb Ridge and start down into Comb Wash. They had it cribbed up. When you get down on the talus slope it's not as bad. The old cowboys used to go out that way onto Cedar Mesa in the wintertime to take care of the cows. That was the only way back and forth through there. That trail was used a lot." (162~)

C. Alfred Frost described the trail as it was in 1932: "The trail on the west side of Comb Reef was very steep and narrow. Many cow bones, bleached white with age were lying around. Large herds of cattle had been driven over this trail. In the narrow places some cows had been crowded and pushed over the ledges, falling to their death." (686~)

The trail was improved by George Perkins in 1930 (1335~) and by the CCC in the mid-1930s (1451~).

DeReese Nielson told a story about the Cowboy Trail: "We'd go out and stay a month at a time with our cows. And we had ten mules and we'd pack grain on them to feed 'em out there. We's goin' down that trail and it was real narrow and we had a sorrel mule that usually always took the lead down the trail. She got a pretty good start down the trail and then she got scared of somethin' and turned around and come back up the trail. She went on

the inside of this brown horse that was carrying a pack of oats. We called him 'Pud.' And she pushed him off 'n that trail and he rolled clear to the bottom of that canyon. Not one bone in his body was left. Everything was just hamburger." (1451~)

—The fourth route is the course of present-day Highway 95. (Bluff NW map.) (See Highway 95.)

—The fifth route is a Navajo trail. It is across from the mouth of Road Canyon (Bluff SW map). It was never used by horses or cattle.

William Henry Jackson of the Ferdinand V. Hayden Survey in 1875 probably used this route: "Started up Epsom Creek [Comb Wash] in an almost due north course.... A high sandstone bluff [Comb Ridge] on our right kept up an equal face as far as we traveled—15m. Camped shortly after noon & after dinner climbed over a dangerous place to the top of the bluff." (950~)

At this point, about fifteen miles up Comb Wash, there are a couple of "Moqui" step routes onto Comb Ridge. These are visible from Comb Wash. The Navajo Trail is not the easiest or most obvious route in the area, but it was certainly the most heavily used. Vaughn Hadenfeldt calls this Jacksons Ladder. (802~, 838~) Winston Hurst noted that it was a part of a Puebloan road. (935~)

After climbing the Navajo Trail, Jackson and his men did not want to reverse the route. Going south along the east side of Comb Ridge, they found another route down. This was the sixth trail.

—The sixth trail, called Navajo Hill, went over Comb Ridge at Navajo Spring (Bluff SW map). (See Highway 163.) William Henry Jackson: "Ret. to camp by a trail that Bob & Harry had found up over the bluffs, much easier and safer." (1335~)

—The seventh trail was San Juan Hill, built in 1880 by members of the Hole-in-the-Rock Expedition. (San Juan Hill map.) (See San Juan Hill.)

—The eighth trail went around the very southern end of Comb Ridge, hard against the San Juan River, and into Butler Wash (San Juan Hill map). (See Butler Wash—San Juan Co.—Comb Ridge—Lower Butler Wash Road.)

There are also many named features along Comb Ridge. From north to south:

—Georges Rock: This prominent white dome is between the northern end of Butler Wash and Comb Ridge (at elevation 6036T on the Hotel Rock map). Clyde Barton: "Old George Lyman worked for us with the sheep for a long time. One time George and me were riding down there and old George says, 'Hey Clyde, what's the name of that rock there? That thing ought to have a name.' And I said, 'that's Georges Rock'"! (162~)

—Highland Lady: (Also called Thumb Rock.) This high knob is seven miles south of Georges Rock (one mile west-southwest of elevation 5127T on the Hotel Rock map). (838~) Winston Hurst: "The name 'Highland Lady' probably came from John Allan, an old-country Scottish Mormon immigrant and Bluff pioneer." (935~)

—Fish Mouth Cave: This appropriately-named cave is near elevation 5432 on the Bluff NW map. It was called Giants Cave by the Illustrated American Exploring Expedition of 1892. They incised their name in the cave. (1105~)

Wirt Jenks Billings and Harry French of the Hyde Exploring Expedition left their names in Fishmouth Cave on December 31, 1893. (249~) James H. Knipmeyer noted that Billings also left this missive on a wall:

> To inhabitants
> of this deserted place!
> Your bodies long ago
> returned unto the dust
> Alas! You all are
> gone to come again
> no more!

Other inscriptions include J.W. Slater, Feb. 3, 1918 and Cardon Jones, Blanding Utah, May 1943. (SAPE.)

—Long Fingers Canyon: (Also called Cottonwood Gulch.) (935~) This is near elevation 4916 on the Bluff NW map. It was named for figures on a petroglyph panel. The Navajo name was "Where the Cottonwoods are Green." A hogan, still extant, at the mouth of Long Fingers Canyon was built by a Navajo named Corn Pollen and his son, Tall Educated One. The Navajo also had a track for horse racing nearby. (1335~)

—Cold Spring Cave: This cave, which has a cold spring in its farthest recesses, is near elevation 4881 on the Bluff SW map. Inscriptions include one that reads: "1892. Cold Spring Cave. IAEE." This refers to the Illustrated American Exploring Expedition. Expedition member Maurice C. Longnecker left this inscription: "M.C.L., 5/11/92, Cinti, Ohio." (1105~, 1384~, SAPE.) Byron Cummings excavated in the cave in 1908. (265~)

—Monarch Cave: This is three-quarters of a mile south of Cold Spring Cave (east of elevation 5405 on the Bluff SW map). Inscriptions include I.A.E. Exped. Monarch's Cave, 1892. This is from the Illustrated American Exploring Expedition.

Comb Wash: (San Juan Co.) Cedar Mesa-Comb Ridge-San Juan River. Hotel Rock, Bluff NW, Bluff SW, and San Juan Hill maps.

Also called Comb Reef Canyon, Comb Reef Wash (218~), Cone Wash (1383~, 1596~), Lacombe Wash (941~), and Valley of the Comb (1389a~).

Robert S. McPherson noted that the Ute name is *Pih-kééviyaagat*, or "Slick Rock Wash." The Navajo name is *Naaghashi Bicho'*, or "Mountain Sheep's Testicles." McPherson noted that in the mid-1800s a group of Navajo were camped at the mouth of Arch Canyon on Comb Wash. They had an argument about who was to lay claim to some prized bighorn sheep testicles. (1335~)

Until the Ferdinand V. Hayden Survey in 1875, Comb Wash was called Epsom Creek. William Henry Jackson of the expedition: "And then comes Epsom Creek, rising among the plateaus farther to the west—so called from the water in one portion of its bed having the effect and tasting like that salt." (951~) Jackson in his diary: "This Epsom water, as we call it, has anything but a cheerful effect upon us." (950~)

B.D. Critchlow of the Denver and Rio Grande Survey of 1880–81 called this McComb Wash, perhaps thinking it was named for Captain John N. Macomb who crossed Comb Ridge in 1860. (490~)

Warren K. Moorehead of the Illustrated American Exploring Expedition of 1892: "Comb Wash is the name given by the early Mormon settlers to a wash which on the map is called Macomb's Creek." (1383~) A USGS expedition led by P. Holman officially renamed the creek in 1884 after Comb Ridge. (774~)

Cone, The: (Emery Co.) San Rafael Desert-Gruvers Mesa. Moonshine Wash map. (4,764')

Also called Red Cone. (1931~)

Confluence, The: (San Juan and Wayne Counties.) Canyonlands National Park-Green River-Colorado River. Spanish Bottom map.

Also called Grand Junction (134~) and The Junction (550~).

This is the joining of the Colorado and Green rivers. It is not labeled on the map.

The Powell Expedition of 1869 was the first to document a visit to The Confluence. George Y. Bradley of that expedition: "Hurra! Hurra! Hurra! Grand [Colorado] River came upon us or rather we came upon that very suddenly and to me unexpectedly.... The cañon looked dark and threatening but at last without warning, no valley or even opening unusual, in broke the Grand with a calm strong tide very different from what has been represented. We were led to expect that it was a rushing, roaring mountain torrent which when united with the Green would give us a grand promenade across the mountains.... The river Colorado formed by the junction of these two is as we can see it (1000 yds.) Calm and wide and very much unlike the impossible unpassable succession of foaming and raging waterfalls and cataracts which have been attributed to it. It is possible we are allured into a dangerous and disastrous cañon of death by the placid waters of this cañon which may be no fair specimen of the whole." (269~)

Francis M. Bishop of the 1871–72 Powell Expedition: "Well, we are at last, after many days of toil and labor, here at the confluence of the two great arteries of this great mountain desert. No more shall our frail boats dash through thy turbid waters, Old Green, and no more shall we press on to see the dark flood from the peaks and parks of Colorado. Grand and Green here sink to thy rest, and from thy grave the *Colorado de Grande* shall flow on forever, and on thy bosom henceforth will we battle with rock and wave. One can hardly tell which is the largest of the two rivers. Neither seems to flow into the other, but there seems to be a blending of both, and from their union rolls the Colorado River." (236~)

Almon H. Thompson of the 1871–72 Powell Expedition: "I think a prettier joining of two streams to form a third was never seen. Neither absorbs or flows into the other, but like two forces of equal strength they mingle and unite." (1877~)

John Wesley Powell climbed to the top of the cliffs to the east of The Confluence: "And what a world of grandeur is spread before us! Below is the canyon, through which the Colorado runs. We can trace its course for miles, and at points catch glimpses of the river. From the northwest comes the Green, in a narrow, winding gorge. From the northeast comes the Grand [Colorado], through a canyon that seems bottomless from where we stand. Away to the west are lines of cliffs and ledges of rock—not such ledges as you may have seen where the quarry-man splits his blocks, but ledges from which the gods might quarry mountains, that, rolled out on the plain below, would stand a lofty range; and not such cliffs as you may have seen where the swallow builds its nest, but cliffs where the soaring eagle is lost to view ere he reached the summit.... Wherever we look there is but a wilderness of rocks; deep gorges, where the rivers are lost below cliffs and towers and pinnacles; and ten thousand strangely carved forms in every direction; and beyond them, mountains blending with the clouds." (1563~)

Frederick S. Dellenbaugh of the 1871–72 Powell Expedition: "No more remote place existed at that time [1871] within the United States—no place more difficult of access." (541~) Dellenbaugh again: "The view from up here is as strange but wild as it is grand—it is in one direction but one wilderness of spins, pinnacles and crags and altogether is a vast terrible desert of barren rock, cut and creviced in all directions." (543~)

Robert Brewster Stanton wrote of the canyons near The Confluence in 1889: "The massive beds of sandstone, of orange, yellow and pink, in places stand in vertical walls from the River's edge, though seldom, if ever, to the full height of the cliffs, and are cut in great alcoves and amphitheatres which form beautiful and impressive scenes, and with every sound send back from their arches most wonderful echos. In other sections, where the rock strata are not so hard and massive, great stretches of talus skirt the bends, and in the wider turns, beautiful flats, covered with bunch grass and greasewood and skirted next to the water by willows, with different shades of green of their foliage, make most charming pictures, as seen from the River against the orange colored cliffs.... The landscape everywhere, away from the river, is of rock—cliffs of rock; plateaus of rock; terraces of rock; crags of rock—ten thousand strangely carved forms ... cathedral shaped buttes, towering hundreds or thousands of feet; cliffs that cannot be scaled, and [upper] canyon walls that shrink the river [canyon] into insignificance, with vast, hollow domes, and tall pinnacles, and shafts ... and all ... colored—yellow, buff, gray red, brown, and chocolate." (1767~)

Inscriptions right at The Confluence included one that used to read: "Sta. 8489+50 D.C.C. & P.R.R., May 4th 1889." This referred to the Stanton-Brown Survey of 1889. Frank C. Kendrick of the expedition is credited with carving the inscription on a "Red Sand Stone." (1305~) From The Confluence Kendrick and crew did not continue down the Colorado River; rather, they rowed and pulled their boats up to Green River Town to meet the main Stanton-Brown Survey. This inscription, probably painted on the rock, is now gone.

Another inscription is from the Kolb Bros, 1911 (referring to the Ellsworth and Emery Kolb trip down the Colorado River in 1911); and JWP, 1891.

Inscriptions on the west side of the Green River at The Confluence include J.W. Wilson, May 17th, 1887; Peter Monnett, 8/96; H.W.C. Prommel, 5/13/26; Pete Mazet, 1931; and Ned L.C.[Chaffin], '34. Another inscription reads "Sta. 8489+50 D.C.C. & P.R.R., May 4th 1889." This is the same content as the Kendrick inscription noted above. Otis "Dock" Marston: "The assumption seems warranted that it was cut by a member of the [Stanton-] Brown party about Memorial Day of 1889 to mark the resumption of the survey approximately at the location where Kendrick had terminated it." (1305~)

Yet another missive is from K. Sawyer, 8-11-14—U.S.R.S.; USRS 1914 elevation 3916.62. This refers to the Eugene Clyde LaRue U.S. Bureau of Reclamation Expedition that was looking for a damsite at The Confluence in 1914. (1106~, 1112~, 1947~, SAPE.)

—Hirams Eye: This prominent sandstone formation is one-quarter mile northeast of Green River mile 8 and is elevation 4874T. It is easily seen from the mouth of Stove Canyon. (See below.) Anderson Thayer told this story to members of the canyon group Cornerstone: "They tell this tale about their grandpa's friend, Hiram. Seems he went to Grand Junction to sell some cattle and ended up falling in love with a barroom gal. Funny thing about her, she'd lost an eye fighting off an overly enthusiastic customer, so she wore a black patch on that blind eye. Hiram wasn't the brightest animal in the farmyard and didn't think twice about marrying her and bringing her home. His father couldn't cotton to a harlot in the family and banished the couple to a life on the mesa. The tale was she turned the blind eye the wrong way one time too many and fell off the edge of the mesa toward the river. Instead of falling all the way down, she died on the rocks you can still see. The story goes those rocks are Hiram's tears turned to stone and Hiram's eye still searches for his lost love. Old-timers say you can still find her bones if you climb down below the Eye." (SAPE.)

—Stove Canyon: This short eastern tributary is at Green River mile 7 (two and three-quarters of a mile upriver from Water Canyon and one-half mile east of elevation 4697T). At the top of the canyon is a uranium-era camp that, among other relics, has a stove. (SAPE.)

In 1928 Edwin T. Wolverton noted that the canyon had a constructed sheep trail going down it. This trail is now cairned and easy to follow to the rim and is often used by river runners. (SAPE.)

Glen Ruby told a story that happened somewhere in this vicinity: "Glen Ruby went out hunting on one of the large bottoms along the river and when he returned he ... arrived on a scene of desolation comparable to that viewed by the fiddling Nero. Slowly and piecemeal the story came out. Chester [Wegemann] and the Chinaman [Tom Wimmer] had landed and started a fire for lunch. They had left the grub box in the boat and while waiting for the fire to burn down to coals suitable for cooking, had decided to

go back to the cliff in search of cliff dwellings.... During their absence a playful wind had whipped the fire into the long dry grass, and the conflagration spread so rapidly that before they were aware of it, they were cut off from the boat. Another gust had blown burning brands into the boat and the leaky cans of gasoline furnished the dense column of black smoke I had seen from the cliffs. The explosions I had heard were the canned goods in the grub box being consumed on the gasoline alter. Never was a sacrificial offering consigned to the flames with more anguish than was exhibited by Chester and the Chinaman." (1663~)

—Powell Canyon: This western tributary of the Green River is one mile upriver from The Confluence (immediately south of elevation 5025T). John Wesley Powell found several routes to the rim of the canyons near The Confluence. One went up what is now known as Powell Canyon. (465~) The route, well-cairned but technical in places, is often used by hikers.

Frederick S. Dellenbaugh of the 1871–72 Powell Expedition: "We succeeded in pulling up the Green a quarter of a mile ... where an attempt to get out of the canyon [up Powell Canyon] was successful. The view from the top was as strange and wild as it was majestic—a vast and terrible desert of barren rock, cut and creviced in all directions. We seemed to be in a new world—a bewildering land of spires, and pinnacles, and crags, and gorges. There was no earth, nothing but naked rock, and the eye returned wearied from the hopeless expanse of forest-like crags, finding relief in the river which over a thousand feet below whirled and twisted and shot on into the increasing depths of Cataract Canyon. Crevices of all sizes and depths ran through the rocks everywhere, and one almost feared to move for fear of slipping into one unawares.... This was the 'Sinave To-weap' of the Indians—the Land of the Evil Spirit." (542~, 662~)

Ellsworth Kolb and party climbed out here in 1911: "The view from the top was overwhelming, and words can hardly describe what we saw, or how we were affected by it." (1124~)

—Cave Cliff: This is the name given by the Powell Expedition of 1871–72 to the cliff a half a mile below The Confluence on the east side of the Colorado River. Powell and George Y. Bradley climbed the cliff. Bradley: "The cliff is a strange one for the soft sandstone on top has worn out in caves and the top is all like honey-comb with them. We paced one of them 75 yds. In a straight line, so high we could walk anywhere in it and many thousand men could be sheltered in that single cliff." (270~)

—Confluence Dam Site: (Proposed.) (Also called Junction Damsite.) (1146~) Bert Loper noted that in 1914 the Reclamation Service, under the direction of John F. Richardson, floated a drill rig to The Confluence to see if a dam could be built there. The actual site was to be about five hundred yards below The Confluence. They did not hit bedrock even after drilling 140 feet. The vague remnants of a building left by the 1914 expedition can still be seen on the west side of the Green River adjacent to The Confluence. (1220~, SAPE.)

Eugene Clyde LaRue of the William R. Chenoweth USGS Expedition of 1921 looked at the site again. Since both the Colorado and Green rivers would have been flooded, the spillway would have been built one-half mile up the Green River and tunnels bored straight through the peninsula (shown at elevation 5127T) into the Colorado River. (1146~)

—Pygmy City: Francis M. Bishop of the 1871–72 Powell Expedition: "It was here [The Confluence] that one 'Steamboat Adams' reported a large and fertile valley, in which he had caused an extensive city to be laid out and offered the lots for sale cheap if he could get a colony to go and settle there. If his city was on a scale with this 'extensive valley' it certainly was a pygmy affair; because there is not valley or soil enough to make a respectable turnip patch, within a radius of thirty miles of the Junction that would admit of cultivation." (237~)

Conical Butte: (San Juan Co.) Navajo Indian Reservation-Monument Valley. Monument Pass map.

Arthur A. Baker: "A circular plug of igneous rock about 200 feet in diameter ... forms a low sharp greenish-gray cone. This conspicuous topographic feature has been named *Tse Ajai* (rock heart) by the Navajo Indians." (100~)

Conservation Spring: (Sevier Co.) Fishlake National Forest-Wasatch Plateau-Corral Canyon. Water Hollow Ridge map.

Stuart Johnson: "That was an important spring for watering livestock. The Forest Service put a storage tank and troughs there years ago. That was back in the 1950s." (1003~)

Cons Knoll: (Garfield Co.) Dixie National Forest-Boulder Mountain. Lower Bowns Reservoir map. (9,283')

Con Tergeson ranched here. (426~, 1487~)

Convulsion Canyon: (Sevier Co.) Fishlake National Forest-Old Woman Plateau-Quitchupah Creek. Acord Lakes map.

Convulsion Canyon marks the top of Quitchupah Creek. (See Quitchupah Creek.)

—Convulsion Canyon Mine: (Also called SUFCO Mine.) This coal mine, now a major supplier for the Castle Dale Power Plant, was started in 1941.

Cookie Jar Butte: (San Juan Co.) Glen Canyon NRA-Glen Canyon. Gunsight Butte map. (4,344')

This is a recent name. It reflects the shape of this sandstone formation.

—Kane Creek: (Also called Kane Wash. Also spelled Cane Creek and Cane Wash.) This creek had three forks. They are shown as part of Lake Powell immediately to the east and west of Cookie Jar Butte. The west fork was called Kane Creek Canyon. The east fork had two heads and the combined canyons were called Kane Wash. All three canyons are now underwater and the names are no longer used.

Edwin G. Woolley, diarist for the Utah Territorial Militia of 1869: "There is a small creek of clear pure water comes out from between the rocks at this point." (2048~)

Frederick S. Dellenbaugh of the 1871–72 Powell Expedition: "It was full of canes when we were there and I believe the name on the maps should be 'Cane' not Kane Canyon. Kane County of course is named after the 'Gentile' [Thomas] Kane who was a good friend of the Mormons, but this little canyon hardly would have been given his name." (544~)

David D. Rust: "Cane Creek was named before Kane County was established. The canes are wild rice." (1678~)

—Movies: *The Greatest Story Ever Told* was, in part, filmed on the Colorado River at the mouth of Kane Creek in 1963. It starred John Wayne and Max von Sydow. (1809~)

—Kane Creek Crossing: A crossing of the Colorado River was located at Kane Creek. David D. Rust: "Cane Creek is a good place to swim animals and that is where the Navahos swam horses when they were in a hurry." (1673~)

—Kane Creek Landing: This river landing, now underwater, was near the downcanyon side of the mouth of Kane Creek (one and one-half miles east-southeast of elevation 4261). A road from Highway 89 to the landing was built in 1957 as an exit point for river runners because of the construction of Glen Canyon Dam twenty-five miles downcanyon. (871~, 1206~)

—Cane Bar: This placer bar, now underwater, was on the north (or west) side of the Colorado River and was one and three-quarter miles south-southeast of Cookie Jar Butte (two miles southwest of elevation 4501). The earliest recorded use of the bar was by the Andrus Military Reconnaissance Expedition of 1866. It was also used by John Wesley Powell as a camp in both 1869 and 1871.

(467~) Inscriptions include J.E. Riding and W.V. Lay, Escalante, 1919. (465~)

Cook Pasture: (Wayne Co.) Dixie National Forest-Boulder Mountain. Government Point map.

Also called Cook Bench and Cook Ledge.

Daniel Cook (1864-1937) and family ran cattle on the bench in the early 1900s. (1865~, 2053~)

—Cook Lake: Unattributed: "Forest of Engelmann Spruce clothes the slopes of this highland recreation area. The lakes are stocked with fingerling and legal-sized trout." (833~)

—Boulder Top Road: Dunk Taylor noted that the road from Cook Pasture up to Boulder Top was built in the 1950s. Before the road, livestock would be brought to Boulder Top from its south end, where there were rolling hills and no steep cliffs. (1865~)

Cooks Mesa: (Wayne Co.) Fishlake National Forest-Thousand Lake Mountain. Torrey and Twin Rocks maps.

Chauncey Harvey Cook (1843-1923) and family moved to Caineville in 1883. They moved to the San Rafael River in 1888 and to Wellington in 1890. (972~, 1591a~)

Cooks Spring: (Iron Co.) Cedar Mountain-Square Mountain. Cedar Mountain and Cedar City maps. PRIVATE PROPERTY.

Moroni Perry: "In the late 1800s there were a group of men who cut trees for lumber just over the top of Square Mountain. They would bring them to the edge of the mountain and push the saw-logs down a steep slope there. Then load the saw-logs on wagons and haul them to Cedar [City]. Mr. Cook was one of the men engaged in this activity." (942~)

Cooley Gulch: (San Juan Co.) Manti-LaSal National Forest-Abajo Mountains-Johnson Creek. Abajo Peak map.

Also spelled Gooley Gulch. (1238~)

—Dream Mine: (Also called Golden Dream Mine.) (1912~) This was on the south side of Cooley Gulch one mile west of Dickson Pass (one-half mile northeast of elevation 8811T). Herbert E. Gregory noted that C.A. Cooley and S.J. Hauser (also spelled Houser and Houseer) founded the Dream Mine in 1893.

Marvin Lyman told the story of the Dream Mine: "About 1890, Mr. Sammy Houseer and his partner by the name of Coolie were camped down at what they called Springfield Spring.... They had been searching for six months or more for gold prospects and were discouraged and ready to leave the mountain. In fact, they figured on leaving the next day.... The next morning Mr. Houseer went up there looking for his stock and he found them up in what is now known as Coolie Gulch which is down off the hill from the

Dream Mine. When he got up there he looked around and the place seemed familiar to him. He finally recalled that he had seen that place in a dream. He saw in the dream how he discovered gold in the sand there that had washed down the mountainside, so he immediately grabbed his pan and started panning and panned out some quite rich gold. He was very excited and came back and got his partner. They went up and traced this gold up the hill for several hundred yards to an outcrop which is known as the Dream Mine. That's why it is called the Dream Mine because he saw this place in a dream." (1258~)

—Marvin Tunnel: This is near the mouth of Cooley Gulch at the "Adit." (2036~) It was named for Marvin Lyman (1894-1972).

Coon Spring: (Emery Co.) Cedar Mountain-Denver and Rio Grande Western Railroad. Cedar map.

This was an important source of water for livestock. (1490~)

Co-op Creek: (Kane Co.) Zion National Park-Clear Creek. Clear Creek Mountain, The Barracks, and Springdale East maps.

William R. Palmer described the advent of the co-op sheep herd in southern Utah: "At first they were driven out in the morning and brought back at night. Then neighbors put their flocks together and took turns in herding them. Finally a community herd developed and they were brought home only once a year to be shorn. The next step was a co-op herd in which sheep were turned in for capital stock. A wool dividend each year supplied the housewife with the wool she needed." (1511~)

Cooper Knoll: (Garfield Co.) Dixie National Forest-Panguitch Lake. Haycock Mountain map. (9,015')

Also called Cooper Peak. (2053~)

Seguine Cooper (1838-1899) ranched in the area in the 1870s. (1445~)

John C.L. Smith of the Exploring Expedition of 1852 may have described the knoll: "We ascended the mountains on the east [of Panguitch Lake], and discovered a very large quantity of pine timber to the east and south of us." (1776~)

—Gould Wiggle: J.J. Porter in 1931: "Steep, rough and crooked road built by Sam and Jake Gould to get from [the east side of] Panguitch Lake to saw mill in Rock canyon." (1346~) This old road goes along the west side of Cooper Knoll.

Cooper Spring: (San Juan Co.) Manti-LaSal National Forest-Dark Canyon Plateau-Dry Mesa. Warren Canyon map.

David M. Cooper and Melvin Martin were the first Euroamerican ranchers known to have used the Dark Canyon Plateau and Elk Ridge areas for grazing their cattle. They came to the area in the mid-1880s. (1821~)

—Cooper Reservoir: Erwin Oliver noted that this small stock reservoir is immediately south of Cooper Spring. (1479~)

—Youngs Reservoir: Erwin Oliver noted that this stock reservoir is one mile northeast of Cooper Spring (immediately west of elevation 8490T). (1479~) (See Youngs Canyon for name derivation.)

Co-op Knoll: (Iron Co.) Cedar Mountain-Kanarra Mountain. Cedar Mountain map. (9,775') PRIVATE PROPERTY.

George Wheeler of the Lieutenant George M. Wheeler Survey of 1872–73: "The cooperative Mormon herd of Cedar grazed in this vicinity." (1997~) The cooperative herd was started in Cedar City in 1857. (516~)

—Co-op Flat: PRIVATE PROPERTY. Moroni Perry: "It is good pasture land as it is fed by several small springs in the area." (942~)

Co-op Valley Sinks: (Iron Co.) Hoosier Creek-Horse Valley Peak. Red Creek Reservoir map.

Also called Co-op Valley (363~) and Hoosier Creek Sink (1931~).

Louella Adams Dalton explained the two parts of the name: "The Co-op Valley got its name from the Parowan Co-op Cattle Company…. Water runs from the Hoosier [Creek] on down the Co-op Valley, forming a big lake at the foot of Sink Hill, where it mysteriously disappears." (363~)

—Blow Up: Luella Adams Dalton described where it was: "Aunt Paulina Lyman ranched at the north end of the Co-op Valley, when the saw mill was there. The blow up was just east of her ranch and over the hill." (516~) Betsy Topham Camp: "The saw mill at Blow Up received its name from the boiler blowing up at the saw mill, killing two men. Pieces from the boiler were found afterwards almost a mile away." (942~)

Coots Slough: (Sevier Co.) Fishlake National Forest-Fish Lake. Fish Lake map.

Max Robinson noted that coots, a duck-like bird in the rail family, frequent the area, especially in the fall. Locally they are called mud hens. (1641~,460~)

Cope Canyon: (Garfield Co.) Bryce Canyon National Park-Pink Cliffs-Paria River. Tropic Canyon map.

Bryce Canyon National Park Superintendent P.P. Paltrow in 1934: "Thomas H. Cope [1853-1930] moved to Tropic in 1896 and settled at the mouth of Tropic Canyon, where he stayed until 1914." (1931~)

Copper Belt Peak: (Piute Co.) Fishlake National Forest-Tushar Mountains. Mount Brigham map. (11,383')

—Copper Belt Mine: This gold and silver mine is one mile east of Copper Belt Peak on the north side of California Gulch (at USMM 2). The mine was started in 1882. (332~)

Copper Canyon: (San Juan Co.) Navajo Indian Reservation-San Juan River. Jacobs Monument, Monitor Butte, and No Mans Mesa North maps.

Also called Copper Creek (1573~) and Copper Gulch (1921~).

Laurance D. Linford noted that the Navajo name is *Tsékooh Béésh Lichíí*. (1204~) Stephen C. Jett noted that the Navajo name is *Beesh Ha'ageed Ch'inili*, or "Metal Mine Outflow." (975~)

Miner Cass Hite discovered copper near the head of the canyon in the early 1880s. (1336~) Charles H. Spencer spent several months mining copper here in the early 1900s. (348~)

Arthur A. Baker in 1936: "Numerous pits have been dug in prospecting these [gold and copper] deposits [in Copper Canyon], but no deposits of commercial value have been discovered." (101~)

Winifred Hawkridge Dixon in 1921: "Copper canyon is … a gorgeous blaze of rich red and deep blue tones." (561~)

—Zahns Camp Road: A road down the canyon provided access from the town of Oljeto to Zahns Camp on the San Juan River. (This is shown as a "4WD" road on the maps.) The road follows the streambed until about three miles from the river. It then follows benches on the west side of the canyon and now ends in Nokai Canyon. (1370~) (See Zahns Bay.)

—Williams Bar and Williamsburg Town: This placer bar, now underwater, was on the east side of the San Juan River and two miles north of Copper Canyon (one-half mile northwest of elevation 4051T on the No Mans Mesa map). Jonathan P. Williams was a trader to the Navajo in the early 1890s in Arizona. In the mid-1890s he started the small gold mining settlement of Williamsburg (now underwater). It was on the south end of the bar and one mile north of Copper Canyon. (472~) Joe Lee: "Trying to recover flour gold he [Jonathan P. Williams] used a steam engine on a flat bottom barge. In the engine he burned crude oil that was carried in five gallon cans from an oil seep up a side canyon." (1157~) Stan Jones noted that a constructed trail, possibly built by Williams, went from Williamsburg to the highlands above. (1022~)

—San Juan Marina: (Proposed.) In the late 1980s a marina, to replace the one at Piute Farms, was considered for Copper Canyon. (599a~)

—Wetherill Trail: This is the "Pack" trail that descends the western cliffs of Copper Canyon (near elevation 5471T on the Jacobs Monument map). (See Appendix Two–Wetherill Trail.) In the 1880s and early 1890s it was called Needles Eye Pass by miners. T.B. "Thad" Duckett in 1891: "Climbed Mesa [Nokai Mesa] west up through what they [miners] call Needles Eye Pass." (575~) The trail was used, and probably improved, by John Wetherill while guiding clients to Rainbow Natural Bridge.

Douglas Preston called it the Moonlight Water Trail: "[The trail] was a gully cut sideways into the cliff, pitched at a good thirty-degree angle.... Nothing but huge boulders and sliding cobbles lying on the top of rotten, canted slickrock." (1573~)

—Organ Rock: (Also called Cabinet Organ Butte, Organ Butte, and Red Organ Rock.) (1370~) This 350-foot tower is a couple of miles east of Copper Canyon (at elevation 5354T on the Oljeto map). It is in the Organ Rock Shale Formation. (SAPE.)

William B. Douglass of the General Land Office noted this in 1909 as *Say-cle-saon* or "red rock standing up." (573~) Arthur A. Baker noted that the Navajo name, which he spelled phonetically *Tse Ealii*, meant "Rock Stick Out." (97~)

The rock was named by a government survey party led by Arthur M. Johnson in 1911. Francis John Dyer of the party: "It stands isolated and apart, stupendous in its majesty, carved by wind and rain and flood into the semblance of a great pipe organ." (587a~)

Charles L. Bernheimer in 1920: "We shall have to climb out of Copper Canyon, descend into Moonlight [Oljeto] Wash, and hope to sleep tonight near Organ Rock.... We had, however, an exquisite view of Organ Rock which stands alone like a huge set of organ pipes resembling an obelisk from the west and an organ screen from the broad south side." (218~)

—Breakfast Table: Charles L. Bernheimer: "On the south side of Copper Canyon as it merged with the plateau on which stands Organ Rock is a cove with rock forms which all resemble the utensils and other outfit we associate with a breakfast table, so we named this cove the Breakfast Table. There was a tea caddy, a perfect sugar

bowl with beehive-like cover, and there was a tea can with handle, spout, and cover." (218~)

—Obelisk: This impressive tower is three miles southwest of Pickrell Mesa (at elevation 5761T on the Jacobs Monument map). Howard B. Carpenter named this impressive tower in 1901: "This is a great square column of stone about 700 ft. high." (345~)

Copper Creek: (Garfield Co.) Henry Mountains-Hansen Creek. Copper Creek Benches map.

—Copper Spring: The cabin at Copper Spring was most likely built by Leverett A. Woodruff. In 1903 he located a mine one-half mile northeast of the spring. (606~) (See Woodruff Canyon.)

Copper Creek: (Garfield Co.) Henry Mountains-North Wash. Mount Ellen and Raggy Canyon maps.

Charles B. Hunt: "[This is a] local name for a stream draining eastward from Mount Ellen and another draining southward from Mount Hillers. There is little or no copper staining along either." (925~)

—Copper Basin Spring: (Mount Ellen map.) Grove Karl Gilbert of the Powell Survey called this Avarett Spring for one of his horse packers, Elisha Averitt. (722~)

Copper Globe: (Emery Co.) San Rafael Swell-Sagebrush Bench. Copper Globe map.

—Copper Globe Mine: (Also called Globe Copper Mine.) This was started sometime before 1900. In the early 1900s Edward Pike became the owner. The mine was never particularly successful and was in use from time to time until World War Two. It is now contained within the Copper Globe Mine Heritage Site. (641~, 710~, 1233~)

Ray Wareham spent a lifetime running livestock on Copper Globe: "They found some copper right where the dome starts.... The only way they could get the ore out of there was to melt it down and high grade it and then take it out with teams and wagons. They needed to build a smelter. Crissy Jensen had a brick kiln down here [in Ferron] and they got a couple of loads of his bricks and took them to the Copper Globe. They didn't have quite enough bricks for the smelter, so they got some mud and finished it up. When they fired it up, the whole thing caved in and they ruined all the ore that was bein' smelted. That big rick of wood [still located near the mine] was cut by Clive Killpack and Fred Zwahlen. You can only see a part of it now.... It used to be a lot bigger rick." (1967~)

—Shepherds End: (Also called Jensen Memorial.) This is at the "Grave" on Copper Globe. A plaque reads: "Henry H. Jensen of Mayfield, Utah was found dead Dec. 16, 1890. Blood and trails in the snow showed he had walked and crawled a mile after he was shot. He still held to his rifle, herding sheep for the Whitbecks. It is said the Robbers Roost gang warned all sheepers to '...stay out of this herding mesa.' He was carried out on a pack mule to the brink of Eagle Canyon to a buckboard 7 miles. He was found by Will and Otto Whitbeck." (1551~, 166~)

Copper Point: (San Juan Co.) Wingate Mesa-White Canyon. Copper Point map. (5,966')

Amasa Lyman filed a copper claim near Copper Point in 1884. He called it Copper Butte. (358~) Willard Luce noted that copper had also been mined from Copper Point during World War One. (1229~)

—Dolly Varden Mine: This is on the north side of Copper Point. James H. Knipmeyer noted that the Duckett brothers (John Baxter and Joseph Alexander) started mining here in 1898. (1115~) They called it the Dolly Varden, whom Pearl Baker noted was the famous singer of the era, Dolly Vardin. (119~)

In 1902 the mine was bought by Alonzo P. Adams, a copper speculator who also bought the nearby Blue Dike (Happy Jack) mine. The mine was not profitable and was abandoned for several years. In 1907 it was owned by a Mr. Bennett. Bert Loper noted it as both Mr. Bennett's Copper Camp and the Dolly Varden Copper Camp. (1215~)

Coral Pink Sand Dunes State Park: (Kane Co.) Moquith Mountains-Block Mesa. Yellowjacket Canyon map. This 3,730 acre park was established in 1963.

The Paiute name is *Atar'uipi*, or "sandy land." (82~)

Arthur F. Bruhn: "Coral-colored grains of sand carried by the wind have piled up into large dunes that reach several hundred feet high in places." (311~)

—Movies: The 1942 film *Arabian Nights,* starring Lief Erickson and Maria Montez, was filmed in part at the dunes (1421~), as was *One Little Indian* (131~).

Cordova Canyon: (Grand Co.) Cisco Desert-Salt Wash. Mollie Hogans map.

Jack Bickers noted that Epemineo Cordova and family, who were ranching at nearby Blue Spring starting in 1916, discovered Cordova Canyon in 1919 and started a ranch at its mouth. They raised livestock as well as vegetables, corn, and alfalfa. Visitors passing by would throw down a rope and the Cordovas would send up a melon or two. The Cordova family abandoned the ranch in the late 1930s. The ruins of the ranch are near the head of the canyon. The "home" spring, in a cave near the ranch house, is prolific and is now choked with poison ivy. (224~, 1977~, SAPE.)

There were three primary access trails to the Cordova Ranch.

—Footman Trail: This "trail" is far up the south end of Cordova Canyon. Chiseled footholds can be seen. This route must not be used. It is an exceedingly dangerous exit.

—Horseman Trail: This stock trail is two miles up Salt Wash from Cordova Canyon.

—Sandslide Trail: This is the easiest and closest stock trail to the Cordova Ranch. It is on the west side of Salt Wash halfway between Cordova and Clover canyons. (SAPE.)

Corn Creek: (Garfield Co.) Dixie National Forest-Escalante Mountains-Main Canyon. Griffin Point map.

Two similar name derivations are given.

First, Philo Allen, Sr. (1818-1909) and his son, Edmund, were the first settlers, arriving in 1875. They built a cabin on the creek and planted corn here. (1655~)

Second: Unattributed: "Corn Creek, so called because Gilbert Adams had once planted corn in this small mountain vale." (381~)

—Bishop Schow Ranch: PRIVATE PROPERTY. Pratt Gates noted that this was at the mouth of Corn Creek. Andrew P. Schow (1839-1913) was an early resident of the Escalante area. (709~) Several buildings remain. (SAPE.)

—Corn Creek Mine: Pratt Gates noted that his brother-in-law, Richard Christiansen, started this coal mine in the mid-1950s. (709~)

—Carl Deuel Mine: Pratt Gates noted that this coal mine in Main Canyon near the mouth of Corn Canyon is shown as adits one-eighth mile east of elevation BM7049. Carl Deuel (1887-1967) worked the mine before World War Two. (709~)

Cornerstone Canyon: (Kane Co.) Glen Canyon NRA-Glen Canyon. Navajo Point and Cathedral Canyon maps.

Katie Lee: "The reason we'd called it that was because on the downstream side of this canyon it looks like a great big building. The sandstone is just cut with a big square edge. Just as square as anything I have ever seen." (1163~)

Corral Canyon: (Emery Co.) Manti-LaSal National Forest-Huntington Creek. Candland Mountain map.

In the early days, livestock was driven into the canyon and a fence across the mouth would keep them in. (2053~)

Corral Canyon: (Emery and Wayne Counties.) San Rafael Swell-Moroni Slopes-Last Chance Wash. The Frying Pan and Caine Springs maps.

Garn Jefferies: "There's a very narrow place in the canyon. As you go up, it opens out a little bit. There's water tricklin' down. They used to chase wild horses up in there and they'd catch them." (959~)

Corral Canyon: (Garfield Co.) Henry Mountains-Straight Creek. Mount Pennell map.

Two similar name derivations are given.

First, Bliss Brinkerhoff: "Boy, that goes back to the real early pioneers. Supposed to be a gold mine up in Corral Canyon. There is a little open spot up in the canyon that they were able to put in a little corral for their sheep. It wasn't for cows. It's just a sheep catchment." (291~)

Second, Garth Noyes: "The fellows that used to run cattle here were from the upper end of Wayne County. The cattle were awful wild. Finding a corral that could hold them was a big deal. They had a good corral in there. They'd chase wild cattle through that country. That's an experience all of its own." (1473~)

Edwin T. Wolverton noted that in the 1880s Ben Bowen and a man named Burke found a rich gold-bearing outcropping in Corral Canyon. They returned to civilization, then came back, but strangely could never find the original location. (2039~)

Corral Canyon: (Kane Co.) Dixie National Forest-Paunsaugunt Plateau-Kanab Creek. Alton map.

Also called Cabin Canyon. (570~, 741~)

Corral Canyon: (Kane Co.) GSCENM-Park Wash. Rainbow Point and Deer Spring Point maps.

Park Wash goes through Corral Canyon.

John H. Watson: "There was a corral built in the gulch or canyon for securing horses and the name was taken from that." (2053~) The old corral is just south of Adair Lake, which is at the head of Corral Canyon. (SAPE.)

Corral Canyon: (Sevier Co.) Fishlake National Forest-Wasatch Plateau-Salina Creek. Water Hollow Ridge map.

Stuart Johnson: "There are some corrals in the lower part of that canyon that we used to use." (1003~)

Corral Creek: (Grand Co.) Uintah and Ouray Indian Reservation-East Tavaputs Plateau-West Willow Creek. Floy Canyon North and Bogart Canyon maps.

Also called Corral Canyon.

Nell Murbarger in 1960: "angled up Corral Canyon, following another clear creek broken by cascading waterfalls." (1414~)

Corral Flat: (Garfield Co.) Dixie National Forest-Sevier Plateau. Junction and Phonolite Hill maps.

Kent Whittaker noted that they had a sheep corral out on the flats. (2002~)

Corral Hollow: (Washington Co.) Zion National Park-Horse Pasture Plateau-North Fork Virgin River. Temple of Sinawava map.

Pioneer ranchers had a horse corral here. (1038~, 1931~)

Corral Point: (Garfield Co.) Henry Mountains-Dugout Creek. Mount Ellen map. (9,850')

Guy Robison noted that they corralled cattle here. (1644~)

Corral Point: (Grand Co.) Book Cliffs-Cisco Wash. Cisco Springs map. (5,425')

This narrow peninsula was used as a corral for livestock. Natural formations kept stock from going north or south and short barb-wire and rock fences kept them from going east or west. (SAPE.)

Corral Ridge: (Kane Co.) Glen Canyon NRA-Kaiparowits Plateau. Navajo Point map. (7,449')

There is an old corral on Corral Ridge near the "Pack Trail" that goes to East End Spring. (SAPE.)

Corry Point: (Washington Co.) Kolob Terrace-West Fork Deep Creek. Cogswell Point and Webster Flat maps. (8,375')

Ann Starr: "Named for Andrew Corry [1846-1933], a sheep rancher and dairyman. Also owned Cook Springs." (942~) Corry was an early resident of Parowan. (516~)

Cottam Bench: (Washington Co.) St. George Fields-Virgin River. St. George map.

Thomas Cottam (1820-1896) and his wife, Caroline (1820-1890), were early settlers of St. George, arriving in 1861. (14~, 273~, 462~)

Cottonwood Bottom: (Grand Co.) Labyrinth Canyon-Low Spur. Mineral Canyon map.

Also called Foote Bottom or North Foote Bottom. (M.78.) (See Tidwell Bottom.)

Cottonwood Canyon: (Carbon Co.) West Tavaputs Plateau-Nine Mile Creek. Bruin Point, Twin Hollow, and Cowboy Bench maps.

Preston Nutter is credited with building the first road up Cottonwood Canyon in the early 1900s to get his livestock to the Range Creek area. (1577~) He had a line cabin at the top of the canyon. (94~)

Inscriptions include S. Groesbeck, Aug. 19, 1867; Horace Larsen, July 30/15; Pete Wilson, 1915; and John Barcock, 1915. (SAPE.)

—Rasmussen Ranch: PRIVATE PROPERTY. This was in Nine Mile Canyon one-half mile east of the mouth of Cottonwood Canyon (Cowboy Bench map). The Oliver Rasmussen family ranched here in the early years. (558~, 725~)

Cottonwood Canyon: (Grand Co.) La Sal Mountains-Dolores River. Fisher Valley map.

Fisher Creek runs through Cottonwood Canyon.

—Constructed Stock Trail: This enters middle Cottonwood Canyon north-northwest of elevation 5629T. It was part of a longer trail that went from Polar Mesa to the Dolores River. (1866~) (See Polar Mesa and Cowhead Hill.) Inscriptions include no name, May 9th, 1897 and W. Morrison, March 27th, 1898. (SAPE.)

Cottonwood Canyon: (Grand Co.) La Sal Mountains-Dolores River. Fisher Towers, Fisher Valley, and Blue Chief Mesa maps.

—Dalton Ranch: This was at the mouth of Cottonwood Canyon. (1931~)

—Top of the World: This is the area between the heads of Cottonwood and Waring canyons (Fisher Towers map). It was named by mountain bike riders and rock climbers. Eric Bjørnstad: "Top of the World is a remote point overlooking Fisher Towers and Onion Creek's colorful gypsum outcrops. North and west is the Colorado River and Richardson Amphitheater. The La Sal Mountains dominate the eastern skyline. It is one of the most spectacular and dramatic overviews on the Colorado Plateau, a sight few have had the pleasure of experiencing." (240~)

Cottonwood Canyon: (Iron Co.) Dixie National Forest-Harmony Mountains-Duncan Canyon. Stoddard Mountain map.

Leslie Pace of New Harmony: "Cottonwood trees growing in the canyon since first explored." (942~)

Cottonwood Canyon: (Iron Co.) Dixie National Forest-Parowan Valley. Little Creek Peak and Cottonwood Mountain maps.

—Upper Cottonwood Troughs: (Cottonwood Mountain map.) This large spring was once developed. (SAPE.)

—Lower Cottonwood Troughs: (Cottonwood Mountain map.) This is a large spring with a no-longer-functioning CCC-style watering trough. (SAPE.)

Cottonwood Canyon: (Kane Co.) GSCENM-Johnson Wash. Skutumpah Creek, Pine Point, and Cutler Point maps.

Nephi Johnson noted that this was named in 1871 by pioneers from the settlement of Johnson for the large cottonwoods found here. (2053~)

—Cottonwood Spring: (Skutumpah Creek map.) This medium-size spring is at the base of a small pour-off. A constructed stock trail provides access from the west. (SAPE.)

—Treasure Canyon: Cottonwood Canyon may also have been called Treasure Canyon, though this is not certain. In 1942 George G. Mace told this story, after noting that the below-mentioned canyon is two miles north and east of Picture Rock in Johnson Canyon. Cottonwood Canyon is actually almost four miles north. Mace: "A man by the name of Fred Crystal, purporting to have come into

possession of an old Spanish map disclosing the deposit of a vast treasure of Spanish gold which had been buried in a cave to save it from Indians, the Spaniards being later all killed but one who mapped the place of deposit, convinced not a few men of Kanab and vicinity that the treasure was surely buried at the above treasure-cave. He said the map was secured from this lone survivor by one of his kin and it had in turn been passed on to him. The apparent sincerity of Mr. Crystal was convincing. About eight or ten men joined him in digging. Curiously enough, what Crystal said developed exactly as he indicated, even to the last chamber in which the gold was to be found. Months of toil was spurred by anticipation, or better, expectation. The only item lacking was the gold." (2053~)

Cottonwood Canyon: (Kane Co.) Moquith Mountains-Kanab Creek. Yellowjacket Canyon, Kanab, and Fredonia maps.

Also called Cottonwood Creek.

Ezra Stevens and William W. Adair in 1941: "This creek runs through Cottonwood Canyon and is named for the cottonwoods along its course." (2053~)

—Riggs Ranch: PRIVATE PROPERTY. (Also called Cottonwood Ranch.) This ranch was located near the top of the canyon. Brigham A. Riggs (1857-1954) had a ranch here starting in the early 1900s. (1027a~)

—Pioneer Road: The Lieutenant George M. Wheeler Survey map of 1872–73 shows a trail going from Mt. Carmel, across the East Fork Virgin River, across the flats, and down Cottonwood Canyon to Wolf Spring. (M.76.) Neil M. Judd in 1919: "Cottonwood Canyon was intimately associated with the settlement of southwestern Utah. Through its winding course ox teams hauled much of the lumber used in construction of the Mormon temple at St. George. Colonists passed through Cottonwood about 1870 bound from an old location on Muddy Creek [Nevada], a western tributary of the Rio Virgin, to new homes in Long Valley. Traffic between this young colony and the older settlements to the west continued over the canyon road—it is still visible in many places—for some years after the founding of Kanab." (1027a~)

Cottonwood Canyon: (Kane and Washington Counties, Utah and Mohave County, Az.) Vermilion Cliffs-Cottonwood Point Wilderness. Hildale and Colorado City, Az. maps.

Also called Sungabi Canyon. (767~)

Cottonwood Canyon: (Mohave Co., Az.) Hurricane Cliffs-Hurricane Wash. Rock Canyon, Az. map.

The Domínguez-Escalante Expedition of 1776–77 camped near the mouth of the canyon. (1357~)

Cottonwood Canyon: (San Juan Co.) Glen Canyon NRA-Wilson Mesa-Glen Canyon. Wilson Creek map.

Also called Cedar Creek Canyon, Cottonwood Creek, and Cottonwood Valley.

This was named by the Hole-in-the-Rock Expedition. Platte D. Lyman provided the first description of the canyon while scouting for the expedition in November 1879: "We found a smooth open Kanyon with water wood and grass in it which we followed up for 3 miles and then began to ascend the bluffs which are at first sandy and afterwards steep solid sandstone hills." (1259~) Lyman returned to the canyon with the main expedition in January 1880: "Moved up to the cottonwoods where the rest of the company are camped." (1259~)

David E. Miller in 1959: "In the spring of the year Cottonwood is indeed a beautiful and peaceful little canyon, not deep and rugged as are most canyons in that country. The stream meanders at a gentle slope along the valley floor, dropping here and there into natural rock tanks which form excellent swimming pools." (1356~)

Eugene L. Controtto in 1961: "Cottonwood Canyon—a delightful anomaly in this country. Instead of being deep and rugged, this canyon is open and rolling. Down its bed flows a bubbling stream of delicious water, and around each bend the traveler is greeted with a stand of green waving cottonwood trees shading soft grassy banks, dancing waters and quiet pools." (447~)

—Cottonwood Hill: The upper part of the canyon became a real challenge for the Hole-in-the-Rock Expedition. They called this section Cottonwood Hill. (1259~) David E. Miller noted it as Little Hole-in-the-Rock. It is one-half mile northwest of Aladdins Lamp Pass. (1356~)

—Register Rocks: This rock, now underwater, was near the mouth of Cottonwood Canyon. It was covered with inscriptions dating to the Hole-in-the-Rock Expedition. David E. Miller in 1953: "I took the liberty of naming the Register Rocks the first time I traversed that part of the old [Hole-in-the-Rock] trail because of several names of the original company found chiseled into the face of the solid stone at that point." (1356~)

Dick Sprang: "The 'Cookie' is what we called the Mormon inscription rock in Cottonwood Valley. It stuck up from the valley floor like a cookie sitting on its broken edge—or like a cookie buried halfway in the valley floor." (19~)

Inscriptions from Hole-in-the-Rock Expedition members included C.E. Walton, Jan. 27, 1880; E.L.L. [Lyman], Jan. 29, 1880; E.Z. Taylor, Jan. 30, 1880; and J.D. Jensen, J.W. Young, and J. Smith, Jan. 30, 1880. (466~)

—Triple Arch: (Also called Pioneer Arch.) (1304~) This arch, now underwater, was behind Register Rock. It was probably first seen, and named, by members of the Hole-in-the-Rock Expedition. Robert H. Vreeland noted that is was also called PT Arch for an inscription that read PT Bridge, with the letters before PT being unreadable. (1954~)

—Pumpkin Rock: Elwyn Blake in 1956: "It was a little below the old road the pioneers used after the crossing at the Hole-in-the-Rock, on the east side of the river [at the mouth of Cottonwood Canyon on the edge of the Colorado River]. We could not locate it last summer and I feel sure that the river may have cut under it, as there is so much land gone that was there in 1921." (255~)

Cottonwood Canyon: (San Juan Co.) Manti-LaSal National Forest-La Sal Mountains-Browns Hole. La Sal West map.

Also called Big Hole Creek.

Cottonwood Creek: (Emery Co.) Wasatch Plateau-Castle Valley-San Rafael River. Rilda Canyon, Mahogany Point, Red Point, Castle Dale, and Hadden Holes maps.

Also called Cottonwood Canyon.

Cottonwood, Ferron, and Huntington creeks come together to form the San Rafael River.

Evelyn Peacock Huntsman: "Cottonwood Creek ... was designated as the 'San Mateo' by the Spanish explorers and as the 'Sivareeche' by the Indians." (931~)

Members of the Elk Mountain Mission of 1855 called this Sweet Cottonwood Creek. (229~, 1500~) Thomas E. Bryson: "Named from cottonwood trees in vicinity of river." (2053~)

—Pioneer Road: (Also called Cottonwood Trail.) Pioneers used Cottonwood Creek to travel from Sanpete County to Castle Valley. (1195~) Montell Seely: "When they had to go along a steep sidehill that was too steep for a wagon to stay upright, they used the hand plow and made a furrow for the upper wheel to 'hang in.' That furrow was the road over that section. When they came to places where the boulders were too close for the wagons to pass through, they would build a fire against the rock and get it as hot as possible, then throw cold water on it. This would cause the rock to crack." (1717~)

—Wilsonville: PRIVATE PROPERTY. (Also called Aikens Ranch.) (1717~) This townsite was on the west side of Cottonwood Creek one and one-half miles downriver from The Breaks (one-half mile north of elevation 5503 on the Hadden Holes map). The town's first residents were brothers Chris, Davis, George, Nick, Silas, and Sylvester Wilson. They arrived in 1878.

Naomi Jensen in 1949: "Wilsonville has been a 'ghost town' for many years. The underlying causes for the decline of this place seems to have been the discarding of the old Gunnison Trail [Old Spanish Trail], the removal of the post office to Castle Dale and the discontinuance of the school." (641~, 1330~, 1734~)

—Old Spanish Trail: The trail went through what would become Wilsonville.

—Racehorse Flat: This is in the "V" formed by the confluence of Cottonwood Wash and Rock Canyon Creek (Hadden Holes map). Lee Mont Swasey: "A fellow named Aikens lived down there and that's where he'd train his race horses." (1853~)

Cottonwood Creek: (Garfield Co.) Dixie National Forest-Sevier Plateau-Johns Valley. Adams Head, Cow Creek, and Grass Lakes maps.

Also called Needle Rock Creek. (764~, 777~)

Clarence Dutton's 1879 Powell Survey map shows this as Joseph Cañon. (584~, 585~)

Scott Robinson in 1942: "It derived its name from the large growth of cottonwood trees which are found along its course." (2053~)

Cottonwood Creek: (Kane Co.) GSCENM-Paria River. Canaan Peak, Butler Valley, Horse Flat, Calico Peak, and Fivemile Valley maps.

Also called Cottonwood Canyon.

Ronald Shofner: "As the name implies, the canyon is lined with the spreading shade of the restful cottonwood tree." (1728~)

The name was in place by 1882. (585~, 1096~)

—Constructed Stock Trail: This goes west from Cottonwood Creek up to the Rush Beds. It starts at a "Corral" on Cottonwood Creek on the Horse Flat map. (SAPE.)

—Constructed Stock Trail: This goes west from Cottonwood Creek up to the Rush Beds. It starts at the "Spring" one mile downcanyon from the abovementioned "Corral." (SAPE.)

—Chynoweth Stock Trail: Ralph Chynoweth had a line cabin in Cottonwood Creek one-half mile up from the mouth of Hackberry Canyon. This is shown on the Calico Peak map. A stock trail goes from the cabin west onto the lower Rush Beds. Ralph Chynoweth: "Somebody burned the old cabin down but there's still a corral there. We built them in 1958." (425~)

—Yellow Rock: This dome of stupendous yellow sandstone is near the junction of Cottonwood Creek and Hackberry Canyon (at elevation 5524 on the Calico Peak map).

—Cottonwood Wash Road: (Also called Cottonwood Cutoff.) (1122~) In 1957 the Cottonwood Wash Road was improved from a poor wagon track to one that would accommodate automobiles. The cost of construction was born locally; adjacent communities were trying to promote the road as a highway between Page and northern Utah. (1658~)

Nell Murbarger in 1961: "Winding through the narrowing canyon that cradles the desultory desert stream, we found ourselves thrilling to a land that grew steadily wilder and more broken.... We rambled on through desert-scapes of most diverse nature—sandstone cliffs, pinnacles, eroded knolls, sage flats, rolling slopes and neat groves of junipers arranged by nature in almost parklike precision, following one upon another." (1415~)

Cottonwood Creek: (San Juan Co.) Manti-LaSal National Forest-Dark Canyon Plateau-San Juan River. Chippean Rocks, Cream Pots, Mancos Jim Butte, Black Mesa Butte, No-Mans Island, and Bluff maps.

(See Cottonwood Wash—San Juan Co. for name derivation.)

Cottonwood Creek: (Sevier Co.) Fishlake National Forest-Pavant Range-Sevier River. White Pine Peak and Richfield maps.

Also called Cottonwood Canyon.

James B. Morrison: "The Pioneers found cottonwoods growing at the mouth of Cotton Wood Canyon." (354~)

Pearl F. Jacobson noted that the first settlers of nearby Richfield took cottonwood saplings from the mouth of the canyon and planted them in the new town. (955~)

—Cottonwood Spring: Springs in the canyon have been developed and water from them is piped to the town of Annabella. (1971~)

Cottonwood Creek: (Sevier Co.) Fishlake National Forest-Wasatch Plateau-Salina Creek. Steves Mountain map.

Jim Crane: "Down in Salina Canyon at the mouth of Cottonwood Creek the old road used to go through a tunnel—the old railroad grade tunnel. That tunnel is no longer there. But, when I was a boy, we used to have to push cows through the tunnel on the way up or down Salina Canyon. The older cows knew where they were going and they would just lead the other cows right through there." (478~)

Cottonwood Creek: (Washington Co.) Dixie National Forest-Pine Valley Mountains-Quail Creek. Saddle Mountain, Washington, and Harrisburg Junction maps.

Jacob Hamblin in 1854: "I rode to Cottonwood Creek, where the town of Harrisburg now stands. I felt exhausted and could go no farther.... Brother Atwood brought some water in the leather holster of his pistol, and put some of it in my mouth and on my head, which revived me." (1210~)

—Cottonwood Aqueduct: This is the "Aqueduct" on the maps. Piping water from Cottonwood Creek to St. George started in the early 1890s. The fifteen-mile-long canal was finished in 1898. (14~)

Cottonwood Creek: (Wayne Co.) Henry Mountains-Town Wash. Dry Lakes Peak and Steamboat Point maps.
Nearby inscriptions include Ernie Steele, 1930 and Rudy Steele, 1932. (SAPE.)

Cottonwood Draw: (Emery Co.) San Rafael Swell-Sids Draw. Drowned Hole Draw and The Wickiup maps.
—Cottonwood Holes: (The Wickiup map.) These are a series of medium-size potholes. A gnarly cottonwood tree is nearby. (SAPE.)
—Wild Dog Reservoir: This stock reservoir is three-quarters of a mile to the south-southeast of Cottonwood Holes. It was built in 1960. (1551~)

Cottonwood Gulch: (Kane Co.) Glen Canyon NRA-Reflection Canyon. Nasja Mesa map.
Also called Cottonwood Creek and Horse Canyon. (M.25.) Edson Alvey noted that there are many cottonwood trees along the gulch. (55~) The name was applied by the USGS in 1951. (1615~)
Katie Lee and friends called this Horse Canyon after finding horse prints in it. Katie told a story about the canyon: "We kept seeing these little pieces of tinsel in the canyon bottom; little pieces no longer than an inch or two. They'd flash at us. We just went crazy trying to figure it out.... About a year later a friend of mine said, 'Oh, haven't you seen that stuff in the canyons before'? I said, 'No, never! Anywhere! Why'? He said, 'Well, the Air Force flies over there and they pull a target and this target has got that tinsel stuff on it so they can see it. It's a firing target.'" (1163~)
Inscriptions include Ed Allen, 1901. (SAPE.)
—Constructed Stock Trail: This enters the north side of middle Cottonwood Canyon (near elevation BM3997). (SAPE.)

Cottonwood Pass: (Garfield Co.) Henry Mountains-Birch Creek. Dry Lake Peak map. (9,800')
Charles B. Hunt noted that this pass between Dry Lakes Peak and Mt. Ellen was called North Pass. (925~)

Cottonwood Ridge: (Carbon Co.) Roan Cliffs-Range Creek. Bruin Point and Patmos Head maps.
Waldo Wilcox: "That was part of Preston Nutter's country.... They took a drill rig into the head of Cottonwood

Canyon. It was an old steam boiler, a cable rig. It is still there. That was in the 1920s." (2011~)

Cottonwood Spring: (Coconino Co., Az.) Vermilion Cliffs National Monument-Hurricane Cliffs-Soap Creek. The Big Knoll, Az. map.
This medium-size spring was once developed. (SAPE.)

Cottonwood Spring: (Emery Co.) San Rafael Swell-Wood Hollow. Sid and Charley map.
This is a developed spring. (780~)
Lee Mont Swasey: "Cottonwoods are there." (1853~)

Cottonwood Spring: (Kane Co.) GSCENM-Escalante Desert-Hole-in-the-Rock Road-Sooner Slide. Sooner Bench map.
This is a large spring with a stock tank set in a small grove of cottonwood trees.
Inscriptions include William Shirts, 18??; Vic Alvey, May 24, 1935; Hugh Chesnut, Feb. 1, 1935; and Mohr Christiansen, March 21, 1936. (SAPE.)
—Capstone Pinnacle: This small pinnacle is at the base of Fiftymile Bench one mile southwest of Cottonwood Spring. Inscriptions include Ken Griffin, 1923 and Vernon Griffin, April 24, 1936. (SAPE.)

Cottonwood Spring: (Kane Co.) Long Valley-Big Hollow. Glendale map.
This is a medium-size spring. An old road goes down to the spring on its west side. (SAPE.)

Cottonwood Tanks: (Garfield Co.) Capitol Reef National Park-Waterpocket Fold-Halls Creek. The Post map.
Dwight Williams: "There was always water in Cottonwood Tanks. I've never in my life seen it what you couldn't push the insects and stuff back and get a drink of water outta Cottonwood Tanks." (2013~) The name was in place by 1908. (1697~)
Inscriptions include Parley Thueson, No. 24, 1892. (1115~)

Cottonwood Wash: (Emery Co.) Cedar Mountain-Price River. Cow Flats, Flattop Mountain, Olsen Reservoir, and Mounds maps.
In April 1901 Watkin James, a sheepherder, was driving his flock from Green River to Price. Losing several head on the desert, he left his other herders and sheep and went looking for the lost band. It wasn't until a couple of weeks later that his nephew, Daniel, went looking for him. He was found on Cottonwood Wash, with the lost sheep around him. He was buried in the old cemetery in Green River. (451~)

Cottonwood Wash: (Emery Co.) San Rafael Swell-Saleratus Wash. Devils Hole, Mexican Mountain, Desert, and Jessies Twist maps.

Also called Cottonwood Gulch and Cottonwood Springs. (1737~)

The name was in place by 1878. (1567~)

The Elk Mountain Mission of 1855 went down the then unnamed wash. Alfred N. Billings of the expedition: "Traveled 5 miles down Dry cannion to the Bench 5 miles to water Smalle Stream of water made By Springs water Breckish very warm." (229~)

Inscriptions include R.A. Hart, Oct. 28, 1879 (1115~); J.A. Smith, 1881; and Jasper Conrad, Sept. 25th, 1881. (SAPE.)

—Old Spanish Trail: The trail went along Cottonwood Wash, though when the wash turns into the San Rafael Reef, the trail continued north parallel to the eastern Reef.

—Rail route: In 1881 the Denver and Rio Grande Western Railroad built a narrow gauge railbed along Cottonwood Wash. Pieces of the railbed can still be seen. Tracks were never laid. (See Denver and Rio Grande Western Railroad.)

—Pinnacle Canyon: This western tributary of Cottonwood Wash is one-half mile downcanyon from where Cottonwood Wash turns abruptly from east to south (one-half mile northwest of elevation 4770 on the Mexican Mountain map). It was named for a prominent pinnacle by Steve Allen. (45~)

Cottonwood Wash: (Emery Co.) San Rafael Desert-San Rafael River. Crows Nest Spring, Spring Canyon, and Horse Bench West maps.

Also called Alkali Pond Gulch.

Cottonwood Wash starts at the junction of Temple Wash and Old Woman Wash near Temple Spring. It then goes into the San Rafael River. Old maps often show this as Temple Mountain Wash. The Cottonwood Wash name was in use by 1897. (1812~)

Inscriptions include W.E Bemus?, Manti and J.S. Hansen, Mayfield, 1891; and JSH [18]91. (1548~)

—Cottonwood Spring: (Crows Nest Spring map.) This is a large spring at the mouth of a small, Entrada-walled canyon. (SAPE.) It was used in the 1890s by miners going from Green River to Glen Canyon and the San Juan River. (915~) The spring is still used by stockmen. The CCC built a water cistern here in 1941. (1779~)

Cottonwood Wash: (Garfield Co.) Henry Mountains-North Wash. Raggy Canyon and Turkey Knob maps.

—Cottonwood Flats: This name, in place by the 1890s, refers to the area around upper Cottonwood Wash. In

1897 Robert Brewster Stanton noted that a road through Cottonwood Flats "will always be sandy & heavy lugging." (1812~)

—Drinking Cup Spring: This is the "Spring" in Cottonwood Wash that is one mile west of its confluence with North Wash (Turkey Knob map). (925~)

—Ekker-Robison Range Camp: Kevin Robison noted that this line camp was on Cottonwood Wash one-quarter mile east of Drinking Cup Spring. A cabin, now gone, was built by Lawrence and Andrew Ekker and Alvin Robison. There are still corrals at the site. (1646~, SAPE.)

Cottonwood Wash: (Grand Co.) Book Cliffs–Grand Valley-Colorado River. Flume Canyon, Antone Canyon, Danish Flat, Agate, and Big Triangle maps.

Also called Desert Wash. (847~)

—Cottonwood Ranch: (See Diamond Canyon—Harms Ranch.)

Cottonwood Wash: (Grand Co.) Dome Plateau-Grand Valley-Salt Wash. Cisco SW and Mollie Hogans maps.

There is a very healthy stand of cottonwood trees in the wash. In pioneer days it was noted that this was a perennial stream. (1931~)

Inscriptions include J.H.W., 1898; M.M., 1906; and many names of Spanish ancestry with dates from the 1920s to the 1940s. It is assumed they were sheepherders. (SAPE.)

Cottonwood Wash: (Kane Co.) Glen Canyon NRA-Warm Creek Bay. Warm Creek Bay map.

—Cottonwood Catchment: This catchment and stock tank are at the head of Cottonwood Wash on Alstrom Point. (SAPE.)

Cottonwood Wash: (San Juan Co.) Manti-LaSal National Forest-Ute Mountain Ute Indian Reservation-Abajo Mountains-San Juan River. Chippean Rocks, Cream Pots, Mancos Jim Butte, Black Mesa Butte, No-Mans Island, and Bluff maps. Some of this canyon is PRIVATE PROPERTY.

Also called Cottonwood Creek and Main Cottonwood. (1389a~)

The Captain John N. Macomb Expedition of 1859 descended Recapture Creek to the San Juan River. Although there is no evidence that the expedition went downriver to Cottonwood Wash, their proximity prompted the Ferdinand V. Hayden Survey in 1877 to name it Macomb Wash (848~, 1269~), a name that did not stick.

Hole-in-the-Rock Expedition members noted it as Cottonwood Creek in 1880. (235~)

The 1881 Rand McNally map of Utah shows it as Hallets Creek (665~), as does the 1883 Utah map by G.F. Cram

(M.13a.). This name remained on maps until at least the early 1920s. (M.73.)

Warren K. Moorehead of the Illustrated American Exploring Expedition of 1892 called it both Hallets Creek and Cottonwood Creek: "So named on account of its immense cottonwood trees." (1383~)

Eliza Marie Partridge Lyman, an early settler of Bluff, in her diary entry for August 20, 1880, told of a huge flood in the canyon: "During the past week we have had a powerful flood which came down the Cottonwood Wash. The water was wider than the San Juan river. It lasted two or three days and nights. The river was also very high and has washed away a good many hundred dollars worth of our brethren's water ditches." (1253~)

Frank McNitt: "[It is] not shady as its name implied, but wide and bare, a naked stretch of white sand and clay parched by the sun, the surface crackled and curling from dried-up moisture, dotted with sagebrush. In the rainy season the wash sometimes carries a foam-flecked runoff flood from the northern slopes into the San Juan." (1334~)

Albert R. Lyman in 1918 noted the lack of good wood for construction in the new town of Bluff in 1880. The settlers had to use cottonwood logs from the canyon: "This famine for lumber induced certain men to slice up cottonwood logs with a whipsaw, but these boards were so determined to warp and twist like a thing in convulsions, they wouldn't lie still after being nailed down." (1240~)

The upper canyon is most famous for its many vanadium and uranium mines. Uranium was discovered in Cottonwood Wash by sheepherder Benito Sanchez of Blanding in 1931. He told Arah Shumway of his discovery. Shumway went on to develop several mining claims in the wash. A vanadium processing plant was built just north of the Cottonwood Wash-Brushy Basin Wash junction during World War Two. It later burned down. (1526~, 1562~, 1730~)

As the vanadium market was dying, the market for uranium strengthened and mining was in full swing by the early 1950s. The height of the uranium boom was in 1958 and by the mid-1980s it had died. (212~)

—Piute Park: (Also called Piute Basin.) This is an area in Cottonwood Canyon near the mouths of Hammond and Allen canyons. Paiute Indians had a settlement here in the early 1900s. (761~) (See Allen Canyon.)

—Car Crossing: This is a road crossing of a narrow section of Cottonwood Wash on the south side of Decker Cove (one-quarter mile northeast of elevation 4757 on the No-Mans Island map). Several old cars were thrown into this slot to build a bridge across it.

—Stock Trail: This enters lower Cottonwood Wash from the east one mile downcanyon from its junction with Black Rock Canyon (three-quarters of a mile south of elevation 4520 on the Bluff map). (SAPE.)

—West Side Sand Dune Stock Trail: This enters lower Cottonwood Wash from Tank Mesa one and one-quarter miles downcanyon from its junction with Black Rock Canyon (one-quarter mile north of elevation 4726 on the Bluff map). Inscriptions in Cottonwood Wash near the trail include B.F.R., 1891 [Benjamin Franklin Redd]; A. 1884; and H. White CCC Co. 3241. (SAPE.)

—Canyon Three: The mouth of this eastern tributary of Cottonwood Wash is two miles (as the crow flies) upcanyon from the mouth of Spring Canyon (immediately north of elevation 4691 on the Bluff map). A constructed stock trail goes through the canyon. (SAPE.)

—Bushwhack Canyon: The mouth of this eastern tributary of Cottonwood Wash is one and one-quarter miles upcanyon from the mouth of Spring Canyon (one-half mile northwest of elevation 4693 on the Bluff map). An interesting constructed stock trail goes through the canyon. (SAPE.)

—Constructed Stock Trail: This remarkable horse ladder enters a short western tributary of lower Cottonwood Wash that is three-quarters of a mile upcanyon from the mouth of Spring Canyon (immediately east of elevation 4805 on the Bluff map).

—Bluff Pond: PRIVATE PROPERTY. (Also called Old Swimming Hole.) This is one-eighth mile west of elevation 4713 on the Bluff map. Brandt Hart: "This is located a short distance up Cottonwood Wash near the town of Bluff. From the early days, this was a farm pond that became the local swimming hole. While fond memories of the pond are common, one tragic event happened in 1956 when several local teenage boys, using dynamite to fish, were killed." (838~)

Albert R. Lyman: "a place where waterbirds sometimes swam, where lithe frogs hid among the rocks on the bank; but more important still, where the young lads of Bluff splashed and ran and leaped for joy: free from all cumbering raiment of any kind whatsoever.... [They were] in love with that 'ole swimmin' hole.' They claimed it was 'up to Jens Nielson's neck,' in the deepest place, for they could go down over their raised hand without touching bottom." (1240~)

Inscriptions include J. Allan Jr., Sept. 2nd, 1886. (838~)

Cottonwood Wash: (Washington Co.) Washington Black Ridge-Virgin River. Harrisburg Junction and Washington Dome maps.

Also called Cottonwood Creek.

Andrew Karl Larson: "So named because of the profusion of broad-leafed cottonwood trees along its margin." (1142~)

Cougar Canyon: (Kane Co.) Pink Cliffs-Muddy Creek. Strawberry Point and Orderville maps.

Kate B. Carter: "Jacob H. Crasly [also spelled Crosby] killed a cougar in this canyon." (384~) John H. Watson noted that the cougar was a very large one, measuring nine feet in length. (2053~)

Cougar Canyon: (Piute Co.) Fishlake National Forest-Tushar Mountains-Order Canyon. Delano Peak map.

Abe McIntosh in 1941: "a small canyon so named because of numerous cougars trapped in that section." (2053~)

Cougar Hollow: (Garfield Co.) Dixie National Forest-Escalante Mountains-Dry Hollow. Pollywog Lake map.

Sonny King: "There was a guy that used to be here by the name of Dean Crab. He was going along and he looked up ahead and saw this old cougar and his tail was going like that. He walked up a little bit and made sure there was no one else around when he went to shoot that cougar. And then Dean up and shot and killed the cougar. That was in the early '60s." (1095~)

Cougar Knoll: (Kane Co.) GSCENM-Kaiparowits Plateau-Lake Canyon. Blackburn Canyon map. (7,606')

Don Coleman: "Cougar Knoll was named after a cougar that used to live in there, a bad one." (441~)

Cougar Ridge: (Garfield Co.) Little Dog Valley-Echard Creek. Circleville Mountain and Fremont Pass maps. (8,967')

The Parley P. Pratt Exploring Expedition to Southern Utah of 1849–50 passed through a gap in Cougar Ridge (Fremont Pass map). John Campbell of the expedition: "Snow 1 foot deep on the level, then pass down narrow hollow." (1762~) The present-day road cuts through the narrow hollow.

Cougar Spring: (Garfield Co.) Dixie National Forest-Sevier Plateau-Mud Spring Creek. Mount Dutton map.

Kent Whittaker noted that in the 1920s his father-in-law, George H. Fox, built a wooden watering trough here by hewing out a large log. (2002~)

Courthouse Rock: (Grand Co.) Tenmile Country-Highway 191. Merrimac Butte map. (5,072')

William T. Tew in 1881: "Court House Rock is a large rock, so large that a man on top looks about 2 ft high & a nice spring bubbles up at its base." (1871~)

Three name derivations are given.

First, Howard Kimball stopped at the rocks in 1914: "This rock was called 'Court House Rock' because at one time a traveling judge held court under it to try a murderer." (1092~)

Second, Joseph F. Anderson in 1915: "This was so called because it became the place where cowboys tried and hanged cattle 'rustlers.'" (62~)

Third, Otho Murphy in 1965: "Someone thought it resembled a court house building." (1420~)

Inscriptions include B.B. Turner, Moab, Ut., July 8th 1879; John Smith, Richfield, Aug. 1882; and M.A. Taylor, Oct. 26, 1890. (1112~, SAPE.)

Courthouse Spring: (Grand Co.) Tenmile Country-Courthouse Wash. Merrimac Butte map.

Also called Upper Courthouse Spring.

(See Courthouse Rock for name derivation.)

—Court House Cattle Company Ranch: In 1912 Charles T. Lupton noted that the ranch was at Courthouse Spring. (1234~)

—Lower Courthouse Spring: (Also called Courthouse Half-way Station [1331~], Courthouse Mail Station [2024~], and Halfway House [1420~].) This is near the junction of Courthouse Wash and present-day Highway 191 (near elevation 4452). In 1848 Orville C. Pratt noted that his expedition traveled about twelve miles from what is now Moab and "passed one small run of living water ... but there was no grass on it." (1572~)

William B. Pace of the Elk Mountain Mission of 1855 called it Iriney Rock Springs, Quiney Rock Springs, and Quincy Rock Springs. (1499~, 1500~) It is assumed that this was in reference to Quincy, Illinois, a place where many Mormons met in the late 1830s and '40s on their sojourn westward.

Until Utah Highway 191 was built, a journey between the rail station at Thompson and Moab would take several days. Courthouse Spring was a favorite stopping spot. It was often just called Courthouse. H.L.A. Culmer in 1905: "Poor meal, fair water." (1822~)

Neil M. Judd in 1907: "Court House Hotel, a two-room stone structure where the stagecoach changed horses and where one could buy a meal of sorts after chasing off the chickens." (1030~)

—Old Spanish Trail: This was a well-known stopping place on the trail.

—Dalton Wells: This was listed on the National Register of Historic Places in 1994. Located at Dalton Spring (near elevation 4401), the well was the site of a large CCC camp from 1935 to 1941. (1225~) From January to April 1943 the camp was used to inter Japanese-Americans. (1226~)

Courthouse Towers: (Grand Co.) Arches National Park-Courthouse Wash. Merrimac Butte, The Windows Section, and Moab maps.

Courthouse Towers are near the mouth of Courthouse Wash. They include the Three Gossips, Park Avenue, The Organ, Tower of Babel, and many unnamed towers, spires, and turrets.

H.L.A. Culmer in 1905: "As we approach we get a glimpse up a distant side canyon of some obelisks or monuments that seem remarkable.... Are of maroon and dark red sandstone—3 of them—close together but quite detached by ½ mile from surrounding buttes, beautiful pedestal of nearly 80 feet. From one view two of them show heads of Egyptian profiles. Are most impressive—standing alone in the great surrounding temples." (1822~)

Court of the Patriarchs: (Washington Co.) Zion National Park-Zion Canyon. Springdale East map.

Also called Three Patriarchs.

Two similar name derivations are given.

First, H. Lorenzo Reid in 1964: "Three of the peaks [of Zion Canyon] reminded President Claude Hirschi of Hurricane of the character-strength of Abraham, Isaac, and Jacob, and hence the names." (1610~)

Second, Eric Bjørnstad: "named in 1916 by Methodist Minister Dr. Frederick Vining Fischer who was so inspired by Zion Canyon that he gave religious names to the monoliths he viewed." (241~) In 1916 Fisher himself wrote of the naming of many of the features in Zion Canyon: "It is not a cañon according to the usual conception so much as a series of nine majestic great inner courts.... Each of these courts grow narrower and more impressive as one passes through them.... We named them in order, the Court of the Wind, the Court of the Sun, the Court of the Patriarchs, the Great Amphitheater, the Court of Music, the Court of Poets, the Court of Many Waters, the Court of Ages and the Voices of the Waters." (1373~)

Cove Canyon: (Garfield Co.) Glen Canyon NRA-The Block-Cataract Canyon. Clearwater Canyon, Sewing Machine, and Bowdie Canyon West maps.

David D. Rust called this Big Cove Canyon in 1935. (1672~)

Otis "Dock" Marston in 1974: "Don't be fooled that Cove Canyon is named for the cove you see from the River. There are coves on top." (899~)

Inscriptions include A. [Andy] H. Miller, De 29, 1900. (SAPE.)

—Cove Spring: (Bowdie Canyon West map.) This medium-size spring was once developed with watering troughs. Ned Chaffin: "Karl Seely had about four hundred tubs up to the Cove Spring ... that he'd hooked up to water his sheep in.... All the way down the damn canyon down there. And had 'em hooked up so the water would flow from one into the other." (411~)

Cove Canyon: (Kane Co.) Pink Cliffs-Long Valley. Orderville map.

Also called The Cove. (349~)

Edward Carroll in 1941: "The farming area comprising two or three hundred acres of land, was so named—The Cove—because it is a miniature valley nestled in a cove, hidden from the view of passers-by until the hills are climbed. A man by the name of Isaac V. Carling (1831–1896) introduced 'dry farming' in this cove in the 1870s." (2053~) The name was in place by 1893. (416~)

Cove Mountain: (Sevier Co.) Fishlake National Forest-Sevier Plateau. Water Creek Canyon and Koosharem maps. (11,047')

Olive N. Gleave: "Cove Mountain ... compares favorably with mountain scenery to be found anywhere in the world. There are beautiful lakes, rushing streams, deep canyons, forest of pine and quaking aspen, and grass to feed cattle, sheep and deer." (1971~)

—First Sawmill: The first sawmill in the Richfield area was set up by Joseph A. Young (son of Brigham Young) on Cove Mountain in 1872. (355~, 955~)

Cowboy Canyon: (San Juan Co.) Dark Canyon Plateau-Gravel Canyon. Jacobs Chair and The Cheesebox maps.

—K-J Spring: This is one mile north of Cowboy Canyon and is two miles east-southeast of Jacobs Chair (one-eighth mile northwest of elevation 5832T on the Jacobs Chair map).

Cowboy Creek: (Sevier Co.) Manti-LaSal National Forest-Wasatch Plateau-Greens Canyon. Heliotrope Mountain and Flagstaff Peak maps.

—Snides Point: This is at the junction of Greens Hollow and Cowboy Canyon (at elevation 8300 on the Flagstaff Peak map). Wayne Gremel: "Years ago the cowboys had a horse named Snide who would always run out onto that point; that is where they'd find him. So they called it Snide Point." (780~)

Cowboy Hat: (San Juan Co.) Navajo Indian Reservation-Douglas Mesa-San Juan River. Slickhorn Canyon East map.

Jack A. Frost: "We passed Cowboy Hat, a balanced rock perched on the canyon rimstone 1500 feet above us." (688~)

Cowboy Mine: (Emery Co.) San Rafael Swell-Coal Cliffs. Mesa Butte map.

Also called Emery Mine.

This coal mine was in operation from 1906 to the 1920s. (570~)

Cowboy Wash: (Montezuma Co., Colo. and San Juan Co., Utah.) San Juan River-Ute Mountain Indian Reservation-Navajo Indian Reservation. Colorado map: Sentinel Peak SW. Utah map: Yellow Rock Point East.

This was most likely named for a line cabin at the mouth of the wash. A nearby inscription is from the USGS (probably in the 1930s) and reads USGS PTBM 4631. (SAPE.)

—Nolands Trading Post: (Also called Four Corners Trading Post and Nolands Four Corners Post.) Established in 1884 by Owen E. (also Edgar O. or Oen E.) Noland, this was on the east side of the San Juan River and one-half mile northwest of the mouth of Cowboy Wash.

The Illustrated American Exploring Expedition of 1892 stopped at Nolands (which they spelled Nolans) and camped a short distance north of it for a couple of days, unfortunately making no other mention of what they found here. (1384~)

Noland sold the store to Arthur Ames and Jesse West before 1900. They sold it to Joseph Heffernan in 1908. The store was in use into the early 1920s. Today, a massive stone structure is still in place, which was apparently used for storage. A log cabin, now gone, provided shelter. Access to the trading post was twofold. First, those coming by saddle stock could come down a constructed stock trail immediately east of the trading post. This is still used by ranchers. Second, a wagon road, with portions now upgraded to a no-longer-used Jeep road, goes along the east bank of the river and up Cowboy Wash. (838~, 1115~, 1121~, 1333~, 1336~, SAPE.)

—River Road: A rough wagon road went along the east side of the river from Nolands to the mouth of McElmo Creek and the Aneth Trading Post. Warren K. Moorehead of the Illustrated American Exploring Expedition of 1892 described traveling the road: "No little difficulty was experienced in getting our heavy baggage through the intervening cañons. We are now past the point where good roads exist.... Our two teams strained every muscle in their attempts to pull the heavy wagons over the rough roads and heavy washouts." (1384~)

—State Line Fence: In this area, the fence was erected by the CCC in 1934.

Cow Canyon: (Carbon Co.) West Tavaputs Plateau-Nine Mile Canyon. Mount Bartles and Wood Canyon maps.

Inscriptions in Nine Mile Canyon near the mouth of Cow Canyon include CW, 1881 and R.B. Clines, Ap 17, 1889. (SAPE.)

Cow Canyon: (Emery Co.) San Rafael Swell-North Fork Coal Wash. The Blocks map.

Lee Mont Swasey: "It has a fence acrost.... When we'd gather cows outta Coal Wash, we'd separate and put Homer Duncan and Ike Nielsen's cows up in Cow Canyon, then we'd take our cows on beyond and then they'd take their cows." (1853~)

Cow Canyon: (Grand Co.) Tenmile Country-Tenmile Canyon. Dubinky Wash map.

Gene Dunham: "There was always cows in it because there is always water there." (580~)

Cow Canyon: (Kane Co.) Glen Canyon NRA-Escalante River-Lake Powell. Stevens Canyon South map.

Edson Alvey noted that wild cattle used to roam the canyon. (55~)

—Rose Canyon: This northern (or eastern) tributary of the Escalante River is the first canyon northwest of Cow Canyon (immediately west of elevation 4491AT). Harlon W. Bement called it Verdant Canyon in the 1950s. (204~) The canyon group EMDC, unaware of its previous designation, named the canyon for its profusion of cliff roses. (SAPE.)

Cow Canyon: (San Juan Co.) Bluff Bench-San Juan River. Bluff map.

Myrtle Hunt: "When Bluff was first settled in 1880, the people had no feed for their milk cows, so they had to find a place for them to graze. They explored the surrounding canyons and found that on the top of Big Bench, north of Bluff, there was good grass, but the only way to get there, and not go five miles around, was to blast a trail through the little box canyon. This they did. They then took turns herding the cows during the day and bringing them in at night, hence the name Cow Canyon." (384~)

Francis F. Kane in 1891: "This bad-land gorge deserves a better name. We rode through it by moonlight and could not help being deeply impressed with the weirdness of our surroundings." (1037~)

Inscriptions include G.B. Waters and G.F. Cloward, 1894. (838~, 1115~)

—Pioneer Road: The road from Bluff to Monticello and on north went through Cow Canyon. Albert R. Lyman: "a narrow defile in the cliff through which rainwater found its way from the bench to the river. It was never intended for a roadway, and every shower wiped it clean of all loose dressing intended to modify the intolerable bumps on the solid rock. Such invincible Road Supervisors as Hyrum Perkins tried one scheme after another, shooting down tons and tons of rock from the cliff above, but it was ground to sand by the wheels and the hoofs, and it went away in the floods. Many a belated teamster thought best to leave his load at the top until morning, and many a load started up from Bluff to stop indefinitely in the canyon." (1240~)

—Ballroom Cave: This large cave on the west side of lower Cow Canyon was used as a gathering place and dance hall by the Bluff settlers. Albert R. Lyman: "Within the towering walls of Cow Canyon ... is an echoing cave which was known to us as Primary Cave, for the many unforgettable picnic parties to which we went." (1242~) The Bluff Primary was the school association.

J. Cecil Alter: "The [cliff dwellings are] located in the mouth of an immense cavern or cave fortuitously split and broken out of the rocks by temperature variations and frosts. The vast amount of loose rock which must have accumulated on the comparatively level floor evidently has been carried to the front and dumped over the ledge by the occupants.... Well back in the cave, is a fine spring of drinking water, making of this a superior estufa or assembly room." (49~)

Inscriptions include Louis Aldun, Nov. 1891; J.H. Poulton, Feb. 22, 1896; M. Van Dyke, Ogden, July 31, 1894; J.B. Duling, 1898; J.W. Hansen, 3-4-99; F.M. Chaplin, 6/3/99; W.W. Ruby, Aug. 14 '07; Dr. Wm J. Schwab, 1910; J.R. Nash, Nov. 2, 1910; Ellis Voorhis, Mar. 21, 1915; and Kumen Jones and L.B. Redd, no date. (838~, SAPE.)

Cow Creek: (Garfield Co.) Dixie National Forest-Sevier Plateau-Johns Valley. Adams Head, Cow Creek, and Grass Lakes maps.
Scott Robinson: "It was so named because of the numerous cows or cattle that graze along its course." (2053~)

Cow Flat: (Garfield Co.) Henry Mountains-Pennell Creek Bench. Ant Knoll map.
Bliss Brinkerhoff: "At the ages of twelve and fourteen my granddad [Willard Brinkerhoff] sent those boys [Willard A. and George Brinkerhoff] with a herd of sheep in the fall of the year [about 1910], down into the lower country. Can you imagine these ladies nowadays lettin' their twelve and fourteen year-old kids take off with a herd of sheep in a camp with horses and mules and not expect to seem 'em for six months? One day down there [on Cow Flat] they didn't get the fire out good in the camp stove. The wind came up and when they came back, the tent was

all burned up with all the supplies. The only thing they had was a case of eggs. They had nothing else to eat ... so they lived on eggs for a month ... and to the day that my dad [Willard A.] died, he didn't like to eat a fried egg or a boiled egg. And bein' in the cow camps a lot of the time one of the cowhands would say, 'All right, Willie, how many eggs this morning?' 'Oh, gosh,' he'd say, 'if I've got to have it, just hand it over to me.' They'd hand him an egg or two and he'd break them into his coffee, stir it up and drink it down. That's the only way he'd eat an egg." (291~)

Cowhead Hill: (Grand Co.) La Sal Mountains-Thompson Canyon. Fisher Valley map. (6,535')
Joe Taylor: "From the air it looks like a cow's head." (1866~)
—Constructed Stock Trail: This starts on the north side of Cowhead Hill (near elevation 6311T) and goes north and west down the cliffs. This was part of a longer trail that went from Polar Mesa to the Dolores River. (1866~, SAPE.) (See Polar Mesa and Cottonwood Canyon–Grand Co.)

Cowley Draw: (Sevier Co.) Fishlake National Forest-Little Lost Creek. Boobe Hole Reservoir map.
Dee Hatch noted that Charles Caesar Cowley, Jr. (1834-1905) and family moved to Venice in the early 1870s. Their son, Joseph C. Cowley (1869-1942), was the first bishop of Venice. (844~, 1971~)

Cowpuncher Guard Station: (Garfield Co.) Dixie National Forest-Boulder Mountain-Pine Creek. Posy Lake map.
The initial location for the guard station was one-half mile north of the present-day Cowpuncher Guard Station, at the "Corral." The station was moved to its present location in 1938. A CCC crew built the buildings. (1655~, 2021~) This former guard station can now be rented from the National Forest Service.
—Cowpuncher Pasture: This is the flat area around the guard station. Two similar name derivations are given. First, cowboys pastured their horses here. (55~) Second, "Old time cowpunchers' headquarters." (1346~)
—CCC Camp: This was near the Cowpuncher Guard Station. The camp, among many projects, helped build the Hells Backbone Road. (2021~)

Cowskin Canyon: (Grand Co.) La Sal Mountains-Dolores River. Dewey map.
Also called Cow Canyon.
Joe Taylor: "That is an old, old name. There used to be a line camp at Cowskin Spring. The water was bad there. The horses could drink it, but people couldn't." (1866~)

Cow Spring: (Grand Co.) Book Cliffs-Right Hand Tusher Canyon. Bobby Canyon South map.

This is a large spring. (SAPE.)

Cow Spring: (San Juan Co.) Mancos Mesa-Cedar Canyon. Mancos Mesa map.

This is a large spring. (SAPE.)

Cow Tank: (San Juan Co.) Cedar Mesa-Dripping Canyon. Moss Back Butte map.

This canyon contains Cow Tank, which is in the upper part of the canyon. Hole-in-the-Rock Expedition scouts discovered this large pothole in 1879, though it wasn't named until later. It became an important watering place for livestock. (257~, 1249~, 1356~) Albert R. Lyman: "It is a big water pocket in the solid rock of the bottom of a gulch where rain stands a long time after any ordinary storm." (1260~)

After I explored the canyon it became clear that either the geology has changed over the years, or the descriptions of the canyon are incorrect. From the Red House Cliffs to its junction with Dripping Canyon, there are a couple of medium-size potholes in Cow Tank. But, a short distance below the confluence, and in Dripping Canyon, is a very large pothole-pond that could realistically be called a cow tank. Access to the tank is not possible by going down Cow Tank, but it is accessible by one of two constructed stock trails from Dripping Canyon. Access from Cow Tank to Dripping Canyon is easy via the "Emigrant Trail." (SAPE.)

—Cow Tank Country: Albert R. Lyman noted the area around the tank as Cow Tank Country (1260~), as did Bert Loper in 1921 (1221~).

Cow Tanks: (Emery Co.) San Rafael Reef-Wild Horse Creek. Temple Mountain map.

Alvin Robison noted that this series of potholes is used by cowboys to water their livestock. (1642~)

Cow Wash: (Wayne Co.) Henry Mountains-Dry Valley. Hanksville map.

Charles B. Hunt noted that this was called Cow Dung Wash and it is shown as that on old maps. (925~)

Cox Hollow: (Kane Co.) Pink Cliffs-Schoppman Hollow. Navajo Lake map.

Orville S. Cox (1814-1888) was an Orderville pioneer. (338~, 379~, 1047~)

Coyote Buttes: (Coconino Co., Az.) Paria Canyon-Vermilion Cliffs Wilderness Area-Coyote Valley. Coyote Buttes, Az. map.

George C. Fraser described Coyote Buttes in 1916: "Nowhere have I seen the cross-bedding so accentuated as here. The weathering of the rock brings the planes of cross-bedding in relief as much as 12 in." (669~)

Coyote Creek: (Garfield Co.) Henry Mountains-Slate Creek. Mount Pennell and Cass Creek Peak maps.

—Coyote Benches: (Cass Creek Peak map.) (Also called Wolverton Benches.) Garth Noyes: "[Edwin T. Wolverton] built the road up over Coyotes Benches. That's the reason they're called Wolverton Benches. The Coyote Benches name came in with the BLM maps. Back when I was a kid herding sheep in there, it was always Wolverton Benches." (1473~) (See Straight Creek—Garfield Co.)

—Turkey Haven Campsite: This BLM campsite is on the road near Coyote Creek one mile southeast of Gibbons Spring (one mile east-northeast of elevation 8638AT on the Mount Pennell map). Garth Noyes: "That used to be called Pine Springs, but the BLM changed it to Turkey Haven. I'll tell you a story about Pine Spring. I was at the Starr Ranch and I was supposed to meet my uncle near Mud Springs. He was with a herd of sheep up there. I got up there on horseback, and I looked everywhere and couldn't find him or the sheep. And night come on me. I was at Pine Springs and didn't have any food and I didn't have anything but my saddle horse. So I hobbled my horse in a little meadow and I set there beside one of those trees all night. I've heard in the movies how you can wrap up in your saddle blanket. That's a bunch of crap. That was one of the worst nights I ever spent in my life." (1473~)

Coyote Creek: (Kane Co.) GSCENM-Kaiparowits Plateau-Wahweap Creek. Horse Flat, Lower Coyote Spring, Nipple Butte, and Glen Canyon City maps.

Also called Coyote Canyon.

Unattributed in 1942: "Named for the animal—Coyote." (2053~)

Ralph Chynoweth: "I had two uncles, and them guys could rope.... Back in the old days they trapped this great big old buck up in Upper Coyote. They decided to rope the buck. So the one that was the best roper tied one end to a tree and told the other one to go up the canyon and flush the buck down to him. As the deer came running past, the roper lassoed the buck and throwed 'im down. Then they put my granddad's [Sampson Chynoweth] ear mark and brand on him.... Then they turned him loose. Now, the Indians used to come into Paria and they'd often stop by granddads to get food. It was two or three years later and this Indian comes into the Paria place, and he says: 'I brought your buck to you.' Granddad said, 'He's not my buck.' And the Indian said, 'He must be because it's got your mark and brand on him'"! (425~)

—Lower Coyote Spring: (Lower Coyote Spring map.) This is a large, developed spring. (SAPE.) Sampson Chynoweth in 1903: "This Spring Shall be known by the name of Coyote Spring. The water up the Wash by the name of Coyote Seeps." (2053~) The official locator was Lew Jepson in 1902.

—White Sands Reservoirs: Ralph Chynoweth noted that these are on lower Coyote Creek one mile south of Chimney Rock (adjacent to elevation 4259 on the Lower Coyote Spring map). (425~)

Coyote Flat: (San Juan Co.) Cedar Mesa-Todie Flat. Cedar Mesa North map.

DeReese Nielson: "They found a bunch of coyotes there, one time, killing some of the new-born calves and that's what they named it, Coyote Flats." (1451~)

—Coyote Canyon: This eastern tributary of Grand Gulch starts on Coyote Flat and goes west (immediately north of elevations 6258T and 6301T on the Cedar Mesa North map). The name was in place by 1907. (1031~)

—Coyote Spring: This is one-quarter mile up Coyote Canyon from its mouth.

Coyote Gulch: (Kane Co.) GSCENM-Glen Canyon NRA-Fiftymile Bench-Escalante River-Lake Powell. Big Hollow Wash, King Mesa, and Stevens Canyon South maps. Also called Coyote Canyon, Coyote Creek, and Coyoto Gulch.

Edson Alvey: "The name was derived from the prevalence of coyotes in the whole region." (55~) D. Eldon Beck: "It was so named because there are hundreds of coyote tracks found along the moist stream beds." (178~)

It is often said that this is the canyon that all others in canyon country are compared to for beauty. Claire Noall in 1957: "This gorge, wide and deep except at the narrow door, and as strangely lovely as any of the vast stone canyons of Southern Utah." (384~)

Tad Nichols in 1971: "A more beautiful place cannot be imagined.... It was the finest canyon walk that I have had. Coyote Gulch is idyllic." (1448~)

Inscriptions include Arnold, 1878. (1115~)

—Headless Hen Canyon: (Also called Topless Turtle.) This northern tributary of Coyote Gulch is east of elevation 4693 on the King Mesa map. A rock formation on the rim of the canyon looks like a headless hen. It was named by The Young Turks. (SAPE.)

—Raven Slot: (Also called Black Newt.) This northern tributary of Coyote Gulch is one-eighth mile west of elevation 4645 on the King Mesa map. Many ravens roost in the small pockets that dot the walls of the canyon. It was named by The Young Turks. (SAPE.)

—Sleepy Hollow: This northern tributary of Coyote Gulch is between elevations 4454 and 4500 on the King Mesa map. Glen Canyon NRA Ranger Bill Wolverton: "Sleepy Hollow was named by Tom and Jennifer Gillette when Tom was the Escalante seasonal ranger." (653~) Tom Gillette: "The place name 'Sleepy Hollow' was born on an April day in 1982. Ranger Glenn Sherrill, wife and volunteer Jennifer and myself spent the day constructing flood gates on the Coyote cattle fence. The wind howled down canyon all day, but we continued to work through the sandblaster till late afternoon. Seeking a break from the wind, we set up camp in an alcove a short ways up [Sleepy Hollow].... The wind took its toll as we laid out our ground sheet and sleeping bags, crawled in and fell asleep, too tired to even make dinner. What a relief! That's my story." (653~)

—Big Tony Fork of Sleepy Hollow: (Also called West Fork of Sleepy Hollow.) This western tributary of Sleepy Hollow is between elevations 5112 and 5142 on the King Mesa map. Steve Allen: "Tony Merten died on his farm in New Mexico in February 1996. His gargantuan size, unlimited physical strength, and unbridled persona perfectly match this slot canyon's character. With his wild red-blond hair and beard, Tony was instantly recognizable to all who encountered him in the canyons or along the windswept desert slickrock he loved so much and worked so hard to preserve. Perhaps all who pass will pay silent homage to Big Tony and to others who have cared about canyon country but can no longer be here to enjoy and be enthralled by it." (47~)

—Long Branch of Sleepy Hollow: (Also called East Fork of Sleepy Hollow.) This eastern tributary of Sleepy Hollow starts at elevation 5020 on the King Mesa map. It was named by The Young Turks. (SAPE.)

—DDI Canyon: The mouth of this northern tributary of Coyote Gulch is east of elevation 4454 on the King Mesa map. DDI is an acronym for "Don't Do It" Canyon, reflecting the fact, unknown at the time, that an unavoidable tangle of poison ivy was waiting at the bottom of the last drop. The canyon was named by The Young Turks. (SAPE.)

—Pintac Canyon: This northern tributary of Coyote Gulch is immediately east of elevation 4978 on the King Mesa map. This is an acronym for "Pain in the Ass Crack," a name given by The Young Turks. (SAPE.)

—Coyote Lake: Ken Sleight: "In recent years a lake inhabited a section of the [lower] canyon when a huge slab of canyon wall broke away and toppled into the canyon. This backed up the water for nearly a mile and nearly made the canyon impassible. In 1965 a huge flood broke the barrier and destroyed the lake. There are many dead cottonwood trees and wide sand 'flats' that attest to the former lake." (1751~) Stephen C. Jett: "We soon found ourselves at the head of a deep green lake. Dead cottonwood trees gave silent testimony to the relatively recent origin of the lake." (976~)

—Icicle Spring: Ken Sleight: "A short distance below Jug Handle Arch [Cliff Arch] a spring continually drips from the canyon wall. During the winter, hundreds of small icicles form and hang from the moist leaves of the Maidenhair Ferns which surround the spring." (1751~)

—Crack-in-the-Wall: This popular hiking route into the lower end of Coyote Gulch goes behind a large fin of sandstone, giving the feature its name. The crack is three-quarters of a mile south-southwest of the mouth of Coyote Gulch (one-quarter mile southwest of elevation 4484T on the Stevens Canyon South map). The trail, once one goes through the crack, continues down a huge and infamous sand dune.

—Detour Trail: Ken Sleight noted that when pack stock was taken down Coyote Gulch to the Escalante River they were not able to make it around the last waterfall in the canyon. Instead, they would pass the fall on the right, then go around a large tower (one-quarter mile northnortheast of elevation 4472AT on the Stevens Canyon South map). Ken: "From this trail can be seen some of the most spectacular and colorful views of the Escalante River Canyon." (1751~)

Coyote Hole: (Kane Co.) GSCENM-Escalante Desert-Hole-in-the-Rock Road. Big Hollow Wash map.

Also called Coyoto Holes, Cyote Seeps (760~), and Thirtyfive Mile (1706~).

Pratt Gates: "The sheepmen used to find a lot of coyotes out there. There used to be seeps there. The coyotes would dig their holes and raise their pups near there, so they called it 'Coyote Holes.'" (709~)

Hole-in-the-Rock Expedition member Platte D. Lyman in 1879: "camped after dark at the Kiota Holes where we had to dig for water and got plenty of it." (1259~, 1356~) Charles P. Berolzheimer in 1920: "We arrived at 'Coyote Holes,' where a little black, rotten water was all we could offer the horses. (222~) James H. Gunnerson in 1927: "a source of poor water along Coyote Creek [Big Hollow Wash]." (797~)

—Coyote Hole Well: Rancher Pole Roundy put the well in. (2051~) At one time there were several wood and stone buildings at Coyote Hole. (SAPE.)

—Coyote Creek: Donald Scott noted in 1928 that Coyote Hole is on Coyote Creek. (1706~) The maps now show this as Big Hollow Wash.

—Panther Seep: One mile west-southwest of Coyote Holes is a large spring with a stock tank. It is at the very bottom of the Upper Trail. In 1918 Herbert E. Gregory called it Panther Seep. (760~) (See Upper Trail.)

—Wilsons Box: The early cattlemen would build large wooden boxes out on the range to store supplies and feed for their cowboys and sheepherders. Wilsons Box was on the Hole-in-the-Rock Road where it branches to Coyote Holes and the base of the Upper Trail. (1068~)

Coyote Hollow: (Garfield Co.) Dixie National Forest-Boulder Mountain-Escalante Mountains-Antimony Creek. Posy Lake, Barker Reservoir, and Pollywog Lake maps.

Also called Coyoto Hollow.

Pratt Gates noted that this was named by early sheepmen. (709~)

—Black Forest: Pratt Gates noted that this area is immediately south of Coyote Hollow: "It was so thick with timber in there that you could hardly ride a horse through it. If you don't know where you are going, you'd better stay out of there. It was just like a jungle. The Forest Service named it not too many years ago." (709~)

Coyote Natural Bridge: (Kane Co.) Glen Canyon NRA-Coyote Gulch. King Mesa map.

(See Coyote Gulch for name derivation.)

D. Eldon Beck in 1943: "We came face to face with a second natural bridge. So suddenly did it loom up before us that we were hardly aware of its presence. Approaching it as we did, and the open arch situated as it was, we were led to think we were looking unobstructed down the canyon." (178~) Beck continued walking downcanyon: "About a mile below the Dutton Bridge [Coyote Natural Bridge], we came into an immense amphitheatre. A tower of rock about sixty feet high created a center of interest. The canyon stream passed through a narrow opening at the base of the tower. With pot-holes, waterfalls, and cliffs blocking our passage we finally found a detour south of the tower. Like Lilliputians of *Gulliver's Travels*, we wandered about in this great Brobdingnagian canyon amphitheatre." (178~)

Edward Abbey: "I walked under the bridge, feeling the sensuous pleasure of moving through a wall of stone, wading the stream that made the opening, standing in shadow and looking back at the upstream canyon bathed in morning light, the sparkling water, the varnished slickrock walls, the fresh cool green of the cottonwoods, the pink and violet plumes of tamarisk." (3~)

Coyote Spring: (San Juan Co.) Manti-LaSal National Forest-La Sal Mountains-Pole Canyon. La Sal East map.
—McCarty Ranch: The Bill McCarty family moved to the La Sal area in early 1878. Their ranch was a short distance south of Coyote Spring. (1750~)

Coyote Valley: (Kane Co., Utah and Coconino Co., Az.) Vermilion Cliffs National Monument-The Cockscomb-Buckskin Gulch. Utah map: Pine Hollow Canyon. Arizona map: Coyote Buttes.
Also called Coyote Wash Valley. (1357~)
—Coyote Spring: (Coyote Buttes map.) The Domínguez-Escalante Expedition of 1776–77 camped at Coyote Spring, calling it *San Juan Capistrano.* (1944~) Father Escalante: "We decided to spend the night here since a little distance away to the east and west there was water and pasturage for the horse herd." (1357~)
C. Gregory Crampton: "The spring, later covered over by drifting sands, was reportedly revealed to ranchers by coyotes who dug down to water." (1357~) Charles D. Walcott noted camping at the already-named Coyote Spring in 1882. (1959~)
Oscar R. Garrett in 1912: "Coyote Spring, running a little stream and which has also been worked over by cattle owners.... The water is piped into a big wooden trough, the overflow running into a small scooped-out depression in the red sand nearby which contains but a pool. The whole is enclosed by a stockade corral fence having an irregular outline of a circle.... Many cow trails center here, and several dim wagon trails likewise come and go." (707~)

Crack Canyon: (Emery Co.) San Rafael Swell-Little Wild Horse Creek. Temple Mountain and Goblin Valley maps.
Joe Bauman: "Deep inside, after the way narrowed and widened again, we reached the crack that gives the canyon its name. Tan walls three hundred feet high seemed nearly to crash together. They were only a couple of feet apart—slick dark brown cliffs with their broken facets and light streaks." (166~)

Crandall Canyon: (Emery Co.) Manti-LaSal National Forest-Huntington Creek. Rilda Canyon map.
Hyrum Oscar Crandall (1844-1904) and family moved to Huntington in 1879. (338~, 1015~) Crandall and William Howard owned a shingle and lath mill in the canyon in the 1880s. (372~)
Ivan W. Young in 1917: "When my little brother George was about 9 years old, he was riding down Crandall Canyon with dad [Frank Albion Young], sitting on a load of lumber.... It [the accident] happened so suddenly, while dad was steering his load down the hill, the left front wheel of the wagon went over a big boulder in the road and threw George off the wagon, just below the boulder, where the wheels had made a big rut. Dad tried desperately to stop the wagon before the rear wheel hit the same boulder and would drop off and crush his boy. However, the momentum carried the wheel over the boulder and up in the air for some distance, completely jumping over George, without harming him. A miracle...." (1014~)

Crater Hill: (Washington Co.) Zion National Park-Virgin River. Springdale West map. (5,192')
Herbert E. Gregory noted that this is an old volcanic cone. (778~)

Crater Lakes: (Sevier Co.) Fishlake National Forest-Mytoge Mountains. Fish Lake map.
Also called The Craters.
Jonathan Wynn: "Sitting atop the Fish Lake Hightop surface is a small basin, with two swampy closed-outlet lakes—not at all true volcanic craters. The small basin is a ... fault-bound graben." (2058~)

Crawford Canyon: (Kane Co.) GSCENM-Meadow Canyon. Podunk Creek and Rainbow Point maps.
E.E. Carter in 1936: "Crawford Creek is a family name and has been is use ever since the early settlers came to this part of the State. An old man named Crawford built the cabin at the head of the canyon." (1931~) This was William Crawford (1842-1913), his wife Carnelia (1851-1933), and family. (388~)

Crawford Draw: (Emery Co.) San Rafael Swell-Eardley Canyon. Twin Knolls and Arsons Garden maps.
The Crawford family, including Edmund, George, James, Nathaniel "Tan," and Quince, moved to the Castle Valley area in the 1880s. (641~, 710~, 970~)
—Crawford Holes: (Twin Knolls map.) These are a series of medium-size potholes. A constructed sheep trail provides access from the north side of the canyon. (SAPE.)
—Crawford Holes Reservoir: This stock reservoir is one mile west of Crawford Holes. It was built in 1960. (1551~)

Crawford Wash: (Washington Co.) Zion National Park-East Fork Virgin River. Springdale East map.
William Robinson Crawford (1842–1913) moved to Rockville in 1862 and to Springdale in 1879. (14~, 1931~) In 1898 the family moved to Oak Creek in Zion Canyon, where they had a ranch for many years. (485~)
George C. Fraser in 1914: "Old Crawford was peculiar and his sons are said to be more so, even to the extent of not having all their wits." (667~)

—Lost Peak: This is one mile north-northeast of the mouth of Crawford Wash (one-third mile north-north-west of elevation 5550). It was named by Courtney Purcell. (1591~)

Cream Pots: (San Juan Co.) Manti-LaSal National Forest-Dark Canyon Plateau-South Elk Ridge. Cream Pots map. John Scorup noted that rock formations in the area look like cream pots. (1821~)

—Cream Pots Trail: (See Hammond Canyon.)

Crescent Butte: (Kane Co.) GSCENM-Vermilion Cliffs. Johnson Lakes map. (5,626')

Also called Dishpan Hill. (1931~)

Francis M. Bishop of the 1871–72 Powell Expedition passed between the Vermilion Cliffs and Crescent Butte while on his way from Johnson to Paria: "Struck across to the east of the high butte at the mouth of the [Johnson] cañon." (236~)

Crescent Canyon: (Grand Co.) Book Cliffs-Thompson Wash. Floy Canyon South, Crescent Junction, and Valley City maps.

Also called Crescent Wash.

(See Crescent Junction for name derivation.)

A short distance up the canyon is an old corral and line camp. Nearby inscriptions include Floyd Dern, Oct. 18, 1923; Ace Bennett, Dolores, Colorado, 1932; and Lino Cordova, March 28, 1936. (SAPE.)

Crescent Canyon: (Wayne Co.) Fishlake National Forest-Thousand Lake Mountain-Sand Wash. Bicknell map.

Martha Mead: "So named by Joe Hickman who thought the name appropriate because of the canyon's shape.... Sometimes called Pipeline Canyon because a line through the canyon supplies water to the town of Bicknell." (2053~) It was also called Sawmill Canyon for a sawmill that was operated here in the early days.

—Constructed Stock Trail: This is the "Pack" trail that goes east from Crescent Canyon and eventually up the East Fork of Red Canyon and onto Thousand Lake Mountain. (291~, 1865~, SAPE.)

Crescent Creek: (Garfield Co.) Henry Mountains-Bromide Basin-North Wash. Mount Ellen and Raggy Canyon maps.

Also called Eagle Creek, Gold Creek, and Pleasant Creek. The name, given by the John Wesley Powell Expedition of 1871–72, used to include the creek from its headwaters in the Henry Mountains to the Colorado River. Today, Crescent Creek refers to the Henry Mountains section of the creek. The lower portion, which runs alongside Highway 95, is now called North Wash. (584~)

Jack Hillers of the Powell Expedition: "went into camp on the bank of a beautiful little creek coming down from the second mt. [Mount Pennell]." (884~)

—Eagle City: (Also called Bromide City.) This was on Crescent Creek two miles west of Lecleed Spring (immediately east of elevation 7909T on the Raggy Canyon map). There was enough mining activity in the Bromide Basin area to support the boom town of Eagle City, which flourished from the 1880s to 1900. At its peak it had a hotel, two saloons, a dance hall, three stores, and a post office. It was called Eagle City because it was perched like an eagle at near the 8,000 foot level on Mt. Ellen. The views from the site are far-reaching and incredible. Little now marks the site of the city. (324~, 604~, 607~, 925~, 1646~, 1881~, SAPE.)

Howard Ritzma noted that only seven thousand dollars worth of gold was removed from the area from 1892 to 1938. (888~)

—Darius Reservoir: (Also called Eagle Pond.) Kevin Robison noted that this pond is immediately south of Eagle City. He and Darius Ekker built the reservoir in the early 1960s. (1646~)

—Eagle Benches: Kevin Robison noted that this area is between Butler Wash and Crescent Creek and to the east of Eagle City (at elevations 6540T and 6921T on the Raggy Canyon map). (1646~)

—Campsite Placer: This was on Crescent Creek one and three-quarters of a mile east of Lecleed Spring (one-eighth mile east of elevation 6110T on the Raggy Canyon map). (1551~)

—Ollie Pysert Cabin: Kevin Robison noted that this is on Crescent Creek two miles east of Lecleed Spring (one-half mile south of elevation 6002T on the Raggy Canyon map). Stu Wylie and Gene Robison built the house in the 1920s. (1646~) (See Pyserts Hole.)

—Crescent Town: (Also called Crescent City.) This small mining settlement on Crescent Creek was one-half mile east of the Ollie Pysert Cabin (near elevation 5553T on the Raggy Canyon map). It was established in the late 1880s and died in the 1890s when the gold boom fizzled. (925~, 1811~)

—Placer Benches: Kevin Robison noted that this area is west and south of Crescent Town and is south and west of Crescent Creek (at elevations 5330T and 5503T on the Raggy Canyon map). (1646~)

—Big Orange Crane: Kevin Robison noted that this well-known landmark on lower Crescent Creek was brought in by Bud Johns in the early 1960s for use in a placer mining operation. (1646~)

Crescent Junction: (Grand Co.) Book Cliffs-Interstate 70. Crescent Junction map.

Also called Crescent and Crescent Station. (M.75.)

Richard A. Firmage noted that the cliffs to the north of town are crescent shaped. This small town was established as a stop on the Denver and Rio Grande Western Railroad in the early 1880s. (644~)

James H. Knipmeyer: "Near the creek, at the foot of the Book Cliffs, is the inscription S.L.S., 1837, dating back to trapper days." (1115~)

—Brendel: (Also called Brendel Station.) This railroad stop, long abandoned, was at Crescent Junction. (1931~)

Crips Hole: (Grand Co.) Tenmile Country-Arths Pasture-Bull Canyon. Gold Bar Canyon map.

Crispen Taylor (1839-1908) brought the first cattle to the area, in 1875. After being forced out by Indians, he returned to stay in 1879. (338~, 1116~)

Crosby Canyon: (Kane Co.) Glen Canyon NRA-Warm Creek Bay. Lone Rock and Warm Creek Bay maps.

Taylor Crosby (1838-1914) first traversed this area in 1859 while on a scouting and Indian mission with Jacob Hamblin. (1639~) Flora Lundquist Heaton: "Taylor Crosby accompanied Jacob Hamblin on many of his trips among the Indians in southern Utah and also to the more war-like Navajo tribes near the Colorado River." (365~)

Taylor Crosby settled in Kanab in 1871. In 1874 he became the "superintendent of stock." (374~) By 1880 much of the good grazing land near Kanab had been grazed off. Ranchers then started pushing their livestock toward the Colorado River and the Wahweap country. Taylor Crosby was one of the first to graze there. (516~)

—Movies: *Maverick,* starring James Garner and Jodie Foster, was shot, in part, in Crosby Canyon. (1421~)

Cross Canyon: (San Juan Co.) Canyonlands National Park-Needles District-The Grabens-Cataract Canyon. Cross Canyon map.

A couple of grabens cross the canyon. (1821~)

—Russian Thistle Meadow: This is at the junction of Imperial Valley and Cross Canyon. Colorado Outward Bound is credited with naming the meadow, which is covered with Russian Thistle.

—Tilted Park: This wide area is one-quarter mile south of the head of Y Canyon (at elevation 5489T). Francis M. Bishop of the Powell Expedition of 1871–72 named it for the pronounced dip or tilt of the cliffs in the area. (465~)

Cross Hollow Hills: (Iron Co.) Cedar Valley-Interstate 15. Cedar City map.

Alva Matheson: "It was so named by sheep and cattle men going from their farms, to and from the mountain, because of the ease it afforded in crossing through the hills from the east side of the valley to the north and west side where most of the farms were located." (942~)

Crossing of the Fathers: (Kane Co.) Glen Canyon NRA-Padre Bay. Gunsight Butte map.

This is not shown on the map. (See Padre Creek–Crossing of the Fathers.)

Croton Canyon: (Kane Co.) GSCENM-Glen Canyon NRA-Kaiparowits Plateau-Last Chance Bay. East of the Navajo and Sit Down Bench maps.

Also called Crotch Canyon.

Crow Creek: (Iron Co.) Dixie National Forest-Coal Creek. Webster Flat and Flanigan Arch maps.

Also called The Gulch. (1012~)

Crow Creek goes through upper Cedar Canyon. Coal Creek goes through lower Cedar Canyon.

—Koal Kreek Mine: (Also called Jones and Bulloch Mine.) (1012~) This coal mine in Coal Creek at the mouth of Crow Canyon was in operation from 1890 to the mid-1960s. It was the largest coal mine in the area. (570~, 888~) The mine property was first owned by Cedar City residents Lehi W. Jones and David Bulloch. The Mormon Church later bought the property. (1012~)

Crows Nest Spring: (Emery Co.) San Rafael Desert-Cottonwood Wash. Crows Nest Spring map.

Also called Hawks Nest Spring.

This medium-size spring is marked by a large, lone cottonwood tree at the base of a small escarpment in the middle of the San Rafael Desert. It is still used by cattle. (100~) Inscriptions include Jake Seely, no date. (SAPE.)

Crow Seep: (Wayne Co.) San Rafael Desert-Robbers Roost Flats. Robbers Roost Flats map. PRIVATE PROPERTY.

Also called Clove Seep. (1735~)

Two name derivations are given.

First, Joe Biddlecome caught a jet black mustang at the seep while it was drinking. He named it Crow. (107~)

Second, Arthur and Hazel Ekker: "As the story goes, the first man to see this seep [probably in the 1890s] found that it had already been staked out by a number of crows and one old horse, thus the name Crow Seep." (1931~)

—Robbers Roost Ranch: (Also called Roost Ranch.) (1311~) The seep is the location of the Biddlecome or Ekker ranch. The ranch was founded by Joe Biddlecome and Millie Scarf Biddlecome in 1909. Pearl Baker: "[Joe Biddlecome] was a cowhand of such competence that he had been invited to leave western Colorado, where his cows always had two calves and sometimes his bulls showed up with calves following." (109~)

Millie Biddlecome: "[in] 1909, we moved out to the Robbers Roost. Ern Wyles and Lew Oleson were out there, and they said it was OK. We had 123 head—roans, blacks, Holsteins, speckled, spotted, streaked, dogies, brockle-faced and a few bald-faced." (227~)

After Joe died following a tonsillectomy in 1928, his daughter, Pearl, and her husband, Mel Marsing, took over the ranch. Pearl Baker: "[My husband Mel] had been leading a horse and the knot of the rope bruised his leg. A deep bone infection set in and he went to a doctor who gave him rheumatism medicine and it spread the infection through his system and he died from it that fall." (119~)

Pearl then ran the ranch with a new husband. They sold the ranch to her sister, Hazel, and her husband, Arthur Ekker, in 1939. The ranch then went to Art's son, A.C. Ekker. Hazel died in 1969; Arthur passed in 1978; Pearl died in 1993; and A.C. died in a plane crash near the ranch in 2000. (119~, 120~, 607~, 1430~)

Alvin Robison told this story about Crow Seep and Arthur Ekker: "The story was that the [black] bear was close to the cabin. He roped that bear and was ajerkin' it and hollerin', 'You'd better get the ax!' He wanted Millie, his wife, to get the ax and hit it on the head while he was keepin' it choked down with that rope." (1642~)

Crystal Geyser: (Grand Co.) Tenmile Country-Green River. Green River map.

Also called Coldwater Geyser and Utah's Old Faithful Geyser.

This geyser, located next to the Green River, is not natural.

Buzz Holmstrom in 1937: "They drilled for oil ... and struck water. Now every thirty-five minutes a geyser of water shoots up into the air, thirty feet high." (903~)

The Writers' Program of 1941: "came into existence when Glen M. Ruby, geologist, began drilling for oil in 1936. Gas flows and a tremendous volume of water forced Ruby to abandon the well at 2,000 feet." (2056~)

Senator Barry Goldwater in 1940: "It erupts every 30 to 60 minutes and seems to have one big eruption then a smaller one and so on. The water comes from a 16" pipe and is shot 75 to 100 feet in the air, the water draining off into the Green River." (738~) Goldwater continued: "Of course we could not resist a temptation to toss every loose rock we saw down the sixteen-inch pipe, so down the tube rattled various large stones. This irresistible urge nearly ended my trip. After the rocks had been dropped into the well [we] decided that the falling waters of the geyser would make an excellent shower bath even though

the water stank to high heaven; consequently, at the next eruption, we dashed under the spray. We had forgotten the rocks we had dropped into the hole, but we remembered them in a hurry when they started bombing around us with loud thumps. One came close enough to the back of my head to shear off the little hair my last barber had left me." (737~)

Crystal Spring: (Grand Co.) Tenmile Country-Blue Hills-Tenmile Wash. Valley City map.

This large spring was once developed using hollowed-out logs for watering troughs. An inscription on one of the troughs is from GB, 1930. (SAPE.)

Crystal Spring: (San Juan Co.) Manti-LaSal National Forest-Beef Basin-North Long Point. House Park Butte map.

This is a large, developed spring. (SAPE.)

Pete Steele: "beautiful water there, just crystal clear." (1821~)

—Constructed Stock Trail: This leads to the spring. (SAPE.)

Crystal Springs Canyon: (San Juan Co.) Glen Canyon NRA-Mancos Mesa-Glen Canyon. Knowles Canyon map. Also called Beaver Canyon, Double Eye Canyon, and Little Ball Canyon. (1298~)

Robert Robertson and Gus Scott were the first to describe the lower canyon, in 1955: "Very brushy near entrance.... After much work get into canyon. About 1/3 mile in is nice pool with beaver dam near. 3 large trees nearby downed by beaver.... Continue up canyon in stream most of time.... Many signs of beaver for 1.5-2 miles.... Robert proposes Beaver Canyon as a name for the canyon.... I would like to suggest that this name be given to the canyon if it is unnamed." (1707~)

Otis "Dock" Marston, though, suggested the name Crystal Springs Canyon. He wanted to avoid what he thought was potential confusion with Cha (beaver in the Navajo language) Canyon north of Navajo Mountain on the San Juan River. (1901~, 466~)

It is noteworthy that Ginger Harmon, THE grandest of great old broads and one of the early day technical canyoneers, deems this as one of her favorite canyons in Utah. (SAPE.)

—Crystal Point: Val Dalton noted that this point is immediately south of the mouth of Crystal Springs Canyon. (517~)

—Little Labyrinth Canyon: This short eastern tributary of Lake Powell is one mile south of Crystal Springs Canyon (one-quarter mile south of elevation 3771T on the Bullfrog map). Katie Lee and friends named the canyon:

"We got back into the canyon about 200 feet and it got so narrow we couldn't even get our heads through. And it was about three hundred feet high and no direct sun in the morning. It was just fascinating. We crawled on our hands and knees because it was a little bit wider at the bottom. I almost got stuck in there and Tad [Nichols] had to pull me out. You had to back out because you couldn't turn around.... It wasn't a labyrinth. It was just a fluted crevice. It was what they call a 'slot canyon' now, a name I can't stand. I hate that name. Slots are in Las Vegas. What an insult to call one of those canyons a slot. I call them sequestered gracilities. I call them erotic sinuosities. I call them flutings, carving, anything but a slot. That's the only name that seemed to come to us at the time, so we called it a labyrinth." (1163~)

Wallace Stegner in 1946: "Most bizarre of all the canyons, the spookiest concession in this rock fun-house, is [Little] Labyrinth Canyon, which narrows down to less than two feet, and whose walls waver and twist so that anyone groping up this dark, crooked, nightmare cranny in the deep rock has to bend over and twist his body sideways to get through. Floor and walls are pocked with perfectly round pockets like nests, full of the pebbles and rocks that have scoured them. Though we cannot see the sky, we know that the walls go up several hundred feet, and though we scramble back in at least a mile and a half, scaling one dry waterfall, we see no sign of an end. The thought of what it would be like to be caught in here in a rain gives us the fantods, and we come out fast." (1827~)

Ann Woodin in 1964: "We stopped at perhaps the most incredible of the many side canyons that we saw, called [Little] Labyrinth.... The walls of the passageway were draped with Venushair fern, red monkey-flower, cliffrose, and the greenest of mosses.... It ended in what is called Fatman's Misery, a constricted, twisted exit. That was only the beginning.... The canyon again narrowed to the most spectacular stretch of sinuous chasm that we had ever seen, an endless winding subterranean passageway, a twisting Gothic catacomb, an interlacing of fluted buttresses made by the rushing torrent twirling rocks around and around. Most of the time no sky was visible, for the canyon walls, stretching up hundreds of feet, never widened or straightened and were seldom more than a few feet apart." (2046~)

—Poison Ivy Canyon: (Also called Ivy Canyon.) This short south-tending eastern tributary of Lake Powell is two miles south of Crystal Springs Canyon (immediately west of elevation 3833T on the Bullfrog map). Katie Lee and friends named the canyon: "We went in this canyon and it was very, very inviting and it was packed with poison ivy.... It had a flowing stream in it but it was just chockfull of poison ivy and we'd only made about three turns and here was this beautiful amphitheater with a stream pouring down the middle of it. Just gorgeous." (1163~)

—Navajo Marbles Canyon: This short eastern tributary of Lake Powell is one-half mile north of Crystal Springs Canyon (one-quarter mile north of elevation 3888T on the Bullfrog map). Katie Lee named the canyon: "In every little depression or ledge are these wonderful Navajo marbles [also called Moqui marbles]. They were of all different sizes. There were some almost as big as tennis balls and then there would be some that were like golf balls, until they got way down to about the size of the end of your little finger, and they were all over the slickrock." (1163~)

—Gerhart Mine: Charles and Rosie Gerhart (also spelled Gearhart) and their son, Elmer, had a uranium mine near the mouth of Navajo Marbles Canyon. They also mined California Bar. Rosie Gerhart was a school teacher in the short-lived town of White Canyon City. (119~, 737~, 1163~)

—Forgotten Point: Val Dalton noted that this is between Forgotten Canyon in the north and Crystal Springs Canyon to the south (at elevation 4121T on the Bullfrog map). (517~)

Crystal Springs: (Iron Co.) Harmony Mountains-Iron Mountain. Stoddard Mountain map.
Leslie Pace: "Named for clear cold water." (942~)

Cuddyback Lake: (Garfield Co.) Dixie National Forest-Boulder Mountain. Jacobs Reservoir map.
Correctly spelled Cuddeback Lake.
Nethella Griffin Woolsey noted that the lake was named for an early stockman. (2051~) This was most likely Lefever Cuddeback (1834-ca. 1904). (388~)

Cummings Mesa: (San Juan Co., Utah and Coconino Co., Az.) Navajo Indian Reservation-Navajo Mountain. Utah maps: Cathedral Canyon, Gregory Butte, and Rainbow Bridge. Arizona maps: Chaiyahi Flat and West Canyon Creek.
Also called Cummings Plateau. This has also been called Fifty-mile Mesa as it is about fifty miles from mile "0" (Lees Ferry) on the Colorado River. (1400~)
Also spelled Cummings' Mesa. (1990~)
The Navajo name is *Tsé Gháá*, or "Top of the Rock." (1931~)
Billie Williams Yost noted that a Navajo name for the mesa was *Nocki-Cummenthi*. (2059~) This name, so like Cummings, seems to actually have been a coincidence

(?). John R. Winslowe in 1966 explained: "According to Navajo clan history, [a gold hunting] party and two others lost heavily in attacks made on them while working the [gold] mine. The story relates that the death of one Spaniard cost the lives of thirty-five to forty Navajos. This seems to have been especially true in an attack made on them after leaving the canyon when they were chased onto Cummings Mesa. It is today known in Navajo as *Nock Cummenthi*, a contraction of words meaning, 'Where the Mexicans were chased up,' ie., into the rocks, where they stood off the Indians." (2033~) William F. Williams: "We went to Nock-Cummenthi where the Navajos chased the Mexicans out of the Navajo Mountain country." (2015~) Byron Cummings led several extended archaeological expeditions into southern Utah starting in 1906. Gary Topping: "The first recorded ascent of Cummings Mesa was made by Byron Cummings and John Wetherill." (1901~) Cummings: "In 1919 John Wetherill and I, first visited the Lofty Narrow Mesa ... that has since been dedicated Cummings Mesa." (502~)

Charles L. Bernheimer in 1921: "To the west of Navajo Mountain was a long Mesa called 'Prof. Byron Cummings Mesa.'" (218~)

The Navajo had been using Cummings Mesa as a grazing area for many years before Cummings' and Wetherill's ascent in 1919 and had established several stock trails to the top of the mesa. (See Dungeon Canyon.)

—Constructed Stock Trail: This is the "Pack Trail" that goes up the east side of Cummings Mesa (West Canyon Creek map). It is still used by the Navajo and is the most common way for hikers to get to the top of the mesa. Charles L. Bernheimer, calling it the Chimney Flue, described ascending the trail in 1924: "A funnel or flume or chimney most nearly describes the place where the mesa could be mounted. Man could do it better than beast; he at least had his hands, but the beasts had experience and strength and hope for grazing on top. It seems to me an Indian trail of this sort is in places more dangerous than no trail. The Indians' ingenuity seems to go asleep at times or to give out, he leaves places of staggering difficulties—or the elements may be responsible for these apparent lapses." (218~) Madelene Cameron noted that the trail was improved as a tribal work project in the 1950s. (335~)

—Airstrip: Myles Headrick in 1959: "On that flight Tex Wright pointed out a small air strip on Cummings Mesa and said they, uranium prospectors, had taken a small bulldozer by air to do the work." (850~) Gus Scott added panache to the story: "Dick [Sprang] wrote me that uranium had been found on Cummings Mesa. A plane landed, got stuck in sand taking off, fouled its engine with sand from the prop wash trying to get unstuck, and will only get off when another plane flies in with a new engine. He said the developers plan to build a road to the top of Cummings. As Dick said, 'the country is swiftly going to hell.'" (1708~)

Cunningham Ranch: (Grand Co.) Book Cliffs-Nash Wash. Calf Canyon map. PRIVATE PROPERTY.

The ranch was started by Harry Bogert in the 1880s. Other owners over the years included Harry Ballard, the Turner family, and Wallace Cunningham. Bill and Joyce Cunningham owned the ranch until they sold it to The Nature Conservancy and the Rocky Mountain Elk Foundation in 1991. It is now managed by the Division of Wildlife Resources. (508~)

Curly Hollow Wash: (Washington Co.) Beaver Dam Mountains-Virgin River. Jarvis Peak and White Hills maps.

Correctly spelled Curley Hollow Wash.

Jedediah Smith of the South West Expedition of 1826-27 went down the Virgin River to where it boxes, then cut west, possibly up Curly Hollow Wash. (1774~)

The Jackson Curley family were early settlers of Washington County, arriving before 1860. (388~)

Currant Canyon: (Duchesne Co.) Bad Land Cliffs-Nine Mile Creek. Currant Canyon map.

Inscriptions in Nine Mile Canyon near the mouth of Currant Canyon include Wittman, 10-11-81; Ben Darling, Orson Stron, 1886; Will Cowan, May 12th, 1888; and J.L. Wilson, Aug. 8th, 1893. (SAPE.)

—Hays Ranch: The Dan Hay Ranch was near the mouth of Currant Canyon in Nine Mile Canyon. (1324~)

Currant Canyon: (Kane Co.) Dixie National Forest-Stout Canyon. Strawberry Point and Long Valley Junction maps.

Also called Currant Creek. (767~)

Thomas Chamberlain in 1893: "The children went to Currant Canyon with a team to gather Currants yesterday. Had a good time." (416~) William Adair in 1942: "The canyon and creek were named for wild currant bushes growing in the canyon." (2053~)

—Currant Canyon Ranch: This was the name given by Thomas Chamberlain to the dairy farm and sheep operation he had in the canyon. (349~, 416~) Mark Chamberlain, the son of Thomas Chamberlain: "We had a little garden there above the carrels [corrals], watered by the spring that came outside of the hill. We got about all the garden stuff that we needed during the summer." (414~)

Curry Canyon: (Emery Co.) Book Cliffs-Big Horn Mountain-Gray Canyon. Three Fords Canyon map.

George Southerland Curry (1864-1900) (also called "Flat Nose" George Curry and Jim King), an outlaw at the turn of the century, was killed by lawmen along the Green River. (200~) George E. Stewart: "He had been kicked in the face by a horse, flattening his nose, and marking him for life. This peculiar facial characteristic was the basis for his sobriquet." (1837~)

Cutler Point: (Kane Co.) White Cliffs-Skutumpah Terrace. Cutler Point map. (6,734')

Also called Singali Point. (767~)

Royal James Cutler (1828–1894) had a sheep ranch near Long Valley Junction in the early years. (349~, 416~)

—Dairy Canyon: This starts one-half mile east of Cutler Point and goes southeast into Dry Lake. (767~)

Cuts Canyon: (Wayne Co.) Capitol Reef National Park-Miners Mountain-Sulphur Creek. Grover, Twin Rocks, and Fruita maps.

Guy Pace noted that Elijah Cutlar "Cut" Behunin (1847-1933) was one of the first to settle in the Fruita area, in about 1885. He had mining claims in the canyon. (1497~, 2013~)

Cyclone Canyon: (San Juan Co.) Canyonlands National Park-Needles District-The Grabens. Spanish Bottom and The Loop maps.

W.G. Carroll in 1956: "named by the cowboys who while searching for stray cattle, had experienced the frequent winds which howl between the high walls." (350~) David Lavender, quoting cowboy Cy Thornell: "The wind gets in here and then rushes round and round trying to find a way out. It never does." (1151~)

Kent Frost: "Because the wind blows through there sometimes, and them grabens they kind of go east and west, and I guess somehow the wind gets blowing up through that part. Sometimes there will be tumbleweed, Russian Thistles, packed up in great big piles in certain places." (690~)

Cyclone Draw: (Wayne Co.) Awapa Plateau-Big Hollow. Jakes Knoll and Moroni Peak maps.

Thaine Taylor: "Anytime the wind blew, why, it was up high enough that it would really snow in there." (1868~)

—Cyclone Co-op Reservoir: (Jakes Knoll map.) Thaine Taylor: "A co-op herd is where all these little bunches of sheep get put together and make a co-op out of it." (1868~)

Cyclone Lake: (Garfield Co.) Dixie National Forest-Boulder Mountain. Posy Lake map.

Scott Robinson: "It was so named due to the fact that the trees in a mile wide swath around the lake had been blown over as though a cyclone had struck here years ago." (2053~)

George C. Fraser in 1915: "We found a spring, much polluted and trampled by cattle ... described by the herders as Cyclone Valley.... We had barely gotten our food out when I noticed a cyclone coming up the valley.... It formed a dense column of dust about 50' high, surmounted by a cloud of dust dispersed like a charge from a shotgun to a height of 150'.... This cyclone ascended the valley quite leisurely, passed directly over the spring.... While we were lunching two smaller cyclones followed ... and ... another large cyclone came along the same route." (668~)

—Clayton: This grazing area is immediately west of Cyclone Lake. (See Clayton Spring.)

D

Dab Keele Spring: (Wayne Co.) Rabbit Valley-Fremont River. Bicknell map.
Dee Hatch noted that Dabney "Dab" Keele (1826-1902) ran livestock in the area. (844~)

Daddy Canyon: (Carbon and Duchesne Counties.) Badland Cliffs-Nine Mile Canyon. Cowboy Bench map.
Also called Big Daddy Canyon.
In the early 1900s Myron Russell had a ranch at the mouth of nearby Dry Canyon. His father was known as Daddy. (558~)
—Constructed Stock Trail: This still-used trail goes up the canyon to Cowboy Bench. (SAPE.)
—Rasmussen Cave: PRIVATE PROPERTY. This famous archaeological site is near the mouth of Daddy Canyon. (1788~) The Rasmussen family had a ranch in Nine Mile Canyon near the mouth of Cottonwood Canyon in the early years. (725~) Inscriptions include E. Shaw, April 12, 1892. (SAPE.)

Daddy Spring: (Carbon Co.) West Tavaputs Plateau-Cold Spring Draw. Bruin Point map.
(See Daddy Canyon for name derivation.)

Dairy Canyon: (Kane Co.) Dixie National Forest-Stout Canyon. Long Valley Junction map.
Also called Dairy Creek. (767~)
Several dairies serving the United Order were at the mouth of the canyon. The first was built in 1874. (1714~, 2053~) This has also been called Hoyts Dairy Canyon for one of the operators of a dairy. (1931~) In 1893 Thomas Chamberlain called it both Dairy Canyon and Covingtons Canyon. A man named Covington had a farm in the canyon. (416~)

Dairy Canyon: (Kane Co.) Wygaret Terrace-Johnson Canyon. Thompson Point map.
B.A. Riggs: "The canyon was named because a pioneer dairy was located there during the early settlement of Kanab." (2053~)
—Alvin Judd Ranch: PRIVATE PROPERTY. This is at the mouth of Dairy Canyon. It was owned by Alfred (or Alvin) Judd. (1831~)

Dairy Creek: (Emery and Sanpete Counties.) Manti-La-Sal National Forest-Wasatch Plateau-Ferron Creek. Flagstaff Peak and Ferron Canyon maps.
Two complimentary name derivations are given.
First, in 1882 Amos and Elmira Stevens started a dairy on Ferron Creek. They took the Dairy Trail up Dairy Creek to get to Dairy Point and Ferron Mountain. (931~)
Second, Ray Wareham: "Joe Wrigley used to have a dairy up on the Ferron Mountain, at Wrigley Spring. He'd come down and bring butter and buttermilk down this trail to town." (1967~)
—Dairy Trail: The "Dairy Trail" is shown on the Ferron Canyon map. It was improved by Hass Fugate and others. It is now a designated hiking trail and is easy to follow. (931~, SAPE.)

Dakota Hill: (Kane Co.) Clear Creek Mountain-Esplin Gulch. Temple of Sinawava map. (6,660')
R.T. Evans, a topographical engineer with the USGS, suggested the name: "So named on account of its capping of Dakota conglomerate gravels." (1931~)

Dalley Canyon: (Iron Co.) Hurricane Cliffs-Parowan Valley. Summit map.
The James Dalley (1822-1905) and William Dalley (ca. 1822-1907) families moved to what is now Enoch in 1854 and helped build Fort Johnson. They moved to Summit Creek in 1859. (338~, 363~, 516~, 921a~)

Dalton Canyon: (Carbon Co.) Roan Cliffs-Range Creek. Patmos Head map.
Waldo Wilcox: "There is an old cattle trail going up that canyon. I think that Barton [See Barton Canyon] built that. I don't know who Dalton was." (2011~)

Dalton Spring: (San Juan Co.) Manti-LaSal National Forest-Abajo Mountains-North Canyon. Abajo Peak map.
Val Dalton noted that this was named for King Henry Dalton. (517~)
—Dalton Trailer Camp: This mining camp near Dalton Spring is noted on several old maps. (2036~)

Dalton Wash: (Washington Co.) Zion National Park-Cougar Mountain-Virgin River. Springdale West and Virgin maps.
—Dalton Town: PRIVATE PROPERTY. John Dalton, Jr. (1801-1885) and family, and others, started a small

community on the north side of the Virgin River at the mouth of Dalton Wash in 1864. Indian troubles forced abandonment in 1866. (258~)

—Duncans Retreat: (Also called Duncan.) Chapman Duncan (1812-1900) and several others settled on the north side of the Virgin River two and one-half miles east of Dalton Town (near elevation 3598 on the Virgin map) in 1861.

Two name derivations are given.

First, Grace M. Twitchell: "The name of the place was suggested from the fact that the first settler, Chapman Duncan (also attributed to John Duncan), retreated to other parts of the country after the floods during the winter of 1861–1862." (371~)

Second, Karl Larson noted that Chapman Duncan moved to the site a short time before it was essentially eradicated by the big flood of 1862, forcing him to retreat to a better location. (1141~)

One of the early settlers of Duncans Retreat was Appleton Harmon and his wife, Elmeda. She described life here in 1862: "We tried to raise foodstuffs, corn, potatoes, etc. in the narrow canyon valley. The river often overflowed and washed our gardens away.... We stayed here a short time but could not raise enough food to live on." (64~)

Appleton and Elmeda Harmon's son, Hosea Frank Harmon, was a small boy in the early 1860s: "All I can remember in that town, which was a very small one, was that we camped on the bank of the river in a big round tent. One night there came a big flood and overflowed the banks and ran into our tent. The folks were very busy taking the things out and forgot me for a while. Someone came into the tent for some more things and found me floating around in a wooden cradle that father had made for me some time before. It was lucky for me that the cradle was water-tight." (64~)

By 1892 the town was abandoned and by 1930 there was little left to see. (273~, 367~, 942~)

Dance Hall Rock: (Kane Co.) GSCENM-Hole-in-the-Rock Road. Sooner Bench map. (4,725')

This huge, flat-floored overhang has also been called Hall Cave, or simply The Hall in honor of Hole-in-the-Rock Expedition member Charles Hall. (182~) The San Juan pioneers danced here during the long winter of 1879–80. (1356~, 1445~, 2051~)

There are many inscriptions dating to the early 1900s on the rock. It is assumed that since the Hole-in-the-Rock Expedition tarried here for several weeks in 1879, members left their names, which have since eroded away. (1115~, SAPE.)

—Dance Hall Rock Spring: This large, developed spring is in a small draw one-half mile west-southwest of Dance Hall Rock. Inscriptions include J. McInelly, April 1906 and ERN, 1930. (SAPE.)

—Unnamed Dome: This small sandstone outcrop is one-half mile west-northwest of Dance Hall Rock at elevation BM4727. Inscriptions include DAR Heaps, 1908 and Angus Barney, 3/15/24. (SAPE.)

Dan Day Reservoir: (Garfield Co.) Dixie National Forest-Escalante Mountains. Antimony map.

Sonny King noted that Daniel Day (1872-1933) and family had a homestead at the mouth of Poison Creek. (1095~, 338~)

Dandelion Flat: (Garfield Co.) Dixie National Forest-Sevier Plateau. Mount Dutton and Junction maps.

Kent Whittaker: "To somebody, there was an awful lot of dandelions around there. There's a pond there. I helped locate that. I went there with a backhoe in the 1950s or '60s." (2002~)

Dandelion Flat: (Garfield Co.) Henry Mountains-Sawmill Basin-Bull Creek. Mount Ellen map.

Guy Robison: "It was just a solid mass of dandelions and they were pretty. They grew up tall and any green thing like that in the mountains looked good. It's mostly grass now." (1644~)

—Lonesome Beaver Campground: This primitive National Forest Service campground is on Sawmill Creek at the south end of Dandelion Flat. (See Sawmill Basin.)

Daniels Canyon: (Emery Co.) Manti-LaSal National Forest-Wasatch Plateau-Rock Canyon. The Cap map.

The Daniels family were early settlers of the Huntington area. (388~)

Daniels Canyon: (Sevier Co.) Fishlake National Forest-Otter Creek. Mount Terrill, Boobe Hole Reservoir, and Burrville maps.

A stretch of Otter Creek goes through Daniels Canyon.

Irvin Warnock noted that Aaron and David Daniels homesteaded in Grass Valley in 1875. (1971~)

Danish Flat: (Grand Co.) Book Cliffs-Grand Valley. Danish Flat map.

—Danish Flat Town: Little is known of this small town. It was settled by Charles Urias Cato (1883-1958) and family, and several other families, in 1908. The town was abandoned in 1920. (644~, 1195~)

Danish Hill: (Wayne Co.) Capitol Reef National Park-Capitol Reef-Cuts Canyon. Fruita map.

Charles Kelly: "Two poor Danishmen were traveling through with a team of poor horses and broken-down outfit. On the hill just east of Fruita a bolt through the doubletree broke and their wagon slid back down the grade, wrecking it. One's name was Swett. The grade has been known ever since as Danish Hill." (1047~)

Dan Leigh Hollow: (Iron Co.) Kolob Terrace-West Fork Deep Creek. Webster Flat map.

Ann Starr noted that Daniel T. Leigh (1852-1927) was an early homesteader. (942~) He moved to Iron County in the 1870s. (388~)

Dan Sill Hill: (Washington Co.) Dixie National Forest-Bull Valley Mountains-Mountain Meadows. Central West map.

Daniel C. Sill was an early resident of St. George. (803~) Nellie McArthur Gubler: "So named because a man by that name had made a road up the canyon and back to get around the deep wash. Today it is better known as the approach to Lytle's Ranch at Mountain Meadows." (1182~)

Dark Angel: (Grand Co.) Arches National Park-Devils Garden. Klondike Bluffs map.

Also called Thumb Rock. (898~)

Harry Reed, onetime custodian of what was then Arches National Monument in the late 1930s: "The monolith looks out southward over a kind of petrified Pandemonium, whereof you can almost smell the brimstone." (1115~) Dick Wilson: "a tall sandstone formation resembling an angel with wings folded." (2019~)

Dark Canyon: (Garfield Co.) Henry Mountains-Slate Creek. Mount Pennell and Mount Ellen maps.

Also called Black Canyon. (1931~)

Bliss Brinkerhoff: "It faces north, it's heavy timber, the sun don't shine in that much. It's just kind of dark to be in it. It's all dark and narrow and deep." (291~)

Dark Canyon: (San Juan Co.) La Sal Mountains-Geyser Creek. Mount Peale map.

—Dark Canyon Lake: Lloyd Holyoak: "Dark Canyon Lake is a crater lake and for many, many years, the bottom was never found. You don't swim in it. The water is so cold. Several people almost drowned in there, trying to swim across it. You just don't do it. It's liquid ice. It was originally called Dark Lake." (906~)

—Unknown Canyon: This is one mile north of Dark Canyon (one-quarter mile south of elevation 10480T). (1664~) Lloyd Holyoak: "It's the kind of canyon that was hidden until we started cutting the trees down in front of it. It's a beautiful canyon." (906~)

—Unknown Ridge: Lloyd Holyoak noted that the ridge is between Dark Canyon Lake and Unknown Canyon (at elevation 10064T). (906~)

Dark Canyon: (San Juan Co.) Manti-LaSal National Forest-Dark Canyon Wilderness-South Elk Ridge-Glen

Canyon NRA-Cataract Canyon. Kigalia Point, Poison Canyon, Warren Canyon, Black Steer Canyon, Indian Head Pass, and Bowdie Canyon West maps.

Also called Vega Canyon. (1860~)

Frank Silvey in 1936: "In 1883 to 1900 [ranchers] Jones Bros., Mel Turner, Dave Cooper, Dave Goudelock and others discovered and named ... 'Dark Canyon.'" (1740~) Two name derivations are given.

First, the ubiquitous story is that the canyon received its name because the lower part of the canyon is so narrow and receives so little sunlight, and is composed of such dark rock, that it is always dark. (873~, 1336~) Buck Lee in 1942: "The canyon is deep and comparatively dark and is probably the reason for its name." (2053~)

Randall Henderson in 1946: "[near the mouth of the canyon] the walls crowded in so close we understood how Dark canyon got its name. I do not know the origin of the name, but it evidently was given by an early-day explorer who came up from the Colorado river and saw only the lower end of the gorge. If his route had been reversed and he had first seen the upper 40 miles of the chasm, I think he would have called it Canyon of the Castles. For it is truly that.... For color and design, Dark canyon is one of the most spectacular in a region where the skyline is never dull or ordinary." (873~)

C. Gregory Crampton: "The mouth of Dark Canyon is narrow and dark.... Direct sunlight reaches the spot only a few hours a day. The immensity of the canyon and the forces of nature that created it are at all times apparent." (465~)

Second, Laverne Powell Tate: "It received its name from the big spring near the [Scorup] cabin where the water flows up dark and red." (1860~) (See Horse Pasture Canyon.)

Fletcher B. Hammond had a different name when he explored the canyon in 1886: "They discovered that Kigalia draw [Dark Canyon] finally descended to the west of the [Elk] mountain to the Colorado and became what was later called Dark Canyon." (821~)

Frederick S. Dellenbaugh of the 1871–72 Powell Expedition provided the first description of Dark Canyon: "A beautiful little brook came down a narrow canyon on the left, and it was up this stream that the Major went for a mile and a half and then climbed on the side. They were obliged to give it up and come back to the bottom. By this time it was too late to make another attempt, so they turned their backs on 'Failure Creek.'" (541~)

Robert Brewster Stanton in 1889: "The upper part of Dark Canyon is covered with Sugar maple trees, and that last fall one man made 3,000 lbs. of sugar from them." (1811~)

Albert R. Lyman: "In the early [eighteen] nineties two men named Dutch and Day made their summer headquarters in Dark Canyon." (1240~) Francis F. Kane reiterated this in 1891: "In Dark Cañon, which is in some way connected with Wooden Shoe Cañon, is Dutch and Day's ranch, which consists of ten or fifteen acres under cultivation." (1037~) Dutch and Day, miners from southwest Colorado, are thought to have been the first Euroamericans to run cattle in Dark Canyon. (820~)

Kane went on to provide the first good description of the upper part of the canyon: "The trail down into Dark Cañon [by way of the Kigalia Trail], in which the only settlers are Messrs. Judd Day and Adam Bashore, familiarly known as Dutch and Day, was about as unpleasant a descent as anything that we had experienced. The trail was very steep and muddy. The cañon at the bottom we found was comparatively flat, and contained splendid pasture, although at this time it was pretty well eaten off. We rode for about three miles through natural meadow land before we reached Dutch and Day's, passing at one place, the mouth as it were of a lateral cañon which has been turned by Messrs. Dutch and Day into a fine horse pasture [Horse Pasture Canyon] by simply fencing in the lower end, the walls of the cañon being so steep that cattle will not stray up into the timber. We found that Messrs. Day and Bashore raised some little corn but with poor success, as it is really too cold for it to mature. They also raised some potatoes." (1037~)

In the mid-1890s (another source says in 1884) Dutch and Day sold their interests to David M. Cooper and Vincent P. Martin of Indian Creek. In 1905 Cooper and Martin sold to the L.H. Redd family, who sold to the Scorup-Somerville Cattle Company in 1926. (820~, 1936~)

Devergne Barber in 1927: "This little canyon, although narrow, is very deep, and a clear water stream cascades its way from the top down to the river. Miniature lakes and waterfalls are abundant.... [We] continued for nearly six miles and found that the farther back we got the wider the canyon became and once again we were in sunshine." (134~)

C. Gregory Crampton in 1964: "The mouth of Dark Canyon is one of the more awesome places in Cataract Canyon. The mouth of Dark Canyon is narrow and dark and the walls of Cataract, approximately half a mile apart, are nearly 2000 ft. high. Direct sunlight reaches the spot only a few hours a day. The immensity of the canyon and the forces of nature that created it are at all times apparent." (465~)

Erwin Oliver aptly described his feelings about Dark Canyon after having run livestock in the canyon for many years: "I didn't like it down in Dark Canyon. I was a guy that liked to look where I was goin', not havin' to be lookin' up to see where I had been." (1479~)

About three miles above Dark Canyon on the Colorado River was, before Lake Powell, an inscription from fur trapper Denis Julien, 1836. (1115~) (See Appendix One—Denis Julien.) William Hiram Edwards of the James S. Best Expedition of 1891 called the inscription location D. Juliens Bend. (597a~)

—Dark Canyon Wilderness: A Primitive Area designation was applied to Dark Canyon in 1970. In 1984 47,116 acres of upper Dark Canyon were designated as a National Forest Wilderness. This includes Dark Canyon from Elk Ridge down to its junction with Woodenshoe Canyon as well as all of Cherry, Deadman, Horse Pasture, Kigalia, Peavine, Poison, Rig, Trail, Warren, and Woodenshoe canyons.

—Cooper and Martin Horse Pasture: Pete Steele noted that this is on the rim of Dark Canyon one and one-half miles south-southwest of Sweet Alice Spring (at elevations 7655T, 7965T, 7824T, and 7580T on the Warren Canyon map). David M. Cooper and Vincent P. Martin had the Dugout Ranch on Indian Creek starting in 1885. They were some of the first ranchers to run cattle on Dark Canyon Plateau. In 1897 they became partners in the Indian Creek Cattle Company. In 1905 they sold their Dark Canyon allotment to Lemuel H. Redd. (73~, 1509~, 1821~)

—The Vagey: (Also called Vega.) Erwin Oliver noted that this was the cowboy name for the upper part of Dark Canyon, above its confluence with Peavine Canyon. (1479~) James H. Knipmeyer: "Probably an Anglization of the Spanish word *vega*, meaning 'meadow.'" (1115~)

—Stock Trail: This went down lower Dark Canyon, from the Sundance Trail to the Colorado River. Charles Kelly noted that the Robbers Roost Gang "did have a sort of trail and crossing at the mouth of Dark Canyon, but it was so rough that any cattle moved over it were almost worthless when they got out." (1059~)

Kent Frost: "Another interesting thing about Dark Canyon is that along in the 1960s and '70s, there were some tremendous floods ... and they absolutely changed that lower Dark Canyon from the Sundance Trail down to the Colorado River. It used to be that if you just went down there and you got down in that lower limestone formation, why you'd go down quite easy and you'd work your way around in the bottom because there were a lot of willows growin' down there, and not many big pools of water. But there was lots of dirt over the whole bottom.... And then after the great floods come down, why it just changed the whole lower part of the canyon and cleaned out all the willows and everything, and left them great big pools that poured off there, down't the Colorado River.... [Before] we didn't have to climb 'way up ... over this here high stuff to get down the pour-offs and down the pools." (690~)

Senator Barry Goldwater buttressed what Kent Frost said in 1940: "The Creek runs over hard limestone that affords walking almost as level and as easy as a sidewalk. At one place this morning we had to go with a rope up to a ledge about 15 ft. outside of that one place the going was very easy, good and fast." (738~)

—Inscription Register: This well-known inscription panel near the mouth of Dark Canyon was used by many generations of river runners, including Harry Aleson, Dr. Russell G. Frazier, Bus Hatch, Buzz Holmstrom, Ellsworth and Emery Kolb, Bert Loper, and Frank Swain. (465~) One inscription reads "Pathe-Bray Colorado River Expedition, Nov. 24, 1927." Another was from Andy Delaney—Gold Prospector, Aug. 2, 1927. (1438~)

—Maidenhair Spring: This spring, now underwater, was a short distance up Dark Canyon from the river and was popular with river runners. (1653~)

—Dark Canyon Dam Site: (Proposed.) (Also called Cataract Canyon Dam Site.) In 1915 the USGS considered a dam on the Colorado River near Dark Canyon. The William Chenowith USGS Expedition of 1921 surveyed one possible location. It would have been two miles above Dark Canyon (one-quarter mile south-southwest of elevation 5366T on the Bowdie Canyon West map). Sidney Paige of the expedition: "Camped last night on bar at mouth of 'damsite' creek." (1503~)

The proposed dam would have been 532-feet high. Eugene Clyde LaRue: "The flowage damage in Cataract Canyon and on Green River would be very small. On Colorado River the small settlement of Moab would be submerged.... The town of Moab could be moved to a higher and better location on Mill Creek." (1146~, 1425~, 1669~, 1985~)

Dark Hollow: (Iron Co.) Dixie National Forest-Sidney Peaks-Second Left Hand Canyon. Brian Head map. Also called Dark Holler. (516~)
William C. Mitchell: "This hollow is so densely covered with trees even at midday the penetration of the sun's rays are so dim it seems only twilight. Almost impossible to ride a horse here unless you follow a trail." (2053~)

Dark Forest: (Coconino Co., Az.) Vermilion Cliffs National Monument-Paria Plateau. One Toe Ridge, Az. map. Compared to the rest of the Sand Hills, this area has a lot of trees. (1083~)

Dark Valley Draw: (Garfield and Wayne Counties.) Dixie National Forest-Boulder Mountain-Pine Creek. Big Lake, Jacobs Reservoir, and Government Point maps. Also called Dark Valley. (670~)
The sun rarely hits the bottom of the canyon.

—Coleman Cabin: PRIVATE PROPERTY. (Also called Snow Cabin.) This is in upper Dark Valley one-quarter mile north of Lava Spring. Ellik Coleman started a dairy farm here in the late 1890s. It was later bought by Charles Snow, Sr., and then by Guy Pace. The original ranch house, built of logs, is near collapse. A cowboy cabin nearby was built with boards from the Torgerson Sawmill on nearby Miller Creek. Guy Pace noted that the cabin has two sides. The Bicknell cowboys would stay in one side, the Torrey cowboys in the other. (1497~, 1865~)

—Dark Valley Pasture: This is the flat area of Dark Valley that is centered on Lava Spring. (1497~)

Dark Valley Shelf: (Garfield Co.) Dixie National Forest-Aquarius Plateau. Jacobs Reservoir and Government Point maps.
—Line Lake: This is on the southeast side of Dark Valley Shelf (at elevation 10709 on the Jacobs Reservoir map). (1865~)

—Doe Lake: This is on the east side of Dark Valley Shelf (one-quarter mile west-southwest of elevation 11001 on the Jacobs Reservoir map). Dunk Taylor: "About every time you go by there you see a doe deer around the edge of it." (1865~)

Dave Canyon: (Garfield Co.) GSCENM-Kaiparowits Plateau-Alvey Wash. Dave Canyon and Canaan Creek maps. Also called Coal Canyon. (1931~)
Edson Alvey: "an eastern tributary of Alvey Wash, named for Dave Mossman [David Daniel Mossman, 1868-1949], who started a homestead at the mouth of the canyon." (55~) There is now no sign of the homestead. (SAPE.)

Daves Canyon: (Kane Co.) Clear Creek Mountain-Meadow Creek. Clear Creek Mountain map.
David Webster Esplin (1868-1960) ran sheep in the area in the early 1900s. (485~)

Daves Hollow: (Garfield Co.) Dixie National Forest-Paunsaugunt Plateau-East Fork Sevier River. Bryce Canyon map. Also called Dave Hollow.

Two name derivations are given.

First, Bryce Canyon National Park Superintendent P.P. Paltrow in 1934: "David O. Littlefield [1845-1898] moved to Cannonville in 1876. He started raising sheep in Daves Hollow in 1880. There he built a house, sheep shearing corral and dug a well." (1931~) Littlefield also had a sawmill here. (1455~)

Second, Robert J. Ott in 1966: "named after Dave Shakespear [1861-1949] who had a sawmill at the head of the draw in the early 1900s." (1931~)

—Daves Hollow Guard Station: (Also called Daves Hollow Ranger Station.) (766~) The original road to the rim of Bryce Canyon went through Daves Hollow and by the guard station. (887~) The first structure was built in 1907. Buildings came and went over the years and in the 1980s the site was redeveloped and is now used by seasonal workers. (2021~)

Dave Teeples Spring: (Garfield Co.) Henry Mountains-Pete Steele Bench. Steele Butte map. PRIVATE PROPERTY.

Keith Durfey noted that Dave Teeples (1877-1945) homesteaded the area around the spring in the early 1900s. Before Teeples, though, Bert Avery had a dugout here. (582~) (See Bert Avery Seep.)

Jack King: "Dave Teeples was a feller that took up the place and they called it the Teeples place and then he lost it. My granddad, [Emory] King, bought it for taxes." (1094~)

Davis Canyon: (San Juan Co.) Canyonlands National Park-Needles District-Indian Creek. South Six-shooter Peak and North Six-shooter Peak maps.

Pete Steele noted that J.J. Davis was an Indian Creek pioneer. (1821~, 388~)

—Davis Canyon Nuclear Waste Dump: (Proposed.) In the early 1980s Davis Canyon was proposed as a repository site for nuclear waste. If the project had gone through, a thirty-seven mile rail line to Davis Canyon for hauling nuclear waste would have been built. As well, buildings and structures would have covered at least five hundred acres, including a coal-fired power plant to run the operation. Water use would have averaged between one and two million gallons a day. (1132~)

Davis Canyon: (San Juan Co.) Manti-LaSal National Forest-Dark Canyon Plateau-North Elk Ridge-Stevens Canyon. Poison Canyon, Chippean Rocks, and Cathedral Butte maps.

(See Davis Canyon above for name derivation.)

Davis Flat: (Garfield Co.) Dixie National Forest-Aquarius Plateau. Big Lake map.

Unattributed: "George Davis who had sheep ranch there in early days." (1346~)

Davis Gulch: (Kane Co.) Glen Canyon NRA-Escalante River-Lake Powell. Davis Gulch map.

Also called Davis Creek. (874~)

Edson Alvey noted that George and John Davis moved to Escalante in the 1870s. They ran sheep in the area. (55~)

George Davis: I had been down Davis Gulch before the Mormons out the Hole [in 1879]. (525~)

Several other features in the Escalante area are named for the Davis brothers, including Georges Camp Canyon and Georgie Hollow. (55~, 2051~)

—Davis Gulch Stock Trail: A constructed stock trail enters middle Davis Gulch on its north side one mile (as the crow flies) upcanyon from LaGorce Arch (one-third mile northwest of elevation 4135AT). (SAPE.) Burnett Hendryx in 1955: "John Black, Philo Allen, and Hayden Church, built that 'trail', and that Allen Cameron, helped them build it." (877~) This was probably in the 1890s.

The trail proved problematic to cattlemen. McKay Bailey is quoted as saying: "This spot is tricky. We had a horse do a two-and-a-half gainer off the cliff here, and once a pack mule landed in the cottonwood trees below." (47~)

Pratt Gates: "I've done it twice and I wouldn't do it again for the life of me…. That trail is just rough and it's spooky. It scares you." (709~)

—Ruess plaque: Toward the end of the slot portion of upper Davis Gulch is a plaque that reads:

> EVERETT RUESS
> I HAVE BEEN THINKING MORE AND MORE THAT I
> SHALL ALWAYS BE ALONE
> WANDERER IN THE WILDERNESS
> *Oh but the desert is glorious now*
> *With marching clouds in the blue sky,*
> *And cool winds blowing.*
> *The smell of sage is sweet*
> *in my nostrils,*
> *And the luring trail leads onward.*

The quotes are from Everett's writings. The plaque was installed in 1984. Davis Gulch was the last known campsite used by Everett Ruess. He inscribed NEMO 1934 on a wall near Bement Arch. The name Nemo was used several times by Everett in his writings. Nemo was either from the Greek word meaning "no one" or from Captain Nemo, who shunned humankind by disappearing under the sea in Jules Verne's *Twenty Thousand Leagues Under the Sea.* (47~)

Many theories have been forwarded about how Ruess died. The person that searched the hardest and longest was Harry Aleson: "After fourteen years of continued interest, considerable questioning, prowling in the area of the disappearance, hearing a great deal said about the affair by Escalante and Boulder folk—I heard firsthand on Pearl Harbor Day this year, some startling statements—from a man of that area, pretty much 'in his cups.' The boy was shot. Killer was named to me. Killer died seven years later. Two others threw the body in the Colorado R.... Nothing re the murder could be proved in court." (34~)

Davis Hollow: (Sevier Co.) Fishlake National Forest-Sevier Plateau-Skueedunk Canyon. Water Creek Canyon map.

Irvin Warnock noted that John Eugene Davis (1845-1935) and family moved to Annabella in the 1880s. (1971~)

Davis Point: (Garfield Co.) Dixie National Forest-Escalante Mountains-Main Canyon. Griffin Point map. PRIVATE PROPERTY.

—Davis Ranch: Pratt Gates noted that Johnny Davis (1881-1960) had a ranch just south of Davis Point (at elevation BM7216). The ranch was initially owned by Martin Liston. Davis sold the ranch to William Henry Gates. It was then called the Toke Gates Ranch. (709~) There are still old buildings at the site. (SAPE.)

Day Canyon: (Grand Co.) Tenmile Country-Colorado River. Gold Bar Canyon map.

Two name derivations are given.

First, the canyon was probably named for Herbert and Mary Day. They arrived in Moab in 1882. Over the years they moved often, living in Castle Valley, Pinhook, and Wilson Mesa among others. Herbert was the sheriff of Moab for several years. (456~, 537~)

Second, Lloyd Holyoak: "That was named after John Day. He did some mining in the area." (906~)

—Two Tortoise Rock: This tower is one mile northwest of the mouth of Day Canyon (at elevation 4865T). (M.1)

Day Spring: (Iron Co.) Cedar Mountain-Pine Spring Knoll. Cedar Mountain map. PRIVATE PROPERTY.

Warren Bullock, who owned the spring: "Information not clear but could have been named for Thomas Day who herded sheep in the area." (942~)

Dead Horse Canyon: (Sevier Co.) Fishlake National Forest-Salina Creek. Gooseberry Creek and Steves Mountain maps.

Also called Browns Hole.

—Wilson Mine: This coal mine is the "Mines" on the north side of Salina Canyon immediately north of the

mouth of Dead Horse Canyon (Steves Mountain map). It was initially called the Nephi Anderson Mine. It was active from 1911 to 1935. (567~, 1794~) W.T. Thom, Jr. in 1923: "Hand-drawn cars transport the coal to the mouth of the mine, where it is dumped through a chute into a small bin from which wagons are loaded. All the coal from this mine is taken to Salina and adjacent towns for domestic use." (1874~)

—Cabin: This was at the mouth of the canyon.

—Constructed Stock Trail: This goes south up the canyon to Browns Hole and eventually to Gooseberry Creek. (SAPE.)

Deadhorse Canyon: (Wayne Co.) Glen Canyon NRA-Canyonlands National Park-Orange Cliffs-Stillwater Canyon. Cleopatras Chair and Turks Head maps.

Also called Beaver Creek.

Edwin T. Wolverton called this Deep Canyon. (619~, 1290~, M.78.) Michael R. Kelsey noted that a couple of stories are told of a horse or horses dying of thirst above the canyon. (1084~)

—Paddys Valley: This is on the west side of the Green River and south of the mouth of Deadhorse Canyon (at elevation 4250 on the Turks Head map). (1301~) Paddy Ross was an early-day river runner. (614~)

—Lower Trail: This constructed stock trail goes from Deadhorse Canyon south along the river into Horse Canyon. (SAPE.) (See Horse Canyon–Wayne Co.)

Dead Horse Point State Park: (Grand Co.) Tenmile Country-Colorado River. Gold Bar Canyon and Shafer Basin maps. (6,067')

Also called Big Point. (354~)

This 5,362 acre park was established in 1959.

Four similar name derivations are given.

First, the point itself has a narrow neck, and with its precipitous sides, it was easy for ranchers to fence the neck and contain their livestock. One year, after a round-up, the less desirable horses were left behind. Although the gate was ostensibly left open, several horses stayed on the point and died.

Second, stockmen left their horses on the point. Desperate for water, several leaped to their deaths. (456~, 1562~, 1855~)

Third, J.D. Dillard, district manager for the Grazing Service: "[In 1890 Bill Snyder] went up toward what is now called Dead Horse Point. He liked the pasturage and using some brush, penned some horses, four or five, up out beyond the neck. There was water and he figured to be right back. The farmers kept him longer than planned and when he was able to return, the horses had choked to death. The water had run out. All that while they could see and smell the Colorado River thousands of feet below but they couldn't get to it. Guess that's really how Dead Horse got its name." (197~)

Fourth, Jean Akens provided an alternate derivation: "If you look down on the White Rim layer of sandstone below the Point, one outcropping near the gooseneck resembles a horse lying on its side, or 'playing dead.'" (12~)

Buck Lee in 1938: "Many who have seen the Great Grand Canyon say that the view from here surpasses that from Bright Angel Trail. At Dead Horse Point the sheer walls of the Canyon's rim drops 3000 feet and over a blue haze for 50 miles one can look out and across a gnarled and twisting world. There are no restrictions governing the reaction one feels here as the imagination goes back into the ages, while these formations were being so roughly broken." (352~)

Jack Breed in 1947: "My first view from Dead Horse Point convinced me that here indeed is another Grand Canyon!... Here in one magnificent vista was one of the largest areas of incompletely explored country remaining in the United States, forbidding, colorful, silent, and inaccessible." (278~)

Les Goates in 1958: "What an obnoxious name for one of the most amazing, stupendous and otherwise indescribable scenic phenomena in all nature—DEAD HORSE POINT." (732~)

—Upper Grand Canyon: This is the local name for the Colorado River gorge below Dead Horse Point. (2056~)

—Movies: *Warlock*, starring Henry Fond and Anthony Quinn, was filmed, in part, on Dead Horse Point. Other movies shot, in part, at the point include *Ten Who Dared*, *Against a Crooked Sky*, *Rio Conchos*, and *The Commancheros*. (12~)

—Deaths: Several deaths have occurred at the point. A woman throwing rocks off of the top leaned over to see where the rocks were hitting 630 feet below. Another was a Boy Scout chasing lizards.

Deadman Canyon: (Carbon Co.) Book Cliffs-Hayes Wash. Deadman Canyon, Helper, and Price maps.

Also called Dead Mans Canyon and Deadmans Creek. (375~)

Annie C. Kimball: "So named because in 1884 the body of a dead man was found in the canyon." (384~)

Deadman Canyon: (San Juan Co.) Manti-LaSal National Forest-Dark Canyon Wilderness-North Elk Ridge-Poison Canyon. Poison Canyon map.

John Scorup: "Seems as how the old cowboys were out there and they found a saddle and a bridle and chaps,

spurs, boots, hat, shirt, everything, and there was nobody around. These had been laying out for a period of time and they figured that whoever it was got mentally ill or something and went off the deep end and walked down that deep canyon and died. That's been called Deadman Canyon ever since." (1821~)

Deadman Hill: (Wayne Co.) Dirty Devil Country-South Fork Robbers Roost Canyon. Robbers Roost Flats map. (6,047')

One of outlaw Cap Brown's men was shot by lawmen in Beaver Box Canyon in the 1880s. The man made it up the Angel Trail, but died and was buried on the hill. (607~)

Frank E. Masland, Jr.: "It was the habit of the Wild Bunch to hole up [at Robbers Roost Spring].... A guard was posted on Deadman Mesa." (1310~)

Deadman Hollow: (Wayne Co.) Awapa Plateau-Riley Canyon. Abes Knoll map.

Dee Hatch: "There were some people comin' across there and they run on to this man. He was already dead, so they finished buryin' him, so they called it Deadman Hollow." (844~)

Thaine Taylor: "From what I've heard, there was a fellow that got lost or disoriented and when they found him, why, he was dead." (1868~)

Deadman Peak: (Emery Co.) San Rafael Swell-Willow Springs Wash. Mussentuchit Flat map. (5,725')

Also called Dead Mans Point. (727~)

Two name derivations are given.

First, Garn Jefferies: "It was a misty day and a fellow had a herd of sheep down there on the desert. He climbed up this little peak to see if he could see where his sheep were. So he set down right on the peak and was poopin' and his feet got out from under him and he slipped and fell down that peak and it killed him. That's the story behind that"! (959~)

Second, Wayne Gremel: "These old-timers told me that some of the Wild Bunch rustled a bunch of horses over in Sevier Valley. One of them got shot. When the posse caught them the next morning, they found a dead guy layin' there, at Deadmans Peak." (780~)

Deadman Point: (Grand Co.) Tenmile Country-Labyrinth Canyon. Mineral Canyon, Dubinky Wash, and Bowknot Bend maps.

James H. Knipmeyer noted that a dead man was found at Deadman Spring by cowboys in the 1890s. (1116~)

Deadman Ridge: (Garfield Co.) GSCENM-Escalante Desert-Hole-in-the-Rock Road. Tenmile Flat map.

Two name derivations are given.

First, Edson Alvey noted that stockman Myron Shurtz was killed on the ridge by lightning in May 1912. (55~) Second, Pratt Gates told a story from the early 1900s: "A man came into Escalante. They didn't know his name or where he came from. He was hungry and he stole some food. He left town and went into the Lower Desert and there was a sheep herd on Deadman Ridge and he went there. The posse caught up with him and he came out of the sheep herder's tent. The posse told him that they were there for him. He turned and started to walk off and one of the posse shot him in the back." (709~)

Deadman Spring: (Grand Co.) Tenmile Country-Spring Canyon. Dubinky Wash map.

This is a large spring with a no-longer-functioning stock reservoir. (SAPE.)

In the 1890s cowboys found a dead man here. (1116~)

Dead Mare Wash: (Garfield Co.) Dixie National Forest-Escalante Mountains-Upper Valley Creek. Upper Valley map.

Pratt Gates: "They found a dead mare there at one time." (709~)

—Spencer Ranch: This was at the mouth of Dead Mare Wash on Upper Valley Creek. The Spencers were Escalante pioneers.

Dead Sheep Pond: (Grand Co.) Book Cliffs-Cisco Desert-Cisco Wash. Cisco Springs map.

This is a still-used stock pond. A sheep corral is nearby. (SAPE.)

Death Canyon: (Garfield Co.) Cedar Point-North Wash. Turkey Knob map.

Alvin Robison: "It's a narrow canyon. It's got a fork on the left-hand side that is so narrow that cattle would get in there and then they couldn't turn around and that's how it got its name. They found 'em dead in there." (1642~)

Inscriptions include W.H. Edwards, R. Travers, and [John] Hislop, 1889. These men were members of the Stanton-Brown Survey of 1889–90. (1548~) Other inscriptions include J. Hugh, 1916; Elmer Thompson, Feb. 27, 1927; and Jim Chappell, March 14, 1941. (SAPE.)

—Green Tree Canyon: Kevin Robison noted that this canyon is immediately south of Death Canyon. A large cottonwood tree grows against a large sandstone wall near its mouth. The tree was the site of a suicide in the early 2000s, giving the canyon a second name, Suicide Canyon. (1646~)

Death Canyon Point: (Uintah Co.) Uintah and Ouray Indian Reservation-East Tavaputs Plateau. Wolf Flat map. (7,303')

In May 1900 two lawmen, Jesse M. Tyler and Sam Jenkins, were killed by the outlaw Kid Curry in response to Tyler's killing of Flat Nose George Curry. (186~)

Death Hollow: (Garfield Co.) Dixie National Forest-Box Hollow Wilderness Area-GSCENM-Escalante River. Roger Peak and Escalante maps.

There are two conflicting stories about the naming of Death Hollow. Old-timers tell the first story, and it is the most believable. They say that an early rancher named Death Hollow after some of his livestock fell off a steep section of the Boulder Mail Trail as they descended into the canyon.

The second story claims that Death Hollow was named for Washington Phipps. He was killed by John Bowington on the Escalante River below Death Hollow. (See Phipps Wash.)

—Boulder Mail Trail: (See Appendix Two—Boulder Mail Trail.)

Lenora LeFevre told of an adventure rancher John King had in 1905 while following the section of the Boulder Mail Trail that crosses Death Hollow: "Storms of sleet and rain had frozen on the trail leaving it a glare of ice. On the edge of the precipice John decided to walk and lead his horse. On the way down the slick narrow canyon trail both feet slipped from under him and off he went over the edge, hanging for dear life to the bridle reins which fortunately were new and strong. Clinching the wall of the chasm with his legs John gradually pulled himself up and over the sandstone to the trail while his horse stood braced against the pull. John promptly mounted his saddle horse and rode on down the steep trail refusing to think of what might have happened." (1168~, 2052~)

George C. Fraser rode the trail in 1922 and wrote about the section dropping into Death Hollow from the east: "The descent from the rim to the Canyon bottom, 750 ft., all over bare rock, with only a small portion of the trail made.... The stream in the bottom of the hollow is beautifully clean, and contains fish, but it is well-nigh undrinkable, on account of the salt." (670~)

—Constructed Stock Trail: This trail, now nearly impossible to find, enters the Right Fork of Death Hollow on its east side one mile southwest of elevation 7933 on the Roger Peak map. There is a sheepers' wing fence at the top of the cliff at the start of the trail. (SAPE.)

—Moonshadow Canyon: The mouth of this western tributary of Death Hollow is one and one-quarter miles (as the crow flies) downcanyon from Sulphur Spring (one-half mile north of elevation 6795 on the Escalante map). It was named for canyon hiker Joe Breddan. He is renowned for his love of moonlit hikes on the slickrock. Of interest in the upper canyon are two square, hand-dug stock ponds. They were most likely built by early sheepmen. Inscriptions include Glen K. Ormand and Preston Porter, Nov. 30, 1936. (SAPE.)

—Death Hollow Spurter Spring: This interesting spring is in the creek of Death Hollow a short distance upcanyon from the Boulder Mail Trail (immediately north of elevation 6630 on the Escalante map). (See Appendix Two—Boulder Mail Trail.) Harry D. Goode noted that water squirts out of the spring about twenty-eight inches. The spring can be most easily seen in low water. (740~, SAPE.)

—OB/Desert Rose Canyon: The mouth of this western tributary of Death Hollow is three-quarters of a mile upcanyon from its mouth (Escalante map). At the spot the Boulder Mail Trail crosses the canyon is an inscription reading "O'Brian," with the "O" and "B" being particularly pronounced. Writer Theresa Williams later named it for its many desert rose bushes. (SAPE.)

Death Hollow: (Garfield Co.) Dixie National Forest-Escalante Mountains-Antimony Creek. Flossie Knoll and Pollywog Lake maps.

Two name derivations are given.

First, Sonny King: "Death Holler comes off the top into a big old basin and then drops off into some ledges. They said that years ago the weather set in and they had a heavy snow and they lost quite a few horses. The next spring they went up there and saw the carcasses of the horses. That was a little after the turn of the century." (1095~)

Second, Dunk Taylor: "I heard that there was a man died there." (1865~) The name was in place by the early 1880s. (1096~)

—Death Hollow Reservoir: (Flossie Knoll map.) Dunk told a story about the reservoir: "That's a place where the pond can be dry and you wake up the next morning and you'll be up to your knees in water if you camp down close to the reservoir. When I'd pull the sheep wagon in there for the sheepherder, I'd leave it up away from the reservoir a bit. Two or so years ago, somebody pulled the sheep wagon right down by the reservoir so he wouldn't have far to lead his horse to water. The next morning his wagon was sittin' in water. That pond collects water from an awful lot of country around there." (1865~)

Death Hollow: (Garfield Co.) GSCENM-Circle Cliffs Basin-Escalante River. Pioneer Mesa, Silver Falls Bench, and Red Breaks maps.

Also called Death Hollow Creek (181~) and Micro Death Hollow (653~).

To differentiate this canyon from the Death Hollow in the upper Escalante, this is most commonly called Little Death Hollow.

—Upper Horse Canyon Trail: This constructed stock trail provides access from the mouth of Little Death Hollow onto Big Bown Bench. The trail starts at the junction of Death Hollow and Horse Canyon and is easy to follow.

An earlier routing of this trail started one-quarter mile below the Death Hollow-Horse Canyon confluence and exited near elevation 5410 on the Red Breaks map. This trail is hard to locate and follow. (SAPE.)

—Pump House: A pump house at the mouth of the canyon contains an old engine and water pump. Several miles of black hose follow the course of the Upper Horse Canyon Trail and go to a couple of watering troughs at the top of the cliff and for a couple of miles beyond. This was built in the 1960s. (1168~) There was a proposal to repair this water project and again graze cattle on Big Bown Bench in 2010.

Death Hollow: (Iron Co.) Kanarra Mountain-Crystal Creek. Cedar Mountain map. PRIVATE PROPERTY.

Warren Pendelton noted that a herd of cattle was poisoned by larkspur here. (1515~)

Death Point: (Washington Co.) Zion National Park-La Verkin Creek. Kolob Arch map. (7,570')

Lucy I. Isom: "One mild winter they [the local cattle cooperative] decided to leave the cattle on the [Kolob] mountain all winter. However, heavy snow fell in January and hundreds of cattle piled up in sheltered spots and on a point and died from starvation. The point is still known as 'Death Point.'" (363~)

Frank Jensen in 1966: "You must have a burning desire to explore the Kolob to take the ride to Death Point.... The view ... however, is magnificent and worth the effort it takes to get there." (966~)

Death Ridge: (Garfield Co.) GSCENM-Kaiparowits Plateau. Death Ridge map. (7,956')

Don Coleman: "One year some cattle got down in there from Lonesome Pine Flat and when they went to get 'em it had snowed a lot and they found a lot of 'em dead. So they call it Death Ridge." (441~)

Death Valley: (San Juan Co.) Wilson Mesa-Navajo Canyon. Alcove Canyon map.

Carl Mahon noted that Erwin Oliver, or his father, Harrison, named this after a bunch of their cattle died there. (1272~)

Erwin Oliver: "That is pretty complicated country down there. There are some rocks that the cattle can't get around. One time they got down in there and there was no water and they couldn't get out, so a lot of them died." (1479~)

Death Valley Draw: (Kane Co.) GSCENM-Hackberry Canyon. Slickrock Bench map.

—Constructed Stock Trail: The lower part of Death Valley Draw is not passable by livestock. To circumvent this area a stock trail leaves the draw on its west side, one-quarter mile east of elevation 6368, and enters the west side of Hackberry Canyon one-quarter mile below the confluence. (SAPE.)

Decker Cove: (San Juan Co.) Black Mesa-Cottonwood Wash. No-Mans Island map.

—Decker Ranch: PRIVATE PROPERTY. This is on the southeast side of Decker Cove and on the east side of Cottonwood Wash (one-quarter mile north of elevation 4657T). Karl Barton noted that the Decker family from Bluff headquartered their ranching operations in Decker Cove. (162~, 1250~) James Bean Decker (1853-1901) was a Bluff pioneer. Albert R. Lyman: "Though he was a cow-man, sheep-man, farmer, and freighter; though he engaged in manual labor on the ditch and in his splendid orchards; and though he acted as one of the Board of Directors of San Juan Co-op, and figured as a valuable diplomat in dealing with the Indians, was yet the greatest choir leader and Sunday School Superintendent within fifty miles." (1240~)

DD Hollow: (Garfield Co.) Graveyard Hollow-Sevier River. Hatch and Panguitch maps.

Correctly spelled Deady Hollow.

Also spelled Deede Hollow and Deedy Hollow. (1931~)

DD Hollow and Graveyard Hollow are the same.

Two name derivations are given.

First, unattributed: "derived its name from Jerry Deady who homesteaded lands in the mouth of this hollow at the south end of Panguitch Valley." (1346~, 2053~)

Second, Ray Tebbs, who used to own a part of the hollow: "DD Hollow is named after a man who used to own some land in that vicinity. It is the first two initials of his name." (1931~)

Dee Pass: (Grand Co.) Tenmile Country-Salt Wash. Dee Pass map. (4,440')

Gene Dunham noted that two men, one named Dee (last or first name?) started a boys' camp in a wash near the pass in the early 1950s. It was called Camp Rustic. They built some rock-walled buildings and some boys did come out, but the camp was not a success. (580~) The remnants of the camp still exist. (SAPE.)

Deep Canyon: (San Juan Co.) Navajo Indian Reservation-San Juan River. Deep Canyon South and Deep Canyon North maps.

Also called Bisha Canyon, Breakneck Canyon, Deza Canyon, and Spring Canyon. (221~, 739~, 975~, 1021~, 1308~)

Deep Creek: (Garfield Co.) Dixie National Forest-Boulder Mountain-Pine Creek. Posy Lake map.

Edson Alvey noted that the creek is in a deep canyon. (55~) Inscriptions include R. Griffin, Sept. 24, 1915. (SAPE.)

—Constructed Stock Trail: This goes down Deep Creek to Pine Creek. (SAPE.)

—Deep Creek Spring #2: This is a large, developed spring. (740~, SAPE.)

Deep Creek: (Garfield Co.) Dixie National Forest-Sevier Plateau-Pine Creek. Mount Dutton and Deep Creek maps.

Kent Whittaker: "It's a deep canyon. Up in the head of the canyon is a real heavy forest. It is a good place to get lost." (2002~)

Albert Delong in 1941: "It is a rough rocky and very deep creek.... It was so named because of the deep rough ledges that border the creek." (2053~)

Deep Creek: (Washington Co.) Zion National Park-North Fork Virgin River. Webster Flat, Cogswell Point, and Temple of Sinawava maps.

Locals called this Crystal Creek or Clear Creek. (1957~)

Deep Creek: (Wayne Co.) Capitol Reef National Park-Waterpocket Fold-Fremont River. Flat Top, Cathedral Mountain, Fruita NW, and Fruita maps.

Don Orton in 1941: "So named for the depth of the stream." (2053~)

—Tunnel Canyon: This is a short northern tributary of a longer unnamed canyon that drops into Deep Creek from the west. Its mouth is one and one-half miles south-southwest of Jailhouse Rock (immediately south of elevation 6063T on the Fruita NW map). A natural bridge, or tunnel, is in the lower part of the canyon. (745~)

—Water Canyon: The mouth of this western tributary of Deep Creek is one and one-half miles northwest of The Notch (at elevation 5459AT on the Fruita map). Guy Pace named the canyon, which is still used for cattle grazing. The canyon has a small spring near its lower end and a large pond, accessible by a short constructed stock trail, in its middle reaches. (1497~, SAPE.)

—Reservoir Canyon: The mouth of this western tributary of Deep Creek is one mile west-northwest of The Notch (at elevation 5513AT on the Fruita map). A stock reservoir at the mouth of the canyon was built by the BLM in 1967. (582~, 745~, 1497~)

—Deep Creek Cabins: These historic cabins were on the south side of the Fremont River (and south of today's Highway 24) opposite the mouth of Deep Creek (one-quarter mile north of elevation 5209T on the Fruita map). All that is left is a long rock wall and a chimney. (SAPE.)

—Short Canyon: This short southern tributary of the Fremont River is southwest of Deep Creek Cabins. It is the second small drainage west of elevation 5209T on the Fruita map. It was named by former Capitol Reef National Park Ranger Fred Goodsell. (745~)

Deep Lake: (Sevier Co.) Fishlake National Forest-Sevier Plateau. Water Creek Canyon map.

Irvin Warnock noted that this is also called Mecham Reservoir. Pioneer Samuel Alvarus Mecham moved to the area in 1883. (1971~)

Deer Creek: (Emery Co.) Wasatch Plateau-Huntington Creek. Red Point and Hiawatha maps.

Mary Guymon: "Frank Woodard of Fountain Green killed a deer there." (384~)

Deer Creek: (Garfield Co.) Dixie National Forest-GS-CENM-Boulder Creek. Deer Creek Lake, Boulder Town, Steep Creek Bench, and King Bench maps.

Unattributed: "Favorite grazing grounds for deer." (1346~)

—Constructed Stock Trails: A couple of constructed stock trails exit lower Deer Creek. The first is three-quarters of a mile (as the crow flies) upcanyon from its junction with Boulder Creek (one-eighth mile southwest of elevation 5520 on the King Bench map) and exits to the east. The second is two and one-half miles (as the crow flies) upcanyon and also exits to the east (three-quarters of a mile west of elevation 6157 on the King Bench map). (SAPE.)

Deer Creek: (Garfield Co.) Dixie National Forest-Sevier Plateau-East Fork Sevier River. Mount Dutton, Adams Head, Cow Creek, Deep Creek, and Antimony maps.

Scott Robinson in 1942: "It was so named because there are so many deer found along this creek and in this vicinity." (2053~)

Deer Creek: (Piute Co.) Fishlake National Forest-Tushar Mountains-Sevier River. Mount Brigham and Marysvale Canyon maps.

Annie C. Kimball: "Pioneers found plenty of deer here." (384~)

Abe McIntosh in 1941: "a small creek running from the mountains to a small flat where deer feed and drink especially in winter months." (2053~)

—Butler and Beck Mine: This gold mine is on Deer Creek one and one-half miles downcanyon from Spring Gulch (near elevation 8228 on the Mount Brigham map). It was discovered by John L. Butler and David Giles in 1889. Later, a share of the mine was sold to John Beck. (1934~)

—Pioneer Road: The road up Deer Creek to Spring Gulch was built in 1896. (1934~)

—Pittsburg Town: This small, short-lived settlement was at the mouth of Deer Creek. (M.68.)

Deer Creek: (San Juan Co.) La Sal Mountains-La Sal Creek. La Sal East map.

Frank Silvey noted that the creek was named by the first settlers, the Thomas Ray family. They arrived in 1877. (1741~, 536~)

Silvey told this story: "The older Indians saw 'the handwriting on the wall' and knew that they were going to lose southeastern Utah to the Whites so decided to kill all deer possible for the hides then drive the balance as far as possible towards their reservation. This they did that summer and the summer of 1883–84. The summer of 1882, the old-timers estimated they killed over three thousand deer for their hides in the La Sal Mountains." (1739~)

Deer Creek Canyon: (Kane Co.) GSCENM-Paria River. Deer Range Point and Bull Valley Gorge maps.

Also called Chua (Snake) Canyon (1931~) and Deer Creek (765~).

Inscriptions include Loran Pollock, June 4, 1929 and Clyde Johnson, June 1, 1930. Inscriptions a short distance up the Paria River from the mouth of Deer Creek Canyon include G.W. Johnson, July 10, 1887; W.E. Hall, 1894; and B.S. Thompson, April 18, 1897. (SAPE.)

Deer Creek Canyon: (Sevier Co.) Fishlake National Forest-Pavant Range-Cottonwood Creek. White Pine Peak map.

Joseph pioneer William Shelton: "Named Deer Creek because the deer were plentiful and the old prospectors used to hunt them for meat while prospecting and digging." (2053~)

Deer Flat: (San Juan Co.) Dark Canyon Plateau-White Canyon. Moss Back Butte and The Cheesebox maps.

Sandy Johnson: "When my dad first come to this country, there were no deer. And then back in about the middle [19]'50s, early '60s, Deer Flat was covered with deer. You could go down there and you could see thousands of head of deer. But in the early days old Al Scorup used to buy the cowboys bullets for 'em to go down and shoot them deer. There were just too many and they were takin' all of the cattle graze." (1002~)

Erwin Oliver: "When I was there, there was thousands of deer. I went out there one morning the last of October when the deer was ruttin'. I was riding over from The Hideout and just as I could see the whole flat I went 'ho-ho-ho Buckskin Bill!' It looked like the whole flat just jumped up and ran. I'll bet there was a thousand deer on there if there was a deer." (1479~)

—Hideout No. 1 Mine: This uranium mine is on the east side of Deer Flat at the "Mine Shaft" (one-quarter mile southwest of elevation 7446T on The Cheesebox map). It was located by J. Wiley Redd of Blanding in 1948. (1872~)

—W.N. Mine: This uranium mine is on the southwest end of Deer Flat at the prow formed by the two forks of K and L Canyon (one-half mile east-southeast of elevation 6170T on The Cheesebox map). It was located by Seth and Lee Shumway of Blanding in 1950. (1872~)

—Hurst Farm: PRIVATE PROPERTY. In 1946 the Hurst family of Blanding started a small dryland farm on the flats. (1936~)

Deer Heaven: (Garfield Co.) Henry Mountains-Cottonwood Creek. Dry Lakes Peak map.

Guy Robison: "The Steele boys called it Deer Haven.... They run onto a lot of deer up there, pretty near any time. So they just called it Deer Haven." (1644~) Alvin Robison: "It was a pretty good Deer Heaven out there in the old days. There was a lot of deer and it's a beautiful place. They done a lot of work on that old trail to git in there, because there's a lot of lava rocks." (1642~)

Deer Range: (Kane Co.) GSCENM-Paria River. Bull Valley Gorge and Deer Range Point maps.

Cal Johnson and Elden Brinkerhoff: "So named because of the large number of deer that ranged there during the summer months." (1931~)

—Riggs Seep: This is at the north edge of Deer Range (immediately south of elevation 6492 on the Bull Valley Gorge map). (766~)

Deer Spring Wash: (Kane Co.) GSCENM-Park Wash. Deer Spring Point and Nephi Point maps.
Also called Deer Springs Canyon. (765~)

In 1932 Julian H. Steward noted this as Wildcat Cañon on his map. (1831~) Alex Findlay in 1942: "Because of the frequency of deer at this spring as a watering place, the spring was so named and the creek took the same name." (2053~)

Deer Trail Mountain: (Piute Co.) Fishlake National Forest-Tushar Mountains. Mount Brigham map. (10,972')

—Deer Trail Mine: PRIVATE PROPERTY. This was the best producer of metals, including gold and silver, in the Marysville area. It was discovered in 1878 by Joseph Smith while he was hunting deer. It was mined intermittently until recently. (332~, 1194~)

—Close In Mine: This alunite mine is one mile northeast of Deer Trail Mine. It was run by Max Krotki in the 19teens. (333~)

Deertrap Mountain: (Washington Co.) Zion National Park-Zion Canyon. Springdale East map. (6,920')
Also spelled Deer Trap Mountain.

This long, thin peninsula was an excellent place to trap deer as it would only take one or two people to guard the "neck" of the mountain. (2053~) Julius V. Madsen in the late 1920s: "In days past, local stockmen came here to hunt deer. By guarding this most narrow strip, the deer were trapped out on the point. It was an easy matter for a hunter or two to kill as many of the animals as might be wanted." (1267~)

Unattributed in 1935: "This is a long promontory extending far out into the canyon from which the finest views of Zion Canyon and Clear Creek Canyon, through which the Zion-Mount Carmel Highway runs, may be had." (2080~)

De Gaulle and his Troops: (San Juan Co.) Valley of the Gods-Lime Creek. Cigarette Spring Cave map.
Also called North Tower. (160a~)

Caricatures of Charles de Gaulle, a French general during World War Two and the President of France from 1958 to 1969, often showed him with a large head and a thin neck. The pinnacle on the south side of the formation has a large block of sandstone standing on a thin pedestal, certainly making it look like de Gaulle if one has a good imagination. (SAPE.)

Delano Peak: (Beaver and Piute Counties.) Fishlake National Forest-Tushar Mountains. Delano Peak map. (12,173')

This is the highest summit in the Tushar Mountains and in both Beaver and Piute counties; its summit is right on the county line. Columbus Delano was President Ulysses S. Grant's Secretary of the Interior from 1870 to 1875. (1444~) The name was in place by 1878. (1567~)

Delicate Arch: (Grand Co.) Arches National Park-Salt Wash. Big Bend map.

Delicate Arch has been called many different names, including The Bloomers Arch, Chaps, The Old Maid's Bloomers, Pant's Crotch, and The Schoolmarm's Pants. (278~, 1977~, 2056~)

Robert H. Vreeland: "There is a story, and it seems to have some foundation, that the National Park Service had intended to label this Landscape Arch because of the view through and beyond it. However, as the story goes, two of the signs became mixed and this arch ended up with the sign 'Delicate Arch.'" (1949~)

An article in a 1909 *Improvement Era Magazine* called it the "Phenomenon in Southern Utah." (60~)

Frank Beckwith of the Arches National Monument Scientific Expedition of 1933-34 is credited with naming the arch. (190~)

Wayne R. McConkie in 1937: "Just across the canyon to the east on the rim of Salt Wash is found the Delicate Arch, the predecessor of all the triumphal arches. This wonder stands alone overlooking the abysmal depth of the canyon below. It rises to an unbelievable height, appearing as only a slim spire when viewed from the side, but from the front one can easily see that it took no fantastic flight of imagination for the cowboys of that range to give it their name of 'The Chaps.'" (1856~)

Catherine Freeman in 1948: "Rising from the sandstone ridge it looks like a giant handle by which the bowl might conceivably be lifted. Soft salmon-pink against a bright blue sky, the arch forms an exquisite frame for the snowy 13,000 foot La Sal Mountains to the south." (676~)

Dick Wilson in 1968: "Delicate is probably the world's most famous and most photographed arch." (2019~)

Donna L. Poulton in 2009: "Delicate Arch is to Utah what the Golden Gate Bridge is to California and the Empire State Building is to New York: it is the symbol by which Utah is recognized as a state." (1559~)

In an atrociously bold proposal in the 1990s, the BLM tried to have oil drill rigs erected so they would be visible through Delicate Arch. Luckily, sane residents beat back the initiative.

Dell Lott Hollow: (Sevier Co.) Fishlake National Forest-Pavant Range-Sevier River. Marysvale Canyon and Antelope Range maps.

Annie C. Kimball: "A group of men were hauling wood from this canyon when Dell Lott's team ran away and wrecked his outfit. This was in 1880." (384~)

Dell Seep: (Wayne Co.) Burr Desert-Poison Spring Canyon. Baking Skillet Knoll map.

Dennis Burdell "Dell" Mecham (1882-1951) ran sheep in the area. Alvin Robison: "He'd leave grain or oats and groceries there for the sheepherders." (1642~)

—Stock Reservoir: A small concrete dam above the seep was built by the BLM in the mid-1940s. (604~, 623~, 1551~)

Delong Creek: (Garfield and Iron Counties.) Dixie National Forest-Threemile Creek. Fivemile Ridge map.

Scott Robinson in 1941: "Named for a Delong family who had a cattle ranch." (2053~) Albert DeLong (1841–1910) was a Panguitch pioneer. He had a ranch on Mammoth Creek and grazed livestock in the area. (363~)

Delores Point: (Grand Co.) La Sal Mountains-South Beaver Mesa. Dolores Point South and Dolores Point North maps.

Correctly spelled Dolores Point.

(See Dolores Point.)

De Mille Peak: (Washington Co.) Vermilion Cliffs-South Mountain. Springdale East map. (6,696')

Also spelled DeMill Peak. (1182~)

Angus M. Woodbury noted that Oliver DeMille (1830–1908) arrived in Shunesburg in 1862. He stayed there for forty-one years, then moved to nearby Rockville. (932~, 2043~)

Oliver Demille's second wife, Fedelia, told this story, which happened while she was living in Shunesburg under DeMille Peak: "In the year 1885 ... the federal officers were after the polygamists.... This frightened my husband, Oliver, very much.... He came home one day and said, 'Fidelia, if these federal officers come here and find two women on this place, they will sure get me.' He told me to get a few things together and he would take me up the canyon and I could stay there until the scare was over. My baby was only eleven days old. He took us up the [Parunuweap] canyon where we camped out. All the shelter we had was a large rock which extended out like a roof. I had my [seven] children with me. After dumping us in this forsaken spot, he then went home and left us to the mercy of the wilds. This being on the fifteenth of February, the weather was yet quite cool. We stayed there, making our bed down on the ground. In the morning we could see the tracks of wild animals all around our beds.... We remained there until the federal scare had quieted down." (1182~)

—First Ascent: Members of the Jesse N. Smith Expedition of 1858 were perhaps the first Euroamericans to ascend the mountain. Certainly they were the first on South Mountain. (469~)

Denmark Wash: (Millard and Sevier Counties.) Pavant Range-Sevier Valley-Sevier River. Beehive Peak and Aurora maps.

Irvin Warnock noted that a large group of Danish families moved to Central in 1881, giving the southwest corner of town the name Little Denmark or Danish Town. The name Denmark Wash reflects the Danish influence in the area. (1970~)

Dennehotso: (Apache Co., Az.) Navajo Indian Reservation-Laguna Creek. Dennehotso, Az. map.

Also spelled Dinehotso.

Two similar name derivations are given.

First, Walter Kennedy noted that *Dennehotso* is Navajo for "'end of a green valley,' because the area used to be under water and was a big lake." (1520~)

Second, *Dennehotso* is Navajo for "where the short grass comes out from the canyon." (1931~)

—Movies: *Stagecoach*, *My Darling Clementine*, and *She Wore a Yellow Ribbon* were filmed, in part, near Dennehotso. (1520~)

—Dennehotso Canyon: (Also called Sahotsoidbeazhe Canyon.) (769~)

—Dennehotso Trading Post: Nancy Peake: "The very existence of ... a trading post, at Dennehotso happened by accident. According to [Walter] Kennedy, a certain Charley Ashcroft 'went broke out at Mexican Water Trading Post ... in about 1923 ... and he was left with no place to go.' So he decided to build another store out in this area so he got Perry Smook and Dutch Taft ... to take a load of building material somewhere further out. They passed Mexican Water, kept on going and about 18 miles across solid rock and sand they got stuck. They were in the Dennehotso area.... Charley said this is close enough.... There was a small spring there.... And that is where Dennehotso stands today." (1520~)

The Dennehotso Post was purchased by Roscoe and Jewel McGee in 1948. Walter Kennedy became the manager. He bought out the McGees in 1953 and ran the post until 1981. Phil Foutz then took over.

Dennett Canyon: (Washington Co.) Zion National Park-East Fork Virgin River. Springdale East map.

Two name derivations are given.

First, John Fabin Bennett (1853-1933) was an early settler of nearby Rockville, arriving before 1870. He started farming in Zion Canyon in 1875 and ran livestock in the area in the early 1900s. (462~, 485~, 1931~, 2043~)

Second, Dave Dennett was an early settler and was the first guide in Zion National Park. He was killed in an accident in 1929. (1931~)

Dennis Cemetery: (Piute Co.) Sevier River-Thompsonville-Highway 89. Marysvale map.

William Taylor Dennis (1810-1894) and his wife, Ann Fullmer (1841-1899), arrived in Marysvale in 1869. They had a ranch near here. (1444~)

Denver and Rio Grande Western Railroad: (Carbon, Emery, and Grand Counties.) Grand Valley-Cisco Desert-Interstate 70-Highway 191. Maps east to west: Westwater, Agate, Cisco, White House, Sagers Flat, Thompson Springs, Crescent Junction, Hatch Mesa, Green River NE, Green River, Jessies Twist, Desert, Cliff, Woodside, Grassy, Cedar, Mounds, Olsen Reservoir, Wellington, and Price.

—Old Railroad Grade: (Grand and Emery Counties.) Maps east to west: Bitter Creek Well, Harley Dome, Agate, Cisco, White House, Sagers Flat, Thompson Springs, Crescent Junction, Hatch Mesa, Green River NE, Green River, Jessies Twist, Desert, Mexican Mountain, Dry Mesa, Chimney Rock, Bob Hill Knoll, and Buckhorn Reservoir.

The railroad from Grand Junction to Price was a part of the Denver and Rio Grande system and was called the Rio Grande Western. The initial route of the railroad was going to be from Grand Junction, through Green River, up the east side of the northern San Rafael Reef along Cottonwood Wash, then under the south end of Cedar Mountain (parallel to today's Green River Cutoff Road) to the Buckhorn Flat area. There it was to divide; one route going north to Ogden, the other going south to Utah's Dixie and beyond. To that end, construction was started and a railbed was built from Grand Junction to Buckhorn Flat. During construction, though, it was decided that a different route should be used. The new route was the same to Green River, but it then went straight up to Woodside, along the Price River to Wellington, and on to Price.

Construction of the tracks was started in 1881 and finished in 1883. The original tracks were narrow gauge. Because the narrow gauge cars could not be used on standard gauge tracks, the tracks were replaced in 1890. In many places the old narrow gauge railbed had to be abandoned and a whole new bed had to be built. (379~, 641~, 710~, 727~)

On the maps one sees the final standard gauge alignment marked as the Denver and Rio Grande Western Railroad, while the abandoned narrow gauge railbed is shown as the Old Railroad Grade. When the narrow-gauge tracks were abandoned, the steel was salvaged, but the creosote-soaked ties, now too short for the standard gauge, were left on the ground. Ranchers were quick to use this rot-proof lumber in constructing fences, outbuilding, and even cabins and line shacks.

Desbrough Canyon: (Carbon and Duchesne Counties.) Badland Cliffs-Nine Mile Canyon. Cowboy Bench and Pinnacle Canyon maps.

A man named Desbrough, and his family, homesteaded in Nine Mile Canyon in the early days. They were only there for a short while. (558~)

Desert: (Emery Co.) Book Cliffs-Highway 191-Denver and Rio Grande Western Railroad. Desert map.

Also called Desert Siding (1931~), Desert Station (1903~), and Desert Switch.

This was the site of the joining of two Denver and Rio Grande Western Railroad construction crews, one coming from the north, the other from the east in March 1883. (834~) The siding was used in the mid-1880s. Lloyd M. Pierson: "A bunk house, section house and a well for engine water were located here." (1547~)

Unattributed: "Desert is appropriate, and not to be contradicted." (606~) (See Denver and Rio Grande Western Railroad.)

Desert Lake: (Emery Co.) Castle Valley-Desert Lake Waterfowl Management Area. Cleveland and Elmo maps.

W.H. Lever in 1896: "Desert Lake, as the name implies, is a veritable lake, forming an oasis in the desert." (1196~)

Mary Henderson Richens: "a reservoir fed by the high water of Huntington Creek and flood waters off Washboard Flats. Alkali from the Cleveland area drains into the lake making the water unfit for human consumption." (2053~)

—Desert Lake Town: Hans P. Marsing, Samuel Wells, and Charley Winders were the first to come to the area, in 1885. In 1888 the town was established by the Thomas Wells family. The town was on a small natural lake that was enhanced by the building of a dam in the early 1890s. It was abandoned by 1910 because of alkaline soil and a broken dam. The town moved essentially en masse to the town of Victor, which is six miles east of Elmo. (346~, 1155~, 1330~) (See Victor Town.)

Desert Mound: (Iron Co.) Neck of the Desert-Swett Peak. Desert Mound map.

Desert Mound became a part of the Iron Mountain mining district in 1871. It is now the site of a defunct open pit iron mine. (469~, SAPE.) (See Iron Mountain.)

Desert Seep Wash: (Emery Co.) Cedar Mountain-Price River. Cleveland, Cow Flats, and Olsen Reservoir maps. Also called Seep Wash. (1233~, 1931~)

Desha Canyon: (San Juan Co.) Navajo Indian Reservation-San Juan River. Navajo Begay and Wilson Creek maps.

Also called Bisha, Cornfield Canyon, and Desha Creek.

Also spelled Descha Canyon, Desh Canyon, and Deshni Canyon. (57~, 1202~, 1204~, 1954~)

Two name derivations are given.

First, *Desha* is Navajo for "curved." (769~) The name was suggested by Herbert E. Gregory in 1915. (1931~)

Second, Stephen C. Jett noted that *Deeshnih Bikooh* in Navajo for "To be Moving the Arm—or hardworking—Canyon." The name refers to a former hardworking resident of the canyon. (975~)

Charles L. Bernheimer in 1925: "We traveled down Desha among exquisite scenery, particularly the lower part of the canyon was of majestic and appalling character." (218~)

—Beverly Arch: This is three-quarters of a mile southeast of the mouth of Desha Canyon (near elevation 4490T on the Wilson Creek map). Beverly Emerton was a hiking companion of Stan and Alice Jones. (1020~)

—Syncline Rapid: Now underwater, this was on the San Juan River just below the mouth of Desha Canyon. C. Gregory Crampton: "The name probably comes from the 'Rapid Syncline' which crosses the San Juan Canyon at this point." (472~) P.W. Tomkins on a Norm Nevills River trip in 1940: "It is a toughy. There's a heavy drag to the right hand wall so it has to be handled very carefully." (1897~)

Desolation Canyon: (Carbon, Emery, Grand, and Uintah Counties.) Tavaputs Plateau-Green River. Maps north to south: Duches Hole, Nutters Hole, Firewater Canyon North, Cedar Ridge Canyon, Steer Ridge Canyon, Chandler Falls, and Three Fords Canyon.

Also called Canyon of Desolation and Green River Wilderness.

The Desolation Canyon section of the Green River starts at the mouth of Sand Wash and ends about sixty-one miles later at Three Fords Canyon. Today, the name "Desolation Canyon" often refers to the combined stretches of Desolation and Gray canyons.

Desolation and Gray canyons were listed on the National Register of Historic Places in 1968 under the name Desolation Canyon.

William Henry Ashley and a party of fur trappers were the first Euroamericans to penetrate Desolation Canyon.

Starting near Green River, Wyoming, the group ran the Green River in small boats into the upper part of Desolation Canyon, exiting near Nine Mile Creek. (74~, 805~) (See Nine Mile Creek for important information.) Ashley: "The country below so far as I descended is entirely mountains of rock destitute of timber (except in places on the border of the river) grass or game, although I was notified that game could not be had in it I expected to find as I had every day in descending the river found geese sufficient for our subsistence." (74~)

The first explorers known to have floated the Green River through Desolation and Gray canyons were members of the William Manly Expedition of 1849. (1150~) Manly: "The rapids were still dangerous in many places, but not so frequent nor so bad as the part we had gone over, and we could see that the river gradually grew smoother as we progressed.... The mountains and hills on each side were barren and of a pale yellow cast, with no chance for us to climb up and take a look to see if there were any chances for us further along.... But these mountains soon came to an end, and there were some cottonwood and willows on the bank of the river, which was now so smooth we could ride along without the continual loading and unloading we had been forced to practice for so long. We had begun to get a little desperate at the lack of game, but the new valley [Gunnison Valley], which grew wider all the time, gave us hope again, if it was quite barren everywhere except back of the willow trees." (1274~)

John Wesley Powell initially called the whole stretch, from the White River through what is now Desolation Canyon, Terrace Canyon. (1023~) Powell: "After dinner we pass through a region of the wildest desolation. The canyon is very tortuous, the river very rapid, and many lateral canyons enter on either side. These usually have their branches, so that the region is cut into a wilderness of gray and brown cliffs.... Piles of broken rock lie against these walls; crags and tower-shaped peaks are seen everywhere, and away above them, long lines of broken cliffs; and above and beyond the cliffs are pine forests, of which we obtain occasional glimpses as we look up through a vista of rocks. The walls are almost without vegetation; a few dwarf bushes are seen here and there, clinging to the rocks, and cedars grow from the crevices— not like the cedars of a land refreshed with rains, great cones bedecked with spray, but ugly clumps, like clubs, beset with spines. We are minded to call this the Canyon of Desolation." (1566~)

Jack C. Sumner of the 1869 Powell Expedition: "Country worthless, though imposing, as there is some fine timber growing on the tops of the mountains." (1847~)

George Y. Bradley, also of the 1869 expedition, did not describe the canyon, but told this brief story: "A terrible gale of dry hot wind swept our camp and roared through the cañon mingling its sound with the hollow roar of the cataract making music fit for the infernal regions. We needed only a few flashes of lightning to meet Milton's most vivid conceptions of Hell." (270~)

Francis M. Bishop of the 1871–72 Powell Expedition provided two descriptions. First, from his diary: "And desolate it is, seen from the summit. Back from the river there is nothing but rocks and cañons. No living or green thing, but all is desolate, dreary and wild.... The river here cuts through an immense plateau [Tavaputs Plateau] and the ridges are steep, sharp and angular. In many places we saw little pedestals supporting monstrous capitals of sandstone, long stalactic columns with a huge boulder on its crest [now called damoselles], high narrow walls surmounting some dividing ridges with deep ragged gorges on either side.... The hills from the summit where I am writing look dreary and desolate. Desolation, indeed, and a cañon full of it." (236~)

Second, from a letter: "The walls are eroded in every direction by the action of the elements, leaving ridges, spurs, buttressed walls, tall spires with bastioned and fluted bases, deep sinuous gorges, dark gulches, frowning cañons, and moraines that they bring in, forming by far too many rapids for our ease and comfort, yet, for scenic beauty unsurpassed." (236~)

Almon H. Thompson of the 1871–72 Powell Expedition: "Climbed the plateau this forenoon.... Very barren and desolate. Not even sage. Very few cacti. I think it merits the name of 'Desolation.' Imagine the ruggedest gully that can be conceived—in fact a great crack; and you have the cañon. Huge columns 500 feet high. Flanked by pinnacles, sectors of arcs with Gothic Buttresses. Sharp crags with their feet in the river and heads in the clouds." (1877~)

E.O. Beaman of the 1871–72 Powell Expedition: The lower part of Desolation is called Cole's [Beaman probably meant Coal] Cañon.... The country here presented no attractive features, being destitute of vegetation, sandy, and desolate, and we left it behind with little regret." (172~)

George F. Flavell in 1896 called it Usher Canyon: "But the mountains [we have been passing through], though not high, have been far more wonderful in their construction than any yet passed on the trip or, in fact, than any

I have ever had the opportunity to witness. They are one continual string of gashes, sliced up and stood on edge. Domes piled on domes." (649~)

Nathaniel Galloway of the Stone-Galloway Expedition of 1909: "Desolation Canyon is a misnomer for of all the canyons thus far it is certainly one of the most luxuriant in foliage; of plant growth the most varied; and of color the most striking." (702~)

Charles Eggert in 1957: "Desolation Canyon was the dismal abyss, the very end of all things. We had reached the very limit of barren bleakness here.... I felt we were traveling on the River Styx. This canyon seemed to be that eternal place between earth and the hereafter. Here time ticked not, nor a sound heard, nor anything felt, we would travel as lost souls—on and on—until the day of judgement when the gates would be opened and we'd be on our way again.... This [canyon] was the test of loneliness; a place so empty of all things, one could look straight into his soul and see the good and evil and judge for himself in the barrenness where he was worthy of traveling nearer to the place he sought. And this place, along the wilderness river trail, was the right one to find that out." (599~)

—Dynamite: (Proposed.) In 1906 James Edwin Birch ran Desolation and Gray canyons. He was studying the feasability of dynamiting the rapids to make the river navigable for steamships. He wanted to boat Gilsonite from the Uintah Basin to the railroad at Green River, Utah. (79~)

—Interesting idea that didn't need dynamite: In 1911 Fred C. Carstarphen also ran Desolation and Gray canyons, exiting near Rock Creek after wrecking his boat. Carstarphen's plan was to float Gilsonite in steel containers down the river where they would be caught at Green River and loaded onto the railroad. (79~)

—Railroad: (Proposed.) Ed F. Harmston led an expedition down Desolation and Gray canyons in 1913 to survey the river for a railroad line along its banks. (833~)

Determination Towers: (San Juan Co.) Tenmile Country-Mill Canyon. Jug Rock map.

The first known description of the Determination Towers (which include Determination Tower, Aeolian Tower, and Echo Tower) was by members of the H.L.A. Culmer Expedition of 1905: "Within eighteen miles of the main line of the Rio Grande Western railroad, in Grand county, Utah, yet off the regular lines of travel and almost unknown because of their location in the midst of a waste of sand and ragged hills, the Culmer exploring party last spring discovered what H.L.A. Culmer, head of the party, regards as the most remarkable monoliths encountered

on the trip.... Mr. Culmer says the rocks are not named, so far as he has been able to learn, and he says he would welcome suggestions of a name.... 'It must be a name of dignity, to fit the mighty grandeur of these lonely rocks,' says Mr. Culmer. 'I consider them as among the finest things in the state. I would be glad to have someone bestow a suitable name on the rocks.... The name, 'Monoliths of the Desert' has occurred to me, but I think some name more striking, yet not less dignified, might be suggested." (1374a~)

The Determination Towers name was applied by the USGS in 1972. (1930~)

Devil Canyon: (San Juan Co.) Manti-LaSal National Forest-Abajo Mountains-Montezuma Creek. Abajo Peak, Blanding North, Devil Mesa, and Bradford Canyon maps. Also called Canyon Diablo (1030~) and Diablo Vallie (575~).

Laurance D. Linford noted that the Navajo name is *Ch'iidii Bikooh*, or "Evil Spirit Canyon." (1204~)

In 1888 Francis A. Hammond noted this as both Summit Canyon and Devil Canyon. (822~)

A couple of similar name derivations are given.

First, in the early days it was a "devil of a canyon" to cross. (801~) Pete Steele: "Nasty canyon"! (1821~)

Second, before the bridge over the canyon was built, freight wagons would occasionally be caught in flash floods in the canyon. (2056~)

—Pioneer Road: The first road from Bluff to Monticello (before the founding of Blanding) went along the south rim of Devil Canyon to its head, across the top of Verdure Creek, then northeast to Monticello. (1240~) (See Verdure Creek.)

—Harry Hopkins Grave: This well-known landmark is the "Grave" at the head of Devil Canyon on the Abajo Peak map. Val Dalton: "The KT cowboys had a camp there and one summertime [in 1887] they were out on the range. Harry Hopkins was the cook and they left him in camp. When they came back that night he'd been shot and he was dead. There were a bunch of unshod horse tracks all around there and they figured the Utes did it, but nobody knows. They buried him right there." (517~)

—Willard Butt Sawmill: In the early days Willard Butt (1858-1919) ran a sawmill and dairy at the head of Devil Canyon. (1240~)

—Devil Canyon Campground: (Blanding North map.) The campground was dedicated in September 1966.

—Dixie No. 1 Mine: This uranium mine in Devil Canyon is one and one-half miles from Montezuma Creek (one-quarter mile north of elevation 5721T on the Bradford

Canyon map). The largest producer in Devil Canyon, it was staked as the Cloudy Day in 1937 and as the Sunny Day in 1952. The mine ran intermittently until the mid-1950s. (921~)

Devils Canyon: (Emery Co.) San Rafael Swell-South Salt Wash. San Rafael Knob, Copper Globe, and Big Bend Draw maps.

Ray Wareham: "It is just a devil of a place to get in and out of." (1967~)

—Devils Canyon Spring: (Big Bend Draw map.) Wayne Gremel: "There are some old sheep troughs there and just above is where the stock trail goes out. That trail has the nicest rock work you've ever seen.... Whoever laid that rock knew what he was doing. In the 1970s they were still running water into those troughs, but no more." (780~, SAPE.)

Devils Garden: (Garfield Co.) GSCENM-Escalante Desert-Hole-in-the-Rock Road. Seep Flat map.

Also called Devils Rock Garden (1659~) and Garden of the Gods (446~).

In 1875 Almon H. Thompson of the 1871–72 Powell Expedition called this The Goblins. (1877~)

There is no evidence that members of the Hole-in-the-Rock Expedition saw the area, though it is unlikely they missed it as they were looking for every scrap of feed they could find for their livestock.

Escalante school teacher Edson Alvey is credited with naming the area. (2051~) But, perhaps David D. Rust suggested the name in 1928: "Run down the desert to little spring at 20 mile (Last Chance). Visit in little canyon not over ½ mile from road the best little garden of statues and natural bridge—a hawk had his nest and one young bird in top of one so we name it Eagle Garden. Perhaps for devils garden." (1672~)

—Metate Arch and Mano Natural Bridge: These spans, both in Devils Garden, were named by Edson Alvey. Metate Arch has a scooped out top, reminiscent of a grinding surface formed when Indians ground their corn. A mano is the rock used to do the grinding. (55~)

Devils Garden: (Grand Co.) Arches National Park-Salt Wash. Klondike Bluffs and Mollie Hogans maps.

Alexander Ringerhoffer explored the arches in 1923 and named what is today's Klondike Bluffs "Devils Garden." Somewhere along the way, the name was shifted to today's Devils Garden. (456~, 1115~)

Harry Reed, onetime custodian of what was then Arches National Monument, in the late 1930s: "It is distinctly a foot and horseback region. Those who know the area say

it is impossible to get lost in it because you have to come out the way you go in." (1115~)

Buck Lee in 1940: "The Devil's Garden, six miles wide and ten miles long, is a conglomeration of forms, both weird and grotesque. Unbalanced rocks, hundreds of feet high, and weighing thousands of tons, seemingly defying the laws of gravity in their apparent unbalanced positions." (354~)

Oliver R. Smith in 1947: "Looking down from the edge of the surrounding table-land one sees—with a bit of imagination—a pit of fire and brimstone right out of Dante's Inferno. It is as if a thousand ruddy tongues of flame were suddenly turned, like Lot's wife, into pillars of stone." (1783~)

Inscriptions include Denis Julien, 9 6re 1844. This was listed on the National Register of Historic Places in 1988. (See Appendix One—Denis Julien.)

—Elbow Hollow: This drainage goes through Devils Garden. The wash makes an "elbow" turn, from north to west. (55~)

Devils Lane: (San Juan Co.) Canyonlands National Park-Needles District-The Grabens. The Loop, Spanish Bottom, and Cross Canyon maps.

Also called Satans Playground. (1403~)

Pete Steele: "The story is that back in the days of yesteryear, old David Goudelock was really a taskmaster and he would sneak down and spy on the cowboys to see if they were doing their job. And so one time he slipped off down t' the Needles where the cowboys was supposed to be working and he camped at this nice little place in one of these grabens where there was nice grass and feed and there was probably a pothole there that he could get some water out." (1821~)

Kent Frost continued the story: "It was a full moonlit night and during the middle of the nighttime, why he heard the clattering of hooves out there, and looked up out of his sleeping bag, and here was the Devil up on the back of his white mule riding back and forth across the little valley. And he was beatin' the mule with his quirt and he was abeatin' the mule, making him run back and forth, and that went on for a long time. And then the Devil stopped over by a tree and tied up the mule and disappeared. And then all things were quiet and nothin' happened the rest of the night. And this Goudelock was scared to death and so the next morning, he saddled up everything, packed up and got out of there, and went over to the ranch and told them he had seen the Devil that night ... and so they called it Devils Kitchen after that. And so the story goes that Goudelock would never go down in that country again, unless he had a lot of his cowboys with him." (690~)

Devils Monument: (Emery Co.) San Rafael Swell-Saddle Horse Canyon. The Blocks map. (6,784')

Also called Brighams Dink. (1853~)

Lee Mont Swasey: "Because they named everything Devils something"! (1853~) (See Devils Racetrack.)

Devils Pocket: (San Juan Co.) Canyonlands National Park-Needles Section-The Grabens. Druid Arch and The Loop maps.

(See Devils Lane for name derivation.)

W. Robert Moore in 1961: "a pleasant hollow lined with green springtime grass and massed patches of flowering beeweed, yellow as mustard. Above and about us soared sheer cliffs and pinnacled walls." (1381~)

Devils Racetrack: (Emery Co.) San Rafael Swell-North Fork Coal Wash. The Blocks map.

Dee Anne Finken noted that the Devils Racetrack was an established cattle route used by the pioneer Swasey family to take their cattle from Sinbad Country north to the lower Coal Wash country. (641~) Monte Clair Swasey: "I guess the only ones worse than the Swaseys was the devil, and so when they'd find a really bad place, they'd name is something after the devil: Devil's Dance Floor, Devil's Canyon, and Devil's Racetrack." (791~)

Lee Mont Swasey, the son of Monte Clair Swasey: "I always knew it as the North Fork Trail." (1853~) (See North Fork Coal Wash—North Fork Trail.) Swasey went on to note that in the old days only a very narrow two hundred yard part of the trail between the heads of North Fork Coal Wash and Bullock Draw was called the Devils Racetrack. The name has now been applied to the whole trail. (1853~)

Near the head of the trail is an inscription from Ned Swasey, March 8, 1950. He is the great grandson of Joseph Swasey who left his inscription at the bottom of the trail in 1875. (SAPE.)

—Pioneer Road: (See Appendix Two—San Rafael Swell Pioneer Road.)

Devils Slide: (Garfield Co.) Dixie National Forest-Boulder Mountain. Grover map.

Dwight Williams: "I'm not sure, but it is so steep that if you ever started, it would be about like sliding down into Hell." (2013~)

Devils Window: (San Juan Co.) Valley of the Gods-Lime Creek. Mexican Hat map.

The name was recommended to the USGS by ranchers Jim and Emery Hunt in 1986. (1931~)

Dewey Seep: (Kane Co.) Glen Canyon NRA-Gunsight Canyon. Warm Creek Bay map.

This is a small, wash-bottom spring.

A small, nearby overhang was used by cowboys as a line camp. (SAPE.)

Dewey Town: (Grand Co.) Colorado River-Dolores River. Dewey map.

Also called The Mail Ford.

This small town was at the junction of the Colorado and Dolores rivers. It was initially called Kingsferry for Samuel King. He built a ferry here in the 1880s.

Two name derivations are given.

First, Dewey Smith prospected in the area in the 1880s. (375~)

Second, it was named in honor of Admiral George Dewey after the Spanish-American War. (1195~)

—Suspension Bridge: (Also called Dewey Bridge.) This one lane swinging suspension bridge was listed on the National Register of Historic Places in 1984. It was built in 1916. The present concrete bridge was built in 1985 and the old bridge was used as a tourist attraction for several years before it was accidently burned down by a boy playing with matches on April 6, 2008. (1987~)

—Dad's Ice Box: This dugout is on the south side of the Colorado River near the old suspension bridge. Verlyn Westwood noted that her grandfather, Dick Westwood, and family had a farm on the north side of the Colorado River in the early years. Dick also had a ferry here. They would store their perishable foods in the Ice Box, and Dick Westwood would ferry the food back and forth along with his passengers. (1987~)

—Dewey Spring: Verlyn Westwood: "Before they [Dewey] had the spring, the [Westwood] family had drunk the river water and gotten typhoid. The kids were so sick several of them almost died. Then one day Grandpa [Dick] Westwood took a stick of dynamite and went up where there was a little bit of moisture seeping out of the sandstone cliff. He blasted out a spring after all those years. From then on they had all the fresh spring water they could use, and only about a block away." (1987~)

—Cato Ranch: (Also called McCarey Ranch.) This was on the west side of the Colorado River directly opposite the mouth of the Dolores River. Charles Cato (1883-1958) ranched here in the early 1900s. (1979~, 1986~)

—Agate Hill: This is one-quarter mile west of the Cato Ranch (at elevations 4413T and 4500T). Agate is found in profusion here. (1979~) Frank C. Kendrick of the Stanton-Brown Survey in 1889: "At mouth of Delores [sic] we ran into a nice bed of Red Agates." (1838a~)

—Salmon Bend: This is the bend in the river immediately downriver from the Dewey Bridge.

—Dewey Dam Site: (Proposed.) The William R. Chenoweth USGS Expedition of 1921 suggested a dam on the Colorado River three miles downcanyon from Dewey. A ladder still hanging from the cliffs on the west side of the Colorado River (one-quarter mile south of elevation 4386AT) is from the dam site survey. It the river had been dammed here, it would have backed water up t Cisco. (644~, 1146~)

Lewis R. Freeman visited the site in 1922: "The Dewey site, on the Grand [Colorado] below the mouth of the Dolores River, was also a very favorable reservoir and had great power possibilities. It was, however, rather too remote from any considerable markets for present development." (679~) The site was under consideration into the 1940s.

—Constructed Stock Trail: This good trail, a short distance downriver from the ladder, goes from the river to the top of the cliffs. It is assumed that it was built for the dam project. The trail can be seen from Highway 128. An old inscription near the trail is from Tom Williams, no date. (SAPE.)

—Cottonwood Bend: PRIVATE PROPERTY. This bend in the Colorado River is between Dewey and Roberts Mesa. The name is taken from the Cottonwood Bend Ranch.

Dials Knob: (Garfield Co.) Henry Mountains-Coal Bed Mesa. Clay Point map. (5,015')
Correctly spelled Dells Knob.
Guy Robison noted that this was named for Dennis Burdell "Dell" Mecham. (1644~) (See Dell Seep.)

Diamond Canyon: (Grand Co.) Roan Cliffs-Book Cliffs-Cottonwood Canyon. Tenmile Canyon South, Preacher Canyon, and Flume Canyon maps.

—Harms Ranch: PRIVATE PROPERTY. (Also called Cottonwood Ranch. Now called Campbell and Hansmire Sheep Ranch.) This is at the junction of Diamond Creek and Cottonwood Wash (one mile north of elevation BM5213 on the Flume Canyon map). German immigrant Louis Harms and family ranched here from the 1890s into the early 1900s. (388~, 1623~)

Diamond Valley: (Washington Co.) Pine Valley Mountains-Red Mountains. Veyo, Saddle Mountain, and Washington maps.
Correctly spelled Dameron Valley.
Also spelled Damran Valley (704~) and Damron Valley (273~).
Andrew Karl Larson: "Dameron Valley was named for William Wallace Dameron, Sr., [also spelled Damron]

one of Washington's first settlers. Somewhere along the line the name 'Dameron' was corrupted to 'Diamond.'" (1141~) Dameron ran livestock in the area starting in the late 1850s. (160~, 2003~)

Albert E. Miller: "Dameron Valley slightly resembles the shape of a diamond and through misunderstanding in the pronunciation of the correct name has become known as Diamond Valley." (2053~) The Diamond name was used early on. Lorenzo Brown in 1863: "drove to diamond valley & camped part of the night." (305~) Sara Jane Rousseau in 1864: "stopped to water the horses at Diamond Valley Springs." (1773~)

George A. Smith in 1869: "The route [to Pine Valley from St. George] leads through the midst of the cones of several extinct volcanoes, some of which look as if they were but recently blown out. These cones render Diamond Valley an interesting locality for the study of geology and the wonderful power of subterranean fires, and give variety and additional interest to the journey."
(1770~)

Orson Pratt Miles noted that his father, William G. Miles, quarried rocks in Diamond Valley that he later shaped into grindstones and whetstones: "The sandstone lay in horizontal layers at about a 45 degree angle and were loosened up with wedges and bars. After the quarrying ... we hauled it with wagons to the factory ... [near] Veyo." (380~)

—Blake Ranch: This was in Diamond Valley one-half mile west of the Diamond Valley Ranch (Saddle Mountain map). B. Blake started the ranch before 1900. The water from the ranch is now used at Snow Canyon State Park. (1931~)

Dianas Throne: (Kane Co.) White Cliffs-The Sand Hills. Mount Carmel map. (6,284')
Also called Heaton Point. (767~)
This dome marks the southern end of the White Cliffs. It was named by William W. Seegmiller in 1920 for the Goddess of the Hunt. (2053~) Local legend has it that Diana, on finding the view from the top of the monolith overwhelmingly beautiful, and unable to bear that much beauty, threw herself off the top.

Dickinson Hill: (Garfield Co.) Dixie National Forest-South Canyon. Panguitch and Fivemile Ridge maps.
Also called Dickinson Ridge. (1931~)
Correctly spelled Dickenson Hill.
James Dickenson (1828-1896) settled at Santa Clara in the early 1860s. He moved to Panguitch in 1871 and later built a sawmill on the hill. (137~, 1346~, 1445~)

Dicks Canyon: (Washington Co.) Dixie National Forest-Pine Valley Mountains-Quail Creek. Signal Peak and Harrisburg Junction maps.

Lucy I. Isom in 1957: "This is Dick's Canyon, named for an Indian, and around the spot where these two streams joined [Dicks Canyon and Quail Creek], the redmen planted corn and squash before the advent of the white men." (384~)

Dickson Gulch: (San Juan Co.) Manti-LaSal National Forest-Abajo Mountains-South Creek. Abajo Peak map.

Correctly spelled Dixon Gulch. (774~)

Frank Dixon and John Duckett had gold mining claims in nearby upper Cooley Gulch in 1892. (1115~, 1407~, 1526~)

Dike, The: (Emery Co.) San Rafael Swell-Muddy Creek. Ireland Mesa, Tomsich Butte, and Copper Globe maps.

—Deweys Arch: Wayne Gremel: "There is an arch out there on The Dike that they call Deweys Arch. That is named for [rancher] Dewey Jensen [1918-1991]." (780~)

Dike Spring: (Emery Co.) San Rafael Swell-Cat Canyon. Big Bend Draw map.

Wayne Gremel noted that there were troughs at the spring: "Used to run quite a little water. It's not real good water." (780~)

Dilly Canyon: (Emery Co.) Roan Cliffs-Range Canyon. Lighthouse Canyon map.

Also spelled Dilley Canyon.

Waldo Wilcox: "Tom Dilly [1864–1900] was an old outlaw who lived there. He came here from Texas. They say that he killed a man over a woman in Texas and he headed north and wound up over here on the west side [of the Green River at Dilly Canyon].... He was a real smooth talker. Probably a real educated man. He went up to Salt Lake and talked some money men into putting up the money to buy Florence Creek [the McPherson Ranch] and then Dilly was going to run the ranch. He told my granddad, Jim McPherson, that he had to go to Thompson and meet the money man and then they'd come back and buy the Florence Creek Ranch. He was gone about a week. When he got back he was alone. He said the guy never showed up. But he paid Granddad McPherson off in gold. After that, they got checking, and the money guy had come to Thompson. Then they left Thompson together. When they built that road up to the Sego Mine [in Sego Canyon north of Thompson Springs], they found the body of that guy. Dilly had shot him and took his money. "I guess he was real cold. Murder was nothing to him. He left there [the McPherson Ranch] and worked for these doctors who had a big ranch up at Patmos Head [in the

Book Cliffs]. He convinced them that they ought to sell the old cows that they had and buy good Hereford cows. So he took a train load of cows back to St. Louis. He wired them and told them that he'd found some Herefords. If they'd send him some money, he'd buy those Herefords and bring them back. They wired him the money, and he's never been seen since.... Those old ladies, when you'd talk to them, they'd still get a twinkle in their eyes when you'd talk about him." (2011~)

Kerry Ross Boren told a slightly different story about Tom Dilly: "Annie's [Annie Thayne] association with [Sanford] Sang Thompson ended abruptly when Tom Dilly decided to stake his claim on her. The two men were partners in a deal to buy cattle from rancher Jim McPherson, but argued over Annie, and parted. A few days later, Tom Dilly lay in the rocks up Thompson Canyon and killed Sang as he rode by. He buried the body in a box, where it was later discovered, the head missing." (263~)

Harvey Hardy: "In later years I have read some uncomplimentary things about Tom Dilly, but when I knew him I always found him to be a pleasant, likeable fellow." (828~)

Dinner Pond: (Emery Co.) San Rafael Swell-Willow Springs Wash. Mussentuchit Flat map.

Also called Lone Tree Wedge Pond. (1551~)

This is a still-used stock reservoir. (SAPE.)

Wayne Gremel: "They used to stop and eat their lunch there." (780~)

Dipping Vat Draw: (Sevier Co.) Fishlake National Forest-Lost Creek. Boobe Hole Reservoir and Rex Reservoir maps.

Dipping vats were primarily used with sheep to get rid of scabies. It was important that every sheep on the range was dipped, as those not dipped would quickly reinfect the treated sheep. Usually the sheep were dipped every year until the scabies were gone, then dipped every couple of years after that. (1380~)

Joseph Harker in 1871: "The greatest difficulty that we have to contend with, in our flocks of sheep, is the scab, which destroys hundreds of sheep and thousands of pounds of wool yearly.... Whenever this takes place there is a loss of from twenty-five to fifty per cent of that flock of sheep.... One scabby sheep put in a thousand, any time in the winter months, will besmear the whole flock." (831~)

Dipping Vat Spring: (Garfield Co.) Dixie National Forest-Escalante Mountains-Cameron Wash. Flake Mountain East map.

(See Dipping Vat Draw for name derivation.)

—Chesnut Ranch: George Hugh Chesnut (1912-1997) and his wife, Orlene (1918-2008), had a homestead at the spring in the early days. (1455~)

Dipping Vat Spring: (Garfield Co.) Dixie National Forest-Sevier Plateau-Burnt Hollow. Mount Dutton map. Kent Whittaker: "It was an old vat made there where they dipped sheep. You can see parts of the vat still there. One time they were dippin' sheep up there. There were a half dozen herders. There was a fellow they called Tex. He was a short feller. And there was a fellow there named Howard Tanner. He was a big man. He was kind of a bully from what I gather. This was before my day. Tex owed Tanner a debt and he kept houndin' him for it. Finally Tex drew his gun and fired two shots into the air. Then he brought the gun down just like he was gonna put it back in his holster and instead he shot that Howard Tanner. My Uncle Tiffer—his real name was Christopher Whitaker and they called him Tiff—was there and he was a United States Marshall. So they grabbed Tex and brought 'im into town along with Howard Tanner. They put Tex in jail and put him right next to Tanner so he could hear him sufferin' all night. They sent him to prison." (2002~)

Dirty Devil Country: (Wayne and Garfield Counties.)

Also called Robbers Roost Country.

This is not named on the USGS maps, but it is a name in common and local use. It is the general area that is east of the Dirty Devil River, south of The Maze Road, west of the Orange Cliffs, and north of the Colorado River.

Dirty Devil River: (Garfield and Wayne Counties.) Maps Hanksville to Lake Powell: The Notch, Point of Rocks West, Angel Cove, Angel Point, Burr Point, Stair Canyon, and Hite North.

Also called Dirty Creek, Dirty Devil Creek, and Fremont River.

The Dirty Devil River starts at the junction of the Fremont River and Muddy Creek at Hanksville and ends at its confluence with the Colorado River (Lake Powell).

Jack C. Sumner of the Powell Expedition of 1869: "We rowed into camp just below a side stream coming in from the north which stinks bad enough to be the sewer from Sodom and Gomorrah, or even hell. I thought I had smelt some pretty bad odors on the battle field two days after action, but they were not up to the standard of that miserable little stream which I dubbed the 'Dirty Devil.'" (450~, 546~)

George Y. Bradley, also of the expedition noted it as Dirty Devil's Creek. (269~)

John Wesley Powell: "As we go down to this point we discover the mouth of a stream which enters from the right.

Into this our little boat is turned. The water is exceedingly muddy and has an unpleasant odor. One of the men in the boat following, seeing what we have done, shouts to [William] Dunn and asks whether it is a trout stream. Dunn replies, much disgusted, that it is 'a dirty devil,' and by this name the river is to be known hereafter." (1563~) While not the actual name derivation, early Blue Valley resident James Nielsen gave an alternate story: "Meandering down the Blue Valley was the Fremont River which the locals all called the 'Dirty Devil' because of the troubles it inflected upon the valley residence [*sic*]. The river afforded an uncertain water supply to a few struggling Mormon families who lived on the rich areas of the delta land bordering its banks.... It was a pain, it drove them to curse and even drove at least one man insane, so even if it wasn't named the Dirty Devil, by all the accounts my ancestors left, it deserved the name." (1453~)

Early Caineville resident George P. Pectol: "a mighty good name for the water in it was muddy and dirty. When it flooded one would think the Devil surely was in it the way it tore its banks and washed land away taking crops, fruit trees, and even homes." (318a~)

Ellsworth Kolb described the Dirty Devil as "muddy and alkaline, while warm springs containing sulphur and other minerals added to its unpalatable taste." (1124~)

Sidney Paige of the William Chenowith USGS Expedition of 1921: "This country at the mouth of the Fremont [Dirty Devil] is very beautiful. Great piles of chocolate-red cliffs rest on the white Aubrey sandstone [today's Cedar Mesa Sandstone]. Shadows and high lights contrast and sharply define the crenulated columns. The sky is pale, clear blue; water brown." (1503~)

Brian Beard in 1975: "At times a roaring chisel of sculpturing wonderment emerging through a broad tree-lined canyon, where water, sand and sky emerge as one. This is the exception, not the rule, for Utah's Dirty Devil has many faces. The face of creation, the face of destruction, the face of oneness, the face of separateness and above all, the face of beauty." (177~)

—Red Monument: (Also called Riverview Butte.) (1230~) This is the conspicuous tower one mile north-northeast of the mouth of the Dirty Devil River (at elevation 4343T on the Hite North map). It was named by John Wesley Powell in 1869: "Had a good view of Red Monument, and the creamy pink rock." (1564~)

—High Devil Reservoir: (Proposed.) This dam, proposed by Robert Brewster Stanton in 1897, would have been two miles up the Dirty Devil from its mouth. Water was to be piped or flumed downriver to use for placer mining. (1812~)

Diversion Hollow: (Emery Co.) Castle Valley-Millsite Reservoir. Ferron map.

Lee Mont Swasey: "That is where they used to divert water into either the North Ditch or the South Ditch." (1853~)

Divide Canyon: (Garfield Co.) Henry Mountains-Tarantula Mesa-Capitol Reef National Park-Sandy Creek. Cave Flat, Bitter Creek Divide, and Sandy Creek Benches maps. Sandy Creek, in its upper reaches, goes down Divide Canyon, which was named after nearby Bitter Creek Divide. (See Bitter Creek Divide.)

Dixie: (Washington Co.) Southwestern Utah.

Dixie is not shown on the maps. It is a term in common use.

(See Washington Co.–Utah's Dixie.)

Dixie Knoll: (Kane Co.) Moccasin Mountains-Block Mesas. Elephant Butte map. (5,840')

This was a good landmark for those following the Elephant Road between Long Valley and Dixie. The name was in place by 1904. (485~) (See Appendix Two—Elephant Road.)

Dixie National Forest: (Garfield, Kane, Iron, Piute, Washington, and Wayne Counties.)

President Teddy Roosevelt proclaimed the Aquarius Forest Reserve in October 1903. It encompassed most of the Aquarius Plateau. He proclaimed the Sevier Forest Reserve in May 1905. This encompassed the Markagunt Plateau. In 1906 the Paunsaugunt Plateau was added to the Sevier Forest Reserve.

In 1905 Dixie National Forest was established. At that time it encompassed the upland areas of Utah's Dixie (Pine Valley Mountains) and went to the Colorado River in Arizona (Arizona Strip country).

In 1908 the name was changed to the Powell National Forest in honor of John Wesley Powell. In 1919 the Paunsaugunt Plateau area of the Sevier Forest Reserve was added to the Powell National Forest and the name was changed to the Powell-Sevier National Forest. The Sevier name was dropped a couple of years later.

In 1944 the Dixie National Forest and Powell National Forest were combined into a single Dixie National Forest. (887~, 2051~) Today the "Dixie," with headquarters in Cedar City, administers over two million acres. It is the largest National Forest in Utah. (2021~)

Dizzy Trail Canyon: (Emery Co.) San Rafael Swell-Muddy Creek. Tomsich Butte, Big Bend Draw, and Ireland Mesa maps.

Wayne Gremel noted that this was named for the access trail that goes from Muddy Creek, across Cat Canyon, and into Dizzy Trail Canyon. The trail starts on Muddy Creek one-half mile above the mouth of Cat Canyon (one-half mile west-southwest of elevation 5651 on the Big Bend Draw map). It then enters Cat Canyon at Dike Spring. From there it goes east out of the canyon, across an area of remarkable badlands, and into Dizzy Trail Canyon (one-quarter mile west of elevation 5963 on the Big Bend Draw map). Wayne Gremel: "In one place the trail is as narrow as this table and the drop is a straight 30 or 40 feet or more. That is why it is called Dizzy Trail, because it is pretty spooky going around there on horseback. Some horses I'd ride across there, but some of them I wouldn't"! (780~)

Wayne told this story: "Mike Hansen and I rode down there one winter. And Mike is a big guy! That trail was frozen. When we got to where it gets narrow and steep, I figured to get off just in case the horses slipped. I jumped off, and when Mike jumped off his, he hit the ground and it was like ice and he just slid out toward the rim and he was rippin' big rocks out of the ground and I got to laughin' ... it could have been serious, he could have slid off, but he finally got stopped just at the edge"! (780~)

In the old days cattlemen would take their livestock from Muddy Creek along this trail and then follow the canyon up to the high country at the top of the San Rafael Swell. Sheepers, on the other hand, could simply take their livestock straight up Dizzy Trail Canyon from its mouth; a small dryfall was easily passed by sheep, but not by cattle. (See Cat Canyon—Emery Co.—San Rafael Swell.)

—Constructed Stock Trail: This exits the very top of the canyon to the south (near elevation 6742AT on the Tomsich Butte map). Inscriptions along the trail date to 1924. (SAPE.)

—Dizzy Trail Stock Pond: This is shown to the northwest of elevation 6128 on the Ireland Mesa map. It is still used, especially by wild horses. (SAPE.)

Doc Lewis Hollow: (Garfield Co.) Dixie National Forest-Threemile Creek. Fivemile Ridge map.

Aaron Lewis (1845-1900) and his wife, Sarah A., arrived in Panguitch in the 1870s. Aaron was a doctor. (388~)

Doctor Canyon: (Sevier Co.) Fishlake National Forest-Fish Lake. Burrville and Fish Lake maps.

Dr. John St. John built a hospital at the mouth of the canyon on Fish Lake in 1889. It closed in 1900. (955, 1641~, 1971~)

—Doctor Creek Campground: In the early days this was called the Tabiona Summer Home Area. Elbert L. Cox: "named in honor of the Utah Indian sub-chief, guide and peace-maker who was instrumental in helping to secure the negotiations preliminary to the ratification of the Friendship Pact with Chief Pah-ga-ne'-a and his little band of Piute Indians." (460~, 749~)

Dodge Point: (San Juan Co.) Great Sage Plain-Montezuma Creek. Devil Mesa and Monticello South maps.

No one has been quite able to put a finger on the naming of this large and important grazing and farming area. The name was in place by the mid-1880s.

First, it is possible that one of the early Texas cattlemen who arrived in the area in the late 1870s was named Dodge.

Second, Mary Anne Dodge was the second wife of James Harvey Dunton, a Hole-in-the-Rock Expedition member. (1195~)

Third, rancher Horace Dodge may have lived in the area. (2069~) His name comes up frequently, though little is known about him.

Brothers Mike and Pat O'Donnel were the first known to have run cattle on this range, starting in 1878. Kumen Jones: "A few stock men first entered the county in the fall of '79. The Odonall's [*sic*] turned cattle loose at the Dodge Spring, two miles south of Verdure Creek." (1016~) By 1888 Bishop Nielson and his sons were running a dairy herd on Dodge Point. (1526~) Joseph B. Harris was the first to patent land on the point, in 1917. (1275~)

Norma Perkins Young: "Pines, pinions and cedar trees grow heavy along the rim of the canyon, then thin out into sage, grassland and cultivated acres. It is recognized as one of the best farming and ranching areas in San Juan County. Since pioneer days it has been known as Dodge Point." (2069~)

—Dodge Spring: PRIVATE PROPERTY. This is in Dodge Canyon two miles south of Verdure (near elevation 6910T on the Monticello South map). The spring was used as a primary camping spot by early settlers and Indians. (1741~, 1855~)

—Perkins Ranch: In 1891 Ben Perkins moved to Dodge Spring and built a ranch there. (1407~, 2069~)

Dog Flat: (Wayne Co.) Awapa Plateau-Deadman Hollow. Abes Knoll and Loa maps.

Thaine Taylor noted that it was named for the ground hogs: "You couldn't hardly ride a horse or the horse would fall in the holes. But they've been eliminated pretty well out there." (1868~, 1914~)

Dog Hollow: (Emery Co.) San Rafael Swell-Red Hole Draw. Short Canyon map.

—Dog Hollow Reservoir: Ray Wareham: "There wasn't even enough water for a dog to git a drink there. They'd always try. There's a pond there. The CC's made that." (1967~)

Dog Lake: (Garfield Co.) Dixie National Forest-Awapa Plateau. Big Lake map.

Dunk Taylor noted that "waterdogs" [salamanders] live in the lake: "They are kind of a thing like a toad, only they're a fish. They can live with water or without water, and when they need water, they burrow in the mud. And they are kind of weird lookin', about eighteen inches long and they have a round mouth. They swim like a fish." (1865~)

—Dog Lake Ditch: This ditch, built by the CCC, brought water into Dog Lake. (1865~)

Dog Ponds: (Emery Co.) Cedar Mesa-Buckhorn Flat. Bob Hill Knoll map.

—Railroad Rocks: These boulders are a short distance west of the Dog Ponds. James H. Knipmeyer noted that this is the local name for several large boulders that have the names of workers on the Old Railroad Grade and of local ranchers inscribed on them. (See Denver and Rio Grande Western Railroad.)

Inscriptions include John H. Averett, June 6, 1881; Adolf Axelsen, June 6, 1881; E. Miller and J.T. Daly, June 7, 1881; Carl E. Jensen, June 17, 1881; Jens Peter Hansen, Nov. 16, 1886; John Justensen, Ern Justensen, April 23, 1906; Warren Allred, 1932; and Preston Wayman, 1951. (1115~, SAPE.)

—Daisy Chain Rocks: These boulders are west of the Railroad Rocks. James H. Knipmeyer: "This name comes from the shape and appearance of one of the prehistoric petroglyphs on the rock." (1115~) Inscriptions include E.D. Brinkerhoff, 1925; Foster Jensen, 1936; and Peter O. Madsen with a note: "Born Sept. 25, 1886." (SAPE.)

Dog Tanks Draw: (San Juan Co.) Dark Canyon Plateau-Comb Wash. Hotel Rock map.

This small, developed spring is no dog. The spring is in a beautiful setting of Gambel oak, large cottonwoods, and pinion and juniper trees. (SAPE.)

Dog Valley: (Garfield Co.) Fremont Canyon-Granite Knolls. Fremont Pass map.

Unattributed: "So named for the many prairie dogs to be seen there." (2053~) The name was in place by 1870. (164~)

The Parley P. Pratt Exploring Expedition to Southern Utah of 1849–50 camped here after a difficult crossing of Fremont Pass in winter. John Brown of the expedition: "Just before sun set we were on the top of the last divide where every team could take its own wagon; we camped in a wide hollow [Dog Valley] that runs west." (1762~) Isaac Haight of the same expedition: "camped as usual without water our cattle almost exhausted for want of feed and water the cold was intense every man froze his feet more or less." (1762~)

—Dog Valley Reservoir: This is at the south end of Dog Valley. James Dalley in 1941: "An early settler built this reservoir and a ditch running for about four miles down to the Dalley ranch." (2053~)

Dogwater: (Garfield Co.) Sandy Creek Benches-Sandy Creek. Sandy Creek Benches map.

South Coleman and North Coleman canyons join to form the short Dogwater, which drains into Sandy Creek. Cowboys use the term "dogwater" to indicate that there was just enough water for a dog to take a drink. (582~, 1821~)

Doll House, The: (Wayne Co.) Canyonlands National Park-Maze District-Spanish Bottom. Spanish Bottom map.

Also called Dolls House and Pregnant Park. (880~)

Emery Kolb climbed out of the canyon in 1911: "The top we were astounded by the magnificent view. Our first view across the country may be compared with looking from N.Y. to Brooklyn at the church steeples as there were hundreds of pinnacles. The rocks were split so that we would step over crevices with hundreds ft. depth below." (1125~)

Edwin T. Wolverton called these The Sentinels in 1904: "Below [The Confluence] we come to a place where a number of gigantic shapes, called the Sentinels, stand out over the west wall of the canon." (1177~, 1429~) Harold W.C. Prommel also called these The Sentinels in the 1920s. (411~, 618~)

In 1957 Randall Henderson went into the Maze area with Kent Frost. He recounted the naming of the Doll House: "Here on three sides we were flanked by a fantastic parade of sandstone gargoyles that rose in ordered array almost as if they were giant dolls on the shelves of a gigantic carnival booth. Since the map-makers had given no special name to this sector of the Standing Rocks region,

I identified them in my notebook as The Doll House." (871~, 1429~)

Mary Beckwith: "Randall's Doll House is called locally the 'Hens and Chickens.'" (192~)

Dolores Point: (Grand Co.) La Sal Mountains-South Beaver Mesa. Dolores Point South and Dolores Point North maps.

Also called Beaver Mesa. (1931~)

(See Dolores River for name derivation.)

Dolores River: (Grand Co.) Colorado River-Dolores River. Utah maps only: Dolores Point North, Steamboat Mesa, Fisher Valley, Blue Chief Mesa, and Dewey.

In 1765 Don Juan María de Rivera, while searching for the Colorado River, reached the Dolores River, which he named *El Río de Nuestra Señora de Dolores*, or "Our Lady of Sorrows." (1363~) The name was also used by the Domìnguez-Escalante Expedition of 1776–77. (1944~)

Dome Canyon: (San Juan Co.) Navajo Indian Reservation-Navajo Mountain-Tsagieto Canyon. Rainbow Bridge map.

This was named by Charles L. Bernheimer in 1922: "Part way toward the Saddle we came across a huge dome, half of which had been broken off. This determined the name 'Half Dome Canyon.'" (221~)

—Half Dome Trail: This is the name Bernheimer used for the trail that went from Rainbow Lodge to Redbud Pass. (445~) Bernheimer: "I call it a trail because in a few places we found stones placed by human hands, at some time in the dim past, on top of rocks where Nature would not have placed them; otherwise there was no trace of path or trail." (219~) (See Cliff Canyon—Sunset Pass.)

Dome Plateau: (Grand Co.) Colorado River-Dolores River. Cisco SW, Big Bend, and Dewey maps. (6,037')

The name was used by the Ferdinand V. Hayden Survey in 1874. (M.30.)

Joe Taylor: "Dome Plateau is also called the 'Back of Beyond.' That was a David Goudelock expression." (1866~) (See Cache Valley Wash.)

James H. Knipmeyer: "Known locally as The Highlands, the plateau was named by early stockmen because it sloped up to such high elevations." (1120~)

Domínguez Butte: (San Juan Co.) Glen Canyon NRA-Glen Canyon. Gunsight Butte map. (4,476')

Also called Domínguez Rock. (596~)

The Domínguez-Escalante Expedition of 1776–77 passed along the east side of the butte on November 6, 1776. (467~)

The name was first used by Stephen C. Jett in a *Desert Magazine* article in 1965: "Another arch lies to the west in one of the rounded masses of Entrada sandstone, which I have called the Domínguez Buttes." (978~)

—Padre Point Marina: (Proposed.) In the 1970s the Navajo Indians proposed building a marina at Domínguez Butte. (1357~)

Domínguez Pass: (Coconino Co., Az.) Vermilion Cliffs National Monument-Paria River. Ferry Swale, Az. map. (4,800')

Also called Domínguez Trail and Sand Trail.

In late October 1776 the Domínguez-Escalante Expedition camped near Lees Ferry and spent several days trying to find a route across the Colorado River. Deep water prevented them from crossing. Instead, the expedition went up the Paria River to the first practical exit out of the canyon to the east. They forged a trail up the cliffs through what was later named Domínguez Pass. They called it *Cuestas De Animas* or "hills that demand courage." (284~, 1020~, 1355~) Father Escalante described the climb: "We spent more than three hours in climbing it because at the beginning it is very rugged and sandy and afterward has very difficult stretches and extremely perilous ledges of rock, and finally it becomes impassable." (261~)

The Antonio Armijo Expedition of 1829–30 most likely used the trail. They certainly were on the top of the cliffs overlooking the Paria River. They called the cliffs the *Coja Colorado*, or "Red Ridge." (69~)

The trail was used by Jacob Hamblin and others in 1858, 1859, and 1860. Thales Haskell in 1859: "Went a short distance further up the [Paria] creek. Turned to the right and climbed a very steep, sandy, rocky mountain some 2 miles from the bottom to the top. Very hard on our pack mules, and in some places very dangerous. We however had no bad luck." (842~, 1357~)

Richard L. Hoxie of the Lieutenant George M. Wheeler Survey of 1872–73: "Trail here is difficult and dangerous, and has been over several rough places today." (917~)

A.H. Jones in 1910: "We took the trail leading up the white sandstone rimrock on the east side of Paria River for about 1½ miles and then worked up a very hard trail over drift sand and rock to the top of the high rim about 1800 ft. above the Paria River." (1010~)

Nora Candell ascended the trail in 1940: "That trail has to be seen to be believed.... Part of it lay along the extreme edge of the first bluff, with a sheer and dizzy drop to one side, so that I had to keep my gaze fixed firmly anywhere but down, in order to prevent peculiar things happening to my inside. Then, after a steep ascent through soft sliding sand that must have been heart-breaking work for the

horses, we started climbing in earnest. Some of the gradients looked utterly unscalable—at one point there was an abrupt step of about four feet in the solid rock—but the animals made it with extraordinarily little fuss." (507~) Nora went on to describe the view from the top: "There, below us, the plain spread out, every shade of blue, purple and grey, while to the north ahead of us, lay the promised land, rose-pink in the distance, the battlements and bastions of impregnable crags, looking like some lost city of dreams." (507~)

The Domínguez Pass name was given by members of the Domínguez-Escalante State/Federal Bicentennial Committee in 1976. (1357~)

Inscriptions along the bottom of the trail include P.W.J. and F.T.J., 1896. Inscription specialist James H. Knipmeyer noted that Price William and Frank Tilton Johnson were the sons of the Warren M. Johnson. He ran Lees Ferry from 1877 to 1895–96. (1111~) Inscriptions along the top of the trail include HEi(?), 1871(?); S.L. Gould, Jan. 25th, 1891; L.A. Willis, Sept. 1st, 1894; and J.E. (or J.L.) Heywood, no date. (SAPE.)

—Animas Plateau: This was the name given by the Domínguez-Escalante Expedition to the area on top of and to the east of Domínguez Pass. (81~)

Donkey Creek: (Wayne Co.) Dixie National Forest-Boulder Mountain-Fremont River. Blind Lake and Torrey maps.

Two name derivations are given.

First, Kate B. Carter: "Early settlers would go to Teasdale for supplies and transport them by pack-burros." (375~) Second, Dwight Williams noted that a herd of wild donkeys lived in the area. (2013~)

Donnelly Canyon: (San Juan Co.) Harts Point-Indian Creek. Harts Point South map.

Also spelled Donnolly Canyon.

John Scorup and Pete Steele noted that there is some historical confusion about the naming of Donnelly Canyon. In the early days, the canyon that now bears the Donnelly Canyon name was called Green Canyon. Henry Green started a ranch at the mouth of the canyon in 1885. (1821~, 1860~) The original Donnelly Canyon was one mile east-southeast of the Dugout Ranch (one-quarter mile north of elevation 6372T). It was here that Joe Donnelly had a ranch at the mouth of the canyon in the early days. (1821~)

—Fringe of Death Canyon: The mouth of this eastern tributary of Indian Creek is one-half mile downcanyon from the mouth of Donnelly Canyon (one-quarter mile south of elevation 6207T). Eric Bjørnstad noted that on the first ascent of a wall in the canyon in 1979, climbing leader Earl Wiggens was unable to place protection for sixty feet. He thought he was on the fringe of death, giving the climb, and the canyon, its name. (239~)

Dons Lake: (Grand Co.) La Sal Mountains-Beaver Creek. Mount Waas map.

Joe Taylor: "It was named for my grandfather, Don Taylor.... The local Fishing and Hunting Club built it. That was in the 1950s. My granddad, Don Taylor, died in 1958 and they built it right about then. We own the water. That is the irrigation water for the Fisher Valley Ranch." (1866~)

Don Spring: (Piute Co.) Manning Creek-Sevier River. Marysvale map.

Correctly spelled Dan Spring.

(See Manning Creek for name derivation.)

This is a large, developed spring. (SAPE.)

Door, The: (Emery Co.) Cedar Mountain-Humbug Flats. Flattop Mountain map.

This low pass between two seven hundred foot mesas is still used by stockmen. (SAPE.)

Dorry Canyon: (San Juan Co.) Manti-LaSal National Forest-La Sal Mountains-Brumley Creek. Mount Tukuhnikivatz map.

Dorry Crouse ran sheep in the area. (456~)

—Chess Ridge: This is between Dorry Canyon and Brumley Creek (at elevations 8550AT and 10597T). (1627~)

—Squaw Spring Ridge: This is three-quarters of a mile south of upper Dorry Canyon (at elevations 8823T and 9370T). (1627~) Lloyd Holyoak: "There were a lot of Indians camped up in the La Sals. It was a summer place, mainly in the years when there was a good crop of pine nuts. The Indians would come and gather them." (906~)

—Squaw Spring: This is the "Spring" on the east side of Squaw Spring Ridge (at elevation 8947T). Faun M. Tanner noted that an Indian woman was killed here in 1881. (1855~)

Double Arch: (Grand Co.) Arches National Park-The Windows Section. The Windows Section map.

Also called Double Windows, The Jughandles, and Twinbow Arch. (262~, 898~)

Frank Beckwith of the Arches National Monument Scientific Expedition of 1933–34: "From one abutment of massive sandstone, two arches arise, and spanning the space to the main wall, each merges in the main block of rock at a different angle." (188~)

James H. Knipmeyer: "One of the most impressive spans in the monument, here two massive arches of reddish-pink sandstone swing outward and downward from the common abutment of the Windows reef." (1120~)

—Movies: Double Arch was used as the backdrop for a short section of *Indiana Jones and the Temple of Doom* in 1989. (1421~)

—Buccaneer Rock: This is immediately south of Double Arch. Unattributed: "named by Frank Beckwith. He said that it reminded him of 'a grizzled Spanish buccaneer, with a pirate cap, a la liberty style.'" (68~)

Double O Arch: (Grand Co.) Arches National Park-Devils Garden. Mollie Hogans map.

Also called Double Arch (898~) and Double Deck Arch (1949~).

Buck Lee in 1940: "the only one yet known with one common base, from which the two project into a second and third series of rock beyond." (354~)

Dougherty Basin: (Garfield Co.) Dixie National Forest-Escalante Mountains. Barker Reservoir map.

Correctly spelled Dority Basin.

Also spelled Daugherty Basin, Dorrity Basin, and Doughertie Basin.

Edson Alvey: "Sam and Marion Dority were early Escalante stockmen." (55~) David Owen noted that in 1888 the Dority family brought five thousand head of sheep and two thousand cows to the Escalante Mountains. (887~)

Dougi Butte: (San Juan Co.) Navajo Indian Reservation-Navajo Mountain-Oak Canyon. Rainbow Bridge map. (5,015')

The name was suggested by Frank E. Masland, Jr. in the early 1960s. He cited two name derivations: One was for a Navajo named Sid (also spelled Cyd) Whiskers, whose family name was Dougi. Whiskers was Zane Grey's guide while he was in the area.

Second, Masland, Jr.: "The original Dougi was the Paiute who gave the Navajo Hoskinnini sanctuary when he successfully avoided [Kit] Carson's raiders." (1931~)

Masland, Jr. continued with a biography of Whiskers: "Sid Whiskers is (in 1961) an ancient Navajo. He hasn't many more years to be with us. He is an old long hair, authentic in every detail. Sid Whiskers was with us in 1956 when we climbed Hill 5014 [now 5015].... It was from this vantage point that I looked to the northeast and noted the most rugged country I had observed. It was Sid Whiskers who through an interpreter gave us the story of the canyons and the fact the Indians considered them impenetrable. Sid Whiskers lives in that general area. He pastures his sheep between Moepitz and what is shown on the map as Oak Canyon. His contribution to our present knowledge of country theretofore unknown is a major one. Hill 5014 [5015] is an important landmark. It should carry a name. I would like to suggest it be officially designated Sid Whiskers Butte." (1931~) Masland, Jr. also called it Dougi Camp Butte. (1309~)

—Moepitz Airfield: This remarkably flat area is one-quarter mile east of Dougi Butte. It was named by Frank E. Masland, Jr. not because aircraft landed on it, but that it was flat enough that they could, a remarkable occurrence in this convoluted country. Masland, Jr.: "Moepitz Airfield is one of the widest, flattest mesa tops in that country. We name it that since helicopters could easily land there and a strip would handle light planes." (1309~)

—Red Top Butte: This is two miles east of Dougi Butte (at elevation 6059 [Rainbow]). It was named by George C. Fraser in 1916. (669~)

Douglas Mesa: (San Juan Co.) Navajo Indian Reservation-San Juan River. Goulding NE, Goulding NW, Slickhorn Canyon West, and Slickhorn Canyon East maps.
Jim Mike noted that the Paiutes call this Sand Grass Hill. (1353~)
Two name derivations are given. The second is most likely correct.
First, William B. Douglass of the General Land Office participated in the Euroamerican discovery of Rainbow Bridge in 1909. (1935~, 1943~)
Second, while prospecting along the San Juan River in 1909 during a period of low water, James Douglas found a gold-filled sand bar. Working quickly, he managed to remove fifteen hundred dollars worth of gold in just a couple of hours. When the river rose, the sand bar was flooded. For twenty years Douglas waited for the water to get low enough to mine the sand bar again. It never did. Tired of the wait, Douglas jumped off the bridge that crossed the San Juan River near Mexican Hat. He left a note behind:
>When this you see
>My old body in the river will be
>There is no one in the world
>To blame for this
>Only me. (2056~)

Douglas Wash: (San Juan Co.) Navajo Indian Reservation-Monument Valley-Halgaitoh Wash. Monument Pass and Mexican Hat SW maps.
(See Douglas Mesa for name derivation.)
—Halgaito Spring: This is in Douglas Wash just above its junction with Halgaitoh Wash (Mexican Hat SW map). (101~)

Downard Spring: (Carbon Co.) West Tavaputs Plateau-Desolation Canyon. Summerhouse Ridge map.
This is a large, developed spring. (SAPE.)
Waldo Wilcox: "There were two or three families of Downards in the area. The spring on Buckskin [Ridge] was Ernest Downard [1899-1964]." (2011~)

Doxford Creek: (Sevier Co.) Fishlake National Forest-Sevier Plateau-Monroe Creek. Koosharem and Monroe Peak maps.
Joseph F. Doxford (1814-1909), an English sailor, arrived in Richfield in 1864. (368~)

DP Spring: (Mesa Co., Colo.) La Sal Mountains-Dolores Point. Dolores Point North map.
Two name derivations are given.
First, Joe Taylor: "That is from the days of the Pittsburgh Cattle Company [pre-1900]. It was for the Denver Pacific I think." (1866~)
Second, the spring is on Dolores Point and the "DP" may refer to that.

Dragerton Town: (Carbon Co.) Book Cliffs-Grassy Trail Creek-Highway 123. Sunnyside map.
This town, located on a part of the old Whitmore Ranch (See Whitmore Canyon), was started in 1942 by the W.E. Ryberg-Strong and Grant Company as a coal mining town to service the Geneva Steel Horse Canyon Mine. (1621~)
In 1973 it combined with another coal mining town, Columbia, to become East Carbon City. (1282~) (See Horse Canyon and East Carbon City.)

Driftwood Canyon: (Kane Co.) Glen Canyon NRA-Glen Canyon. Navajo Point and Cathedral Canyon maps.
Katie Lee had several descriptions of the canyon. First: "I spotted a narrow, mysterious gap in the right bank with a tiny cove at its mouth.... The entrance, not twenty-five feet wide, was piled head high with driftwood.... Under it ran a crystal stream and just ahead in the only spot of sunlight stood a radiant redbud tree, backed by a rose-colored wall dripping with desert varnish. Paradise.... We called it Driftwood Canyon." (1162~)
Second: "Great alcoves, ceilings several hundred feet up, overhang giant thumbs that poke from the snaking canyon's opposite side. It is dizzying to look up at a winding blue river in the sky, see a paint-spill of darker colors dripping from the rim over rose-colored walls.... We called it Driftwood Canyon. Turned out aptly named. Only one year in ten thereafter did I see its entrance minus the old Colorado's woodpile." (1162~)
Third: "And also, it had redbud trees in it that would make you cry. They were so beautiful and right up against the wall. You'd wonder how in the name of God they ever

stayed there.... It was just beyond description, just like being in some damn fairyland. Everything came together. It had everything all the other canyons had had, plus more." (1163~)

Joseph L. Dudziak in 1962: "Found much driftwood in a large pool at entrance—a rather forbidding and certainly uninviting wading job. Entered a second pool for a long swim and entered a great amphitheatre about as big as Music Temple. Very impressive." (577~)

Otis "Dock" Marston in 1962: "Very fine.... DON'T MISS IT"! (1298~)

—Klondike Bar: (Also spelled Klondyke Bar.) This placer bar, now underwater, was on the north side of the Colorado River immediately west of the mouth of Driftwood Canyon (one-eighth mile south of elevations 4060 and 4082 on the Cathedral Canyon map). Klondike Bar was one of the most extensive mining sites in Glen Canyon during the gold rush years of the 1890s.

Two name derivations are given. First, C. Gregory Crampton: "The first location was made here December 22, 1897 by Louis M. Chaffin, Seth Laugee [also spelled Longee], and William B. Hay [Billy Hay] who commemorated the contemporary gold rush to Yukon Territory by calling their discovery the Klondike Placer Mining Claim, though it is recorded as the 'Clondike.'" (467~)

Second, David D. Rust: "Bill Rust and [Nathaniel] Galloway traded a pack horse and supplies to Ed Meskin.... Ed Meskin started for the Klondyke so they named it Klondyke Bar." (1674~)

—Klondike Trail: (Also called Louis M. Chaffin Trail and Slickrock Trail.) (19~) A constructed stock trail, built by Louis M. Chaffin, led from Klondike Bar to the benches between the river and the Kaiparowits Plateau. It starts one-quarter mile northeast of elevation 4082 on the Cathedral Canyon map. During the gold mining boom of the 1890s, supplies were brought to the bar from Escalante. After following the Hole-in-the-Rock Road, the route turned generally west and followed a bench at the base of the Kaiparowits Plateau to Klondike Bar. Some of this trail still exists. (408~, 1928~, SAPE.)

—Quaking Bog Canyon: (Also called Klondike Cove.) (675~) This northern (or western) tributary of Lake Powell is three-quarters of a mile east of the mouth of Driftwood Canyon (one-quarter mile east of elevation 4070 on the Cathedral Canyon map). Katie Lee and friends named the canyon: "We went through a tamarisk thicket. We practically had to get a machete to get in there. It was murder gettin' in there, another one of those where you just bushwhack and when you finally got there, there

was this beautiful pool and this amphitheater with all the moss and the maidenhair fern growin' around ... the reason for the 'quaking bog' is because it was so muddy." (1163~)

—Klondike Cove: This is a recent name for the lake area at the mouth of Quaking Bog Canyon. (1857~)

—Spring Pool Canyon: This short northern (or western) tributary of Lake Powell, now submerged, was one-eighth mile east of the mouth of Driftwood Canyon (one-quarter mile south-southeast of elevation 3856 on the Cathedral Canyon map). It was named by Katie Lee and friends. (1163~)

Drift Trail Canyon: (San Juan Co.) Manti-LaSal National Forest-Dark Canyon Plateau-North Elk Ridge-Dark Canyon. Poison Canyon map.

—Drift Trail: John F. Vallentine noted that the Drift Trail was the primary access used by cowboys to herd their livestock from Dark Canyon to Elk Ridge. (1936~) John Scorup: "It hasn't been used for years and years, but in the old days, they used to gather all the TY cattle and bring them in down Peavine Canyon and down Dark Canyon and then they'd take them back on top, take them out of Drift Trail Canyon." (1821~) The TY cattle were owned by Al and Jim Scorup. They ran thousands of head of cattle on Elk Ridge and the Abajo Mountains in the 1890s and early 1900s. (1131~)

Erwin Oliver: "The year I went out was the last year they ever ran cattle up Drift Trail Canyon. From then on, they used trucks. That was in 1954." (1479~)

Drinks Canyon: (Grand Co.) La Sal Mountains-Colorado River. Rill Creek and Big Bend maps.

Lloyd Holyoak and Joe Taylor agreed that this is a newer name provided by river runners. (906~, 1866~)

Dripping Canyon: (San Juan Co.) Cedar Mesa-Grand Gulch. Moss Back Butte and Pollys Pasture maps.

Also called Dripping Spring Canyon.

Hole-in-the-Rock Expedition members named this in 1880. (1356~)

Al and John Wetherill, while with the Hyde Exploring Expedition, left their names in the canyon in 1894. (249~)

—Dripping Spring: (Also called Drippin.) (560a~) This is one-half mile upcanyon from its mouth (Pollys Pasture map).

Dripping Spring: (Garfield Co.) Dirty Devil Country-The Big Ridge-Happy Canyon. The Pinnacle map.

Also called Drip Spring. (100~)

This is a large, developed spring. (SAPE.)

Some older maps have confused Dripping Spring with nearby Two Pipe Spring, wrongfully swapping names.

Barbara Ekker, paraphrasing Ned Chaffin: "Dripping Springs also has a good corral. Good place to camp in summer as it was cool there and in the winter you were out of the North winds." (411~)

—Constructed Stock Trail: This goes to the spring. (100~, SAPE.)

Dripping Spring: (Grand Co.) Tenmile Country-Tenmile Canyon. Dubinky Wash.

Lorin Milton: "It [Dripping Spring] had good, but little, water that dripped out of a seam in the rock.... It was a pretty good little cow camp ... right there handy and in a bunch of cottonwood trees. Water dripped into a bucket afixed to the canyon wall and was used for people, not cattle." (1430~)

Although it is known that ranchers and sheepherders have used Dripping Springs since the 1880s, Chris and Henry Halverson were the first to have their names associated with it when they bought land here in 1929. (1780~) Alton Halverson, Chris's son, and family, built the two cabins (now ruins) here in 1942–43. (580~, 1084~)

—Old Spanish Trail: (Variation.) A variation of the Old Spanish Trail crossed the top of Tenmile Canyon near Dripping Spring. Gene Dunham noted that the Spanish left a line of tall cairns on the top of high points as they worked their way from Moab to Green River Crossing. One could look through a carefully constructed hole at the top of the cairn and in the distance one would see the next cairn. The cairns with their sighting holes led over the heads of the many canyons encountered in Tenmile Country. Forty years ago one could still do this. Today most of the cairns have either been knocked down or reconstructed without the sight holes. (580~, SAPE.)

Dripping Spring: (Piute Co.) Sevier Plateau-Steens Canyon. Phonolite Hill map.

This is a medium-size, wash-bottom spring. (SAPE.)

Dripping Spring: (San Juan Co.) Hatch Point-Colorado River. Shafer Basin map.

Val Dalton: "It's more or less seeping out of the rock. When I first went up there years ago there was a cliff face there about ten foot high. Now it's about two foot high. It's filled up with silt and dirt and sand." (517~)

Dripping Spring: (San Juan Co.) Wingate Mesa-Mahon Canyon. Mancos Mesa NE map.

Carl Mahon noted that he named this while working for the BLM. It was developed for use by bighorn sheep. (1272~)

Dripping Springs: (Grand Co.) Uintah and Ouray Indian Reservation-Coal Creek. Lion Canyon map.

This large spring issues from a long, crumbling wall. (SAPE.)

Drips, The: (Emery Co.) San Rafael Swell-Coal Wash. Horn Silver Gulch map.

This large spring consists of water dripping from an overhang. In good years, it flows from the rock as though out of a hose. (SAPE.) Ray Wareham: "The water comes and goes, but it's always there. It isn't good water. The cows won't drink it. It must have a bad taste." (1967~)

Inscriptions include J. Killpack, 188?; S. Hanson, 1897; JAZ, 1907; and Seely Peterson, no date (probably in the 1930s). (1115~, SAPE.)

—Pioneer Road: (See Appendix Two—San Rafael Swell Pioneer Trail.)

Drip Tank Canyon: (Kane Co.) GSCENM-Kaiparowits Plateau-Last Chance Creek. Ship Mountain Point map.

Also called Dripping Spring. (984~)

—Drip Tank: This is a large, wash-bottom spring in a pretty setting. (SAPE.) Volney King noted the tank in 1890. (1096~)

Drip Tank Canyon: (Kane Co.) GSCENM-Kitchen Canyon. Deer Range Point map.

A small spring in the canyon fills several potholes. (SAPE.) Ralph Chynoweth noted that this is a name from the early days. (425~)

Drowned Hole Draw: (Emery Co.) San Rafael Swell-San Rafael River. Drowned Hole Draw map.

Also spelled Drownded Hole Draw. (1931~)

Guy and Nina Robison noted that a man drowned in this small canyon. (1645~)

—Drowned Hole: The "Drowned Hole" as shown on the Drowned Hole Draw map does not exist. The drainage itself does contain a series of large, and very pretty, potholes. (SAPE.)

Druid Arch: (San Juan Co.) Canyonlands National Park-Needles District-Elephant Canyon. Druid Arch map.

The first Euroamerican credited with seeing Druid Arch was rancher David Goudelock in 1915. (1950~)

Tug Wilson, son of Canyonlands National Park Superintendent Bates Wilson, was the first to bring the arch to the public's attention. He noted that he initially saw the arch from the air in 1959. He later led a group to it on foot: "I went around a high point on a natural bench formed by the white layer of sandstone, I saw a massive arch loom before me. Excited, I called to John [Levering] and dad [Bates Wilson]. Throwing them a rope, I pulled them from the narrow canyon up to the same bench from where the arch is viewed today. A photograph was later sent to Robert Dechert [a cousin of Bates Wilson].... He was asked what he thought the name of this wonderful arch should be. Bob replied that it should be called Druid Arch, after the builders of Stonehenge in England." (2017~)

Dry Camp Valley Spring: (Iron Co.) Dixie National Forest-Markagunt Plateau-Tippets Valley. Henrie Knolls map.

This is a large, developed, and still-used spring and stock reservoir. (SAPE.)

Dry Canyon: (Carbon Co.) West Tavaputs Plateau-Nine Mile Creek. Twin Hollow and Cowboy Bench maps.

Also called Dry Fork Canyon. (1788~)

This is one of the best watered and most beautiful canyons on the West Tavaputs Plateau. (SAPE.)

Inscriptions include Myron Russell, May 9, 1917. Myron had a ranch at the mouth of the canyon. (558~)

A rumor, unsubstantiated, claims that there was an inscription at the mouth of the canyon from 1839. If so, it would have been from a fur trapper of that era. The inscription seems to have disappeared. (558~)

Dry Canyon: (Carbon and Emery Counties.) Roan Cliffs-Range Creek. Lighthouse Canyon map.

Waldo Wilcox: "It is dry. There is a spring but it is way, way up there." (2011~)

Dry Canyon: (Iron Co.) Hurricane Cliffs-Parowan Canyon. Red Creek Reservoir and Parowan maps.

Also called Spring Creek. (1931~)

LaVar Taylor noted that the canyon was dry. (1515~)

Dry Canyon: (Kane Co.) Alton Amphitheater-Kanab Creek. Alton map.

Also called Dry Hollow. (741~)

Unattributed: "Called Dry Canyon because no continuous stream is there." (2053~) The name was applied in 1872.

—Seegmiller Ranch: Daniel Seegmiller (ca. 1836-1899) and family had a ranch on Kanab Creek at the mouth of Dry Canyon. They moved here in about 1885. (1716~) Seegmiller was killed in Kanab over a water rights issue. His killer committed suicide. (388~)

Dry Canyon: (Sevier Co.) Fishlake National Forest-Sevier Plateau-Sevier River. Monroe Peak and Antelope Range maps.

Also called Dry Creek.

Most of the water that goes down the canyon sinks into the ground. (1971~)

—United Order Sawmill: The first sawmill in Sevier County was built in what was then called Dry Creek Canyon by the United Order in the mid-1870s. (381~, 1418~)

—Monkeytown: This once prosperous ranch community was on Dry Creek. (1971~) The town was noted by Volney King in 1892. (1096~)

Dry Creek: (Piute Co.) Fishlake National Forest-Sevier Plateau-Sevier River. Marysvale Peak, Malmsten Peak, and Piute Reservoir maps.

Also called Dry Creek Canyon and Dry Wash.

Newel Nielson: "It goes dry in the fall." (1458~) Edward Sudweeks: "It was so named because it is dry most of the season." (2053~) E.C. Bird: "was so named because it is dry three months out of the year." (2053~)

—Dry Creek Guard Station: (Marysvale Peak map.) This was once staffed by rangers patrolling the Sevier Plateau. The station is no longer in use.

Dry Fork Coyote Gulch: (Kane Co.) GSCENM-Cat Pasture-Escalante Desert-Coyote Gulch. Basin Canyon, Big Hollow Wash, and King Mesa maps.

Also called Twenty-five Mile. (709~)

Edson Alvey: "The name is derived from the fact that it lacks water throughout most of its course." (55~)

—Peek-a-boo Canyon: This popular short slot canyon is a northern tributary of Dry Fork Coyote Gulch that is one and one-quarter miles upcanyon from the mouth of Brimstone Gulch (one-quarter mile east of elevation 4988 on the Big Hollow Wash map). Edson Alvey named the gorge in the 1930s: "The name was derived from several small natural bridges and the extremely narrow, meandering pattern of its course." (55~) The two bridges were called the Peek-a-Boo Bridges. (1955~) The USGS: "Mr. Alvey took his daughters hiking through the canyon and they would play 'Peek-a-boo' throughout the intricacies of the feature." (1931~)

—Spooky Gulch: This popular short slot canyon is a northern tributary of Dry Fork Coyote Gulch. It is three-quarters of a mile upcanyon from the mouth of Brimstone Gulch (immediately east of elevation 4754 on the Big Hollow Wash map). Edson Alvey named the gorge: "The name was derived from the 'creepy' feeling one gets in traveling through it." (55~) (See Brimstone Gulch.)

—Box Elder Canyon: This short northern tributary of Dry Fork Coyote Gulch is three miles (as the crow flies) downcanyon from the mouth of Brimstone Gulch (immediately east of elevation 4744 on the Big Hollow Wash map). A dense tangle of box elder trees are at the mouth of the canyon. It was named by Glen Canyon National Recreation Area Ranger Bill Wolverton. (653~)

—Grove Canyon: This short northern tributary of Dry Fork Coyote Gulch is one mile downcanyon from the mouth of Box Elder Canyon (immediately east of elevation 4587 on the Big Hollow Wash map). A large grove of cottonwood trees block the mouth of the canyon. (SAPE.)

Dry Fork Rock Creek: (Garfield Co.) Dixie National Forest-Johns Valley-Sevier River. Cow Creek map.
Also called Little Rock Creek and South Fork Rock Creek. (1931~)
Ward Savage: "always dry except for snow and heavy rain fall runoff." (1931~)

Dry Hollow: (Garfield Co.) Dixie National Forest-Escalante Mountains-Antimony Creek. Pollywog Lake map.
Sonny King noted that there is an Upper Dry Hollow and a Lower Dry Hollow. Upper Dry Hollow is near Wildcat Reservoir; Lower Dry Hollow is near Poison Creek Reservoir #1. (1095~)

Dry Hollow: (Garfield Co.) GSCENM-Boulder Mountain-Boulder Creek. Boulder Town and Calf Creek maps.
Burns Ormand noted that they used to call this Water Hollow because of the running water in the lower part of the canyon. It was named Dry Hollow because the upper end had no running water. (1487~)
—Boulder Mail Trail: (See Appendix Two—Boulder Mail Trail.)
—Claude V. Cutoff Road: This historic road crosses Dry Hollow three-quarters of a mile above its junction with Boulder Creek (one-quarter mile south of elevation 6263 on the Calf Creek map). (See Highway 12 and Haymaker Bench.)

Dry Lake: (Garfield Co.) Dixie National Forest-Boulder Mountain. Jacobs Reservoir map.
Pratt Gates: "When the snow falls deep, you get a lot of water and when it doesn't, it's dry." (709~)

Dry Lake: (Kane Co.) Wygaret Terrace-Johnson Canyon. Cutler Point map.
Unattributed: "The Dry Lake was so named because much of the year it was dry." (2053~)
From a water document dated June 1884: "The following claim was granted to Justin M. Johnson and Benjamin Hamblin for the surface water flowing down from Skumpa Canyon into what is known as Dry Lake above Johnson, for agricultural purposes." (2053~)

Dry Lake: (Piute Co.) Fishlake National Forest-Sevier Plateau. Marysvale Peak map.
This is a natural lake. (1458~)
Edward Sudweeks in 1941: "It derived its name because it goes dry during the late fall months. The water covers about ten of the three hundred acres." (2053~)

Dry Lake: (Piute Co.) Sevier Plateau-Forshea Mountain. Piute Reservoir map.
E.C. Bird: "was so named because it is dry three months out of the year." (2053~)

Dry Lake Reservoir: (Wayne Co.) Awapa Plateau-Balsam Hollow. Smooth Knoll map.
This is locally called Meeks Lake. Dunk Taylor: "Meeks was the guy that built a ditch clear up by Smooth Knoll. They brought it down around and dumped it off into Mitts Reservoir and then over Upper Balsam and then they dumped it into Meeks Lake." (1865~)

Dry Lakes: (Iron Co.) Parowan Canyon-Third House Flat. Brian Head and Parowan maps.
Warren Pendleton noted that the lakes dried up by the end of summer. (1515~)
Cartographer C.C. Myers in 1959: "feature name refers to a region or area, and not to a dry lake. The name … is well established, and is very much in use by local residents." (1931~)

Dry Lakes Peak: (Garfield Co.) Henry Mountains-Birch Creek. Dry Lakes Peak map. (10,451')
—Dry Lake Area: This is just north of Dry Lakes Peak. Don Orton in 1941: "a depression that has water for only a short period during the year." (2053~)
Garth Noyes: "When my father, Hyrum, was a teenager he lost his saddle horse. He went into Green River and there was a crystal ball reader there, charging twenty-five cents for a fortune. My father went in and thought he'd trick the fortune teller. He asked her, 'Where's my saddle horse'? The woman went through all of her gyrations and looked at her crystal ball and she says, 'Your saddle horse is in Dry Lakes in the Henry Mountains.… ' My father didn't think much about it; he just laughed. A week or so later he was riding up in the Dry Lakes country and, sure enough, there was his saddle horse"! (1473~)

Dry Lake Swale: (Garfield Co.) Henry Mountains-Trachyte Point-North Wash. Black Table and Turkey Knob maps.
—Jacks Knob: (Also called Buffalo Rock.) Kevin Robison noted that this sandstone knob is on the east side of Dry Lake Swale and adjacent to the east side of Highway 276. It is two miles north of Trachyte Creek (immediately west of elevation 4841T on the Black Table map). Alvin Robison named it in the 1950s for rancher Jack King. Robison and King and their cowboys used the rock as a meeting place. (1646~) Inscriptions include D.? Cook, 1912; E. Cook, 1914; and Sam Allen, 1926. (SAPE.)

Dry Lake Wash: (Emery Co.) Horse Bench-Green River. Horse Bench East and Green River SE maps.

Also called Dry Lakes Wash. (M.78.)

Pearl Baker in 1973: "This is a fine location for a thermo-nuclear power plant as there is only one small ranch between this location and Lake Powell 100 miles below." (123~)

—Sunrise Mine: This manganese mine, consisting of several shallow pits, is in the South Fork of Dry Lake Wash (southeast of elevation 4478 on the Horse Bench East map). It was first mined in the early 1900s. (104~)

Dry Mesa: (San Juan Co.) Manti-LaSal National Forest-Dark Canyon Plateau. Indian Head Pass, Woodenshoe Buttes, Warren Canyon, and Kigalia Point maps.

—Fuller Reservoir: Erwin Oliver noted that this is the stock reservoir below the southwest side of Dry Mesa and is one and one-half miles west-southwest of Cooper Spring (at elevation 8106 on the Warren Canyon map). It was named for rancher Lude Fuller. (1479~)

—Government Pasture Pond: Erwin Oliver noted that this stock reservoir is two and one-half miles southeast of Cooper Spring (at elevation 8194T on the Woodenshoe Buttes map). The pastureland surrounding the pond is called Government Pasture. (1479~)

Dry Mountain: (Emery Co.) Manti-LaSal National Forest-Wasatch Plateau-Ferron Creek. Flagstaff Peak and Ferron Canyon maps. (7,913')

Ray Wareham noted that in the early years this was a favorite spot for gathering wood and cutting lumber. (1967~)

Dry Oak Spring: (Grand Co.) Cisco Desert-Yellow Cat Mesa. Mollie Hogans map.

This is a medium-size, developed spring. (SAPE.) Jack Bickers: "This spring is now called 'Dead Oak Spring,' and has facilities for a large cattle operation, presently unused. The spring is nearly dry now, but for a long time served many head of cattle—and probably will again." (224~)

Dry Pond: (Emery Co.) San Rafael Swell-Big Flat. Devils Hole map.

Wayne Smith noted that this was also called Rufus Wilberg Reservoir for a previous owner. (1931~) Rufus was the son of prominent Castle Dale rancher Carl Wilberg. (2009~) (See Wilberg Wash.)

Dry Red Canyon: (Sevier Co.) Fishlake National Forest-Pavant Range-Sevier River. Beehive Peak and Aurora maps.

Also called Red Canyon. (1931~)

Dry Rock Creek: (Kane Co.) Glen Canyon NRA-Kaiparowits Plateau-Glen Canyon-Rock Creek Bay. Navajo Point and Mazuki Point maps.

(See Rock Creek for name derivation.)

—Cowboy Camp: This line camp in upper Dry Rock Creek is at the junction of Spencer and Lake canyons (one-quarter mile east of elevation 6047 on the Navajo Point map). It is on the Talus Trail. (See Appendix Two—Talus Trail.) Inscriptions include SRS, 1927; Wells Woolsey on Robin, Jan. 12th, 1944; Harvey Liston, Jan. 16, 1944; and Bob Woolsey, Dec. 24, 1955. (SAPE.)

—Madonna Arch: This is on the east side of Dry Rock Creek one and one-half miles upcanyon from its junction with Middle Rock Creek (one-quarter mile west of elevation 4740 on the Mazuki Point map). Stan Jones: "I named that because it's a formation that to me looks like a lady with a veil." (1020~)

Dry Valley: (Kane Co.) Dixie National Forest-Markagunt Plateau-Midway Creek. Henrie Knolls map.

William L. Crawford called this area The Drys while herding sheep here in June 1903. Crawford told this story in his diary: "Some thing run the sheep off in the night so I had to bring them back. I see from the tracks this morning it was a Bear." (485~)

Dry Valley: (San Juan Co.) Great Sage Plain-Harts Draw. Photograph Gap, Church Rock, Hatch Rock, and Sandstone Draw maps.

Also called Pusley Valley. (1532~)

This lowland area is between the La Sal Mountains to the north and the Abajo Mountains to the south.

William Henry Jackson of the Ferdinand V. Hayden Survey in 1875 noted this as "a valley like expansion." (950~)

The valley was initially called Hudsons Valley for rancher Joshua B. "Spud" Hudson. He arrived in the area in 1879. (1037~)

Francis F. Kane in 1891: "There is, however, a good deal of grammar [grama] grass, and this whole country—the Dry Creek Valley as it is called—is considered good winter range.... At present it supports about seventeen thousand head of cattle." (1037~)

H.L.A. Culmer in 1905: "But for lack of water this would be one of the finest valleys in Utah but the thirsty soil drinks up the rain and the grass that is disposed to grow freely is stamped out by the sheep." (494~)

David Lavender in 1943: "[it] looks exactly as it sounds.... A few fat lumps of sandstone sat glumly under the brassy sky. The distant forest of piñon was like a black skullcap pulled tight on a wrinkled forehead." (1151~)

—Old Spanish Trail: The trail traversed Dry Valley.

Dry Valley: (Wayne Co.) Henry Mountains-Highway 95. Bull Mountain and Hanksville maps.

Alvin Robison noted that it is not always dry; there is live water in the lower end of the valley. (1642~)

—Step Reservoir: This was in Dry Valley Wash about a hundred yards east of Highway 95 on the Hanksville map. The reservoir was blown up to keep it from filling with sand. (1931~)

Dry Valley Creek: (Garfield Co.) GSCENM-Rock Springs. Henrieville and Slickrock Bench maps.

Two name derivations are given.

First, Charles G. Mace and Ed Swapp in 1941: "Named because of dryness of locality, there being no available water from streams and springs." (2053~)

Second, Ralph Chynoweth: "There's water all of the way! It's got a live stream in it, pretty much year 'round. The middle fork of Dry Creek is where they get the water for Kodachrome Basin State Park." (425~) The name was in place by the 1880s. (2053~)

Ralph Chynoweth told these stories about Dry Valley: "My dad [Harvey Chynoweth] told me that when it's dry, it's one of the worst places in the whole world. He told me that the cattle used to get a disease out there that's called 'wooden tongue.' The tongue of the cow goes paralyzed and they can't eat or drink and they just die. Dad told me that they went for years and years trying to figure out what caused that. In the upper end of the valley the water is really good. But when you come down a little farther into the lower Dry Valley, it seeps up and the water's real alkali. The cows have to drink, so they drink this water that's real alkaline. Dad figured it was a combination of the alkali and the black greasewood that is in the upper part of Dry Valley that would cause these cattle to get this wooden tongue. Dad used to pull their tongue way out and use a corn cob and rub that over the tongue back and forth and then they could eat. When I was a kid I'd stand there for hours doing that. I'd go down to the field and get an arm full of alfalfa and poke it in them cows' mouths. Then they could chew it and swallow it. They couldn't pick it up off the ground and they couldn't drink." (425~)

Ralph continued the story: "Once when I was a little kid dad and I went out to Dry Valley. He'd already lost a whole bunch of cattle to wooden tongue and we needed to take them to the upper part of the valley. Two of the cows were blind from the wooden tongue and I told my dad, 'these cows are blind, dad. They can't see where they are going.' 'Well,' he said, 'Just leave 'em.' So we drove the other cattle up into Dry Valley Creek. There was a big old high bank there and the trail went around it and off the bank. Dad told me, 'You stay down in the bottom and I'll go up above and keep the cattle from going over and we'll take them on up the creek.' I was sitting down in the creek and I looked up there and here comes one of them blind cows. She was following the other cows and her front feet slid off the high bank and I just held my breath. A little of the bank caved off and all of a sudden she come over and plopped down there and didn't move. I was really upset and I though, 'Man, I hope that other one don't come.' And in just a few minutes, here come the other one. She done the very same thing. Both of them fell off." (425~)

Dry Wash: (Emery Co.) Cedar Mountain-Desert Seep Wash. Cleveland and Cow Flats maps.

Inscriptions include Joe Hadden, 8-89 and Alford Hadden, 1899. (1115~)

—Dormans Gulch: This small southern tributary of upper Dry Wash is one-half mile east of CCC Pond (immediately east of elevation 5797 on the Cleveland map). Lee Mont Swasey: "J. Eldon Dorman. He was an Indian rock art fanatic. Started out as a coal camp doctor. Really nice old guy. He took [rock art specialist and author] Kenneth Castleton down there and showed him the rock art. So, Castleton named it Dormans Gulch." (1853~)

—Dry Wash Pictographs: These were added to the Utah State Register of Historic Sites in 1975.

Dry Wash: (Emery Co.) Manti-LaSal National Forest-Wasatch Plateau-Millsite Reservoir. Flagstaff Peak and Ferron maps.

—Dry Wash Trail: This constructed stock trail is the "Pack" trail that goes up Dry Wash (on both maps). (SAPE.)

Dry Wash: (Emery Co.) San Rafael Swell-North Salt Wash. Emery East, Short Canyon, and Sid and Charley maps.

Lee Mont Swasey: "It is dry most of the time." (1853~)

—Olsens Corral: This is on Dry Wash one mile west of Rochester Reservoir (near elevation 6020 on the Short Canyon map). Lee Mont Swasey: "That's a fairly modern corral. I would say 1950s or 1960s. The Olsens live in Moore." (1853~) Ray Wareham noted that it was Travis, Boyd, and Clayton Olsen. (1967~)

Dry Wash: (Garfield Co.) Dixie National Forest-Asay Creek. Asay Bench and George Mountain maps.

Also called Goat Pen Creek. (1931~)

Dry Wash: (Garfield Co.) Henry Mountains-Sweetwater Creek. Mount Ellen, Steele Butte, and Stevens Mesa maps.

Also called Little Creek.

Dry Wash: (Garfield and Piute Counties.) Awapa Plateau-East Fork Sevier River. Flossie Knoll, Angle, and Antimony maps.

Abe McIntosh in 1941: "A small spring is situated at the mouth of the canyon. But before it gets very far the water seeps into the ground leaving the lower end of the canyon dry." (2053~)

Dry Wash: (Grand Co.) Cache Valley-Colorado River. Big Bend map.

—Constructed Stock Trail: This incredible trail goes down Dry Wash from Cache Valley to the Colorado River. (1866~, SAPE.) (See Cache Valley and Stearns Creek.)

Dry Wash: (Kane Co.) Black Mountain-Long Valley. Glendale map.

Also called Flume Canyon. (767~)

Dry Wash: (Kane Co.) GSCENM-Kaiparowits Plateau-Last Chance Creek. Petes Cove and Needle Eye Point maps.

Unattributed: "Name was given because of the nature of the canyon which was applied by the [Almon] Thompson Survey Party in 1872. (2053~) Edson Alvey noted that there was no water in the wash. (55~)

—Constructed Stock Trail: This starts at the "Y" formed by two small forks of upper Dry Wash (one-quarter mile south-southeast of elevation 6066 on the Petes Cove map). (SAPE.)

Dry Wash: (San Juan Co.) Cedar Mesa-Comb Wash. Bluff NW map.

Also called Dry Creek.

—Matheny Canyon: The mouth of this short western tributary of Dry Wash is one and one-half miles south of its junction with Picket Fork (northwest of elevation 5641). Archaeologist Ray T. Matheny of Brigham Young University discovered Anasazi relics here.

Dry Wash: (San Juan Co.) Manti-LaSal National Forest-Abajo Mountains-Cottonwood Wash. Mount Linnaeus, Mancos Jim Butte, and Cream Pots maps.

Also called Dry Canyon Wash and Dry Wash Canyon. (761~)

Marvin Lyman: "There was a stream of water that comes out of the west of the Abajo Mountain up here and goes down Cottonwood and they call it Dry Wash. There was a real nice stream of water there ... and it was a beautiful stream." (1257~)

—Nizhoni Campground: This National Forest campground is two miles west-southwest of the point where Cherry Creek turns into Johnson Creek (one-quarter mile west-southwest of elevation 7824T on the Mount Linnaeus map). *Nizhóní* is Navajo for "something that is beautiful or attractive." (2072~)

—Dry Wash Reservoir: This is one-half mile south of Nizhoni Campground (one-quarter mile northwest of elevation 7681 on the Mount Linnaeus map). It is fed by a ditch, built in the late 1940s, coming from Dry Wash. In one place a tunnel was dug through an escarpment. (835~)

—Little Valleys: Early settlers called a trio of canyons—Dry Wash, Allen Canyon, and Hammond Canyon—the Little Valleys. The Paiutes claimed these valleys as their own for many years. (1237~, 1249~) (See Allen Canyon.)

Dry Wash: (Sevier Co.) Fishlake National Forest-Tushar Mountains-Clear Creek Canyon. Marysvale Canyon map.

—Dry Wash Trail: This constructed stock trail went up Dry Wash to Sage Flat and First Spring. (M.68., SAPE.)

Dry X Res: (Emery Co.) Castle Valley-Molen Seep Wash. Short Canyon map.

Wayne Gremel noted that Dry X was homesteaded in the 1890s by Willie Black: "They farmed out there and then they had to quit. They just didn't have enough water. There is an old cabin out there on the Dry Wash road. It is called the Willie Black House. They call everything around there the Dry X." (780~)

—Dry Wash: This is the small wash the comes out of the east side of Dry X Reservoir. (1233~)

Dubinky Wash: (Grand Co.) Tenmile Country-The Needles-Hell Roaring Canyon. Dubinky Wash and Mineral Canyon maps.

Also spelled Dewbenky Wash, Dobink Wash, and Doobinky Wash.

Guy Robison: "It was named after Dubinky Anderson. His first name was Albert." (1430~) Dubinky ran cattle in the area in the 1920s and '30s. The surrounding country was important for cattle grazing and became known as both Tenmile Country or simply as "Dubinky." (See Tenmile Country.) Pearl Baker: "Dubinky over near Dead Horse Point was named because there was a little spring there. Dubinky Anderson had a still there." (124~)

—Ekker Ranch: In 1936 Arthur Ekker (1911-1978), who would later buy the Biddlecome Ranch at Crow Seep on Robbers Roost Flats, had a house built of railroad ties next to Dubinky Wash one and one-quarter miles south of Dubinky Well (Dubinky Wash map). The remnants of this ranch still remain and include the house and a unique corral made with one inch cable. (197~, 1430~, SAPE.)

Guy Robison worked for Arthur Ekker at the ranch. He told a couple of stories about his time there: "It started to storm and snow. I didn't think anything about it. The snow wasn't too cold, but it came down fast enough that it laid about four or six inches on the ground. I got on my horse and started for home, to Dubinky. And the sun came out and the glare just blazed, and I didn't have a pair of glasses. The first thing I knew I was plumb blind. I couldn't see nothin'. I couldn't even see the head of my horse. I thought, well, the best thing for me to do is just get ahold of that saddle horn and give 'im his head and he'll go home. I knew the trail good and I knew when we dropped off into the wash. We'd drop off of quite a little jump down into it and then we'd be in the gravel. I remember when we hit that.

I knew we weren't very far from home. When I got there, the old pony stopped at the granary and I hollered to Art [Ekker]. He come out and wanted to know what the matter was and I said, 'I'm blind.' And he come over and helped me off m' horse and took me in the house and it hurt, hurt like a son of a gun. I was absolutely blind. I just went to bed and stayed there for three days. I was hurtin' to beat the band. Art'd come and get hold of me and help me out when I had to go out. I finally started to glimmerin' a little bit and seein' just a little bit and, of course it kept gettin' better. But now my eyes were blue. And they'd been brown for my whole life. But now they were blue. And they've stayed blue." (1644~)

The second story concerned Arthur Ekker: "[He] had a band of horses runnin' out there and he had a mare he wanted to get. The horse was four or five years old. She'd been broke to lead, but she was a little wild. We had quite a hard run to gettin' the horses rounded up and into a corral. We got a halter on this mare, and since she was supposed to be broke, Art got to thinking, 'Well, I've rode my old horse pretty damn hard. I'll just get on this little mare and let my horse rest.' So Art got on this little mare and had the other horse on the end of his lariat. When we got out the gate, this bronco horse saw the gate open and the other horses goin' out and he just run by and scared that little mare and she started to buckin'. Somehow or other, the rope caught 'round Art's spur and Art went sailing off'n the buckin' mare. But he was caught up on the spur and he was being drug along. By the time I got my rope off the horse I was leading, and got after him, he had quite a start on me, but I caught up with him. But my horse was scared of him adraggin' and I couldn't get close enough. About that time, he come loose and I'll tell you it was a relief! And he was shook up. So was I. He was skinned, but not really hurt." (1644~)

—Dubinky Well: This well, drilled by the CCC in 1937, is no longer in use. (142~)

Duches Hole: (Uintah Co.) Uintah and Ouray Indian Reservation-Desolation Canyon. Duches Hole map.

This was also called Bens Hole. Jean Bennett in 1965: "Ben's Hole was first settled by Ben Morris ... locally known as Wild Horse Ben, who came from Oklahoma. He chased wild horses, raised pintos and made whiskey." (209~)

Ken Sleight: "He was quite a bootlegger and also enjoyed his own liquor extremely so. At one time while drunk he beat up two Greeks quite soundly. One of the Greeks in desperation pulled a gun on Ben causing each to shoot at the other. The Greek was seriously wounded and taken to the hospital. He recovered but they sent Ben to prison for the shooting. While Ben was in prison a man by the name of Carmen jumped his claim but he in turn sold it to another fellow named Dutch Buetell before Ben was released from prison. Whiskey making was the main industry at Ben's Hole. Ben used to 'age' his whiskey by placing the barrels of charged liquid on top of his pack mules and carrying them the thirty miles to 'civilization.' He said it was equal to 10 years of aging." (1754~)

Duchesne County:

The county seat is Duchesne City.

The county was established in 1914 from the eastern part of Wasatch County. (1194~)

Duchesne, a French word, was probably introduced by French trappers to the Uintah Basin in the early 1800s. (1148~)

Duck Creek Sinks: (Kane Co.) Dixie National Forest-Markagunt Plateau. Henrie Knolls map.

Julius S. Dalley: "During early settlement of Kane County, 1872, and years following many ducks swarmed the lakes and streams of this section." (2053~) Water from Duck Lake and Duck Creek flows into the sinks and goes underground here, marking the end of Duck Creek. (2020~)

—Movies: *Drums Along the Mohawk* was filmed, in part, along Duck Creek. (421~)

Ducket Crossing: (San Juan Co.) Dark Canyon Plateau-White Canyon. Mancos Mesa NE map.

Correctly spelled Duckett Crossing.

This is one of the four named crossings of White Canyon. (The others are Gravel Crossing, Soldier Crossing, and Outlaw Crossing.)

John Baxter Duckett (1849-1910) and his brother, Joseph Alexander Duckett (1848-1933), first mined gold in the Abajo Mountains and then started the Dolly Varden Copper Mine in lower White Canyon in 1898. (1115~)

Francis F. Kane in 1891: There are no more than two known crossings [of White Canyon]. One of these two is unknown except to two or three cattlemen who range their cattle in the winter in this part of the country. The other is better known and is called Soldier's Crossing." (1037~) It is assumed that then the unnamed crossing was Duckett Crossing.

Duckett Crossing was also called Fifteen Mile Crossing. It was fifteen miles from the old town of Hite. (324~) W.W. Dyar in 1904: "They camped the first night at Fifteen Mile Crossing, which is about three miles beyond Copper Point. Fifteen Mile is a small wash or gulch opening into White Canyon, and like all the smaller water courses in that region, is entirely dry most of the year." (587~)

James H. Knipmeyer noted that the original stock trail and, later, wagon road from Hite on the Colorado River to Blanding and Monticello did not follow the present course of Highway 95. Rather, it went from Hite, along the north side of White Canyon, over the head of Fort-knocker Canyon, and crossed White Canyon at Duckett Crossing. It then followed the south side of White Canyon, cut up through the Bears Ears, and went on to the towns. (1115~)

—Duckett Canyon: Carl Mahon identified this as the short canyon immediately southwest of Duckett Crossing. (1272~) James H. Knipmeyer noted that it is very likely that the Duckett brothers base camped in this small canyon while working at their Dolly Varden Copper Mine. (1115~) (See Copper Point.)

Duckett Ridge: (San Juan Co.) Manti-LaSal National Forest-Abajo Mountains. Mount Linnaeus map.
(See Duckett Crossing for name derivation.)

The ridge was extensively mined during the gold rush years of the 1890s by brothers John Baxter and Joseph Alexander Duckett.

—Duckett Mine and Cabin: The Duckett brothers' mine and cabin are on the north end of Duckett Ridge (near elevation 10263). The cabin is still extant. (1115~)

Duck Lake: (Kane Co.) Dixie National Forest-Markagunt Plateau. Henrie Knolls map.
Also called Duck Creek Pond. (2020~)

Lieutenant George M. Wheeler of the Wheeler Survey of 1872–73: "Clambering over the rough lava by the aid of a blind Indian trail, we suddenly emerge upon a handsome glade-like valley, in which springs up, as if by magic, a creek fully 25 feet wide. Duck on their migrations southward (September 20) were noted in large numbers." (1997~)

George C. Fraser in 1915: "The contrast of the verdant hillsides, the flesh colored ribbon of shore and the pinkish tinge of the beach under water, with the blue depth of the center, makes a very beautiful picture." (668~)

—CCC Camp: This was near Duck Lake and was in operation for three years. They built the Duck Lake Ranger Station. (2021~)

—Duck Lake Ranger Station: This still-used ranger station is adjacent to Duck Lake. The first buildings were erected in 1908. In 1933 the CCC constructed new buildings. Other buildings have been added and old buildings updated over the years. (2021~)

—Movies: An area two miles east of Duck Lake, called Movie Ranch, was the site for filming *My Friend Flicka*. (1658~)

Duck Lake: (San Juan Co.) Manti-LaSal National Forest-Dark Canyon Plateau-North Elk Ridge. Poison Canyon map.

—Gooseberry Guard Station: (Also called Gooseberry Ranger Station.) This ranger station is one mile north of Duck Lake at elevation BM8558. Randall Henderson: "Gooseberry Station was well named. Great patches of wild Gooseberries grow here…. They are more palatable in pies than eaten raw." (866~)

Dugout Creek: (Carbon Co.) Book Cliffs-Clark Valley-Grassy Trail Creek. Pine Canyon and Sunnyside Junction maps.

Kate B. Carter: "Some of the early settlers lived in dugouts." (375~) Tom McCourt: "There is a very old, but fairly well preserved dugout cabin near the mouth of Dugout Canyon…. I suspect that the canyon might have been named Dugout because of this old cabin." (1323a~)

Dugout Creek: (Garfield Co.) Henry Mountains-Sweetwater Creek. Mount Ellen, Steele Butte, and Stevens Mesa maps.

Charles B. Hunt: "presumably named for a range camp dugout." (925~) Hunt noted that Grove Karl Gilbert of the Powell Survey called this Cache Creek after caching supplies here in 1875–76. (925~, 723~)

Barbara Ekker: "Early ranchers lived in dugouts along the creek while herding their cattle." (607~) Guy Robison: "A fella by the name of Bert Avery had a dugout there, just above that spring. I think you can still see where it was. That's how come it's named dugout." (1644~)

—Sarvis Bench: This is between Dugout Creek and McClellan Spring (at elevations 8556T and 8590T on the Mount Ellen map). (1537~)

Dugout Ranch: (San Juan Co.) Abajo Mountains-Indian Creek. Harts Point South map.
Also called Indian Creek Ranch and Scorup Ranch.

There is some confusion as to the exact dates and who settled exactly when and where. This is the best reconstruction I can provide.

The first Euroamerican known to spend time in the area was George Washington Johnson (aka George Johnson Wilbourne), sometimes known as "Indian Creek" Johnson. He arrived in the early 1880s.

D.M. Cooper and Mel Turner made an effort to settle in the Dugout area starting in the fall of 1885. Others, including Harry G. Green, Lee Kirk, and V.P. Martin then moved to the area. John E. Brown, arriving from the Glen Canyon area in 1887, was the first to try and make a real go of it, planting an orchard, stringing fence, and constructing irrigation ditches. At that time the L.D.S. Church contemplated establishing a town at Indian Creek, but the idea didn't go forward.

Al Scorup, one of the later owners of the ranch, noted that these early settlers lived in dugouts, providing the name. In about 1888 Thomas Pink Trout bought the Dugout Ranch. In the early 1900s D.M. Cooper, David Goudelock, Harry Green, and V.P. Martin bought out Trout and combined their own ranches to form the Indian Creek Cattle Company. They sold it to Al and Jim Scorup and Bill and Andrew Somerville in 1919. These men formed the famed Scorup-Somerville (S&S) Cattle Company. Redd Ranches bought the property in 1965 and sold it to The Nature Conservancy in 1997. (143~, 536~, 774~, 1508~, 1526~, 1741~, 1960~)

Francis F. Kane in 1891: "Our ride after lunch took us over a plateau covered with pinion and then finally down into a cañon which we subsequently found to be the cañon of [North] Cottonwood creek. At the bottom of this there seemed to be a poor winter range. The first fence that we struck was that of [Thomas] Ray's ranch.... We learned that it was ten miles further to [John E.] Brown's, we pushed on down the valley, reaching Gillegan's ranch [Dugout Ranch] some time after dark.... Gillegan's Ranch on Indian Creek. D.P. Martin, who works Gillegan's ranch, says he has been on Indian creek for four or five years and that there were scarcely anybody who came here before him.... Leaving Gillegan's we rode up the valley to Cooper and Turners' ranch which is two miles above Gillegan's, and adjoining John Brown's.

"After leaving Turner's we passed on into Brown's enclosure. We found his farm to be much the finest in the whole district.... He says he was the earliest settler on Indian Creek, coming here five winters ago (1886). That he also has a place on Salt Creek." (1037~)

Jack Breed in 1952: "Hidden in a remote canyon, accessible by an unmarked road that is passable only when dry, Dugout has one of the most dramatic locations I have ever seen. The entrance trail twists down through Indian Creek until the canyon itself widens into a flat-bottomed oasis half a mile wide and perhaps ten miles long. Fields of grass and alfalfa, bordered by gently swaying cottonwoods, surround the ranch, while the background rise ruddy sandstone cliffs a thousand feet high." (277~)

—Movies: *City Slickers II* was filmed, in part, at the Dugout Ranch. (1421~)

—Fringe of Life Canyon: This eastern tributary of Indian Creek is one mile southeast of Dugout Ranch (one-quarter mile south of elevation 6201T). The original name was Donnelly Canyon. (See Donnelly Canyon.) Rock climbers recently renamed it Fringe of Life Canyon. (239~) Pete Steele, when told what climbers had renamed the canyon, said: "Oh, Yea. Can you imagine some old cowboy tellin' you that!" (1821~)

—Paragon Prow: This jutting prow is immediately south of the Dugout Ranch (at elevation 6289T). It was named by rock climbers.

—Scurrilous rumor: Kent Frost in 1957: "There is a rumor going around here that the Dugout Ranch in Indian Creek has been sold to the army and will be made into a Jet and guided missile airbase with the big Wingate Ledges to be hollowed out for the hangers and air raid shelters.... This makes us very sad as we hate to see this happening to our country." (691~)

Dugout Wash: (Emery Co.) San Rafael Desert-Sweetwater Reef-San Rafael River. The Flat Tops, Jacks Knob, and Spring Canyon maps.

This long shallow wash was named for its two springs, Upper Dugout Spring and Dugout Spring (Jacks Knob map).

Two name derivations are given.

First, water was procured by digging a trench in the sand and building a watering trough at ground level. Old maps show these as Trough (for Upper Dugout Spring) and Dugout Trough (for Dugout Spring). (100~, 623~, 1642~)

Second, Martin Robison noted that rancher Andy Moore dug out part of a hillside when building a cabin at the spring, giving the spring and wash its name. (1931~)

Pearl Baker: "Dugout flowed freely a few miles of bitter alkaline fluid that, while it didn't seem to bother horses and cattle, acted an instant purgative to man." (120~)

Alvin Robison told this story about Andy Moore: "They had a little old log cabin there at Dugout Spring. It wasn't very big and it had a little lean-to on one side of it. When

I was a kid, we was out there with the Moores and Arthur Ekker. We were all ridin' and Arthur Ekker had a new horse, a paint horse, and we was cuttin' cattle. And what happened, that horse kinda run away with 'im and took 'im under that lean-to and pretty near knocked him off. Art laid plumb down on the side of that horse and the horse went under that porch and out the other end without knockin' him off." (1642~)

Millie Biddlecome told the story of seeing a black bear in the wash in 1921: "It was awful hot and the bear, a little yearling brown one, ran across the wash and up under a little ledge on the other side where it was shady." (226~)

Dugway Hollow: (Emery Co.) Manti-LaSal National Forest-Wasatch Plateau-Ferron Creek. Flagstaff Peak and Ferron Mountain maps.

Before the modern road up Ferron Canyon's north side was built by the CCC in the late 1930s, the old road went up the south side of the canyon and then up Dugway Hollow. Ray Wareham noted that the road up Dugway Hollow was difficult for the early settlers. (1967~) One can still walk the old road up the hollow. (SAPE.)

Duma Point: (Grand Co.) Tenmile Country-White Wash. Dee Pass map. (4,800')

The small manganese mines on and around Duma Point were located in the early 1900s and were used sporadically through World War Two. (104~)

Duncan Mountain: (Iron Co.) Dixie National Forest-Harmony Mountains. Stoddard Mountain map. (7,743')

Homer Duncan (1815–1906) arrived in St. George in 1863. (462~) He had a ranch on Duncan Creek in the Leach Canyon area starting in the 1870s. (516~, 1184~)

Duncan Mountain: (Sevier Co.) Fishlake National Forest-Wasatch Plateau. Acord Lakes map. (9,251')

John Duncan (1846-1931) started running cattle on the mountain in 1877. (931~) John, his wife Theressa (1853-1935), and family moved to the town of Quitchupah in 1882. (710~)

Dungeon Canyon: (San Juan Co.) Navajo Indian Reservation-Cummings Mesa-Glen Canyon. Cathedral Canyon and Gregory Butte maps.

Katie Lee described river runner Tad Nichols' naming the canyon in 1955: "The entrance [to the canyon] was a missing tooth in the wall. Dark, very narrow, no growth inside, a flat mud-sand-gravel floor. We named it (or Tad did) when we found him tightly huddled into himself, soaking up the only spot of sun near its mouth, and chattering ... 'Brr-rrr ... this place is like a ... DUNGEON'"! (1162~) Again, Katie Lee: "And then we started up the dry throat of this incredible peristalsis canyon. It drew you in

just like peristalsis in your throat. You just couldn't stop. You just kept going. It had an entirely different feeling from any of the other canyons that we'd ever been in. It was colder than a witch's tit in there. The walls were at least three hundred feet high, all with magnificent flutings and overhangs. It was a ventriloquist canyon. You could say a whispering word down at one end of this one long hall and it would be heard at the other end. But as soon as you turned around a corner you couldn't hear a thing. In this particular hall I could envision prisoners shackled to the wall, almost hear the clank of chains as you walked through there. It was very, very mysterious." (1163~)

Joseph L. Dudziak in 1962: "We entered a long corridor with over-hanging walls which produced a twilight occasionally penetrated by brilliant shafts of sunlight—like spot lights on a stage; beautiful color patterns in subdued light.... Being almost blue with cold, we made a fire to thaw out before turning back." (577~)

—Constructed Stock Trail: This trail goes up upper Dungeon Canyon onto Cummings Mesa (immediately north of elevation 4454 on the Gregory Butte map). Improved as a work project in the 1940s, the trail, though it has slumped in places, is still easy to follow. (1021~, SAPE.)

Dunham Wash: (Kane Co.) Pink Cliffs-Deer Wash. Skutumpah Creek and Deer Spring Point maps.

Cal Johnson: "Old Joe Dunham. He had a little house up there. He had quite a reputation. You couldn't help but like that man. He was an old rough cowboy." (984~)

Durfey Butte: (Garfield Co.) Henry Mountains-Dry Lake Flat. Mount Ellen map. (9,580')

Also called Little Ragged.

George Durfey moved his family to Notom in 1919 and started a major sheep-raising operation on the north side of the Henry Mountains. He had a cabin to the northwest of the butte. (582~, 700~, 1419~, 1537~)

Durfey Creek: (Garfield Co.) Dixie National Forest-Boulder Mountain-Oak Creek. Lower Bowns Reservoir map.

Keith Durfey noted that Alma Durfey (1844-1924) had a dairy on Durfey Creek in the late 1800s. (582~)

Durfey Creek: (Garfield Co.) Dixie National Forest-Boulder Mountain-West Fork Boulder Creek. Jacobs Reservoir and Deer Creek Lake maps.

Mrs. Mac LeFevre noted that Alma Durfey lived in the area in about 1885. (1931~)

Durffey Mesa: (Garfield Co.) GSCENM-Boulder Creek. Calf Creek, King Bench, and Boulder Town maps. (6,848')

Correctly spelled Durfey Mesa.

(See Durfey Butte for name derivation.)

Durkee Creek: (Piute Co.) White Hills-Sevier River. Marysvale map.

Also spelled Durke Creek.

The Miles and Eliza Durkee family arrived in Marysvale in 1865. They had a ranch near the mouth of the canyon. (1444~)

—Durkee Reservoir: This stock pond was built in 1963. (1526~)

—Durkee Springs: This is a large spring. (SAPE.)

—Bullion Hill: This hill, part of the Marysvale Uranium District, is to the north and east of the mouth of Durkee Creek and is centered on elevation 6848 (Nipple). The name was applied by miners. (1088~)

—Twin Hills: These hills, part of the Marysvale Uranium District, are to the south of Durkee Creek and immediately north of elevation 6850. The name was applied by miners. (1088~)

Dutch Flat: (Emery Co.) Castle Valley-Molen Reef. Molen map. PRIVATE PROPERTY.

Evelyn Peacock Huntsman: "Ferdinand Behling [1864-1925] and family arrived in Ferron from Germany in 1899.... Because the Behlings were from what was then known as Deutschland (Germany) and lived on the large area of the flat land east of town the people in Ferron referred to the area as Deutsch Flat. The spelling changed over the years and it became known as 'Dutch Flat.'" (931~)

—Dutch Flat Reservoir: This still-used stock reservoir was built in 1936. (1551~)

—Old Spanish Trail: The trail crossed Dutch Flat. (1551~)

Dutch Fork Reservoir: (Sanpete Co.) Manti-LaSal National Forest-Wasatch Plateau. Ferron Reservoir map.

This was built in the early 1950s. (1330~)

Dutchman Arch: (Emery Co.) San Rafael Swell-Head of Sinbad. San Rafael Knob map.

Also called Dutchmen's Arch (1551~) and Sinbad Arch (1956~).

Dee Anne Finken noted that a Dutchman was employed by pioneer rancher John Seely. (641~) Lee Mont Swasey noted that the Dutchman worked for Earl Seely. (1853~)

Inscriptions include an unreadable name with the date 1898. Other inscriptions are E. Jeffs, 1915 and Warren Allred, Feb. 20, 1931. (SAPE.)

Dutchmans Wash: (Emery Co.) Castle Valley-Cottonwood Creek. Hadden Holes map.

Lee Mont Swasey: "There were lots of Dutchmen in this country. They got crowded out of Sanpete." (1853~)

—Dutchmans Wash Stock Pond: PRIVATE PROPERTY. This pond is in Dutchmans Wash.

Dutton Pass: (Washington Co.) Vermilion Cliffs-Gould Wash. Smithsonian Butte map. (5,400')

Also called Dutton Notch.

(See Smithsonian Butte for name derivation and Towers of the Virgin for Clarence Dutton's description of the views from the pass.)

—Dutton Pass Spring: This large, developed, and still-used spring is on the west side of Dutton Pass. (SAPE.)

Dwarf: (San Juan Co.) Manti-LaSal National Forest-Dark Canyon Plateau-South Elk Ridge. Cream Pots map.

Three name derivations are given.

First, Pete Steele: "Once upon a time there was a little Navajo pony that was a dwarf and it used to run right in that area. And that's why it's called Dwarf." (1821~)

Second, Albert R. Lyman noted that it was named for a small spring: "Up along the narrow backbone, hidden by the trees, and then along the shelf to what is known as Dwarf Spring." (1239~)

Third, Al Scorup: "The Elk Mountain cattle [in the 1890s] were Texas Dwarfs from an original 2000 that came from Texas. A fellow saw the calves of these cows and asked John [Ernest] Adams what kind of bulls he had the calves from. Adams said, 'those are just little mavericks that run wild, they don't have no fathers'"! (1701~)

Nearby inscriptions date to 1891. (SAPE.)

Dyches Draw: (Piute Co.) Fishlake National Forest-Sevier Plateau-Dry Creek. Marysvale Peak map.

Newel Nielson noted that Milo T. Dyches worked for the Forest Service in the early 1900s. (1458~)

E

Eagle Canyon: (Emery Co.) San Rafael Swell-North Salt Wash. San Rafael Knob, Copper Globe, and Sid and Charley maps.

Two name derivations are given.

First, Dee Anne Finken: "Eagle Canyon got its name when one day Rod and Joe Swasey rode up to the point where the canyon suddenly boxes, and Rod exclaimed 'God, an eagle couldn't fly out of here!'" (641~)

Second, Kate B. Carter: "So named by first settlers because they found a pair of eagles nesting in the ledges." (384~, 2053~)

Inscriptions include John Justensen, 1889; Warren Allred and Orson Justensen "camped for night, going to Sinbad, Deep Snow and Cold," 1898; and Seely Peterson, Aug. 15, 1932. (SAPE.)

—Swasey Cabin: (Also called Joe Swasey's Cabin.) This historic cabin is shown but is not named on the San Rafael Knob map. It is at the top of Eagle Canyon and is one mile west of Forked Post Pond. It was listed on the Utah State Register of Historic Places in 1971.

Rodney Degrasse Swasey (1832-1898) moved to the Castle Valley area in 1874. A rancher, he and his four sons—Charlie, Sid, Rod, and Joe—were soon running cattle throughout the San Rafael Swell.

Initially the family used caves at the head of Eagle Canyon as their home. They called one of the caves Joe's Office for Joe Swasey and they called the whole complex Cliff Dweller. In 1921 they built a cabin, hauling Douglas fir logs from Eagle Canyon. (122~, 511~, 641~, 727~, 1853~) Lee Mont Swasey: "In the early days the ranchers could run their stock anywhere they wanted. They had free rein. Later on, when things started tightening up, I think that they decided 'We'd better start homesteading.' I think that the Swasey Cabin was built as part of a homestead." (1853~) The cabin has been stabilized by the BLM.

Inscriptions in the area include ? Seely, 1907 and C.P. Pilling, April 21, 1920. (SAPE.)

—Amasy Spring: Lee Mont Swasey noted that this was the Swasey name for the good spring near the cabin and that it may mean "jackass" in the Paiute language. (1853~)

—Broken Cross Pinnacle: Dee Anne Finken noted that this pinnacle, which is behind the Swasey Cabin, was given its name by rancher Seely Peterson. (641~)

Pearl Baker noted that it was called Cliff Dweller Peak: "Mr. Hartsell followed the ancient traces up south Temple, over Cliff Dweller Spring, past Cliff Dweller Peak where Joe and Central Swasey had a cabin." (114~)

Nedra Swasey Humphrey, the great great granddaughter of Joe Swasey, wrote a letter to Steve Allen in 1992: "I stayed in the [Swasey] cabin several times growing up and loved the area.... I feel I must tell you that all the Swaseys called the rock Grizzly Bear Rock.... As you go up the road take a good look and you tell me what it should be called"! Lee Mont Swasey: "Bull Pucky! That's the Broken Cross. You can look at it and see that it's a cross that the arms are broken off." (1853~)

—Eagle Canyon Road: This started as a stock trail and was improved in the 1920s by an oil company. (1853~)

—South Fork Eagle Canyon: The mouth of this southern tributary of Eagle Canyon is one and one-quarter miles (as the crow flies) downcanyon from the Swasey Cabin (north of elevations 7355 and 7735 on the San Rafael Knob map). (1853~)

—Eagle Canyon Arch: This is the "Natural Arch" that is one-half mile downcanyon from the junction of Eagle Canyon and South Fork Eagle Canyon (at elevation 7082 on the San Rafael Knob map). Cowboys called it the Needles Eye. (1956~) Lee Mont Swasey noted that it was called Jug Handle Arch. (1853~) Dottie Grimes noted it as Beer Stein Rock. (791~)

—Deer Canyon: This small southern tributary of Eagle Canyon is one-third of a mile downcanyon from Eagle Canyon Arch (immediately west of elevation 7260 on the San Rafael Knob map). (1853~)

—Upper Eagle Canyon Spring and Troughs: These are at the mouth of Deer Canyon. Lee Mont Swasey: "That spring is incredibly high in sulphur. You could stick your arm in the water, pull it out, and by the time you got back to camp, your arm would just be black! It smells nasty." (1853~)

—Horse Canyon: The mouth of this small southern tributary of Eagle Canyon is one-quarter mile west of Deer

Canyon (south of elevation 7285 on the San Rafael Knob map). (1853~)

—Lower Eagle Canyon Spring: This is at an abandoned meander in Eagle Canyon four miles southeast of Sid and Charley (one-quarter mile southeast of elevation 6022 on the Sid and Charley map). (780~)

Eagle Crags: (Washington Co.) Vermilion Cliffs-Horse Valley Wash. Springdale West map.

Almon H. Thompson of the 1871–72 Powell Expedition most likely called this Virgin Temple: "Virgin Temple—on the other side of the river and above Rockville." (1877~)

Jonreed Lauritzen in 1947: "Eagle Crags ranges a sober Monks' Procession of colossal statuary on the southern horizon." (1149~)

Eagle Gate Arch: (Kane Co.) GSCENM-Johnson Canyon. Johnson Lakes map.

Frank Jensen: "Eagle Arch, so named because of its resemblance to an eagle perched on a nest." (964~)

Francis M. Bishop of the 1871–72 Powell Expedition: "Yesterday went over to Eagle Gate [Johnson]." (236~)

—Movies: *Dude Ranger* was filmed, in part, with Eagle Gate Arch in the background. (131~)

Eagle Mesa: (San Juan Co.) Navajo Indian Reservation-Monument Valley. Goulding and Monument Pass maps. (6,541')

Also called Eagle Rock, Eagle Rock Mesa (1204~), Wide Butte (101~), and Wide Mesa (1197~).

The Navajo believe that spirits go here after death. (1204~)

Joseph Miller: "This great stone image requires little play of the imagination to suggest a likeness to the great American eagle on its perch." (1359~)

James H. Knipmeyer: "The name of Eagle Rock came from its resemblance to an eagle perched on a ledge. The mesa was then named for the rock, located at its western end." (1115~)

Joyce Muench called this Pop's Mesa in 1941: "a long stretch of unadulterated mass, flat on the top and impenetrable. It sheers off at either end and looks vast and mysterious." (1404~)

Eardley Canyon: (Emery Co.) San Rafael Swell-Straight Wash. Arsons Garden map.

The name was given to the canyon in 1973 in honor of Dr. Armand J. Eardley (1901-1972), a Utah geologist who went through the canyon in 1930. He was the Dean of Mines and Mineral Industries at the University of Utah for many years. (1470~)

Eardley described the canyon in his field notes: "Find descent and arrive bottom of canyon.... Descent thru short

tributary.... Locate probable emergency outlet. Making good process down stream on tail end of flood (we hope) which had occurred the day previously. Having to wade almost continually. Find many extremely narrow gorges which permit of no escape should flood occur." (589~)

Earl Canyon: (Washington Co.) Dixie National Forest-Pine Valley Mountains-Santa Clara River. Central East map.

Sylvester Henry Earl (1815–1872) arrived in the Pine Valley area in 1861. (462~, 1803~)

Earls Draw: (Emery Co.) San Rafael Swell-Road Draw. San Rafael Knob and Twin Knolls maps.

Dee Anne Finken noted that Earl Seely (1884-1931) was an early cattleman. (641~) Lee Mont Swasey noted that Earl Seely was an early sheepman. (1853~)

—Deep Reservoir: This stock reservoir is in a small southern tributary of Earls Draw that is one mile east of Forked Post Pond (one-quarter mile northeast of elevation 7125 on the San Rafael Knob map). It was built in 1958. (1551~)

—Square Reservoir: This stock reservoir in Earls Draw is one and three-quarters of a mile east of Forked Post Pond (one-quarter mile northeast of elevation 7041 on the San Rafael Knob map). It was built in 1958. (1551~)

—Earls Draw Reservoir: This stock reservoir in Earls Draw is two miles east of Forked Post Pond (adjacent to elevation 6875 on the San Rafael Knob map). It was built in 1964. (1551~)

Early Weed Bench: (Kane Co.) GSCENM-Escalante Desert-Hole-in-the-Rock Road. Sunset Flat and Egypt maps.

Edson Alvey noted that the bench was named by ranchers who noticed that since it tips to the south it warms up quickly in the spring, allowing plants to bloom earlier than in other areas. (55~)

Ear of the Wind: (Navajo Co., Az.) Navajo Indian Reservation-Monument Valley. Mitten Buttes, Az. map.

Robert de Roos in 1965: "The valley winds swirl through it and sing an eerie song." (556a~)

East Bench: (Garfield Co.) Sevier River-Highway 89. Panguitch and Panguitch NW maps.

The bench is immediately east of Panguitch. Construction of the Hatchtown Reservoir in 1909 allowed the otherwise dry East Bench to be irrigated for the first time, opening the area to settlement. (65~)

East Canyon: (San Juan Co.) Dry Valley-Hatch Wash. Eastland NW, Sop Canyon, and Church Rock maps.

Orville C. Pratt described the then unnamed canyon in 1848: "We began descending one of the longest and steepest mountains yet passed over. But we got down it with safety. After reaching the bottom the scenery in the valley was the most rugged and sublime I ever beheld." (1572~)

John Strong Newberry of the Captain John N. Macomb Expedition of 1859: "From the vivid colors of the walls of the cañon where we entered it, it was named by our party Cañon Pintado [Painted Canyon]. Its walls are precipitous, generally almost perpendicular, the lower half composed of strata which are bright red, green, yellow or white; soft but massive beds weathering, as such materials are so prone to do in this region, into arches, domes, spires, towers, and a thousand other imitations of human architecture, all on a colossal scale." (1266~)

Charles H. Dimmock of the same expedition called it Valley of the Cañon de las Pañitas, or "The Valley of the Canyon of Little Rocks." (559~) Dimmock went on to write about finding "Saurian fossils of exceeding interest." These dinosaur fossils were a major find for the expedition. (1269~)

East Carbon City: (Carbon Co.) Book Cliffs-Grassy Trail Creek-Highway 123. Sunnyside map.

In 1973 the small towns of Dragerton and Columbia combined to form East Carbon City. (1282~)

East Cedar Mountain: (Emery Co.) San Rafael Swell-Moroni Slopes. The Frying Pan map. (7,066')

Early maps label this Heeps Mountain. (727~)

East Clark Bench: (Kane Co.) Paria Canyon-Vermilion Cliffs Wilderness Area-Paria Canyon-Cedar Hollow-Highway 89. Bridger Point map.

The bench is east of the Paria River. (984~)

In 1871 three families of Clarks helped start the town of Skutumpah, which was also known as Clarkdale. John Wesley Clark (1818-1869) bought out John Doyle Lee's interest in Lees Ferry on the Paria River in about 1872 and ran livestock in the area. (885~, 1639~)

Edwin G. Woolley, diarist for the Utah Territorial Militia of 1869, noted that expedition scouts got a bit confused while trying to cross the bench: "The guides admitted that they were slightly turned around.... We had wandered around 3 hours, coming 5 miles from where we started. We had considerable amusement with all our trouble. We were all certain that we were right and all the rest wrong. Some thought that we were not lost, but it was the Pah Reer [Paria River] was wandering, and we were all positive that we knew exactly where we were, but we did not known exactly where we wanted to get to." (476~)

East Coyote Wash: (San Juan Co.) La Sal Mountains-La Sal-Coyote Wash. La Sal West, La Sal East, Lisbon Valley, and Lisbon Gap maps.

(See West Coyote Wash for name derivation.)

The Don Juan María Antonia de Rivera Expedition of 1765, on its way home to Santa Fe from the Moab area, crossed through this area. (953~)

—Old Spanish Trail: (Variation.) G. Clell Jacobs: "East Coyote Branch was a favored section of the Spanish Trail during the heyday of the large caravans from Los Angeles to Santa Fe during the 1830s and 1840s because of the abundance of water and grass for the large herds and because that branch was not a 'heavy trail' as compared to the trail through Dry Valley. A trail through sand and soft earth, on undulating ground can increase the loads of burden on pack animals, pound their hooves, and shorten their lives as useful animals." (953~)

East Creek: (Garfield Co.) Dixie National Forest-Paunsaugunt Plateau-East Fork Sevier River. Bryce Point and Bryce Canyon maps.

This is east of the East Fork Sevier River.

—Syrett Sawmill: This was on East Creek one mile north-northeast of Whiteman Spring (at elevation BM7824 on the Bryce Point map). (766~) Reuben C. "Ruby" Syrett (1884-1945) started ranching in the area in 1916. (311~) (See Rubys Inn.)

East End Spring: (Kane Co.) Glen Canyon NRA-Kaiparowits Plateau-Navajo Point. Navajo Point map.

This medium-size spring was once developed. (SAPE.)

It is the spring that is furthest east on the Kaiparowits Plateau. Albert Twitchell officially located the spring in 1903: "The said springs are situated on the southeast rim of the Fifty Mile Mountain." (2053~)

Easter Pasture Canyon: (Garfield Co.) Glen Canyon NRA-Waterhole Flat-Cataract Canyon. Clearwater Canyon and Teapot Rock maps.

Ned Chaffin: "Faun [Chaffin] first found his way into here on a Easter Sunday, so we called it Easter Pasture." (606~, 615~)

—Constructed Stock Trail: This short trail enters the east side of Easter Pasture Canyon one mile north of the Colorado River (one-quarter mile southwest of elevation 5352T on the Teapot Rock map). The trail, with little construction, continues down to the river. (SAPE.) It is possible that John Hislop of the James S. Best Expedition of 1891 used the general course of this trail (most likely not in existence at the time) to hike to Dandy Crossing for dynamite to help them blow up a rock that was pinning one of their bolts at Capsize Rapid at the mouth of Range Creek. (1320~) (See Range Creek—Mile-Long Rapid.)

—Chimney Rock: Noted by early river runners, this is one of several chimney-like pinnacles on the Colorado River within a mile of the mouth of Easter Pasture Canyon. (1574~)

—Chimney Rock Bend: This is the bend in the river at Chimney Rock. It starts at Gypsum Canyon and ends at Easter Pasture Canyon. (1574~)

East Fork Sevier River: (Garfield and Kane Counties.) Dixie National Forest-Paunsaugunt Plateau-Piute Reservoir. Maps south to north: Podunk Creek, Tropic Reservoir, Bryce Point, Bryce Canyon, Tropic Canyon, Flake Mountain East, Cow Creek, Sweetwater Creek, Grass Lakes, Antimony, Deep Creek, Phonolite Hill, Junction, and Piute Reservoir.

Also called East Canyon, East Fork Creek, and Rock Canyon. (2032~)

(See Sevier River for name derivation.)

Gwinn Harris Heap of the Lieutenant Edward F. Beale Expedition of 1853 called this *San Pasqual*. (854~) Joseph Fish, a member of the Andrus Military Reconnaissance Expedition of 1866, used the East Fork Sevier River name. (645~) The Lieutenant George M. Wheeler Survey map of 1872–73 shows it as East Fork Canyon. (M.76.) The East Fork Sevier River name was in place by 1874. (312a~)

Clarence Dutton of the Powell Survey: "About midway between the middle and southern eruptive centers the Sevier Plateau is cut completely in twain by a mighty gorge called the East Fork Canyon.... It is not a narrow chasm, but a valley walled by ledge upon ledge.... The total depth varies in different parts from 1,400 to 3,700 feet." (584~)

—Old Spanish Trail: (Variation.) The Old Spanish Trail—Fish Lake Route—went along Otter Creek, by today's Otter Creek Reservoir, and then turned west along East Fork Sevier River to join the main Old Spanish Trail at Junction. (477~)

East Fork Virgin River: (Kane and Washington Counties.) Zion National Park-Parunuweap Canyon. Long Valley Junction, Glendale, Orderville, Mount Carmel, The Barracks, Springdale East, and Springdale West maps.

(See Parunuweap Canyon for name derivation.)

East Fork Virgin River flows through Parunuweap Canyon.

The Jedediah Smith Expedition of 1826 traveled up the Sevier River, over the divide at today's Long Valley Junction, and down East Fork Virgin River, probably leaving it near Sixmile Turn (See below) at the head of Parunuweap Canyon. They rejoined the river near Hurricane. (2044~) Stephen Vandiver Jones of the 1871–72 Powell Expedition called this the Long Valley Branch of the Virgin River. (1023~) Richard L. Hoxie of the Lieutenant George M.

Wheeler Survey of 1872–73 called it South Fork of Virgin. (916~) The 1881 Rand McNally Utah map shows it as the main fork of the *Rio Virgin* and the North Fork as the Springdale Fork (665~), as does the H.H. Hardesty map of 1882 (M.29.).

Inscriptions along the original road cut across the river near Mount Carmel Junction include N.S., April 1907; I.W. Blake, 1911; Carl Dennis, April 20, 1917; and Dale Brimhall, April 1921. (SAPE.)

—Sixmile Turn: This turn in the upper part of East Fork Virgin River at the head of Parunuweap Canyon is one-half mile west of the mouth of Bay Bill Canyon (one-half mile southeast of elevation 5205 on The Barracks map). It is shown as part of a "Jeep Trail." The turn is six miles from Mount Carmel and is on the Elephant Road. (See Appendix Two—Elephant Road.)

Priddy Meeks in 1852: "[We went down] the Rio Virgen and down through Long Valley to what is called the 'Elephant' where the creek is closed upon by impassable high rocks on each side [Parunuweap Canyon]. We passed on down in the bed of the creek we supposed six miles before a chance appeared for us to leave the creek which we gladly embraced." (1343~)

The Jesse N. Smith Expedition of 1858 took the same route. Smith: "The course of the stream being westerly we turned out on the left hand or south side of the canyon [at Sixmile Turn]." (1775~)

Stephen Vandiver Jones of the Powell Survey took the turn in 1872 and called the hill out of the canyon Elephant Hill. (1023~)

The Lieutenant George M. Wheeler Survey of 1872–73 went down the East Fork Sevier River as far as they could with horses and exited to the south at Sixmile Turn. They then continued on to Shunesburg. (775~)

East Gate Reservoir: (Wayne Co.) Henry Mountains-Goatwater Point. Bull Mountain map.

This is a still-used stock reservoir. (SAPE.)

East Mitten Butte: (Navajo Co., Az.) Navajo Indian Reservation-Monument Valley. Mitten Buttes, Az. map. (6,226')

Also called Coffee Pot Rock and Tea Pot Rock. (556a~, 856~)

Laurance D. Linford noted that the Navajo name is *'Álá Tsoh*, or "Big Hands." (1204~, 556a~) The GLO (General Land Office) map of 1899 shows these as The Pinnacles. (M.23.) In 1901 Howard B. Carpenter called the East Mitten "Ragged Top Monument." (345~) Stewart M. Young noted it as The Mitten in 1911. (2074~)

Arno Nell in 1922: "At sunset I paused to marvel at two rock formations resembling a right and a left-hand mitten. Both of them are several hundred feet high, pointing skyward and standing opposite each other." (1431~)

Richard E. Klinck: "Like two gigantic hands they point skyward, silent and omnipotent. According to the Navajos, the Mittens are the Big Hands, signs of a great power that was once present upon earth, but is now dormant and still." (1099~)

Margaret G. Wood in 1948: "There were several 'Mittens' so-called because the tall, oblong, massive-rock-butte forms the hand and a long, slender spire at one end resembles the thumb which does give the effect of a mitten. And each mitten stands high against the sky on a symmetrically terraced base of rock fragments sloping in and up to a perfect fit at the wrist." (2042~)

East Moody Canyon: (Garfield Co.) Glen Canyon NRA-Circle Cliffs-Escalante River. Deer Point, Stevens Canyon North, and Scorpion maps.

(See Moody Creek Canyon for name derivation.)

East Mountain: (Emery Co.) Manti-LaSal National Forest-Wasatch Plateau. Rilda Canyon map. (10,743')

East Mountain is the highest point in Emery County.

East of the Navajo: (Kane Co.) GSCENM-Kaiparowits Plateau. East of the Navajo and Needle Eye Point maps.

This highland area is east of Navajo Canyon.

East Rim Trail: (Washington Co.) Zion National Park-Echo Canyon. Temple of Sinawava map.

Also called Bend Trail or Big Bend Trail because it starts at the Big Bend of the North Fork Virgin River. (481~, 485~)

This was listed on the National Register of Historic Places in 1987.

This old Indian trail was improved into a fair horse trail by John Winder in 1896. (2043~) Winder told this story: "One of the most regrettable spills I ever had occurred while I was taking a bunch of horses onto the mountain.... Right here where the old trail was steep and slick on the bare rock, the crevice at the side is unusually deep. Refusing to go over this bad stretch of trail, the crazy nag went to bucking.... Downward he leaped over the slick rock floor, nearer and nearer to the edge of the crevice; and just as I was thinking that even a mad horse had sense enough to avoid danger to itself, he disappeared into that crack, like a bee in a jug.... I could hear his body striking the walls and my new saddle scraping the rocks. The crack at this point is nearly two hundred feet deep, and we had to go about a half mile to get into the end of it. We

finally found the horse with a hundred holes in his skin and his breath gone forever." (50~)

The trail became the standard route between the Rockville-Springdale area and the communities in Long Valley. (485~) It was improved from time to time. William L. Crawford in 1901: "Went to the [Big] Bend to work on the [East Rim] trail for J.A. Winder.... We worked on the two lower ledges, put in two blasts and drilled several more holes.... We fired two blasts this forenoon." (484~)

The trail was improved again in the mid-1920s by the National Park Service. It is now a popular hiking trail. (311~) Julius V. Madsen in the late 1920s: "The trail engraves a letter 'M' in its upward trend. With each bend comes a new and more startling panorama." (1267~)

Eivind T. Scoyen in 1931: "The most spectacular trail is that known as the East Rim Trail. It rises to the rim of the main canyon at a point where the climber may look down into the colorful depths, with an unbroken view of the entire length of Zion." (1710~)

East Spring: (Carbon Co.) Book Cliffs-Grassy Trail Creek. Sunnyside map.

Also called Big Spring.

In the early days water from East Spring was pumped to the railroad siding at Cedar. (1490~)

East Spring Canyon: (Sevier Co.) Fishlake National Forest-Old Woman Plateau-Convulsion Canyon. Acord Lakes map.

—Jack Addley Monument: This is at the junction of East Spring and Mud Spring canyons. Jack Addley (1918-1938) was killed here by lightning while chasing cattle. (1931~)

East Squaw Canyon: (Uintah Co.) Uintah and Ouray Indian Reservation-Hill Creek. Flat Rock Mesa and Agency Draw NW maps.

—Webster City: PRIVATE PROPERTY. (Also called Webster Cattle Company Ranch and Webster Ranch. Now called the V. Jenks Ranch.) This famous ranch was at the mouth of East Squaw Canyon on Hill Creek. The Webster City Cattle Company was started by a group of investors from Webster City, Iowa in the 1880s. It became one of the largest ranches in the Book Cliffs area, running up to thirty-five thousand head of cattle. It began selling out in the 1890s. (186~)

Waldo Wilcox told this story about the outlaw Tom Dilly and the Webster Cattle Company: "They branded as the Flying V. Tom Dilly would skin that center out and make it into a 'T.' Then he called his brand the Big T. Then he'd take them to the coal companies out here." (2011~)

East Temple, The: (Washington Co.) Zion National Park-Zion Canyon. Springdale East map. (7,709')

Also called Eastern Temple. (668~)

This is on the east side of Zion Canyon. Clarence Dutton of the Powell Survey named the East Temple: "Just behind them [Temples of the Virgin], rising a thousand feet higher, is the East Temple, crowned with a cylindric dome of white sandstone." (584~)

Robert Frothingham in 1932: "majestic East Temple, with its massive truncated peak winged on either side by a cone-shaped peak and an elongated pyramid of lesser altitude—an impressive mass of exquisite proportions." (698~)

—First Ascent: This monolith was first climbed by a Sierra Club group led by Glen Dawson in 1938. (532~)

East Tidwell Canyon: (Sevier Co.) Fishlake National Forest-Short Canyon-Forsyth Reservoir. Geyser Peak and Forsyth Reservoir maps.

Also called Forsyth Valley. (1931~)

(See Tidwell Valley for name derivation.)

East Valley: (Garfield Co.) GSCENM-Tropic Valley. Tropic Canyon and Cannonville maps.

Also called Losee Valley. (2053~)

—Losee Town: (Also called Looseville, Loseeville, and New Clifton.) This town was two miles east of Tropic in East Valley (near the "Cemetery" on the Tropic Canyon map). Isaac Losee and Orville Cox settled here in 1886. The town was abandoned by 1900. (772~, 1445~)

—Pasture Canyon: W.J. Shakespear: "Is located east of Tropic and approximately 3 miles northeast of Losee Valley. It has a small stream along its coarse which is fenced off into a pasture, this being how it derived its name. This canyon is used for watering cattle during the spring and fall months." (2053~)

Echard Canyon: (Piute Co.) Fishlake National Forest-Tushar Mountains-Dog Valley. Circleville Mountain and Fremont Pass maps.

Thomas Thomas in 1941: "It is a large canyon about two and one-half miles long with a few aspen trees, chokecherry and other shrubbery growing along its course. It opens into Big Dog Valley. Origin of name unknown." (2053~)

Echo Canyon: (Washington Co.) Zion National Park-Zion Canyon. Temple of Sinawava map.

Also called Box Canyon. (482~)

George C. Fraser in 1915: "There is tremendous echo here, so distinct as to be uncanny. A word shouted into the depths is not reverberated, but about two seconds after its utterance is repeated plainly and so with pistol shots.... For convenience it may be designated Echo Canyon." (668~)

Julius V. Madsen in the late 1920s: "All of a sudden, the downward view is cut off. We find ourselves enveloped within the bosom of a deep and unbelievably narrow defile, not unlike an aisleway in some mammoth old world cathedral. The shoes of the horses, striking upon the rocks, sound out sharp and clear, echoing up and down the long corridor. This is Echo Canyon.... Every sound has its answer, not once, but several times. No other name would suit it quite so well.... We come to a place in this narrow gorge where the walls are extremely close together. The Park Service had to blast out a half-tunnel to make sufficient space for a horse to pass between. At this place, by looking up through the slit that separates the two walls, it is possible to see the stars during the daylight hours." (1267~)

—Echo Canyon Trail: (Also called Deer Trap Trail.) (1267~) Julius V. Madsen in the late 1920s: "The Deer Trap Trail takes off into a wild and rugged country, following an old, abandoned route. We climb out of the rugged valley by way of Shelly Point (elevation 6595)." (1267~)

Echo Cliffs: (Coconino Co., Az.) Navajo Indian Reservation-Colorado River. Lees Ferry and Explosive Rock, Az. maps.

The Navajo name is *Tsé K'aan Dahsitáni*, or "Rocks Standing Up Ridge." (857~)

Frederick S. Dellenbaugh of the 1871–72 Powell Expedition: "For amusement I tried to shoot into the river with Cap.'s 44 Remington revolver. As I pulled the trigger the noise was absolutely staggering. The violent report was followed by dead silence. While we were remarking the intensity of the crash, from far away on some distant cliffs northward the sound waves were hurled back to us with a rattle like that of musketry. We tried again with the same result.... We could call the place nothing but Echo Peaks, and since then the name has been applied also to the line of cliffs breaking to the south." (541~)

—CCC Trail: Harvey Butchart noted that the "Pack" trail going up the Echo Cliffs immediately south of the Echo Peaks (Lees Ferry map) was built by the CCC. (321~)

—Buzzard Highland Trail: Harvey Butchart noted that this is the extension of the CCC Trail. It goes east down the backside of the Echo Cliffs and down a sand dune. (321~)

—Badaway Country: In the early days this was the Paiute name for the country between today's Highway 89 and the Colorado River, which includes the Echo Cliffs.

Ed Lamb Point: (Kane Co., Utah and Mohave Co., Az.) Vermilion Cliffs-Moquith Mountains. Utah map: Yellowjacket Canyon. Arizona map: Kaibab. (7,058')

Nell Murbarger noted that Edwin R. Lamb (1831-1924) and family moved to the town of Virgin in 1861. Lamb and his brothers ran a sawmill on nearby Pine Valley Mountain and were known for the kegs and barrels they made. (1416~)

Edmunds Hole: (Garfield Co.) Dixie National Forest-Boulder Mountain-Stair Canyon. Lower Bowns Reservoir map.

Edmund Rice King (1882-1953) was a pioneer from the Teasdale and Bicknell areas. (388~, 426~, 582~)

Edna Peak: (Piute Co.) Fishlake National Forest-Tushar Mountains. Mount Brigham map.

Also spelled Aetna Peak. (332~)

Several alunite mines operated on the flanks of Edna Peak starting in the 19teens. These included the Christmas, Sunshine, and Aetna Peak mines. (332~)

—Wedge Mine: PRIVATE PROPERTY. This gold mine is one-eighth mile north of the summit of Edna Peak at 11,000 feet. Geologist Eugene Callaghan: "In spite of a relatively small production, the Wedge Mine, discovered in 1898, was a spectacular gold occurrence; large pea-sized nuggets were recovered." (332~)

Edward Spring: (Iron Co.) Dixie National Forest-Cottonwood Canyon. Little Creek Peak map.

Also called Edward Trough. (1931~)

Ann Walton, the daughter of David Edwards (1857-1919), noted that he was a Hole-in-the-Rock pioneer. After suffering setbacks in Bluff, the family moved to Paragonah in 1884: "Here father used his homestead right and filed on 160 acres of good farming land out to Little Creek." (1964~)

Egg Canyon: (Garfield Co.) GSCENM-The Gulch. Lamp Stand and Steep Creek Bench maps.

Also called Egg Box Canyon. (1168~)

Burns Ormand: "Whoever called it Egg Canyon had eggs on the pack mule and broke 'em, agittin up there. That's the way I understand it.... We used to put our eggs in the grain bags as we was fillin' them ... and then as we took grain out of the sacks to grain our horses, why we'd get the eggs outta there." (1487~)

Eggnog: (Garfield Co.) Henry Mountains-Bullfrog Creek. Ant Knoll map.

Two name derivations are given.

First, Charles B. Hunt: "[Eggnog is] a good spring and favorite stopping place for stockmen. The name is said to refer to the liquid refreshment, other than spring water, consumed there." (925~)

Second, Keith Durfey: "It was just such good, pleasant water, it was like drinking eggnog ... it was tasty." (582~)

Dwight Williams: "The old sheep herders and the old cattlemen, when they got to that little spring of water there at Eggnog, that was such good water that they just thought that it was as good as eggnog." (2013~)

Bliss Brinkerhoff, who has owned the range rights to Eggnog since the 1940s: "Back in the old days, there were very few places that you could find drinkin' water out on the desert, and that was one of 'em. It's probably not one of the better ones, but when your other choice is to pack water in five gallon wooden kegs to your sheep or cow camp, that is quite a chore. Eggnog happens to be one of the places that you can drink the water and it won't kill ya. My granddaddy [Willard Brinkerhoff] lived to be eighty-one years old and it finally got him. But the Bureau of Land Management has a sign hangin' on it now, 'Unfit for Human Consumption.' People were tougher back in those days. The taste is actually just a little bit of alkali, just a kind of a tart taste to it. And them old-timers would say: 'Oh, that water down there tastes just like eggnog.'" (291~)

—Bliss Brinkerhoff Cabin: PRIVATE PROPERTY. (Also called Riddle Cabin.) Bliss Brinkerhoff: "The guy's last name was Riddle and he built a little cabin down there [at Eggnog].... When I first went down there, if you didn't have a tent, you went over and throwed your bed down inside that little cabin. And the mice, my word.... I never did have one get clear down in bed with me, but they were on top of me and runnin' across my forehead. The cowboys would be stacked in there, just like sardines, trying to get out of the weather.... It was a landmark. It was burned down in the 1960s." (291~) Bliss built a new cabin here in 1999. (291~, 582~)

Egypt: (Garfield Co.) GSCENM-Glen Canyon NRA-Escalante River. Sunset Flat, Silver Falls Bench, and Egypt maps.

Edson Alvey noted that the area is reminiscent of the Egyptian desert. (55~)

—Constructed Stock Trail: This starts three-quarters of a mile down the Escalante River from the mouth of Harris Wash and goes generally southwest up to Egypt. It is just north of elevation 5056T on the Silver Falls Bench map. (SAPE.)

—Constructed Stock Trail: This starts on the Escalante River one and one-quarter miles (as the crow flies) downriver from the mouth of Fence Canyon and goes generally west up to Egypt. It is across the river from the mouth of Neon Canyon (one-half mile east of elevation 5045T on the Egypt map). (SAPE.)

—Egypt Slots: (See Twentyfive Mile Wash.)

Eight Foot Rapids: (San Juan Co.) San Juan River-The Narrows. Mexican Hat map.

Hugh D. Miser of the Kelly W. Trimble USGS Expedition of 1921: "Here are several small rapids, of which the largest, with a fall of 8 feet, runs over a boulder bar at the mouth of a southern tributary half a mile above The Narrows." (1370~)

Famed war correspondent Ernie Pyle described going through the rapid with Norm Nevills in 1939: "going through was just like having an automobile accident. It was a blur. It was all over so quickly I never caught any details at all. I only know that even right in the middle of it, I was disappointed. For it wasn't bad at all." (1592~)

Eightmile Bar: (Coconino Co., Az.) Glen Canyon NRA-Glen Canyon. Ferry Swale, Az. map.

Lil Diemler in 1946: "We camped at 8-mile camp. Eight miles above Lee's Ferry." (557~)

Eightmile Gap: (Kane Co.) Shinarump Cliffs-Johnson Run. Thompson Point map.

Walter Clement Powell of the 1871–72 Powell Expedition noted that the gap is eight miles from Kanab. (1570~)

—Eightmile Spring: This is near Eightmile Gap. The spring stopped discharging water in the 1930s. (1931~) The Paiute name is *Kanavatsi*, or "Willow Spring." (82~) The Powell Survey had a temporary base camp here in 1872. Almon Thompson of the Survey: "Camped at 'Eightmile Springs.'" (1877~)

—Honeymoon Trail: The spring was a popular camp spot for those following the Honeymoon Trail. (2053~) (See Appendix Two—Honeymoon Trail.)

Eightmile Pass: (Kane Co.) GSCENM-Vermilion Cliffs. Eightmile Pass map. (5,800')

Ralph Chynoweth noted that the pass is eight miles from the old town of Paria. (425~) A stock trail goes through the pass. (SAPE.) Cal Johnson: "It is a good shortcut if you are going from the Rock House or Nipple Ranch to the Paria. We use that a lot. The old pioneer trail went through there." (984~)

—Long Butte: This large butte is directly south of Eightmile Pass (at elevation 6537 [Kimball]). (765~) Cal Johnson noted that it was called Eightmile Pass Butte. (984~) Herbert E. Gregory noted it as Lone Butte. (M.27.) It is shown, without a name, on maps as early as 1886.

Eightmile Rock: (San Juan Co.) Hatch Point-Threemile Creek. Eightmile Rock map. (6,400')

Also called Lone Rock. (906~)

This dome is eight miles from the historic Hatch Ranch. (See Hatch Ranch Canyon–Hatch Ranch.) It is the site of an Indian encampment and has been used as a line camp since the late 1800s. (SAPE.)

Ekker Butte: (Wayne Co.) Glen Canyon NRA-Orange Cliffs. Turks Head map. (6,227')

Also called Castle Butte.

Ned Chaffin: "Dad [Louis M. Chaffin] called it Wolverton Butte." (411~) This was for explorer, miner, and river runner Edwin T. Wolverton.

Canyonlands National Park Superintendent Bates Wilson named it for Cornelius Ekker (1884-1952), the father of Arthur Ekker and the grandfather of A.C. Ekker. They were members of a ranching family from Hanksville. (411~, 1429~)

Elaterite Basin: (Wayne Co.) Glen Canyon NRA-Orange Cliffs. Elaterite Basin map.

Also called Laterite Basin, Laterite Country, and Literite Basin. (103~, 1322~)

The basin contains Big Water Canyon and was initially called Big Water by cattlemen. Elaterite is a soft mineral resin that oozes out of the rocks in the basin. It is used as a substitute for rubber. (607~, 1430~, 1621~)

—Elaterite Butte: (6,552') Also called Bagpipe Butte (120~) and Jack and His Family (411~).

Elba Flat: (Grand Co.) Book Cliffs-Interstate 70. Sagers Flat and White House maps.

—Elba Siding: (Sagers Flat map.) (Also called Elba Station.) This was a siding on the Denver and Rio Grande Western Railroad in the 1880s. Some maps show it as Pinto as it is near Pinto Wash. (1623~) (See Denver and Rio Grande Western Railroad.)

Elbo Spring: (Kane Co.) Sink Valley Wash-Fisher Canyon. Bald Knoll map.

Correctly spelled Elbow Spring.

This very nice medium-size spring is difficult to locate. It is on a short tributary to Sink Valley Wash that is called Old Elbow. (570~, 741~, SAPE.)

Elbow, The: (Piute Co.) Fishlake National Forest-Sevier Valley. Malmsten Peak and Piute Reservoir maps.

Abe McIntosh in 1941: "a large bend around in the hills shaped like an elbow, where crops are successfully grown because of the protection from frost by the hills." (2053~)

Elbow of the Sandy: (Garfield Co.) Sandy Creek Benches-Sandy Creek. Sandy Creek Benches map.

This is a tight, elbow-shaped turn in Sandy Creek.

—Chocolate Hill: This is the chocolate-colored hill on the road just north of the Elbow of the Sandy. Keith Durfey: "It's bentonite clay ... and it's chocolate colored and it [the road] used to be steeper than heck. Exxon Oil Company a few years ago went in and took a lot of the grade out of it and put gravel on it." (582~)

Elbow Ranch: (Piute Co.) Sevier River-Manning Creek. Marysvale map. PRIVATE PROPERTY.

This historic eight hundred acre ranch is now abandoned. It was bought by the Utah Division of Wildlife Resources.

Elbow Spring: (Sevier Co.) Fishlake National Forest-Little Lost Creek. Boobe Hole Reservoir map.

This is a large, developed, and still-used spring.

The spring is at the "elbow" or sharp turn of Little Lost Creek, where the creek turns from west to north.

Inscriptions include one that reads: "Elbow Spring—Little Lost Creek." (SAPE.)

Electric Lake: (Emery Co.) Manti-LaSal National Forest-Huntington Creek. Scofield and Candland Mountain maps.

—Connellsville: This tiny coal mining town, now under Electric Lake, was added to the Utah State Register of Historic Sites in 1973. The town was established in 1875. Coal was hauled from here by pack animals as far away as Salt Lake City. Montell Seely: "The town ... was named for a large and famous coking center in Connellsville, Pennsylvania." (1717~)

Elephant, The: (Kane Co.) Vermilion Cliffs-Kanab Creek-Tiny Canyon. Kanab map.

This small sandstone formation bears a resemblance to an elephant's head and trunk when viewed from the east. Priddy Meeks used the name in 1852. (1343~)

Elephant Butte: (Grand Co.) Arches National Park-The Windows Section. The Windows Section map.

Also called The Massif (898~) and Stone Elephants (278~).

—Archaeological Cave: This is on the south side of Elephant Butte. Frank Beckwith of the Arches National Monument Scientific Expedition of 1933–34: "has been visited previous to this expedition and it was reported to us that cedar bark, a few squash seeds, and some bone awls had been taken from it. Our party found four pit holes, evidencing visitations by the whites, and whatever of value the cave might once have held, nothing remained." (190~)

—Movies: The opening scenes of *Indiana Jones and the Last Crusade* were filmed, in part, at Archaeological Cave. (68~)

—Aunt Emma: This formation is east of Archaeological Cave. Unattributed: "named by Frank Beckwith. To him, the rock resembled a very proper, aristocratic grande dame." (68~)

Elephant Butte: (Kane Co.) White Cliffs-Block Mesas. Elephant Butte map. (6,812')

Also called Elephant Mountain. (485~)

This large sandstone butte bears a resemblance to an elephant. (1639~) Hattie Esplin: "The Elephant is a large mountain of heavy sand and there is a natural gap through it, the trail through it being called the Elephant Gap." (363~)

—Elephant Road: (See Appendix Two—Elephant Road.)

Elephant Canyon: (San Juan Co.) Canyonlands National Park-Needles District-Colorado River. Druid Arch and The Loop maps.

Two name derivations are given; the first is most widely accepted.

First, Kent Frost noted that this was named after Elephant Hill by cowboys who thought the surrounding domelands looked like a herd of elephants. (697~)

Second, Bill Barnard: "According to legend Elephant Hill was named by a pioneer who decided the only way to cross it was like Hannibal crossed the Alps, on an elephant." (136~)

—Elephant Hill: This is part of a famous road that leads from Squaw Flat into the heart of Needles country. The road started as a constructed stock trail that was in use for many years. Pete Steele noted that in about 1947–48 Dugout Ranch owner Al Scorup had the stock trail widened and made suitable for vehicles. He needed to get heavy equipment up to the toplands to construct stock reservoirs. This became part of the first vehicle road that provided access to Beef Basin. (1821~)

Kent Frost told of driving his Model A up the hill. Over the years the road has deteriorated and is now suitable only for four-wheel-drive vehicles. (697~)

W.G. Carroll in 1956: "Elephant Hill is a high narrow ridge with steep broken faces of this red sandstone, separating two equally narrow canyons. Gnarled juniper and pinyon cling sparsely to its side.... This is the first real barrier to the Needles and crossing it on horseback or by Jeep is an adventure." (350~)

Alice Higgins in 1965: "I had been warned back in Moab that Elephant Hill was a thriller, and as we inched and backed and slid over its loose rocks I regretted that I had not bought and filled out one of the Last Will and Testament forms that were on sale at the checkout counter in the supermarket where we provisioned. When we were safely through this ordeal-by-Jeep I had to use my left hand to unclench my right from the door handle." (880~)

Dick Wilson in 1968: "Elephant Hill is presently the barrier that separates the men from the boys, as far as jeeping is concerned. The trail is a good one—good and rough"! (2019~)

—Silver Stairs: This is on the "4WD" road that provides access to Devils Pocket from Elephant Canyon. It is one mile northwest of Elephant Hill (one-eighth mile east-southeast of elevation 5095T on The Loop map). Fran Barnes: "The Silver Stairs is a length of Jeep trail that ... could easily have acquired an expletive for a name rather than the lovely name it has. But perhaps the beauty of the setting charmed those who first traveled and named this rugged stone stairway." (141~)

Elephant Rock: (Iron Co.) Dixie National Forest-Hurricane Cliffs-Little Valley. Cottonwood Mountain map.

—Old Spanish Trail: The trail went a short distance east of Elephant Rock. (1551~)

Elias Wells Hollow: (Wayne Co.) Fishlake National Forest-Mytoge Mountains-Row of Pines Bench. Fish Lake map.

Thaine Taylor: "It was named after Elias H. Blackburn [1827-1908]." (1868~) He settled in Loa in 1879. (248~)

Elliker Basin: (Iron Co.) Hurricane Cliffs-Interstate 15. Summit map.

Gordon R. Staker, the BLM area manager in 1971: "The name referring to the man who homesteaded and cleared the timber in the basin." (1931~) This was Heinrich "Henry" Elliker (1828-1914). He and his family moved to Cedar City in 1856. Lydia Fielding: "He was one of the best farmers in southern Utah." (639~)

This was initially called Bolly Basin. Herbert E. Gregory: "Bolly Basin is a circular valley thickly floored by alluvium and in absence of drainage outlets becomes at times a shallow pond from which water seeps westward underground. It is entirely surrounded by lavas and thus has the superficial appearance of a volcanic crater." (768~)

Elliott Mesa: (Emery Co.) Beckwith Plateau-Gray Canyon. Cliff, Butler Canyon, and Jenny Canyon maps. (6,946')

(See Big Spring Ranch for name derivation.)

Elmo Town: (Emery Co.) Castle Valley-Timothy Wash. Elmo map.

Also called St. Elmo. (2053~)

The Eagle Extension of the Cleveland Canal was completed in 1904, bringing water to the Elmo area and opening it for farming. Several residents from nearby Cleveland started the town in 1908. The first postmaster, Thursa

Olsen, noted in 1908 that the town was originally known as Carson "presumably after Kit Carson." (2053~)

Two name derivations are given.

First, Edward A. Geary: "There are differing accounts of how the community gained its name, but the prevailing local tradition holds that Elmo was formed from the initials of four pioneer families, Erickson, Larsen, Mortensen, and Oviatt." (710~)

Second, Lucile Richens noted that the town was named for "the book 'St. Elmo' written by either John Fox, Jr. or E.P. Roe." (2053~)

Elsies Nipple: (Wayne Co.) Awapa Plateau-Sage Flat Draw. Moroni Peak map. (8,368')

Interviewer: Do you know who Elsie was? **Rancher**: "Elsie Mc.... She was pretty well formed." **Interviewer**: "Say no more." **Rancher**: I'm not goin' to." (SAPE.) The Elsie was Elsie McCllellan, the daughter of Hugh J. McCllellan, the first settler to Rabbit Valley. (1931~)

Elsinore Town: (Sevier Co.) Sevier Valley-Highway 89. Elsinore map.

Also spelled Elsenore.

The first settlers of Elsinore, James C. Jensen, Charles H. Nielson, Niels Erickson, and others arrived in 1874. Nora Jensen Christensen: "President [Joseph A. Young of Richfield] said, 'I have passed by there several times, coming from Clear Creek Canyon, and every time I turn on that bend of the road I think of my visit to Denmark and the little site of Elsinore situated on the right hand Oressund.' So it was decided to call the new town 'Elsinore.'" (1970~, 1932~) Since most of the townspeople were of Danish ancestry, the town was often called Little Denmark. (954~)

A *Deseret News* article from February 25, 1885 noted: "Elsinore is a village of Sevier County, containing about forty families, mostly Scandinavians, who, in point of enterprise will, we think, compare favorably with those of any other place in the mountains. None of the inhabitants are really wealthy; indeed, it is not so long since they were all, or nearly all, quite poor; but they are industrious, thrifty, temperate people, who bid fair to soon become comparatively independent." (1186~)

Dona S. Hansen and Neta Davidson told this remarkable story: "Mr. and Mrs. Shaw and [their seven-month-old daughter] Illeene were in their buggy ready to go to Elsinore when some pigs went by on the road. The pigs frightened the horse, and it started running. The buggy wheels passed over some lumber ... causing the buggy to tip over. The occupants were thrown out. Mr. Shaw landed on his feet and probably could have stopped the horse, but he saw the baby fly out of the arms of Mrs. Shaw and go down the well. He ran to the well, grasped the rope and slid down to the water.... He reached under the water about a foot and grasped Illeene. He put her over one arm and, holding the rope with the other arm, climbed up the rocks.... The family doctor always called Illeene 'Miss Miracle' after that." (954~)

—Elsinore Canal: This was constructed by the first settlers in 1874–75. Nora Jensen Christensen described how it was done: "The plowing was done in the following manner: One span [pair] of mules and one span of horses were used. Three men were needed, one to drive, one to hold the plow, and one to stand on the doubletree holding onto the mules' tails. The plow would often buck when it struck a large rock, throwing the rider off the implement." (1970~)

—Brooklyn Town: The town of Brooklyn was one mile south of Elsinore. Two name derivations are given. First, one of the town's first residents was John Brooks Wasden (1844-1908). He arrived in 1873. (384~, 1970~) Second, Ezlan Jackman noted that it was named for Brooklyn, New York. (2053~)

—Brooklyn Canal: The canal was built in the mid-1880s. (384~)

Emerald Lakes: (Sevier Co.) Fishlake National Forest-UM Plateau. Hilgard Mountain map.

Wayne Gremel: "When you look down on it, it is the greenish color of an emerald." (780~)

Emerald Pools: (Washington Co.) Zion National Park-Zion Canyon. Temple of Sinawava map.

The Writers' Program of 1941: "The Emerald Pools are small pockets of water formed by ribbon-like waterfalls that plunge hundreds of feet down the face of steep cliffs." (2056~)

—Emerald Pools Trail: This was listed on the National Register of Historic Places in 1987.

Emery County:

The county seat is Castle Dale.

The county was established in 1880 from Sanpete and Sevier counties by the Utah Territorial Legislature. It was named for the Territorial Governor of Utah, George W. Emery (1875–1880). Residents of Castle Valley wanted to call it Castle County. (1330~, 1932~)

Emery Town: (Emery Co.) Castle Valley-Muddy Creek-Highway 10. Emery West and Emery East maps.

(See Emery County for name derivation.)

The initial townsite was three miles north of the present town (one-quarter mile south of elevation 6406 on the Emery East map). The first settler, Casper Christensen,

arrived in 1881. At that time the town was called variously Muddy, Muddy Creek, Upper Muddy Creek, Camp Muddy Creek, or Casper. (380~, 710~, 1330~, 1853~, 2056~) The first townsite was not adequate. In 1885 residents began working on a canal to take water from Muddy Creek to the more favorable present location of the town. A Daughters of Utah Pioneers plaque tells the story of the construction of the Emery Canal: "From 1885 to 1889, the pioneers who located on the Muddy three miles northeast from Emery built in their poverty a tunnel 1200 feet long through blue slate rock to bring water to the town. Their only tools were pick and shovel and blasting powder. They hauled dirt out in a two wheeled cart and sank three shafts to hoist dirt in wooden buckets by horse power. Their living quarters were dugouts along the creek." (1551~) Wayne Gremel: "It isn't a tunnel anymore. They took the top off it. That was later with heavy machinery." (780~)

—Upper Muddy Cemetery: This small cemetery is near the first townsite. The one gravestone still readable is from Pleasant Minchey, 1820–1900. (SAPE.)

—Moore Mine: This coal mine is four miles east of Emery on Muddy Creek (immediately south of elevation 6206 on the Emery East map). It was started by Thomas Thompson of Ferron in 1905. (567~, 1233~)

—Emery to Hanksville Pioneer Road: (See Appendix Two—Emery to Hanksville Pioneer Road.)

Emery Valley: (Garfield Co.) Paunsaugunt Plateau-East Fork Sevier River. Bryce Canyon map.

Also called Flakey Bottom. (1931~)

Also spelled Emory Valley. (M.60)

This, and the southern part of Johns Valley, were called the Panguitch Hayfield by Clarence Dutton of the Powell Survey in 1880. (586~) J.J. Porter in 1931: "Named by surveyors while making original survey about 1876." (1346~)

Emigrant Pass: (Sevier Co.) Fishlake National Forest-Interstate 70. Old Woman Plateau map. (7,980')

Also called Salina Pass, Salina Summit Station (328~), Wasatch Gap (M.10.), Wahsatch Pass (M.20.), and Wah Satch Pass (M.66.).

(See Ivie Creek.)

This marks the saddle between Ivie Creek, which flows east into Muddy Creek, and Meadow Creek, which flows west into Salina Canyon. It was a landmark for pioneers from the earliest days of the Old Spanish Trail and was heavily used by settlers of Castle Valley. (477~)

Captain John W. Gunnison passed through the pass in 1853. (1411~) He called it Wasatch Pass. (1696~)

Gwinn Harris Heap of the Lieutenant Edward F. Beale Expedition of 1853: "The divide is broad, level, and smooth, and the descent on the western side [Salina Canyon] easy." (855~)

Emigrant Spring: (Garfield Co.) Glen Canyon NRA-Silver Falls Creek. Silver Falls Bench map.

Also called Immigrant Spring.

This medium-size spring is on the backside of an abandoned meander in Silver Falls Creek. It was used by travelers on the Halls Road, which went up Silver Falls Creek. (See Appendix Two—Halls Road.) Charles P. Berholzheimer noted in 1920 that a sign in the canyon noted "Good Water Here." (222~)

Edson Alvey noted that at one time nearby inscriptions dated to 1893. (55~) Ken Sleight found those older inscriptions in the early 1960s: Emerson Peterson, May 9, '99 and Hartley Black, Nov. 8/20. (1753~) Many inscriptions have disappeared and now the oldest inscription is from J.F. Younger, 1907. (SAPE.)

—Emigrant Butte: This monolith is in the middle of the abandoned meander at Emigrant Spring. (1753~)

Emmett Hill: (Coconino Co., Az.) Vermilion Cliffs National Monument-Vermilion Cliffs-Alt. Highway 89. Emmett Hill and Emmett Wash, Az. maps.

Also spelled Emett Hill.

The Domìnguez-Escalante Expedition of 1776–77 camped here, calling it *San Bartolemé*. Father Escalante: "Here there is extensive valley land but of bad terrain." (1944~) There is now a highway rest area near the site.

James Simpson Emmett (1850-1923) and family lived at Lees Ferry from 1896 until 1909. (364~) Rowland W. Rider: "The ranch at Lee's Ferry, owned and operated by Jim Emett [*sic*], was isolated in either direction by more than ninety miles of ungraded road from the nearest towns. Mr. Emett, by virtue of controlling the water, thereby controlled the cattle range in the area.... Now this man Emett was quite a character. He stood six foot four and I tell you he had steel gray eyes. He'd look right through you.... He was the master of that entire range for hundreds of miles." (1629~)

Inscriptions include F.M., March 14, 1919. (SAPE.)

—Emmett Spring: (Emmett Wash map.) This medium-size, developed spring was the main source of water in House Rock Valley. It was used by James Emmett's ranching operations from the 1890s into the 1900s. (1629~, SAPE.)

Englestead Hollow: (Kane and Washington Counties.) Clear Creek Mountain-Orderville Canyon. Temple of Sinawava map.

This was originally called Bull Hollow. (1931~)

The name was recommended by R.T. Evans, a topographical engineer with the USGS, for a local stockman. (1931~) Rasmus Madsen Englestead (1823–1896) and family were early settlers of Mount Carmel. (803~, 1714~)

Enoch Town: (Iron Co.) Cedar Valley-Interstate 15. Enoch map.

Also called Elk Horn Springs (942~, 1715~) and Johns Fort (360~).

Joel Hills Johnson noted in 1853 that the Indian name was "Pakwwoots, signifying a cluster of springs." (991~)

The town was named in 1884 in honor of the Order of Enoch, a Mormon United Order. (369~, 942~)

In 1844 John C. Fremont called it *Ojo de San Jose*, or "St. Joseph Spring." (1830~) Orville C. Pratt called it St. Jose Spring in 1848. Pratt described it as "one of the finest fountains and streams of water on the entire route. Good land, & a beautiful country all day today." (1572~)

The Parley P. Pratt Exploring Expedition to Southern Utah of 1849–50: "On this hill comes out large Springs making several acres of very rich bench land on its immediate sides. Black soil, clothed with grass & canes." (1762~)

—Fort Johnson: In 1851 Joel Hills Johnson (1802-1882) claimed "Johnson Spring [Enoch]." He built a stockade and what would become known as Fort Johnson, with nine-foot-high walls that were over two feet thick. The fort was one-half mile northwest of Enoch, and is marked on the map. (1013~)

Thomas D. Brown of the Southern Indian Mission of 1854: "Stayed all night at Johnson's Spring with Joel H. Johnson—good spring—a good range for cattle and many Indians around him." (306~) Abandoned in 1853 because of Indian troubles, the area was repopulated starting in 1854. Today little remains of the fort. (SAPE.)

—Old Spanish Trail: The trail went through what would become Enoch.

Enterprise Town: (Washington Co.) Escalante Valley-Shoal Creek-Highway 18. Enterprise map.

Also called Shoal Creek.

Anson P. Winsor and others started the town of Enterprise in 1896. Kate B. Carter: "Early settlers considered their settlement an enterprising community. First called Hebron for a town in Palestine." (375~) Andrew Jenson: "The new settlement (Enterprise) is known for its beautiful gardens, fine orchards and numerous shade trees." (972~)

John W. Young described the area in 1868, before the town was settled: "This place is much like Mountain Meadows, an excellent place for stock raising and dairying, having plenty of range and good hay land; but not very great facilities for grain raising. Father Zera Pulsipher and his sons and sons-in-law comprise the largest share of the inhabitants, but the place is growing and will by and by become quite a settlement.... In some places this wash is very narrow, being bounded on either side with perpendicular rocks looming up hundreds of feet high; and these deep cuts will, in some cases, continue for miles, and then open out into a beautiful little valley, with springs of water, and beautiful patches of meadow lands." (2066~)

—Old Spanish Trail: The trail went by what would become Enterprise.

Eph Hanks Tower: (Wayne Co.) Capitol Reef National Park-Capitol Reef. Golden Throne map.

Ephraim K. Hanks (1826-1896) was the first settler at Pleasant Creek. Charles Kelly: "[Ephraim Hanks was] the husband of many wives.... [He] maintained a still and consumed most his own product." (1047~) Hanks died at Pleasant Creek and was buried in Caineville.

Solomon F. Kimball told this story of Hanks' voyage to America in 1842: "During a heavy storm, he and two of his companions were thrown from the fore-royal yard into the rigging below. One of his mates was instantly killed and the other fell overboard, the big, blue sharks eating the body. Eph ... grabbed a dangling rope, and amid shouts and cheers from his companions below, slid to the trembling fore-top, where he calmly waited for further orders." (358~)

Inscriptions near the tower include Eph Hanks, no date. (SAPE.)

Ernie Canyon: (Emery Co.) San Rafael Swell-Iron Wash. Twin Knolls, Arsons Garden, Old Woman Wash, and Crows Nest Spring maps.

Inscriptions include Rulan Dahl and Warren Allred, 1/12/37. (SAPE.)

—Ernies Reservoir: This stock reservoir is near the mouth of Ernie Canyon (Old Woman Wash map). It was built in 1968. (1551~)

Ernies Country: (Garfield Co.) Canyonlands National Park-Maze District-Main Flat. Cross Canyon, Teapot Rock, Spanish Bottom, and Elaterite Basin maps.

Also called Big Flat.

Also spelled Erney Country. (797~)

Hazel Ekker in 1965: "As to Ernie Country that name came from Ernie Larsen. He was the first one in there with sheep so I was told.... I saw his name and date on rocks or in one of the caves ... it was in the [18]90s. [Edwin T.] Wolverton called it Nequoia Basin on one of his maps and shows it as such. He said it meant Standing Rock." (617~)

Joseph L. Dudziak in 1962: "and then came to the complicated jumble known as 'Ernies Country.' A series of box canyons completely enclosed in great walls and domes extended for miles to the south. The floor of these canyons were smooth and would be easily traversable with a Jeep—If you could get a Jeep down." (576~)

—Clells Spring: This large spring is at the northwest edge of Ernies Country and is one-half mile southeast of Whitmore Arch (one-quarter mile west of elevation 5321T on the Elaterite Basin map). It is developed with a CCC-style trough. (SAPE.) Richard F. Negri noted that the spring was named for Clell Chaffin (1907-1968), son of pioneer stockman Louis M. Chaffin. (1430~) It was named by George Franz. (411~) Ned Chaffin: "a very small spring, but always reliable for a drink of water." (606~)

—Horse Heaven: Ned Chaffin: "No one ever calls that flat, right up from the right of the Clell's Spring ... what we called it, Horse Heaven. You turn your horses loose over there and that's the first place they'd head for." (411~)

—The Chute: This stock route, now a part of the "Foot" trail, is one-quarter mile east-southeast of Clells Spring. (615~) Ned Chaffin: "a narrow canyon thru the rocks. The pathway here is very narrow and high on both sides." (606~)

—Sunken Valley: This graben valley is on the north (or west) side of the Colorado River and is on the south edge of Ernies Country. It is three-quarters of a mile west of the mouth of Cross Canyon (at elevations 4841T and 5044T on the Cross Canyon map). Michael R. Kelsey named the valley. (1084~)

—Sand Tank Canyon: This western tributary of the Colorado River is the lower end of Wide Valley and is the first canyon east of Range Canyon (one-quarter mile west of elevation 5165T on the Teapot Rock map). Barbara Ekker: "Water wouldn't last in it long as it had a sand bottom." (617~) Ned Chaffin: "Big Sand Tank Canyon is named from the big sand tank located in the canyon." (411~) The tank is just above the big drop to the river and is often full of very muddy water. (SAPE.)

Escalante Canyon: (Garfield Co.) Dixie National Forest-Escalante Mountains-Sweetwater Creek. Sweetwater Creek map.

(See Escalante River for name derivation.)

Also called Little Escalante Canyon and Little Last Chance Canyon. (1931~)

Do not confuse this short canyon with the main Escalante Canyon which contains the Escalante River. Sweetwater Creek runs through Escalante Canyon.

—Escalante Summit: (Also called Escalante Divide.) (See Main Canyon—The Top.)

Escalante Canyon: (Kane Co.) GSCENM-Kaiparowits Plateau-Last Chance Wash. Death Ridge, Horse Mountain, and Petes Cove maps.

Do not confuse this short canyon with the main Escalante Canyon which contains the Escalante River.

Inscriptions include Jero Reynolds, Dec. 11, 1915. (SAPE.)

Escalante Desert: (Beaver and Iron Counties.)

Also called Escalante Valley, Muddy Desert (1762~), and West Desert (1512~).

The Indian name is *Taw-gu-Uav,* or "Thirsty Desert." (1512~)

The Domìnguez-Escalante Expedition of 1776–77 skirted along the edge of this forbidding desert, which they called *Nuestra Señora de la Luz,* or "Our Lady of Light." (805~) Bogged down in a snowstorm that made the clay soil a muddy mess, the expedition rested here for a day. Father Escalante: "We were in great distress, without firewood and extremely cold, for with so much snow and water the ground, which was soft here, was unfit for travel." (261~)

Jedediah Smith of the South West Expedition of 1826–27: "To my great Surprise instead of a River an immense sand plain was before me where the utmost view with my Glass could not embrace any appearance of water. The only exception to this interminable waste of sand was a few detached rocky hills that rose from the surrounding plain and the stunted sedge that was thinly scattered over its surface." (1774~)

The United States Exploring Expedition of 1838–1842 gave a general description of the area on their map: "This Plain is a waste of Sand, with a few detached Mountains, (some of which rise to the region of perpetual Snow), whose positions are unknown; from these flow small streams that are soon lost in the sand. A few Indians are scattered over the plain, the most miserable objects in creation." (M.77.)

Robert Campbell of the Parley P. Pratt Exploring Expedition to Southern Utah of 1849–50: "look to the NW to

the eye can see no farther, very extensive valley good deal larger than Salt Lake." (1762~)

Escalante Mountains: (Garfield Co.) Dixie National Forest-GSCENM. Antimony, Barker Reservoir, Grass Lakes, Griffin Point, Pollywog Lake, Sweetwater Creek, and Upper Valley maps.

(See Escalante River for name derivation.)

Almon H. Thompson of the 1871–72 Powell Expedition called this Table Mountain. (1877~) Dr. J.D.M. Crockwell called these the Sevier Mountains in 1871. (492~) Hole-in-the-Rock Expedition member James Monroe Redd called this the Wasatch Range in 1879–80. (1356~)

Escalante National Monument:

This is not shown on the maps. It was a 1936 proposal to turn 6,968 square miles (8 percent of the total area of the state) of southern Utah—from Moab to the Navajo Indian Reservation—into a national monument. The Director of the Utah State Planning Board, Ray B. West, sent a letter to then Governor Henry H. Blood describing the advantages of the proposed park: "The principal advantages that will accrue from the designation of this area as a national monument will be the preservation for all time and under proper control of the many scenic wonders and areas of archaeological importance.... It is reasonable to expect that the proceeds due directly or indirectly to tourist business will mean more to Southern Utah than those from any other use to which this barren and almost unproductive area may be put." (1981~) The idea was dropped because of pressure from local groups and extractive industries. (699~)

Wallace Stegner: "Once in the 1930s, Harold Ickes and others were proposing that almost all of southern Utah be made into one vast national park. That never came to pass; if it had, I suspect that the southern Utah economy would be stronger than it is now, and the wilderness would be more intact." (1827a~)

Escalante Natural Bridge: (Garfield Co.) GSCENM-Escalante River. Calf Creek map.

Also called Arch Bridge. (181~)

Robert H. Vreeland noted that the arch was named after the river: "A few local people call it Outlaw Arch because a man (John F. Boynton) shot and killed his partner (Washington Phipps) in the general vicinity of the arch, on November 30, 1878." (1953~) (See Phipps Wash.)

—Lady Arch: (Also called Lady Bridge.) This is the "Natural Arch" that is one-quarter mile upriver from Escalante Natural Bridge. It was named by D. Elden Beck in 1939. (181~)

—Osborne Canyon: (Correctly spelled Osborn Canyon. Also spelled Osbourne Canyon.) This is the first canyon east of the mouth of Sand Creek and it is directly north of Escalante Natural Bridge. William Osborn (1848-1931) and family moved to Escalante in 1873. (1168~, 1487~, 2051~)

Escalante Petrified Forest State Reserve: (Garfield Co.) Escalante River-Pine Creek. Escalante map.
(See Escalante River for name derivation.)
Also called Escalante Petrified Forest State Park.
This park was established in 1964 and was enlarged to 1,350 acres in 1972. Edson Alvey noted that the area was initially called Bailey Dump, named for the John Bailey family. (55~) A dump is a pasture area.
—Bailey Wash: This small drainage goes through the middle of Escalante Petrified Forest State Reserve. It is immediately west of the Black Hills. (55~) In the early days the pioneers found the Escalante Indians living at the mouth of Bailey Wash. (1181~)

Escalante Rim: (Garfield Co.) GSCENM-Straight Cliffs. Dave Canyon map.
(See Escalante River for name derivation.)
Although this is shown as a single point (elevation 7133) on the rim of the Straight Cliffs, the name is used locally to describe the rim between Escalante Town and the Cedar Wash area. This is a fairly new name. (1931~)

Escalante River: (Garfield and Kane Counties.) GSCENM-Escalante Mountains-Glen Canyon NRA-Glen Canyon. Escalante, Calf Creek, King Bench, Red Breaks, Silver Falls Bench, Egypt, Scorpion Gulch, King Mesa, Stevens Canyon South, and Davis Gulch maps.
Also called Boulder Creek, Dirty Devil River, Escalante Gulch, Potato Creek, and Potato Valley Creek.
Also spelled Escalant, Escalanta, Escalanti, Escalantis, Eskalantie, and Esklanty.
The Escalante River was discovered in August 1866 by the Andrus Military Reconnaissance Expedition. Captain James Andrus had been assigned the task of locating Indian trails between Utah's Dixie (southwestern Utah) and the Colorado River and hunting for a group of Indians who had been harassing and stealing from Mormon settlers during the Black Hawk War. Andrus called the Escalante River "Birch Creek." (475~)
Andrus provided the first description of the Escalante River area: "The whole of this country from the mountains [Boulder Mountain] to the [Colorado] river is cut up in all directions by these narrow deep perpendicular crevices, some of which are hundreds of feet in depth and but a rod or two in width." (475~)

Joseph Fish was with Andrus: "August 30th we traveled down a stream which was about the size of the creek at Parowan. There were some cottonwoods along its banks. We soon came to a nice open valley, with good soil where we found some wild potatoes from which we named the valley Potato Valley." (1128~)
The next Euroamerican to visit Potato Valley was Jacob Hamblin, the famous Mormon explorer and missionary to the Indians. He passed through the area in 1871 while trying to carry supplies to the mouth of the Dirty Devil River for John Wesley Powell's second Colorado River Expedition. Thinking he was on the Dirty Devil River, Hamblin led his group down the Escalante River for about fifty miles. The trip was described as a terrible one and the group was finally stopped by quicksand and boulders.
After Hamblin's failure to reach the Dirty Devil River, Frederick S. Dellenbaugh and Almon H. Thompson, members of the Powell Expedition, were assigned the task of finding the Dirty Devil River and getting supplies to Powell. They worked their way over what are now called the Escalante Mountains and dropped into Potato Valley. Dellenbaugh called it Big Boulder Creek (543~) while Thompson called it Potato Valley Creek (1877~).
Like Hamblin, Dellenbaugh and Thompson thought the stream running through the valley was the Dirty Devil River. They followed it downcanyon to the mouth of what they called Rocky Gulch (Harris Wash) and camped. Dellenbaugh: "Prof. [Almon H. Thompson] and Dodds then climbed to where they could get a wider view.... Prof. perceived at once that we were not on the river we thought we were on, for by this explanation he saw that the stream we were trying to descend flowed into the Colorado far to the south-west of the Unknown [Henry] Mountain, whereas he knew positively that the Dirty Devil came in on the north-east. Then the question was, 'What river is this?' for we had not noted a tributary of any size between the Dirty Devil and the San Juan. It was a new river whose identity had not been fathomed." (541~) The Dellenbaugh-Thompson party left Potato Valley by skirting along Boulder Mountain. They eventually did find the Dirty Devil River.
In 1935 Dellenbaugh recalled their naming of the river: "We named it the Escalante because its mouth was not a great distance up from the place where Escalante crossed the Colorado." (548~) Franciscan Friars Silvestre Vélez de Escalante and Francisco Atanasio Domìnguez were the first Euroamericans known to have traversed the canyons of southern Utah. They passed south of the Escalante

River in 1776 while searching for a route from Santa Fe to Los Angeles. (See Appendix One—Domínguez-Escalante Expedition of 1776–77.)

John Wesley Powell: "It heads in the Aquarius Plateau and flows into the Colorado. Its course, as well as that of all its many tributaries, is in deep box-canyons of homogeneous red sandstone, often with vertical walls that are broken by many beautiful alcoves and glens. Much of the region is of naked, smooth, red rock, but the alcoves and glens that break the canyon walls are the sites of perennial springs, about which patches of luxuriant verdure gather." (1563~)

Clarence Dutton of the Powell Survey described the Escalante River area from the summit of the Aquarius Plateau: "The view to the south and southeast is dismal and suggestive of the terrible.... The rocks are swept bare of soil and show the naked edges of the strata. Nature has here made a geological map of the country and colored it so that we may read and copy it miles away." (584~)

Claire Noall in 1957 wrote about the Escalante River near the mouth of Davis Gulch: "The natural etchings of the walls bespoke the arabesques of exquisite Persian art. But no influence had entered this canyon by way of the Ottoman Empire or the Moslem conquest. Yet the nature of the bas-reliefs in rose-colored sandstone—tall as some of the friezes were, more than a hundred feet—reminded us constantly of the patterned design of the long-sustained arts of Egypt, Iran, and Spain. However, only the waters springing from the Aquarius, the Kaiparowits, and the skies, aided by the sands and the winds, have here wielded the tools of the artist." (384~)

Before the lower part of the Escalante River was inundated by the waters of Lake Powell, several old inscriptions were found near its mouth. They included L. Harris 1894 April 22 and T. Williams Dec. 25 1885. (466~, 737~)

—Bowington Road: (See Appendix Two—Bowington Road.)

—Emma Bar: This placer bar, now underwater, was on the east side of the Colorado River one-half mile below the mouth of the Escalante River (The Rincon map). It was mined by Edward Mesken in about 1889. (466~)

—Walking Rock Canyon: This short eastern tributary of Lake Powell is east of Emma Bar (one-eighth mile south of elevation 3922T on The Rincon map).

Escalante Town: (Garfield Co.) Escalante River-Highway 12. Escalante map.

Also called Escalanta (1096~) and Eskalanty (209~).

Locally pronounced Escalant.

(See Escalante River for name derivation.)

While Captain James Andrus had "discovered" the Escalante River and Potato Valley, he made no mention of its suitability for settlement. The first to do so was William Derby Johnson of the 1871–72 Powell Expedition. He was with Frederick S. Dellenbaugh and Almon H. Thompson on their trek to the Dirty Devil River in support of Powell. Johnson: "The valley is six miles long by two wide, and with generally smooth surface, well situated for farming and irrigation. A large stream of water, enough to water at least 1000 acres, runs through it. Plenty of grass and wood near at hand, and altogether a good and suitable place for farming community, but not so good for stock." (1004~)

In 1875 Almon H. Thompson returned to Potato Valley with the Powell Survey. He ran into a group of Mormons from Panguitch who were interested in settling the valley. One of that group, James Schow, described the meeting. His group was working on an irrigation ditch when they noticed a billow of dust down on the Escalante Desert. Afraid that the dust signaled Indians and possible trouble, they watched warily. The dust cloud approached Potato Valley, then disappeared over a hill. Waiting for nightfall, the Mormons sneaked up the hill to where they could see that it was a company of white men. They joined the group.

Thompson had already designated the area they were in as the Escalante River Basin several years earlier. Thompson: "Saw four Mormons from Panguitch who are talking about making a settlement here. Advised them to call the place Escalante." (1877~)

The first permanent Euroamerican residents of Escalante arrived in July 1875. These were William Alvey, Thomas Heaps, Andrew Peter Schow, Don Carlos Shirts, David Stevenson, and Isaac Turnbow. They quickly laid out the townsite and assigned farm and pasturelands. Their first houses consisted of cellars dug into the ground topped with poles and branches covered with dirt. By the spring of 1876 the first log cabins had been erected and rough roads had been built to the nearby canyons.

The town expanded quickly as others heard about the fine land in Escalante. It was incorporated in 1903. Initially the primary industry was dairy farming. Over the years this was supplanted by sheep and cattle ranching. In 1880 the town had a population of 623; by 1923 it had risen to 1,010. Since then the town has decreased in population and at present it has about eight hundred residents. (47~, 466~, 1655~)

—First Holler: Pratt Gates noted that this small canyon is just off Highway 12 to the south of town (immediately south of elevation 6039). Pratt: "The CCC went in there and made some caves for dynamite and they got some steel doors on them." (709~)

—Second Holler: Pratt Gates noted that this is the first side canyon to the south of First Holler (immediately east of elevation 5773). The Old Road used to go up this canyon and onto Big Flats. (709~)

—Third Holler: Pratt Gates noted that this is immediately south of Second Holler (immediately north of elevation BM5768). (709~)

Esplin Gulch: (Kane Co.) Vermilion Cliffs-Orderville Canyon. Temple of Sinawava map.

Zion National Park Superintendent P.P. Patraw in 1934 noted that Henry Webster Esplin (1854–1943) and family were early settlers of Orderville. (1931~, 366~) Herbert E. Gregory noted that they arrived in the area in 1872. (762~)

Esplin Spring: (Kane Co.) White Cliffs-Block Mesas. Elephant Butte map.

David Esplin (1868-1960) ran livestock in this area in the early 1900s. (485~)

Everett Hollow: (Kane Co.) Dixie National Forest-Markagunt Plateau-Swains Creek. Strawberry Point map.

Correctly spelled Averett Hollow.

Also called Everett Canyon.

Kate B. Carter noted that Elijah Averett was killed while chasing Indians in 1866. (384~) (See Averett Canyon.)

Everstein Ridge: (Iron Co.) Kolob Terrace-Sherratt Point. Webster Flat map. (9,010')

George L. Everstein (also spelled Everstine) arrived in Cedar City in the 1870s. (388~, 516~)

Explorer Canyon: (Kane Co.) Glen Canyon NRA-Escalante River-Lake Powell. Stevens Canyon South and Davis Gulch maps.

Also called Fence Canyon. (1953~)

A group of Explorer Scouts visited the area in the early 1950s. Scout leader Rulon W. Doman: "A recent exploration trip by some of our leaders and older Explorer young men has resulted in discovery of an unnamed canyon and lake adjoining the Escalante River. At least as far as we are able to determine there is no known name attached to these places. We would therefore like to request naming them Explorer Canyon and Explorer Lake." (1931~) The name was approved by the USGS in 1957. Walter Meayers Edwards in 1967: "We hiked to the far end, splashing through crystal pools ... drink from a cool, sweet spring. Here 500-foot-high walls merged in a gigantic alcove. Water trickled down into an inviting pool. Vines entwined a chaos of rocks under the overhang. The great alcove acted like an orchestra shell, reflecting the chirps of swooping violet-green swallows and the sweet descending notes of canyon wrens. We left the miniature Shangri-La reluctantly." (596~)

—Zane Grey Arch: This is near the head of Explorer Canyon on its north rim. It was named by Escalante school teacher Edson Alvey "for want of a better name." (1021~)

—Garces Island: This is a recent name for an island in the Escalante River at the mouth of Explorer Canyon (at elevation 3970T on the Davis Gulch map). (675~)

—Twin Alcove Canyon: This eastern tributary of the Escalante River is the first canyon north of Explorer Canyon (at elevation 4169AT on the Stevens Canyon South map).

Eye of the Whale: (Grand Co.) Arches National Park-Herdina Park. The Windows Section map.

The arch, which looks like a large eye, was named by former Arches National Park Ranger Lloyd Pierson and his family. (1949~, 1977~)

Ezra Mc Bench: (Kane Co.) Glen Canyon NRA-Escalante River. King Mesa map. (5,167')

Also called Ezra Bench.

Edson Alvey noted that Ezra McInelly (1882-1949) ran livestock in the area in the early years. (55~)

F

Fable Valley: (San Juan Co.) Dark Canyon Plateau-Beef Basin-Gypsum Canyon. Fable Valley and Bowdie Canyon East maps.

Also called Big Fable Valley (1821~) and Fabled Valley (1001~).

Pete Steele: "After you've been out on the desert and all of a sudden you come out of the rocks and here's this beautiful valley. And it's like coming into a fabled land." (1821~)

Jacob R. Young trailed livestock into Fable Valley in the early 1900s. He recounted this story: "We had a stockade house that we lived in. We forgot to shut the door before we left. Next time I went up there, my horse kept snorting and blowing, and I couldn't imagine what was the matter. I got up there within about fifty yards of the house, and tied my horse up. I went over and opened the door, a big old lion jumped into my face. He had been in there all winter. He had gathered bones and killed deer and calves. He had the most stinking outfit I ever saw. We had to take a whole day to clean it out.... He just missed me and spit in my face as he came out." (2064~)

Gordon C. Baldwin in 1945: "This is a very broad valley hemmed in by high sandstone cliffs; the valley floor is thickly covered with sage, while clumps of juniper and piñon dot the upper slopes. A number of springs in the short side canyons form an excellent water supply." (127~)

—Little Fable Valley: This short western tributary of upper Fable Valley has a "Pack Trail" starting at a "Corral" going through it. The "Corral" is two miles southwest of Wild Cow Spring (at elevation 7240 on the Fable Valley map). This spectacular constructed stock trail, probably built by Cooper and Martin in the mid-1880s, was one of the main routes into Fable Valley. (1821~)

—Fable Spring: (Fable Valley map.) This used to be called Cow Tanks. (1821~)

—Wild Cow Canyon: This short eastern tributary of Fable Valley contains Fable Spring. A "Pack Trail" goes through the canyon. The trail was rough and was not often used by cowboys. (1821~)

—Fable Valley Trailhead: The trail starts as a "Pack Trail" at the head of Gypsum Canyon (one mile northwest of South Spring on the Fable Valley map). It goes generally west above the inner gorge of Gypsum Canyon into Fable Valley. John Scorup noted that the trail was probably built by Cooper and Martin in the late 1800s. (1821~)

—Aesops Arch: Robert H. Vreeland: "This arch is near the base of the cattle trail into the canyon on the opposite wall." (1955~)

Nell Murbarger named the arch in 1959: "I suggested we call it Aesop's Arch for it seemed to me that the old Greek maker-of-fables should have some recognition in Fable Valley." (1413~)

Face Canyon: (San Juan Co.) Navajo Indian Reservation-Glen Canyon NRA-Glen Canyon. Face Canyon, Gregory Butte, and Gunsight Butte maps.

C. Gregory Crampton: "Face Canyon, named by river men in recent times for the face-like figures which can be seen on the right wall of the canyon at the entrance." (467~)

Joyce Muench: "Face Canyon wears a heavy rock profile at its entrance." (1400~) The faces are now underwater.

Factory Butte: (Wayne Co.) North Caineville Mesa-Upper Blue Hills. Factory Butte map. (6,321')

Also called The Factory. (1233~)

Grove Karl Gilbert of the Powell Survey called this Needle Butte. (722~, 723~)Early area resident Charles Hunt noted that Factory Butte was named in 1882 by a group of settlers from Rabbit Valley who were looking for a route between Loa and the Colorado River. They called it Provo Factory because they thought it resembled the profile of a Provo woolen mill. (970a~, 1412~, 1419~) Volney King of the expedition: "I made up a wash that led northward towards the Provo Factory (as it is called). It has a similar appearance at a distance to that building." (1096~)

Joyce Muench: "Smoke-grimed, bulky and solid, it is the epitome of all factories, seen from this western side. On the south, Factory Butte's pediment pinches out to scarcely door-width, and from the north is no more than a finger-thick column, topping the dusty slopes. Below, soft hills of the lifeless gray are ferruled with arrow-straight furrows in a spacious badland, without a stick of vegetation." (1397~)

—Factory Butte Coal Mine: This is near Factory Butte. (925~) (See Coal Mine Wash.)

—Movies: *Dark Blood*, starring River Phoenix, was filmed, in part, near Factory Butte. Phoenix died before filming was complete and the movie was never released. (1809~)

Fairyland Canyon: (Garfield Co.) Bryce Canyon National Park-Pink Cliffs-Campbell Creek. Bryce Canyon map.

The name was applied by Bryce Canyon National Park Superintendent P.P. Paltrow. (1931~) Eivind T. Scoyen in 1931: "In the section of Bryce, known as Fairyland, you find the old familiar figures of childhood." (1710~)

Ward J. Roylance: "Fancy can run riot here and still be at a loss, but the character of the area can be suggested by saying that it is a three-dimensional Arabian Nights. In the foreground are walls and columns, rose-colored below and with cream colored capitols; in the center is a huge crumbling monument that looks like a thousand tons of disintegrating copper; and beyond to the right and left are acres of ruins. They stand in barbarously eroded abutments and terraces, their gaunt and wind-beaten skeletons softened by the play of sunlight upon the deep rose and red, and yellow and gold, of the stone." (1658~)

Falls, The: (Kane Co.) Skutumpah Terrace-Sink Valley Wash. Bald Knoll map.

This is a twenty-foot waterfall in upper Kanab Creek. A large spring is below the fall. (SAPE.)

—Elbow: This refers to the junction of Kanab Creek and Sink Valley Wash. (570~, 741~)

Family Butte: (Emery Co.) San Rafael Swell-Tan Seep. San Rafael Knob map. (7,393')

This is locally called Seven Sisters as it has seven distinct pinnacles along its crest. Lee Mont Swasey noted that Family Butte is the older name. (1853~) It represents the Swasey family: Joe, Charley, Sid, Rod, and others. (624~)

—Green Vein Mesa: This long, thin mesa starts one-half mile north of Family Butte (at elevations 7595 and 7745). It is most well known for several uranium mines along its sides. They were located in 1950 by Ferron residents Frank Blackburn and Irvin Olsen. (845~, 988~, 1618~, 1967~)

—Turkey Tower: This spectacular tower is two miles north of Family Butte (at elevation 7595). It was named by Steve Allen for its similarity to the head of a turkey when seen from a distance.

—Family Butte Pond: (Also called Family Butte Reservoir.) This stock reservoir is three-quarters of a mile south-southeast of Family Butte (one-half mile southeast of elevation 7128). (1931~)

Far End Canyon: (Coconino Co., Az.) Navajo Indian Reservation-Navajo Creek. Oak Springs and Chaiyahi Rim SE, Az. maps.

James H. Knipmeyer: "Named because it is the easternmost tributary of Navajo Canyon." (1115~)

Carl I. Wheat noted that the Navajo name is *Jad-yo-eeka-haza*, or "Lost Leg Canyon." Wheat heard this story from Navajo Whitehat: "Many years ago (before 1864) food became scarce and the women were out picking berries for food. A certain man had a rifle in his Hogan, far up on the rim, and his child accidentally shot the father in the knee. When the women returned they did their best to cure the wound, but it became constantly worse.... Gangrene set in, and finally the entire leg rotted off." (1995~)

Farley Canyon: (San Juan Co.) Glen Canyon NRA-Glen Canyon. Copper Point and Hite South maps.

Also called Parley Canyon.

C. Gregory Crampton: "According to Frank A. Barrett, long a resident of Glen Canyon ..., the canyon derives its name from Tom Farley who ran cattle in the region in the 1880s and 1890s." (465~)

David D. Rust noted in 1958 that outlaws would not use the ferry at Hite and Dandy Crossing, but would cross at Farley Canyon as they could not be as readily seen. (1680~)

—Woody's Store: G.W. "Woody" Edgell, who ran the Hite Ferry from 1961 to 1963, had a home and a small store one mile up Farley Canyon. (1795~)

Farm Canyon: (Kane Co.) Vermilion Cliffs-Cottonwood Canyon. Yellowjacket Canyon and Kanab maps.

Neil M. Judd in 1919: "Wild hay, and at times grain, have been grown here as winter feed for cattle. The larger of the areas cultivated lies at the junction of the canyon's two branches." (1027a~)

Farmers Knob: (Garfield Co.) Henry Mountains-Taylor Ridges. Cass Creek Peak map.

Also called Farmers Knoll. (1229~)

Bliss Brinkerhoff: "That's because when they started to dig in the uranium out there, the ones that was diggin' was just a bunch of old farmers just diggin' part-time." (291~)

This area was the site of a uranium and vanadium mining operation owned by Cornelius Ekker. The minerals were found embedded in petrified logs. (1043~) Willard Luce noted that uranium mining started here in the early 1940s, early for the area. (1229~)

Farnsworth Reservoir: (Sevier Co.) Fishlake National Forest-Niotche Creek. Gooseberry Creek map.

Stephen Martindale Farnsworth, Jr. (1847-1928) and family moved to Gooseberry in the mid-1870s. His daughter, Flossie Farnsworth Hartman: "One morning the children were getting dressed and the little girl, Effie, crawled under the bed for her shoe. She cried out and said a sliver was in her knee. It turned out to be a rattlesnake sting. Within 24 hours she was dead. The children had left Ozy Vern, 9 months old, for just a few moments at their play and he crawled over the boards of a summer well and after a search for him, he was found down in the well. The folks were broken hearted and decided to leave Gooseberry." (841~, 888a~) (See Farnsworth Tanks for the rest of the story.)

Farnsworth Tanks: (Emery Co.) San Rafael Reef-Swazy Seep. Old Woman Wash map.

Also called Farnsworth Reservoir. (1551~)

(See Farnsworth Reservoir for the start of the story.) After leaving the Gooseberry area, Stephen Martindale Farnsworth, Jr. and family moved to Giles in Blue Valley in the early 1890s. Unattributed: "This brought them nothing but trouble. The wild bunch from Robbers Roost was stealing their cattle and the floods took the whole valley every spring while they lived there." (888a~, 841~) The family moved to Lyman in 1896.

—Farnsworth Canyon: This is one-quarter mile northeast of Farnsworth Tank. Joe Bauman called it Doorway Wash: "This is a canyon of modern art. The north cliffs are cubist sculptures with roughly chiseled facets, harsh shadows backing each block that pops from the glassy face. To the south, the sensuous wall glows, smooth and slanting, decorated with dimples, seams, scratches. There were potholes in the shaded parts. A chalk white Henry Moore masterpiece of layered swirls is displayed in the runoff channel. It's as big as a coffee table, lounging on brown gravel and chipped stones." (166~)

Farrell Pond: (Sevier Co.) Fishlake National Forest-Thousand Lake Mountain. Geyser Peak map.

Dee Hatch noted that Boyd Farrell was the owner of the first farm in Paradise Valley. (844~) Garn Jefferies: "Boyd Farrell was from back east and he was playin' the stock markets real heavy and made lots of money. He came around and bought what they call Paradise [Ranch] now, and the Solomon Ranch." (959~)

Farview Point: (Garfield Co.) Bryce Canyon National Park-Paunsaugunt Plateau-Pink Cliffs. Bryce Point map. (8,819')

Bryce Canyon National Park Superintendent P.P. Paltrow noted in 1935 that the point provides the most comprehensive view of the park. (1931~)

Fault Point: (Garfield Co.) Glen Canyon NRA-The Cove. Bowdie Canyon West map. (5,773')

Geologist Howard R. Fitzma: "a prominent point in which faulted Permian Cedar Mesa and Organ Rock strata are conspicuously and colorfully exposed on the point's southwest face." (648~)

Fence Canyon: (Garfield Co.) Glen Canyon NRA-Escalante River. Egypt map.

Also called Upper Fence Canyon.

Edson Alvey noted that the canyon used to have a fence across its mouth. (55~)

—Fence Canyon Line Shack: (Also called Lloyd Gates Cabin.) (1729~) A couple of hitching posts and a small concrete foundation near the river are all that remain of a line shack that was burned to the ground in April 1990 by an arsonist. On the same day this line shack flared, another one at the mouth of Silver Falls Creek was torched. Twenty-one head of cattle were killed a short distance upriver. Although a ten thousand dollar reward was posted, the perpetrators were never found. (47~, 441~)

—Constructed Stock Trail: This goes down the point that divides the two forks of Fence Canyon. (SAPE.)

Fence Canyon: (Kane Co.) Glen Canyon NRA-Escalante River-Lake Powell. Stevens Canyon South map.

Also called Little Cow Canyon (183~) and Lower Fence Canyon.

Edson Alvey noted that a fence across the mouth of the canyon held cattle in. (55~)

—Necktie Bend: This was David D. Rust's name for the curve of the Escalante River at the mouth of Fence Canyon. (1672~)

Ferns Nipple: (Wayne Co.) Capitol Reef National Park-Capitol Reef. Golden Throne map.

Charles Kelly noted that Cass Mulford named this for area resident Fern Graham. (1047~)

Ferron Creek: (Emery and Sanpete Counties.) Manti-La-Sal National Forest-Wasatch Plateau-Castle Valley-San Rafael River. Ferron Reservoir, Ferron Canyon, Flagstaff Peak, Ferron, Molen, Horn Silver Gulch, and Hadden Holes maps.

(See Ferron Town for name derivation.)

Ferron, Cottonwood, and Huntington creeks come together to form the San Rafael River.

In 1848 Orville C. Pratt called this by its Indian name *Garambuya*, a name also used by the Fremont Expedition of 1853. (166~, 710~) Pratt: "Found good grass & water. Country the same as heretofore, rocky and barren." (1572~)

The Colonel William Wing Loring Expedition of 1857-58 called it Garamboyer Creek. Loring: "where there is a good camp." (1276~)

Inscriptions include one at the mouth that reads "Welcome" and is dated August 10, 1899. (SAPE.)

—Old Spanish Trail: The trail crossed Ferron Creek in the vicinity of the town.

—Ferron Canyon Road: The first road up the canyon was built by settlers in 1883. Evelyn Peacock Huntsman: "They had no dynamite so they built fires on the large rocks to make them crumble. It was winter and they had to build fires first to thaw the ground enough to work it." (931~) The CCC built the modern road up the canyon in the 1930s. (1330~)

Ferron Mountain: (Sanpete Co.) Manti-LaSal National Forest-Wasatch Plateau. Heliotrope Mountain, Ferron Reservoir, Flagstaff Peak, and Ferron Canyon maps. (10,678')

Also called The Mountain. (1967~)

(See Ferron Town for name derivation.)

Wayne Gremel: "The natives all called it Big Mountain when they first came into this country. Then, up the Muddy [Creek] we run stock on what the Emery [town] people call the 'North Side' and the Ferron [town] people call the 'South Side.'" (780~)

—The Great White Wall: This is the incredible wall on the mountain's southwest end.

Ferron Reservoir: (Sanpete Co.) Manti-LaSal National Forest-Wasatch Plateau. Ferron Reservoir map.

(See Ferron Town for name derivation.)

This natural lake was turned into a reservoir in 1888 with the addition of a twenty-five-foot dam and spillway. Other improvements have been added over the years. (1330~)

—Petty Resort: In the 1930s George Petty, who had been running a sawmill near the reservoir for many years, leased land and started a small resort. Petty sold the resort in 1947 to Elmer Dean and Florence Petty. Riedel George bought the resort in 1973. (931~)

Ferron Town: (Emery Co.) Castle Valley-Ferron Creek-Highway 10. Ferron and Molen maps.

Also called Ferron Creek (328~) and Ferrons City (M.29.). The town, founded in 1877, was named for Augustus David Ferron, a surveyor for the General Land Office. He led an expedition to the area in the early 1870s. (710~, 925~, 1531~, 1561~)

Unattributed: "When [land surveyor Augustus Ferron] and his helpers were surveying land in Castle Valley prior to settlement, the suggestion was made that if Ferron would allow the crew to duck him in the creek which they were on, it would henceforth bear his name. And so his finished plat shows the creek by his name." (606~, 931~)

Stella McElprang described what the first settlers saw when they arrived at the Ferron townsite: "Much of the valley was flat, covered with Castle Valley Clover and shad scale. Nestled under the cliffs of the mountain were giant formations that seemed to be abandoned windowless castles with stumps of chimneys still intact. The rolling hills were covered with a mat of prickly pear and greasewood so thick that only rabbits, prairie dogs and the dust colored snakes and lizards could penetrate. An abundance of bunch grass and cottonwoods along the creek beds and flat meadows made this look like a good place to stay." (1330~)

The original location of the town, near the banks of Ferron Creek, became water soaked as the area was developed, forcing the pioneers to move their houses to the present townsite on higher ground. (931~)

—Kings Canal: John Edson King (1856-1921) was the originator of the King Canal. He arrived in Ferron in 1878. (1196~)

Ferry Swale Canyon: (Coconino Co., Az.) Glen Canyon NRA-Colorado River. Ferry Swale, Az. map.

The Domínguez-Escalante Expedition of 1776–77 crossed the upper edge of Ferry Swale on their way from Domínguez Pass to Glen Canyon. Father Escalante: "We went down the other side [from Domínguez Pass] through cliff-lined gorges as we headed north and after one league turned east for half a one over a stretch of red sand which was quite troublesome for the horse herds." (261~)

Inscriptions near the mouth of Ferry Swale Canyon include F.G. Faatz and G.M. Wright, Nov. 16, 1892. (467~)

—Ferry Swale Tank: This is a still-used stock reservoir. (SAPE.)

Fiddler Butte: (Garfield Co.) Dirty Devil Country-Hatch Canyon. Fiddler Butte map. (6,027')

Barbara Ekker: "A sheepman who ran his herds on these red benches was a fiddle player and would lull his herd nightly with his melodies." (607~)

—Fiddler Cove Canyon Stock Trail: This constructed stock trail enters Fiddler Cove Canyon from the south one mile upcanyon from its mouth (Stair Canyon map). (SAPE.)

—Bathtub Butte: Eric Bjørnstad noted that this tower is one and one-half miles east of Fiddler Butte (at elevation 6224T on the Fiddler Butte map). (241~)

Fiddlers Canyon: (Iron Co.) Hurricane Cliffs-Windy Ridge-Cedar Valley. Flanigan Arch and Cedar City maps. Janet Burton Seegmiller noted that in the early years four of the men building a road up the canyon happened to play the fiddle. (942~, 1715~, 2053~)

Fiddlers Green: (San Juan Co.) White Mesa-Recapture Creek. Big Bench map.

Peter Minnerly Shumway and family moved to this meadow on Recapture Creek in 1910. Helen N. Shumway: "There do not seem to be any stories about where the name Fiddler's Green came from, except for one reference made by J. Glen [Shumway] in an interview. He says, 'We lived at a place we called Fiddler's Green,' giving one the feeling that they had chosen the name. Leland Shumway believed it may have come from the green sandstone hills surrounding the canyon." (1731~) In 1887 Charles Eugene Walton mentioned a "Fiddlers Grove" near Recapture Creek. (1965~)

Fiery Furnace: (Grand Co.) Arches National Park-Salt Valley. The Windows Section and Mollie Hogans maps.

After visiting the area with Canyonlands National Park Superintendent Bates Wilson and Ed Abbey in 1959, Cecil M. Ouelletee wrote: "Stretching for five mile north was the jumbled landscape of stone pinnacles, slabs and huge towers of the Fiery Furnace, so named because in bright sunlight this land appears to glow as if heated by a nighty underground fire." (1494~)

Fife Creek: (Iron and Kane Counties.) Kolob Terrace-Deep Creek. Webster Flat and Cogswell Point maps.

Peter Muir Fife, an early resident of Cedar City, was one of the first settlers to start a coal mine in Coal Creek, near Martins Flat. (768~, 1727~)

Paul Fife provided this short history: "Peter Muir Fife [ca. 1805–1875] was one of the pioneers of the Iron Mission, living most of his life as a farmer at Hamilton's Fort. One of Peter's sons, Joseph Smith Fife [1863–1939], homesteaded some land in 1885 around the headwaters of the Virgin River, which flows into Zion National Park. That high country was called 'Cedar Mountain.' Joseph's ranch was in the area now called 'Three Creeks,' where Fife Creek, Deep Creek, and Shoppman Creek merge to become Deep Creek. His principal business was dairying, including cheese production. This was also true of most of the other ranchers on Cedar Mountain. Later they nearly all sold their dairy cows and went into sheep ranching. Fife also built a small reservoir on his land, called Aspen

Lake, which was later enlarged. The ranch cabin was situated near the west shore of the lake." (640~)

Fiftymile Bench: (Kane Co.) GSCENM-Kaiparowits Plateau. Maps north to south: Basin Canyon, Big Hollow Wash, Blackburn Canyon, Sooner Bench, and Navajo Point.

This bench runs for somewhat less than fifty miles. It is sandwiched between the Lower Desert and the top of the Kaiparowits Plateau, and just under the Fiftymile Cliffs.

Fiftymile Creek: (Kane Co.) Glen Canyon NRA-Escalante River-Lake Powell. Davis Gulch map.

Also called Fifty Gulch, Fiftymile Gulch, and Soda Gulch. This is fifty miles from the town of Escalante.

Bering Monroe described the canyon in 1945 while looking for Gregory Natural Bridge: "After about 3/4 mil. Up this canyon we come to the most beautiful amphitheatre that God could ever have created—it is a perfect Jewel of God's work 400 ft. long in perfect semi-circle 100 ft. high—100ft. deep with Maiden Hair Ferns growing out of the cliff side all the way around the bowl and a beautiful pool in the center—It is far more beautiful than 'Music Temple' and when I saw 'Music Temple' I thought God had thrown away the pattern when finished! But lo!—he had only begun." (1375~)

—First Known Descent: Members of a National Geographic Society expedition in 1949 accomplished the first known descent of Soda Gulch. They found the upper part of the canyon wide and easy, but the lower part—now under Lake Powell—was a four-foot-wide constriction. Trip members described it as a "nightmare"; quicksand forced them to abandon their horses and they had to swim or chimney across long stretches of cold water. (275~)

Inscriptions include Al Morton, Burnett Hendrix, and Gail Bailey, 1922 and Emit Porter, Dec. 4, 1927. Another inscription reads "E Reus Hunters, June 6, 1935." This refers to the disappearance of Everett Ruess. (SAPE.) (See Davis Gulch.)

—Fiftymile Spring: (Sooner Bench map.) (Also called The Sodie.)

The Hole-in-the-Rock Expedition stopped here. Expedition member Platte D. Lyman in November 1879: "We drove 10 miles over the roughest country I ever saw a wagon go over and camped at the 50 miles spring." (1259~, 1356~)

—Button-Bailey Cabin: Fiftymile Spring was an often-used camping area for cowboys in the old days. In the 1940s Clark Veater moved a pioneer cabin, in pieces, from Escalante to Fiftymile Spring and reassembled it there. (1467~) This historic building was burned by an arsonist in 1996. Several rows of "Moqui" type steps can be seen on the cliffs behind the cabin site. They were chiseled by cowboys, not Indians. Inscriptions include A. Allen, 1903; Eugene Allen, May 12, 1908; and Milton Twitchell, May 12, 1908. (SAPE.)

—Rock Corral: (Also called Corral Seep.) (1672~) This is the cliff-bound corral near the spring. Charles Kelly: "The Rock corral was another large cave in which the pioneers kept their stock, a few poles being sufficient to close the entrance." (1068~)

—Gregory Natural Bridge: This bridge, now underwater, was near the mouth of Fiftymile Creek. It was named by a group led by Norm Nevills in 1940 for Herbert E. Gregory (1869-1952), geologist and explorer, who did extensive geologic exploration in canyon country from 1909 to 1929. Gregory's books and articles were an essential resource used in compiling this book. (1021~, 1283~, 1382~, 2051~, 2056~)

Senator Barry Goldwater in 1940: "[Norm Nevills] has named it *Nijani* but we insist on Gregory in honor of Dr. Gregory." (738~) Mildred Baker in 1940: "Norm [Nevills] asked about naming it, suggesting we call it the 'Doris May [the name of Nevill's wife].' Hoots of disgust greeted this, so nothing further along that line was mentioned. One of the party suggested naming it the 'Gregory' bridge, but Norm turned it down emphatically. While they had been measuring the span, I rested in the shade and had been thinking how peaceful it was there, so thought it would be a good idea to call it 'Hozhoni' or Bridge of Peace, that being Navajo for Peace. In submitting this later, Norm, who claims to know Navajo, said he knew of no such word and thought 'Nizhoni' or Beautiful might be the word I alluded to. So we decided to call it 'Nizhoni.'" (106~)

John Southworth, present at the "discovery" of the bridge in 1940: "I was wholly unimpressed by the bridge.... Saw lots of tin cans from cow camps. And lots of signs of cows. Frankly the whole thing bored me and I nearly walked under it without seeing it." (632~)

There was some controversy about who did "discover" the bridge. Gregory and Norm Nevills both claimed to have been the first there. Southworth's note of cans nearby helps make the case that stockmen knew of the bridge. Peter Orin Barker said that he'd seen the arch in 1922, if not before. (19~)

William R. Chenoweth of the William R. Chenoweth USGS Expedition of 1921: "This Bridge is across the creek and forms a perfect Bridge, and not an arch." (1992~)

Norm Nevills to Chenoweth: "Please don't feel that we have attempted to discredit your find, but actually the bridge was seen even before your visit in 1921. The important thing was to bring to public attention this bridge, in order to stimulate and further interest in the proposed Escalante Monument area, in which this bridge lies." (1440~)

Charles Larabee in 1948: "It is one of nature's masterpieces, and deserves a better fate than to be hidden from appreciative eyes in this inaccessible hinterland." (1133~)

Stephen C. Jett in 1963: "This massive bridge is, incredibly, eclipsed by the magnificence of its setting. Great cliffs enclosing unbelievably constricted and contorted canyons, strange, twisted rock formations, and great caves and alcoves strain one's credulity. But all this grandeur and beauty was slightly tarnished by the depressing thought that Gregory and most of its surroundings will soon be sacrificed on the altar of the great god 'Reclamation.'" (976~)

Fiftymile Mountain: (Garfield and Kane Counties.) GS-CENM-Glen Canyon NRA-Kaiparowits Plateau.
(See Kaiparowits Plateau.)

Fiftymile Point: (Kane Co.) Glen Canyon NRA-Kaiparowits Plateau. Nasja Mesa and Davis Gulch maps. (5,947')

This is fifty miles from the town of Escalante. In 1928 Clyde Kluckhohn called this Bridge Buttress in reference to Hole-in-the-Rock Arch which is on the east side of the point: "Bridge Buttress presented many geological problems. Its surface was like an ancient sea beach with shells, with bright-colored, rounded pebbles, with petrified logs and stumps and with hollow rocks which looked as if they had been blown up with gas so that they seemed like egg shells." (1100~)

—Hole-in-the-Rock Arch: This is on Fiftymile Point and is clearly visible from Hole-in-the-Rock Well. (See Hole-in-the-Rock Well.)

—Sixty Point: The long peninsula that projects south from Fiftymile Point (and contains elevations U78-5623 and 5825T on the Nasja Mesa map) has never had a formal name. Clyde Kluckhohn in 1928: "Gothic Buttress, shaped like the slim cathedrals of the French twelfth century, its steep sides carrying pilaster shapes, its lofty spires supported by Caryatides." (1100~)

In 1952 Ida Chidester noted it as both Sixty Mile Point and Arm of the Point. (379~) Harry Aleson called it Sixty Point, a name that he got from stockmen. (26~) P.T. Reilly noted it as 60 Mile Point. (1612~)

Inscriptions at the base of the southern tip of the point (near elevation BM4241 on the Nasja Mesa map) include L. Harris, Feb. 24, 1887 and A. Allen, May 24, 1907. (1115~, SAPE.)

—Airstrip: This was constructed on the point during the uranium boom of the 1950s. (441~)

Findlay Ranch: (Kane Co.) White Cliffs-Meadow Canyon. Deer Spring Point map.

Also called Deer Springs Ranch and Meadows Ranch.

Also spelled Findley Ranch and Finley Ranch.

Alexander Duncan Findlay (1853-1935) started the ranch in the late 1870s. In the 1880s he sold it to John Kitchen of the Nipple Ranch. (1083~, 1638~, 1639~)

—Ted Ford Ranch: Cal Johnson noted that Ted Ford had a homestead one mile down Deer Spring Wash from the Findlay Ranch. (984~)

Fin Little Wash: (Kane Co.) GSCENM-Clay Hole Wash. Nephi Point map.

Also called Finn Little Cañon. (1831~)

Also spelled Finn Little Wash. (765~)

Julius S. Dalley in 1942: "Named for a man by the name of 'Fin' Little." (2053~) Cal Johnson: "Finley Little ran cattle up in there. That was in the 1870s and 1880s." (984~)

—Fin Little Spring: This was developed in 1980 by the BLM. A constructed stock trail leads from the highlands down to the spring. (1551~, SAPE.)

Fins, The: (Garfield and Wayne Counties.) Canyonlands National Park-Maze District-Land of Standing Rocks. Elaterite Basin and Spanish Bottom maps.

Also spelled The Finns. (619~)

Arthur Ekker and Leon Moynier noted in 1953 that these were "named after the vertical standing rocks in the area." (1931~)

James H. Knipmeyer: "named for the resemblance of the long, narrow, parallel sandstone blades of rock to the dorsal fins on fish." (1115~)

Firepit Knoll: (Washington Co.) Zion National Park-Lower Kolob Plateau. The Guardian Angels map. (7,265')

Also called French Knoll. (778~)

The USGS: "Name derived from a large extinct crater on the south slope of The Knoll near the summit." (1931~)

Firewater Canyon: (Uintah Co.) Uintah and Ouray Indian Reservation-East Tavaputs Plateau-Desolation Canyon. Firewater Canyon South and Firewater Canyon North maps.

Old maps show this as Cunepah Canyon. George Stewart noted that *Cunepah* is Ute for "firewater." (199~, 833~, 859~)

Waldo Wilcox added to the story: "It was NOT named after Ben Morris's still [See Big Canyon].... It was named by the early people who went in there. That was Jick Taylor. Jick had a boy and he ran in Wild Horse Basin.... Just

before he died, Jick Taylor's boy, Bud Taylor, was in a nursing home over in Fruita [Colorado]. I went and talked to him. I asked him where Firewater got its name. Bud told me that when his dad, Jick Taylor, first went into Wild Horse Basin, there were some Indians there. And the head Indian's name was Firewater. And that is where Firewater got its name." (2011~)

Jean Bennett told this story about a near disaster at the mouth of Firewater Canyon: "Vern Muse and a friend were riding horses above the ledge on the right bank when the friend's horse slipped throwing both horse and rider into the rapids. The horse was able to gain footing and, by hanging onto the horse, Muse's friend was pulled to safety." (209~)

Ed F. Harmston told a similar story that happened near Firewater Canyon in 1913: "After going about a mile 'Black Tiger' [a horse] falls [from the] trail into the river with his pack, but is rescued without any damage." (833~) (See Cedar Ridge Canyon and the Black Tiger for the rest of the story.)

First Canyon: (Coconino Co., Az. and San Juan Co., Utah.) Navajo Indian Reservation-Navajo Mountain-Tsagieto Canyon. Arizona map: Chaiyahi Flat. Utah map: Rainbow Bridge.

Also called To-Hi-Ling Canyon. (867~)

This is the first canyon crossed while following the trail from Rainbow Lodge to Rainbow Natural Bridge. The name was given by archaeologist Charles L. Bernheimer. (221~)

Bernheimer in 1922: "We were joined a little later by our Indian, Hosteen Chee, a Navajo whose hogan is not far from our camp which we named 'Sagi-To,' or 'Waters in the Rocks.' The Indian's name is 'Sag-nini-jazi' which translated means, 'the little man who lives among the rocks.'" (218~)

First Lake: (Iron Co.) Hurricane Cliffs-Summit Mountain. Flanigan Arch map.

Warren Pendleton noted that this is the first lake one reached on the road to Dry Lakes. (653~)

First Left Hand Canyon: (Iron Co.) Dixie National Forest-Parowan Canyon. Red Creek Reservoir and Parowan maps.

Also called Grand Castle Canyon. (2053~)

Bowery Creek runs through First Left Hand Canyon.

John C.L. Smith of the Exploring Expedition of 1852 was the first to use the name: "We went up Centre Creek [Parowan Canyon], took the first left hand fork." (1776~)

—The Bowery: This was at the head of First Left Hand Fork. It was used by early residents of Parowan for celebrations. (2053~)

First Mound: (Iron Co.) Hurricane Cliffs-Parowan Creek. Parowan map.

Also called Black Knob. (484~)

In the early days, those traveling from Parowan to Summit would mark their progress as they passed First Mound, then Second Mound.

—Old Spanish Trail: The trail went just north of First Mound.

First Narrows: (Washington Co.) Virgin River-Big Round Valley. White Hills map.

Jedediah Smith of the South West Expedition of 1826-27 went down the Virgin River through First Narrows and on to Beaver Dam: "the river ... entered the mountain which we could see from and that we could not follow the River through the Mt. Unless we traveled in the water as the Rocks rise from the water perpendicularly on both sides.... Early the next morning we started down in the bed of the general shallowness of the water. By the meanderings of the stream it was about 12 m through the rocks rising perpendicularly from the waters edge in most places to a height of 3 or 400 feet.... At one place I was obliged to unload and swim the horses." (1774~)

Gwinn Harris Heap of the Lieutenant Edward F. Beale Expedition of 1853 described going through the First Narrows: "The river bottom was hemmed in by bluffs.... The road which followed down the bottom, was at times through deep sand, as was mostly the case since leaving the Vegas de Santa Clara. The scenery was gloomy and forbidding, and gave indication that we were approaching a wild and desolate region." (854~)

First Point Spring: (Kane Co.) GSCENM-Skutumpah Terrace. Skutumpah Creek map.

This is a large, developed spring. (SAPE.)

First Spring: (Iron Co.) Hurricane Cliffs-Summit Creek. Summit map.

This is a small spring. (SAPE.)

There are three numerically named springs in a row: First Spring, Second Spring, and Third Spring. The First Spring is closest to Summit, the Third Spring, the furthest away.

First Spring Hollow: (Sevier Co.) Fishlake National Forest-Tushar Mountains-Clear Creek. Marysvale Canyon map.

Ezlan Jackman in 1942: "Called First Spring Hollow because the first spring to be reached on the road to the mountains." (2053~) The road starts at Sage Flat and goes south up Sargent Mountain to the spring.

Fish Creek: (Sevier Co.) Fishlake National Forest-Tushar Mountains-Clear Creek Canyon. Trail Mountain map.

Inscriptions include ?A.H., Cook 1881. (SAPE.)

Fish Creek: (Piute and Sevier Counties.) Fishlake National Forest-Tushar Mountains-Clear Creek. Mount Belknap and Trail Mountain maps.

In the late 1800s pioneers built a road up Fish Creek to access timber and for gold mining. (1934~)

—Jim Long Reservoir: This stock reservoir is in the middle of Fish Creek Meadows (Mount Belknap map). Jim Long discovered the Breckinridge Mine to the south of Tip Top in 1895. (1934~)

—Handspike Creek: This is the first eastern tributary of Fish Creek to the north of Wilson Creek (Mount Belknap map). (1934~)

Fish Creek: (Wayne Co.) Dixie National Forest-Boulder Mountain-Fremont River. Blind Lake, Torrey, and Twin Rocks maps.

Dwight Williams noted that there have always been fish in the creek. (2013~)

—Fish Creek Trail: This is the "Pack Trail" at the head of Fish Creek that ascends Fish Creek Point (Blind Lake map). The Great Western Trail goes up this trail and down the Bowns Point Trail. (337~)

—Fish Creek Lake: (Blind Lake map.) (Also called Fish Creek Reservoir.) John Campbell: "one of the North Slope Lakes rated a World Class fishery." (337~)

Fish Creek Cove: (Wayne Co.) Dixie National Forest-Boulder Mountain. Blind Lake map.

James H. Knipmeyer: "It was at one time known as Bullard Cove, as between 1880 and 1884 the Bullard brothers, Will and Ezra, pastured their cattle here." (1119~)

In the late 1890s the Fred Noyes and Cutlar Behunin families moved to Fish Creek. (1891~) By the late 1920s the land was owned by D.N. Covington. (1392~)

Dwight Williams: "In the early days of the Mormon Church, the Church took, and they still do, their tithing as they call it, in kind. If people wanted to pay their tithing in kind, they paid it in livestock or cattle. The Church gathered up quite a herd of cattle and they had to have someplace for them to run and feed. So they would take them to Fish Creek Cove." (2013~)

James H. Knipmeyer noted that Albert King Thurber inscribed his name in the canyon in 1877. (1105~) Other inscriptions include HMB, 1878; G. Holliday, 11th June 1880; N. Sheffet, April 17, 1881; F.M. Works, April 23, 1885; D.J. Stewart, 1887; Lewis Adams, May 2nd, 1887;

John D. Adams, July 16, 1887; and Benjamin Perkins and Mary Ann Perkins, May 1st, 1887. (1112~, 1115~, SAPE.)

Fish Creek Canyon: (San Juan Co.) Cedar Mesa-Comb Wash. South Long Point, Snow Flat Spring Cave, and Bluff NW maps.

Also called Fish Canyon.

Buck Lee in 1942: "It has thousands of little minnows in it about 2 inches or less long and takes its name from these minnows." (2053~, 697~, 1451~) The name was in place by 1908.

The canyon was visited by William Henry Jackson of the Ferdinand V. Hayden Survey in 1875: "went up side canyon [Fish Creek] 8 or 10 miles. Found ruins plenty." (950~)

Fisher Canyon: (Kane Co.) Pink Cliffs-Bald Knoll Hollow. Alton and Bald Knoll maps.

Also called Finger Canyon. (1658~)

—Fisher Spring: (Bald Knoll map.) This is a large spring with two sets of watering troughs. (SAPE.)

Fisher Spring: (Coconino Co., Az.) Vermilion Cliffs National Monument-Vermilion Cliffs-Johnson Point. Navajo Bridge, Az. map.

Also called Parker Spring. (469~)

This is a medium-size spring in an incredible setting. (SAPE.)

This may have been named for George Fisher. He was in the area in the 1940s. (1070~) It has also been called Twomile Canyon; the spring is two miles from Lees Ferry.

Inscriptions include C.E. Holladay, C.A. Huntington, and I.D. Watson with the date 1857. The three men were in the Lees Ferry area in the 1890s. It is unclear why they used the 1857 date. (1076~, 1115~, SAPE.)

—Constructed Stock Trail: This drops to Fisher Spring on its west side. (SAPE.)

Fisher Towers: (Grand Co.) La Sal Mountains-Richardson Amphitheater. Fisher Towers and Fisher Valley maps.

Also called Colorado River Organ. (1658~)

(See Fisher Valley for name derivation.)

Joe Taylor: "We called them, as a group, the Pipe Organs. Now the bird watchers and rock climbers have named each individual tower. They were always called the Pipe Organs. I was fairly grown before I saw the name Fisher Towers." (1866~)

The towers range from eight hundred to seventeen hundred feet in height and have names that include King Fisher, Ancient Art, The Oracle, and Cottontail Tower. (239~)

Merel S. Sager of the National Park Service in 1937: "From a distance, these red sandstone formations suggest the skyline of Manhattan.... Some have dominant, unbroken vertical lines of the modern skyscraper, while others resemble Gothic cathedrals with delicate carvings." (2056~)

Buck Lee in 1940: "a grand array of the most fascinating and grotesque formations one can ever imagine. These great rock spires and pinnacles rise out of a broken and twisted world to the unbelievable heights of over 1700 feet, in sheer walls on all sides. One need have no imagination to see pictures and sculptures made by the Master Painter and Sculptor in the many towering cliffs, where color and formation vie with each other in an effort to enchant." (354~)

—Movies: In 1967 *Blue*, starring Terence Stamp and Ricardo Montalban, was filmed, in part, with the Fisher Towers as a backdrop. (1806~) John Ford's *Wagonmaster* was filmed, in part, in Professor Valley with the Fisher Towers in the background. (1421~)

Fisher Valley: (Grand Co.) Manti-LaSal National Forest-Fisher Creek. Fisher Valley map.

Two name derivations are given.

First, James H. Knipmeyer: "Here was a pastoral paradise completely surrounded by cliffs and towering peaks.... Locally known as Forbidden Valley because of its inaccessibility, it was named Fisher after an early-day rancher." (1120~, 2056~)

George Amasa Larsen, a pioneer Castle Valley rancher: "Fisher Valley was named for the first white to be there. Fisher talked so much about what a fine place it was that his friends always called it Fisher Valley." (935a~)

Huntley Ingalls reinforced the idea that a family named Fisher lived here: "In the Fisher Towers, named for an early rancher, nature has created a pink, red, and orange skyscraper city in nightmare Gothic. In few areas of the Southwest can one find more bizarre masterpieces of erosion." (939~) William Gladstone Steel also noted a reference from 1926 to an early settler named Fisher. (1819~)

Second, Joe Taylor, whose family has lived in the area since the 1880s: "I've never heard of a Fisher family living there. The one thing that I heard from my grandfather, Don Taylor, was him quoting an old-timer. This fellow told him that it was supposed to be Fissure, like a hole in the ground, not Fisher like a person's name." (1866~)

To bolster this argument, it is known that early diarists, including Jacob Hamblin, used the term "fissure" as a synonym for a canyon or defile. In a diary entry from 1858 Hamblin described the Glen Canyon country: "after climbing dangerous cliffs and crossing extensive fissures." (235~)

—Fisher Valley Ranch: Joe Taylor noted that his grandfather, Don Taylor, and family bought the Fisher Valley Ranch: "In the old days ranchers would homestead different areas. The big ranches would put their hired men on a ranch. On this ranch they put a hired man there in the fall and when they went back the next spring, there were other families there. They said that there had been nobody there so they just took up the homestead. Years later the house burned down and there was a skeleton of a person buried under the foundation. My granddad always said that the family always felt that the homesteaders had killed their hired man and jumped the claim." (1866~)

Fisheye Arch: (San Juan Co.) Canyonlands National Park-Needles District-Salt Creek. South Six-shooter Peak map.

This was named for Frank "Fisheye" Masland, Jr. (1896-1994) by former Canyonlands National Park Superintendent Bates Wilson. He received his nickname while on a river trip in 1948. Masland, Jr. and Otis "Dock" Marston discovered the arch in 1962. (1429~, 1948~)

Masland, Jr. told the story: "[my] companions started calling me 'Fish-Eyes.' It seems the usual way for the person riding the stern of the boat to go through a rapid is sitting up, but being blissfully ignorant of the approved technique, I stretched out face down with my head overhanging the stern. Since the boats go through the rapids stern first, I was under water most of he way.... After two or three trips in this submerged position, they began talking about the fish-eye view I had of the water, and soon 'Fish-Eyes' was my name." (4~)

Fish Lake: (Sevier Co.) Fishlake National Forest-Fishlake Hightop Plateau. Fish Lake map.

In 1848 Orville C. Pratt called this Washach Lake. (1572~)

Thomas D. Brown of the Southern Indian Mission of 1854 called it both Pangwitch Lake and Fish Lake. (307~)

George Washington Bean wrote a letter dated October 13, 1871: "The monster of Fish Lake is only 300 ft. long, no nascent. Formerly raised great havoc with papooses." (175~)

The 1874 Frank A. Gray map mistakenly labels this as Gunnison's Lake and shows it as the headwaters of the Fremont River. (M.26.)

Barbara Ekker: "Elias Blackburn was chairman of [a] group that met March 1, 1889 with representatives of the Indian tribe who fished in Fish Lake and negotiated the purchase of the outlet of Fish Lake for the price of 'nine horses, 500 pounds of flour, 1 good beef steer, and one suit of clothes.' An unofficial story is that the group met *Pogneab*, the fishing Chief of the Indians, took a liking to the suit of clothes one of the irrigation company representatives was wearing and insisted that he be given that suit before he would sign. To obtain the agreement, the negotiator gave his suit to *Pogneab*, and went home in his underwear." (607~, 1047~)

Clarence Dutton of the Powell Survey: "No resort more beautiful than this lake can be found in Southern Utah. Its grassy banks clad with groves of spruce and aspen; the splendid vista down between its mountain walls, with the massive fronts of Mounts Marvine and Hilgard in the distance; the crystal-clear expanse of the lake itself, combine to form a scene of beauty rarely equaled in the West." (584~)

Irvin Warnock: "No matter the number of times one comes to the first glimpse of beautiful shimmering Fish Lake from the turn of the road at hill top, the sight is quietly inspiring. A sense of calmness and serenity pervades the soul; 'God is in his heaven, all is well with the world.' That is the charm and promise of Fish Lake." (1971~)

George Albert Adams told this story that happened at Fish Lake in the mid-1870s: "Will Wilcox, a young fellow about fifteen years old, in his fun, grabbed an automatic revolver, which we had in camp and deliberately placed it against my head, pulling the trigger in rapid succession with a command to surrender. Knowing the revolver was not loaded, I refused to so surrender, which caused the repeating of the automatic snap. Henry Wilcox, an older brother, came up and grabbed the gun and reprimanded his brither fir such a desperate act, warning him that the gun was loaded. Of course this brought an absolute silence ... and after we got over the scare I took the gun to my amazement, I found four bullets which had been snapped several times without exploding. In order to learn the cause of the non-explosion, I fired one shot, which exploded in the usual way." (6~)

—Old Spanish Trail: (Variation.) The Old Spanish Trail—Fish Lake Route—went along the west shore of Fish Lake. (477~)

—Fish Lake Resort: Although pioneers had been coming to Fish Lake for many years to fish and vacation, it wasn't until Charles Skougaard arrived in 1911 that a true resort was built. In 1914 the first car was driven to the resort. (357~) (See Skougaard Canyon.)

—Fish Lake Dam: (Proposed.) The first dam proposed for Fish Lake was by a committee of Rabbit Valley pioneers in 1878. (592~)

Fish Lake Hightop Plateau: (Sevier Co.) Fishlake National Forest. Burrville, Fish Lake, and Mount Terrill maps. (11,633')
Also called Fishlake Mountains and Fishlake Plateau.
This is the highest summit in the Fishlake Mountains and in Sevier County.

Fishlake National Forest: (Beaver, Emery, Garfield, Iron, Juab, Millard, Piute, Sevier, and Wayne Counties.) President Grover Cleveland designated Fishlake Reserve in 1891. It was expanded incrementally over the years and was designated as Fishlake National Forest in 1923. It now covers over 1.5 million acres. (2063~)

Fish Seep Draw: (Grand Co.) Cisco Desert-The Highlands-Lost Spring Canyon. Cisco SW and Mollie Hogans maps.
Joe Taylor: "There is no water or fish in Fish Seep Draw. It is dry. There are willows, though, and there probably used to be water there back in the days when this whole country was wetter." (1866~)

Fitzgerald Park: (Sevier Co.) Fishlake National Forest-Sevier Plateau. Monroe Peak map.
The Richard Collings family moved to Monroe in 1872 and were the first to run livestock on Monroe Mountain. (369~)
Sylvia Collings Musig in 1965: "There is an old quaking aspen tree at Fitzgerald's Park, on the west slope of Monroe Mountain quite near the peak, that bears this inscription in its rough bark, 'W.R.C. [William Richard Collins], Sept. 1872.' Men who have ridden on that range for many years have said that these are the oldest initials carved on the Monroe Mountain." (369~)

Five Canyon: (Garfield Co.) Henry Mountains-Tarantula Mesa-South Creek. Cave Flat and Steele Butte maps.
Early ranchers noted that the canyon has five arms.
—Constructed Stock Trail: This goes out a lower western tributary of Five Canyon. It is two and one-half miles southwest of the junction of Five Canyon and Sweetwater Creek (one-half mile north of elevation 6411T on the Steele Butte map). (291~, 582~, SAPE.)

Fivemile Valley: (Kane Co.) GSCENM-The Cockscomb. Fivemile Valley map.
Ralph Chynoweth noted that this is five miles from the old townsite of Paria. (425~)
In 1869, the Mormon Territorial Militia called it Great Gulch. (476~) Herbert E. Gregory noted it as Robinson Creek. (M.27.)
—Fivemile Spring: This is a large, developed, and still-used spring. (SAPE.)

—Fivemile Ranch: This is shown as a ruin at the "Spring" one mile south of Fivemile Spring. The ranch was started by John Magnum and family in the early 1930s. (1083~) There are house and corral ruins at the site. (SAPE.)
—Robinson Creek: This starts in the northern end of Fivemile Valley and goes south to join Sand Gulch. (765~)

Fivemile Wash: (Emery Co.) San Rafael Desert-Green River. Jessies Twist and Green River maps.
Ted Ekker noted that this is five miles from the railroad line in Green River. (623~)
—Wheeler Ranch: (Also called Wheeler Brothers Ranch.) Ross Wheeler (See Ruby Ranch) had a small ranch on the west side of the Green River just above the mouth of Fivemile Wash. Hazel Ekker: "Ross had a small frame house ... a small garden that he watered with a bucket. An Anderson ... was farming on the other side of the river and had been having Wheeler help him with some of his work.... When Ross didn't come over to his boat, Anderson worried and finally thought he could tell the cabin was burned. So he [and others] went to investigate.... These people found Wheelers body, too badly burned to tell if he'd been shot or not. There were bullet holes in his water bucket which was salvaged from the ashes." (612~) Ross died in 1920.

Fivemile Wash: (Garfield Co.) Capitol Reef National Park-Capitol Reef-Sandy Creek. Bear Canyon, Sandy Creek Benches, and Notom maps.
Keith Durfey noted that the wash is five miles from Notom. (582~)

Flag Point: (Kane Co.) GSCENM-Vermilion Cliffs. Johnson Lakes map. (6,498')
Also called Navajo Wells Point.
Francis M. Bishop of the Powell Expedition of 1871–72: "Stopped when opposite the flag point at Navajo Wells." (236~) Flag Point can be seen from Navajo Wells. (SAPE.) The Powell Survey erected several flags on the point to help with their survey work. (2053~)

Flake Mountain: (Garfield Co.) Dixie National Forest-Paunsaugunt Plateau. Flake Mountain East and Flake Mountain West maps. (8,317')
Mathew Evans in 1941: "This mountain derived its name from a man named Flake who settled in this area." (2053~) In 1949 Mrs. Irvin Warnock noted that William J. Flake (1839-1932) explored the area in 1875. (1972~) He was one the first group to explore Potato Valley, or what would become the town of Escalante. (1188~)
—Flake Swale: (Also called Flake Bottoms [363~] and Flake Meadow [2063~].) Isaac Jimeson Riddle: "It was

on these Flake Bottoms that the Panguitch People were at that time [mid-1870s] raising much of their hay." (1314~)

—Squaw Spring: This is shown as a stock pond on the south side of Flake Mountain (one-quarter mile south-southeast of elevation 8044 on the Flake Mountain East map). Unattributed: "This spring derived its name from the locally known squaw brush that surrounded it." (2053~, 1346~)

Flanigan Arch: (Iron Co.) Coal Creek-Ashdown Creek. Flanigan Arch map.

Also called Ashdown Bridge. (1956~)

Also spelled Flannigan Arch.

Herbert E. Gregory noted that naturalist William Flanigan (1877-1961) of Cedar City discovered the arch in 1916. (768~) Alva Matheson, who knew Flanigan, noted that there used to be a sawmill at the mouth of Ashdown Gorge. By 1916 timber for the mill was becoming scarce. The owners, knowing that William Flanigan had built the cable lift down Cable Mountain near Zion Canyon (See Cable Mountain), asked him to determine if they could do the same at this location. Flanigan and others discovered the arch while exploring the canyon walls for a route to the top of the canyon. (1313~)

Flat Canyon: (Carbon Co.) West Tavaputs Plateau-Desolation Canyon. Patmos Head, Summerhouse Ridge, Twin Hollow, Steer Ridge Canyon, and Cedar Ridge Canyon maps.

Also called Flat Canyon Creek. (106~)

Two name derivations are given.

First, Waldo Wilcox: "When you look at it, there are little flat terraces on both sides of the canyon." (2011~)

Second, William Gladstone Steel in 1926 noted that it is "a canyon with a flat bottom." (1819~)

—Constructed Stock Trail: This goes up Flat Canyon. Inscriptions near the trail include a date from 1921 and EHVW, 7-13-26. (SAPE.)

Flat Canyon: (Piute Co.) Fishlake National Forest-Sevier Plateau-Durkee Creek. Marysvale Peak and Marysvale maps.

—Flat Canyon Trail: This is the "Pack" trail that starts on the north side of Marysvale Peak (Marysvale Peak map) and goes west down the canyon to the Willow Springs area (Marysvale map).

Flat Canyon: (Sevier Co.) Fishlake National Forest-Pavant Range-Sevier Canal. White Pine Peak and Elsinore maps.

The clay in Flat Canyon was used to build many of the pioneer houses in Elsinore. (364~)

Flatiron Lakes: (Wayne Co.) Dixie National Forest-Boulder Mountain. Torrey map.

Barbara Ekker: "There are a cluster of small lakes, two of which have the triangular shape of a flatiron." (607~)

Flat Iron Mesa: (Carbon Co.) West Tavaputs Plateau-Cold Spring Draw. Bruin Point map. (8,834')

Two similar name derivations are given.

First, Howard C. Price: "cowboys who ran cattle in the area and named it such because of its unique shape and flat open top." (1931~)

Second, Waldo Wilcox: "That was because it is shaped like a flat branding iron." (2011~)

Flat Nose George Canyon: (Grand Co.) Roan Cliffs-Rattlesnake Canyon. Floy Canyon North and Bobby Canyon North maps.

A couple of stories are told about the death of the outlaw George Southerland Curry (1864-1900), also called "Flat Nose" George Curry and Jim King).

First, Edward M. Kirby noted that Flat Nose George Currie (also spelled Curry), a member of Butch Cassidy's Wild Bunch, was killed in nearby Range Canyon on April 17, 1900. (1098~)

Second, Waldo Wilcox: "The story that I heard, and I've heard several ever since, was that Flat Nose George had the Range Valley Cattle Company. He'd ordered some boots in town. So he went to get the boots and he lost his horses and the horses swum the river. So he was building himself a raft to get back to his camp and his horses. There is a big rock there and my dad [Ray 'Budge' Wilcox] showed me and where my granddad, Jim McPherson, had showed him. He was trying to build him a raft in that drift pile. There were two posses looking for Joe Walker. One on each side of the river. The ones on this side [west] run onto him first. He started shooting at them behind this rock. He was sitting on a little rock next to the big rock when they shot him and killed him. Supposedly, when the posse from the other side came and looked, one of the guys from that posse shot him again! I'm sure that is right, because there are bullet holes in the rock. There was a big monument on that rock, then the Bureau of Land Management kicked it over because it wasn't natural." (2011~)

—Constructed Stock Trail: This goes up Flat Nose George Canyon. Construction is most visible going around falls. (SAPE.)

—Flat Nose George Canyon Line Camp: This was under an overhang one-half mile upcanyon from its mouth (Bobby Canyon North map). (SAPE.)

Flats, The: (Garfield Co.) GSCENM-Circle Cliffs Basin. Lamp Stand map.

Also called Burr Flats and Flats Field. (1401~)

Although The Flats is only shown on one USGS 7.5 Minute Series map, local usage dictates that it is all of the pasturelands encompassed by the Circle Cliffs. (56~, 1487~)

Flat Top: (Emery Co.) San Rafael Swell-Sinbad Country. Temple Mountain map.

Also called Flat Top Mesa and Shinarump Mesa. (846~) The mesa was heavily, and productively, mined during the uranium boom of the 1950s. (988~)

Flat Top: (Garfield Co.) Dixie National Forest-Escalante Mountains-Cherry Creek. Griffin Point map. (7,843')

Also called Flat Top Mountain.

Jack Justett in 1941: "It is a large, flat, thickly timbered mountain and was so named because of its levelness." (2053~)

Flat Top: (Wayne Co.) Fishlake National Forest-Thousand Lake Mountain. Flat Top map. (11,306')

This small flat-topped mesa marks the highest point on Thousand Lake Mountain. (SAPE.)

Flat Tops, The: (Emery Co.) San Rafael Desert-Maze Road. The Flat Tops map. (6,089')

Also called Flat Butte (1779~) and Twin Buttes (1750~).

The Flat Tops consist of three distinct buttes. The northern butte is labeled on the map as Little Flat Top. The middle butte is called Mid Top. The southern butte is called South Flat Top or Big Flat Top. (100~, 569~)

—Moore Line Camp: Barbara Ekker noted that rancher Andy Moore (1894-1968) had a line camp at Little Flat Top in the early years. (606~) (See North Spring.)

Flax Lakes: (Kane Co.) Long Valley-Black Mountain. Long Valley Junction map.

Herbert E. Gregory noted that Johanas Flax used the lake for irrigation. (1931~)

Flint Flat: (Garfield Co.) Glen Canyon NRA-Big Ridge. Gordon Flats and Clearwater Canyon maps.

Wiladeane Chaffin Wubben Hills: "The Flint Trail and Flint Flats were given those names because there were so many chips of flint laying around. The ground used to be covered with pieces of jasper and flint, but starting in the 1940s people began getting into the area and picked up most of the artifacts." (1430~)

—Flint Seep: (Gordon Flats map.) Louis M. Chaffin built a road to the seep for hauling water. (411~)

—Flint Trail: (Also called Flint's Trail.) (871~) This "4WD" road starts on Flint Flat (Gordon Flats map) and descends twelve hundred feet in two miles through the Orange Cliffs. It ends in Flint Cove (Teapot Rock map).

The road started as an Indian trail and was later used as a stock trail. Outlaws used the trail at the turn of the century. The trail was upgraded into a wagon road by Edwin T. Wolverton, Pat Brown, Faun L. and Louis M. Chaffin, and others for the Nequoia Oil Company in 1919. They used it to bring a Keystone Rig into Elaterite Basin to test drill for oil. In the mid-1950s the road was improved by the Atomic Energy Commission into its present configuration. (100~, 404~, 871~, 1429~) The National Park Service now maintains the road.

Old maps often show this as Middle Trail, which is between the North Trail down North Trail Canyon and the South or Squaw Trail into Hatch Canyon. Unattributed: "The party went down the Middle Trail into Brooders Hole [probably upper Range Canyon] and journeyed as near as possible to the Standy Rocks [Land of Standing Rocks]." (617~)

—Flint Cabins: (Also called Wolvertons Cabins.) These cabins were near the head of the Flint Trail (one-quarter mile south-southeast of Flint Seep on the Gordon Flats map). They were built by Edwin T. Wolverton, Louis M. and Fawn L. Chaffin, Dubinky Anderson, and Paul Solgauer. Wolverton started the Nequoia Oil Company and the others were his employees. After the oil company folded, Louis M. Chaffin used the cabins as his headquarters for ranching operations. (411~, 1430~, SAPE.)

—Harness-up Spring: This is on the west side of Flint Flat and is three-quarters of a mile west-southwest of Flint Seep (one-quarter mile northwest of elevation 6723T on the Gordon Flats map). A constructed stock trail leads to this medium-size, developed spring. Richard F. Negri noted that the spring was used by the Chaffin family while they pushed livestock over the Flint Trail in the early to mid-1900s. (1430~, SAPE.)

Barbara Ekker, paraphrasing Ned Chaffin: "Harness Up was where your horse was 'traded' for a winded and lame horse—not stolen—just traded or borrowed by parties unknown." (411~) Ned Chaffin: "Harness Up is permanent water. Clell and Faun [Chaffin] built a trail into the spring and troughed it up." (606~)

Inscriptions include LM, Jan. 19, 1936. (SAPE.)

Floating Island Lake: (Sevier Co.) Fishlake National Forest-Thousand Lake Mountain. Geyser Peak map.

—Burnt Springs: Garn Jefferies noted that this is immediately north of Floating Island Lake. (959~)

—Johnson Cabin: This was on the north side of Floating Island Lake. It was a well-known landmark in the 1890s. (1931~)

Flood Canyon: (Emery Co.) Manti LaSal National Forest-Huntington Creek. Candland Mountain map.

In the early years Abe Day and Alma Staker had a sawmill here. It washed away in a spring flood. (1330~)

Flood Canyon: (Kane Co.) GSCENM-Johnson Wash. Johnson Lakes map.

George G. Mace: "Terrific floods have originated in this dry canyon and so flooded the town that it became known as Flood Canyon." (2053~)

—Pioneer Road: The "4WD" road in Flood Canyon was built in pioneer days. (765~)

Florence Creek: (Grand Co.) Uintah and Ouray Indian Reservation-East Tavaputs Plateau-Desolation Canyon. Walker Point, Lion Canyon, Moonwater Point, Three Fords Canyon, and Chandler Falls maps.

There are several stories about the naming of the creek. The first derivation is correct.

First, Waldo Wilcox: "By golly, I know where that name came from! It was named after Florence [Lorene Harris] Fuller [1866–1930]. When my granddad, Jim McPherson, and his uncles went into Florence Creek to settle it, Florence was their cook." (2011~) Sylvia Harris Ekker noted that Florence Fuller was her aunt: "[She] became known as the Cattle Queen of the Colorado Plateau…. She went to Texas, where I believe she entertained in saloons and dealt cards. When she returned home she had many beautiful dresses…. She brought 500 head of cattle back to Utah, given her by a man named Tom Horn. It was an agreement to get her out of Texas. I never knew just what was behind it, but I suspect it was a payoff over a poker game…. She ran her cattle around Woodside, on the San Rafael, and up in the Book Cliff Mountains." (622~)

Second, Waldo Wilcox: "One story is that it was named by the men at the Range Valley Cattle Company for one of their girlfriends. That is absolutely not correct. I got the story from the people who were actually there." (2011~)

Third, James M. Aton noted that Joseph Wing claimed it was named for his future wife, Florence. (79~)

Fourth, the creek was named by members of the Powell Expedition in the early 1870s. (1808~)

Charles Eggert in 1957: "The creek was a disappointment. It was a small stream and choked with tumbleweeds." (599~)

Nell Murbarger in 1960: "The canyon walls began to narrow and grow progressively more sheer. Scores of times the twisting gorge appeared to end only a few hundred yards ahead, but a sharp bend would reveal more canyon and trail. Stone pinnacles and promontories appeared on the rimrock. Great stone arches high on the skyline stood out in silhouette against the last bright glow of the day." (1414~)

—McPherson Ranch: (Also called Cradle M Ranch and Florence Creek Ranch.) Trapper Jack had squatter's rights to lower Florence Creek and had a home on the creek at the mouth of Slough Canyon (Lion Canyon map). (79~) Waldo Wilcox: "My granddad, Jim McPherson, [and two uncles] bought the place from Trapper Jack. He actually paid Trapper Jack to show him Florence Creek." (2011~) Jim McPherson moved with his uncles to Florence Creek in 1887. They built a thriving ranch operation. (1780~)

Waldo Wilcox continued the history of the ranch: "My mother was a McPherson. My dad, Ray 'Budge' Wilcox; my uncle, Hap Wilcox; and my granddad, Carlos Wilcox; bought it from the Jim McPherson family. That was sometime around 1930. We left there in 1941 after selling it to the Utes. We leased it back from the Indians for a year or so and then left." (2011~)

Owen McCook, a Ute, took over the ranch, but abandoned it after arsonists burned several buildings to the ground in the mid-1940s. (79~) In later years the Utes built a small resort here. It has since been abandoned. (200~) Jean Bennett in 1965: "The Indians refused to live at the ranch because they thought it was haunted. They called it the Ghost Ranch." (209~)

Waldo Wilcox described the construction of the rock houses at Florence Creek: "My granddad, Jim McPherson, hired a rock mason from up to Provo. He was a Frenchman. The farther along he got the prettier the work was. Seems like he was slowing down to keep the job going. So granddad fired him. The Seamounts [at Rock Creek] told granddad to let him finish the Florence Creek house, then they'd hire him to build the Rock Creek buildings. The Florence Creek house cost five thousand dollars to build…. Granddad McPherson always said up to the time he died that that house was his downfall. That is what broke him." (2011~)

Emery Kolb in 1911: "saw a fine looking ranch and stopped for information. It proved to be James McPherson's, a cattle raiser. A large swing suggested the man was a home man and on meeting him found him of the best western type." (1125~)

Elwyn Blake in 1926: "The hospitality of the McPhersons is one of the striking reminders of the Old West, as contrasted with some of the present day ranchers." (253~)

—McPherson Ranch Stock Trail: This constructed pack trail goes from the McPherson Ranch south along the east side of the Green River to Green River Town. In many places construction is apparent and is often quite well done. (1985~, SAPE.)

Florence Spring: Uintah and Ouray Indian Reservation-East Tavaputs Plateau-Florence Creek. Walker Point map.

Also called McPherson Spring.

(See Florence Creek for name derivation.)

Nell Murbarger in 1960: "We were now in the country once ranged by the outlaws of Butch Cassidy's 'Wild Bunch.'" (1414~)

Flossie Knoll: (Wayne Co.) Awapa Plateau-Deer Hollow. Flossie Knoll map. (8,940')

Guy Pace: "It was kind of an odd story. The way I remember it Flossie [Flossie Allred Pace] was left out to the sheep camp for a couple of weeks. [Her husband] Jeff [Pace] probably came to town for supplies and something happened and Flossie was left out there without ever seein' anybody. I guess when they got back, she named the area." (1497~)

Thaine Taylor noted that they called it Flossies Nipple: "The old-timers when you asked 'Why do they call it that?' they'd say they fenced it to keep their calves from suckin." (1868~)

—Flossie Lake: Alfonzo Turner: "It's a natural pond and we went out there in the early '60s and dug it out so it'd collect more water." (1914~)

Floy Wash: (Grand Co.) Roan Cliffs-Book Cliffs-Little Grand Wash. Floy Canyon North, Floy Canyon South, Crescent Junction, and Hatch Mesa maps.

Also called Rio Grande Wash (M.69.), Saleratus Creek (1623~), and Saleratus Wash (646~).

The Ferdinand V. Hayden Survey in 1876 called this Bitter-water Creek. (849~, 1931~) The Floy Wash name was not used until the railroad (See below) started using the name Floy. (1931~)

Sylvia Harris Ekker, who's father, Gilmore Anderson "Ink" Harris, used to run cattle in the canyon, noted that they called it Paradise Canyon. (622~)

Inscriptions include Simon Trujillo, 1943 and J.W. Caywood, 1947. (SAPE.)

—Old Spanish Trail: The trail crossed lower Floy Wash. (1544~)

—Floy: (Hatch Mesa map.) (Also called Floy Junction, Floy Station, and Little Grande.) This was a stop on the Denver and Rio Grande Western Railroad starting in the early 1880s. (644~) (See Denver and Rio Grande Western Railroad.)

Arthur A. Baker noted that in 1952 there was still a small settlement here. (104~)

—Shinnville: This settlement was part of a manganese mining operation developed by Colonel James A. Shinn in 1917. The camp was to the south of Floy. The exact location is unknown. (1781~)

—Moore Ranch: PRIVATE PROPERTY. This is at the "Corral" two miles west of Crescent Butte in Floy Wash (Floy Canyon South map). (646~)

—Harris Ranch: PRIVATE PROPERTY. This is one-half mile north of the Moore Ranch on Floy Wash. (646~) Sylvia Harris Ekker, the daughter of Gilmore Anderson "Ink" Harris (1873-1958), noted that he first bought a half interest from Thompson Town entrepreneur Harry Ballard in the early 1900s. Later he bought Ballard out. The Harris family sold the ranch in 1922. They called it the Paradise Ranch. (622~)

Flu Knolls: (Uintah Co.) Uintah Basin-Eightmile Flat. Crow Knoll map. (5,220')

This refers to the malady. (1931~)

Fools Canyon: (Kane Co.) Glen Canyon NRA-Escalante River. King Mesa map.

Also called Fools Creek. (874~)

Edson Alvey: "The name was derived from the fact that there was no accessible route into it." (55~) Don Coleman: "It fooled a lot of people. They figured they could get out of it up in the head, and there's only one trail and if you missed it, it made a fool out of ya. That's what they said." (441~) The name was in place by 1908. (M.27.)

—Fools Canyon Stock Trail: A constructed stock trail crosses Fools Canyon one and one-half miles upcanyon from its mouth (at the first "N" in "Canyon"). The northern section, onto Ezra McBench, can be very difficult to follow. The southern section is well-constructed and is easy to find and follow. Pratt Gates noted that the southern trail was built in the 1950s. Big improvements were done to it about forty years ago. (441~, 709~)

Forbidding Canyon: (San Juan Co.) Navajo Indian Reservation-Navajo Mountain-Glen Canyon. Chaiyahi Flat and Rainbow Bridge maps.

Aztec Creek flows through Forbidding Canyon. (See Aztec Creek.)

The Navajo call this '*Altíí'Àl í Bikooh*, or "Canyon Where Bows are Made." (1204~)

The naming of the canyon is a bit confusing as it has had several names.

James Black, a gold miner on the Colorado River in the 1890s wrote of the initial naming of the canyon: "[We] climbed off the [Navajo] mountain into what was then known as Broken Leg Canyon. We then followed through into Under-the-arm Canyon to the [Rainbow] natural bridge. As the canyon then had no name given by white men we decided to call it Aztec canyon, which we did. For a good many years thereafter prospectors in that region called it by the name we gave it." (1595~) Black's name was found inscribed at the mouth of the canyon, with a date of Feb. 1894?. (1707~)

Hank Hassell provided a derivation for the Aztec Canyon name: "The creek was named for a group of mysterious structures at the mouth of the canyon, which early prospectors mistakenly attributed to the ancient Aztecs." (843~)

Two derivations for the Forbidding Canyon name are given.

First, it was named Forbidding Canyon in 1921 by the Charles L. Bernheimer Expedition: "Forbidding Canyon proved impassable for a pack-train.... It was too rugged and snarly; it was blocked by steep shelves that could not be descended, necessitating detours on trailless mountain sides, often dangerous to man and beast." (219~, 1901~)

Zeke Johnson was with the Bernheimer Expedition. When asked about who named it Forbidding Canyon, Johnson said: "Just a crowd of us in camp—we wanted it called 'forbidding' because we could not get there at first—after the [Redbud] pass was open we called it Forbidding." (1006~)

Second, Ann Woodin in 1964: "Forbidden Canyon, so named by the Navajos because of a landslide, a sign they interpreted to mean that their gods did not want them to trespass further." (2046~) Lil Diemler echoed the derivation: "The story of Forbidden Canyon is that it was put there to guard the Bridge and Indians were forbidden to enter." (557~)

Some early maps show this as Forbidden Canyon. Stan Jones remarked on the change of Forbidden to Forbidding: "I talked to the superintendent [of Glen Canyon National Recreation Area] about that, and I said, 'I'd like to use another name on the map that I'm going to do because 'Forbidden' means you can't go in there, and that isn't true.' And so we picked the word 'Forbidding' instead of 'Forbidden' and that's why on old maps, it's Forbidden Canyon and on the newer maps it's Forbidding Canyon." (1020~)

Frank Wright summed it up in 1955: "Forbidden, Forbidding, Aztec ... dernit, why don't they make up their minds? I'll tell you why. The creek was named Aztec—by prospectors probably, who thought the ruins here at the mouth were built by Aztec Indians. The Navajo, who knew about Rainbow Bridge long before white men came into this country, considered it sacred. At Mexican Hat,

where Norm [Nevills] knew many of the Navajos, they said it was mysterious, full of uneasy spirits, a forbidding kind of place." (1162~)

To clear up any confusion about duplicate names, Forbidding Canyon contains Aztec Creek. A small side canyon, Bridge Canyon, contains Rainbow Natural Bridge. Forbidding Canyon is shown on early maps, including Cass Hite's map of 1890, as West Canyon. (M.32.) The name Aztec first showed up on maps in 1922. Early Euroamerican explorers on the river called it Bridge Canyon for the word "Bridge" chipped on a cliff near the mouth of the canyon. (See Rainbow Bridge National Monument.)

Earl Morris in 1922: "An adequate conception of the ruggedness of this particular region cannot be conveyed in words.... In looking from the foot of Cummings Mesa toward Navajo Mountain, the foreground [the breaks of Aztec Creek] might be likened to a sea driven in the teeth of a hurricane, the waves of which at their height had been transfixed to salmon-colored stone." (1390~)

Ervin S. Cobb in 1940: "I'm reasonably sure none of our species will ever get down into Forbidden Canyon or, having got down there, ever get out again. So you see it also is appropriately named. Were it not that bandings of sunshine and cloud-play splash it with shifting pastel hues—dun, ecru, soft brown, blush-pink, dulled lavender—what lies cupped in there would be like a giant paint-bucket scraped clean. It's the sensational coloring that makes the pageantry. Otherwise, the desolation would be so complete, the utter wastefulness of it all so depressing that you could imagine anyone who for very long stared down into that dreary pit going sick at the stomach." (438~)

Alfred M. Bailey in 1947: "Massive overhanging cliffs black against patches of sunlight; glistening pools of crystal-clear water which constantly beckoned; the fluttering of ash-throated flycatchers against the blue as they sailed from one scraggly limb to another; and the echoing calls of the canyon wrens." (93~)

Tad Nichols: "Water flowed all along the way. Little rivulets streamed across the bedrock, formed by springs that bubbled out of the canyon floor. You could get down on you hands and knees and drink from these cool bubbling springs—refreshing on a hot day. Here and there the water came down in little cascades over layered rocks, rippling down over the edges, creating beautiful patterns. The scene changed around each corner." (1449~)

Inscriptions include Geo. Emmerson and M.S. Foote, Dec. 28th, 1881 and J.P. Williams, 6/2 82. Stan Jones: "Jonathan Patterson Williams was a trader and prospector whose zeal for gold prompted him to build and operate the first small dredge on the lower San Juan River in 1890. Prior to that useless endeavor he had probed many canyons at the foot of Navajo Mountain." (1019~)

A "JW" inscription above a short but sheer drop on a boulder marks how far down the canyon John Wetherill, after entering Forbidding Canyon near its top, was able to get in either 1911 (1019~, 1115~) or 1920 (218~). Two explanations are given. First, Stan Jones: "probably carved in 1911 when Wetherill explored the gorge seeking a new and shorter south route to Rainbow Bridge." (1019~) Second, on July 18, 1920 the Charles L. Bernheimer Expedition was stopped by overwhelming obstacles in Forbidding Canyon as they tried to make their way down. John Wetherill left the group and headed downcanyon, afoot. Bernheimer: "One cannot remain in the Canyon bottom long because of high shelves caused by hard lime stone at the lower end of which are deep water pools. The animals cannot go down these shelves.... Wetherill turned up worn out. He had scouted for a way out. It was easy enough to get out of West Canyon [Forbidding Canyon] but well nigh impossible to get down with our animals." (218~)

In 1922 Wetherill again joined Bernheimer in exploring the Rainbow Plateau country. This time they approached the bridge from the south by going down Cliff Canyon. After working out a route through Redbud Pass (See Redbud Pass), the group split: Wetherill continued past Rainbow Bridge and down Bridge Canyon to Forbidding Canyon. He then turned up that canyon. At the same time, Bernheimer was going down Cliff Canyon to its mouth, then down Forbidding Canyon. They found a prominent "five or six foot thick blackened iron stained rock layer." As well, they noted several obstacles that would need some work to get their stock around. Obstacle number four, though, stopped them cold. Bernheimer: "The fourth we decided as well nigh-impossible without considerable time-consuming, trail-making, and bridge-building.... At obstacle no. 4, the canyon brook had a deep gash, on the other side a five foot stick indicated that some Indian at one time had gone through and used it to reach the top of the ledge. We decided that the thing could not be done." Wetherill in the meantime had succeeded in coming up Forbidding Canyon and met Bernheimer at obstacle no. 4. Here he engraved his initials "JW" and the date, 1922. (218~, 221~, SAPE.)

Inscriptions, now underwater, included E. Howard/ Wesley Powell, January 14, 1881 (693~); Hislop, 1891 (1920~); G.M. Wright, Nov. 1892 (628~); Jas [James] Black, 1894; and Cummings-Douglass Expedition members Don Beauregard 1909 and N. [Neil] M. Judd, 8/14/09. (18~, 1115~)

—Constructed Stock Trail: This drops from Chaiyahi Flat (one-eighth mile south of elevation 5966) into upper Aztec Creek (one-quarter mile south of elevation 5470 on the Chaiyahi Flat map). (SAPE.) The trail does not continue down Aztec Creek.

—Constructed Stock Trail: Once below the slot at the very top of Aztec Creek (See Ferguson Canyon below), a remarkable constructed sheep trail runs all the way through the canyon. It is apparent that if the water was high, there were several places where sheep would have to swim. (SAPE.)

—Ferguson Canyon: The Charles L. Bernheimer Expedition of 1921 made their way up Jayi Canyon, over a "plateau," by The Kettle (See The Kettle), down Ferguson Canyon, and into what they called West Canyon (Aztec Creek). Bernheimer described their route: "Coming from Jay-i [Canyon] we trailed up a sandy, old creek bed until we came to what looked like a plateau. All of a sudden to our right hand a deep one hundred feet hole appeared. That was called by Wetherill the West Canyon Kettle; it is black, too. We struck off to the left for it was evident, although our road led to West Canyon [Aztec Creek], no one could climb down a kettle's side. This took us to Ferguson Canyon which empties into West Canyon and has good water and feed.... We found a rough at times dangerous trail never visited by white man between Jay-i and West Canyon." (218~)

Unfortunately neither Bernheimer, nor other expedition members, clearly described or mapped their route, making the location of Ferguson Canyon a bit of a mystery. Bernheimer was notorious for getting his directions wrong, his names wrong, or providing little detail, making an accurate assessment of their route all the more difficult.

Their route went up Jayi Canyon and crossed the head of the upper inner gorge of Aztec Creek. At this point there is a small saddle/flat/plateau (one-quarter mile north-northwest of elevation 5605 on the Chaiyahi Flat map). Here, going down Aztec Creek is not an option because of a section of deep slot canyon.

The route continued northeast up to the very head of Aztec Creek. This one-mile-long section of canyon (immediately south of elevation 5470) is fast and easy and ends on the top of the high cliffs at the junction of several drainages (one-eighth mile south of elevation 5270). The junction far below is The Kettle. (See The Kettle.) This also marks the head of Goldenrod Canyon. (See below.)

The expedition could not see a way down the walls of The Kettle. (They did find a way down into The Kettle on the Bernheimer Expedition of 1924. [See The Kettle.])

Now, following the rim of Goldenrod Canyon northwest for one-half mile, an obvious break in the cliffs was found to the west (one-quarter mile south of elevation 5505 on the Chaiyahi Flat map). Today this canyon/pass contains a constructed stock trail that drops right into Aztec Creek. There are a couple of hogans along this part of the trail. (SAPE.) Bernheimer: "We finally descended into Ferguson Canyon to its junction with West Canyon [Aztec Creek].... With the exception of Wetherill, [Earl] Morris, myself, and a man by the name of Ferguson, who had carved his name on a rock, I believe no white men have been in this vicinity." (221~)

Harvey Leake and Dick Sprang, on their map of the area, show this obvious break in the cliffs. And, they show Ferguson Canyon as being simply the upper end of Aztec Creek as it is marked on the Chaiyahi Flat map. (1156~)

—Goldenrod Canyon: (Also spelled Golden Rod Canyon.) This eastern tributary of Aztec Creek is mentioned by Charles L. Bernheimer. James H. Knipmeyer: "Harvey [Leake, the great grandson of John Wetherill] believes that what Bernheimer called Goldenrod Canyon may be this unnamed eastern tributary [which he located as the canyon one-half mile south of elevation 4991 and one-half mile north of elevation 5452 on the Chaiyahi Flat map]." (1115~)

Bernheimer: "In this canyon a lightning change occurred. There was plenty of grass, twenty inches high; there were acres of poison oak [ivy] and goldenrod. We call this Goldenrod Canyon rather than Poison Oak Canyon, as the latter would have been ungrateful." (221~)

Bernheimer then wrote about their exit route out of Goldenrod Canyon: "We started to get out of Goldenrod Canyon, not a difficult performance at first, but at the top we met with obstacles in the form of ugly slick-rock, the worst of which we had to cross sidewise with a drop of a hundred feet or more to the left of us. In case of a mishap there would have been no anchorage between us and eternity. The stretch was short but perilous. Often the only break to slipping was a microscopic particle of quartz, a mere speck of sand strongly imbedded in its matrix." (221~) The route they took could very well follow what is today a constructed stock trail that starts one mile up Goldenrod Canyon from its mouth and ends at Round Rock. (SAPE.)

—Kansas Pass: This rugged break or pass in the cliffs between upper Aztec Creek and upper Goldenrod Canyon is one-quarter mile north of elevation 5470 on the Chaiyahi Flat map. It was named by the canyon group Kansas. (SAPE.)

—Ruths Camp: This superb campsite in the narrows of Aztec Creek (one-quarter mile east of elevation 4921T on the Rainbow Bridge map) was named for Ruth Graham Allen, the mother of Steve Allen. She died in April, 2011 while Steve and the Kansas group were camped here.

—Sandal Cave: (Also called Bernheimer Cave and Upper Bernheimer Cave.) This huge cave is a short distance up Forbidding Canyon from its junction with Cliff Canyon (Rainbow Bridge map). Charles L. Bernheimer in 1922: "We named it Sandal Cave because of the large number of sandals we uncovered." (221~) Bernheimer and Earl Morris left a "Bernheimer Expedition, 1922" inscription in the cave. (SAPE.)

—Charcoal Cave: (Also called Bernheimer Cave and Lower Bernheimer Cave.) This large cave is a short distance down Aztec Creek from its junction with Cliff Canyon (Rainbow Bridge map). It was named by Charles L. Bernheimer in 1922: "At a cave which we named Charcoal Cave because of its many fireplaces, we turned back, after digging for remains in the refuse piles." (219~) Earl Morris was with Bernheimer: "I rode down stream [from the mouth of Cliff Canyon] to the bend above the limit of travel for stock & tethered my horse in an inlet at E. side of canyon where there was shade & grass, then continued on foot to Bernheimer Cave." (1389a~) Bernheimer left an inscription on the wall of the cave that read: "C.L. Bernheimer, New York, American Museum of Natural History Expedition, 1922." (812~, SAPE.)

—Constructed Stock Trail: This goes along intermediate benches from Aztec Creek, under the east side of Cummings Mesa, over the heads of Cathedral and Little Arch canyons, and in the old days, down into Glen Canyon. (SAPE.)

—Rainbow Bridge Marina: This floating marina, one of the first on Lake Powell, was several miles up Forbidding Canyon. The marina was moved—docks and all—to Dangling Rope in the 1990s.

—Firelight Island: Now underwater, this was on the south (or east) side of the Colorado River one-half mile north of the mouth of Forbidding Canyon (one-quarter mile northwest of elevation 4030T on the Rainbow Bridge map). Katie Lee and friends named the island: "We built a block-long driftwood pyre and just lit it. In the days when we were running the Grand Canyon we were initiated into the DWB, that was the 'Driftwood Burners' Society.' The way to belong to the Driftwood Burners' Society was that you had one match to set a whole driftwood pile on fire. No stacking, no nothing. If you couldn't do it with one match you were not a member. We were asked to do this by the park service, to burn all of the driftwood piles that we saw along the river. They didn't want it clogging Lake Mead. If I had thought about it, I'd have told them to go kiss my ass. We burned that thing and we danced around it all night. I'm sure you could have seen it from outer space. It was immense." (1163~)

Apparently Dick Sprang didn't know that it was okay to build these driftwood fires: "One thing I found highly disgusting ... was encountering several of the broad shoreline bars ... in a burned condition. How it's beyond dispute that some of these bars were burned by the horde of let's-see-everything-in-a-hurry river travelers of that era who were down there to see what Glen Canyon looked like when it was too late to save it. One particular outfit ... actually set fire to some of the bars to provide spectacular Kodachrome photographs for these dear souls who were roaming down the river. This is as utterly disgusting as anything I can think of and yet it's quite fitting. You might as well cremate the damn place because it was dying." (1797~)

—Bridge Canyon Dam Site: (Proposed.) John A. Widtsoe in 1922: "At Bridge Canyon is perhaps the best damsite yet seen, but the walls are lower than elsewhere, so that a really large storage reservoir would be impossible." (2007~)

—Bridge Canyon Rapids: This rapid at the mouth of Forbidding Canyon, now underwater, was one of the few in Glen Canyon that proved challenging to river runners. Lewis R. Freeman in 1922: "Troublesome was hardly the word to describe that tumbling wall of rock-churned water. Indeed, annihilative would come nearer to conveying my first impression, for I had known quieter-looking and quieter-sounding rapids that were toothed to grind up a twenty-foot bateau. Far from appearing possible ... that rolling patch of boulder-strewn foam looked quite capable of swamping a boat that tried to run down its tossing combers." (679~)

Ford Pasture: (Kane Co.) Skutumpah Terrace-Highway 136. Bald Knoll map.
Edwin Ford (1831-1909) arrived in Upper Kanab in 1865. (59~) He moved to Kanab in 1873. (1187~)
—Gypsum Wash: This long, wide, western tributary of Johnson Wash is one mile south of Ford Pasture and runs east-west along Highway 136 (near elevations 6091, 6297, and 6329). (766~)

Forebay, The: (Iron Co.) Hurricane Cliffs-Parowan Canyon. Parowan map.
Warren Pendleton: "It got its name from the water works there. The water goes into the pipeline there to come into Parowan Power Plant." (1515~)
—Benson Sawmill: Nathan Benson, Sr. (1826-1916) had a sawmill at The Forebay from 1880 to 1896. (1551~)

Forest Creek: (Garfield Co.) Fishlake National Forest-Sevier Plateau-East Fork Sevier River. Mount Dutton, Deep Creek, and Antimony maps.
Two name derivations are given.
First, Henry Forrest arrived in Antimony in 1873. (380~, 1969~)
Second, E.C. Bird: "Is a large creek and tributary of Pole Canyon running in a northerly direction. It was so named because of the dense timber growth along its course." (2053~)
The name was in use by 1887. (1096~)

Forgotten Canyon: (San Juan Co.) Glen Canyon NRA-Mancos Mesa-Glen Canyon. Knowles Canyon map.
Also called Moqui Canyon, North Gulch, and Second Canyon.
Katie Lee: "The canyon ... was called Forgotten Canyon by Dudy Thomas and Dick Sprang of Sedona, Arizona, because it was left entirely off the old Plan & Profile maps." (1162~) Dudy Sprang is quoted as saying: "Let's say the canyon has been forgotten, and for our purposes call it that." (1795~)
Harry Aleson in 1952: "We clear space under oak trees for kitchen, 2 others outside for bedrolls and campfire. North edge of oak grove nearest entrance to canyon opposite Smith Fork. Since '45 I've called this 'No Name' Canyon. On their 1951 Glen Canyon trip, Dudy [Sprang] suggested calling this 'Forgotten Canyon.' It is a good name. Let us hope it may become known as Forgotten Canyon." (17~)
Harry Aleson described the canyon and its exploration in October 1952: "Dick [Sprang] and I go up into narrows, The Slot, and I wade into cold water to my chest, to where I see deeper water in last pool.... We go down canyon a bit to check on a possible passage on a ledge, L.B. [Left Bank], that Dick had spotted last year. Elmer Purtymun [also spelled Purtyman], in party, had climbed up, but reported slickrock impassable. But Dick was right on possibility. He had brought tools from Sedona for cutting 'Moki Steps'.... Dick and I take ropes, tools and canteens up into Forgotten Canyon. We take equipment onto ledge and begin job of cutting transverse 'Moki Steps' on the same level we had spotted ancient ones, three of them.... With the aid of safety lines on three varying points for pins, we

alternately cut a series of steps with a stone-facing tool and heavy hammer. Between cuttings, we climb down for rest. For over half the day we worked on slickrock slope averaging sixty degrees. About 4:30, Dick gets across traverse with the line, anchoring it to boulder." (19~)

—Defiance House Ruin: This was listed on the National Register of Historic Places in 1978. The aforementioned Aleson party discovered what they called the Three Warriors Ruin in Forgotten Canyon, named for a nearby pictograph panel depicting three warriors, which later visitors thought looked "defiant" since they carried clubs and shields. The structures were used from about AD 1250 to AD 1285. The ruin is on the north side of the canyon and is two and one-half miles east of its mouth (one-eighth mile south of elevation 4126T). (539~, 1901~)

Harry Aleson: "There are three large, white paintings, figures holding raised shields. Directly, I spot a Cliff Dwelling or Moki House to left of paintings.... We see 2 rooms in complete condition and a Kiva with a partial roof hole. Several hundred pounds of rock have fallen off wall and dropped onto portion of roof. Main cross-log has decomposed, dropping one end onto floor.... Floor is undisturbed, but covered with sand and light wind-blown rubbish. Many cobwebs. Rock deflector for firepit is in place. Entrance to draft shaft is open.... Roof entrance to Kiva has been fitted with flat, carefully-shaped, thick sandstones. A few feet away stood the well-preserved Moki House, with a rounded S-E corner. Between the house and back wall was a well-built granary. Closing stone for granary door lay in four pieces outside entrance. Nearby, a broken metate. Ruins of three other rooms and walls. Dim red and white painting also on the wall of overhang. A perfect metate and mano on a section of fallen retaining wall. Many shards about." (19~)

—45 Degree Canyon: This short southern tributary of Forgotten Canyon is three-quarters of a mile east of its mouth (between elevations 4035T and 4088T). It was named by Frank E. Masland, Jr. in 1947. Derivation is unknown but can be guessed at. (1309~)

—Bobtail Canyon: The mouth of this eastern tributary of Glen Canyon is one-eighth mile north of the mouth of Forgotten Canyon (immediately north of elevation 3847T). Gus Scott noted that it was named by Dick Sprang and Harry Aleson in the 1950s. (1709~)

Forked Post Pond: (Emery Co.) San Rafael Swell-Head of Sinbad. San Rafael Knob map.
This stock reservoir was built in 1958. (1551~) Lee Mont Swasey: "I asked dad [Monte Clair Swasey] and he said,

'Well, there was a post that they planted there and it had a fork in it.'" (1853~)

—Pulley Reservoir: This stock reservoir is one-eighth mile northwest of Forked Post Pond. It was built in 1958. (1551~)

—Puny Pond: This small stock reservoir is one-eighth mile south of Forked Post Pond. (1931~)

—Sinbad Erosion Control Reservoirs: These two stock reservoirs are one mile south of Forked Post Pond. They were built in 1958. (1551~) Lee Mont Swasey noted that these are called Twin Ponds. (1853~) They are also called Head of Earls Draw Ponds. (1931~)

—Chimney Rock: Lee Mont Swasey noted that this large Navajo Sandstone tower is one mile south-southwest of Forked Post Pond (one-eighth mile east of elevation 7762). (1853~)

Forshea Mountain: (Piute Co.) Fishlake National Forest-Sevier Plateau. Phonolite Hill and Malmsten Peak maps. (9,793')
Also spelled Forshey Mountain. (318a~)
Correctly spelled Forshee Mountain.
James Edward Forshee arrived in Antimony in 1873. (1444~, 1969~) Betty Ann Larsen: "His legacy lives on in Piute County as Forshee Mountain (misspelled on maps as Forshea).... The Forshee Draw, Forshee Point, Forshee Spring and Forshee Reservoir are located in the lower Parker Mountain Range." (1135~) Volney King in 1885: "I hunted cattle at the ... Forshee mountains." (1096~)

—Forshea Spring: (Malmsten Peak map.) (Also called Forshea Corral Spring.) This is a large, developed spring and stock pond. (SAPE.) Edward Sudweeks noted that the spring is near the top of Forshea Mountain and was used for watering stock: "It was named from Forshea, the man who built the corral around the spring." (2053~) Inscriptions near the spring on aspen trees date to the early 1930s. (SAPE.)

Forshea Point: (Piute Co.) Awapa Plateau-Parker Mountain. Angle map. (9,428')
(See Forshea Mountain for name derivation.)
Thaine Taylor: "A man by the name of Forshee built some troughs there and when the spring dried up, they built a big pond below it and when the troughs run over the water filled that pond, so they had water the year 'round." (1868~) There are still troughs, an aspen pole corral, and a stock pond. (SAPE.)

Forsyth Creek: (Washington Co.) Dixie National Forest-Pine Valley Mountains-Santa Clara River. Saddle Mountain and Central East maps.
Also spelled Forsythe Creek. (355~)

Thomas R. Forsyth (1813-1898) had a sawmill in Pine Valley starting in 1863. (887~, 1803~) Lorenzo Brown called it Forsyth Kanyon in 1863. (305~)

In the early days the creek was logged. George C. Fraser in 1915: "All along were stumps of large pines and the stones paving the road showed marks of heavy wagon wheels.... In places the canyon was V-shaped between steep cliffs with only a few places where trees could grow and the sculpture was fine." (668~)

Forsyth Reservoir: (Sevier Co.) Fishlake National Forest-Highway 72. Forsyth Reservoir map.

This was named for Forsyth Spring, which was covered when the reservoir was built. George Forsyth was a pioneer rancher. Construction of the reservoir started in 1902 and was completed in 1917. A flash flood destroyed the initial dam in 1921. It was rebuilt in 1925. (844~, 1419~, 1786~)

Fort Bottom: (San Juan Co.) Canyonlands National Park-Labyrinth Canyon. Horsethief Canyon map.

A fort-like cliff dwelling is on top of a prominent hill overlooking this bottomland. It is visible from the river. (197~)

William Hiram Edwards of the Stanton-Brown Survey of 1889–90: "We come in sight of an ancient Aztec fort on a high point commanding a view up and down the river of twenty miles. We climbed up to it and found that at some time it had been a two-story structure ... the whole built of flat stones laid up with mortar.... Around the base of the ledge of rock where the fort stood were the ruins of many houses and below these was a tract of land of 400 or 500 acres with a small lake in the center. This land had evidently been farmed by these people by means of irrigation as we could trace the lines of the main ditch and several small laterals. It must have been many hundreds of years ago as the head of the ditch was at least 75 feet above the present river bed." (597~)

The bottom was named by the James S. Best Expedition of 1891. James A. McCormick of the expedition noted that the hilltop ruin was called Aztec Fort. (1320~)

Lute H. Johnson in 1896: "The fort commands a view of the river for several miles, and the wars of extermination must have been all but a Gibraltar for the Aztecs.... As to the probably time the Aztecs dwelled here, it is no more possible to say than it is to say how old are the rocks themselves." (996~)

P.A. Leonard stopped at the bottom in 1904, calling it Fort Harbor. (1177~) Bert Loper called it Fort Hill in 1907. (1215~)

Charles Russell in 1907: "At Fort Point is situated an interesting cliff dwelling, located on a high knoll about 600 feet above the river, and, as the river makes a bend here, it commands a view both up and down the river." (1670a~)

C.A. Peet in 1909: "This place was probably the rendezvous of some ancient tribe of Indians. It occupies a commanding position and overlooks the river for miles in each direction. At the base of the cliff upon which the fort is located, we found the remains of many stone building, built under the overhanging cliffs and resembling Cliff Dwellers' houses. These are mostly very small, with low ceiling, and look more like quarries or store houses than dwellings." (1523a~)

Devergne Barber of the Pathe-Bray Expedition of 1927, in a fit of hyperbole wrote: "The climb was exceptionally dangerous, as it had probably been hundreds of years since any sort of a trail had led to it, therefore it was necessary for us to search for a way in which the ascent might be made without too great a risk. The better part of two hours was consumed in making the top.... The descent was much faster than the climb, in fact Val [Woodbury] descended for about fifty feet at a high rate of speed. His injuries were limited to bruises and abrasions but his clothing will require some attention with a sail needle and canvas when he returns to camp." (134~)

Clyde L. Eddy in 1929: "Two or three of the men climbed up to the house on the hilltop and found that it actually was an ancient block-house or look-out, built of heavy, flat stones and commanding an excellent view of the surrounding country." (593~)

Buzz Holmstrom in 1937: Visited first cliff dweller's house on the mesa in Horseshoe Bend—not too hard to get to. [The outlaw] Cabin on bottom below has been visited by many people.... The view is splendid." (903~)

Senator Barry Goldwater in 1940: "Between mile 41 and 37 there is an isthmus around which the river bends. Again at the narrows of the isthmus the river is separated by only a few hundred yards of red sandstone which if it weren't there would make an island out of this isthmus. On a high mesa at the end of this strip of land is an old watch tower used by Indians of old to watch both approaches of the river—probably an outpost of Cliff Dwellers. It having no name on the map, we named it 'Watch Tower Butte.'" (738~) Mildred Baker, on the expedition with Barry Goldwater, called it Indian Watchtower. (106~)

Nearby inscriptions include GSHATT? 1894; John Wey? 18??; and K. Saye, 8-7-14.

—Outlaw Cabin: (Also called Walker Cabin.) This is on Fort Bottom. Del Taylor: "Mark Walker was one of the early settlers coming to Moab in 1883 with the Taylors. He ran cattle on the east side of the Green River and on the White Rim south of the Fort Bottom where he built the cabin in the early 1900s. I'm not certain as to the date but would say not later than 1906–1907." (1864~) Pearl Baker noted that the cabin was used by Butch Cassidy and the Wild Bunch. (111~) There is no evidence of this. Leland Tidwell described the cabin as it was in 1921: "The cabin was clean, it had a table and couple of benches in it, and we built a good fire in the fireplace and put the benches along the wall and sort of leaned back and went to sleep…. The cabin was good and snug, and had a sort of brush roof out in front for a lean-to porch sort of thing." (1890~)

Names inscribed on the cabin include L.Y. Moore, Nov. 1913 and A.J. Tadje Moving Pictures, Oct. 11-1914, Gone to the NEEDLES. (1112~, SAPE.)

—Walker Cut: This road goes up the peninsula of land that juts into Fort Bottom. It started as a stock trail built by rancher Mark Walker. (1085~)

—Tent Bottom: This is on the west side of the Green River one-quarter mile southeast of Fort Bottom (one-quarter mile east of elevation 4050T). H. Michael Behrendt noted that after World War One several of the bottoms along the Green River were settled: "Tent Bottom was a settlement. The plan failed because the Green River was undependable, the farms too isolated." (197~)

—Tent Bottom Stock Trail: This cairned stock trail follows intermediate ledges from Tent Bottom to Millard Canyon. The trail is still easy to follow. (SAPE.)

Fort Johnson: (Iron Co.) Cedar Valley-Johnson Creek. Enoch map.

(See Enoch Town for name derivation.)

Fortknocker Canyon: (San Juan Co.) Dark Canyon Plateau-White Canyon. Indian Head Pass and Copper Point maps.

Jim and Al Scorup noted that in the early days this was called Meadow Canyon. (1931~)

Several excellent and complimentary stories are told about the naming of the canyon.

First, Pete Steele and John Scorup noted that the canyon was correctly called Fart Knocker, a cowboy term that refers to the condition of a horse or cow falling down and getting air—from both ends—knocked out of it. (1821~)

Second, Sandy Johnson: "And the story is that Al Scorup got throwed out there and it knocked the fart out of 'im, so they called it Fartknocker Canyon." (1002~)

Third, Carl Mahon: "The cowboys were telling me that they used to wean calves off the cows out in the Horse Tank country and up around the Squaw and Papoose Rock. They'd take them down this sand slide. They could go down it, but it was so steep they couldn't come back up it. So after they'd wean them, they could take them out on another trail. One time they were starting down the sand dune and were trying to get the calves to go, and they didn't want to go. And old Franklin Jacob Adams grabbed a couple of calves around the neck. He was a big old guy and kind of fat, and he grabbed a couple of them calves and started off down this sand slide and they got their feet tangled up and they just rolled down to the bottom. And one of the cowboys said to the other one, 'I'll bet that knocked the fart out of old Jacob!'" (1272~) The name was changed by the USGS from Fartknocker to Fortknocker for appropriate reasons.

Fort Pearce Wash: (Mohave Co., Az. and Washington Co., Utah.) Little Valley-Virgin River. Arizona map: Rock Canyon. Utah maps: The Divide, Washington Dome, Yellowhorse Flat, and St. George.

Also called Pearce Wash.

The Domínguez-Escalante Expedition of 1776–77 camped near the junction of Hurricane and Fort Pearce washes. Father Escalante: "We halted by the time the sun had set, in an arroyo where we found good and large waterholes with sufficient pasturage for the horse herd. We named the place San Donulo or Arroyo del Taray." (1357~)

The Antonio Armijo Expedition of 1829–30 called this Stinking Water Canyon. (855a~)

—Fort Pearce: (Washington Dome map.) (Also called Pearce's Ranch.) (M.70.) This was listed on the National Register of Historic Places in 1975. In 1861, after the town of St. George was settled, there was a need for grazing ground for surplus livestock. Fort Pearce Wash was chosen as the appropriate place. A fort was built in 1866 by Frederick Foremast in response to the Black Hawk War. Captain John David Lafayette Pearce (1837–1909) was put in charge. Frederick S. Dellenbaugh of the Powell Expedition of 1871–72: "Fort Pierce was merely a house with loopholes built of blocks of sandstone." (550~)

Juanita Brooks: "The building is not large, and its thick stone walls are held together by mud mortar. There are no windows, only portholes form tiny openings along the sides, which its one door is now just an open place in the walls on the east. On alternate sides small appendages jut out from the main walls, whose portholes give a clear sweep of the full length and width of the building, so that no Indian could shelter himself close against the wall." (364~)

Albert E. Miller: "Some herd houses were built here and a large rock corral constructed which was for holding the stock through the night. A gate faced the east, and on a bluff, or ledge of rock overlooking the corral, a rock fort was built.... The walls, of which were about eight feet high, but had no roof. The fort was fashioned in the shape of a red cross with portholes in the front of each of the four projecting ends, and one porthole in each side of each projection, making in all sixteen portholes. This arrangement gave the guards a crossfire from all directions." (1354~) The fort was in use for about four years. (1142~, 1354~) It has been partially restored.

Inscriptions include William Swapp, 1865; E.E. Spencer, 1871; B.F. Goates, 1873; G.A. Lytle, 1874; ?A. Brown, 1877; and J.B. McDonald, April the 10th, 1879. (SAPE.)

Fortress Arch: (San Juan Co.) Canyonlands National Park-Needles District-Horse Canyon. South Six-shooter Peak map.

W. Robert Moore helped name the arch in 1961: "Erosion has carved an opening, perhaps 80 to 90 feet wide, through a heavy humped spur that rears above a rock-strewn defile. The battlemented appearance of the sandstone layer capping the arch, as well as the big columnar end of the rock spur, suggested a crumbling mountain stronghold. We named it Fortress Arch." (1381~)

Forty Caves Canyon: (Coconino Co., Az.) Navajo Indian Reservation-Segito Canyon. Chaiyahi Rim SE, Az. map.

Charles L. Bernheimer in 1924: "The other [canyon] we called Canyon of the Forty Caves ... so named because ... I counted on one ledge as we came out on the plateau between the two branches twenty caves." (218~)

Fortymile Gulch: (Kane Co.) GSCENM-Glen Canyon NRA-Fiftymile Bench-Willow Gulch. Sooner Bench and Davis Gulch maps.

Also called Fortymile Canyon and Fortymile Wash.

Fortymile Gulch is forty miles from the town of Escalante. Stephen C. Jett, ca. 1963: "[we went] through a section so narrow at the bottom that we had to straddle the stream higher up the walls by placing our feet on one side and our hands on the other." (976~)

—Fortymile Spring: (Sooner Bench map.) (Also spelled Forty-mile Spring.) The Hole-in-the-Rock Expedition, finding the best water they had encountered since leaving Escalante at Fortymile Spring, tarried here for three weeks in 1879 while a scouting party explored the route ahead. This pause in the trek allowed new members to catch up to the main group. (47~, 1356~, 2051~)

Expedition member Charles Eugene Walton: "We went on to 40 mile Spring out on the Desert.... There the company were altogether, and explorers were sent out a route. They returned and reported that a bird could not fly over the route let alone taking wagons." (1965~) Undoubtedly Hole-in-the-Rock Expedition members left their names on nearby rocks, but they have been obliterated by more recent inscriptions. (1115~)

—Hidden Waterfall: Edson Alvey noted that this is the extremely pretty twenty-foot waterfall in Fortymile Gulch. (56~)

Found Mesa: (San Juan Co.) Dark Canyon Plateau-White Canyon. Jacobs Chair and The Cheesebox maps. (7,055')

Carl Mahon: "They called it Found Mesa because they had some mining claims on it that they called the Found Claims." (1272~)

Fountain Tanks: (Garfield Co.) Capitol Reef National Park-Waterpocket Fold-Halls Creek. Deer Point map.

Samuel Rowley called these the Grand Tanks in 1882. (1014~) Dwight Williams noted that ranchers called them The Tanks. Fountain Tanks is a recent name. (2013~)

These large potholes were used by those traveling the Halls Road. (See Appendix Two—Halls Road.) In 1882 Josephine Catherine Chatterly Wood was in the first large group that followed the Halls Road. At one point they camped near a pool, which is assumed to have been the Fountain Tanks. Arriving in the night, they scooped up the water and brought it back to camp where they drank it. In the morning they found two dead sheep in the tank. Wood in her diary described the value of the water: "Water is one of the greatest blessings we can have while traveling. It is so priceless we pour a cup of it in one man's hands, and another holds his hands under that, and four or five people wash with one or two cups of water." (2041~)

Inscriptions include John Allen, July 10, 1881; G.B. Hobbs, May 7th, 82; W.J. Robbins, May 7, 1882; D. Edwards, Nov. 21st, 82; H.D. Bayles, April 22, 1888; T. [Thomas Burk] Foy, Mar. 21, 1889; J.R. Stratton, June 10, 1892; F.A. Baker, June 14th, 1917; and Ed Kinon, 8/19/21. (1112~, SAPE.)

Four-Foot Rapids: (San Juan Co.) San Juan River-Chinle Creek. San Juan Hill map.

The rapid drops four feet over its length. (89~)

—Prospector Loop: This loop of the river is one-half mile south of Four-Foot Rapids (at elevation 4665). Gold miners were active on the loop in the 1890s. The remnants of their rock houses can still be seen. (838~, SAPE.)

—Chimney Rock: This is the river runners' name for the prominent tower in the middle of Prospector Loop (immediately north of elevation 4665). (838~)

—Constructed Stock Trail: This exits San Juan Canyon to the south up a point that is immediately east of Prospector Loop (toward elevation 4763). (SAPE.)

—The Rincon: This is on the north side of the San Juan River and is one mile north of Four-Foot Rapids (at elevation 5031). A constructed stock trail goes up the cliffs to Lime Ridge on the northeast side of The Rincon. (SAPE.) This was called Rincon Canyon by miners in 1890. (838~, 1548~)

—Midway Canyon: This northern tributary of the San Juan River is one mile west of The Rincon (immediately east of elevation 4890 on the Mexican Hat map). (838~)

—Hell Hole: This is one-eighth mile south of the mouth of Midway Canyon (one-eighth mile northeast of elevation 4963 on the Mexican Hat map). A constructed stock trail, visible only in a short middle section, goes up the cliff to the west. (838~, SAPE.)

Fourmile Bench: (Garfield Co.) GSCENM-Glen Canyon NRA-Circle Cliffs Basin. Horse Pasture Mesa map.

Don Coleman: "It's approximately four miles from where the cattle could get to water from any direction. They figure it was four miles on horseback." (441~)

Fourmile Bench: (Kane Co.) GSCENM-Kaiparowits Plateau. Petes Cove, Fourmile Bench, and Ship Mountain Point maps.

—Power Plant: (Proposed.) In the 1970s, as part of a Kaiparowits Power Project, a coal-fired electrical generating station was proposed for this location. (See Smoky Mountain—Andalex Coal Mine.)

Fourmile Canyon: (Garfield Co.) Glen Canyon NRA-Glen Canyon. Clay Point, Mount Holmes, and Hite South maps.

Also called Fourmile Creek. (1812~)

This is four miles downcanyon from the old townsite of Hite. The name dates to at least 1893. (465~)

Harry Aleson in 1952: "Huge blocks of Shinarump, much-tumbled, all but choke canyon mouth, transversely.... Fine pools and trickles of delicious, cool water." (17~)

—Constructed Stock Trail: This went from the Colorado River, up Fourmile Canyon, and between Mount Holmes and Mount Ellsworth. The only construction still visible is where the trail exits the north fork of Fourmile Canyon (three-quarters of a mile west-northwest of elevation 5313T on the Mount Holmes map). (SAPE.)

Alvin Robison: "They had one place that was so tight they had to take the saddle and gear off to get the horses

through and then they'd redo 'em on the other side. And because of the way that trail went up there, they could spend a half a day goin' and still throw a rock back across to where they was in the morning." (1642~) Alvin also noted that this was not used for cattle, just for horses.

—Illinois Bar: This placer bar, now underwater, was on the east side of the Colorado River one-half mile north-northeast of the mouth of Fourmile Canyon (three-quarters of a mile northwest of elevation 3848T on the Hite South map). The bar was first mined in 1897. (465~)

—Beaver Tail Tower: This pretty, two-hundred-foot tower is one-eighth mile east of Illinois Bar.

—Camp Mills: This gold miners' camp was just above the mouth of Fourmile Canyon (Hite South map). It was named by Robert Brewster Stanton in 1897. (1812~)

—Big Rock Rapid: This small rapid at the mouth of Fourmile Canyon, now underwater, was formed by a large boulder in the river and was a well-known hazard on the Colorado River before Lake Powell. (1812~)

Fourmile Canyon: (Garfield Co.) Henry Mountains-Clay Point-Bullfrog Creek. Clay Point map.

Bliss Brinkerhoff noted that it is four miles from upper Fourmile Canyon to Eggnog and it is four miles from lower Fourmile Canyon, up Bullfrog Creek, to Eggnog. (291~)

—Fourmile Stock Trail: This trail/road starts one-third mile north-northeast of Fourmile Spring (one-quarter mile south of elevation 4725T) and goes down to Fourmile Spring and to Bullfrog Creek. Bliss Brinkerhoff noted that this was originally a stock trail built by the BLM. Later, the upper part of the trail was improved by a seismograph crew. (291~, SAPE.)

—Fourmile Spring: This large spring area is gorgeous. (SAPE.)

Fourmile Canyon: (Kane Co.) GSCENM-Kaiparowits Plateau-Tommy Canyon. Horse Mountain and Fourmile Bench maps.

Also called Fourmile Wash.

—Fourmile Water: (Horse Mountain map.) This is a medium-size spring. A still-used line shack and corral are nearby. (SAPE.) Old maps show it as Cow Camp. (1931~)

Fourmile Hollow: (Kane Co.) Glendale Bench-Kanab Creek. Glendale map.

This is four miles from the town of Glendale. (2053~)

—Constructed Stock Trail: This enters the west fork of upper Fourmile Hollow on its east side one and three-quarters of a mile west-southwest of Black Knoll (one-quarter mile north-northeast of elevation 6346). (SAPE.)

Fourmile Wash: (Uintah Co.) West Tavaputs Plateau-Green River. Crow Knoll and Moon Bottom maps.

There is an old cabin and corral on the bottom. Inscriptions include Brownie, 4/1924. (1756~, SAPE.)

—Indian Pasture: This is one mile west of Fourmile Bottom (between elevations 4633T and 5156T on the Moon Bottom map). (833~, 1756~)

Four Springs: (Coconino Co., Az.) Vermilion Cliffs National Monument-Vermilion Cliffs-House Rock Valley. House Rock Spring, Az. map.

There are four springs high on the Vermilion Cliffs. They have been developed and at one time the water was piped to House Rock Valley Ranch. (SAPE.)

—House Rock Valley Ranch: This was one mile southwest of Four Springs (at elevation 5547T).

Foy Bench: (Sevier Co.) Fishlake National Forest-Highway 72. Forsyth Reservoir and Geyser Peak maps.

Charles Kelly: "The Foy family came to Caineville [in the early 1890s] from Beaver county. Later moved to the Blue Mountains near Moab." (1073~, 962~) This was William B. Foy (1837-1920) and his wife, Lucinda (1848-1924), and their oldest son, Thomas.

France Canyon: (Kane Co.) Dixie National Forest-Sunset Cliffs-Sevier River. George Mountain map.

Unattributed: "So named because France Henrie made plans to homestead lands at mouth of this hollow while working for the Panguitch Livestock Company." (2053~, 1346~)

Freckles Canyon: (Grand Co.) Tenmile Country-Tenmile Canyon. Dubinky Wash map.

Gene Dunham noted that there are brown spots, or freckles, on the walls of the canyon. (580~)

—Constructed Stock Trail: This goes up and out the canyon on its north side. (SAPE.)

Freddies Cistern: (Garfield Co.) Glen Canyon NRA-Andy Miller Flat-Cataract Canyon. Bowdie Canyon West and Sewing Machine maps.

—Constructed Stock Trail: This enters upper Freddies Cistern canyon on its south side (one-quarter mile north of elevation 5305T on the Bowdie Canyon West map). (SAPE.)

Fredonia Town: (Coconino Co., Az.) Shinarump Cliffs-Kanab Creek-Highway 389. Fredonia, Az. map.

Andrew Jenson: "The name, Fredonia, is a contraction of the English 'free' and Spanish 'dona' and signifies 'a free woman,' the name being suggested by Apostle Erastus Snow." (972~) The Fredonia area was first considered for settlement in 1884. The first settlers arrived in 1887. (972~)

Freds Ridge: (Garfield Co.) Little Rockies-Mount Ellsworth. Mount Holmes map.

Garth Noyes: "Freds Ridge is named after my uncle, Frederick F. Noyes [1847-1922]. He was from Torrey. He used to bring his herd of sheep up there and stay on that ridge all winter long. That was between the turn of the century and about 1920." (1473~)

Lula Parker Bentenson, the sister of Butch Cassidy, told a story that happened to Fred Noyes' wife. In short, Butch rode up to the Noyes Ranch and found a crying woman. She told Butch that the mortgage holder for the ranch was coming that day to foreclose unless she could come up with five hundred dollars. Butch went out to his horse, retrieved the money from his saddle bag, and gave it to Mrs. Noyes, telling her to pay off the debt and to make absolutely sure to get a receipt and a release on the ranch. The banker came, she paid him, got the proper documentation, and then he left. The legend goes that Butch was waiting along the road and robbed the banker, retrieving his money and at the same time ensuring that the Noyes Ranch was debt-free. (223~)

Fremont Canyon: (Garfield and Iron Counties.) Dog Valley-Little Salt Lake. Fremont Pass, Burnt Peak, Kane Canyon, Buckhorn Flat, Cottonwood Mountain, and Paragonah maps.

The lower end of the canyon is called Fremont Wash.

The Parley P. Pratt Exploring Expedition to Southern Utah of 1849–50 called this Little Salt Lake Hollow. (1762~) Caught in bad weather and bitter cold, the expedition stopped to camp after a difficult battle up Chokecherry Creek. John Brown of the expedition: "I took two or three men and went to examine a pass [Fremont Pass] to the right we road [*sic*] all day and found a pass over which I thought we could go, it was a long way through the mountain and very difficult…. It was a great undertaking and a very hazardous one." (1762~) Since Brown discovered the pass, expedition member Benjamin F. Stewart called it Browns Pass. (1762~)

John Brown provided a further description: "We aimed for a gap in the mountains [Fremont Pass], where we supposed the road passed thru…. We carried a shovel with us to clear the snow to make fires and to make our beds. The next day we found the snow very deep, as we neared the gap in the mountains two animals gave out and were left…. The snow was waist deep and every man and every animal stepped in the same tract…. It was dark before we camped and our animals were so tired, they could not hunt the grass that night, but stood among the cedars and ate bark, a thing I never saw before." (301~)

—Summer Gate: The Pratt expedition continued down the canyon, stopping to camp near today's Sand Cliff Spring (Kane Canyon map) in an area of tall conglomerate sandstone cliffs. They called this the Summer Gate.

John Christopher Armstrong of the expedition, in summation of the experience: "We have fought with the storms and the tempests and it must have been by and through the divine interposition of providence of God who led Nephi of old, that we were brought over these mountains. To look at them it would be said that no white man could do it or be rash enough to undertake it, or have the enterprising spirit enough to attempt it. The Mormons are the boys for such expeditions. They fear neither canyon, mountains, snowstorms, gulleys or rivers, because they know they are led by the mighty God of Jacob." (71~)

John Steele expanded on the problems the Pratt expedition faced: "Commence to come across the mountain.... Just had to let the wagons down into some deep ravines with ropes and help our cattle up out the same way. Had to shovel through the snow in dozens of places.... The snow two feet deep and drifted in heaps.... Stormed continually.... With much labor and toil we got our wagons all together upon the summit of the mountain.... Our cattle almost exhausted for want of feed and water. The cold was intense. Every man froze his feet more or less.... Came down the canyon which is quite narrow with perpendicular rocks some hundred feet high of the most curious formation called the Pass Summer Gate." (808~) Steele called this both Fremont Canyon and Bakers Canyon. (1820~)

John Christopher Armstrong left his name on a wall at Summer Gate (J.C. Armstrong 1849). Armstrong: "About three and 3/4 miles from camp we passed through the summer gate. It is a place where rocks of the mountains rise perpendicular above our heads as if bidding defiance to man. After passing through the canyon it began to widen all the way down. At about one-half mile farther, the rocks at some sides [look] very much like the ramparts of some Baronial castle such as was used in feudal times.... One fourth mile farther there was a range of stupendous rocks. One was named the 'Cornish Rock,' on account of its resemblance to a Cornice work done by stone masons and cut to put over doors. I cut my name on the face of these rocks." (71~)

In February 1854 John C. Fremont's fifth expedition went through the pass on their way to Parowan. (1444~) Solomon Nunes Carvalho of that expedition: "By noon we were in a defile of the mountains [Fremont Pass] through which was a dry bed of a creek. We followed its winding course, and camped ... in a valley, with plenty of grass.... We had now triumphantly overcome the immense mountain, which I do not believe human foot, whether civilized or Indian, had ever before attempted." (385~) Carvalho did not realize that the Pratt expedition had crossed the pass in winter conditions several years before, and with wagons.

Jack Justett in 1941: "It was at first a small pass or trail which was founded by a scout named Fremont who led the early settlers into Panguitch valley. Now there is a road built there which is used as a short cut between Panguitch and Beaver." (2053~)

Inscriptions include A.H., 1-54. This was most likely from a member of the John C. Fremont Expedition of 1854. Other inscriptions include J.H. Skin?, April 21, 1861; J. Wiley, 1866; C.W. Simkins, 1881; H. Wiley, 1881; and J.R. Williams, 1886. (SAPE.)

—Fremont Spring: (Burnt Peak map.) This is a large spring. (SAPE.)

—Gentry's Upper Fremont Ranch: (Burnt Peak map.) PRIVATE PROPERTY. This still-used ranch is in Fremont Canyon one mile northwest of Fremont Spring. Nearby is a small cemetery. One of the gravestones reads: "Homesteader Milton H. Gentry. 1889–1962. He loved and defended truth." (1551~)

—Gentry's Lower Fremont Ranch: (Kane Canyon map.) PRIVATE PROPERTY. This still-used ranch is in Fremont Canyon two miles west of Sand Cliff Spring. (1551~)

Fremont Indian State Park: (Sevier Co.) Tushar Mountains-Pavant Range-Clear Creek-Interstate 70. Marysvale Canyon map.

This 889 acre park was established in 1985.

The extensive ruins and rock art found along the walls of Clear Creek Canyon were noted by early explorers. But, it wasn't until the construction of Interstate 70 in the 1970s that several of the major sites were found and a true grasp of the importance of the canyon in Fremont Indian history was recognized. Over four thousand years of prehistoric use are represented here. (2063~) This is one of Utah's finest state parks. (SAPE.)

Fremont Pass: (Garfield Co.) Fremont Canyon-Dog Valley. Fremont Pass map. (7,522')

(See Fremont Canyon for name derivation.)

Fremont River: (Sevier and Wayne Counties.) Fishlake National Forest-Johnson Valley Reservoir-Capitol Reef National Park-Dirty Devil River. Fish Lake, Forsyth Reservoir, Lyman, Bicknell, Torrey, Twin Rocks, Fruita,

Caineville, Town Point, Steamboat Point, and Hanksville maps.

Also called Big Sandy. (1548~)

Barbara Ekker: "This river originates at Johnson Valley Reservoir, north of Fish Lake, and drains southeast to combine with Muddy Creek [at Hanksville] to form the Dirty Devil River that flows into Lake Powell." (607~)

In 1853–54 John C. Fremont led an expedition across what would become the Thousand Lake Mountain and Fish Lake areas. Local lore noted that Fremont followed what would become the Fremont River from Fish Lake down to the present townsite of Fremont, where he carved his name on a tree. (340~)

Fremont, though, did not recognize the river as a major feature and did not note it on his maps. Perhaps this was because the expedition was in dire circumstances. Deep snow made travel difficult. The expedition ran out of food. Caching their equipment, the expedition headed west. Before reaching Parowan, the group was reduced to eating their horses. One man died. (1563~)

On July 27, 1869 the Powell Expedition discovered an unknown river coming into lower Narrow Canyon from the north. They named it the Dirty Devil (See Dirty Devil River), but they did not know that the upper Dirty Devil River had two major branches, now named the Fremont River and Muddy Creek. Powell would later name the east-west running branch of the river for John C. Fremont. (607~, 1047~)

In the mid-1870s Albert King Thurber, founder of the town of Bicknell, noted this as Lake Creek. (1887~) It is shown as that on the Froiseth map of 1871. (M.20.) That name comes from the fact that the river—before the construction of Johnson Valley Reservoir—started at Fish Lake.

In a *Deseret News* article in 1871 J.D.M. Crockwell called it Sanwan (derivation unknown) and noted that it started at a lake. (492~) A Gray's Atlas map of 1873 shows it as the West Fork of the Dirty Devil River. (M.40.) Both the 1874 Asher and Adams map (M.2.) and the 1876 Colton map (M.43.) show it as the Lake Fork.

Albert R. Lyman noted that Josephine Catherine Chatterly Wood and party went down the Fremont River below Capitol Wash in 1882. She described one of the river crossings: "You would pity us if you could see us today. Our team was first, and when the poor horses came to the bank they had to drop straight down into the water, and when they pulled the wagon in, it came to the bottom with a bump. Standing almost straight up and down towards the other side we came to a dead stand-still, the team couldn't pull the two wagons while they jumped up the stream bank.... With much whipping and shouting we got the first wagon up the bank and pulled to one side. The horses didn't want to go in the water again, but they went and were hitched on the other wagon and finally got it to the bank." (1242~)

—Fremont River Gorge: This is the very narrow stretch of the Fremont River a short distance west of Fruita. The National Park Service called it Palisade Canyon in 1934. (699~) In 1939 Herbert E. Gregory noted that it was known as Granite Gorge. (776~)

—Split Fork Wash: The mouth of this southern tributary of the Fremont River is two-thirds of a mile (as the crow flies) downriver from the mouth of Fish Creek (Twin Rocks map). The forks split two and one-half miles north of the Pioneer Register (one-eighth mile south of elevation 5670T on the Golden Throne map). It was named by former Capitol Reef National Park Ranger Fred Goodsell in 1997. The canyon splits many times over its course from the top of the Waterpocket Fold to its end at Pleasant Creek. (745~) Keith Durfey told a story that happened in the canyon: "She was a beautiful collie, yellow coat, and she'd been run over when she was young, and so she was kind of gimpy in one leg. He followed him [Golden Durfey] all over the place. Called her 'Queenie.' It was foggy and she was following him from scent, and he rode out to the edge of the ledge and looked around to see if he could see any sheep and then turned around. She walked out and took a step too far before she realized it, and then she couldn't pull herself back up ... fell to her death from there." (582~)

Fremont Town: (Wayne Co.) Rabbit Valley-Fremont River-Highway 72. Lyman map.

(See Fremont River for name derivation.)

Andrew J. Allred, William Wilson Morrell, William Henry "Hen" Maxfield, and families moved to Fremont in April 1876, settling first on nearby Spring Creek and later in what is now Fremont. (1047~, 1786~) George C. Fraser in 1915: "A more trifling and miserable village I have not seen." (668~)

—Fremont Spring: George Washington Bean: "Just outside the outskirts of the little village of Fremont is a large spring for arid Utah flowing as much as 10 cubic feet per second. This is named on the early survey plat as 'Fremont' spring, and the creek flowing from it on the hill side of the grove was Fremont Creek." (174~, 1737~)

—Fremont-Loa Ditch: This started as the Westside Ditch, which was built in the late 1870s. (373~)

—Center Canal: (Also called Center Ditch.) This ditch, one of the first built in Fremont, went from the river to Allred Point. The canal has been abandoned. (1188~)

French Spring Fork: (Wayne Co.) Dirty Devil Country-Happy Canyon. Gordon Flats map.

Also called Frenchie's Spring Fork.

Don Orton noted that the canyon and a nearby spring were named for French sheepherders in the early days. (2053~)

—French Spring: (Also called French Seep, Frenchs Spring, and The Frenchy.) This large spring was developed by Joe Biddlecome in about 1910. Water was piped into troughs. (119~, 120~, 1311~, SAPE.) Frank E. Masland, Jr. in 1963: "This is probably the best and most water in that country." (1311~)

—French North Trail: (Also called North Trail.) This amazing constructed stock trail goes up a western tributary of lower French Spring Fork that is one mile north-northeast of its junction with Happy Canyon (at elevation 5125T). The trail exits the upper east side and ends near elevation 6003T. It was most likely built by sheepherders in the early 1900s. It was last used to run livestock in the mid-1970s. (120~, 607~, 1430~, SAPE.)

Freshwater Spring: (Grand Co.) Arches National Park-Salt Wash. The Windows Section map.

James H. Knipmeyer: "So named because of the contrast between its waters and the brackish, alkaline flow of nearby Salt Wash." (1115~)

Inscriptions include J.E.D., 1860. It is thought that this was a member of a military company from Camp Floyd, near Salt Lake City. They were on their way to Santa Fe. J.E.D. was most likely scouting for water for the expedition. (1105~)

—Freshwater Canyon: This is the local name for the canyon that contains the spring. (1115~)

Friendship Cove: (Kane Co.) Glen Canyon NRA-Glen Canyon. Gregory Butte map.

Also called Cottonwood Wash. (467~)

Stan Jones: "Every year the Rotary Club would have a cook-out and members in Page who had boats would invite Rotary Club members from throughout Arizona to come and go out on the new Lake Powell with them. They'd go out overnight and drink a little and burn steaks. They called that a 'Friendship Meeting.' I said, 'Well, that place doesn't have any name. We'd better put in on the map and we'll call it Friendship Cove.'" (1020~)

Katie Lee and friends called it Cattail Canyon before Lake Powell: "We named it first Pussy Willow Canyon because I didn't know the difference between pussy willows and cattails. There weren't any cattails in that canyon. None. But one day we came out of Driftwood and we had a bunch of cattails from Smith Fork. We were just about to take off and one of the cattails I picked up burst! And I said, 'Hey! Hmmm. You know what we could do. We could grease me all over, up and down, in and out, everything but my hair, and we could find a nice place to take some photos, and bust these things loose and I'll look like a plucked chicken and you can take some photos.'" So that is what we did." (1163~)

Frisky Creek: (Garfield Co.) Dixie National Forest-Boulder Mountain-Deer Creek. Lower Bowns Reservoir, Steep Creek Bench, and Boulder Town maps.

—Frisky Flat: This meadow is at the head of Frisky Creek. (1931~)

—Frisky Creek Trail: This is the "Pack" trail that drops off the west side of Bowns Point (Lower Bowns Reservoir map). (1094~, SAPE.)

Frog Hollow: (Washington Co.) Hurricane Cliffs-Hurricane Fields. The Divide and Hurricane maps.

—Constructed Stock Trail: This enters the east side of lower Frog Hollow, above the lowest falls (Hurricane map). With only one way, easily fenced, into this small, well-watered pasture area, ranchers found it convenient to leave their horses here.

Fruita Town: (Wayne Co.) Capitol Reef National Park-Capitol Reef-Highway 24. Fruita map.

Also called Sand Creek. (164~)

Fruita was initially called Junction for its location at the junction of Sulphur Creek and the Fremont River. The first person to stake a squatter's claim to the area was Franklin W. Young in 1879. He quickly passed his claim on to Samuel Rogers, who then passed it to Nels (also spelled Neils) Johnson. Johnson, Leo R. Holt, and the father and son Elija and Hyrum Behunin were the first to file for homesteads in the valley. Johnson built a cabin in 1886 and started an ongoing tradition of growing fruit trees.

At its largest, the town supported eight to ten families consisting of about 108 residents. When the town applied for a post office in about 1900, homesteaders discovered that another town had already been named Junction, Utah. They changed the name to Fruita to reflect its primary crop of fruit. The National Park Service bought the town in 1955 and it was abandoned by 1960. (346~, 721~, 1786~, 1884~, 2056~)

Inscriptions include J.B. Waters, March 4 1880; Earl Behunin, no date; and Rudolph Pace, no date. (1105~)

Fry Canyon: (San Juan Co.) Moss Back Butte-Highway 95-White Canyon. Moss Back Butte, Fry Spring, and Jacobs Chair maps.

Also called Frey Canyon Camp (1037~), Fry Canyon Branch (114~), Fry Canyon Cave (761~), Fry's Cabin (758~), and Fry's Cove (1260~).

Fry Spring is PRIVATE PROPERTY.

It is unclear exactly when or which pioneer was the first to find and use what would become Fry Canyon and the spring located in the middle of the canyon. Cass Hite entered Glen Canyon by way of White Canyon in 1883 and may have had a passing knowledge of the spring. The gold rush that Hite is credited with starting in Glen Canyon lasted sporadically for a couple of decades and brought a constant trickle of prospectors down White Canyon to Glen Canyon. Certainly the spring was known to some of them.

Cattle grazing in the canyon was most likely started by Texas cowboys in the late 1870s or early 1880s. John E. Brown, credited with starting the Dugout Ranch on Indian Creek, ran livestock in Glen Canyon near the mouth of White Canyon (Browns Rim) as early as 1883. He must have known of this strategic spring.

Claude Sanford and a man named Smelzer also started running cattle in White Canyon in the early 1880s. Sanford, a rancher from Grass Valley, and Smelzer, had a herd of longhorns in White Canyon. Sanford would start what would later be called the Gibbons or Cat Ranch in the Henry Mountains. He was also responsible for helping Al Scorup get started in the cattle business in White Canyon.

Charlie Fry, a Kentuckian, arrived in the White Canyon area to do some prospecting sometime before 1891. Herbert E. Gregory noted that Fry had a camp at Woodenshoe Springs on Deer Flat before settling at Fry Spring. (761~)

Albert R. Lyman: "In the solitudes of Elk Mountain and White Canyon, a gray bearded hermit appeared every now and then, always alone, always armed to the teeth, and always in rags and dirt beyond description. He gave the name of Charley Frye, and while he lived, good horses, especially stock horses, disappeared in a very remarkable way." (1240~)

At the spring Fry set up a base camp, building a small house under an overhang near an existing Anasazi cliff dwelling and a corral for his horses.

Albert R. Lyman provided an interesting description of a fictional Charley Spy in his book *Voice of the Intangible*. This was certainly Charlie Fry: "Spy never cared to get very far from the thick timber. He loitered always near it like an old mossback steer. You might see him looming up a ghastly apparition among the oak brush, and the next minute you might not be able to find so much as his track. The forest was to him what water is to a frog.... No one followed nor sniffed his tracks, for he carried a veritable cannon of a Winchester under his leg, and a wicked old Colt's forty-five on his hip.... His teeth were few and scattering.... His white whiskers hung wavy and thin on each side, and under his wrinkled skin the lean muscles revealed the dry hinge and socket of his jaws. His laugh was a weather-beaten cackle ... and his blood-shot, storm-battered eyes ... looked painfully like twin kidney sores on a cayuse." (1249~)

Al and Jim Scorup found Charlie Fry at the spring when they first arrived in the White Canyon area in 1891 with a herd of Claude Sanford's cattle. Over a period of years the Scorup brothers were to dominate the White Canyon range with their "Lazy TY" cattle and later with the Scorup-Somerville Cattle Company, often using Fry Springs as a base. A small settlement arose as prospectors and settlers trickled into Glen Canyon.

Somewhere along the line Charlie Fry disappeared from the scene, though Albert R. Lyman provided what may or may not have been a fictional end, telling of finding Charlie dead in a cave somewhere out on Mancos Mesa. (1249~)

W.W. Dyar, while visiting the bridges of White Canyon in 1904, camped at the spring: "The travelers camped at a place called Fry Cabin. The cabin has entirely disappeared, but a fine spring welling from the foot of an overhanging ledge of rocks marked the spot where a lonely ranchman had had for a time his ephemeral dwelling in the desert." (587~)

In 1918 the Scorups sold their range rights and Fry Springs to Franklin Jacob Adams, who died in an accident in White Canyon in 1940. (See Jacobs Chair.)

During the uranium years from the late 1940s to the early 1960s the settlement of Fry Spring boomed and a post office was established, though it remained running for only a short period.

Hardy and Charlie Redd bought the rights to Fry Springs in the early 1960s. They in turn sold it to Sandy Johnson in 1978. Sandy still uses this as one of his bases of operation. (1002~)

Inscriptions include F.E. Horton, April 23, 1899. (1115~)
—White Canyon Mine No. 1: This uranium mine is on Fry Mesa two miles southwest of The Cheesebox (near elevation 6282T on The Cheesebox map). Robert E. Thaden:

"The claim was originally located by Shumway Bros. [A.E. and Seth], Blanding, Utah, and was purchased from them by the White Canyon Mining Co. in 1951." (1872~)

Frying Pan, The: (Emery Co.) San Rafael Swell-Moroni Slopes. The Frying Pan map.

Garn Jefferies noted that this is shaped like a frying pan. (959~) Wayne Gremel noted that it looks like a frying pan from the air. (780~)

—Frying Pan Catchment: Wayne Gremel: "The Bureau of Land Management built that in the '50s or '60s. I've never been out there when the tank wasn't full of water." (780~)

Frying Pan Flat: (Sevier Co.) Fishlake National Forest-Johnson Valley Reservoir. Fish Lake map.

Thaine Taylor: "It's a meadow that's shaped just like a frying pan. Got a handle on it and a big round area." (1868~) In the early years John Peterson and the Frands [also spelled Franz] families had houses on the Frying Pan. (1191~)

—CCC Camp: This was located on the flat in 1933. (238~)

Frying Pan Flat: (Sevier Co.) San Rafael Swell-Highway 72. Johns Peak map.

Wayne Gremel: "That is Krantz Country. They built that pond up there and when they got done, it looked like a frying pan." (780~)

Jim Crane noted that this was originally named Sign Board Flat. The Frying Pan Flat name was mistakenly put on this feature when the USGS made their original maps of the area in 1966. Jim Crane: "When they first put the road through here, they had a little sign there and it said,

'Last Chance Truck Trail.' It was on an iron post. The CCs built the road and put up the sign [in the 1940s]." (478~)

Fugate Ditch: (Emery Co.) Castle Valley-Ferron. Molen map.

Lee Mont Swasey: "It was probably named for Tom Fugate [1866-1940]." (1853~) Fugate was an early resident of Castle Valley. (388~)

Fuller Bottom: (Emery Co.) San Rafael Swell-San Rafael River. Buckhorn Reservoir and Sids Mountain maps.

Two name derivations are given.

First, Stella McElprang noted that Tom Fuller had a ranch here in the late 1880s. (1330~)

Second, Muriel Smith noted that it was Bob Fuller. (1780~) Ben R. Hite, a brother of Cass Hite, in 1893: "Where the San Rafael river cuts through the reef there is a little bar formed on the east side ... and Bob Fuller, a ranchman of good reputation in that country told me just a week ago that they had found good placer gold on that bar." (889~) Sylvia Harris Ekker noted that Florence Harris (See Florence Creek) married Bob Fuller in about 1884. He was killed in a shoot-out over a bull. (622~)

Funnel Falls: (Grand Co.) Colorado River-Westwater Canyon. Big Triangle map.

Ellsworth Kolb and Bert Loper called this Double Pitch Rapid in 1916. (1362~)

Furniture Draw: (Emery Co.) San Rafael Swell-Buckhorn Wash. Bob Hill Knoll map.

—Old Spanish Trail: The trail passed over the head of Furniture Draw. (1270~)

Gahew Spring: (Sevier Co.) Fishlake National Forest-Fish Lake. Burrville map.

Dee Hatch noted that the area around the spring was logged for railroad cross ties in the 1880s. (844~)

Gap, The: (Garfield Co.) Dixie National Forest-Escalante Mountains. Barker Reservoir map. (9,840')

Pratt Gates noted that this is a tough pass with a difficult trail going through it that was used by stockmen. It used to be a rough wagon road. (709~)

Gap, The: (San Juan Co.) Dry Valley-Highway 191. Church Rock map. (6,116')

Highway 191 goes through a gap formed by two two-hundred-foot-tall mesas.

In 1765 the Don Juan Maria de Rivera Expedition camped here. Rivera: "There was little pasturage, bad shelter, but much firewood. That night we suffered a furious storm of wind and rain; because of that ... we called this campground El Purgatorio." (1172~, 953~)

Gap, The: (San Juan Co.) Navajo Indian Reservation-Oljeto Mesa-Rock Door Mesa. Goulding map.

Also called Big Rock Door.

This gap between sheer rock cliffs provides a shortcut from Goulding to Oljeto. (1204~)

Joyce Muench in 1941: "High above the tiny patch that we know to be the [Gouldings] Trading Post, stand the 'Sentinel' and 'Baldy,' guarding 'The Gap' which opens a small but interesting region that has a stone bridge and picturesque side-canyons and ridges." (1404~)

Gap, The: (Wayne Co.) Canyonlands National Park-Maze District-Elaterite Basin. Elaterite Basin map. (5,863')

Also called The Saddle. (M.44.)

This is a pass on the ridge that divides Elaterite Basin from The Maze. Arthur Ekker noted in 1966 that it was called Windy Pass. (618~)

—Nipple Trail: Ned Chaffin described the trail through The Gap: "You just went and climbed over the rocks where you could and if one of 'em got in your way and if it wasn't too big, you rolled it off.... We didn't use it a lot. I only remember puttin' cattle over there just a time or two." (411~)

Gap Spring, The: (Garfield Co.) Dixie National Forest-Boulder Mountain. Posy Lake map.

This is a developed spring. (740~)

The spring is in what is locally called The Gap. The road through The Gap to Cyclone Lake was built by the CCC in the 1930s. (887~)

Garden Basin: (Garfield Co.) Henry Mountains-Raggy Draw. Mount Ellen map.

Guy Robison: "They had a little water seepin' there and planted a patch of potatoes and so they called it the Potato Patch. That's Garden Basin." (1644~)

Garden Basin: (Sevier and Wayne Counties.) Fishlake National Forest-Thousand Lake Mountain. Geyser Peak map.

Garn Jefferies: "There was a couple who moved in up there in the early 1900s. There's a natural spring there and there is not much area. So instead of making it a farm, they raised a nice big garden. They only stayed a few years. They started to build a house, but never finished it. They lived in tents." (959~)

Garden of Eden: (Grand Co.) Arches National Park-Salt Wash. The Windows Section map.

Also called The Fingers, King Row, and Toadstools. (898~)

Unattributed: "So named because early visitors thought they saw rock formations resembling Adam and Eve, complete with Adam holding an apple to take the first bite." (68~)

—Owl Rock: This was in the Garden of Eden. It fell from its perch in March 1941. (898~)

Garden Spring: (Garfield Co.) Dixie National Forest-Escalante Mountains-Water Canyon. Upper Valley map.

Edson Alvey noted that the Henry Heaps, Sr. family planted a garden here in the 1880s. (55~, 2051~)

Gardner Draw: (Washington Co.) Dixie National Forest-Bull Valley Mountains-Moody Wash. Central West map. (See Gardner Peak for name derivation.)

Gardner Hollow: (Kane Co.) Pink Cliffs-Long Valley. Orderville map.

Henry Gardner (1848-1930) arrived in Mount Carmel in 1865. (349~)

Gardner Peak: (Washington Co.) Dixie National Forest-Pine Valley Mountains-Pine Ridge. Grass Valley map. (9,488')

Robert Gardner, Jr. (1819–1906), a lumberman, arrived in Pine Valley in 1861. (160~, 462~, 1141~)

In 1855 Isaac Riddle lost a cow in the area. He followed it up a creek—sleeping in his saddle blankets at night—until he finally followed the cow's hoof prints to the top of a ridge. Isaac wrote about looking from the ridge across to Gardner Peak: "There stretching before me was the most beautiful sight I had ever beheld on God's green earth. Huge pines grew down to the floor of the valley which was carpeted with dew-drenched grass waving as high as a horse's knee; quaking aspen bordered the giant pines, stretching their arms up to reach the sunlight, filled the gulch below.... Giant pines and quaking aspens grew along each creek bed from where they left the foot of the mountains until they joined the main creek. The only sign of life in the whole valley was the lost cow peacefully grazing in the virgin meadow." (1182~)

Garfield County:

The county seat is Panguitch.

Garfield County was established in 1882 from Kane and Sevier counties. It was initially to have been named Snow County in honor of southern Utah pioneer Erastus Snow. But, President James A. Garfield had recently been assassinated and Governor Eli H. Murray felt that Garfield County was a more appropriate name.

Garnet Ridge: (San Juan Co.) Navajo Indian Reservation-Chinle Wash. Moses Rock and Mexican Water maps. Donald L. Baars: "a volcanic neck (diatreme) south of the San Juan River along Comb Ridge; a well-known source for garnets." (86~) These pyrope garnets are locally called Arizona Rubies. (769~)

Gate Canyon: (Duchesne Co.) Badland Cliffs-Nine Mile Canyon. Gilsonite Draw, Cowboy Bench, and Currant Canyon maps.

Unattributed: "[About one and one-quarter miles up Gate Canyon], a stone arch once spanned the ravine. It was destroyed about 1905. Some people ... were afraid of the arch someday falling and killing people. Newt Stewart was hired to destroy the arch. Gate Canyon receives its name from the arch, which resembled the entrance or gate to a western ranch." (1465~)

Lela N. Fackrell in 1905: "Here travel was never safe during July or August as there was no undergrowth on the barren cliffs to hold moisture should a flash flood occur. It was not uncommon to have the creek swell fifteen feet in as many minutes and the road went winding down the creekbed! No one stopped for lunch on this stretch of road. Skies were constantly watched. Taut nerves could not be relaxed until the safety of open plains was reached." (1182~)

Enid C. Howard in 1971: "This road through Gate Canyon to Myton was one of the first roads in the Territory of Utah, and a killer for the teams freighting supplies from Price to the settlers in the Uintah Basin and the Military Post at Fort Duchesne. The road was built by cavalry troops after the Meeker Massacre at White River, Colorado in 1879." (912~)

Inscriptions include Max Leonard Explorer Trapper Passing here in 1860; H.L. Leonard, 1886; J. Nelson, 1886; D.M. Fairbanks, April 23, 1887; HAP, 1887; Frank Jones, Alf Moore, Jan. 4, 1888; WR Powell, Lot Powell, 1889; Jess Barruetabena, Tuby Spain, 1889; J.O. Fielding, May 23th, 89; Abe Powell, 1890; JK Scott, BK Scott, Aug. 17, 1891; B. Geary, 1892; Jo. Bell, 93; JF Snyder, Aug. 19, 94; Harmon Noble, 1896; J. Spencer, June 26, 1896—Packer By God; Elmer Powell, 1918; and Nellie Smith, June 24, 1927. (SAPE.)

—Outlaw Point: This is one mile up Gate Canyon from its mouth (one-half mile west-northwest of elevation 6801 on the Cowboy Bench map). Unattributed: "A group of outlaws intended to ambush the soldiers escorting the army payroll and Indian annuities.... The army was told of the plan by an informant and the guard was doubled to 40 soldiers. The Outlaws hiding on the ledges hastily called off the ambush." (1465~)

Gates Canyon: (Kane Co.) GSCENM-Kaiparowits Plateau-Sunday Canyon. Blackburn Canyon map.

Also called Gates Draw.

Pratt Gates noted that William Henry Gates, Sr. (1860-1896) and Moriah Gates were Escalante pioneers. (709~)

—Back of Gates: Pratt Gates noted that this is the area between the heads of Gates Draw and Monday Canyon. Back of Gates extends to Rogers Canyon. Pratt: "It's rough, rough country down in there." (709~)

Gates Creek: (Sevier Co.) Fishlake National Forest-Gooseberry Creek. Gooseberry Creek map.

George Gates (1812-1896) and his wife, Mary (1829-1903), and family were early settlers of Salina. (388~)

Gates Spring: (Garfield Co.) Dixie National Forest-Escalante Mountains-Holbys Bottom. Barker Reservoir map.

Pratt Gates: "That is where my great grandfather, William Henry Gates, homesteaded. They had a two-room big cabin there from the early '20s to the early '30s." (709~)

Gates Tank: (Kane Co.) Glen Canyon NRA-Fools Canyon. King Mesa map.

Don Coleman: "[Rancher] Floyd Gates and his son, Len, used to camp there all the time." (441~)

Gemini Arch: (Grand Co.) Tenmile Country-Arths Pasture. Gold Bar Canyon map.

Also called Gemini Bridge.

This was initially named Stewart Twins for the daughters of Clive Stewart, who saw the arch in the early 1930s. The bridge was rediscovered by guides Lin Ottinger and Fran Barnes in 1957. Ottinger is credited with naming the arch for the Gemini twins of Roman mythology. Fran Barnes submitted the name to the USGS in 1968. (1931~, 1952~) Fran Barnes: "We, their discoverers, have called these vast rock bridges the 'Gemini Bridges,' not because of any similarity between them and the Roman mythological characters, Castor and Pollux, nor from any official right to name new and outstanding geological formations, but out of a simple need to call them SOMETHING until such time as the proper authorities have assigned a name to our bridges." (150~)

Gentry Mountain: (Emery Co.) Manti-LaSal National Forest-Wasatch Plateau. Hiawatha and Wattis maps. (10,142')

Bill Gentry arrived in Castle Valley in 1875. Mary Guymon noted that Gentry ran cattle on the mountain. (369~, 380~, 384~) Lou Jean S. Wiggins: "Gentry ... had a wide, red beard that was so long he could tuck it under his belt." (1195~)

—Starr Point: This is the north end of Gentry Mountain. William Starr (1856-1927) and family ran livestock here in the early days. (1195~)

George Rock: (San Juan Co.) Dry Valley-Highway 211. Church Rock map. (6,621')

Also called The Alligator.

James H. Knipmeyer noted that George R. Adams (1864-1935) ran livestock here in the 1890s. (1116~)

—Christiansen Pasture: PRIVATE PROPERTY. This pastureland is to the south and west of George Rock. Alfred C. Christiansen and family patented the land in 1936. (1936~)

Georges Draw: (Emery Co.) San Rafael Swell-Reid Neilson Draw. San Rafael Knob and Twin Knolls maps.

Two name derivations are given.

First, Dee Anne Finken noted that George Crawford was an early cattleman. (641~)

Second, Lee Mont Swasey: "I would imagine that it was probably George Wareham [1875-1958]. They had a homestead here below town [Ferron]." (1853~)

—Sinbad Erosion Control Pond: This stock reservoir is in upper Georges Draw two miles southeast of Forked Post Pond (immediately south of elevation 6921 on the San Rafael Knob map). (1551~)

—Rods Cabin: This was one-half mile west-northwest of Sinbad Erosion Control Pond (one-quarter mile west of elevation 6921 on the San Rafael Knob map). Built by Rod Swasey (1832-1898), all that is left are a couple of difficult-to-find log corrals. (1853~, SAPE.) Lee Mont Swasey: "We spent a lot of time there when I was a kid. The [cattle] allotment is right there.... There was a little shack there and we'd spend two weeks at a time.... It was a little one-room cabin ... had a stove, cupboards, a bed in there." (1853~)

—Georges Draw Well: (Twin Knolls map.) (Also called Sinbad Well.) (1931~) Lee Mont Swasey: "If you've ever smelt the water that comes out of Georges Draw Well ... it's really high in sulphur and it stinks bad." (1853~)

Georgetown: (Kane Co.) Paria River-Yellow Creek. Cannonville map.

The town was established in 1886 by Seth Johnson and others. It was named for Apostle George Q. Cannon (1827-1901). The town, which once boasted a population of over 200, was abandoned by the early 1900s because of a lack of water and the destruction of the fields by floods. (346~, 489~, 777~, 1445~)

Georgie Hollow: (Kane Co.) GSCENM-Kaiparowits Plateau-Lake Canyon. Sooner Bench map.

Don Coleman: "Georgie Hollow was named after Georgie Davis [1861-1951]." Don told a story about Georgie: "Up on top of the Kaiparowits Plateau one time, the fog was real bad. You can't see plants in front of you when it sets in. They's an old guy, name of Georgie Davis who used to live up here and help chase cattle. One morning he was riding on the Plateau and all of a sudden he was looking straight down at the Escalante River. And Georgie says: 'I had to spur the horse like hell to get back on the mountain 'afore the fog lifted'"! (441~)

Geyser Pass: (San Juan Co.) Manti-LaSal National Forest-La Sal Mountains-Mount Mellenthin. Mount Peale map. (10,538')

Rancher Al Geyser used the area between 1878 and 1889. (1546~, 2056~) The name was in place before 1900. (792~)

—Geyser Reservoir: This was three miles east-northeast of Dark Canyon Lake (one-eighth mile west of elevation 8567T). An attempt to build the reservoir in 1910 failed when the dam, under construction, washed out. It was never rebuilt. (926~)

—Scorups Pasture: (Also called Geyser Pasture.) (1936~) This is one-half mile east of Geyser Pass (at elevation 10290T).

Lloyd Holyoak noted that the Indian Creek Cattle Company owned most of the east side of the La Sal Mountains and used the area for running their cattle. (906~) In 1942 the Indian Creek Cattle Company built two line cabins at the pasture. (1703~)

Geshi Canyon: (Coconino Co., Az.) Navajo Indian Reservation-Navajo Creek. Oak Springs, Shonto NW, and Inscription House Ruin, Az. maps.

Also spelled Gishi Canyon. (1995~)

Two similar name derivations are given.

First, Carl I. Wheat in 1954: "*Gish* (cane) [or walking stick], *ih* (he who has), *aboko* (canyon), or the canyon of the man called he who has a cane." (1995~, 1962~)

Second, Laurance D. Linford noted that *Gishì Bikèyah* refers to the upper crossing of Navajo Canyon and literally translates as "Mr. Cane's Field." (1204~)

In 1910 Jesse Walter Fewkes called this Toen Le Shu She Canyon. (638a~, 1392a~)

Geyser Peak: (Sevier Co.) Fishlake National Forest-Thousand Lake Mountain. Geyser Peak map. (10,597')

It is postulated that the peak was named for John Geiser. He arrived in Rabbit Valley in 1876. (1412~, 1641~)

Ghost Ridge: (Garfield Co.) Henry Mountains-Gold Creek. Copper Creek Benches map.

Two name derivations are given.

First, Charles B. Hunt: "[This is] a ridge near the Starr Ranch. The name recalls a range-camp prank." (925~) Garth Noyes expanded on the story: "With sheepherders, whenever a new guy comes out, they'll pull a joke on him if they can. They told this new guy that there were ghosts on the ridge. This fellow said he wasn't scared because he didn't believe in ghosts. So, one moonlit night the old-timers camouflaged one of the guys and set him up on the ridge. Then, they sent the new fellow out to check on the sheep. The camouflaged guy came riding down the ridge like he was a spirit or something and just about scared the pants off of the new guy. After that, they called it Ghost Ridge." (1473~)

Second, Guy Robison: "This is where Arthur Crockett committed suicide." (1644~) (See Taylor Ridges—Crockett Ranch.)

Ghost Rock: (Emery Co.) San Rafael Swell-Head of Sinbad-Interstate 70. San Rafael Knob map.

Dee Anne Finken: "Ghost Rock was named on a day when fog in the Head of Sinbad hid the base of the rock from view and gave it the appearance of a ghost floating in the air." (641~)

Lee Mont Swasey: "Now people have told me that there are two Ghost Rocks, one on each side of the Interstate. That is wrong. The only Ghost Rock is on the south side. The one on the north side is just another rock." (1853~)

Gibbons Springs: (Garfield Co.) Henry Mountains-Slate Creek. Mount Pennell map.

Charlie Gibbons (1860-1952) started the Fairview Ranch (See Collie Wash—Fairview Ranch), and his brother, Ben Gibbons (1867-1946), started the Cat Ranch (See Taylor Ridges—Cat Ranch). Charlie and his two daughters, Dora and Edna, caught a spectacular wild mustang named Wildfire on the Burr Desert. This became the basis for the Zane Grey novel *Wildfire* (1916). (507~, 604~, 1473~, 1644~)

Doc Inglesby expanded on the story: "Chas [Charlie] Gibbons and Rufe Stoddard caught a stallion that [Butch] Cassidy gang stole and which got loose. This was the basis for Grey's WILDFIRE story." (940~) Pearl Baker noted that Charlie Gibbon's daughter, Edna, was the model for Grey's character Lucy in the novel. (1643~)

Grey described Wildfire: "Wildfire was as red as fire. His long mane, wild in the wind, was like a whipping, black-streaked flame. Silhouetted there against that cañon background he seemed gigantic, a demon horse, ready to plunge into fiery depths." (788~)

Gibbs Spring: (Piute Co.) Fishlake National Forest-Tushar Mountains-Gold Gulch. Delano Peak map.

Josiah F. Gibbs (1845-1932) was an early resident of Marysvale. (717~)

Gibex Point: (Wayne Co.) Dirty Devil Country-Sams Mesa Box Canyon. Burr Point map. (5,390')

Also called Ibex Point.

Barbara Ekker: "The origin of the name is complex because the Ibex animal is not a native of North America. Some say Indian goats often escaped captivity to run and interbreed with the wild desert sheep. The horns of the off-spring had a more gradual curve making them look similar to what was thought was the South American Ibex. But the Ibex was not a native of South America but of Asia, Africa, and parts of Europe." (607~)

Arthur, Hazel, and Ted Ekker told this story: "Many years ago when the Spanish Conquistadores were looking for the Seven Lost Cities of Cibola, they had no pack animals. Some of the Indians of the Central American countries were using Ibex (a member of the goat family) for beasts of burden, so the Spanish got a herd of them and brought them as far as the Colorado River where a bunch got loose and went back to their wild way of life. Many years later, Clyde Scharf, a brother-in-law of Joe Biddlecome, an early settler of the Robbers Roost country, heard this story from some sheepherders and they swore that there were still some of the Ibex down in the canyon (Twin Corral Box). Clyde made a trip into the canyon and all he found were some mountain sheep [bighorn sheep] but not Ibex. When he came out he told the herders that they should call the point Gibex because they guyed him into going in there on the pretext of seeing some Ibex. This point has been known by this name among the local residents ever since; this happened around 1911." (1931~)

Gifford Canyon: (Washington Co.) Zion National Park-Pine Creek. Springdale East map.

The USGS noted that Samuel Kendall Gifford (1821–1907) and his son, Oliver DeMille Gifford (1854–1932), moved to Shunesburg in 1862 and then to Springdale in 1874. Oliver Gifford was the bishop of the Springdale Ward from 1895 to 1913. (1192~, 1931~)

—Constructed Stock Trail: This rugged trail, now very hard to find, goes out the top of the canyon. The upper part of the trail is now gone and the route is dangerous. (SAPE.)

—Rock Pasture Plateau: This high area divides Clear Creek from Parunuweap Canyon. It encompasses the high points that lie between Checkerboard Mesa and Bridge Mountain and includes the elevations listed below. (1267~)

—Jenny Peak: **NO TRESPASSING.** This is in a Research Natural Area and is closed to all. The peak is east of Gifford Canyon and is elevation 6310. It was named by Steve Ramras. (1591~)

—Red Jenny: **NO TRESPASSING.** This is in a Research Natural Area and is closed to all. The peak is east of Gifford Canyon and is one-quarter mile east of elevation 5787. It was named by Steve Ramras. (1591~)

—The Triplets: These three summits are one mile east of Jenny Peak (one-eighth mile west of elevation 6531). They were named by Steve Ramras. (1591~)

—The Fin: This is immediately east of The Triplets and is elevation 6531. It was named by Courtney Purcell. (1591~)

—Nippletop: This is one-quarter mile northeast of The Fin (at elevation 6715). (1591~)

—Separation Peak: This separates Nippletop and Crazy Quilt Mesa. (1591~)

—Crazy Quilt Mesa: **NO TRESPASSING.** This is in a Research Natural Area and is closed to all. The mesa is immediately east of Separation Peak and includes elevation 6537. (1591~)

Giles Hollow: (Wayne Co.) Dixie National Forest-Boulder Mountain-Dark Valley Draw. Smooth Knoll and Government Point maps.

Dunk Taylor noted that there have been members of the Giles family living in the area since the 1880s. (1865~, 1419~, 1914~) (See Giles Town.)

Giles Town: (Wayne Co.) Blue Valley-Fremont River-Highway 24. Steamboat Point map.

The town was settled by Hyrum W. Burgess before 1883, giving it its first name, Burgess. It was also called Burgess Blue Valley or Blue Valley. (1781~)

In 1895 the town was renamed for resident and Bishop Henry Giles (?-1892). The town was divided by the Fremont River, with the larger population on its south side. By 1900, the town had two hundred residents. Giles was abandoned in 1919 after drought, flash floods, and accumulated salts ruined the crop land. Still visible are the foundations of many houses, corrals, and a couple of hand-dug wells. The Giles Cemetery is nearby. (346~, 607~, 1537~, 1786~, 2056~, SAPE.) (See Caineville.)

James W. Nielsen told the story of the death of Bishop Giles: "[He] was thrown from a horse and received a compound fracture of his right leg. They got a horse doctor from Grass Valley, sixty miles away, to come down. Gangrene had set in and they sawed his leg off with an ordinary cross cut saw. No sedative, no nothing. He rolled a newspaper into a cone and hollered through it while they did the job. He died the next day." (1453~)

—Abbott House: This pioneer boarding house is about all that is left of Giles. Owned by Edward C. and Elizabeth Abbot, the shell of this stone house still stands next to Highway 24 at the Giles townsite. (804~, 1194~)

—Berthas Rock: This prominent pinnacle, on the cliffs one-half mile west of Giles, was named for a daughter of Bishop Giles. (2053~)

—Kitchentown: (Also spelled Kitchen Town.) Kitchentown was on the north side of the Fremont River three miles east of Giles at mile 112 on Highway 12 (one-quarter mile west-southwest of elevation 4364). The town, founded by Bert Avery in March 1887, was initially called Clifton for the nearby cliffs. (925~, 1419~, 1537~) Mary Henderson Richens: "Named by Willis E. Robinson for the surrounding cliffs…. It was settled by four families who moved away prior to 1900 because of the many numerous floods." (2053~) (See Caineville.)

Gilson Butte: (Emery Co.) San Rafael Desert-Highway 24. Gilson Butte map. (5,553')

Also called Gilson Castle (M.72.) and Gilson's Castle (M.73.).

Three name derivations are given. The first is not correct. First, Caineville pioneer David D. Rust in about 1920: "Jane Gilson, cattle queen of San Rafael." (1672~)

Second, Robert Brewster Stanton called it Gibson's Butte in 1889. G.W. Gibson was a member of the Stanton-Brown Survey of 1889–90. (1811~)

Third, in the early 1880s T.H. Wigglesworth, a surveyor with the Denver and Rio Grande Western Railroad, discovered a new type of mineral which was initially called either asphaltum or Uintaite. The Uintaite name came from the fact that it was discovered on the Uintah and Ouray Indian Reservation. (520~) Irene Branch Keller: "When it burned it gave off dense clouds of black smoke with a peculiar odor, and instead of reducing to ashes, the material melted.... It is used in industrial work such as water proofing materials, paints and varnishes and asphalt." (379~)

The commercial importance of the mineral was first recognized by Samuel Henry Gilson (1836-1913) in 1884. Herbert F. Kretchman: "More than anyone else, Sam Gilson was responsible for its early development and certainly deserved to have his name indelibly attached to the mineral. Not only did he buy up claims and locate others himself, but he sought uses for the mineral and cleared up complications of mining rights." (1130~)

Gilson initially settled in Price in the mid-1870s and was a cowboy for the Samuel R. Bennion family and the Ireland Cattle Company in the San Rafael Swell starting in 1875. He also ranched in what became known as Gilson Valley near Salina Canyon. (See Gilson Valley.) The Gilson Butte name was in place by 1889. (213~, 379~, 1186~, 1766~) Nearby inscriptions include Stuart Wyll, 1904. (SAPE.)

—Little Gilson Butte: (Also called Little Butte.) (1931~) An inscription from JLS and FLS, 1861 is a mystery; there were no known Euroamericans in this country at that time. (1115~)

—Gilson Butte Well: In the mid-1960s the military fired Pershing missiles from Gilson Butte Well to White Sands, New Mexico. At the time there were a thousand troops living in a tent city near the well. (1419~, 1642~)

The well itself was built by Andy Denny. Alvin Robison: "I helped put that in. Alton Morrell was the instigator of it. The well actually was drilled by an oil company that wanted to drill for oil. But they hit water. Then the cowboys came in—and that was Alton Morrell—and put some sucker rods in and fixed it up and used it. That was in the 1950s." (1642~, 623~)

Gilsonite Draw: (Duchesne Co.) Ashley National Forest-Wells Draw. Gilsonite Draw map.

Gilsonite, a coal-like substance, was first discovered in Gilsonite Draw in the early 1880s. (See Gilson Butte.)

Gilson Valley: (Sevier Co.) Old Woman Plateau-Mill Hollow. Walker Flat and Old Woman Plateau maps. PRIVATE PROPERTY.

This is shown on the 1871 Froiseth map as Gunnison Valley. Captain John W. Gunnison went through the valley in 1853. (M.20.) William B. Pace of the Elk Mountain Mission of 1855 called it Gunison [*sic*] Valley. (1500~) Samuel Henry Gilson (1836-1913) ran livestock and had a coal mine in the area starting in the mid-1870s. In the late 1870s Gilson had a ranch here. (584~, 722~, 1186~, 1877~) (See Gilson Butte.)

—Poplar Knob: PRIVATE PROPERTY. This small hill is in Gilson Valley one and one-half miles north-northeast of Oak Spring Ranch (three-quarters of a mile north-northeast of elevation 6625 on the Old Woman Plateau map). Dee C. Taylor: "It was named Polar Knob after dead poplar trees which surround an abandoned ranch cabin on the northeastern side of the ridge." (1863~)

Glass Eye Canyon: (Kane Co.) GSCENM-Flood Canyon. Johnson Lakes map.

Also called East Branch Flood Canyon. (765~)

Cal Johnson: "It has been Glass Eye all my life. There's a spring right up in there and a guy by the name of Lester Little went and developed that and ran cattle there. He had a ranch right at the mouth of the canyon." (984~)

Glen Canyon: (Garfield, Kane, and San Juan Counties, Utah and Coconino Co., Az.) Glen Canyon NRA-Colorado River.

The Glen Canyon section of the Colorado River starts at the mouth of the Dirty Devil River and ends 169 miles later at Lees Ferry.

Father Escalante of the Domìnguez-Escalante Expedition of 1776–77 provided the first, though short, description of Glen Canyon while traversing the area near Waheap Creek: "a large number ravines, hillocks and peaks of red earth, which at first sight look like the ruins of a fort." (81~)

Thales Haskell, who crossed the Colorado River at the Crossing of the Fathers with Jacob Hamblin in 1859, provided an early, albeit short description of Glen Canyon: "wandered lazily over the rocks a while and gazed at the Colerado and the high rocky cliffs on each side through which it wound its zigzag course." (842~)

John Wesley Powell provided the first detailed description of the canyon in 1869: "Now we had come again to the red and orange sandstone, and the walls were of beautiful bright rock, low at first, but as we cut down through the strata, rising higher and higher. Now and then, on this and that side, the rocks were vertical from the water's edge; but usually they were cut into mounds and cones and hills of solid sandstone, rising one above the other as they stretched back in a gentle slope for miles. These mounds have been cut out by the showers from the bright orange rock, and glitter in resplendent beauty under the mid-day sun. Hour after hour have we gazed entranced on them, as they faded in the perspective, and retreated to the rear; for the river was gentle, though swift, and we had but to steer our boats, and on we went through this land of beauty and glory." (1564~)

Powell called the section of the Colorado River from the Dirty Devil River to the San Juan River "Mound Canyon." Jack Hillers of the 1871–72 Powell Expedition: "Called this Mound Canon. The top of the plateau is curiously eroded. Looks like huge mounds closely joined, like a grave yard." (884~)

The section from the San Juan River to the Paria River Powell called Monument Canyon. (1565~) E.O. Beaman of the 1871–72 Powell Expedition: "We came to Monument Cañon, where the walls are eight hundred feet high on either side, with an occasional butte or monument towering above to the height of two thousand feet.... So named from the round-topped cliffs and mountains bordering it." (172~)

In his diary entry for 1871 Powell hinted at the name he would later use formally in his writings: "There are many glens along the walls.... Glens with springs and oak trees; now and then a cottonwood. There are cañons, shelves, and steps up to them. The river nearly fills the channel from wall to wall.... Thompson, Steward, and I climb at night into one of the 'oak glens'.... The Oak glens still continue as a characteristic of the cañon." (662~)

After his second expedition in 1871–72, Powell combined the two canyons into a single Glen Canyon: "So we have a curious ensemble of wonderful features—carved walls, royal arches, glens, alcove gulches, mounds, and monuments. From which of these features shall we select a name? We decide to call it Glen Canyon." (1563~)

John A. Widtsoe in 1922: "The scenery is sublime. Great cliffs of majestic proportions and vivid red, and of infinite variety. Immense arches, auditoriums, stadiums, amphitheatres, temples, palaces, nature's writing on the walls. There are hanging gardens, groves and glens, apparently blind alleys that turn everywhere as you come nearer. Occasionally mighty rocks tower out of the river. There is an overpowering quality in the feeling induced by the scenes along the River." (2007~)

Lewis R. Freeman in 1924: "Glen Canyon is in many ways the most beautiful of all the gorges of the Colorado. Less spectacular scenically than some of the ampler dimensioned chasms of the upper and lower river, for beauty that allures rather than staggers, the tapestried walls of Glen Canyon are without a rival." (681~)

Devergne Barber in 1927: "The walls are ever changing and the white granite which I show topping the inner gorge, resembles snow at a distance and the great spires, temples, cathedrals, buttes and cliffs pass us by in a never ending procession." (134~)

Wallace Stegner in 1946: "Awe was never Glen Canyon's province. That is for the Grand Canyon. Glen Canyon was for delight.... Seen from the air, the Glen Canyon country reveals itself as a bare-stone, salmon-pink table land whose surface is a chaos of domes, knobs, beehives, baldheads, hollows, and potholes, dissected by the deep corkscrew channels of streams." (1827~)

Ann Wooden in 1964: "This is a place of texture: the slippery shining surface of the river, the sandstone walls, the feathery fringes of the willows and tamarisks, the smooth pebbles scattered on sand bars, the dried, cracked mud. It is a place of color: burnished copper and gold, sand beige and pink, metallic black patches of shadow, soft greens. It is a place of form: flowing curves in slit side canyons, sweeps of domes and cave lips, pools of water in pockets, scraggly limbs of a dead sycamore. It is a place of reflections: bits of smooth water everywhere imprisoning pieces of sky, of cliff, or green leaves." (2046~)

Katie Lee provided a superb description of the canyon: "I don't know when the *harmony* of the Glen began to dawn on me. Everything fit. The willows hanging over the water, the banks of young shoots running parallel to the water's edge in strips, as if planted there by hand instead of a receding tide. The heron roosts where leaves and branches were splotched white with years of birdshit. The way sandstone walls curved gently down, or stabbed into the river's edge: the immense talus slopes acting as buttresses for the varnished cliffs rising hundreds of feet to a cobalt sky. Row upon row of multicolored green trimmed the base of massive orange walls. Pink and white sand islands, like dabs of artist's paint, looked to be floating on strips of blue or coffee-colored ribbon, and rock fingers poked into the water, ruffling its flow. The eye was led from one faultless design to the next, moving in beauty, no colors colliding—a 360-degree cyclorama with a soundtrack from the river, narrating." (1162~)

Bruce Berger in 1962: "What we found was nothing: nothing palpable, nothing made visible, nothing multiplied to vastness. For miles and miles we saw only sky and hellishly swirling stone. Here was a world as void as our imaginings of creation. It was inchoate with an angry beauty—as if a mad potter had whirled sandstone on spool after spool and set it spinning like gyroscopes out to a sandstone infinity. And in all this semblance of motion was something so still that it made us seem negligible, invisible, and immensely satisfied." (216~)

Glen Canyon City: (Kane Co.) East Clark Bench-Wahweap Creek-Highway 89. Glen Canyon City map.

The Glen Canyon City name is no longer used; it is now called Big Water.

In 1957 Rincon Builders and Developers bought 120 acres at this site. They were planning on building a city of ten thousand to accommodate construction workers on Glen Canyon Dam. The town was established in 1957, but the city never blossomed. (861~)

The Antonio Armijo Expedition of 1829–30 passed by what would become Big Water. (855a~)

Glen Canyon Dam: (Coconino Co., Az.) Glen Canyon NRA-Lake Powell. Page, Az. map.

Also called The Tombstone.

The damming of the Glen Canyon section of the Colorado River was seriously investigated as early as 1915. At that time the USGS looked at seven different dam sites. Two were considered the most practical. Damsite #1 (also called Lower Damsite) was four miles above Lees Ferry (at elevation 4271T on the Lees Ferry map) on a loop in the river. Spillways would have been drilled through the narrow part of the loop. John A. Widtsoe in 1922: "The rock looks solid on both sides. Great vertical fissures are observed…. This looks by all odds the most promising site that we have seen." (2007~)

Damsite #2 (also called Upper Damsite) was on a loop nine miles above Lees Ferry (at elevation 4060T on the Ferry Swale map). Again, spillways would have been drilled through the narrow part of the loop. (1146~) The final location is fifteen miles above Lees Ferry.

President Dwight Eisenhower signed a bill authorizing the construction of the dam in 1956. Construction started in 1957, with completion in 1965. (1008~) The dam is 580 feet above the original flow of the Colorado River and 700 feet above bedrock. The approximate cost of the dam was one billion dollars. (2057~)

—Glen Canyon Bridge: The bridge is immediately downriver from Glen Canyon dam. Construction started in 1957 and was completed in 1959. (1008~)

Glendale Town: (Kane Co.) Long Valley-Sevier River-Highway 89. Glendale map.

The first settlers arrived in 1864 and initially named the town Berrys Spring or Berryville for the John, Robert, and William Berry families. (1141~, 1639~)

The Berrys were killed in an Indian raid in 1866, giving Berry Knoll its name. The town name was changed in 1871 by Bishop James Leithead. He noted that the area reminded him of his hometown of Glendale, Scotland. (1639~) The Berryville and Berry Springs names were still used by many for several more decades.

Lydia Ann Nelson Brinkerhoff described her family's experience in Glendale in 1871: "The first year our crops were almost a failure on account of an early frost, and again we had a hard time finding something to sustain life. I remember father sold our last cow; she was a large cow and gave a lot of rich good milk. We received her value in frost-bitten corn. How we disliked the bread made from that corn." (292~)

—Glendale Bench: The bench was often mentioned by pioneers. Thomas Chamberlain in 1893: "I went with Ben Hopkins out on the Glendale 'Bench' & staked off some dry land for farming." (416~)

Glenwood Town: (Sevier Co.) Sevier Valley-Mill Creek-Highway 119. Sigurd map.

Also spelled Glennwood.

In 1863 Brigham Young sent a group that included Robert Wilson Glenn (1813-1873) to explore the area. Leila Oldroyd described their first views of the townsite: "When they first came upon this little cove they were greatly impressed by its beauty. Green grass in abundance stood as high as the horses' knees and two cool, clear springs sent a large, willow-lined stream of water flowing down through the center of the valley below." (1971~)

In the summer of 1864 Robert Glenn, Isaac Robert Sampson, George Pectol, Peter M. Oldroyd, Sr., and others moved to the area. The first townspeople called it Glencove, Glenn's Cove, or Glenco. Apostle Orson Hyde, on a visit in November 1864, named the town Glenwood. Indian troubles forced abandonment in 1867.

Andrew Jenson in 1891: "Glenwood is noted for it s beautiful location, good water, good mill sites, rich land and industriuos people." (974a~)

Lucile S. Powell told a story of the trouble: "[In July 1865] Merrit Stanley, a blacksmith, went out after coal to start a fire in his shop. As he raised up with a bucket of coal, he was fired upon by an Indian who lay concealed under the creek bank. One bullet went through his right breast, one seared his lip under his nose, and still another grazed his forehead. He was taken to the home of the bishop and cared for by Mrs. Peter M. Olyroyd who was one of the noble pioneer nurses. The bullet had gone through the body, and great skill was needed. The faithful woman took a white silk handkerchief and drew it back and forth through the wound, thoroughly cleansing it, and kept it open while it healed." (1970~) The town was resettled in 1870. (955~)

—Glenwood State Fish Hatchery: The hatchery was started in 1921. (1971~)

Goat Park: (Wayne Co.) Robbers Roost Flats-Horseshoe Canyon. Head Spur, Sugarloaf Butte, and Robbers Roost Flats maps.

Arthur Ekker in 1964: "The name is believed to have derived from a herd of wild goats which used to roam this park area." (1931~)

Goat Spring: (Emery Co.) Cedar Mountain-Bull Hollow. Cleveland map.

This medium-size spring was once developed. (SAPE.)

Goat Springs: (Kane Co.) Vermilion Cliffs-Cottonwood Canyon. Hildale map.

This is a small spring with no-longer-functioning troughs. The line shack marked on the map has burned down. (SAPE.)

Goatwater Point: (Wayne Co.) Henry Mountains-Granite Wash. Bull Mountain map. (5,368')

Guy Robison: "And somebody was huntin' for a goat and found him there." (1644~)

—Goatwater Spring: This is a medium-size spring. (SAPE.)

—Pioneer Road: One can still see and follow the pioneer road between the Granite Ranch (See Granite Wash) and Goatwater Point. (SAPE.)

Goblin Valley State Park: (Emery Co.) San Rafael Swell-Eastern Reef. Goblin Valley map.

Also called Goblin Gulch (1562~) and Valley of Goblins (1401~).

In 1954 the State of Utah bought 3,654 acres for a state park, which was established in 1959.

This magical valley of hoodoos and pinnacles, formed in Entrada Sandstone, was first seen by the settlers of Hanksville in the early 1880s; the original wagon road from Hanksville north to Green River went close to the valley.

Arthur Chaffin is credited with being the first to bring the valley to the attention of outsiders: "Lost Valley of the Goblins. This valley I saw first in about 1921 while looking out for a road from Greenriver to Caineville so as to miss the desert sands. I was accompanied by Boyd Ivie, another County Commissioner, and Dell Mecham." (401~) Chaffin did not advertise the valley's presence until 1949. At that time he brought photographer P.W. Tompkins and guide Elley Robinson to the area. Although Chaffin initially called it Mushroom Valley, the three men decided to rename it Goblin Valley. (1047~)

Jack Breed in 1952: "This amazing little valley, about eight square miles in area, looks like a convention of freaks. Crowded into its galleries and amphitheaters are hundreds of crazily carved sandstone figures, in inspiration somewhere between the bizarre creations of a Dali and the prehistoric statues of Easter Island." (277~)

Charles Kelly in 1952: "If Dante had visited Goblin Valley ... he would have found in stone all the grotesque forms needed to illustrate his *Inferno*. There, with in the space of a few hundred acres he would have been face to face with a fantastic array of goblins, monsters and demons—surrounded by the faces of tortured souls. All sense of reality is lost as one wanders among the thousands of strangely eroded formations where no imagination is required to see shapes resembling mythical beasts, dragons, prehistoric monsters, giants, dwarfs, cartoon characters, well-known animals and historic faces." (1056~)

Joyce Muench in 1957: "The name told you what to expect, but no one is ever prepared for the limits to which Nature will go for a laugh. Neither grass nor any other self-respecting plant lives there. It's just Entrada sandstone and clay, baked to pavement hardness with thousands upon thousands of silly, slightly malicious characters assembled around courtyards.... I had the distinct sensation several times, that one of the Goblins behind me had moved. It was just a flicker of movement, caught out of the corner of my eye, and he was back in position when I whirled to face him. I wondered if there were not a glimmer of some emotion in his deepset eye-sockets." (1401~)

Keith Wright in 1964: "There are single goblins, goblins in groups, goblins in the form of animals, goblins in the form of people, goblins staring at the visitors, goblins staring at each other, little goblins, big goblins, goblins standing high on the far rim looking superciliously upon subordinates below, goblins with bases of rocks, goblins (whose claim to fame will be comparatively fleeting) with bases of earth, goblins of infinite sizes and shapes." (2055~)

—Movies: *City Slickers* and *Galaxy Quest* were, in part, filmed in Goblin Valley. (1421~)

Gold Bar Canyon: (Grand Co.) Tenmile Country-Colorado River. Gold Bar Canyon map.

Gold Bar Placer is immediately across the Colorado River from the mouth of Gold Bar Canyon. (999~) Lloyd Holyoak: "During the depression, in the 1920s, they had placer mines there. They used high pressure water. They took a lot of gold off that bar." (906~)

—Culvert Canyon: (Also called Cameltoe Canyon.) This northern (or western) tributary of the Colorado River is the first canyon east of Gold Bar Canyon (between elevations 4293T and 4672T). It was named by writer and climber Eric Bjørnstad. (242~) Matt Moore: "It's also called Dragonfly Canyon by many locals. We spun off the Dragonfly theme and called it Odonata Canyon." (653~)

—Monticello Rock: This butte, which looks like Thomas Jefferson's Monticello home, is one and one-half miles north-northwest of the mouth of Gold Bar Canyon (at elevation 4965T).

Gold Basin: (San Juan Co.) Manti-LaSal National Forest-La Sal Mountains-Brumley Creek. Mount Tukuhnikivatz map.

Traces of gold were found in the basin in 1898. (456~)

Gold Creek Spring: (Garfield Co.) Henry Mountains-Mount Hillers. Cass Creek Peak map.

Leverett A. Woodruff filed for a mining claim near here in 1901. (606~)

Golden Gate: (Emery Co.) San Rafael Swell-North Fork Coal Wash. The Blocks map.

This feature, two impressive pinnacles, is formed from gold-colored Navajo Sandstone. Lee Mont Swasey noted that he had also heard it called Horsecock Rock by locals. (1853~)

—Golden Gate Trail: Lee Mont Swasey noted that this stock trail starts in South Fork Coal Wash at Pipe Spring (one-quarter mile north of elevation 6242). It then crosses Bullock Draw, goes to the west side of the Golden Gate, and joins the North Fork Trail. (1853~) (See North Fork Coal Wash—North Fork Trail.)

Golden Stairs, The: (Garfield Co.) Glen Canyon NRA-Orange Cliffs-China Neck. Elaterite Basin map.

This constructed stock trail was built in the 1890s. Ted Ekker noted that the name was given because of the stair step nature of the topography and the golden color of the rock. (623~) Ned Chaffin: "The Golden Staircase, that was a son-of-a-gun for cattle." (411~)

Inscriptions include Ned Chaffin, May 6th, 1934. (SAPE.)

—Constructed Stock Trail: An older trail drops through the same cliffs as the Golden Stairs, but two miles to the west-southwest. The only construction found today is near the top (one-eighth mile east-southeast of elevation 6039AT). (SAPE.)

Golden Throne: (Wayne Co.) Capitol Reef National Park-Capitol Reef. Golden Throne map. (7,042')

This spectacular monolith was named for its gold color at sunrise and sunset.

—Blowout Flat: Keith Durfey noted that this wind-catching depression is one-quarter mile northeast of the Golden Throne. (582~)

Gold Gulch: (Piute Co.) Fishlake National Forest-Tushar Mountains-Sevier River. Delano Peak and Piute Reservoir maps.

Abe McIntosh in 1921: "A main trail leads to this Gulch where prospectors have traveled and found rich samples of ore." (2053~)

Gold Hole: (Uintah Co.) Uintah and Ouray Indian Reservation-Desolation Canyon. Duches Hole map.

Also called Blue Grass Hole. (209~)

Jean Bennett in 1965: "[Rancher] Vern Muse states that gold was panned here and that the gold seekers located a campsite here." (209~)

Ed F. Harmston in 1913: "The cliffs at Gold Hole are very high and picturesque, resembling Queen Anne gables, Ionic and Doric columns, Mansard roofs, with domes and towers galore." (833~) It is unclear here if Harmston is writing about Gold Hole, which is pretty, but is not significant, or about Sumners Amphitheater which is a couple of miles downriver. (See Maverick Canyon—Sumners Amphitheater.)

—Constructed Stock Trail: This goes from Gold Hole up the cliffs to the northwest (one-quarter mile southeast of elevation 5323T). (SAPE.)

Gold Queen Gulch: (San Juan Co.) Manti-LaSal National Forest-Abajo Mountains-South Creek. Abajo Peak map.

The Gold Queen Mine, a large gold mining operation that lasted from 1896 until 1903, was at the top of the gulch (at elevation 10860T). (774~, 1526~)

Clyde Barton: "They had big ricks of wood cut and stacked up at the mine at a place they called the Wood Yard. They fired their smelting furnaces with wood. They had a dance in Monticello one night and as I was leaving, somebody came in and said there was a huge fire on the mountain. Somebody set those ricks of wood on fire. You could see it in town here." (162~)

—Danish Girl Mine: This gold mine is in upper Gold Queen Basin one-quarter mile northeast of the Gold

Queen Mine. Marvin Lyman: "It was built by a bunch of Swedes who came into Monticello during the [gold] boom." (1258~)

Good Hope Mesa: (Garfield Co.) Glen Canyon NRA-Little Rockies. Ticaboo Mesa and Good Hope Bay maps.

Two river historians, Otis "Dock" Marston and Arthur Chaffin, noted that the mesa was named for a gold miner named Goodhope who had a placer mine on nearby Good Hope Bar starting in the late 1880s or early 1890s. (1285~) The name was in place by 1893. (M.5)

In a small side canyon on the west side of Good Hope Mesa is an inscription from Cass Hite's brother, who lived with him at both Ticaboo and Hite. It reads: "John P. Hite. Late of Potosi Mo. Now of Dandy X [Hite Crossing], 1891." Wm. [Billy] Bright, an early miner, left his name alongside Hite's. (SAPE.)

—Pioneer Placer: (Also called Ticaboo Placer.) This placer bar, now underwater, was on the west side of the Colorado River and on the east side of Good Hope Mesa one and one-half miles south of the mouth of Ticaboo Creek (one-quarter mile southeast of elevation 4222AT on the Good Hope Bay map). The placer was discovered by J.R. Bush and Allen Osment in 1889. (465~)

—Bessie Bar: This placer bar, now underwater, was on the west side of the Colorado River and on the east side of Good Hope Mesa two miles south of the mouth of Ticaboo Creek (three-quarters of a mile south of elevation 4222AT on the Good Hope Bay map). It was initially called the Ann S. Bar by Robert B. Stanton in 1897. (465~, 1812~) Later is was named for Bessie, the wife of Glen Canyon miner Bert Seabolt. (1672~)

—Good Hope Bar: This placer bar, now underwater, was on the west side of the Colorado River and the southeast side of Good Hope Mesa and was three miles south of the mouth of Ticaboo Creek (one and one-half miles south of elevation 4222AT on the Good Hope Bay map). The bar was first worked by George and Frank Gillam and Cass and John Hite in 1887. (465~, 925~) David D. Rust, who mined the bar in 1898 along with about twenty other workers for the Good Hope Mining Company: "The mining company ... were operating a sluice box arrangement about two hundred yards long and used a forty foot water wheel to hoist the water into the flume and carry it back into a small reservoir where the water was stored to use in sluicing gravel bars." (1682~) Later, Bert Seabolt patented the claim and Andrew Hunt built an airstrip here. (17~)

—Seabolt Point: In both 1935 and 1939 David D. Rust mentioned going to the "top of Seabolt Point above

Goodhope Bar." (1672~) It is believed that this was a point, perhaps now underwater, that was just a short distance above the bar, not on the top of Good Hope Mesa. It was named for miner Bert Seabolt.

—The Rincon: (Also called Little Rincon or Upper Rincon to differentiate it from The Rincon [The Rincon map] further down the lake.) (465~) This rincon, now underwater, was on the east side of the Colorado River and was two miles southeast of Good Hope Mesa (one-half mile northwest of elevation 3765T on the Good Hope Bay map). William D. Lipe noted that this is not a true rincon: "Unlike the Rincon proper, which is an abandoned meander of the Colorado ... the Little Rincon is merely an unusually wide (up to 1 ½ mi.) part of the canyon." (1207~) This area, accessible by way of a stock trail from Red Canyon, was used by cowboys from the late 1800s on for cattle grazing. (465~)

—Constructed Stock Trail: This trail went up the south side of Little Rincon to Mancos Mesa. It was one-quarter mile southwest of elevation 4812T on the Good Hope Bay map. It is unclear if this was a regularly used trail as there is essentially nothing left of it. (SAPE.) Unattributed in 1937: "Left Red Canyon 6 a.m. traveled S'ly 6 miles along the Colorado River thence SE'ly 8 miles up over Ring Cone [Little Rincon], thence SE'ly 8 miles to Cedar [Canyon]." (560a~)

Good Water Canyon: (Emery Co.) San Rafael Swell-San Rafael River. Bottleneck Peak map.

Owen McClenahan: "This canyon is named for the good water tanks near its head. During prohibition days the water was used to make whiskey. Cowboys used it for a swim and a bath." (1318~)

Gooseberry Canyon: (Carbon Co.) Roan Cliffs-Range Creek. Summerhouse Ridge, Lighthouse Canyon, and Lila Point maps.

Waldo Wilcox: "There are gooseberries up in there. Back in the early days, when we first went into Range Creek, the main trail was up Gooseberry Canyon. I doubt anybody has been over it for a hundred years." (2011~)

Gooseberry Canyon: (San Juan Co.) Canyonlands National Park-Island in the Sky District-Colorado River. Monument Basin map.

Also called Small Buck Canyon. (1631~)

—Gooseberry Trail: (Also called Government Trail.) This "Foot Trail" goes from Grand View Point down to the White Rim Trail and to the head of Gooseberry Canyon. It was built by the Works Progress Administration (WPA). (534~)

Gooseberry Creek: (Sevier Co.) Fishlake National Forest-Salina Canyon. Gooseberry Creek and Steves Mountain maps.

Gooseberry Creek flows through Gooseberry Valley.

Kate B. Carter: "a prolific growth of wild gooseberries in the vicinity." (375~)

In 1853 Captain John W. Gunnison called this by its Indian name, *Un-got-tah-li-kin*. (474~) The Lieutenant George M. Wheeler Survey of 1873 map shows it as Gunnison Valley, since the Captain John W. Gunnison Expedition of 1853 went through it. (M.76.)

Clarence Dutton of the Powell Survey: "A noble valley opens into the middle of Salina Cañon.... This lateral valley is named, locally, Strawberry Valley." (584~)

George C. Fraser in 1915: "The valley bottom affords fine pasture and is cultivated in small patches.... The soil is black, apparently rich.... Gooseberry Creek is a fine stream of clear, cold water." (668~)

—Gooseberry Ranger Station: This was initially the location of the settlement of Gooseberry, which was founded in 1878 (or 1882) by Peter Rasmussen and others, and consisted of a couple of ranch families who started a school. The "town" folded in 1890. (972~, 2053~) The ranger station, built in 1908, was also used over the years as a CCC camp, an experimental station, and a youth camp. (2022~)

George C. Fraser described the location of the ranger station: "a pleasant cottage on a southerly facing hillside in a grove of quaking aspen." (668~)

—Old Spanish Trail: The trail went through Salina Canyon, but if wagons were being used, or the weather was poor, a bypass to the south was essential. Going east, the bypass went up Soldier Canyon and Gooseberry Creek, over the top, down Antone Hollow to Niotche Creek, and back into upper Salina Creek. (1003~, 1734~)

Gooseberry Hollow: (Emery Co.) Cedar Mountain-Huff Hollow. Chimney Rock map.

—Gooseberry Spring: The spring area under a huge overhang is surrounded by gooseberries. Because of the difficulty of access, livestock never grazed here. (SAPE.)

Gooseberry Mountain: (Washington Co.) Vermilion Cliffs-Highway 59-Virgin River. Virgin, Little Creek Peak, and Springdale West maps. (5,485')

Also called Gooseberry Mesa.

The Jesse N. Smith Expedition of 1858 traveled under the south side of Gooseberry Mountain. (469~)

—Cornelius Wash: The mouth of this southern tributary of the Virgin River is one-half mile east of Virgin. It starts on Gooseberry Mountain near elevation 5203 and runs north-northeast, going by elevations 4412 and 3666 on the Virgin map. (767~)

—Jepson Butte: This northern extension of Gooseberry Mountain is three miles southeast of Virgin (at elevation 4970 on the Virgin map). (767~)

Goose Neck: (San Juan Co.) Canyonlands National Park-Colorado River. Musselman Arch and Shafer Basin maps. Also spelled Goose-neck. (218~)

This extreme bend in the Colorado River is shaped like a goose's neck.

—Goose Neck Stock Trail: Lloyd Holyoak noted that he helped build the trail from the river to the top of the Goose Neck. "There is a place we called the Narrows. When we started work there, I had to crawl around on my hands and knees. It was only yea wide, and we had to build it up. We drove stakes in the rock and built it out so we could take horses around there. There's a limestone ledge almost at the top. The trail is pretty clear up to that point. We had to do some blasting to get the horses up over that limestone ledge. Limestone is the hardest thing to drill with a hand drill and an old hammer. There are some tanks up there that hold water pretty much year 'around and that's what we counted on for water for our horses." (906~)

—Horse Bottom: This is on the north side of the Colorado River and immediately north of the Goose Neck (at elevation 4010T on the Shafer Basin map). It is believed that John Jackson was the first to run livestock on the bottom, in the early 1900s. Karl Tangren ran horses here starting in the 1950s.

Two access trails exist. The first was by way of a trail along the river from Oil Well Bottom. (See Pyramid Butte.) (1084~) The second, noted by Lloyd Holyoak, starts near elevation 4495T and goes southwest on the Shafer Basin map. Lloyd said that he used to run horses on the bottom. (906~)

—Alvey Holyoak Camp: This line camp was at the very southwest side of the Goose Neck next to the river. Except for a small stone fence and an old mattress spring, there is little left. (906~, SAPE.)

Gooseneck Point: (Kane Co.) Glen Canyon NRA-Glen Canyon. Gunsight Butte and Gregory Butte maps. (4,695')

Theron Liddle called this Miskin Point in 1946. (1200~) (See Gregory Butte—Mesken Bar.)

Stockmen named it for its "long narrow crooked shape." (1931~)

Gooseneck Ridge: (Carbon Co.) West Tavaputs Plateau-Rock Creek. Summerhouse Ridge map.

Waldo Wilcox: "Henning Olsen, a one-legged Danishman, had a homestead there. He was a rancher. He got his leg shot off down at the Pump Station." (2011~) (See Trail Canyon—Carbon Co.—Pump Station.)

Goosenecks, The: (San Juan Co.) Navajo Indian Reservation-San Juan River. The Goosenecks map.

Also called Great Goosenecks (73~, 1658~) and Goose Neck Bend (744b~).

Charles L. Bernheimer in 1929: "We reached the shore of the San Juan at one of its goose necks. The river takes a turn around what is now an island one thousand feet high in a ragged sort of a circle." (218~)

Hoffman Birney in 1931: "In tracing the course of the [San Juan] river, the Saints [Mormons] came upon a spot where the stream virtually doubled upon its course, cutting a great circular amphitheater in the exact center of which there rose a huge terraced cone of sandstone more than eight hundred feet in height. A dike of rock scarcely ten feet in thickness separated the point of the river's entrance from that where it left the loop.... It was—and is—a spot overpowering in its impressive grandeur.... They christened the place 'The Twist.' Later it came to be known by the title it now bears, one of equal poetic charm—'the Gooseneck.'" (235~)

Norm Nevills in 1936: "The river at times enters veritable tunnels which for almost half a mile will confine the stream to a gorge fifty feet across and with shiny black rocks of glassy smooth limestone almost converging five hundred feet above. Then, with startling suddenness the color scheme is changed to many shades of red. And it's color, color, color all the time"! (1437~)

Famed war correspondent Ernie Pyle in 1939: "[Goosenecks] isn't a very good term, for the thing resembles a goose's neck about as much as mine does.... This thing is sort of a drunken edition of the Grand Canyon.... It loops back and forth, as evenly as tho the loops had been made by a machine." (1593~)

Randall Henderson in 1945: "The San Juan meanders between its canyon walls in a series of dizzy turns resembling the gyrations of a mammoth sidewinder." (860~)

Alfred M. Bailey in 1947: "Today the river makes five majestic bends between these towering walls, twisting back on itself so that it journeys 25 miles to cover an airline distance of five.... Known to geologists as a magnificent example of 'entrenched meander,' the Goosenecks present a truly remarkable spectacle in a land of scenic splendors." (93~)

Helen Kendall in 1948: "Passed the world's most famous goosenecks, but they were *all* goosenecks to me. Just one curve after another which was closed at both ends with towering cliffs on all sides. The only direction in which we could see any distance was up." (1086~)

Goosenecks: (Wayne Co.) Capitol Reef National Park-Sulphur Creek. Twin Rocks map.

This is a particularly winding section of Sulphur Creek that from above looks like the curve of a goose's neck.

Goosenecks State Park: (San Juan Co.) Valley of the Gods-San Juan River. The Goosenecks map.

(See The Goosenecks for name derivation.)

This ten acre park was established in 1962. It does not actually contain The Goosenecks of the San Juan River; rather, it is a point of land that provides a terrific view of them.

—Goosenecks Dam Site: (Proposed.) This dam on the San Juan River was suggested by the Bureau of Reclamation in 1946. (78~)

Gordon Creek: (Carbon Co.) Castle Valley-Price River. Pinnacle Peak and Price maps.

Mae Grames Brown: "Albert [James Grames] went to Price landing on January 1, 1881.... He purchased a squatters rights in the mouth of Gordon Creek from James Gordon for $30." (305a~)

Charles Gorley provided an early description: "Gordon Creek was a small creek ravine into Price River about one mile above Price.... Gordon Creek was very shallow and some times would flood the farms. So my dad and uncle [Charles Grames] made a canal through the [Al] Nelson ranch when he was not there to drain their ground and before Nelson came back it had made a deep wash so he got real mad and left and never came back. The wash got so deep that they could not keep the water out of the creek on the farm. So my father and uncle eventually moved over on Price River." (747~)

—Gordon Creek Town: This "town," organized as the Gordon Creek Branch of the Carbon Stake, was started in 1930. It was not a true town, just an organization that included the families living along Gordon Creek. (972~)

Gordon Flats: (Wayne Co.) Glen Canyon NRA-Orange Cliffs. Gordon Flats map.

Also called Flint Garden (M.44.) and Tater Patch (814~).

Ned Chaffin: "Today's maps use the word 'Gordons,' but according to old-timers the area was named the French Gardens because it was so pretty and the French sheepherders grazed it a lot. Someone couldn't understand the French accent and 'Gardens' came out 'Gordons.'" (1430~)

—Bull Seep: This small spring is one and one-half miles south-southwest of French Spring (one-half mile south of elevation 6548T on the Gordon Flats map). (100~, SAPE.)

Gordon Reservoir: (San Juan Co.) Abajo Mountains-Great Sage Plain-Clay Draw. Monticello Lake map.

Famed pioneer and cowboy Willard Eugene "Latigo" Gordon helped build the reservoir, which was completed in 1902. (2069~) Zane Grey modeled the Lassiter character in his novels *Riders of the Purple Sage* and *The Rainbow Trail* after Latigo. (784~, 1508~) A story illustrates why. H.L.A. Culmer in 1905: "The cabin is full of holes from guns. [Latigo] Gordon in one fray stood off 3 men in the East cabin [See Spring Creek–Carlisle Town], beat two of them till they ran and was on the other beating him over the head with a sixshooter when help came. Meantime Gordon had 9 wounds, one thro the lungs.... Got doctor from Denver who gave him one week to live. He replied 'G–d–- you I'll be riding the range when you are dead.' 2 years later the doctor died." (494~, 1822~)

Norma Palmer Blankenagel: "He could keep a tin can rolling constantly under a fusillade of revolver shots. In a corral filled with wild horses racing madly to keep from being caught, Gordon could lay the loop of his lariat over his foot and with a quick toss of his leg rope any designated horse by the forelegs." (257~)

Gothic Arch: (San Juan Co.) Canyonlands National Park-Needles District-Horse Canyon. South Six-shooter Peak map.

This was named by Canyonlands National Park Superintendent Bates Wilson in 1957. Robert H. Vreeland: "The name probably comes from the fact that the viewer is reminded of medieval architecture with its characteristic flying buttresses and pointed arches." (1950~, 1429~)

Gothic Creek: (San Juan Co.) Navajo Indian Reservation-San Juan River. Toh Atin Mesa West, Gray Spot Rock, Boundary Butte, White Rock Point, and San Juan Hill maps.

This is named after Gothic Mesa, which is immediately across the San Juan River from the mouth of Gothic Creek. The Captain John N. Macomb Expedition of 1859 applied the Gothic Mesa name to the cliffs surrounding what would become the town of Bluff. (769~, 1266~) Donald L. Baars noted that it was named for its weirdly eroded walls that looked gothic. (86~)

Gottfredsen Creek: (Sevier Co.) Fishlake National Forest-Sevenmile Creek. Mount Terrill map.

Correctly spelled Gottfredson Creek.

Brothers Hans Gottfredson (1848-1917) and Peter Gottfredson (1846-1934) were pioneers of Glenwood and Sigurd, arriving in about 1871. (238~, 1971~)

Gould Wash: (Washington Co.) Hurricane Cliffs-Virgin River. Smithsonian Butte, Little Creek Mountain, The Divide, and Hurricane maps.

Also called Goulds Wash (469~) and Little Creek Wash (1931~).

The Jesse N. Smith Expedition of 1858 called this Willow Creek. (469~)

Samuel J. Gould (1778–1869) and family arrived in Cedar City in 1851. They moved to St. George in 1861. (160~, 1727~)

—Gould Ranch: PRIVATE PROPERTY. (Also called Workmans Ranch or Workmans Spring [667~]. Also spelled Ghools [1842~], Goolds [2048~], Gools [773~], Goulds [775~], and Gould's Ranche [170~].)

This historic ranch is two and one-half miles east of Mollies Nipple (one-quarter mile southeast of elevation 4088T on the Hurricane map). The Samuel Gould family started the ranch in Goulds Wash in the mid-1860s. It became a stopping place for those heading to the Arizona settlements. It was mentioned by the Andrus Military Reconnaissance Expedition of 1866. (475~, 1141~)

—Gould Spring: (Little Creek Mountain map.) This is the location of Goulds Shearing Corral. From 1910 to the early 1930s, legend has it that more sheep were sheared here than anyplace in the world. It is estimated that up to one hundred fifty thousand sheep a year were brought here in the spring. Two thousand to three thousand sheep a day would be sheared. Cattlemen, unhappy with the sheep controlling the range, burned the corrals and outbuildings a couple of times. By the mid-1930s transportation became easier and the shearing corrals were shut down. (1544~, 1608~)

An article from the *Washington County News*, May 6, 1914: "Manti Workman was killed ... shortly after leaving Goulds wash, by a load of wool tipping over on him. His brother Nephi came along behind him and extracted him, but he was smothered." (1843~)

—Little Man Bend: This prominent bend in the Virgin River is one-half mile northwest of the mouth of Gould Wash (one-eighth mile east of elevation 2992T on the Hurricane map). It was named for a small Indian petroglyph found on a boulder. (514~)

Goulding Town: (San Juan Co.) Navajo Indian Reservation-Oljeto Mesa. Goulding map.

Also called Goulding Trading Post.

Goulding Trading Post was listed on the National Register of Historic Places in 1980.

Harry Goulding (ca. 1897-1981) and his wife, Mike, moved to Monument Valley in 1924. For the first year or so they lived in a tent while building a rock-walled trading post. Because of this, Navajo called it Tent Water. (1057~) The Navajo also called it *Tségiizh*, or "Rock Gap." The town is near a gap—now called The Gap—in a high cliff. (1943~, 2016~) The Gouldings ran the trading post for more than thirty years. (875~)

Harry Goulding: "Long about 1920 me and another old boy come ridin' through here with a pack outfit. And I made up my mind right then I'd hogtie a piece of this valley." (1999~) Here he homesteaded 640 acres. Later, the Gouldings gave much of the land as an endowment to the Navajo. The Seventh Day Adventists and Knox College of Galesburg, Illinois then built a school and church under the leadership of Marvin and Gwendolyn Walter. (1607~) Charles Kelly described the view from Goulding Trading Post in 1935: "[It] is situated in what I consider the most picturesque spot in America. Perched high on a cliff it overlooks the western half of Monument Valley, with a view extending from forty to eighty miles in three directions. Against the northeastern skyline in the center of the flat sandy valley stands a row of those magnificent sandstone monuments which give the place its name. Behind them the sun rises each morning, painting the desert with innumerable delicate tints, never twice alike." (1075~)

—Old Baldy: This rounded sandstone buttress is immediately west of Goulding. (1127~) Joseph Miller: "According to legend, [Old Baldy] is the north portal of the rock door to the old main trail from the Indian country to the white man's country." (1359~)

Government Bird Rock: (San Juan Co.) Navajo Indian Reservation-Douglas Mesa-San Juan River. Slickhorn Canyon West map.

Brandt Hart noted that this rock formation looks like a bird and is above Government Rapids. (838~)

Government Creek: (Wayne Co.) Dixie National Forest-Boulder Mountain-Fremont River. Bicknell map.

Don Orton in 1941: "So named because it was used by a group of government surveyors who used the site as a camping ground." (2053~)

Government Point: (Wayne Co.) Dixie National Forest-Boulder Mountain. Government Point map. (10,359')

This was named after the Government Point Trail, which was built by the government.

—Government Point Trail: (Also called Forest Service Trail #140 and Ranger Trail.) This is the "Pack" trail that goes down the west side of the point. Dunk Taylor: "That's an old trail that the rangers, back in the 1920s or so, would ride to see that the stock was where it was supposed to be. It was his job to try and keep everybody honest. They'd hire people to clean out the trails and he'd ride from the Wildcat Ranger Station on the east side of Boulder Mountain around to the Aquarius Ranger Station and then over to Jubilee [Ranger Station] and back to Teasdale to make his circuit." (1865~) The trail was heavily used until the modern road was built in the mid-1950s. (1094~)

Government Rapids: (San Juan Co.) Glen Canyon NRA-San Juan River. Slickhorn Canyon East map.

The standard story about the naming of the rapids is that two boats on a government survey trip wrecked here in 1921. This story has been repeated in several river guides. (93~) Randall Henderson in 1945: "Two government survey boats are reported to have gone on the rocks here during an early period when boats were not as well designed for this kind of water as they are today." (860~)

The government survey was the Kelly W. Trimble USGS Expedition of 1921. The party did indeed have problems on one rapid. Expedition member Arthur A. Baker: "One of the boats containing two members of the party not only narrowly missed striking the canyon wall but struck a boulder and was burst on one side from bow to stern. The boat was nearly filled with water by the time a landing place was reached." (1370~) This happened not at Government Rapid, but several miles upriver, above Johns Canyon. (1370~) Apparently Norm Nevills made up the story about Government Rapids to make it seem more difficult to his clients. (1976~)

In 1940 P.W. Tomkins, while on a Norm Nevills river trip, noted that they called this Nevills Rapid: "The rapid was a bit mean." (1897~)

Grabens, The: (San Juan Co.) Canyonlands National Park-Needles District. The Loop, Spanish Bottom, and Cross Canyon maps.

Geologist Eugene D. Foushee defined a graben: "'Graben' is the German word for grave, referring to an old grave that has sunken; a graben valley is formed by a fault on each side of the valley—the valley floor being the downthrown block." (659~) The Graben name was officially applied in the late 1960s. (1931~)

David Lavender in 1943: "Wide, flat-bottomed valleys bordered by abrupt walls ran every which way. They crossed each other, paralleled each other, started and stopped with no apparent excuse. You enter the head of one—or the foot; the distinction is meaningless for they are apt to slope either way at any given point." (1151~)

Graff Point: (Iron Co.) Hurricane Cliffs-Blue Valley. Cedar Mountain map. (9,047') PRIVATE PROPERTY.

—Graff Coal Mine: P. Arnold Graff (1869-1956) started a coal mine here in the late 1880s. The mine was on the south end of Graff Point (one-quarter mile northwest of elevation 8851). (570~)

—Pollock Mine: This coal mine was on the north slope of Graff Point and is the western of the two "Coal Mines" shown on the map. The mine was active in the 1920s. (570~, 1715~)

—Kleen Koal Mine: This was one of the major coal mines in the area and is the eastern of the two "Coal Mines" shown on the map. It was in operation between 1937 and 1952. A one and one-half-mile-long aerial tramway was used to move coal down the mountain. (570~)

—Kanarraville Mine: This is one of the earliest coal mines in the area, opening in 1873. It was at the south end of Graff Point (one-quarter mile west of elevation 8851). (570~)

Grafton Mesa: (Washington Co.) Vermilion Cliffs-Virgin River. Springdale West map. (4,775')

(See Grafton Town for name derivation.)

—Grafton Mesa Road: The road from Grafton to the top of Grafton Mesa was completed in the late 1890s or early 1900s. It was often called the Wood Road because locals got their wood from the mesa top. (751~) George C. Fraser ascended the road in 1914 and described the view from the top: "To the east the entire upper Virgin Valley was spread before us with all the temples brought out in sharp relief by the light of the setting sun; the colors of the rocks of every shade, from the light shales at the base of the Permian through the chocolate at the summit, the vermilion cliffs above and the brilliant white of the jura, capped and streaked by the gypsiferous layers above, were accentuated and changed chameleon-like, as the sun moved down, and finally its light reflected from the clouds struck them. In the maze of color and sculpture, interest in the appreciations of details was lost.... This view was a picture framed by nature in the rain-bow, that only disappeared when the sun's rays passed. Whether this view was more beautiful than any other I have ever seen is not subject to determination; it is, however, one of a very few to be remembered as the most magnificent." (667~) Inscriptions include K.H., 10/1916. (SAPE.)

Grafton Town: (Washington Co.) Vermilion Cliffs-Virgin River-Highway 9. Springdale West map.

Also called Old Grafton (363~) and Wheeler (667~, M.72., M.74.).

Also spelled Graeton.

Three name derivations are given.

First, Charles Slaughter, who moved to Grafton in 1861, is credited with naming the town after the town of Grafton, West Virginia. (375~)

Second, it was named for a town in England. (1932~, 2053~)

Third, from the Church Chronology: "The name was evidently taken in honor of a family by the name of Graff who settled there." (2053~) The Jacob Johannes Graf family arrived in Santa Clara in 1861. (462~)

The town was settled by Nathan C. Tenney, James McFate, Benjamin Platt, and others in 1859. The original townsite was one mile south of the present site of Grafton. (1611~) Flash floods proved problematic. Angus M. Woodbury told the story of the first flood encountered by the new residents: "Rain started on Christmas day, 1861, and continued for forty days. The Virgin became a raging torrent.... As the waters swirled around the wagon box home of Nathan Tenney, several men picked it up with his expectant wife in it and carried it to higher ground north of the river, where a son was born. He was named, appropriately enough, Marvelous Flood Tenney." (2043~)

Alma Barney was there for the flood: "There were about eight houses in the little berg [Grafton] on the bank of the river. The morning after the big flood found all the people of the town marooned on the side of the mountain with but one house left standing, and that one house was ours." (138~) The town was relocated to its present site and for a short while was called New Grafton. (972~)

Inscriptions include Valentine Sleut, May 14, 1879; Justin M. Johnson, 1879; and Joseph Hilton, Nov. 20th, 1881. (1112~, 1115~)

—Movies: The town was abandoned by the mid-1940s, but was often-used by the motion picture industry. *The Electric Horseman, Son of Flicka, Arizona Kid,* and *Butch Cassidy and the Sundance Kid* were, in part, filmed here. (354~, 1552~, 1639~, 1932~)

—Adventure Town: This small town was between Grafton and Rockville. Established in 1860 by Philip Klingensmith and others, it was soon found that the area was too small to support growth. A new townsite, now Rockville, was selected and Adventure was abandoned. (371~) C. Gregory Crampton: "The name was chosen because it was regarded as an adventure to attempt a settlement along the Virgin River." (469~)

Grafton Wash: (Washington Co.) Vermilion Cliffs-Virgin River. Smithsonian Butte and Springdale West maps. Also called Old Grafton Wash. (163~)
(See Grafton Town for name derivation.)

Gramse: (Sevier Co.) Sevier Valley-Highway 89. Richfield map.
Correctly spelled Grams.
Rudolph Grams (1863-1923) and his wife, Anna, were Richfield pioneers. (388~)

Granary Spring: (Wayne Co.) Robbers Roost Flats-Bluejohn Canyon. Robbers Roost Flats map.
Arthur Ekker noted that until about fifteen years ago (1940s then) Upper Blue John Spring was the common name for this spring. Then the Ekker family stopped providing grain storage for the seasonal sheep herders, so Carl Seeley and other sheepmen brought several granaries (large, metal, mouse-proof boxes) and a cabin to the spring. The name Granary Spring came into use to refer to the spring and sheep camp, and the name has been in local use ever since. (100~, 1084~, 1931~)

Grand Bench: (Kane Co.) Glen Canyon NRA-Glen Canyon. Gregory Butte, Gunsight Butte, Sit Down Bench, and Mazuki Point maps.
Edson Alvey: "A large, elevated, flat-topped bench on the west side of Fifty Mile Mountain, between Rock Creek and Last Chance. The name was derived from its large size." (55~)
In 1945 Arthur L. Crawford called it Wild Horse Bench: "a lofty platform covered with a fine growth of bunch grass.... Before us stretched a pageant of splendid desolation. Ineffably haunting and mysterious, the reaches of the river, with the beautiful side glens, revealed the rock heart of the chasmed desert.... To me this was the sublimest view ever experienced." (479~)
—Grand Neck Bench: (Blackburn Canyon and Mazuki Point maps.) This narrow jetty of land provides access to Grand Bench from the north. Inscriptions include J. Rix Heaps, 1939 and Arnold Davey, June 6, 1949. (SAPE.)

Grand Castle: (Iron Co.) Dixie National Forest-First Left Hand Canyon. Parowan map. (8,572')
Inez S. Cooper: "Grand Castle names the beautiful formations of rocks in Parowan's First Left Hand Canyon, about one-half mile beyond the Vermillion Castle Recreation area. It was named by Dr. James Talmadge. The rock formations remind one of two guards standing at the bottom of a large elaborately formed Grand Castle. Red,

pink, and grey rocks make up this unusual and beautiful formation." (942~)

Grand County:
The county seat is Moab.
Grand County was established in 1890 from Emery and Uintah counties. The county takes its name from the Grand (Colorado) River, which runs through it. (456~, 1932~)

Grand Flat: (San Juan Co.) Cedar Mesa-Highway 95. Kane Gulch map.
David E. Miller: "As the company [Hole-in-the-Rock Expedition of 1879-80] approached the base of Elk Ridge, the cedar [pinion and juniper] forest became more and more dense, requiring a crew of choppers to go in front to blaze a trail for the wagons. Natural clearings in this huge forest were called 'Flats,' such as Grand Flat." (1356~)

Grand Gulch: (Garfield Co.) Capitol Reef National Park-Glen Canyon NRA-Glen Canyon. Bitter Creek Divide, Wagon Box Mesa, The Post, Deer Point, Stevens Canyon North, and Hall Mesa maps.
Also called The Gulch (2013~) and Strike Valley (1374~). Halls Creek runs through Grand Gulch.
(See Halls Creek.)

Grand Gulch: (San Juan Co.) Cedar Mesa-San Juan River. Kane Gulch, Cedar Mesa North, Pollys Pasture, Red House Spring, and Slickhorn Canyon West maps.
Also called Box Canyon (1356~), Grand Cañon, and Grand Gorge (250~).
Also spelled Grande Gulch. (574~)
Kate B. Carter noted that this was named by Hole-in-the-Rock Expedition scouts George B. Hobbs, George Morrill, Lemuel Redd, and George Sevy in 1879. (352~) The Mormon pioneers noted that the canyon was so long and had so many arms that it took them far out of their way to get around it.
Platte D. Lyman of the Hole-in-the-Rock Expedition provided the first description of the canyon, in March 1880: "We found gulches with perpendicular banks 1000 feet high running from the extreme north 30 miles into the San Juan on the south ... we can make a passable road by following an old Indian trail." (1259~)
Richard Wetherill in 1896: "It is the most tortuous cañon in the whole of the Southwest, making bends from 200 to 600 yards apart almost its entire length or for 50 miles and each bend means a cave or overhanging cliff, all of these with an exposure to the sun had been occupied by either cliff houses or as burial places.... Ingress or egress is very difficult. There being not more than 5

or 6 places where even footmen can get in or out of the Cañon." (1993~)

H.L.A. Culmer in 1905: "The cliffs uprose higher than any we had yet seen on the trip—500, 800, 1000 ft. sheer, and the canyon so tortuous that we sometimes traveled half a mile to make 100 feet of direct distance. Strange shapes and grotesque faces varied the forms and huge cottonwood trees, hoary with age, twisted and bent in dragon writhings to add to the effect.... We have been in many canyons but Grand Gulch seems to have character of its own. It is rarely more than 200 feet wide at the bottom, sometimes only 15 feet and it winds like a wounded worm.... Today we rode many miles up Grand Gulch amid bewildering arrangements of crags and gorges, the lines growing heavier as we ascend, until they are cyclopean, titanic rather than fantastic. Cliffs with holes through them, cap rocks like tam-o-shanters, rim rocks far overhanging, cave seams with Moqui houses not all in ruins." (494~)

Nels C. Nelson of the Cartier American Museum of Natural History Expedition of 1920: "One of the least frequented and probably also one of the most inaccessible parts of the United States. A great rift in the earth, tortuous and fantastic, with mushroom or toadstool rocks, monuments of standing, seated, and bust figures, hats atilt, and every conceivable form and shape on which imagination seizes or turns into semblance of life." (1334~)

Hugh D. Miser hiked in the lower canyon in 1921: "[It] presents some of the wildest scenery along the San Juan. It is a dark, narrow canyon with vertical red walls several hundred feet in height at whose base lie heaps of huge boulders and great piles of driftwood. At the mouth of the gulch there stands a castle-like column of brown sandstone 400 feet high, whose position and form suggest that it is an ancient fortress guarding the approach to the gulch." (1370~)

Edward Abbey in 1989: "Reserved now as a refuge for wildlife, as a reservoir of clean air and water, as a preserve for human pleasure and adventure—true multiple use, in my opinion—Grand Gulch meanders for fifty miles through the sandstone off of Cedar Mesa to its outlet on the San Juan River. Within those fifty miles of slickrock walls, stone arches, rock art both natural and human, overhanging alcoves, and grassy benches of alluvium is one of the greatest displays of ancient cliff dwellings in the entire American Southwest." (2~)

James H. Knipmeyer: "Names and dates of many relic and pot-hunters were carved and written in charcoal in many of the prehistoric archaeological sites scattered along the length of the canyon including those of Charles McLoyd and C.C. Graham, the various Wetherill brothers, as well as members of the two expeditions to the canyon led by Richard Wetherill." (1115~)

—Primitive Area: Grand Gulch was designated as a Primitive Area in 1971, which ended all grazing in the canyon. (1901~) The Grand Gulch Archaeological District was listed on the National Register of Historic Places in 1982. These administrative designations do not give Grand Gulch permanent protection.

—Junction Spring: This is at the junction of Grand Gulch and Kane Gulch (Kane Gulch map).

—Stimper Arch: This is the "Natural Arch" that is in Grand Gulch just below the mouth of Kane Gulch (Kane Gulch map). James H. Knipmeyer: "Named in 1973 by a Bureau of Land Management ranger named Steve, along with a companion named Jim, and a dog called Pepper. A combination of parts of the three names forms 'Stimper.'" (1116~)

—Todie Canyon: The head of this eastern tributary of Grand Gulch is two miles southeast of Long Flat (south of elevation 6444T on the Cedar Mesa North map). (See Todie Flat—Todie Canyon.)

—Lion Track Spring: This is in Grand Gulch one and one-quarter miles (as the crow flies) downcanyon from the mouth of Todie Canyon (one-quarter mile northeast of elevation 6247T on the Cedar Mesa North map).

—Coyote Canyon: The mouth of this eastern tributary of Grand Gulch is two miles upcanyon from its junction with Bullet Canyon (one-half mile southeast of elevation 6109 on the Pollys Pasture map). (See Coyote Flat—Coyote Canyon.)

—Coyote Spring: This is a short distance up Coyote Canyon.

—The Thumb: This is on the north side of Grand Gulch one-quarter mile upcanyon from Sheiks Canyon (Pollys Pasture map).

—Sheiks Canyon: This eastern tributary of Grand Gulch is one mile upcanyon from its junction with Bullet Canyon (one-half mile north of elevation 6221 on the Pollys Pasture map). (See Sheiks Flat—Skeiks Canyon.)

—Green Mask Spring: This is a short distance up Sheiks Canyon. (See Sheiks Flat—Green Mask Spring.)

—Totem Pole: This is on the north side of Grand Gulch halfway between Green House and Step canyons (Pollys Pasture map).

—Bullet Canyon Spring: This is at the junction of Bullet Canyon and Grand Gulch (Pollys Pasture map). (See Bullet Canyon—Bullet Junction Spring.)

—Cow Tank Canyon: This northern tributary of Grand Gulch is the first canyon west of Dripping Canyon (Pollys Pasture map). Fred Blackburn noted that a stock trail ran the length of Cow Tank Canyon. The section near a large pour-off has disappeared. (250~) There is a constructed stock trail, though certainly not used by cattle, leading to large potholes and to the Cow Tank Spring area. (SAPE.)

—Cow Tank Spring: This is in the lower part of Cow Tank Canyon (one-quarter mile east of elevation 5528 on the Pollys Pasture map).

—Government Trail: This is the "Pack Trail" that enters the east side of Grand Gulch just south of the mouth of Pollys Canyon (Pollys Pasture map). The trailhead for the Government Trail is at a stock pond one-half mile east-southeast of elevation 5575. Eric Bayles: "The government built it, the government shot it in there." (168~) Brandt Hart noted that the trail is not quite drawn correctly on the map. (838~)

—Deer Canyon: This is the first eastern tributary of Grand Gulch that is south of Pollys Canyon (one-quarter mile east-northeast of elevation 5328T on the Red House Spring map). Deer Canyon is also north of elevation 5383 on the Pollys Pasture map.

—Big Pour Off Spring: This is in Grand Gulch three miles below the mouth of Pollys Canyon (one-quarter mile east-northeast of elevation 5455T on the Red House Spring map).

—Banister Spring: (Also spelled Bannister Spring.) This is in Grand Gulch one mile (as the crow flies) upcanyon from the mouth of Collins Canyon (one-quarter mile northwest of elevation 5338AT on the Red House Spring map). A nearby ruin has a banister.

—Red Man Canyon: This small northern tributary of Grand Gulch is one-half mile (as the crow flies) downcanyon from Water Canyon (immediately south of elevation 4932T on the Red House Spring map). The name comes from a nearby pictograph.

—Shangri-La Canyon: This eastern tributary of Grand Gulch is one and one-half miles (as the crow flies) upcanyon from the San Juan River (immediately north of elevation 4882 on the Slickhorn Canyon West map). (838~)

—Long-gone Rapid: Bert Loper: "In 1894 when I made this same trip [down the San Juan River] there was an impassable rapid at this place [the mouth of Grand Gulch] and I had been telling the boys that we were going to have much trouble ... now all we had to do was just drift peacefully past the canyon for all the huge boulders had disappeared." (1221~)

—Trimble Camp: This was at the mouth of a small southern tributary of the San Juan River one and one-half miles downriver from the mouth of Grand Gulch (north of elevation 4776 on the Slickhorn Canyon West map). The Kelly W. Trimble USGS Expedition of 1921 used this campsite. (1650~) Over the years it became a popular river camp. It was destroyed by a flash flood on Memorial Day, 2009. Energetic river runners have re-established the camp. (838~, SAPE.)

Grand Gulch Plateau: (San Juan Co.) Cedar Mesa-Grand Gulch. Kane Gulch and South Long Point maps. Although Grand Gulch Plateau is labeled on only two maps, by common usage it is a much larger area that goes from the Red House Cliffs to the west, Highway 95 to the north, Comb Wash to the east, and the San Juan River to the south. Locally, the Grand Gulch Plateau and Cedar Mesa names are interchangeable.

Grand Staircase: (Garfield, Iron, Kane, and Washington Counties, Utah and Coconino and Mohave Counties, Az.) Also called Giant Stairway. (1148~)

The Grand Staircase is a geological and geographic feature consisting of alternating bands of cliffs that start at the rim of the Grand Canyon in Arizona and end at the top of the Paunsaugunt Plateau in southern Utah. Each cliff band, of up to two thousand feet in height, is separated by a flat area or bench of from a couple of miles to close to twenty miles in width. The major cliff bands and flats, from south to north, include: Kaibab Plateau, Chocolate Cliffs, Shinarump Flats, Vermilion Cliffs, Wygaret Terrace, White Cliffs, Skutumpah Terrace, Gray Cliffs, Podunk Terrace, Sunset Cliffs, Pink Cliffs, and at the top, the Paunsaugunt Plateau. (1472~)

Francis M. Bishop of the 1871–72 Powell Expedition described the view as he traveled generally west from House Rock Valley to the Eightmile Gap area: "As we gained the summit and emerged from the timber a picture no artist's pencil could paint burst suddenly upon our vision. Down the dark green slope of Kaibab [Mountains] in undulating forests stretched away miles of pinon and cedar blending almost insensible with the valley stretching along north and south at the foot of the Mts. Across the valley some six or eight miles from out the silent plain rose line after line of cliffs, at first a series of pine and cedar hills; then a grander line of vermilion cliffs some four or five miles back, lifting their deep red walls a thousand feet or more and yet above and beyond these rose line after line of broken vert, ridges of buff, gray, red or vermilion cliffs variegated with long lines of dark green forest with a frost work of glittering snow, until all seemed to unite and center in the Skum-pah Mountains." (236~)

John Wesley Powell in 1873: "The faulting and folding of the rocks have, together with erosion, produced long lines of cliffs of a magnitude that is believed to be elsewhere unknown. These cliffs are bold escarpments, often hundreds or even thousands of feet high, great geographical steps, scores or hundreds of miles in length, presenting steep faces of rock, often quite vertical. Having climbed such a step, you descend by a gentle, sometimes imperceptible, slope to the foot of the next. There are thus presented several series of terraces, the steps to each of them being well-defined escarpments of rock." (1566~)

Frederick S. Dellenbaugh: "I shall never fail to see distinctly the wonderful view from the summit we had of the bewildering cliff-land leading away northward to the Pink Cliffs. The lines of cliffs rose up like some giant stairway." (551~)

John Wesley Powell described the Grand Staircase, a term he coined: "Place a book before you on a table with its front edge toward you, rest another book on the back of this, place a third on the back of the second, and in like manner a fourth on the third. Now the leaves of the books dip from you and the cut edges stand in tiny escarpments facing you. So the rock-formed leaves of these books of geology have the escarpment edges turned southward, while each book itself dips northward, and the crest of each plateau book is the summit of a line of cliffs." (1563~)

Leonard Herbert Swett in 1880: "Looking back across the ashy waste of Sage desert over which we had come [south from Kanab], the bright cliffs of Utah loomed up like frozen waves one above another, there being four layers in sight. The first, the Red, which Surround Kanab, The Second 8 or 10 miles beyond being white. The third, still farther being the Pink Cliffs of upper Kanab. Then rising sharp and blue just Beyond rises the divide whose summit forms a water shed between Salt lake Basin and the district drained by the Colorado." (1349~)

H.M. Cadell in 1887 called this The Terraces: "All the great physical features imprinted by the *subterranean* forces on the Grand Cañon District cross it in an approximately north and south direction. There is, however, another and equally distinct system of cliff lines at right angles to the first. These are cliffs of erosion, which have not been elevated into their present forms, but are the result of the long-continued action of subaërial agencies. As we go northwards from the brink of the Grand Cañon, parallel to the ledges that separate the minor plateaux, the land begins after a while to rise in a series of terraces

which form a great stair up to the High Plateaux of Utah." (328~)

Dr. Russell G. Frazier in the early 1940s: "For several years I have shouted from the mountain tops, 'this area should be set aside as a national monument,' in order that our children and children's children may have the pleasure of a pack trip through this beautiful desert country.... These wonders could be brought to all America with a little careful planning.... Where in all the world can so many of Nature's wonders be seen in so short a time." (674~)

Wallace Stegner in 1942: "Step by step, cliff-line by cliff-line, the terraces break off to the Colorado. Layers of rock thousands of feet thick have come off as neatly as layers of paint before a scraper. The further you get back from the Grand Canyon the more recent the layer, until you meet the top in the Bryce Canyon formations of the Paunsaugunt Plateau. You stand and contemplate that vast wreckage, and the wind blows sand against your ankles and you yell and step back as if the wind were a mower blade." (1826~)

Jonreed Lauritzen in 1947: "From the highest rim of Pink Cliffs to the bottom of the Grand Canyon the whole history of the earth's billion years is written plainly for geologists to read in the faces of the cliffs. But for us who seek a purely esthetic experience it is a magnificent tapestry woven in bright colors held together by the golden ecru threads of the Colorado River and its tributaries. Nowhere on the earth is there a wilder pattern of dramatic coloring and majesty than this." (1149~)

Grand Staircase Escalante National Monument: (Garfield and Kane Counties.)

Drawing on provisions of the Antiquities Act of 1906, President Bill Clinton proclaimed the Grand Staircase Escalante National Monument in September 1996. The monument encompasses three distinct physiographic areas: the Escalante Canyons, the Kaiparowits Plateau, and the combined Paria River drainages and the eastern section of the Grand Staircase. Breaking from tradition, President Clinton decided that the Bureau of Land Management, rather than the National Park Service, would have oversight of the new monument. The main headquarters are in Kanab, with smaller contact stations in Big Water, Tropic, and Escalante.

The first paragraph of the establishment proclamation, by President Bill Clinton, reads: "The Grand Staircase-Escalante National Monument's vast and austere landscape embraces a spectacular array of scientific and historic resources. This high, rugged, and remote region, where bold plateaus and multi-hued cliffs run for distances that defy human perspective, was the last place in the continental United States to be mapped. Even today, this unspoiled natural area remains a frontier, a quality that greatly enhances the monument's value for scientific study. The monument has a long and dignified human history: it is a place where one can see how nature shapes human endeavors in the American West, where distance and aridity have been pitted against our dreams and courage. The monument presents exemplary opportunities for geologists, paleontologists, archeologists, historians, and biologists."

Grand Valley: (Grand Co.) Colorado River-Book Cliffs.

The Grand Valley name is not used on the USGS 7.5 Minute Series maps, but it is used on larger scale USGS maps. It refers, in general, to the area between the Colorado River and the Book Cliffs and runs from Grand Junction, Colorado to Cisco, Utah. It is the seemingly endless flats on either side of Interstate 70. (See Cisco Desert.)

Grand View: (Grand Co.) Manti-LaSal National Forest-La Sal Mountains-Horse Mountain. Warner Lake map. (10,895')

Also called Grand View Mountain and Horse Mountain. (1931~)

Grand View Point: (San Juan Co.) Canyonlands National Park-Island in the Sky District. Monument Basin map. (6,297')

Arthur Ekker noted in 1951 that the original name was Grand River Point. (1931~)

The first time the name was used was in a 1961 article in *Desert Magazine* by Alfred Nestler: "On this 'island' [Island in the Sky] are hundreds of grand view points overlooking a vast sea of towering buttes, spires, mesas, canyons and distant mountain ranges in three states, filling the vast purple distance in every direction." (1435~)

—Government Trail: The trail from Grand View Point to the White Rim started as a sheep trail. It was named Government Trail after the area became a National Park in 1964. (239~, 277~)

Grand Wash: (Wayne Co.) Capitol Reef National Park-Capitol Reef-Fremont River. Fruita map.

Charles Kelly noted that the wash was named for its grand scenery and spectacular surroundings. (1047~)

Anne Snow noted that until E.C. Behunin built a road through nearby Capitol Wash in 1882, travel to the "lower country" (Blue Valley) was through Grand Wash and then along the Fremont River. (1786~)

—Singing Rock: Charles Kelly noted that this is "a large, but shallow concavity in the cliff in Grand Wash, giving

an unusual acoustical effect similar to that in the Mormon Tabernacle." (1047~) When Capitol Reef National Monument was designated, the ceremony was performed here.

—Cassidy Arch: This is the "Natural Arch" in Grand Wash that is one and one-half miles (as the crow flies) upcanyon from The Narrows. The outlaw Butch Cassidy is rumored to have had a cabin near here in the 1890s. (699~, 1072~, 1657~)

—Cassidy Cabin: This is on the north side of Grand Wash in the vicinity of elevation 5381. (SAPE.)

—Oyler Tunnel: (Also called Oyler Mine.) This was listed on the National Register of Historic Places in 1999. It is at the head of Grand Wash. H.J. McClellan and Thomas Pritchett filed for the original claim in 1901, calling it the Nightingale Claim. The next owners were Jack Butler and Tom Nixon. They worked the mine and built a couple of still-standing rock-walled buildings between 1904 and 1911. T.J. Jukes and Jacob Young bought the claim, but failed to keep up with the yearly development work. Michael Valentine "Tine" Oyler took over the mine in 1913. (700~, 1047~, 1671~)

—Behunin Cabin: This pioneer cabin is along Highway 24 one and one-half miles east of the mouth of Grand Wash (one-quarter mile east of elevation 5155). A plaque near the cabin tells the story of Elijah Cutlar Behunin (1847-1933) and family. The ten member family built the cabin in 1882. Several stayed in the house, others under nearby overhangs. (1551~) Ruby Noyes Tippets: "It was dobbed with mud and would withstand the rains and winds of this rough country. Poles were secured for the roof beams and rough boards were placed over these poles.... [Jane Behunin's] post bed almost filled one complete side of the room and the children had to sit outside on the sandy bank of the river to play. The family ate meals outside.... This was a life of luxury for the Behunin family ... a roof over their heads, a fireplace to cook in, and a water supply right by the door." (1891~) They stayed for about two years. After floods wiped out their garden, the family moved to Notom, a town they had already briefly lived in. (1657~)

—Corral Canyon: Charles Kelly: "[It is] a short blind canyon opening on the Dirty Devil [Fremont] River below the mouth of Grand Wash. Outlaws from Robbers Roost, including 'Silver Tip' used to corral their horses here when passing through the country." (1047~) There are a couple of possible locations for this canyon.

Grange Hole: (Emery Co.) Manti-LaSal National Forest-Huntington Creek. Rilda Canyon map.

Also called Ray Grange Canyon.

Ray Grange (1885-1927) ran livestock in the canyon in the early days. (1330~)

Granite Creek: (Garfield and Wayne Counties.) Henry Mountains-Beaver Canyon. Mount Ellen, Raggy Canyon, Bull Mountain, and Baking Skillet Knoll maps.

Also called Granite Wash.

Barbara Ekker: "This stream originates on the northeast slopes of Mount Ellen in the Henry Mountains south of Hanksville. It drains northeast into Granite Wash and receives its name from the granite ridges near its source." (607~)

—Granite Ranch: PRIVATE PROPERTY. (Also called Buhr Ranch.) This is on Granite Creek at Granite Spring one and one-quarter miles northwest of Goatwater Spring (one-half mile north of elevation 5178T on the Bull Mountain map). Barbara Ekker: "This historic ranch on the northeast side of the Henry Mountains was originally a 'way station' for travelers going to the Colorado River in search of gold or to the mineral outcroppings in the Henry Mountains." (607~) Granite Spring was the only reliable water source along the forty mile route.

The ranch was started by J.B. Buhr in about 1889. Buhr was friendly with the local outlaws, giving the ranch the transient name of Robbers Roost. (1750~) Buhr left the area and the ranch went to Cornelius and Edna Ekker. Nelius was a mail rider from 1910 to 1914 for the high wage of one dollar a day. He sold the ranch in 1926. It is now owned by a group from Idaho. (607~, 1644~) (See Burr Desert.)

—The Jump: Charles B. Hunt: "Named for ledge crossed by Granite Creek." (925~) The ledge is on upper Granite Creek (northwest of elevation 7882 on the Raggy Canyon map). (SAPE.)

Granite Knolls: (Garfield Co.) Dog Valley-Granite Valley. Fremont Pass map.

—Granite Pond: Lying just south of the appropriately-named Granite Knolls, Granite Pond is a still-used stock reservoir. (SAPE.)

Granite Mountain: (Iron Co.) Swett Peak-Iron Springs. Cedar City NW map. (6,725')

Indians call this *To-no-quitch-i-wunt*, or "Little Black Mountains." (1512~)

Grapevine Pass: (Washington Co.) Virgin River-Interstate 15. Harrisburg Junction map. (3,200')

Also called Grapevine Sand. (1447~)

The 1873 H.H. Lloyd map shows this, mistakenly, as "Grape Vineyard." (M.40.)

This was the site of the pioneer road across the Black Dike (usually called Washington Black Ridge), a major obstacle to early settlers. (1142~) The area was a nightmare to cross with wagons. Albert E. Miller: "To cross the Grapevine sand, one wagon could be left while its team was hooked onto another outfit, then both teams going back for the wagon left behind. In this way the deep sand could be crossed." (1354~)

Grace Woodbury: "Later the family living at Grapevine Springs built a road across the sands, of logs, bark, clay and straw and charged persons who used it, twenty-five cents for the privilege." (353~)

—Grapevine Spring: (Also spelled Grape Vine Spring.) (704~) This spring is in Grapevine Pass. John D. Lee in 1851: "These springs boil up at the foot of a large sand mound and moisten about one acre of land, which is completely interlocked with vines." (2043~) Thomas D. Brown of the Southern Indian Mission of 1854 called it Grapevine Spring. (306~) Mary Minerva Dart Judd on a trip in 1856: "We passed a spring where wild grapevines were growing luxuriantly. The spot has since been known as Grapevine Springs." (367~)

George Peter Pectol: "The next summer 26 July 1869 my father [George Pectol] walked from Washington to Toquerville and back, a distance of about 70 miles. On his return home he drank water from a cool spring known as Grapevine spring. This was the beginning of his last illness as it affected him immediately.... He died." (318a~)

Grapevine Spring: (Washington Co.) Zion National Park-Left Fork Great West Canyon. The Guardian Angels map.

This is a very large spring. (SAPE.)

Grapevine Wash: (Washington Co.) Pine Valley Mountains-Virgin River. Pintura and Hurricane Wash maps.

Wild grapes grow in the canyon. (1038~)

This was also called Dipping Pen Wash. The dipping vats, used by sheep to eliminate scabies, were in upper Grapevine Wash. (1931~)

Grasshopper Mine: (Piute Co.) Fishlake National Forest-Tushar Mountains. Mount Belknap map.

The Grasshopper Mine was located in 1890.

—Grasshopper Creek: The Grasshopper Mine is at the head of Grasshopper Creek on Grasshopper Flat. (1934~)

Grass Lakes: (Garfield Co.) Dixie National Forest-Escalante Mountains. Grass Lakes map.

Sonny King: "In the spring the Grass Lakes have quite a lot of water. Later on in the summer, the cattle graze out there on that old lake bottom." (1095~)

Grass Valley: (Iron Co.) Hurricane Cliffs-Parowan Canyon. Parowan map.

William Lowder noted that lots of grass could be found here. (1515~) William G. Rowley noted that in the early years the small boys from Parowan would herd their cattle to Grass Valley in the spring. (363~)

Grass Valley: (Piute and Sevier Counties.) Grass Valley-Otter Creek. Burrville, Koosharem, Greenwich, Abes Knoll, and Parker Knoll maps.

Also called Coyote.

Also spelled Grassvalley.

Anne Snow noted that the valley was traversed by the William Wolfskill Expedition of 1830–31. (1786~)

The Utah Territorial Militia reconnoitered the area in 1866. William B. Pace of the expedition: "We came out into Grass Valley. This valley is about 50 or 60 miles long runing North and South by 8 or 10 wide, and was reported as the headquarters of all Maurading Indians." (1501~)

The Franklin B. Woolley map of 1866 shows this as Otter or Grass Valley Creek (475~) and the Froiseth map of 1871 shows it as Grass Valley. (M.20.)

George Washington Bean was with an exploring party sent by Brigham Young in 1873: "We camped on the spot where Burrville is now located. Here we noticed the prettiest natural meadows that I ever saw and there was bunch-grass all over the hills. Hence we named the place Grass Valley." (749~)

The first to settle the area were George Washington Bean and Albert King Thurber. In 1940 George Bean's son, George T., wrote of the initial settling of the area: "At the closing of the Indian war [the Black Hawk War] affecting this portion of the State, some of the Indians were more or less restless and dissatisfied, particularly the young Indians, and they longed to eat some more 'Mormon' Beef and ride Mormon horses, and continued to commit more depredations against the settlers, thereby making all uncertain and it was feared a general outbreak might again occur, thereby compelling the people to abandon their homes and move away again for an indefinite period. Whereupon PRESIDENT Brigham Young called my father, Geo. W. Bean and A.K. Thurber as missionaries to come and settle near and labor among them in the interest of Peace and harmony, and suggested Grass valley a

good place to settle, at least for a time, as there was 3 or four bands of Indians within easy reach of that section who were obstreperous and threatening." (173~)

In the 1870s Grass Valley was also called Co-op Valley because a couple of cooperative herds were grazed here. (469~)

Jean S. Greenwood: "There is a bit of magic in the term 'Grass Valley,' an allure of inviting romance, a touch of daring, yet with an undercurrent of peace and security." (1194~)

Garn Jefferies told this story about his grandfather, Thomas Jefferies, trailing sheep through Grass Valley in the early days: "He took [his sheep] to Grass Valley, which is pretty high country, on a Sunday. He had his herder ring the sheep in there. And here came a snowstorm and he kept pushin' and pushin' them. There was a lot of tall brush in there and the sheep piled up and he lost 298 sheep there that night. Smothering." (959~)

—Grass Valley Massacre: Leland Hargrave Creer: "A party of young Navajo in 1873 went to the east fork of the Sevier River to trade with some Utes in the neighborhood. In Grass Valley they encountered a severe storm and took refuge in a vacant home belonging to a rancher named McCarty. The Navajo, becoming hungry because of the delay, killed a small calf belonging to the ranch, who in turn, without giving the Indians an opportunity of explaining their circumstances, killed three of them and wounded a fourth." (487~) The Indians, ready to retaliate, were stopped by Jacob Hamblin.

—Old Spanish Trail: (Variation.) The Old Spanish Trail—Fishlake Route—descended from Fish Lake into Grass Valley. Following Otter Creek, the trail then joined the East Fork Sevier River and went on to Junction. (477~)

Grass Valley: (Washington Co.) Dixie National Forest-Pine Valley Mountains. Grass Valley map.

Andrew Jenson: "From the earliest time Grass Valley was used as a pasture for the stock belonging to the settlements of the surrounding country." (972~)

—Rencher Ranch: Umpstead Rencher (1823-1881) was one of the first to farm and ranch in Grass Valley. He arrived in the mid-1860s. (1141~)

Grassy Hollow: (Kane Co.) Pink Cliffs-Long Valley. Strawberry Point, Long Valley Junction, and Glendale maps.

Also called Grass Canyon (767~) and Grassy Canyon.

Julius S. Dalley in 1942: "Named for nature of pasturage—abundance of grass." (2053~) The United Order owned land in the canyon in the 1880s. (349~)

Grassy Trail Creek: (Emery Co.) Book Cliffs-Cedar Mountain-Price River. Sunnyside, Sunnyside Junction, Mounds, Cedar, and Grassy maps.

Also called Cottonwood Creek. (1931~)

(See Whitmore Canyon for name derivation.)

The name was in place by 1878. (1567~)

—USGS Mistake: It should be noted that on the Mounds map Grassy Trail Creek is shown, incorrectly, as Cottonwood Creek.

—Grassy Trail Reservoir: (Sunnyside map.) This stock reservoir was built in 1952. (1490~)

Grassy Trail Oil and Gas Field: (Emery Co.) Cedar Mountain-Highway 191. Mounds map.

This field was brought online in 1961.

Grassy Wash: (Emery Co.) Book Cliffs-Price River. Lila Point, Cedar, Grassy, and Woodside maps.

This is a different wash than the Grassy Trail Creek noted above.

Unattributed: "A broad valley and a few springs of grass is good for the name of GRASSY." (606~) The name was in place by 1878. (584~)

—Grassy: (Grassy map.) (Also called Grassy Trail.) This was a switching station on the Denver and Rio Grande Western Railroad. In the 1880s, the rail route from Green River to Price was often termed the "Grassy Trail" route, named for the nearby creek. (710~) (See Denver and Rio Grande Western Railroad.)

Gravel Canyon: (San Juan Co.) Dark Canyon Plateau-White Canyon. Black Steer Canyon, The Cheesebox, and Jacobs Chair maps.

Gravel is found throughout the canyon's lower end. (1821~)

Ginger Harmon described a descent of the canyon in 1992: "I clawed, contorted, chimneyed, groveled, grabbed, giggled, got belayed, pressed, paddled, prayed, raced, rappelled, raved, swam, squeezed, slithered, slipped, slid, shimmied, straddled, stemmed, sometimes actually walked, saw the reliquiae of the ancient ones, and emerged from the mouth of the canyon worn-out, ragged, and happy." (46~)

—Gravel Crossing: (Jacobs Chair map.) This is one of four named crossings of White Canyon. (The others are Duckett Crossing, Soldier Crossing, and Outlaw Crossing.) It was in use by cowboys by the early 1880s. A very old building near the crossing, now a ruin, was used by cowboys as a line camp from the earliest days. (690~) Inscriptions include HML. It is believed that these are the initials of Henry M. Lyman. (1115~, SAPE.)

Gravel Spring: (Kane Co.) Dixie National Forest-Highway 89. Long Valley Junction map.

Discovered by Royal Cutler in 1881, the spring is in a gravel bed. (2053~)

—Gravel Spring Ranch: This historic ranch was near Gravel Spring. Although not started by Allen Joseph Stout, he was the owner in the mid-1890s. (1191~)

Gray Canyon: (Emery and Grand Counties.) Book Cliffs-Green River. Three Fords Canyon, Butler Canyon, Tusher Canyon, and Blue Castle Butte maps.

The Gray Canyon section of the Green River starts at Three Fords Canyon and ends at Green River Town. It is about thirty-five miles long. (200~, 551~, 1821~)

The canyon was named by John Wesley Powell for the dominant color of its walls. Other names came first. In 1869 Powell called it Coal Canyon for coal beds found there. In 1871 he changed the name to Lignite Canyon and, in 1872, to its present name of Gray Canyon. (269~)

Jack Hillers of the 1871–72 Powell Expedition: "It is God's country, for man don't want it." (884~)

Emery Kolb in 1911: "While the 1st part of the canyon is well named [Desolation Canyon] I do not approve of the name being carried down the whole 97 miles as from the middle of it to the end [Gray Canyon] is one of the finest of all the series in scenic beauty. Innumerable forms of every conceivable creature could be seen with the use of very little imagination." (1125~)

—Gray Canyon: This is the name used by Senator Barry Goldwater for the stretch of the Green River from Green River Town to the start of Labyrinth Canyon: "The river from Green river to LABYRINTH Canyon below here is very quiet, wide and in some places quite shallow. It runs in Gray Canyon which isn't much of a canyon—walls slope back and rise to a height, so far, of about 200 feet." (738~)

Gray Knoll: (Washington Co.) Little Creek Mountain-Little Creek. Little Creek Mountain map. (5,511')

Herbert E. Gregory: "A group of springs that issues from the base of the Shinarump conglomerate south of Gray Knoll feeds a wooden pipe 4 miles long with 14 gallons a minute." (767~)

Grays Pasture: (San Juan Co.) Canyonlands National Park-Island in the Sky District. Musselman Arch map.

Ken Allred: "Gray's Pasture, out beyond the Neck, is named that because the [Delbert] Taylors had a big gray stud who ran there." (197~, 1429~)

Gray Whiskers: (Navajo Co., Az.) Navajo Indian Reservation-Mitchell Mesa. Mystery Valley, Az. map. (6,385')

Also called Gray Whiskers Butte.

Laurance D. Linford noted that the Navajo name is *Dághaa' Libái,* or "Gray Whiskers." (1204~)

Greasewood Draw: (Emery Co.) San Rafael Swell-San Rafael River. Arsons Garden and Greasewood Draw maps.

Greasewood, or *Sarcobatus vermiculatus,* is a bush that was used by pioneers for firewood. It is a member of the pigweed family, which also counts shadscale as a member. It is an important forage plant for cattle. (887~, 1341~)

—Hatts Pond: This stock pond is one-half mile north of Greasewood Draw and two miles east-northeast of Greasewood Tank (one-eighth mile west of elevation 4302 on the Greasewood Draw map). The historic Hatt Ranch is nearby. (See San Rafael River—Hatt Ranch for name derivation.)

—Shinarump Canyon: This northern tributary of Greasewood Draw is three-quarters of a mile north of Greasewood Tank (at elevation 4582T on the Greasewood Draw map).

—Three Finger Canyon: This northern tributary of Greasewood Draw is two miles north Greasewood Tank (one-eighth mile south of elevation 5133T on the Greasewood Draw map).

Greasewood Flat: (Emery Co.) Castle Valley-Cedar Mountain. Cleveland map.

(See Greasewood Draw for name derivation.)

Great Arch, The: (Washington Co.) Zion National Park-Pine Creek. Springdale East map.

Also called Great Arch of Zion. (2080~)

This is not a true arch, but a "blind" arch; there is no gap at the top of the arch. (481~)

—Canyon Overlook Trail: This short trail goes from Highway 9 to the top of The Great Arch. It was built in 1932. (1038~)

Great Bend: (San Juan Co.) Glen Canyon NRA-Navajo Indian Reservation-San Juan River. Alcove Canyon map.

This is the longest loop on the San Juan River. The Writers' Program of 1941: "At the Great Bend the river makes a nine-mile loop and returns to within a half a mile of its starting point. At the west end of this loop the Colorado [River] is only 5 miles away, but the San Juan travels 34 miles before the two streams meet." (2056~)

—Great Bend Dam Site: (Proposed.) This dam on the San Juan River was proposed by the Bureau of Reclamation in 1946. (78~)

Greatheart Mesa: (Washington Co.) Zion National Park-Guardian Angel Pass. The Guardian Angels map. (7,405')

Unattributed: "Named for Christiana's guide in the story of Pilgrims Progress." (2053~)

—Rams Peak: This is three-quarters of a mile north of the top of Greatheart Mesa. It was named for canyon hiker Steve "Ram" Ramras. (1591~)

—The Hourglass: This is one mile east of the top of Greatheart Mesa (at elevation 7205). (1591~)

Great Sage Plain: (San Juan Co., Utah and Dolores and San Miguel Counties, Colo.)

This huge area has no official border. It is generally the comparatively flat area between the San Juan Mountains of Colorado and the Abajo Mountains of Utah. It is not shown on USGS maps, but the name was and is in common use and is used in this book.

The first to use the name was John Strong Newberry of the Captain John N. Macomb Expedition of 1859: "As we stood on its threshold we looked far out over a great plain, to the eye as limitless as the sea; the monotonous outline of its surface varied only by two or three small island-like mountains, so distant as scarcely to rise above the horizon line. Here we were to leave the lofty sierras of the Rocky Mountain system, which had so long looked down on our camps and marches ... and take our weary way across the arid expanse of the great western plateau; a region whose dreary monotony is only broken by frightful chasms, where alone the weary traveler finds shelter from the burning heat of a cloudless sun, and where he seeks, too often in vain, a cooling draught that shall slake his thirst. To us, however, as well as to all the civilized world, it was a *terra incognita,* and was viewed with eager interest, both as the scene of our future explorations and as the possible repository of truth which we might gather and add to the sum total of human knowledge.... It is called the Great Sage-plain." (1266~)

Ferdinand V. Hayden of the Hayden Survey of 1872–74 noted this as the Great Sage Plain on his expedition map: "This whole portion of the country is now and must ever remain utterly worthless. It has no timber, very little grass, and no water." (848~)

In 1885 R. McDonald used the name Piute Mesa: "Piute Mesa extends from the eastern base of the Blue Mountains [Abajo Mountains] in Utah to the Canyon of the Dolores in Colorado, and from Dry Valley to the breaks of the San Juan.... The Mesa is covered with a sort of blue grass and mountain bunch grass, and all cattlemen have to do is to fence a section and they have the finest hay meadow on the Pacific slope. The Mesa at present supports 50,000 head of cattle, 15,000 of these belong to Carlisle Bros." (1328~)

Ward J. Roylance: "Monotonously level and gently rolling to the eye, the vast plain is incised by a network of shallow to deepening channels draining into the canyons of Montezuma, McElmo and Recapture creeks.... It is used as winter range for livestock and much of it is dry-farmed, with pinto beans and grains being important crops." (1658~)

—Books: Zane Grey used the Great Sage Plain country, in part, as the backdrop for his novel *Riders of the Purple Sage*. (784~, 1336~)

Great Wall, The: (Grand Co.) Arches National Park-Arches Road. The Windows Section map.

This is named for its four mile length. (898~)

There are three distinct formations along the Great Wall.

—The Lovers. This is toward the south end and looks like two people standing next to each other.

—The Poodle: This is toward the north end near the "Natural Arch" (southeast of elevation 4965T). It looks like a poodle.

—The Phallus: This is immediately north of The Poodle. (898~)

Great West Canyon: (Washington Co.) Zion National Park-Left Fork North Creek. The Guardian Angels map.

The upper part of Left Fork North Creek goes through Great West Canyon. (See North Creek—Washington Co.)

Great Western Trail:

This trail picks a tortuous route from Mexico to Canada. Along the way it goes through Arizona, New Mexico, Utah, Wyoming, Montana, and Idaho. Different pieces of the trail are open to hikers, mountain bikers, horseback riders, and off-road vehicles. (337~) The trail is not shown on the USGS 7.5 Minute Series maps. One does see signs along the highways in southern Utah pointing to access points along the trail.

Great White Throne, The: (Washington Co.) Zion National Park-Zion Canyon. Temple of Sinawava map. (6,744')

Angus M. Woodbury noted that this was named by Dr. Frederick Vining Fischer in 1916. Fischer in a letter to Woodbury: "Never have I seen such a sight before. It is by all odds America's masterpiece. Boys, I have looked for this mountain all my life but I never expected to find it in this world. This mountain is the Great White Throne." (2043~)

Clarence Dutton of the Powell Survey: "Directly in front of us a complex group of white towers, springing from a central pile, mounts upwards to the clouds. Out of their midst, and high over all, rises a dome-like mass, which dominates the entire landscape. It is almost pure white, with brilliant streaks of carmine descending its vertical walls.... It is impossible to liken this object to any familiar shape, for it resembles none. Yet its shape is far from being indefinite; on the contrary, it has a definiteness and individuality which extort an exclamation of surprise when first beheld. There is no name provided for such an object, nor is it worth while to invent one. Call it a dome; not because it has the ordinary shape of such a structure, but because it performs the function of a dome." (585~)

LeRoy Jeffers in 1922: "In nobility it ranks among the world's greatest rocks." (960~)

R.B. Gray in 1927: "Most spectacular of all of Zion's temples of stone and 'one of the world's great rocks,' is the Great White Throne, often called El Gobernador in honor of a former governor of Utah. This colossal butte, hewn completely away from the east wall of the canyon rises from a base of maroon and vermilion sandstone that fades into a rosy buff, while the upper half of the structure is ivory, pale buff and white. From some viewpoints its shape suggests a truncated pyramid or an immense wedge; from the north its appearance is that of a flattened dome." (754~)

—First Ascent: In 1927 W.H.W. Evans made a solo ascent of the monolith, becoming the first person to make the climb. On the way down, he slipped and fell, knocking himself unconscious. Rangers found him several days later and were able to rescue him.

Juanita Brooks described the first ascent: "a seasoned mountain climber proud of his achievements in the Alps and other high mountains of the world. He would win added fame by being the first to reach the top of this for one night his signal fire glowed on top of the crest, and that was all. Searching parties were sent out, airplanes flew over. It was futile, for the man had disappeared completely and the mountain stood in silent disdain of their puny efforts." (293~)

Green Hollow: (Iron Co.) Cedar Mountain-Interstate 15. Cedar Mountain and Cedar City maps. PRIVATE PROPERTY.

Zella B. Matheson noted that a Cedar City doctor, Earnest F. Green, used the water from the lake to irrigate his fields. (942~)

Green Lake: (Garfield Co.) Dixie National Forest-Boulder Mountain. Deer Creek Lake map.

Pratt Gates: "There's a lot of undergrowth in it that makes it look thick and dark green." (709~)

Green River: (Utah counties north to south: Daggett, Uintah, Carbon, Emery, Grand, Wayne, and San Juan.) The Green River starts on Fremont Peak in the Wind River Mountains of Wyoming and ends where it joins the Colorado River at The Confluence.

The river has had many names.

The Navajo name is *Tó Dootl'izhi*. (983~)

The Ute name for the upper Green River is *Ka'na*, or "bitterroot." (1175~)

The Domínguez-Escalante Expedition of 1776–77 noted that Crow Indians called it the *Seeds-Kee-dee Agie*, or "Prairie Hen River," a name in common use until about 1840. (1175~, 2049~)

The Spaniards gave it the name *Rio San Buenadventura*, or "River of Good Travel." They also called it *Rio Santa Cruz*. (48~, 261~, 463~) An article in the *Missouri Gazette* of May 15, 1813 noted it as the Colorado or Spanish river. (2049~)

Rufus Wood Leigh: "Green River was generally known to Americans during the trapper era—1820–1839—as the Spanish River." (1175~)

The General William Henry Ashley Expedition of 1825 gave a now disavowed derivation. C.B. Coutant in 1899: "Ashley ... with his little band he pushed forward to Spanish River, the name of which he promptly changed to Green River, after one of his St. Louis partners. It has been claimed by several historians that the name of this river comes from the color of its waters; be that as it may, General Ashley named it." (458~)

Trapper Daniel Potts called it the *Leichadu* in 1827. (1385~)

John C. Fremont traversed the area in 1848: "The refreshing appearance of the broad river, with its timbered shores and green-wooded islands, in contrast to its dry sandy plains, probably obtained for it the name of Green River, which was bestowed on it by the Spaniards, who first came into this country to trade some twenty-five years ago. It was then familiarly known as the Seeds-kedèe-agie, or Prairie Hen (Tetrao urophasianus) River; a name which is received from the Crows, to whom its upper waters belong, and on which this bird is still very abundant. By the Shoshone and Utah Indians, to whom belongs, for a considerable distance below, the country where we were now traveling, it was called the Bitter-root River, from the great abundance in its valley of a plant which affords them one of their favorite roots. Lower down, from Brown's Hole to the southward, the river runs through lofty chasms, walled in by precipices of *red rock*; and even among the wilder tribes who inhabit that portion of its course I have heard it called, by Indian refugees from the Californian settlements, the *Rio Colorado*." (683~)

While Fremont attributed the name to the green plant life, Hiram Martin Chittenden noted in 1902 that "This does not seem unreasonable, although some who are well acquainted with the characteristics of the river are more inclined to attribute the name to the appearance of the water, which is a very pronounced green, than to the foliage of the valley, which is in no marked degree different from that along other streams in this locality." (422~)

The Lieutenant Edward F. Beale Expedition of 1853 called it both the Upper Colorado and the Green River Fork of the Great Colorado. Gwinn Harris Heaps of that expedition, while camped near present-day Green River, Utah: "The scenery on its banks was grand and solemn." (855~)

The Captain John W. Gunnison Expedition of 1853 called it both the Green River and by its Indian name, *Akanaquint* (1089~), a name that was in use until at least 1875. (M.65.)

The H.H. Lloyd map of 1872 shows it as the Green River Fork of the Colorado River. (M.40.)

The Writers' Program of 1941: "It is a wolf in sheep's clothing, hiding behind a bland and limpid surface its turbulent upstream past, and giving no hint of its crashing, thrusting, downstream future." (2056~)

Green River Cutoff Road: (Emery Co.) San Rafael Swell-Cedar Mountain. Maps west to east: Hadden Holes, Buckhorn Reservoir, Bob Hill Knoll, Chimney Rock, Dry Mesa, and Cliff.

Also called Dry Mesa Truck Trail.

This road between Castle Dale and Green River ran under the south side of Cedar Mountain. It was fifty percent shorter than taking the main road through Price. The road, a rough track dating from the early days, was improved by the CCC in 1938. (710~, 2053~) Although the road has been steadily improved over the years, it is still a dirt road that can be impassable when wet.

—Old Spanish Trail: The route of the Green River Cutoff Road was a part of the Old Spanish Trail. Bert J. Silliman noted that the Elk Mountain Mission of 1855 was told of this route by the Ute Indians. It was called the Old Trail as it probably predated the Old Spanish Trail. (1734~)

Green River Desert: (Emery and Grand Counties.) (See Gunnison Valley.)

Green River Gap: (Grand Co.) Book Cliffs-Gunnison Valley. Hatch Mesa map.

This pass between Hatch Mesa to the south and Horse Mesa to the north was used as a shortcut by stockmen going from the Floy Wash/Trough Springs area to Green River. A well-worn stock trail goes through the gap. (SAPE.)

The Colonel William Wing Loring Expedition of 1857-58 went through the gap. (1545~) Loring: "Road runs between two rocky buttes, and strikes the [Old Spanish Trail]." (1276~)

Green River Overlook: (San Juan Co.) Canyonlands National Park-Island in the Sky District. Upheaval Dome map. (6,000')

—Movies: A short scene from *The Greatest Story Ever Told* was filmed at Green River Overlook. (1421~)

Green River State Recreation Area: (Emery Co.) Gunnison Valley-Green River. Green River map.

Also called Green River State Park.

This fifty-three acre park was established in 1965. Besides a campground, the park provides boat access to the Green River.

Green River Town: (Emery and Grand Counties.) Green River-Gunnison Valley-Interstate 70. Green River map.

Also called Green River Crossing, Green River Station, Green River Village, Gunnison Crossing, Old Trapper Ford, and Spanish Crossing.

Also spelled Greenriver.

The site of Green River Town was first used in 1876 when H. Elwyn Blake, Sr. established a mail relay station on the east side of the river. Blake also operated a ferry from that location. The first permanent resident was John Thomas "Tom" Farrer, Sr. whom, with family, arrived in 1879. May Belle Dahling Harper Phillips, paraphrasing the daughter of John Thomas Farrer, Sr., Beatrice Farrer Dahling: "[She] talked of building their homes of willows, when they first came into the Green River Valley. They called it Willow Boweries, and most houses had a double wall in some part of the house as a hide-out against outlaws and Indians." (1536~)

The town was initially called Blake, Blake Station, or Blake City, as was its counterpart on the west side of the river. (366~, 1780~) In 1895 the town was renamed. West Blake was named Greenriver. The one word spelling was to distinguish it from Green River, Wyoming. East Blake was named Elgin by resident George W. Durant who came from Elgin, Illinois. By the early 1920s the town of Elgin was all but abandoned. The old townsite is one mile

to the southeast of the present-day bridge in Green River Town. (125~, 1780~)

The coming of the Denver and Rio Grande Western Railroad in 1881–83 helped bolster the town's economy. It became a center for rail crews and a railroad bridge across the river made the town important to commerce. (346~, 580~, 606~, 644~, 710~, 1563~) During the gold boom in Glen Canyon and the San Juan River in the 1890s the town was called the Gateway to San Juan.

Buzz Holmstrom in 1937: "[it] is the most miserable dilapidated one-horse town I ever saw." (903~)

—Riverside Siding: This siding was used by work crews during the construction of the original railroad bridge across the Green River in 1883. The site has disappeared. (1547~) (See Denver and Rio Grande Western Railroad.)

—Railroad Bridge: The first bridge across the Green River was completed in 1883. Joanne Ekker: "The bridge ... was somewhat under-constructed for the weight of the steam engines so the engine would drop its passenger cars and they would be physically pushed across the bridge and reconnected to another engine on the other side"! (621~)

—Green River Crossing: (Also called Gunnison Crossing, Old Spanish Trail Crossing, Old Ute Crossing, and Ute Crossing.) This prehistoric and historic crossing of the Green River was a short distance north of town. The exact crossing location can only be guessed at. The river channel has changed considerably over the past one hundred or more years. (In 1938, there was a boundary dispute in Green River between Grand and Emery counties because the river channel had changed from a half to a full mile over the years.)

William Lewis Manly, after running the Green River from Flaming Gorge, exited the canyon here in 1849. (1274~) Other notable early explorers crossing here included William Wolfskill and George C. Yount in 1830–31, trapper Denis Julien in the mid-1830s, and John C. Fremont in 1848.

Captain John W. Gunnison in 1853: "The river is 300 yards wide, with a pebbly bottom, as we forded it, but with quicksands on either side of our path. The water, rising just above the axletrees of our common wagons, flows with a strong current, and is colored by the red sandstone of the country through which it passes.... A fine field of blue-grass in a grove of cottonwood just above the ford." (1089~)

Frederick S. Dellenbaugh of the 1871–72 Powell Expedition: "Gunnison Crossing was the great Indian highway. All trails converged with that place because they couldn't cross the river farther down, except at the Crossing of the Fathers." (552~, 580~)

The first ferry across the river was built by the town's first settler, John Thomas Farrer, Sr., in 1879. In the early 1880s Robert Hatrich also built a ferry across the river. The ferry operations continued under various owners until the first highway bridge was built in 1910–11. (468~)

—First Utah Oil Well: In 1891 the first oil well drilled in Utah was just south of Green River Town on the east side of the Green River. (471~)

—Butterfly Bend: This bend of the Green River is two miles south of Green River Town (one-half mile east of elevation 4362T on the Green River map). (121~)

—Butterfly Bar: This river bar or bottom is on the east side of Butterfly Bend. (1462~)

—Green River Melons: Green River Town is justifiably famous for its melons. An unattributed government document from 1913 presaged this: "The Green River city fruit belt has long been famed for its peaches, pears, apples, grapes and other fruit. However, the enterprising citizens of this section have found a new field for their energy and are giving especial attention to the growing of cantaloupes and watermelons, particularly winter melons. A person who has ever had the privilege of eating a Green River cantaloupe has had his taste spoiled for life—that is, for eating a cantaloupe grown elsewhere." (1815~)

Greens Canyon: (Sevier Co.) Manti-LaSal National Forest-Wasatch Plateau-Muddy Creek. Heliotrope Mountain and Flagstaff Peak maps.
Also called Greens Hollow.
Wayne Gremel: "It was named for someone named Green from Sanpete County. They ran cattle there." (780~)

Green Spring: (Washington Co.) Virgin River-Mill Creek. Washington map.
Also called The Green.
John D. Lee told Brigham Young about the spring and how good it was. (329~) Andrew Karl Larson: "Its waters were on relatively high ground and could be stored up with a minimum effort." (1141~) Water from the spring was ditched to the Mill Ponds on Mill Creek for use at the Cotton Factory and gristmill. (329~)

Greenwater Spring: (San Juan Co.) Mancos Mesa-Castle Wash-Highway 276. Clay Hills map. PRIVATE PROPERTY.
(See Irish Green Spring for name derivation.)
The Hole-in-the-Rock Expedition used the spring in 1880, calling it Green Water. Expedition member George B. Hobbs: "after traveling about 15 miles to the so-called Green Water." (1356~)

Charles L. Bernheimer noted in July 1929 that the spring was named "because there was [some] green vegetation." (249~) Val Dalton noted that a nearby overhang was used by generations of cowboys as a line camp. (517~)
Inscriptions include one that states: "This is the Country Where the Coyotes Bark at Strangers." (1115~, 1451~)

Greenwich Town: (Piute Co.) Grass Valley-Box Creek-Highway 62. Greenwich map.
Also called Box Creek (1458~) and Greenville (M.56.).
Also spelled Greenwick. (972~)
A. Vernaldo Hatch: "Greenwich is an Indian name and is the home of the few remaining tribesmen." (1970~) Mary N. Porter Harris: "The name Greenwich is recorded as an anglicized version of an earlier Indian name." (1194~)
Tom Box and his family moved to what was called Boxville on Box Creek in the mid-1870s. At the same time the nearby settlement of Greenwich was being developed. Newel Nielson described the combining of the two small towns of Boxville and Greenwich: "There was a post office there [near the mouth of Box Creek] and as the area grew, people built on the creeks more and that post office gradually moved this way [toward Greenwich] and made two or three stops before it got here and the name come with it, so that's how we got to be Greenwich." (1458~)

—Old Spanish Trail: (Variation.) The Old Spanish Trail—Fish Lake Route—went along Otter Creek and by what would become Greenwich. (477~)

Gregory Butte: (San Juan Co.) Glen Canyon NRA-Lake Powell. Gregory Butte map. (4,651')
This thousand-foot-tall monolith was called Church Rock by early river runners. (708~) It was named for geologist and explorer Herbert E. Gregory (1869-1952). The name was given after lake water had drowned Gregory Natural Bridge in Fiftymile Creek Canyon and a new geologic feature was needed to honor Gregory. (1021~) (See Gregory Butte—Washington Co.)

—Navajo Bar: This placer bar, now underwater, was on the south (or east) side of the Colorado River one mile north-northwest of Gregory Butte. (1163~) In the 1890s a Mr. Rothschild mined here and at that time it was called Rothschild Bar. (1812~)

—Dove Canyon: The mouth of this short eastern tributary of Lake Powell, now mostly underwater, is one and one-half miles northeast of Gregory Butte (immediately west of elevation 3771). Katie Lee in 1955: "a cool, short labyrinth. The delicate pink stone at the entrance looks soft and easy to imprint, like real dunes of real sand, but once inside we are caught between pillars of eternity—rippled, silver-grey walls that we can touch with both hands in some places.... There comes a soft and plaintive call from above the pools, one I know by heart but have not heard before inside the canyons. Coo-loou Coo-coo-coo. The mourning, or rain, dove. DOVE CANYON." (1162~)

Again, Katie Lee: "The reason it's called Dove Canyon is we went into it and found it fascinating as usual. Its colors were like the wings of a dove; you could see a sheen on them. Kind of a deep purple, then a sort of milky grey and the colors reminded me of a dove ... and on the way out I heard a dove. I know I heard doves time and time again, but I had never heard one down in a canyon that echoed like that. So that's why we named it Dove Canyon. The canyon had the same colors as a dove's wings, the same iridescent strangeness about some of the rocks, and then on top of all that, we get the absolute and we hear a dove calling." (1163~)

—Happy Canyon: The mouth of this short eastern tributary of Lake Powell, now mostly underwater, is one mile east-northeast of Gregory Butte (west of elevation 3721). Katie Lee and friends named the canyon in 1959: "We tried so often to get in it and it was always covered with a gooey mud and we couldn't get anywhere in the thing. Finally, once we did, we changed its name from Mud Swamp Canyon to Happy Canyon. We finally made it in there." (1163~)

—Marigold Bar: This placer bar, now underwater, was on the west side of the Colorado River one mile south-south-west of Gregory Butte (one-quarter mile west of elevation 3729). A nearby inscription was from Leo Campbell, March 13, 1913. (467~)

—Trail Spring Canyon: (Also called Spring Canyon and Spring Trail Canyon.) This short eastern tributary of Lake Powell, now mostly underwater, is two and one-half miles south of Gregory Butte (immediately west of elevation 3784). (1163~)

—Mesken Bar: (Also called Diamond Bar.) (1851~) (Also spelled Mescan Bar, Mexican Bar, and Miskin Bar.) This placer bar, now underwater, was on the west (or north) side of the Colorado River one-half mile west of the mouth of Trail Spring Canyon (one-half mile north-west of elevation 4349). Gold prospector Edward Meskin located a placer claim here in 1885. He called it the Diamond Placer. The Meskin name was applied in 1896. (467~, 470~, 1047~, 1795~) Charles Kelly noted that Meskin first came to Glen Canyon before 1879 as a fur trapper. (1350~) Jerry Johnson noted that Meskin came to the canyons to escape an unrequited love. (1350~)

David D. Rust: "Nice old Dutchman. Could sing and play guitar. Good company. Nice old boy—pleasant man."

(1677~) Louis M. Chaffin in 1888: "Ed Meskin was a little Dutchman, although he talked plain enough and he laughed a lot. He wore chin whiskers and a moustache." (405~)

In 1889 Robert Brewster Stanton ran into Meskin on the bar: "an old trapper and prospector and his dog Sport." (1811~) Arthur Chaffin: "Meskin did some trapping on the River—a very short man—had mustache & goatee—had dog named 'Fido' & taught him to trim ship on command." (390~)

Charles Kelly told of the possible final demise of Ed Meskin when a prospector from Richfield found a skeleton of a man and a dog in a small cave to the south of Green River. It was believed that this was Ed Meskin. (1350~)

Access to the bar was either by river or by a road from the town of Paria that went down Wahweap Creek, by Gunsight Butte, to the Crossing of the Fathers. (1812~) Inscriptions at the bar included Hislop, 1891. (1070~)

Gregory Butte: (Washington Co.) Zion National Park-La Verkin Creek. Kolob Arch map. (7,535')

Herbert E. Gregory was a pioneer geologist in southern Utah. His first venture into canyon country was a geologic study of the Navajo Indian Reservation in Utah and Arizona in 1907. His last study was of Zion and Bryce Canyon national parks in 1951. In between he wrote papers on the geology of the Kaiparowits Plateau, the Paunsaugunt Region, and the San Juan country.

Gresham Spring: (Garfield Co.) Dixie National Forest-Boulder Mountain. Deer Creek Lake map.

Cal Gresham and family moved to Boulder in 1895. (1168~, 1487~)

Grey Cliffs: (Kane Co.)

Also spelled Gray Cliffs.

These are not shown on the USGS 7.5 Minute Series maps.

John Wesley Powell in 1873: "The rock is of white homogeneous sandstone; above, we have 200 feet of light-gray limestone, containing Jurassic fossils. For this line [of the cliffs of the Grand Staircase] we have also adopted the English translation of the Indian name, Gray Cliffs." (1566~)

Clarence Dutton of the Powell Survey: "The Gray Cliffs are nearly white, and are merely toned with gray." (584~)

Grey Mesa: (San Juan Co.) Glen Canyon NRA-Wilson Mesa. Wilson Creek, The Rincon, Deep Canyon North, and Alcove Canyon maps.

Also called Rustlers Flat (34~, 774~) and Slick Rock Bench (1238~).

Also spelled Gray Mesa.

In 1879 Hole-in-the-Rock Expedition scouts noted that the mesa top was grey in contrast to the surrounding red cliffs.

—Lookout Point and The Slick Rocks: After crossing the mesa, the scouts were at first unable to find a route down the cliffs. Scout George B. Hobbs called the edge of the mesa Lookout Point, and its steep sides The Slick Rocks. Hobbs told this remarkable story: "Just before reaching these rocks [Lookout Point] a herd of Llamas [bighorn sheep] ... came up and followed us for some distance.... I tried to catch it [a bighorn sheep] with a pack rope, but it was very active in dodging the lasso.... I followed it for some distance. It seemed to draw me off down in the rocks until I finally got to the bottom of the rocks.... I climbed back up the rocks and soon learned that Bro. Sevy and Morrell who had been trying to find a way to get down these rocks, but had returned to camp, reporting that we could go no farther. I told them that I had already been clear to the bottom.... This seemed to be the only passage down these slick rocks." (1356~) This route (near elevation BM4374 on the Alcove Canyon map) was improved into a rough and remarkable road which can still be followed. This section does not follow the "Emigrant Trail" shown on the map. (SAPE.)

Hole-in-the-Rock Expedition member Elizabeth Morris Decker called the descent Harrys Slideoff: "It's the roughest country you or anybody else ever seen; it's nothing in the world but rocks and holes, hills and hollows. The mountains are just one solid rock as smooth as an apple." (1356~)

Griffin Creek: (Garfield Co.) Dixie National Forest-Escalante Mountains-North Creek. Barker Reservoir map. (See Griffin Top for name derivation.)

—Island in the Sky: This flat area on a ridge at the north end of Griffin Creek is two miles east of Lower Barker Reservoir (one mile northeast of elevation 8918). (1551~)

Griffin Point: (Garfield Co.) Dixie National Forest-Escalante Mountains. Griffin Point map. (10,389')
(See Griffin Top for name derivation.)

Griffin Ranch: (Garfield Co.) GSCENM-Boulder Mountain-Hog Ranch Spring Canyon. Wide Hollow Reservoir map.
This was started by George Riddle. He sold it to Varney Griffin (1888-1922) in 1915. (2051~)

—Griffin Spring: The ranch was at the spring. (55~)

Griffin Top: (Garfield Co.) Dixie National Forest-Escalante Mountains. Grass Lakes, Griffin Point, Barker Reservoir, and Sweetwater Creek maps. (10,748')

Edson Alvey noted that Charles E. Griffin, Sr. (1836–1900) moved to the Escalante area in 1879. He and his sons ran sheep in the area. (55~, 2051~) George Coombs: "I helped Griffins' take their sheep out on Griffin Top (Boulder Mt.) about the first time sheep were ever taken out there—that was about 1890. I remember the grass was so high that you could hardly see the sheep for it." (810~)

Donald Scott in 1928: "On Griffin Top, a point on the Aquarius Plateau, [our guide Mr. Christensen] said there had been a great battlefield, for on a mound there he had picked up quantities of arrow and spear points as well as stone axes and hammers." (1705~)

—Griffin Top Road: The road across the plateau was built by the CCC in the 1930s. (887~)

Grimes Creek: (Garfield Co.) Dixie National Forest-Boulder Mountain-Sand Creek. Roger Peak map.
Burns Ormand noted that his uncle, Joseph Allen Grimes, ran livestock in the area. (1487~)

Grimes Wash: (Emery Co.) Wasatch Plateau-Cottonwood Creek. Red Point map.
William and Carrie Grimes were Orangeville pioneers. (388~)

—Swasey Ranch: This was on Cottonwood Creek near the mouth of Grimes Wash (at elevation 5997). (M.68.)

Gripe Reservoir: (Wayne Co.) Awapa Plateau-West Fork Cedar Peak Draw. Flossie Knoll map.
Two name derivations are given.
First, locals asked that no names be used to protect the guilty from embarrassment: The person the reservoir was named after was well-known for griping about absolutely everything. (1497~)
Second, this is the only water in a large area and it took a lot of griping by ranchers to have the reservoir built. (1865~)

Grosvenor Arch: (Kane Co.) GSCENM-The Cockscomb-Cottonwood Creek. Butler Valley map.
Otis "Dock" Marston noted that this was called Butler Arch and Butler Valley Arch. (1288~, 1728~)
Jack Breed in 1949: "What we saw was an arch—a new arch, uncharted and unnamed! This striking natural bridge is carved from creamy rock, a rarity in a land of brilliant reds. Actually it is a double arch, with the larger span on the end of a buttress that juts from the main sandstone butte. Near the anchor end wind has blasted a smaller hole through the buttress.... As far as we could

learn, we were the first to find it. We named this feature 'Grosvenor Arch' in honor of Dr. Gilbert Grosvenor [1875-1966], President of the National Geographic Society, the man who, we all agreed, had done more than any other person to arouse public interest in geography." (275~)

Nell Murbarger in 1961: "Cattlemen of the region, who had known of the arch for some 70 or 80 yeas were understandably 'amused' when the arch was 'discovered' [by the National Geographic Society expedition] in 1949." (1415~)

—Gilgal: Ward J. Roylance: "A mile south of the Grosvenor Arch turnoff, just east of the main road, is a grouping of large alabaster stones known as Gilgal. Superficially a Stonehenge in miniature, the stones are arranged systematically and purposefully into two concentric circles of 12 stones each, one within the other, with a center stone or 'altar table' in the exact center.... The monument was created in 1978 under the supervision of Dallas J. Anderson, a professor of art at Brigham Young University, who was its originator." (1658~)

Grotto Canyon: (San Juan Co.) Navajo Indian Reservation-Cummings Mesa-Glen Canyon. Gregory Butte map.

Katie Lee named the canyon in 1955: "Like many other canyons, this half-mile beauty ends at a deep sand-rimmed pool. Above it a twisting purple-pink grotto trickles clear water, all surrounded by forty-foot banks of maidenhair fern—shimmering emeralds.... The pool holds bouquets of watercress, sweet but tangy.... What sets this canyon we named Grotto apart from others? The time of day? Weather? The yellow brightness, canyon wren music, and flowers, all at the same time? Water whispering secrets from above the grotto"? (1162~)

Joseph L. Dudziak in 1962: "a most beautiful box canyon with a small lake, lined with brilliantly green vegetation—principally Venus-fern, poison ivy and red bud." (577~)

Grotto Springs: (Washington Co.) Zion National Park-Zion Canyon. Temple of Sinawava map.

Also called The Grotto.

The first Zion National Park Visitor Center and campground were below The Grotto. They opened in 1928. (481~)

—Grotto Trail: This was listed on the National Register of Historic Places in 1996.

Grover Town: (Wayne Co.) Boulder Mountain-Carcass Creek-Highway 12. Grover map.

Also called Carcass or Carcass Creek. (887~, 1972~)

Will Bullard and Alex Keele were the first to settle in the area, in 1880. The town was established in the mid-1880s and was named for President Grover Cleveland. Now just a collection of ranches, Grover used to be a real town with a school. People found they couldn't make a living here, so many gradually moved away. (426~, 607~, 699~)

Veola Clark in 1953: "Grover is more than just a settlement of a few ranches, it is a quiet, peaceful, little green valley knit together by good neighbors." (1786~)

—Grover Wagon Road: (Also called Miners Mountain Road and Old Grover Road.) This historic nine and one-half-mile-long road starts at a Park Service sign reading "Old Wagon Road" on the Capitol Reef National Park Scenic Drive. This is one and three-quarters of a mile south of Ferns Nipple (one-eighth mile southeast of elevation BM5897 on the Golden Throne map). Then road skirts along the north side of Capitol Wash and goes over Miners Mountain where it joins what are now Jeep roads (near elevation 7841 on the Grover map). It ends at the town of Grover. It was constructed in the mid-1880s and was used until the 1930s. (1476~)

Dwight Williams told a story about the road, which he traveled as a boy: "In later years there was a man here by the name of Clare Okerlund. He ran sheep out on Parker Mountain in the summertime. He would take his sheep herd to the desert or down in the Hanksville area in the wintertime. In the spring he would drive them back to Parker Mountain. One spring, after Capitol Reef Park had been designated, he was trailing his sheep up through that area. He got to where this old road [Grover Wagon Road] takes off and he was met by a Park official. The Park official said they were tired of him trailin' the sheep up through Fruita and up through the Park; they'd like him to go over this old road over Miners Mountain.

"Clare Okerlund finally agreed to take his sheep up over this Miners Mountain Road. It was a lot of work for Clare because his sheep didn't know that route. Well, it came time in the fall for 'im to take his sheep back to the desert. So he went to get a permit from the Park. The Park people said, 'Well, Clare, we'd like to have you go back down acrost the Miners on that old road.' And Clare said to the Park people, 'Let me tell you,' he said, 'I had a tough time getting up over that Miners Mountain with my sheep herd last year.' He said, 'I prayed to the Lord that if He did let me make it through there, I'd never ask Him to help me back through there again. Now,' he says, 'you don't want me to break my promise to the Lord, do you'? So he didn't go back down that old road." (2013~)

Groves Creek: (Iron Co.) Harmony Mountains-Cedar Valley. Stoddard Mountain and Kanarraville maps.

Elisha Hurd Groves (1797–1868) arrived in Iron County in 1850. He helped build the original Fort Harmony in

1852. (369~) He was also one of the first to commercially cut logs in the area. (887~)

Gruvers Mesa: (Emery Co.) San Rafael Desert-Moonshine Wash. Moonshine Wash map. (4,822')

The old name for this was Red Reef or Red Dome. (M.72.) Marion Gruver was an early rancher from the Green River area. (1645~)

—Gruvers Canyon: This southern tributary of the San Rafael River starts at the west end of Gruvers Mesa (at elevation 4821T) and goes north-northeast. It was named by David Pimental. (1548~)

Gulch, The: (Garfield Co.) GSCENM-Escalante River. Steep Creek Bench, King Bench, and Red Breaks maps. Also called Big Gulch (222~) and Seep Creek (777~).

The Gulch is normally divided into two parts: The Upper Gulch is to the north of the Burr Trail; the Lower Gulch is to the south of the Burr Trail.

Inscriptions include W.E.H., Sp. 1887. (SAPE.)

—-Indian Trail Gulch: The mouth of this western tributary of the Upper Gulch is three-quarters of a mile upcanyon from the mouth of Egg Canyon (one-eighth mile west of elevation 6912 on the Steep Creek Bench map).

—Lamanite Arch: Indian Trail Gulch contains Lamanite Arch, which is one mile upcanyon from its mouth (one-quarter mile southeast of elevation 6992 on the Steep Creek Bench map). It was named by Tropic resident Herman Pollack in the mid-1960s. (1956~) Mormons believe that Lamanites were the ancestors of the American Indians. (1115~) Albert R. Lyman: "The Book of Mormon deals with the history of ancient Americans and in particular with two opposing nations, who contended a thousand years for supremacy. From 600 BC to AD 400 it was a question of which one was to prevail. One of these peoples, known as the Lamanites, were the aggressors, the attackers, robbers, outlaws. They were trying to enslave and rule over the other people, the Nephites. The Nephites were the peaceful ones, subsisting by their own industry, and getting their living from the soil. A tremendous war in 400 AD resulted in the destruction of all the Nephites but those who descended over to the Lamanites to save their lives. It is generally taken for granted by Book of Mormon readers, that these descenters [*sic*] lost their identity as Nephites." (1248~)

Several constructed stock trail exit Lower Gulch.

—The first trail is at the confluence with Long Canyon and exits to the east onto King Bench (one-quarter mile north of elevation 6224 on the King Bench map). (SAPE.)

—The second trail exits to the east onto King Bench three-quarters of a mile downcanyon from the junction with Long Canyon (one-quarter mile south-southwest of elevation 6224 on the King Bench map). (SAPE.)

—The third trail exits to the east onto King Bench one and one-third miles downcanyon from the junction with Long Canyon (one-quarter mile west of elevation 5893 on the King Bench map). (SAPE.)

—The fourth trail is shown as a hiking trail that crosses the Lower Gulch three miles downcanyon from the junction with Long Canyon (one-quarter mile southeast of elevation 5762 on the King Bench map. (SAPE.)

—The fifth trail comes down a short western tributary at a "Tank" that is one and one-half miles downcanyon from the fourth trail (hiking trail) (to the east of elevation 5973 on the King Bench map). (SAPE.)

—The sixth trail exits to the east onto King Bench two miles upcanyon (as the crow flies) from the mouth of Halfway Hollow (one-eighth mile west of elevation 5322 on the King Bench map). (SAPE.)

—The seventh trail exits to the west onto Brigham Tea Bench one and one-half miles upcanyon (as the crow flies) from the mouth of Halfway Hollow (one-quarter mile north of elevation 5363 on the King Bench map). There are a line shack and corral at the base of the trail. (SAPE.)

—Sand Holler Trail: This eighth trail goes west up Sand Holler onto Brigham Tea Bench. It is three-quarters of a mile upcanyon from the Escalante River (one-quarter mile south of elevation 5184 on the Red Breaks map). (1487~, SAPE.)

Gunlock Town: (Washington Co.) Santa Clara River-Gunlock Reservoir. Gunlock map.

The Parley P. Pratt Exploring Expedition to Southern Utah of 1849–50 passed here. Robert Campbell of the expedition: "Continued up the [Santa Clara] river thro' some fertile and good bottoms well timbered with Cotton wood." (1762~)

The town was founded by William Haynes Hamblin (1830-1872), Dudley Leavitt, Isaac Riddle, and George A. Smith in 1855 (or 1857). The four men and their families first looked at Santa Clara, but decided there wasn't enough water and land for farming. In 1862 a flood destroyed the town and a new location about three miles up the Santa Clara River was found. (1646a~)

Three complimentary name derivations are given.

First, William Hamblin's nickname was Gunlock. (14~, 296~, 375~) Apparently Hamblin was good at fixing gunlocks. (1481~)

Second, James Samuel Page Bowler in the early 1880s: "Gunlock appeared to be a war-like name and aroused my curiosity and upon inquiring I learned that Apostle George A. Smith so named it as a kind of Memento of events connected with William Hamblin and Pioneer life." (267~)

Third, Andrew Jenson: "William Hamblin was known among the pioneers as an expert hunter and splendid marksman, and was frequently referred to as 'Gunlock Will.'" (972~)

Hamblin, slated to be an expert witness in a mining dispute in Nevada, was poisoned. He died trying to get home to Gunlock.

—Old Spanish Trail: The trail went by what would become Gunlock.

—Gunlock Reservoir State Park: (Gunlock and Shivwits maps.) (Also called Gunlock State Park.) This six hundred acre park was established in 1970.

Gunnison Butte: (Emery Co.) Book Cliffs-Green River. Blue Castle Butte and Tusher Canyon maps. (5,034')
Also called Gunnison Point (665~) and Gunnison's Point (M.49).

This prominent tower is visible from Green River Town. Stephen Vandiver Jones, a member of the 1871–72 Powell Expedition: "A very irregular hill rises nearly opposite camp. The elements have eroded all the upper strata of rocks, except in one spot, leaving the hill nearly square, the highest point resembling the steeple of a church.... We name it 'Cathedral Butte.'" (1023~)

Almon H. Thompson, also of the Powell Expedition, renamed it Gunnisons Butte Cathedral in his original diary. (1879~) Thompson: "One butte opposite our camp is like a Gothic church, spire on one end and buttresses along the side." (1877~)

Raymond Austin Cogswell of the Stone-Galloway Expedition of 1909 called it both Table Butte and Sentinel Butte. (440~)

Charles Eggert in 1957: "The butte was like some Romanesque Cathedral, and surrounding it, tier upon tier, were small chapels formed by talus, and great stone buttresses. It was one of the most imposing sights along the river and it remained long in view as the river twisted and turned, seemingly lost in the flats of the desert." (599~)

—Brighams Butte: This pinnacle was on the west side of Gunnison Butte (near elevation 5034 on the Blue Castle Butte map). The butte toppled in 1956. (1931~) Waldo Wilcox noted that while Brighams Butte stood, locals called Gunnison Butte "Brighams Wives." (2011~)

—Gunnison Butte Damsite: (Proposed.) In 1963 the Bureau of Reclamation considered a dam at Gunnison Butte on the Green River.

Gunnison Valley: (Emery and Grand Counties.) Green River-Book Cliffs-Interstate 70. Green River, Green River NE, Blue Castle Butte, and Tusher Canyon maps.
Also called Green River Valley.

This large valley is centered around Green River Town and is bound on the north by the Book Cliffs and in the south by the San Rafael Desert.

Captain John W. Gunnison led an expedition through the area in 1853. He described the valley which would later bear his name: "Except three or four small cotton-wood trees in the ravine near us, there is not a tree to be seen by the unassisted eye on any part of the horizon.... And to the south, mass after mass of course conglomerate is broken in fragments, or piled in turret-shaped heaps, colored by ferruginous cement from a deep black to a brilliant red, whilst in some rocks there are argillaceous layers, varying to gray or glittering with white. The surface around us is whitened with fields of alkali, precisely resembling fields of snow." (1089~)

Jacob H. Schiel, a geologist with Gunnison: "in the vicinity of Green River.... They form isolated hills of curious shape and often considerable size. Many have almost the shape of great churches or houses with colossal chimneys towering nearby. Where the dirty black shapes stand close together, one thinks he sees the ruins of a city whose inhabitants are buried under their fallen adobe houses or else flown from the awful, desolate region." (1696~)

Members of the 1869 Powell Expedition called it Castle Valley. (236~) John Wesley Powell later named it in honor of Captain John W. Gunnison. He and several of his men were killed to the west of the valley, near Sevier Lake, by Ute Indians. (584~, 644~, 710~, 1563~)

Powell also described the valley: "Extensive sand plains extend back from the immediate river valley as far as we can see on either side. These naked, drifting sands gleam brilliantly in the midday sun of July.... Plains and hills and cliffs and distant mountains seem to be floating vaguely about in a trembling, wave-rocked sea, and patches of landscape seem to float away and be lost, and then to reappear." (1563~)

Almon H. Thompson of the Powell Expedition of 1871–72: "The valley is desolate, a barren waste of sand.... It is an eroded valley with cliffs all around, castellated in fairy turrets, pinnacles, towers, and bastions." (1877~)

Arthur A. Baker in 1946: "Areas covered by dune sand are interspersed with bare-rock surfaces, badlands, and broad soil-covered valleys. Broad areas of low relief are commonly bordered by cliffs 100 feet or more high; and large and small mesas, rounded domes or sharp spires of bare rock, and shallow canyons are common surface features. The lowland in the vicinity of the town of Green River is a desolate, nearly barren area of wide shallow valleys, low isolated hills and knolls, and long low hogbacks." (100~)

Unattributed in 1950: "Trying to make a living raising cattle on the Green River Desert or driving an automobile across its deep sandy wastes on a hot afternoon, one suffers the torments of hell, and curses the country and the reasons that brought him there. However, as the purple shadows begin to lengthen across the gold and red sands, as the towering buttes take on a rosy hue, and distant purple mountains are silhouetted against a royal blue sky, it becomes a dream world of marvelous beauty." (1425~)

—Gunnisons Trail: Gunnison's route became known as the Gunnison Trail. Stella McElprang: "[Gunnison] came to the Green river just south of where the White [Price] River enters it, then west to Cedar Mountain and south to the point of the Big Cedar and west again to the San Rafael river. Probably he came up the Buckhorn Draw and along the present Castle Dale-Greenriver road [Green River Cutoff road], crossing Huntington, Cottonwood and Ferron creeks. It is definitely known that he was on Ferron creek where it breaks into The Box, east of Molen.... He followed the Molen reef to a point east and south of Emery, thence over the mountain [Wasatch Plateau] along the trail used by the early settlers [the Old Spanish Trail]." (1330~)

Gunsight Butte: (Kane Co.) Glen Canyon NRA-Lake Powell. Gunsight Butte map. (4,678')
Also called Castle Butte, Chimney Rock (476~), The Gunsight (80~), and Gun Sight Mountain (488~).
The Domínguez-Escalante Expedition of 1776–77 went around the south side of the butte and camped. They called their camping area *San Vicente Ferrer*. (1357~)
Edwin G. Woolley, diarist for the Utah Territorial Militia of 1869, called it Steamboat Rock. (476~, 2048~)
The Lieutenant George M. Wheeler Survey of 1872–73 called it Gunshot Mountain. Wheeler: "The scene is one of remarkable grandeur and almost unique in its loneliness." (1997~)
Arthur L. Crawford: "Gunsight Butte was probably named by Jacob Hamblin who passed many times beneath its majesty as he trekked his mysterious way teaching peace to the Navahos." (479~)
George C. Fraser in 1923: "The trail to the Crossing [of the Fathers] from the west is blocked by a rocky spur jutting to the cañon rim from the heights bounding the river plain. The notch in the center ... affords a pass, steep of

approach and barely wide enough to accommodate packs. It is shaped like the rear sight of a rifle and when looked through ... reveals a distant knob analogous to the front sight of a gun; hence the name." (671~)
Nora Candell in 1940: "Ahead of us, Gunsight Point stood up sharply, cold and inimical. Never have I seen a landscape that looked so utterly, actively cruel and relentless as that one. (Wyoming can look passively pitiless, but this is some work): sun-baked, alkaline and waterless; no sign of any living thing; no hope at all for any lost traveler.... And yet it had a sort of weird beauty of its own." (507~)
—Gunsight Tank: This is a still-used stock pond. (SAPE.)
—Gunsight Bar: This placer bar, now underwater, was on the north (or west) side of the Colorado River directly north of the mouth of Labyrinth Bay.

Gunsight Canyon: (Kane Co.) Glen Canyon NRA-Gunsight Bay. Warm Creek Bay and Gunsight Butte maps.
Also called Cottonwood Canyon. (467~)
(See Gunsight Butte—Kane Co. for name derivation.)
In 2006 a National Park Service crew found an inscription from Don Bernard de Miera, the cartographer for the Domínguez-Escalante Expedition of 1776–77, reading "Paso por Aqui ano de 1776." (1115~)
—Gunsight Spring: (Warm Creek Bay map.) A spectacular "Pack Trail" goes to this medium-size spring. The trail is incorrectly marked on the map, but is easy to follow from the top. The trail leads to the spring, but does not continue down the canyon. (SAPE.)

Gunsight Pass: (Kane Co.) Glen Canyon NRA-Glen Canyon. Gunsight Butte map. (3,640')
(See Gunsight Butte—Kane Co. for name derivation.)
Andrew Smith Gibbons of the Jacob Hamblin Expedition to the Hopi of 1858 called this the Devil's Gate, "a place where the trail passes between steep, perpendicular rocks." (714~)
Jacob Hamblin, Thales Haskell, and others passed this way in 1859. Haskell: "Came to a pass in a mountain just wide enough for the mules to single file, perpendicular rocks very high on each side." (842~)
Edwin G. Woolley, diarist for the Utah Territorial Militia of 1869: "This Gunsight is a cleft in the solid rock mountain, wedge shaped about a foot wide at bottom, in the narrowest place, and two hundred feet through, and a hundred feet high. Twenty men could guard this pass against an army. We passed through Gunsight, and down a steep rock into an opening or valley in rocks. Whichever way we look there is nothing but rock mountains, in fantastic shapes. It is rock around, rocks above, rocks

beneath, rocks in chasms, rocks in towers, rocks in ridges, rocks everywhere; it is, in fact, all rock." (476~, 2048~)
Inscriptions included H.M. Roper, Salem Utah, and E.P. Pectol and M. Grundy, Oct. 18, 1896. (1115~)
—Constructed Stock Trail: Now underwater, this went through Gunsight Pass.

Guss Knoll: (Wayne Co.) Hell Hole Swale-Dirty Devil River. Angel Cove map. (4,760')
Correctly spelled Gus Knoll.
Guy Robison noted Gus Williams herded sheep in the area. (1644~)

Gut, The: (Kane Co.) GSCENM-The Cockscomb. Butler Valley map.
Ralph Chynoweth: "The old road cuts down the cliffs and into a hole and then up and out of there and it is narrow and tight. And it is just below 'The Neck' [Butler Valley Neck], and below that is 'The Crotch' [Cads Crotch]. That is why they call it 'Gut.'" (425~)

Guymon Pond: (Emery Co.) Cedar Mountain-Buckhorn Flat. Buckhorn Reservoir map.
This is a small, still-used stock reservoir. (SAPE.)
William Albert Guymon (1849-1922) first came to the Castle Valley area in 1877 while looking for cattle stolen by Indians. Guymon and family moved to the Huntington area in 1879. (1014~, 1195~)

Guymon Wash: (Emery Co.) Castle Valley-Huntington Creek. Huntington map.
(See Guymon Pond for name derivation.)

Gypsum Canyon: (San Juan Co.) Dark Canyon Plateau-Glen Canyon NRA-Beef Basin-Cataract Canyon. Fable Valley, Bowdie Canyon East, and Teapot Rock maps.
John F. Steward, a geologist on the 1871–72 Powell Expedition, named the canyon for the beds of gypsum found here. Others on the survey called it Stewards Gulch. (465~, 1877~)
Powell and men hiked up the canyon. Powell: "We soon come to pools of water; then to a brook, which is lost in the sands below; and, passing up the brook we find the canyon narrows, the walls close in, are often overhanging, and at last we find ourselves in a vast amphitheater, with a pool of deep, clear, cold water on the bottom." (1563~)

—Geology: The oldest exposed rock strata in Canyonlands National Park are these gypsum beds, which are about 290 million years old. (87~)
—Goudelock Trail: This constructed stock trail allows access to the lower end of Gypsum Canyon from Imperial Valley. The trail starts on the west end of Imperial Valley (one mile west of elevation 5372T on the Teapot Rock map) and ends one mile north of the mouth of Gypsum Canyon. It is unclear when the trail was built. Almon H. Thompson of the 1871–72 Powell Expedition noted seeing horse sign in the canyon. Pete Steele noted that the trail was built by David Goudelock in 1915: "Back in the heyday of the S.S. [Scorup-Somerville] Cattle Company, they used to have a lot of horses.... They would take some of their extra horses down through and off down, and put 'em on the river bottom, down at the mouth of Gypsum Canyon. [They would leave them] for two or three months." (1821~, 465~, 690~, SAPE.) It is likely that a rough Indian trail was later improved by cowboys. Today this is a hard trail to find and follow. (SAPE.) Inscriptions include Al Trulliner and Mavky(?) Shelley, 2/15/56. (SAPE.)
—Gypsum Canyon Rapid: This was often described as a "whirlpool" by early river runners. Ethan Allen Reynolds in 1889: "We were unaccountably swept into a small but vicious whirlpool.... Around and around we spun, and although I rowed with all my might, we drew steadily nearer the vortex. Finally my end of the boat began to sink.... Finding we were going down, I let go of the oars and hung on to the seat of the boat." (1619~)

Gypsum Creek: (Navajo Co., Az. and San Juan Co., Utah.) Navajo Indian Reservation-San Juan River. Arizona maps: Mitten Buttes and Rooster Rock. Utah maps: Mexican Hat SW, Mexican Hat SE, and Mexican Hat.
The name was in place by 1893. (M.5)
—Gyp Creek Rapid: Famed war correspondent Ernie Pyle in 1939: "Gyp Creek rapids, usually placid, had for some reason turned into a maelstrom. The sand-laden waves reared up ahead of us like a painting of a furious sea. There were great holes in the water, and much sound and spray and fury." (1592~)

H

Hackberry Canyon: (Kane Co.) GSCENM-Paria River. Slickrock Bench and Calico Peak maps.

Also called Hackberry Creek.

Netleaf hackberry trees are common in the lower canyon.

—Upper Trail: (Also called Upper Death Valley Trail.) Ralph Chynoweth noted that this constructed stock trail goes west out of Hackberry Canyon to lower Upper Death Valley. It is one and one-quarter miles north of the mouth of Stone Donkey Canyon (one-half mile north of elevation 5607 on the Calico Peak map). (425~) (See Stone Donkey Canyon below.) Inscriptions include Wm. Chynoweth, 1892; Eldorado Mg. Co., Aug. 4, 1912, Ed Griffin, L.D. Watson; V. Raplee, no date; Art Chynoweth, 1921; Ray Willis, 1921; Bill LeFevre, 1924; and Virg. Pollock, 1930. (SAPE.)

—Twin Knolls: Ralph Chynoweth noted that these knolls are immediately north of the "V" formed by Hackberry and Stone Donkey canyons. The southern knoll is elevation 5607 on the Calico Peak map. (425~)

—Stone Donkey Canyon: (Also called Big Canyon.) The mouth of this western tributary of Hackberry Canyon is one and three-quarters of a mile northeast of Sam Pollock Arch (one-quarter mile southwest of elevation 6634 [Cottonwood] on the Calico Peak map). Ralph Chynoweth: "There's a rock down there that somebody thought looked like the head of a donkey." (425~)

—Stone Donkey Line Camp: There are line shacks at the mouth of the canyon. (SAPE.)

—Lower Trail: (Also called Lower Death Valley Trail.) Ralph Chynoweth noted that this constructed stock trail goes west from Hackberry Canyon, across Lower Death Valley, to the Paria River. It starts one mile south of the mouth of Stone Donkey Canyon (one-half mile south of elevation 5582 on the Calico Peak map). It then goes west across Lower Death Valley and drops to the Paria River between Hogeye and Kitchen canyons. Some of the trail over the uplands is difficult to find and follow. Inscriptions include S.T. Graff, Dec. 12, 1925. (425~, SAPE.)

—Lower Rush Beds Trail: Ralph Chynoweth noted that this constructed stock trail goes east from Hackberry Canyon to the Rush Beds. It starts immediately upcanyon from the Rockfall (See below) and one-quarter mile south of the Lower Trail (Calico Peak map). (425~, SAPE.)

—Rockfall: (Also called The Jump-up.) This rockfall in Hackberry Canyon is one and one-quarter miles south of its junction with Stone Donkey Canyon. This landmark is familiar to cowboys and hikers.

Ralph Chynoweth: "Where that rockfall is now, there was a jump-up that was about five feet high.... In 1987 a friend and I went deer hunting down in that country. We climbed out on the Lower Rush Beds Trail and there is a bit of a point and there is a little place where the grass is pretty good, so we camped. It was the 25th of October and we were taking our packs off the horses. I heard this bad rumble and I asked my friend, 'My word, what was that?' It rumbled down in Hackberry Canyon right under us and then pretty quick the dust boiled up outta there. That dust kept boilin' up outta that canyon even after it got dark. And that's when that wall caved off and formed the rockfall." (425~)

—Watson Cabin: This is on the lower west side of Hackberry Canyon one and three-quarters of a mile south-southeast of Sam Pollock Arch (one-quarter mile southeast of elevation 5767 on the Calico Peak map). Ralph Chynoweth: "His name was Frank Watson. There's a good stream of water down there. Back in those days all people had to worry about was something to wear and something to eat. This old man, Watson, didn't have a family. So he went down to that old cabin.... He dammed off the creek and he raised a garden.... That was in the 1890s." (425~)

Inscriptions on the logs of the cabin include Geo. Thompson, 1921; Reed Thompson, 1923; and L.P. Chynoweth, 1926. (SAPE.)

—Watson Cabin Trail: This constructed stock trail goes east from the Watson Cabin up the cliffs to the south end of the Rush Beds. Inscriptions include Geo. F. Thompson, 1921; Lawrence Chynoweth, 1927; and Reed Goulding, 1928. (SAPE.)

Hackberry Tank: (Coconino Co., Az.) Glen Canyon NRA-Highway 89. Ferry Swale, Az. map.

This still-used stock reservoir has a couple of netleaf hackberry trees nearby. (SAPE.)

Hadden Holes: (Emery Co.) Castle Valley-Cedar Hollow. Hadden Holes and Buckhorn Reservoir maps.

These are a series of natural potholes in the slickrock bottom of the canyon. Short stretches of constructed stock trail join several of the holes. (SAPE.)

Alfred E. Hadden (1884-1969) was a resident of the town of Victor. (388~, 1551~)

Hal Canyon: (Grand Co.) La Sal Mountains-Colorado River. Big Bend map.

Joe Taylor noted that this is a name given by river runners. (1866~)

Halchita Town: (San Juan Co.) Navajo Indian Reservation-Halgaitoh Wash. The Goosenecks and Mexican Hat SW maps.

Doris Valle noted that *Halchita* is Navajo for "in the midst of the red." (1935~) This small town's claim to fame is that astronaut uniforms were sewn in a small factory here. (838~)

Haley Canyon: (Carbon Co.) Castle Valley-Porphyry Bench-South Gordon Creek. Wattis and Pinnacle Peak maps.

—Haley Siding: This railroad siding was two and one-half miles south-southwest of the mouth of Haley Canyon (one-half mile south of elevation 6537 on the Pinnacle Peak map). (428~) The siding has been removed.

Halfway Bench: (Wayne Co.) Burr Desert-Highway 95-Meadow Gulch. Hanksville map.

Charles B. Hunt: "The bench is about midway between Hanksville and the Poison Spring Benches." (925~)

—Sorrel Butte: This small butte is two miles southeast of Halfway Bench (at elevation 5026). Charles B. Hunt noted that the name came from the color of the butte: sorrel is a light chestnut brown. (925~)

Halfway Hollow: (Garfield Co.) GSCENM-Escalante Desert-Hole-in-the-Rock Road-Harris Wash. Tenmile Flat map.

Also called 15 Mile. (1672~)

Pratt Gates: "When the cowboys and the sheepmen went down on the lower desert [Escalante Desert], you went to the Tenmile [Wash]. Then you went to the Twentymile [Wash]. Halfway Hollow was in between. They figured it was fifteen miles from town." (709~)

Halfway Wash: (Wayne Co.) Henry Mountains-Meadow Gulch. Bull Mountain and Hanksville maps.

Guy Robison noted that in the old days travelers knew they were halfway to the Granite Ranch from Hanksville when they reached Halfway Wash. (1644~)

Halgaitoh Wash: (San Juan Co.) Navajo Indian Reservation-Monument Valley-Gypsum Creek. Goulding NE,

Monument Pass, Mexican Hat SW, and Mexican Hat SE maps.

Also called Monument Wash.

Also spelled Halgaito Wash, Hokito Wash, and Hulkito Wash. (101~, 1931~)

Two name derivations are given.

First, Mary Foushee noted that *Hailgaito* is Navajo for "valley of white water." (660~)

Second, Laurance D. Linford noted that it is Navajo for "plains water." (1204~)

—Red Spring: This is one mile downcanyon from the very top of Halgaitoh Wash (one-quarter mile southeast of elevation 5491 on the Goulding NE map). (101~)

Hall Creek: (Garfield Co.) Dixie National Forest-Escalante Mountains-Main Canyon. Barker Reservoir and Griffin Point maps.

(See Hall Ranch for name derivation.)

—Griffin Point Trail: (Also called Green Ranger Station Trail.) This is the "Pack Trail" that goes up Hall Creek to Griffin Top (Griffin Point map).

Hall Divide: (Garfield Co.) Capitol Reef National Park-Waterpocket Fold-Halls Creek. Deer Point map.

Also called Halls Divide.

(See Halls Creek for name derivation.)

The divide is a small valley that allowed early settlers to bypass the narrows of Halls Creek, which were not negotiable by pack stock or wagons. The Halls Road went over Hall Divide. (See Appendix Two—Halls Road.)

John A. Widtsoe in 1922: "Crossed Hall's Divide. Bad Road." (2007~)

—The Narrows: This is a narrow, three-mile-long gorge in Halls Creek. In 1875 Grove Karl Gilbert of the Powell Survey called it variously Horseshoe Cañon and Horseshoe Bend: "The traveler who follows down Waterpocket Canyon [Halls Creek] now comes to a place where the creek turns from the open canyon of the shale and enters a dark cleft in the sandstone. He can follow the course of the water (on foot) and will be repaid for the wetting of his feet by the strange beauty of the defile. For nearly three miles he will thread his way through a gorge walled in by the smooth, curved faces of the massive sandstone, and so narrow and devious that it is gloomy for lack of sunlight, and then he will emerge once more into the open canyon." (699~)

John A. Widtsoe: "Half of party went through canyon of Hall Creek. Wonderful they declare. Called it Canopy Gorge from overhanging rock. Vast amphitheatre there with perfect acoustics. About six miles of rounding narrow gorge—in places only 30 feet across." (2007~)

Hall Mesa: (Garfield Co.) Henry Mountains-Halls Creek. Hall Mesa, Deer Point, and Clay Point maps. (5,244') (See Halls Creek for name derivation.)

Dr. William H. Schock mentioned going down Halls Creek to the Baker Ranch and by Monument Mesa in the 1890s. It is believed that Schock's Monument Mesa is Hall Mesa. (1697~)

Hall Ranch: (Garfield Co.) Escalante Mountains-Escalante River-Highway 12. Wide Hollow Reservoir map.

Job Pitcher Hall (1820-1888)—the brother of Charles Hall—and family homesteaded here starting in 1875. (2051~) James Varley Roe, paraphrasing Robert Franklin Hall, the son of Job Pitcher Hall: "The first house built on the farm was made by first digging a trench the size of the room, two feet deep. Then they took cedar posts, peeled off the bark, put them around in the trench, first, the big end of the post down, then the little end down. The post stood about seven feet above the ground. They were put close together, leaving some posts out for a doorway, to let the light in. A piece of canvas was dropped down over the opening when it was cold and rainy. Poles were put over the top, creek willows and cedar boughs were placed in the large cracks, then cedar bark over all the top, then dirt. The ground was the floor. They did their cooking on a fire out in the front of the house." (1646a~)

Halls Creek: (Garfield Co.) Capitol Reef National Park-Waterpocket Fold-Glen Canyon NRA-Glen Canyon. Bitter Creek Divide, Wagon Box Mesa, The Post, Deer Point, Stevens Canyon North, and Hall Mesa maps.

Also called Halls Canyon, Halls Wash, and Waterpocket Canyon.

Halls Creek runs through Grand Gulch.

This was initially called Hoxie Creek for Richard L. Hoxie of the Lieutenant George M. Wheeler Survey of 1872–73. It was still known by that name as late as 1924. (1028~, 1901~)

In 1882 both Volney King and Sam Rowley called it Grand Gulch. (1014~, 1096~) This name is still in use.

Charles Hall (1823-1904) was a scout on the Hole-in-the-Rock Expedition. Realizing that the Hole-in-the-Rock route was too difficult, another and easier way was found. (See Appendix Two—Halls Road, and Hall Ranch below.) John A. Widtsoe in 1922: "There is so much magnificent scenery that in spite of our best desires, we are not appreciating it as we should. Marvelous how man becomes callous"! (2007~)

—Lake Mead: This large stock reservoir is at the junction of Bitter Spring Creek and Halls Creek (at elevation 5187T on the Bitter Creek Divide map). A lake this large in a dry country seemed to be "Lake Mead" in size to ranchers. (582~, 745~)

—Color Canyon: The mouth of this small western tributary of Halls Creek is one and three-quarters of a mile north of Brimhall Double Arch (at elevation 4525T on the Deer Point map). Former Capitol Reef National Park Ranger Fred Goodsell: "Color Canyon refers to the unusual rainbow of colors and shades of rock that radiate from the Chinle Formation in the center portion of the canyon." (745~)

—FW Canyon: This western tributary of Halls Creek is three-quarters of a mile south of Halls Creek Overlook (immediately south of elevation 5224T on the Deer Point map). An inscription that appears very old and reads "FW" gives the canyon its name. It is likely that Grove Karl Gilbert of the Powell Survey called this Pa-runa-weap Canyon: "The gulch in which we find water is Pa-runa-weap of the narrowest type. The horses can go only within 200 ft. of the water on account of the narrowness and we have to carry it to them. The walls rise about 400 ft. and the gulch ends abruptly." (722~, 723~)

—Road: A uranium-era mining road goes partway up FW Canyon.

—Hopsage Canyon: The mouth of this crooked western tributary of Halls Creek is two miles downcanyon from the Fountain Tanks (three-quarters of a mile southwest of elevation 5123T on the Deer Point map). Fred Goodsell: "The name of the canyon comes from a plant species growing in the canyon. They are typically located in the Mojave desert, but are rare in Capitol Reef." (745~) Inscriptions include R. Baker, March 30, 1934. (SAPE.)

—Spiderwart Meander: (Also called Spiderwart Canyon.) The mouth of this small western tributary of Halls Creek is two and one-quarter miles (as the crow flies) north of Millers Creek (one-half mile north of elevation 4333T on the Hall Mesa map). Fred Goodsell named it in 1973 for the many spiderwart flowers he found here. (745~)

—White Toad Canyon: The mouth of this small western tributary of Halls Creek is two miles (as the crow flies) north of Millers Creek (one-quarter mile south of elevation 4333T on the Hall Mesa map). Fred Goodsell named it in 1973 after finding what at first appeared to be a dead bleached toad in the canyon. While reaching for it, he was surprised to find that the "dead" toad was in fact alive and was a normally white Great Basin spadefoot toad. (745~)

—South Canyon: The mouth of this small western tributary of Halls Creek is one and one-half miles north of Millers Creek (one-quarter mile west of elevation 4330T on the Hall Mesa map). Fred Goodsell named the canyon in 1973. It is on the southern border of Capitol Reef National Park. (745~)

—Hall Ranch: (Also called Halls Ranch.) This historic ranch on Halls Creek was two and one-half miles downcanyon from Millers Creek (one-quarter mile south of elevation 3741AT on the Hall Mesa map). In 1881 Charles Hall established a small farm here. From the farm he ran a ferry that was one mile north of the mouth of Halls Creek and eight miles from his farm. In order to see if he had ferry customers, Hall would climb a high ridge on the Waterpocket Fold near the farm to a vantage point where he could see the ferry crossing. It is speculated that he had a signaling system. (See Halls Crossing.)

Hall abandoned the ferry in 1884 when the railroad was built to Green River. Wagon roads dropping south from the railroad provided easier access than the arduous Halls Road.

The National Park Service closed the road down Halls Creek to vehicles in 1974 and the whole canyon to cattle in 1988. (303~, 470~, 699~, 745~, 925~, 1476~)

Inscriptions include one that reads "C. Hall Camped here with his family." (1115~)

—Baker Ranch: (Also called Smith Ranch and Smiths Ranch.) This ranch, now underwater, was two miles downcanyon from Hall Ranch (one mile west-southwest of elevation 4131T on the Hall Mesa map). In 1907 what was to become the historic Baker Ranch was established by Thomas Smith. In 1908 Dr. William H. Schock noted it as Smith's Cabin. By 1910 Smith had eight hundred deeded acres in valley. He sold the ranch to Eugene Baker (1878-1942) and family in 1919. John A. Widtsoe described the ranch as it was in 1922: "Small three roomed shanty, cistern and corrals." (2007~)

The Bakers made a go of it until the mid-1940s when poor grazing and an uncertain water supply for crops forced them to vacate the ranch. Eugene Baker's son, Carlyle, then purchased a ranch to the east of Thousand Lake Mountain, in 1946. (See Rock Springs Wash—Baker Ranch.)

In 1946 the Halls Creek Cattle Association took over the land, though they did not have anyone living at the ranch. In 1965 the federal government bought the land (303~, 1697~) and soon thereafter it was flooded by the rising waters of Lake Powell.

—There were four ways to get to the ranch. First, go down Halls Creek. Second, cross Bullfrog Creek and go around the southern end of Hall Mesa and up Halls Creek. Third, follow the Baker Trail from the Waterpocket Fold. (See

Stevens Canyon–Baker Trail.) Fourth, take the Loco Trail. (See Halls Creek Overlook—Loco Trail.)

Harry Aleson and Arthur Chaffin tried to tow a boat down Halls Creek in 1957. Aleson: "Slowgoing down Hall Creek—scouting afoot—bog-downs in quickie [quicksand] spots—brushing rocks—snaking boat trailer thru with long rope—finding and losing (due to washouts) trail—ploughing and fighting deep, dry sands—left trailer and boat." (39~)

—Whiskey Creek: The mouth of this small western tributary of Halls Creek is at the Baker Ranch (immediately south of elevation 4013 on the Hall Mesa map). Dwight Williams: "Evidently it must've been where they cached the whiskey." (2013~) The Baker Ranch used the water as well. Lenard E. Brown: "Water from Whiskey Creek was brought down in a concrete ditch to the vineyard and orchard.... Cooking and drinking water was stored in a cistern about 150 feet east of the main ranch house. Holding two or three thousand gallons, it was filled from Whiskey Creek." (303~)

Halls Creek Overlook: (Garfield Co.) Capitol Reef National Park-Waterpocket Fold-Halls Creek. Deer Point map.

Also called Brimhall Overlook.

—Loco Trail: (Also called Brimhall Trail and Ticaboo Trail.) This is the "Pack Trail" that goes from Halls Creek Overlook into Halls Creek. Dwight Williams: "We nicknamed [that] the Loco Trail because loco weed is a problem down in that area. Some years it makes the animals crazy if they eat it.... We went off this trail and killed three or four cows because they were locoin' and a few of 'em went off the trail." (2013~)

The trail went unused for years. In 1972 Capitol Reef National Park Ranger Fred Goodsell was told about the trail. All he could find, though, was an inscription panel partway down the cliffs. Taking a pick and shovel, Fred, doing his best guesswork, reestablished the trail. Since then the trail has been reworked several times and is now a popular hiking trail. (745~)

Halls Crossing: (San Juan Co.) Glen Canyon NRA-Lake Powell-Highway 276. Halls Crossing map.

Also called Halls Crossing Marina, Halls Landing, Halls Old Ferry (1215~), and Halls Upper Ferry (162a~).

(See Halls Creek for name derivation. See Appendix Two—Hall Road for more information on the crossing.)

The Halls Crossing shown on the map is not the location of the original Halls Crossing. It is the present location of Halls Crossing Marina. On the west side of the river the actual Halls Crossing was one-quarter mile east of elevation 3877T. On the east side of the river the crossing was adjacent to elevation 3967T.

In 1882 Josephine Catherine Chatterly Wood was with a group that crossed here: "Now it is our turn—O pray for us! We drove on to this raft, and the wagon was securely tied to it with ropes. The men started to rowing, and down the raft and all went into the water with a splash. My heart went faint. I went blind and clung to my babies. I shall never forget my feeling as we went down into the water and my fear of the wagon going off into the swift-flowing water. Before we started I asked Fred [Jones] to nail the cover down on all sides [of the wagon] so that if we were drowned we would all go together, and he did. When the treacherous river was safely crossed, we did thank our Heavenly Father." (2041~)

Inscriptions near the crossing included R. Hall, 1887; W.S. Rust, Dec. 12/88; Wm. Bright came to river, 1889; J.L. Foy, May 5, 1890; Otto Lind, Ouray Colo., Ja 26-93; and W.R. Carrell, July 29, 1897. (466~)

—Big Bar: (Also called High Bar.) This placer bar, now underwater, was on the south (or east) side of the Colorado River and was one mile north of Halls Crossing Marina (one-half mile north-northwest of elevation 3744T). Big Bar was first mined in 1888. (466~)

Hamblin Spring: (Washington Co.) Dixie National Forest-Cove Mountain-Holt Canyon. Pinto map.

This medium-size spring was once developed. (SAPE.)

—Hamblin Town: (Also called Fort Hamblin, Jacob Hamblin Fort, Jacob Hamblins Fort, Jacob Hamblin's Town, and Mountain Meadows.) This small town was a couple of hundred yards south of Hamblin Spring. Jacob Hamblin (1819-1886) and his two brothers settled here in 1856, picking the location because it was on the Old Spanish Trail. After a couple of years Jacob Hamblin was called by Brigham Young to help settle other areas in Dixie. Overgrazing and gullying caused the abandonment of the town by the early 1900s. Today there is little left but stone foundations. (371~, 1551~, SAPE.)

George C. Fraser in 1915: "[Hamblin Town] is marked by two deserted frame houses and a stone house, all of them built subsequent to Jacob Hamblin's time." (668~)

—Hamblin Cemetery: This is labeled on the map.

Hambrick Bottom: (Emery Co.) Castle Valley-San Rafael River. Hadden Holes map.

Thaddeus Hambrick (1845-1904) and family moved to the area in the late 1880s. (1330~) Millie Biddlecome: "He lived down on the Bottoms, they called it, and his family had very little to go on. He raised horses." (227~)

Hambrick acquired the land through the Desert Land Act. (791~)

Hamiltons Fort: (Iron Co.) Cedar Valley-Shurtz Creek-Interstate 15. Cedar City NW map.

Also called Ham's Fort (360~) and Shirts Fort (1658~). Also spelled Hambleton Fort. (M.50.)

Dixie pioneer Peter Shirts started a ranch near Hamiltons Fort in 1852. (369~, 1013~) At that time it was variously called Fort Sidon after Sidon in Phonecia, Asia (942~, 2053~) and Walker's Fort because of the troubles with Ute Chief Walker (369~, 1715~).

Shirts offered half of the creek to his friend John Hamilton, Sr. if he would move his family here, which he did in 1853. In 1857 the present site of the fort was picked by George A. Smith, who then named it in honor of John Hamilton, Sr. (369~)

Hammond Canyon: (San Juan Co.) Manti-LaSal National Forest–Ute Mountain Ute Indian Reservation-Dark Canyon Plateau-South Elk Ridge-Cottonwood Wash. Kigalia Point and Cream Pots maps. There is some PRIVATE PROPERTY in this canyon.

The lower part of the canyon is on Ute Indian land and access is denied. The rest of the canyon, from the Cream Pots Trail up, is National Forest Service land and has been proposed as the Hammond Canyon Archaeological Area.

Fletcher B. Hammond: "This canyon with abundant lower country that could be used as winter range seemed to catch the eyes of the Hammonds [Fletcher A. Hammond and his son, Fletcher B. Hammond]; and they said they would pre-empt this part of this new and beautiful country for their herd. After consultation the group said, 'If you are sure you like this part of this new country, probably the first white men ever to set foot on these parts [in 1886], it is proper and fit that we should call this canyon HAMMOND CANYON'; and that is how it got its name. Fletcher B. Hammond soon built a log cabin some little distance in it from Cottonwood [Wash], and that became the headquarters of the Hammond cattle company." (821~)

The canyon still shows many signs of occupation, from structures made from axe-cut trees to inscriptions dating to the late 1800s. A diversion dam, check dam, water works, and several corrals in the lower canyon give evidence that this canyon, with its year-around stream, was once heavily used.

—Posey Trail: (Also called Forest Service Trail #012.) This constructed stock trail starts at Little Notch on Elk Ridge and goes east down a southern fork of Hammond

Canyon (Kigalia Point map). It was built by the Utes and Paiutes who lived at the mouth of Hammond Canyon. (See Posey Canyon.)

—Blue Ice Fork: This short southern tributary of upper Hammond Canyon is one and one-half miles east-north-east of Little Notch (one-eighth mile south of elevation 6983T on the Kigalia Point map). Blue ice runnels are common in the canyon in winter. (SAPE.)

—Hammond Canyon Arch: This pretty arch is on the north side of upper Hammond Canyon and is two and one-half miles east-northeast of Little Notch (near elevation 7525T on the Kigalia Point map). Byron Cummings in 1910: "In Hammond Canyon we came upon a natural arch that in its proportions and form was beautiful and attractive, but ... it will no doubt be many years before this arch will become as well known as the natural bridges of White and Armstrong canyons." (505~)

—Lunch Canyon: This northern tributary of Hammond Canyon is four miles downcanyon from Little Notch (at elevation 6327T on the Cream Pots map). (799~)

—Guymon Canyon: The head of this northern tributary of Hammond Canyon is one and one-half miles south-southeast of East Point (just north of elevation 6109T on the Cream Pots map). Pete Steele noted that Willard Guymon lived in Blanding. (1821~) In 1959 he helped James H. Gunnerson during an archaeological survey of the canyon. (799~)

—Olsen Canyon: This northern tributary of Hammond Canyon is one-quarter mile downcanyon from Guymon Canyon (west of elevation 6287T on the Cream Pots map). (799~)

—North Trail: This goes generally up the ridge between Guymon and Olsen canyons. It is surmised that this route was constructed in the 1940s. (SAPE.)

—Cream Pots Trail: (Also called Forest Service Trail #005.) This road, now a hiking trail, goes from the Cream Pots north into Hammond Canyon between Guymon and Olsen canyons (Cream Pots map). It was a stock trail until the late 1950s or early '60s when it was upgraded into a logging road. (1451~, 1821~)

—Jess Posey Farm: In 1927 Herbert E. Gregory mentioned this farm being five miles up Hammond Canyon (immediately east of elevation 6405T on the Cream Pots map). (761~)

Ham Rock: (Grand Co.) Arches National Park-Garden of Eden. The Windows Section map.
John F. Hoffman noted that this is shaped like a ham. (898~)

—Pothole Arch: This is on the north side of Ham Rock. It was named by Stanley W. Lohman of the Denver office of the USGS. (898~)

Hancock Canyon: (Garfield Co.) Dixie National Forest-Sevier Plateau-Casto Canyon. Casto Canyon and Flake Mountain West maps.
Cyrus Alonzo Hancock (1845-1905) was the first person to build a home in what is now Panguitch, in 1871. (138~) He grazed sheep in the canyon in the mid-1890s. (1346~)

Hancock Flat: (Sevier Co.) Fishlake National Forest-Fish Lake. Burrville map.
Dee Hatch noted that Albert Hancock and family were early settlers of the Grass Valley area. (844~) They were dairy farmers. (1191~)

Hancock Peak: (Iron Co.) Dixie National Forest-Mammoth Creek. Brian Head map. (10,598')
Also spelled Handcock Peak. (516~)
Two name derivations are given.
First, Dixie National Forest Ranger Frank W. Seaman noted that a man named Hancock was lost here for several days in the early years. (2053~)
Second, Ernest Hancock ranched on nearby Mammoth Creek starting in the mid-1870s. (363~)

Hancock Spring: (Coconino Co., Az.) Vermilion Cliffs National Monument-Vermilion Cliffs. Emmett Hill, Az. map.
This medium-size spring was once developed. Inscriptions include the date 7/31/11, no name and G.(?) Hancock, July 19, 1925. (SAPE.)

—Constructed Stock Trail: This goes up the drainage immediately north of Hancock Spring to the top of the Vermilion Cliffs. It was probably just used as a sheep trail. Inscriptions include July 17, '11, no name. (SAPE.)

—Bonelli Spring: This is the "Spring" near the top of the Vermilion Cliffs four miles west-northwest of Hancock Spring (one-quarter mile west of elevation 7097 [Jacob] on the One Toe Ridge map). A sheepman named Bonelli developed the spring in the early 1930s and pumped water up to tanks on the rim. A crack in the upper wall provides access to the Sand Hills. (1083~, SAPE.)
Inscriptions include Ben Hamblin, no date; D.E. Hoyt, July 14, 1942; and Fred J. Benally, 1966. (SAPE.)

—Black Hills Spring: This small spring is one mile southeast of Bonelli Spring (one-eighth mile southwest of elevation 5587 on the One Toe Ridge map) at the base of a jumble of intriguing black hills. Nearby stock reservoirs and corrals were built by the CCC. (SAPE.)

Hancock Spring: (Garfield Co.) Henry Mountains-Dark Canyon. Mount Pennell map.

Guy and Nina Robison noted that this developed spring was named for rancher Riley Hancock. (1645~)

Hang Dog Creek: (San Juan Co.) Manti-LaSal National Forest-La Sal Mountains-Twomile Creek. Mount Peale and La Sal East maps.

Unattributed: "Hang Dog is a good one—a dog was left tied in a shed and accidentally hanged himself before its owner returned." (456~)

Hanksville Airport: (Wayne Co.) Muddy Creek-Highway 24. The Notch map.

This was built in 1946 as an emergency airstrip. Miriam B. Murphy: "The emergency landing strip proved its worth many times. In 1951 a DC-8 with forty-two passengers and crew members had to land in Hanksville, and in 1959 a TWA Constellation en route to Los Angeles with fifty-four aboard made an emergency landing. Bad weather and low fuel contributed to the forced landing of many small aircraft over the years." (1419~)

Hanksville: (Wayne Co.) Henry Mountains-Fremont River-Dirty Devil River-Highways 24 and 95. Hanksville map.

Also called Hanks Place (2053~) and Hankstown (1075~). There has been some confusion as to the derivation of the original name of Hanksville, which was Graves Valley. Three name derivations are given.

First, Barbara Ekker: "Some older folks say it was called Graves first because of mounded Indian graves outside of town." (607~)

Second, again Barbara Ekker: "Others say an old hermit by the name of John Graves was here when Ebenezer Hanks and his family arrived in 1882." (607~, 469~) Barbara Ekker also noted that the hermit Graves, upset by the intrusion of newcomers, moved to the Colorado River for more solitude. (607~)

Unattributed: "People of Hanksville have a legend concerning this man Graves, who lived the life of a hermit there, having a large band of horses. Eventually, Cass Hite, a prospector, joined him as a partner. Their prospecting ground was around Mt. Pennell in the middle Henry Mountains. Meeting with little success.... Graves mysteriously faded from the picture and has since been referred to as the ghost of Mt. Pennell." (1186~)

Charlie Gibbons, who moved from Loa to Hanksville in early 1882: "When the first people moved there [to Hanksville] there was a hermit by the name of Graves who lived there and it's how it got its name. The people began to settle and he left and went to Mt. Pennell and

was there for a long time. They called him the Evil Spirit of Mt. Pennell. He later disappeared and no one knew where." (1288~)

Third, the Powell expeditions used both the names Groves Valley (as in a grove of trees) and Meadow Valley. (1186~) In 1882 Elias H. Blackburn of Loa noted it in his diary as Groves Valley and provided one of the first, albeit brief, descriptions: "a good valley about 4,000 acres of bottom land." (248~) Blackburn expanded on this description later: "It Seems that almost any thing Can be raised here. Weather Warm. Vegetation Grass & Starting Green. It is all that I Expected." (1412~)

Fourth, Charles B. Hunt surmised that the town was named for a Walter H. Graves. He was a topographer with Grove Karl Gilbert of the Powell Survey of 1875–76. (925~, 1537~)

Fifth, Franklin A. Nims of the Stanton-Brown Survey of 1889–90 called it Grouse Valley: "At Grouse Valley we stopped and got a few supplies at a little store. The town is Mormon and located in a nice valley at the foot of the Henry Mountains on the Dirty Devil River." (1461~)

It is known how Hanksville got its final name. Albert King Thurber visited the area while looking for a route from Rabbit Valley to Glen Canyon in 1881: "It contains 5,000 to 6,000 acres of good lands, with the Fremont River running through it. The Curtis Creek [Muddy Creek] comes in at the lower end of the valley ... soil very rich." (1888~) Ebenezer Hanks (1815–1884), told of the area by Albert King Thurber, was looking for a place where he could support his polygamous family. Hanks, joined by the Goulds, McDougalls, and Sylvesters moved to the area in 1882. Hanks died after only two years. It wasn't until a post office was established in 1884 that the town was named Hanksville for him. (607~, 1047~)

Robert Brewster Stanton in a fit of whimsy in 1898: "We timed our journey so as to stop in Grave's Valley overnight, and thus we approached it in the evening. Looking across from the southwest to the terraces beyond, just before the twilight, there is laid out, against the pale amethyst sky, a city of immense proportions, with streets and avenues, parks and pleasure grounds, cathedrals with towering domes and spires, palaces and halls, battlements and towers, monuments and minarets. And as the sun begins to sink behind the western hills, the bright rosy red rays, flashing back from the polished ledges of rock, bring out more clearly into view, first one and then another, the great carved palaces with their windows all aglow; while the domes of majestic cathedrals burst forth in one ruby mass, and the towers upon the battlements one by one raise their beacons of flashing fire. Then, gradually, and sometimes suddenly, each light is extinguished, and the evening shades, in veilings of pink and lilac, are drawn over the seemingly perfect, yet weird metropolis, blotting out the scene and leaving but a single, rugged, and regretful mountain sky line." (1767~)

Leland Hargrave Creer: "One of the dreariest and loneliest sites in Utah is Hanksville.... Isolated and secluded." (489~)

Jack Breed in 1952: "Hanksville itself proved to be a sad spot. Once knee-deep in rich prairie grass, the region around it is now unimaginably barren and desolate." (277~)

Robert Coughlan in 1954: "One comes upon it with disbelief; a speck of stubborn protoplasm amidst the vastness of the desert, surrounded by drifting sands, stupendous buttes, grotesque red sandstone shapes and arid washes filled with loose, bone-dry pebbles." (457~)

—Emery to Hanksville Pioneer Road: (See Appendix Two—Emery to Hanksville Pioneer Road.)

Hansen Creek: (Garfield Co.) Henry Mountains-Glen Canyon NRA-Glen Canyon. Cass Creek Peak, Copper Creek Benches, Ant Knoll, Lost Spring, and Bullfrog maps.

Also called Squaw Creek.

Also spelled Hanson Creek.

Two possibly related name derivations are given.

First, Charles Kelly noted that a man named Hansen tried to drive an ox team down the creek in about 1882. (925~, 1049~)

Second, C. Gregory Crampton noted that in 1888 N. Hansen and Theodore Hansen were the first to establish a mining claim at the mouth of the creek. (466~)

Hansen Creek was often called Copper Creek for copper deposits found along one of its upper tributaries on Mt. Hillers. (466~)

Buzz Holmstrom called it Billy Hay House Creek in 1937, with a note: "He went thru three years ago for relics." (903~)

Herbert E. Gregory in 1918: "Sandstone in Hansen Canyon wonderful, overhanging, arched, & grand alcoves—overhang of one estimated 120'." (760~)

Katie Lee in 1955: "We have to walk through the willows and along the Kayenta ledge to enter its mouth. The most beautiful array of tapestry walls I've yet to see are in this canyon. Every bend shows another and each is a work of art." (1162~)

Inscriptions include Moroni Hunt, 12-17-15; Oral King and Victor Goodwin, 3/28/39; and Grant Maxfield and Ellis Pritchett, Dec. 18, 1949. (SAPE.)

—Mining Road: This wagon road down Hansen Creek was built in the 1890s to service mining claims in the area. (466~, 470~, 925~)

—Smith Bar: (Also called Smith Brothers Bar.) This placer bar, now underwater, was on the west side of the Colorado River and was bisected by the mouth of Hansen Creek (Bullfrog map). The earliest miners prospected the bar in 1888. The Smith brothers are known to have mined here. (466~, 1766~) (See Smith Fork.)

Inscriptions included A.W. Allen, 1889; Byron Cook, 1898; and Ira Behunin, Feb. 3, 1913. (466~)

—Moqui Bar: (Also called Dr. Schock Bar and Gressman Bar. Also spelled Moki Bar and Moquie Bar.) Moqui Bar, now underwater, was on the west side of the Colorado River one mile downcanyon from the mouth of Hansen Creek (one-quarter mile northeast of elevation 3724T on the Bullfrog map). Prehistoric pecked hand and foot holds, often called Moqui steps, went up the cliffs behind the bar. They were noted by early miners and gave the bar its name. (466~)

This large gravel bar was also known as Chaffin Bar for Louis M. Chaffin. He was one of the locators in 1895. Louis M. Chaffin: "The Moki Bar produced more gold than any other bar on the river." (405~)

Robert B. Stanton in 1897: "The flat in front is finest farm below Good Hope, 200 or 300 acres, perhaps, easily watered." (1812~)

Pearl Baker, when asked the question, "What amounts of money were required to buy a bar such as the Moki?" replied: "There weren't any sales, much. Some fellow would come in and make big plans and would be right back in two weeks with all the equipment needed—then borrow a dollar to get home on." (108~)

—Noble Canyon: This short, western tributary of Glen Canyon is two miles downcanyon from the mouth of Hansen Creek (northwest of elevation 3818T on the Bullfrog map). Derivation of the name is unknown, but it was in use in the 1890s. (466~)

—Elbow Bar: (Also called Moki or Moqui bar.) This placer bar, now underwater, was on the west side of the Colorado River at the mouth of Noble Canyon. C. Gregory Crampton: "The inside bend of the Colorado River ... is suggestive of the shape of an elbow." (466~)

Hans Flats: (Wayne Co.) Glen Canyon NRA-Millard Canyon. Head Spur map.

Also called Harris Flat. (1672~)

Hans Anderson was an employee of the Biddlecomes at their ranch at Crow Seep. (See Crow Seep.) Pearl Baker: "Hans Andersen was a small, red-headed Irishman, droll and sweet-tempered.... He was a good stockhand, tended to business, and was completely reliable." (120~, 607~)

Happy Canyon: (Garfield and Wayne Counties.) Dirty Devil Country-Dirty Devil River. Gordon Flats, The Pinnacle, and Burr Point maps.

Four similar name derivations are given.

First, Ned Chaffin: "The old-timers said it was named 'Happy Canyon' because you were very 'Happy' to get out of the canyon." (413~)

Second, Mary Beckwith: "Happy Canon was named from a remark made by a ranch hand who was sent into the canyon to retrieve some stock. He floundered around for a considerable period of time and remarked upon getting out, '...that he was damned HAPPY to finally find his way out.'" (192~)

Third, Ted Ekker: "The reason that they called it Happy Canyon was because they could take in two or three herds of sheep and ... just go home and leave them there ... leave them for a month." (623~)

Fourth, Hazel Ekker: "A sheep herder was in there with sheep from Hanksville. Owner had sent him to Hatch Canyon. Went to Hatch Canyon and searched for him. He was found in the next canyon down and he said, 'I knew I wasn't in Hatch Canyon but I was in another canyon and I am sure happy to get out of there.'" (616~)

Ned Chaffin noted that in the early days Sam "Broomtail" Adams ran wild horses in upper Happy Canyon. (411~)

The Happy Canyon name was in place by 1909. (1523a~)

—South Fork Happy Canyon: (Clearwater Canyon map.) (Also called Big Fork.) (100~) Ted Ekker noted that a mining road constructed by the Simplots during the uranium years in the 1950s starts one-half mile northwest of Lands End (at elevation 6927T). It goes northwest into the canyon. An airstrip in the canyon (two miles east of The Pinnacle at elevation 4934T on The Pinnacle map) was also constructed by the Simplots. (623~)

Happy Jack Mine: (San Juan Co.) Wingate Mesa-White Canyon-Highway 95. Copper Point map. PRIVATE PROPERTY.

James H. Knipmeyer noted that in 1899 the Blue Dike Mine was filed on by six individuals. Alonzo P. Adams bought the mine in 1902. Thereafter the mine went through many hands and was then abandoned for several years until the uranium boom. It then became the Happy Jack. (1115~)

Gary Topping: "In the San Juan country, the most profitable uranium mine by far was the Happy Jack.... In 1946 a Moab road contractor ... bought the mine for $500. The mine was unprofitable because the low-grade copper ore was too contaminated with uranium to be economically refined. They were about to sell the mine for back taxes when the government announced its uranium-buying program.... During its peak in the 1950s, the Happy Jack produced thirty tons of ore per day, and netted its owners over $25 million." (1901~) The owners were Joe Cooper and Warren Bronson. (246~)

Sandy Johnson told the story of his grandfather's near miss with the Happy Jack: "Joe Cooper come down here and filed on that. He wanted my granddad to come down and help him mine it. And at that time money was pretty hard to get ahold of and my granddad says that all he had to come up with was two hundred and fifty dollars. And he couldn't come up with that two hundred fifty dollars. So Cooper got [some other folks] and they came up with the two hundred fifty dollars. And when they sold out they each got seventeen million out of it." (1002~)

—Uranium Ore Buying Station: In 1955 the Atomic Energy Commission built a buying station at the foot of the Happy Jack Mine on Highway 95. (246~)

Happy Valley: (Wayne Co.) Dixie National Forest-Boulder Mountain-Sulphur Creek. Grover map.

Some of this land is PRIVATE PROPERTY.

Also called Covington Ranch. (1931~)

Sulphur Creek runs through Happy Valley.

Emmett Clark noted that the valley was named by June Covington. He spent his honeymoon here in about 1920, and came back calling it Happy Valley. (426~)

Hardhead Water Spring: (Kane Co.) GSCENM-Kaiparowits Plateau-Big Sage. Carcass Canyon map.

Also called Hard-head Spring.

This is a large, developed spring. (SAPE.)

Edson Alvey noted that the name derivation is unknown. (55~)

Hardscrabble: (San Juan Co.) Cedar Mesa-Pollys Canyon. Pollys Pasture map.

Two name derivations are given.

First, DeReese Nielson: "The cowboys had a hard scrabble making a go of it.... Rough times." (1451~)

Second, S.G. Daniel of the USGS in 1986: "Hardscrabble is a term referring to an area of rocky sandy ground that does not support vegetation." (1931~)

Hardscrabble Bottom: (San Juan Co.) Canyonlands National Park-Labyrinth Canyon. Horsethief Canyon map.

Also called Granite Bottom. (M.78.)

Michael R. Kelsey noted that the trail used to get into and out of Hardscrabble Bottom was difficult, giving the bottom its name. (1085~)

—Hardscrabble Camp: This is the "Campground" on the bottom.

—Mule Bottom: This is on the north (or west) side of the Green River and is immediately west of Hardscrabble Camp (one-half mile southeast of elevation 4020T). Ken Allred named the bottom for a couple of mules he found here. (1085~) The remnants of a rock house are near the northeast end of the bottom.

—Constructed Stock Trail: This goes from Mule Bottom up the initial cliff band to the north. Another constructed stock trail traverses along the river to the west and goes to Tent Bottom. (SAPE.)

Hare Valley: (Wayne Co.) Awapa Plateau-Antelope Spring Draw. Smooth Knoll map.

Alfonzo Turner: "I presumed and always thought it was named after Harvey Mangrum." (1914~)

—The Homestead: This line camp is at the "Corral" in Hare Valley. Alfonzo Turner: "A fellow by the name of Hyrum Brinkerhoff homesteaded that up there and had a bunch of sheep. He hauled water on a wagon from Antelope Spring out there in the summer and homesteaded that ground. He had a sheep wagon there." (1914~) Alfonzo also noted that Claire Okerlund later obtained the property. The corral and a cabin ruin are still at the site. (SAPE.)

Harley Dome: (Grand Co.) Book Cliffs-Grand Valley-Interstate 70. Harley Dome map. PRIVATE PROPERTY. This small community was named for oilman Harley Basker. He lived in the area in the 1920s. (644~, 1195~)

—Harley Dome Gas Field: This gas field contains natural gas that is rich in helium. In the 1920s the wells were capped and the area was set aside as a federal gas reserve. Limited production has occurred from time to time. (1658~)

Harmon Canyon: (Carbon Co.) West Tavaputs Plateau-Nine Mile Canyon. Currant Canyon map.

—Harmon House: PRIVATE PROPERTY. (Also called Hanks Ranch and Old Rock House.) (558~, 725~) Edwin L. Harmon (1854-1933) and family built a rock house in Nine Mile Canyon one-quarter mile west of the mouth of Harmon Canyon in the late 1880s. It was a stage stop along the route from Price to Myton. (558~, 1788~) The Hanks family owned the property until at least the mid-1930s. (725~)

—Sky House Ridge: This prominent north-south ridge is directly south of the Harmon House. (725~)

—Harmon Canyon Junction: This is where Harmon Canyon meets Nine Mile Canyon. (912~) The old pioneer road up the canyon has now been improved into a good road used by gas and oil industry trucks.

Harmon Creek: (Washington Co.) Dixie National Forest-Pine Valley Mountains-South Ash Creek. Signal Rock and Pintura maps.

Appleton Milo Harmon (1820–1877) and family moved to Toquerville in 1862. He supervised the construction of the cotton mill on Mill Creek near Washington in 1865–66, built a furniture factory in Toquerville, and a woolen mill in Washington Town. (160~, 363~, 1141~)

Harmonica Point: (Sanpete Co.) Manti-LaSal National Forest-Wasatch Plateau. Ferron Reservoir map. (10,513')

—Petty Peak: This is the highest summit on Harmonica Point (at elevation 10513). In 1997 the USGS named the peak for George Albert Petty (1861-1944), an early settler. (260~, 1930~)

Harmony Flat: (San Juan Co.) Cedar Mesa-Highway 95. Kane Gulch map.

Hole-in-the-Rock Expedition member Kumen Jones in 1880: "So called for a party of original [Hole-in-the-Rock] pioneers who came from New Harmony and laid over a few days hunting for horses that strayed off." (1018~)

Harpole Mesa: (Grand Co.) Manti-LaSal National Forest-La Sal Mountains-Pinhook Valley. Warner Lake map. (7,039')

Joseph Harpole (1801-1908) had a ranch in Castle Valley from 1886 to 1908. He was the oldest man in the state when he died. (456~, 1546~)

Harrisburg Town: (Washington Co.) Virgin River-Quail Creek. Harrisburg Junction map.

Also called Cottonwood Creek. (1572a~)

George A. Smith visited what would become Harrisburg: "This little settlement is located in a desert spot, which I first visited in 1857, and did not even suspect, what is now [1870] a fixed fact, that a thriving village with blooming orchards and vineyards containing a great variety of fruit would so soon ornament a spot so desolate and barren." (1771~)

Moses Harris (1789–1890) and family moved from San Bernardino, California to an area near present-day Harrisburg, or what they called Harrisville, in 1859. The original site was abandoned and the residents moved three miles up Cottonwood Creek to the present site of Harrisburg, changing the name along the way. A little town blossomed and by 1868 there were over one hundred people living here. Flash floods, a grass hopper invasion, and water problems forced abandonment by the early

1890s. Most of the families moved to the nearby town of Leeds. (258~, 354~, 371~)

Priddy Meeks: "I moved to Harrisburg and while there I saw more trouble than I ever saw in all my life before. I went there well off and left there miserably broke up and through the rascality of the people." (1343~)

Charles Roscoe Savage described Harrisburg country in 1870: "All around us the earth looks like as though it had been calcimined, broken up and desolate looking." (372~)

—Harrisburg Dome: An oil well, shown on the top of the dome as a "DH" (Drill Hole), was drilled in the early 1920s. (163~)

Harris Flat: (Kane Co.) Dixie National Forest-Markagunt Plateau. Long Valley Junction map.

Also called Harris Claim Pasture (485~), Harris Claim Ranch (416~), and The Ranger Station (1191~).

Julius S. Dalley that this was named for Moses Harris (1798-1890), a Glendale pioneer. (2053~, 388~)

—Harris Flat Ranger Station: This was built after 1912. The station closed in the early 1950s. (2021~)

Harris Fork: (Grand Co.) Uintah and Ouray Indian Reservation-East Tavaputs Plateau-Big Dogie Canyon. Chicken Fork map.

Gilmore Anderson "Ink" Harris (1873-1958) of Green River ran livestock in the Book Cliffs and on the East Tavaputs Plateau. (622~)

Harris Mountain: (Kane Co.) White Cliffs-Block Mesas. Elephant Butte map. (6,666')

Kate B. Carter noted that a Harris family ranched here in the 1880s. (384~) June R. Roundy: "[there] is a mountain named Harris Mountain. Below the mountain lies a flat that is called the Harris Flat, then midway between the mountain and the sand dunes we find the Harris Springs. It is not known how they received the name of Harris. Llewellyn [Harris] records having lived in that area at least from 1862 to 1865." (1656~)

—Joe Creek: The exact location of this is unclear. One source noted that the creek was "under the south bluff of 'Harris Mountain' and was '... named for Indian Joe.'" (2053~)

Harris Springs: (Kane Co.) White Cliffs-Block Mesa. Yellowjacket Canyon map.

(See Harris Mountain for name derivation.)

This is a large, still-used spring with troughs. (SAPE.)

Thomas Chamberlain mentioned Harris Spring in 1893. (416~)

Harris Wash: (Garfield Co.) GSCENM-Glen Canyon NRA-Escalante Desert-Escalante River. Tenmile Flat, Red Breaks, and Silver Falls Bench maps.

(See Llewellyn Gulch.)

Harris Wash is the lower part of Alvey Wash. The name changes at Tenmile Spring (Tenmile Flat map).

There are two conflicting stories about the naming of the canyon. First, the dominant story is that Llewellyn Harris (1832-1908), one of the earliest settlers in the area, had a farm at the head of the wash in the late 1870s. (2051~)

Second, Edson Alvey noted that Jimmy L. Harris (1866-1930) was an early stockman. (55~, 388~)

The Powell Expedition of 1871–72 called this both Rock Gulch and Rocky Gulch. They later renamed it False Creek after at first thinking they were on the Dirty Devil River. (1877~, 2051~) In 1926 William Gladstone Steel noted, incorrectly, that the False Creek name came from the fact that the water "rises and sinks in the sand." (1819~)

The Lieutenant George M. Wheeler Survey map of 1872–73 shows this as False Creek, with the note "Dry" tacked on. (M.76.)

Charles P. Berolzheimer in 1920: "The canyon grew narrower and steeper, its red sides rising above to a height of four hundred feet. The canyon twisted back and forth, forming little sand benches and at other places, running in under the cliff.... In the canyon walls were many caves and small holes, some of which contained cliff dwellings or grainaries." (222~)

Inscriptions include George Gunn, Nov. 12, 1888. (1115~)

—Halls Road: (See Appendix Two—Halls Road.) Two variations of the Halls Road went down Harris Wash. One version went from the town of Escalante and down Harris Wash. Another version went across Spencer Flat and down the Lower Sandslide. The routes then joined and went up Silver Falls Creek.

In 1920 the Ohio Drilling Company improved the old wagon road through Harris Wash and up Silver Falls Creek to Wagon Box Mesa in Circle Cliffs Basin, making it passable for trucks. In 1968 the State Road Department looked seriously at improving the old wagon and uranium mining road into a paved road if the Trans Escalante Federal Parkway over the Waterpocket Fold was not built. (See Stevens Arch—Trans Escalante Federal Parkway.) The road was, supposedly, closed permanently after the area was included in Glen Canyon National Recreation Area. (777~, 1168~) In 2007 the possibility was again raised of opening the road and turning it into a highway.

—Zebra Slot: (Also called Unique Slot.) This northern tributary of Harris Wash is north of its junction with

Halfway Hollow (immediately west of elevation 5579 on the Tenmile Flat map). Scott Patterson: "The first time we went there the stripes made it look zebra-like. On a sunny day it looks more like a Candy Cane and that name is more appropriate. I wish we would have named it Peppermint, but the name Zebra is the one that stuck." (653~)

—Constructed Stock Trail: This starts in Harris Wash at a corral (not shown on the map) that is one-quarter mile south of elevation 5312 on the Red Breaks map and goes southwest towards Seep Flat. Inscriptions include George Gunn, Nov. 12, 1888, Parowan City. (SAPE.)

—Constructed Stock Trail: This starts in Harris Wash at a "Corral" and "Spring" (at elevation 5059 on the Red Breaks map) and goes south to Buckaroo Flat. Inscriptions include the date May 8, 1891. (SAPE.)

—Harris Wash Trailhead: This is in Harris Wash three-quarters of a mile downcanyon from the aforementioned "Corral" and "Spring" on the Red Breaks map.

—Devils Gate: This narrow area in Harris Wash is three miles (as the crow flies) downcanyon from the Harris Wash Trailhead (near elevation 5007 on the Red Breaks map). (1760~) In 1952 Allen Cameron called it Hells Gate: "The full fury of summer flash floods is channeled through this narrow passageway." (334~)

—Emigrant Steps: This horse ladder is on the north side of Harris Wash one and one-third miles (as the crow flies) up from the Escalante River (near "2-134" on the Silver Falls Bench map). The steps were used as a shortcut for those following the Halls Road. (1760~) Don Coleman: "I don't know how it got its name. Only that it was from the old-timers. They was tryin' to get off from up here on The V down to the Escalante River. So they cut them steps to get their horses up and down.... An old rancher named Lloyd Gates told me that the Indians had a trail there first." (441~)

Burns Ormand noted that the trail was built in the 1880s and was used by cowboys herding livestock on The V and to avoid the willow thickets in Harris Wash. (1487~) Another source noted that wagons were lowered down the cliffs into Harris Wash here. (384~)

Harrison Peak: (Washington Co.) Dixie National Forest-Bull Valley Mountains-Grassy Flat. Central East map. (7,729')

Richard Harrison (1807–1882) was a Pinto pioneer. (388~)

Harrison Spring: (San Juan Co.) Mancos Mesa-Moqui Canyon. Mancos Mesa map.

Sandy Johnson noted that Harrison Spring and Harrison Canyon were named for TY Ranch foreman Harrison Oliver. He was here in the 1950s. (1002~)

Eric Bayles: "Harrison Oliver was a small man and seriously hard of hearing. Harrison was a terrible driver because he couldn't hear the engine. He would rev the engine up until he could hear it, then dump in the clutch, with all kinds of comical consequences and abuse of the equipment." (167~)

—The Crack: This is a particularly narrow section of the old cattle trail that went by Harrison Spring and up the cliffs to the north. Carl Mahon: "When we went out there the first time, it was pretty rough and usually if the horse didn't mind what he was doing or hadn't been there before, there was a good chance he would fall down because there are some bad places there. And during the uranium boom ... there were some fellows from Dove Creek went out there and they ended up killing two horses there.... Then in the mid-1960s we took a portable generator and drill out there and we drilled and shot and then cribbed that up. We spent maybe four or five days, maybe a week, there on that Crack to get that shot out and make it safe to go up and down." (1272~)

Erwin Oliver, the son of Harrison Oliver: "We was comin' off of Mancos Mesa one time and I had probably sixty head of cattle with me. This was before they had that road up there. We'd camped up on that little point right near The Crack where we could hold them. The next morning we started down into Moqui Canyon and there is a narrow little chute you had to go down for a short ways to the next level and you'd have to turn there or if you kept going straight it was quite a ways over the cliff. And there was only so much room in that chute. We were puttin' these cattle down there and I was riding this bronco. I hadn't rode him very much. There was some slickrock right on top, sloped just a little. This one cow broke away and I didn't want him to go. So I kinda jumped that colt out there to head the cow off. He turned the cow all right, and when he did, his hind feet stepped out on this slickrock a little too far and he went over this edge with me. It was a long way to the ground. And I looked up and I could see that colt's feet above me and I was right under him, still in the saddle.

"This all happened in a split second. And you won't believe what happened. We was falling a long ways and I was still in the saddle and we was upside down and all of a sudden I felt a hand reach out and grab me and set me back on that ledge. It was the hand of God that grabbed me and saved my life. You can't tell me there isn't a God.... He picked that horse up and set him down on his feet." (1479~)

The crack was widened by construction of a road in 1971 by an oil company. (1002~) (See Mancos Mesa—Exxon Road.)

Harry Colwes Spring: (Kane Co.) GSCENM-Kaiparowits Plateau-Indian Gardens. Blackburn Canyon map.
Correctly spelled Harry Cowles Spring.
This is a medium-size spring. (SAPE.)
Don Coleman: "Henry [Newell] Cowles [1868-1938] was an old cowboy that ran cattle out there." (441~) (See Hole-in-the-Rock—Fort Hall.)

Hartnet, The: (Wayne Co.) Capitol Reef National Park-South Desert. Cathedral Mountain and Fruita NW maps.
Also called Hartnet Country. (1931~)
David Hartnet developed a difficult trail between Rabbit Valley and Caineville in the early 1900s. The route went across Thousand Lake Mountain and down Polk Creek for a short distance to South Desert Spring. It then crossed The Hartnet and Hartnet Draw and went by Acklin Spring to Rockwater Spring. Miriam B. Murphy: "From there, [it] went east to Willow Spring, and then down Caineville Wash to Caineville." (1419~)
The route was used to avoid the often impassable Capitol Wash (Capitol Gorge) route between Torrey and Caineville. The Hartnet Trail was improved into the Hartnet Road in the mid-1940s (1476~) or in 1954 (1419~).
—Slickrock Reservoir: This stock reservoir, now abandoned, is on Hartnet Draw one-half mile west of its junction with Pierce Draw (one-quarter mile south-southeast of elevation 6236 on the Cathedral Mountain map).
—Acklin Spring: This is the "Spring" in Hartnet Draw that is three miles west of the Temple of the Moon (one-half mile south of elevation 6202 on the Fruit NW map). Although used from the early days, it was not developed until 1955. A corral is nearby. (1497~, SAPE.)
—Hyrum Williams Bench: This is on The Hartnet one mile south of Acklin Spring (at elevation 6263T on the Fruita NW map). Keith Durfey noted that Hyrum Williams (1870–1928) ran sheep here in the early days. (582~)

Harts Draw: (San Juan Co.) Harts Point-Indian Creek. Monticello Lake, Photograph Gap, Hatch Rock, Harts Point South, and North Six-shooter Peak maps.
Also called Hart Canyon (761~), Hart Draw, and Hart Draw Canyon.

Jim Scorup in 1957: "The feature [was named] for an early cattle rustling homesteader in the draw, by the name of Charlie Hart." (1931~) Frank Silvey noted that the name was in place by 1883.

Francis F. Kane in 1891: "The trail continued along Hart's Wash.... This Hart's Wash, as it is called, seems to contain first rate winter pasture." (1037~)

Margaret Perkins: "The first known record of any white man passing through the country was made by the U.S. Topographic Engineers Expedition in 1859. Under the leadership of [Captain John N.] Macomb, this expedition passed east of the Abajo Mountains and descended 'Cañon Colorado' to its juncture with the Grand (Colorado) River." (1526~, 1443~) Fran Barnes established that Macomb's *Cañon Colorado* was in fact Harts Draw. (146~)

John Strong Newberry of the Macomb Expedition: "We reached the brink of a large cañon 1,200 feet in depth, which we called, from the prevailing color of its walls, Cañon Colorado, into which with great difficulty we descended." (1443~)

Charles H. Dimmock was with the Macomb Expedition: "To accomplish a descent of some 600 feet to the valley beneath, the trail turns somewhat North of East & winding around the intricacies of the bluff, by a path the trembling mule hesitates to pursue, follows up the side, slowly descending from ledge to ledge, for 3 ½ miles, ultimately reaching the bottom of the gorge [Harts Draw]. It may be proper to state that this descent is deemed impracticable for a train of packed mules & that the train with the military escort were left at Camp ..., and a small armed party of nine pushed on to seek the junction of the Grand & Green Rivers." (559~) The *Cañon Colorado* name was in use until at least 1868. (M.19.)

Arthur A. Baker told this story in his Field Notes of 1927: "Chub [a horse] was killed by falling off a ledge into boulders. Goldman had ridden him down Hart Draw and tied him to limb of tree. While Goldman was absent Chub reared back, broke off the limb and apparently became frightened by dragging limb and fell backwards over cliff." (98~)

—Harts Spring: (Photograph Gap map.) PRIVATE PROPERTY. The Scorup-Somerville Cattle Company patented the spring in 1940. It now belongs to Val Dalton. (517~, 1936~)

—Macomb Canyon: This eastern tributary of Harts Draw is one and three-quarters of a mile south of the head of Little Water Creek (one-eighth mile southwest of elevation 6096AT on the Harts Point North map). Until 1988 it was unclear how the Macomb Expedition of 1859 actually got from Harts Point into Harts Draw. At that time Tom Budlong discovered the route down what he called Macomb Canyon. This rugged route, which Macomb took livestock down, starts on the north side of the canyon. (143~, 146~, SAPE.)

—Frost Canyon: This northern tributary of Harts Draw is one mile west of the head of Little Water Creek (immediately south of elevation 5965T on the Harts Point North map). (143~) A constructed stock trail leads partway down the canyon to a good spring and a hand-dug stock pond. The trail starts one-eighth mile east of elevation 5965T. Nearby is an inscription from Joel Redd, no date. (SAPE.)

—Last Chance Water: This spring on Harts Point is one-quarter mile southwest of elevation 6210T on the Harts Point North map. It was the last reliable water as one went north on Harts Point. A constructed stock trail leads to the spring. (99~, SAPE.)

—Last Chance Well and Sheep Corral: These are one-half mile south of Last Chance Water (at elevation 6373T on the Harts Point North map). The well is no longer in use. (SAPE.)

—Aqueduct Arch: This is the "Natural Bridge" in a western tributary of Harts Draw that is two and one-half miles southeast of Last Chance Well (near elevation 6358 on the Harts Point North map). Robert H. Vreeland: "The name comes from the appearance of the arc of rock." (1951~)

Harts Spring Draw: (San Juan Co.) Dry Valley-Harts Draw. Photograph Gap map.

(See Harts Draw for name derivation.)

Val Dalton: "There's a story of a lost gold or silver mine associated with Hart Springs Draw because it was one of the routes in and out of that lower country from the Dugout Ranch. The story has it, there was a guy getting ready to quit the Dugout and they asked him to take a bunch of horses when he left and leave them at corrals there at the old homestead at Harts Spring. He had an old bag that he carried on his saddle that he filled with rocks to throw at the horses when they'd get in a narrow place on the trail. When he got done moving the horses, he threw this bag of rocks down right there by the corral. Nobody paid any attention to it. A year or two later, somebody noticed that bag of rocks and picked them up and noticed they looked like there was some metal in them. He had them assayed and one story says they were gold and one story says they were silver." (517~)

Harveys Fear Cliff: (Kane Co.) GSCENM-Kaiparowits Plateau. Navajo Point map.

Two similar name derivations are given.

First, Don Coleman: "There was a man with the last name of Harvey. He was chasin' wild cattle up on the Kaiparowits Plateau. He roped one and the cinch broke and he fell off his horse and he wouldn't let go of the rope to the cow. And it was a mean cow, and it was after him. And so he got knocked over the edge of the cliff and he grabbed onto a bush and hung on. The rope was still on the cow and every time Harvey would try to crawl back over the edge of the cliff, it would run at him, which would slacken the rope. He would slide down, and then the cow, not seeing Harvey, would walk away and at the same time pull him back up. Back and forth went the cow, and up and down went Harvey. And that's a big steep ledge down off'n there. That's how it got the name Harveys Fear." (441~)

Second, David Roberts told a slightly different story: "Way back in the early years of the last century, a ranch hand named Harvey Watts was chasing cattle in the vicinity. An ornery old cow suddenly reversed direction and pushed Harvey's horse off the edge. Harvey managed to grab a small bush and dangled there, a slip away from a fatal fall, while the cow deliberated whether to finish the job or go back to munching grass. Since then the cliff has been named for the cowpoke's terror." (1636~, 1931~)

—Harveys Fear Horse Trail: (See Appendix Two—Talus Trail.)

Hastiin Yazhi Bito: (Coconino Co., Az.) Navajo Indian Reservation-Rainbow Plateau. Face Canyon, Az. map.

Leon Wall noted that *Hastiin* is Navajo for "a man"; *Yázhí* is "small" or "little"; and *Bito'* is "water," or something along the lines of "Small Man Water." (1962~) Jesse C. Dyer of the USGS noted the translation as "Littleman's Water Pockets." (588~)

The name refers to a large pothole with a constructed stock trail going down to it on the west side of Hastiin Yazhi Bito (one-quarter mile south of elevation 4328T). (SAPE.)

Hatch Canyon: (Garfield Co.) Dirty Devil Country-Dirty Devil River. Clearwater Canyon, Fiddler Butte, and Stair Canyon maps.

Ned Chaffin: "Two canyons here. We always called the canyon on the north and west 'North Hatches Canyon' and the fork on the south and east we called 'South Hatches.'" (413~)

Two name derivations are given. The first is believed to be correct.

First, Pearl Baker in 1966: "[Edwin T.] Wolverton ... said that [Hatchie] was the old Indian name for that canyon." (109~) Hazel Ekker: "Roy Whitehorse (Navajo man) ... says that *atchee* means a red color—then he places both hands carefully together making every finger match and says, '... there is a little difference but I can't tell it *atchee*—say it that way (and I can't find even a hint of difference) means high cliff. How about that for Hatchie Canyon. I'll bet it was once *atchee atchee*—like high red cliff.'" (109~)

Second, Guy and Nina Robison noted that it was named for rancher Ren Hatch. This was either Lorenzo Hatch (1854-1926) or his son, Lorenzo, Jr. (1877-1931). (1645~)

—South Trail: (Also called Squaw Trail.) (287~) This is the "Pack Trail" that starts on The Big Ridge and goes south into North Hatch Canyon (Clearwater Canyon map). Ted Ekker noted that it started as a constructed stock trail and was improved to a vehicle road during the uranium boom of the 1950s by the Simplots. The road is now closed to vehicles. (100~, 623~) (See Two Pipe Spring.)

—Pass: This unnamed pass, a part of the South Trail, is between North and South Hatch canyons and is two and one-half miles west-northwest of Sunset Pass (between elevations 5383T and 5492T on the Clearwater Canyon map). Inscriptions include Mont Caldwell and Roy Blackburn, April 26, 1932. (SAPE.)

—Old Spanish Trail: (Variation.) The Old Spanish Trail—Winter Route—went through Hatch Canyon. (1737~)

Hatch Canyon: (Piute Co.) Awapa Plateau-Otter Creek. Abes Knoll map.

Dee Hatch noted that George Andrew Hatch, Sr. (1847-1910) and family moved to Greenwich in 1877. (844~, 1972~)

Hatch Mesa: (Grand Co.) Book Cliffs-Interstate 70. Hatch Mesa map. (5,586')

—Hatch Ranch: PRIVATE PROPERTY. This was one mile east of Hatch Mesa and two miles north-northeast of Floy (near elevation 4745). The ranch was started by Lorenzo "Ren" Hatch, Jr. (1877-1931). (1780~, 646~) For several years in the late 1920s and early 1930s the Bill Tomlinson family rented the ranch. (1898~) There is little left. (SAPE.)

—Ascent Route: A route to the top of the mesa is on the north side of the projecting east-trending southern peninsula. Although there are other routes to the top, this was apparently the most commonly used. It is unclear if this was used for stock. Inscriptions along the route include

H.L. Moon, 1904; W.D., Aug. 13, 1905; H.C. Reynolds, 1929; and Duck Tomlinson, 1934. (SAPE.)

Hatch Mountain: (Garfield Co.) Dixie National Forest-Limerock Canyon. Hatch and Haycock Mountain maps. (8,292')

Abie J. Haycock: "Ira W. Hatch [1852-1936], one of the very prominent citizens of Panguitch in early days, did a great deal to develop the country all up the Mammoth Creek and in beautiful Castle Valley." (363~)

Hatch Point: (San Juan Co.) Canyonlands National Park-Needles District. Shafer Basin, Lockhart Basin, Trough Springs Canyon, North Six-shooter Peak, and Harts Point North maps.

(See Hatch Ranch Canyon–Hatch Ranch for name derivation.)

Lloyd Holyoak: "There's a trail that goes out of Hatch Wash onto Hatch Point. One day we were gathering cattle in Hatch Wash and dad posted me at its head while he went looking for cattle. While he was gone I went to sleep under a tamarisk tree. He woke me up and he says, 'Oh, I see you found a snake!' Right next to me was a really big rattlesnake laying out its full length.... It was about five feet long and had thirteen rattles. Luckily I rolled away from him! I killed him. I remember that like it was yesterday." (906~)

—Silveys Pocket: Frank Silvey: "In 1887 [Jack Will and Frank Silvey] discovered 'Silvey Pocket' on Hatch Point, overlooking the Colorado River." (1740~) The location is unknown.

—Minor Overlook: This small butte and overlook are on the west side of Hatch Point three miles south of Hurrah Pass (at elevation 5579T on the Trough Springs Canyon map). From a plaque at the overlook: "David C. Minor. 1939–1990. NPS and BLM Recreation Planner cheerfully worked for the public in the Needles and Canyon Rims areas from 1968 to 1990." (1551~)

—Wineglass: This small arch is one mile south-southeast of Minor Overlook (one-quarter mile south-southwest of elevation 5569T on the Trough Springs Canyon map). Shaped like a wine glass, it was named by local cowboys. (1951~)

Hatch Ranch Canyon: (San Juan Co.) Hatch Point-Hatch Wash. Hatch Rock map.

Also called Hatch Wash Canyon. (1931~)

This was initially known as Hudson Wash for rancher Joshua B. "Spud" Hudson. He had a winter camp at Hatch Rock starting in the late 1870s or early 1880s. (1741~)

—Hatch Ranch: This was on the west side of Hatch Ranch Canyon one-half mile upcanyon from its junction with

Hatch Wash (near elevation 5645T). Frank Silvey noted that Alonzo Hatch started ranching in the canyon in 1881. Later, Henry Wood ranched this for the Carlisle Cattle Company. In the late 1880s the Silveys bought the ranch. Silvey described the ranch as it was in 1881: "[they] soon reached a fine large spring with a nice, natural meadow surrounding it." (1741~)

John Frank Sleeper in 1890: "We reached the Hatch Ranch which is a rendezvous house for all of the horse thieves in the country, and they were all on the dodge for some stealing or killing that they had been in. When we came in sight they sneaked off up in the hills thinking we were officers." (509~)

Inscriptions include Faleen, 1886; Jas Lewis, 1887; and M.C. Carson, Oregon, 7-27-1890. (1112~, SAPE.)

—Ojo Verde: (Also called Green Spring.) Fran Barnes noted that the spring near the now abandoned Hatch Ranch was on the route of the Old Spanish Trail. The Spanish called it *Ojo Verde*, or "Green Eye" because the clear spring pool was surrounded by green grasses. (142~)

John Strong Newberry of the Captain John N. Macomb Expedition of 1859: "The Ojo Verde is a copious spring in a cañon cut out of the red sandstone, ten miles west of La Teneja [Casa Colorado Rock]. The surrounding country is very sterile ... but about the spring the bottom of the cañon is covered with the greenest and most luxuriant grass." (1266~)

Hatch Town: (Garfield Co.) Sevier River-Highway 89. Hatch map.

Also called Hatche's Ranch, Hatch Ranch, Hatch's Ranch, Hatchtown, Mammoth, Mammoth Old Hatch Town, and Mammoth Ranch.

Meltiar (also spelled Meletiah) Hatch (1825-1895) and his two wives were part of the Eagle Valley Mission in Nevada. When Nevada demanded back taxes from the Mormon settlers, they abandoned the state and many of those from the Eagle Valley Mission resettled near Panguitch. The Hatch family chose land near the junction of Mammoth and Asay creeks on the Sevier River in 1872. By 1877 a small town had developed and the Hatch name had been applied. After a flood in 1900, the town was moved one mile north to its present location. (373~, 832~, 1445~, 1551~)

—Big Hill: This is the hill on the southwest edge of town (at elevation 7145). (832~)

—Hatchtown Dam: This dam on the Sevier River near the mouth of Mammoth Creek was built in 1907–08. The dam burst on May 26, 1914, sending a torrent of water sixteen feet deep through the town of Circleville. Although there was a real fear that the high water would cause the dams at Otter Creek and Piute reservoirs to burst, they held. No lives were lost, though there was significant damage to houses, farms, and roads. (1516~)

Hatch Trading Post: (San Juan Co.) Navajo Indian Reservation-Montezuma Creek. Hatch Trading Post map. PRIVATE PROPERTY.

It is believed that Roy Rutherford started a trading post near here in 1903. Joseph Hatch bought the trading post in 1924 (or 1926 depending on source). He built a new trading post—today's Hatch Trading Post—in 1926. His brother, Ira, took over in 1927, and Ira's son, Sherman, took over in 1949. It is now owned by Laura Hatch. (217~)

Hatch Wash: (San Juan Co.) Dry Valley-Hatch Point-Kane Springs Creek. Church Rock, Sandstone Draw, Hatch Rock, La Sal Junction, Eightmile Rock, and Trough Springs Canyon maps.

(See Hatch Ranch Canyon for name derivation.)

—Constructed Stock Trail: This crosses Hatch Wash one-half mile (as the crow flies) above its confluence with Little Water Creek. The trail starts at a "Corral" on the west side of the canyon and goes east into the canyon and out by way of an unnamed side canyon shown to the south of elevation 5640T on the La Sal Junction map. (SAPE.)

Hat Rock: (Grand Co.) Book Cliffs-Bitter Creek. Bryson Canyon map.

The name was given by oil and gas field personnel in the early 1960s. (1931~)

—Number Four Point: This prominent point is one mile north-northeast of Hat Rock. It overlooks the B.W. Hancock No. 4 Hancock-Federal Gas Well. (1634~)

—Robs Canyon: This western tributary of Bitter Creek goes northwest between Number Four Point and Hat Rock (immediately south of elevation 6192). (1634~)

—Apex Point: This is one mile west-northwest of Hat Rock (at elevation 6494). (1634~)

Hattie Green Mine: (Kane Co.) GSCENM-The Cockscomb. Fivemile Valley map.

Two conflicting stories are told.

First, Thomas W. Smith: "Peter Shirts and Ezra Meeks were the first white men to settle on the Pahreah Creek. They were mining men and were interested in a claim located about three miles east of Rock House, known as 'the Hattie Green Copper Mine.'" (1783~)

Second, this copper mine was started by George J. Simonds in 1893. It was abandoned by the 1920s. (1083~, 2053~)

Hatt Reservoir: (Emery Co.) San Rafael Desert-San Rafael River. Jessies Twist map.

(See San Rafael River—Hatt Ranch for name derivation.)

Hawkeye Natural Bridge: (San Juan Co.) Navajo Indian Reservation-Deep Canyon. Deep Canyon South map.

Charles L. Bernheimer in 1925: "[Zeke] Johnson had been there in 1925 and carved his name on the side ... it should be noted that the matrix is in process of forming a second bridge back of the free-standing one, and in doing so it has a deep recess in the center resembling an eye. As there is a similarity between a hawk's eye and this bridge ensemble, we decided to name the bridge 'Hawk's Eye Bridge,' the free standing part being the eyebrow, the matrix part the eye slit and eye balls." (218~)

Frank E. Masland, Jr.: "It is actually a double arch with a complete narrow break-through above the cave in the background." (1308~)

Senator Barry Goldwater in 1951: "Hawkeye is a magnificent arch—not so imposing as Rainbow, but worthy of more attention than it has received.... It has amazing symmetry, and the soft texture of the stone enhances the beauty of its structure." (739~)

Hawkins Canyon: (Garfield Co.) Circleville Canyon-Sevier River. Fremont Pass and Bull Rush Peak maps.

William R. Hawkins arrived in Greenwich in the 1870s. (388~)

Haws Pasture: (Garfield Co.) Dixie National Forest-Boulder Mountain-Bear Creek. Deer Creek Lake and Boulder Town maps.

Lenora Hall LeFevre noted that John Franklin Haws (1864–1919) established a dairy farm here in 1885. (1168~)

Hay Canyon: (Grand Co.) Roan Cliffs-Westwater Creek. Cedar Camp Canyon, Preacher Canyon, and Dry Canyon maps.

—Old Trappers' Trail: Hay Canyon was part of the old fur trapper route from the Grand Junction area to the Uintah Basin in the 1830s-40s. The actual trail in Hay Canyon paralleled the present-day road going up the West Fork of the canyon, but on the east side of the canyon. (See Appendix Two—Old Trappers' Trail.)

Inscriptions include D. Julien, 18??. (SAPE.) (See Appendix One—Denis Julien.)

—Old U.S. 6 and 50: The old highway from the south side of the Book Cliffs-East Tavaputs Plateau to the north side went through Hay Canyon.

Hay Canyon: (Kane Co.) Pink Cliffs-North Fork Virgin River. Strawberry Point and Straight Canyon maps.

Kate B. Carter: "Hay was cut in this canyon during the early settlement of Kanab." (384~) The name was in place by 1895. (416~)

Haycock Mountain: (Garfield Co.) Dixie National Forest-Panguitch Creek. Haycock Mountain map. (9,047')

Linda King Newell noted that Albert Haycock (1856-1937) had a ranch on Haycock Creek starting in the 1870s. (1445~) Maurice Newton Cope: "After many years in the sheep business Haycock came out with about the same amount as he started with." (453~)

Haycock Point: (Kane Co.) GSCENM-Kaiparowits Plateau-Wahweap Creek. Glen Canyon City and Nipple Butte maps. (5,331')

Samuel Haycock (ca. 1832-1904) was an early settler of Sink Valley. (59~)

Hayes Wash: (Carbon Co.) Book Cliffs-Price River. Deadman Canyon, Wellington, and Price maps.

Also called Sand Wash. (1931~)

—Dead Horse Crossing: This pioneer crossing of the Price River was a short distance downriver from the mouth of Hayes Wash and four miles south of Price. Albert Barnes: "This Dead Horse Crossing received its name from the fact that so many horses had died from drinking the water which had formed in clear pools but was so extremely alkaline that it caused their deaths." (1621~)

The area near Dead Horse Crossing was also the initial location of Wellington Town. (1621~)

Hay Lakes: (Garfield Co.) Dixie National Forest-Awapa Plateau. Big Lake and Pollywog Lake maps.

Dunk Taylor: "There was lots of sheep out there in the early days and there was lots of grass growing in them. Now cows would wade out and pretty well eat the grass off them shallow lakes. But the sheep wouldn't go in the water. And that is how it got its name." (1865~)

Haymaker Bench: (Garfield Co.) GSCENM-Calf Creek-Highway 12. Calf Creek map.

Nethella Griffin Woolsey noted that Charles Haymaker moved to the Escalante area in 1886. For a couple of years he lived in a cabin at the mouth of Calf Creek and raised sugar cane. (2051~)

—Claude V. Cutoff Road: This historic road starts one mile northeast of Calf Creek Recreation Area (mile 77.5 or one-eighth mile west of elevation 5863 on Haymaker Bench). It then crosses Dry Hollow and Boulder Creek and ends in Boulder. Jerry Roundy noted that the road was built in 1924 as a shortcut from the Boulder Road into lower Boulder Town. Claude V. Baker (1881–1945) had a ranch near the road. (1655~)

Haystack Rock: (Coconino Co., Az.) Navajo Indian Reservation-Navajo Mountain. Chaiyahi Flat, Az. map. (6,111')

Also called The Haystacks. (1919~)

Frank E. Masland, Jr.: "two great conical slickrock heaps that are so aptly named." (1308~)

This was the first proposed site for Rainbow Lodge. (See Rainbow Lodge.) The site, though, lacked water. (843~)

Head of Bullfrog: (Garfield Co.) Henry Mountains-Bullfrog Creek. Mount Ellen map.

(See Bullfrog Creek for name derivation.)

Bullfrog Creek heads at Head of Bullfrog.

Head of Sinbad: (Emery Co.) San Rafael Swell-Interstate 70. The Blocks, San Rafael Knob, Twin Knolls, and The Wickiup maps.

Also called Red Hills, Sinbad Plateau, Swasey Flats, and Wild Horse Country.

Also spelled Head of Sin Bad. (728~)

Clarence Dutton of the Powell Survey called this high area in the middle of the San Rafael Swell both the Red Amphitheatre and the Valley of Rasselas. (584~) Bert J. Silliman: "It may be explained that the Valley of Rasselas was a vale of peace and plenty protected from adversity by rock girt walls. And those sandstone vertical precipices that ring the Sindbad [*sic*] are the points of similarity with the Valley of Rasselas." (1734~)

It is believed that the Sinbad name was given by early Spanish explorers as they followed the Old Spanish Trail, perhaps after reading the stories of *The Arabian Nights* (published in English in 1706). (641~, 1330~)

LaMont Johnson: "Sinbad ... so named because of its massive collection of tinted peaks, cliffs, buttes, pinnacles, ledges and summits, looking like the ruins of an ancient city from a distance in the rays of the early morning sun or the late afternoon sun. The origin comes straight from the Arabian Nights, since travelers of every nationality, including Arabs, followed the Spanish Trial." (995~)

Bert J. Silliman: "Just how the name of Sindbad was transferred from Arabia to these inaccessible, rock walled, inhospitable valleys must be an interesting story, but at this time, its details can only be guessed at." (1734~) (See Roc Creek for more on the name derivation.)

Harry Aleson in 1960: "This Sinbad Country surely is spectacular, deep and rugged, and more fabulous than much or most of the Grand Canyon." (37~)

—Head of Sinbad Pictographs: These were added to the Utah State Register of Historic Sites in 1971.

—Old Spanish Trail: (Variation.) The Old Spanish Trail—Winter Route—crossed the Head of Sinbad. (1734~)

—Wood Holler Road: This went from Ferron, down Horn Silver Gulch, through Coal Wash, to Sinbad Country. It was the first road into Head of Sinbad and was built before 1928. (727~, 1318~)

Inscriptions in various places on the Head of Sinbad include James Watt, May 26th, 1893, Manti, Utah; Warren Allred, 1895; and Royal Allred, 1924. (SAPE.)

—Pasture Pond: This stock reservoir is on the Head of Sinbad one mile north of Forked Post Pond (at elevation 7012 on the San Rafael Knob map). (1853~)

—The Pasture: This is the pasture area around Pasture Pond. Lee Mont Swasey: "We had a couple of fences there [about one-quarter mile northwest of Pasture Pond]. That made it a nice pasture to turn saddle horses loose and you could find 'em again." (1853~)

—Swasey Cabin: The foundation of a very old log cabin is one-quarter mile northeast of Pasture Pond. Lee Mont Swasey: "The Swaseys built a cabin there and you can still find the foundation out there." (1853~, SAPE.)

Headquarters Valley: (Kane Co.) GSCENM-Kaiparowits Plateau-Wahweap Creek. Canaan Peak and Butler Valley maps.

—Headquarters Cabin: (Butler Valley map.) Ralph Chynoweth: "There's an old cabin up in the head of Headquarters. The ranchers had a headquarters for their operations up there." (425~) The cabin is still there. (SAPE.)

Head Spur: (Wayne Co.) Glen Canyon NRA-The Spur. Head Spur map.

(See The Spur for name derivation.)

This was called Head of Spur by ranchers. (604~)

—The Beehives: Ted Ekker noted that this dome is on the northwest side of Head Spur two miles north-northwest of Outlaw Spring (at elevation 6070T). (623~)

Heaps Canyon: (Garfield Co.) Dixie National Forest-Escalante Mountains-Main Canyon. Griffin Point, Upper Valley, and Wide Hollow Reservoir maps.

Also spelled Heppes Canyon. (1559~)

(See Heaps Ranch for name derivation.)

Heaps Canyon: (Washington Co.) Zion National Park-Zion Canyon. Temple of Sinawava map.

Also called Emerald Pool Canyon. (2080~)

Also spelled Heeps Canyon and Hepes Canyon.

Nancy C. Crawford: "William Heaps farmed land near the mouth of Emerald Pool canyon and built a cabin near by [in 1884]. For many years this little canyon was known by the settlers as Heaps Canyon." (482~, 2043~) J.L.

Crawford noted that Heaps bought his land from early resident Isaac Behunin for two hundred bushels of corn. (480~)

Heaps Ranch: (Garfield Co.) Kaiparowits Plateau-Escalante River-Upper Valley. Wide Hollow Reservoir map. PRIVATE PROPERTY.

Nethella Griffin Woolsey noted that Willard Heaps (1862–1934) and family homesteaded here in the 1880s. (2051~)

Hearthstone Flat: (Sevier Co.) Fishlake National Forest-Scorups Meadows. Rex Reservoir map.

—Hearthstone Spring: This is a large spring. (SAPE.)

Heath Wash: (Washington Co.) Dixie National Forest-Pine Valley Mountains-Cottonwood Wash. Signal Peak and Harrisburg Junction maps.

This was most likely named for St. George pioneer Henry Heath (1828–1908). He arrived here in 1862. (462~)

Hebes Mountain: (Emery Co.) San Rafael Swell-Mussentuchit Flat. Ireland Mesa and Mussentuchit Flat maps. (6,312')

Pearl Baker noted that Hebe Wilson ran cattle in the area in the 1890s. (122~)

—Constructed Stock Trail: This trail helped stock get around a dry fall in Hebe Canyon that is west of the south end of Hebes Mountain (one-eighth mile southwest of elevation 5855 on the Ireland Mesa map). (SAPE.)

—Hebe Canyon Stock Pond: This pond, still used by wild horses, is in Hebe Canyon one-half mile west-northwest of Slaughter Slopes Reservoir (Ireland Mesa map). (SAPE.)

Hebron Town: (Washington Co.) Flat Top Mountain-Shoal Creek. Hebron map.

Also called Shoal Creek. (1262~)

This small town was started by John and Charles Pulsipher in 1862. Because of Indian troubles, a fort was built in 1866. Erastus Snow visited the town in 1868 and suggested the name "after the ancient Hebron in Palestine." (972~) The town, never large, slowly vacated and by the late 1890s most of its residents had moved to nearby Enterprise. (972~)

Heliotrope Mountain: (Sanpete Co.) Manti-LaSal National Forest-Wasatch Plateau. Heliotrope Mountain map. (11,130')

Two name derivations are given.

First, Wayne Gremel: "Heliotrope is a type of purple flower that grows up there on that mountain." (780~)

Second, Hugh F. O'Neil in 1940: "So named because in early days a heliograph station was established there by the United States Geographic Survey and the name

'Heliotrop' was a local corruption of 'heliograph.' Now renamed Wasatch peak by the geographic survey, after the Wasatch range of mountains." (1484~) The Heliotrope Mountain name was retained.

Hell Canyon: (San Juan Co.) Manti-LaSal National Forest-La Sal Mountains-Pack Creek. Mount Tukuhnikivatz map.

Jose Knighton noted that this is considered the most rugged canyon in the La Sal Mountains. (1103~) Lloyd Holyoak: "Everybody who has hunted in Hell's Canyon has named it that because trying to carry a deer outta Hell's Canyon is a long, drawn-out affair. It's a rough canyon. If you have stock down in there you have to walk in to get them. You can't get a horse in there. It was hell being down in that canyon." (906~)

Hell Hole: (Garfield Co.) Circleville Canyon-Sevier River. Fremont Pass and Bull Rush Peak maps.

Kent Whittaker: "There's pretty rough goin' up through there." (2002~)

Hell Hole Canyon: (Piute Co.) Fishlake National Forest-Sevier Plateau-The Elbow. Malmsten Peak map.

Edward Sudweeks in 1941: "The name is descriptive of the rough, deep, rocky canyon." (2053~) Newel Nielson: "You get in there, you can't get out." (1458~)

Hell Roaring Canyon: (Grand Co.) Tenmile Country-Labyrinth Canyon. The Knoll, Jug Rock, and Mineral Canyon maps.

Also spelled Hell Rorin Canyon.

Two similar name derivations are given.

First, Julius Stone of the Stone-Galloway Expedition of 1909: "A few miles below Bowknot Bend a tributary entering the Green from the east has cut through the massive red sandstone a sharp gorge known by the expressive name of Hell Roaring Canyon. At ordinary times the roar is not terrifying. But the undercut rocks and their water-polished surfaces are mute reminders that there are times when the canyon has not [a] peaceful aspect.... During storms such gorges hold roaring torrents of muddy water sweeping in terrifying fury down their rock-ribbed troughs. These are fed by the rain-born cascades which plunge over the brink from the rock shelves above where they have gathered chocolate, amber, and red sand and boulders." (1840~)

Second, Norm Nevills in 1938: "Canyon well named as the wind causes a roar." (1442~) William Cook: "a side canyon named for the roar of the strong wind that often blows through it." (449~)

Senator Barry Goldwater in 1941: "That is a terrible name to put on such a beautiful side canyon, and the man who so named it must have been in a bad mood that day for I could easily think of nicer names for this spot." (736~)

Guy Robison told a story about winter in Hell Roaring Canyon: "I went down there one Christmas eve. Art and Hazel [Ekker] went to Hanksville to his mother's place for Christmas, and Art says, 'You just as well go down and see if the water's still runnin' there. There's a spring in Mineral Canyon and see if it's froze.'

[At that time, the only access to Mineral Canyon was by way of the Hell Roaring Stock Trail. (See below.)] It was pretty cold weather. And I did and the water was runnin' good but the [Green] river was so solid that during the night it would 'boom' like a cannon.... I knew it was going to be a cold night and I drug up quite a little pile of cottonwood where I had my camp. Along in the night, I froze out. I didn't have a bed enough and so I lit the fire and made a good, big fire. I had two horses, and both of 'em come up to that fire. They were both white ... had frost on 'em ... and one of 'em was a sorrel and the other was brown and they both looked the same. But they stood right there by that fire, just like a man would, warm one side and then turn around and warm the other and they never left it. As quick as daylight come, I got my stuff together and on 'em and outta there. They told me later that it got forty below that night." (1644~)

Hellroaring Canyon contains one of the oldest inscriptions along the Green River. Nathaniel Galloway of the Stone-Galloway Expedition of 1909: "M. Stone find 3 hundred yards up the [Hell Roaring] canyon the inscription D. Julien, 3 Mai 1836." (701~) (See Appendix One— Denis Julien.) Other inscriptions include Edwin T. Wolverton, Mart. Baker, N.E. Wolverton, 7/1/1905. (1112~)

—Jewell Tibbetts Arch: This is at the head of Hell Roaring Canyon (The Knoll map). Jewel Tibbetts (1903–1969) was the wife of rancher Bill Tibbetts. He ran livestock in the area in the 1920s. (1322~, 1931~)

—Hell Roaring Stock Trail: This constructed stock trail enters Hell Roaring Canyon on its north side one and one-half miles south of Jug Rock (one-eighth mile southeast of elevation 5178T on the Jug Rock map). It was built about 1900 and was later improved by Loren Milton, a cowboy for Arthur Ekker, in 1936–37. (1084~, 1430~)

Gene Dunham: "I saw an article a few years ago in the [Moab] paper about a wonderful discovery. They had discovered a trail into Hell Roaring Canyon! The cowboys had used that for a hundred years before. But some tourist found this trail and it was just like it had dropped out of the sky." (580~)

—Kachina Towers: These pinnacles are on the south side of Hell Roaring Canyon one and one-half miles south-southwest of Jug Rock (at elevation 5130 on the Jug Rock map). Eric Bjørnstad named them "because they looked like Kachina dolls." (243~)

—Uranium Road: Mining access to Hell Roaring Canyon was by way of a road along the banks of the Green River starting at Mineral Bottom.

Hellroaring Canyon: (Grand Co.) La Sal Mountains-Richardson Amphitheater-Professor Creek. Fisher Towers map.

"Hellroaring" Tom Wilson Branson was a lumberman in the La Sal Mountains starting in the early 1890s. Unattributed: "Few men played a greater part in the building and development of Grand County than did Thomas W. Branson. Many of the houses built in Moab in the early days were constructed of lumber sawed by the Branson Sawmill.... In those days there were practically no roads and the transportation of lumber to Moab from the La Sal Mountains was a big problem. Mr. Branson with his indomitable energy, overcame this problem to a great extent by floating lumber down the Colorado River from Castle Valley." (2030~)

Hells Backbone: (Garfield Co.) Dixie National Forest-Boulder Mountain-Hells Backbone Road. Roger Peak map.

Jerry Roundy noted that early Escalante resident Henry Baker is credited with naming this narrow strip of land that divides upper Death Hollow and Sand Creek. (1655~)

—Hells Backbone Road: In 1933 the "upper road," now called the Hells Backbone Road, was built by the CCC. Winding for nearly forty miles through what was then Powell National Forest, the Hells Backbone Road was the first automobile road to connect Boulder and Escalante. But, it was not open in winter. It was not until Highway 12 was completed in 1940 that the towns were permanently linked by a year-around automobile road.

The construction workers called the section of the road that crossed the head of Death Hollow the Poison Road, declaring "one drop sure death." The first bridge across the backbone, built by the CCC, was replaced in 1960, and it was replaced again in the early 2000s. (47~, 2051~)

Hells Bellows: (Kane Co.) Vermilion Cliffs-Johnson Canyon. Johnson Lakes map.

Lester Little: "So named because the combination of wind and sand (or snow) at the mouth of Johnson's Canyon creates an exceptionally unpleasant condition of drifting, biting sand in dry weather and bitter cold blizzards in the winter." (2053~) Vaydes Brueck: "named it Hell's

Bellows because the wind blew all the time.... Still does, too." (308~)

Inscriptions include one that reads "Buy your Gasoline Oil Supplies from Jenson and Brooks by Fredonia Arizona." In the early days this was the primary road between Long Valley, Kanab, and the Arizona Strip country.

—The Sand: This is the area at the mouth of Johnson Canyon, including Hells Bellows. Nephi Johnson: "Known as The Sand from the time of first travel that way in 1870. The name was derived because of the heavy sand making travel difficult. Sand formation conferring 1 mile from side to side of the Johnson Canyon." (2053~)

Hells Half Acre: (San Juan Co.) Dark Canyon Plateau-Highway 95. Kane Gulch and South Long Point maps.

Albert R. Lyman: "Hell's Half-acre is but an open space made by some ancient fire in the thick cedars, and it has a rude corral in the center where cowpunchers camp when they have business in that vicinity." (1249~)

DeReese Nielson: "There is just a small acre in the trees.... They was holdin' the cattle there one time and they was noonin' the cattle, and the cattle got scared and stampeded out there, and after that, all the old cowboys called it 'Hell's Half Acre.'" (1451~)

Hells Hole: (Carbon Co.) West Tavaputs Plateau-Gooseneck Ridge-Bear Canyon. Summerhouse Ridge map.

Waldo Wilcox: "That was hell when you got cows down in there trying to go down to Desolation Canyon and you couldn't get through and they didn't want to come back out." (2011~)

Hells Hole: (Wayne Co.) Fishlake National Forest-Thousand Lake Mountain. Flat Top and Torrey maps.

Dunk Taylor: "It's just a hell of a hole down in there." (1865~)

Guy Pace: "Hells Hole is just an old black hole, black lava. It's difficult to even ride a horse in there. But the cows get in there and we have to get them out." (1497~)

Hells Hole Canyon: (Wayne Co.) Hell Hole Swale-Guss Knoll-Dirty Devil River. Angel Cove map.

Also called Hell Hole Swale. (1931~) The area at the mouth of Hells Hole Canyon and at the base of the Upper Sand Slide was called Hells Hole by early cowboys.

In 1930 Zane Grey described a "Hell Hole" tributary of the Dirty Devil River, noting that the Dirty Devil was the "hell" and the canyon out of it was the "hole." (785~) It is unclear if Grey was writing about this specific canyon or just the sentiment of getting out of the Dirty Devil Canyon.

—Outlaw Trail: Pearl Baker noted that a route used by cattlemen went across the top of Hells Hole, down the

Upper Sand Slide, down the Dirty Devil River, and up the Angel Trail to Robbers Roost Flats. (122~) This was a variation of the Angel Trail used by the Robbers Roost outlaws. (1311~) (See Angel Cove—Angel Trail.)

Henderson Canyon: (Garfield Co.) Dixie National Forest-GSCENM-East Valley-Paria River. Pine Lake, Tropic Canyon, and Cannonville maps.

Also called Henderson Creek and Henderson Valley.

Bryce Canyon National Park Superintendent P.P. Patraw in 1935 noted that William Jasper Henderson (1840-1919) moved to Cannonville in 1876. Henderson and family lived at Henderson Spring in Henderson Canyon in 1891–92. (1931~, 2051~)

Henderson Hill: (Iron Co.) Dixie National Forest-Parowan Canyon. Parowan map. (8,722')

John Henderson (1831-1915) was a Parowan pioneer. (363~) He had a sawmill in Parowan Canyon in the early days. (516~)

Hendrickson Lake: (Iron Co.) Dixie National Forest-Second Left Hand Canyon. Brian Head map.

Max Clark Hendrickson: "In the olden days Hiram Ackley Hendrickson [1834-1921] carried fish from Panguitch Lake to this lake ... and planted the first fish there. It is a well-known, well-liked fishing spot today." (1515~)

Hendrick Spring: (Emery Co.) San Rafael Swell-Sand Bench. Horn Silver Gulch map.

This is a large, wash-bottom spring. (SAPE.)

Henrie Knolls: (Garfield Co.) Dixie National Forest-Markagunt Plateau. Henrie Knolls map. (9,256')

Samuel Henrie (1836-1910), his wife Hannah, and family moved to Panguitch in 1871. Later, the family had a ranch in nearby Blue Springs Valley. (363~, 877a~)

Henrieville Creek: (Garfield and Kane Counties.) GSCENM-Kaiparowits Plateau-Paria River. Canaan Peak, Upper Valley, Pine Lake, Henrieville, and Cannonville maps.

Also called Big Creek (425~) and East Branch Paria River (972~).

(See Henrieville for name derivation.)

Almon H. Thompson of the Powell Expedition of 1871–72 called this Table Cliff Creek. (1445~, 2051~) Herbert E. Gregory called it the Henrieville Fork of the Paria River. (766~)

—Smith Ranch: Ralph Chynoweth: "Right where the bridge crosses Highway 12 [one-quarter mile below the mouth of Shurtz Bush Creek at elevation BM6645 on the Henrieville map] the Smiths had a ranch and they called that the Smith Ranch. There was a bunch of Smiths that lived there in the early years." (425~)

Henrieville: (Garfield Co.) The Cockscomb-Highway 12. Henrieville map.

The town was established in the mid-1870s by residents of nearby Wooden Shoe and Clifton. Wooden Shoe was named for its Dutch settlers and Clifton for the surrounding cliffs. These tiny towns were abandoned in about 1878 because of water problems. Many of their residents moved either to Cannonville or Henrieville. James Henrie (1827-1916) was the president of the Panguitch Stake from 1877-1882. (421~)

—Butlerville: This settlement, established in about 1880 by a family named Butler, was a short distance south of Henrieville. Little is known about the town. (2053~)

Henry Mountains: (Garfield and Wayne Counties.) Bull Mountain, Cass Creek Peak, Copper Creek Benches, Lost Spring, Mount Holmes, Mount Pennell, Raggy Canyon, and Ticaboo Mesa maps.

The USGS mistakenly left the Henry Mountains designation off of the Mount Ellen map.

Also called Dirty Devil Mountains (1877~) and Mount Henry (561~).

The Navajo name *Dzil bishi' adinii*, or "Mountains Without a Name," is in reference to the fact that the mountains were not part of Navajo lands. (1231~)

The Andrus Military Reconnaissance Expedition of 1866 noted that the Indian name was the *Pot-Se-Nip* Mountains. (475~, 1655~)

Almon H. Thompson of the 1871–72 Powell Expedition noted that the Paiute name is *A wish a chog*. (1877~)

John Wesley Powell initially called these the Unknown Mountains. (551~) Charles B. Hunt noted that they were named in 1869 by Powell for Professor Joseph Henry. At the time of the Powell Expedition Henry was the Secretary of the Smithsonian Institution and was an ardent supporter of Powell. (925~)

Walter Clement Powell of the Powell Expedition of 1871-72: "Maj. [John Wesley Powell] told me that he had named one of the Dirty Devil Mountains 'Mount Clement'; I wore the new honor with becoming dignity." (1570~) It is not known which summit received the name, which did not stick.

Grove Karl Gilbert of the Powell Survey: "No one but a geologist will ever profitably seek out the Henry Mountains.... The Henry Mountains are not a range, and have no trend; they are simply a group of five individual mountains, separated by low passes and arranged without discernible system.... Springs abound upon their flanks, and their upper slopes are clothed with a luxuriant herbage and with groves of timber." (723~)

Clarence Dutton of the Powell Survey described the Henry Mountains from a viewpoint on the Aquarius Plateau: "Directly east of us, beyond the domes of the flexure [Waterpocket Fold], rise the Henry Mountains. They are barely 35 miles distant, and they seem to be near neighbors. Under a clear sky every detail is distinct and no finer view of them is possible. It seems as if a few hours of lively traveling would bring us there, but it is a two days journey with the best of animals. They are by far the most striking features of the panorama, on account of the strong contrast they present to the scenery around them. Among innumerable flat crest-lines, terminating in walls, they rise up grandly into peaks of Alpine form and grace like a modern cathedral among catacombs—the gothic order of architecture contrasting with the elephantine." (584~)

Clarence Dutton, again, in 1875: "If we stand on the Eastern verge of the Wasatch Plateau and look Eastward, we shall behold one of those strange spectacles which are seen only in the Plateau Province, and which have a peculiar kind of impressiveness, and even of sublimity.... It is not the wonder inspired by great mountains, for only two or three peaks of the Henry mountains are well in view; and these, with their noble Alpine forms, seem as strangely out of place as Westminister Abbey would be among the ruins of Thebes." (584~)

Albert King Thurber in 1881: "A peculiarity of the country in and about the Henry mountain is that no animal life is there; no game of deer, antelope or sheep, although fine feed, springs and shade. This is accounted for by the water being poisonous. It will do to travel up on but not dwell on." (1888~)

In 1882 Volney King called these the South Mountains as they were south of his location in Blue Valley. (1096~)

Ben Wetherill in 1897: "The Henrys are almost destitute of timber & while such scenery may be grand in its way it seems to show up some of Natures Warring spirit while the timber clad mountains of ours [La Platas in Colorado] shows up Nature in a more peaceful mood." (1988~)

Charles B. Hunt: "In the 1930s the area still was frontier—a long distance from railroads, paved roads, telephones, stores, or medical services. It was the heart of an area the size of New York State without a railroad, and a third of that area was without any kind of a road. This was not Marlboro country; it was Bull Durham country." (922~)

Joyce Muench in 1962: "The colors, which would task the best stocked artist's palette, may be brilliant to blinding, or soft and mellow—depending on time of day, season, or weather conditions. It's a canvas untouched by man, as primeval and amazing as when early explorers registered their surprise by calling the range, 'the Unknown Mountain.'" (1399~)

—Henry Mountain Cattle History: Cattle were being grazed by Indians in the Henry Mountains by the early 1870s, and perhaps decades earlier. Jack Hillers of the 1871–72 Powell Expedition wrote about finding Indian cattle here. (884~)

Barbara Ekker wrote about the first known use by Euroamericans: "The first known attempt to make a living from the Henry Mountain region was by two stockmen, Bean and Forest, who were believed to be from Colorado. They introduced cattle to the north part of the Henry Mountains in about 1878 but made no attempt to settle.... They sold the range to [John] Tescher of Moab (in 1881).... About this time Quimby Oliver 'Cap' Brown, generally believed to be a renegade, moved to the creek that now bears his name on the east side of Mount Pennell. The region later became a haven for renegades but this appears to be the first use of it as a hideaway." (609~)

—Josephine Gold Mine: This fictional mine concerns Spanish gold in the Henry Mountains. Two versions of the story are given. First, Nina Robison: "The story about the Josephine was that it was a lost Spanish gold and silver mine that was supposed to have been rediscovered in the 1880s by two prospectors. The mine was rumored to have been cursed by Indians who provided slave labor to the Spaniards who operated the mine. The curse said that anyone who tried to work the mine would become very sick. One of the prospectors who rediscovered the mine died, and the other was scared out. That's the story." (1430~)

Second, Charles Kelly: "Following the Old Spanish Trail into Utah they [a group of explorers] crossed the Colorado River at the old Ute ford [Crossing of the Fathers], then turned north into the Henry mountains, where they discovered rich gold ore. They mined it, built a crude smelter, made charcoal from mountain cedars and reduced the ore. They called their mine the Josephine. After working a year or more, living on deer and mountain sheep, they decided to return to Santa Fe. But a Quarrel arose over division of the gold. To settle this quarrel they decided to cast it all into an image of the infant Jesus and let courts settle their argument. This was done and the image loaded on a pack mule when they started back. While crossing over Fifty Mile mountain [Kaiparowits Plateau] they were attacked by Indians. While some of the men fought, others found a cave and buried the golden image. Four men survived to reach Santa Fe. They made a map of the country, showing where the gold was buried, but none ever returned to claim it." (1046~)

Hens Hole Peak: (Wayne Co.) Fishlake National Forest-Thousand Lake Mountain. Flat Top map. (10,805')

Two name derivations are given. Both involve William Henry "Hen" Maxfield, a sheepman in the late 1800s.

First, Henry was very tall and lanky and had a bad back. In order to more comfortably shear his sheep, he dug a waist-deep hole and stood in it so the sheep would be at a convenient level.

Second, Henry broke his leg on the slopes of the peak. (844~)

Hepplers Ponds: (Sevier Co.) Sevier River-Bull Claim Hill. Richfield and Annabella maps.

Irvin Warnock noted that Andrew Heppler (1838-1906), his wife Louisiana (1846-1926), and family moved to Prattsville in 1873. (1971~) Heppler developed the ponds by building the low dams. (1931~)

Hepworth Wash: (Washington Co.) Zion National Park-Pine Creek. Springdale East map.

Two related name derivations are given.

First, Squire Hepworth, Sr. (1843–1921) and family moved to Springdale by 1870. (462~)

Second, Squire Hepworth, Sr.'s son, Thornton Hepworth (1864-1926) was appointed bishop of the Springdale Ward in 1914, a post he held until 1926. (1931~) Thornton Hepworth's son, Thornton Hepworth, Jr. was killed by lightning while on the top of Cable Mountain in 1908. (2043~)

—Stevens Canyon Constructed Stock Trail: This goes from East Fork Virgin River to the top of the first cliff band near the mouth of Hepworth Wash. It is one-quarter mile south of the mouth. The trail allowed access to upper Stevens Wash and upper Hepworth Wash. (SAPE.) It is unclear if the trail continued on up the cliffs and eventually to Long Valley. William L. Crawford in 1900: "I came home via Stevens Wash. We found it to be about as practical as the Bend [East Rim Trail], which is the best route yet found." (483~) After much searching, the canyon group EMDC was unable to locate the upper portion of the trail, or to find any possibility of such a trail that could be used by horses. (SAPE.)

—Destination Peak: This is on the east side of Hepworth Wash and is one-eighth mile west of elevation 6408. It was named by Tanya Milligan and others. (1591~)

—Gifford Peak: This is on the east side of Hepworth Wash and is one-half mile south-southwest of elevation 6408. It was named by Courtney Purcell. (1591~)

—Hepworth Peak: This is at the head of Hepworth Wash. (1591~)

—Roof Peak: This is one-eighth mile south of Hepworth Peak (at elevation 6542). Courtney Purcell: "Roof Peak is one of the most impressive, obscure peaks in the backcountry of eastern Zion National Park." (1591~)

Herdina Park: (Grand Co.) Arches National Park-Willow Flats. The Windows Section map.

Also called Herdina Arch (898~) and Leaping Arch (1977~).

Vicki Webster: "Herdina Park was named after the amateur fossil hunter Jerry Herdina. A Chicago steel engineer, Herdina was an avid explore of this part of the country." (1977~)

—Beckwith Arch: This is the "Natural Arch" that is on the north side of Herdina Park. Frank A. Beckwith led the Arches National Monument Scientific Expedition of 1933–34.

Herring Flat: (Emery Co.) Ferron Creek-Zwahlen Wash. Ferron map.

Lee Mont Swasey noted that Joseph Herring (?-1913) and family were early settlers. (1853~, 388~) Ray Wareham: "They just took their cows up there and that was their flat…. I would say it had to be 1910, 1915 and probably before that." (1967~)

—Herring Flat Debris Basin: This large pond is in the middle of Herring Flat (at elevation 6073). (780~) Lee Mont Swasey noted that the Soil Conservation Service built the Debris Basin at the same time as Millsite Reservoir, in 1968–69. (1853~)

Heward Creek: (Garfield Co.) Dixie National Forest-Sheep Creek. Bryce Point map.

Also spelled Howard Creek. (777~)

Herbert Heward was a Cannonville pioneer. (388~)

Hey Joe Canyon: (Grand Co.) Tenmile Country-Labyrinth Canyon. Tenmile Point map.

Also called Buck Canyon. (M.78.)

—Hey Joe Mine: This uranium mine was started in the early 1950s. There are still mining relics in the canyon.

—Access Road: Access to the canyon for heavy equipment was by way of the road into Spring Canyon and then along the edge of the Green River.

—Hiking Trail: Gene Dunham noted that a constructed and cairned hiking trail starts behind Hey Joe Mine and goes up the south side of Hey Joe Canyon. The trail was used by uranium miners, who lived on the rim of the canyon. It is now used by mountain bikers. (580~, SAPE.)

Hiawatha Town: (Carbon Co.) Wasatch Plateau-Gentry Mountain. Hiawatha map. PRIVATE PROPERTY.

Also called Black Hawk. (375~)

A man named Smith is credited with being the first to settle in the area. In 1908 Fred E. Sweet (also spelled Sweats) started the Hiawatha Mine (shown on Middle Fork). He is credited with naming it Camp Hiawatha.

Two similar name derivations are given.

First, Sweet's favorite poem was Henry Wadsworth Longfellow's "Hiawatha."

Second, it was named after a famous Pennsylvania coal mine, which was named for Longfellow's "Hiawatha."

The townsite itself was not initially called Hiawatha, but rather, Greek Town. The name was officially changed to Hiawatha in 1915. (375~, 1195~, 1801~)

William Stackaleman lived in Hiawatha: "By 1915 a company store, a four-room schoolhouse, and about three hundred two and four room houses, not modern, were built to accommodate approximately one thousand population…. Mining was done by hand; pick, shovel and hand drill…. The mine employed about two hundred fifty men…. In 1926 the towns of East and West Hiawatha became ghost towns when the mines were shut down and the buildings were sold to Ketchum's Building and Supply Company of Salt Lake City." (1802~)

The town had a resurrection of sorts and boomed during the 1940s and '50s and hung on until the United States Fuel Company folded in 1991.

Hickman Canyon: (Piute Co.) Sevier Plateau-East Fork Sevier River. Phonolite Hill map.

Also called Hickman Holler.

Kent Whittaker noted that Thomas Hugo Hickman (1832-1907) was an early resident of the Antimony area. (2002~) Hickman had a farm in the canyon. (2053~)

Hickman Natural Bridge: (Wayne Co.) Capitol Reef National Park-Capitol Reef. Fruita map.

Also called Broad Arch, Broad Arch Bridge, Fruita Bridge, Fruita Natural Bridge, and Holt Natural Bridge.

Joseph S. Hickman (1887-1925) was born in the area. He became a state legislator and taught at Wayne High School in Bicknell for many years. He was a promoter of designating Capitol Reef as a national monument. Hickman drowned when a sudden storm hit while he was boat fishing on Fish Lake. Leo Holt, an early settler, is said to have discovered the bridge. (699~, 1047~, 1476~, 1884~, 2056~)

Don Maguire provided the first description in 1892: "I saw the great natural bridge that lies north of the Grand Wash. It spans a chasm about twelve-hundred feet above the hollow of the cañon and forms a perfect arch over a cañon or gorge about seventy feet wide." (1271~)

J. Cecil Alter in 1927: "The Hickman Natural Bridge is the largest and most graceful among the bridge forms in this wonderland.... Not a line, face or surface is awry.... It is oriented toward the wilderness of upstanding rocks, and it rises out of the edge of the jungle itself like a wide-striding beast." (50~)

—Whiskey Spring: This was just above the bridge. It was used by moonshiners during prohibition years. The spring was eradicated by a landslide in 1979. Archaeologist Mary E. Mulroy: "[Whiskey Spring] is a persistent seep at the base of a cliff. The locale was probably important in prehistoric times but the only remains noted there are from the pioneer period when the spring was used as a watering place for cattle." (1410~)

—Hickman Natural Bridge Trail: This was a rough path before 1940 when it was improved by the CCC.

—Bridge Canyon: (Also called Cove Canyon.) This is the historic name for the canyon that contains Hickman Natural Bridge. (776~)

—Navajo Dome: This monolith is one-third of a mile northeast of Hickman Natural Bridge (halfway between elevations 5526T and 6489T). (1657~)

—Capitol Dome: This monolith is immediately east of Navajo Dome. (1657~) Joyce Muench: "from which a resemblance to the Washington Capitol has inspired the name." (1401~)

—Walker Peak: This dome is one-half mile north of Hickman Natural Bridge (at 4-54). Chief Wakara (also called Walker) was a prominent Ute leader in the late 1800s. (1657~)

—Sharks Tooth: This is an appropriately-named sandstone monolith that is three-quarters of a mile northwest of Hickman Natural Bridge and is elevation 6821T.

Hickman Pasture: (Wayne Co.) Dixie National Forest-Boulder Mountain-Fish Creek. Blind Lake map.

Dwight Williams noted that William Hickman (1878-1961) and family fenced the pasture and used it as a dairy pasture in the summertime. (2013~)

Hickman Spring: (Wayne Co.) Fishlake National Forest-Thousand Lake Mountain. Flat Top map.

Anne Snow noted that William Hickman (1878-1961) ran cattle in the area in the early 1900s. (1786~)

Hidden Canyon: (Washington Co.) Zion National Park-Zion Canyon. Springdale East and Temple of Sinawava maps.

Julius V. Madsen in the late 1920s: "Into a veritable hanging canyon you wander, crawling over moss-covered

boulders, through dense clumps of undergrowth, between smooth-faced, sheer walls that rise hundreds of feet above you. Very little was known of this enchanted gorge until 1927 when Park Rangers explored it in search of a lost mountain climber. It is now becoming very popular as a rendezvous for venturesome mountaineers." (1267~)

J. Cecil Alter in 1927: "The crevice between Cable Mountain and the Great White Throne [Hidden Canyon] is an awesome trench extending a mile due south. It is from four hundred and fifty to five hundred and fifty feet wide at the top and from eighteen hundred to two thousand feet in depth, the lower two hundred feet consisting of an unlighted saw kerf. This singular gully is as straight and symmetrical as if cut with a trenching machine." (50~)

—Hidden Canyon Trail: This hiking trail was listed on the National Register of Historic Places in 1987. It was constructed in 1925. (311~) In the early days, before construction of the trail, a route up the canyon was problematic. George C. Fraser in 1914 noted that the route from the floor of Zion Canyon, up Hidden Canyon, to Cable Mountain "involv[ed] labor and mountaineering skill." (667~)

Hidden Lake: (Grand Co.) La Sal Mountains-Beaver Creek. Mount Waas map.

Joe Taylor: "There are two Hidden Lakes. The one named on the map is what we call the Old Hidden Lake. It was built by the local Hunting Club.... That was in the 1950s. You can't see it from the road. You can ride back and forth by it and never know it's there." (1866~)

—New Hidden Lake: Joe Taylor: "Then there is the New Hidden Lake above Taylor Flat." (1866~) It is one mile west of the south end of Taylor Flat (one-quarter mile north of elevation 8987AT).

—Tin Roof Draw: PRIVATE PROPERTY. Charles B. Hunt noted that this is one mile northwest of Hidden Lake (one-half mile southwest of elevation 8504AT). (924~) Joe Taylor: "There used to be a big two-story log cabin there that had a tin roof on it. It was a ranch and now it's on my ranch. That's where I run my mares and colts." (1866~)

Bette L. Stanton supplied some of the history: "The [Tom] Larsens also purchased a place on the north end of the La Sals [in 1909] where they spent the long hot summers. They called it the 'tin roof' house." (1805~)

—Shafer Creek: Joe Taylor noted that this stream goes through Tin Roof. (1866~)

Hidden Lake: (Kane Co.) Long Valley-Highway 89. Glendale map.

Also called Chamberlain Farm and Harris Lake.

Herbert E. Gregory: "An Indian legend tells that a horse crossing this spot left its hoof print in the soil. The track grew deeper, and water accumulated in the depression until it became a beautiful lake." (758~)

Wayne K. Platt: "[Rancher] Mr. Marcellus Johnson has records dated 1896 referring to this water as Chamberlain Spring, but for many years it has been known as Hidden Lake." (1931~)

Emma Carroll Seegmiller in 1939: "The pretty little lake nestling at the foothills and entirely hidden from view by trees and dense foliage that surrounds it, furnished a bathing resort and a place of recreation. Then the [woolen] factory furnished a name for both farm and lake—Factory Lake—Factory Farm.... The farms are known [now] by the more prepossessing titles of 'Lake Farm' and 'Hidden Farm.'" (1714~) The woolen factory was established in 1882 by members of the United Order and led by Thomas Chamberlain. It ran until 1898. (349~)

Hidden Passage Canyon: (Kane Co.) Glen Canyon NRA-Glen Canyon. Nasja Mesa map.

Also called Crevice Canyon. (1321~)

John Widtsoe in 1922: "It is a narrow, high winding gorge, with a small stream trickling down it. Near the entrance are dense groves of scrub oak, and large patches of poison oak. As we enter, the gorge narrows, a blue rift above is the sky. Where the gorge widens a vast overhanging canopy wholly shuts out the light. A little further on the gorge narrows and water fills the passageway.... In this twilight-lighted, moist nook, vegetation is profuse climbing up the rocky slopes and fastening itself in really impossible places as it seems to us.... We name the place Maidenhair Gorge." (2007~)

Senator Barry Goldwater was with Norm Nevills in 1940: "We stopped in Hidden Passage Canyon which is most well named.... Its mouth is completely hidden by brush." (738~) Randall Henderson noted that it was named by Norm Nevills. (869~)

Lil Diemler in 1946: "The canyon is narrow enough in places to span it with out stretching ones arms.... A stream of cold water flows thru the canyon and we drank from it frequently.... It was necessary to cross this stream at intervals and where there were no stepping stones we waded, at one place hip deep.... In one place we were taken up the face of a cliff on a rope.... A second rock was also negotiated with a rope.... Farther up the canyon there is a rock ledge which must be negotiated on hands and knees

and in one place on the abdomen, wriggling along for about ten feet ... with nothing but several 100 feet of very thin air between them and the canyon floor." (557~)

Weldon F. Heald in 1948: "Behind a well-camouflaged entrance a narrow, twisting corridor between vertical walls leads back into a maze of cliffs, domes and knobs.... Within the enclosing walls was an utter confusion of smooth barren rocks with precipitous sides dropping into unseen depths. I could think of nothing it resembled on earth or elsewhere unless it might be a corral full of pink, hairless monsters of Gargantuan proportions. But what I will always remember about Hidden Passage is the upper waterfall at the head of the Canyon. There the corridor widens out into a vaulted hall at the head of which a slender thread of water falls into a clear pool. From the twilit room we looked up to the overhanging walls far above us, enclosing a narrow slit of sky between. There in the deep blue midday sky shone one brilliant star." (1521~)

Cid Rickets Sumner in 1957: "Hidden Passage—it was well-named. I could not make it stand forth to be seen.... I looked ahead to where both walls drew in upon each other, curving away into what must be yet another mighty coil beyond my sight, and walked slowly on." (1846~)

Unattributed in 1958: "a fantastically tortuous narrow canyon, carved in solid sandstone, with sheer walls and an often level floor. As you walk in or alongside its narrow rivulet, each turn of the way seems to lead to a blank wall, beyond which you will be able to go no farther—but then another bend shows a way out." (730~)

Katie Lee: "Hidden Passage. Exactly. If the shadow that reveals the passage isn't there—if you come upon it in bright morning sunlight, or late afternoon, or on a cloudy day—you'll miss it, most likely." (1162~)

Bruce Berger in 1962: "Hidden Passage, a canyon whose entrance from many viewpoints is lost in a sweep of solid sandstone. Set like a stage between two monolithic walls, it threads its way back and forth through successive backdrops as if through a scenery loft." (216~)

Wallace Stegner, after Lake Powell started filling: "Worst of all is the loss of places I remember.... I look over my shoulder and recognize the swamped and truncated entrance to Hidden Passage Canyon.... The old masked entrance is swallowed up, the water rises almost over the shoulder of the inner cliffs. Once that canyon was a pure delight to walk in; now it is only another slot with water in it, a thing to poke a motorboat into for five minutes and then roar out again." (1825~)

—Scraggly Juniper Camp: Located along the Talus Trail (See Appendix Two—Talus Trail), this is near the head of

Hidden Passage Canyon (near elevation 4352T). Named for a scraggly juniper tree, the camp was near a series of seasonally large potholes accessible to livestock. Nearby inscriptions include Philo E. Allen, no date. (SAPE.)

—Hidden Passage Crossing: There was a documented Indian crossing of the Colorado River at the mouth of Hidden Passage Canyon. (126~)

Hidden Valley: (San Juan Co.) Wingate Mesa-Blue Notch Canyon. Mancos Mesa NE map.

Carl Mahon: "They did a bunch of mining out there during the uranium boom and it isn't a canyon that is real noticeable when you're going down through there, and they just called it 'Hidden Canyon.'" (1272~)

Hideout Canyon: (San Juan Co.) Dark Canyon Plateau-White Canyon. Woodenshoe Buttes and The Cheesebox maps.

—The Hideout: (Woodenshoe Buttes map.) PRIVATE PROPERTY. The Hideout is a cluster of buildings at a spring near the top of Hideout Canyon. It has been used by cattlemen, and, at times, by outlaws, from the 1880s to the present. Sandy Johnson noted that there are buildings of different ages there, including an old cabin used by the outlaws. Sandy Johnson: "Al Scorup wouldn't stay there because he was scared that them outlaws would come there." (1002~)

Erwin Oliver: "I didn't like The Hideout. The rats was terrible in the little shack there. You couldn't sleep for the rats." (1479~)

John Scorup: "One story I hear about my granddad [Jim Scorup] was when Old Posy and his band of Utes were out raising Hell with all the white people. Grandpa and Uncle Tom came into camp one night and were cooking supper. And they had their beds down and grandpa always carried a .45 six-shooter. He had it laying on his bed. He was busy cooking supper and all of a sudden the doorway darkened up and in came Old Posy and about ten of his band of Utes and he says, 'We're going to take all your flour. We're gonna take all your sugar. We're gonna take all your coffee. And we're going to take all your groceries. Maybe we'll kill you white men.' Grandpa walked over to his bed, picked up his six-shooter and he says, 'I've got six bullets in here.' He says: 'Which one of you wants to be the first to die'? He says, 'I'll feed you supper, and give you some flour, sugar, and some coffee to go on your way, but you're not taking anything that I don't give you.' Old Posy clapped his hands, 'Ah, brave white man!' he says. 'Pretty good man. No bother you. I see your cows out there. I won't kill your cows anymore.' So grandpa had

a pretty good relationship with Old Posy after that. He wasn't going to take any crap off of 'im." (1821~)

Hideout Canyon: (Grand Co.) La Sal Mountains-Fisher Creek. Fisher Valley map.

Also called Cottonwood Canyon. (1931~)

Joe Taylor: "It was called The Hideout because there was a dugout there where the outlaws hid out. It is a name from the very early days." (1866~)

—Hideout Wall: Eric Bjørnstad noted that this cliff is to the east of upper Hideout Canyon and is one mile southwest of Cowhead Hill (immediately west of elevation 6704T). Spliff Spire is at the north end of the wall. (240~)

Hideout Mesa: (San Juan Co.) Manti-LaSal National Forest-La Sal Mountains-La Sal Creek. Ray Mesa map. (7,560')

Outlaws Tom and Bill McCarty and others used to hide out on the mesa in the late 1880s and early 1890s. McCarty built a shelter under the south rim of the mesa near the Blue Cap Mine. (456~, 754~, 1750~)

Highlands, The: (Grand Co.) Cisco Desert-Dome Plateau. Mollie Hogans and Cisco SW maps.

Charles J. Scott: "The Highlands is appropriately named because it is reminiscent of Scotland, especially during the early weeks of spring. These splendid domed ridges, with their soft greenishy hues and dramatic slopes, remind me of my wanderings in Glen Tilt and the Orkneys a decade ago." (1704~)

Highline Ditch: (Wayne Co.) Rabbit Valley-Fremont River. Bicknell and Lyman maps.

This canal was built to bring water to Lyman and Bicknell. It was high enough to bypass Fremont and Loa, which had their own ditches. (373~)

—Tanner Backbone: Dunk Taylor: "When they were putting in the Highline Ditch, my dad [William G. Taylor] spent one whole winter with the plow team and the scrapers and dug out a section of the canal through what they call Tanner Backbone. That was about eighty years ago." (1865~) Tanner Backbone is near the mouth of Lime Kiln Hollow (one-eighth mile west of elevation 7434 on the Highline Ditch on the Lyman map).

High Mountain: (Iron Co.) Dixie National Forest-Sugarloaf Mountain. Flanigan Arch map. (9,937')

Also called High Knoll. (768~)

High Point Rock: (Coconino Co., Az.) Navajo Indian Reservation-Rainbow Plateau. Tse Esgizii, Az. map. (5,421')

This Navajo Sandstone dome stands high above the surrounding country. It is an excellent landmark. (SAPE.)

High Spur: (Wayne Co.) Glen Canyon NRA-The Spur. Head Spur and Sugarloaf Butte maps.

(See The Spur for name derivation.)

This was called High Part of the Spur by early ranchers. (120~)

Highway 9: (Kane and Washington Counties.)

Also called Zion-Mount Carmel Highway.

This goes east from La Verkin, by Rockville and Springdale, through Zion Canyon, to Mount Carmel. It was built in 1927–30 at a cost of two million dollars. This included the cost of the one-mile-long Zion-Mount Carmel Tunnel. At the time it was the longest tunnel in the United States. (262~)

Highway 10: (Carbon and Emery Counties.)

This goes south from Price, through Castle Dale and Ferron, to Fremont Junction on Interstate 70. The initial road was laid out and built from 1882 to 1885. By 1929 the road had been graveled from Price to Ferron and in 1930 the gravel was continued to Emery. Highway 10 was paved by 1954. (710~)

Highway 12: (Garfield and Wayne Counties.)

This used to be Utah Highway 117.

This goes south from Torrey to Escalante and then generally west to Highway 89 a couple of miles south of Panguitch. Along its course it passes through Boulder, Escalante, Henrieville, Cannonville, and Tropic. In 1990 it was designated a Scenic Byway. (337~)

—Torrey to Boulder: (Also called the East End or Grover-Boulder Road.) Much of this section of the highway was constructed by the CCC in the late 1930s and early '40s. At that time it was a dirt road. (2021~, 2051~)

—Boulder to Escalante: (Also called Calf Creek Road and Lower Boulder Road.) The first road between the towns of Boulder and Escalante was the Old Boulder Road. It started as a rough trail that was slowly improved over a period of years to the point that wagons and, later, automobiles could use it. Starting from Escalante, the Old Boulder Road crossed Big Flat and dropped to the Escalante River just below the mouth of Calf Creek. The road then went downriver for several hundred yards, exited the canyon, and followed a tortuous path up the cliffs to Haymaker Bench. After crossing the bench, the Hogback, and New Home Bench, the road descended into Boulder.

The difficulties the pioneers had in traveling this road were enormous. Early users planned on four to seven days from Escalante to Boulder, camping en route. To negotiate the roughest sections, wagons were unloaded or even taken apart. Bad weather often delayed passage.

One pioneer, Sally May King, is quoted as saying, "The man who found the route for this road should have a medal, or else be killed." A companion then exclaimed: "Kill him, damn him. That's what I say." (1168~)

By 1914 an alternate route from Haymaker Bench across Dry Hollow and Boulder Creek to lower Boulder had been established. In 1924 this rough path was improved into a good wagon road. It was called the Claude V. Cutoff road, named for Claude Vincent Baker (1881-1945), a Boulder rancher. This road shortened the trip from Escalante to Boulder by a day and became the standard route for several years.

Burns Ormand noted that the road crew was directed by Purse Levitt and the road was also called the Levitt Cutoff, or just The Cutoff. (1487~)

As the towns of Escalante and Boulder grew, both the Old Boulder Road and the Claude V. Cutoff proved inadequate. In 1934 the CCC started work on an all-weather, one lane "lower road" between the two towns. This road, which became Highway 12, followed some sections of the Old Boulder road but diverged from it by following lower Calf Creek and then going directly up the steep cliffs to Haymaker Bench. A one-lane bridge across the Escalante River cost five thousand dollars to build. The road was a huge undertaking and was not finished until 1940. Widening and paving occurred in spurts and the present paved configuration was not completed until 1985. The original one-lane bridge across the river was replaced by a two-lane bridge in 1995. (2021~)

This section of Highway 12 was deemed one of the most beautiful drives in America by *Car and Driver* magazine. In 2010 the State of Utah proposed upgrading this bucolic road into a high speed highway.

—Escalante to Henrieville: The original pioneer road from Escalante west went up Main Canyon, over the Escalante Mountains, and down Sweetwater Creek to Widtsoe. In 1952, the Utah State Road Commission decided to reroute the road through Upper Valley to Henrieville. This was completed in 1958. (47~, 1168~, 2051~)

Highway 14: (Iron and Kane Counties.)

Also called Markagunt High Plateau Scenic Byway.

This goes east from Cedar City, over the Markagunt Plateau, to Long Valley Junction.

Highway 20: (Garfield and Iron Counties.)

This short highway runs from Highway 89 north of Panguitch at Bear Valley Junction to Interstate 15 about fifteen miles north of Paragonah. The highway follows one of the old pioneer routes from Dixie to Panguitch. It was designated Highway 20 in 1927.

Highway 22: (Garfield and Piute Counties.)

Also called the Johns Canyon Road.

This goes south from Otter Creek Reservoir, through Johns Valley, to Bryce Canyon. The initial road was built in the early 1920s. (2063~) The highway was not finished until the 1990s.

Highway 24: (Emery, Sevier, and Wayne Counties.)

This goes south from Green River to Hanksville, then turns generally west and northwest and goes through Torrey, Bicknell, Loa, and Sigurd and ends in Salina.

—Green River to Hanksville: In the pioneer days there were three main routes travelers used between Green River and Hanksville.

The first route went directly below, and parallel to, the east face of the San Rafael Reef. Much of this road is still used by recreationists. During the gold mining boom of 1892–93, the road was realigned and upgraded. As well, a railroad spur was proposed that would have run along the face of the reef to Hanksville and down Trachyte Creek to the Colorado River. (889~) (See Trachyte Creek.)

The second route started in Green River and went south to the Chaffin Ranch on the San Rafael River. It then went by Keg Knoll, over the head of Horseshoe Canyon, between the Flat Tops to Jeffery Well, and south to Hanksville. This is now called the West Canyonlands Road or the Maze Road. This old trail was updated and improved into a good vehicle road by Louis M. Chaffin and George Franz in 1927. (1781~)

The third route somewhat followed the present course of Highway 24, though there were innumerable variations. In 1898 the Hoskinnini Mining Company, under the direction of Robert Brewster Stanton, constructed part of the road. (See Hoskinnini Road.) Charles B. Hunt in 1935: "The road between Hanksville and Green River was little more than a pair of tracks and the position of the tracks shifted with every storm. The 15 miles from Green River to the San Rafael River was across shale— good in dry weather but slippery as grease and hub-deep in mud in wet weather. The 40 miles from the San Rafael to Hanksville was in sand—good in wet weather but loose and tractionless in dry weather. These conditions served to separate the optimists from the pessimists; to the optimists part of the road always was good, and to the pessimists part always was bad." (922~)

Gene Dunham described the road during the uranium boom years of the late 1940s and early '50s: "There were ore trucks everywhere. No pavement. That was a terrible, terrible road. From Jessies Twist you go down the hill and across the San Rafael River. They had a fairly good bridge across the San Rafael. And then up across that long old hill on the other side. Then you'd get up on top of that hill onto the sand flats just before you'd get to Temple Junction. There would be five roads. You'd just take your pick. Because everyone would say 'this is no good' and start a new road. The other guy would go the other way. And I mean it was a mess. And there were broken-down trucks and spare tires and radiators just strewn from one end to the other. The main job here in town [Green River] was putting radiators on at night so they could haul ore the next day." (580~) In 1952, at the urging of the Atomic Energy Commission, a new oiled road was started between the two towns.

—Hanksville to Torrey. The original pioneer road, built in 1883, went from Hanksville, through Kitchentown, Giles, Elephant, and Caineville, and across the Blue Flats. The section of road to the west of Caineville through the bentonite clays of the Morrison Formation was called the Blue Dugway (also Blue Dug-Way) and was considered most treacherous; the clay when wet was slick as oil and wagons, men, and beasts all had problems negotiating it. Several descriptions give an idea of the hardships travelers faced.

Ethel Jensen: "a treacherous stretch of gouged out road, which topped a blue clay hill. In wet weather it was extremely slippery and difficult and there also was the Dirty Devil [Fremont] River crossing." (962~)

Dwight L. King: "On the left-hand side of the Blue Dugway, the hill sloped precipitously for several hundred feet. On the right-hand side, it sloped to the sandstone cap rock. There was no room for freighters to turn around, stop, or make any kind of an adjustment once they started up or down the Blue Dugway. On cloudy, rainy days it was dismal. The dark blue clay and overcast sky blended to make it seem a hellish place." (1093~)

Jack King: "It was a hell of a good road except when it was wet. You had a lot of storm on it and that old glue would build up on your tires and make it damn near impossible to get through." (1094~)

James Nielsen: "We had to let the wagons down part of the way by hand into a box canyon with sheer red sandstone cliffs on both sides. At its bottom was the Fremont River, with a quicksand bottom, meandering crookedly through its entire length." (1453~)

The original alignment of the road down the Blue Dugway can still be seen in several places. (SAPE.)

As the road continued west, it went along the Fremont River. But, there were more than fifty river crossings. (304~) The road was rerouted up Capitol Wash and on to Torrey. The locals had an expression for that stretch: "It's six mile to it and six miles through it," referring to the six miles through Capitol Wash and six miles to Torrey. (844~) (See Capitol Wash.) A variation, longer but easier, went up the Fremont River to Grand Wash, which it ascended to Fruita.

In 1962 the highway through Capitol Wash was rerouted back to the present Fremont River corridor. By that time all of Highway 24 had been paved. (962~, 1419~)

Highway 56: (Iron Co.)

This starts in Cedar City and goes west to the Utah-Nevada border near Modena.

—Cedar City to Beryl Junction: The original road, designated Highway 56, went from Cedar City, by Desert Mound, to Beryl Junction. In 1945 the highway was realigned to go through Iron Mountain.

—Beryl Junction to State Line: This section became Highway 18 in 1927.

Highway 72: (Sevier and Wayne Counties.)

This goes south from Fremont Junction on Interstate 70 to Loa.

It was designated as Highway 72 in 1933. Richard F. Madole of the USGS: "Prior to the late 1980s, Utah Highway 72 was a rough, narrow two-lane dirt road." (1352~)

Highway 89: (Utah counties north to south: Rich, Cache, Boxelder, Weber, Davis, Salt Lake, Sanpete, Sevier, Piute, Garfield, and Kane.)

This federal highway goes from Yellowstone National Park south to Flagstaff, Arizona. Until 1925 what would become the Utah section of Highway 89 was a minor road that went from Thistle, Utah to Flagstaff, Arizona. In 1934 much of the road was upgraded and a totally new section was built through Marysvale Canyon.

Highway 95: (Garfield, San Juan, and Wayne Counties.)

Also called the Bicentennial Highway.

This highway goes generally west from Blanding to Hanksville. It is part of the Trail of the Ancients National Scenic Byway.

The route was laid out over time first by ranchers and later by miners. Trails were developed slowly with use and over the years many variations existed.

—The initial road from Blanding to Natural Bridges went over Elk Ridge, through the Bears Ears, and down Maverick Point. Heavy snows would close the road in winter. In the early 1950s the highway was rerouted to cross Comb Ridge three miles north of where the highway now cuts through. Money for the rerouting was provided by the Atomic Energy Commission. They wanted to make access easier to the many uranium mines in the area.

This is now called Old Highway 95. After crossing Comb Wash, the Old Highway went along the south rim of Arch Canyon and joined the present-day highway alignment. The next iteration was the realignment of the highway through the present-day "big gash" in Comb Ridge in the early 1970s.

—The section of highway from Natural Bridges to the ferry at Dandy Crossing (Hite) was started in the mid-1940s and was finished in September 1946. Arthur Chaffin, then the owner of the ferry at Dandy Crossing, had pushed for the road construction for years and had helped on much of it. In the early 1950s the rough road, with help from the AEC, was graded and improved. Even though the uranium and tourist traffic was up, this was still a serious road. At that time a large sign was erected along the road which told visitors about the remoteness and seriousness of driving it in those early days:

DRIVE CAREFULLY

This road is safe when dry and if driven at reasonable speeds not exceeding 30 miles per hour.

Carry Ample Water—Check Gas and Oil.

Use low gear on steep Grades.

REDUCE TO LOW OR SECOND GEAR BEFORE DRIVING THROUGH SAND DO NOT STOP IN SAND.

Sound Horn on Curves and Dugways.

Do not park in washes—Stop only on High Ground.

Gas, meals, Lodging available at Hite & Hanksville.

The construction of the bridges over the Colorado and Dirty Devil rivers forced a realignment of the highway away from Dandy Crossing. They were finished in 1964. The highway bridge over White Canyon was dedicated in 1966.

—The section from Dandy Crossing, up North Wash, to Hanksville was also a major hurdle. The road wasn't very good: One early traveler noted that he crossed North Wash seventy-six times in thirty miles!

The highway, though unpaved, was completed in 1969. Final paving was finished in 1976, which is why it is called the Bicentennial Highway. (212~, 277~, 647~, 1730~)

Highway 128: (Grand Co.)

Also called River Road.

This goes generally southwest from Interstate 70 near Cisco to Moab, after first going through Dewey and by Castle Valley.

The initial route between Moab and Castle Valley went up to 8,000 feet in the La Sal Mountains, making it unreliable in winter. (See Negro Bill Canyon.) Construction on the route along the river was started in 1897 by Samuel

King. Over a period of several years King established a ferry at Dewey and improved the road from Cisco to Castle Valley. For a short while it was called the King Road (also Grand River Toll Road) until it was purchased by the county. In 1920, the roadbed was raised above high water level. It was designated as Highway 128 in 1921 and it was paved in the 1960s. (456~, 644~, 1984~)

An inscription along the road near Big Bend reads "Kings Toll Road." (1115~, SAPE.)

Highway 163: (San Juan Co.)

This short highway goes generally southwest from Bluff, through Mexican Hat, and ends in Kayenta, Arizona. For many years this was part of the main highway (then Highway 47) that ran between Thompson and Flagstaff.

—Bluff to Mexican Hat: The road between Bluff and Mexican Hat had to cross Butler Wash, go over or around Comb Ridge, and cross Comb Wash. A poor stock trail into Butler Wash was improved in 1888 when the county spent seventy-five dollars on upgrades. From there the road went down the wash (See Butler Wash—San Juan Co.—Lower Butler Wash Road) to the San Juan River and to The Rincon (See San Juan Hill–The Rincon) where it joined the Hole-in-the-Rock Road.

The oil boom of 1908–1910 in Mexican Hat forced the rerouting and building of a good road from Bluff, across Butler Wash, over Comb Ridge by way of Navajo Pass, across Comb Wash, up Snake Canyon, and across Lime Creek Valley to Mexican Hat.

The route over Comb Ridge at Navajo Pass and down Navajo Hill to Navajo Spring had been used by the Navajo for years. The first to mention a trail here was William Henry Jackson of the Ferdinand V. Hayden Survey in 1875: "[from Bluff] our trail took back until it got on the bed rock, following along the upturned edges of white and red sandstone that had been tipped up. Crossing a deep rock cut & then up higher still following the goat tracks of the Indians who had passed us the day before until we came down into the San Juan at the mouth of Epsom Creek [Comb Wash]." (950~)

Hole-in-the-Rock Expedition scout George B. Hobbs told of the trail up Navajo Hill in 1879: "The next day we came to a break in this cliff [Comb Ridge] where the cliff dwellers [undoubtedly local Navajo] had previously done a vast amount of work in making a trail leading up the side to the top." (1356~)

H.L.A. Culmer in 1905: "It is one of the dizziest things on earth—narrow, steep, and rocky." (1822~)

In 1910 Bluff townspeople and the State of Utah paid fifteen hundred dollars to build a very rough road over

Navajo Pass. (1335~) Albert R. Lyman: "At least it was called a road, and will perhaps continue by that name though it becomes impassible to the most acrobatic burro that ever carried a pack." (1240~)

The road was improved a little bit at a time. Doris Valle: "Lynn Palmer told of scraping the surfaces on the switchbacks atop Comb Ridge [Navajo Hill] with almost half his blade hanging over the side, nothing below it but thin air." (1935~) The first automobile traversed the hill in 1917, though it had to be hauled up with a team of horses. (1335~)

Charles Kelly described Navajo Hill as it was in 1928: "The road down the west side of Comb Ridge is known as Navajo Hill, without doubt the steepest, most dangerous hill to be found in the whole desert. It dropped straight down over a narrow dugway so steep we never expected to get the car back up again." (1075~)

The present highway follows the approximate route of the old trail over Navajo Hill. The highway was rerouted, widened, and graveled in 1953, with a final alignment done in the early 1970s. (774~, 1356~, 1713~, SAPE.)

One of the big obstacles on the road south from Mexican Hat was crossing the San Juan River. Cornelia Perkins described the evolution of the several bridges over the river: "Mr. Hennasey erected the first bridge about 1910 but an ice floe took it out. The next two structures could very well be called the oil and uranium bridges. A 190-foot span went up in 1913 when oil activity was at its peak in the Goodridge Field. Wire cables were strung and soon a wooden bridge capable of carrying one-way traffic was finished. It gave way under the beating of the heavy uranium traffic and was reduced to the role of a foot bridge in 1954. Taking its place in 1954 was a new steel structure resting on large concrete abutments." (1526~) This is the present bridge.

Brandt Hart on the collapse of the old swinging bridge from the uranium days: "I asked a ... Navajo ... named Harlin ... just what happened to the old swinging Goodridge bridge. Harlin, a World War Two vet, doesn't speak much English, but I understood that a truck coming from the Halchita Uranium Mill was carrying sulfuric acid or some such. It came down the hill, crossed the bridge, and crashed into the wall spilling the acid which ate away the cables on the old bridge. That may have been 1957." (838~)

Highway 191: (Carbon, Emery, Grand, and San Juan Counties.)

This highway goes generally south from Flaming Gorge Reservoir in Wyoming to Wilcox, Arizona. The section we are interested in goes south from Price to Bluff.

—Price to Green River and Crescent Junction. The initial road was built in 1914. In 1934 this road would become the paved Highway 6/50 before the construction of Interstate 70. (644~)

—Crescent Junction to Moab: (Formerly Highways 160 and 450.) Members of the Elk Mountain Mission of 1855 were the first Euroamerican settlers (as opposed to exploring expeditions or transient travelers) to travel the route between Thompson and Moab. They were faced with a severe obstacle in Moab Canyon: the Jumping-off Place (or Moab Dugway or Old Mormon Dugway). Oliver B. Huntington of the mission: "The jumping-off place is a perpendicular ledge twenty-five feet high, down which Wm. Huntington [Oliver's brother] and Jackson Stewart, the year previous, let five wagons with their loads by ropes, taking their wagons to pieces. The knowledge of this induced President Billings to take a company of twelve horsemen in the morning and move rapidly to the canyon; all the way down these men fixed the road, and at the 'jump-off' they worked a road over a point of the mountain covered with very large rocks; in half a day they completed a very passable road where in the morning it had seemed impossible to pass with wagons." (229~)

Mary Day traversed the road in 1882. She noted it as the "drag-up and slide-down road." (2029~)

The route remained a rough track, even as other roads in the area were improving. Frequent flash floods continually erased the road, giving locals little impetus to try and improve it.

The first ferry, located where the present bridge across the Colorado River is now routed, was operated by Norman Taylor in 1881. It was in use until a bridge was built over the river in 1912. (2056~)

In 1919 the road was rerouted and graded, with convicts providing the man power. It was then designated US Highway 450. The road was paved in 1940 and the name was changed to Highway 160. (518~, 644~, 1331~)

—Moab to Bluff: (Formerly Highway 160 from Moab to Monticello and Highway 47 from Monticello to Bluff.) Although Indian and Spanish trails existed in the vicinity of present-day Highway 191 between Moab and Bluff, it wasn't until after the Hole-in-the-Rock Expedition of 1879–80 that a wagon road was constructed. As new towns were settled (such as Monticello in 1886 and

Blanding in 1905), the road was realigned in order to take them in.

In the 19teens the Forest Service, in order to attract visitors, gave names to specific sections of road. The stretch from Thompson to Bluff was called the Sandrock Road. The section from Moab to La Sal and on to Paradox in Colorado was named the Rainbow Route.

The section from Moab to Monticello was called the Navajo Trail. Howard Kimball described the Navajo Trail as it was in 1914: "In those days there were no paved roads, just ones of mud, sand, and rock, with lots of mud during the spring thaw. It took about a week and a half for them to make the [sixty mile] trip [from Moab to Blanding]. At times they would have to hook up all four horses to one wagon to pull it out of the mud." (1092~)

By 1924 the whole route from Thompson to Bluff and beyond was graded. Paving started in 1938 and the road was completely paved in the 1950s. (644~, 1397~, 1530~)

Highway 211: (San Juan Co.)

This short highway goes west from Highway 191 at Church Rock, past the Dugout Ranch at Indian Creek, to the Needles Section of Canyonlands National Park.

When Al Scorup bought the Dugout Ranch on Indian Creek in 1918 he noted that there was no road to his property and the trail crossed the creek fourteen times. To remedy the situation he built a road along the north side of the valley in 1929. The road was graded and improved in 1944. Glendon Black ran the road grader: "I took the grader and eye-balled the road across that flat and through the sagebrush to the pass between the two hills [Photograph Gap] on the west horizon." (1911~)

The road was paved in 1965 and became Highway 211. (152~)

Highway 276: (Garfield, Kane, and San Juan Counties.)

This starts on Highway 95 near Natural Bridges National Monument and goes generally northwest and ends about twenty miles south of Hanksville at Highway 95. Along the way it crosses Lake Powell between Halls Crossing and Bullfrog marinas.

—Natural Bridges to Halls Crossing: This stretch of highway follows or closely parallels sections of the old Hole-in-the-Rock Road (Emigrant Road). Over the years the road slowly improved, with major improvements in the mid-1950s during the uranium boom. It was designated as Highway 263 in 1969. The designation was changed to Highway 276 in 1985 when the ferry service started at Lake Powell.

—Bullfrog Basin to Hanksville: This section of highway paralleled an old county road for some of its length, but other sections were through entirely new country. It was built in 1965 as access to the new marina at Bullfrog Basin.

Highway 313: (Grand and San Juan Counties.)
Also called Dead Horse Point Mesa Scenic Byway.

This short highway goes west and south from Highway 191 about twenty miles north of Moab to the Island in the Sky District of Canyonlands National Park and Dead Horse Point State Park.

Gene Dunham noted that the highway section up Sevenmile Canyon was constructed by the CCC. They had a camp at Dalton Springs near the mouth of the canyon. (580~, 278~) (See Little Mountain Spring for the original route to Deadhorse Point.) The highway alignment followed local roads that were upgraded in the mid-1970s.

—Movies: The opening scenes from *Breakdown*, starring Kurt Russell, were shot along the highway.

Highway Reservoir: (Garfield Co.) Little Rockies-Highway 276. Lost Spring map.

This still-used stock pond is next to Highway 276. (SAPE.)

Hildale Town: (Washington Co.) Vermilion Cliffs-Short Creek-Highway 59. Hildale map.

Also called Maxwell Spring. (294~)

This area, located right on the Arizona and Utah border, was settled by William Bailey Maxwell in the early 1860s. (See Maxwell Canyon.) It remained a grazing land until about 1912 when several families moved to the area. By the mid-1920s the town had become known for its acceptance of polygamy and was called Short Creek. In 1962 the Arizona side of the town was incorporated as Colorado City and the Utah side was incorporated as Hildale. The towns are still the center for polygamy and were featured in Jon Krakauer's book *Under the Banner of Heaven: A Story of Violent Faith.* (311~)

—Holmes Point: This was the name given by Herbert E. Gregory to the prominent point one mile northwest of Hildale (at elevation 6375). William Henry Holmes was a member of the Ferdinand V. Hayden Survey in the 1870s. (767~)

Hilgard Mountain: (Sevier Co.) Fishlake National Forest-Sheep Valley. Hilgard Mountain map. (11,533')

Also called Hill-guard Peak (369~), Mount Hilgard (584~, 1567~), and Mount Hilgram (M.73.).

In 1875 Almon H. Thompson and Grove Karl Gilbert of the Powell Survey climbed the peak and named it Mount Hilgard. (722~, 723~, 1877~) J.E. Hilgard was the head of the Naval Observatory at the time of the Powell Expedition of 1871–72. (1824~)

George C. Fraser in 1915: "Mt. Hilgard is a disappointment. It is even less of a mountain than [Mount] Terrill, really a table top." (668~)

—Old Spanish Trail: (Variation.) The Old Spanish Trail—Fish Lake Route—went under the west side of Hilgard Mountain. (477~)

Hill Creek: (Grand and Uintah Counties.) Uintah and Ouray Indian Reservation-East Tavaputs Plateau-Willow Creek. Floy Canyon North, Walker Point, Chicken Fork, Black Knolls, Flat Rock Mesa, Agency Draw NW, and Big Pack Mountain NW maps.

John Wesley Powell called this Kwzant Creek in 1878. (1567~) G.B. Richardson noted it as Kwiant Creek in 1908. (1623~)

Two derivations for the Hill name are given.

First, cattleman Adams "Charley" Hill arrived in the area in 1894. (520~, 1931~)

Second, the Don Hill family had property on nearby Willow Creek. (110~)

—Webster City: This famous ranch was on Hill Creek. (See East Squaw Canyon–Webster City.)

Hillsdale Town: (Garfield Co.) Sevier River-Highway 89. Hatch map.

Also spelled Hinsdale. (887a~)

Linda King Newel noted that the town was settled in 1871. One of the first to arrive was Joel Hills Johnson (1802-1882). Local tradition noted that the town was named either for Johnson or in memory of his mother, who's maiden name was Hills. (65~, 832~, 1445~) In a *Deseret News* article in 1872 Hills wrote: "I am forming a new settlement in Iron County ... which I call Hillsdale." (990~) Later he provided the real derivation in his diary: "I call it Hillsdale it being a valley between the hills, Hills also being a part of my own name." (989~)

Drought, flash floods, and a lack of economic opportunities forced the abandonment of Hillsdale by the late 1920s. (65~)

Hiram Corral Spring: (Emery Co.) San Rafael Swell-South Sand Bench. Short Canyon map.

Also called Hyrums Pond.

Correctly spelled Hyrum Corral Spring.

This is a large, developed spring. (SAPE.)

The corral is one-quarter mile south of the spring (near elevation 6150). Lee Mont Swasey: "Hyrum was Hyrum Nelson [1860-1949]." (1853~) He arrived in Ferron in the early 1880s. (931~) Ray Wareham: "Hyrum lived right there. He had a corral and he run a lot of horses down there and sold 'em to the government.... It was a good spring and he had it all troughed up." (1967~)

—Hyrums Pond Draw: Hiram Corral Spring is in this draw. (369~)

—Devils Dance Floor: This is the flat area to the east of the spring. Lee Mont Swasey: "It is just a big flat Entrada Sandstone opening. Don't know who gave it that name." (1853~) (See Devils Racetrack.)

Hi Spring: (Sevier Co.) Fishlake National Forest-Fishlake High Top Plateau-Na-Gah Flat. Fish Lake map.

Max Robinson noted that this is probably misspelled. It should be "High" Spring, since it is near the top of a hill. (1641~)

Hite: (San Juan Co.) Glen Canyon NRA-Glen Canyon-Highway 95. Hite South and Hite North maps.

Also called Canyoneers Marina and Hite Marina. (1659~) This marina, constructed in 1964, is not at the same location as the original townsite of Hite. (See Hite Town and Dandy Crossing.)

—Browns Bar: (Also called Browns Bottom.) This placer bar, now underwater, was on the east side of the Colorado River and was one-half mile west of present-day Hite Marina (Hite North map). John E. Brown started running livestock in the area in the late 1870s. (465~) (See Browns Rim.)

—Phoebes Castle: This tower is on the south side of Highway 95 one and one-quarter miles northwest of Hite (one-half mile south of elevation 4234 on the Hite North map). Barbara Ekker: "Arthur Chaffin was coming from Hite and there was a flood coming down [North Wash], so he put his wife [Phoebe] up in the rocks to save her. He made it clear up to Granite [Ranch] and Grandma said he came in there and sat with them and told them what a horrible flood it was and stayed with them for a couple of days, and then it dawned on him that he had left his wife, Phoebe, down there at Hog Seep." (604~)

Hite Town and Dandy Crossing: (Garfield Co.) Glen Canyon NRA-Lake Powell-Trachyte Creek. Hite South map.

Also called Brinkerhoff Ferry, Chaffin Ranch, Hite City, Hite City Bottom, Moqui Crossing, Old Moquise Crossing, and Trachyte Crossing.

Also spelled Hyte.

These entries are not shown on the map.

The old town of Hite, now underwater, was not near the present site of Hite Marina. It was at the mouth of Trachyte Creek on the west bank of the Colorado River (one-half mile north-northeast of elevation 4003T).

Although the town was named for miner Cass Hite (1845-1914), other settlers used the crossing before he arrived in 1883. Rancher John E. Brown ran cattle in the area

starting in the late 1870s. Albert King Thurber and an exploring party used Dandy Crossing, and explored White Canyon, in 1881. (381~, 1888~)

Born to wander, Cass Hite was a miner in Montana and Colorado before entering canyon country. Arthur Chaffin in 1955: "Cass Hite came to the Colorado in September of 1883. I knew Cass when I was a young fellow and many, many times I went up river by boat, by horse back and by walking, to get the mail which came from Hanksville and Green River, Utah each week on horseback to Hite. Cass Hite came to San Juan River in the early '80s and hunted for the *Peso-La-Ki* silver mine [supposedly near Navajo Mountain]. Hoskinnini [Chief of the Navajos] befriended Cass and got him to leave the reservation lest he might get killed [for sticking his nose in their silver business]. He then came to Hite with a 'pack outfit' and several other men—when arriving at the river he was in the lead and rode across, called back to the other boys saying 'Come on boys, she's a Dandy Crossing.' It took that name for several years, until Cass got a mail route established from Green River to Hite—then they named it 'Hite' after Cass." (1162~, 1402~)

Pearl Baker quoted Cass Hite as saying: "The little band [of Indians] brought me to White Canyon, and we came down the canyon to the mouth. I called the crossing from White Canyon to where Hite is now 'Dandy Crossing.' I carved my name on the rock the next day after I got there, September 19, 1883." (121~) This inscription was flooded by Lake Powell. It actually read Sep 19 AD 1883. (17~)

Another claim for naming Dandy Crossing came from Blanding resident Albert R. Lyman in 1963: "My father [Walter C. Lyman] discovered and named Dandy Crossing in 1884. Later Cas [*sic*] Hite began a ferry there, and changed the name to Hite." (1162~)

Cass Hite started the small settlement of Hite and provided a ferry service across the Colorado River. (470~, 1162~) George F. Flavell described Hite as it was in 1896: "We made camp and went over to the village [of Hite], it being small, only a post office, hotel, and restaurant, all in a room 14 x 16 feet." (649~)

Vern Lyman noted that the ferry at Dandy Crossing was run by George Brinkerhoff, Louis F. Brown, and Amasa Mason Lyman, Jr. in 1885. Joseph Franklin Barton was the first to use the new ferry: "The crossing on the Colorado river is beautiful, with nice bottoms on either side, and it is not at all difficult to get to and from the river. (162a~) The ferry washed away. (34~)

Hoffman Birney described the route of the ferry: "The old ford apparently ran from the north bank of Trachyte

Creek diagonally across the river to the south bank of White Cañon. She must have been a mean one, particularly for horses, for many of the bars and banks are pretty deep quicksand." (231~)

C. Gregory Crampton: "Dandy Crossing ... was located up- or downstream some distance, depending on the stage of water in the river.... [It] was not a ford.... Most of those who crossed in the horse and buggy days had to swim their animals." (465~)

John Frank Sleeper in 1890: "I started in to see how deep it was and kept on until I was across on the other side, and the water only reached the saddle skirts. Father tied the pack horses together and led them across without wetting a pack." (509~)

Ben Wetherill had difficulty crossing the river in 1897: "We camped opposite & I lost my appetite worrying how we were to get the boat over—for a river a 1/4 mile wide strikes terror to the heart of one to whom a full irrigation ditch is a big stream.... I nearly drowned two horses before deciding that they knew less about water than we did." (1172~)

In 1891 Hite was convicted of killing Adolph Kohler. Although he claimed self-defense, Hite was convicted and thrown into jail. The residents of the area, though, thought that Hite was innocent. A *Deseret Weekly* article in 1893 noted that "A petition is being circulated ... asking the unconditional pardon of Cass I. Hite, who is now confined in the penitentiary for the killing of a man at Blake [Green River Town]. Already the names of 1200 citizens are enrolled." (1446~)

Cass was freed, but did not return to Hite. Instead, he started a ranch at the mouth of Ticaboo Creek on the Colorado River and lived out his years there. (1446~) (See Ticaboo Creek for the rest of the story.)

The ferry was abandoned for many years, though the crossing was still used by ranchers and prospectors. Herbert E. Gregory noted that Charlie Gibbons ranched at Hite from 1905 to 1914, probably on a part-time basis. (758~)

Prospector and cowboy Frank Lawler took over in 1912. (118~) Barbara Ekker: "Frank Lawler got his draft call, sold the place, and got to his draft board and found the Armistice had been signed and so had lost Hite.... [He then] went to work for Arthur Chaffin ... he got bitten by a rabid coyote [near Hite] and walked to Hanksville. He was bitten in the hand or arm.... Franz Weber took him by wagon to Green River where he boarded the train to Salt Lake and medical care (shots into the belly daily)." (606~)

Darrys Ekker: "Frank was an old fella that came out in Missouri or somewhere, he was an old batch.... He was awful nice, but never did marry. He come here, he was just a lone prospector, an old bachelor, hermit you might say." (610~) Louis M. Chaffin: "Frank Lawler was the crookedest fellow I ever met." (408~)

The next owner was Tom Humphries (also spelled Humphrey). Frank Lawler told this story: "Tom Humphrey and I picked grapes at Hite—smashed grapes in barrels—Humphrey reached for grapes—rattler bit him on wrist. Covered it with towel and cow manure—2 hours. And no bad effects." (1153~)

David D. Rust told this story about Tom Humphries: "In 1923 [I] found Tom flat with sun-stroke. He had a glass eye and got up to wash his face. 'Is my eye straight'? He wanted it to look good and had no mirror." (1674~)

Charles Kelly told a story that happened in 1932: "Here we found John Young, an old prospector. His two partners, Sam Gates and Harry Correll, had attempted to cross the river some days previous on a raft. The raft had struck a rock and gone to pieces. Sam Gates attempted to swim to shore, but disappeared. Correll remained on the rock two days, then caught a floating log and drifted down stream ten miles. Landed on same side of the river, and walked back opposite camp." (1049~)

Humphries sold Hite to the Snow brothers of Richfield. They, in turn, sold it to Arthur Chaffin in 1934. Chaffin told the story of why he moved to Hite: "In 1934 I returned to Hite to work my mining claims again.... I built a boat and went down the river to my claims, when I returned my gas and tools had been taken from my truck.... So I borrowed some gas and went out to get other tools. Made another trip down the river after caching my gas and supplies in the sand dunes.... I returned in a few days and some one had found my caches and I was stripped once more.... I could see that I was going to have to establish a head quarters at Hite in order to operate my mining claims. Oren Snow of Richfield Utah owned the old squatter's right—so I bought his relinkishment and made an application for a home-stead." (398~)

Senator Barry Goldwater in 1940: "In 1935 A.L. Chaffin and his wife came to this place, which was then nothing but a sandy waste. Here they built a home and a ranch that are a monument to Mr. Chaffin's ingenuity, enterprise, and ambition. He has developed his own water system, and has trees and truck growing. They live in a pleasant ranch house built of logs and driftwood plastered with mud, and with a mud roof.... He has built a stern-wheeler, powered with an old auto,—not just its motor—which plies up and down the river with supplies for the few placer miners in the area. In all, they have a wonderful place." (737~)

Harry Aleson: "Here completely isolated from the rest of the world in a cozy nook on the river bank [Arthur Chaffin] raised semitropical fruits along with vegetables and farm crops.... For years Arthur Chaffin's ranch was unquestionably the most isolated in the United States. He lived 120 miles from the nearest railroad and his nearest neighbor downstream on the Colorado was at Lee's Ferry, 162 miles away." (20~)

Aleson also told this story: "The year I met A.L. Chaffin, 1945, at the Chaffin Ranch on Trachyte Creek, Art told me this story. The Navajos, coming to trade, wanted liquor. Art didn't have it. To prove it, one day he would stoop in the rear of the counter, raise a gallon jug partly into sight. After much coaxing on the part of the old Navajo, for a drink, Art brought the Navajo in alone, for a drink, to help himself to the jug. Suddenly, he came up gagging and splurting vinegar around the place." (19~)

Willard Luce in 1946: "The small house was set back in the shade of Russian Olive, Catalpa and Honey Locust trees. Forming a hedge across one side of the yard was a row of fig trees, with fruit as large as a big apricot. Cherries, too, and they were ripe. And apricots and apples and pears. He has several trees of Chinese or Oriental dates." (1229~)

Until 1946 the crossing at Hite was primarily used by livestock and wagons; the road along the south rim of White Canyon and through North Wash was too rugged for automobiles. At that date, a reasonably good road was established (See Highway 95) and the first ferry to carry automobiles across the river was built by Arthur Chaffin. Other families moved to the tiny settlement. Martin and Pearl Guymond and Claude Simonds arrived in 1944, Aaron Porter and family in 1947, and the Dan Miller and Jack Perhoson families in 1948. (403~)

In 1947 Chaffin tried to sell the ranch. He ran an ad in the *Salt Lake Tribune*: "Beautiful Chaffin Ranch at Hite, 160 miles north Lees Ferry on Colorado River. New power ferry now opens travel from Salt Lake City and Richfield through Wayne Wonderland to Blanding and scenic Utah. Ranch contains 274 acres. On maps as HITE, UTAH and plans are to become townsite. Raise fruit and vegetables. Price with cattle setup $35,000. Without cattle $25,000." (397~)

He sold the ranch to Reed Maxfield and Clyde Konold in 1956. Because of default, Chaffin got the ranch back in 1957. (397~)

Arthur wrote this story in 1950: "We ... were standing on the west bank of the Colorado River ... and some of us saw Dannie Miller and Harold Martin thrown from a boat into the river by hitting an over head cable. We all saw them swimming and before Mr. [E.J.] Guymont [Guymond] and Chaffin could get to them with a row boat from the Ferry, Harold Martin was drowned. We were able to pick up Mr. Miller before he drowned." (397~)

Arthur Chaffin received this letter from the Treasury Department: "An inspector from this office discovered last week that your place of business was selling beer at retail, and our records do not show that you have ever paid tax as retail beer dealer." (397~) Chaffin had to pay five dollars and fifty cents in taxes and a penalty of eighty-three cents.

During the uranium boom of the 1950s-60s, Guy and Nina Robison ran the ferry at Hite. Guy Robison: "They had a uranium mill across the river [at White Canyon City]. There was a little traffic to be crossin' several times a day and that was the damnest ferry you ever seen. It was run with a Model A Ford engine and the ferry held on a solid cable, but you had another cable that run on a belt around the engine and that towed you across.... We crossed people, crossed horses, crossed anybody that'd come along. Made a little bit of money. We made expenses ... and we had a rock house up above and had a little farm, and a little orchard and one time some fellas came down there and planted a lot of tomatoes and he had an airplane and he figured they could raise tomatoes early enough and get 'em out with this airplane and make some money, but they didn't. They raised the tomatoes all right but.... " Nina Robison finished the story: "They crashed the airplane." (1644~)

Nina Robison: "I can tell you about the setting. It was in between the canyon walls. The climate was absolutely semi-tropical. So we harvested pomegranates and figs and nuts of all kinds. We had lots of peaches, apricots, pears. We enjoyed it." (1644~)

The ferry was abandoned when the bridges over the Colorado and Dirty Devil rivers were completed in 1964. (470~, 1162~)

C. Gregory Crampton: "The formal ceremonies for the opening of the Hanksville-Blanding road [now Highway 95] and the inauguration of the ferry were held at the Chaffin Ranch on September 17, 1946." (465~)

Hittle Bottom: (Grand Co.) Richardson Amphitheater-Colorado River. Dewey map.

Also spelled Hittel Bottom. (1931~)

A plaque at Hittle Bottom Recreation Site (one-half mile upriver from Hittle Bottom) reads: "In the early 1900s the Tom Kitsen family lived here. Tom carried the mail with his team of horses from the Cisco Post Office. He used his place as a halfway stop to change his teams. All that remains of his homestead is the rock walled dugout [still visible]. The grave site [shown as 'Grave' on the map] south of the remaining dug-out is his mothers. Evidently she went to the river to get water, fell in, caught pneumonia and died. The site is named for a later resident." (1551~)

Joe Taylor: "The Hittles had a farm and the floods came and just covered that farm with mud and rocks and they left." (1866~)

Hodge Ranch Spring: (Piute Co.) Sevier Plateau-Forshea Mountain. Phonolite Hill map.

This large spring was once developed. (SAPE.)

—Hodge Ranch: Kent Whittaker noted that the George Hodge family had a small ranch here in the early days. (2002~)

Hogan Pass: (Sevier Co.) Fishlake National Forest-Thousand Lake Mountain. Geyser Peak map. (8,800')

Garn Jefferies noted that a man named Hogan was the first to ranch in nearby Paradise Valley in the late 1890s or early 1900s. (959~) This was probably Jim Hogan. (931~)

Hogansaani Spring: (Apache Co., Az.) Navajo Indian Reservation-Walker Creek. Hogansaani Creek map.

Also called Ojo de Casa. (769~)

Hogansaani is Navajo for "Lone House in the Desert." (769~)

Hogan Spring: (Grand Co.) Grand Valley-Danish Wash. Cisco map.

This is a large, developed spring. Remnants of a line shack are nearby. (SAPE.)

Hogback, The: (Garfield Co.) GSCENM-Dry Hollow-Calf Creek. Calf Creek map.

Also called The Hogsback. (55~)

Highway 12 runs the high ridge of The Hogback between Calf Creek on the west and Dry Hollow on the east. (See Highway 12.)

Hog Canyon: (Garfield Co.) Henry Mountains-North Wash. Black Table and Hite North maps.

(Also see Hog Spring.)

Barbara Ekker: "There are many 'hog' stories about this place. One of the most reliable took place in the early 1900s when Lee Brinkerhoff [another source says Tom Humphries] was moving a load of hogs from Hite on the Colorado River when a wheel on his wagon broke,

forcing him to unload his hogs at this spring where there was good grazing and ample water. This spring was also an overnight camp for freighters headed to the [Stanton] gold dredge and the community at Hite. Cameron Brinkerhoff, who owned the Trachyte Ranch at one time, also wintered pigs at the spring." (607~)

—Boss Hawg Canyon: (Also called Boss Hog, Hog 1, and West Fork Hog Canyon.) The top of this northern tributary of Hog Canyon is one-quarter mile west of elevation 5079AT on the Black Table map. It was named by David Black and Jim Wright. Stefan Folias: "HOG THEME: based on Hog Canyon/Hog Springs." (653~)

—Hog 2: (Also called Middle Fork Hog Canyon.) This northern tributary of Hog Canyon is one-quarter mile east of Boss Hawg Canyon (one-eighth mile west of elevation 4895T on the Black Table map). (653~)

—Razorback Canyon: (Also called East Fork Hog Canyon and Hog 3.) This northern tributary of Hog Canyon is one-quarter mile east of Hog 2 and Hog Spring is at its mouth. It was named by Steve Ramras. Stefan Folias: "Named for the iron concretion-studded walls which are frequently chimneyed." (653~)

—Moqui Queen: This is the local name for an oft-visited Barrier Canyon Style pictograph in a cave near the mouth of Hog Springs Canyon. (663~)

Hog Canyon: (Kane Co.) Wygaret Terrace-Kanab Creek. Thompson Point and Kanab maps.

Julius S. Dalley: "So named because the residents of Kanab turned their hogs into the canyon during the fall of the year to fatten on the acorns growing there." (2053~)

Cal Johnson: "They said that some old boy run a bunch of pigs up in there and they called it Hog Canyon." (984~)

—Hog Canyon Spring: (Thompson Point map.) In the early days water was piped from the springs to Kanab.

—Gristmill: Adonis Findlay Robinson noted that a gristmill operated at the mouth of the canyon in the early 1880s. (1639~)

Hog Canyon: (San Juan Co.) Harts Point-Indian Creek. Photograph Gap and Harts Point South maps.

Pete Steele noted that the canyon was fenced with knit wire (sheep wire) to hold the pigs that used to pasture in the canyon. The fence still stands. (1821~)

Hogeye Creek: (Kane Co.) GSCENM-Paria River. Calico Peak map.

Ralph Chynoweth: "It's a big deep canyon that comes into the Paria. You can only go up it so far and it closes up and there is a jump-up that is 25 feet high or so. They [Sam Pollock and others] went in there with some dynamite and blasted a trail up and around that jump-up. There's some pretty trees down there and a pretty stream with some of the best water you ever saw in the middle of Hogeye." (425~)

Ralph told this story about Hogeye Canyon: "There's a pretty stream going in there and there's a ledge where the old cowboys used to camp. This one guy used to live there. He's dead now. He told me a story about when he got outta the Army in 1946. He came home and bought a bunch of cattle and took them down into the Hogeye. It was along toward evening, not quite dark. He told me: 'I heard one of the most blood-curdling sounds you ever heard in your life.' And he said, 'Boy, it just made the hair stand up on the back of your neck. I really didn't know what it was or where it came from. But it sounded bad.'

"Now this fellow was out alone and without a gun. He had a short handle axe and that was it. The fellow told me: 'I heard that sound again and I didn't even dare go to bed. I built a great big fire and set around it all night with that little stub hatchet.' Next day the fellow went out and checked tracks and found that it was a wolf. There's a guy that lived here in town, his name was Sears Willis. He went out and caught that wolf in a trap and he said it was one big animal. It was the last wolf in this country." (425~)

—Hogeye Creek Butte: This low butte is at the mouth of Hogeye Creek. (1083~)

—Hogeye Ranch: This was at the mouth of Hogeye Creek and to the north of Hogeye Creek Butte. It was probably occupied from the mid-1870s until the mid-1880s. All that is left of the ranch is a stone foundation. A nearby inscription is from Effil G?ffal, 1899. (425~, SAPE.)

Hog Ranch Spring: (Garfield Co.) Dixie National Forest-Boulder Mountain. Posy Lake map.

Two similar name derivations are given.

First, Pratt Gates: "A lot of the old pioneers and farmers would take their hogs from Escalante and drive them clear up here to Hog Ranch Spring and turn them loose for the summer. Then in the fall, the men would go up there and gather the hogs and drive them back to Escalante." (709~)

Second, unattributed: "Rancher turned his hogs loose and they went wild; Hog Wild." (1346~)

—Hog Ranch Spring Canyon: (Also called Dry Fork North Creek.) This goes from Hog Ranch Spring south to the Griffin Ranch (Posy Lake and Wide Hollow Reservoir maps).

Hogs Back: (Garfield Co.) Henry Mountains-Highway 276. Black Table map.

—Pulpit Bulge: This is one-quarter mile southeast of the Hogs Back (at elevation 5752T). It was named by Grove Karl Gilbert of the Powell Survey: "The Pulpit Bulge is no more sketchable than the Maze, which it resembles." (722~, 723~)

Hogs Heaven: (Washington Co.) Kolob Terrace-Deep Creek. Cogswell Point map.

Frank Jensen noted that a rancher raised hogs here. (967~)

Hog Spring: (Garfield Co.) Henry Mountains-North Wash. Black Table map.

Also called Hog Canyon Spring. (1796~)

Also spelled Hogg Spring. (797~)

(See Hog Canyon—Garfield Co. for name derivation.)

Charles Cutler Sharp in 1909: "About noon we came to Hog Canyon, a branch creek from the south which delivered about a three inch stream of nice sparkling water over a sandstone ledge about fifteen feet high into North Wash." (1720~)

Donald Scott in 1928: "Hog Spring, an easily distinguished rill of clear water coming out of the solid rock face about fifteen feet high." (1705~)

Tom McCourt: "The spring itself was a pipe driven into the sandy creek bank from which splashed a weak but steady flow of cold, sweet water. The old spring isn't there anymore. Road construction and attempts to 'enhance' the flow killed it in the 1970s." (1325~)

Inscriptions include a date of 1883 with no name; G. Miller, March 29, 1913; Elmer Jeffs, April 12, 1929; Darys F. Ekker, Aug. 14, 1935; F.G. Wilson, Aug. 14, 1935; A. Ekker, Aug. 17, 1935; Roy Despain, Sept. 1, 1941; and Brig Larsen, Moab Utah, May 21, 1947. (SAPE.)

Holbys Bottom: (Garfield Co.) Dixie National Forest-Escalante Mountains-Twitchell Creek. Barker Reservoir map.

Correctly spelled Holtby Bottom.

Edson Alvey noted that rancher John Nelson Holtby moved to the Escalante area in the 1880s. (55~, 2051~)

Holding Pond: (Grand Co.) Book Cliffs-Cisco Desert-Death Valley. Cisco Springs map.

This is a still-used stock pond. Sheep were held in a nearby corral. (SAPE.)

Hole in the Rock: (Iron Co.) Squaw Hollow-Parowan Canyon. Parowan map.

Dixie National Forest Ranger Frank W. Seaman noted that one can crawl through this natural rock formation. (2053~) Robert H. Vreeland: "The local people know of this arch and occasionally drive to it, but it is virtually unknown to the rest of the world." (1956~)

Hole-in-the-Rock: (Kane Co.) Glen Canyon NRA-Glen Canyon. Davis Gulch map.

This was listed on the Utah State Register of Historic Sites in 1971 and on the National Register of Historic Places in 1975.

(See Appendix Four–The Hole-in-the-Rock Expedition for the story of the expedition and of the Hole.)

The story of the Hole didn't end with the expedition. In 1898 twenty-six employees of the Hoskinnini Mining Company, under the direction of Nathaniel Galloway, improved the Hole, making it easier to traverse. They were improving access to their extensive mining claims in Glen Canyon. The mining company is credited with cutting the steps (horse ladder) near the top of the Hole, which made the route much easier for pack animals, but made it impossible for wagons. (466~, 1812~) (See Hoskinnini Road.)

Vern Lyman was interviewed by Harry Aleson in 1953. Aleson: "[Vern Lyman] mentioned seeing Navajos easily trotting down the cut steps carrying 100 pound bags of sugar." (34~)

Rockfall into the Hole in 1956 made it impossible for even horses to descend the route. (1812~)

Modern day hikers can only get a taste of what the Hole-in-the-Rock was really like. Several large boulders now choke the upper sections and the fill that smoothed the ramp has long since washed away. A careful search, especially ten to twenty feet above the present floor, will reveal signs of the old trail.

Inscriptions at the Hole-in-the-Rock include Decker, 1880; O.F. Hunter and C.A. Quiqley, Oct. 23/1896; J.V.L., 1894; A.E. Sherman, Feb. 13/[18]99; and "The first car to the hole, HSR." (466~, 1112~, 2007~, SAPE.)

—Hole-in-the-Rock Commemorative Plaque: This brass plaque, now found at the top of the Hole-in-the Rock, was placed at the bottom of the Hole in 1939 by D. Eldon Beck. (184~) The plaque was moved during the filling of Lake Powell.

—Hole-in-the-Rock Creek: The Hole-in-the-Rock was at the top of Hole-in-the-Rock Creek. Apparently the creek had an adequate flow of water that was used by the expedition and was well-known to later miners and river runners.

—Fort Hall: (Also called Hall's Trading Post and Rock House Trading Post.) Henry "Harry" Newell Cowles, Joseph T. Hall (no relation to Charles Hall), and Edward Wilcock operated a popular Indian trading post and ferry

service at the foot of the Hole-in-the-Rock from 1900 to 1902. (34~, 466~)

—Jackass Bench: (Also called Jackass Bar and Jackass Mesa.) (1356~) Jackass Bench, now underwater, was on the west side of the Colorado River just north of the Hole-in-the-Rock (one-half mile southwest of elevation 4164T on The Rincon map). It was used by the Hole-in-the-Rock Expedition for grazing, as it was later by ranchers. (466~)

—Jackass Bench Trail: This starts one and one-half miles northeast of Hole-in-the-Rock (one-eighth mile north of elevation 4252T on the Davis Gulch map) and goes east down the cliffs to Lake Powell. The trail was built by the Hole-in-the-Rock scouts looking for a route across Glen Canyon. In November 1879 Platte D. Lyman went down the approximate route of the trail: "We took our wagons 2 miles farther up the river [from the Hole-in-the-Rock] to where the banks are not so abrupt but are still solid sandstone, and took the front wheels from under the boat and lowered it down about 1 mile onto a sandy bench [Jackass Bench]." (1259~) Lyman in December 1880: "Today put our horses down over a trail which we have made to a bench [Jackass Bench] next to the river where there is a little feed and water." (1259~) The trail, like the Hole-in-the-Rock, was improved by the Hoskinnini Mining Company. (466~)

—Hole-in-the-Rock Marina: (Proposed.) When Lake Powell was filling, this was one of several possibilities for a marina. (1400~)

Hole-in-the-Rock Road: (Garfield and Kane Counties.) GSCENM-Glen Canyon NRA. Maps Highway 12 to the Hole-in-the-Rock: Dave Canyon, Tenmile Flat, Seep Flat, Sunset Flat, Basin Canyon, Big Hollow Wash, Blackburn Canyon, Sooner Bench, and Davis Gulch.

Also called Desert Road, Emigrant Road, Emigrant Trail, Escalante Short-cut, Hole-in-the-Rock Trail, and Old Desert Road.

The Hole-in-the-Rock Trail was listed on the National Register of Historic Places in 1982.

This road is not labeled on the maps. It starts at elevation 5740 on the Dave Canyon map and ends at the marked Hole-in-the-Rock on the Davis Gulch map.

The Hole-in-the-Rock Road was built by members of the Hole-in-the-Rock Expedition of 1879–80. (See Appendix Four–The Hole-in-the-Rock Expedition.) The automobile road, following the general path of the original pioneer road, was completed in 1941.

—Escalante Desert: (Also called Desert Field, Little Desert, and Lower Desert.) This is the almost-level pasture area on either side of the Hole-in-the-Rock Road between the town of Escalante and Glen Canyon and between the Escalante River and the Kaiparowits Plateau. (663~)

In the early days pioneers had private land in and around Escalante Town, but lands below, or south of, Alvey Wash were regarded as being communal, or able to be used by all.

Frederick S. Dellenbaugh of the Powell Survey: "The country to the ... south [of Escalante Town] is a terrible country, terrible mixture of canyons and cliffs; it is very difficult to traverse; I suppose it is easier now, because the trails have been worked out." (552~)

Hole-in-the-Rock Well: (Kane Co.) Glen Canyon NRA-Hole-in-the-Rock Road. Davis Gulch map.

Don Coleman noted that the well was drilled for oil in the 1960s, but they hit water instead. (441~) It is still used by livestock.

A plaque near the well was installed in 1957 by the Utah Pioneer Trails and Landmarks Association. It reads:

> **The naming of this arch honors**
> **the historic trek of the MORMON PIONEERS**
> **called by**
> **BRIGHAM YOUNG**
> **To Colonize San Juan County**
> **in 1879–1880**.

The plaque refers to Hole-in-the-Rock Arch, which is on Fiftymile Point and is visible from the well.

Holeman Spring Basin: (San Juan Co.) Canyonlands National Park-Island in the Sky District. Upheaval Dome map.

Correctly spelled Holman Spring Basin.

Del Taylor: "Holman Spring was named for Al Holman who ran cattle on the White Rim after Mark Walker left there. Holman and my father [A.T. "Del" Taylor] ran cattle in Greys Pasture in the summers and on the Green River in the winter." (1864~)

—Deer Canyon: Ned Chaffin noted that Holman Spring is in Deer Canyon. (413~)

—The Jug: This prominent tower is at the head of Holman Spring Basin and is one-half mile south of Holman Spring (at elevation 5826T). (1351~)

—Wilhite Trail: This constructed stock trail is the "Foot" trail that cuts generally east-west from Island in the Sky to the top of the White Rim. It was built by the CCC. Along the trail is an inscription reading "Wilhite Trail." It is not known who this was. (SAPE.)

Hole Spring: (Garfield Co.) Henry Mountains-Woodruff Canyon. Mount Holmes map.

This is a large spring. A corral is nearby. (SAPE.)

Hole Trail: (Emery Co.) Manti-LaSal National Forest-Wasatch Plateau-Muddy Creek. Ferron map.

This constructed stock trail is only labeled on the Ferron map. From the south it starts on Muddy Creek near the "Gaging Station" on the Emery East map. It goes north through what is called The Hole of Bills Fork, which is one-quarter mile northwest of elevation 7285 on the Ferron map, and then goes west to Sage Flat (Flagstaff Peak map). (M.68., SAPE.)

Holiday Mesa: (San Juan Co.) Navajo Indian Reservation-Oljeto Wash. Oljeto map. (5,515')

Correctly spelled Halliday Mesa.

Byron Cummings noted that Navajo Tom Halliday (also known as Navajo John) and family lived near the mesa in the early 1900s. (501~)

—Little Oljeto Mesa: This is immediately south of Holiday Mesa (at elevation 5297). (1197~)

Holly Oak Spring: (Iron Co.) Dixie National Forest-Upper Bear Valley. Little Creek Peak map.

Correctly spelled Holyoak Spring.

Betsy Topham Camp: "One spring in the area is called 'Holyoak Spring.' The [Henry] Holyoak homestead was an early-day stage stop." (336~)

A contingent of the Hole-in-the-Rock Expedition stopped here for a couple of days in 1879 to regroup. Expedition member Maggie Nielson: "spent two days and three nights in this beautiful little valley [Bear Valley] getting our drinking water from Halyoak [*sic*] Springs, which we thought was the best water in the world." (1456~, 1356~)

—Old Spanish Trail: The trail went by Holly Oak Spring.

Holt Canyon: (Washington Co.) Dixie National Forest-Mountain Meadows-Escalante Valley. Pinto and Enterprise maps.

—Holt Cemetery: (Enterprise map.) This is in Holt Canyon. James Holt (1804–1894) is buried here.

—Holt Town: (Also called Holts Ranch.) (972~) This small town was a couple of hundred yards south of Holt Cemetery on the west side of the road. It was started by John and William Pulsipher in 1862. (283~) James Holt: "In the month of February 1867, I moved to the Mountain Meadows.... In a few years I took up a ranch that was about six miles north of the Mountain Meadows [the Pulsipher Ranch]. Here we all worked, making a new home, planting trees, putting in crops, making a reservoir, tending the sheep and etc." (905~)

—Old Spanish Trail: The trail went through Holt Canyon. (1828~)

Holt Draw: (Wayne Co.) Fishlake National Forest-Thousand Lake Mountain-Sulphur Creek. Torrey and Twin Rocks maps.

Also called Holt Hollow and Holts Draw.

Guy Pace and Max Robinson noted that William Holt (1842-1920) moved first to the Escalante area in 1886 (another source says 1884) and, shortly thereafter, to the Torrey area. He homesteaded in Holt Draw. (1497~, 1641~, 1522~)

—Bingo Ranch: PRIVATE PROPERTY. This is near the mouth of Holt Draw north of Torrey (at elevation 6822 on the Torrey map). The ranch marks the end of the Torrey Canal. Bingo Ranch owner Guy Pace: "There was a song about a dog, Bingo was his name." (1497~)

—Flatiron Point: This summit is between lower Sand Creek and Holt Draw and is three miles northwest of Torrey (at elevation 7972 on the Torrey map). (1497~)

Home Base: (Emery Co.) San Rafael Swell-Lone Man Draw. Twin Knolls map.

Lee Mont Swasey noted that, pre-1900, this was the horse catchers' headquarters: "There's a horse trap right there (one-half mile northeast of elevation 6847). They would chase the [wild] horses and catch them in this trap.... This one is built out of slab and cable. We know that the cable came from the [oil] well at Twin Knolls. After the wells were drilled, they had the cables to hold the tower. The old-timers would go and scrounge the cables, untwist it to make it go farther, and then weave it through the boards.... This was in the 1920s. That is what the Swaseys did; to make an income they would go out and gather in the wild horses and then take 'em for sale." (1853~, 641~)

Home Valley Knoll: (Washington Co.) Upper Kolob Plateau-Blue Springs Reservoir. Kolob Reservoir map. (8,160')

Also called Home Valley. (363~)

—Lamoreaux Ranch: PRIVATE PROPERTY. This is one-quarter mile southwest of Home Valley Knoll (one-eighth mile west of elevation 7860).

Homewater Spring: (San Juan Co.) Dark Canyon Plateau-Beef Basin. Fable Valley map.

Also called Home Spring. (1664~)

Pioneer rancher John Adams noted that the only live water on Beef Basin was at what he called House Spring. (758~)

John Scorup noted that these are two large, developed springs in a small canyon. Cowboys had a semi-permanent camp here for many years, making it a "home." A rough road leads to the springs. (1821~, SAPE.)

Honaker Trail: (San Juan Co.) The Goosenecks-San Juan River. The Goosenecks map.

In 1894 Augustus C. Honaker (1840-1905) and his brother, Henry, had a placer claim at the bottom of what is now the Honaker Trail. Honaker used a rough trail that followed the approximate course of the present Honaker Trail to gain access to his claims. Frank H. Hyde noted that Honaker lowered his supplies, and himself, over the cliff with a rope. (936~, 1985~)

Bert Loper, who worked for Honaker, told about the rough trail: "There was two or three of us young fellows at that time carried the stuff down from ledge to ledge until we got to the last big ledge, was about one hundred and thirty or one hundred and forty feet, we had to let the stuff over with ropes, and then when we got our stuff let over the cliff we would go out to the point where the trail now goes over and climb down a rope ladder, and then came back to the ledge and went down to the river." (1220~)

On another occasion Loper expanded on the story: "Just a word about Honaker trail—the placer claim at the foot of the trail was the same one that I was interested in in 1894 ... at the time there was no trail down into the canyon where the Honaker trail is now situated so we had to carry all our stuff down on our backs to the big ledge and then let it over with ropes but there was a 60 foot ledge at the point where the trail now comes over was the only place that we had to get down but there was a crevice and by tying a rope to a rock and letting it hang over we could manage to get up and down at this place and on our first trip into the canyon [we had] to carry a four horse load of provisions down to the big ledge which at this place was about 120 feet thick.... Our next job was to get Mr. Honaker over the crevice and it was sure some job for he was deathly afraid of anything high and we tried to persuade him to try it but of no avail and as it was growing late and all our stuff [was at] the foot of the ledge including our beds George and I in our desperation jumped on Mr. Honaker and tied him up and put him on the end of the rope and in that way got him onto camp for the night." (1221~)

Loper also claimed that the trail was not actually built by Honaker: "The trail is called Honaker trail but Mr. Honaker never even saw the trail it having been built after Mr. Honaker had quit the canyon." (1221~) Other sources agreed with Loper, noting that it was later-day gold miners who completed the trail in 1904. The name was attributed to Honaker because of his placer claim at its foot. (1370~, 1985~)

Several sources noted that the first horse that tried to negotiate the trail fell to its death. It is said no pack animal after that made the round trip successfully. (88~, 1370~) Other diarists, though, noted that it was an often-used pack trail. (1901~)

The trail is still in excellent condition and hikers marvel at the extensive work and cribbing needed to build it. Painted numbers along the trail provided orientation for geologists studying the cliff in recent years.

Whether the trail was actually built by Honaker or not, legend has it that Honaker found little gold along the San Juan River—just enough to fashion a wedding ring for his wife. (1935~)

It is interesting to note that the Honaker Trail was justifiably famous almost from the moment it was built. Several magazine articles extolled its ruggedness and remoteness. A *Montezuma Journal* article from Sept. 2, 1909 called it the "celebrated Honaker trail."

—Horn Point: This small promontory about halfway down the Honaker Trail is a favorite rest place for hikers. Hugh D. Miser called it The Home in 1921. (1368~)

—Constructed Stock Trail: This follows the San Juan River south from the bottom of the Honaker Trail. It goes for several miles and construction is visible here and there along the river. Brandt Hart noted that this trail may have joined up with the Mendenhall Trail. (See Mendenhall Loop.) Inscriptions include W.P. Brooks and Sam L. Simon, June 23, 1891, and W.S. Martin, Jan. 29, 1911. (838~, SAPE.)

Hondu, The: (Emery Co.) San Rafael Swell-Muddy Creek. Ireland Mesa map.

Also called Beer Stein Rock (791~) and Hondoo on the Muddy (1401~).

Also spelled Hondoo Arch. (1956~)

Arthur Chaffin: "The Hondu is on the Muddy River, was first discovered by Ole Sorensen of Emery, Utah, in the year 1877, when he started to run cattle there at that time." (401~)

Two name derivations are given.

First, Dee Anne Finken: "Hondoo Country and Hondoo Arch along the Muddy River derive their names from the likeness of the arch to the small loop knot on the end of a cowboy's lariat." (641~)

Second, Robert H. Vreeland: "It was so named because the shape of its pillar resembles that of a cowboy's twirling lasso rope." (1956~)

—South Canyon: Wayne Gremel noted that this short western tributary of Muddy Creek is two miles south of The Hondu (at elevation 5265): "Neils Morrison told me

that there is a horse trail off of Johns Hole, down South Canyon to Muddy Creek." (780~)

Honishoosh Attin: (Coconino Co., Az.) Navajo Indian Reservation-Rainbow Plateau. West Canyon Creek, Az. map.

This formation includes elevations 5964T and 6275T.

Jesse C. Dyer of the USGS noted that *Honish'oosh Atiin* is Navajo for "Shadow Trail." (588~) Paul Fife: "Warren tells us that *'atiin'* means 'way' or trail,' so that designation might refer to the trail which runs along the Carmel Bench at the base of the cliffs. I looked in a dictionary and found that *'shoosh'* means 'to lay alongside or parallel to' and *honoogi'* (the only word I could find starting with *'hon'* means 'rough'—so maybe the whole thing means trail next to a rough place." (653~)

Charles L. Bernheimer called the whole ridge The Crouching Camel in 1921 (elevation 5964T is the head of the camel, elevation 6275T is the body): "a dike-like rock chain in the north which I named, as it had to be christened, Crouching Camel.... Our trail led us to the very base."

Bernheimer, looking from the Camel toward Navajo Canyon: "Every few hundred feet opened yawning six hundred feet deep rock throats, without a vestige of vegetation. Deep down beyond was a surface of humps, tubercles, and whalebacks, bare and grey, the typical windswept slickrock—a sea of them. Beyond was a narrow green vein-like looking crinkly curling thread that is Navajo Canyon." (218~)

—Constructed Stock Trail: This very good trail is shown as the "Pack Trail" crossing under the south side of Honishoosh Atiin. In places it is not correctly shown on the map. (SAPE.)

—Constructed Stock Trail: The "Pack Trail" noted above is not the original trail below the west side of Honishoosh Atiin. The original trail was a short distance to the south of elevations 5151T and 5501T. (SAPE.) This is the trail Bernheimer's expedition used.

—Garden Snail: This prominent tower is immediately north of elevation 5964T. Charles L. Bernheimer in 1921: "A nameless mesa which, because of resemblance, we called 'Garden Snail Mesa.'" (218~) Inscriptions include M.S. Foote, Mar. 8, 1882; M. [Mike] Murphy, March 10, 1882; and [Charles] Beatty, 1882. (1115~, SAPE.)

Hooch Spring: (Wayne Co.) San Rafael Desert-North Spring Wash. Whitbeck Knoll map.

The spring was developed in 1929. Illicit liquor was brewed here. (1551~)

Hoodle Creek: (Garfield Co.) Dixie National Forest-Sevier Plateau-Pole Canyon. Mount Dutton and Deep Creek maps.

Also called Noodle Creek.

George W. Dobson in 1941: "derived its name because an old settler, Joseph Crowe, hunted deer with his hound dog along this creek and would urge his dog after the deer with the words, 'oodle them up.'" (2053~)

Hook and Ladder Gulch: (San Juan Co.) Dry Valley-Hatch Wash. Sandstone Draw and Hatch Rock maps.

Two name derivations are given. The first is believed to be correct.

First, Karl Barton: "That's a brand. Hook 'n Ladder Brand." (162~)

Second, James H. Knipmeyer: "It received its name from the trail that led out of the head of the draw to the ranch at La Sal. The cowboys claimed that you needed a fireman's hook and ladder to get up over it." (1115~) There are many stock trails into and out of Hook and Ladder Gulch and all are very easy with little or no construction. (SAPE.)

—Dry Valley CCC Camp: Fran Barnes noted that this CCC camp, which was in operation from 1940 to 1942, was at the mouth of Hook and Ladder Gulch (one-eighth mile west of elevation 5649T on the Hatch Rock map). (143~)

—CCC Reservoir: This stock reservoir is two miles north of the Dry Valley CCC Camp (one-quarter mile south-southwest of elevation 5950T on the Hatch Rock map).

Hoosier Creek: (Iron Co.) Hoosier Lake-Co-op Valley Sinks. Red Creek Reservoir map.

Also called Hoosier Meadows. (363~)

—The Hoosier: This was a ranch on Hoosier Creek. (942~) John H. Pendleton: "An old man from Indiana (the Hoosier State) camped at these meadows in the early days and to locate this camp it was referred to as 'The Hoosier.'" (2053~) Luella Adams Dalton noted that Neils Mortenson was the first owner of the meadow. It was later sold to John Henderson. (516~, 363~)

—Hoosier Lake: (Also called Hoosier Reservoir.) Brothers James, Hugh, Thomas, and William Adams built a dam across Hoosier Meadow in the 1870s, forming Hoosier Lake. (516~)

—The Narrows: Hoosier Creek goes through this narrow area between two low hills that are immediately north of Red Creek Reservoir. (516~)

Hoover Peak: (Piute Co.) Tushar Mountains-Marysvale Canyon. Marysvale Canyon map. (7,082')

—Hoovertown: In 1936 Kenneth Holdaway and Ada Steele Hoover moved to the Sevier River directly under what would become Hoover Peak. They started a honkey-tonk named Hoovers on the east side of the road opposite the mouth of Deer Creek. The area was called Hoovertown. Ken's daughter, Joan Anderson, noted that in its heyday, the bar would sell three hundred kegs of beer a week to the miners. They closed the bar in 1944 and re-opened it in 1953 as a café specializing in southern fried chicken. The café continues to operate to this date. Kenneth died in 1972; Ada died in 2003. (61~)

—Winkleman Town: (Also spelled Winkelman.) This was on the west side of the Sevier River at the mouth of Deer Creek, where a Rest Stop is now located. William Winkleman started the town, which housed mostly miners, in 1919. They worked at the Winkleman Mine (also called Copper Butte Mine) a couple of miles up Deer Creek. By the mid-1930s the town had all but disappeared. (61~, 332~)

Joan Anderson noted that her father, Ken Hoover, tried to build a tramway from the Winkleman Mine to the mouth of the canyon. They erected twelve towers and strung the cable, but the grade was too great and the cars went out of control, zipping down the cable, and demolishing themselves at the bottom of the run. The tramway was not rebuilt. (61~)

Hop Creek: (San Juan Co.) La Sal Mountains-La Sal Creek. Mount Peale, Buckeye Reservoir, and Ray Mesa maps.

Wild hops grew along the bank of the creek. (456~)

—Taylor Corral: In 1881 the Taylors (See Taylor Flat) and John Shafer built a corral at the top of the creek. (1741~)

Hop Creek: (San Juan Co.) Manti-LaSal National Forest-Abajo Mountains-North Cottonwood Creek. Shay Mountain and Cathedral Butte maps.

Mary N. Porter Harris: "Hop Creek has wild hops on its bank." (1195~)

Val Dalton: "According to Wade Shupe ... there's a lost silver mine in Hop Creek. A guy by the name of Woodruff was camped down there by where the Cottonwood Ranger Station is now. He was an old hermit and when he'd come to town he'd buy his groceries with almost pure grade silver ore. He supposedly sold the mine to a bunch of investors from up north that got wind of it. They rode up Hop Creek to where the mine was and they camped for the night and they said something that made this old hermit mad. So during the night, he just got up and left them. They said it took them two or three days to find their way out of there. And to this day, nobody's ever located any semblance of his mine." (517~)

Hops Spring: (Kane Co.) Long Valley-Spencer Bench. Long Valley Junction map. PRIVATE PROPERTY.

Also called Hop Spring.

Unattributed: "Named for hops found there and which were picked by early settlers of Long Valley." (2053~)

Hop Valley: (Washington Co.) Zion National Park-Firepit Knoll. The Guardian Angels and Kolob Arch maps. Part of Hop Valley is PRIVATE PROPERTY.

Ron Kay noted that wild hops used to grow here. (1038~) Frank Jensen in 1966: "Hop Valley is another phenomenon of the Kolob [Terrace]. At one time ... it was a crooked, narrow canyon like all the rest of Zion. Then the mouth of the canyon was blocked by a landslide and filled with sand. Hop Valley is so different from the other canyons of Kolob Terrace that the sight is startling." (966~)

—Straton Ranch: Frank Straton had a cattle ranch in Hop Valley in the early years. (363~)

—Constructed Stock Trail: This trail, now a road, is shown as a "Pack Trail" on the map.

Horn, The: (Garfield Co.) Glen Canyon NRA-Glen Canyon. Hite South map.

The Horn, a jutting ridge of rock that forced the Colorado River into a tight bend, was a well-known landmark on the river before Lake Powell. Robert Brewster Stanton called it Camp Horn in 1889. (1811~) Cass Hite's map of 1890 shows it as Cape Horn. (M.32.) The ridge at its narrowest place was called The Notch or Cape Horn Notch. (1812~)

In 1909 Raymond Austin Cogswell rounded The Horn and was prompted to write that he was entering the "Portal to the Isle of Death." (439~)

—Stanton Road: (See Twomile Canyon—Garfield Co.—Stanton Road.)

—Lonesome Flat: This placer bar, now underwater, was on the south (or west) side of the Colorado River immediately north of the saddle to the west of The Horn (one-eighth mile north of elevation 3820T). The bar was noted as early as 1897. (465~)

—The Horn: The large unnamed mesa directly to the north and across the Colorado River from The Horn was also called "The Horn." It includes elevations 4607T, 4990T, and 4738T. A road around The Horn was built during the 1950s uranium years. Inscriptions include E.W. Grove, 1916; A.G. Turner, 1917; and K. Rosequist, 1954. (SAPE.)

—Horn Spring: This small spring was once developed. It is on the west side of The Horn at the "Spring." A sheep corral is nearby. (SAPE.)

Horn, The: (Garfield Co.) Henry Mountains-Pennellen Pass. Mount Pennell and Mount Ellen maps.

This sheer granite outcropping was called both Sentinel Butte and Pass Butte by Grove Karl Gilbert of the Powell Survey. Gilbert provided its first, brief description: "The bald face spur of Pennell that faces the pass [The Horn] and is close at hand shown horizontality on top as though it might be a conformable dike." (722~)

The Horn has now become a popular rock climbing area. (723~, 925~, SAPE.)

Hornet Point: (Washington Co.) Kolob Plateau-The Pillars. Kolob Reservoir map. (9370') PRIVATE PROPERTY.

In 1930 Captain Maurice Francis Graham, a famous World War One pilot, while carrying mail from Los Angeles to Cedar City, crash landed on Hornet Hill in a snowstorm. Although both he and his airplane survived the crash, he was found dead—mail in his arms—in nearby Crystal Creek Canyon. (1551~)

Horn Silver Gulch: (Emery Co.) San Rafael Swell-North Salt Wash. Horn Silver Gulch map.

Joe Bauman noted that hornsilver is a type of silver ore. Although silver was probably not found here in economic quantities, Horn Silver did become the name of a copper mine in the gulch. The name was in use before 1920. (166~)

Inscriptions include Lan. Wareham, July 1, 1917; Glen Pettey, June 10, 1920; and W.M. Heath, Sept. 14, 1934. (SAPE.)

—Dead Mule Flat: Lee Mont Swasey noted that this is on the north side of Horn Silver Gulch one and one-half miles south-southeast of Oscars Pond (between elevations 5661, 5735, and 5828). (1853~)

—Pioneer Road: (See Appendix Two—San Rafael Swell Pioneer Trail.)

Horse Bench: (Emery Co.) San Rafael Desert-Dry Lake Wash. Moonshine Wash, Horse Bench East, and Horse Bench West maps.

—Horse Bench Reservoir: (Horse Bench East map.) The reservoir is a surprise; it is very pretty in an austere and subtle way. A man-made earthen dam forms a reservoir in an area of colorful bentonite hills. When the reservoir was built by the CCC in the early 1940s, it covered what was locally called Tank Spring. (1234~, 1779~, SAPE.)

A small dome on the edge of Horse Bench overlooking the San Rafael River has an inscription from B. Tomlinson, 1893. The Tomlinson family ran cattle throughout the area. (SAPE.)

—Big Ben Mine: This open pit vanadium and uranium mine is at the "Open Pit Mine" on the west side of Horse

Bench (at elevation 4304T on the Horse Bench West map). It was in operation in the 1950s. (1906~)

Horse Bench: (Garfield Co.) Dixie National Forest-Sevier Plateau. Casto Canyon map.

Albert Delong in 1941: "It is a large flat bench thickly covered with trees and is used as a range for horses." (2053~)

Horse Canyon: (Carbon Co.) Book Cliffs-The Cove. Lila Point map.

—Geneva Mine: (Also called Horse Canyon Geneva Mine and Horse Canyon Mine.) Lucile Richens noted that it is a "small canyon east of Sunnyside containing the horse barns and pasture for the horses used in Sunnyside Number Two Mine." (2053~) The Geneva Steel Company opened this coal mine in Horse Canyon in 1944. At one time it was the largest producer of coal west of the Mississippi. The company built the nearby town of Dragerton for its employees. (1621~, 1974~)

Horse Canyon: (Emery Co.) Manti-LaSal National Forest-Huntington Creek. Rilda Canyon map.

Mary Guymon noted that Alma Staker's horse died in the canyon. (1330~)

Horse Canyon: (Garfield Co.) GSCENM-Escalante River. Lamp Stand, Pioneer Mesa, King Bench, and Red Breaks maps.

Also called Horse Creek. (777~)

Burns Ormand: "At one time there was a lot of wild horses run out there in the Circle Cliffs. These guys built some corrals down in Horse Canyon and was gonna run the horses down in there and catch 'em. After they got the corrals built, a big rain storm came and washed their fences down. They named it Horse Canyon after that." (1487~)

—King Bench Trail: This constructed stock trail, shown as a hiking trail on the King Bench map, exits Horse Canyon to the west one-half mile below its confluence with Wolverine Creek (east of elevation 5678). (SAPE.)

—Horse Canyon Trail: (Also called Upper Horse Canyon Trail.) This constructed stock trail, often used, exits Horse Canyon to the east onto Big Bown Bench. It starts immediately below the mouth of Little Death Hollow in Horse Canyon (Red Breaks map).

Burns Ormand: "One time, my brother and I was goin' up that trail and it got dark on us. There was a crack that went through this big rock. We had this old horse with a pair of homemade rawhide packbags on 'im and he jumped up in there and hung himself with the packbags. There he was, just his feet agoin' like that and he couldn't get out, like a car spinning its wheels. We had to take that

pack off'n 'im and carry it up the trail a ways and put it back on 'im again." (1487~, SAPE.)

—Windless Trail: This constructed stock trail, seldom used, starts one mile (as the crow flies) up Horse Canyon from the Escalante River and goes west up to King Bench. It starts one-quarter mile west of elevation 5410 on the Red Breaks map. Burns Ormand noted that the small side canyon the trail ascends is notably windless. (1487~, SAPE.)

Horse Canyon: (Grand Co.) Book Cliffs-Gunnison Valley-Browns Wash. Floy Canyon South, Bobby Canyon South, and Hatch Mesa maps.

Lloyd M. Pierson noted that the Colonel William Wing Loring Expedition of 1857-58 camped at what they called 13 Mile Spring in what was probably Horse Canyon. (1545~) Loring: "Good grass a mile to the east of camp." (1276~)

—Tomlinson Ranch: In the early days Mirt Tomlinson had a ranch at the mouth of Horse Canyon. The Milton family bought out Tomlinson. They used Horse Canyon for winter range and Cub Valley and Tom Farrer Valley (Floy Canyon South map) as summer range. (1430~)

Horse Canyon: (Grand Co.) Roan Cliffs-Flat Nose George Canyon. Walker Point, Floy Canyon North, and Bobby Canyon North maps.

Ranchers kept their horses in the canyon with a fence near its mouth.

Horse Canyon: (San Juan Co.) Alkali Point-Montezuma Creek. Bradford Canyon map.

The name was recommended to the USGS by ranchers Max Dalton, Ashton Harris, and Jesse Grover in 1980. (1931~)

Horse Canyon: (San Juan Co.) Canyonlands National Park-The Needles District-Indian Creek. South Sixshooter Peak map.

The Scorup-Somerville Cattle Company had a line camp in the canyon and would fence in the riding horses here. (1936~)

Inscriptions include Art Burrows, 1878; C. Melvin Turner, 1890 (or 1893); and Trout (referring to early resident Thomas Trout), no date. (1105~, 1115~)

—Trail Fork: Michael R. Kelsey noted that the mouth of this eastern tributary of Horse Canyon is three-quarters of a mile northeast of the Thirteen Faces (See Thirteen Faces) and is between elevations 6050T and 6207T. A rugged route goes out of the canyon here. (1084~)

Horse Canyon: (San Juan Co.) Navajo Indian Reservation-Navajo Mountain-Tsagieto Canyon. Rainbow Bridge and Chaiyahi Flat maps.

Marion A. Speers in 1931: "The first canyon is 'Horse Pasture Canyon' so named because they [at Rainbow Lodge] keep the idle horses and mules in there. The only fencing required is a hundred yards or so at the lower end." (1790~)

Horse Canyon: (Wayne Co.) Canyonlands National Park-Maze District-Orange Cliffs-Stillwater Canyon. Elaterite Basin, Cleopatras Chair, and Turks Head maps.

An 1893 Rand McNally map shows this as Beaver Creek (M.58.), as does the Edwin T. Wolverton map of 1928 (M.78.).

Frank A. Brewer called it Elaterite Canyon and noted that Eph Moore used it to run livestock. Brewer also noted that Fawn Chaffin called it Cow Canyon and that the early National Park rangers called it Maze Canyon. (281~)

Louis M. Chaffin noted in a 1959 interview that Horse Canyon was used by outlaws: "There was a lot of activity in Horse Canyon [by] the Robbers Roosters. They had a cabin down at the mouth of it on Green River that must have been beautifully furnished. I have seen the arms of overstuffed chairs, as well as women's clothing around where it stood. Joe Bush burned it down. The only way they could get into the canyon was down over a rock slide. When the Roosters left the country they left some horses in Horse Canyon. There were two gray mares and a bay mare ... that bay mare could outrun anything that ate grass for 100 miles." (405~)

Inscriptions include Ernest Reid, March 1903. (SAPE.)

—Horse Canyon Trail: This is the "Pack Trail" that is on the south side of Horse Canyon near its head (Elaterite Basin map). (SAPE.)

—Big Bend: This is the obvious north to south bend in Horse Canyon one mile below the South Fork (Turks Head map). (615~)

—Main Water: (Also called First Water.) Hazel Ekker noted that the spring is at the lower end of Big Bend. (615~)

—Lorax Canyon: The head of this short eastern tributary of lower Horse Canyon is one-half mile north-northwest of elevation 5271T on the Turks Head map. It was named by the canyon group Kansas for a sandstone formation near its mouth with a fancied similarity to a Dr. Seuss character. (SAPE.)

—Lower Trail: This constructed stock trail goes from Horse Canyon to Deadhorse Canyon along a narrow bench between the river and the upper cliffs. The section that goes up the initial cliff band in Horse Canyon

is three-quarters of a mile east of elevation 4958T on the Turks Head map. (SAPE.)

—Harvest Scene Pictograph Panel: (Also called Bird Site.) (387~) This was listed on the National Register of Historic Places in 1975. This famous Barrier Canyon Style rock art panel is in a tributary of the South Fork of Horse Canyon and is one-third of a mile southeast of the Chocolate Drops (near elevation 4953T on the Spanish Bottom map). The name was suggested by archaeologist Dean Brimhall who thought that a couple of figures looked like they were harvesting grain. (387~)

Frank A. Brewer, in a 1968 interview with Pearl Baker, claimed he discovered the Harvest Scene Panel in the early 1900s. "I saw a big overhang that cattle used a lot for shade and shelter.... If some vandal has not spoiled that stuff it may prove that there was civilization here long before any other and I would like to have my name credited with the discovery—call it Brewer's Find something like that 'Brewer's Picture Gallery.'" (280~) Cowboys, chasing Brewer's aforementioned cattle, had certainly seen the panel first.

Horse Collar Ruin: (San Juan Co.) Natural Bridges National Monument-White Canyon. Moss Back Butte map. Also called Water Jar Cave. (1931~)

Marian G. Nielson in 1949: "The doors of this particular ruin are shaped like horse collars, whence the name." (1457~)

—Cathedral Rock: This is an old name for a prominent formation in White Canyon approximately one-eighth mile south of Horse Collar Ruin. (1872~)

Horsecorn Canyon: (Uintah Co.) Uintah and Ouray Indian Reservation-East Tavaputs Plateau-Hill Creek. Wolf Flat, Dog Knoll, and Agency Draw NW maps.

A ranch at the mouth of the canyon used to grow horse corn (a field corn grown specifically for livestock).

Horse Creek: (Garfield Co.) Dixie National Forest-Escalante Mountains. Sweetwater Creek and Grass Lakes maps.

William Gladstone Steel in 1926: "Wild horses had a good summer range there." (1819~)

—Steed Ranch: Pratt Gates noted that the Newell Steed family had a ranch on Horse Creek. (709~)

Horse Flat: (Kane Co.) GSCENM-The Cockscomb. Horse Flat and Butler Valley maps.

—West Bench: Ralph Chynoweth noted that the area between Cads Crotch on the west and Wahweap Creek on the east is known as West Bench. This includes Horse Flat, a name that is unknown to local ranchers. (425~)

Horse Fork: (Sevier Co.) Fishlake National Forest-Clear Creek. Johns Peak map.
Also called East Fork of Clear Creek.
Jim Crane: "They used to run hundreds of horses in that area. People ran horses then like they do cattle now." (478~)

Horse Haven: (Carbon Co.) West Tavaputs Plateau-Flat Canyon. Twin Hollow and Summerhouse Ridge maps.
Waldo Wilcox: "Wild horses like that up there. Heaven for horses up on that high bench." (2011~)

Horsehead Peak: (San Juan Co.) Manti-LaSal National Forest-Abajo Mountains. Abajo Peak map. (11,212')
Fred W. Keller: "On an otherwise naked slope of the Blue Mountain, spruce trees grow in the outline of a horse's head. This physical feature is very distinct in winter, and at distances of as great as thirty miles, looking over the mesas. From the earliest times the cowboys have considered the 'Horse Head' a scenic wonder." (1039~)
Norma Perkins Young: "In the center of a rounded symmetrical mountain peak, was the startling likeness of the neck and head of a great horse. The face was blazed. The neck, ears and sides were formed by a dense growth of tall balsams and pines." (2069~)
—Copper Queen Mine: This famous mine is on the west side of North Canyon below Horsehead Peak (one-quarter mile southeast of elevation 11025T).

Horsehead Point: (San Juan Co.) Great Sage Plain-Horsehead Canyon. Eastland, Horsehead Point, and Northdale maps.
Carl Mahon: "You can see Horsehead Peak (Abajo Peak map) from the [Horsehead] point." (1272~)
—McCabe Ranch: In the early 1900s the Henry McCabe Ranch had their main cow camp at Horsehead Spring (Eastland map). (1504~)
—Horsehead: This little settlement on Horsehead Point was started by farmers in the early 1920s. (42~)

Horse Heaven: (Emery Co.) San Rafael Swell-Mexican Mountain. Mexican Mountain, Chimney Rock, Dry Mesa, and Devils Hole maps.
This pastureland was a favorite for wild horses. They were often seen here. (1764~)
—The Grotto: The head of this canyon starts at the south end of Horse Heaven (one-half mile north of elevation 5530 on the Mexican Mountain map). The mouth of the canyon is at elevation BM5073. It was named by Steve Allen. (45~)

Horse Heaven: (Emery Co.) San Rafael Swell-Moroni Slopes. Caine Springs and The Frying Pan maps.
Garn Jefferies: "It's a really good place for horses. They trail down the wash quite a ways and get a drink." (959~)
Wayne Gremel: "Wild horses used to like to stay out there. Used to be lots of grass. They'd water in Corral Canyon." (780~)
—Horse Heaven Canyon: This northern tributary of Salt Wash starts on the west side of Horse Heaven and goes southwest, then south, down the Moroni Slopes. The head of the canyon is immediately south of the Moroni Slopes Catchment (immediately south of elevation 6366 on The Frying Pan map).

Horse Heaven: (Piute Co.) Fishlake National Forest-Tushar Mountains-Edna Peak. Mount Brigham map.
William E. White described the Horse Heaven area in 1920: "In ten thousand nooks and corners flowers of wondrous hue and beauty, acres of bluebells like segments of sky dropped to earth, clumps of sego lilies, smiling demurely on their slender stems, fair tinted columbines, with their delicate, fragile beauty, bright red wild roses twice the usual size perfume the air with their sweet fragrance, yellow primrose and purple larkspurs nod at each other in the mountain breeze, stately goldenrods, fluffy Indian biscuit and Indian paint brushes galore, blood-red prickly pear blossoms flaunt their radiant colors, wild arbutus vines climb the bushes and load them with white, puffy blossoms.... And in the secluded nooks often under some giant pine where water oozes and mosses grow are mountain lilies red as ox blood, and on the mountain top in Horse Heaven are purplish red flowers shedding a strong sleep-producing odor." (2006~)

Horse Hollow: (Kane Co.) Dixie National Forest-Paunsaugunt Plateau-Robinson Canyon. Alton and Podunk Creek maps.
George C. Mace named the canyon in the early 1900s. He and George Greenhalgh used the canyon for pasturing horses. (2053~)

Horsehoof Arch: (San Juan Co.) Canyonlands National Park-Needles District-Butler Flat. Cross Canyon map.
Robert H. Vreeland: "The name comes from the resemblance of the arc of rock to a horse's foreleg in shape, with the hoof clearly outlined." (1950~)

Horse Mesa: (Grand Co.) Book Cliffs-Interstate 70. Hatch Mesa map. (5,498')
—Horse Mesa Stock Trails: Two constructed stock trails lead to the top of Horse Mesa. The first starts at a stock pond in The Basin and goes west toward elevation 5470.

The second starts in Horse Canyon and goes east up the cliffs and ends near elevation 5470. (SAPE.)

Horse Mesa: (Wayne Co.) Capitol Reef National Park-Capitol Reef. Fruita map. (6,402')

It is rumored that this small mesa was used by outlaws to pasture their horses. It is known that sheepers used the mesa. (1497~)

—North Horse Mesa: This small mesa is one-half mile northwest of Horse Mesa (at elevation 6592T). (745~)

—Constructed Stock Trail: This trail, now very difficult to find and follow, starts at the east end of a short peninsula shown one-quarter mile northeast of elevation 6303T and goes east down to South Desert. (582~, 1047~, 1497~, SAPE.)

Horse Mountain: (San Juan Co.) Manti-LaSal National Forest-Dark Canyon Plateau-North Elk Ridge-Beef Basin. House Park Butte and Poison Canyon maps. (9,242')

Herbert E. Gregory in 1927: "Horse Mt. Gives magnificent view of everything." (761~) David D. Rust considered this one of the top fourteen viewpoints on the Colorado Plateau. (677~) Rust in 1935: "one of the sweeping glorious panoramas of the west—or the world." (1672~) Joyce Muench described the view from the top in 1954: "It was an 'earthscape': never to be forgotten—too big to grasp except in bold outlines. An air view of this panorama would show a sublime simplicity." (1403~)

—Constructed Stock Trail: This starts in the west fork of Paradise Canyon near the "Seep" and goes east and then north up to Horse Mountain. (SAPE.)

Horse Mountain: (San Juan Co.) Manti-LaSal National Forest-La Sal Mountains. Warner Lake map. (11,130')

This was part of what used to be called North Mountain, along with Mount Waas and Green Mountain.

Horse Pasture: (San Juan Co.) Dark Canyon Plateau-Youngs Canyon. Bowdie Canyon East map.

—Horse Canyon Line Shack: This shack, shown in upper Horse Pasture (at elevation 6934T), was a popular cowboy camp. The cave that contains the living area started out three feet high. Stories are told of cowboys spending claustrophobic nights tucked into the tight space. In about 1960 an air compressor and rock drill were used to carve the cave to its present configuration. (1821~, SAPE.)

Horse Pasture Canyon: (San Juan Co.) Manti-LaSal National Forest-Dark Canyon Wilderness-North Elk Ridge-Dark Canyon. Poison Canyon map.

Ranchers would run their cattle in Dark Canyon, but would put their horses in Horse Pasture Canyon. (1821~) The earliest mention of the canyon came from Francis

F. Kane who visited the Dutch and Day Ranch in Dark Canyon in 1891: "We rode for about three miles [down Dark Canyon] through natural meadow land before we reached Dutch and Day's, passing at one place, the mouth as it were of a lateral cañon which has been turned by Messrs. Dutch and Day into a fine horse pasture by simply fencing in the lower end, the walls of the cañon being so steep that cattle will not stray up into the timber. (1037~) (See Dark Canyon for more on Dutch and Day.)

—Horse Pasture Stock Trail: (Also called Forest Service Trail #025.) The Horse Pasture Trailhead is at the head of Horse Pasture Canyon (one-eighth mile southeast of elevation 8596T). This spectacular trail follows the rim of the canyon south for one mile before dropping into the canyon. (SAPE.)

—Redd Cabin: This was on the north side of Dark Canyon one-quarter mile west of the mouth of Horse Pasture Canyon. It was built by Lemuel H. Redd (1836-1910), a Blanding stockman who ran cattle in Dark Canyon starting in 1905. It is unclear if the cabin burned down (1451~, 1829~) or if excessive gullying toppled the cabin into Dark Canyon. One can still find logs from the cabin and other detritus on the hillside above the creek. Inscriptions include Harve Williams, 6/6/30. (SAPE.) It is unclear if this was also the location of the Dutch and Day Ranch.

—Scorup Cabin: (Also called Dark Canyon Camp.) (560a~) The site of the Scorup Cabin is shown in Dark Canyon just east of the mouth of Horse Pasture Canyon. The Scorup Cabin was built after the Redd Cabin and is still standing. John Scorup: "There's two different buildings put together. One building and a room added on. The original building, moved in from Rig Canyon, was a cook shack for the oil company when they drilled the well [there] ... they skidded that cabin up there to the spring ... in the '40s." (1821~)

—Erosion Control Dams: Fletcher B. Hammond mentioned that Cooper and Martin built erosion control dams in Dark Canyon near the Scorup Cabin in the 1890s. One can still see pieces of the dams. (820~, SAPE.)

—Little Horse Pasture: This short northern tributary of Dark Canyon is the first canyon to the southeast of Horse Pasture Canyon (immediately south of elevation 7930). Erwin Oliver noted that there were a couple of cabins in the canyon and that the cowboys would hold their horses here overnight as it was easier than holding them in Horse Pasture Canyon. (1479~) The cabins are now gone. (SAPE.)

Horse Pasture Mesa: (Garfield Co.) GSCENM-Circle Cliffs. Horse Pasture Mesa map. (5,807')
Don Coleman noted that ranchers kept horses on the mesa.
—Constructed Stock Trail: This goes up the northwest side of the mesa. (441~, SAPE.)

Horse Pasture Plateau: (Washington Co.) Zion National Park-Upper Kolob Plateau. Kolob Reservoir, Temple of Sinawava, and The Guardian Angels maps.
Early settlers used this as a horse pasture. (1038~) LeRoy Jeffers in 1922: "The view from the final point of Horse Pasture Plateau is rugged in the extreme. Great temples and buttes of varied architecture and coloring are isolated by narrow V-shaped canyons impossible to cross, while far below in the distance we catch a glimpse of the green floor of Zion Canyon." (960~)
R.B. Gray in 1927: "Horse Pasture Plateau, prosaic name for one of the salient mesa promontories of the strange Kolob Plateau." (754~)
J. Cecil Alter in 1927: "The Horse Pasture Peninsula on Kolob's lofty south rim might better be rechristened Pegasus Point, for the pasture is inclosed with some of the park's most forbidding scenery, allowing only our imaginations to roam." (50~)
—Never Done Mountain: This is on Horse Pasture Plateau at the head of Imlay Canyon (at elevation 7370 on the Temple of Sinawava map). (1570a~)

Horse Ranch Mountain: (Washington Co.) Zion National Park-Tucupit Point. Kolob Arch map. (8,726')
This is the highest point in Zion National Park.
—Larson Cabin: This was one mile east of Horse Ranch Mountain (one-quarter mile east of elevation 8124).

Horseshoe Bend: (Emery Co.) San Rafael Swell-Interstate 70. The Blocks and The Wickiup maps.
The cliffs bend in a horseshoe shape.
—Devils Backyard: This pasture area is a couple of miles north and east of Horseshoe Bend (centered on elevation 6322 on The Wickiup map). The name is derived from a tower with two pronounced "ears" that from a distance looked like the head of the Devil to the cowboys.
—Devils Tower: This is on the west side of Devils Backyard (one-eighth mile northwest of elevation 7028 on The Blocks map). (1853~)

Horseshoe Canyon: (Wayne Co.) Canyonlands National Park-Horseshoe Canyon Detached Unit-Hans Flats-Labyrinth Canyon. Head Spur, Sugarloaf Butte, Keg Knoll, and Bowknot Bend maps.
Horseshoe Canyon contains Barrier Creek, which was a barrier to travelers. The Barrier Creek name was in place by 1878. (1567~) The canyon was later named for a butte in the abandoned meander at its mouth that forms a horseshoe-shaped canyon. The butte is called The Frog. A frog is a horseman's term for the bottom of a horse's hoof. Randall Henderson: "It is an amazing gorge—a great chasm big enough to carry a stream like the Colorado River, and yet for the most part as dry as a typical desert arroyo." (871~)
Inscriptions include Bill Tibbetts, September 15, 1924. (1322~)
—Deadman Trail: This constructed stock trail, shown as a "Foot Trail," enters Horseshoe Canyon from The Spur one and one-quarter miles upcanyon from the mouth of Water Canyon (one-half mile southwest of elevation 5100T on the Sugarloaf Butte map). Ted Ekker: "I don't know why it was called Deadman Trail. Whether ... somebody died on the trail or whether maybe somebody who was working for Chuchuros [local sheepmen] got blowed himself up or something when he was building that trail." (623~)
David D. Rust noted going up the Deadman Trail to 'Rustler's Flat' in 1935. (1672~)
—Great Gallery Rock Art Panel: This was listed on the National Register of Historic Places in 1972. The Great Gallery is a stupendous Barrier Canyon Style pictograph panel. Archaeologist James H. Gunnerson in 1969: "The Great Gallery of Barrier Canyon, is probably the most spectacular pictograph site in Utah if not in the entire United States. Perhaps the most surprising thing about this site is that none of the figures have been significantly damaged by vandals as have so many other pictographs." (797~)
Leland Tidwell, who ran livestock in the area in the 1930s and '40s, though, related this story to Richard Negri: "Once when I was ridin' in the canyon I heard a loud explosion. I gave my horse the spurs and wound up at the big panel. There were a couple of oil men there and they had just blasted off a piece of the wall with dynamite— just to the left of what you call the 'Holy Ghost.' They had destroyed several of the figures and you can see what's left of them on the ground. I'd brought my old 30-30 saddle gun with me and I jerked it out. I told them to get the hell out of there or I'd let them have it. They left without any trouble." (1428~)
Betty L. Tipps: "The Great Gallery is devoid of prehistoric cultural remains other than rock art." (1892~) Tipps noted that paint from the figures dates to 1900 BC or older.
—Johns Hole: (Also called Johns Canyon.) This small eastern tributary of Horseshoe Canyon is one-third of a

mile downcanyon from Water Canyon (Sugarloaf Butte map). Ned Chaffin: "The only Johns Hole I know was in Barrier Canyon [Horseshoe Canyon] just up the canyon from the Philips Oil Co. Road, in a small canyon coming in from the east side of the Canyon. John Rumjue made a little bit of 'Hooch' there. A real nice spring of water and a pretty place." (413~) Chaffin: "Uncle John's whiskey wasn't nothin' but good.... His whiskey was considered the best in the country." (411~) The water was piped into a covered box. (100~)

—Phillips Petroleum Mining Road: This "4WD" road crosses Horseshoe Canyon one-half mile downcanyon from Water Canyon. The west side of the road is the Horseshoe Canyon and Great Gallery Trailhead. The road, now closed to vehicles, was built by Louis M. Chaffin and his son, Arthur, for Phillips Petroleum in 1928–29. They followed the general route of an old stock trail down what was then called The Slide or The Sandslide Trail. The road crosses Horseshoe Canyon and goes to a "DH" (Drill Hole) near Sugarloaf Butte. The well was not successful. (120~, 1430~) (See Sugarloaf Butte.)

In 1940 artist Elzy J. Bird drove down the road: "I still suck in my breath when I think of this access into Barrier Canyon. Scraping the cliff with your vehicle on the one side and with only inches to spare on the other you look down into almost infinity and feel something like a small ant on a tall flag pole." (230~)

Dick Sprang in the early 1960s: "There's a gut-buster road down both sides of [Horseshoe Canyon].... This road, today, separates the men from the boys." (1799~)

—Low Spur Canyon: This southern (or eastern) tributary of Horseshoe Canyon is north of elevation 5187T on the Keg Knoll map. It was named by Michael R. Kelsey. (653~)

—Angel Trail: This constructed stock trail enters lower Horseshoe Canyon on its east side two and one-half miles upcanyon from its mouth (one-quarter mile southwest of elevation 5036AT on the Bowknot Bend map). Stories vary about its construction. It may have been built by the Tidwells, one of the early ranch families, or by the CCC in the mid-1930s. (1644~, SAPE.)

—Frog Trail: This constructed stock trail enters lower Horseshoe Canyon on its west side, behind The Frog (which is elevation 4587T on the Bowknot Bend map). The top of the trail starts one-eighth mile north of elevation 4919 and ends one-half mile north-northwest of elevation 4587T. Ted Ekker noted that the Tidwells built the trail in the early 1900s. The Angel Trail and Frog Trail were often used together to cross the canyon. (623~, SAPE.)

—Aboriginal Route: Leland Tidwell: "Go up Horseshoe about 1 1/4 miles and on the left-hand [east] side going up, there is a set of notches carved in the rock to get out on top. The notches are deep and have a little lip on the fronts of them." (1890~)

—Constructed Stock Trail: This runs along the Green River between the mouths of Horseshoe and Twomile canyons. (SAPE.)

—Hanging Rock Bottom: (Also called Elevation Bottom.) (111~) This is on the west side of the Green River one mile downriver from the mouth of Horseshoe Canyon. (1462~)

Horseshoe Lake: (Garfield Co.) Dixie National Forest-Boulder Mountain. Deer Creek Lake map.

This is shaped like a horseshoe. The name was in place by 1920. (222~)

Horseshoe Ridge: (Garfield Co.) Henry Mountains-McClellan Wash. Dry Lakes Peak map. (10,003')

Guy Robison noted that the ridge is shaped like a horseshoe. (1644~, 925~)

Horse Spring Canyon: (Garfield Co.) GSCENM-Kaiparowits Plateau-Alvey Wash. Canaan Peak, Death Ridge, and Canaan Creek maps.

Two name derivations are given.

First, Don Coleman: "They used to run horses up on there. There is a spring and that is where they got their water. They had a little fence and they put the horses up in there and they let 'em graze and when they needed extra horses they'd go up and git 'em and bring 'em out." (441~)

Second, unattributed in 1931: "Band of horses were snowed in and starved to death there." (1346~)

—Horse Spring: (Canaan Peak map.) This is a large spring with a watering trough in a beautiful setting. Nearby are the remnants of old hollowed out logs that at one time were used as troughs. (SAPE.)

Horse Tanks: (San Juan Co.) Dark Canyon Plateau-White Canyon. Copper Point map.

—Horse Tank: The actual horse tank is two miles north-northeast of the marked Horse Tank and is on the south side of the road between elevations 5019T and 5088AT. Sandy Johnson: "Right here at Horse Tank is a big tank underneath the rock. And right up there is where the cowboys stayed." (1002~) Carl Mahon noted that Monroe Redd raised horses and camped here in the late 1800s. (1272~)

John F. Vallentine told this story: "It was during this winter (1900–01) that Jim Scorup and Henry Noall encountered Butch Cassidy and the Robbers Roost Gang at Horse Tank. The gang had stolen some 200 head of horses from parties unknown and had three cattle carcasses dressed out. The encounter was amicably settled when Jim requested that they only kill what cattle they could eat and humbly departed." (1936~)

—Hour House: C. Gregory Crampton: "Located near a spring [Horse Tank] ... are the ruins of a one-room slab-rock house built against an overhang.... Nearby a weathered and broken wagon stands on a sheet of bare rock. The history of the place is altogether a mystery." (471~) At the overhang is an inscription reading "Nov. 1 1891, Hour House The Lanlord [*sic*]." A skull and crossbones have also been carved on the rock. (SAPE.)

—Scorup Reservoir: This is the stock reservoir at the marked Horse Tanks (immediately north of elevation 5007T). Al Scorup ran livestock in the area in the early days. (1002~) (See Scorup Canyon.)

—Horse Tank Canyon: Horse Tank is at the top of this northern tributary of White Canyon.

—Constructed Stock Trail: This enters upper Horse Tanks Canyon on its west side (immediately north of elevation 5022T). (SAPE.)

Horsethief Point: (Grand Co.) Tenmile Country-Labyrinth Canyon. Bowknot Bend, Upheaval Dome, and Mineral Canyon maps.
Also called Deer Mesa. (1227~)
In 1871 John Wesley Powell noted this as Tower Cliffs. (662~)

—Horsethief Ranch: PRIVATE PROPERTY. (Also called Robbers Roost.) Horsethief Ranch is on Horsethief Point at Horsethief Spring (Mineral Canyon map). The area around Horsethief Ranch, and a nearby spring, were used by stockmen and outlaws starting in the late 1800s. The first building was not constructed until 1930. Gene Dunham: "Art Murray [also spelled Murry] was the one that founded the Horsethief [Ranch]. He ran cattle out there and had many run-ins with the people from Moab and other areas. He finally got disgusted with the whole thing and moved to Canada. He was running five or six hundred cows. He just left. He lived with his cows and took good care of them and lived in caves and alcoves and built cedar fences—piled up cedar brush and so forth. He lived like an Indian." (580~)
Later owners included Ken Allred (1951–1958); Bill and Jewel Tibbets (1959–1965); Mac and Alice McKinney (1965–1973); Dick and Nancy Eckert (1973–1981); and Michael Behrendt (1981–). (197~)

—Horsethief Trail: (See Horsethief Canyon—Wayne Co. below.)

Horsethief Canyon: (Wayne Co.) Glen Canyon NRA-The Spur-Labyrinth Canyon. Horsethief Canyon map.
—Horsethief Trail: This famous trail was used by outlaws starting in the 1880s. Pearl Baker noted that the trail was used by Butch Cassidy and the Wild Bunch. (123~)
Several descriptions of the trail are given.
First, the trail crossed Horsethief Point (Bowknot Bend map) and went down to Horsethief Bottom. Following the river downcanyon across Point Bottom, it went up Horsethief Canyon where a constructed trail on its upper west side (one-eighth mile northeast of elevation 5105T) led up to The Spur. The Horsethief Trail out of Horsethief Canyon, probably very rugged at first, was improved by the Tidwell family in the 1920s. (197~, 623~)
Second, Del Taylor: "As far as I ever knew the trail came off the end of Horsethief Point and it was a rugged trail to say the least, then down the east side of the Green to Millard or maybe should say the lower end of Potato Bottom. I have crossed there several times and in low water was not to bad." (1864~)
Third, Pearl Baker: "The old Horsethief Trail came off the north side of Horsethief Point to the river, and down to across from the head of Island Bottom [Saddle Horse Bottom], where the crossing was on a good gravel bottom. The trail then followed the west side of the river down to Horsethief Canyon which comes in from the Spur, up that canyon to where Clyde's Spring Fork comes in and out just about there onto the High Part of the Spur." (123~)
Frank E. Masland, Jr. in 1963: "For 500 feet, it switchbacks so steeply those in the lead get a crick in their necks looking up at the strung out [pack] string. It wasn't only steep, the footing (if it may be called that) was rough, loose rock and it had been unused so long that in a number of places it was blocked by slides. It was, in fact, an abrupt talus slope.... I never had to achieve such agility as I did to stay on this two foot trail.... You don't really walk on a trail like this. You leap from rock to rock, wishing you were a mountain goat." (1311~)
Inscriptions at the top of the trail include Martin Wall, Dec. 1900 and Leland Tidwell, 1920. Inscriptions near the mouth include D.K. Winders, 1895 and Leland Tidwell, 1921. (1115~, SAPE.)
—Sheep Trail: This now all-but-gone constructed sheep trail exited Horsethief Canyon via a short eastern side canyon that is two miles (as the crow flies) down from the head of the canyon (one-eighth mile north of elevation 5018T). (SAPE.)

Horse Valley: (Emery Co.) San Rafael Swell-McKay Flat. Horse Valley map.

Also called Bubbs Valley. (1931~)

Horse Valley: (Garfield and Kane Counties.) GSCENM-Kaiparowits Plateau-Dry Valley Creek. Henrieville map.

Also called Rozencrans Pasture. (2053~)

Unattributed: "Named because of ranging or pasturing horses here." (2053~)

—Horse Valley Ranch: PRIVATE PROPERTY. Ralph Chynoweth noted that James Smith and family built a ranch in Horse Valley in the late teens or early 1920s. The ranch was at the end of the "Jeep Trail" that comes into the valley from the west. (425~)

—Constructed Stock Trail: Ralph noted that a stock trail goes from the ranch east to the top of the cliffs. (425~)

Horse Valley: (Wayne Co.) Rabbit Valley-Cedar Creek. Lyman map.

Anne Snow noted that the valley was settled by the Tidwells, a reclusive family, in the early 1870s. They left their name on many features in this country. (1786~)

Horse Valley Peak: (Garfield Co.) Dixie National Forest-Sevier Plateau. Bull Rush Peak map. (8,571')

Betsy Topham Camp: "It derived its name from the wild horses that were found in the valley, some were white and some black and white." (942~) The government had the wild horses killed. (1515~)

—Horse Valley: Albert DeLong in 1941: "It serves as a range for a numerous amount of horses." (2053~) E.C. Bird in 1941: "It was so named because one of the old settlers, William Kettleman, who homesteaded on the outskirts of Circleville, ranged his horses in this vicinity." (2053~)

Hoskinnini Mesa: (Kane Co.) Glen Canyon NRA-Glen Canyon. Bullfrog map. (4,295')

Also spelled Hoskaninni Mesa.

This was named for Robert Brewster Stanton's Hoskinnini Mining Company. In 1898–1900 Stanton built a road from Green River, through the Henry Mountains, across the Cane Spring Desert, and along Hoskinnini Mesa to Stanton Canyon. (1812~) (See Stanton Canyon.)

Hoskinnini Mesa: (San Juan Co.) Navajo Indian Reservation-Oljeto Wash. Oljeto, Jacobs Monument, Big Point, and Boot Mesa maps. (6,715')

(See Hoskinnini Monument for name derivation.)

Also spelled Hoskaninni Mesa.

The Navajo Year Book, 1961: "Haskinnini Mesa ... is named after a headman called *Hashke Neiniihii*, or "The one who distributes them in an angry way." (1929~)

William F. Williams noted that in 1885 Navajo Chief Hoskinnini lived on the mesa. (90~)

Harry Goulding noted that Navajo ran sheep on top of the mesa. They would put old clothing on the sheep to act as scarecrows to keep the coyotes away. (1380~)

C. William Harrison in 1979: "It is a land of junipers and cactus, of big skies and restless breezes, of brooding silences and lost Indian ruins waiting to be discovered." (836~)

—Constructed Stock Trail: The "4WD" trail up the mesa (Big Point map) closely follows the original stock route used by Chief Hoskinnini. (443~)

Hoskinnini Monument: (Garfield Co.) Glen Canyon NRA-Little Rockies-Swett Creek. Mount Holmes map.

Also called Hoskinnini Pillar (1569~) and Hoskininni Rock (1402~).

Also spelled Haashkeneinii, Hashkéneinii, Hashkeniini, Hashkéniinii, and Hoskaninni.

Harry Aleson in 1965: "Hoskinnini Monument is a pillar of Wingate [Sandstone] at least 250 feet high—a bold Indian face like unto [Navajo] Chief Hoskinnini—standing with his blanket wrapped high about his body—and in a red sunset his strong face is a striking likeness of the old chief who never surrendered to the Whiteman. Even the detail of headdress and bushy eyebrow is very lifelike.... And Arthur Chaffin, who was a friend of the old Chief, named the monument Hoskinnini because of a good likeness to the Indian." (27~)

Arthur Chaffin: "The first time I saw this monument was in 1934 while chasing wild horses. It stood up there in the image of old Hoskinnini, with his back so straight, his profile so true, that it made me think of the old Navajo chief who used to trade at my trading post down the Colorado River at Camp Stone in 1903–4. The old chief was about 105 years old at that time." (401~) (See Appendix One—Navajo Long Walk.)

Hoskinnini Road: (Garfield and Wayne Counties.) San Rafael Desert-Burr Desert-Henry Mountains-Glen Canyon. Cass Creek Peak, Copper Creek Benches, and Ant Knoll maps.

Also spelled Hoskaninni Road.

(See Hoskinnini Mesa for name derivation.)

Although the road is only named on the three maps listed above, the road went from Green River to Glen Canyon. It was built by Robert Brewster Stanton in 1898–1900 to take a dredge, in pieces, from the rail yard in Green River to placer claims in Glen Canyon. (See Stanton Canyon for the full story.)

Since roads in the area were either rudimentary or non-existent, Stanton had to either rebuild much of a pioneer road or construct long sections of new road.

The route went southwest from Green River and joined the existing road that ran south under the east face of the San Rafael Reef. Near Temple Wash it cut across the desert, passing Mollys Castle on its west side. It then went near Brigham Butte and through The Notch to Hanksville. From Hanksville the road went south by Goatwater Point to the Granite Ranch and on south by Little Egypt before turning southwest and going through Stanton Pass between Bulldog and Cass Creek peaks. The road then went down Hansen Creek to Cane Spring. It exited the creek and cut overland to Stanton Canyon. At this point Charlie Gibbons and crew, under the direction of J.W. "Jack" Wilson, constructed a road down the cliffs of the canyon about one mile up from the Colorado River. They had to use a large steel cable to help lower the equipment. (19~, 466~)

David D. Rust: "Charlie Gibbons brought the [Stanton] dredge in for $5,000 from Green River." (1676~) Louis M. Chaffin noted that the dredge weighted about 180 tons. Arthur B. Starr helped Gibbons bring equipment down the road and helped construct several sections: "The heaviest pieces of machinery were on especially equipped wagons pulled by sixteen of the biggest horses I ever saw. And they were having their work cut out for them, too.... From [Hanksville] we went through a pass [Stanton Pass] in the Henry Mountains.... I remember that parts of this section of the road had to be made by Mr. Stanton's men. Particularly where deep washes had to be crossed entrance and egress slopes had to be dug. I remember one place where rock had to be blasted away to make a slope up to a mesa." (1814~)

Hosteen Tso Canyon: (San Juan Co.) Navajo Indian Reservation-Chinle Creek. Mexican Water and Moses Rock maps.

Hastiin is Navajo for "man." *Tsoh* is Navajo for "big" or "large," or "Big Man Canyon." (2072~) The "Big Man" lived about four miles south of the canyon. (1931~)

Hotel Mesa: (Grand Co.) Colorado River-Dolores River. Blue Chief Mesa and Dewey maps.

Also called Hotel de Stone. (575~)

Hotel Mesa, at the juncture of the Colorado and Dolores rivers, is known as both the Dolores Triangle and Picture Gallery. (1195~)

Three name derivations are given for Picture Gallery.

First, unattributed: "From the top of this [Hotel] mesa ranches can be seen, with beautiful green fields and lakes or ponds surrounded by trees. This is Picture Gallery." (456~)

Second, William Gladstone Steel in 1925: "So named because of its resemblance to a large mirror." (1819~)

Third, Jack Kruckenberg and family leased Picture Gallery Ranch in the 1960s. Mrs. Kruckenberg thought that the Picture Gallery name was because a former owner of the ranch had decorated the ranch house with pin-up pictures. (840~)

—Hotel Bottom: (Dewey map.) George White noted that this was named "from one of the former owners who made a small fortune operating a hotel in the area of Boulder Dam during the construction period." (1931~)

—Wolverton Ranch: This was on the east side of the Colorado River one-half mile north of Hotel Bottom (at elevation 4125T on the Dewey map). (1931~)

Hotel Rock: (San Juan Co.) Dark Canyon Plateau-Little Baullie Mesa. Hotel Rock map. (6,259')

This isolated dome, visible from Highway 95, stands high above the pinyon and juniper of Little Baullie Mesa. Kent Frost: "It has all those rooms [Anasazi cliff dwellings] around on the rock, the reason the cowboys call it [Hotel Rock]." (690~)

—Old Road: An old road, not shown on the map, goes along the north rim of Arch Canyon to Hotel Rock. The road is now closed.

Houchen Hollow: (Iron Co.) Kolob Terrace-West Fork Deep Creek. Webster Flat map.

Henry Houchen (1837-1915) moved to Cedar City in the 1870s. (388~)

House Park Butte: (San Juan Co.) Dark Canyon Plateau-Beef Basin. House Park Butte and Fable Valley maps. (7,318')

This high, rugged butte was named for a homestead on its northeast side. Built by rancher Mel Turner in the late 1800s, remnants of a house and corrals still stand. A nearby spring provided water. (143~, 1084~, SAPE.)

—Bow Hunter Arch: This splendid arch is high on the east side of the butte. The name comes from a nearby pictograph. (SAPE.)

House Rock: (Coconino Co., Az.) House Rock Valley-Alt. Highway 89. House Rock, Az. map. PRIVATE PROPERTY.

Also called Rock House.

The small settlement of House Rock or House Rock Ranch was first developed by the Canaan Cooperative Stock Company and the Orderville Co-op in 1877. At that time William Bailey Maxwell built the stone ranch house. The ranch was sold to John W. Young in 1887 and to B.F.

Saunders and the Grand Canyon Cattle Company (Bar Z) in 1896. Saunders then sold his share of the ranch to the Grand Canyon Cattle Company and E.J. Marshall in 1907. (1140~)

President Theodore Roosevelt stayed at House Rock in 1913 while on his way to the Grand Canyon. (1140~)

In 1930 Genaro Fourzan and Henry S. Stephenson purchased the ranch. They had a gas station and grocery store here. (1140~)

Stephenson sold the ranch to Roy Woolley and a consortium from the Kanab area in 1945. Woolley sold the ranch to Rubin Broadbent, Mel and John Schoppman, and others in 1955. Today this is the headquarters for a private ranch.

Inscriptions on the house include those of the builders, J.M and W.B. Maxwell, 1877. (1115~) Other inscriptions include E.P. Adair; J.G. [James Godson] Bleak; and Ephraim [K. Hanks], no date. (1140~)

House Rock Spring: (Coconino Co., Az.) Vermilion Cliffs National Monument-Vermilion Cliffs-House Rock Valley. House Rock Spring, Az. map.

Also called Deer Spring, Rockhous Springs (58~), and Rock House Spring (437~).

The Domínguez-Escalante Expedition of 1776–77 procured water from the spring. Father Escalante: "Here at the base of the valley's eastern mesa [Vermilion Cliffs] are three runoffs of good water, but there was not enough for the horse herd." (1357~)

Frederick S. Dellenbaugh of the 1871–72 Powell Expedition: "At sunset we arrived at a spring in a narrow gulch of the cliffs. Grass grew in abundance in the valley below, and hundreds of dead pines and cedars scattered among the living ones which cover the foothills supplied fuel for a roaring fire ... this was House Rock Spring and the valley was House Rock Valley.... The spring had received its name from the fact that a Mormon party [led by Jacob Hamblin] once took refuge from a storm under some huge broken rocks, and wrote facetiously upon the face of one of them with charcoal, 'Rock House Hotel.' For want of a better name the place was always referred to as the House Rock Spring, till it became firmly fastened." (542~)

At a different time, Dellenbaugh provided more details: "About sunset we passed two large boulders which had fallen together, forming a rude shelter, under which [a local guide named] Riggs or some one else had slept, and then had jocosely printed above with charcoal the words 'Rock House Hotel.'" (541~)

In 1872 John D. Lee and several others built a small building at the spring to secure it for the Mormon Church. John D. Lee: "About noon reached the House Rock Springs ... then commenced putting a Rock House to Secure the Ranch.... Finished the house and wrote on the Door the date of location." (437~)

Frihoff G. Nielson in 1876: "House Rock Springs are 2 small streams running out of the rocks. It takes a long time to water 50 head of oxen. Here is a Corral and 2 houses built by the Church." (1452~)

Ida Hunt Udall noted that Jed Adair and family lived at House Rock Spring in 1882. (1925~)

Scores of inscriptions are found at House Rock Spring. The oldest include J.D. Lee, Dec. 25, 1871; W.H. Solomon, May 12, 1873; Joseph Adams from Kaysville to Arizona ANT. Busten on June A.D. 1873; C.C. Allen, June 2, 1873; J.M. Alstrom, Mar. 17, 1876; and K[umen] Jones of Cedar City, no date. (1115~, SAPE.)

—Honeymoon Trail: With its good water, this was an important stop on the trail.

—House Rock Cemetery: Frank Beckwith of the Arches National Monument Scientific Expedition of 1933–34: "Just talked to an old woman who went to Lee's Ferry in an ox team in the spring of 1889; stopped at House Rock Valley and there were a lot of graves there, and she was scared—of people who had died on the way." (189~)

Today, only one gravestone still stands. It reads: "Daughter of Edwin and Mary Whiting. 1862–1882. Died at Houserock AJ." (1551~) Ida Hunt Udall told the story: "The day before our arrival there they had buried a young lady 20 years of age, Miss May Whiting from Brigham City, Arizona. She had for some years been troubled with dropsy [tuberculosis], and had got this far on the road to Utah in company with her mother and brothers when she died. Poor Girl! My heart ached to think of her being buried in that lonely place." (1925~) The grave was mentioned by Lorenzo Brown in his diary in 1882. (305~) Another grave did exist here. It was for Susan N. Robbins who died here as a nine-day-old infant in 1873. (1787b~)

House Rock Wash: (Coconino Co., Az.) House Rock Valley-Colorado River. House Rock Wash, House Rock, Emmett Hill, Emmett Wash, and Bitter Springs, Az. maps.

Also called Rock House Valley. (487~)

House Rock Wash goes through House Rock Valley.

(See House Rock Spring for name derivation.)

House Rock Wash, in its lower end, goes through Rider Canyon.

The Paiute name for House Rock Valley is *Aesak*, or "basket-like," referring to the cliffs on either side of the valley forming a basket shape. (82~)

The Domínguez-Escalante Expedition of 1776–77 crossed House Rock Valley at the south edge of the Vermilion Cliffs. Escalante called this "troublesome country." (261~)

William Bailey Maxwell, returning from California after being released by the Mormon Battalion, came through House Rock Valley in 1847.

—Stone Wall: M.C. Tunison in 1905: "The Indians pointed to its [House Rock Valley's] west wall and said, 'Stone Wall.' We found our way westward blocked by almost a sheer wall of red sandstone [Vermilion Cliffs], some 2500 ft. high, with a capping of white sandstone showing here and there adding beauty and grandeur to the picture." (1909~)

Houston Flat: (Garfield Co.) Dixie National Forest-Markagunt Plateau. Asay Bench map.

Joseph Houston (1851-1912) and family ranched on Rock Creek near Mammoth Creek starting in the 1870s. (363~) (See Red Desert—Houston Mountain.)

Howes Cemetery: (Piute Co.) Sevier River-Tenmile Creek. Piute Reservoir map.

William Howes (1826-1900) and his wife, Sarah (1828-1903), had ranch here in the early years. They were buried in the cemetery. (388~, 1551~)

Hub, The: (Navajo Co., Az.) Navajo Indian Reservation-Monument Valley. Mitten Buttes, Az. map.

James H. Knipmeyer: "This small butte is so named because it rises in the approximate center of the main portion of the Monument Valley buttes and mesas. They seem to circle around it." (1115~)

Huber Wash: (Washington Co.) Zion National Park-Virgin River. Springdale West map.

Edward Huber (1813-1869) and his wife, Mary Ann (1813-1861), moved to Rockville in the early 1860s. (1141~)

Huff Hollow: (Emery Co.) Cedar Mountain-Humbug Canyon. Chimney Rock and Bob Hill Knoll maps.

Edward A. Geary noted that starting in about 1912 several families maintained dry farms on Huff Bench. They lived here during the growing season, but returned to their homes in the winter. This lasted until about 1930 when drought and other factors forced abandonment of the area. (710~)

—Huff Bench: (Chimney Rock map.) PRIVATE PROPERTY.

Humbug Canyon: (Emery Co.) Cedar Mountain-Price River. Bob Hill Knoll, Cow Flats, Flattop Mountain, and Grassy maps.

—Jump Trail: (Also called Humbug Trail and The Jump.) This old road goes from the southeast side of Lucky Flats into Humbug Canyon. Its top is one-eighth mile north of elevation 6034 on the Cow Flats map.

Hungry Creek: (Garfield Co.) Dixie National Forest-Boulder Mountain-Pine Creek. Posy Lake map.

Three name derivations are given.

First, Don Coleman: "I've heard stories but I think it was 'cause people get mighty hungry tryin' to make a livin' there." (441~)

Second, Edson Alvey noted that an old trail crossed the creek and travelers would stop here for lunch. (55~)

Third, unattributed in 1931: "Man by name of Deuel became lost there while hunting cattle and nearly starved." (1346~)

—CCC Camp: The CCC had a camp on the creek from 1933 to 1934. (2051~) Members of the camp are credited with building the Hells Backbone Road. (887~) One can still find the ruins of the camp. (SAPE.)

Hunt Canyon: (Grand Co.) Roan Cliffs-Westwater Creek. Preacher Canyon map.

Unattributed: "Canyon was site of a hunting camp during drilling operations in area in 1960–1961 and is still a popular hunting area." (1634~)

Hunt Creek: (Garfield Co.) Johns Valley-East Fork Sevier River. Flake Mountain East map.

Hyrum Barton in 1941: "It is a small creek used for watering stock and was at one time a water source for a sawmill that was located near its mouth. It derived its name from a man named Hunt who homesteaded along this creek." (2053~)

Hunt Draw: (Emery Co.) San Rafael Swell-Muddy Creek. Hunt Draw map.

—Muddy Ranch: Charles A. Hunt [1883-1952] and family built a house (still extant) near the mouth of the draw in about 1920. (604~, 1642~) They also built a brush and rock dam across Muddy Creek and a ditch to the ranch site. There they grew vegetables and sugar cane. After many years, Hunt sold the ranch to Alton Morrell. It is now owned by the BLM. (804~)

Rulon Hunt: "Dad [Charles Hunt] started Muddy Ranch. We'd travel back and forth from Caineville. Floyd [brother] and I planted the fields. He didn't care to work the horses so I'd plow and harrow and care for the team. Floyd hand sowed the seed and did all the cooking, an arrangement I liked and I guess he did too." (927~)

—Stinking Spring Creek: This wash runs from Hunt Draw on the east, under the south end of the San Rafael Reef, to Muddy Creek (near elevations 4725T and 4802T). The only spring in the wash is at the mouth of Quandary Canyon (directly north of elevation 4802T). This is Stinking Spring. (845~, SAPE.) (See Cistern Canyon—Quandary Canyon.)

Hunters Canyon: (Grand and San Juan Counties.) Behind the Rocks-Kane Springs Canyon. Kane Springs, Trough Springs Canyon, and Moab maps.

Also called Smith Canyon. (99~)

Lloyd Holyoak noted that this is an old name: "There's a trail that goes out the top and there used to be good deer hunting in there. People would slip down there and poach a few deer, so it was named Hunter Canyon." (906~)

—Rotary Rock: This monolith is at the top of a southern tributary of Hunters Canyon (one-quarter mile southeast of elevation 5481T on the Trough Springs Canyon map). (2019~)

Hunter Spring: (Garfield Co.) Sevier Plateau-Table Mountain. Phonolite Hill map.

Kent Whittaker: "There was an old fellow from Antimony whose name was [Archie M.] Hunter. He ran horses out on Table Mountain in the early days. In fact, he had that draw where the spring is fenced off up in its head." (2002~, 1444~)

Gary Dean Young: "A.M. Hunter, who was not a Mormon but well-liked by them all. He imported purebred trotting horses into the valley from Scotland [in the early 1880s]." (2063~)

Huntington Canal: (Emery Co.) Castle Valley-Danish Bench. Red Point and Castle Dale maps.

(See Huntington Creek for name derivation.)

This was built between 1879 and 1884. It brought water from Huntington Creek to Lawrence and to the flatlands south of town. (710~, 1330~, 1561~)

Huntington Creek: (Emery Co.) Wasatch Plateau-Castle Valley-San Rafael River. Fairview Lakes, Scofield, Candland Mountain, Rilda Canyon, Hiawatha, Red Point, Huntington, and Hadden Holes maps.

Also called Huntington River. (361~)

Huntington, Cottonwood, and Ferron creeks come together to form the San Rafael River.

In 1848 Orville C. Pratt called this the San Rafell River. (1572~)

Gwinn Harris Heap of the Lieutenant Edward F. Beale Expedition of 1853 called it the East Fork of the San Rafael River: "At our encampment, the creek was seven yards in breadth and eighteen inches deep. The water was cool and sweet, and good pasturage on its banks." (854~)

Lieutenant E.G. Beckwith of the Captain John W. Gunnison Expedition of 1853 called it both the San Rafael and the Garambulla River (187~), a name also used on the Colton map of 1876 (M.43.). Beckwith: "There is not a tree at the point where we crossed this stream; a narrow bottom is covered with dry grass and willow bushes, intermixed with the buffalo berry bush thickly covered with fruit." (187~, 710~)

William D. Huntington (1818-1887) led a Mormon exploring party through the area in 1854 while on their way to the San Juan River area. Edward A. Geary: "It seems likely that Huntington Creek received its present name on this occasion." (710~)

William B. Pace of the Elk Mountain Mission of 1855 noted it as Huntington's Creek. (1500~) The Colonel William Wing Loring Expedition of 1857-58 used the Spanish name *San Marcus* or the Indian name of Taveajo Creek. (166~, 710~, 931~) Loring: "where there is good grass and water, with sage." (1276~)

The 1881 Rand McNally Utah map shows the lower portion of the creek as Shangint Creek. (665~)

—Old Spanish Trail: This crossed Huntington Creek near the Black Hills and south of today's Green River Cutoff Road (Buckhorn Reservoir and Hadden Holes maps).

Huntington Lake: (Emery Co.) Huntington Creek-Highway 10. Huntington map.

Also called Huntington North Reservoir.

(See Huntington Creek for name derivation.)

The lake was created by building the Huntington North Dam and building the East and West dikes. The project was completed in 1966.

—Huntington State Park. (Also called Huntington Lake State Beach and Huntington Lake State Park.) This 237 acre park is at Huntington Lake.

Huntington Reservoir: (Sanpete Co.) Manti-LaSal National Forest-Wasatch Plateau. Huntington Reservoir map.

(See Huntington Creek for name derivation.)

Before the reservoir, this was called Erickson Flat for a Castle Valley pioneer. (1014~) The original reservoir was finished in 1898. (2053~) The dam height was raised in 1919–20 and its final configuration was completed in 1966. (2049~)

—Ann Marie Canyon: This small canyon comes into Huntington Reservoir from the north. (1014~)

—Day Sawmill: Ira A. Day, Sr. (1855-1933) had a sawmill in the canyon in 1884. (1717~)

Huntington Town: (Emery Co.) Castle Valley-Highway 10. Huntington map.

Also called Hunting. (818a~)

(See Huntington Creek for name derivation.)

A Daughters of Utah Pioneers plaque tells the story: "In 1875 Leander Lemmon and James McHadden, seeking a good range for their horses, found feed plentiful at the mouth of Huntington Canyon and vicinity. Mr. Lemmon brought sheep and cattle from Cottonwood, Salt Lake County. In the autumn of 1876 he built the first log cabin on Huntington Creek." (1551~, 380~, 1014~)

The town started to grow in 1877 with the arrival of William H. Avery, Elam Cheney, Elias and Jehu Cox, Frederick Fenn, Benjamin Jones, Heber Jones, and Elam and Rilda McBride. (1014~)

Hunt Reservoir: (Wayne Co.) Awapa Plateau-Cedar Peak Draw. Flossie Knoll map.

Alfonzo Taylor noted that this was named for George Hunt (1886-1948). (1914~)

Hunts Lakes: (Sevier Co.) Fishlake National Forest-Sevier Plateau. Monroe Peak map.

Moroni Hunt (1852-1919) and his brothers settled in Monroe in 1871. They built the lake for water storage for their sheep in the 1880s. (1971~)

Hunts Mesa: (Navajo Co., Az.) Navajo Indian Reservation-Monument Valley. Mitten Buttes, Az. map. (6,376')

Jim and Emery Hunt were longtime residents and owners of a trading post and small motel in Mexican Hat during the post oil boom years. Doris Valle: "In every settlement there is one early day family who is a basic part of the framework through the growing years. In Mexican Hat it was the Hunts." (1935~)

Stephen C. Jett in 1968: "Perhaps the greatest experience of all, though, is ascending Hunts Mesa and looking out across the monuments [of Monument Valley] from the Rim, where one has a full view of one of the great scenic treasure houses in the world." (977~)

—Clara Bernheimer Natural Bridge: This is on the east side of Hunts Mesa. A plaque at the bridge reads: "Clara Bernheimer Natural Bridge. Discovered June 8th, 1927 by the VI Bernheimer Expedition of the American Museum of Natural History, New York." Clara was the wife of Charles L. Bernheimer. The plaque was installed by John W. Wetherill and others in 1937.

Hurrah Pass: (San Juan Co.) Hatch Point-Kane Springs Canyon. Trough Springs Canyon map. (4,200')

Lillian McCormick: "The 'Notch' was a pass through which cattlemen drove their herds up from the east side of the [Colorado] river bottom into Kane Creek. It was a hard climb for the cattle, but the cowboys were able to count them as they passed through the notch. As the last cow went through, a shout of 'hurrah' echoed from canyon wall to canyon wall because all the cattle got through and were accounted for. This cattle trail was later bladed into a roadway by miners, and is known today as Hurrah Pass." (2027~)

—Predator Tower: This sharp buttress is one mile north-northeast of Hurrah Pass (one-eighth mile southeast of elevation 4588T).

Hurricane Cliffs: (Iron and Washington Counties, Utah and Mohave Co., Az.) Fremont Canyon, Utah-Mount Trumbull, Az. Utah maps only: Kane Canyon, Burnt Peak, Buckskin Flat, Cottonwood Mountain, Paragonah, Parowan, Summit, Enoch, Cedar City, Cedar Mountain, Kanarraville, Kolob Arch, Smith Mesa, Pintura, Hurricane, and The Divide.

Also called Wasatch Lift (1646a~) and Wah-Satch Mountains (282~).

(See Hurricane Town for name derivation.)

This escarpment, some two hundred miles long, starts at Fremont Canyon at the very south end of the Tushar Mountains and ends at Mount Trumbull in Arizona. It marks the edge of the Colorado Plateau where it joins the basin and range country to the west.

Jedediah Smith of the South West Expedition of 1826–27 went down the Virgin River, noting the imposing cliffs to his east: "the country off from the River Rough Rocky and Red hills no timber or game." (1774~)

Thomas D. Brown of the Southern Indian Mission of 1854 provided one of the first descriptions of the Hurricane Cliffs: "But see over Ash Creek to the east, what table lands are these broken off so abruptly? By some floods of water, what lofty spires! What turrets! What walls! What bastions! What outworks to some elevated forts! What battlements are these? What inaccessible ramparts? From these no doubt are often heard Heaven's artillery cannonading. What guards patrol these elevated walls"? (306~)

Frederick S. Dellenbaugh of the 1871–72 Powell Expedition: "We were now on what the inhabitants of the region called Hurricane Hill, and from this we applied the name Hurricane Ledge to the long line of sharp cliffs we had followed, which begin at the Virgin River and extend, almost unbroken and eight hundred to a thousand feet high, south to the Grand Canyon, forming the western boundary of the Uinkaret Plateau." (541~)

H.M. Cadell in 1887: "The Hurricane Ledge presents an almost impassable barrier to the traveler across the plateaux. It may be crossed where occasional narrow gullies have gashed its front, or where old volcanoes on the plateau above have poured over the brink streams of lava, and formed rugged slopes which may be climbed with difficulty." (328~)

Leo A. Borah in 1936: "We took a new road that passes through Hurricane, named for the mighty Hurricane Cliff, formed by faulting, which towers across Utah's southern boundary as a sheer red wall in some places fully 2,000 feet high. The view from the top is stupendous. Volcanic forces perhaps millions of years ago broke the earth's crust here and tilted a portion of it so high that it is an eyrie from which the visitor gazes spellbound. The fancy came to me that once when Mother Nature left her most talented but erratic children alone with paint pots and sculpturing chisels, they wrought this topsy-turvey scene out of pure mischief." (262~)

Hurricane Hill: (Washington Co.) Hurricane Cliffs-Hurricane Town. Hurricane map.

Also spelled Hariken Hill. (58~)

(See Hurricane Town for name derivation.)

A road up Hurricane Hill provided access through the Hurricane Cliffs to other areas in southern Utah. As such, it was often described in the early literature.

Edwin G. Woolley, diarist for the Utah Territorial Militia of 1869: "Camped at foot of Hurricane Hill ... started up the hill; we had got part way up, when we saw something across dugway. Came nearer, and found it to be a barricade built of rock about 4 feet high. A noble piece of work. We suppose it to have been built for protection of frontier against Indians." (476~)

James A. Little in 1871: "To the top of Hurricane hill, the road is as difficult as any piece I ever traveled of about the same distance, and is easily described as follows: rock, rock and sand mixed, heavy sand, more rock, &c." (1209~)

Charles Roscoe Savage in 1875: "This is a bad road for nervous people." (1690~)

Mary Woolley Chamberlain in the early years when she was a young girl: "All went well till we reached a very steep, short turn near the top of the hill. This was the most dangerous part.... Con (a fourteen year old) realized that it would take an extra large rock to block the wheel when it stopped on this curve.... While he was tugging at it, the wagon began rolling back down the hill ... the precipice was hundreds of feet deep at this point.... I was unable to [put the brake on] from the high spring-seat. As I felt the wagon rolling towards the edge of the road I jumped for my life. Con succeeded in getting a smaller

rock under the wheel when it was within about three feet of the brink." (415~)

—Rockhouse Wash: This short drainage is immediately north of Hurricane Hill (one-eighth mile south of elevation 3544). It was named for a still-extant rock-walled building in the upper wash.

Hurricane Hollow: (Garfield Co.) Dixie National Forest-Escalante Mountains-Horse Creek. Sweetwater Creek map.

—Birch Hollow: This small southern tributary of Horse Creek is one-half mile west of Hurricane Hollow. (1931~)

Hurricane Mesa: (Washington Co.) Hurricane Cliffs-Smith Mesa. Virgin and Smith Mesa maps. Some of Hurricane Mesa is PRIVATE PROPERTY.

Also called Pioneer Mesa (767~, 1931~) and Smith Mesa (448~).

(See Hurricane Town for name derivation.)

In 1955 a private contractor working for the United States Air Force built a test facility on top of Hurricane Mesa. This included a twelve thousand foot railroad-type track that led to the rim of the cliff. It was used for testing ejection mechanisms for jet airplanes. A rocket-powered sled would be sent down the track at speeds up to eighteen hundred miles per hour and the ejection seat would be deployed at the rim, letting a dummy or a monkey parachute fifteen hundred feet to the ground. The base was closed in 1961. (40~)

—Belted Cliffs: Herbert E. Gregory used this name for the cliffs on the southeast side of Hurricane Mesa. (767~)

Hurricane Town: (Washington Co.) Virgin River-Hurricane Cliffs-Highways 9, 17, and 59. Hurricane map.

Andrew Karl Larson told the story of the naming of Hurricane: "They asked Nephi Johnson if it was possible to get down over the hill (the Hurricane Fault).... Johnson thought that if they got some men on horseback with ropes, the light vehicle could be eased down by way of this trail. They accomplished their object; when they had got over the worst part of the trail to the base of the hill, a whirlwind came up and tore the top off the buggy. [Mormon Apostle] Erastus Snow exclaimed, 'Well, that was a hurricane! We'll call this place Hurricane.'" (1141~)

The town was started with the completion of the Hurricane Canal in 1904, which opened the land on Hurricane Bench to farming. A local tongue-in-cheek story says that the wind blows so hard in Hurricane that the farmers feed lead shot to their turkeys to hold them down.

Wilhelmina Hinton described the town in 1950: "The panorama of beauty and industry that unfolds before the eye from the top of the Hurricane hill is not duplicated anywhere in Utah. The patch-work of orchards, grain fields and alfalfa fields, as they spread before one in their varying shades of green and in varying sizes, remind one of a crazy patch quilt. Only a quilt of such size and magnitude must have been fashioned by the gods." (273~)

—Hurricane Canal: This was listed on the Utah State Register of Historic Sites in 1971 and on the National Register of Historic Places in 1977. This amazing and historically significant seven-mile-long canal was started in 1893, finished in 1904, and was abandoned in 1985 when the ditch was replaced by pipe. (14~, 273~, 1552~) Ward J. Roylance: "Dixie people dug and blasted from the Virgin River's cliffs a canal eight feet wide, four feet deep, and nearly eight miles long. Using nothing more complicated than a wheel barrow, they built dams (two of which were destroyed by floods), trestles to support high flumes, and nine tunnels through solid rock." (1658~)

Arthur F. Bruhn added detail: "The work was challenging from the outset. The available tools were primitive, consisting of picks, shovels, handmade drills, crowbars, and wheelbarrows.... Few of the workers, which included young boys, were skilled with explosives; as a consequence, several men were accidentally killed.... Lack of capital and good equipment forced the men to construct some sections atop unstable rock fills. They frequently had to excavate tunnels to avoid costly detours and, in some places, wooden flumes were necessary to carry water across tributary canyons." (311~)

The canal was updated and reinforced from time to time with concrete and rebar. It is now no longer in use. A terrific hiking trail goes along sections of the canal. (SAPE.)

—The Narrows: (Also called Timpoweap Canyon.) (767~) This narrow section of the Virgin River is two miles west of the town of Virgin (immediately south of elevation 3558 on the Virgin map).

—Narrows Dam: Two dams, used to provide water for the Hurricane Canal, were built in The Narrows in the mid-1890s. They quickly washed away. A third dam lasted until 1910. The next dam, built with concrete, lasted until 1985. The present dam no longer directs water into the Hurricane Canal, but to a canal taking water to Quail Lake. (1551~)

—Hurricane Bridge: This spans the Virgin River between the towns of Hurricane and La Verkin. Before the bridge, a ford at this point was called the Crossing of the Fathers. (448~)

Hurricane Wash: (Kane Co.) GSCENM-Glen Canyon NRA-Escalante Desert-Coyote Gulch. Big Hollow Wash and King Mesa maps.

Also called Hurricane Hollow. (1382~)

Edson Alvey: "The name is derived from the strong winds that sometimes blow in the area." (55~)

Hyatt Canyon: (Iron Co.) Hole in the Rock-Parowan Canyon. Parowan map.

John Hyatt (1832-1911) was a Parowan pioneer. (388~)

Hydes Bottom: (Uintah Co.) Uintah and Ouray Indian Reservation-Green River. Moon Bottom map.

Also called Cooper Bottom. (209~)

Jean Bennett in 1965: "Hydes Bottom is sometimes called Long Bottom. Upstream from the island is Frank Hyde's place. Frank sold whiskey in Vernal." (209~) James M. Aton noted that Hyde had a still on an island in the river near the bottom. (79~)

Iceberg Canyon: (San Juan Co.) Glen Canyon NRA-Wilson Mesa-Glen Canyon. Alcove Canyon and The Rincon maps.

This was initially called Wilson Canyon for either Alva Wilson or for a rancher locals referred to as Old Man Wilson. (1795~) (See Wilson Mesa—San Juan Co.)

Charles L. Bernheimer, during an archaeological expedition in 1929, called this both Slickhorn Canyon and Filius Canis Canyon: "The box canyon which took us two hours to cross has no name, but as the men gave it a name which is not fit to repeat, I translated it into Latin and it sounds better that way. *Filius Canis* is its name henceforth." (218~) Their name of course was "son of a bitch." Two complimentary name derivations are given.

First, Tad Nichols in 1955: "We called this one Iceberg because the pool you had to go through was so cold that unless you had a rubber raft or an inner tube, or something, it was hard to get across." (1449~)

Second, Katie Lee: "There's no iceberg in [the canyon], but it looks as though a glacier had carved out the canyon and the twenty-foot drop-off into it.... Intermittent seeps and stream (now dry) have left variegated ribbons in the middle of the bowl-like floor and down the walls—colored maroon in the center, edging into purples and violets outlined in chalk white. Again, that feeling of ice ... icicles. Like a toboggan run through an ice cave.... Iceberg Canyon was its name from then on." (1162~)

—Access Road: Access to Iceberg Canyon was from an extension of the old mining road that went from Lake Canyon into The Rincon. From The Rincon a road, now underwater, traversed benches above the river. (466~) (See The Rincon—Uranium Mining Road.)

—Constructed Stock Trail: This ascends the wall on the south side of the canyon three-quarters of a mile above its mouth. (1519~) James H. Knipmeyer noted an inscription along the trail: "Notice: Please Don't Take Our Horses. Also Look Out For Your Cattle So The Indians Don't Drive them Out The San Juan River." (1115~)

—Fizzle Canyon: This short western tributary of the Colorado River is two miles north of Iceberg Canyon (one-half mile north of elevation 4493 on The Rincon map). Katie Lee and friends noted that the canyon was short and "fizzled." (1163~)

—The Reef: This is on the west side of the Colorado River across from the mouth of Iceberg Canyon. From the lake it is an obvious wide, tall, uniformly steep sandstone slab that is at the very end of the Waterpocket Fold (immediately west of elevation 4172T on The Rincon map). (See Annies Canyon–Abandoned Road.) The old name is The Reef. (56~) In 2004 a new name, The Slope, was proposed by Alan Silverstein. It was accepted by the USGS Board on Geographic Names in 2005. (1138~, SAPE.)

Icelander Creek: (Carbon and Emery Counties.) Book Cliffs-Highway 191-Grassy Trail Creek. Sunnyside and Cedar maps.

—Whitmore Spring: This is one-half mile south of Dragerton. It is the source of water in Icelander Creek. (1490~) (See Whitmore Canyon for name derivation.)

Ida Gulch: (Grand Co.) La Sal Mountains-Richardson Amphitheater-Colorado River. Big Bend map.

Also called Idas Gulch. (75~)

Joe Taylor: "Mrs. Stearn was named Ida." (1866~) (See Stearns Creek.)

—Movies: *Rio Grande* and *Battle at Apache Pass* were filmed, in part, in Ida Gulch. (1809~)

Imlay Canyon: (Washington Co.) Zion National Park-North Fork Virgin River. Temple of Sinawava map.

James Havens Imlay (1815–1890) arrived in Harmony in 1863 and moved to Panguitch in 1871. (437~, 462~) He ran sheep in the area. The name was applied to the canyon in 1934. (1445~, 1931~)

Dennis Turville noted that he called it Troll's Treat: "since we felt like trolls ferrying our packs through all of the obstacles, especially with that damned 300-foot rope." (653~)

—Elephant Temple: This is on the south side of the mouth of Imlay Canyon (at elevation 5510). (430~)

Imperial Valley: (San Juan Co.) Glen Canyon NRA-Dark Canyon Plateau-Cross Canyon. Teapot Rock and Cross Canyon maps.

John Scorup: "it was so wide and lush, it'd get the proper moisture, the grass would grow up. It was just a big, lush, majestic valley. Like a king's." (1821~)

—Imperial Canyon: This wide drainage goes west from Imperial Valley to the Colorado River (between elevations 4884T and 5468T on the Teapot Rock map).

—Cranberry Point: This is on the west side of the Colorado River immediately north of the mouth of Imperial Canyon (one-eighth mile northeast of elevation 3982T on the Teapot Rock map). William Hiram Edwards ran the river with the James S. Best Expedition in 1891: "A few days later we camped for the night at a place we named Cranberry Point at the head of Hell's Half Mile.... When the [Stanton-] Brown party passed through here they found a half barrel of cut loaf sugar.... While digging around in the sand and driftwood one of the men ... found ... a case of a dozen quart jars of cranberry jam." (597~)

Impossible Peak: (Garfield Co.) Dixie National Forest-Boulder Mountain. Steep Creek Bench map. (7,767')
Cowboys noted that the peak is impossible to ascend.

Inclined Temple: (Washington Co.) Zion National Park-Ivins Mountain. The Guardian Angels map. (7,150')
Unattributed: "So named because its broad top has a decided incline." (1931~)

Indian Canyon: (Kane Co.) Vermilion Cliffs-Cottonwood Canyon. Yellowjacket Canyon and Kanab maps.
Pre-historic Indians frequented the canyon. (1027a~, 1694~)
Harvey Butchart in 1968: "went up Indian Canyon and walked to the end, a most impressive smooth grassy floor with a couple of pools from the seeps with sheer red walls all around." (319~)

Indian Canyon: (Sevier Co.) San Rafael Swell-Willow Springs Wash. Willow Springs map.
—Constructed Stock Trail: Jim Crane noted that the CCC built the stock trail that goes up the prow between Indian Canyon and the North Fork. It is still in use. (478~, SAPE.)

Indian Creek: (San Juan Co.) Manti-LaSal National Forest-Abajo Mountains-Canyonlands National Park-Needles District-Colorado River. Abajo Peak, Mount Linnaeus, Shay Mountain, Harts Point South, Harts Point North, North Six-shooter Peak, The Loop, and Monument Basin maps.
Also called Indian Canyon (863~) and Indian Valley (1406~).
Members of the Captain John N. Macomb Expedition of 1859 dropped off Harts Point into Harts Canyon and then to its junction with today's Indian Creek. John Strong Newberry of the expedition had another name for it: "Soon after issuing from the mouth of Cañon Colorado [Harts Canyon] ... we were soon buried in a deep

and narrow gorge, which is then continuous till it joins the greater cañon of Grand [Colorado] River. The cañon, from its many windings and the many branches which open into it, we designated by the name of Labyrinth Cañon [today's Indian Canyon].... The bottom is occupied with cotton-woods, and thickets of narrow-leaved willow, cane, and salt-bush; all of which, with fallen rocks, quicksands, and deep water-holes, made the passage through it almost impossible." (1266~)

Charles H. Dimmock was with Newberry: "The trail winds through its devious mazes ... crossing Labyrinth Creek [Indian Creek], flowing through the narrow gorge, one hundred & twenty-seven times in 16 miles." (559~)

William Henry Jackson of the Ferdinand V. Hayden Survey in 1875 called it *Canon Colorado*. (950~)

Frank Silvey: "In June, 1881 John E. Brown, Tom Peppers, Green, Robinson and others, following Piute Indians, discovered and named Indian Creek." (1739~)

Albert R. Lyman in 1884: "The Utes had often told about a fine valley northwest of Blue Mountain [Abajo Mountains].... Bishop Nielson, Thales Haskel and others went with a pack outfit to find the wonderful valley, and see whether it was a fit place to re-establish the San Juan Mission [which had settled in Bluff in 1880 but was having a hard go of it because of water problems]. The valley, since known as Indian Creek, impressed them favorably in a general way, but its patches of land were badly scattered to be safely farmed in an Indian country, so the proposition was dropped." (1240~)

Inscriptions include J.D. Powers, Mar. 23, 1885; J.E. Rogerson, Apr. 1, 1887; Jack Cottrell, no date (but most likely pre-1900); Ralph Hurst, J. 24, 1911; Hill Dalley, 1911; S.G. Peay, 1911; Wilford L. Draper, April 9, 1919; Truman Wilcox, 7-11-26; and Salli (?) Gentry, no date. (838~, 1112~, SAPE.)

—Indian Creek Guard Station: This Forest Service guard station, now gone, was one and one-half miles south of Twin Peaks (one-quarter mile south of Indian Creek near elevation 9240 on the Mount Linnaeus map).

—Kelly Ranch: (Correctly spelled Kelley Ranch.) This was immediately south of Newspaper Rock (near elevation 6161 on the Shay Mountain map). All that remains are a cabin ruin and old corrals. (SAPE.) Nearby inscriptions include J.G. Kelley and T.W. Kelley, 1892. (883~, 1115~, SAPE.)

—Newberry Butte: This is one mile south of the mouth of Indian Creek (at elevation 4907T on the Monument Basin map). It was named in 1987 by Ray Wheeler. (144~)
John Strong Newberry of the Captain John N. Macomb

Expedition of 1859, and party, reached the summit. (143~) Newberry: "On every side we were surrounded by columns, pinnacles, and castles of fantastic shapes.... South of us, about a mile distant, rose one of the castle-like buttes, which I have already mentioned.... This butte was composed of alternate layers of chocolate-colored sandstone and shale ... its side nearly perpendicular, but most curiously ornamented with columns and pilaster, porticos and colonnades, cornices and battlements, flanked here and there with tall outstanding towers, and crowned with spires so slender that it seemed as though a breath of air would suffice to topple them from their foundations. To accomplish the object for which we had come so far [to find the confluence of the Colorado and Green rivers], it seemed necessary that we should ascend this butte.... Stripping off nearly all our clothing, we made the attempt, and after two hours of most arduous labor succeeded in reaching the summit. The view which there burst upon us was such as amply repaid us for all the toil. It baffles description, however, and I can only hope that our sketches will give some faint idea of its strange and unearthly character. The great cañon (Grand Canyon) of the Lower Colorado, with its cliffs a mile in height, affords grander and more impressive scenes, but those having far less variety and beauty of detail than this. From the pinnacle on which we stood the eye swept over an area some fifty miles in diameter, everywhere marked by features of more than ordinary interest; lofty lines of massive mesas rising in successive steps to form the frame of the picture; the interval between them more than 2,000 feet below their summits. A great basin of sunken plain lay stretched out before us as on a map. Not a particle of vegetation was anywhere discernible; nothing but bare and barren rocks of rich and varied colors shimmering in the sunlight. Scattered over the plain were thousands of the fantastically formed buttes to which I have so often referred in my notes; pyramids, domes, towers, columns, spires, of every conceivable form and size. Among these by far the most remarkable was the forest of Gothic spires [The Needles].... Nothing in nature or in art offers a parallel to these singular objects, but some idea of their appearance may be gained by imagining the island of New York thickly set with spires like that of Trinity Church, but many of them full twice in height." (1266~)

Charles H. Dimmock was with Newberry: "The summit of a columnar sandstone pile, lifted high above the top of the left wall of the canyon & about two miles distant from the point of interruption, was ascended with much difficulty, and from it the turbid stream of the Grand

River—twelve to fifteen hundred feet below—was visible; passing in devious & contorted course between sandstone walls, from one thousand to twelve hundred feet in height, whose pilastered faces, in light & shadow, through all the changes of the sandstone series, from deepest red to lightest yellow, presented an appearance wonderful in the beauty of its originality.... South of the stand point [Newberry Butte] described, many miles distant, the barren plain, arid and trembling from intensity of heat, is covered by mesas broken into isolated pinnacles & clustered castled summits [The Needles], so architectural in effect that among spires, turrets & battlements the eye seems wandering over the ruined glories of a heavened-burned city." (559~)

—Oil Road: A road partway down Indian Creek was built to support the oil drilling activities of Utah Petroleum at the Ellie Well site in the mid-1920s. (1928~) Al Scorup, the owner of the Dugout Ranch, noted that they put in a road on the north side of Indian Creek in 1928 and improved it to a good graded road in 1944. (1703~) (See Highway 211.)

—Forest Service Trail #019: This constructed stock trail starts in upper Indian Creek at the "Headgate" and ends at Aspen Flat (Mount Linnaeus map). (SAPE.)

Indian Creek: (Kane Co.) Glen Canyon NRA-Escalante River-Lake Powell. Davis Gulch map.

Also called Indian Gulch. (183~)

Two name derivations are given.

First, Edson Alvey noted that Indian remains were found in the canyon. (55~)

Second, D. Elden Beck noted that Jess Barker of Escalante told him in 1939 that "It was in this gulch that the early white men and the Indians came to barter." (182~)

Indian Gardens: (Kane Co.) GSCENM-Kaiparowits Plateau-Lake Canyon. Blackburn Canyon map.

Don Coleman: "The Indian Gardens is named after Llewellyn Harris. He was married to an Indian woman and he had a garden in there. He has his name in there; Llewellyn Harris, 1883 or so." (441~) The inscription reads: "L. Harris, April 9, 1889." (SAPE.)

Seth Ohms, a descendent of Llewellyn Harris, added to the story: "Llewellyn and his family lived with a tribe of Indians on the mountain for one or two years. There he planted a garden in a narrow wash near the head of a seep." (1656~)

Indian Gulch: (Garfield Co.) Dixie National Forest-Boulder Mountain-The Gulch. Lower Bowns Reservoir and Steep Creek Bench maps.

Edson Alvey noted that Fremont Indian remains were found here. (55~)

An inscription high in the canyon is from Hartley Black, June 2, 1917. (SAPE.)

Indian Head Pass: (San Juan Co.) Dark Canyon Plateau-Dark Canyon. Indian Head Pass map. (5,660')

A small sandstone formation on the west side of the pass bears a resemblance to a man's profile.

—Constructed Stock Trail: This trail, no longer used, goes through Indian Head Pass. (SAPE.)

Indian Hollow: (Emery Co.) Castle Valley-Ferron Town-Ferron Creek. Ferron map.

Also called Indian Holler. (931~)

Ray Wareham: "There was a man named Nelson that owned a farm there. He got really sick and passed out right on Ferron Creek. He figured he was just going to die there, and a couple of days later he wakes up and here's this old Indian that's been doctorin' 'im. And he got completely better, and that's why that's called Indian Hollow." (1967~)

Indian Hollow: (Garfield Co.) Dixie National Forest-Threemile Creek. Fivemile Ridge map.

Koz K. Richards in 1941: "It was named Indian Hollow because of the large number of Indians that used to be around in that vicinity. There has been many signs of Indians and a few Indian graves found there." (2053~)

Indian Hollow: (Kane Co.) GSCENM-Sheep Creek. Bryce Point, Cannonville, and Bull Valley Gorge maps.

Also called Indian Creek. (777~)

Early stockmen found Paiute Indians living in the area. John H. Davies: "I saw the [Paiute] tribe coming south out of another canyon called Indian Hollow. Viewing them from a distance it was a rather picturesque sight. They had no domesticated animals. The squaws were plodding single file along a narrow trail. Most of them were fat and short in stature. Each of them carried on her back a large bag containing all her family belongings; and some of them were even carrying babies as well.... The men and the older boys were scattered out on either side of the squaws and children hunting rabbits and other small game." (523~)

Indian Hollow: (Washington Co.) Dixie National Forest-Pine Valley Mountains-Mahogany Creek. Saddle Mountain and Central East maps.

On December 27, 1866 Pine Valley settler Cyrus Hancock was attacked by Navajo Indians on nearby Mahogany

Creek. Impaled in the arm by an arrow, Hancock fled down Indian Hollow. (1447~)

Indian Peak: (Sevier Co.) Fishlake National Forest-Sevier Plateau. Koosharem map. (9,830')

Two complimentary name derivations are given.

First, Ezhan Jackman in 1942: "Called Indian Peak because it is the highest peak in this range of mountains.... The Indians used this peak to signal from and send messages from one side of the mountain to the other." (2053~)

Second, Joseph F. Parker: "The Indians had a trail up Indian Creek where they traveled to and from the old Indian Peak." (2053~)

Indian Spring Benches: (Garfield Co.) Henry Mountains-Hansen Creek. Copper Creek Benches map.

—Indian Spring: Two similar stories surface about this developed spring. First, Charles B. Hunt: "Named for the abundant flint and pottery chips that are found in the vicinity of the spring." (925~)

Second, Garth Noyes: "My uncle [Frank Noyes] told me that at one time ... he saw where the Indians had killed two or three hundred deer. They'd tanned the hides while they were there. He said that is was obvious that they had been there for quite a long time and got a lot of deer meat out of that area." (1473~)

Indian Springs: (Sevier Co.) Sevier Valley-Glenwood. Sigurd map.

Leila Oldroyd: "On March 21, 1867, Jens Peter Peterson, his wife, and a neighbor girl, Mary Smith, left Richfield to do some trading in Glenwood. At the Black Ridge east of the Sevier River, they were attacked by Indians, all three being killed and their bodies mutilated. The Glenwood boys, Joseph Hendrickson and Joseph Frankum, were gathering cows in a nearby field and saw the Indians. They ran to town and gave the warning and a group of ten or more men answered the call to pursue the Indians. The Indians made a stand when they reached a spot northeast of town, now called Indian Creek, and fought there for some time, finally pulling off into the hills." (1971~)

Ingram Hollow: (Garfield Co.) Dixie National Forest-Paunsaugunt Plateau-East Fork Sevier River. Bryce Point and Tropic Reservoir maps.

W.J. Shakespear: "It was named for Joseph Ingram [1846-1921] who ranched there in early days." (2053~)

Inscription House Ruins: (Coconino Co., Az.) Navajo Indian Reservation-Navajo National Monument-Navajo Canyon. Inscription House Ruin, Az. map.

These ruins have been closed to all visitors since 1968.

Ts'ah Biis Kin is Navajo for "House in the Sagebrush." (1204~, 2072~)

These famous ruins are a part of Navajo National Monument. They were "discovered" by Dr. Byron Cummings in 1909. He initially called it Adobe House. (830~, 975~) Cummings returned to excavate the ruins in 1914-16. (265~) The Inscription House name was given by Cummings and John Wetherill in 1911. (856~)

Charles L. Bernheimer: "Inscription House takes its name from some markings in Spanish, practically illegible, but the date of 1661 is readily discernible." (221~) It has been determined that the 1661 date is actually from 1861 and was put there by a member of an expedition to Hopi country led by Jacob Hamblin. (1105~) This, of course, made Cumming's "discovery" of the ruins nearly a half a century late.

Byron Cummings in his 1909 diary: "This seems to be a structure between the oldest structures of Saga ot Sosa [today's Tseyi-hatsosi] and the best structures of the cliff dwellers. The walls are very well built and enough grass or twigs used, left long and laid lengthwise, to make the walls very strong. This building is in a fairly good state of preservation and must have been a very important community among them. It is an excellent place for study.... The flats of this part of the canyon made excellent cornfields and must have supported quite an extensive population." (499~)

Elizabeth Compton Hegemann in 1963: "Inscription House cliff dwelling is not large and sprawling like Keet Seel nor strikingly beautiful like Betatakin, but it is intimate and charming in its own gracefully curved promontory. The cave is perfectly located, easy of access, and looks out over the grass- and brush-filled valley between the smooth red sandstone walls of Neetsin Canyon." (856~)

Hal K. Rothman detailed why Inscription House Ruin was closed: "Self-guiding trail markers had been uprooted and tossed aside, picnic fires had been built, vandals had rolled large boulders through the protective fence, and a number of prehistoric ceiling beams were used for campfire fuel." (1654~)

Inscriptions include C.M. Cade, A.D. 1882; N.C. Young, 1882; W. Brockway, May 10, 1883; John Hadley, Nov. 17, 1885; and W. Williams, 1885. (1112~, 1115~)

Inspiration Point: (Garfield Co.) Bryce Canyon National Park-Paunsaugunt Plateau-Pink Cliffs. Bryce Point map. (8,143')

Ward J. Roylance from Inspiration Point: "The first impression may be of a mountainside of thousands of segmented columns; the second of countless joined monuments standing row on row from the floor of the canyon to the rim; but the third and most satisfying summary is of all the finest cycloliths of ancient times, brought to this amphitheater to be preserved unto posterity." (1658~)

—Movies: In 1927 two films, *The Shepherd of the Hills* and *Ramona* were filmed, in part, here. (1715~)

Interplanetary Airstrip: (Carbon Co.) West Tavaputs Plateau-Nine Mile Canyon. Currant Canyon map.

This airstrip is now almost completely grown over and is difficult to see. (SAPE.)

Les Porter in 1998: "According to [Dennis] Willis [a BLM employee], this airstrip was used by various oil and gas companies to move crews in and out of the work areas in this Stone Cabin Gas Field vicinity. The story goes that one employee, a 'Buck Rogers' fan, waiting for the airplane on various occasions inscribed the words 'Interplanetary Airstrip' in the rock near the airstrip. Mr. Willis confided that he believed this to have been done any time from the 1930s thru 1950s." (1931~) The inscription, though very faint, survives. (SAPE.)

Interstate 70: (Utah counties east to west: Grand, Emery, Sevier, and Millard.)

This Interstate section through Utah is about 232 miles long. One unique aspect about it is that, unlike most other sections of the Interstate Highway system, little of this was built on top of or parallel to other U.S. highways; long stretches of this part of the interstate were built through country that had no roads whatsoever.

—Grand Junction to Green River: (Also called Dinosaur Diamond Prehistoric Highway.) This section was developed starting in 1913. Some of the road followed the old narrow gauge railroad bed which was built in 1883 and abandoned for a standard gauge track nearby in 1890. (See Denver and Rio Grande Western Railroad.) This became a part of a national road system called the Midland Trail. It later became Utah Highway 50/6. (1542~)

—Green River to Salina: This section goes over the San Rafael Swell. Construction started in 1963 and was partially opened in 1970, though the road was not completed until 1990.

There were three major obstacles. One was cutting through the San Rafael Reef twelve miles west of Green River through Spotted Wolf Canyon. The canyon was only a couple of feet wide before construction and had to be blasted into a gap that would accommodate four lanes of traffic.

The second problem was building two bridges over Eagle Canyon. These are the highest bridges on the Interstate Highway system. (710~)

The third problem was in constructing the highway through Salina Canyon. Here the construction crew followed the course of an old railroad grade from the 1880s that was never used. They had to destroy two of the old tunnels during construction.

—Salina to Interstate 15 at Cove Fort. The Interstate took a completely new route through Sevier Valley, bypassing the cities of Salina and Richfield and several smaller towns.

Ipson Creek: (Garfield Co.) Dixie National Forest-Panguitch Lake. Red Creek Reservoir and Panguitch Lake maps.

Also spelled Ispon Creek. (1931~)

Neils Peter Ipson (1833-1910) homesteaded at the mouth of the canyon in 1873–74. Legend says that he traded Indians a steer for the creek. He spent forty summers at the lake. (365~, 1191~, 1445~, 1931~)

Ireland Mesa: (Emery Co.) San Rafael Swell-Muddy Creek. Ireland Mesa map. (6,770')

Mining engineer E.A. Ireland came into the Salina Canyon country in 1878. He bought three ranches in the Salina Canyon area—Mountain Ranch, Oak Springs Ranch, and the Christianson Ranch—and started the Ireland Cattle Company. (186~, 369~, 606~, 710~, 1330~, 1968~)

Irish Green Spring: (San Juan Co.) Mancos Mesa-Castle Wash-Highway 276. Clay Hills map. PRIVATE PROPERTY.

Two name derivations are given.

First, Charles L. Bernheimer in 1929: Our camp site ... was called Irish Green,—I suppose because there was some vegetation and good water." (218~)

Second, Carl Mahon was told this story: "There was an Irishman by the name of Green and he was trapping out in that country and he camped there." (1272~)

The spring was discovered by members of the Hole-in-the-Rock Expedition in 1880. It was, and still is, the headquarters for several ranching outfits, including the Scorup-Somerville and the Lazy TY. (1901~)

Eric Bayles noted that until the 1970s the cowboys would sleep outdoors or under an overhang. When Kent Schmitt bought the Lazy TY, he brought in trailers and made it a comfortable line camp. (167~)

Inscriptions include R. Fey, Dec. 19, 1885. (1115~)

Iron County:

The county seat is Parowan.

Iron County was established in 1852 from previously undesignated lands. It was named by Brigham Young for its plentiful supply of iron ore. (1727~, 1932~)

Iron Mountain: (Iron Co.) Harmony Mountains-Neck of the Desert. Desert Mound map. (7,831')

Also called Iron Buttes. (1211~)

The mountain became the base for the Iron Mission of 1851. Although the mission was not successful, in later years (the 1940s) iron production was ramped up and became very successful. (469~)

John C. Fremont in 1854: "Iron here occurs in extraordinary masses, in some parts accumulated into mountains, which come out in crests of solid iron thirty feet thick and a hundred yards long." (683~)

Iron Peak: (Iron Co.) Dixie National Forest-Hurricane Cliffs. Cottonwood Mountain map. (8,158')

Also called Iron Point. (1931~)

Betsy Topham Camp: "prominent peak ... is called Iron Peak because of the rich iron ore in the area." (336~)

Iron Spring Draw: (Garfield Co.) Dixie National Forest-Escalante Mountains-Coyote Hollow. Barker Reservoir map.

Two name derivations are given.

First, J.J. Porter in 1931: "Man named Irons grazed sheep on this flat about 1890." (1346~)

Second, Pratt Gates: "There are some little springs up in there that have a lot of iron in them. You can touch it but you can't drink it." (709~)

Iron Springs: (Iron Co.) Granite Mountain-Iron Springs Creek. Cedar City NW map. PRIVATE PROPERTY.

The Indian name is *Pan-ag-up* or *Pan-ag-a-pa*, or "Iron Springs." (1512~)

The Domínguez-Escalante Expedition of 1776–77 passed the springs.

In 1849 the Captain Jefferson Hunt Party traveled through the area while following the Old Spanish Trail. It is believed that Hunt was the first to recognize the importance of the iron deposits he saw here. One of his companions, Addison Pratt, called this Cedar Spring: "Near this spring is immense quantities of rich iron ore." (1571~)

John D. Lee, the diarist for the Iron Mission in 1851: "Pres. [George] Smith in co. with some 10 others ... ascended one of those hills or small mountains of Iron Ore distance about ½ mile found large quantities of ore. Some appeared to have been subject to the action of heat & was pronounced by some to be dead. However specimens of the ore rock & to be tested by regular and proper process." (1159~)

In 1855 Thomas D. Brown of the Southern Indian Mission described the first iron smelted at Iron Springs: "The first iron this day [January 25] from Trial Furnace of Iron Company, was slightly rolled and squeezed on [a] hearth, instead of being puddled it was wrought into a slightly malleable iron rod, part of it sent to Pres. Young and some nails made out of the balance." (306~)

Louisa Barnes Pratt in 1857: "They had been trying five years to make iron, till every person engaged in the enterprise was reduced to poverty. The old iron works spread a gloom over the whole place." (360~)

—Pioneer Road: A road was built from the new town of Cedar City to Iron Springs in 1852 and surface mining for iron ore started. (1715~, 1839~)

—Old Spanish Trail: The trail went by Iron Springs, which was an important stop.

—Iron City: This town was started in 1869 by Homer Duncan and Ebenezer Hanks in support of the Iron Mission. (376~)

—Iron Springs Gap: (Also called Iron Springs Pass.) This is two miles southeast of Iron Springs. It is a gap between two hills (elevations 5669 and 5774). (1012~)

Iron Top Mesa: (Kane Co.) Glen Canyon NRA-Waterpocket Fold. Halls Crossing and The Rincon NE maps. (4,381')

Three name derivations are given.

First, Keith Durfey noted that they used to call black brush, which is the dominant plant on the mesa, iron brush. (582~)

Second, Dwight Williams noted that there were signs of iron ore on the mesa top. (2013~)

Third, there was an Iron Rock Island on the north side of the Colorado River and under the south side of Iron Top Mesa (one-half mile south of elevation 3998T on the Halls Crossing map). The island received its name by 1889. (466~) Perhaps Iron Top Mesa received its name from Iron Rock Island.

—Schock Trail: (Also called Bare-Rock Trail [1797~] and Miners Stairs [1672~].) This constructed stock trail, which goes to the top of Iron Top Mesa, starts on the southeast side of the mesa (one-half mile southeast of elevation 3998T on the Halls Crossing map), at lake's edge. Before the lake, the trail started on the now-submerged Anderson Bar. Today the lower part of the trail is well-cairned and goes generally northwest to the top of Iron Top Mesa. From there the it went to Halls Ranch [Baker Ranch] near the mouth of Halls Creek, staying between the face of the Waterpocket Fold and the Colorado River.

(466~) (See Appendix Two—Lower Desert to Halls Creek Trail.)

There is some question about who built the trail. A gold miner named Anderson located the first mining claim on the bar in 1889 and many believe he built the trail. Several years later Dr. William H. Schock (1846-1927) mined extensively in the area, eventually building a cabin one-half mile west of the trail on what had earlier been called Anderson Bar. The trail was later improved by area stockmen and uranium miners and was in use until Lake Powell filled. (1795~, SAPE.)

Inscriptions included C.N. Sorensen, May 18, 1894; Peter Gregerson, May 25, 1894; D. Dunsire, Jan the 13, 1898; F.A. Baker, 3-9-21; J.I. Mulford, Notom Utah, no date; and William Black, no date. (466~)

—Irontop Trail: A constructed stock trail went from the southeast end of Iron Top Mesa to the top of the Waterpocket Fold. From there it is presumed to have joined the Baker Trail, which goes to Halls Creek, or the Bowns Trail, which goes to Bowns Canyon and the Escalante River. (2013~)

—High Bar: This placer bar, now underwater, was on the west side of the Colorado River opposite the mouth of Lake Canyon and under the east rim of Iron Top Mesa (Halls Crossing map). The bar was mined as early as 1889. (466~)

Iron Wash: (Emery Co.) San Rafael Swell-San Rafael Reef-San Rafael River. San Rafael Knob, Twin Knolls, Temple Mountain, Old Woman Wash, Crows Nest Spring, Greasewood Draw, and Horse Bench West maps. In 1889 Robert Brewster Stanton noted this as Iron Springs Wash. (1811~) Lee Mont Swasey: "I'm assuming that it was named for the iron oxide color on the ledges." (1853~)

Inscriptions include B?, Dec. 18, 1892; R. Larson, 1892; J.A. Watt, March 28, 1894; Glen Stewart, Delta Utah USA, 1910; Nels Brotherson, Jan. 11, 1912; Ed Gillies, 5-26-16; Mr. R.F. Drake, March 23, 1924; F.J. Hatt, 6/1/31; and M.E. Kingon, Warren Allred, 1941. (SAPE.)

—Iron Spring: Many early diarists mention an Iron Spring. It is assumed that this is the spring area a short distance below the mouth of Iron Wash as it comes out of the San Rafael Reef (at elevation 4860 on the Old Woman Wash map). It is also possible that the Iron Spring of old is the well-known Lost Spring, which is in lower Iron Wash (Old Woman Wash map). (See Lost Spring—Emery Co.)

—Taylor Allotment Reservoir: This stock reservoir is to the south of Iron Wash and two miles southwest of Lone

Parson Hole (immediately north of elevation 6849 on the Twin Knolls map). It was built in 1962. (1551~) (See Taylor Flat for name derivation.)

—Iron Wash Trail: Lee Mont Swasey: "Iron Wash was one of the main thoroughfares from the big [San Rafael] desert, up through the Reef in Iron Wash, and then on up to Home Base [Sinbad]." (1853~) There is no longer a trail here, but one can piece together a route livestock could have taken. (SAPE.)

Isaac: (Washington Co.) Zion National Park-Court of the Patriarchs. Springdale East map. (6,381')

(See Court of the Patriarchs for name derivation.)

—Isaac Canyon: This is between Isaac and Abraham. (1548~)

Island in the Sky: (San Juan Co.) Canyonlands National Park-Island in the Sky District. Musselman Arch, Monument Basin, Turks Head, and Upheaval Dome maps.

Canyonlands National Park Superintendent Bates Wilson: "The March 1961 *Desert Magazine* on Page 28 has an article by Alfred Nestler entitled 'Our Island in the Sky' and describes the area. We believe this was the first use of that name." (1931~) Nester, in the article: "Imagine a lonely rugged island with more than a hundred miles of shoreline with long peninsulas, points and promontories, as well as many beautiful coves, bays and harbors.... 6000 feet in elevation perched atop sheer sandstone cliffs more than 2000 feet above the mighty Colorado River." (1435~)

Ivie Creek: (Emery and Sevier Counties.) Old Woman Plateau-Muddy Creek. Old Woman Plateau, Walker Flat, and Mesa Butte maps.

Also spelled Ivy Creek. (854~, 1567~)

Two name derivations are given.

First, James Ivie (1830-1906) and his brother, John (1833-1909), were members of the Elk Mountain Mission of 1855. The expedition, on their way to Moab, traversed Ivie Creek. (1105~)

Second, the H.S. Ivie family lived in the area in the early years. The name was in place by 1875. (722~)

Jedediah Smith of the South West Expedition of 1826–27 followed the creek from Castle Valley over the Wasatch Plateau, noting only that "I determined to strike westward to a low place in the [Wasatch] Mountain and cross over." While following the creek Smith's party met an "old squaw." Giving her a badger to eat, Smith noted that she "immediately tore it in pieces and laid it on the coals. When it was about half cooked she commenced eating making no nice distinction between hair pelts entrails and meet." (1774~)

In 1875 Grove Karl Gilbert of the Powell Survey found an inscription along Ivie Creek that read: "D. Eulien, 10 May 1832." This refers to fur trapper Denis Julien. The inscription is now gone. (See Appendix One—Denis Julien.)

In 1848 Orville C. Pratt called this the *Rio Del Puerto*, or the "River of the Pass," in reference to Emigrant Pass at the top of Ivie Creek. (1572~) (See Emigrant Pass.)

Gwinn Harris Heap of the Lieutenant Edward F. Beale Expedition of 1853 traveled up the canyon: "[we] came to a gap, giving issue to a small stream [Ivie Creek], which we ascended three miles. The aridity of the country continued unchanged; the looseness of the soil, constantly kept shifting by rains, prevented much vegetation except in bottom lands.... In the valley in which we encamped was good grass, which increased in quantity and improved in quality as we ascended it.... Resumed our journey before sunrise, and went up the [Ivie] creek seven miles. This gorge, for it is almost too narrow to be called a valley, affords a good pass through the range. It narrows from one hundred feet to thirty-five feet, with lofty and perpendicular rocks on either side.... The hills were clothed, from their summits to their base, with a thick growth of pine trees, cedars, and aspens, and the brook was swarming with trout." (854~)

The Captain John W. Gunnison Expedition of 1853 also traveled through the area. Gunnison called it *Akanaquint*. (477~) It is also shown as Akanaquint Creek on the Lieutenant George M. Wheeler Survey map of 1872–73. (M.76.)

The Colonel William Wing Loring Expedition of 1857-58 called this St. Rafael Creek. (166~)

Clarence Dutton of the Powell Survey mistakenly labeled it as Ivy Creek. (584~)

James H. Knipmeyer noted that members of the Elk Mountain Mission—I.M. Behunin, A.N. Billings, and Joseph S. Rawlins—inscribed their names in the canyon in 1855. (1105~, SAPE.) Mike Molen also left an inscription in 1876. (SAPE.)

—Old Spanish Trail: The trail went along Ivie Creek.

—Old Ranch: This now abandoned ranch is immediately north of Interstate 70 and is on the south side of Ivie Creek (one-quarter mile east-northeast of elevation 6247 on the Walker Flat map). A canal, with flumes, goes upstream for a mile. (SAPE.)

No one quite knows to whom the ranch belonged. Stuart Johnson noted that he thought the Mecham family had the ranch: "I can't imagine how they had enough perseverance to eke out a living on that kind of land." (1003~)

Wayne Gremel thought that Chris Jensen owned the ranch and added: "Chris Jensen farmed it for a long time, but who homesteaded it I have no idea." (780~)

—Ivy Creek Bench Reservoir: This still-used stock reservoir is on the south side of Ivie Creek Bench one and one-half miles west-northwest of Windy Peak (near elevation 6643 on the Walker Flat map). It was built in 1939. (1551~)

Ivie Canyon: (Sevier Co.) Fishlake National Forest-Mytoge Mountains-Fremont River. Fish Lake and Forsyth Reservoir maps.

Dee Hatch noted that Will Ivie was an early resident of the area. (844~)

Ivins Mountain: (Washington Co.) Zion National Park-Inclined Temple. The Guardian Angels map. (7,019')

Also called Mount Ivins.

The USGS noted that Apostle Anthony Woodward Ivins (1852–1934) was a pioneer and was "an outstanding character in the history of the Mormon Church." (1931~) His father, Israel Ivins, arrived in St. George in 1861 when Anthony was nine years old. The mid-1870s saw Ivins leading the Mormon colonization in the Mexican states of Chihuahua and Sonora. In 1890 Anthony Ivins was elected mayor of St. George. (160~, 235~, 945~)

Milton R. Hunter: "Anthony W. Ivins was a cattleman during much of his life. The statement has been made that he '... probably loved the time that he spent on the range as well, if not better, than any other time of his life. He did much for the development of the cattle business in southern Utah.'" (929~) Hoffman Birney in 1931: He is also the most widely known and the best-loved man in Utah." (235~)

Ivins Town: (Washington Co.) Red Mountains-Santa Clara River-Highway 8. Santa Clara map.

The area around Ivins was initially called Santa Clara Bench and was used by farmers and ranchers. A lack of water was problematic and, in 1914, a canal was built. In 1918 a reservoir was constructed and in 1922 Alden Gray and family became the first to settle here. The town was named after Apostle Anthony W. Ivins. (273~, 311~, 375~) (See Ivins Mountain.)

Mrs. Harmon Gubler, Jr. described the town and surrounding country in 1950: "As you travel north and west of the Santa Clara Valley, you suddenly come upon a view that defies all nature to surpass. There is the snow-capped Pine Valley Mountain rising in the distance in its majesty of sapphire blue. Underneath, in a gradual slope, God has lavishly bestowed his colors of purple, black, gray, and red. Then comes an abrupt decline of red cliffs that tower for a hundred of feet in the air.... To the west and south high mountains raise their towering peaks in the distance and in the center of all this, lies a flat open bench land known as the Santa Clara Bench. To the north and nestled underneath these perpendicular cliffs, lies the town of Ivins." (273~)

—Upper Santa Clara Canal: This was built from 1911 to 1914.

—Ivins Reservoir: Construction started in 1917 and was finished in 1918. Over the years the dam has been raised and repaired a couple of times. (273~)

Jackass Benches: (Emery Co.) San Rafael Swell-San Rafael Reef. Spotted Wolf Canyon and Drowned Hole Draw maps.

Dee Anne Finken noted that burros are still found on the benches. Locals believe that they are the descendants of burros from the Old Spanish Trail years. (641~)

—Project Number 486 Pond: This stock pond on Jackass Benches is one mile east of Drowned Hole (one-quarter mile south of elevation 6003 on the Drowned Hole Draw map). (1551~)

Jackass Flat: (Emery Co.) San Rafael Swell-Box Flat Wash. Devils Hole map.

(See Jackass Benches for name derivation.)

—Jackass Flat Line Camp: This was on the northeast side of Jackass Flat. (SAPE.)

Jackass Spring: (Garfield Co.) Dixie National Forest-Aquarius Plateau. Pollywog Lake map.

Dunk Taylor: "There's a little live water there and the sheepherders back in the old days knew where to find their mules." (1865~)

Jackass Spring: (Garfield Co.) Henry Mountains-Bullfrog Creek. Ant Knoll map.

This is a small, developed spring. (SAPE.)

Bliss Brinkerhoff: "There used to be a lot of wild horses and jackasses down in that country and that's one of the places where it was heavily populated with jackasses." (291~)

Jackass Wash: (Emery Co.) Wasatch Plateau-Sand Wash. Poison Spring Bench map.

Also called Sand Wash and Shorty Wash. (1931~)

—Windy Ridge: This long, prominent ridge is immediately west of middle Jackass Wash and is one and three-quarters of a mile south of Cottonwood Spring (at elevations 6402 and 6167).

Jack Creek: (Carbon Co.) West Tavaputs Plateau-Desolation Canyon. Patmos Head, Bruin Point, Twin Hollow, Cedar Ridge Canyon, and Firewater Canyon North maps.
Bill Seamount: "[Trapper Jack] had a ferry below McPherson Ranch." (1712~) (See Three Fords Canyon—Grand Co.)

Inscriptions include J.R. Goldsbrough, J.H. Lunt, and ? Sperry, Jan. 12, 1889. (1575~)

—Lighthouse Rock: This tower, visible from the river, is on the west bank of the Green River two miles upcanyon from Jack Creek (one-quarter mile west of elevation 4603AT on the Firewater Canyon North map). (200~) A sketch of Lighthouse Rock is in John Wesley Powell's *The Exploration of the Colorado River of the West and its Tributaries*. (1563~)

—1st Horse Ford: This is one mile below the mouth of Jack Creek. The Ed F. Harmston Expedition of 1913 used this ford to cross the Green River with their horses. (833~)

Jackrabbit Canyon: (San Juan Co.) Navajo Indian Reservation-Piute Mesa-Piute Canyon. Chaiyahi Rim NE, Navajo Begay, and Deep Canyon South maps.

Also called Jackrabbit Fork (101~) and Zane Grey Canyon (1931~).

Charles L. Bernheimer in 1926: "The canyon or pass proved as picturesquely rough as I have ever seen. The space between the walls was about 50–75 feet and their own height 1500 feet.... We promptly called this nameless avenue of travel Rock Narrows Pass." (218~, 1116~)

Jackrabbit Wash: (Iron Co.) Red Hills-Long Hollow. Parowan Gap and Enoch NE maps.

Also called Spanish Treasure Wash. (1875~, 1930~)

Jack Riggs Bench: (Kane Co.) GSCENM-Kaiparowits Plateau-Wahweap Creek. Horse Flat, Lower Coyote Spring, and Nipple Butte maps.

Ralph Chynoweth: "This guy from Panguitch put his cattle down in Wahweap Creek. He built some of the trails that come up outta Wahweap Creek onto the bench. His name was Jack Riggs [1888-1959].... He's an old-timer." (425~)

—The Cheese Box: This prominent prow is on the northwest side of Jack Riggs Bench (at elevation 6212 on the Horse Flat map).

—Constructed Stock Trail: This old trail goes from Wahweap Creek to the top of Jack Riggs Bench on its east side. Its mouth is five miles down Wahweap Creek from its junction with Tommy Smith Creek (one-eighth mile north-northeast of elevation 5087 on the Horse Flat map). (SAPE.)

—Jack Riggs Point: This is two and one-half miles south-southeast of the head of Jack Riggs Canyon (at elevation 5925 on the Lower Coyote Spring map). (1931~)

Jacks Hole: (Emery Co.) Gray Canyon-Last Chance Canyon. Three Fords Canyon map.

Waldo Wilcox: "Jack was a horse thief or horse trader back in the very early years. He spent the winter there." (2011~)

Jacks Knob: (Emery Co.) San Rafael Desert-Sweetwater Reef. Jacks Knob map. (5,442')

Two name derivations are given.

First, Guy and Nina Robison noted that John "Jack" Cottrell ranched in the area in the 1890s. (1645~) Ned Chaffin: "a very good place to look over a large part of the San Rafael Desert. Believe it was named for Jack Cottrell." (413~) (See Collie Wash—Fairview Ranch.)

Second, Alvin Robison noted that rancher Andy Moore employed Jack Baker in the 1950s. (1642~)

Inscriptions include CW, 1893 and Warren Beebe, May 19, 1912. (SAPE.)

Jackson Hole: (Grand Co.) Amasa Back-Colorado River. Gold Bar Canyon and Moab maps.

Also called Jackson Canyon and MGM Bottom.

Rancher John Jackson lived in Moab from 1891 to about 1917. (198~, 456~) Lloyd Holyoak: "John Jackson was quite a rich guy. He was an old rancher and was here for many years." (906~)

Val Dalton: "The only story I've heard is that Jackson supposedly went up into Dry Valley and stole cattle. He'd bring them down that Jackson Ladder Trail to hide them. Then when the heat cooled off on them, he'd swim them across the river and either take them over Hanksville way, or Cedar City, or sometimes up to Green River to sell them. He had ties with what they called the old outlaw bunch that was running in there. He'd just take them a little ways and then the other guys would take them the rest of the way and then they'd split the money." (517~)

—Jacksons Ladder: (Also called Jacobs Ladder.) This constructed stock trail, built by John Jackson, exits the cliffs behind Jackson Hole and goes up to Amasa Back. Jackson ran both horses and cattle on Jackson Bottom. The trail is now used by mountain bikers. Val Dalton noted that cattlemen stopped using the trail when a pipeline was built along it. (517~)

Jackson Point: (Iron Co.) Kolob Terrace-West Fork Deep Creek. Webster Flat map. (8,780')

James Jackson, Jr. (1826-1897) and his brothers (John and William) arrived in Toquerville in the early 1860s. James was a prominent sheepman. (947~)

Jackson Ridge: (San Juan Co.) Manti-LaSal National Forest-Abajo Mountains. Abajo Peak and Mount Linnaeus maps. (11,164')

(See Camp Jackson Reservoir for name derivation.)

—Indian Creek Pass: This is at the northeast end of Jackson Ridge (near elevation BM9691 on the Mount Linnaeus map). The name was used by miners in the 1890s and early 1900s. (1115~, 1489~)

Jackson Spring: (San Juan Co.) Manti-LaSal National Forest-Abajo Mountains-Harts Draw. Monticello Lake map.

Pete Steele noted that John Jackson was a sheepherder. He had a cabin at the spring at the turn of the century. The ruins of the cabin are still here. (1821~)

—Jackson Trail: This constructed stock trail leads from the spring into Harts Draw. It is now difficult to follow. (517~, 1821~, SAPE.)

Jack Spring: (San Juan Co.) Manti-LaSal National Forest-Abajo Mountains-Allen Canyon. Mount Linnaeus map.

This is a large spring. (SAPE.)

Grant Bayles noted that Jack was an old sheepman. (1931~)

Jacks Rock: (Emery Co.) Desolation Canyon-Green River. Three Fords Canyon map.

Waldo Wilcox noted that Trapper Jack kept his traps here in the late 1880s. (2011~) (See Florence Creek—McPherson Ranch.)

Jacob: (Washington Co.) Zion National Park-Court of the Patriarchs. Springdale East map.

(See Court of the Patriarchs for name derivation.)

Jacob Hamblin Arch: (Kane Co.) Glen Canyon NRA-Coyote Gulch. King Mesa map.

Also called Cliff Arch, Cliff Hamblin Natural Arch (1931~), and Coyote Arch (1672~).

This was originally named Lobo Arch by early ranchers for a wolf that roamed the area. The Jacob Hamblin Arch name was suggested to guide Burnett Hendricks by a man measuring silt on the Escalante River. Hendricks later mentioned the name to members of a National Geographic Society expedition down Coyote Gulch in 1955. (19~, 47~, 1931~)

Jacob Hamblin (1819-1886) was the first Mormon missionary to visit the general area and to befriend the Indians. He was also a scout and explorer who proved invaluable to John Wesley Powell during the latter's Colorado River adventures. (47~, 546~)

Powell traveled with Hamblin in 1870: "This man Hamblin speaks their language well, and has a great influence over all the Indians in the region round about. He is a silent, reserved man, and when he speaks, it is in a slow, quiet way that inspires great awe. His talk was so low that they had to listen attentively to hear, and they sat around him in death-like silence." (1565~)

Frederick S. Dellenbaugh of the 1871–72 Powell Expedition: "On landing we were met by a slow-moving, very quiet individual, who said he was Jacob Hamblin. His voice was so low, his manner so simple, his clothing so usual, that I could hardly believe that this was Utah's famous Indian-fighter and manager." (541~, 2051~)

Jacob Hamblin in 1873: "I have spent the last nineteen years of my life mostly attending to Indian matters; have spent more nights under cedar and pine trees than in a house; though I do not regret it." (813~)

D. Eldon Beck: "[In 1939] I had visited this same canyon and had seen this bridge, naming it at that time the 'Dutton Natural Bridge.' I named it in honor of the great western geologist, Captain Clarence E. Dutton, who studied and traversed these deserts and plateaus of southern Utah years ago." (178~)

W. Robert Moore in 1955: "It looked to us as if a giant had thrust a fist through the rock wall to provide a peep-hole through which he might view the canyon beyond." (1382~)

—Dripping Spring: Tad Nichols named this large spring which is immediately downcanyon from Jacob Hamblin Arch. (1448~, SAPE.)

Jacobs Chair: (San Juan Co.) Dark Canyon Plateau-White Canyon. Jacobs Chair map. (6,805')

Local lore says that Jacobs Chair was named for cattleman Franklin Jacob Adams (1872-1940) after he died within sight of the tower in 1940. (See story below). But, the Herbert E. Gregory map named Jacobs Chair in 1938. (774~) It is most likely that it was named for Franklin Jacob Adams before he died; he ran cattle in the area for many years.

DeReese Nielson told the story of Adams' death on October 5, 1940: "And this Mr. Adams, he was just a tough old cowboy, and he was just the kind that everything had to go and be right. I rode with him many a year and he treated me real good. But he was really a stubborn and bull-headed old man. He just was. I come to Blanding one time and Jacob Adams took two cowboys, Clyde Lyman and Mark Goodmanson, down to their winter range to bring some calves to the [Elk] mountain. They got down to White Canyon, close to Fry Canyon, and they camped on the east side of White Canyon [at Duckett Crossing]. The next morning there was a big flood in the canyon.

They had to get across some way and Jacob Adams told Clyde Lyman, 'Clyde, you take your horse and make 'im go across that flood and we'll bring the mules right behind ya.' And Clyde tried to make his horse go in the water and it wouldn't.

"Adams said, 'Mark, make your mule go over. That mule will go over there.' It was a terrible flood, rocks and mud, and everything going down the creek. Mark couldn't make his mule go in the creek, so Jacob Adams said, 'Boy, what'n the hell is wrong with you?' He was on a big horse and I remember this horse and they called him 'Sam.' And Jacob got on this horse and he took him to the edge of the water and then he hung the spurs to 'im and the horse jumped in the water and the rocks and the mud was rollin' down there and it took him down the creek. And these two boys, they was young boys and they didn't know what to do. So they started following him down the creek. And a hundred yards down the creek, the horse got out. And they could see Adams but there was nothing they could do.

"So one of the boys went back to Kigalia on Elk Mountain. There was a telephone there. He called Blanding for some help and they sent help out there. I went with them and we went down that canyon in the night looking for Mr. Adams, after the floods had gone down. One of the gentlemen from Blanding, his name was Charlie Saubs, went about five miles down White Canyon. He found his body washed to the side of the creek.... This Clyde Lyman was a good friend of mine, and he told me in detail just what happened. This old man, he was a good old man, a good hearted old man, but he was just stubborn, just an old stubborn cowboy." (1451~)

—Stevens Knob: Carl Mahon noted that Walt Stevens (1883-1955) "spent quite a lot of time out there prospecting and trapping and exploring. He found uranium up there and he leased it to some company or sold it to some company. The story is that it has good ore all the way under it and the roof wouldn't hold up and, of course, the more they took out, the more chances of something happening. So they wanted to shoot the whole knob off of it and the government wouldn't let them and there is still a lot of ore under that. And he used to have a camp right there, close." (1272~)

Jacobs Pool: (Coconino Co., Az.) Vermilion Cliffs National Monument-Vermilion Cliffs. Emmett Hill, Az. map.

This is a large spring.

Also called The Pools. (1570~)

The Paiute name is *Timarepaxante*, or "place with a lot of Indian spinach." (82~)

The spring was discovered during the Jacob Hamblin Expedition to the Hopi in 1858. Expedition member Andrew Smith Gibbons called it Cane Spring. (714~)

Hamblin and party returned to the pools on October 26, 1859. Trip member Thales Haskel: "Brs. Hamblin, Crosby, and myself dug out and walled up this spring and named it Jacob's Pool.... Good feed and water here but not much wood." (842~)

Frederick S. Dellenbaugh of the 1871–72 Powell Expedition: "Jacob's Pools were so named because Jacob Hamblin, a sort of Mormon Leatherstocking, was one of the first and few white men who had camped beside them, and as he was always called Jacob, the pools when it was necessary to mention them were spoken of as his pools. This is the way names are fastened on a country by the first travelers through it." Dellenbaugh went on to describe the pool: "We came to Jacob's Pools, two basins, in the clay of some foothills on the right of the valley, which hold the water of a fine spring that issues just above them." (542~)

John Hanson Beadle in 1872: "The pool is a clear, cold spring, at the head of a gulch, sending out a stream the size of one's wrist, which runs two or three hundred yards down the plain before it disappears.... John D. Lee has pre-empted the pool, and has his wife Rachel living there in a sort of brush tent, making butter and cheese from a herd of twenty cows.... I found this wife at the Pool like the one at the river [Lees Ferry], favorable to the Gentiles and a disbeliever in polygamy." (170~) Lee and family called it The Pools. (294~)

Andrew Amundsen was here with Jacob Hamblin in 1873: "We got to Jacobs Poolls ... vary bad water good feed." (58~)

James S. Brown in 1875: "a desolate and forbidding place." (300~)

Minnie Peterson Brown may have called the pools Buffalo Ranch in 1884: "We went by way of Jacob's Pool or Buffalo Ranch and we saw our first buffalo there." (382~)

Herbert E. Gregory camped near the pools in 1900: "Beautifully cut up into towers, cathedrals and many great bowlders have fallen down slope and rest on pinnacles of soft rock which has been left by erosion [now called damoselles].... Pools has fairly good alkali water formerly used by Moki Indians who have built terraces here and irrigated them." (773~)

—Honeymoon Trail: This was an important stop on the trail. In 1876 George Dabling noted that Jacobs Pool was used to rest and strengthen livestock before or after crossing the Colorado River at Lees Ferry. (513~)

—Lees Ranch: (Also called Doyle's Retreat, Lee's Retreat, and Rachel's Pools.) Wesley P. Larsen noted that John D. Lee and part of his polygamist family moved to Jacobs Pool in 1872. It is believed that the stone base for the Lee home is just above the highest spring above Jacobs Pool. The home was called Rachel's House. In 1873 Lee and family were forced to abandon the home when the military came looking for Lee for his part in the Mountain Meadows massacre. (52~, 1140~)

Charles Kelly noted that Rachel had been brought up by Lee from the age of five. He married her at age fourteen and she became one of his favorite wives, living with him at Lees Ferry and Jacobs Pools. (1160~)

John D. Lee described building his home at the pools on May 27, 1872: "We commenced building a Shelter to shield us from the burning Elements of the Sun, Rachel Andora, and Amorah and I pining and setting the posts ready to receive the willows, while James and the little Boys were cutting and hauling the willows, and my daughter Amorah weaving the willows in to form the sides." (388~) Lee would later build a stone house with two bedrooms and a kitchen. (170~)

—Rock House: This stone house, still standing below the lower springs, was built by John W. Young for use as a line camp in the 1880s. Wesley P. Larsen noted that some of the stones from Rachel's House were used to build Young's rock house. (1140~, 1787b~)

Oscar R. Garrett in 1912: "I come to a watering place for a bunch of cattle.... There is a deserted one-story one-room stone house here well preserved ... while one hundred feet distant on the northwest is a reservoir nearly full of water. At the upper northeastward corner sets a large wooden tank trough for the cattle. A three-inch iron pipe runs a small stream into this tank." (337~)

The house is covered with inscriptions that include Roy Frank, May 12th, 1910; Mabel Cook, Alice Crandell Woodruff, July 4, 1918; and H.B. Spencer, March 7, 1926. (SAPE.)

Jacobs Reservoir: (Garfield Co.) Dixie National Forest-Aquarius Plateau. Jacobs Reservoir map.

Also called Jacobs Lake.

Scott Robinson in 1941: "It was built by a man by the name of Jacobs who ranched there and ran sheep using this reservoir for watering purposes and also irrigation." (2053~) Charles Kelly noted that this was Reuben and John C. Jacobs. They had a ranch near Torrey. (1047~) Edson Alvey: "a large snow-fed lake enlarged by a dam built by John Jacobs." (55~) The dam was built in 1900. (2051~)

Jacobs Spring: (San Juan Co.) Mancos Mesa-Cedar Canyon. Mancos Mesa map.

Also called Zane Grey Tank. (761~)

Val Dalton, Sandy Johnson, and Carl Mahon noted that the Jacobs Spring marked on the map is not correct. There is no spring there; it is a very large tank or pothole that has been called Janes Tank (also called Jane Tank) for many years by cattlemen. The tank and a nearby overhang were the headquarters for cowboys on Mancos Mesa. (517~, 1002~, 1272~)

Carl Mahon: "There was an old mule and whenever she came up missing, wherever they were camped, they soon found out that they could find old Jane down at this tank, so they just named it Janes Tank." (1272~)

Charles L. Bernheimer in 1929: "a waterhole about 10 feet square with a squawking frog whom we moved ... the hole was very deep." (218~) Bernheimer provided perhaps the first description of the "Neon" effect: "A stone thrown into the [Janes Tank] pool threw curious ripple shadows against the back wall of the hole." (218~) From his writing, Bernheimer implied that the Janes Tank name was in use before 1910.

Eric Bayles told this story about cowboys Harrison Oliver and his son, Erwin: "Harrison was kind of a little short fellow, and Erwin was big and tall.... Harrison come in early one day choking to death and went up there and crawled in [Janes] tank and got a drink, and when Erwin come home, back to Janes Tank, he just started supper and tended stuff and wondered where his dad was. Finally he went to get some water and there wasn't no bucket, so he went up there and his dad was in the tank, been in there all afternoon. He said, 'Hell, kid, took you long enough to get here'! He was too short and he couldn't get out of the tank"! (168~)

—Jacobs Spring: The real Jacobs Spring is on the south side of the canyon one mile downcanyon from Janes Tank and is several hundred feet up the hillside. There are a set of old watering troughs here. Franklin Jacob Adams ran livestock in the area. (1002~)

Jacobs Tanks: (Kane Co.) Paria Canyon-Vermilion Cliffs Wilderness Area-East Clark Bench-Highway 89. Glen Canyon City map.

The tanks are a series of large potholes in a beautiful setting of sublime slickrock. (SAPE.) They were probably named for Jacob Hamblin. (See Jacob Hamblin Arch.)

Jacobs Valley: (Garfield Co.) Dixie National Forest-Boulder Mountain. Jacobs Reservoir map.

(See Jacobs Reservoir for name derivation.)

—Stringham Pasture: This is at the north end of Jacobs Valley. Dunk Taylor noted that the Stringham family had a dairy here in the summers in the early years. (1865~)

Jahu Flat: (Wayne Co.) Fishlake National Forest-Thousand Lake Mountain. Flat Top map.

Correctly spelled Jehu Flat.

Guy Pace noted that Jehu John Blackburn (1824-1879) and his son, Jehu Thomas Blackburn (1848-1931), were early ranchers. (1497~, 388~)

Jailhouse Rock: (Wayne Co.) Capitol Reef National Park-South Desert. Fruita NW map.

Also called Court House. (1657~)

Guy Pace noted that this was named by Cass Mulford. He caught wild horses here. (1497~)

—Mining Road: This road, built in the mid-1900s, goes from the Hartnet Road west down the cliffs to Jailhouse Rock. It was initially a stock trail. (1497~)

—Temple Rock: (Also called The Steeple.) (1119~, 1401~) This small tower is one and one-half miles west-northwest of Jailhouse Rock (at elevation 5987T). (745~)

Jail Rock: (San Juan Co.) Great Sage Plain-Dry Valley. Hatch Rock map.

Faun McConkie Tanner: "In Dry Valley there is one dome rock called Jail Rock (there were a number of these dome-like rocks which have water in them). They were well known to cowboys and ranchers. In some, such as Jail Rock, it was necessary to have help to get in and out of the hole in the rock. One of the Dry Valley ranchers one day wanted to go to Moab. His wife objected. The husband then found one of these water holes that would keep his wife under control, yet furnish water to slake her thirst, while he went to town to savor the beverage at the local saloon. He dropped her into one of these tanks, and from that time forward it has been called Jail Rock." (1855~)

Pete Steele embellished the story: "John Jackson ... would go to town to get drunk and party with the boys. Before he left, he'd drop his wife in there with a little groceries and water, and he'd go to town, and the cowboys riding by would hear somebody screaming and ranting and raving and they'd go up there 't the top of the rock and look down in there and there would be the wife. 'What's the matter'? 'I'm out of food and water. And that old son of a bitch is gone'! So the cowboys would drop some more food and water into it and ride on. They didn't want to get crossways of John Jackson." (1821~)

Otho Murphy added to the story: "Jug Rock [Jail Rock] was so named because of its unusual appearance. A lone rock, setting out there in the desert sands, which nature had hewn with a deep jug-like tank halfway up the side...."

It was later re-named Jail Rock, after a couple of unusual happenings took place there. The first one was when a sheriff's posse was chasing a group of five outlaws, capturing three of them and lowered them into the jug for safe keeping while they rounded up the other two.... Later, a certain local cowboy used this same rock to hide his wife and children in when he went into town for supplies and a little red-eye. One time he left them there for three days while he was in town on a drunken spree." (1420~)

An unnamed source changed the story just a bit, noting that Cowboy John "was riding by the hole rock one day wondering how to get away [from his wife and kids] for a short spell when he got the big plan.... And spurring his horse he rode into camp shouting, 'Come on honey, the redskins are coming!'.... John led his family to the rock and lowered them in the hole ... then chuckling all the way he headed for town and the nearest drink ... it was several days later before he sobered up enough to remember his family in the rock. With some misgivings he rode back and called to them. He was answered with a shot. For two days he pleaded and begged but his wife answered only with a shot.... When at last she decided she had pushed luck far enough she tossed her gun up to John and allowed him to help her out of the hole.... Fellow cowboys hearing about the incident howled and promptly dubbed the rock 'Jailhouse Rock.'" (1560~)

Jake Hollow: (Garfield Co.) Dixie National Forest-Escalante Mountains-North Creek. Griffin Point map.
The lower canyon contains a no-longer-used stock pond and other water diversions.
Edson Alvey noted that Jacob "Jake" Butler was an early Escalante stockman. (55~, 1346~)
Inscriptions include Reed Wooley, 7/17/39. (SAPE.)

Jakes Knoll: (Wayne Co.) Awapa Plateau-Big Hollow. Jakes Knoll map. (9,079')
Thaine Taylor: "[Jake White] lived over here in Lyman. He had sheep and he had a camp down right under the knoll. He used it so much that everyone just called it Jakes Knoll." (1868~)
Alfonzo Taylor told the story of moving several hundred sheep from Hanksville to the Awapa Plateau for Jake White: "Then me and Jake's boy, Orrin, drove them sheep from Hanksville. Of course we didn't do it all in a day. We took the sheep and went out there to the end of Big Holler and started to lamb those sheep. That was in the last part of May and that is the only knoll in the area that has any quakies [aspens] for building a corral. We went up there and cut quakies and built a corral and used it to catch the lambs and to dock them. We camped there for a week. I

think we had about eight hundred head of ewes. So, that's how Jakes Knoll got its name." (1914~)

Jarvis Peak: (Washington Co.) Beaver Dam Mountains-Blakes Lambing Grounds. Jarvis Peak map. (6,529')
Zora Smith Jarvis noted that George Jarvis (1823-1913) was a Dixie pioneer in 1861. (958~) His son, Brigham Jarvis (1850-1933), was responsible for the construction of the Jarvis Ditch in 1896. It started at the headwaters of Cottonwood Creek and ran for eighteen miles to St. George. (361~)

Jason Creek: (Sanpete Co.) Manti-LaSal National Forest-Wasatch Plateau-Horse Creek. Flagstaff Peak and Heliotrope Mountain maps.
—Jason Cabin: (Flagstaff Peak map.) The cabin is gone. There are a large, developed spring and several corrals at the site. (SAPE.)

Jasper Canyon: (Wayne Co.) Canyonlands National Park-Maze District-Land of Standing Rocks-Stillwater Canyon. Spanish Bottom map. **NO TRESPASSING.** Although this area is public property, the upper part of the canyon, from the big pour-over near the Colorado River up, has been closed by the National Park Service in order to protect its fragile environment. It is one of the few places in southern Utah that has never been grazed.
Jasper Canyon was named in the early 1960s for its jasper outcroppings by University of Utah archaeologist Dr. Dean R. Brimhall. (287~) Hazel Ekker in 1965: "We agreed with Dean who explored that first canyon east of Pete's Mesa afoot with Walter Cottam to call it Jasper Canyon because of the large beds of jasper within it." (618~)
Kent Frost called this Defiance Canyon. (697~) An article in the *San Juan Record*, April 14, 1966 related Kent's experiences: "'Defiance is a box canyon with a 300-foot waterfall at its mouth on the Green River and sheer walls at its head in Robbers Roost,' said Frost in describing the challenge that thwarted his many earlier attempts at entry.... Defiance Canyon had never been visited in modern times, until Frost figured out a complicated way to climb down into it in April of 1963, after many failed attempts. 'On that first visit, Defiance had the pure, untouched look of a place no human had previously disturbed,' Frost said. 'The desert moss crust [cryptobiotic soil] on the ground was unbroken. There were no large animal tracks. The only signs of life were birds, a few rodents and lizards. There were remnants of prehistoric Indians camped there, also.'" (1429~, 697~)
In 1964 Rosalie Goldman joined Frost on a trip to the canyon. She described his first descent: "Finally, he

[Frost] appeared one day at another new spot on the rim, alone but equipped with climber's gear—pitons, a ring and rope. The wall seemed to offer a switchback route, if he could pass an overhang. He let himself down on his rope, negotiated the overhang and found the rest of the way so quickly he was at the bottom in twenty minutes. Twenty minutes for a canyon that had resisted him for years." Goldman went on to describe the canyon: "Desert varnish made bold vertical stripes on the pink sandstone. We admired the graceful spires that rose fifty feet and more from the floor.... There were three verdant springs along the way. As we clambered along, the canyon widened to a quarter of a mile in some places, where vast cottonwood trees shaded banks that sloped down to the thickets of tamarisk and willow." (735~)

Francis M. Bishop of the 1871–72 Powell Expedition camped near the mouth of Jasper Canyon and in an apparently reflective mood wrote: "I would you could see some of the beautiful things that are here in this eternal solitude—but once fore [the 1869 Powell Expedition] ever startled by the voice of humanity. Lying here scorched by the fire's heat of summer, frozen and chilled by the bitter tempests of winter, scenes of wonderful beauty and sublimity grown old.... All these great mountains must fall, must crumble, and on to the sea." (236~)

The Powell Expedition spent a day here. Some of the members climbed to the rim and left an inscription reading "CEEX 1871." Expedition members called themselves the Colorado Exploring Expedition. (1115~, SAPE.)

Jayi Canyon: (Coconino Co., Az.) Navajo Indian Reservation-Navajo Creek. Chaiyahi Flat and Chaiyahi Rim SW, Az. maps.

Two similar name derivations are given.

First, in Navajo history Blind Salt Clansman is credited with being the first Navajo to discover Rainbow Bridge, sometime between 1863 and 1868. In 1908 he informed trading post owner Louisa Wetherill of its existence, leading to its "discovery" by Euroamerican explorers in 1909. His Navajo name was *Jaa'í Biye'* (Jayi Begay) or "Son of Mr. Ears." (975~, 1231~)

Second, James H. Knipmeyer: "The Navajo word *jaa'í* also refers to the white man's coffee pot, the handle resembling an 'ear.' One source says that somewhere in the Jayi drainage is a formation known as Coffee Pot Rock." (1116~)

Charles L. Bernheimer in 1921: "We are to reach Navaho Canyon for camp tonight at a place Wetherill pronounced as 'Jay-I.'" (218~)

Jeffery Reservoir: (Sevier Co.) San Rafael Swell-Last Chance Desert-Temple Wash. Solomons Temple map. Also spelled Jeffry Reservoir.

Garn Jefferies noted that his grandfather, Thomas Jeffery, had the pond built back in the old days. (959~)

Jeffery Well: (Emery Co.) San Rafael Desert-Blackburn Draw. Gilson Butte map.

The well was drilled by the Des Moines Oil Company in 1912. (641~) It was initially known as the Tasker Well for Green River resident and oil drill operator Charles P. Tasker. (1781~) A Star Rig, the largest oil rig available at the time, was hauled to the well site by ten teams of horses. (1931~)

Two name derivations are given.

First, Alvin Robison noted that the well was named for Orrin Jeffery: "They were cattle people from the upper end of Wayne County." (1642~)

Second, Barbara Ekker: "[The well] was named for Alford Jeffery of Salina who was a sheep man with his base ranch at the base of Thousand Lake Mountain. He came to Burdell 'Dell' Mecham with a proposition. Jeffery would put a water pump on a well on Dell's homestead if he could have the privilege of watering his sheep west of the well. Dell would retain the right to use the equipment to pump water for his sheep. So in early spring after the snow was gone they started pumping water for the sheep at the Flat Tops. The well was 450 ft. deep and the engine that Jeffery brought proved to be too small. Clive Mecham had to go back to Hanksville and bring out a Fordson tractor to run the pump. This was in 1930." (606~)

Garn Jefferies: "They put a pump with a little platform there and we'd drive a car up on the platform and the hind wheels would turn the pump." (959~)

—CCC Camp: This side (satellite) camp, associated with the CCC camp in Green River, was at Jeffery Well. They built what was then called the Flat Butte [Flat Top] Truck Trail, which connected the Green River-Hanksville road and the Robbers Roost road. (1779~)

—Henry Mountain Buffalo Herd: Barbara Ekker: "Buffalo were planted at Robbers Roost in April of '41 by the Fish and Game Club in Price, Utah. There were 18 two year old cows and 3 bulls from Yellowstone National Park. The animals were transported in individual crates and released at Jeffery Well near the Flat Tops north of the famed Robbers Roost. The bulls headed north in the fall of '41—headed back home. A second trip to Yellowstone to get five more bulls was in April '42. The herd migrated south across the Burr Desert to the Henry Mountains. The first hunt was in 1950." (606~, 1748~)

Jekes Hole: (San Juan Co.) Black Mesa-Cottonwood Wash. Black Mesa Butte map.

This is misspelled on the map. (See Zekes Hole.)

Jennings Wash: (Washington Co.) Zion National Park-Coalpits Wash. The Guardian Angels and Springdale West maps.

Henry Jennings (1812-1876) arrived in Rockville in 1862. (462~, 2053~)

Jenny Canyon: (Emery Co.) Beckwith Plateau-Elliott Mesa-Price River. Jenny Canyon map.

This was most likely named for a Jenny, or mule.

Jensen Canyon: (Sevier Co.) Fishlake National Forest-Sevier Plateau-Sevier River. Annabella map.

Several Jensen families lived in Elsinore in the early years. Jens Iver Jensen (1846-1936) was the earliest, arriving in 1874. (954~)

Jensen Seep: (Emery Co.) San Rafael Swell-South Salt Wash. Short Canyon map.

Ray Wareham noted that this is correctly called Justensen Seep, named for a ranch family from Castle Valley. (1967~)

Jericho Ridge: (Iron Co.) Cedar Breaks National Monument-Cedar Breaks. Navajo Lake map.

—Wall of Jericho: (Also called Walls of Jericho.) This is at the upper end of Jericho Ridge. Robert H. Vreeland noted that geologist Frederick Pack thought the opening looked like a gateway in an artificial wall. (1956~)

Jerrys Flat: (Emery Co.) San Rafael Swell-Cliff Dweller Flat. Drowned Hole Draw map.

—Jerry Flat Reservoir: This stock reservoir is on the northwest end of Jerrys Flat (immediately south of elevation 6525). It was built in 1960. (1551~)

Jessies Twist: (Emery Co.) San Rafael Desert-Ninemile Wash. Jessies Twist map.

This section of the now abandoned highway from Hanksville to Green River was named for Jesse Knight. Ted Ekker: "Prior to the road going down Jessies Twist, it went to the north and hit the San Rafael River. There is a kind of a bench that runs all of the way around to the San Rafael River. Where the Interstate [70] goes now was probably the original road to Hanksville, the old wagon road. It went right straight out through the Blue Country, turned to the south on the east side of the San Rafael [Reef], went to where Hatts have their ranch right now, turned and went out towards the Reef and then along the Reef. And the purpose of that was to stay out of the sand as much as they could. The old freighters and the cattlemen and sheepmen that traded across the desert stayed closer to the Reef because there wasn't that much sand

there and they could make a better road. And up until the automobile days it was used. Then along comes Jesse. He said: 'I know an easier way to get down off of that rim. We'll just go right straight south and I'll build a road down off that rim.' And that is how Jessies Twist got its name." (623~)

Jet Basin: (Wayne Co.) Henry Mountains-Table Mountain-Coaly Wash. Dry Lakes Peak map.

Also called Blue Basin (925~) and Jet Basin (1055~).

Jet is a mineral found in coal beds. It looks like black obsidian; it has a smooth surface that breaks conchoidally and it is often carved and polished into jewelry. The largest jet deposit in the nation is here. (567~, 604~)

—Kell Mine: In the mid-1920s Jack Kell had a jet mine in the basin. It was in use for just a couple of years. No signs of the mine remain. (1055~, SAPE.)

Jewkes Hollow: (Emery Co.) Wasatch Plateau-Castle Valley. The Cap and Castle Dale maps.

Samuel R. Jewkes (1823-1900) and family arrived in Orangeville in 1878. They are credited with bringing both the first threshing machine and gristmill to Castle Valley. (710~)

Joseph H. Jewkes: "One morning Sam R. was putting lumber on the head blocks to square it up.... He pressed the lever which turned on the power and started the saw, not knowing that his little son, Sam, was lying 'Belly Boost' across the belt. I was just underneath the belt but could do nothing to prevent the accident as it happened so suddenly. As soon as the water was turned on, Sam R. noticed the boy, but it was too late to prevent his being hurled through the air for about forty feet.... Sam R. ran and picked up his son whose head was mashed flat like two hands pressed together.... In three days, without medical attention, he was walking around completely healed through the power of the priesthood and the faith of his parents." (982~)

Jim Larsen Reservoir: (Wayne Co.) Dixie National Forest-Boulder Mountain-Spring Branch. Blind Lake map.

Dwight Williams noted that Jim Larsen built the reservoir in about 1900. (2013~)

Jim Little Canyon: (Uintah Co.) Uintah and Ouray Indian Reservation-Willow Creek. Big Pack Mountain NW map.

Uintah Ute Jim Little and his wife, Carrie, lived in the area in the early days. (388~)

Inscriptions include a very old series that includes the initials JJ and possibly the date 1811. (SAPE.) (See Appendix Two—Old Trappers' Trail.)

Jimmie Canyon: (Garfield Co.) GSCENM-Escalante Mountains-Dry Creek. Pine Lake and Henrieville maps. Ralph Chynoweth noted that this is a name from the early days. (425~)

—Davies Mine: This is on the upper west side of Jimmie Canyon (immediately south of elevation 6998 on the Pine Lake map). It was probably started by James Davies of Escalante and was active in 1952–53. (570~)

—Pollock Mine: This is on the upper west side of Jimmie Canyon (one-eighth mile east-northeast of elevation 6998 on the Pine Lake map). Almon H. Thompson of the 1871–72 Powell Expedition: "Found a seam of coal 2 feet wide in the cliffs." (1877~) This was what would become the Pollock Mine in the 1920s. (570~)

Jimmy Keen Flat: (Grand Co.) Manti-LaSal National Forest-LaSal Mountains. Warner Lake map.
Bathalee Lawley: "Above Castle Valley and the Pinhook battleground is an area called Jimmy Keen Flat. James [Murry Stocks, 1890-1953] had homesteaded there in his early years. His former homestead bears his nickname, 'Jimmy Keen.'" (2026~)

Jims Farm: (Sevier Co.) San Rafael Swell-Deer Peak. Johns Peak and Willow Springs maps.
Jim Crane: "It was a grazing area used by somebody named Jim. I don't think anybody ever homesteaded it. I think it was kind of a little gag. To the old-timers traveling through there it looked like a farm. It's flat and it's open and to a cowboy it looked like a farm." (478~) Carrie Lou Gremel: "That was Elliot and Wanda Krantz. Their son was Jim." (780~)

Jim Wilson Reservoir: (Emery Co.) Cedar Mountain-Buckhorn Flat. Buckhorn Reservoir map.
James Wilson ran livestock in the area in the early 1900s. (388~)

J J Reservoir: (Emery Co.) Castle Valley-Hadden Flat. Buckhorn Reservoir map.
This is a still-used stock reservoir. (SAPE.)
A rancher named Jenkins used the pond. (1931~)

J L Eddy: (Grand Co.) Colorado River-Jackson Hole. Gold Bar Canyon map.
James H. Knipmeyer speculates: "The name may have a connection with a test well drilled by the Mid-West Oil Exploration Company during the 1920s. Soon after, another well was drilled across the river for Snowden and McSweeny. Both wells were in the John L. (J.L.?) Shafer Dome (structural dome). A river 'eddy' would be a good place for a boat landing." (1116~)

Job Corps Pond: (Emery Co.) Cedar Mesa-Buckhorn Flat. Buckhorn Reservoir map.
This is a large, still-used stock reservoir. (SAPE.)

Jobs Head: (Washington Co.) Zion National Park-Firepit Knoll. The Guardian Angels map. (7,233') PRIVATE PROPERTY.
Also called Jebs Head.
Zion National Park Superintendent Paul R. Franke noted in 1958 that the name is from early settlers who referred to the bible for the name. (1931~)

—Windy Peak: This is one mile east of Jobs Head (at elevation 7888). It was named by Courtney Purcell. (1591~)

Joe and His Dog: (Emery Co.) San Rafael Swell-Sids Mountain-Saddle Horse Canyon. The Blocks map. (6,690')
This fin of sandstone at the crest of a ridge was named for early Castle Valley and San Rafael Swell pioneer Joe Swasey (1861-1930). Stella McElprang: "The life story of Joseph Swasey is very colorful and interesting. He feared nothing, (was not reckless, however). He was capable of handling situations that might cause most of us to lose our nerve. He was a successful horse raiser and prospector, having located some very valuable mineral mining claims." (1330~)
One story is told of Joe roping a wildcat and attempting to tame it. (511~)

Joe Hole Wash: (Emery Co.) San Rafael Swell-Lost Spring Wash. Chimney Rock and Dry Mesa maps.
Also called Joes Hole Wash.
(See Joe and his Dog for name derivation.)

—Joes Holes: (Chimney Rock map.) A constructed stock trail leads to two large ponds in Joe Hole Wash. (SAPE.) In the early days William A. Thayn ran sheep in the Joe Hole Wash area. (1974~)

—Rancho Not So Grande: PRIVATE PROPERTY. This historic ranch on Joe Hole Wash is just south of the Green River Cutoff Road (one-quarter mile south of elevation 5307 on the Dry Mesa map). Wayne and Betty Smith bought the land from a Mr. Nottingham in the early 1940s and built a small cabin here. Betty is credited with naming the ranch: "Dick and Edith Gardner—we called her 'Pete,'—came from California during the uranium boom and they went out there and staked a claim at El Rancho and they lived in a tent. We had a cabin out there and so they decided that they wanted to built this rock house. All of us got together, Wayne and I and Pete and Dick, and gathered rocks, and gathered rocks for months and finally had enough that we thought we'd start

construction ... and we finally got it together." (1764~)
The rock building still stands.

Betty Smith's granddaughter, Donna Dinkens, told a story about her and Betty standing in the doorway of the rock house at Rancho Not So Grande during a storm. A bolt of lightning went right between them and knocked the back wall out of the house! (1764~)

Betty Smith, at age eighty-four, related this poem about the ranch:

> El Rancho, you are the sweetest place this side of heaven to me.
>
> The Chimney Rock and cedar tree.
>
> When I die I want to rest upon the Cedar Mountain so high,
>
> 'Cause that's where God will look for me.

Betty Smith: "I wrote a note [that we posted in the house] that said: 'this is a fun place to come and stop and get out of the weather and stay overnight if you need to, but please leave it as you find it.' Nobody every did. They just make a big mess." (1764~)

The final insult to the ranch happened recently. Betty Smith: "We went there one time, Wayne and I, and there was two big semi-trucks and two men with chain saws and you know there's a little cabin to the side of the rock house? They were gonna saw it in two and take it"! (1764~)

At the age of 80 Betty starting writing this poem. She has added to it every year:

> I say I'm Old and Ruff and Dirty and Tough
>
> and I never can get drunk enough.
>
> When I was 80 I was an old lady.
>
> When I was 81 I wasn't having much fun.
>
> When I was 82 I had to tend too [to Betty's husband Wayne].
>
> When I was 83, Wayne had died and I just had to tend to me.
>
> When I was 84 I didn't want to do it any more.
>
> When I was 85 I was still alive.
>
> When I was 86 I was in a Hell of a fix.
>
> When I was 87 I was supposed to be in hell or heaven.
>
> Now I'm 88, I should have met St. Peter at the Pearly Gates!
>
> When I was 89 I went shopping up at Penny and Duane's Mellon Vine [the local grocery store].
>
> When I was 90 I went to the Cowboy Caucus [a yearly event in Green River] and
>
> I said, 'Come on all you cowboys if you want to flirt
>
> Here comes Betty Smith in a hobbled skirt.
>
> You can hug her and kiss her as much as you please,

> but you can't get her hobbles above her knees'!
>
> When I was 91 and I got in my pretty red Lincoln Town Car
>
> and picked up a man and dragged main and had fun!
>
> When I was 92, I went to the cemetery and waited for you
>
> to come and dig a hole and throw me in.
>
> When I was 93, I just had to tend me.
>
> Now I'm 94 and I don't want to do it any more.
>
> On July 20 [2009] I'll be ninety-five and I
>
> hope I won't still be alive.
>
> I'm now ninety-six and I'm in a heck of a fix.
>
> Now that I'm ninety-seven nobody wants me in heaven or hell or in the cemetery, so I don't know what to do. (1764~)

Joe Hutch Canyon: (Emery Co.) West Tavaputs Plateau-Desolation Canyon. Chandler Falls map.
(See Joe Hutch Creek for name derivation.)
—Three Islands: These are the three small islands just above Joe Hutch Canyon Rapids. (833~)

Joe Hutch Creek: (Grand Co.) Uintah and Ouray Indian Reservation-East Tavaputs Plateau-Desolation Canyon. Moonwater Point and Chandler Falls maps.
Waldo Wilcox: "I think I'm the only man left who knows that. Joe Hutch came from back east somewhere. He had tuberculosis. He was looking for a dry place to settle because that was supposed to be good for tuberculosis. Whether he died there or someplace else, I don't know. He is probably buried there someplace." (2011~)
—Cow Swim: This crossing of the Green River is near the mouth of Joe Hutch Creek. The cowboys at McPherson Ranch, one mile downriver, used to swim their cattle across the river here. (200~) Waldo Wilcox: "If the river was high, if you could cross anywhere, that was the place. It was just like a raceway there. If you fell off your horse, you'd still be floating! It was called Joe Hutch Ford and Joe Hutch Bottom on both sides." (2011~)
—Joe Hutch Rapid: (Also called Ledge Rapid.) This is on the Green River at the mouth of Joe Hutch Canyon (Chandler Falls map).

Joe Jensen Spring: (Emery Co.) Cedar Mountain-Bob Hill Flat. Bob Hill Knoll map.
This spring rarely has a flow of water. (SAPE.)
Joseph Wilford Jensen (1885-1919) was an early resident of Cleveland. (388~)

Joe Lay Reservoir: (Garfield Co.) Dixie National Forest-Escalante Mountains-North Creek. Barker Reservoir map.
Nethella Griffin Woolsey noted that Joe Lay moved to the Escalante area in 1884. (2051~)

—Old Lady Young Ranch: Pratt Gates noted that this was one-eighth mile south of Joe Lay Reservoir on what they called Old Lady Young Flats. (709~) A campground is now near the ranch site.

Joe Lott Creek: (Piute and Sevier Counties.) Fishlake National Forest-Tushar Mountains-Clear Creek Canyon. Mount Belknap, Mount Brigham, and Marysvale Canyon maps.

Also called South Joe Lott Creek.

(See Clear Creek Canyon—Lott Ranch for name derivation.)

Joe Lott Creek: (Sevier Co.) Fishlake National Forest-Pavant Range-Clear Creek Canyon. Marysvale Canyon map.

Also called North Joe Lott Creek.

(See Clear Creek Canyon—Lott Ranch for name derivation.)

—Alma Christiansen Trail: This is the "Pack" trail that goes north between Joe Lott and Whiskey Spring creeks. Alma Christiansen had a farm at the bottom of the trail from 1917 to 1944. (1551~)

Joes Tank: (Coconino Co., Az.) Vermilion Cliffs National Monument-Paria Plateau-Sand Hills. The Big Knoll, Az. map.

—Joes Ranch: (Also called Joseph Hamblin's Cow Camp [1027a~] and The Ranch.) Joseph Hamblin (1854-1924), a son of Jacob Hamblin (See Jacobs Pools), established a ranch here in 1884. Neil M. Judd in 1920: "Joseph Hamblin waters his cattle from a reservoir that catches such rains as fall on 15 acres of bare white sandstone." (1027a~)

In 1926 John Adams bought the ranch. He sold it to A.T. Spence in 1941 (another source said 1944). Merle Findlay bought the ranch in 1944 and sold it to John Rich in 1962. The Two Mile Corporation bought the ranch in 1980. (1083~) It is now owned by The Nature Conservancy.

Joes Valley: (Emery Co.) Manti-LaSal National Forest-Wasatch Plateau. Joes Valley Reservoir map.

Three stories are given. The first is the most reliable.

Evelyn Peacock Huntsman: "The Spanish name for the valley was St. Joseph's Valley which has become Joe's Valley." (931~)

Second, Mrs. Emeline Cox Jewkes noted that in the early days a group of Mormon settlers saw a big Indian chasing a little Indian into a cave. The big Indian then left and the Mormons helped the little Indian. This Indian became a friend of the Mormons and his name was Indian Joe. (1330~)

Third, Wesley R. Curtis noted that Joe Swasey (1861-1930) was one of four brothers who settled in the valley

in 1874. The Swaseys were famous for their courage and their tall tales. Curtis: "Sid [Swasey] had engaged a young bear in hand-to-hand combat within the confines of a small log cabin at Joe's Valley. On that memorable occasion, Charlie [Swasey] had his money riding on the bear. He figured it to be a safe bet, but knowing Sid as well as he did, he felt it was only prudent to issue the ground rules as he locked the cabin door behind his brother; 'Fight 'em fair Sid! Fight 'im fair.'" (511~) The Swasey family had interests in Joes Valley starting in the late 1870s. (931~) But, the name is shown on the Lieutenant George M. Wheeler Survey map of 1872–73. (M.76.)

—Joes Valley Reservoir: Construction on the dam started in 1963 and was completed in 1965. (1747~)

Joe Wilson Canyon: (San Juan Co.) Dry Valley-Hatch Wash. La Sal West, La Sal Junction, and Hatch Rock maps.

In the early 1880s brothers Ervin and Joe Wilson, young cowboys from Moab, were attacked by Indians while looking for stray horses on the southern slopes of the La Sal Mountains. Joe was badly injured, but escaped. (1526~, 1530~)

Lloyd Holyoak knew Joe and Ervin Wilson: "They were running their milk cows up on Wilson Mesa. Joe and Ervin Wilson were in charge of them. The Indians attacked and they tried to outrun them. Joe's horse was shot out from under him. Joe decided that he was going to play dead and told Ervin to go to town for help. So Ervin took off and Joe laid there and an Indian came by and shot him in the head with the rifle and figured he was dead. Ervin got some help and came back and Joe was still alive. He lost his left eye." (906~)

John Thomas Farrer, Sr.: "That was one of the worst sights I ever saw and to recover without the aid of a doctor. They doctored his wounds with cactus 'Prickle Pears,' as we termed it, that grows on the desert." (634~)

—Wilson Arch: (La Sal West map.) Joe Wilson homesteaded here. The early name was Second Looking Glass, the "second" reference being to nearby Looking Glass Arch. While drawing maps, the USGS mistakenly renamed it Window Arch. Local residents protested, forcing the USGS to change the name back to Wilson Arch. (1855~, 2023~, 2068~)

—Joe Wilson Ranch: Lloyd Holyoak noted that the ranch was in Joe Wilson Canyon near Wilson Arch: "I remember as a kid stopping there when we went through with the wagon to water the horses because there was a spring. That was Joe's cabin. He lived there for a long time. I remember him living there as a little teeny boy, when we went to Monticello several times. So he must've moved out of there probably around, oh, maybe '38, '39, somewhere in that neighborhood." (906~)

Johansen Pond: (Emery Co.) Castle Valley-Black Hills. Hadden Holes map.

Edward A. Geary noted that Peter "Pete Joe" Johansen (1861-1936) homesteaded in Huntington Canyon in 1889. He later made Castle Dale his base of operations for raising cattle. (710~, 369~)

John Allen Bottom: (Garfield Co.) Dixie National Forest-Boulder Mountain-Deep Creek. Posy Lake map.

Edson Alvey noted that John Allen moved to the Escalante area in the late 1870s (55~, 2051~) and had a ranch here (1346~).

John Brown Creek: (Grand Co., Utah and Mesa Co., Colo.) La Sal Mountains-Kirks Basin. Utah maps: Dolores Point South and Dolores Point North. Colorado map: Gateway.

Joe Taylor: "There was a man named John E. Brown (1861-1951) and he had a ranch there. He had the Kirks Basin Ranch and he had Sinbad and he was a big cattleman." (1866~) James H. Knipmeyer noted that John E. Brown was in this area from 1897 to about 1910. (1115~) (See Browns Rim.)

John Cameron Troughs: (Garfield Co.) Dixie National Forest-Rock Canyon. Haycock Mountain map.

This large spring was once developed. (SAPE.)

John Cameron (1847–1926) was a Panguitch pioneer. He ran livestock in the area. (388~)

John Henry Canyon: (Kane Co.) GSCENM-Kaiparowits Plateau-Warm Creek. Fourmile Bench, Nipple Butte, and Tibbet Bench maps.

Also called Middle Warm Creek. (1931~)

—John Henry Spring: (Tibbet Bench map.) This is a large, wash-bottom spring. (SAPE.)

—Kaiparowits Coal Field: (Proposed.) A coal mine, part of the Kaiparowits Power Project, would have been located in and around John Henry Bench. (920~) The mine was stopped by the proclamation of Grand Staircase-Escalante National Monument in 1996.

John McDonald Hole: (Emery Co.) Castle Valley-Short Canyon Reservoir. Short Canyon map.

Lee Mont Swasey: "John McDonald was a wood cutter in the early 1900s and that's who that was named after." (1853~)

Johnnies Hole: (San Juan Co.) Nokai Dome-Castle Creek. Nokai Dome map.

Also called Bull Valley (1248~) and John's Hole (761~). Also spelled Johnny Hole.

The canyon was most likely named for John Ernest Adams (1866-1936). He moved to Bluff in the early 1880s. (1116~)

—Constructed Stock Trail: This very rugged and hard-to-find trail, still in use, provides access to Johnnies Hole. (168~, 517~, SAPE.) Herbert E. Gregory in 1925: "Very difficult trail into canyon." (761~)

—Windmill: The windmill near the top of the canyon was erected in the 1960s. (168~)

—Half Track: This abandoned World War Two-era half track vehicle has become a landmark on the rough road that goes from Highway 276, over the heads of Lake Canyon and Johnnies Hole, and onto Nokai Dome. It is at elevation BM4717 on the Halls Crossing NE map. Eric Bayles: "I understand it belonged to Calvin Black.... I guess they used it to haul water when they were drilling around here." (168~)

—Books: Louis L'Amour mentioned Johnnies Hole in *The Haunted Mesa*. (1336~)

Johnny Benal Canyon: (San Juan Co.) Bug Park-Montezuma Creek. Bug Canyon and Hatch Trading Post maps. Correctly spelled Johnny Benow Canyon.

—Benows Band: This is the name used in government documents for a band of Ute Indians whom, under the leadership of Johnny Benow, had a settlement at Bug Park (Bug Canyon map). In the early 1900s several ranchers complained about Benow's Band over a conflict about grazing rights. Although the Utes were the first to have livestock in Montezuma Creek, many ranchers felt that the Indians should be eliminated.

In response, another rancher, L.L. Morrison wrote: "I am well acquainted with ... John Benow, and all their band of Indians living ... in what is known as Bug Park. I consider them as good Inds. as I have ever known. I do not believe they steal a little bit. They live by working for cattlemen and what they get from their rations and sheep. They are farming a little and have goats, sheep and horses." (1602~)

Inscriptions include Allen K. Neal, 1937. (SAPE.)

Johnny Coldwater Spring: (San Juan Co.) Mancos Mesa-Cedar Canyon. Mancos Mesa map.

This is a large spring. (SAPE.)

Two name derivations are given.

First, Carl Mahon noted that Johnny Coldwater was an old Indian who camped there. (1272~)

Second, the following stories all relate to pioneer cattleman John Ernest Adams (1866-1936). He started running livestock in the area in the 1880s. Jacob R. Young: "I used to get a kick out of old John Adams. He used to take a ten pound bucket and boil a lot of potatoes. In the morning he would wrap them up in his jumper, and he would go all day. He would eat on the cold potatoes and drink cold water. If we were driving and wanted to stop and get something to eat, he would get mad and say, 'Oh, come on, let's go.' We used to call him Cold Water Johnny." (2064~)

Barbara Thompson Dorigatti: "Because John Adams always drank cold water instead of coffee when he camped with them, they nicknamed him 'Cold Water Johnny.'" (1195~)

Unattributed: "As a cowboy John was called 'cold water John' because he always kept his church's Word of Wisdom. At mealtime when the other cowboys had their coffee, he drank water." (1911~)

Erwin Oliver told a story that happened near Johnny Coldwater Spring: "I was out on Mancos Mesa near Johnny Coldwater the spring they set off the big atomic bomb in Nevada. That downwind come across the Mancos.... It was just like a big old dust cloud coming up, like a whirlwind.... And our faces and hands just burned. There were big blisters all over our faces and hands. The hair come off the horses and lots of the cattle died. Nobody ever said nothing. The government tried to cover it up for years. I was there with my dad, Harrison, and Dan and Willie Lehigh, and Old Man Cunningham and I think Brig Stevens." (1479~)

—Johnny Coldwater Canyon: The spring is in this canyon. At one time there were a couple of constructed stock ponds here; they have disappeared. It was an important watering hole for cattle. (517~, 1901~)

John R Canyon: (Kane Co.) Wygaret Terrace-Kanab Creek. Cutler Point and White Tower maps.

Also called John R Creek. (741~)

Four name derivations are given. The first is most accepted, but all three are certainly possible.

First, John R. Young (ca. 1837-1920) was the nephew of Brigham Young. He first explored the Kanab area in 1868 and visited in 1871. In 1874 Young moved to Kanab and became the president of the United Order. (1639~) George G. Mace in 1941: "Named for John R. Young who held claims there in the early settlement of Kanab." (2053~)

Second, John R. Rider was one of the first settlers of Kanab, arriving in 1870. Notably, in the early 1870s, Rider helped build a road up Kanab Canyon to Three Lakes. From there the road went up John R. Canyon, back into Kanab Canyon, and eventually to Long Valley. Later, the long detour up John R. Canyon was eliminated and a road was forced directly up Kanab Canyon. Rider, as well, located the first ditch in Kanab, and was a justice of the peace and a judge. (349~, 1639~)

Third, John R. Stewart was the head of the Co-op Stock, Horse, and Sheep Herd in 1871. (312a~)

Fourth, John R. Findlay arrived in Kanab in 1884. Findlay carried mail from Kanab to Panguitch, the route taking him right through John R. Canyon. He was also in the cattle business and became the president of the first bank in Kanab. (373~, 1639~)

Johns Canyon: (San Juan Co.) Cedar Mesa-San Juan River. Cedar Mesa South, Slickhorn Canyon East, and Goulding NE maps.

Also called Zahns Canyon. (See Zahns Bay.)

Several stories are given for the naming of Johns Canyon. The first is correct; the second and third are added for color.

First, historians for the most part agree that the canyon was named for early rancher John Ernest Adams. Lisle Adams: "Johns Canyon was named after my grandpa. His name was John Ernest Adams [1866–1936] and that's where he run cattle." (7~) Adams ran cattle in the canyon starting in the 1880s.

Doris Valle: "Bluff cattleman John [Ernest] Adams was probably the first to herd his cattle along the narrow ledge into that cow paradise. The canyon is now officially called John's Canyon. Almost certainly the name refers to Adams' time there." (1935~)

Second, Buck Lee of the nearby W-L Ranch in 1941: "This canyon was originally settled by a man by the name of [gold miner] Jim Douglas and was first called Douglas Canyon but later a geology professor from Indiana spent several summers exploring in there. The professor's first name was John but has forgotten his last name. The name of the canyon was changed from Douglas to John's Canyon." (2053~)

Third, Ann Zwinger in 1978: "Johns Canyon is named after John Oliver, who with is brother, Bill, ran cattle here in the 1930s." (2081~) Robert S. McPherson also noted that the canyon was named for John Oliver. (1336~) John Oliver did run a small trading post in Mexican Hat in the early 1920s. Charles L. Bernheimer in 1920: "a cheerful, pleasing, if filthy personality.... He had a fine head on his shoulders, though. He looked like the best looking U.S. senator and almost conversed as well, only a bit more 'rough necky.'" (218~) It is not known if he had any connection to Johns Canyon.

Several sources told about and incident that happened in Johns Canyon on February 28, 1934. DeReese Nielson:

"[Jimmy Palmer] got mixed up with a gambler in Texas and he got in trouble and this gambler had a daughter and Jimmy Palmer told this girl, 'Your dad's in trouble and he's gone to Monticello, Utah, and we've got to go up there to meet 'im.' And so this girl went with him. Then he went down on the [Navajo] reservation to Gouldings [Trading Post] and started herding sheep for [Harry] Goulding. Then Goulding told 'im to bring the sheep over into Johns Canyon. So he brought the sheep over there.

"The guy who owned Johns Canyon at the time, William Edward Oliver, had trouble with this Jimmy Palmer and told him to get out and never come back again. Jimmy Palmer got mad at him and shot him and his nephew, Norris Shumway. Then he cut off the head of Shumway with an axe. Jimmy Palmer put the old man's body in the trunk of a car and crashed it over a ledge a couple three miles outta Johns Canyon. Then the law went down there. So Jimmy Palmer took off with this girl back to Texas. The law finally caught 'im there.... And they found out then that he'd killed this girl's father, too." (1451~, 1935~)

—Constructed Stock Trail: This enters upper Johns Canyon via a short northern tributary that is between elevations 6397T and 6438T on the Cedar Mesa South map. The trail does not continue to the middle section of the canyon; there are ledges that can be hiked, but that livestock could not negotiate. (SAPE.)

—Cottoways Land: This is the large pasture area in the wide middle section of Johns Canyon (all on the Cedar Mesa South map). The name is shown on a "Map of the San Juan Oil Fields" from the early 1900s. (1859~)

—Johns Canyon Line Camp: Located at the north end of Cottoways Land, this cabin was built in the early 1900s. All that remains are a chimney and a few logs. Inscriptions include W.E., 5/11/96. This could date from the days of the cabin, but it is unclear if this is an old or new inscription. (SAPE.)

—Slickhorn Gulch Trail: (Also called Goodridge Road and Johns Canyon Trail.) This road runs from the top of the Honaker Trail generally west under the south rim of Cedar Mesa, across the middle section of Johns Canyon (Cottoways Land) to the mouth of Slickhorn Gulch. Some sections are shown as a "Foot Trail" on the maps.

Alfred Wetherill described following the trail into Johns Canyon in 1895: "As we go along the trail between the point [Cedar Mesa] and the head of the cañon, the horses have to lean a little toward the uphill side before they feel safe.... We worked our way around the fallen cliffs, with the San Juan [River] roaring along below us, and came

into the little valley of Willow Creek [Johns Canyon].... The water here was splendid and lots of it." (651~)

Botanist Alice Eastwood in the mid-1890s: "The bluff [Cedar Mesa], at the foot of which we rode for many miles before reaching Willow Creek, consists really of a series of bluffs, each receding behind its predecessor and forming a serrated chain extending for miles. Late in the afternoon we reached the head of Willow Creek [actually the middle part of Johns Canyon, or Cottoways Land], a paradise in this awful desert. For some distance from the big spring the water flows in a continuous stream, finally settling in deep pools in the rocky basin of the wash." (590~)

The trail was later improved into a road. Hugh D. Miser: "The road ... was constructed many years ago [sometime between 1908 and 1910] by E.L. Goodridge [See Mexican Hat] for the purpose of lowering drilling machinery to the bottom of the [Slickhorn] canyon, where there are large oil seeps. An engine, after being brought across the desert for a distance of more than 175 miles, (taking 30 days to haul by mule from Gallup, New Mexico) was safely taken down the canyon wall to a point within a stone's throw of the drilling site, but at that point, owing to an unfortunate accident, the engine tumbled from the road and over the cliffs to the bottom of the canyon and was thus broken beyond repair." (1370~)

The road was improved by Don Danvers in the early 1950s. He drilled two wells near the mouth of the canyon. (88~) From the mouth of Slickhorn Canyon one can still see the remnants of both the Goodridge and the Danvers roads. (838~, SAPE.)

It is noteworthy that the Slickhorn Gulch Trail follows the course of an old Indian route; many Anasazi pictographs and petroglyphs are found near it. As well, it was also used as a pack route by miners during the San Juan gold rush years of the 1890s. S.W. Honaker, one of several Honaker brothers who prospected in the area, left his name on a rock next to the old trail in about 1895. (SAPE.)

—Constructed Stock Trail: This impressive trail enters the north side of middle Johns Canyon (Cottoways Land) from Point Lookout via a short side canyon that is one-quarter mile east of elevation 6266T on the Slickhorn Canyon East map. It was built during the San Juan gold rush in the 1890s. (1451~, SAPE.) E.M. Butterworth camped in Johns Canyon in 1920 and followed the trail out of the canyon: "We spent the night in John's Canyon with one Adam Louis, a relic of the old scraps with the Utes who undoubtedly had some wonderful experiences, but who is the most magnificent liar I have ever had the pleasure to encounter.... The trail over the rim rock out of John's Canyon is very steep and dangerous but once at the [Cedar] Mesa is good going." (327~)

—Constructed Stock Trail: This rough trail enters the middle section of Johns Canyon (Cottoways Land) from its south side. The trail, vague in places, enters one-half mile west of elevation 6337T on the Cedar Mesa South map. (SAPE.) It is believed that this was the first trail used to bring stock into middle Johns Canyon.

—Constructed Stock Trail: This short trail provides access to the lower middle section of Johns Canyon. It is on the east side of the canyon one-eighth mile southwest of elevation 5152T on the Slickhorn Canyon East map. (SAPE.)

—Johns Canyon Mining Trail: (Also called Wetherill Trail.) This impressive trail enters Johns Canyon near its mouth. From the top, it starts one-eighth mile west of elevation 5185T on the Slickhorn Canyon East map. It goes southwest along a high ridge before dropping into Johns Canyon one-half mile upcanyon from its mouth. The trail then goes down Johns Canyon, exits to the west, and follows a cliff band above the San Juan River for one-quarter mile before ending at a sheer drop.

The Wetherill brothers had a placer mining operation at the mouth of Johns Canyon during the gold boom years in the 1890s. Alfred Wetherill described the trail in 1895: "A few miles down [from the top of the inner gorge of Johns Canyon], along the edge of Willow Creek Cañon [Johns Canyon], was the trail our outfit had made a few years before down to a lower level, but not all the way to the river bottom.... At the bottom of the ledge we had to fasten a rope to a chunk of slide rock, and go down the last section like circus performers.... The last fifty feet was over broken ledges and you had to edge along the rocks and grab for hand holds and places for your feet. If you kept it up long enough, you would finally reach level ground, or rocks, or 'otherwise.' This place is where we let our bunch down when we were working placer ground." (651~, 1901~)

John Wetherill called this the Bishop Trail and suggested that the trail crossed the river: "The horse trail went only to the last rim. From there we went down on ropes. We had a boat at the foot of the trail to cross the river when the spring thaws began." (1989~) The Bishop may have been Ben Bishop who was known to have been in the area in the 1890s.

—Navajo Trail: This is the name given by Stewart Aitchison to the Wetherill Trail after it crossed the San Juan River. (9~) The trail went upriver for one-half mile before

exiting by way of a large southern tributary to the top of Douglas Mesa. Al Wetherill left his name on the cliff face near the bottom of the trail. The trail itself was a difficult endeavor and one that stock did not use. In several places vertical walls were overcome with stacks of logs and crude ladders. The top of the trail exits onto Douglas Mesa a short distance south of elevation 5743 on the Goulding NE map. Today, because the ladders are gone, the lower trail is nearly impossible to follow. The upper part of the trail is still in good condition and provides access down from the top to the pasturelands in the main canyon. (838~, SAPE.)

—Sulphur Spring: This is on the east side of the San Juan River and is three miles downcanyon from the mouth of Johns Canyon (three-quarters of a mile north-northwest of elevation 4738T on the Slickhorn Canyon East map). It was noted that the spring contained hydrogen sulphide by the Kelly W. Trimble USGS Expedition of 1921. (1370~)

Johns Hole: (Emery Co.) San Rafael Swell-Slaughter Slopes. Hunt Draw, Ireland Mesa, and The Frying Pan map.

—Constructed Stock Trail: This trail, most likely just used by sheep, provided access from the Slaughter Slopes into Johns Hole. It starts three-quarters of a mile south of the very head of Ireland Mesa Canyon (one-quarter mile west-northwest of elevation 6685 on the Ireland Mesa map). (SAPE.)

Johnson Bench: (Emery Co.) Wasatch Plateau-Castle Valley. Castle Dale map.

Brothers Joseph E. Johnson (1858-1908) and Milas Edgar Johnson (1851-1933) arrived in Castle Valley in 1879. (1000~)

Johnson Bench: (Garfield Co.) Paunsaugunt Plateau-East Fork Sevier River. Wilson Peak and Bryce Canyon maps.

Joseph Hills Johnson (1866-1908): "I bought a place in Bryce Canyon and we lived there and dairied there for five or six years and most of my family were born and raised there on the ranch. We just lived there during the summer, when fall came, when school started, we moved back into town." (992~, 1346~)

Johnson Canyon: (Garfield Co.) Dixie National Forest-Paunsaugunt Plateau-Sevier River. Wilson Peak map.

(See Johnson Bench—Garfield Co. for name derivation.)

Johnson Canyon: (Kane Co.) Dixie National Forest-Long Valley-East Fork Virgin River. Long Valley Junction map. Warren M. Johnson (1838-1902) and family had a land claim here in 1875. (259~)

Johnson Canyon: (Kane Co., Utah and Coconino Co., Az.) GSCENM-Vermilion Cliffs-Kanab Creek. Utah maps: Bald Knoll, Skutumpah Creek, Pine Point, Cutler Point, Thompson Point, and Johnson Lakes. Arizona maps: Shinarump Point, Muggins Flat, Fredonia, and Clear Water Spring.

Also called Johnson Wash and Kimball Valley. (1357~) (See Johnson Town for name derivation.)

Before the first settlers arrived this was called both Hay Canyon (374~) and White Sage Creek (1800~).

The Domínguez-Escalante Expedition of 1776–77 camped near the mouth of Johnson Canyon, calling the site *Camp Santa Barbara*. (1357~) The Andrus Military Reconnaissance Expedition of 1866 called it Kanyon Ranche Kanyon. (475~)

The Utah Territorial Militia came through the area in 1869 and called it both Twelve Mile Canyon because it was twelve miles from Kanab, and Scoom Pah Canyon, a name that is now used for a tributary of Johnson Canyon. (476~)

Jesse N. Smith called it Ranch Canyon in 1870 (1775~), as did Francis M. Bishop of the 1871–72 Powell Expedition (236~). Pioneers also called it Spring Canyon or Spring Ranch Canyon. (541~, 1639~)

Inscriptions include Jack Hamblin, no date; A? Hamcluff, no date; and W.L. Cluff, Nov. th 1, 1892. (SAPE.)

—Movies: *Westward the Women*, *The Lone Ranger*, *Buffalo Bill*, and *War Drums* were filmed, in part here. A western townsite, now on PRIVATE PROPERTY, was built for the films in Johnson Canyon near the mouth of Dairy Canyon (near elevation 5348T on the Thompson Point map). (1421~, 1955~)

Johnson Creek: (Iron Co.) Fort Johnson-Cedar Valley-Rush Lake. Enoch map.

(See Enoch Town for name derivation.)

Johnson Creek: (San Juan Co.) Manti-LaSal National Forest-Abajo Mountains-Recapture Creek. Abajo Peak, Mount Linnaeus, Mancos Jim Butte, and Blanding North maps.

Ezekiel "Zeke" Johnson (1869-1957) arrived in Blanding in 1906. (1241~, 1562~)

—Johnson Creek Ditch: The ditch, started by Walter C. Lyman in 1887 and finished in 1903, ran from Johnson Creek to White Mesa near the Edge of the Cedars. A 420-foot tunnel was excavated to complete the ditch. It provided the first reliable source of water for the new town of Blanding. (1526~)

Johnson Draw: (Uintah Co.) East Tavaputs Plateau-Hill Creek. Agency Draw NW and Big Pack Mountain maps. This was most likely named for Nine Mile Canyon pioneer Don C. Johnson. (558~, 1788~)

Johnson Hole: (Kane Co.) GSCENM-Paria River. Calico Peak, Slickrock Bench, and Deer Range Point maps.

Ralph Chynoweth noted that this is a name from the old days. (425~) Cal Johnson thought, but wasn't sure, that is was named for Hart Johnson from the Tropic area. (984~)

Johnson Hollow: (Emery Co.) Cedar Mountain-Humbug Canyon. Bob Hill Knoll map.

(See Johnson Bench—Emery Co. for name derivation.)

—Winder and Weber Stock Pond: This is at the top of the southeastern fork of Johnson Hollow. Written in the concrete of the dam: "Built by ?Winder and Louis E. Weber, June 26, 1967." (SAPE.)

Johnson Hollow: (Garfield Co.) Dixie National Forest-Paunsaugunt Plateau-East Fork Sevier River. Bryce Point and Bryce Canyon maps.

(See Johnson Bench—Garfield Co. for name derivation.)

Johnson Lakes Canyon: (Kane Co.) GSCENM-Flood Canyon. Nephi Point, Pine Point, and Johnson Lakes maps.

(See Johnson Town for name derivation.)

—Lambs Point: This south-facing point stands over the west side of Johnson Lake (Johnson Lakes map). (742~)

—Needle Rock Canyon: This small northern tributary of Johnson Lakes Canyon is immediately west of Lambs Point (between elevations 5659T and 5682T on the Johnson Lakes map). (742~)

Johnson Mountain: (Washington Co.) Zion National Park-East Fork Virgin River. Springdale East map. (5,875')

Zion National Park Superintendent P.P. Patraw noted that Nephi Johnson, Sr. (1833–1919), a Virgin Town pioneer, was the first Euroamerican known to have visited Zion Canyon. The name was applied in 1934. (1931~)

Johnson Point: (Coconino Co., Az.) Glen Canyon NRA-Paria River. Lees Ferry and Navajo Bridge, Az. maps. (3,792')

Warren M. Johnson (1838–1902) operated Lees Ferry from 1876 to 1896. (2053~)

—Constructed Stock Trail: This goes up the western wall of a short drainage that is two miles west of Lees Ferry (northwest of elevation 3334T on the Lees Ferry map). Warren M. Johnson built a trail up to the point in the 1880s. (2053~, SAPE.)

Johnson Ranch: (Garfield Co.) GSCENM-Sheep Creek. Bryce Point map.

(See Johnson Bench—Garfield Co. for name derivation.)

Johnson Run: (Kane Co., Utah and Coconino Co., Az.) GSCENM-Vermilion Cliffs-Kanab Creek. Utah maps: Johnson Lakes and Thompson Point. Arizona maps: Muggins Flat, Shinarump Point, and Fredonia.

(See Johnson Town for name derivation.)

This area takes the run-off from Johnson Canyon. (2053~) The name was in place by 1874. (1787~)

The Domínguez-Escalante Expedition of 1776–77 crossed this area. (1611~)

Johnson Spring: (Carbon Co.) West Tavaputs Plateau-Steer Ridge Canyon. Steer Ridge Canyon map.

Waldo Wilcox: "I think that was Nick Johnson. He had a homestead there. There was an old cabin near there last I knew." (2011~)

Johnson Store Butte: (Kane Co.) GSCENM-Paria River. West Clark Bench map.

(See Johnson Town for name derivation.)

Two name derivations are given.

First, the Johnson brothers had a store in Kanab starting in 1891. (1639~) James H. Knipmeyer noted that the butte's name came from its supposed resemblance to the Johnson Brothers Store. (1116~)

Second, Angus Swapp noted that the Johnson brothers would store their supplies at the butte when they were out on the range. (1931~)

Johnsons Up On Top: (Grand Co.) LaSal Mountains-Spanish Valley. Rill Creek map.

Lloyd Holyoak: "It was named for a guy by the name of Johnson. He ran his cows up there." (906~) This was Joseph Horace Johnson (1850-1935). He ran livestock here in the early 1900s. (1420~)

Johnson Town: (Kane Co.) Vermilion Cliffs-Johnson Canyon. Johnson Lakes map. PRIVATE PROPERTY.

Also called Johnson's, Johnson City, Johnsons Settlement, and Kanyon Ranche.

Jesse N. Smith was on a trip with Brigham Young and John Wesley Powell in 1870: "Reached a spring in Ranch Canyon, or more properly a seep under the rocks ... afterwards the site of Johnson." (1775~)

George Washington Johnson noted in 1870 that this was called Johnson Hey: "During the Summer of 1870 it was thot best to have a reunion of the Johnson's and invitations were circulated throughout the territory.... Here I met with four brothers and one sister and many more of our kindred.... During the winter [of 1870] we went to Kanab, also to a little stream 12 miles above which we

called Johnson Hey. We made arrangements to colonize the Johnson familey [sic]." (986~)

Joel Hills Johnson (1802-1882) and family settled here in 1871. Joel Hills Johnson: "On January 23, 1871, I was in the home of Brigham Young in St. George. President Young suggested that the Johnson family take over what was called Spring Canyon Ranch ... for a stock ranch.... We went and found a beautiful canyon half a mile wide and several miles long covered with grass, with small springs coming out at the foot of the bluffs on each side and plenty of building rock and fire wood." (989~, 1188~)

The Lieutenant George M. Wheeler Survey map of 1872–73 shows this as Johnson's Rock Spring. Several early diarists simply called it Rock Springs. (1423~)

Vaydes Brueck: "It used to be called the Spring Canyon Ranch because it had so many springs in it, and my great great grandfather [Joel Hills Johnson] was one of the first settlers and so it was eventually named Johnson because of him." (308~)

The large Johnson family started the town and by the 1880s it boasted a variety store and a school house. Overgrazing led to flash floods, and drought, forced abandonment of the town by 1915. (300~, 712~, 716~, 765~, 1639~)

Enid Supernaw described the town as it was in the early days: "It was a beautiful area, you went up a big, big land and trees on both sides and up against the cliff was a little house and then over a little farther from that was a spring that we always had to go and get a drink of water, 'cause you could open the old door and walk right out there and dip your dipper in and oh that's the best water coming right out the side of the mountain." (308~)

Oscar R. Garrett in 1912: "The settlement consists of only a dozen houses or so built of adobe brick and strung along both sides of the arroyo." (707~)

—Granary Ranch: PRIVATE PROPERTY. (Also called James Bunting Ranch.) This historic ranch site is in Johnson Canyon one-quarter mile north of the mouth of Long Canyon (Cutler Point map). (1115~)

—Pictograph Rock: PRIVATE PROPERTY. (Also called Picture Rock.) This is located at the Granary Ranch. It is covered with Indian pictographs and petroglyphs as well as many historic inscriptions. (2053~) Inscriptions include F.B.W., 1866. Franklin B. Woolley was a member of the Andrus Military Reconnaissance Expedition. W.D.J. Jr., 1871 refers to William Derby Johnson, one of the pioneers of Johnson Canyon and a member of Powell's second expedition down the Colorado River in 1871–72. (1105~) Other inscriptions include D.J. Willson, Apr.

11, 1871; F. Perkins, 1877; G.B. Hobbs, 1879; Gib Hunt, 1884; and James Henrie, Dec. 1890. (1115~, SAPE.)

Johnson Valley Reservoir: (Sevier Co.) Fishlake National Forest-Fremont River. Fish Lake map.

Also called Johnson Reservoir.

Before the reservoir it was known as Johnson Flat. (365~, 1191~)

In 1874 George Cloward became the first settler to build a home at what would become Johnson Valley Reservoir. Rebecca M. Hales: "The second summer his family lived there the roof caved in, killing the mother and two children." (365~)

Barbara Ekker: "This reservoir is located one and a half miles north of Fish Lake where John Johnson ran a dairy during the summer." (607~) Johnson arrived in Salina in 1864. He moved to Redmond in the 1870s and then to what would become Johnson Valley Reservoir. The reservoir was built between 1890 and 1899. (974~, 1419~, 1786~, 1970~)

—Old Spanish Trail: (Variation.) The Old Spanish Trail—Fish Lake Route—went through Johnson Valley. (477~)

Johns Valley: (Garfield Co.) Paunsaugunt Plateau-Emery Valley-East Fork Sevier River. Bryce Canyon, Tropic Canyon, Flake Mountain East, Cow Creek, Sweetwater Creek, Grass Lakes, and Antimony maps.

Also called Emery Valley. (363~, 1314~, 1455~)

The Lieutenant George M. Wheeler Survey map of 1872–73 shows this as Plateau Valley. (M.76.) Clarence Dutton of the Powell Survey called the southern part of Johns Valley (and Emery Valley) the Panguitch Hayfield. (584~, 585~)

The first to use the John name in print was Volney King in 1883. He called it simply "Johns." (1096~)

It is unclear which John should be given credit for the name of the valley. There have been several claims, but most of the dates for them are later than 1883.

First, the first survey of the Johns Valley area was done in 1876. At that time Mrs. John D. Lee had squatter's rights near the mouth of Sweetwater Creek. (1455~)

Second, early resident Oscar J. Adair: "Named after John Campbell, John Hammeker and John Hunt. (1455~)

Third, Gary Dean Young: "In 1893–94, Robert S. Mangum worked for a cattleman in the north end of the valley named John Williams.... At the same time, mention is made of land on Thumb Creek being farmed by John Hunt. John Hammeker is said to have lived on Sweetwater Creek.... John H. Davies was foreman from 1874 to 1900 for the Kanarra Cattle Co-op.... John Steele helped him. Two of the earliest homesteaders in the north end of

the valley in about 1894 were John Campbell and John Wesley 'Dick' Young. It is no wonder that the name of Emery Valley evolved to John's Valley." (2063~)

John R. Campbell arrived in Johns Valley in 1907. (1972~) Daisie Campbell Johnson: "A few years later [my father John Richard Campbell] built a little home in Johns Valley—the first home built. It was located up against the hill. Because of this, the valley was called 'John's Valley'—named after John R. Campbell." (1455~)

Fourth, John Duncan noted that Emery Valley was "also called John's Valley after the Apostle John A. Widtsoe." (2063~)

Gilbert Reed Beebe, an early resident of Widtsoe, paraphrased his stepfather, who traversed Johns Valley in 1909: "He told of the wonderful meadows of tall bluegrass (as he called it) and how it was belly-deep on the horses; that unused water ran from several side canyons, that a small river flowed the entire length of the valley—cold, pure, and clear; how sage hens were in abundance; cottontail and jackrabbits were fat and plentiful; that bands of wild horses dotted the landscape; that it was a veritable Garden of Eden." (1455~)

Johns Peak: (Sevier Co.) Fishlake National Forest-SB Ridge. Johns Peak map. (9,540')

John Wesley Powell called this Mt. Alice in 1878 (1567~) and Clarence Dutton of the Powell Survey noted it as that on his map of 1879 (584~).

Two possible name derivations are given.

First, Dee Hatch noted that John Albrecht was an early settler. (844~)

Second, Wayne Gremel noted that John Christianson herded sheep on the peak in the early days. (780~)

—Poverty Flat: Jim Crane noted that this is the large pastureland to the southeast of Johns Peak (between elevations 8433 and 8699).

John Wills Bench: (Kane Co.) GSCENM-Kaiparowits Plateau-Wahweap Creek. Nipple Butte map.

John W. Wills ran livestock here in the early 1900s. (388~)

Jolley Gulch: (Kane Co.) Zion National Park-Clear Creek. Temple of Sinawava and Springdale East maps.

Also called Grassy Canon and Grassy Meadow. (1931~)

Also spelled Jolly Gulch.

Henry Bryant Manning Jolley (1813-1896) and family were some of the first settlers of southern Utah, arriving in the early 1850s. They moved to Washington County in 1862, then to Mount Carmel in the late 1860s. (1141~, 1639~)

Jolley Hollow: (Garfield Co.) Bryce Canyon National Park-Pink Cliffs-Tropic Canyon. Tropic Canyon map.

Bryce Canyon National Park Superintendent P.P. Patraw in 1934: "Jesse L. Jolley settled in Tropic in 1894. He ran sheep in the hollow." (1931~)

Jolly Mill Hollow: (Sevier Co.) Fishlake National Forest-Old Woman Plateau-Convulsion Canyon. Acord Lakes map.

—Lower Spring: This medium-size, developed spring is a short distance up the hollow under an overhang. A short constructed stock trail leads to the spring. (SAPE.)

—Upper Spring: This large, developed spring is one mile up the hollow. An inscription on an aspen tree near the spring is from William Peacock, Oct. 1935. (SAPE.)

Jones Bench: (Sevier Co.) Capitol Reef National Park-Fishlake National Forest-Thousand Lake Mountain. Solomons Temple and Geyser Peak maps.

(See Last Chance Ranch for name derivation.)

Jones Canyon: (Mesa Co., Colo. and Grand Co., Utah.) Wrigley Mesa-Colorado River. Colorado map: Sieber Canyon. Utah map: Westwater.

Sam Jones was a rancher from nearby Unaweep Canyon in Colorado. He was murdered in West Creek in 1891. (1363~)

Jones Corral Draw: (Garfield Co.) Dixie National Forest-Sevier Plateau-Rocky Ford Creek. Mount Dutton and Junction maps.

Edward Sudweeks in 1941: "It is a large spring used for watering stock. It was named for a man named Jones who built corrals at the head of this spring [in about 1885]." (2053~, 1346~) M.D. Allen in 1969 (on his 86th birthday): "It should be noted that a Mr. Jones had 'the best land' in Center Valley north of Antimony (now owned by Herbert Gleave and Homer Savage)." (44~)

—Jones Corral Guard Station: (Mount Dutton map.) This was used as a pasture by the Forest Service starting in 1908. The guard station was built in the 1930s, but is no longer in use. (2021~) The main house can now be rented from the National Forest Service. A campground is adjacent to it.

—Jones Corral District: This is the area around Jones Corral. (1346~)

Jones Hill: (Iron Co.) Hurricane Cliffs-Eagle Peak. Flanigan Arch map. (9,003')

This was most likely named for Lehi Willard Jones (1854-1947), a pioneer rancher from Cedar City. He was part owner of a coal mine at the mouth of nearby Crow Creek. (1012~)

This peak may have been climbed in 1852. Matthew Carruthers: "scaled one of the highest mountains on the left of the [Coal Creek] kanyon as you go up and discovered a vast quantity of timber and poles." (351~)

Jones Hollow: (Washington Co.) Dixie National Forest-Pine Valley Mountains-Leeds Creek. Signal Peak map.

This was most likely named for William Edward Jones (1830-1897). He moved to Leeds in 1868. (462~)

Jones Spring: (Iron Co.) Hurricane Cliffs-Cedar Valley. Enoch map.

This was most likely named for Enoch pioneer Sylvester F. Jones (1848-1934). He moved from Missouri to Cedar City in the 1860s and to Enoch in the 1890s. (388~)

Jones Well: (San Juan Co.) Black Mesa-Cottonwood Canyon. No-Mans Island map.

Karl Barton noted that Vint Jones drilled the well. (162~)

Jorgensen Pond: (Emery Co.) Castle Valley-Favorite Hills. Buckhorn Reservoir map.

This is a still-used stock pond. (SAPE.)

Stella McElprang noted that John S. Jorgensen (1855-1933) moved to the Wilsonville area in 1890. (1330~)

Jorgenson Creek: (Sevier Co.) Fishlake National Forest-Fish Lake-Lake Creek. Fish Lake map.

Leah Jane Jorgensen Carter noted that Johan Gustav Jorgensen (1837-1901) homesteaded here in 1878–79. (2063~)

Jorgenson Flat: (Garfield Co.) Dixie National Forest-Boulder Mountain. Lower Bowns Reservoir, Golden Throne, Grover, and Bear Canyon maps.

Also called Jorgey Flat (1094~)or Yergy Flat (1931~); both are contractions of Jorgenson.

Charles Kelly noted that the Jorgenson family were early settlers of Fruita. (1047~)

Joseph Canyon: (Kane Co.) White Cliffs-East Fork Virgin River. Mount Carmel map.

William L. Crawford mentioned herding sheep and camping to the west of Monument Knoll, at the headwaters of Joseph Canyon, with both Joseph Heaton and Joseph Esplin in April and May 1903. (485~)

Joseph Peak: (Sevier Co.) Fishlake National Forest-Pavant Range. Joseph Peak map. (9,325')

Irvin Warnock noted that Joseph F. Parker (1841-1936) "was one of the ranchers who opened the Joseph Mountain to the livestock industry. One of the mountain peaks is named for him." (1971~)

Joseph Town: (Sevier Co.) Sevier Valley-Sevier River-Highways 89 and 118. Antelope Range map.

Also called Joseph City and St. Joseph. (584~)

The town was settled by Charles Green, John Pine, Daniel Brown, and others in the spring of 1864. The town was initially called Jericho. Indian troubles forced abandonment in 1865.

Resettlement started in 1871 with William M. Carter, Christian Johnson, Beason Lewis, and Tarlton Lewis. Stake President Joseph A. Young, visiting in 1872, renamed the town in honor of himself. (1970~)

Revo Morrey: "At that early date the settlement of Joseph was not inviting. There were no trees, fences, nor road, only shadscale, rabbit brush, and willows. The few homes consisted of wagon bows set upon the ground, with a cellar or dugout having a brush shed over the entrance. Some people made 'Bull' fences around their houses, by interweaving brush and sticks." (1970~)

Josiah Spring: (Sevier Co.) Fishlake National Forest-Scorup Meadows. Rex Reservoir map.

This is a large, developed, and still-used spring. (SAPE.)

Jubilee Guard Station: (Garfield Co.) Dixie National Forest-Aquarius Plateau-Pine Creek. Big Lake map.

Pratt Gates: "The government put a guard station up there. They'd send a man up there and he stayed there in the summer and watched for fires and this and that." (709~)

The original building was constructed by the Torgersons of Bicknell in 1905. The site was abandoned in the late 1920s. Richa Wilson: "In 1989, the State Historic Preservation Office ... [determined] that the site ... was eligible for listing in the National Register of Historic Places. It was deemed significant as one of the oldest remaining guard stations in Utah.... The Forest [Service] restored the cabin in 1989–90.... [The building is also significant as it] is the only log guard station remaining on [Dixie National] Forest." (2021~)

Judd Hollow: (Kane Co.) Paria Canyon-Vermilion Cliffs Wilderness Area-Paria River. Glen Canyon City, Bridger Point, and Wrather Arch maps.

Zadok Knapp Judd, Sr. (1827–1909) and family moved to Kanab from Iron County in the early 1870s.

—Judd Hollow Spring: (Glen Canyon City map.) This is a large, developed, and still-used spring. (2053~, SAPE.)

Judd Pasture: (Garfield Co.) Dixie National Forest-Sevier Plateau-Carter Creek. Flake Mountain West map.

J.J. Porter in 1931: "Named by J.B. Showalter for a man by the name of Judd who herded sheep for Showalter." (1346~)

—Constructed Stock Trail: This goes northwest from Judd Pasture Troughs for one and one-half miles (over elevation 9586) and down the Hancock Fork of Hancock Creek. Inscriptions found on trees along the trail include Jack Talbot, 1913 and Stan LeFevre, June 4, 1919. A cryptic message reads "The Cowboy. The Roan Goddass [sic]. Rode This Trail." (SAPE.)

Judd Spring: (Garfield Co.) Dixie National Forest-Rock Canyon. Haycock Mountain map.

This large spring was once developed. (SAPE.)

J.J. Porter in 1931: "Arza Judd, a cattle man, discovered the spring and used to camp at the spring about 1885–1905." (1346~)

Jug Handle, The: (Grand Co.) Tenmile Country-Colorado River. Gold Bar Canyon map.

Also called Jug Handle Arch. (2019~)

Named for its shape, it is readily visible from the Potash Road.

Jug Rock: (Grand Co.) Dome Plateau-Winter Camp Ridge. Cisco SW map.

Joe Taylor: "You can always get water there. When my kids were young, we were moving cows out there. I told them, 'You can always get a drink on that rock.' So, we went over there, tied up the horses, climbed up that rock, and there wasn't a drop. So it's really that there is almost always water there"! (1866~) Three large potholes on the top of the rock have water only after recent rains. (SAPE.)

Jug Rock: (Grand Co.) Tenmile Country-Bartlett Flat. Jug Rock map. (5,301')

Water held in potholes gave this monolith its name. (SAPE.)

Inscriptions include A. Thatcher, Payson, March 1895. (SAPE.)

Jumping Off Point: (Grand Co.) East Tavaputs Plateau-Pipeline Canyon. Preacher Canyon map. (8,410')

Unattributed: "[The] ridge has precipitous sides." (1930~)

Jump-up Canyon: (Kane Co.) Dixie National Forest-Pink Cliffs-Long Valley. Long Valley Junction map.

Jump-up is a pioneer term for a short, steep cliff or obstruction that livestock must "jump up" to get over.

Junction Butte: (San Juan Co.) Canyonlands National Park-Island in the Sky District. Monument Basin and Turks Head maps. (6,400')

Frank E. Masland, Jr.: "Junction Butte marks the wedding of the Green and the Grand [rivers]." (1310~)

—White Crack Trail: This 1950s uranium-era road has deteriorated into a hiking trail. It starts two miles south of Junction Butte at the "Campground" at the end of a "4WD" road on the Monument Basin map. Once through the White Crack, the trail continues to the top of Stove

Canyon, a short tributary to Stillwater Canyon. (SAPE.) (See Stillwater Canyon—Stove Canyon.)

Junction Town: (Piute Co.) Circle Valley-Sevier River-Highways 62 and 89. Junction map.

Also called City Creek. (1444~, 1972~)

The town is near the junction of the Sevier River and East Fork Sevier River. (1187~) It was established in 1876 by the Jolley family. They had a burr mill here. (324~)

—Old Spanish Trail: The trail went through what would become Junction. As well, a variation of the Old Spanish Trail, the Fish Lake Route, after coming from the upper Salina Canyon area, joined the Old Spanish Trail at Junction. (477~)

Junes Bottom: (Emery Co.) Labyrinth Canyon-Green River. Tenmile Point map.

This was used as a grazing area by Andy Moore in the 1930s. In 1933 he allowed June Marsing of Green River to build a ranch on the bottom where he farmed and watched Moore's livestock. The Marsings stayed until 1937.

A story is told that before Marsing built the wagon road to the bottom, he would have to lower his children to the bottom on ropes. Gene Dunham: "That has been a bit embellished. It is a little ledgy." (580~) Marsing did build a couple of cabins on the bottom. Several walls and other relics remain. (580~, 1430~, SAPE.)

—Ricks Canyon: This is on the east side of the Green River directly across from Junes Bottom (at Point 5-101). Rick Schmidt's father was the commander of the Utah Launch Complex near Green River in the 1970s. (580~) (See Utah Launch Complex—White Sands Missile Range.)

—Constructed Stock Trail: This enters Ricks Canyon one-half mile from the river on its south side. It was built by Gene Dunham in the 1970s. (580~)

Justensen Flats: (Emery Co.) San Rafael Swell-Interstate 70. Copper Globe map.

Also spelled Justenson Flats.

Dee Anne Finken noted that Orson and Buck Justensen were early-day sheepherders. (641~)

K

Kachina Bridge: (San Juan Co.) Natural Bridges National Monument-White Canyon. Moss Back Butte map.
Also called Caroline Bridge and The Senator. (774~)
(See Natural Bridges National Monument for name derivation.)
H.L.A. Culmer noted that in 1905 he found an inscription "W.C. McLoyd and C.C. Graham, 1892–3" near the bridge. (494~)
—Ruin Rock: This is immediately north of Kachina Bridge (at elevation 5939T). (1872~)

Kadachrome Flat: (Kane Co.) Paria River-Little Creek Wood Bench. Henrieville map.
Correctly spelled Kodachrome Flat.
(See Kodachrome Flat.)

Kaiparowits Plateau: (Garfield and Kane Counties.) GSCENM-Glen Canyon NRA.
Also called Fifty Mile Mesa, Fiftymile Mountain, and The Kaiparowits. (70~, 218~, 221~)
Also spelled Kaiparowitz Plateau. (1356~)
Steve Allen: "The many names used for the Kaiparowits Plateau are often confusing to the first-time visitor. The whole upland area is commonly called the Kaiparowits Plateau even though the actual plateau is several miles west of the near-vertical cliffs facing you as you drive down the Hole-in-the-Rock Road. These near-vertical cliffs are called the Straight Cliffs, though the section between Escalante and the Collet Top Road is also called the Escalante Rim. Beyond Collet Top, the highlands above the Straight Cliffs are called Fiftymile Mountain." (47~, 2051~)
The Andrus Military Reconnaissance Expedition of 1866 called this Sandstone Point. (475~) The Lieutenant George M. Wheeler Survey map of 1872–73 shows it as Linear Plateau. (M.76.) The Gray's Atlas map of 1873 shows is at Broken Alkaline Mountains (unexplored). (M.40.) Almon H. Thompson of the Powell Survey noted that the plateau had also been called Marshalls Peak, named for Lieutenant William L. Marshall of the Wheeler Survey. (1116~, 1877~)
Walter Clement Powell of the 1871–72 Powell Expedition: "So far as I have been able to ascertain, we were the first white men to visit the plateau. The Indian name for a small elevation near the north end [now named Canaan Peak] is *Kia-par-o-wits*, so we called the whole plateau by that name." (1570~)
Four name derivations are given.
First, Charles Kelly, the first superintendent of Capitol Reef National Park, is credited with gleaning the meaning of *Kaiparowits* as "Big Mountains Little Brother," referring to Navajo Mountain to the east, from Paiute Indians. This is now the accepted definition.
Second, Herbert E. Gregory received a slightly different definition from Don Shurtz in 1918, noting that *Kaip* means "Mountain" and *wits* means "son." Shultz concluded that it meant "Son of Table Cliff." (760~)
Third, Navajo linguist Richard Van Valkenburgh: "Piute: *Kaiparowits; Kapiapowitz.* Navajo: *Tsèndoolzhah*, or Rock Point Descending Jaggedly (refers to point projecting down towards the juncture of the San Juan and Colorado Rivers)." (1943~)
Fourth, Hulbert Burroughs in 1938: "Although the origin of this [name] is uncertain, some believe it came from the name given by the Indians to the daring pioneer, Major Powell.... Powell had lost his right arm in the civil war, so the Pahutes called him *Kai-par-uts*, or 'one arm.'" (315~)
Early writers called the plateau Wild Horse Mesa, a name that was used as the title of a novel by Zane Grey in 1928. (789~) Grey in 1924: "Where it got the felicitous name we could not learn; perhaps from the Mormon wild-horse hunters. Wild stallions with bands were known to disappear and not be seen again; and it was certainly a thrilling and satisfying assumption to believe they had a way to surmount this mesa." (782~)
Ervin S. Cobb in 1940: "This noble barrier, with its base in the blended shadows and its top palings in the clouds, is so-called [Wild Horse Mesa] because stray mustangs that have gone wilder than any deer are said to frequent it." (438~)
Clyde Kluckhohn led an expedition to the top of the Kaiparowits Plateau in 1928: "Our first glimpse of this fair valley [the Kaiparowits Plateau] as we climbed over the Mesa rim was a moment of ecstasy, one of those fleeting instants, treasured forever in memory, when the soul's longing is completely satisfied and the spirit soars, when

all the dark corners of one's mind and all the unhappy tangents of thought are for a time blotted out and washed into oblivion, when there is a place only for rapture. We had expected Inferno, but we found Paradise." (1100~)

Kluckhohn again: "Of all the splendid skyward cliffs which cast their shadows over an uninhabited, little-known region of southeastern Utah none are so grand, none so siren in their mystery as those of Wild Horse Mesa. Its formidable battlements, once glimpsed, cannot be forgotten. The imagination continues to lay siege to them, for they seem (as indeed they are) the ramparts of another world, a world infinitely desirable but unattainable." (1100~)

Randall Henderson in 1951: "Its top surface is slashed by numerous arroyos. Domes and small-scale ridges and buttes outcrop in every direction. The rise above the pinyon and juniper forest, which covers much of the top of the plateau, like temples and fortresses of cream-colored Wahweap sandstone. Tens of thousands of years of rain and wind have scooped out great caverns in the sidewalls of these buttes." (872~)

One published warning about a trip to the Kaiparowits Plateau stated: "This is a several weeks' pack-trip and should not be attempted without competent guides and adequate equipment." (2056~)

John Phillips in 1996: "The plateau here looked like the artwork for a Windham Hill album cover: buff-green tumbleweed, pinyon pines, needle-sharp yuccas, and 10-foot-tall one-seed junipers, many of them a century old. 'Gnarly' does not adequately describe their trunks. More like a combination of Lake Superior driftwood and Keith Richard's forehead." (1535~)

Harvey Halpern in the 1990s: "We call it the Cowcrapairowits Plateau. There is little left of the glory so eloquently written about by such luminaries as Zane Grey and Clyde Kluckhohn. Overgrazing has brought this once special place to its knees; the springs have been trampled into uselessness, caves and overhangs are packed with shit and dead cows, the once-fertile pasturelands of grasses are now just extensive swaths of sagebrush and sand, and the famous myriad of archaeological sites are, for the most part, just more dust and dirt. What a shame. For all of us." (812~)

—First Euroamerican ascent: Almon H. Thompson of the Powell Survey made an ascent of the Kaiparowits Plateau from its east side and spent a couple of days on top, from August 2 to August 4, 1875. From Thompson's diary: "[From Potato Valley we] Came about 25 miles down the valley, climbed the first bench [Fiftymile Bench] and up

about 350 feet of the second, when we came to a place we could not get over. Worked on it and got the mule, Net, up. Came down to the lower bench and camped.... Finished our trail and got to the top of the plateau." (777~)

—Books: Zane Grey titled a book, *Wild Horse Mesa*, after the Kaiparowits Plateau. (247~, 789~) Clyde Kluckhohn's book, *Beyond the Rainbow*, is about his adventures there.

K and L Canyon: (San Juan Co.) Dark Canyon Plateau-White Canyon. The Cheesebox map.

The Carnegie Museum Archaeological Expedition of 1945 named the canyon for J. Leroy Kay, the head of the expedition, and Henry Lyman, a local guide. (1721~)

Kaibito Creek: (Coconino Co., Az.) Navajo Indian Reservation-Navajo Creek. Kaibito, White Hills, Horsethief Mesa, and Cedar Tree Bench, Az. maps.

Kaibito Creek and all of its side canyons are closed to all visitors.

Kaibito Creek runs through Chaol Canyon.

K'ai' Bii' Tò is Navajo for a "spring in the willows." (769~, 2072~)

—Constructed Stock Trail: This exits the middle part of Kaibito Creek to the west one mile south of Tse Esgizii Canyon (immediately east of elevation 5221T on the Cedar Tree Bench map). (SAPE.)

—Constructed Stock Trail: This incredible trail, used only by sheep, exits the middle part of Kaibito Creek to the east. It goes along the west side of a dome (elevation 4458T on the Cedar Tree Bench map). An inscription along the trail is from Aug. 1951. (SAPE.)

—Constructed Stock Trail: This trail, used only by sheep, exits middle Kaibito Creek to the west (one-eighth mile south of elevation 4042 on the Cedar Tree Bench map). (SAPE.)

—Constructed Stock Trail: This trail, used only by sheep, exits lower Kaibito Creek to the west one mile south of Piñon Waterfall (at elevation 4011 on the Cedar Tree Bench map). (SAPE.)

—Constructed Stock Trail: This excellent trail is the "Pack Trail" on the west side of Kaibito Creek two miles up from its confluence with Navajo Creek (Cedar Tree Bench map). (SAPE.)

Kanab Creek: (Kane Co., Utah and Coconino and Mohave Counties, Az.) Vermilion Cliffs-Colorado River. Utah maps: Alton, Bald Knoll, Glendale, White Tower, and Kanab. Arizona maps: Fredonia, Clear Water Spring, Gunsight Point, Findlay Tank, Jumpup Point, Grama Spring, Fishtail Mesa, and Kanab Point.

Also called Kanab Canyon, Kanab River (1556~, 1894~), Kanab Wash, and Main Canyon (324~).

Also spelled Kanabe Creek (1804~) and Knab Creek (M.8.).

Rose H. Hamblin: "Kanab gets its name from the Indian baby's *Khan*, the willow basket in which the tiny papoose is carried on its mother's back. The word comes from *Kanaw* meaning willow; so Kanab is 'the place of the willows,' so named by the Piute Indians, long before white men set foot on the red soil, because of the willows growing along the bank of the creek." (349~)

The 1829–30 Antonio Armijo Expedition crossed Kanab Creek, probably in the vicinity of Fredonia. They called it *Carnero*, or "Ram Creek." (69~, 805~) In 1869 the Utah Territorial Militia, while chasing Navajo, called it Grand Gulch. (476~)

H.M. Cadell in 1887: "The Kanab Plateau ... is a simple monotonous expanse of desert, with only one salient point of interest. This is the Kanab Cañon, a magnificent side gorge which runs through the centre of the plateau, and opens into the heart of the Grand Cañon." (328~)

—Movies: The 1924 movie *Deadwood Coach*, starring Tom Mix, and the 1944 film *Buffalo Bill*, were filmed, in part, in Kanab Canyon. Other movies filmed, in part, here included *The Lone Ranger* (1938), *Calamity Jane and Sam Bass*, *Westward the Woman*, *War Drums*, *Duel at Diablo*, and *The Outlaw Josie Wales*. (131~)

Popular television shows *Have Gun Will Travel*, *Death Valley Days*, and *Gunsmoke* were also shot, in part, here. (1421~)

—Big Lake: (Also called Big Lake Reservoir.) This reservoir was in a small western tributary of Kanab Creek just south of The Sand Hills (one-half mile west of elevation 5617T on the White Tower map). It was built by Kanab pioneers in the early 1870s and was the town's first reservoir. (1639~) John Henry Standifird in 1873: "Big lake is ... something like ½ mile long and on an average about 600 feet wide and fed by Springs. Affording a nice irrigating stream, there has been a few trout planted here." (1804~)

Kanab Town: (Kane Co.) Vermilion Cliffs-Kanab Creek-Highways 11 and 89. Kanab map.

Also called Fort Kanab and Lower Kanab (Alton was Upper Kanab).

Also spelled Canab, Cannab (294~), and Kanabe (475~). (See Kanab Creek for name derivation.)

This is the county seat of Kane County.

The first settlers arrived in 1858. Construction of a fort near Kanab Creek was started in 1865 and was finished in 1867. It was abandoned during the Black Hawk Indian War. Jacob Hamblin reestablished the fort in 1869 and by 1870 a real town had been started. (349~, 369~, 470~) Hamblin called this both Cannan and Kanab. (814~)

Jacob Hamblin in September 1869: "We found upon our arrival, after communicating our business to the red brethren that they were not only willing but very anxious to assist in making place of security for ourselves and for them. We have now an area of eleven rods square enclosed with a substantial cedar stockade, and thirteen log houses for us and the native brethren. There are two good stone guard houses, and one snug commissary house." (817~)

Frederick S. Dellenbaugh of the 1871–72 Powell Expedition: "The village ... was laid out in the characteristic Mormon style with wide streets and regular lots fenced by wattling willows between stakes.... Fruit trees, shade trees, and vines had been planted and were already beginning to promise near results while corn, potatoes, etc. gave fine crops.... The entire settlement had a thrifty air, as is the case with the Mormons.... Not a grog-shop, or gambling saloon, or dance-hall was to be seen; quite in contrast with the usual disgraceful accompaniments of the ordinary frontier town." (541~)

John Hanson Beadle in 1872: "Kanab sits back in a beautiful cove in the mountains, something like a crescent in shape, the mountain peaks east and west of the town putting out southward to the Arizona line. All the land within the cove appears rich." (171~)

Maurine Whipple in 1949: "The Kanab country is part of what is actually the wildest and most desolate section of North America. Not a tidy land where the eye measures distance in terms of human habitation, but a vastness where the adobe house of the white man clinging to the crumbling banks of a wash seems as futile as the ancient pueblo under a cliff. A country as unknowable as the mountains of the moon." (1998~)

—Cedar Flats: Neil M. Judd in 1915: "In the broad valley extending from Kanab to Johnson Run and on its low dividing ridge, known locally as the 'Cedar Flats.'" (1027a~)

—Sand Hollow: This was the local name for a section of the Honeymoon Trail that was one mile east of Kanab. Unattributed: "early named Sand Hollow because of the coarse, deep sand carried to the site by floods, causing travel between Kanab and Johnson to be difficult over the sandy stretch of road." (2053~)

—Movies: With its beautiful setting and juxtaposition to nearby scenic wonders such as the Grand Canyon and Zion and Bryce Canyon national parks, Kanab became a center for film making starting in the 1930s. It was often called Little Hollywood. Such films as *Drums Along the Mohawk*, *The Lone Ranger*, and *Union Pacific* were, in part, filmed here. (349~)

Kanarra Creek: (Iron Co.) Kanarra Mountain-Hurricane Cliffs-Ash Creek. Cedar Mountain, Kanarraville, Kolob Arch, and New Harmony maps. Some of Kanarra Creek is PRIVATE PROPERTY.

Also called Summit Creek. (469~)

Also spelled Canara Creek and Kannarah Creek.

Arthur F. Bruhn noted that Paiute Chief Kuanar (also Quan-ar) lived on the creek. (311~) He died near Enoch after being thrown from his horse. (1512~)

William R. Palmer: "During the early days of the settlement of the country, when there were many more Indians than white men, a great chief named Kanarra reigned supreme over his tribe. He was very unfriendly toward the white people who were coming into the country to take up the land and kill the game which the Indians for generations had regarded as their own.... In order to protect themselves from this hostile tribe, the people built a fort on what is now the public square. Because this fort was built as a protection against Kanarra and his tribe, the town was called Kanarra." (1013~)

The Domínguez-Escalante Expedition of 1776–77 called this *Rio de Nuestra Señora del Pilar de Zaragoza* or "Our Lady of the Pilar of Zaragoza." (261~) The Parley P. Pratt Exploring Expedition to Southern Utah of 1849–50 called it Summit Creek. (1762~)

John C.L. Smith of the Exploring Expedition of 1852 was the first to mention the name: "The old chief Awannap, or as [Chief] Walker calls him, Quinnarrah, requested me from time to time, to go over and visit them at the Pangquick [Panguitch] Lake." (1776~)

Kanarraville: (Iron Co.) Cedar Valley-Hurricane Cliffs-Interstate 15. Kanarraville map.

(See Kanarra Creek for name derivation.)

The Holdredge map of 1866 shows this as Kanawa. (M.31.) Joseph F. Smith noted it as Kanarra in 1867. (1777~) The George F. Cram map of 1875 shows it as Kanary. (M.12.)

The town was settled in 1861 by former residents of nearby New Harmony, including John Davies, Elisha H. Groves, and William James. They initially settled on Kanarra Creek one mile northeast of the present townsite. Several years later a group from Toquerville moved to the present townsite and in 1866 the two towns consolidated at the present site. (2063~)

Charles Roscoe Savage in 1870: "Kanarra ... a cold and cheerless place. This place is almost directly on the rim of the basin, as the water runs in two directions, to the Sevier sink and the Pacific, it is wonderful how folks do so well in such looking places." (1691~)

Don Maguire in 1878: "The natural scenery around Kanarrah is very interesting. Great peaks of red sandstone rise in the mountains to the east [Hurricane Cliffs], and give the soil ... a pinkish hue. The country is very rugged and very much of it is yet unknown to white men." (1902~)

Kane County:

The county seat is Kanab.

Kane County was established in 1864 from Washington County and areas of land that had no previous designation. The county was named for Brigadier General Thomas L. Kane. Although not a Mormon, he helped the Mormons with their difficulties with the federal government. (1639~, 1932~)

On Kane's death in 1883, George Q. Cannon wrote: "There is no man outside of Utah who holds a warmer place in the hearts of the 'Mormon' people than the hero who has just departed.... General Kane was small in stature but possessed a great and magnanimous soul. He was a brilliant writer and an impressive speaker. His views of all public matters and religious and philosophical principles were broad and strongly marked, and the qualities of the statesman, the warrior, the independent thinker, the poetic writer and the generous philanthropist were thoroughly established in his character." (1185~)

Wallace Stegner wrote about the Kane County area in 1942: "The tiny oases huddle in their pockets in the rock, surrounded on all sides by as terrible and beautiful a wasteland as the world can show, colored every color of the spectrum even to blue and green, sculptured by sandblast winds, fretted by meandering lines of cliffs hundreds of miles long and often several thousand feet high, carved and broken and split by canyons so deep and narrow that the rivers run in sunless depths and cannot be approached for miles. Man is an interloper in that country." (1826~)

Kane Gulch: (San Juan Co.) Cedar Mesa-Grand Gulch. Kane Gulch map.

Also called Kane Canyon. (1389a~, 2081~)

Kane Spring was used by the Hole-in-the-Rock Expedition in 1880. They called it Cane Spring for the stand of canes around it. Expedition member Platte D. Lyman called it Canebrake. (1259~) Later, the name was misspelled "Kane." (1356~, 1451~)

James H. Knipmeyer noted that this was also called Wetherill Canyon for the well-known relic hunter John Wetherill. He started exploring the region in the 1890s. He left an inscription near the mouth of the canyon in 1920. (1115~, 1389a~, 2081~)

Charles L. Bernheimer in 1929: "We entered Kane Canyon. A more thrilling, concentrated bit of travel in exquisite, weird scenery I have not come across. The canyon is narrow, tortuous." (218~)

—Constructed Stock Trail: The "Pack Trail" going down Kane Gulch was built by members of the Whitmore Exploring Expedition, an archaeological reconnaissance led by Richard Wetherill, in 1896–97. Wetherill: "One animal fell off the trail where it wound about a ledge going into the canon and was killed instantly." (250~) Over the years the trail has been realigned and improved into a very good hiking trail.

Kane Spring: (Kane Co.) White Cliffs-Block Mesas. Elephant Butte map.

Also spelled Cane Spring. (483~)

This is a large, still-used spring with a CCC-style trough. (SAPE.)

Kane Spring Draw: (Washington Co.) Dixie National Forest-Bull Valley Mountains-Santa Clara River. Central East and Central West maps.

This is a large spring. (SAPE.)

James H. Martineau called this Resting Spring in 1857. (1306~)

William B. Smart noted that it was named for Thomas L. Kane. (1762~) (See Kane County.)

The John C. Fremont Expedition of 1843–44 noted the then unnamed spring as a "small run of water." (1762~)

—Old Spanish Trail: Mary Esther Staheli noted that Kane Spring was a stopping place on the Old Spanish Trail. (1803~) It was also an often-used stopping place by the Mormon pioneers who were going from Salt Lake City to Las Vegas, Nevada and San Bernardino, California. Sara Jane Rousseau in 1864: "Left camp [at Mountain Meadows], went … to Cane Springs where we watered the horses and ate a luncheon." (1773~)

Kane Springs Canyon: (San Juan Co.) La Sal Mountains-Black Ridge-Colorado River. Kane Springs, Trough Springs Canyon, and Moab maps.

Also called Caine Springs Station. (1739~)

Also spelled Caine Spring. (377~)

This was initially called Hudsons Wash for Joshua B. "Spud" Hudson. He ran livestock in the area starting in the late 1870s. (M.72., M.74.) Hudson received his

nickname for his well-known propensity for always carrying a potato in his pocket. (536~)

It was historically spelled Cane Spring for the many canes along its course. For some unexplained reason map makers started spelling the name with a "K" sometime after 1926. (99~)

Inscriptions included Jack Lavender, 1884; George Ipson, 188?; and Chas Patten, Apr. 9, 1889. These were destroyed when the road was built. (1115~)

—Kane Springs: (Kane Springs map.) This is in upper Kane Springs Canyon and was a well-known stopping place on the Old Spanish Trail. In 1848 Orville C. Pratt called it *Corasito* or *Corisite*, perhaps referring to a type of orchid-like plant. Later the spring was used by stagecoaches and mail carriers. Located along Highway 191, it is now a roadside park. (456~, 1538~, 1572~)

—Seraph Rock: This 45-foot pinnacle near Kane Springs was named by rock climbers. Eric Bjørnstad: "Seraph is a diminutive tower with a celestial name. Seraph is one of the six-winged angels standing in the presence of God." (240~)

—Saint Louis Rock: C. Gregory Crampton noted that this was the name used by the Elk Mountain Mission of 1855 for the huge rock mesa that stands above and behind Kane Springs. (477~) Ethan Pettit of the expedition: "to St. Louis rock … very rough and rocky road." (1532~)

—Hole N' the Rock: PRIVATE PROPERTY. This popular tourist attraction is one-eighth mile south of Kane Springs (at elevation 5060T on the Kane Springs map). Steven Davis noted that this is a five thousand square foot home and business excavated from solid sandstone. It was built by Albert Christensen over a twenty year period in the 1940s and '50s. (527~)

James H. Knipmeyer noted that there are over 150 inscriptions at the site, including P. Maxwell, 1878; D.A. Johnson, 1883; W. McConkie, 1888; and Joe Wilson, Jan. 10, 1899. (1105~, 1112~)

Tom McCarty, who would become the famous outlaw who ran with Butch Cassidy, left his name on the rock in 1878, most likely while on his way to visit his brother Bill, who was one of the first residents of La Sal. (1750~)

—Blue Hill: C. Gregory Crampton noted that this is the hill to the north of Kane Springs that north-bound travelers had to negotiate to get up to Spanish Valley. The top of the hill is three miles from the spring. (474~) It proved problematic. Wilma Galbraith went down the hill in 1916 and later told her children that, to paraphrase: "The road was nothing more than a trail cut from the side of the canyon and littered with rocks and boulders that had fallen from the cut. One of their horses was only 'green' broke and became frightened and began bucking and kicking trying to get loose. Dad told Mother to take the boys to the side of the wagon away from the canyon to help balance the wagon. Mother said there were times when one wheel would be running on air. Each time it seemed the wagon would go over the side they would hit a boulder and be bounced back onto the road." (1911~)

—Lower Kane Spring: This is the "Spring" in lower Kane Spring Canyon that is one mile (as the crow flies) upcanyon from the Colorado River (one-quarter mile southwest of elevation 4672T on the Moab map).

—Gatherer Canyon: This eastern tributary of lower Kane Springs Canyon goes east from Kane Spring. The name derivation is unknown. It is a recent name. (M.55.)

Kasov Spring: (Sevier Co.) Fishlake National Forest-Dipping Vat Draw. Rex Reservoir map.

This large spring was once developed. (SAPE.)

Kathys Canyon: (San Juan Co.) Glen Canyon NRA-Red Canyon. Mancos Mesa NE and Good Hope Bay maps.

Carl Mahon noted that Kathy Irvine's husband, Chuck Irvine, did bighorn sheep research in the area with Utah State University in the mid-1960s. (1272~)

Keesle Country: (Emery Co.) San Rafael Swell-Muddy Creek. Hunt Draw map.

Also called Lost Forever Country.

Wayne Gremel noted that the Keesle family ran sheep here. Carrie Lou Gremel thought that they came from Manti or Ephraim. (780~) The family name may be Kessel, Keasel, or Keisel. (388~)

—Mud Canyon: This western tributary of Muddy Creek drains part of Keesle Country. It is one mile downcanyon from the mouth of Chimney Canyon (north of elevations 5030T and 5168AT). Steve Allen named the canyon for its relentless mud walls formed from the Moenkopi Formation.

Keet Seel Ruin: (Navajo Co., Az.) Navajo Indian Reservation-Navajo National Monument-Skeleton Mesa-Keet Seel Canyon. Keet Seel Ruin, Az. map.

Also spelled Kiet Siel (265~) and Kitsel (499~).

Three similar name derivations are given.

First, Herbert E. Gregory noted that *Kit sil* is Navajo for "broken pottery." (769~)

Second, Robert W. Young noted that *Kits'iili* is Navajo for "shattered house." (2072~)

Third, Laurance D. Linford noted that *Leets'aats'iil* is Navajo for "broken pottery house." (1204~)

Richard Wetherill and Charlie Mason are credited with discovering Keet Seel Ruin in 1895. They spent several days digging here. Realizing its potential, Wetherill returned with C.E. Whitmore and George Bowles for more extensive digging in 1897.

The first somewhat scientific expedition to the ruin was led by Byron Cummings in 1909. (1204~, 1654~) In his notes Cummings had little to say about Keet Seel: "It is a community house containing about 148 rooms, with several kivas. The walls are made of dressed stone and clay for the most part, a few are constructed by setting up poles and sticks on end and then plastering them within and without with clay." (499~)

Cummings in a letter to his wife: "To get to the Keetseel ruins I had to be helped by my three guides with a rope securely tied around my waist. Two held it above and one climbed along with me placing my feet. There was no risk whatever with the three giants who are watching over me. The feat was worth all the trouble." (218~)

Keg Knoll: (Emery Co.) Antelope Valley-Maze Road. Keg Knoll map. (5,317')

Also called Keg Butte and Monument Hill.

Keg Knoll is a major landmark on the east side of the San Rafael Desert. Its abundance of caves attracted Puebloan Indians and, later, cowboys.

Two name derivations are given.

First, Barbara Ekker noted that a moonshiner once lived here and delivered his product in kegs. (604~) (See Old Man Spring.) Ned Chaffin: "a favorite place for the bootleggers to make 'Hooch.'" (413~)

Second, Ted Ekker noted that from a distance, the knoll looks like a keg laid on its side. (623~)

Nearby inscriptions include My Home - Bill Tibbets, Sept. 1924 and Tom Perkins, 1924. (SAPE.)

Keg Point: (Emery Co.) San Rafael Desert-Labyrinth Canyon. Tenmile Point map. (4,865')

—Register Rock: This rock, which is covered with historic inscriptions, is on the north (or east) side of the Green River and is one and one-half river miles upriver from the mouth of Hey Joe Canyon (one-quarter mile east-southeast of elevation 4606T). It was also called the Post Office Register and Registration Rock. Famous names inscribed on the rock include Barry Goldwater, Ellsworth and Emery Kolb, and Eugene Clyde LaRue. (123~, 1947~, SAPE.)

An inscription across the river from Register Rock reads: "Howland Brothers. Dealers in Divided Skirts and Panty Wear. 11-12-16. Babe Howland - Sign painter and hair dresser." (SAPE.)

Keg Spring Canyon: (Emery Co.) Antelope Valley-Labyrinth Canyon. Keg Knoll, Bowknot Bend, and Tenmile Point maps.

(See Keg Knoll for name derivation.)

—Keg Spring: (Bowknot Bend map.) This large spring sits in a very pretty box canyon. On older maps it is called, correctly, Keg Knoll Spring. This differentiates it from the Keg Spring on the Keg Knoll map.

—Wolverton Trail: (Also called Copper Miners Trail.) This constructed stock trail on the east side of Keg Spring Canyon is one-half mile north of Keg Spring and leads to the spring (Bowknot Bend map). The trail was built by Edwin T. Wolverton. He mined copper near Keg Knoll in the early 1900s. (619~)

—Andy Moore Trail: This constructed stock trail enters the west side of a small western tributary of Keg Spring Canyon. It is one and one-quarter miles south of Keg Spring (one-quarter mile northwest of the "Cave" on the Bowknot Bend map). Ted Ekker noted that it was built by rancher Andy Moore (1894-1968) in the 1920s. (623~)

—Chuchuru Sheep Trail: This constructed stock trail enters the middle part of the canyon on its west side at the end of a marked road (one-eighth mile northeast of elevation 4510T on the Bowknot Bend map). Ted Ekker noted that the trail was built by the Chuchuru family in about 1945. The Chuchurus were also responsible for building a pumphouse and small dam in Keg Spring Canyon a short distance below the sheep trail in 1962. Water was pumped to tanks on the rim of the canyon. (623~)

—Buck Canyon: This western tributary of Keg Spring Canyon is two and one-quarter miles up Keg Spring Canyon from the Green River (immediately south of elevation 4518T on the Tenmile Point map).

—Buck Canyon Trail: A trail down Buck Canyon was initially a constructed stock trail. Michael R. Kelsey noted that the trail was later improved into a uranium mining road by Bill Moore and others in the 1950s. (1084~)

—Wolverton Canyon: This small western tributary of the Green River is one-eighth mile north of the mouth of Keg Spring Canyon (one-half mile north of elevation 4623 on the Tenmile Point map).

—Wolverton Canyon Trail: This constructed stock trail enters Wolverton Canyon on its upper north side. It was named by Michael R. Kelsey for Edwin T. Wolverton (1862-1930). He had a copper mine near Keg Knoll in the early 1900s. Copper ore from the mine was carried down the trail that he built in the canyon. The ore was then boated upriver to his ranch on Wolverton Bottom, just below today's Ruby Ranch. (604~, 1084~)

—Big Bull Bottom: This is the name ranchers gave to the small, tamarisk-choked bottom on the Green River at the mouth of Keg Spring Canyon.

Keller Canyon: (Kane Co.) Pink Cliffs-Muddy Creek. Orderville map.

Stephen Vandiver Jones in 1872: "camped at 3 beautiful springs, surrounded by rough hills." (1023~) Dale L. Morgan noted that two of the springs were "Rubes Spring and Kellers Springs, which once supplied water for considerable areas of meadow lands, have been destroyed by erosion along Muddy Creek." (1023~)

Keller Knoll: (Garfield Co.) Dixie National Forest-Boulder Mountain. Lower Bowns Reservoir map. (9,612')

George Keller was one of the few black men in southern Utah. Born in 1880 in Manti, George was adopted by an Euroamerican family named Keller. They moved to Emery County in 1882. (368~)

Keller became a sheep and ranch foreman and worked for the King Ranch on Tarantula Mesa. Keith Durfey: "He was up on top of the Boulder [Mountain]. He used to go up there with the sheep in late July and August. The top of Boulder [Mountain] is famous for lightning storms and I'm quite sure he had a real close call and I think it was that his camp jack (he was the herder—they always had a herder and a camp jack, the guy who moved camp and did the cooking and stuff like that)—and they were just going to have a noon meal. They had sourdough in a pan. They had a bitch that had had a litter of pups and they'd had them just inside of the tent for protection of the pups, and lightning struck right by and killed all the pups and fried the dough, so they say. Where the nails were in their boots, it burned their feet. And that was the last time George Keller ever went on top of Boulder [Mountain]." (582~)

Burns Ormand, who knew George Keller as a youth, told a variation of the story: "They said that him [George Keller] and his brother came out here and herded sheep for Emory King. One day lightning hit and killed his brother because he was up on top. And George never would herd sheep on top again because of that." (1487~)

Keller Reservoir: (San Juan Co.) Great Sage Plain-Spring Creek. Monticello North map.

Also called Bailey Reservoir. (1144~)

Fred W. and Mabel Keller and family started a farm on South Canyon Point to the north of Keller Reservoir in the early 1920s. Val Dalton: "[Keller] was a judge here for years, a lawyer, and he raised horses and he built that Keller Reservoir to store his water out of Spring Creek." (517~)

Keller was famous for writing the locally well-known song "Blue Mountain" in 1929. The chorus went:

Blue Mountain, your azure deep
Blue Mountain with sides so steep
Blue Mountain with horsehead on your side
You have won my love to keep. (2069~)

Kelsey Mare Hollow: (Iron and Washington Counties.) Dixie National Forest-Harmony Mountains-Bumblebee Canyon. Stoddard Mountain map.

Orrin Kelsey (1840-1892) moved to Harmony by 1870. He started a farm a couple of miles south of New Harmony in the 1880s. (462~)

Kens Lake: (San Juan Co.) La Sal Mountains-Spanish Valley. Kane Springs map.

This reservoir was finished in 1977 and was named for former Moab mayor Ken McDougald in 1981. It had been called Mill Creek Reservoir. Water for the reservoir came from Mill Creek through the 645-foot Sheley Tunnel, which was named for Horace Sheley. He started construction of the tunnel in the early 1900s. (644~) Tom McCourt noted that the waterfall issuing from the tunnel is called Faux Falls. (1323~) The fall can be seen from Highway 191.

—Poverty Flat Town: The site for this town was in the general area west of Kens Lake. The town was also called Bueno, Bueno Vista, Plainfield, or sometimes just The Flat. By 1879 Poverty Flat had a post office. The settlement received its name after drought forced the farmers to abandon their farms. Poverty Flat was slowly abandoned as residents moved north to Moab. (456~, 1526~, 1530~)

Kettle, The: (Coconino Co., Az.) Navajo Indian Reservation-Navajo Mountain-Aztec Creek. Chaiyahi Flat, Az. map.

Also called Stew Kettle and West Canyon Kettle.

The Kettle is incorrectly marked on the map. The exact location is a bit of a mystery, but it is known that The Kettle is a specific area of a canyon, not a generic sandstone ridge.

According to historians and explorers Harvey Leake [great grandson of John Wetherill] and James H. Knipmeyer, The Kettle is the upper eastern tributary of Goldenrod Canyon (immediately east of elevations 5270 and 5710). (1115~, 1156~) (See Forbidding Canyon—Ferguson Canyon for the Charles L. Bernheimer Expedition's discovery of The Kettle in 1921.)

The Charles L. Bernheimer Expedition of 1921 explored the area. One of the participants, archaeologist Earl Morris, described The Kettle as "a maze of tortuous cañons winding in and out among dumpling-like knobs of rock, too hopelessly rough to be crossed by a pack train." (1389~)

Bernheimer noted that expedition member John Wetherill called it The Kettle because the bottom of it "was quite black." (221~)

Gary Topping: "The outlet, a narrow slit, is barely detectable from the rim and gives the impression that the sides form a continuous bowl." (1901~)

While the Charles L. Bernheimer Expedition of 1921 skirted The Kettle and found a way into Aztec Creek, the Bernheimer Expedition of 1924 went right up its bottom. As with their earlier expedition, the 1924 trip took them up Jayi Canyon from Navajo Creek and crossed the head of the upper inner gorge of Aztec Creek. At this point there is a small saddle/flat/plateau (one-quarter mile north-northwest of elevation 5605 on the Chaiyahi Flat map). Their route continued northeast up to the very head of Aztec Creek. This one-mile-long section of canyon (immediately south of elevation 5470) is fast and easy and ends on the top of the high cliffs at the junction of several drainages (one-eighth mile south of elevation 5270). The junction far below is The Kettle. This also marks the head of Goldenrod Canyon. (See Forbidding Canyon–Goldenrod Canyon.)

Now, following the rim of Goldenrod Canyon northwest for one mile, they found a rugged stock trail going down into upper Goldenrod Canyon (one-quarter mile northeast of elevation 5505). They then went southeast up Goldenrod Canyon, and then up The Kettle over very rugged terrain, and finally onto Chaiyahi Flat. Bernheimer, mistakenly called Goldenrod Canyon "Forbidding Canyon" in his diary: "The ride through [up] Jay-i Canyon is uninteresting, but when we reached The Kettle the aspect changed. Deep down lay Forbidding [Goldenrod] Canyon. All about it is ruthlessly savage. Our descent, after we had found an old little used trail, was on hand and foot. I for one did not bother with my mule. When we were down we thought one of those ledges so well known to us appeared necessitating our climbing up a canyon shelf and finding a final descent that way. We followed Forbidding [Goldenrod Canyon] east, very frequently through thick brush of oaks, willows, live-oak, cedar and pinon, a precarious and disagreeable way of moving. The snapping branches have a way of scratching, the tree trunks a way to meet vigorously one's knees and shins. We followed Forbidding [Goldenrod] Canyon in its course to its beginning. Its whole life history is like its birth place. Rough, threatening life and limb. Comparatively narrow though

The Kettle is, it was difficult to pick a way which did not necessitate retracing." (218~, 1156~, SAPE.)

Keyhole Arch: (San Juan Co.) Navajo Indian Reservation-Cummings Mesa-Wetherill Canyon. Cathedral Canyon map.

This very beautiful arch was named by the National Geographic Society for its keyhole shape. It was discovered from the air by Royce Knight in the early 1960s. It is difficult to see except from the air or from the rim of Cummings Mesa. (1021~, 1954~, SAPE.)

Keystone Arch: (San Juan Co.) Manti-LaSal National Forest-Dark Canyon Plateau-Arch Canyon. Kigalia Point map.

Robert H. Vreeland: "keystone for the arch of rock is missing." (1955~) The name was in place by 1927. (761~)

Kiahtipes Reservoir: (Emery Co.) Book Cliffs-Highway 191. Woodside map.

Dino Kiahtipes: "My grandfather [Gust Kiahtipes, 1894-1967] and father [Nick Gust Kiahtipes, 1931-1985] ran sheep in the Woodside area. I believe they had the reservoir built to hold water for the sheep. I don't know who actually named the reservoir." (1090~, 388~)

Kigalia Point: (San Juan Co.) Manti-LaSal National Forest-Dark Canyon Plateau-South Elk Ridge. Kigalia Point map. (8,574')

Robert S. McPherson noted that Kigalia Canyon was called *Naahootso* by the Navajo. This means "Place Across the River to Escape from the Enemy," referring to the roundup of Navajos by Kit Carson during the Long Walk of 1863–64. (1338~)

Navajo Chief K'aayelii (also spelled Kigalia or Kigaly) was born in 1801 near Kigalia Spring. (455~) By the early 1860s K'aayelli was herding livestock from Elk Ridge to the Henry Mountains. Kigalia was not caught by Kit Carson and lived here over the duration of the Navajo imprisonment. He died in 1894 and was buried at Montezuma Creek near Blanding. (1562~) (See Appendix One—Navajo Long Walk.)

Albert R. Lyman: "old Kigaly—now people have kind of anglicized that word—they call it Kigalia and a lot of other things, but I knew Kigaly.... When the Forestry Service took it up they tried to change the name of it, so now people don't know anything about it. They think that it may be Kigalia, but it wasn't that at all, it was Kigaly." (1250~) Although named for a person, two name derivations are given for the word itself.

First, *K'aayelii* is Navajo for "Torch." (983~)

Second, David D. Rust in 1935: "Learned meaning of Kigalia—a Navajo word for arrow pouch." (1672~)

—Kigalia Canyon: This southern tributary of Dark Canyon is between Kigalia Point and Little Notch.

—Kigalia Spring: This is the "Spring" in the upper part of Kigalia Canyon that is one and one-quarter miles south-southwest of Little Notch (one-quarter mile west of elevation 8395T). Chief Kigalia used it as the base of his sheep and horse operation. (369~) Fletcher B. Hammond in 1886: "a wonderful stream of about 20 degrees year round." (821~)

Albert R. Lyman: "When we came into the country the Paiutes claimed the Elk Mountain as their exclusive territory, and when our explorers went there in the early [eighteen] eighties and bought of them the right to use the mountain for our cattle, they had made some arrangements with the Navajo. Kigaly, who was camped with his sheep at that time by the spring which has gone by his name ever since. But neither Kigaly nor any other Navajo ever went again with sheep on Elk Mountain." (1236~)

—Kigalia Guard Station: (Also called Kigalia Forester Station and U.S. Forester Station.) (218~) This is adjacent to Kigalia Spring. It is no longer in use.

Killian Hollow: (Sevier Co.) Sevier Plateau-The Brink. Water Creek Canyon map.

James Laman Killian (1845-1903) moved to Glenwood in 1864 and married Rachel Powell. He was known to be particularly adept at establishing good relations with local Indians. In 1896 they moved to Orangeville and remained there for the rest of their lives. (1937~)

Killpack Canyon: (Emery Co.) Manti-LaSal National Forest-Wasatch Plateau-Rock Canyon. The Cap map.

J.D. Killpack arrived in Ferron in 1879. (710~) He had a mine near the head of the canyon in the early years. (M.68.)

—Mine Road: This went up Killpack Canyon to the Killpack Mine and to the nearby Axel Anderson Mine. (M.68.)

Kimble and Turner Peak: (Garfield Co.) Henry Mountains-Crescent Creek. Mount Ellen map. (11,115')

Correctly spelled Kimball and Turner Peak. (1115~)

In the late 1880s miners F.A. Kimball and Alonzo G. Turner developed the Oro Mine on the flanks of the peak. They mined for gold and copper. (923~, 1795~, 1881~)

Bliss Brinkerhoff: "My dad [Willard A.] said that old Kimball and Turner were mean: 'Boy, if we let our sheep get to pokin' their head over the top into Bromide Basin, they was there with their rifles and tellin' us, 'Boy, the first sheep that gets into Bromide Basin is dead. And after we get the sheep, maybe we'll get the herders, too.'" (291~)

Kimball Draw: (Emery Co.) San Rafael Swell-Muddy Creek. Copper Globe and Big Bend Draw maps.

Ray Wareham noted that Kimball Rasmussen was a pioneer rancher. (1967~) Dee Anne Finken noted that the draw was used by cowboys to take their cattle from Copper Globe to Muddy Creek. (641~)

Inscriptions include JN, 1905 and Mont Swasey, 1950. (SAPE.)

Kimball Valley: (Kane Co.) GSCENM-Vermilion Cliffs. Eightmile Pass map.

Cal Johnson: "It is an old name." (984~) It was in place by 1881. (665~)

—Sand Gulch Reservoir: This large stock reservoir is on the north side of Kimball Valley one and one-half miles southeast of Eightmile Pass (near elevation 5563T). It was built by the BLM in the 1960s or '70s. (984~)

King Bench: (Garfield Co.) Dixie National Forest-Boulder Mountain. Roger Peak map.

(See King Mesa for name derivation.)

King Bench: (Garfield Co.) GSCENM-Circle Cliffs. Lamp Stand, King Bench, Steep Creek Bench, and Red Breaks maps.

Also called Kings Bench.

(See King Mesa for name derivation.)

—The Diadem: This is the northeast end of King Bench immediately south of, and above, the Long Canyon Overlook (at elevation 6380T on the Lamp Stand map). Joyce Muench: "Because of its resemblance to a monarch's crown, this finely sculptured battlement has been called the Diadem." (337~) A diadem is a crown.

King Ditch: (Emery Co.) Castle Valley-Ferron Creek. Ferron map.

The ditch was engineered by John Edson King (1856-1921). He moved to Ferron in 1879. (1531~) This is not the same person as John King below.

King Mesa: (Kane Co.) Glen Canyon NRA-Escalante River. King Mesa map. (5,294')

John King (1862-1949) and his wife, Sally (also spelled Saley or Sallie), arrived in Escalante in 1893 and moved to Salt Gulch (near the town of Boulder) in 1896. (700~, 1168~) Another source noted that King moved to Boulder in 1888. (356~) Don Coleman: "John King come across there and he camped there for several days in a bad snowstorm, and so that's where it got its name." (441~)

—King Spring: The spring was improved about forty years ago. (441~)

King Mine: (Kane Co.) GSCENM-Kitchen Corral Wash. Eightmile Pass map.

This manganese mine was started by John H. Brown in 1939. After going through a couple of owners, it was abandoned by the mid-1950s. (1083~)

—Mine Gulch: The King Mine is in Mine Gulch. (765~)

King-on-his-Throne: (San Juan Co.) Navajo Indian Reservation-Monument Valley. Monument Pass map.

Also called Emperor on His Throne (1359~) and Emperor's Throne (252~).

Joyce Muench in 1941: "There is a rigid back of a chair and the imagination has no difficulty in investing the erect figure that sits there, with kinghood." (1404~)

King Ranch: (Garfield Co.) Dixie National Forest-Boulder Mountain-Sweetwater Creek. Roger Peak map. PRIVATE PROPERTY.

This was started by John and Sally King in 1894. (See King Mesa.) They moved to the ranch permanently in 1899. Nethella King Griffin Woolsey: "The [King] homestead was in a pleasant little circular valley entirely surrounded by wooded hills. The soil there is deep and rich, and now after forty years, is still very productive." (2052~)

Kings Bottom: (Grand Co.) Spanish Valley-Colorado River. Moab map.

Samuel N. King started a farm on the bottom in the early 1890s. (2024~)

Lloyd Holyoak: "Kings Bottom was one of the areas we ran our horses and cattle in the early years. That was our main winter range. Every spring and fall we'd trail our cattle in and out of there. We'd go from Hatch Point, down Hunter Canyon, through Kane Springs Canyon, to Kings Bottom." (906~)

—Moonflower Canyon: This very short eastern tributary of the Colorado River is east of the north end of Kings Bottom (at elevation 3965). Eric Bjørnstad: "Moonflower Canyon is named for the moonflower proliferus in the area (as in much of canyonlands country). The plant is also known as jimsonweed and [sacred] datura." (239~)

James H. Knipmeyer noted that there are many old inscriptions dating to the early 1900s just outside the mouth of the canyon. (1115~)

—Movies: *Warlock* and *The Comancheros* were filmed, in part, on Kings Bottom. (1809~)

Kings Canyon Bottom: (Uintah Co.) Uintah and Ouray Indian Reservation-Green River. Moon Bottom map.

—Smiths Suspension Bridge: The bridge went between the south end of Kings Canyon Bottom and Fourmile Bottom. A man by the name of Smith built the bridge for use by sheep and horses when a ferry was unable to operate in the winter because of ice on the river. (1756~)

Kings Crown: (Emery Co.) Castle Valley-Molen Reef. Molen map.

This small hill has a capstone that forms what looks like a king's crown. Ray Wareham noted that it was a good landmark used by ranchers. (1967~)

—Indian War Camp: Lee Mont Swasey noted that this is an area one-half mile north of Kings Crown. (1853~, 931~)

Nearby inscriptions include Waggen, 1909 and Helen Mae Swasey, 1945. (SAPE.)

—Ball Field: This is one-half mile northwest of Kings Crown (between elevations 6055 and 6075). Lee Mont Swasey: "Every Easter the Church would sponsor an Easter egg hunt. The whole town would go out there and hunt Easter eggs and have a big town picnic." (1853~)

Kings Meadow Canyon: (Sevier Co.) Sevier Plateau-Rainbow Hills. Water Creek Canyon and Sigurd maps. PRIVATE PROPERTY.

Peterson Creek goes through Kings Meadow Canyon.

The name was in use by 1873. (173~)

—South Meadow: This is the southern portion of Kings Meadow that is near Mud Spring. (1551~)

—Kings Meadow Ranch: (Also called Nebeker Ranch.) George W. Nebeker and family had a ranch on Kings Meadow in the late 1870s. (1971~)

Ethel Jensen: "The roads were soft from the recent spring thaw, but the boys found no serious difficulty until they reached what was called the 'Willow Patch' in Kings Meadow Canyon. Here, a spumy little creek poured in from the east, and finding no where to go, spread over the area of the heavy willow copse, making of it a veritable bog." (962~)

Kings Pasture: (Garfield Co.) Dixie National Forest-Boulder Mountain. Deer Creek Lake map.

(See King Mesa and King Ranch for name derivation.)

Kingston Canyon: (Piute Co.) Sevier Plateau-Sevier River. Phonolite Hill and Junction maps.

Also called East Fork Canyon. (1931~)

(See Kingston Town for name derivation.)

East Fork Sevier River flows through Kingston Canyon.

Kingston Town: (Piute Co.) Circle Valley-Sevier River-Highway 62. Junction map.

The original town of Kingston was immediately east of the present townsite, on the east side of East Fork Sevier River. For a short time the town was called East Fork. (469~)

Town pioneer M.D. Allen noted that Thomas Rice King (1813-1879) and his wife, Matilda Robison (1811-1894), and their five sons and their families settled here and started a United Order. They built a mill, a tannery, and a fort. (44~, 374~)

In 1883 the United Order was disbanded and the townsite became the property of the King family. Other families then moved to the present townsite, which became today's Kingston. For a short while it was also called East Junction. (374~)

—Peterson Hill: This is one mile northwest of Kingston (at elevation 6400). Zella B. Matheson: "Alfred Christian Peterson and his wife, Confederate American Kenner Peterson, owned a farm on the ground sloping up the hill on the southeast and a certain amount of the hill, thus the hill is known as Peterson Hill." (1931~)

Kings Valley: (Iron Co.) Dixie National Forest-Horse Valley. Red Creek Reservoir map.

Also called Horse Valley. (1931~)

Bishop H.L. Adams noted that in the early years the valley was owned by John King Paramore (1860-1928). (2053~) He ran sheep here. (516~)

Kinneys Peak: (Sevier Co.) Fishlake National Forest-Clear Creek. Johns Peak map. (9,464')

The Kinney family were early residents of the Richfield, Monroe, and Elsinore areas. (388~)

—Duck Pond: Jim Crane noted that this stock pond is one mile south of Kinneys Peak (one-half mile southwest of elevation 8957). (478~)

—Kinney Meadow Spring: Jim Crane noted that this is one mile southwest of Kinneys Peak (one-eighth mile north of elevation 8957): "That's a good little spring and because of the reference to the Kinney Meadow we got to calling it that." (478~) Kinney had an eighty acre homestead near the spring. (1931~)

—Willow Basin: Jim Crane noted that this is immediately north and west of Duck Pond. (478~)

—Hippie Camp Spring: Jim Crane noted that this is in the first draw to the east of Duck Pond (one-quarter mile south-southeast of elevation 8957): "Ralph Lund ran sheep in the Clear Creek area for years and years. In the [19]60s or '70s he always camped there and he actually had some hippies living with him. They were a grubby bunch." (478~)

—Sampsons Hole: Jim Crane noted that this is one-half mile south of the Duck Pond: "It's a big hole, a hole as big as Sampson." (478~)

—Elk Mountain: Jim Crane noted that this is three-quarters of a mile southeast of the Duck Pond (at elevation 9723). (478~)

Kinnikinnick Spring: (Sevier Co.) Fishlake National Forest-Lost Creek. Rex Reservoir map.

This is a large spring. In the early days, someone dug a hole deep into a cliff face to develop the spring. It has great water. (SAPE.)

Two name derivations are given.

First, kinnikinnick is an eastern name for a dogwood, which are common in the area.

Second, James H. Knipmeyer noted that it was an Algonquian term for a leaf and bark mixture smoked by the Indians. (1115~)

Kirby Pond: (Emery Co.) Antelope Valley-Maze Road. Keg Knoll map.

Ted Ekker noted that Swanee Kirby was a BLM employee. (623~)

Kirbys Point: (Kane Co.) GSCENM-Kitchen Canyon. Deer Range Point map. (5,958')

Also called Kirby Ridge.

Correctly spelled Kerby Point.

Francis Kerby (1847-1925) and family were early settlers of Paria Town. They lived here from 1877 into the early 1880s. (388~, 1181~)

Kirk Arch: (San Juan Co.) Canyonlands National Park-Needles District-Salt Creek. House Park Butte map.

Rensselaer Lee Kirk, Sr. (1859-1945) homesteaded below the arch in the late 1880s. (1084~) The arch was rediscovered by Ross Musselman and his daughter in 1940. It was called Musselman Arch for many years. (1950~) Canyonlands National Park Superintendent Bates Wilson and his son, Tug, renamed the arch in 1950 for Kirk. (1429~)

In 1961 a National Geographic Society expedition visited the area and called it Corleissen Arch for Harley J. Corleissen, a former chairman of the Utah State Road Commission. (1381~)

Kirks Basin: (Grand Co.) LaSal Mountains-Taylor Flat. Dolores Point South map.

Kirk Puckett ran cattle in the area starting in 1880. He lived here for a couple of years and moved on. (1526~, 1741~)

Kitchen Canyon: (Kane Co.) GSCENM-Paria River. Deer Range Point and Calico Peak maps.

Also called Mollys Nipple Cañon (1831~) and Nipple Canyon (984~). John Green Kitchen (1830-1898) arrived in Kanab in 1873. In 1879 he moved his family to Kitchen Canyon where they built what was called the Nipple Ranch for its location under Mollies Nipple. The Kitchens abandoned the ranch by 1898. (275~, 1612~, 1639~, 1831~)

Cal Johnson: "[John Kitchen] had an old man there that worked with him, a man named Joe Honey. He got involved with old man Kitchen's wife and she had a son from him. And so they moved out." (984~)

George C. Fraser told a different story: "Because of his [John Kitchen's] drinking habits, he had trouble with his wife, who obtained a divorce from him.... [He] came to Lee's Ferry to live with [Jim Emmett].... [Emmett] brought with him 5 gals. of whiskey, which Kitchen attacked without moderation and soon had the D.T.s. Emmett sought to quiet Kitchen by giving him laudanum and Kitchen, who at the time was well over 60, died." (669~) Inscriptions include Wallace and David S. Johnson, 1893 and Anna Hendricks and Minnie Wall, August 10, 1893. (SAPE.)

—Nipple Ranch: PRIVATE PROPERTY. (Also called Kitchen Ranch.) This was on the south side of Kitchen Canyon one and one-quarter miles east of Nipple Lake (one-eighth mile south-southeast of elevation 5442 on the Deer Range Point map). Stone foundations, fireplaces, and log walls are all that remain of the ranch. (SAPE.) Cal Johnson, who owns the Nipple Ranch, noted that the Kitchens were not the first to settle here; ranchers from the Tropic area, including the Cannons and Smiths, were here first. (984~) Richard L. Hoxie of the Lieutenant George M. Wheeler Survey of 1872–73 visited the area and wrote that there were "two or three milk ranches" in the vicinity. (916~)

—Averett Ranch: PRIVATE PROPERTY. Ralph Chynoweth noted that this was on the north side of Kitchen Canyon and immediately east of the mouth of Parley Hollow (Deer Range Point map). All that is known is that the Averett family ranched here. There are two chimneys in the general area. It is unclear which was the actual Averett Ranch. (425~, 1831~, SAPE.)

—Monkey House: PRIVATE PROPERTY. This ranch was on the north side of Kitchen Canyon at the mouth of Wilsey Hollow (Deer Range Point map). (See Wilsey Hollow.) The ranch was built by Dick Woolsey in 1896.

Two name derivations are given. First, Cal Johnson: "Right there in Woolsey Hollow there is a big rock. It has the profile of a monkey's head. Old man [Peter] Shirts and the Shirts family settled here. In the back of the rock was a sort of a cave. It was half as big as this room, here. He built a lean-to, a porch out in front, put in a couple of trees, and he lived there. That was sometime after 1860." (984~)

Second, Jack Breed in 1949: "When [Dick] Woolsey and his wife settled in this area, they brought a large monkey.... He was kept in a small cupola atop a post near the cabin. Whenever he noticed anyone approaching, he would chatter loudly to warn his master." (275~)

George C. Fraser in 1922: "Woolsey was a pioneer in the country 25 years ago, and from frequent attacks of delirium tremens, was referred to as 'the man with snakes in his boots.'" (670~)

Inscriptions include J.W. Mano?, June 1917; ? Twitchell, May 1918; and Layton Smith, March 13, 1933. (SAPE.)

—Kitchen Canyon Constructed Wagon Road: This road went from the Nipple Ranch down the north side of Kitchen Canyon to the Paria River. A rubble slope on the lower part of the route has collapsed, making the road impassable, even to most hikers. (SAPE.)

Cal Johnson noted that the trail was built by the earliest settlers of the town of Paria as Kitchen Canyon was the closest place for good clear, clean water. Johnson: "The Paria—the old-timers called it the 'Pah-rear'—because it had such bad water that they'd get the 'back door johnnies.'" Although Cal tried to keep the road open for stock for many years, a huge flash flood permanently closed the road in the 1980s. (984~)

—Dripping Cave: (Also called Big Drip.) This is the large waterfall in the lower part of Kitchen Canyon, just above the mouth of Drip Tank Canyon. Cal Johnson: "I used to tell my family that if they ever dropped an atomic bomb, why, I knew of a place where we'd all be safe—the Dripping Cave. You could ride a horse right behind the waterfall into that cave and we'd be safe and have some water and we could survive." (984~)

—Kitchen Canyon Sheep Trail: This trail, much of it now gone, starts at the mouth of Kitchen Canyon and goes northwest up the cliffs to Deer Trails. Inscriptions include Jim Henderson, 1926 with the notation "Stop and talk to the sheepherders"; and Kay Clark and M.G. Clark, May 7, 1930. (SAPE.)

Kitchen Corral Spring: (Kane Co.) GSCENM-Park Wash. Eightmile Pass map.
(See Kitchen Canyon for name derivation.)
The concrete cistern at the spring was built by the CCC. (984~)
The spring was likely visited by Richard L. Hoxie of the Lieutenant George M. Wheeler Survey of 1872–73. He noted that there were several milk ranches in the area and "water good & grass." (916~)

—Kitchen Corral: This is the "Corral" that is one-quarter mile north of Kitchen Corral Spring. Cal Johnson: "That is the old Kitchen Corral. The old cowboys built that. Kitchen did not build that corral. (984~)

—Kitchen Creek Canyon: This short canyon is immediately east of the Kitchen Corral. The name was noted by archaeologist Julian H. Steward in 1941. (1831~) The canyon contains a large, developed spring. A constructed stock trail, now vague, exits the canyon to the north. (SAPE.)

Kitchen Corral Wash: (Kane Co.) GSCENM-Vermilion Cliffs-Buckskin Gulch. Eightmile Pass map.
(See Kitchen Canyon for name derivation.)
Herbert E. Gregory noted that this used to be called Kaibab Wash, which was the joining of Deer Spring Creek and Park Wash. Downcanyon this becomes Buckskin Gulch. (765~, 984~)

—Pioneer Road: This branched north from the Honeymoon Trail and went up Kitchen Corral and Park washes to the ranches at Swallow Park. (See Appendix Two–Honeymoon Trail.)

—Elmos Spring: This is just below the confluence of Park Wash and Deer Spring Wash. (765~) Cattleman Elmo Cope inscribed his name nearby in 1922. (SAPE.) The name is no longer in use.

—Cal Johnson Rock House: PRIVATE PROPERTY. (Also called Rock House.) This line cabin is on upper Kitchen Corral Wash immediately south of Kitchen Corral Point. The CCC built a line camp here in the 1930s. Cal Johnson: "The sheep and goat men furnished the supplies, lumber and the tent and all that stuff and the CCs used native rock to build that rock house. They built it with four separate rooms so each of the sheepmen in the area could have a room. There was Sam Graff and John Johnson and a man named Houston. They stored their supplies there. I put up that cabin there. The area around there is called Rock House Pasture." (984~)

—Hun Got Toh Pass: This name was used by the Mormon Territorial Militia of 1869 in reference to Kitchen Corral Wash as it breaks through the Vermilion Cliffs. (476~)

Kitchens Tank: (Coconino Co., Az.) Vermilion Cliffs National Monument-Paria Plateau-House Rock Valley. House Rock Spring, Az. map.
(See Kitchen Canyon for name derivation.)
This is a still-used stock reservoir. (SAPE.)

Klondike Bluffs: (Grand Co.) Arches National Park-Salt Valley. Klondike Bluffs map.
Also called The Klondike. (758~)

The Klondike Bluffs are considered the remotest and least visited area of Arches National Park. Initially it was called Devils Garden, a name given it by rancher Alexander Ringhoffer on December 24, 1922. Other names have included The Palisades and Red Bluffs. (898~) This area was not a part of the original Arches National Park. It was added by President Franklin D. Roosevelt in 1938. (1115~)

Two related name derivations are given.

First, Vicki Webster: "The Klondike name was thought to have been used by miners in reference to the Alaska Gold Rush." (1977~)

Second, James H. Knipmeyer: "Supposedly the ridge was crossed by an early stagecoach run between Thompson, Utah, and Moab. The weather along this ridge can be cold and windy during the winter months, and it is said that the stagecoach operators dubbed this 'Klondike Ridge' because it was the coldest place on the route. It was only natural that the higher rock landmark atop it would assume the name Klondike Bluffs and that during modern times the 'ridge' would lose its significance." (1120~)

Knoll, The: (Iron Co.) Hurricane Cliffs-Cedar Valley. Cedar City map.

Myron A. Shirts noted that the first settlers to arrive in Cedar City, in 1851, initially camped on the north side of The Knoll at what was called Wagon-Box Camp. The settlers took their wagon boxes off and used them for temporary shelter until permanent structures could be built. (1727~)

—Big Field: This six thousand acre field is west and north of The Knoll. It was noted in John D. Lee's diary entry for February 17, 1849 (436~) and is also shown on a map from the early 1850s (1727~). The Big Field was set aside as a communal farming area by the Parowan pioneers. (1715~)

Knowles Canyon: (San Juan Co.) Glen Canyon NRA-Mancos Mesa-Glen Canyon. Knowles Canyon map.

Also called Calamity Canyon. (8~)

Also spelled Knolls Canyon. (1510~)

Carl Mahon: "Ray Redd was quite a historian ... and he told me that there was a family named Knowles that lived in Grand Junction. They ran cattle over in that country and they were looking to find a place to run some more cattle. I don't know if they knew somebody or if they just went exploring. But they found this Knowles Canyon and they brought a bunch of cattle in there and ran them for a few years and then they sold out to Scorup. That was in the late 18s or early 19s." (1272~)

James H. Knipmeyer filled in some of the pieces by noting that brothers Emery and Henry Knowles had a ranch near the lower end of Westwater Canyon before moving to San Juan County in the early 1890s. (1115~) The name was in place by 1915. (M.72.)

Val Dalton told a story about Knowles Canyon: "We've had cattle stolen and butchered in Knowles Canyon right down there by the lake [Lake Powell] by people in boats!" (517~)

—Constructed Stock Trail: This goes right out the upper end of Knowles Canyon. (SAPE.)

—Olympia Bar: (Also called Bennetts Bar, Double Day, Gold Coin Placer, Olympic Bar, and Santa Rosa Bar.) This placer bar, now underwater, was on the east side of the Colorado River three-quarters of a mile north of the mouth of Knowles Canyon.

The bar was first mined by David Lemmon, Timothy O'Keefe, J.J. Ryan, and Michael Ryan in 1886. They called it the Lone Star Placer. At one time a water wheel, built by Frank Bennett, was mounted on a cliff above the bar. (465~, 1812~)

—Sundog Bar: This placer bar, now underwater, was on the west side of the Colorado River one mile south of Knowles Canyon (one-half mile east of elevation 3808T). (465~)

Kodachrome Flat: (Kane Co.) Paria River-Little Creek Wood Bench. Henrieville map.

Incorrectly spelled Kadachrome Flat.

Ralph Chynoweth: "When I was a kid, this was called Chimney Rock Flat." (425~)

Jack Breed of the National Geographic Society in 1949: "It was a beautiful and fantastic country. A mile to the left near the base of the cliff I could see red pinnacles thrust up from the valley floor. The few natives who had been here called this area 'Thorny Pasture,' but we renamed it 'Kodachrome Flat' because of the astonishing variety of contrasting colors in the formations. Huge rocks, towers, pinnacles, fins, and fans surrounded us. Everywhere the results of erosion could be seen in all stages." (275~)

The Thorny Pasture name may have been a misunderstanding on the part of the National Geographic members. One source noted that the pasture was called not "Thorny" but "Thorleys" Pasture for Henrieville bishop Thorley Johnson. (311~, 421~)

Nell Murbarger in 1961: "Kodachrome Flat—a name that irks me terrible. From the time this region was first settled by pioneering Mormon cattlemen, this lovely hidden valley had been known to all as 'Thorny Pasture,' a nomenclature as rustic and guileless as the men who bestowed it. But due, presumably to high coloring of the formations studding and ringing the valley, the aforementioned National Geographic explorers had seen fit to discard that time-honored designation in favor of a copyrighted tradename of the Eastman Kodak Company." (1415~)

Ward J. Roylance in 1965: "a secluded basin featuring fluted cliffs and unique formations. Its singular formations may be 'petrified geyser holes'—upright cylindrical columns of white stone rising high from bases of red rock: possibly they are remnants of ancient 'plugs' that once filled deep circular holes in a different type of material. Over the ages, enclosing stone eroded away and left the much harder cores to stand alone as enduring monuments to a world that used to be." (1659~)

Robert F. Leslie in 1967: "The colorful Kodachrome Flat ... pales any of the so-called painted deserts. It would be impossible to exaggerate the miles of leafy greens, blood reds, royal blues, and jonquil yellows." (1179~)

Ronald Shofner in 1970: "Once known as Thorny Pasture to the rugged cattlemen who have ranged here since the turn of the century, this area is one of mystery and beauty.... There are small pockets and flats between them which can be roamed freely. The mystery, which has yet to receive an adequate explanation, is how the numerous tall, gray, totempole-like spires sprinkled liberally throughout the Flats came into being." (1728~)

—Eagles View Trail: This is the "Pack Trail" that goes north from Kodachrome Flat toward Henrieville. Now a popular hiking trail, it was initially a stock trail built before 1900. The WPA improved the trail in the 1930s.

Ralph Chynoweth: "When I was a little kid me and my nephew rode up to the top of the trail. There's a tree right there at the saddle. When we got there, there was a rope tied to the tree. We were wondering, so we looked over the edge and a horse was hangin' off the edge and it was dead. Some guys went up there with this horse, it was an old mare, and it gave out and wouldn't go any further. So they tied the horse to the tree. It got muckin' around and somehow went over the edge." (425~)

—Kodachrome Basin State Park: (Also called Kodachrome Basin State Reserve and Kodachrome State Park.) This 2,240 acre park, located on Kodachrome Flat, was established as Chimney Rock State Park in 1962. Apparently that name, coming from a nearby tower, was used for fear of a lawsuit from the Kodak company. The name was changed in the mid-1960s. (1658~)

Kolob Arch: (Washington Co.) Zion National Park-La Verkin Creek. Kolob Arch map.
(See Kolob Plateau for name derivation.)
With a span of 287 feet, this is the fourth longest arch in the world.
—Arch Canyon: The trail to Kolob Arch goes up Arch Canyon. (966~)

Kolob Creek Canyon: (Washington Co.) Zion National Park-North Fork Virgin River. Kolob Reservoir, Cogswell Point, and Temple of Sinawava maps.
Also called Big Creek, Kolob Creek, and Oak Creek. (363~)
Also spelled Colob Creek Canyon. (585~, 1035~)
(See Kolob Plateau for name derivation.)
In 1840 Captain Joseph R. Walker was the first to see upper Kolob Creek. He described it to an unattributed newspaper writer: "On the upper Virgin [Kolob Creek] are two very remarkable falls. One of them ... is the most stupendous cataract in the world; it falls in an almost unbroken sheet a distance of full one thousand feet! At the fall the stream is narrowed to thirty or forty yards, while the canon rises on either side in almost perpendicular cliffs.... The pent up stream rushes on to the brink of the precipice, leaps over and falls with scarce a break into the vast abyss beneath. Capt. Walker describes the sight as grand beyond description." (1469~)
—Boundary Canyon: (Also called Dry Fork Kolob Creek.) This starts north of Gooseberry Creek Knoll and goes generally east into Kolob Creek. (1548~)

Kolob Peak: (Washington Co.) Upper Kolob Plateau-The Hardscrabble. Kolob Reservoir map. (8,933')
Also called White Butte.
(See Kolob Plateau for name derivation.)

Kolob Plateau: (Kane and Washington Counties.) Hurricane Cliffs-North Fork Virgin River. Kolob Reservoir, Smith Mesa, and The Guardian Angels maps.
Also called Kolob Terrace and North Fork Country. (984~)
Although Kolob Plateau is labeled on only three maps, by common usage it a much larger area that goes from the Hurricane Cliffs on the west to the Pink Cliffs on the east, and from Kanarra Mountain on the north to Zion Canyon on the south. George W. Brimhall of Grafton was perhaps the first to use the term in writing, in 1864: "on a mountain called Kolob." (288~)
Three similar name derivations are given.
First, Elizabeth Kane, the wife of Thomas L. Kane, in 1872: "The Mormons called it 'Kolob' in allusion to some celestial mountain referred to in the Book of Mormon;

but as United States Government Explorers have been here recently it is probably re-christened by the mundane title of some Representative or Senator, whose vote next year may be hoped for to increase the Survey Appropriation." (1035~)

Second, Kevin J. Fernlund: "Kolob ... was a Mormon term from *The Pearl of Great Price*, which meant a place close to where God lives." (639~, 50~)

Third, George C. Fraser in 1914: "'Kolob' in Mormon theology signifies the place of abode—a separate world or planet—of the Supreme Ruler of the Universe." (667~)

Fourth, William R. Palmer in 1942: "Kolob as given in the book of Abraham (Book of Mormon) is a great star around which all other stars revolve. Some people think eventually this plateau will be more beautiful than Zion." (2053~)

Jack Hillers of the Powell Expedition of 1871–72: "The scenery is grand of its kind and affords fine subjects for the camera. The formation is homogenous sandstone. The top had been overflowed with lava.... Pinnacles innumerable, forming an immense harrow upside down. Here and there are scattered peaks, overlooking the others by a thousand feet, or like giants among dwarfs. All bare rock no vegetation on the towers." (884~)

Clarence Dutton of the Powell Survey: "It is a veritable wonderland. If we descend to it we shall perceive numberless rock-forms of nameless shapes, but often grotesque and ludicrous, starting up from the earth as isolated freaks of carving or standing in clusters and rows along the white walls of sandstone ... the land here is full of comedy. It is a singular display of Nature's art mingled with nonsense." (965~)

Jonreed Lauritzen in 1947: "Now on every side the eye can drink of fiery stuff and the imagination runs loose like a wild stud colt. Mountains swirl and pile up in forms so dynamically shaped that they seem to drift and toss in the wind and only a steadiness of eye can hold them to their bases. The scene below, the canyon itself, is like something dropped from paradise and left dragging on the clouds. There is no peace from the stillness that smites the ears; all else is chaos, sublime and weird and awesome." (1149~)

Dale L. Morgan in 1949: "The hurried survey by [Stephen Vandiver] Jones [of the Powell Expedition of 1871-72] of the [Kolob Plateau] recorded for the first time the remarkable features of the Kolob Terrace, stretches of relatively flat land into which are incised many closely spaced deep canyons and above which rise volcanic cones and sheets of basaltic lava. In the [18] seventies the abundant palatable herbage attracted cattlemen, who established summer homes, tended their stock, and made butter and cheese for market. Though its forage has been seriously depleted, the Kolob still is an important grazing district." (1023~) Herbert E. Gregory in 1950: "The Kolob Terrace ... is an area of subdued topography in a region of sharply accentuated relief. In contrast with the discordant valley profiles and the elaborately dissected interstream spaces of adjoining regions the surface of the Kolob is characterized by rounded hills that slope gently downward to broad valley floors. Every part of the surface is covered by organized drainage and many square miles are so thickly mantled with soil that rock outcrops are rare." (768~)

—Zion National Park: In 1923 some of Kolob Plateau was designated as Zion National Monument. It was added to Zion National Park in 1956. (965~)

Kolob Reservoir: (Washington Co.) Upper Kolob Plateau-Kolob Creek. Kolob Reservoir map.
(See Kolob Plateau for name derivation.)
—Spillsbury Ranch: PRIVATE PROPERTY. This is one-half mile north of the north end of Kolob Reservoir. It was started by Rhone Spillsbury of Toquerville in the early days. (363~, 570~)
—Sevy Ranch: PRIVATE PROPERTY. This is one mile north of the north end of Kolob Reservoir. (570~)

Koosharem Town: (Sevier Co.) Grass Valley-Otter Creek. Koosharem and Burrville maps.
Also called Grassburg, Grass Valley, and Red Clover.
Also spelled Coosharem (584~, M.27.), Cousharem (1567~), and Koosharm (1970~).
Three similar name derivations are given.
First, A. Vernaldo Hatch: "'Koosharem' is derived from an Indian name meaning 'Clover Blossom.'" (1444~, 1970~)
Second, the Utah Federal Writer's Project of 1938: "Believe to have derived its name from a carrot-like plant, the roots of which were eaten by Indians." (1932~, 1193~)
Third, Hugh F. O'Neil in 1939: "Name means 'roots that are good to eat,' is derived from wild red clover plants flourishing in the vicinity, which were cooked and eaten." (1482~, 1512~)
The town was settled in 1874 by John Christensen, Karen Nielson, and Frands Peterson. (1970~)
—Koosharem Cemetery: (Koosharem map.) One story, told on a tablet at the Koosharem Cemetery, warrants special attention. The following is paraphrased: "Mary C. Parsons. 1849–1911. Handcart Pioneers. At age 6 or so her parents died in Kansas on the way to Zion. Adopted by another couple, they continued on their journey. In Wyoming the company was caught in a snow storm.

Mary's legs were frozen and had to be amputated. Walking on knees, she continued on in life, getting married and raising 7 children." (1551~)

—Koosharem Reservoir: (Burrville map.) Before the reservoir was built, the area was called The Plateau. (357~) J. Leland DeLange: "The construction of the [Koosharem Reservoir] dam got underway the fall of 1897. A wide trench was dug across the meadow and then the trench was filled with rocks to make the foundation of the dam. Wagons, with dump boards, were loaded at traps located on the west side of the reservoir. Men with teams and scrapers loaded the wagons and spread and compacted the dirt in the dam. The outlet pipe was man-made of tarred lumber, and the gate was purchased from Salt Lake City." (1971~)

—Kishera: It is unclear if Kishera was a town or an Indian settlement. Located near Koosharum on today's Highway 89, it is mentioned by John D. Lee in his diary of 1858. (436~)

—Plateau Town: Very little is known about this "town." Harry Aleson, while trying to track down the history of Glen Canyon's Dr. William H. Schock, interviewed Mrs. June Hansen: "As a child she remembers living on Dr. Schock's ranch while her Mother did the cooking for the crew on the cattle ranch—at PLATEAU. Checking a present-day road map, I find Plateau exactly on the spot near the Koosharem Reservoir.... Very likely, Dr. Schock called his ranch, PLATEAU." (35~)

L

Labyrinth Bay: (Coconino Co., Az. and San Juan Co., Utah.) Glen Canyon NRA-Lake Powell. Arizona map: Wild Horse Mesa. Utah map: Gunsight Butte.

Also called Catacomb Canyon, Labyrinth Canyon, Liiki-izh Shijei, and Maze Canyon.

Harry Aleson called this Little Heaven in 1958. (25~)

Otis "Dock" Marston: "Labyrinth was a sweetie for [river runner Norm] Nevills. At the time of a previous discovery it was designated Catacomb but Ros Johnson was such an enthusiast and promised so much business to Nevills, he wisely permitted her to discover it again." (1289~)

Wallace Stegner in 1948: "Most bizarre of all the canyons, the spookiest concession in this rock fun-house, is Labyrinth Canyon, which narrows down to less than two feet, and whose walls waver and twist so that anyone groping up this dark, crooked, nightmare cranny in the deep rock has to bend over and twist his body sideways to get through.... The thought of what it would be like to be caught in here in a rain gives us the fantods, and we come out fast." (1823~)

Katie Lee in 1954: "We had a great time ... got up Labyrinth via a method it isn't even nice to say out loud let alone in print, but it was really something!!!! Lawd"! (1164~)

Katie Lee at a later date: "They walked about three miles [up the canyon] until it ended in a crevasse—an exit for ravens only. They decided to call it 'The Devil's Corkscrew,' but Norm [Nevills], who liked doing the naming jobs himself, insisted on 'Labyrinth,' though there's a repeat in the lower Grand. It isn't a labyrinth. You can't get lost—one way in, one way out—but simple walking is not the mode of locomotion ... we crawl up through a little bitty hole called Fat Man's Misery, after which is a very long 200-foot-deep, shoulder-width, fluted rift that slants so much you need your hands, as well as feet, to negotiate it." (1162~)

Bill Thompson wrote of Fat Man's Misery in 1957: "Upper convoluted canyon is utterly unbelievable as ever. I consider it one of the truly great wonders of the Southwest on a par with the Rainbow Bridge and Monument Valley." (1880~)

—Circle Pool: Mary Beckwith noted in 1958 that this was the river runner namefor a large pool at the mouth of the canyon. (195~)

Labyrinth Canyon: (Emery and Grand Counties.) Green River. Maps north to south: Green River SE, Tenmile Point, Bowknot Bend, and Mineral Canyon.

Also spelled Labarinth Canyon.

The Labyrinth Canyon section of the Green River starts at its confluence with the San Rafael River and ends at the Emery/Wayne County line at Saddle Horse Bottom. The end of Labyrinth Canyon is somewhat artificial and these days river runners commonly use Mineral Bottom as the dividing line between Labyrinth and Stillwater canyons, since that divides these popular slow-water sections evenly and the takeout for Labyrinth and the put-in for Stillwater is at Mineral Bottom.

George Y. Bradley of the Powell Expedition of 1869: "The whole country is inconceivably desolate, as we float along on a muddy stream walled in by huge sand-stone bluffs that echo back the slightest sound. Hardly a bird save the ill-omened raven or an occasional eagle screaming over us; one feels a sense of loneliness as he looks on the little part ... bound on an errand the issue of which everybody declares must be disastrous." (270~)

John Wesley Powell in 1871: "Gradually the walls rise higher and higher as we proceed, and the summit of the canyon is formed of the same beds of orange-colored sandstone.... The course of the river is tortuous, and it nearly doubles upon itself many times." (1563~)

Frederick S. Dellenbaugh of the 1871–72 Powell Expedition: "This seemed the most fantastic region we had yet encountered. Buttes, pinnacles, turrets, spires, castles, gulches, alcoves, canyons and canyons, all hewn 'as the years of eternity roll' out of the verdureless labyrinth of solid rock, made us feel more than ever a sense of intruding into a forbidden realm." (541~)

Dellenbaugh also described the canyon in a letter home: "The river turns through rather low land almost a valley until the banks gradually rise to walls and the walls form Labyrinth Cañon. This Cañon well deserves its name for such a twisting and bending I never saw before. At one place we had to travel six miles on the river, and got back to the place we started from—except that there was a thin wall about five hundred yards across between us and the starting point [Bowknot Bend]." (550~)

Frank C. Kendrick of the Stanton-Brown Survey in 1889: "The river is like an immense snake that is stretched out taking a sun bath and has not room to stretch out strait [*sic*]. It must be fully 3 times as long as in a direct line." (1838a~)

Lute H. Johnson in 1893: "After miles of this uncertainty the walls, as though at last deciding to hide this river from the droughting sun, rise on both sides at once, gradually for a distance, until gaining an even 1,300 feet, and having attained that, stand bare and formidable. The river with ever changing degrees of swiftness, turning from bank to bank in mad rebellion against such perfect confinement, twists and bends for hundreds of miles between these huge walls of rock, a mad, fretting and foaming current at times, and again a limpid, placid stream, as though the very exertions demanded their seasons of rest. These red sandstone walls, so straight that they often lean backwards are castellated with the light yellow rocks of another age, glacial-polished, wind carved, now and then broken by a sister cañon opening back from the river; their faces broken into shadow and light by the inclining rays of the sun are grotesque, fantastical. A never ending panorama of such mighty walls, picturesque palisades, a narrow slit of liquid blue sky, with floating islands of feathery white clouds above.... Miles and miles this ever-changing scenery, unsurpassed for variety, grandeur and beauty, stretches out until the mind of man is awed, subdued and inundated with the sublime." (998~)

Unattributed in 1891: "In Labyrinth cañon the water is in many places a seething cauldron, the dark waters whirling around in great eddies, tossing the boat of the party about as if a feather." (1907~)

A Mr. Minnich of the Green River Mining and Improvement Company provided a hallucinatory description of Labyrinth and Stillwater canyons in 1895 while trying to attract homesteaders to the bottoms along the river: "The climate is partially semi-tropical, so mild and equitable that the natural changes in the atmosphere cause no irritations to diseases.... The winters are mild. It seldom snows; ice never forms upon the rivers.... The summers are warm, but the atmosphere is so dry that the heat is never oppressive.... Rheumatism, Catarrh [an inflamation of the mucous membranes] and kindred diseases cannot exist there. We have taken over twenty persons so afflicted, down in row boats during the past three years and not one but that was relieved in a very short

time.... There is no scum on the water, or moss on the trees or rocks. Germ life cannot exist here.... The air is so rare that nothing ever decays.... The Products of these bottom lands are of the very finest.... The openings offered for fine fruit farms are not to be equaled outside of California or Florida. Late spring and early fall frosts are not known.... For raising sweet potatoes, peanuts and tobacco, this country cannot be excelled.... For the tourist there is no brighter place, no grander place, on earth. There are no mountains, but walls of rock, whose beauty of color no pen can describe nor artist's brush do justice to. Among these the river so twists and turns that there is ever a shifting panorama before the eye.... Thousands of canary birds and tropical birds of variegated plumage add joy and beauty to the scene.... It is today a paradise for the poor man. It will soon be a haven of beauty and rest for the wealthy." (1365~)

P.A. Leonard in 1904: "At the base of these frowning walls of red sandstone, quartzite and porphyry beautiful fertile bottoms lie along the river, free from overflow at highest watermark by a comfortable margin of several feet, and further protected by an extraordinary growth of willows, forming a green fringe, giving a grateful contrast to the deep red, black and gray colorings of the canyon walls. These bottoms are in some cases a mile or two in length and half a mile or more wide, and usually consist of a sandy loam, which represents the best type of fertile soil in Utah.... Luxuriant growths of bunch grass, blue grass and wild cane are found, together with cottonwood and oak trees." (1178~)

Chas. T. Leeds of the Corps of Engineers in 1910: "There is no point of the compass toward which the river does not flow in some part of its length." (1281~) Amos Burg in 1938: "Named for its winding course, also for its dry lateral canyons, arches, grottoes and buttes that resembled ruined masonry. Barren rock wilderness but very interesting, varied in form and color, red at midday, orange tinted at sunset." (313~)

Senator Barry Goldwater in 1940: "We entered Labyrinth Canyon—this masterpiece of nature started right out to show us that she was well named. Back and forth the river twisted and turned—Red Sandstone walls rising 2 to 400 ft. hemmed us and the river in—What a quick change— from open country into a canyon—But still the river remained quiet and smooth." (738~)

Colin Fletcher in 1997: "Above all, Labyrinth was labyrinthine. On the map it writhed with the exaggerated, improbable sinuosity of a sidewinder rattlesnake scaling a sand dune, and in rockbound reality that meant its constant corkscrews were flanked by alternate cliff and flatland. Cliffs on the outside of each sweeping curve, where the swirling river bit into solid rock. Flatland on the curve's inner flank, where at high water the slower-moving current had deposited silt.... Because no bottomland was the same as the last, no cliff identical to its predecessor, the river kept playing me variations on these, its current prime themes: sheer red rock faces; then flat green-fringed bottomland. And because of our labyrinthine path the light was always changing key." (650~)

Lackey Basin: (San Juan Co.) Manti-LaSal National Forest-La Sal Mountains. La Sal West map.

"Uncle" Bensham F. Lackey lived in the area from the late 1800s into the early 1900s. (388~, 1526~)

—Trough Springs Creek: This is one of several creeks that drain Lackey Basin. It is at elevation 6749T and it ends near the "Hecla Shaft."

Ladder Canyon: (Kane Co.) GSCENM Clay Hole Wash. Nephi Point map.

—Ladder Trail: Herbert E. Gregory noted that this constructed stock trail goes from the Petrified Hollow area north up Ladder Canyon to Nephi, near the head of Nephi Wash. (765~) (See Nephi Pasture—Nephi.) Cal Johnson: "It is a rough trail coming down there. It's just like a ladder going down those rocks." (984~)

Lady in the Bathtub: (San Juan Co.) Valley of the Gods-Moki Dugway. Cedar Mesa South map. (5,552')

Also called Angel's Fear (160a~) and Balanced Rock (266~).

The name was given by tour guides in the early 1960s. (1931~)

Doug Williams in 1965: "After examining 'Lady in a Bathtub,' ... at some length, you get the sneaking suspicion that Walt Disney, not mother nature, supervised the sculpturing process." (2012~)

Lady Mountain: (Washington Co.) Zion National Park-Zion Canyon. Temple of Sinawava map. (6,945')

Also called Mount Zion. (50~, 698~, 2080~)

Zion National Park Superintendent P.P. Patraw in 1934: "The name Lady Mountain was the first one applied so far as known and was given because of the figure of a woman to be seen near the top of the mountain. However, this figure is very indistinct and even when one sees it, after much difficulty in having it pointed out, it requires considerable imagination to form a figure out of it." (1931~)

Juanita Brooks from the summit of Lady Mountain: "There are no words coined to describe the magnificence of the view from here, the expanse of unexplored land that opens to the west, the labyrinth of peaks whose tops are on a level with the high plateau, but separated from each other by abysmal chasms, so many of them huddled together like giants. Beyond them the view stretches out as though to the end of the earth." (293~)

—Lady Mountain Trail: The trail to the top of the mountain was built in 1925. (2043~) Unattributed in 1935: "The trail itself is unique and provides thrills for even experienced climbers. One thousand four hundred steps have been cut in the solid rock along this trail, and 2,000 feet of cable is used to steady the climber." (2080~)

—Cliff Dwelling Mountain: This summit is immediately west of Lady Mountain (at elevation 6945). (2080~)

LaGorce Arch: (Kane Co.) Glen Canyon NRA-Davis Gulch. Davis Gulch map.

Also called Moqui Arch and Moqui Window.

Also spelled LaGarce Arch.

Bering Monroe hiked to the bridge in 1945. Unaware of its previous designation, he called it Roosevelt Natural Bridge, noting that he was at the bridge when the former president died. (1375~)

In honor of Bering Monroe, Harlon Bement called it the Window of Bering Monroe or Bering Monroe Arch.

Dr. John Oliver LaGorce (1880-1949) was an editor at *National Geographic* in the mid-1950s. W.L. Rusho of the USGS: "Although used extensively, the name 'LaGorce' is inappropriate, since Mr. LaGorce was merely an official of the National Geographic Society who had no personal association with either the arch or the general surrounding area." (1931~, 1382~, 1953~)

Before its near-inundation by Lake Powell, an inscription by rancher Peter Orin Barker, dated 1895, was found on the arch. (1021~)

Lake Bottom: (Grand Co.) Colorado River-Amasa Back. Gold Bar Canyon map.

Lloyd Holyoak: "Lake Bottom is just what it is; there is a lake there. Lake Bottom was a placer mine. They placer mined the bar and dredged it out, forming the lake. That is where Lake Bottom comes from." (906~)

—Wild Horse Inn: Now gone, this establishment was on Lake Bottom. (1931~)

Lake Bottom: (Grand Co.) Hotel Mesa-Dolores River. Dewey map.

In the early 1900s Jim Waring homesteaded the bottom. It was called Waring Bottom until 1910 when the name was changed to Lake Bottom. (456~)

—Dolores River Ford: This ford of the Dolores River went between Roberts Bottom and Lake Bottom. Jean Akens: "This ford was used frequently by cowboys, outlaws and others." (13~, 456~)

Lake Canyon: (Kane Co.) GSCENM-Kaiparowits Plateau-Dry Rock Creek. Blackburn Canyon, Sooner Bench, and Navajo Point maps.

Also called Duck Lake (1100~), Lake Draw, Lake Pasture, and The Lakes (1706~).

Don Coleman: "It was a little lake, and then they went in with a team and scraper and made it bigger and put a little dam on it." (441~) Herbert E. Gregory in 1918: "'the Lakes' two ponds in valley each 3000 sq. ft.... Lake formerly fenced. Third lake 6000 sq. ft. below." (760~) The lake is still here and is used by stockmen. Inscriptions include Ken, 1925.

—Line Cabin: A still-used line cabin is on the upper east side of Lake Pasture (Blackburn Canyon map). A large, developed spring is nearby. (441~, SAPE.)

Lake Canyon: (San Juan Co.) Glen Canyon NRA-Lake Powell. Nokai Dome, Halls Crossing NE, and Halls Crossing maps.

Also called Lake Wash. (1259~)

Ranchers from the 1880s called this Lake Canyon or Lake Gulch for a large lake formed by a dam of natural debris and sand several miles up the canyon from the Colorado River. (1249~) (See Lake Pagahrit below.)

Miners during the gold rush days at the turn of the century called it Mystery Canyon or Mysterious Canyon. (466~, 1356~) Buzz Holmstrom: "Up here Lake Creek is called the Mysterious Canyon, as there are many dwellings up there, some very inaccessible & several mummies have been taken out." (560~)

The Eugene Clyde LaRue map of the William R. Chenoweth USGS Expedition of 1921 shows this as Redd Lake in honor of Lemuel H. Redd, a Hole-in-the-Rock Expedition member. He ran livestock in the area. (1145~) Albert R. Lyman in 1936: "The mouth of Lake Gulch is an imposing sight, and always, even to the accustomed eye, it calls men down from the saddle and holds them with rapt awe and admiration; the massive cliffs towering straight to the sky, the broad Colorado river reaching from wall to wall, the voice of the water, the echo, the mystery of this chasm deep in the solid rock—the human mind is lost in contemplation." (1249~)

In a fit of hyperbole, an unattributed *Sunset Magazine* writer said this about Lake Canyon in 1958: "Beautiful waterfalls; extensive cliff dwellings reminiscent of Mesa Verde." (730~)

Dick Sprang spread the ashes of his wife, Dudy, over Lake Canyon, writing: "There were no services, no pagan rites. Her ashes will be released over the lovely and beautiful plateau between the Colorado and San Juan rivers at a point in East Lake Canyon where the low walls retreat and form a rincon floored by wild roses and dogwood and shaded by great cottonwoods. She loved this spot above all others." (1798~)

In a letter to Gary Topping in 1985, Sprang noted that he found inscriptions in a Lake Canyon tributary dating to 1911. One stated: "This is the damndest country God ever put rock on." Another noted: "Be Ware Ye Thieves—Goddam You." (19~, 1115~)

An inscription, in Glen Canyon directly across from the mouth of Lake Canyon, read "Ian ce V. Lay, 1837." There was quite a hullabaloo when this inscription was discovered since it was such an early date. But, the consensus was that it was either being mis-read or it was a fake. The date was most likely 1887. (21~, 1115~) C. Burt, a Colorado prospector, left his name and a date of 1896 near the 1837 inscription, giving rise to the thought that he may have left this bogus number. (1115~)

—Lake Country: This is an area that is defined by White Canyon to the north, Glen Canyon to the west, the San Juan River to the south, and the Red House Cliffs to the east. It was named by local cattlemen who also called it The Lakes, Land of Pagahrit, Lost Cowboy Country, and Pagahrit Country. (6~, 1238~, 1243~)

Erwin Oliver: "A new man is not very good to you in the red rock country. They get lost so many times. We called that country from Halls Crossing to Lake Canyon 'Lost Cowboy' because they got lost out there so much." (1901~) Herbert E. Gregory called it the Red Rock Plateau: "It is an isolated region and difficult of access." (774~)

Albert R. Lyman in 1890: "a country of drifting sand and bald rocks, a country of dry desolation gashed deeply with crooked gulches. Its surface had been carved by the winds into knobs and pinnacles and figures of fantastic patterns. The hellish howl of coyotes echoed back and forth in the darkness of its nights, and long green lizards raced over its hot hills in the day." (1901~)

—East Fork: (Also called East Lake Canyon.) This is the long east fork of the canyon. Its upper end is immediately west of elevation 4727T on the Nokai Dome map. (1523~)

—The Fortress: (Also called Spanish Fort.) This large Anasazi ruin is on the east side of the East Fork one mile (as the crow flies) upcanyon from its junction with Lake Canyon, at a "4WD" road on the Nokai Dome map. It is mentioned in many accounts of the area. Hole-in-the-Rock Expedition member Platte D. Lyman in February 1880: "On a point of rock jutting into the lake is the remains of an old stone fortification, built probably several hundred years ago." (1356~)

Neil M. Judd in 1923: "One ruin passed was built with apparent haste, of bluish slate.... Consisted of five rooms along cliff edge with 30 x 50' enclosed court to E. Not a sherd visible; no refuse; stones carelessly placed and no mud." (1033~)

Archaeologist Floyd W. Sharrock: "Because of its formidable appearance it is locally known as 'The Fortress.' There are, however, no other characteristics to indicate a possible defensive arrangement.... The enclosure is more likely a plaza than a defensive retreat." (1722~)

—Lyman Headquarters: (Also called Lake Canyon Camp.) This huge cave was listed as the Lost Canyon Cowboy Camp on the National Register of Historic Places in 1988. It is in Lake Canyon two and one-quarter miles (as the crow flies) upcanyon from the "Emigrant Trail" (which is shown on the Halls Crossing NE map). It is one-eighth mile southwest of elevation 4321T on the Nokai Dome map. The cave has been used by generations of cowboys as a line camp, including those of the Lazy TY and Scorup-Somerville cattle outfits. (1936~)

John Ernest Adams, Platte D. Lyman, and Wayne Redd were the first to trail cattle into the Lake Pagahrit region, bringing in 225 head in January 1884. They are known to have used the cave. (1260~, 1861~) Lyman called it the Wind Camp. (1259~)

Inscriptions include George Lyman, Blanding Utah, May 1934 and Clyde Lyman, May 6, 1939. (SAPE.)

—Bobtail Fork: (Also called Bobtail Creek.) The "Emigrant Trail" runs along the north side of this eastern tributary of Lake Canyon (one-quarter mile south of elevation 4100T on the Halls Crossing NE map). (1523~, 1795~)

—Lake Canyon Line Cabin: Val Dalton: "It was where the ["Emigrant"] road crosses the canyon [Halls Crossing NE map]. Scorups owned it and Tim Smits burned it down. What happened was, he put a pot of beans on to boil and went out to ride and when he came back, his house and bed and everything was burned up." (517~) This was in the 1970s.

—Lake Pagahrit: (Also called Hermit Lake.) This lake in Lake Canyon no longer exists. The "Emigrant Trail" on the Halls Crossing NE map crossed just above the lake. Albert R. Lyman noted the derivation of the name: "To them [Paiute Indians] we are indebted for the name, which means 'standing water,' and is pronounced paw-GAH-rit.... They said the lake used to have in it a monster which raised its head above the surface in the stillness of the night, and sang a bedeviling song to lure men within its reach." (1245~)

Other names have been used. Hole-in-the-Rock Expedition member William Naylor Eyre: "We found a beautiful lake in a rock basin. We named it Henry Lake." (1356~) Neil M. Judd in 1923: "known both as Red Lake and, to the Navaho, as Black Lake." (1033~)

The Hole-in-the-Rock Expedition crossed the dam of Lake Pagahrit in 1880. Expedition member Platte D. Lyman in February 1880: "a beautiful clear sheet of spring water ½ a mile long and nearly as wide, and apparently very deep. Cottonwood, willow, canes, flags, bulrushes and several kinds of grass grow luxuriantly, and it would make an excellent stock ranch." (1356~)

Albert R. Lyman visited the lake in 1891 as a young boy: "The Pagahrit welcomed me in from the burning desert with joyous sights and sounds and cooling breath from every living thing—the green groves, the grass, the flowers, the happy birds singing exultantly from the trees and the willows. The gentle echo of it came back to me from the gray cliffs enclosing the garden from the wild outside." Lyman described one of the unique feature of the lake: "And wonder of wonders: Pagahrit had three floating islands! Covered with tall rushes as sails on a ship, they sailed with every change of the wind from one side to the other of their little ocean." (1245~)

Pete Steele told a story about his uncle, Perry Steele, and the formation of the islands: "[It] was full of water and there was a lot of vegetation growing around the edge of this lake, and it had been doing so for many years. It was kind of what he referred to as 'peat.' They had this big roan steer that my great grandfather was very proud of and this steer went out to get him a drink of water and he fell through this peat into the lake.... Every time it would try to crawl up [the peat], it would give 'way and he was getting tired. So great-grandpa told him, 'You boys better go out there and help that steer and get him out.' They tied a log on his head so he wouldn't go under the water.... So they took an ax and a shovel and they cut a lane out through that peat to the solid ground to where they could bring that steer back up that lane.... And they got the steer out. Well, they sat there that night and a little wind came up like it does in San Juan County.... The next day, where they had dug that canal, had broken across from the short end to another place and it became an island. And it floated out on Lake Pagahrit and he says that a lot of the cowboys thereafter, they always called that the 'Floating Island' of Lake Pagahrit." (1821~)

The lake no longer exits. Cattleman Al Scorup recalled the bursting of the dam: "To the best of my recollection, the Hermit Lake [Lake Pagahrit] went out Nov. 1st, 1915.

My brother and I were there with a bunch of cattle, and it rained so hard, there was an awful flood and the lake went out." (1702~)

—Lower Lake Pagahrit: Geologist Joel Lawrence Pederson discovered an ancient lakebed two miles below Lake Pagahrit, which he named Lower Pagahrit. (1523~)

—Wasp House: Now underwater, this huge ruin was a popular stop for river runners in Glen Canyon and is often mentioned in historical records. It was one mile up Lake Canyon from its mouth. (708~) Harry Aleson noted that he found an inscription at Wasp House Ruin from R. Collett, May 21, 1881. (19~)

—Long Bottom: This placer bar, now underwater, was on the west side of the Colorado River one mile south of the mouth of Lake Canyon (adjacent to elevation 3868T on the Halls Crossing map). It was being used by 1889. (466~)

—Bedrock Dam Site: (Proposed.) This was on the Colorado River one mile below the mouth of Lake Canyon (Halls Crossing map). The William R. Chenoweth USGS Expedition of 1921 proposed the dam. It would have butted up against the east face of Iron Top Mesa. It was the only place where the river had scoured the canyon down to bedrock. (774~, 1146~, 2007~)

Lake Hollow: (Garfield Co.) Dixie National Forest-Mammoth Creek. Haycock Mountain and Asay Bench maps.
This is a large spring with still-used troughs. (SAPE.)
Unattributed: "Named by sheepherders on account of being a trail via this hollow to Panguitch Lake from Mammoth Creek." (2053~, 1346~)

Lake Louise: (Sevier Co.) Fishlake National Forest-Fish Lake Hightop Plateau-Tasha Creek. Mount Terrill map.
This was named by Elbert L. Cox in the 1930s for his wife, Louise. (1641~)

Lake Philo: (Garfield Co.) Dixie National Forest-Aquarius Plateau. Big Lake map.
This was most likely named for Philo Allen, Sr. (See Allen Dump.)

Lake Powell: (Garfield, Kane, and San Juan Counties, Utah and Coconino Co., Az.)
This man-made reservoir was named for Major John Wesley Powell who led the first expeditions down the Green and Colorado rivers in 1869 and 1871–72. (See Glen Canyon Dam.)
Otis "Dock" Marston in 1966: "With both ends of the Canyon dedicated to the memory of murderers [Cass Hite on the north end and John D. Lee on the south end] and in recognition of the destruction of the Glens of Glen

Canyon, we can suggest the name Gruesome Gulch as Glen now is incongruous." (1293~)

One serious suggestion for a name was Lake Nevills for famed river runner Norm Nevills. (1283~)

Pearl Baker: "We people who have lived at White Canyon and Hite and on the river are heartbroken that so much was lost beneath the lake. Nothing that Lake Powell can ever give to the visiting public can even begin to compare with the damage that it did in the wonderful, wonderful, fabulous places it covered." (119~)

Homer L. Dodge in 1965: "Glen Canyon, one of the beauty spots of the world, has been destroyed and in its place we find Lake Powell, a sorry substitute, good only for motor boats and water skiers for whom there are already plenty of lakes.... If we hurry, we can see and enjoy these natural wonders. But what about our children and the coming generations? Will we leave them any wilderness in which to renew their souls." (563~)

Eliot Porter wrote a eulogy to Glen Canyon in 1969: "This is the monument men have built—you and I—not to the lost Eden so few knew, but to their engineering ingenuity and ruthless ability to transform the land, to remake it simply for the sake of remaking it, thoughtlessly, providently. Gone is indeed an Eden, an Eden of wondrous canyons, some deep, dark, and narrow, some cut in bare rock and boulder-strewn, some green and sunlit. They all bore names suited to their particular attributes: Mystery, Twilight, Dungeon, Labyrinth, Cathedral, Hidden Passage. And one, because of difficult access, was called Lost Eden—a name that now speaks the fate of Glen Canyon." (1555~) (See Lost Eden Canyon.)

Lambs Knoll: (Washington Co.) Lower Kolob Plateau-Smith Mesa. The Guardian Angels map. (6,353')
Edwin Ruthven Lamb (1831–1924) arrived in Virgin in 1862. In 1870 Lamb and family moved to Toquerville. (355~, 462~, 879~)

—Moqui Peak: This is one mile south-southeast of Lambs Knoll (one-quarter mile south of elevation 6040). It was named by Courtney Purcell for the many Moqui marbles (small round sandstone concretions) found on the summit. (1591~)

Lamp Stand: (Garfield Co.) GSCENM-Circle Cliffs Basin. Lamp Stand map. (6,590')
Charles P. Berolzheimer in 1920: "[We] had been told to look for a large natural feature shaped like a lamp stand." (222~, 1396~)

—Natural Tank: An unnamed pothole is one mile northwest of the Lamp Stand (one-eighth mile south-southeast of elevation 6495T). (SAPE.) Charles P. Berolzheimer in

1920: "The water was rather hard to get at. One had to climb up a series of steps hewn of the rock till the first hole came in sight. Above this, also in the solid rock, was another tank, and still another over this. To water the horses we had to throw buckets of water down from the first hole into a little depression in the ground." (222~)

Land of Standing Rocks: (Wayne Co.) Canyonlands National Park-Maze District. Elaterite Basin and Spanish Bottom maps.

Also called Land of Standing Men (851~) and Standy Rocks (617~).

The Land of Standing Rocks area is dotted with pinnacles, towers, and fins formed in the Moenkopi and Organ Rock Shale formations. Over the years many have been given names, including Candlestick Rock, Lizard Rock, Standing Rock, Totem Pole, and The Wall. One formation, The Gong and Gavel, was named by photographers Josef and Joyce Muench in 1957. (871~)

George Y. Bradley of the Powell Expedition of 1869: "And though a thousand spires point Heavenward all around us yet not one sends forth the welcome peal of bells to wake the echoes of these ancient cliffs and remind us of happier if not grander scenes." (270~)

Frederick S. Dellenbaugh of the 1871–72 Powell Expedition: "The Major and [Stephen Vandiver] Jones discovered a series of parks enclosed by pinnacles and thin walls.... We found them both strange and interesting. Made a sketch looking out into the Sinare-to-weap (Land of the Evil Spirit) as the Major calls it." (543~)

John Wesley Powell: "We are now down among the buttes, and in a region the surface of which is naked, solid rock—a beautiful red sandstone, forming a smooth, undulating pavement. The Indians call this the *Toom'pin Tuweap'*, or 'Rock Land,' and sometimes the *Toom'pin wunear' Tuweap'*, or 'Land of Standing Rock.'" (1563~, 465~)

Almon H. Thompson of the 1871–72 Powell Expedition: "To the west was 'Sinar-too-weep', or 'Ghost Land' composed of columns of grey and red sandstones, often 300 feet high with a base for 170 feet of grey, then 100 of red, then orange, and a cap sometimes of red, sometimes of grey, sometimes sharp pinnacles, sometimes round towers." (1877~)

John F. Steward of the 1871–72 Powell Expedition: "We enter these adamantine forests and are hedged in on every side with walls and with lines of needle-like buttes. Passing on we find park after park containing from 200 to 300 acres. They are like natural gardens, but wanting in one essential element—fertility. The dry sandy soil affords sustenance only for pines and cedars. Each of these park-like alcoves is drained by the deep gully to which their origin was due. Often, where the rocks are stripped of the sandy soil, little depressions have become eroded in the rock. In these water has collected, which is very pure and clear." (1830~)

E.O. Beaman of the 1871–72 Powell Expedition: "As far as the sight can reach, a smooth, flat rock spreads out in every direction in unbroken monotony, save when here and there, a butte or pinnacle looms up like some stern guardian of the stony waste. Many of these pinnacles are from three hundred to one thousand feet high, composed of the most exquisite party-colored sandstone, and cut and washed by the sandstorms into the most grotesque and fantastic forms. On some portions of the plain they are grouped so as to present the appearance of a grove; others resemble ruined cities and castles in the distance, and still others are like the mammoths and saurians of by-gone ages browsing quietly." (172~)

Amos Burg in 1938: "This is the most inaccessible part of the United States. Scaling a thousand-foot cliff [from the river], our eyes swept the 'Land of Standing Rocks,' dome-shaped and pinnacled, weird and fascinating in shape and color. Here were limitless leagues of silence. In all directions extended uninhabited, waterless wastes, with a jumble of mesas, buttes, peaks and mountains that shoulder above this plateau of naked rocks. The sight awed and inspired me." (314~)

Landscape Arch: (Grand Co.) Arches National Park-Devils Garden. Mollie Hogans map.

Also called Delicate Arch.

(See Delicate Arch—Grand Co. for name derivation.)

This is the third longest natural arch in the world, having a span of 290 feet. Although discovered in the late 1800s, the arch was named by Frank Beckwith of the Arches National Monument Scientific Expedition of 1933-34: "Wind-blown sand rises behind it in a steep slope, covered with cedars [junipers], giving this arch somewhat the appearance of a landscape painted within a frame cut to an arch effect." (898~)

Dick Wilson in 1968: "Landscape is said to be a scientific impossibility violating the laws of physics, engineering, and rigid-body dynamics. Its 291-foot thread of rock is suspended delicately through space and gently attached at both ends. The slightest earth tremor would probably date its end." (2019~)

Since 1991 several large chunks of rock have fallen from the arch.

Lands End: (Garfield Co.) Glen Canyon NRA-Big Ridge. Clearwater Canyon and Teapot Rock maps. (7,151')
Also called Lands End Plateau. (1658~)
This area marks the end of The Big Ridge. Early maps often called all of The Big Ridge "Lands End." (473~) David D. Rust in 1930: "Ride 3 miles to 'Lands End' for master view." (1672~)
Ward J. Roylance described the view from Lands End: "Cataract Canyon, Standing Rocks, the Needles, Salt Creek mesas and canyons, Dark Canyon, Gypsum Canyon, and the great eastern wall of Indian Creek are plainly visible across the basin from Lands End. So also are the La Sals and Abajos, Dead Horse Point area, and Junction Butte." (1659~)
—Lands End Peak: (Also called Lands End Butte.) (100~)
This is on the southwest side of Lands End (at elevation 7151 [Lands End] on the Clearwater Canyon map). In 1960 Harry Aleson noted that in 1955 the USGS put a triangulation station at Lands End Peak. (30~)

Langston Mountain: (Iron Co.) Zion National Park-La Verkin Creek. Kolob Reservoir and Kolob Arch maps. (7,408')
John Langston (1822–1882) arrived in Rockville in 1862. His son, John H. Langston (1863-1930), is credited with being the first child born in Rockville. The family later moved to Springdale. (14~, 273~, 482~)

Larb Hollow: (Garfield Co.) Dixie National Forest-Boulder Mountain-Spring Gulch. Lower Bowns Reservoir and Grover maps.
Several old cowboys noted that Larb was a browse grass for livestock.

Lark Canyon: (Washington Co.) Dixie National Forest-Pine Valley Mountains-Santa Clara River. Saddle Mountain and Central East maps.
This was most likely named for Washington County pioneer William Lark (1819–1889). (1134~)

Larry Canyon: (Wayne Co.) Dirty Devil Country-Dirty Devil River. Angel Point and Burr Point maps.
Guy Robison noted that the canyon was probably named for Larry Thompson, the first person to fence the canyon. (1644~)
—Constructed Stock Trail: This enters lower Larry Canyon on its south side one-half mile upcanyon from its mouth. Ted Ekker noted that it was built by Joe Biddlecome before 1920. (623~)
Guy Robison: "It's a hell of a trail. It's awful.... Lots of bedrock and steep and narrow." (1644~)

La Sal Creek: (San Juan Co., Utah and Montrose Co., Colo.) Manti-LaSal National Forest-Old La Sal-Dolores River. Utah maps: Mount Peale, La Sal East, Ray Mesa. Colorado map: Paradox.
(See La Sal Mountains for name derivation.)
In 1875 the Ferdinand V. Hayden Survey called this Tukuhnikavats Creek. (420~)
—La Sal Guard Station: This was on La Sal Creek one and one-half miles north-northwest of Old La Sal (one-quarter mile northeast of elevation 7407T on the La Sal East map). There is nothing at the site now. (1931~)

La Sal Junction: (San Juan Co.) Highway 191-West Coyote Creek. La Sal Junction map.
This is the junction of Highways 191 and 46.
—Old Spanish Trail: The trail crossed what is now La Sal Junction. (474~)

La Sal Mountains: (Grand and San Juan Counties.)
Also called Live Lassell Mountains, Livi Lasell Mountains (818a~), Sierra la Sal (M.20.), and Sierra Le Sal (M.60.). Also spelled Lasalle Mountains, La Salle Mountains, and Lasal Mountains.
The Navajo name for the La Sal Mountains is *Dzil Ashdlá'ii. Dzil* is Navajo for "mountain" and *Ashdlá'* means "five," or "five mountains" for the major peaks of the La Sals. (983~, 1962~)
Two name derivations are given. The first is correct.
First, *La Sal* is "The Salt" in Spanish. The mountain range was noticed by Spanish traders as early as 1750 and by 1765 the name *Sierra de La Sal* was on the maps. Frey Silvestre Veliz de Escalante, after passing through the area in 1776, wrote in his diary: "It [the Dolores River] runs northwest and west until it joins the Rio de la Sal because close to it there are salt beds where according to what we are told, the Yutas who live hereabout get their salt." (1526~)
John C. Fremont in 1854: "Salt is abundant on the eastern border [of Utah], mountains—as the *Sierra de Sal*— being named from it." (683~)
Second, a 1908 *Wasatch Wave* newspaper article noted: "La Salle National Forest is named after the famous French explorer Robert Cevalier de la Salle, who in 1669 set out upon a tour of western exploration." (556~)
Orville C. Pratt called these the California Mountains in 1848. At that time California had no eastern border, leading to some confusion. (1572~)
Jacob H. Schiel of the Captain John W. Gunnison Expedition of 1853 noted them as the Elk Mountains. (1696~)
It is unclear if he knew the name in 1853, or if he learned of that name later: his book of 1859 is a mix of his diaries

and narrative. It is difficult to distinguish between the two.

The Elk Mountain Mission of 1855 called these the Elk Mountains, a name that was used by other expeditions and diarists until the late 1800s. (1855~) William B. Pace of the expedition called them both Elk Mountains and East Mountains. (1500~) Rusty Salmon noted that the Ute Indians were the ones who named the range the Elk Mountains for the "herds they hunted there." (1687~)

The Ferdinand V. Hayden Survey in 1875 referred to them as the Salt Mountains. Hayden: "The Salt Mountains consist of about thirty peaks, forming a range about 15 miles in length and about 5 miles wide." (848~)

The Colonel William Wing Loring Expedition of 1857-58 called them Gray Mountain. (1276~)

La Sal Pass: (San Juan Co.) Manti-LaSal National Forest-La Sal Mountains-Hell Canyon. Mount Tukuhnikivatz map. (10,160')

This is the pass between Mount Tukuhnikivatz and South Mountain. It used to be called South Pass. (1627~) It was an often-used camping area by Paiute Indians. (1741~)

La Sal Town: (San Juan Co.) La Sal Mountains-Highway 46. La Sal East map. PRIVATE PROPERTY.

Also called New La Sal. (2029~)

The Ferdinand V. Hayden Survey in 1875 noted this as an area of Ute Farms. (M.30.)

The town of Old La Sal was established in 1877 by the Thomas Ray family. Cornelia Perkins: "August 6, 1901, the post office was officially moved from La Sal [now Old La Sal] to the new headquarters ranch at that time called Coyote [now called La Sal]. The post office retained the name La Sal and the new ranch and townsite gradually took that name also." (1526~, 122~, 1530~)

David Lavender in 1943: "It is not a town. It is a sheep company: store, garage, warehouses, boardinghouses, barns, networks of corrals, and mile after mile of fodder-producing fields set like bright emeralds in the gray sage. It is a good Mormon concern run in a good Mormon way by its horse-trading boss, Charlie Redd." (1151~) The "town" is now the headquarters for Redd Ranches. (1750~)

—La Sal Canal: This went from La Sal Creek, across a divide, to Coyote Flats. It was finished in 1889 with construction overseen by Jon Cunningham of the Pittsburgh Cattle Company. (1741~)

Last Chance Canyon: (Emery Co.) West Tavaputs Plateau-Gray Canyon. Three Fords Canyon map.

Waldo Wilcox: "The Last Chance Bench lays in the sun. If you are snowed in over on that range, it was the last chance you had and if you didn't make it there, your cows died." (2011~)

Last Chance Canyon: (Iron Co.) Hurricane Cliffs-High Mountain-Cedar Canyon. Flanigan Arch map.

Also called Log Hollow. (768~)

Jess Guymon: "With just the one outlet if you missed that it was the 'Last Chance' for escape." (2053~)

—Pioneer Road: A road used to go up Last Chance Canyon. (1931~)

Last Chance Creek: (Kane Co.) GSCENM-Kaiparowits Plateau-Glen Canyon NRA-Last Chance Bay. Petes Cove, Ship Mountain Point, Needle Eye Point, Smoky Hollow, and Sit Down Bench maps.

The Lieutenant George M. Wheeler Survey map of 1872–73 shows this as Cotton Creek. (M.76.) The Last Chance Creek name is shown on the 1887 J. Barthalemew map. (328~) Volney King noted it as Last Chance Cannon in 1890. (1096~)

Two name derivations are given.

First, Arthur L. Crawford in 1945: "For years during early pioneer history this canyon was the last chance for anyone entering from the south to get out of the chasms, over the [Kaiparowits] plateau, and across to the cow towns to the north and west." (479~, 1346~)

Second, Edson Alvey noted that this remote canyon was the last chance for livestock to water. (55~)

In 1938, a *St. Louis Post-Dispatch* article described the canyon with absolutely no accuracy: "In Last Chance Canyon ... they found thousands of cliff dwellings lining the canyon walls for 15 miles. Smoke-blackened walls told of the cooking fires of generations." (1927~)

Nora Candell in 1940: "A creek runs through it, and it seemed strange and rather pleasant, to be splashing along in the water after all the arid miles we had traveled. After a while it widens out into a broad valley with enormous towering cliffs on either side; wonderful, stupendous scenery ... even in thought, one runs out of adjectives." (507~)

Dr. Russell G. Frazier described Last Chance Creek as seen from the river in 1955 as "a spectacular knife slash through the rocks." (672~)

Joyce Muench, from Last Chance Bay in 1964: "Great buttes stand back on their rolling peneplain of slickrock, and the horizon is high, along the tops of mesas which stretch clear off into the distance." (1400~)

—Rogers Grave: Near the road crossing on the lower part of Last Chance Wash (Sit Down Bench map) is a gravestone simply marked "Rogers." (SAPE.)

Last Chance Creek: (Emery, Sevier, and Wayne Counties.) San Rafael Swell-Salt Wash. Johns Peak, Willow Springs, Solomons Temple, Salvation Creek, and Caine Springs maps.

Also called Last Chance Wash and Middle Desert Wash. (567~)

Garn Jefferies: "When you were going from Paradise Valley down to the [Last Chance] desert, this was the last chance for water before you dropped over the Limestone Cliffs." (959~)

—Doris Basin: Jim Crane noted that this drainage is to the north of Last Chance Creek and is two miles west of Round Spring (one-half mile north of elevation 8614 on the Johns Peak map). (478~)

—Cow Pond Draw: Jim Crane noted that this northern (or western) tributary of Last Chance Creek is immediately north of Doris Basin and is one mile south of Johns Peak (immediately south of elevation 8517 on the Johns Peak map). (478~)

—Last Chance Dugway: This steep section of road goes up the cliffs three miles north-northeast of Last Chance Ranch (one-quarter mile west-northwest of elevation 6223 on the Willow Springs map). Inscriptions include Leroy Allred, March 1, 1910. Jim Crane: "Those inscriptions are interesting because the dugway there didn't exist until the CCs built it in the 1940s." (478~, SAPE.) (See Willow Springs Wash.)

—Piano Hill: This is one-half mile east of Last Chance Dugway. Jim Crane: "When the CCs had the camp over at Willow Springs, all the boys got together and bought a piano and had that at the CCs camp. When they disbanded the camp, they didn't know what to do with the piano. Since they couldn't decide, they hauled it over to the [Last Chance] Dugway and kicked the sucker off the hill. You can still see the keys and such at the bottom of the cliff. We call that Piano Hill now." (478~)

Last Chance Desert: (Emery Co.) San Rafael Swell-Limestone Cliffs. Solomons Temple and Willow Springs maps.

(See Last Chance Creek for name derivation.)

Last Chance Ranch: (Sevier Co.) San Rafael Swell-Last Chance Desert. Willow Springs map. PRIVATE PROPERTY.

Also called Sorensen Ranch.

Garn Jefferies: "Tom Jones and Tom Clark started the Last Chance Ranch. After a few years Tom Jones parted with Tom Clark. Tom Clark stayed there and Tom Jones went up on the bench south of the [Jefferies] ranch. He was going to start a farm up there. He went up and got

some water from some springs and brought it down to the bench, but he just didn't have enough water. He finally sold it. Irwin Robison bought it. They had the Paradise Valley Ranch and the Last Chance Ranch. The Sorensen brothers bought it [in the late 1940s]." (959~)

Jim Crane, the present owner of the ranch, noted that his father, Elliot Crane, bought the property in 1958. Jim still uses the ranch as the base of his operations on the Last Chance Desert. (478~) Jim Crane on the name: "That ranch has been called a lot of things. It was the Robison Ranch, then when Sorenson bought it, it was the Sorenson Ranch. Every time it changed ownership, it was called something else. I remember when dad [Elliot Crane] bought it. The Bureau of Land Management asked him, 'What're you going to call it, the Crane Ranch?' Dad said, 'Heck no I'm not going to call it the Crane Ranch. It's going to be the Last Chance Ranch because the Last Chance Creek comes down through it and that's exactly what it needs to be named.' Now I suppose its name is going to stay with it, no matter what happens." (478~)

Last Chance Rapid: (Grand Co.) Colorado River-Westwater Canyon. Big Triangle map.

For those running Westwater Canyon, Last Chance Rapid is the last chance to flip a boat; there are no more rapids after Last Chance. (1363~)

Lathrop Canyon: (San Juan Co.) Canyonlands National Park-Island in the Sky District-Colorado River. Musselman Arch and Monument Basin maps.

—Lathrop Canyon Sheep Trail: This is the "Foot Trail" at the top of Lathrop Canyon (Musselman Arch map). Howard Lathrop is credited with building the trail. He ran sheep in the area in the 1940s. The lower part of the trail, from the White Rim to the Colorado River, is shown as a "4WD" road. This part of the trail was upgraded to a road during the uranium boom of the 1950s. Howard's wife, Marguerite, described the building of the trail in 1940: "After much foot work, surveying and engineering, with dynamite he blasted a path through the rocks. He had two men with picks and shovels clear away the debris." (1147~, 1429~)

—Sheep Camp: At least until the mid-1960s, an old cabin and storage building used by sheepherders were at the top of the Lathrop Canyon Sheep Trail. (1435~, SAPE.) Inscriptions include Rusty Allen, Oct. 30, 1926. (1112~)

Lava Point: (Washington Co.) Zion National Park-Upper Kolob Plateau. Kolob Reservoir map. (7,822')

Besides its location on a lava rock outcrop, it is also the highest drivable point in Zion National Park.

Lava Spring: (Wayne Co.) Dixie National Forest-Boulder Mountain-Dark Valley. Government Point map.

This is a large, beautiful spring that issues from a boulder field of lava rocks. (SAPE.)

Lavender Canyon: (Iron Co.) Cedar Breaks National Monument-Columbine Ridge-Ashdown Creek. Brian Head map.

Also called Rattle Canyon. (768~)

Lavender is a light purple color, which accurately describes the walls of this canyon.

Lavender Canyon: (San Juan Co.) Canyonlands National Park-Needles District-Indian Creek. Cathedral Butte, South Six-shooter Peak, and Harts Point South maps.

Also called Lavender Creek.

Ed Lavender was a Colorado rancher from the Paradox area. He was also the stepfather of noted western author David Lavender. Richard Negri: "During the 1920s Ed Lavender was buying cattle from the Scorup-Somerville Cattle Company. When the S/S sold a batch of cattle to Ed, they rounded them up and held them in the closest box canyon near the Dugout Ranch until Ed's drovers would arrive and drive them off; hence, that canyon became known as Lavender's Canyon." (1429~)

—Lavender Mesa: This small mesa is sandwiched between Lavender and Davis canyons (at elevations 6950 and 6738T on the South Six-shooter Peak map). (911~). Edwin T. Wolverton called the Lavender Mesa area Rock Island in 1928: "the place we called Rock Island.... Some of the valleys near the heads of the canyons are beautiful, with their streams of clear water and luxuriant vegetation. Some time, some day, people who love such things will go to look at the district, but they can not take easy chairs with them, and they will be beyond the sound of a locomotive whistle." (2037~)

La Verkin Creek: (Iron and Washington Counties.) Zion National Park-Upper Kolob Plateau-Ash Creek. Kolob Reservoir, Kolob Arch, Smith Mesa, Pintura, and Hurricane maps.

Also spelled Levearskin River (469~, 2043~), Le Virken Creek (1023~), and Lavearskin River (1161~).

(See La Verkin Town for name derivation.)

La Verkin Town: (Washington Co.) Virgin River-Hurricane Cliffs-Highway 17. Hurricane map.

Also spelled Leverkin. (437~)

Three name derivations are given. The first two are similar.

First, Thomas Judd in 1895: "The La Verkin Creek name doubtless arose from a corruption of the pronunciation of the Virgen [Virgin] River.... In the course of time our American use of the Spanish name and sound La Virgen, (using the hard sound for the 'g') became corrupted in our spelling from the proper letters to 'La Verkin,' retaining, rudely, the Spanish sound, but sacrificing the Spanish spelling." (1931~)

Second, Arthur F. Bruhn: "Some people believe that the Paiute Indians who lived here could not pronounce the Spanish word for the creek, *La Virgin* (pronounced La Verheen), leading to the corruption of the world as La Verkin." (311~)

Third, Kate B. Carter noted that *Laverkin* was an Indian word for "Beautiful Valley." (380~)

The area was settled in 1888 by Thomas Judd, Morris Wilson, and several others. In 1895, after first building a canal to bring water to the area, a town was established. (273~, 311~, 324~)

George C. Fraser in 1914: "A small town with little land under cultivation. Floods in the Virgin have created havoc with the old farms. There was growing some grain, many peaches and apricots and grapes." (667~)

—La Verkin Canal: (Hurricane and Virgin maps.) To make the town of La Verkin viable, the first settlers had to dig a canal to carry water from the Virgin River into the town, a massive undertaking. Thomas Cottam and Thomas Judd spearheaded construction, which started in 1888. After much work, they found that water would sink into the gypsum soil. It was only after the introduction of cement in the early 1900s that the canal worked well. (14~)

—La Verkin Hot Springs: (See Pah Tempe Spring.)

Lawrence Town: (Emery Co.) Castle Valley-Huntington Creek. Huntington map.

This town, initially named Lower Huntington Creek, was settled in 1879 by David Dimmick, Simeon Drollinger, H.S. Loveless, William Alma Staker, and others. It was named in 1889 in honor of Mormon Stake President C.G. Lawrence. (972~, 1933~, 2053~)

—Stakersville: This was an area just to the south of Lawrence. (1717~) (See Staker Canyon and Staker Spring for name derivation.)

Leach Canyon: (Iron Co.) Harmony Mountains-Duncan Creek. Desert Mound map.

Duncan Creek goes through Leach Canyon.

Also called Leaches Canyon. (1931~)

—Leach's Cut-off: In 1855 James Leach (1815–1911) built what would become Leach's Cut-off, a road that took a direct route from Cedar City to Pinto and Mountain Meadows, avoiding the original wagon road from Cedar City through Iron Springs, Antelope Springs, and Newcastle. (1256~)

Lean-to Canyon: (San Juan Co.) Dark Canyon Plateau-Dark Canyon. Bowdie Canyon East, Black Steer Canyon, and Indian Head Pass maps.

Two similar name derivations are given.

First, John Scorup: "The lean-to actually is just a little small alcove, just real tiny, and its got cedar and pinyon posts comin' down through the front and one little door in it." (1821~)

Second, Carl Mahon: "When the Youngs [See Youngs Canyon] were over there, they built a camp out on a point along the rim of the canyon and they took and cut a whole bunch of trees and leaned them up against a ledge and put cedar bark on them and kind of fixed it up like a hogan and they camped there. So it just went by the name of Lean-to because the lean-to was in that canyon." (1272~)

Jim Scorup: "The name originated from an old lean-to shelter the cowboys used when herding cattle in this area. It is near the NE end of the point in the small clearings." (1931~)

—Big Cave: This well-known line camp cave is on the upper east side of Lean-To Canyon (one-eighth mile north of elevation 6012T on the Bowdie Canyon West map). (1821~)

—Lean-to Trail: There are credible stories about a stock trail going all the way down Lean-to Canyon. Carl Mahon noted that he believes that the trail actually dropped into the canyon near its mouth from the north and went down a steep slope. (1272~)

Leap Creek: (Washington Co.) Hurricane Cliffs-Ash Creek. New Harmony and Pintura maps.

(See Peters Leap for name derivation.)

Lebaron Creek: (Beaver Co.) Tushar Mountains-East Fork Iant Creek. Shelly Baldy Peak and Circleville Mountain maps.

Unattributed: "Named for Alonzo, Dan, and William LeBaron, sheepmen, prospectors and trappers in the 1870s." (260~, 1930~)

Leche-e Rock: (Coconino Co., Az.) Navajo Indian Reservation-Antelope Creek. Leche-e Rock, Az. map. (5,900')
Lichíí' is Navajo for "red." This is Red Rock. (2072~)

Lecleed Spring: (Garfield Co.) Henry Mountains-Crescent Creek. Raggy Canyon map.

Guy Robison noted that a fellow named Lecleed lived in the area. (1644~) Kevin Robison said he knew it as McCleets Spring. (1646~)

Leeds Town: (Washington Co.) Hurricane Cliffs-Interstate 15. Hurricane and Pintura maps.

The first settlers, Richard Ashby and John S. Harris, arrived in 1866. The town was initially named Bennington (also spelled Benington) for Elder Bennington Stringham. He changed the name to Leeds in honor of the town in England where he served a mission. (375~, 382~, 1277~)

The discovery of silver at nearby Silver Reef in 1875 brought prosperity to the town until the mid-1880s. With the longest growing season of any town in Utah, Leeds has now become famous for its orchards. (311~)

Martha Mills told of an incident of travel just before getting to Leeds in 1870: "We went about 3 miles and the tire on the wagon I drove broke and we had to camp. Martin [Mills] walked two miles and found a blacksmith at the settlement.... He got the wheel fixed and got about a mile and a half and the tire broke again. He took it back and got it patched.... We started again and got about six miles from everybody and the tire broke again." (383~)

—Road Valley: Marietta M. Mariger: "Leeds is a pretty little town situated on Highway 91 [now Interstate 15], in a valley originally called Road Valley.... [It] was a welcome place to the freighters, as it was neither a sand patch nor a bed of boulders." (1277~)

Lee Pass: (Washington Co.) Zion National Park-Beatty Point. Kolob Arch map. (6,000')

Frank Jensen in 1964: "Lee Pass, incidentally, was named for John D. Lee [1812-1877] of the infamous Mountain Meadow Massacre." (965~) Jensen in 1966: "Lee Pass is the finest viewing platform for the Finger Canyon area." (966~)

Lee Point: (Iron Co.) Hurricane Cliffs-Blue Valley. Cedar Mountain map. (8,400') PRIVATE PROPERTY.

Herbert E. Gregory noted that Willis T. Lee of the USGS studied the geology of Iron County in the early 1900s. (768~)

Leers Canyon: (Duchesne Co.) Bad Land Cliffs-Argyle Creek. Wood Canyon map.

This is most likely named for the Ed Lee family. They had a ranch along Argyle Creek from the early days to 1919. (558~)

Lees Backbone: (Coconino Co., Az.) Navajo Indian Reservation-Echo Cliffs. Lees Ferry, Az. map.

Also called Hell's Back Bone. (294~)

Early explorers and settlers found that after crossing the Colorado River at Lees Ferry, a route was needed up the initial cliff band. In the spring of 1873 a large group of Mormons on their way to settle on the Little Colorado

River crossed at Lees Ferry. John D. Lee and the leader of the settlers, John W. Young, helped build a road up the cliffs at what was then called Devil's Backbone. (437~, 2065~) Andrew Amundsen, one of the group: "We then comenst cosing over Wagons, all over sef and sound.... In the Morning we stared op the hill verry rokky and steep ... no track ner road ever made, for we wass the first ones that ever crosed the Cllored with Wagons, so we hed to break over road all the way, and in som places very rough so that we hed to woke it." (58~)

The road proved problematic for travelers and several diarists mentioned their travails on its steep and rugged slopes. Jesse N. Smith in 1878: "We came to the celebrated Lee hill over a bold point of mountain that came to the river on the eastern side. The ascent was bad and the descent difficult and dangerous, the worst road I ever saw traveled with vehicles." (1775~)

Minnie Petersen Brown in 1884: "The road led up a rocky mountain and once the wheels got in a groove there was no turning out until the top of the mountain was reached. Those tracks in the rocks looked as though they had been chiseled out." (382~)

A.H. Jones in 1910: "had quite a lot of work to do on the dugway along the River to get our wagons over, and almost lost the boat over the edge." (1009~)

Not only was the route up Lees Backbone difficult, the route down the south side of the cliffs was also hard. Bert M. Fireman: "The descent toward the south was a frightening experience, on a road so narrow and impeded by rocks and sheer cliffs that the finest horsemanship was necessary, with locked wheels and safety ropes often needed to prevent wagon and teams from tumbling to death. It was a 350-foot descent, extended over about four miles, every bit dangerous and harrowing." (644~)

Inscriptions include one that reads "Dec. 4, 1878. This Rock Sentinel to Passing of First Mesa Company Under the Command of Hyrum Smith Phelps." Others include I.T. Kempton, Oct. 82; Isaac Miller, 24 Jul 1885; Val. Wightman, May 10, 95; and Jack Rowe, Jov. 13/96. (1019~, 1111~)

Lees Ferry: (Coconino Co., Az.) Glen Canyon NRA-Colorado River. Lees Ferry, Az. map.

Also called Lee Ferry, Pahreah Ferry, Paria Crossing, and Pa Weep.

Also spelled Luis Ferry. (915~)

The Navajo term for Lees Ferry is *Tsinaa'eel Dahsi'á* or "Boat Placed Above." (983~) The Paiute name is *Parove*, or "crossing." (82~)

Lees Ferry was historically one of the few good fords of the Colorado River between Moab and the mouth of the Grand Canyon. The other good crossings were at Hite and the Crossing of the Fathers.

The first Euroamerican explorers known to have seen the area were members of the Domínguez-Escalante Expedition. They camped at the mouth of the Paria River in October 1776. Staggered by the immensity of the surrounding cliffs, which they knew they would have to somehow climb on their march to the east, they called their camp *San Benito Salsipuedes*. *San Benito* refers to a "garish white cassock with colored markings that was worn by errant brothers as a mark of punishment." (1357~) *Salsipuedes* means "get out if you can." Together they refer to the predicament the expedition found itself in. Escalante: "We were surrounded everywhere by plateaus and inaccessible peaks." (81~, 284~) The expedition did not cross the Colorado River at Lees Ferry; rather, they struggled up the cliffs via the Domínguez Trail and crossed the river at the Crossing of the Fathers. Don Bernardo de Miera, the cartographer for the expedition, called the Lees Ferry area *Saint Bartolome*. (48~)

William B. Maxwell and members of the Mormon Battalion were the first Euroamericans known to have crossed the Colorado River at Lees Ferry. They were returning from California in 1847 when they crossed the river here. (See Appendix One—William Bailey Maxwell.)

Jacob Hamblin and party, bound for the Hopi towns to the south, passed by the mouth of the Paria River in 1858. Although they crossed the Colorado River at the Crossing of the Fathers, Hamblin reconnoitered enough to realize that a crossing of the Colorado at the Paria River would save several days of hard travel. Hamblin returned in 1859 and again crossed at the Crossing of the Fathers. In 1860, determined to force a crossing at the Paria, his party carried a small boat from Santa Clara. Although they carted the boat over Hurricane Hill and the Buckskin Mountains, they were defeated by the deep sands near Jacobs Pool and abandoned it on the desert. Without the boat, but determined to cross, the group built a raft, which unfortunately didn't float well enough to allow passage. (1612~)

John Steele described the country at the mouth of the Paria River while on an expedition with Jacob Hamblin in 1862: "The rock stands up biding defiance to wind and weather in all manner of shapes. It looks as though nature had some wonderful freaks about this river." (1820~)

The Jacob Hamblin Expedition to the Hopi of 1864 was able to cross the Colorado River at the mouth of the Paria, becoming the second group of Euroamericans to do so. Noting that the area of the crossing was exceedingly remote, Hamblin named it Lonely Dell. Other settlers called it Jacobs Crossing in honor of Hamblin. (475~, 1612~)

By 1869 a small settlement near the crossing had been started by the Mormon Church. Jack C. Sumner of the 1969 Powell Expedition: "It is desolate enough to suit a lovesick poet." (1847~)

John D. Lee (1812-1877) was sent by the church to run the ferry and to trade with the Indians in 1871. Recollecting Hamblin's name, Lee called his ranch at the mouth of the Paria River "Lonely Dell." (551~, 737~, 1612~) Lee in 1872: "In return for the kind reception & affable Manner in which they had been entertained since their arrival at this place, they & Maj. Powell adopted My Name for the place, Lonely Dell & so ordered it to be printed U.S. Mapped." (437~)

Henry C. DeMotte of the 1871–72 Powell Expedition described Lee and Lonely Dell: "a strange eccentric character whose true biography would record many thrilling adventures and hair-breadth escapes, and possibly throw light on many mysterious passages of Mormon history. This peculiar man, generally considered an outlaw, even by his own people, gave us a cordial welcome to his home, and served us to the best his larder could supply.... The house of logs, and innocent of floor, whose foundations were not laid with square and compass, stood with gable pointing toward the south of east; along one side a shade, composed of leafy boughs, served well the purpose of a verandah." (553~)

George Cannon Lambert described Lee in the early 1870s: "He may have been a fanatic, although he did not have the air of one. He impressed me as being a man of sound sense and good judgment; of independent thought and action, who would not easily be swerved from what he conceived to be the right course by anything that others might say or do." (361~)

John Hanson Beadle visited the area in 1872: "The view was one for the poet, the painter, and the novelist. The lofty mountains which wall in the Colorado, here gave back a few rods from the water's edge. From the mountain summits, forty miles northward, Pahreah Creek plunged down by a series of wild cascades into a deep gorge, which meandering across the plateau, grew into a rugged cañon, and here, at its junction with the Colorado, widened its granite jaws to inclose a small plat of level land. On all sides rose the red and yellow hills, by successive 'benches,' to a plateau five thousand feet above; on that again red buttes rose thousands of feet higher,

their wind-worn and polished summits very inaccessible to man, and barely brushed by the bald eagle in his loftiest flights." (171~)

John D. Lee was convicted of participating in the 1857 Mountain Meadows Massacre and was executed twenty years later, in 1877. After his death, Lee's wife, Emma, sold the ferry to the Mormon Church for three thousand dollars in cash, cattle, and a wagon. Joseph L. Foutz and Warren Johnson were assigned to run the ferry. (1475~)

Anthony W. Ivins told this story in 1878: "For the first time since people have lived here [at Lees Ferry] the Colorado is frozen over at the ferry from shore to shore ... in the still water where the ferry boat crosses there is a natural bridge of ice over which teams have been crossing for several days.... We unhitched the team, tied a rope to the end of the tongue, and the two of us easily pulled the wagon to the south bank. We then led the horses over singly.... Some of the cattle we were obliged to throw down and hog tie and drag them across. The ice was so smooth that a man could drag an animal over without trouble." (945~)

Lydia Ann Nelson Brinkerhoff, Warren Johnson's sister-in-law, lived at Lees Ferry in the early 1880s: "Our home was in a narrow deep canyon; in the summertime the heat became intense. Fishing was good in the river during flood season; I remember cleaning one that weighed thirty-five pounds.... The weather was warm and ... they had an abundance of vegetables, melons, grapes and other kinds of fruits." (292~)

Minnie Petersen Brown in 1884: "This was a haven for the weary traveler.... Everything looked so good. They still had apples on the trees and there were pumpkins, squash and potatoes.... A clear stream of water ran through the little village and on to join the mighty Colorado River." Brown went on to describe the crossing: "The method of ferrying was planned very carefully. The men first took over one wagon and a span of horses. The horses were blindfolded and before they led them on the boat, they removed all the harness except the halter, this left them free to swim if necessary. The owner stood by their heads—talked to them so they would not get excited." (382~)

Warren Johnson turned the ferry over to James Simpson Emmett and family in 1895 or 1896. Prior to Emmett, the ferry boat had been operated with oars. Emmett installed a cable across the river, making the ferry much more efficient. (364~, 1629~)

Emmett sold the Lees Ferry Ranch (also called Emmett Ranch) and ferry to the Grand Canyon Cattle Company in 1909. (1629~) George C. Fraser in 1914: "Jim Emmet [*sic*] formerly lived at Lee's Ferry.... He was driven out of Lee's Ferry by the Grand Canyon Cattle Company people, with whose superintendent he had quarreled. The two men had guns out for each other for some time. Emmet was accused of stealing cattle up in that country." (667~) In 1910 Coconino County took over the operation of the ferry, which they did until 1928 when the bridge over Marble Canyon six miles downriver was built. (1629~)

A.H. Jones in 1910: "The ranch [Lees Ferry] is a very pretty little place with a fine lot of fruit trees, grapevines, etc. There are about 14 acres of alfalfa and they cut about 150 tons making five cuttings. They irrigate from a ditch out of the Pahria. It is a real garden spot." (1009~)

Oscar R. Garrett in 1912: "I want to continue looking about the historical place—a little isolated community all to itself and far from the World's commotion, situated in the heart of a vast region of a most interesting character ... containing more marvels than any other part of the globe of equal extent." (707~)

John A. Widtsoe in 1922: "The surroundings in Lee's Ferry, while barren, are very colorful and entrancing.... The morning coloring of the cliffs was extraordinarily beautiful. The vermillion glow illuminated the valley. Then the changes came one after another. The gamut thrilled our souls." (2007~)

Helen C. Fairley: "The final ferry crossing took place on June 7, 1928, and it ended in tragedy. Two passengers and ferryman Adolph Johnson were drowned when their boat was torqued and flipped in a whirlpool." (629~)

Harry Aleson described the area in the 1950s: "Here Nature has flung her hues with extravagant hand, red and blues blending into a myriad of shades between, held back in their riotous display by the somber, practical grays alone." (34~)

Inscriptions include E. Kane, Aug. 20, 91; McCormick, Aug. 18, 91; LH Jewel, Sept. 20, 91; G.M. Wright, Nov. 17, 1892; J.A. Tepples, Sept. 10th, 92; I.T. Kempton, Oct. 92; Annie Hunt, 1892; and Alice and Jack Rowe, Nov. 13/96. (1111~, SAPE.)

There were two crossing of the Colorado River near Lees Ferry.

—Upper Crossing: (Also called Lees Ferry and Upper Ferry.) The original crossing was one-half mile above the present-day boat ramp (at elevation BM3148). This crossing led to the hard pull up Lees Backbone. Ruins are still visible at the ferry site. (629~, 1612~, SAPE.) Inscriptions include A.K. Thurber, no date and E.A. Burk, Nov. 21, 89.

—Lower Crossing: (Also called Lower Ferry.) The Lower Crossing was just below the Paria Riffle. It was used in low water and was popular as it avoided the Lees Backbone route. It was established in 1878–79. Inscriptions include J.C.K., Mar. 21, 88; O.F. Graham and J.A. Teeples, Sept. 10, 92; and Ella Schooler, Mar. 26, 1898. (629~, 1115~)

—Honeymoon Trail: This crossed the Colorado River at Lees Ferry.

—Books: Zane Grey immortalized Lonely Dell in his book *Heritage of the Desert*, calling it the Garden of Eschtah. (712~)

—Blue Lake: Julia Emmett (daughter of James Simpson Emmett): "The river often backed up into the Paria's mouth, to create a wide shallow lake, which, as it settled, became blue as the hot desert skies.... There was always good hunting on the Blue Lake." (364~)

—Charles H. Spencer Mining Camp and the Spencer Trail: Charles H. Spencer arrived at Lees Ferry in May 1910 as the managing director of the American Placer Corporation. He had been led to believe that gold was in the Chinle Formation mud- and siltstones, which are prevalent in the area. Valeen Tippets Avery: "The plan was to force water under pressure into the silts of the Chinle, then pipe the resulting slurry across corrugated plates coated with mercury in an amalgamator. Mercury absorbs gold too fine to be collected from rockers, pans, or sluice boxes, and the gold is easily retorted from the mercury later." (84~)

Spencer set up quite an operation at Lees Ferry, building a dozen or more buildings for his crew and equipment. Needing a steady supply of coal, Spencer found a source in a branch of Warm Creek Canyon twenty-eight miles up the Colorado River in Glen Canyon. (See Warm Creek—Warm Creek Cabins.) Spencer initially thought the best way to transport the coal was by mule. Although he knew about the Domìnguez Trail (See Domìnguez Trail), he deemed it too difficult. An old Indian trail went up the cliffs immediately behind his sluicing operation and in the fall of 1910 he had his men improve it into a good pack trail. The trail is shown but is not named on the Lees Ferry map. It starts immediately east of Lees Ferry and goes up the cliffs to the northeast.

Otis "Dock" Marston: "I have information that this trail was built by Eugene Spencer with a crew of about fifty Indians and they had plenty of blasting powder ... we talked with him in L.A. [Los Angeles, California]. He states that the trail was built about 6› wide and on an even grade." (1284~)

The trail became the standard route for those going between the settlement of Lees Ferry to the towns of the upper Paria River. Oscar R. Garrett in 1912: "On leaving the settlement of Lee's Ferry the trail zig-zags up the rugged vertical wall back of the rock houses and somewhat to the east also. At present, the mail is brought in that way." (707~)

Herbert E. Gregory in 1915: "trail up Colorado Canyon cliff. Very long & difficult. Greybird and Rat [horses] fell and rolled into dangerous position." (760~)

John A. Widtsoe on Sunday, September 17, 1922: "It was the steepest yet the best trail of its kind tried by me. We climbed to the top.... A panorama of astounding proportions lay on all sides of us.... To the north and east we could see the windings of the Colorado, along which we had come. It seems a bit awful; and we had to shake ourselves and say, we have been down in it, and it's very pleasant there.... The colors are not in the chasm, but they riot above and beyond, for wherever the eye ranges, it sees red and yellow, and brown and gray and grayish green in a complexity of combinations.... The scene is one of brilliant immensity. This is the Lord's Day, and we worship Him this day through his works.... Then we moved up to the highest point, named by us *Panorama Point*, where the view is even larger." (2007~)

Inscriptions near the trail include G.M. Wright, Nov. 17, 1892. (1112~)

It turned out that hauling coal on mules was not practical. Spencer then had a ninety-two-foot stern-wheel paddle boat built in San Francisco. He had it shipped in pieces to Marysvale, Utah by train and then on wagons to the mouth of Warm Creek Canyon, where it was reassembled. The boat, though, used as much coal as it carried to transport the coal down the river to Lees Ferry and return to Warm Creek Canyon. It was abandoned at Lees Ferry where its remains can still be seen in low water.

Spencer abandoned the project. The buildings at Lees Ferry were used on and off by various groups, including the USGS, until the building of Glen Canyon dam. By 1965 a ranger was living at Lees Ferry, and in 1967 many of the original buildings erected by Spencer and his men were razed. (84~, 348~, 1612~)

Lees Ranch: (San Juan Co.) Valley of the Gods-Moqui Dugway. Cedar Mesa South map. PRIVATE PROPERTY.
Also called Garden of the Gods Bed and Breakfast and X-Bar-L Guest Ranch.
Ward J. Roylance: "Still standing in the valley is the ruin of an imposing ranch house built by Clarence and William 'Buck' Lee in the 1920s. The rock mansion contained

nine rooms, four of them with fireplaces. Water was piped from a spring.... [Buck Lee] was an artist and a teller of marvelous tales who provided guided tours to area attractions." (1658~)

Another source noted that the ranch was built in 1933 after the Lee Ranch on the Piute Strip was designated as part of the Navajo Indian Reservation. Walter Ford noted that the Lees were the grandsons of John D. Lee. (654~)

Lees Spring Wash: (Beaver and Iron Counties.) Coyote Bench-Fremont Wash. Kane Canyon, Burnt Peak, and Buckhorn Flat maps.
John Percival Lee had a ranch on nearby South Creek starting in the late 1850s. (271~, 1447~, 1931~)

Lee Valley: (Washington Co.) Zion National Park-Lower Kolob Plateau. The Guardian Angels map.
The Lee brothers had a farm in Lee Valley in the early years. (363~)

Le Fevre Creek: (Iron Co.) Dixie National Forest-Upper Bear Valley. Little Creek Peak map.
Also spelled LeFevre Creek and Lefever Creek.
William LeFevre (1833–1920) arrived in Paragonah in 1851. (336~) He had a ranch at the mouth of the canyon in the early years. Maggie Nielson in 1879: "Moved to the LeFeore [*sic*] Ranch mouth of Bear Creek Canyon." (1456~)

Left Hand Canyon: (Kane Co.) Sunset Cliffs-Kanab Creek. Alton map.
Also called North Hollow. (741~)

Left Hand Collet Canyon: (Kane Co.) GSCENM-Kaiparowits Plateau-Escalante Desert-Twentymile Wash. Petes Cove, Collet Top, and Seep Flat maps.
(See Collet Top for name derivation.)
John Phillips of *Car and Driver Magazine* in 1996: "Through Left hand Collet Canyon—arguably 13 of the most scenic off-road miles in America." (1535~)

Left Hand Tusher Canyon: (Grand Co.) Roan Cliffs-Book Cliffs-Green River. Floy Canyon North, Bobby Canyon North, Bobby Canyon South, and Tusher Canyon maps.
(See Tusher Canyon—Grand Co.—Book Cliffs for name derivation.)

Lehi Canyon: (San Juan Co.) Navajo Indian Reservation-Anasazi Canyon. Rainbow Bridge and Nasja Mesa maps.
Also called East Fork Mystery Canyon. (1915~)
Frank E. Masland, Jr. suggested the name in 1959 after Paiute Dan Lehi led an expedition through the area. Lehi was born at nearby Haystack Rock and was raised in the canyon. Masland, Jr: "This, however, was Dan Lehi's country. He had been raised here but left as a boy and

had not been back for twenty-five years. He remembered every bush and rock. There was never a moment's hesitation. It was truly a remarkable demonstration." (1309~, 1919~) Daniel Perkins, a horse wrangler for the original 1909 Rainbow Bridge Expedition: "The Lehi family are fine people." (1528~)

—Constructed Stock Trail: This enters the very upper end of the canyon from the north (Rainbow Bridge map). (SAPE.)

—Constructed Stock Trail: This enters the canyon from the south. The trail skirts the dome of elevation 4683T on its east side (Rainbow Bridge map). (SAPE.)

Lemmon Spring: (Kane Co.) Clear Creek Mountain-Echo Canyon. Temple of Sinawava map.
Also spelled Lemon Spring. (1931~)
James A. Lemmon (1815-1882) arrived in Springdale in 1862. (482~, 1891~) He had a logging operation at Lemmon Spring in the early days. (1931~)

Lemon Flats: (Emery Co.) Cedar Mountain-Lucky Flats. Cow Flats map.
Correctly spelled Lemmon Flats.
Leander Lemmon (1839-1907), one of the first settlers of Huntington, arrived in 1875. He ran livestock in Castle Valley and on the San Rafael Swell. (380~, 641~, 710~, 1318~)

Lems Draw: (San Juan Co.) White Mesa-Recapture Creek. Blanding North and Blanding South maps.
Lemuel H. Redd (1836-1910) was a Hole-in-the-Rock Expedition member and a Blanding pioneer. (1526~)

Lens Canyon: (San Juan Co.) Canyonlands National Park-Needles District-Lower Red Lake Canyon. Spanish Bottom map.
Len Woodruff was a cowboy for one of the local ranches in the early years. (1116~)

Les George Point: (Kane Co.) Glen Canyon NRA-Escalante River. Stevens Canyon South and King Mesa maps. (4,861')
Rancher Leslie George (1876-1955) was the Garfield County assessor in the 1930s. (55~, 2051~)
—The Bobway: This constructed stock trail provides access to Les George Point from the Escalante River. It is in a short side canyon that is two miles (as the crow flies) upriver from the mouth of Coyote Gulch (east of elevation 4404T on the Stevens Canyon South map). (SAPE.)

Le Vanger Lakes: (Kane Co.) Dixie National Forest-Long Valley. Long Valley Junction map.
Also called Swapp Lakes.
Correctly spelled Levanger Lakes.
Also spelled Levengar Lakes. (1639~)

Julius S. Dalley noted that Nils J. Levanger (1845–1931), an Upper Kanab and Glendale pioneer, built dikes to help impound more water in natural lakes. (2053~)

Levi Well: (Grand Co.) Tenmile Country-Blue Hills. Dee Pass map.
Also called Cook Levi Well and Levi Well #1. (417~)
This oil well was drilled in 1912 by the British American Petroleum Co. Geologist Charles T. Lupton: "A fairly strong flow of water was struck at 350 feet and a little gas with a small quantity of oil is reported to have been encountered near the bottom of the hole." (1234~) The well is now used for filling stock watering troughs. (SAPE.)

Lews Hole: (Emery Co.) San Rafael Swell-Joe Hole Wash. Chimney Rock map.
—Constructed Stock Trail: This trail on the south side of Joe Hole Wash leads to the large pond in Lews Hole. (SAPE.)

Lichii Niahi: (Coconino Co., Az.) Navajo Indian Reservation-Rainbow Plateau. Face Canyon, Az. map.
Jesse C. Dyer of the USGS noted that *Lichíí Ní'ahí* is Navajo for "Red Ridge." (588~)

Lick Creek: (Kane Co.) Pink Cliffs-Skutumpah Creek. Skutumpah Creek map.
George G. Mace: "Because of salt or saline deer and cattle 'licks' in the canyon, it became known as Lick Canyon." (2053~)

Lick Wash: (Kane Co.) GSCENM-Park Wash. Rainbow Point and Deer Spring Point maps.
Cal Johnson: "We call that Lick Country. There is a little salt in the dirt and the cattle would lick that dirt." (984~)
—Constructed Stock Trail: This goes down Lick Wash from the Skutumpah Road to Park Wash. There is only one very short section of construction and there is a fence. (SAPE.)

Lighthouse Canyon: (Emery Co.) Roan Cliffs-Range Creek. Lighthouse Canyon map.
—Lighthouse Canyon Trail: Waldo Wilcox: "In the early days [early 1880s] the Range Creek Cattle Company had that. The trail they used to get up to Range Valley Mountain [from Range Creek], up on top, went up Lighthouse Canyon. They built a cabin right up at the top there at the end of the trail and they'd hold the cattle so they could keep them from coming off too quick. There was no door in the cabin; you had to come in from the roof. There were no windows in it. So that was the lighthouse right at the top of the canyon, and that is where the canyon got its name.... I bet my brother, Don and I, were the last ones to use that trail. We took a bunch of cows down there.

Where they'd cribbed up over a ledge, a log broke and we just barely got over that trail." (2011~)

Lightning Draw: (Garfield Co.) Dixie National Forest-Paunsaugunt Plateau-Coyote Hollow. Bryce Canyon map.
Unattributed: "Lightning killed a bunch of sheep owned by N.C. Neilson about 1908 in the head of this hollow." (2053~, 1346~)

Lightning Hollow: (Garfield Co.) Dixie National Forest-Sevier Plateau-Deer Creek. Adams Head and Cow Creek maps.
E.C. Bird in 1941: "So named because lightning strikes there so often and it is believed it is due to the presence of magnetic iron in the ground." (2053~)

Liilkiizh Shijei: (Coconino Co., Az.) Navajo Indian Reservation-Rainbow Plateau-Lake Powell. Wild Horse Mesa, Az. map.
Liílkiizh is Navajo for "spotted horse." *Shijéí* is Navajo for "heart." (1962~) This is a newer name. It is most commonly called Labyrinth Canyon. (See Labyrinth Bay.)

Lila Canyon: (Carbon Co.) Book Cliffs-The Cove-Grassy Wash. Lila Point map.
—Tunnel: Between 1942 and 1946 a one and one-half-mile-long tunnel was excavated between the Horse Valley Mine and Lila Canyon. (1621~)

Lime Creek: (San Juan Co.) Cedar Mesa-Valley of the Gods-San Juan River. Cedar Mesa North, Cedar Mesa South, Snow Flat Spring Cave, Cigarette Spring Cave, Mexican Hat, and San Juan Hill maps.
Also called Limestone Creek. (472~)
This was initially called Epsom Creek because much of the water was alkaline. (774~) It is shown as that on the 1881 William M. Bradley map. (M.8.) The bedrock of much of Lime Creek Valley is limestone, which gave the canyon its present name. (774~)
Alfred Wetherill in 1895: "In the bottom of [the creek], a beautiful, clear, cold spring was gushing up. We got down to sample it and it was a mere sample! As the saying goes, we were spitting cotton for hours. It was fortunate that we did not empty our canteens beforehand. The spring was rank and vile with magnesia, or 'gyp' water." (651~)
Inscriptions include John Scott, May 9, 1894 and Henry Honaker, May 12, 1894. James H. Knipmeyer: "The names 'Frog Creek' and 'Pool Creek' are printed in charcoal near the Honaker and Scott names, and very likely were their names for the creek"! (1112~)
—Constructed Stock Trail: This goes a short distance down the upper north fork of West Fork Lime Creek to a cave used as a line camp by cowboys. It is one-half mile

southeast of elevation 6507T on the Cedar Mesa South map. (SAPE.)
—The earliest known Indian site in San Juan County is on Lime Ridge. The Clovis Paleo-Indian site dates to about 9,000 BC. (529~)
—Upper West Fork Lime Creek Spring: This is the "Spring" that is one mile northeast of Rooster Butte (at elevation 4808 on the Cigarette Spring Cave map). A constructed stock trail leads down the west side of the canyon to the spring. (SAPE.)
—Upper East Fork Lime Creek Spring: This is the "Spring" that is one mile northeast of Pyramid Peak (at elevation 4837 on the Cigarette Spring Cave map). This large spring was often used by stockmen: two horse corrals and an old line shack (ruin) are nearby. Inscriptions include Stephen Perkins, no date. (SAPE.)

Lime Kill Hollow: (Wayne Co.) Rabbit Valley-Highline Ditch. Lyman map.
Correctly spelled Lime Kiln Hollow.
According to Wayne Blackburn, most of the early houses in Rabbit Valley were made of adobe. They used lime from the hollow to make mortar. (844~)
—Tanner Backbone: This is on the Highline Ditch one-half mile northwest of the mouth of Lime Kiln Hollow (one-eighth mile west of elevation 7434). (1865~)

Limekiln Creek: (Garfield Co.) Sevier Plateau-East Bench. Casto Canyon and Panguitch maps.
The first lime kilns in Panguitch were built here in the late 1870s. (1445~, 2053~)
—Lons Knoll: This is one-eighth mile north of North Fork and is one and one-half miles north-northwest of Birch Spring (at elevation 8024 on the Casto Canyon map). J.J. Porter in 1931: "Alonzo Hancock ranged horses on this knoll about 1900." (1346~)

Limestone Bench: (Emery Co.) San Rafael Swell-Oil Well Flat. The Wickiup and Bottleneck Peak maps.
—Sinbad Erosion Control Reservoirs: These stock reservoirs are on the south end of Limestone Bench and are two and one-half miles northwest of Sids Holes (one-half mile northeast of elevation 5930 on The Wickiup map). They were built in 1958. (1551~)

Limestone Cliffs: (Sevier Co.) Fishlake National Forest-Highway 72. Geyser Peak, Willow Springs, and Johns Peak maps.
Garn Jefferies noted that the cliffs are made of limestone. Garn told this story about the old cattle trail that drops from the Paradise Valley area, through the Limestone Cliffs, to the Last Chance Desert: "My dad said he went to the Foy Ranch one time and they had him take a bronco

down to the [Jefferies] ranch house to break it. It was a really pretty bronco. He was leading that bronco down the trail and all of a sudden it spooked and lunged back, broke the rope, and rolled down that hill. He said later that he was glad it wasn't his horse that went over, or he would have gone, too"! (959~)

—Jim Crane Stock Trail: Jim Crane: "We had a trail that went from The Frying Pan [this is Clay Flats on the Willow Springs map] down over the Limestone Cliffs to South Bench [at the head of Mussentuchit Wash]. We built that trail in 1991 or so and we had to zigzag that sucker." (478~)

—Levi Draw: Jim Crane noted that this northern tributary of Last Chance Wash drops east from the Limestone Cliffs immediately north of elevation 6304 on the Willow Springs map. Jim Crane: "That is what the Sorensons [local ranchers] called it. They'd say: 'It's only natural. You got Solomon and Levi.'" (478~)

—Richardson Bench: Jim Crane noted that this bench is between the Limestone Cliffs and upper Solomon Creek (at elevations 6952 and 7157 on the Geyser Peak map). (478~)

Limestone Creek: (Garfield Co.) Dixie National Forest-Hatch Mountain-Sevier River. Haycock Mountain and Hatch maps.
Also called Limestone Canyon.
Limestone Creek goes through Limerock Canyon.
Early residents of Panguitch used lime from the canyon to help build their homes. (832~)

—West Bench Fields: This open area is between the mouths of Limestone and Mammoth creeks (centered around elevation 7022 on the Hatch map). (832~)

Line Canyon: (Grand Co.) La Sal Mountains-Dolores River. Fisher Valley and Blue Chief Mesa maps.
Joe Taylor: "I asked my dad [Lester Taylor] when I was a teenager, 'was it Line or Lion, or Lyon?' There was a family in Gateway [Colorado] named Line and I suspect that they were involved in that somehow." (1866~)

Line Canyon: (Piute Co.) Fishlake National Forest-Tushar Mountains-Picnic Creek. Mount Belknap map.
In the old days cowboys had a line camp at the junction of Picnic Creek and Line Canyon.

—Constructed Stock Trail: This is shown on the map.

Link Canyon Wash: (Emery and Sevier Counties.) Old Woman Plateau-Quitchupah Creek. Emery West map.
Also called Link Creek. (1931~)
Wayne Gremel noted that this was named for the Link Canyon Mine. Locally it was known as Wildcat Canyon. Carrie Lou Gremel: "It was a wildcat to go up: straight

up." Wayne Gremel: "In the old days they'd have to rough-lock the wheels on their wagons to go down there." (780~)

—Link Canyon Mine: This was a coal mine. (567~)

Link Flats: (Emery Co.) San Rafael Swell-Copper Globe. Copper Globe map.
Ray Wareham, who had the Copper Globe allotment for many years, said that this is misspelled. This should be Lynx Flats, named for the cat. (1967~)

—The Window: This break in the upper cliffs is on the northeast side of Link Flats and is one and one-quarter miles northeast of the Lucky Strike Mine (one-quarter mile north-northwest of elevation 6038). The Window provides a dramatic view of the San Rafael Swell with the Henry Mountains in the background. (1853~, SAPE.)

Lion Bench: (Grand Co.) Book Cliffs-Bitter Creek. Bryson Canyon map.
This was a name given by sheepherders who camped here in the early years. (1931~)

Lion Hollow: (Carbon Co.) West Tavaputs Plateau-Desolation Canyon. Chandler Falls map.
Waldo Wilcox: "The only thing I can tell you about Lion Hollow was that back in the early days when they wanted to steal cattle, that is where they would put them." (2011~)

Lion Mountain: (Wayne Co.) Dixie National Forest-Boulder Mountain. Grover map. (8,871')
Also called Lion Mesa.
Grove Karl Gilbert of the Powell Survey called this Square Butte. (722~)
Don Orton in 1941: "So named because it seemed to be a favorite haunt for mountain lions." (2053~)

Lipiquino Water: (Grand Co.) Dome Plateau-Winter Camp Wash. Cisco SW map.
This pretty, narrow canyon contains both a small spring and a long series of potholes that often have water in them. (SAPE.) They were used by sheepherders.

Lisbon Mine: (San Juan Co.) La Sal Town-West Coyote Wash. La Sal West map.
This uranium mine was developed in the 1950s. It is now seeing some limited activity.

Lisbon Valley: (San Juan Co.) La Sal Town-Three Step Hill. Lisbon Valley, Lisbon Gap, and Summit Point maps.
Jack Silvey noted that the valley was named for the town of Lisbon, Portugal. (257~) The name was in place by 1885 and the area was called "the winter range of Coyote [La Sal area] cattlemen." (1328~)
The Don Juan María Antonia de Rivera Expedition of 1765 crossed Lisbon Valley. (953~)

In 1880 a miner picked up a piece of gold in the valley, setting off a small gold rush. Since absolutely no other gold was found, it is surmised that the gold had dropped out of a previous explorer's pack. (1741~)

In the 1950s uranium was discovered in the valley, starting a huge boom that continues to this day.

Liston Flat: (Garfield Co.) Dixie National Forest-Kaiparowits Plateau. Upper Valley map.

Rufus Liston (1848-1923) moved to the Escalante area in 1883. (2051~) He had a ranch on the flat. (1931~)

Liston Seep: (Kane Co.) GSCENM-Escalante Desert-Hole-in-the-Rock Road-Big Hollow Wash. Big Hollow Wash map.

This is a small, wash-bottom seep with a no-longer-functioning stock tank. (SAPE.)

Martin Liston moved to Escalante in 1877 and ran livestock in the area. (2051~)

Little Arch Canyon: (San Juan Co.) Navajo Indian Reservation-Cummings Mesa-Glen Canyon. Cathedral Canyon map.

Katie Lee and friends initially called this Fern Glen Canyon (1163~), and it is sometimes shown as that on older maps.

David and Gudy Gaskill went up the canyon in 1949 from the river: "Travel was difficult beyond the plunge pool—up past the waterfall on a few slippery steps hewn by someone in the sandstone and through an increasingly tortured labyrinthe, seemingly into the womb of the earth." (708~)

Katie Lee named the canyon in 1955: "Halfway back we noticed a deep, worn-to-velvet sluiceway. Eyeing its track upward we saw a beautiful little arch, a skylight to the outer gorge, where the water actually comes from. Millions of years ago it was just a pothole. When we walked up a talus slope to take pictures, we could see where the canyon's old watercourse ran before it broke through. Lying on our backs, we marked the eons of time, felt the earth turn, walked down our *renamed* canyon, Little Arch, very satisfied with our venture." (1162~)

Otis "Dock" Marston in 1962: "Must see! Try HARD to get into it! Short and sweet"! (1298~)

—Notch Canyon: This was the very short canyon, now underwater, that was one-quarter mile northeast of Little Arch Canyon. (M.25.)

Little Baullie Mesa: (San Juan Co.) Dark Canyon Plateau-Arch Canyon. Hotel Rock map. (6,621')

(See Baullies Mesa for name derivation.)

Little Black Mountains: (Emery Co.) San Rafael Swell-Salvation Creek. Salvation Creek map. (6,939')

Garn Jefferies noted that the mountains are made of black lava rock. (959~)

—Between the Mountains: Garn Jefferies noted that this pasture area is between Little Black Mountain and the cliffs to the north. (959~)

Little Bown Bench: (Garfield Co.) GSCENM-Glen Canyon NRA-Escalante River. King Bench, Silver Falls Bench, Pioneer Mesa, and Red Breaks maps.

(See Bowns Canyon for name derivation.)

Little Bridge Canyon: (San Juan Co.) Canyonlands National Park-Island in the Sky District-Colorado River. Musselman Arch and Shafer Basin maps.

Also called Shady Canyon. (1084~)

James H. Knipmeyer noted that the Little Bridge Canyon name was originally applied to the next side canyon upriver. It contains a small bridge in its upper end. The name was given by John Shafer and Ross Musselman in the early 1900s. (1116~)

—Hermit Canyon: This eastern tributary of the Colorado River is directly across from Little Bridge Canyon (which is shown on the Musselman Arch map). Hermit Canyon is south of elevation 4340T on the Shafer Basin map. Jack Milling moved to the bottom in 1947 and tried to farm here. (1085~)

—Hermit Canyon Stock Trail: This constructed stock trail goes up Hermit Canyon and exits a small side canyon to the north (immediately east of elevation 4340T on the Shafer Basin map). (SAPE.)

—Hermit Bottom Trail: This goes south along ledges on the east side of the Colorado River to the Tangren Line Camp. That camp is in a small side canyon immediately west of elevation 4441T on the Lockhart Basin map. The camp was built by Karl Tangren in the 1950s. The trail then continues south to the mouth of Lockhart Canyon. (1084~, SAPE.)

Little Canyon: (Grand Co.) Tenmile Country-Colorado River. Gold Bar Canyon map.

Dick Wilson: "Little Canyon does not exactly live up to its name." (2019~)

—Bride Canyon: Eric Bjørnstad noted that this short, eastern tributary of Little Canyon is two and one-half miles upcanyon from its mouth (as the crow flies) and is immediately north of elevation 5288T. It was named by rock climbers who called climbs in the canyon Shotgun Wedding, Cold Feet, and Honeymoon. (242~)

—The Bride: This tower is on the north side of middle Bride Canyon (one-half mile southwest of elevation

5288T). (242~) Shaped like a bride, with a bouquet and a tiara, it was first ascended by Fred Beckey and Eric Bjørnstad in 1971. (145~)

—Gooney Bird Rock: This tower is immediately south of the mouth of Bride Canyon (one-quarter mile northeast of elevation 4728T). Eric Bjørnstad: "Gooney Bird is named for the black-footed Albatross of the South Sea Islands." (242~)

Little Creek: (Iron Co.) Dixie National Forest-Hurricane Cliffs-Parowan Valley. Red Creek Reservoir and Cottonwood Mountain maps.

Also called Little Creek Canyon. (1456~, 1579~)

Upper Little Creek runs through Mortensen Canyon.

Paiute Indians call this *Saw-on-quint*, or "Sage Brush Creek." (1512~)

LaVar Taylor: "The creek is much smaller than others so the old-timers called it Little Creek." (1515~)

—Old Spanish Trail: This was the route the Old Spanish Trail took to get through the Hurricane Cliffs.

—Pioneer Road: Betsy Topham Camp noted that a rough road was built up the canyon in 1864. (942~) Pioneers used it to get to Panguitch and beyond. (1579~) John C.L. Smith of the Expedition of 1852: "We traveled up Little Creek kanyon which is a rough, rocky place." (1776~)

—The Swamps: William Lowder: "The swamps are at the head of Little Creek. Every summer it would get really swampy and that is why they call it the Swamps." (1515~)

—Movies: Betsy Topham Camp: "Some scenes from the movie 'Brigham Young' were filmed [in Little Creek Canyon] to depict the pioneers entering the Salt Lake Valley. Wagons were lowered over cliffs and other exciting filming was done." (336~)

Little Creek Mountain: (Washington Co.) Hurricane Cliffs-Highway 59. Little Creek Mountain and The Divide maps. (5,912')

Also called Little Creek Terrace. (767~)

—Trough Spring: This was on the northeast side of Little Creek Mountain one-half mile north of Gray Knoll (one-quarter mile northeast of elevation 5163 on the Little Creek Mountain map). It is unclear if this is the correct location for this spring. A ground check was not successful in locating a spring or a hint of a spring here. (SAPE.) The spring was a popular and important stopping place for travelers. (767~) Jesse N. Smith, while on a trip with Brigham Young and John Wesley Powell in 1870: "We stayed over night at the Sheep Troughs, a little seep of water." (1775~) James A. Little called it the Sheep Troughs in 1871. (1209~) Stephen Vandiver Jones of the Powell Expedition of 1871–72 called it Sheep Trough Spring.

(1023~) The Lieutenant George M. Wheeler Survey map of 1872–73 shows it as Trough's Spring. (M.76.) Andrew Amundsen called it Sheeptroves in 1873. (58~)

—Tough Spring Canyon: Trough Spring (?) is located in this canyon. A constructed stock trail, starting on the west side of Gray Knoll, goes into the canyon. (SAPE.)

—Rattlesnake Spring: PRIVATE PROPERTY. This is on the north side of Little Creek Mountain three miles northwest of Gray Knoll (one-quarter mile northwest of elevation 5447 on the Little Creek Mountain map). (767~)

Little Creek Peak: (Iron Co.) Dixie National Forest-Markagunt Plateau-Threemile Creek. Little Creek Peak map. (10,140')

This is the highest summit on the Markagunt Plateau. The name was in place by 1879. (M.60.)

—Pioneer Trail: Alma Barney: "In 1864 ... a band of sturdy pioneers ... made their way [from Parowan Valley] up Little Creek Canyon, crossing the divide at a point where the road now crosses." (137~)

Little Creek Wood Bench: (Garfield Co.) GSCENM-Paria River. Henrieville map.

Ralph Chynoweth: "The old-timers built a road from Little Creek to the top of Little Creek Wood Bench with a team and wagon and an old scraper. That's where they got their winter wood to stay warm. There is a lot of wood out there." (425~) The road is on the northeast side of Little Creek Wood Bench.

Little Deer Peak: (Sevier Co.) San Rafael Swell-Post Hollow. Johns Peak map. (7,881')

Jim Crane: "Little Deer Peak looks just like Deer Peak, but it is only about one-third the size." (478~)

Little Dog Valley: (Garfield Co.) Dog Valley-Cougar Ridge. Fremont Pass and Circleville Mountain maps.

The Parley P. Pratt Exploring Expedition to Southern Utah of 1849–50 crossed the valley. Robert Campbell of the expedition: "Get next into a small Basin [Little Dog Valley], no outlet." (1762~)

Little Dolores River: (Grand Co., Utah and Mesa Co., Colo.) Snyder Mesa-Westwater Canyon. Sieber Canyon, Westwater Canyon, and Agate maps.

Also called Rio Dolores Chiquito. (847~)

Little Dry Valley: (Kane Co.) GSCENM-Paria River. Cannonville and Bull Valley Gorge maps.

Ivan Willis and Sam Graff in 1963: "The Little Dry Valley is separated from Big Dry Valley by a ridge of hills.... The area is void of water causing the name." (1931~)

—Shakespear Arch: This is on the northeast side of Little Dry Valley one and one-half miles southwest of Chimney Rock (one-eighth mile northwest of elevation 6071 on the

Henrieville map). Kodachrome Basin State Park Superintendent Tom Shakespear discovered the arch in 1979. (1658~)

Little Duncan Mountain: (Sevier Co.) Fishlake National Forest-Wasatch Plateau. Acord Lakes map. (9,022') (See Duncan Mountain for name derivation.)

Little Eccles Canyon: (Emery Co.) Manti-LaSal National Forest-Huntington Creek-Electric Lake. Huntington Reservoir and Candland Mountain maps.

David Eccles had a sawmill in the canyon in the early years. (1330~)

Little Egypt: (Garfield Co.) Henry Mountains-Highway 95. Raggy Canyon map.

Also called Egypt and Little Goblin Valley.

Charles B. Hunt noted that the area was named for its "grotesque erosion forms in sandstone." (925~) He also described it as "a collection of curious erosion remnants." (923~)

Littlefield Town: (Mohave Co., Az.) Beaver Dam Mountains-Interstate 15. Littlefield, Az. map.

Also called Millersburg.

Henry W. Miller and others settled the town in 1865. It was abandoned in 1866 because of Indian troubles and was repopulated starting in 1875. (972~) The town was initially called Beaver Dams for the creek the town is located on. Although the name of the creek predates the name of the town by fifteen years, it is noteworthy that the new settlers had problems with beavers continually damming their irrigation ditches. (1319~) The name was changed in 1894 to reflect the fact that the farms were all little. (154~)

—Old Spanish Trail: The trail went by what would become Littlefield.

Little Forest Creek: (Garfield Co.) Dixie National Forest-Escalante Mountains-Antimony Creek. Antimony map.

This is a perennial creek. Locals added "Little" to the name to distinguish it from nearby Forest Creek to the west. (1931~)

Little Gap: (Iron Co.) Parowan Valley-Little Salt Lake. Parowan Gap map.

It is a little gap as compared to the bigger Parowan Gap one mile to the north.

Inscriptions include H.S., April 11, 1905. (SAPE.)

Little Grand Canyon: (Emery Co.) San Rafael Swell-San Rafael River. Bottleneck Peak and Sids Mountain maps.

The San Rafael River runs, in part, through the Little Grand Canyon. It received its name from the fanciful comparison of this canyon's beauty to that of the Grand Canyon in Arizona.

Little Grand Wash: (Grand Co.) Tenmile Country-Green River. Crescent Junction, Hatch Mesa, Green River NE, and Green River maps.

Also called Little Valley. (1205~)

Unattributed: "Little Grand remains as the contradictory name of a wash." (606~)

—Old Spanish Trail: The trail crossed Little Grand Wash.

—Oil Field: John Thomas Farrer, Sr. noted that in 1884 he found oil in Little Valley: "found a small spring. They cleaned it out so as to water horses as they came back. But to their surprise it was covered with black oil.... Now was the first discovery of oil in the Territory of Utah." (634~) Nothing came of the discovery.

—Little Valley: This large meadow is on the east side of the Green River and two miles west-southwest of Little Grand Wash (at elevation 4034T on the Green River map). (M.78.) The name was in place by 1884. (634~)

—Little Valley Farms: PRIVATE PROPERTY. There are a couple of historic farms on the Green River at the mouth of Little Grand Wash (Green River map). Brothers Arthur, Roswell, and Wallace Wheeler had a ranch at Little Valley starting in 1884. After two of the brothers left for the Yukon in 1898, Roswell built a cabin across from Little Valley on the west side of the river and just above the mouth of Fivemile Wash. Roswell, a bachelor, died in a fire in his cabin under mysterious circumstances in 1920. (1780~)

The Halverson Ranch was started by Henry Halverson (1865-1940) in the late 1880s. He sold the ranch to Mrs. Lens Perkins in 1905. (1780~)

Otis "Dock" Marston noted that the Gilmore Anderson "Ink" Harris family ranched on Little Grand Wash next to the Green River starting in 1888. (1734~) Bert J. Silliman in 1957: "They had a cabin and an orchard and a small alfalfa field." (126~)

Pearl Baker noted that the area was called Peacharosa: "It was once vast peach orchards and called Peacharosa; the orchards were wiped out by a severe winter, and it is now called Little Valley." (123~)

—Auger Bar: This was a gravel bar at the mouth of Little Grand Wash on the Green River. William Glen Hoyt: "The bar at the Auger was formed largely by boulders brought into the river from Little Grand Wash." (918~, 121~)

—Devils Auger: (Also called The Auger and Auger Hole.) This rapid is just below the mouth of Little Grand Wash (Green River map). The Stanton-Brown Survey of 1889 wrecked one of their boats here. (1462~) They called it both The Whirlpool and Devils Anger. (1767~)

Unattributed in 1892: "The river, ordinarily 300 yards wide, here is contracted to 100 yards in width, and there is an abrupt turn.... Just before this is reached the bank becomes an immense mass of boulders.... The danger is in passing these rocks. The swift current dashes against this concave shore and is thrown back with considerable violence. It is as rough and treacherous a piece of water as anyone cares to tackle in a rowboat. A number of men have been wrecked there, and all who know the place dread it." (1818~)

Lute H. Johnson in 1893: "A rapid called the Devil's Auger offers the first formidable barrier to navigation. A sudden drop in the river bed causes a quickening of the current and a sharp turn in the channel forms a twisting, boiling rapid that calls forth the boatman's keenest senses and threatens destruction to any manner of craft." (998~)

—Farrer Bar: This is on the south side of the mouth of Little Grand Wash (Green River map). John Thomas Farrer, Sr. (1831-1917) arrived in Green River in 1879. (1462~)

—Farrer Riffle: This small rapid is one mile downriver from of the Auger Bar (Green River map). (912~)

—Cable Bar: This sand bar is one mile west of Farrer Riffle at a distinct west to south bend in the river (Green River map). (912~, 1462~)

—Black Bird Mining Claim: This manganese mining area is one-half mile south of Little Grand Wash (near elevation 4381T on the Green River NE map). Charles R. Hanks owned the claims in the early 1940s. (104~)

Little Hole: (Grand Co.) Grand Valley-Westwater Canyon. Agate map.

Mike Milligan noted that a copper mine was located here in the 1920s and that the canyon was used by bootleggers during prohibition. (1362~)

—Constructed Stock Trail: This enters the canyon on its west side. (SAPE.)

Little Holes: (Emery Co.) San Rafael Swell-Buckhorn Flat. Bob Hill Knoll map.

Also called Little Water Holes (2053~) and Water Pocket (584~).

These are a series of large potholes in a shallow canyon. (SAPE.)

The Elk Mountain Mission of 1855 camped here. Oliver B. Huntington of the expedition: "[we] clambered down the overhanging rock and drawed up water with lassos and then passed it from hand to hand until it reached the top. This was very dangerous work, occupied ten men. A little after dark all the stock got a taste of water and very few all they wanted." (1270~)

Alfred N. Billings of the expedition: "It took 8 or 10 men to get the water up to the cattle. About one hundred and (150 feet) we had to draw the Water with Laraets [lariats]." (229~)

—Old Spanish Trail: The trail went by the Little Holes, which were a reliable source of water.

—Conquistador Pinnacles: These short pinnacles are three-quarters of a mile west of Little Holes. The name reflects the fact that the Spanish camped in the area. (45~)

Little Horse Bottom: (Carbon Co.) Desolation Canyon-Green River. Duches Hole map.

—Constructed Stock Trail: This exits Little Horse Bottom on its east side. (SAPE.)

Little Jim Canyon: (Grand Co.) East Tavaputs Plateau-Kelly Canyon. Tenmile Canyon North map.

—Stock Trail: A still-used cattle trail goes through the canyon. (SAPE.)

Little Meadow: (Piute Co.) Sevier Plateau-Grass Valley. Greenwich map.

Newel Nielson: "There is a small spring there and it is a very small meadow." (1458~)

Little Meadow Creek: (Kane Co.) Clear Creek Mountain-Meadow Creek. Clear Creek Mountain map.

William Adair and John H. Watson in 1942: "The place received its name from the Little Meadows, the place of its source." (2053~)

A water rights notice stated: "Henry B. Jolley, a citizen of Mount Carmel, Utah, was on the 6th of September A.D. 1881 adjudged entitled to Primary Right of the natural supply known as Little Meadow Spring, near Mount Carmel." (2053~)

Little Mountain Spring: (Grand Co.) Tenmile Country-Dubinky Wash. Dubinky Wash map.

This developed spring is on what is called Little Mountain. It is not a real mountain, just a high hill.

—Little Mountain Road: This is shown, but is unnamed, on the map. Gene Dunham noted that it was the first road to Dead Horse Point, before Highway 313 was built up Sevenmile Canyon. The road started on Klondike Flat and went west to the Blue Hills. It then went south, up Little Mountain, by Little Mountain Spring and Dubinky Well, across Bartlett Flat, over The Knoll, and to Dead Horse Point. (580~)

—Gustavus Manganese Claims: These were on the south side of Little Mountain and were worked in 1918. (104~)

Little Notch: (San Juan Co.) Manti-LaSal National Forest-Dark Canyon Plateau-South Elk Ridge. Kigalia Point map.

The Little Notch is a thin ridge that divides the tops of Hammond and Kigalia canyons. In the early 1950s the Atomic Energy Commission had a base camp at Little Notch which they used while test drilling for uranium. (212~)

—Kigalia Canyon: This goes northwest from Little Notch and intersects Peavine Canyon. (See Kigalia Point.)

—Little Notch Trail: (Also called Forest Service Trail #026.) The road from Little Notch down Kigalia Canyon was built by the Midwest Refining Company in 1926–27. It continued down Peavine Canyon into Dark Canyon and to a drill pad in Reservoir Canyon (now called Rig Canyon). (774~, 1829~)

Little Ocean Draw: (Emery Co.) San Rafael Swell-Chute Canyon. San Rafael Knob and Horse Valley maps.

Lee Mont Swasey: "I asked Smokey Hawkins, who was the foreman for the Price Stake, about Little Ocean Draw. He said that once you get out there, those rolling hills look like waves." (1853~)

Little Park Wash: (Emery Co.) Book Cliffs-Trail Canyon. Lila Point, Woodside, Turtle Canyon, and Jenny Canyon maps.

—Saddlehorn: This prominent knob on the top of the Book Cliffs is on the west side of Little Park Wash and is one and one-half miles east-northeast of Kiahtipes Reservoir (at elevation 6669 [Saddlehorn] on the Woodside map). (SAPE.)

Little Pine Creek: (Piute Co.) Fishlake National Forest-Tushar Mountains-Big Pine Creek. Circleville Mountain and Circleville maps.

Thomas Thomas in 1941: "It is a very small creek running from a spring in a southeast direction emptying into Big Pine Creek. It is so named because of the Pine trees that grow along its course." (2053~)

The Parley P. Pratt Exploring Expedition of 1849–50 crossed the head of the canyon. Robert Campbell of the expedition called it 1st Kanyon as it was the first the expedition had to cross after ascending nearby Birch Creek to the north. Campbell: "the snow so deep the Rocks covered—then descend sideling steep Rocky hollow, men with ropes hold back [the wagons], ascend, & strike to the right, steep, Rocky, & snow drifted very deep. Then descend, Steep Rock pitch to 1st Kanyon.... Ascend nearly perpendicular, snow drifted very deep on the ascent side of the hill." (1762~)

Little Purgatory: (Washington Co.) Hurricane Cliffs-Virgin River. Hurricane map.

George C. Fraser in 1914: "There is little grass and without water no prospect of improvement. A portion of it is appropriately called 'Purgatory Flats.'" (667~)

Little Rainbow Bridge: (Grand Co.) Tenmile Country-Poison Spider Mesa-Bootlegger Canyon. Moab map.

Although the USGS still shows this as Little Rainbow Bridge, its local name, Corona Arch, is used in most literature and on trail signs.

—Bowtie Arch: This is within sight of Little Rainbow Bridge. Robert H. Vreeland noted that its original name was Paul Bunyans Pottie, a name that was later applied to an arch in Canyonlands National Park. Vreeland also noted that nothing about the arch resembles a bowtie. (1952~)

Another source noted that it was initially named Paul Bunyan's Shit Hole by early ranchers. When Canyonlands National Park Superintendent Bates Wilson was trying to have the area turned into a National Park, he changed the name. (1116~)

Little Rock House Canyon: (Uintah Co.) Uintah and Ouray Indian Reservation-East Tavaputs Plateau-Desolation Canyon. Firewater Canyon North map.

—Gold Hole Rincon: (Also called Gold Hole.) This abandoned meander on the east side of the Green River is two miles north of Little Rock House Canyon (at elevation 4857T). (200~, 2049~)

—Stampede Flat: This river bottom is on the east side of the Green River immediately south of the mouth of Little Rock House Canyon. (200~, 833~)

—Split Rock: (Also called Hole-in-the-Ledge.) Ed F. Harmston in 1913: "at lower end of Stampede Flat pass through the split rock, a crevice in a mass of rock which having fallen from the ledges above, fills the space between the foot of the ledge and the river." (833~)

Little Rockies: (Garfield Co.) Henry Mountains-Glen Canyon NRA. Ticaboo Mesa, Mount Holmes, Lost Spring, and Copper Creek Benches maps.

Also called Little Raggies. (17~)

The Little Rockies are often considered a part of the Henry Mountains. They consist of two peaks (Mount Ellsworth and Mount Holmes) that are substantially lower than the other three summits (Mount Ellen, Mount Pennell, and Mount Hillers) in the range. Grove Karl Gilbert of the Powell Survey called these the South Mountains in 1876 as they are south of the main, and higher, peaks. (925~)

Little Salt Lake: (Iron Co.) Parowan Valley-Fremont Wash. Paragonah and Parowan Gap maps.

Also called Parowan Lake.

For early travelers going south from Salt Lake City, this was reminiscent of the Great Salt Lake, though much smaller.

Orville C. Pratt in 1848: "In the center of it [Parowan Valley] was a fine lake full of fish, with gravelly banks, and into which run 4 fine mountain streams." (1572~)

Addison Pratt of the Jefferson Hunt Party in 1849: "The lake appeared about a dozen miles long and the water appears to be more impregnated with saleratus than salt.... There were plenty of wild geese and ducks about it, and in the bottoms were plenty of hares and sage hens." (1571~)

William Lewis Manly of the Jayhawker Party in 1849: "[we] passed Little Salt Lake, which was almost dry, with a beach around it almost as white as snow. It might have had a little more of the dignity of a lake in wet weather, but it was a rather dry affair as we saw it." (1274~)

C. Gregory Crampton noted that in the early days, before nearby streams had been tapped for water, the area around the lake was a lush pasture and marsh area. (469~)

—Old Spanish Trail: This was a well-documented landmark on the trail.

Little Sand Flat: (Wayne Co.) Capitol Reef National Park-Waterpocket Fold. Cathedral Mountain map.

—Little Sand Flat Canyon: This goes from Little Sand Flat to the South Desert. It is immediately south of elevation 6422. Former Capitol Reef National Park Ranger Fred Goodsell named the canyon. (745~)

—Oil Well Road: An abandoned oil well road runs along the north rim of Little Sand Flat Canyon, crosses Little Sand Flat, and ends at a drill hole and airstrip near elevation 7086 on the Twin Rocks map. The road was constructed in 1955 by Golden Durfey and two of his sons for Phillips Petroleum. (582~, 745~)

Little Triangle: (Grand Co.) Colorado River-Westwater Canyon. Big Triangle map.

This is immediately south of the Big Triangle. It is the point at the junction of Renegade and Ryan creeks.

Little Valley: (Garfield Co.) GSCENM-Escalante Desert-Twentyfive Mile Wash. Sunset Flat map.

Also called Little Red Valley. (1931~)

Edson Alvey noted that this was named by early stockmen and that it was also called Sunset Valley for the "variable colored rockstacks." (55~, 56~)

Little Valley: (Iron Co.) Dixie National Forest-Hurricane Cliffs-Upper Bear Valley. Cottonwood Mountain and Little Creek Peak maps.

—Old Spanish Trail: The trail went through Little Valley. (1551~)

Little Valley: (Kane Co.) GSCENM-Glen Canyon NRA-Kaiparowits Plateau-Last Chance Bay. Mazuki Point, East of the Navajo, Blackburn Canyon, Gunsight Butte, and Sit Down Bench maps.

Also called Little Valley Creek. (1931~)

Edson Alvey noted that this remote canyon was the last chance for livestock to water before heading either west along the rim of the Colorado River or north onto the Kaiparowits Plateau. (55~)

—Constructed Stock Trail: This leads out of the inner gorge of Little Valley to Rock Creek Bench and eventually up Mudholes Canyon to the top of the Kaiparowits Plateau. At the bottom it starts near elevation 4744 and at the top it ends one-quarter mile southeast of elevation 5664 on the Blackburn Canyon map. (SAPE.)

—Wild Horse Ranch: (Also called Little Valley Line Camp.) This is at a medium-size spring where the Grand Bench Road crosses Little Valley (one-quarter mile west of elevation 4276 on the Sit Down Bench map). In 1946 Theron Liddle, while on an expedition following the bench above Glen Canyon and below the Kaiparowits Plateau (See Appendix Two—Talus Trail), made his way to what he called Wild Horse Ranch. He described it as "a narrow bunch-grass covered ledge between the cliffs of the Kaiparowits Plateau and the chasm of the Colorado." (1200~)

Little Wedge: (Emery Co.) San Rafael Swell-San Rafael River. Sids Mountain map.

—Sorrel Mule Mine: This copper and silver mine is on the east side of Little Wedge on the San Rafael River and is just upriver from the mouth of Salt Wash (one-eighth mile south-southeast of elevation 5584). Owen McClenahan noted that it was mined by Jack Montis in 1898. (1318~, 606~)

By 1900 the mine was owned by the Denver-based San Rafael Mining Company. Unattributed in 1900: "The property comprises seven lode claims and is being developed by a tunnel now into the mountain about 1100 feet." (1364a~)

Little Wild Horse Canyon: (Emery Co.) San Rafael Swell-Muddy Creek. Horse Valley and Little Wild Horse Mesa maps.

Also called Little Wild Horse Creek.

(See Wild Horse Butte for name derivation.)

Joe Bauman described a descent of Little Wild Horse Canyon many years ago: "Tall sides bound us most of the way. We had to jimmy ourselves through sometimes, depending on our arms. Devoid of life, the narrow canyon had walls as dark as limestone. Their slanting strata were worn into curve after indentation after swerve. Arms outstretched, we could let our fingers glide along both sides as we walked in the shade on round stones and gravel. The walls were clean, smooth, deeply scored for the first five feet. Higher, where the floods didn't polish them, they were gnarled. In the sunlight, the gullies were pink at the bottom, fading into gray above." (166~)

Little Wild Horse Mesa: (Emery Co.) San Rafael Swell-Muddy Creek. Little Wild Horse Mesa map. (5,417')
(See Wild Horse Butte for name derivation.)
Dee Anne Finken noted that uranium and vanadium mining on Little Wild Horse Mesa started in 1904. (641~)
Henry S. Johnson, Jr.: "[J.M.] Boutwell reports that as early as 1904 a shipment of 30,000 pounds of carnotite ore [from Little Wild Horse Mesa] had been made to Germany. The producers had not received payment for this ore ..., however, and probably did not feel encouraged to continue production." (987~)

Lizard Rock: (Wayne Co.) Canyonlands National Park-Maze District-Land of Standing Rocks. Elaterite Basin and Spanish Bottom maps. (5,807')
This was called Moon Rock or The Moon by Arthur and Hazel Ekker. (618~)
Richard Negri: "Cowboys, including Ned and Faun Chaffin who were moving cattle, stopped for lunch in the shadow of the rock. They watched two large, multi-colored lizards fighting there, and called it Lizard Rock. The year may have been either 1922 or 1923." (1429~)
Ned Chaffin: "And one of 'em, the yellow one, had the other one's tail in his mouth and wouldn't let go. And I mean, boy they was fightin' and squirmin' around there and kickin' up the dust." (411~)
—The Train: Otis "Dock" Marston in 1966: "Northerly from Lizard Rock is a much smaller formation known locally as The Train." (1291~)

Lizonbee Springs: (Sevier Co.) Fishlake National Forest-Wasatch Plateau. Acord Lakes map.
Correctly spelled Lisonbee Spring.
Also spelled Lisonber Springs.
William W. Lisonbee (1842-1909) and his wife, Mary (1846-1925), and family were early settlers of the Aurora and Annabella areas, arriving before 1900. (388~)

Lizzie Creek: (Garfield Co.) Dixie National Forest-Boulder Mountain-Frisky Creek. Boulder Town map.
Burns Ormand thought, but was not positive, that this was named for Elizabeth "Lizzie" Gilmore McInelly (1882-1930). (1487~)

Llewellyn Canyon: (Kane Co.) GSCENM-Kaiparowits Plateau-Mudholes Canyon. Blackburn Canyon map.
Also called Llewellyn Draw. (664~)
Llewellyn Harris (1832-1908) lived in the area in the 1880s. (441~) (See Llewellyn Gulch.)
—Window Wind Arch: (Also called Moqui Window.) This large arch is at the head of Llewellyn Canyon on the rim of the Straight Cliffs. James H. Knipmeyer: "[it] was named for the 'window-like' opening ... [and] ... for the winds which often rush around the inside of the hollowed-out rock mass before streaming through the opening and down over the rim of the plateau." (1115~) Inscriptions include L. Harris, April 14, 1888; J. Cox, '05; William M. Shirts, June 7, 1918; C.H. Baker, July 20, 1919; Orlow Goulding, 1923; and Orland Porter, May 22, '25. (SAPE.)

Llewellyn Gulch: (Kane Co.) Glen Canyon NRA-Glen Canyon. Nasja Mesa map.
There are many stories about Escalante pioneer and rancher Llewellyn Harris.
Alma Barney was a Dixie and Escalante pioneer: "I remember once seeing a man by the name of Llewylen [*sic*] Harris stripped to the waist one cold winter day, tied to a post, and given 20 lashes to appease the Indians for striking one of their number." (138~)
Thomas D. Brown of the Southern Indian Mission of 1854 told the whole story: "Llewellyn Harris struck Joseph the Indian living at Patriarch Groves with the barrel of his gun and cut him on the Forehead. L. Harris put in chains to await the result." (306~)
Arthur Chaffin, a river runner and Glen Canyon explorer, recounted a story about Llewellyn Harris. Apparently a friend of Harris's, gold miner Jack Butler, lent a burro to Harris, who used it on a trip into Waterpocket Fold country. Caught in a snow storm and unable to move, Harris camped in a large cave for six weeks and ended up eating the burro. When asked about Llewellyn Harris years later, Butler told Chaffin: "That's the son-of-a-bitch that ate my burro!" (19~, 2051~)
Van Verbeck fleshed out the story: "[Harris] had started over the Circle cliffs to Escalante for grub, came a snow that stayed on a couple of months. He was on top of those cliffs. You can imagine about how slick these slopes can be with an inch of snow. He ate Jack Butler's mule, it was sixteen years old." (1945~)

Inscriptions in the canyon include two from L. Harris with dates of March 29, 1888 and March 2, 1896. An earlier date of 1884 is seen, but no name is associated with it. A. Allen also left his name May 2, 1907. (SAPE.)

—Arch Trail: This constructed stock trail provides access to the canyon on its south side. It goes by a small natural arch that is one mile upcanyon from Lake Powell (one-eighth mile west-northwest of elevation 3940). (SAPE.)

—Bonnie Little Arch: This small, exquisite arch in lower Llewellyn Gulch was named for James H. Knipmeyer's wife, Bonnie. Bonnie means "pretty" and the arch is small, or "Pretty Little Arch." (SAPE.)

—San Juan Placer Claim: (Also called San Juan Bar.) This placer bar, now underwater, was on the west side of the Colorado River two miles south of the mouth of Llewellyn Gulch (one-half mile southeast of elevation 3900T). It was staked by Robert Brewster Stanton in 1889. (466~)

—New York State Placer Claim: (Also called New York Bar.) This placer bar, now underwater, was immediately south of the San Juan Placer Claim. Franklin A. Nims of the Stanton-Brown Survey of 1889: "Hislop, Richard Gibson and myself staked out a placer claim of 80 acres, and named it 'the New York State Placer mine [in July 1889].'" (1462~) Nims noted that a couple of the crew members were New York "Tenderfeet."

—Llewellyn Gulch Marina: (Proposed.) In the early 1960s, as part of the Trans-Escalante Federal Parkway, a marina was planned at Llewellyn Gulch. The parkway proposal failed and the marina was never built. (446~) (See Stevens Arch—Trans-Escalante Federal Parkway.)

Lloyd Creek: (Washington Co.) Dixie National Forest-Pine Valley Mountains-Santa Clara River. Saddle Mountain and Central East maps.

Also called Lloyd Canyon and Love Creek. (1931~)

Robert Lewis Lloyd (1822-1892) arrived in Washington in 1857 (462~) and moved to Pine Valley in 1862 (1803~). Reed Snow Gardner: "The annual berry hunt up Lloyd Canyon in September was looked forward to by all the kids in town.... These raspberries had probably been growing there for centuries.... The air was pure and clean, and it was rugged country; ledges of granite rock covered one side of the canyon and a few tall trees, together with shrubbery of oak, maple, etc. covered the other side. Cold springs of water oozed out of the side of the canyon floor and then disappeared into the ground." (1803~)

—Brown Sawmill: John and Ben Brown and James Jacobsen ran a sawmill in Lloyd Canyon in the 1880s. (367~)

Loa Town: (Wayne Co.) Rabbit Valley-Fremont River-Highways 24 and 72. Loa map.

This is the county seat of Wayne County.

John C. Fremont passed through the Loa area in February 1854.

The first settlers were Hugh J. McClellan and family. They moved to the Loa area in 1875. In 1879 the extended Blackburn family, headed by Elias Hicks Blackburn, moved to the area. Miriam B. Murphy: "So many Blackburns took up land in and around Loa, in fact, that the settlement was sometimes called Blackburn." (1419~, 248~) Elias Hicks Blackburn on May 10, 1879: "I take my wife and her small children and started to Fremont or Rabbit Valley." (248~)

The town was named by John R. and Franklin Young. They had both been Mormon missionaries in Hawaii. Many years later Lloyd Young noted that their original name for the town was to be "Aloha" but they then decided the area resembled Hawaii's Mauna Loa volcano. (607~, 699~, 1047~, 1786~) Hugh F. O'Neil noted that the town was indeed named by Franklin Young, but "because of the volcano-like appearance of a Mt. Pooneke?, near the settlement." (1485~)

—Loa Town Ditch: Anne Snow noted that the construction of the ditch, which runs from the north of Fremont to the west of Loa, was started in the late 1870s. (1786~)

Lockerby Town: (San Juan Co.) Highway 666-Cottonwood Canyon. Northdale map.

This tiny town, settled in 1912, was named for A.E. Lockerby. (375~, 1336~)

Lockhart Basin: (San Juan Co.) Hatch Point-Colorado River. Eightmile Rock and Lockhart Basin maps.

Also called Lockhart Gulch. (761~)

Also spelled Lock Heart Basin. (694~)

James H. Knipmeyer noted that Ollie Lockhart left an inscription, "Ollie Lockhart Feb. 8th, 1888 Silverton Colorado," near the mouth of the canyon. Other inscriptions include John E. Brown and James C. Blood, Jan. 9, 1887. (1112~, SAPE.)

—Oil Well Road: The road into Lockhart Basin was built for an oil well drilled by Utah Southern in 1927. (98~, 761~)

—Miner's Cabin: This cabin, once a well-known landmark at the mouth of the canyon, was built in 1926 for use by the abovementioned oil exploration crew. The cabin is now gone. (517~, SAPE.)

—Charlie Redd Sheep Trail: This constructed stock trail goes from Lockhart Basin up to Hatch Point (between elevations 4542T and 5882T on the Lockhart Basin map).

(SAPE.) Val Dalton: "Charlie Redd [1889-1975] always wanted to use that country for his sheep and he brought the sheep off of a trail off Hatch Point. Mostly he brought bucks down there. The cowboys supposedly found the sheep there one spring when they went down to gather their cows. So they shot them all until they ran out of bullets and then they roped them all until they give out their horses and then they just had to let the rest of them go. And so during the summer the cowboys went up and blasted the trail off. The story has it that Charlie went to bring his sheep back down there the next year and some of those sheep that he had salvaged the year before headed right down the trail and—you know how sheep are—they got to that blasted part and I guess he lost the whole herd." (517~) The trail was built in the early 1900s.

—Constructed Stock Trail: This also goes from Lockhart Basin to Hatch Point. It is two miles north of the Redd Sheep Trail. It goes east up the cliffs from marker 3-139 on the Lockhart Basin map. (517~, SAPE.)

—Lockhart Basin Gold Mine: Val Dalton told the story of this "lost" mine: "The story has it that Les Young was cowboyin' and he saw a bighorn sheep and he was hungry and he was going to go up and try to kill it. So he chased that bighorn sheep and he came by this cave and it supposedly had an old wooden wheelbarrow and a bunch of other stuff in it. He picked up some rocks by this old wood wheelbarrow and put them in his chap pocket and went ahead to chase that sheep.

"One story has him on the north side of Lockhart Canyon and the other story has him on the south side of Lockhart Canyon. [His nephew Jake Young's] source said he was on Hatch Point and he chased the sheep off the top of the point.... Les quit cowboyin' for a bit and when he went back to cowboyin', he felt these lumps in his chaps pocket and he pulled those rocks out and they had got all shiny and he had them assayed and they were close to fifty percent gold. And nobody's ever been able to find this old gold mine and every story has the wheelbarrow and the cave." (517~)

Lockhart Wash: (Emery Co.) San Rafael Swell-San Rafael River. Drowned Hole Wash and Devils Hole maps.

A man named Lockhart tried ranching near the San Rafael River in Lockhart Box (Devils Hole map). Many old maps show the Lockhart Cabins. (727~, 1318~)

Locomotive Point: (Emery Co.) San Rafael Swell-Head of Sinbad. The Blocks map. (7,404')

Also called Locomotive Rock.

Lee Mont Swasey noted that the buttress looks like a train locomotive. (1853~)

—The Gap: This low point is near the east end of Locomotive Point. Inscriptions include C.H. McDonald, June 8, 1907. Stockman Warren Allred left an inscription that reads: "Warren Allred: 1898 to 12-18-36. First-last." Lee Mont Swasey described Allred as "the most writingest person on the Sinbad. He was a sheepman from Spring City. I don't think a day went by that he didn't write his name on a rock, somewhere"! (1853~, SAPE.)

—Orchard Draw: This small draw is one mile west of Locomotive Point (one-eighth mile east of elevation 7084). Lee Mont Swasey: "The cedar trees were lined up so it looked like an orchard.... The Swaseys started to build a cabin at Orchard Draw, but by that time the Head of Sinbad had become established as a livestock driveway, so they were denied the homestead application." (1853~) Inscriptions include Warren Allred and Owen Justensen, 1937. (SAPE.)

Log Cabin Rapids: (Carbon Co.) Desolation Canyon-Green River. Steer Ridge Canyon map.

—Log Cabin: This rock tower is on the ridgetop one and one-half miles southeast of Log Cabin Rapids (at elevation 7207T). It looks like a log cabin and gives the rapid its name. It is visible from the river.

Almon H. Thompson of the 1871–72 Powell Expedition: "Beaman got a view of what I think is the highest nearly vertical cliff that we have seen. It is nearly 2800 feet above river. Called it Log Cabin Cliff on account of some shales that present the appearance of a Log Cabin." (1877~)

Jack Hillers of the same expedition: "Opposite our camp is the most highest vertical cliff we have seen on the river. It is some 2800 feet high. On the top is a very singular rock. It resembles the cabins of the country. We called it Cabin Cliff." (884~)

—Surprise Rapid: This is the "Rapids" one mile upriver from Log Cabin Rapids. Ed F. Harmston in 1913: "Larsen shoots the Boat-wreck Rapids [Surprise Rapids] successfully this morning (over ½ of the boats that attempt these rapids are wrecked)." (833~)

Logging Grove Draw: (Wayne Co.) Dixie National Forest-Boulder Mountain-Dark Valley Draw. Smooth Knoll and Government Point maps.

Also called Logging Grove Mountain. (357~)

Kate B. Carter noted that early settlers used logs from the grove to build their houses. (375~) Thaine Taylor: "They did lots of loggin out there. Big old ponderosa pine. That's quite a grove of 'em, just wonderful logs." (1868~)

Dunk Taylor: "They logged a lot of ponderosa logs outta Logging Grove. That was in the middle '40s. They pretty well had it logged out. There's been a little logging in there since. Then everybody got one of these wood-burning stoves and there was lots of Yellow Pine in there. Everybody hauled wood out of the Logging Grove." (1865~)

Lone Butte: (San Juan Co.) Dark Canyon Plateau-White Canyon. The Cheesebox map. (7,074')

Sandy Johnson noted that this butte is not labeled correctly on the map. The actual Lone Butte is between Ram Mesa and Cheesebox Canyon (at elevation 7350T). Sandy Johnson: "That is what my dad and all the old-timers called it." (1002~)

Lone Cedar Draw: (San Juan Co.) Dry Valley-Harts Draw. Photograph Gap map.

—Lone Cedar Stock Trail: Val Dalton noted that the trail goes down Lone Cedar Draw into Harts Draw. (517~)

Lone Cedar Flat: (Garfield Co.) Henry Mountains-Highway 95. Turkey Knob map.

Dee Hatch noted that there was a lone cedar [juniper] on the otherwise barren plains. It was an often-used landmark. (844~) Garth Noyes: "There's only one cedar tree on the whole flat. They built a reservoir there now, and you've got a lot of tamarisk close by, but there was that one lone cedar tree out there. That's why it's called Lone Cedar Flat." (1473~) The name was in place by the early 1900s. (1928~)

Lonely Spring: (Kane Co.) Bryce Canyon National Park-Pink Cliffs-Bull Valley. Rainbow Point map.

—Lonely Park: This is the area around Lonely Spring. It is an old sheepherder name. (1931~)

Lone Man Draw: (Emery Co.) San Rafael Reef-Iron Wash. Twin Knolls and Old Woman Wash maps.

—Lone Man Butte: (Twin Knolls map.) Dee Anne Finken noted that the butte looks like a lone man. (641~)

—Constructed Stock Trail: This goes from Iron Wash, up Lone Man Draw, into Ernie Canyon. (SAPE.)

Lone Parson Hole: (Emery Co.) San Rafael Swell-Iron Wash. Twin Knolls map.

These are a series of sandstone potholes that are easily accessible to livestock. (SAPE.)

Lee Swasey noted that they are called the Box Tanks. When asked "why?" Lee responded: "Mainly there used to be a sign right here that said 'Box Tanks!'" (1853~)

Lone Pine Canyon: (San Juan Co.) Glen Canyon NRA-Mancos Mesa-Forgotten Canyon. Knowles Canyon map.

—Lone Pine Spring: This is a large pothole. (SAPE.)

Lone Pine Point: (Kane Co.) GSCENM-Swap Canyon. Cutler Point map. (6,505')

Unattributed: "One lone pine tree on Point of Ridge, thus called Lone Pine Point." (1931~)

Lone Rock: (Kane Co.) Glen Canyon NRA-Lake Powell. Lone Rock map. (4,005')

This 334-foot free-standing tower was in the middle of a favorite grazing area in the 1880s and '90s. (464~)

The Domínguez-Escalante Expedition camped near here in November 1776. (1020~)

Edwin G. Woolley, diarist for the Utah Territorial Militia of 1869, called it Capitol Rock: "This rock stands in the bottom, and is about 300 feet in diameter the longest way, and 200 feet the shortest, is full 200 feet high; composed of white sand stone. If the deserts of Arabia or Africa are any worse then this place we don't think we should like traveling in those countries." (2048~)

Volney King noted it in his diary of 1882 as Lone Rock. (1096~)

Arthur L. Crawford in 1945: "At sunset we reached Lone Rock, sentinel of the wilderness, a gigantic monolith rising abruptly from the dune-covered bed of the Wahweap, a landmark that can be seen for miles up and down the drainage." (479~)

Lone Rock: (Kane Co.) GSCENM-Dance Hall Rock. Sooner Bench map. (4,594')

This small Entrada Sandstone dome was used by cowboys to escape wind and rain.

Inscriptions include J.A.H., 1906; Morris Shirts, Dec. 14, 1917; and Smith Alvey, Nov. 19, 1925. Another inscription from Lamon Griffin in 1937 reads "Filthy Swine." (SAPE.)

Lone Tree Crossing: (Emery Co.) San Rafael Swell-Muddy Creek. Mesa Butte map.

Two related name derivations are given.

First, there was a lone tree here and old maps often show this as The Lone Tree. (727~)

Second, Wayne Gremel noted that it was named after the Lone Tree Cattle Company. Wayne didn't know, though, which was first, the tree or the cattle outfit. Wayne: "They had a camp there at one time, the way I understand it.... When I first came into this country there were still posts in the ground where they had their corral. That was in the late 1800s. And, there was a lone pine tree a little bit farther south and to the west a bit." (780~)

Ranchers used a portable bridge during the winter grazing season to avoid quicksand. They removed it during the flash flood season. (1931~)

Lone Tree Mountain: (Iron Co.) Hurricane Cliffs-Cedar Mountain. Cedar City and Cedar Mountain maps. (9,391')

This has also been called Mount Henry. In 1851 Henry Lunt led the first group of pioneers to Cedar City. (375~)

William R. Palmer noted that there was just one lone tree on the mountain. (2053~)

—Corry Mine: This is the "Mine" on the west side of Lone Tree Mountain one-half mile east-northeast of Green Lakes (near elevation 8345 on the Cedar City map). Andrew Corry (1846-1933) started the coal mine in 1885. From 1900 to 1910 it supplied most of the coal for Cedar City. A rail tram on the northeast side of the mountain took coal from the top of the mountain to the road below. It ran until the 1920s. (570~, 1715~)

Lone Tree Reservoir: (Emery Co.) San Rafael Swell-North Salt Wash. Short Canyon map.

Also called Lone Tree Pond.

The reservoir was built in 1962. (1551~)

Lone Tree Wedge: (Emery Co.) San Rafael Swell-Muddy Creek. Ireland Mesa map.

Also called The Wedge. (780~)

This wedge of land is between Willow Springs Wash and Muddy Creek.

—Blackum Trail: This constructed stock trail still provides access from Lone Tree Wedge to Muddy Creek. It is one-quarter mile downriver from the mouth of Cat Canyon and goes west. The trail also crosses Muddy Creek and goes east up the cliffs. "Red" Blackum (Blackham?) was an early rancher. (641~, SAPE.) (See Cat Canyon.)

—BLM Project 453: This stock pond, no longer functioning, is on Lone Tree Wedge near elevation 5565. It was built in 1968. (1551~)

Long Canyon: (Coconino Co., Az.) Kaibab Plateau-Coyote Valley. Coyote Buttes, Az. map.

—Winter Road: This is immediately north of Long Canyon. C. Gregory Crampton: "an alternate road across the Kaibab, used in the 1930s (?) When U.S. Highway 89 was closed by snow." (1357~)

Long Canyon: (Coconino Co., Az.) Navajo Indian Reservation-Navajo Creek. Chaiyahi Rim SE and Chaiyahi Rim SW, Az. maps.

Pyramid and Segito canyons join to form Long Canyon.

Charles L. Bernheimer called this by its Navajo name *Neskla-nizadi*, or "Long Corner." (218~)

Carl I. Wheat noted that the Navajo name is *Nuz-daat-hashklaha*, or "Box Canyon": "And its course is marked by numerous very large old cottonwoods and occasional surface water." (1995~)

—Billy Goat Spring: William C. Miller noted that this was in the middle section of Long Canyon. (1360~)

Long Canyon: (Emery Co.) Beckwith Plateau-Elliott Mesa-Gray Canyon. Cliff, Jenny Canyon, Blue Castle Butte, and Tusher Canyon maps.

—Swasey Ranch: Charles A. Swasey, Sr. (1851-1923) had a ranch at the mouth of the canyon. Three sources give different dates for when he started ranching here: 1880s (200~), 1906 (1780~), or the early 1920s (79~). He and his son, Charles, Jr., built the present ranch house in the 1920s. Swasey died near here, at Swasey Spring, in 1923. (1780~) (See Short Canyon—Emery Co.—Beckwith Plateau.) Lee Mont Swasey: They [Charley Swasey and wife] moved to Green River for his wife's health. Green River is a lower climate. I don't know if he homesteaded or bought the ranch [at the mouth of Long Canyon]." (1853~)

—Constructed Stock Trail: This goes up Long Canyon to a spring, but does not continue up and out of the canyon. (SAPE.)

Long Canyon: (Emery Co.) Beckwith Plateau-Elliott Mesa-Price River. Cliff and Jenny Canyon maps.

Waldo Wilcox noted that there is an old rock house at the mouth of the canyon and that someone had a farm here. (2011~) The rock house is still here with an inscription from Cesario Martinez, 1944. (SAPE.)

—Constructed Stock Trail: This good trail starts a short distance west of the rock house and goes generally west up the initial cliff band. It is unclear if the trail continued to the top of Elliott Mesa. An easy route to the top is available. (SAPE.)

—Constructed Stock Trail: This faint trail starts a short distance east of the rock house and goes generally south up the initial cliff band. It is unclear if the trail continued to the top of Elliott Mesa. An easy route to the top is available. (SAPE.)

Long Canyon: (Garfield Co.) GSCENM-The Gulch. Lamp Stand, Steep Creek Bench, and King Bench maps.

Edson Alvey noted that this is a long canyon. (55~)

Ward J. Roylance: "The Wingate here is highly fractured in places, and some of it has been bleached to a whitish shade in contrast to its normal dark red.... The cliffs display intriguing erosional patterns and beautiful tonal designs effected by desert varnish." (1657~)

—Long Canyon Road: The road through the canyon was built for uranium miners in 1950 to provide access to Circle Cliffs Basin. (1168~) Before the road was built, the only vehicle route to the Circle Cliffs Basin was by going down Harris Wash, crossing the Escalante River, and going up Silver Falls Creek.

Long Canyon: (Grand Co.) Tenmile Country-Colorado River. Gold Bar Canyon map.

—Pucker Pass: This steep section of road is at the upper end of Long Canyon (one-eighth mile west of elevation 5842T). Fred Radcliffe: "In the early days, the pass was known as Shipman's Cutoff." (1594~)

James H. Knipmeyer: "The 'official' version is that it received its name from the fact that a person's mouth and face would 'pucker up' in disbelief upon first seeing the precipitous declivity down which they were expected to descend. 'Unofficially,' however, it was not a person's mouth and face that would pucker up in fear, but their —." (1115~)

Lloyd Holyoak: "When they built the potash mills down at Potash, the first route to that area was down Pucker Pass. That was before the road along the river from Moab was built. They took all of their construction materials and equipment through the pass. The new truckers that drove the pass would get to the top and look down and say: 'No way am I going to go down there.' Then they'd just unhook the trailer and come back to Moab and let somebody else take it down." (906~)

Dan Julien in 1967: "Wow! What a pass! They meant it when they put up the sign, 'Jeep Trail Only.'" (1031~)

—Maverick Buttress: This splits upper Long Canyon into a North and South forks (at elevation 5842T). (242~)

Long Canyon: (Kane Co.) Dixie National Forest-Long Valley-McDonald Lake. Long Valley Junction map.
—Jolly Ranch: In the early days Reuben Jolley (1853-1923) and family had a ranch at the mouth of Long Canyon. (1639~)

Long Canyon: (Kane Co.) Glen Canyon NRA-Glen Canyon. The Rincon NE and The Rincon maps.
Also called Navajo Canyon.
Navajo Creek runs through Long Canyon.
Edson Alvey noted that this is a long canyon. (55~) According to Casey Bown, the Navajo used the canyon to graze their sheep in the late 1800s and early 1900s. (47~)

Long Canyon: (Kane Co.) GSCENM-Johnson Wash. Pine Point and Cutler Point maps.
George G. Mace: "Some of the canyons tributary to Johnson are too short almost to be considered canyons so this one, being five or more miles in length, received the name Long Canyon." (2053~)
—Bunting Corral: Julian H. Steward noted that James Bunting (1832-1923) had a corral at the mouth of the canyon in the early days. (1831~)
—Long Canyon Spring: This is the "Well" in the upper canyon (Pine Point map). It is a still-used stock reservoir. A corral is nearby. (SAPE.)

Long Canyon: (Kane Co.) GSCENM-Paria River. West Clark Bench map.
Also called Ash Creek. (765~)

Long Canyon: (San Juan Co.) Dark Canyon Plateau-White Canyon. The Cheesebox, Indian Head Pass, and Jacobs Chair maps.
This is a long canyon, especially when compared to nearby Short Canyon. (162~)
—Constructed Stock Trail: This enters Long Canyon on its east side one-half mile up from its mouth (Jacobs Chair map). The trail continues downcanyon into White Canyon. Sandy Johnson: "I think old Butch and Sundance mighta hid some horses 'way back in there when they were coming across that country. There's good tank water [See Duckett Tanks below] in there, at the bottom.... I take bulls in there. In the old days they'd use that trail in the summer for the water." (1002~)
—Duckett Tanks: These large potholes a short distance up Long Canyon from its mouth (Jacobs Chair map) were named for John Baxter Duckett (1849-1910) and his brother, Joseph Alexander Duckett (1848-1933). They were the locators of the nearby Dolly Varden, a copper mine started in the 1890s. (1115~) (See Copper Point-Dolly Varden Mine.)
Herbert E. Gregory in 1927: "Ducketts [Tank] ... can be reached by entering [White Canyon at Gravel Crossing] & walking down 3 miles." (761~) David D. Rust mentioned going to the tanks in 1935: "find plenty of tank water in canyon where trail has been cut down the rock." (1672~)
—Commission Butte: This is one-half mile north of the mouth of Long Canyon (at elevation 5742T on the Jacobs Chair map). (215~)

Long Canyon: (San Juan Co.) Manti-LaSal National Forest-Abajo Mountains-Dodge Canyon. Abajo Peak, Blanding North, and Devil Mesa maps.
Karl Barton: "Long Canyon got its name because it's long. Just a long canyon." (162~) Karl noted that the large stock pond in Long Canyon was built by Vint Jones in the late 1960s. Jones owned the private land here.

Long Flat Canyon: (Kane Co.) GSCENM-Kaiparowits Plateau-Wahweap Creek. Butler Valley and Horse Flat maps.
Ken Goulding, Sr.: "The canyon starts at the lower end of Long Flat. Thus the name Long Flat Canyon." (1931~)

Long Hollow: (Garfield Co.) Dixie National Forest-Paunsaugunt Plateau-East Fork Sevier River. Tropic Reservoir map.
Don Orton in 1941: "This hollow is the longest hollow leading back from East Fork Creek to rim of Paunsaugunt Plateau on the east side." (2053~, 1346~)

Long Hollow: (Iron Co.) Dixie National Forest-Ashdown Creek. Webster Flat and Flanigan Arch maps.

Warren Pendleton noted that it is a long, narrow hollow between hills. (1515~)

Long Hollow: (Wayne Co.) Awapa Plateau-Spring Creek. Jakes Knoll, Moroni Peak, and Loa maps.

Thaine Taylor: "It comes clear from Parker Mountain right down to the [Loa] Bottoms." (1868~)

Longleaf Flat: (Wayne Co.) Capitol Reef National Park-Capitol Reef. Twin Rocks and Fruita maps.

Also called Sleeping Ute Flat.

Charles Kelly noted that longleaf pines are found on the flat. (1047~)

—Constructed Stock Trail: The present-day hiking trail to Hickman Natural Bridge and the Navajo Knobs was once a constructed stock trail that went as far as Longleaf Flat. (SAPE.)

Long Neck: (Garfield Co.) Dixie National Forest-Boulder Mountain. Steep Creek Bench and Boulder Town maps.

This was named for its shape when viewed from above. (1930~)

—Long Neck Cabin: This is labeled on the Steep Creek Bench map. It was built by the Ormands, a ranch family from Boulder, in the mid-1920s. (1487~)

Long Valley: (Kane Co.) Dixie National Forest-East Fork Virgin River. Long Valley Junction, Glendale, Orderville, and Mount Carmel maps.

Also called The Valley, Lone Valley (665~), Parunuweap Valley (72~, 1023~, 1141~), Virgin River Valley (1023~), and Upper Virgin Valley (777~).

Also spelled Longvalley. (363~)

The Indians call this *Pawau,* referring to "water" (91~), or *O-wat-ie,* or "Yellow Valley" (1512~).

Thora Pearce: "So named because it is twenty miles long and only one mile wide." (2053~)

The first Euroamericans to visit the valley were members of the John C.L. Smith Exploring Expedition of 1852. Smith: "There can be a good wagon road got from the Sevier country to this point [Long Valley]. There are plenty of hops and timber, and some handsome places for settlements in the narrow but fertile bottom of the stream." (1776~)

In 1853 Captain Joseph Walker visited the area while crossing from the headwaters of the Virgin to the Sevier rivers. He noted that the country was "torn all to pieces with kanyons." (1469~)

The Jesse N. Smith Expedition of 1858 called this Enchanted Valley. (469~)

In 1864 the first settlers, including brothers John and William Berry, called it Berry Valley, a name that was used until at least 1869. Because of Indian troubles, the area was abandoned until 1871. It was repopulated with settlers from the Muddy Creek Mission in Nevada. (349~, 2048~)

James W. Watson in 1871: "The hills are low, covered with cedars, and at the top afford plenty of range and grass for stock. The land appears to be very rich. A bountiful stream of water runs through the valley, affording plenty for all purposes." (1973~)

Edward M. Webb in 1878: "The explorers entered the valley Christmas day, 1870, and found it to be simply a canyon from 100 yards to three-fourths of a mile in width and about 15 or 20 miles in length. Through it flows a River, affording scarcely sufficient water to irrigate the 1,300 acres of tillable land the valley contains.... The soil of the valley is generally a heavy clay; the climate mild and adapted to the growth of small grain." (374~)

Inscriptions included J.C.L. Smith, June 16, 1852. Smith led the John C.L. Smith Expedition. Other inscriptions included members of the Jesse N. Smith Expedition of 1858. (469~) All of the inscriptions are now gone.

Long Valley: (Sevier Co.) Sevier River-Antelope Range. Antelope Range map.

—Black Knoll: This hill, part of the Marysvale Uranium District, is on the southwest edge of Long Valley (one-quarter mile north of elevation 6189). The name was applied by miners. (1088~)

Long Valley Junction: (Kane Co.) Dixie National Forest-East Fork Virgin River-Sevier River. Long Valley Junction map.

Also called The Divide, Gravel Pass, Gravel Springs Junction, Long Valley Divide, and Long Valley Summit. (311~, 349~, 1659~)

This marks the divide between the headwaters of East Fork Virgin River and the Sevier River. (349~)

Brigham Stowell told of going over the pass in 1884: "We found the snow three and a half feet deep and no trace of a road. We first sent all the spare men afoot, with their feet and legs wrapped in gunny sacks, to lead. They marked the road for the horses to follow.... There was much difficulty in getting to the summit both with the stock and the road, as there was always someone having trouble with either wagons or teams. Many of the men called were not used to handling a team, which made more work for those who were.... There was much timber that had fallen and was covered up with snow, and we had to cut it out before we could move on." (359~)

—The Buttermilk: Royal J. Cutler had a sheep ranch at The Divide in the early years. He called it The Buttermilk. (349~)

Long Willow Bottom Reservoir: (Garfield Co.) Dixie National Forest-Escalante Mountains-Twitchell Creek. Barker Reservoir map.

Before the dam was built, this was called Long Willow Bottom. Pratt Gates: "The Long Willow Bottom used to have a lot of willows up around the head of it." (709~) Edson Alvey noted that the reservoir was built by The New Escalante Irrigation Company. (55~)

Looking Glass Rock: (San Juan Co.) Highway 191-Joe Wilson Canyon. La Sal Junction map.

Also called Vulcan's Tomb. (1954~)

Spanish travelers called this *La Ventana*, or "The Window." (1115~)

The Writers' Program of 1941: "It is so named because the view through the opening seems to be a reflection of the opposite wall." (2056~) The arch was named by rancher John Silvey in 1889. (1741~)

In 1855 Ethan Pettit of the Elk Mountain Mission mentioned the then unnamed Looking Glass Rock: "cross revine to right to big rock with hole through it to right of [the Old Spanish] trail." (1532~)

Ellen Scarborough in 1911: "Many years ago nature brought down her best sculptors, painters and artists to entertain, on sandstone, every passer-by. For centuries they have been busy changing her stage settings to please her various troupes. On Looking Glass rock, near the stage road, she has set in a perfect mirror. She knows that a woman couldn't go a whole day without trying to look pretty, so she made it for our convenience.... But I never knew before that a looking glass could be made in sandstone out of pure atmosphere and bright sunlight." (1695~)

Inscriptions include N. Pryne, Jan. 3, 1887 and J.H. Fullmer, 1899. (1112~)

—Old Spanish Trail: The trail passed the east side of Looking Glass Rock. (1532~)

Lookout Peak: (Wayne Co.) Dixie National Forest-Boulder Mountain. Government Point map. (11,124')

Also called The Button (722~) and Lookout Point (2053~).

Don Orton in 1941: "So named because it was much used as a control station for forest fires." (2053~)

Lookout Point: (Emery Co.) Antelope Valley-Maze Road. Keg Knoll map. (4,597')

Pearl Baker: "I never thought to see the time that I could stand on Lookout Point at Keg [Knoll] and not see a horse—I have seen as high as ten or twelve big bands from that vantage point." (120~)

Lookout Point: (Emery Co.) San Rafael Swell-South Salt Wash. Short Canyon map. (6,250')

Lee Mont Swasey: "On the 1920s geologic maps they call that Drunken Man's Point. You can look at it and it looks like a drunken man leanin' up against the wall." (1853~, 727~)

Ray Wareham: "Vern Kofford from Castle Dale was chasin' horses out along there. He was comin' up from the west and his horse stepped in a badger hole. The horse fell with a broken leg, and it killed Kofford right there. Before we finally found him, the sand had blowed over him and you couldn't even see his head. The fall broke his neck. That was in late 1934. So we think of Lookout Point as Dead Horse Point because he died just a half a mile west of it or so." (1967~)

Lookout Point: (Navajo Co., Az.) Navajo Indian Reservation-Monument Valley. Mitten Buttes, Az. map.

Also called Monument Pass.

This is the location of the Monument Valley Visitor Center and The View, a large hotel.

Loop, The: (San Juan Co.) Canyonlands National Park-Needles District-Colorado River. The Loop map.

This section of river is actually a double loop; the river doubles back on itself twice. Early explorers called it Double Bow Knot.

Frank C. Kendrick of the Stanton-Brown Survey in 1889: "A grand & gloomy place." (1838a~)

Emery Kolb in 1914: "three rounded loops, very symmetrical in form, with an almost circular formation of flat-topped rock, a mile or more in diameter in the center of each loop." (1124~)

Devergne Barber described climbing to the saddle in 1927: "Hanging on by our fingernails, falling rocks menacing us from above, we worked upward. Two hours and 45 minutes later we reached the saddle, a scant 400 ft. away from where we had left the boats. But in that 400 ft. many a life had been in jeopardy." Barber then described climbing down the other side: "By crawling on our hands and knees under an overhanging ledge, and then hanging by our hands and dropping about 12 feet, we found a place where descent to the river was possible." (133~)

Inscriptions near The Loop include Dee Higgins, 10-20-12. (1112~)

—Loop Canyon: This short southern (or eastern) tributary of the Colorado river is at the southeast end of the lower loop and is immediately west of elevation 4692T. It was named by Michael R. Kelsey. (1084~)

—The Grotto: This short southern (or eastern) tributary of the Colorado River is at the very south end of the lower loop (immediately west of elevation 4761T). The mouth of the canyon, a deep recess, is a popular camp for river runners. (SAPE.)

—Anasazi Bottom: This is on the south (or east) side of the Colorado River immediately below the lower loop and adjacent to The Grotto (one-eighth mile south of elevation 4291T). It was named by Michael R. Kelsey. There are Anasazi ruins nearby. (1084~)

—Railroad Tunnels: (Proposed.) The chief engineer of the Stanton-Brown Survey of 1889, Frank Clarence Kendrick, proposed drilling railroad tunnels through The Loops. (1305~, 1460~)

Lopez Gulch: (San Juan Co.) Dry Valley-Hatch Wash. Sandstone Draw map.

Unattributed: "named for Fermin R. Lopez (1881-1962), a pioneer cowboy who herded cattle and sheep in this area for many years." (1931~) The name was proposed to the USGS by La Sal resident Hardy Redd in 1975. (1931~) Lopez worked as foreman for Charlie Redd and his La Sal Livestock Company for many years. Leonard J. Arrington: "Tall, bald, blue-eyed, 'F.R.' Lopez was both witty and handsome.... An all-around hand, Lopez could build a house, construct a corral, swing the lariat, rope a steer, break a bronco, and was deadly as a hunter." (73~)

Losee Canyon: (Garfield Co.) Dixie National Forest-Sevier Plateau-Casto Wash. Casto Canyon map.

Correctly spelled Lossee Canyon.

Isaac Lossee (1816-1891) and family were early settlers of Panguitch. A story is told of Henry Lossee carrying mail one winter. While trying to cross East Fork Sevier River something happened and he froze to death. (1346~, 1445~, 1455~)

Lost Canyon: (San Juan Co.) Canyonlands National Park-Needles District-Salt Creek. Druid Arch and The Loop maps.

During the early years there was a cowboy camp in the canyon. David Lavender in 1943: "The spot is a favorite cowboy hostelry, equipped with the familiar cache of grain and grub. Decorated, too. Using charcoal as a medium, many a lonely guest has expressed himself by writing or drawing on the smooth stone.... The writings were mainly names and dates, followed by succinct remarks on the weather, pinto beans, gnats, and life in general." (1151~) Later, the cowboys abandoned the camp and started using the Cave Spring camp since it had better vehicle access. (1821~) (See Cave Spring—San Juan Co.)

Inscriptions include Ellis Hatch, 1919; James Scorup, 6/25/28; and Rufus Allen, Oct. 3, 1921. (1115~, SAPE.)

Lost Canyon: (San Juan Co.) Dark Canyon Plateau-Dark Canyon. Black Steer Canyon and Indian Head Pass maps.
—Ginshu Canyon: This very short southern tributary of Dark Canyon drops from Lost Canyon Point (immediately west of elevation 6016AT on the Indian Head Pass map). The name was applied by Colorado Outward Bound trip leaders.

Lost Creek: (Garfield Co.) Dixie National Forest-Boulder Mountain-Lost Spring Creek. Posy Lake and Wide Hollow Reservoir maps.

Two name derivations are given.

First, Edson Alvey: "The name was given because of the stream of water that is lost by seeping into the streambed." (55~)

Second, unattributed in 1931: "Mike Shurtz, one of the first settlers, was lost there for three days." (1346~)

Lost Creek: (Garfield Co.) Dixie National Forest-Sevier Plateau-Circle Valley. Mount Dutton map.

E.C. Bird in 1941: "This creek is supplied with water from the numerous springs that spring up along its head. The water that seeps up runs a short distance and sinks into the ground and is lost, never coming up again to the surface, this being why it was named Lost Creek." (2053~)

Lost Creek: (Sevier Co.) Fishlake National Forest-Sevier River. Mount Terrill, Gooseberry Creek, Rex Reservoir, Salina, and Aurora maps.

The Lieutenant George M. Wheeler Survey map of 1872–73 shows this as Los Bellos Valles Creek. (M.76.) Clarence Dutton's 1879 Powell Survey map shows it as Los Creek. (584~) The 1881 Rand McNally Utah map shows it as Lost Creek. (665~)

Max Robinson: "That was not Lost Creek. It was 'Loss,' L-O-S-S. It was named after a man named Loss. Elbert L. Cox said that the people in their map making got mixed up and put, instead of Loss Creek, they put Lost Creek.... This man by the name of Loss was in livestock up there." (1641~)

—Lost Creek Town: In 1877 several families moved to the mouth of Lost Creek. They called their settlement Lost Creek. (1971~)

—Lost Creek Ranch: PRIVATE PROPERTY. The headquarters for this historic ranch is just south of the mouth of Lost Creek (near elevation 5187 on the Aurora map). The ranch was started by Peter C. Scorup. In 1918 San Juan County's Al Scorup bought the ranch. He called it Loss Creek. (1703~, 1936~) (See Scorups Meadows.)

—Salina Grazing Pasture: This is the large area around the head of Lost Creek (Mt. Terrill map). It was a part of the Lost Creek Ranch and the Salina Land and Grazing Company owned by Christian C. and Al Scorup. Al Scorup was the president of the Salina Land and Grazing Company from 1928 to 1951. Al's daughter, Alberta Fairbourn, then took over and owned the business until 1984. (1936~)

Lost Eden Canyon: (Kane Co.) Glen Canyon NRA-Waterpocket Fold-Glen Canyon. The Rincon NE and Halls Crossing maps.

Also called Little Eden Canyon. (31~)

(See Lake Powell—Eliot Porter quote.)

Katie Lee believes that this was named by famed river runner and explorer Harry Aleson. Harry married Dorothy Donaldson Keyes in the canyon. (1336~) Otis "Dock" Marston: "There is a little alcove in there and I went with him and a wedding party from Hite on down to where he was to be married.... [The Minister] performed the ceremony up in this little alcove, which after that we called it The Temple.... That is pretty much all submerged now." (31~)

P.T. Reilly noted that the marriage location was called The Chapel. (1615~) Harry and Dorothy listed the location of their wedding as The Chapel "near Mile One Hundred Eighteen" on their wedding invitation. Ken Sleight to Otis "Dock" Marston: "The CHAPEL sounds good Dock, but I kinda like Little Eden. It certainly was a Garden of Eden to a couple we know." (1755~)

David and Gudy Gaskill: "Beneath the sheer, sandstone cliffs of this canyon the reservoir indeed conceals an eden, lost beneath the waters. Cool, damp and tranquil alcoves here were once gardens of life, wreathed with maidenhair fern and adorned with delicate necklaces of lobelia and columbine. The chambers seemingly glowed from reflections in hues of orange and pink. The sterile, often over-hanging, rock walls that one sees today in Lost Eden only hint at the curve of these flooded alcoves and the life that flourished there." (708~)

Katie Lee: "It was just a picture book. Each turn was a different color, a different striation, a different arrangement of the petrified dunes.... You could see how the world was being put together and torn apart. It was wonderful, and beautiful.... Mother Nature. She just softly molds everything in sandstone." (1163~)

—Burro Bar: (Also called Borough Placer Bar.) This placer bar, now underwater, was on the west side of the Colorado River at the mouth of Lost Eden Canyon (Halls Crossing map). Carlo Shirts prospected Burro Bar in 1882. It is not known if he found gold. (466~, 925~, 999~, 2053~)

—Endless Eden Canyon: This is the first canyon north of Lost Eden Canyon (The Rincon NE map). It was named by the canyon group EMDC in the early 1990s. (SAPE.)

—Halls Bar: (Also called Captain Jack Placer, Halls Crossing Bar, and Watkins No. 2.) This placer bar, now underwater, was on the north (or west) side of the Colorado River one mile east of the mouth of Lost Eden Canyon (one-half mile south of elevation 3842T on the Halls Crossing map). The Boston Placer Mining Company was here from 1899 to 1900. (466~)

—Boston Bar: (Also called Little Anderson Bar and Little Giant Bar.) (466~, 2053~) This placer bar, now underwater, was on the east side of the Colorado River one-quarter mile southeast of the mouth of Lost Eden Canyon (Halls Crossing map). The Boston Placer Mining Company operated here in 1899–1900. The president of the company, Dr. C.E. Watkins, was from Massachusetts. (466~, 1812~)

—Slime Gulch: The mouth of this western tributary of Lake Powell is one mile south of the mouth of Lost Eden Canyon (one-eighth mile north of elevation 3972T on the Halls Crossing map). It was named by a team of canyoneers from the Telluride Guide and Mountaineering School in 1969. (SAPE.)

—Two Deer Spring: This spring, now underwater, was at the mouth of Slime Gulch. Katie Lee and friends named it in 1962: "We saw these two deer along the right wall. We got out of the boats when we saw the deer and we hiked up to see where they had gone. When we got up there we found two beautiful pools surrounded by lush growth.... I remember that I immediately stripped and jumped in and I almost froze my ass off! Oooooo! It was just ice cold." (1163~)

Lost Lake: (Garfield Co.) Dixie National Forest-Awapa Plateau. Pollywog Lake map.

Dunk Taylor: "Lost Lake is kind of a hidden lake. You come out around the flats and through the trees, and all at once, there's that little lake. Lost Spring is just down the draw from it. They did have sheep troughs there but later they went in with a Cat and made a pretty good pond there. It's live water. It's always got water in it." (1865~)

Lost Park: (Wayne Co.) Robbers Roost Flats-Lost Park. Robbers Roost Flats map.

—Lost Park Canyons: These start to the east of Lost Park and go north into Horseshoe Canyon. They were named by Michael R. Kelsey. (653~)

Lost Spring: (Emery Co.) San Rafael Desert-Iron Wash. Old Woman Wash map.

Also called Red Rock Spring. (1551~) This may have also been called Iron Spring. (See Iron Wash—Iron Spring.) This large, excellent spring was a major watering place for livestock on the San Rafael Desert. (SAPE.)

Elwyn Blake in 1949: "It was while camped at Lost Spring that Mr. and Mrs. [Bert] Loper went to Greenriver for provisions. On the way back Bert thought how I would appreciate a few watermelons. He bought a sack of them at the San Rafael ranch, sixteen miles from Greenriver, and ruptured his appendix while lifting them into the wagon. Mrs. Loper took him to Greenriver and they went by train to Grand Junction, the nearest hospital, where he was operated on." (254~)

Inscriptions include Earl Hatch, 189?; Andrew Ekker, June 12, 1910; ? Wimmer, 6/16/12/; and J. Simmons, 1-7-1914. (SAPE.)

—Red Rock Storage: These watering troughs were built by the BLM in 1940. (1551~)

—Old Spanish Trail: (Variation.) In 1951 Bert J. Silliman noted that the Old Spanish Trail—Winter Route—passed by Lost Spring, "which is a small spring of good water in a most unlikely place for a spring." (1734~)

Lost Spring: (Wayne Co.) Dirty Devil Country-South Fork Robbers Roost Canyon. Robbers Roost Flats and Angel Point maps.

Note that there are two Lost Springs: one on each map. The drainages they are each in come together just above the South Fork of Robbers Roost Canyon. The drainages are called the Lost Spring canyons. They were named by Michael R. Kelsey. (653~)

Lost Spring: (Wayne Co.) Henry Mountains-Table Mountain. Dry Lakes Peak map.

This is a developed spring. (SAPE.)

Nina Robison: "My story is that somebody was lost and they found the spring. And that is why they called it Lost Spring." (1644~)

Lost Spring Canyon: (Grand Co.) Cisco Desert-The Highlands-Salt Wash. Mollie Hogans map.

—Lost Spring: This is a large, developed spring. Nearby are a couple of corrals. A line shack, shown on some maps, has been moved. An inscription at the spring is from The Davis's, 1958. (SAPE.)

Lost Spring Creek: (Garfield Co.) GSCENM-Boulder Mountain-Pine Creek. Wide Hollow Reservoir map.

Pratt Gates: "Lost Spring is a little stream of water that comes out of a little lake below Posy Lake and it runs down through the trees and pretty soon it disappears. It gets lost." (709~)

Lost Spring Knoll: (Garfield Co.) Dixie National Forest-Awapa Plateau. Pollywog Lake map. (9,787')

—Lost Lake: Sonny King noted that this stock pond was built in the 1950s or '60s. (1095~)

Lost Spring Wash: (Emery Co.) San Rafael Swell-Saleratus Wash. Dry Mesa, Mexican Mountain, Desert, and Jessies Twist maps.

Big Hole and Joe Hole washes join to form Lost Spring Wash.

—Lost Spring: Ted Ekker: "[The spring] is in a situation there that you could ride right over the top of it and not find it." (623~) The CCC improved the spring in 1934. (623~)

—Old Spanish Trail: The trail went up Lost Spring Wash to Cement Crossing before going on to Big Holes. (1270~)

Lost Spring Wash: (Garfield Co.) Henry Mountains-Shitamaring Creek. Copper Creek Benches and Lost Spring maps.

—Lost Spring: This is a large, developed, and still-used spring.

Charles B. Hunt: "[The] name probably signifies difficulty of finding this spring which is hidden in an obscure tributary wash." (925~, SAPE.)

Lost Spring Wash: (Kane Co., Utah and Coconino Co., Az.) Vermilion Cliffs-Kanab Creek. Utah map: Thompson Point. Arizona maps: Shinarump Point and Fredonia.

Lost Spring is in Lost Spring Gap (Thompson Point map). Unattributed: "Named because it was discovered and lost again." (2053~)

Lost Water: (Grand Co.) Dome Plateau-Squaw Park-Tub Canyon. Cisco SW map.

Joe Taylor: "I named that. There is a spring there and you can't find it. That's why it is lost. Literally. All the country around there looks the same. It's cedar trees and sagebrush for twenty-five miles. When I was a little kid of about eleven I went there with one of the old cowboys. We got a drink and the water was good. Later, when I was a teenager, my brother and I were riding out there and it was hot. I said, 'there's some water here, someplace. I've been to it.' He said, 'Oh, hell, there's no water out here.' We didn't find the water that day. We were out there a year or so later. It had bothered me that we couldn't find it. And that time we did. That's why we call it Lost Water." (1866~)

The spring is difficult to find; it is deep in a rock-walled canyon.

—Constructed Stock Trail: A short trail leads around boulders as one comes up Tub Canyon to the spring. (SAPE.)

Low Canyon: (San Juan Co.) Wingate Mesa-Red Canyon. Chocolate Drop map.

Correctly spelled Lowe Canyon.

Carl Mahon noted that Dr. Jess Lowe of Cooperative Wildlife Research at Utah State University conducted bighorn sheep research in the canyon in the mid-1960s. (1272~)

Lowder Creek: (Iron Co.) Dixie National Forest-Brian Head-Mammoth Creek. Brian Head map.

Also spelled Louder Creek. (749~, 768~)

(See Tebbs Hollow for name derivation.)

—Lowder Creek Ranger Station: This was at the upper end of Lowder Creek and three-quarters of a mile west-northwest of Long Flat (one-eighth mile west of elevation 10317). The station was built in the early 1900s at the site of the original Lowder Ranch. (768~, 887~) It was closed in the early 1950s. Eleanor G. Bruhn, granddaughter of John L. Lowder: "No prettier spot can be found anywhere." (516~)

Lower Barker Reservoir: (Garfield Co.) Dixie National Forest-Escalante Mountains-North Creek. Barker Reservoir map.

Also called Little Barker Reservoir. (1931~)

(See Barker Reservoir for name derivation.)

This was built by the New Escalante Irrigation Company. (55~)

Lower Bear Valley: (Iron Co.) Showalter Mountain-Bear Creek. Little Creek Peak and Burnt Peak maps.

(See Upper Bear Valley for name derivation.)

The Paragonah Co-op Cattle Company was the first owner of Lower Bear Valley. They ran about three thousand head of cattle here from 1870 to 1895. John Topham then became the owner. (336~)

—Old Spanish Trail: The trail went through Little Bear Valley.

Lower Black Box: (Emery Co.) San Rafael Reef-San Rafael River. Spotted Wolf Canyon map.

(See Black Box for name derivation.)

The Lower Black Box is a long, narrow section of the San Rafael River. It starts at Swazys Leap and ends where the river exits the San Rafael Reef at Tidwell Bottoms.

The John C. Fremont Expedition of 1853-54 came up the San Rafael River from its confluence with the Green River. They then pushed up through the Lower Black Box into Mexican Bend. From there they tried to ascend the Upper Black Box, turning around in failure. They noted that they had to swim their horses in places. (166~)

H.L.A. Culmer presaged the naming of the canyon in 1909: "As for going up the San Rafael Canyon, that is considered quite an achievement on foot or horseback at the lowest stage of the stream, and it is quite impossible in the Spring time. It involves leaping your horse from rocky ledges into deep water and many a quick pitapat over quicksand down in the dark boxes of the canyon. The trip is said to contain more thrills to the mile than any other trail in the universe." (496~)

Frank L. Hess of the USGS in 1911: "San Rafael River ... has cut a deep canyon with nearly perpendicular walls a thousand feet or more high which are in places impressively beautiful. Broad and narrow bands of red, white, and buff alternate with the sedimentary rocks of the walls, and with the bright blue of the sky and the green of the cottonwoods and brush on the floor of the canyon produce very striking color effects." (166~)

—Lower Black Box Dam: (Proposed.) Over the years there have been several proposals to construct a dam at the mouth of the Lower Black Box. One, in 1906, would have entailed building a dam 350-feet high. The water would have backed up twelve miles into Mexican Bend. (2049~)

Lower Blue Hills: (Wayne Co.) Skyline Rim-Factory Bench. Skyline Rim and Steamboat Point maps.

—Mars Society Encampment: This is in the Lower Blue Hills and is one-half mile northwest of elevation 4679T on the Skyline Rim map. The Mars Society has a research station here. Blaine Harden: "The modules parking space is in a barren corner of the West that bears an astonishing resemblance to actual pictures of Mars that have been transmitted back to Earth by various unmanned space agencies. They go outside in white canvas space suits trimmed in duct tape. Their helmets are made from plastic light fixtures and white bullet-shaped trash-can lids." (826~)

Lower Browns Reservoir: (Garfield Co.) Boulder Mountain-Oak Creek. Lower Bowns Reservoir map.

Correctly spelled Lower Bowns Reservoir.

George C. Fraser in 1915: "The reservoir is formed by building two dams in a small valley, out of which into another valley the water is ditched." (668~)

Lower Calf Creek Falls: (Garfield Co.) GSCENM-Calf Creek. Calf Creek map.

This stunning 125-foot waterfall is a popular hiker's destination. It is the lower of two major falls along Calf Creek. (See Upper Calf Creek Falls.) D. Elden Beck visited what he called the Rainbow Falls in 1939: "Words of mine cannot describe it adequately." (180~)

Lower Death Valley: (Kane Co.) GSCENM-Hackberry Canyon. Calico Peak map.

(See Upper Death Valley for name derivation.)

—Lower Death Valley Trail: (See Hackberry Canyon—Lower Trail.) Inscriptions include S.T. Graff, Dec. 12, 1925. (SAPE.)

—Carlos Ridge: Ralph Chynoweth noted that this is the ridge between the Paria River and Hackberry Canyon near their confluence (at elevations 6033, 6018, and 5969). It was named for a Mr. Carlo and family who had a ranch on the Paria River. Ralph Chynoweth: "Old man Carlo … would climb out of the Paria Canyon and he'd go over the top of the ridge and into Hackberry and visit with old man Watson [See Rock Springs Creek-Watson Ridge] and that's why they called it Carlos Ridge." (425~) Herbert E. Gregory noted on his map of 1908 that this was an "Unsurveyed Sandstone Badlands." (M.27.)

Lower Group: (Wayne Co.) Capitol Reef National Park-Middle Desert. Fruita NW map.

Also called East Cathedral Valley (1077~) and Lower Valley.

Charles Kelly, who helped name Cathedral Valley, described the Lower Group of Cathedral Valley in 1945: "About two miles distant was a pink cliff running several miles east and west, beautifully sculptured into what appeared to be architectural forms—pillars, columns, spires and decorative statuary—resembling the ruins of a thousand Greek temples. On the flat sandy desert half a mile from this cliff stood two large natural structures and two smaller ones, eroded to architectural forms resembling great cathedrals." (1077~)

—Sculptured Cliff: These are the cliffs immediately south of the Lower Group. They were named by Charles Kelly.

Lower Horse Flats: (San Juan Co.) Dark Canyon Plateau-Dark Canyon. Black Steer Canyon map.

Sandy Johnson: "The name was given to a series of small natural clearings where wild horses were found in the early 1900s." (1931~)

—Sandy Johnson Line Shacks: Sandy Johnson had a couple of line shacks on Lower Horse Flats. Vandalism made him remove the cabins. (1002~)

Lower Jump: (San Juan Co.) Canyonlands National Park-Needles District-Salt Wash. The Loops map.

This is a 250-foot pour-off or waterfall. It is the last, or "lower" jump in Salt Wash. The views from the top of Lower Jump are spectacular.

Lower Kimberly: (Piute Co.) Fishlake National Forest-Tushar Mountains-Mill Creek. Mount Belknap map.

(See Upper Kimberly for name derivation.)

Lower Kolob Plateau: (Washington Co.) Zion National Park-Cave Valley. Smith Mesa and The Guardian Angels maps. Most of Lower Kolob Plateau is PRIVATE PROPERTY.

(See Kolob Creek Canyon for name derivation.)

Lower Pasture: (Wayne Co.) Horseshoe Canyon-Spur Fork. Head Spur map.

The name was given by the Joe Biddlecome family sometime after 1909. (117~) Biddlecome used it as a cattle pasture. (120~)

Lower Podunk Creek: (Kane Co.) GSCENM-Lick Wash. Rainbow Point and Deer Spring Point maps.

Also called Riggs Canyon. (766~)

(See Podunk Creek for name derivation.)

—Podunk: This was on Lower Podunk Creek near the "Spring" one-quarter mile below the mouth of Horse Hollow (Rainbow Point map). (766~)

—Brown Ranch: PRIVATE PROPERTY. This was on Lower Podunk Creek one and one-half miles downcanyon from its junction with Horse Hollow (near the "Spring" at elevation 6841 on the Rainbow Point map). (766~) Cal Johnson noted that it was owned by Johnny Brown: "He had a sawmill up in the Podunk country." (984~) This was most likely John Franklin Brown (1858-1944) or his son, John Hyrum Brown (1884-1961).

Lower Red Lake Canyon: (San Juan Co.) Canyonlands National Park-Needles District-The Grabens-Cataract Canyon. Spanish Bottom map.

Also called Powell Canyon (618~, M.78.) and Red Wash (114~).

Otis "Dock" Marston noted that it was called Red Canyon, Red Lake Canyon, and Butler Canyon. (405~)

Two name derivations are given for the Butler name.

First, Mont Butler ran livestock in the area in the 1890s. (1743~)

Second, P.T. Reilly noted that Jack Butler was a mining partner of Jack Sumner of the Powell Expedition of 1869. (1613~)

James H. Knipmeyer: "In the early days there was a small natural lake near the south end of this canyon. The red limestone in the canyon gave the waters a reddish color." (1116~) Several diarists from the early days mentioned this "waterhole" in the canyon. (433~)

Inscriptions near the mouth of the canyon include Denis Julien, 1836. This inscription site was listed on the

National Register of Historic Places in 1988. (See Appendix One—Denis Julien.)

—Old Spanish Trail: (Variation.) The Old Spanish Trail—Winter Route—may have crossed the Colorado River at Spanish Bottom. The western half of the route is discussed under Spanish Bottom. The eastern half of the route is discussed below.

In 1871 John Wesley Powell mentioned seeing a trail going up the cliffs in the vicinity of Lower Red Lake Canyon: "found an Indian trail for horses, and campfires that were probably made last winter. No doubt but that horses can be taken down to the Colorado at this point." (662~)

Powell's Indian Trail was not the present "Pack Trail" shown going up Lower Red Lake Canyon. That trail was not in existence until the early 1960s. Several historians in the 1950s thoroughly explored Lower Red Lake Canyon and found not a hint of a trail down the cliffs. Otis "Dock" Marston in 1956 explored this route and found that there were several drops that would require construction: "Near the head of Red Lake Canyon is a drop of about 30 feet which could be by-passed by stock with some trail building. A half mile closer to the River some first rate drops which aggregate 550 feet or more. It is possible to by-pass these drops on foot but we saw no sign of trail beyond some very faint deer trails." (1734~)

Kent Frost also explored for a stock trail down the canyon in the 1950s and did not find one. (1734~)

C. Gregory Crampton also noted in the late 1950s that there was no trail up Lower Red Lake Canyon from the river: "An examination was made of the lower reaches of Red Lake Canyon and the open bank along the Colorado for 3/4 mi. above the mouth of the canyon. No sign of stock or of a stock trail was seen in Red Lake Canyon." (465~)

Powell's Indian Trail, now sometimes called the Julien Inscription Trail, started at the mouth of Lower Red Lake Canyon and went southeast up a prominent thin ridge and over elevation 4427T. It then went east for one-quarter mile before going up a steep slope and ending at the top of the cliffs near elevation 5102T. Although much of the trail has disappeared, there are several definite sections of construction.

In a letter to Otis "Dock" Marston in 1953 Bert J. Silliman provided a brief description of the trail: "On the other side of the river [from Spanish Bottom] a mile or so lower down, a water course comes down the canyon wall by means of which the Old [Bear's Ears] Trail [Julien Inscription Trail] ascended to a sunken valley or graben

between parallel faults that characterize that region. (619~, SAPE.)

It is impossible to definitively say that a variation of the Old Spanish Trail crossed here; there is no hard evidence. That a very old trail did cross here is axiomatic. Denis Julien was obviously following a trail when he left his name in 1836. To the argument that the country is too difficult, one only has to follow the Domínguez-Escalante route at the Crossing of the Fathers and across Navajo Canyon to realize that the Spanish in 1776 crossed terrain that was as difficult, if not more so, than that at Spanish Bottom.

To the argument that the crossing, just above the first rapid in Cataract Canyon, would prove too dangerous, it must be remembered that the river, certainly as far down as The Confluence, used to freeze in the winter.

There is an argument that once across the river and in The Grabens, there was no easy way through them. After a careful examination of all of the grabens, it becomes apparent that, although serpentine, there are a couple of easy ways through them. (SAPE.)

This conundrum, much like many mysteries in canyon country, is unlikely to ever have a definitive conclusion; it is best that way.

Lower Sand Slide: (Wayne Co.) Hell Hole Swale-Dirty Devil River. Angel Cove map.

This cliff dune is still used by stockmen to get cattle from Hells Hole Swale down to the Dirty Devil River. (SAPE.)

Lower Trail Canyon: (Kane Co.) GSCENM-Kaiparowits Plateau-Left Hand Collet Canyon. Collet Top map.

Edson Alvey noted that cattle were trailed through the canyon. (55~)

Lowrey Spring: (Coconino Co., Az.) Vermilion Cliffs National Monument-Vermilion Cliffs-Cathedral Wash. Navajo Bridge, Az. map.

This medium-size spring was once developed.

David "Buck" Lowrey built Marble Canyon Lodge in 1927. (1551~)

Water from the spring was piped for several miles to the lodge. (SAPE.)

Lucky Flats: (Emery Co.) Cedar Mountain-Lucky Flats Wash. Flattop Mountain and Cow Flats maps.

Lamont Johnson: "[Bill Gentry] was chasing cattle when his horse knocked over a rock that glistened in the sunlight. He thought it was gold, so he gave it that name." (1190~)

Lucky Strike Mine: (Emery Co.) San Rafael Swell-Reds Canyon. Copper Globe Mine.

This successful uranium mine was started in 1949 by Frank Blackburn and Irvin Olsen of Ferron and a

University of Utah geologist named Staker. (641~, 845~, 1318~, 1967~)

Lundell Spring: (Iron Co.) Dixie National Forest-Kolob Terrace. Webster Flat map.

Albert and Hilma Lundell were early residents of Glendale and Upper Kanab. They moved to Cedar City in the early 1900s. (388~)

Lunts Horse Pasture: (Carbon Co.) West Tavaputs Plateau-Desolation Canyon. Cedar Ridge Canyon map.

Also called Lunt Pasture (1575~) and Lunts Pasture (79~).

Two name derivations are given.

First, Howard C. Price, Jr. noted that J.H. Lunt was thought to have been the first cowboy in the area. (1575~)

Second, Shed Lunt (1875-1959) was the original owner of the Rock Creek Ranch. (2011~)

Lydias Canyon: (Kane Co.) Pink Cliffs-Long Canyon. Strawberry Point, Orderville, and Glendale maps.

Also spelled Liddies Canyon. (349~)

Allen Joseph Stout (1815-1889) and family moved to the mouth of Lydias Canyon in 1864. Lydia (1849-1888) was the Stout's oldest daughter. The family only stayed for a couple of years. (1572a~)

—Sawmill: A sawmill was located here for several years in the early 1870s. (1639~)

Lyges Fork: (Wayne Co.) Fishlake National Forest-Thousand Lake Mountain-Pole Canyon. Lyman map.

Dunk Taylor noted that Lyge Morrell an early resident of the area. (1865~)

Lyman Canyon: (San Juan Co.) Dark Canyon Plateau-Hells Half Acre-Kane Gulch. South Long Point and Kane Gulch maps.

Platte D. Lyman (1848-1901) was the second in charge of the Hole-in-the-Rock Expedition. He crossed the mouth of the canyon in March 1880. (1241~, 1356~)

—Constructed Stock Trail: An old stock trail that was improved during the 1950s uranium boom into a road has now deteriorated back into a still-used stock trail. It goes up the south side of the east fork of Lyman Canyon to South Long Point. (SAPE.)

Lyman Town: (Wayne Co.) Rabbit Valley-Fremont River-Highway 24. Lyman map.

Also called Wilmoth.

The town was settled in 1876 by the James P. Sampson family. Sampson first visited the area as a surveyor in 1874. (1194~)

Two name derivations are given.

First, Barbara Ekker: "This settlement was originally named East Loa, then in 1893 it was changed to honor Apostle Francis M. Lyman (1840-1916) who had suggested they move their settlement to higher ground." (607~, 1419~, 1786~)

Second, Andrew Jenson: "named Lyman in honor of Theodore Lyman, who the previous year [1882] had taken up land in the vicinity." (972~)

Lynns Pond: (Emery Co.) Castle Valley-Cedar Hollow. Buckhorn Reservoir map.

This is a still-used stock reservoir. (SAPE.)